KT-434-603

The **Rough Guide** to

Chile

written and researched by

Melissa Graham and Andrew Benson

with additional contributions by
Alex Stewart

ROUGH
GUIDES

NEW YORK • LONDON • DELHI

www.roughguides.com

Contents

Food and drink specialities insert following p.120

Adventure sports insert following p.312

Wildlife insert following p.504

3

◄◄ Isla Negra ◄ Chilote church

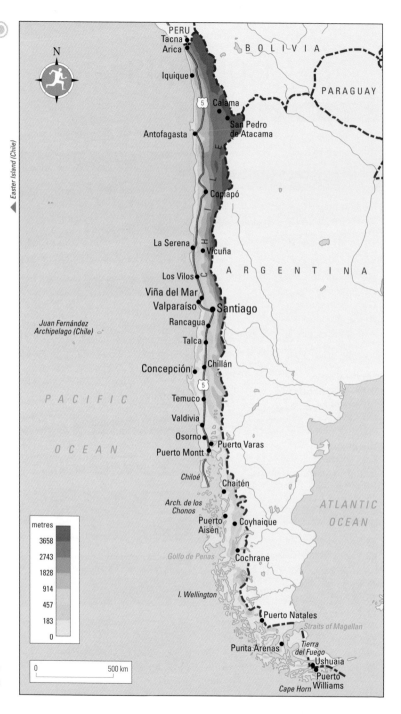

N

PERU
Tacna
Arica
Iquique
5 Calama
San Pedro
de Atacama
Antofagasta
Copiapó
La Serena
Vicuña
A R G E N T I N A
Los Vilos
Viña del Mar
Valparaíso   Santiago
Rancagua
Juan Fernández
Archipelago (Chile)
Talca
Concepción   Chillán
5
P A C I F I C   Temuco
Valdivia
Osorno
O C E A N   Puerto Varas
Puerto Montt
Chiloé
Chaitén
Arch. de los
Chonos   ATLANTIC
Puerto   Coyhaique   OCEAN
Aisén
Golfo de Penas   Cochrane
I. Wellington
Puerto Natales
Straits of Magellan
Punta Arenas   Tierra
del Fuego
Ushuaia
Puerto
Cape Horn Williams

BOLIVIA

PARAGUAY

metres
3658
2743
1828
914
457
183
0

0   500 km

Introduction to

Chile

A long, narrow sliver of land, clinging to the edge of a continent, Chile has often drawn attention to itself for its wholly implausible shape. Seen in the pages of an atlas, the country's outline strikes you as aberrant and fantastical; almost 4000km in length (the equivalent of Norway to Nigeria), and with an average width of just 180km, the very idea of it seems absurd. Once you're on Chilean soil, however, these boundaries make perfect sense, and visitors quickly realize that Chile is a geographically self-contained unit. The Andes, the great mountain range that forms its eastern border, are a formidable barrier of rock and ice that cuts the country off from Argentina and Bolivia. The Atacama Desert, a thousand-kilometre stretch of parched wasteland, separates it from Peru to the north. And to the west, only a few islands dotted in the Pacific Ocean break the waves that roll onto Chile's coast from Australasia.

All this has created a country distinct from the rest of South America and one that defies many people's expectations of an Andean country. It is developed, relatively affluent, and – with the exception of the infamous military Pinochet regime of the 1970s and 1980s – boasts a long tradition of political stability and orderly government. It is, without doubt, one of the safest and most relaxing South American countries to travel in. Its buses are comfortable and run on time. Its people are polite, respectful and discreet. And, by regional standards, its police are honest.

5

Fact file

• One of Chile's most outstanding features is its **shape** – a long thin strip stretching almost 4000km in length that takes in an extraordinary diversity of terrains.

• Some **15.6 million people** live in Chile, around one third of them in Santiago. It has a fairly homogenous mestizo population of mixed Spanish and indigenous ancestry. Very few indigenous groups remain, only the Mapuche of the south (numbering around 300,000) and the smaller population of Aymara in the far north (around 40,000).

• Chile is **one of the most developed countries in Latin America**, with the steadiest growth in the region. According to figures produced by Transparency International, a non-governmental organization associated with the United Nations, Chile also has the lowest level of corruption in Latin America, and is less corrupt than a number of wealthier countries such as France and Japan.

• Although known throughout the world for its infamous military dictatorship during the 1970s and 1980s, Chile has a long history of parliamentary democracy, and is today probably the **most politically stable country in South America**.

◀ Castro craft market

Above all, though, it is for its remote and dizzyingly beautiful landscapes that visitors head to Chile. With its population of fifteen million largely confined to a handful of major cities, and a land area three times greater than the UK's, much of Chile is made up of vast tracts of scarcely touched wilderness – places where you can be days from the nearest tarred road, and where it's not unusual to stumble upon steaming hot springs, gleaming white salt flats or emerald lakes, and have them all to yourself. Few countries, moreover, can match the astounding contrasts of scenery you'll find here, ranging from the driest desert in the world to immense ice fields and glaciers. Spread between these extremes is a kaleidoscope of panoramas, taking in sun-baked scrubland, lush vineyards and orchards, virgin temperate rainforest, dramatic fjords and bleak Patagonian steppes. Towering over it all is the long, jagged spine of the Andes, punctuated by colossal peaks and smouldering volcanoes.

You can experience this wilderness in whatever style you choose – Chile is not a developing country, and you don't have to slum it while you're here. There are plenty of modest, inexpensive accommodation options and camping facilities up and down the country, while those on a more generous budget will find increasing numbers of luxurious, beautifully designed lodges in spectacular locations, particularly in the south. Whatever your budget, you'll

> Chile is, without doubt, one of the safest and most relaxing South American countries to travel in

probably want to take advantage of the numerous possibilities for outdoor activities, whether it be jeep rides, bird-watching, skiing, horse trekking, wine tours, hiking, volcano climbing, sea kayaking, white-water rafting or fly-fishing – all offered by a large number of local outfitters, and comprehensively detailed in this guide. If you have less active plans in mind, you can sit back and take in Chile's scenery from various ferry rides in the south, on reasonably priced flights or on organized tours from most of the main cities. However you do it, you won't be disappointed.

▲ Baqueanos, Torres del Paine

Altiplano driving

The south of Chile may have the monopoly on outdoor activities, but the north offers one of South America's most exciting adventures: driving across the altiplano. Shared with neighbouring Argentina, Bolivia and Peru, the altiplano is a high plateau connecting the eastern and western ranges of the Andes, sitting at an altitude of up to 4500m. Beautiful and desolate in equal measure, it's a land of bleak, sunburnt plains dotted with gleaming white salt flats, turquoise lakes and snow-capped volcanoes. Huddled in their shadows are the tiny, semi-abandoned villages of the indigenous Aymara, who've herded llamas and alpacas up here for many centuries. You can visit the altiplano on organized tours from Chile's northern cities, but far and away the best way to do it is by renting a sturdy 4WD, loading it up with a tent, a stove and gallons of fuel and water, and heading up solo – an experience that allows you to truly appreciate the wilderness, the solitude and the sheer majesty of the place. Naturally, this is a serious journey and you'll need to take sensible precautions; for more on driving through the altiplano, see Basics, p.51, and the box, p.259, in the El Norte Grande chapter.

Where to go

Given Chile's great size, and the huge distances that separate the main attractions, it's important to give careful thought to your itinerary before you go. If you want to experience both the northern and southern extremes, you should invest in a LAN air pass (⊛ www.lanchile.com), unless you're prepared to spend many hours sitting on a bus, or are in the country for an extended period. Otherwise, most visitors with just two or three weeks to play with tend to choose between heading north or south from Santiago, even then singling out a few chosen targets, rather than trying to fit everything in. Something else to bear in mind is that, on the whole Chile's cities are not that exciting, and are best used as a jumping-off point to get out into the backcountry. In light of this, you should seriously consider renting a vehicle for at least part of your trip, as public transport to some of the most beautiful areas, including many national parks, is non-existent. We discuss each region's highlights in greater detail in the chapter introductions; what follows is a brief summary of attractions in each area.

▲ Aymara woman

Santiago, though boasting some fine monuments, museums and restaurants, is not to everyone's taste, with its ceaseless noise and traffic and heavy pollution, and two or three days here is enough for most visitors. The capital is handy for visiting some of the country's oldest **vineyards**, while a string of splendid beaches as well as the quirky port city of **Valparaíso** and the fashionable seaside resort of **Viña del Mar** both sit on its doorstep.

North of Santiago, highlights include the handsome colonial city of **La Serena**, the lush, deeply rural **Elqui Valley**, and another succession of idyllic **beaches** along the dazzling fringe of the **Norte Chico**, a region that mostly comprises semi-arid landscapes and brittle vegetation. At the northern edge of this region, the tidy little city of **Copiapó** serves as a springboard for excursions to the white sands and turquoise waters of **Bahía Inglesa**, one of the country's most attractive seaside resorts, and east into the cordillera, where you'll find the mineral-streaked volcanoes of **Parque Nacional Nevado de Tres Cruces** and the radiant

> Few countries match the astounding contrasts of scenery, from the driest desert in the world to immense glaciers

Laguna Verde. Further north, the barren **Atacama Desert**, stretching over 1000km into southern Peru, presents an unforgettable, if forbidding, landscape, whose sights number ancient petroglyphs (indigenous rock art), abandoned nitrate ghost towns and a scattering of fertile, fruit-filled oases. Up in the Andes, the vast plateau known as the **altiplano**, as high and remote as Tibet, encompasses snow-capped volcanoes, bleached-white salt flats, lakes speckled pink with flamingoes, grazing

Chile's regions

Administratively, Chile is divided into thirteen regions, numbered one to twelve (with the addition of the Metropolitan region). We've listed each region by number and name below, followed by the regional capital in parentheses.

I   Tarapacá (Iquique)
II   Antofagasta (Antofagasta)
III   Atacama (Copiapó)
IV   Coquimbo (La Serena)
V   Valparaíso (Valparaíso)
VI   Libertador General O'Higgins (Rancagua)
VII   Maule (Talca)
VIII   Bío Bío (Concepción)
IX   Araucanía (Temuco)
X   Los Lagos (Puerto Montt)
XI   Aisén (Coihaique)
XII   Magallanes y Antártida Chilena (Punta Arenas)

llamas, alpacas and vicuñas, tiny whitewashed churches and native Aymara communities. The best points to head for up here are **Parque Nacional Lauca**, reached from the city of Arica, and **Parque Nacional Volcán Isluga**, near Iquique.

South of Santiago, the chief appeal of the lush **Central Valley** is its swaths of orchards and vineyards, dotted with stately haciendas, while further south, the famous, much-visited **Lake District** presents a picture-postcard of perfect, conical volcanoes (including the exquisite **Volcán Osorno**), iris-blue lakes, rolling pastureland and dense native forests, perfect for hiking. A short ferry ride from Puerto Montt, at the southern edge of the Lake District, the **Chiloé** archipelago is a quiet, rural

▲ Lago Yelcho

backwater, famous for its rickety houses on stilts, old wooden churches and rich local mythology. Back on the mainland, south of Puerto Montt, the **Carretera Austral** – a 1000-kilometre long unpaved "highway" – carves its way through virgin temperate rainforest and past dramatic fjords, one of which is the embarkation point for a 200-kilometre boat trip out to the sensational **Laguna San Rafael glacier**. Beyond the Carretera Austral, cut off by the **Campo de Hielo Sur** (southern ice field) lies **Southern Patagonia**, a country of bleak windswept plains bordered by the magnificent granite spires of the **Torres del Paine** massif, Chile's single most famous sight, and a magnet for hikers and climbers. Just over the easily crossed border in Argentina are two of the region's star attractions: the **Fitz Roy Sector** in the north of the **Parque Nacional Los Glaciares**, a favourite for trekkers, and, to the south, the awe-inspiring **Glaciar Perito Moreno**. Across the

Magellan Strait, **Tierra del Fuego**, shared with Argentina, sits shivering at the bottom of the world, a remote land of a harsh, desolate beauty.

Finally, there are Chile's two Pacific possessions: remote **Easter Island**, famed for its mysterious statues and fascinating prehistoric culture; and the little-visited **Isla Robinson Crusoe**, part of the Juan Fernández Archipelago, sporting dramatic volcanic peaks covered with dense vegetation.

▼ Magellanic penguins

When to go

The **north** of the country can be comfortably visited at any time of year, though if you're planning to rent a 4WD and tour the altiplano, note that the unpredictable weather phenomenon known as the **Bolivian Winter** (or invierno altiplánico) can produce heavy, sporadic rainfall between December and February (the height of summer), washing away roads and disrupting communications.

In the **centre** and **south** of the country, you should avoid the months of June to September (unless you plan to go skiing), when heavy snowfall often blocks access to the mountains, including many national parks. The peak summer months are January and February, but as accommodation rates and crowds increase in equal measure, you'd be better off coming in November, December or March, when the weather is often just as good.

Daytime temperatures and average rainfall

	Jan	Feb	Mar	Apr	May	Jun	Jul	Aug	Sep	Oct	Nov	Dec
Antofagasta												
Max (°C)	24	24	28	21	19	18	17	17	18	19	21	22
Max (°F)	75	75	82	70	66	64	63	63	64	66	70	72
Min (°C)	17	17	16	14	13	11	11	11	12	13	14	16
Min (°F)	63	63	61	57	55	52	52	52	54	55	57	61
rainfall (mm)	0	0	0	0	0	3	5	4	0	3	0	0
rainfall (in)	0	0	0	0	0	.11	.19	.15	0	.11	0	0
Arica												
Max (°C)	26	27	25	24	22	19	18	18	19	20	22	24
Max (°F)	79	80	78	75	71	67	65	65	66	69	72	76
Min (°C)	20	20	19	17	15	14	14	14	15	15	17	18
Min (°F)	68	68	66	63	60	58	57	58	59	60	62	65
rainfall (mm)	1	0	0	0	0	0	0	3	0	0	0	2
rainfall (in)	.03	0	0	0	0	0	0	.11	0	0	0	.07
Punta Arenas												
Max (°C)	14	14	12	10	7	5	4	6	8	11	12	14
Max (°F)	57	57	54	50	45	41	39	43	46	52	54	57
Min (°C)	7	7	5	4	2	1	-1	1	2	3	4	6
Min (°F)	45	45	41	39	36	34	30	34	36	37	39	43
rainfall (mm)	38	23	33	36	33	41	28	31	23	28	18	36
rainfall (in)	1.5	.90	1.3	1.4	1.3	1.6	1.1	1.2	.90	1.1	.70	1.4
Santiago												
Max (°C)	29	29	27	23	18	14	15	17	19	22	26	28
Max (°F)	84	84	81	73	64	57	59	63	66	72	79	82
Min (°C)	12	11	9	7	5	3	3	4	6	7	9	11
Min (°F)	54	52	48	45	41	37	37	39	43	45	48	52
rainfall (mm)	3	3	5	13	64	84	76	56	31	15	8	5
rainfall (in)	.11	.11	.19	.51	2.5	3.3	2.9	2.2	1.2	.59	.31	.19
Valdivia												
Max (°C)	23	23	21	17	13	11	11	12	14	17	18	21
Max (°F)	73	73	70	63	55	52	52	54	57	63	64	70
Min (°C)	11	11	9	8	6	6	5	4	5	7	8	10
Min (°F)	52	52	48	46	43	43	41	39	41	45	46	50
rainfall (mm)	66	74	132	234	361	550	394	328	208	127	125	104
rainfall (in)	2.6	2.9	5.1	9.2	14.2	21.6	15.5	12.9	8.1	5	4.9	4.1

things not to miss

It's not possible to see everything Chile has to offer in one trip – and we don't suggest you try. What follows is a selective taste of the country's highlights: outstanding scenery, picturesque villages and dramatic wildlife. They're arranged in five colour-coded categories, which you can browse through to find the very best things to see and experience. All highlights have a page reference to take you further into the guide, where you can find out more.

01 Parque Nacional Torres del Paine Page **513** • Without a doubt, this spectacular park is what draws most visitors to southern Chile, and it does not disappoint even after all the photos and build-up.

02 Valparaíso Page **147** • This remarkable perched city drapes over a jumble of steep hills around a wide bay.

04 Churches of Chiloé Page **431** • The archipelago's beautiful wooden churches rise over the heart of almost every small village.

03 Chinchorro mummies Page **271** • Gape at these prehistoric, remarkably intact mummies, pulled from a seven-thousand-year-old burial site near Arica.

15

05 **Cemetery at Punta Arenas** Page **498** • Discover this fascinating necropolis in Punta Arenas, the main transport hub of the far south.

06 **Valle de la Luna** Page **244** • Trek across this aptly named moonscape, just south of San Pedro de Atacama.

07 Bahía Inglesa Page **217** • Dip into turquoise waters and soak up rays on the relatively unspoilt beach.

08 Lapis lazuli
Pages **78** & **128** • For a lovely Chilean souvenir, pick up jewellery made from lapis, the cool blue stone mined throughout the country and sold in local crafts markets.

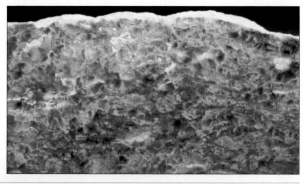

09 Penguins Page **503** • Head to the thriving sanctuaries at Isla Magdalena and Seno Otway for an up-close look at penguins.

17

10 Southern Patagonia Page **489** • Explore the tip of the Americas, where the country splinters into granite towers, glaciers and fjords.

11 **Mercado Central, Santiago** Page 112 • Tuck into a tasty lunch at the market's bustling fish markets, serving the freshest catch.

12 **The moai of Easter Island** Page 570 • It's remote and expensive to get to, but once there you'll surely get caught up in the game of, "Who built these giant moai? How? Why?"

14 Pisco Elqui Page **204** • Take a tour of a distillery, followed by a taste of a pisco sour, Chile's national cocktail.

13 Geoglyph at Cerro Unitas Page **260** • The world's largest geoglyph is appropriately known as the "Gigante de Atacama".

15 Termas de Puyuhuapi Page **462** • Isolated and largely inaccessible, the resort here is home to steaming hot springs, and is one of the great getaways along the Carretera Austral.

16 San Rafael glacier Page **471** • Embark on an exhilarating boat ride alongside this stunning ice formation.

17 Rodeos and huasos Page **287** • Witness expert horsemanship and a slice of national culture at the rodeos in the Central Valley.

18 Sea lions in the Beagle Channel Page **546** • If you make it all the way down to Tierra del Fuego, a trip through the Channel to see these delightful creatures is a near requisite.

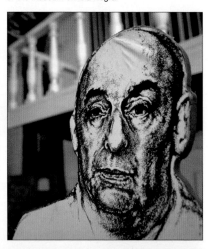

20 Tracking Pablo Neruda

Pages **113, 156** & **161** • The Nobel Prize-winning poet is one of Chile's best-known literary exports. Visit any of the three houses he lived in: La Chascona in Santiago, La Sebastiana in Valparaíso, or the museum on Isla Negra.

19 Fly-fishing Page 464 •

The gin-clear waters of the rivers off the Carretera Austral hold some of the world's top spots for fly-fishing.

21 Hiking Volcán Villarrica Page 360 •

Take a guided hike up this active volcano, the focal point of a park with excellent opportunities for trekking and camping.

22 Laguna Verde Page **215** • Massive active volcanoes surround these richly hued waters, making for an almost surreal landscape – the perfect spot to enjoy the bubbling lakeside hot springs.

23 Teleférico over Santiago Page **115** • Dangle high above the sprawling capital, surrounded by the snow-capped Andes.

24 Pre-Columbian art Page **105** • Santiago's Museo Precolombino is the capital's best museum, home to striking pieces of pre-Columbian art, from urns to incense burners to ancient Andean textiles.

25 **Flowering desert** Page **208** • You may well miss it, because it only happens once every four years, but if the parched desert happens to be covered by a carpet of flowers during your visit, you're sure to be awed by the sight.

26 **The night sky** Page **202** • Chile's northern skies are the most transparent in the southern hemisphere, as testified by the many international observatories stationed here. Head to the Elqui Valley's Cerro Mamalluca observatory to play astronomer and gaze up at the stars.

Basics

Basics

Getting there

Nearly everyone flies into Chile, arriving at Santiago's modern international airport, though some will travel by land from a neighbouring country and even fewer will arrive on a ship. Note that relatively few airlines have scheduled flights to Santiago (not to be confused with namesake cities in Spain, Cuba, Dominican Republic and elsewhere), and prices have risen recently as fuel fares have rocketed.

Airfares always depend on the **season**. You'll pay the highest fares in December to February, and June to August, the southern and northern hemisphere's summer holiday months. Fares drop slightly during the "shoulder" months – March and November – and you'll get the best prices during the low seasons: April, May, September and October. Note also that flying on weekends ordinarily adds around 10 percent to the round-trip fare; price ranges quoted below assume midweek travel.

You can often cut costs by going through a **specialist flight agent** – either a consolidator, who buys up blocks of tickets from the airlines and sells them at a discount, or a **discount agent**, who in addition to dealing with discounted flights may also offer special student and youth fares and a range of other travel-related services such as travel insurance, rail passes, car rentals, tours and the like. Some agents specialize in **charter flights**, which may be cheaper than scheduled flights, but have fixed departure dates and high withdrawal penalties.

Another possibility is arranging a **courier flight**, although you'll need a flexible schedule and preferably be travelling alone with very little luggage. In return for shepherding a parcel through customs, you can expect to get a deeply discounted ticket. You'll also be restricted in the duration of your stay.

If Chile is only one stop on a longer journey, you might want to consider buying a **Round-the-World** (RTW) ticket. Some travel agents can sell you an "off-the-shelf" RTW ticket that will have you touching down in about half a dozen cities (Santiago is on many itineraries). Alternatively, you can have a travel agent assemble a RTW ticket for you; in this case the ticket can be tailored to your needs but is apt to be more expensive. Figure on around £900 or US$1600 for a RTW ticket that includes a stopover in Santiago de Chile.

Air passes

LAN offers special coupon **air passes**, called **Visit Chile**, available to anyone who's not a resident of Chile, flying into the country on a LAN or Iberia flight only. These must be bought outside the country and can be used for most internal, mainland flights. The price is US$312 for the first three coupons, then US$104 for each additional coupon. A total of six tickets is permitted per air pass. There's a maximum stay of one month and the first coupon must be used within fourteen days of arrival in Chile. In view of all these restrictions and the fact that you may find promotional fares in Chile, you might not find the air pass worth it. If you plan to visit Easter Island, note that your flight there from Santiago will also be far cheaper if the ticket is bought in conjunction with a LAN international flight (see p.47), but Visit Chile coupons cannot be used.

Booking flights online

Many airlines and discount **travel websites** offer the opportunity to book your tickets, hotels and holiday packages online, cutting out the costs of agents and middlemen; these are worth going for, as long as you don't mind the inflexibility of non-refundable, non-changeable deals. There are some bargains to be had on auction sites too, if you're prepared to bid keenly. Almost all airlines have their own websites, offering flight tickets that can sometimes be just as cheap, and are often more flexible.

Online booking agents and general travel sites

Ⓦ **www.cheapflights.co.uk** (in UK & Ireland), Ⓦ **www.cheapflights.com** (in US), Ⓦ **www.cheapflights.ca** (in Canada). Flight deals, travel agents, plus links to other travel sites.

Ⓦ **www.cheaptickets.com** (in US), Ⓦ **cheaptickets.co.uk** (in UK). Discount flight specialists. Also in US at ☏ 1-888/922-8849.

Ⓦ **www.ebookers.com** (in UK), Ⓦ **www.ebookers.ie** (in Ireland). Efficient, easy to use flight finder, with competitive fares.

Ⓦ **www.etn.nl/discount** A hub of consolidator and discount agent links, maintained by the nonprofit European Travel Network.

Ⓦ **www.expedia.co.uk** (in UK), Ⓦ **www.expedia.com** (in US), Ⓦ **www.expedia.ca** (in Canada). Discount airfares, all-airline search engine and daily deals.

Ⓦ **www.flights4less.co.uk** Does just what it says on the tin.

Ⓦ **www.flyaow.com** "Airlines of the Web" – online air travel info and reservations.

Ⓦ **www.flynow.com** Simple to use independent travel site offering good-value fares.

Ⓦ **www.gaytravel.com** US gay travel agent, offering accommodation, cruises, tours and more. Also at ☏ 1-800/GAY-TRAVEL.

Ⓦ **www.geocities.com/thavery2000** An extensive list of airline websites and US toll-free numbers.

Ⓦ **www.hotwire.com** Bookings from the US only. Last-minute savings of up to forty percent on regular published fares. Travellers must be at least 18 and there are no refunds, transfers or changes allowed. If you're looking for the cheapest possible scheduled flight, this is probably your best bet.

Ⓦ **www.kelkoo.co.uk** Useful UK-only price-comparison site, checking several sources of low-cost flights (and other goods and services) according to specific criteria.

Ⓦ **www.lastminute.com** (in UK), Ⓦ **www.lastminute.com.au** (in Australia), Ⓦ **www.lastminute.co.nz** (in New Zealand), Ⓦ **www.site59.com** (in US). Good last-minute holiday package and flight-only deals.

Ⓦ **www.opodo.co.uk** Popular and reliable source of low UK airfares. Owned by, and run in conjunction with, nine major European airlines.

Ⓦ **www.orbitz.com** Comprehensive web travel source, with the usual flight, car hire and hotel deals but also great follow-up customer service.

Ⓦ **www.priceline.co.uk** (in UK), Ⓦ **www.priceline.com** (in US). Name-your-own-price website that has deals at around forty percent off standard fares.

Ⓦ **www.qixo.com** A comparison search that trawls through other ticket sites – including agencies and airlines – to find the best deals.

Ⓦ **www.skyauction.com** Bookings from the US only. Auctions tickets and travel packages to destinations worldwide using a "second bid" scheme, just like e-Bay. You state the maximum you're willing to pay, and the system will bid only as much as it takes to outbid others, up to your stated limit.

Ⓦ **www.ticketplanet.com** California-based site that claims to be the first to sell consolidator fares over the web. Especially good for circle-Pacific and round-the-world fares.

Ⓦ **www.travelocity.co.uk** (in UK), Ⓦ **www.travelocity.com** (in US), Ⓦ **www.travelocity.ca** (in Canada), Ⓦ **www.zuji.com.au** (in Australia), Ⓦ **www.zuji.co.nz** (in New Zealand). Destination guides, hot web fares and best deals for car hire, accommodation and lodging as well as fares. Provides access to the travel agent system SABRE, the most comprehensive central reservations system in the US.

Ⓦ **www.travelshop.com.au** Australian site offering discounted flights, packages, insurance, and online bookings. Also on ☏ 1300/767 908.

Ⓦ **travel.yahoo.com** (in US), Ⓦ **ca.travel.yahoo.com** (in Canada), Ⓦ **uk.travel.yahoo.com** (in UK), Ⓦ **au.travel.yahoo.com** (in Australia). Incorporates some Rough Guides material in its coverage of destination countries and cities across the world, with information about places to eat and sleep, and a flight finder.

Ⓦ **www.travelzoo.com** Great resource for news on the latest airline sales, cruise discounts and hotel deals. Links bring you directly to the carrier's site.

Flights from the US and Canada

While US travellers are not exactly spoiled for choice, they shouldn't find it too hard to get a fairly convenient flight to Santiago. Several airlines offer **daily non-stop flights**, and typical APEX fares from the US are US$800 (low season) or US$1000 (high season) from Miami or the New York region, at least half as much again from California or the Mid-West; you can also stop over in Panama or Lima. There's even less choice if you're flying from Canada to Chile, though you shouldn't have much problem finding a connecting flight with a US carrier or with LAN via

Newark, Miami or Los Angeles. Sample fares from Toronto are Can$1100 (low season)/Can$1500 (high season); fares are about 20 percent more from Vancouver.

Approximate **flying times** from the US to Santiago are: from Miami, 8 hours; from LA, 13 hours; and from the New York area, 10 hours. Approximate flying times from Canada to Santiago are: from Toronto, 11 hours; from Vancouver, 16 hours or more.

Airlines

Air Canada ☎1-888/247-2262, ⊛www.aircanada.com.
American Airlines ☎1-800/433-7300, ⊛www.aa.com.
Continental Airlines Domestic ☎1-800/523-FARE, International ☎1-800/231-0856, ⊛www.continental.com.
Copa Airlines US ☎1-800/FLY-COPA, ⊛www.copaair.com.
Delta International ☎1-800/241-4141, ⊛www.delta.com.
LAN US ☎1-800/735-5526, Canada ☎416/862-0807, ⊛www.lan.com.
United Airlines International ☎1-800/538-2929, ⊛www.united.com.

Courier flights

Air Courier Association ☎1-800/282-1202, ⊛www.aircourier.org. Courier flight broker. Membership (US$35 for a year) also entitles you to twenty percent discount on travel insurance and name-your-own-price non-courier flights.
International Association of Air Travel Couriers ☎308/632-3273, ⊛www.courier.org. Courier flight broker. One year's membership costing US$45 in the US or Canada (US$50 elsewhere).

Discount travel agents

Air Brokers International ☎1-800/883-3273, ⊛www.airbrokers.com. Consolidator and specialist in round-the-world and circle-Pacific tickets.
Airtech ☎212/219-7000, ⊛www.airtech.com. Standby seat broker; also deals in consolidator fares.
Educational Travel Center ☎1-800/747-5551 or 608/256-5551, ⊛www.edtrav.com. Low-cost fares worldwide, student/youth discount offers, and Eurail passes, car rental and tours.
High Adventure Travel ☎1-800/350-0612 or 415/912-5600, ⊛www.airtreks.com. Round-the-world and circle-Pacific tickets. The website features

an interactive database that lets you build and price your own round-the-world itinerary.
STA Travel US ☎1-800/329-9537, Canada ☎1-888/427-5639, ⊛www.statravel.com. Worldwide specialists in independent travel; also student IDs, travel insurance, car rental, rail passes, and more.
TFI Tours ☎1-800/745-8000 or 212/736-1140, ⊛www.lowestairprice.com. Well-established consolidator with a wide variety of global fares; less competitive on the US domestic market.
Travel Avenue ☎1-800/333-3335, ⊛www.travelavenue.com. Full-service travel agent that offers discounts in the form of rebates.
Travel Cuts US ☎1-800/592-CUTS, Canada ☎1-888/246-9762, ⊛www.travelcuts.com. Popular, long-established student-travel organization, with worldwide offers.
Travelers Advantage ☎1-877/259-2691, ⊛www.travelersadvantage.com. Discount travel club, with cash-back deals and discounted car rental. Membership required ($1 for 3 months' trial).
Travelosophy US ☎1-800/332-2687, ⊛www.itravelosophy.com. Good range of discounted and student fares worldwide.
Worldtek Travel ☎1-800/243-1723, ⊛www.worldtek.com. Discount travel agency for worldwide travel.

CHILE
tailormade by specialists

TRIPS worldwide
ORDER YOUR BROCHURE FROM TRIPS WORLDWIDE

telephone 0117 311 4400
web www.tripsworldwide.co.uk

Tour operators

Adventure Center ☎ 1-800/228-8747 or 510/654-1879, ⓦ www.adventurecenter.com. Hiking and "soft adventure" specialists offering a seventeen-day "Absolute Chile" tour.

Adventures Abroad ☎ 1-800/665-3998 or 604/303-1099, ⓦ www.adventures-abroad.com. Adventure specialists offering two-week tours to Patagonia, and very long trips throughout Argentina and Chile.

Adventures on Skis ☎ 1-800/628-9655 or 413/568-2855, ⓦ www.advonskis.com. Offers package trips to Portillo, Chile's top ski resort.

Anglatin, Ltd, ☎ 1-800/485-7842 or 541/344-7023, ⓦ www.anglatin.com. Offers ten-day tours of Patagonia and the Lake District and a few educationally oriented packages such as the ten-day "Wineries, Wine and Cuisine" tour.

Ecosummer Expeditions ☎ 1-800/465-8884 or 250/674-0102, ⓦ www.ecosummer.com. A British Columbia–based company offering expeditions and kayaking and trekking holidays in South America and elsewhere.

4th Dimension Tours ☎ 1-800/343-0020, ⓦ www.4thdimension.com. City breaks, cruises, ski packages and so on. Highlights include the nine-day "The Best of Chile" tour (land/air); skiing in Valle Nevado (land/air); seven-night cruise on the Terra Australis (cruise and local air from Santiago).

Globus and Cosmos ☎ 1-866/755-8581, ⓦ www.globusandcosmos.com. Specializing in Antarctica and two-week South American "samplers". Request brochures online, by phone or via a travel agent.

Holidaze Ski Tours ☎ 1-800/526-2827 or 732/280-1120, ⓦ www.holidaze.com. Skiing in South America during the northern summer.

International Market Place ☎ 1-800/641-3456, ⓦ www.imp-world-tours.com. Magellan and Patagonian cruises are among the offerings.

Journeys International ☎ 1-800/255-8735 or 734/665-4407, ⓦ www.journeys-intl.com. Runs Antarctica trips and a "Chile-end-to-end" fourteen-day tour.

Mountain Travel–Sobek, ☎ 1-888/687-6235, ⓦ www.mtsobek.com. Trips include a "Patagonia Explorer" adventure package.

Nature Expeditions International ☎ 1-800/869-0639, ⓦ www.naturexp.com. The sixteen-day Chile tour takes in Torres del Paine.

Ponce de Leon Travel ☎ 305/266-5827 or 1-800/826-4845. Ski, spa, cruise and customized packages, including a three-day "Classic Santiago, Valparaíso and Viña del Mar" tour (with optional horseback riding, river rafting and wine tasting), and a four-day trip to Easter Island.

REI Adventures ☎ 1-800/622-2236, ⓦ www.rei.com. Climbing, cycling, hiking, cruising, paddling and multi-sport tours, such as trekking in Patagonia.

Safaricentre ☎ 310/546-4411 or 1-800/624-5342 in California, 1-800/223-6046 rest of US, 1-800/233-6046 in Canada, ⓦ www.safaricentre.com. Wide range of packages, including a four-day Patagonian cruise and six days in the Atacama Desert.

Saga Road Scholar Tours ☎ 1-800/621-2151, ⓦ www.sagaholidays.com. Learning adventures for senior travellers, such as "Chile: From Glacial Peaks to Pacific Shores", with optional three-night extension to Easter Island.

Wilderness Travel ☎ 1-800/368-2794, ⓦ www.wildernesstravel.com. Specialists in hiking, cultural and wildlife adventures. Offers include the Futaleufú Trail, and sixteen days in Patagonia plus an Iguazú Falls extension.

Worldwide Quest Adventures ☎ 1-800/387-1483, ⓦ www.worldwidequest.com. Their name is self-explanatory and one of their packages is a two-week discovery of the "history and mystery" of Peru and Chile.

Flights from the UK and Ireland

Several airlines offer regular scheduled flights from London to Santiago de Chile; a few airlines also offer flights from Dublin. None of them is direct, and as a rule you'll have to choose between flying **via another European or Latin American city** or **via the US** (the latter trips can be marginally cheaper, but are usually longer). In general, high-season fares cost upwards of £800. An important point to consider when shopping for tickets is that if you go directly through an airline you'll be offered what they call their "published fares", which are usually vastly more expensive than the "net fares" they sell to certain flight agents (known as consolidators).

In short, it's nearly always cheaper to book your flight through a specialized or **discount flight agency**. We've listed several below, but it's also worth checking the travel sections of London's *Time Out* and the national Sunday newspapers, or phoning the Air Travel Advisory Bureau (☎ 020/7636 5000) for a list of discount agents. You should always shop around, though, as some agencies can offer exceptionally good one-off deals.

In addition to fares, it's also worth paying attention to the **routings** used by the different airlines – in particular, check how many stops are involved, and how long you'll have to spend in transit (note that transit in the US can be especially uncomfortable, often with no access to the airport shops). Even the shortest and most convenient routings via Madrid or Buenos Aires entail a total travelling time of over 16 hours. Apart from trying to minimize the length of the flight, another reason to scrutinize the routings is that many airlines allow you to break your journey and take stopovers on the way – sometimes for free, sometimes for a surcharge of around 10 percent. Interesting **potential stopovers** include Buenos Aires (Air France and Aerolíneas Argentinas), Bogotá (Avianca) and São Paulo and Rio (British Airways and Varig) in South America; Newark, Boston, Chicago, Miami, Dallas and Washington (American, Continental and United) in the US; and Madrid (Iberia, LAN) and Paris (Air France) in Europe.

Airlines

Aerolíneas Argentinas UK ☎0845/601 1915, 🖳www.aerolineas.com.ar.
Air France UK ☎0845/359 1000, Republic of Ireland ☎01/605 0383, 🖳www.airfrance.com.
American Airlines UK ☎0845/778 9789, Republic of Ireland ☎01/602 0550, 🖳www.aa.com.
British Airways UK ☎0870/850 9850, Republic of Ireland ☎1800/626 747, 🖳www.ba.com.
Continental Airlines UK ☎0845/607 6760, Republic of Ireland ☎1890/925 252, 🖳www.continental.com.
Iberia UK ☎0845/601 2854, Republic of Ireland ☎01/407 3017, 🖳www.iberiaairlines.co.uk.
LAN UK ☎0800/917 0572, 🖳www.lan.com.
Lufthansa UK ☎0845/773 7747, Republic of Ireland ☎01/844 5544, 🖳www.lufthansa.com.
Varig UK ☎020/8321 7170, 🖳www.varig.co.uk.

Courier flights

International Association of Air Travel Couriers UK ☎0800/074 6481 or 01291/625 656, 🖳www.aircourier.co.uk. Agent for lots of companies.

Flight and travel agents

In the UK

Bridge the World UK ☎0870/814 4400, 🖳www.bridgetheworld.com. Specialists in long-haul travel, with good-value flight deals, round-the-world tickets and tailor-made packages, all aimed at the backpacker market.
British Airways Holidays ☎0870/240 0747, 🖳www.baholidays.co.uk. An exhaustive range of package and tailor-made holidays around the world, using British Airways and other top-quality international airlines.
Co-op Travel Care UK ☎0870/112 0085, 🖳www.travelcareonline.com. Flights and holidays around the world from the UK's largest independent travel agent. Non-partisan and informed advice.
Flynow UK ☎0870/066 0004, 🖳www.flynow.com. Large range of discounted tickets; official South African Airways agent.
Major Travel ☎020/7393 1060, 🖳www.majortravel.co.uk. Reliable discount agent, often with very low fares to Santiago.
North South Travel UK ☎01245/608 291, 🖳www.northsouthtravel.co.uk. Friendly, competitive travel agency, offering discounted fares worldwide. Profits are used to support projects in the developing world, especially the promotion of sustainable tourism.
Passage to South America ☎020/8767 8989. Good South American specialist, offering low-cost fares and helpful advice.
Premier Travel Derry ☎028/7126 3333, 🖳www.premiertravel.uk.com. Discount flight specialists.

Visit our website
1000's of photos
100's of itineraries
numerious hotel and regional descriptions

www.newworlds.co.uk
⁺⁴⁴(0)20 8445 8444

International flight emissions offset with Climate Care
Dedicated to responsible tourism

New Worlds

Specialists in Chile

Our experienced team will be delighted to create your tailor-made itinerary

Tailor-made itineraries

Bolivia | Chile | Costa Rica | Cuba | Ecuador | Galapagos | Peru

Quest Travel UK ☎ 0870/442 3542, ⓦ www
.questtravel.com. Specialists in round-the-world
tickets and discount fares and package holidays to
Australia and New Zealand.

Rosetta Travel Belfast ☎ 028/9064 0304,
ⓦ www.rosettatravel.com. Flight and holiday agent,
specializing in deals direct from Belfast.

South American Experience ☎ 020/7976 5511,
ⓦ www.southamericanexperience.co.uk. Mainly a
discount flight agent, but also offers a range of tours,
plus a very popular "soft landing package", designed
to make arrivals pain-free.

STA Travel UK ☎ 0870/160 0599, ⓦ www
.statravel.co.uk. Worldwide specialists in low-cost
flights and tours for students and under-26s, though
other customers are welcome.

Trailfinders UK ☎ 0845/058 5858, ⓦ www
.trailfinders.com, Republic of Ireland ☎ 01/677
7888, ⓦ www.trailfinders.ie. One of the best-
informed and most efficient agents for independent
travellers.

In Ireland

Aran Travel International Republic of Ireland
☎ 091/562 595, ⓦ homepages.iol.ie/~arantvl
/aranmain.htm. Good-value flights to all parts of the
world.

CIE Tours International Republic of Ireland
☎ 01/703 1888, ⓦ www.cietours.ie. General flight
and tour agent.

Joe Walsh Tours Republic of Ireland ☎ 01/241
0800, ⓦ www.joewalshtours.ie. Long-established
general budget fares and holidays agent. Also
pilgrimages to Lourdes, Rome, Santiago de
Compostela and others.

Lee Travel Republic of Ireland ☎ 021/427 7111,
ⓦ www.leetravel.ie. Flights and holidays worldwide.

Trailfinders UK ☎ 0845/058 5858, ⓦ www
.trailfinders.com, Republic of Ireland ☎ 01/677 7888,
ⓦ www.trailfinders.ie. One of the best-informed and
most efficient agents for independent travellers.

USIT Northern Ireland ☎ 028/9032 7111, Republic
of Ireland ☎ 01/602 1904, ⓦ www.usit.ie.
Specialists in student, youth and independent travel
– flights, trains, study tours, TEFL, visas and more.

Tour operators

Austral Tours ☎ 020/7233 5384, ⓦ www
.latinamerica.co.uk. Small company offering a
seventeen-day tour in northern and southern Chile,
plus tailor-made itineraries. Especially good at
organizing special-interest holidays based around
wine tours, fishing, trekking or archeology.

British Airways Holidays ☎ 0870/240 0747,
ⓦ www.baholidays.co.uk. Offers an exhaustive range
of package and tailor-make holidays around the world,
including a tour of Patagonia. Flights are on British
Airways and other top-quality international airlines.

Dragoman UK ☎ 01728/861 133, ⓦ www
.dragoman.co.uk. Extended overland journeys in
purpose-built expedition vehicles; shorter camping
and hotel-based safaris, too. Destinations include
Chile.

Exodus UK ☎ 0870/240 5550, ⓦ www.exodus
.co.uk. Adventure tour operator taking small groups
for specialist programmes, including walking, biking,
overland, adventure, and cultural trips. Among its long
tours is a five-week exploration of Patagonia.

Explore Worldwide UK ☎ 0870/333 4001, Ireland
(c/o Maxwell's Travel) ☎ 01/677 9479, ⓦ www
.exploreworldwide.com. Small-group tours, treks,
expeditions and safaris. Offers three-week tours of
the fjords and Patagonia, with accommodation mostly
in small local hotels. Some supplements for single
travellers.

Intrepid Travel UK ☎ 020/8960 6333, ⓦ www
.intrepidtravel.com. Small-group tours with the
emphasis on cross-cultural contact and low-impact
tourism.

Journey Latin America UK ☎ 020/8747 3108,
ⓦ www.journeylatinamerica.co.uk. Specialists
in flights, packages and tailor-made trips to Latin
America, with excursions and cruises in Chile.

Kumuka Expeditions UK ☎ 0800/389 2328,
Ireland ☎ 1800/798 637, ⓦ www.kumuka.co.uk.

CHILE

**Bespoke trips for the more
independent and
adventurous
traveller**

Desert, vineyards,
volcanoes,
Easter Island,
lake district,
glaciers, national parks
and fjords. Wildlife,
culture, cruises, walking,
food and wine, self-drive
options. Combine with
Argentina, Peru & Bolivia.
Direct flights from Europe.

t: 020 8758 4774
for advice and colour brochure

w: www.sunvil.co.uk
with downloadable pdf's

e: latinamerica@sunvil.co.uk

ATOL protected 808

Sunvil
LATIN AMERICA

AITO LATA

Independent tour operator specializing in overland expeditions, as well as local and private transport tours, **Kuoni Travel** UK ℡01306/747 734, ⓦwww .kuoni.co.uk. Flexible package holidays to Chile and elsewhere; good family offers.

Tailored Expeditions ⓦwww.tailoredexpeditions .com. Argentina-based company specializing in individual customised trips to select destinations in Argentina, Chile, Peru and Uruguay.

Thomas Cook UK ℡0870/750 5711, ⓦwww .thomascook.co.uk. Long-established one-stop travel agency for package holidays, city breaks or flights, with bureau de change issuing Thomas Cook branded travellers' cheques, plus travel insurance and car rental.

Tucan Travel ℡020/7370 4555, ⓦwww .tucantravel.com. Group holidays in southern Chile and Argentina, plus a range of overland expeditions in South America.

Wildlife Worldwide UK ℡020/8667 9158, ⓦwww.wildlifeworldwide.com. Tailor-made trips for wildlife and wilderness enthusiasts.

World Expeditions UK ℡020/8870 2600, ⓦwww.worldexpeditions.co.uk. Australian-owned adventure company offering a two-week Jesuit-route trip and fifteen days in Torres del Paine. All expeditions are graded by difficulty. Challenging trips available for hardcore adventurers; special offerings for over-fifty travellers.

Flights from Australia and New Zealand

Although there are only a couple of airlines that fly to Santiago, the going is pretty straightforward – all follow the same route across the Pacific and cost much the same – with Qantas, Air New Zealand, Air Tahiti, LAN and Aerolíneas Argentinas offering several flights a week between them via Auckland, Papeete and/or Easter Island (LAN only). As total **flying time** is around twenty hours, you may want to take advantage of the free stopover allowed each way.

Tickets purchased direct from the airlines can often work out more expensive than a round-the-world (RTW) fare. Travel agents offer the best deals and have the latest information on limited special offers, such as free stopovers and fly-drive/accommodation packages. Flight Centres and STA (which offer fare reductions for ISIC card-holders and under 26s) generally offer the lowest fares and can also assist with visas.

Airfares vary throughout the year and depend on both the season (defined as high

from December to February, and low the rest of the year) and duration of stay (tickets are available for 21 days, 45 days, 90 days, 6 months and one year, with 45- and 90-day tickets the best value. Seat availability on most international flights out of Australia and New Zealand is often limited, so it's best to book several weeks ahead.

Most **Australian** flights are out of Sydney (you'll pay the same from Melbourne, Canberra and Brisbane, but expect to pay ten percent more from Cairns, Adelaide and Hobart, and twenty percent more from Perth and Darwin). The **lowest fares** for 45-day tickets cost upwards of Aus$2000 depending on season, with 90-day tickets costing at least 20 percent more.

Flights out of **New Zealand** generally leave from Auckland, with 45-day fares starting at NZ$1600, while the best 90-day deals will come to at least NZ$2200.

Airlines

Aerolineas Argentinas Australia ℡02/9317 3018, New Zealand ℡09/275 9914, ⓦwww .aerolineas.com.

Air New Zealand Australia ℡13 24 76, ⓦwww .airnewzealand.com.au, New Zealand ℡0800/737 000, ⓦwww.airnewzealand.co.nz.

Air Tahiti Nui Australia ℡02/9244 2899, New Zealand ℡09/308 3360, ⓦwww.airtahitinui -usa.com.

LAN Australia ℡1300/361 400 or 02/9244 2333, New Zealand ℡09/309 8673, ⓦwww .lan.com.

Qantas Australia ℡13 13 13, New Zealand ℡0800/808 767 or 09/357 8900, ⓦwww .qantas.com.

Travel agents

Flight Centre Australia ℡13 31 33, ⓦwww .flightcentre.com.au, New Zealand ℡0800/243 544, ⓦwww.flightcentre.co.nz. Rock-bottom fares worldwide.

Northern Gateway Australia ℡1800/174 800, ⓦwww.northerngateway.com.au.

STA Travel Australia ℡1300/733 035, ⓦwww .statravel.com.au, New Zealand ℡0508/782 872, ⓦwww.statravel.co.nz. Worldwide specialists in low-cost flights, overlands and holiday deals. Good discounts for students and under-26s.

Trailfinders Australia ℡1300/780 212, ⓦwww .trailfinders.com.au. One of the best-informed and most efficient agents for independent travellers.

travel.com.au and travel.co.nz Australia
☎1300/130 483 or 02/9249 5444, ⓦwww.travel
.com.au, New Zealand ☎0800/468 332, ⓦwww
.travel.co.nz. Comprehensive online travel company,
with discounted fares.

Specialist agents

Adventure Associates Australia ☎02/9389
7466, ⓦwww.adventureassociates.com.au.
Long-established operator with tours and cruises to
Antarctica and South America.
Adventure World Australia ☎02/8913 0755,
ⓦwww.adventureworld.com.au; New Zealand
☎09/524 5118, ⓦwww.adventureworld.co.nz.
Agents for a vast array of international adventure
travel companies that operate trips to South America.
Austral Tours Australia ☎1800/620 833 or
03/9600 1733, ⓦwww.australtours.com. Central
and South American specialist covering the region
from Ecuador to Easter Island and Tierra del Fuego.
Australian Andean Adventures Australia
☎02/9299 9973, ⓦwww.andeanadventures.com
.au. Trekking specialist offering cross-country skiing in
Patagonia and an explorers' trek in Patagonia.
Kumuka Expeditions Australia ☎1800/804
277 or 02/9279 0491, ⓦwww.kumuka.com.
Independent tour operator specializing in overland
expeditions, such as a one-month "Pure Patagonia"
trip.
South America Travel Centre Australia
☎1800/655 051 or 03/9642 5353,

ⓦwww.satc.com.au. Large selection of tours and
city accommodation packages throughout the region.
Travel.com Australia ☎1300/130 482 or 02/9249
5444, ⓦwww.travel.com.au; New Zealand
☎09/359 3860, ⓦwww.travel.co.nz.
Travelplan Australia ☎1300/130 754 or 02/9958
1888, ⓦwww.travelplan.com.au. Holidays in the
snow worldwide.

Tour operators

Classic Safari Company Australia
☎1300/130 218 or 02/9327 0666, ⓦwww
.classicsafaricompany.com.au. Luxury, tailor-made
safaris to India, Africa and South America.
Contours Australia ☎1800/331 378, ⓦwww
.contourstravel.com.au. Specialists in tailored city
stopover packages and tours, including self-drive
tours through the Lake District and a ten-day budget
tour of Patagonia using local buses and cheap to
mid-range hotels.
Peregrine Adventures Australia ☎03/9663
8611, ⓦwww.peregrine.net.au; in New Zealand,
contact Adventure Travel Company ☎03/364 3400.
Adventure tours including South America.
World Expeditions Australia ☎1300/720 000,
ⓦwww.worldexpeditions.com.au, New Zealand
☎0800/350 354, ⓦwww.worldexpeditions.co.nz.
Offers a number of adventure walking holidays. Based
in Sydney but also branches in Adelaide, Auckland,
Brisbane, Melbourne and Perth.

Red tape and visas

Most foreign visitors to Chile do not need a visa. The exception are citizens of a
small number of countries including Cuba, Russia, all Middle Eastern countries,
except Israel, and all African countries, except for South Africa. But check with
your local Chilean consulate. If you do need one, you'll have to submit an application to your consulate, along with your passport and a full written itinerary.
Remember that you will need a multiple entry visa if you plan to leave Chilean
territory and re-enter it.

Visitors of all nationalities are issued with a
tourist entry card (*Tarjeta de Turismo*) on
arrival in Chile, which is valid for ninety days,
and can be extended once for an additional
ninety days. It will be checked by the International Police at the airport or border post

when you leave Chile – if it's expired you
won't be allowed to leave the country until
you've paid the appropriate fine at the nearest Intendencia (up to US$100, depending
on the number of days past the expiry date).
If this happens when you're trying to fly out

of the international airport in Santiago, you'll have to go back downtown to Moneda 1342 (Mon–Fri 9am–1pm; ☎2/6725320).

If at any time during your stay in Chile you **lose** your tourist card, you should ask for a duplicate immediately, either from the Fronteras department of the Policía Internacional, General Borgoño 1052, Santiago (☎2/698 2211) or from the Extranjer's department of the Intendencia in any provincial capital (addresses are listed below). There's no charge for replacing lost or stolen cards.

If you want to **extend** your tourist card, you've got two choices. You can either pay US$100 at the Intendencia of Santiago or any provincial capital, or you can simply leave the country and re-enter, getting a brand-new ninety-day *Tarjeta de Turismo* for free. The latter option is usually far cheaper and certainly more interesting – from Santiago, for instance, you could take the very scenic seven-hour bus ride to Mendoza in Argentina – and there are many other opportunities for border crossing up and down Chile.

Note that a tourist card does not allow you to undertake any **paid employment** in Chile – for this, you need to get a work visa before you enter the country, which can either be arranged by your employer in Chile or by yourself on presentation (to your embassy or consulate) of an employment contract authorized by a Chilean public notary. You can't swap a tourist card for a work visa while you're in Chile, which means that legally you can't just go out and find a job – though many language schools are happy to ignore the rules when employing language teachers. Other

points to note are that **under-18s** travelling to Chile without parents need written parental consent authorized by the Chilean Embassy, and that minors travelling to Chile with just one parent need the written, authorized consent of the absent parent.

Intendencias

Antofagasta: Arturo Prat 384 ☎55/281260, ☏266055.
Concepción: Aníbal Pinto 442 ☎41/225347, ☏230247.
Copiapó: Los Carrera s/n ☎52/212727, ☏212460.
Coyhaique: Plaza 485 ☎67/231000, ☏231494.
Iquique: Costanera s/n ☎57/426106, ☏424244.
La Serena: Arturo Prat 350 ☎51/224421, ☏212190.
Puerto Montt: Décima Región 480 ☎65/252720.
Punta Arenas: Bories 901 ☎61/221675.
Rancagua: Plaza de los Héroes ☎72/225781, ☏222528.
Santiago: Moneda 1342 ☎2/6725320, ☏698 0510.
Talca: 1 Oriente 1190 ☎71/225965, ☏225060.
Temuco: Bulnes 590 ☎45/212616, ☏213064.
Valparaíso: Melgarejo 669, 18th Floor ☎32/213047, ☏212679.

Chilean embassies and consulates abroad

Australia

Embassy: 10 Culgoa Circuit, O'Malley, Canberra ACT 2606 ☎02/6286 2430, ✉chilemb@embachile-australia.com, ⊛www .embachile-australia.com.
Consulate: Level 18, National Mutual Building, 44 Market St, Sydney 2000 ☎02/9299 2533.

Canada

Embassy: 50 O'Connor St, suite 1413, Ottawa, ON K1P 6L2 ☎613/235-4402, ✉echileca@chile.ca, ⊛www.chile.ca.
Consulates: 2 Bloor St W, #1801, Toronto, ON M4W 3E2 ☎416/924-0106; 1010 Sherbrooke St W #710, Montréal, PQ H3A 2R7 ☎514/499-0405; 1185 W Georgia St, #1250, Vancouver, BC V6E 4E6 ☎604/681-9162.

New Zealand

Embassy: 19 Bolton St, Wellington ☎04/471 6270, ☏04/472 5324, ✉echile@embchile.co.nz, ⊛www.embchile.co.nz.

Arrival tax

Chile levies an **arrival tax** for **US, Canadian, Australian and Mexican** citizens in reciprocation of similar taxes levied on Chilean citizens arriving in these countries. This means you must pay **US$100, US$55, US$34 or US$15 respectively** upon arrival at Santiago or Easter Island airports (check with a Chilean consulate for the latest amount). However, the payment is valid for the lifetime of the passport and is not levied upon crossing land borders.

Consulates: PO Box 612, Auckland ☎ 09/373 4602, ✉ pbex@ihug.co.nz. PO Box 359, Christchurch ☎ 03/366 5096, ✉ petert@cecc .org.nz.

UK

Embassy and Consulate: 12 Devonshire St, London W1N 2DS ☎ 020/7580 6392, ✉ embachile @embachile.co.uk, ⊛ www.echileuk.demon.co.uk.

US

Embassy: 1732 Massachusetts Ave NW, Washington, DC 20036 ☎ 202/785-1746 or

785-1747, ✉ embassy@embassyofchile.org, ⊛ www.chile-usa.org.
Consulates: 1732 Massachusetts Ave, Washington, DC 20036 ☎ 202/785-3159; Public Ledger Building, Suite 444, Chestnut & Sixth Sts, Philadelphia, PA 19106 ☎ 215/829-9520; 1360 Post Oak Blvd, Suite 2330, Houston, TX 77056 ☎ 713/963-9066; 875 N Michigan Ave, Suite 3352, Chicago, IL 60611 ☎ 312/654-8780; 1110 Brickell Ave, Miami, FL 33131 ☎ 305/373-8623; 866 United Nations Plaza #302, New York, NY 10017 ☎ 212/355-0612; 870 Market St #1062, San Francisco, CA 94102 ☎ 415/982-7662.

Information, websites and maps

The only Chilean tourist office maintained abroad is in Madrid, Spain (Rafael Calvo 18, 5o., D ☎ 913082095, ☎ 914350413, ✉ turismochile@telefonica.net). You can, however, get limited tourist information, including a glossy manual, at the Chilean Embassy in many countries. Alternatively, some of the tour companies who specialize in the region prepare fact sheets on the countries they visit, and their brochures will at least give you an idea of what the main tourist attractions look like. Another good source of information is the Chile Information Pack produced by South American Explorers (a US-run non-profit organization that provides services to travellers in South America); it costs US$6.50 for non-members and US$4.50 for members, and can be paid for by credit card using the club's online order form (⊛ www.samexplo.org) or by fax (☎ 607/277 6122). One of the best sources of pre-trip information is the Internet, with a number of websites offering hard facts, titbits and question-and-answer forums. Finally, you can buy maps before you go (see p.38 for a list of retailers), though you'll find a better selection in Santiago.

Tourist information

Chile's government-run tourist board is called **Sernatur** (short for Servicio Nacional de Turismo). There's a large and very helpful office in Santiago (see p.95), plus branches in every provincial capital in Chile. They produce a huge amount of material, including themed booklets on camping, skiing, national parks, beaches, thermal springs and so on; for some reason these are often kept out of sight, so you'll have to specifically ask to see everything they've got. In smaller towns you're more likely to find a municipal **Oficina de Turismo**, sometimes attached

to the Municipalidad (town hall) and usually with a very limited supply of printed information to hand out. If there's no separate tourist office it's worth trying the **Municipalidad** itself – they sometimes stock a few maps and leaflets, and at the very least can deliver over-the-counter advice. Another source of information is the excellent series of **TurisTel guidebooks**, published annually by the Chilean phone company, CTC, and available at numerous pavement kiosks in Santiago, and CTC offices in Chilean cities. They come in three volumes, covering the north, the centre and the south, and give extremely detailed information on even the tiniest of places, with comprehensive street plans and road maps. The English translation, available at many kiosks, suffers from infrequent updating.

Online information

Chile has embraced the **Internet** with much enthusiasm, and any Web search on "Chile" will produce thousands of matches. We've listed a few of them below, but these are really just a starting point for what can easily turn into hours of surfing.

Government websites

Australian Department of Foreign Affairs ⓦ www.dfat.gov.au. Advice and reports on unstable countries and regions.
British Foreign and Commonwealth Office ⓦ www.fco.gov.uk. Constantly updated advice for travellers on circumstances affecting safety in over 130 countries.
Canadian Foreign Affairs Department ⓦ www.dfait-maeci.gc.ca/menu-e.asp. Country-by-country travel advisories.
Government of Chile ⓦ www.segegob.cl. Official government website, with email links to various ministries.
Sernatur ⓦ www.sernatur.cl. The national tourist board's site, with pages on national parks, major tourist attractions, history, culture and food.
US State Department Travel Advisories ⓦ http://travel.state.gov/travel_warnings.htm. Website providing "consular information sheets" detailing the dangers of travelling in some countries.

Other useful websites

Chilean Patagonia ⓦ www.chileaustral.com. Easy-to-use site dedicated to tourism in Chilean Patagonia, including city guides, national parks, hotels, weather forecasts and lots more.
Easter Island ⓦ www.netaxs.com/~trance/rapanui.html. A short introduction to Easter Island's history and attractions, with great pictures and lots of links.
El Mercurio ⓦ www.emol.com. The long-established, rather conservative daily newspaper, online in Spanish.
Chip Travel ⓦ www.chiptravel.cl. First-rate site (partly funded by the government) with a vast range of useful information, from bus timetables to nightlife listings. Make this your first stop.
Chile Hotels ⓦ www.chile-hotels.com. A long list of Chilean hotels, with online booking facilities, plus brief descriptions of the towns and cities.

LAN ⓦ www.lan.com. Check out timetables and fares on the Lan national flight network.
South American Explorers ⓦ www.samexplo.org. Excellent site belonging to the long-established non-profit organization providing services for scientists, explorers and travellers in South America. Offers travel advisories and warnings, trip reports, a bulletin board and sensibly indexed links with other sites.
Sunsite Chile Weblink ⓦ sunsite.dcc.uchile.cl. Very useful page set up by the Universidad de Chile with links to many other sites, grouped in categories such as news, government, law, tourism, weather and so on.
Turismo Chile ⓦ www.turismochile.cl. Descriptions of the major attractions in each region, with some historical and cultural background.

Maps

No two **road maps** of Chile are identical, and none is absolutely correct. The bulk of errors lie in the representation of dirt roads: some maps mark them incorrectly as tarred roads, some leave out a random selection of dirt roads altogether, and some mark them quite clearly where nothing exists at all. Most drivers end up using two or three different maps, cross-referencing them to spot the errors.

You'll find a number of reliable country maps, including the **Rough Guides'** detailed, waterproof Chile map. The comprehensive **TurisTel** map is printed in the back of its guides to Chile (see opposite) and also published in a separate booklet. **Sernatur** produces a good fold-out map of the whole of Chile, called the *Gran Mapa Caminero de Chile*, on sale at the main office in Santiago, and an excellent map of the north, called the *Mapa Rutero Turístico Macroregión Norte*, free from Sernatur offices in Santiago and the north (ask, as they're rarely on display). Other useful maps include **Auto Mapa's** *Rutas de Chile* series, distributed internationally. Outside of Chile, also look for the **Reise Know-How Verlag** and **Nelles Verlag** maps of Chile, which combine clear road detail along with contours and colour tinting.

You can pick up free and usually adequate **street plans** in the tourist office of most cities, but better by far are those contained in the Turistel guidebooks, with a map for practically every town and village you're likely to want to visit. Bookshops and kiosks sell street-indexed maps of Santiago, but the most comprehensive A–Z of Santiago appears in the back of the CTC phone directory.

The Instituto Geográfico Militar produces 1:50,000 **topographic maps**, but these can only be bought from its office at Dieciocho 369 in Santiago (℡2/4606800, 🖷2/4608294, 🖳www.igm.cl, 📧clientes@igm.cl). They're very expensive too, at about US$15 each – a cheaper alternative is to photocopy A4-size sections of them in the map room of Santiago's Biblioteca Nacional (see p.109). Another problem with the IGM maps is that footpaths are rarely marked. Instead, the best ones to use for **hiking** are the new series of JLM maps (📧jmattassi@interactiva.cl), which cover some of the main national parks and occasionally extend into neighbouring Argentina. They're produced in collaboration with Conaf and are available in bookshops and some souvenir or outdoor stores. In most cases, a general map is accompanied by detailed maps of particular areas within a region. The maps are usually contoured and have elevation tinting. Note that latitude and longitude information is indicated but ought to be treated with caution as errors have been detected.

An alternative set of trekking maps, primarily for the southern tip of the country, is available from the Argentinean cartographers **Zagier y Urruty**.

Map outlets

In the US and Canada

110 North Latitude US ℡336/369-4171, 🖳www.110nlatitude.com.

Book Passage 51 Tamal Vista Blvd, Corte Madera, CA 94925 and in the historic San Francisco Ferry Building ℡1-800/999-7909 or ℡415/927-0960, 🖳www.bookpassage.com.

Complete Traveller Bookstore 199 Madison Ave, New York, NY ℡212/685-9007, 🖳www.completetravellerbooks.com.

Distant Lands 56 S Raymond Ave, Pasadena, CA 91105 ℡1-800/310-3220, 🖳www.distantlands.com.

Elliot Bay Book Company 101 S Main St, Seattle, WA 98104 ℡1-800/962-5311, 🖳www.elliotbaybook.com.

Globe Corner Bookstore 28 Church St, Cambridge, MA 02138 ℡1-800/358-6013, 🖳www.globecorner.com.

Longitude Books 115 W 30th St, #1206, New York, NY 10001 ℡1-800/342-2164, 🖳www.longitudebooks.com.

Map Link 30 S La Patera Lane, Unit 5, Santa Barbara, CA 93117 ℡805/692-6777 or 1-800/962-1394, 🖳www.maplink.com.

Map Town 400 5 Ave SW #100, Calgary, AB T2P 0L6 ℡1-877/921-6277 or ℡403/266-2241, 🖳www.maptown.com.

Travel Bug Bookstore 3065 W Broadway, Vancouver, BC V6K 2G9 ℡604/737-1122, 🖳www.travelbugbooks.ca.

World of Maps 1235 Wellington St, Ottawa, ON K1Y 3A3 ℡1-800/214-8524, 🖳www.worldofmaps.com.

In the UK and Ireland

Stanfords 12–14 Long Acre, London WC2E 9LP ℡020/7836 1321, 🖳www.stanfords.co.uk. Also at 39 Spring Gardens, Manchester M2 2BG ℡0161/831 0250, and 29 Corn St, Bristol BS1 1HT ℡0117/929 9966.

Blackwell's Map Centre 50 Broad St, Oxford OX1 3BQ ℡01865/793 550, 🖳maps.blackwell.co.uk. Branches in Bristol, Cambridge, Cardiff, Leeds, Liverpool, Newcastle, Reading and Sheffield.

Easons Bookshop 40 Lower O'Connell St, Dublin 1 ℡01/858 3800, 🖳www.eason.ie, plus other branches around Ireland; call or check the website for details.

John Smith & Son Glasgow Caledonian University Bookshop, 70 Cowcaddens Rd, Glasgow G4 0BA ℡0141/332 8173, 🖳www.johnsmith.co.uk. For details of other branches in Scotland and England, call or check the website.

The Map Shop 30a Belvoir St, Leicester LE1 6QH ℡0116/247 1400, 🖳www.mapshopleicester.co.uk.

National Map Centre 22–24 Caxton St, London SW1H 0QU ℡020/7222 2466, 🖳www.mapstore.co.uk.

National Map Centre Ireland 34 Aungier St, Dublin 2 ℡01/476 0471, 🖳www.mapcentre.ie.

Ordnance Survey Ireland Phoenix Park, Dublin 8 ℡01/8025 300, 🖳www.irlgov.ie/osi.

Ordnance Survey of Northern Ireland Colby House, Stranmillis Ct, Belfast BT9 5BJ ℡028/9025 5755, 🖳www.osni.gov.uk.

The Travel Bookshop 13–15 Blenheim Crescent, London W11 2EE ℡020/7229 5260, 🖳www.thetravelbookshop.co.uk.

Traveller 55 Grey St, Newcastle-upon-Tyne NE1 6EF ℡0191/261 5622, 🖳www.newtraveller.com.

In Australia and New Zealand

Mapland (Australia) 372 Little Bourke St, Melbourne, Vic 3000 ℡03/9670 4383, 🖳www.mapland.com.au.

Map Shop (Australia) 6–10 Peel St, Adelaide, SA 5000 ℡08/8231 2033, 🖳www.mapshop.net.au.

Map World (Australia) 280 Pitt St, Sydney, NSW 2000 ☏ 02/9261 3601, ⓦ www.mapworld.not.au. Also at 900 Hay St, Perth, WA 6000 ☏ 08/9322 5733, 65 Northbourne Ave, Canberra, ACT 2601 ☏ 02/6230 4097.

Map World (New Zealand) 173 Gloucester St, Christchurch ☏ 0800/627 967, ⓦ www.mapworld.co.nz.

Insurance

You'd do well to take out an insurance policy before travelling to cover against theft, loss and illness or injury. Before paying for a new policy, however, it's worth checking whether you are already covered: some all-risks home insurance policies may cover your possessions when overseas, and many private medical schemes include cover when abroad. In Canada, provincial health plans usually provide partial cover for medical mishaps overseas, while holders of official student/teacher/youth cards in Canada and the US are entitled to meagre accident coverage and hospital in-patient benefits. Students will often find that their student health coverage extends during the vacations and for one term beyond the date of last enrolment.

After checking out the possibilities above, you might want to contact a specialist travel insurance company, or consider the travel insurance deal we offer (see box). A typical travel insurance policy usually provides cover for the loss of baggage, tickets and – up to a certain limit – cash or cheques, as well as cancellation or curtailment of your journey. Most of them exclude so-called dangerous sports unless an extra premium is paid: in Chile this can mean scuba-diving, whitewater rafting, windsurfing and trekking, though probably not kayaking or jeep safaris. Many policies can be chopped and changed to exclude coverage you don't need – for example, sickness and accident benefits can often be excluded or included at will. If you do take medical coverage, ascertain whether benefits will be paid as treatment proceeds or only after you return home,

Rough Guides travel insurance

Rough Guides has teamed up with Columbus Direct to offer you **travel insurance** that can be tailored to suit your needs.

Readers can choose from many different travel insurance products, including a low-cost **backpacker** option for long stays; a **short break** option for city getaways; a typical **holiday package** option; and many others. There are also annual **multi-trip** policies for those who travel regularly, with variable levels of cover available. Different sports and activities (trekking, skiing, etc) can be covered if required on most policies.

Rough Guides travel insurance is available to the residents of 36 different countries with different language options to choose from via our website – ⓦ www.roughguidesinsurance.com – where you can also purchase the insurance.

Alternatively, UK residents should call ☏ 0800/083 9507; US citizens ☏ 1-800/749-4922; Australians ☏ 1-300/669 999. All other nationalities should call ☏ +44 870/890 2843.

and if there is a 24-hour medical emergency number. When securing baggage cover, make sure that the per-article limit – typically under £500/$750 and sometimes as little as £250/$400 – will cover your most valuable possession. If you need to make a claim, you should keep receipts for medicines and medical treatment, and in the event you have anything stolen, you must obtain an official statement from the police.

Health

On the whole, Chile is a fairly risk-free country to travel in, as far as health problems are concerned. No inoculations are required, though you might want to consider a hepatitis-A jab, as a precaution. Check, too, that your tetanus boosters are up-to-date. Most travellers experience the occasional stomach upset while adjusting to unfamiliar micro-organisms in the food and water, however. Sun poisoning is also quite common, especially at high altitudes.

Pharmacies and hospitals

Chile is well endowed with **pharmacies** (*farmacias*) – in Santiago and other major cities, you'll find one on just about every street corner, and even smaller towns usually offer at least a handful to choose from. They're invariably stocked with a vast range of medicines, many of which can be purchased over the counter with no doctor's prescription; if you anticipate having to buy medication, make a note of its generic name, as brand names are likely to be different. If you need to see a doctor, your best bet is to make an appointment at the outpatient department of the nearest **hospital**, usually known as a *clínica*. The majority of *clínicas* are private, and expensive, so it's essential to ensure that your travel insurance provides good medical cover. An initial consultation will set you back around CH$15,000–20,000, and the cost of treatment can be astronomical. As with North American hospitals, you can pay for it by credit card, but make sure you get all the details you need to claim it back on your travel insurance.

Disease

Although it's highly unlikely that you'll contract any of the following diseases, it's important that you are, at least, aware of them, and take appropriate precautions where necessary. For up-to-date information on disease outbreaks, check the US Centers for Disease Control's website ⓦ www.cdc.gov.

Rabies, though only a remote risk, does exist in Chile. If you get bitten or scratched by a dog, you should seek medical attention *immediately*. The disease can be cured, but only through a series of stomach injections administered before the onset of symptoms, which can appear within 24 hours or lie dormant for months, and include irrational behaviour, fear of water and foaming at the mouth. There is a vaccine – a course of three injections that has to be started at least a month before departure – but it's expensive and doesn't prevent you from contracting rabies, though it does buy you time to get to hospital.

Cholera – transmitted through contaminated water – occasionally breaks out in rural areas, but tends to be very localized, restricted to communities living in poor conditions with inadequate sanitation facilities and limited access to health care. As a tourist, it's unlikely you'll go anywhere near these places, but if you suspect you're infected (symptoms include watery diarrhoea, explosive vomiting and fever) it's easy to treat, provided you get to a doctor immediately and keep drinking large quantities of bottled or boiled water. There's no point getting a cholera inoculation, as the cholera germ has become resistant to the vaccine, which is generally acknowledged to be worthless.

Hantavirus – a rare virus with a high fatality rate carried by long-tailed rats – has been around for years, but wasn't identified until 1993 in the Southwest US. It's now recognized to be a pan-American virus and has been monitored in Chile since 1995. Since then 273 cases have been recorded, of which 110 were fatal. Most of the cases were in rural areas of the south. In general there are about 60 cases of hantavirus infecton each year in Chile, about half of them fatal. After 25 cases broke out in 1997, the government mounted a massive public health campaign to control the spread of the disease, which is contracted by inhaling or swallowing dust contaminated with infected rats' faeces or urine, and whose symptoms include fever, headache, intestinal pain and acute respiratory problems.

Thanks to increased public awareness and a huge research programme carried out by the US Centers for Disease Control, hantavirus is not a serious threat in Chile, but as the disease is still incurable it pays to follow the Ministry of Health's guidelines. In short, if you're camping, always do so in areas free of rubbish, dense weeds or heaps of logs or firewood (places where rats tend to nest and breed); use a hermetically sealed tent with no holes in it; keep all food completely sealed and out of reach of rats; and don't leave unwashed dishes lying around. If you're renting a rustic *cabaña* that looks as if it hasn't been inhabited for a while, open all doors and windows and let it ventilate for thirty minutes before you occupy it, then check carefully for any signs of rat excrement (while covering your mouth with a handkerchief). If you find any, all surfaces should be sprayed with disinfectant, before being swept, dusted and aired – the virus does not survive on exposure to chlorine and sunlight.

HIV and AIDS are not widespread in Chile, and are mainly concentrated in the poorer suburbs of Santiago and Valparaíso, Chile's largest port. Condoms (*condónes*) are available in some supermarkets and pharmacies. In both state and private hospitals, all blood is screened and only disposable needles are used to give injections.

Food and water

In general, food is hygienically prepared in Chile, posing no threats to your health. Until recently, restaurants were prohibited from serving uncooked vegetables that grow at ground level (like lettuce and beetroot), because they were considered at risk of being irrigated with contaminated water. This ban has been lifted as the risk has been virtually eliminated. However, many people (particularly middle-class Santiago housewives) still take the precaution of disinfecting their raw vegetables at home with special products specifically designed for this purpose sold alongside fruit and vegetables in supermarkets. You may want to do likewise, but there's no need to go overboard, as the risk of buying contaminated food is extremely small. As long as you wash all fresh produce thoroughly, you shouldn't have any problems.

Shellfish, on the other hand, should be treated with the utmost caution. Every year, a handful of people die in Chile because they inadvertently eat bivalve shellfish contaminated by red tide, or *marea roja*, an alga which becomes toxic when the seawater temperature rises. The Chilean government monitors the presence of *marea roja* with extreme diligence and bans all commercial shellfish collection when the phenomenon occurs. There is little health risk when eating in restaurants or buying shellfish in markets, as these are regularly inspected by the health authorities, but it's extremely dangerous to collect shellfish for your own consumption unless you're absolutely certain that the area is free of red tide. Note that red tide affects *all* shellfish, cooked or uncooked.

Tap water almost everywhere is clean and safe, but can occasionally cause diarrhoea in unfamiliar stomachs. Most travellers prefer to avoid this by drinking bottled mineral water, which is widely available in restaurants, grocery stores and supermarkets. If you're travelling in remote areas, you may find that only well water or stored rainwater is available; it should be boiled for a minimum of five minutes (ten minutes at high altitudes) or treated with chemical sterilization tablets. The same applies to stream water that may have been contaminated by animals or humans.

Altitude sickness

Anyone travelling in Chile's northern **altiplano**, where altitudes commonly reach 4500m – or indeed anyone going higher than 3000m in the cordillera – needs to be aware of the risks of **altitude sickness**, locally known as *soroche* or *apunamiento*. This debilitating and sometimes dangerous condition is caused by the reduced atmospheric pressure and corresponding reduction in oxygen that occurs around 3000m above sea level. Basic symptoms include breathlessness, headaches, nausea and extreme tiredness, rather like a bad hangover. There's no way of predicting whether or not you'll be susceptible to the condition, which seems to strike quite randomly, affecting people differently from one ascent to another. You can, however, take steps to avoid it by ascending slowly and allowing yourself to acclimatize. In particular, don't be tempted to whizz straight up to the altiplano from sea level, but spend a night or two acclimatizing en route. You should also avoid alcohol and salt, and drink lots of water.

If you want to be really sure, you can also take a preventive drug called **acetazolamide** (125mg twice daily), starting a day before you ascend and continuing for a further three or four days. This effectively speeds up acclimatization, but has the added effect of making you urinate a lot, and produces a tingling sensation in your fingers and toes. You might prefer to carry it only as a precaution, as it also relieves symptoms once you've developed them at altitude. Though available over the counter in pharmacies in Santiago and the north, note that acetazolamide is in most countries a prescription-only drug, as it can be dangerous for people with heart conditions. If in doubt, stick to the bitter-tasting **coca leaves** chewed by most locals in the altiplano (where they're widely available at markets and village stores), to ease the headaches and sense of exhaustion.

Although extremely unpleasant, this basic form of altitude sickness is essentially harmless and passes after about 24 hours (if it doesn't, descend at least 500m). However, in its more serious forms, altitude sickness can be dangerous and even life-threatening. One to two percent of people travelling to 4000m develop **HAPO** (high altitude pulmonary oedema), caused by the build-up of liquid in the lungs. Symptoms include fever, an increased pulse rate, and coughing up white fluid; sufferers should descend immediately, whereupon recovery is usually quick and complete.

Rarer, but more serious, is **HACO** (high altitude cerebral oedema), which occurs when the brain gets waterlogged with fluid. Symptoms include loss of balance, severe lassitude, weakness or numbness on one side of the body and a confused mental state. If you or a fellow traveller display any of these symptoms, descend immediately and get to a doctor; HACO can be fatal within 24 hours.

Sunstroke

In many parts of Chile, **sunburn** and **dehydration** are major threats. They are obviously more of a problem in the excessively dry climate of the north, but even in the south of the country, it's easy to underestimate the strength of the summer sun. To prevent sunburn, take a high-factor sunscreen and wear a wide-brimmed hat. It's also essential to drink plenty of fluids before you go out, and always carry large quantities of water with you when you're hiking in the sun. As you lose a lot of salt when you sweat, add more to your food, or take a rehydration solution (if you don't have any, add half a teaspoonful of salt and four tablespoons of sugar to a litre of bottled water). Too much sun can often lead to diarrhoea, and it's always a good idea to carry an over-the-counter treatment like Imodium.

Hypothermia

Another potential enemy, especially at high altitudes and in Chile's far southern reaches, is **hypothermia.** Because early symptoms can include an almost euphoric sense of sleepiness and disorientation, your body's core temperature can plummet to danger level before you know what has happened. Chile's northern deserts have such clear air that it can drop to -20ºC (-4ºF) at night, which makes you very vulnerable to hypothermia while sleeping if proper precautions aren't taken. Patagonia's average summer temperatures of 15ºC (59ºF), with occasional highs of 28ºC

(82°F), can give a false sense of security in an area where it snows and rains without warning. Even in clear weather, winds can exceed 100kph and it only takes an inadvertent soaking while crossing a stream for the wind chill factor to induce hypothermia within a matter of minutes. Even if you're just going out for a short walk, be prepared for the worst the weather can throw at you and carry an emergency supply of high-energy food as well as a dry change of clothes. Always take suitable clothing and equipment if travelling in the desert or altiplano – down clothing and sleeping bags are ideal, as they pack up small and light during the heat of the day, but provide lots of warmth when you need it. Also, avoid camping alone – there's safety in numbers. If you get hypothermia, the best thing to do is take your clothes off and jump into a sleeping bag with someone else. This is absolutely serious – sharing another person's body heat is the most effective way of restoring your own. If you're alone, or have no willing partners, then get out of the wind and the rain, remove all wet or damp clothes, get dry, and drink plenty of hot fluids.

Medical resources for travellers

Websites

Ⓦ **www.cdc.gov/travel** US Department of Health and Human Services travel health and disease control department, listing precautions, diseases and preventive measures by region, as well as a summary of cruise ship sanitation levels.

Ⓦ **health.yahoo.com** Information on specific diseases and conditions, drugs and herbal remedies, as well as advice from health experts.

Ⓦ **www.cdc.gov/travel** The US government's official site for travel health.

Ⓦ **www.fitfortravel.scot.nhs.uk** Scottish NHS website carrying information about travel-related diseases and how to avoid them.

Ⓦ **www.istm.org** The website of the International Society for Travel Medicine, with a full list of clinics specializing in international travel health. Publishes outbreak warnings, suggested inoculations, precautions and other background information for travellers.

Ⓦ **www.tmvc.com.au** Contains a list of travel clinics in Australia, New Zealand and South Africa, plus general information on travel health, including information tailored to your destination.

Ⓦ **www.travelvax.net** Everything you ever wanted to know about diseases and vaccines.

In the US and Canada

Canadian Society for International Health 1 Nicholas St, Suite 1105, Ottawa, ON K1N 7B7 ☎613/241-5785, Ⓦwww.csih.org. The website has an extensive list of travel health centres across Canada.

Centers for Disease Control 1600 Clifton Rd NE, Atlanta, GA 30333 ☎1-800/311-3435 or 404/639-3534, Ⓦwww.cdc.gov. Publishes outbreak warnings, suggested inoculations, precautions and other background information for travellers. Useful website plus International Travelers Hotline on ☎1-877/FYI-TRIP.

International SOS Assistance 3600 Horizon Blvd, Suite 300, Trevose, PA 19053, USA 19053-6956 ☎1-800/523-8930, Ⓦwww.intsos.com. Members receive pre-trip medical referral info, as well as overseas emergency services designed to complement travel insurance coverage

MEDJET Assistance ☎1-800/963-3538 or ☎205/595-6626, Ⓦwww.medjetassistance.com. Annual membership program for travellers ($205 for individuals, $325 for families) that, in the event of illness or injury, will fly members home or to the hospital of their choice in a medically equipped and staffed jet.

Travel Medicine ☎1-800/872-8633, Ⓦwww .travmed.com. Sells first-aid kits, mosquito netting, water filters, reference books and other health-related travel products; there's a travel clinic directory, too.

In the UK and Ireland

British Airways Travel Clinics 213 Piccadilly, London W1J 9HQ (Mon–Fri 9.30am–5.30pm, Sat 10am–3.30pm, no appointment necessary; ☎0845/600 2236); 101 Cheapside, London EC2V 6DT (Mon–Fri 9am–4.30pm, appointment required; ☎0845/600 2236); Ⓦwww.britishairways.com /travel/healthclinintro/public/en_gb. Vaccinations, tailored advice from an online database and a complete range of travel healthcare products.

Dun Laoghaire Medical Centre 5 Northumberland Ave, Dun Laoghaire, County Dublin ☎01/280 4996, Ⓕ01/280 5603. Advice on medical matters abroad.

Hospital for Tropical Diseases Travel Clinic 2nd floor, Mortimer Market Centre, off Capper St, London WC1E 6AU (Mon–Fri 9am–5pm by appointment only; ☎020/7388 9600, Ⓦwww .thehtd.org; a consultation costs £15, which is waived if you have your injections or buy your malaria pills here). A recorded Health Line

43

(☏0906/133 7733; 50p per min) gives hints on hygiene and illness prevention as well as listing appropriate immunizations.

Liverpool School of Tropical Medicine Pembroke Place, Liverpool L3 5QA ☏0151/708 9393, ☜www.liv.ac.uk/lstm/about/TravelClinic .htm. Walk-in clinic Mon–Fri 9am–noon; appointment required for yellow fever, but not for other jabs.

MASTA (Medical Advisory Service for Travellers Abroad) Clinics around the UK (log on to ☜www.masta.org or call ☏0870/606 2782 for the nearest). Also sends out a health brief tailored to the country you are visiting and your standard of accommodation for £3.49, and operates a pre-recorded 24-hour Travellers' Health Line (UK ☏0906/550 1402, £1 per min), giving written information tailored to your journey by return of post.

Nomad Pharmacy surgeries: 52 Grosvenor Gardens, London SW1W 0AG; 40 Bernard St, London, WC1N 1LE; and 3-4 Wellington Terrace, Turnpike Lane, London N8 0PX (☏020/7833 4114 to book vaccination appointment). They give advice free if you go in person, or their telephone helpline is ☏0906/863 3414 (60p per minute). They can give information tailored to your travel needs.

Trailfinders Immunization clinic (no appointments necessary) at 194 Kensington High St, London W8 7RG (Mon–Fri 9am–5pm except Thurs to 6pm, Sat 10am–5.15pm; ☏020/7938 3999).

Travel Health Centre Department of International Health and Tropical Medicine, Royal College of Surgeons in Ireland, Mercers Medical Centre, Stephen's St Lower, Dublin 2 ☏01/402 2337. Expert pre-trip advice and inoculations.

Travel Medicine Services PO Box 254, 16 College St, Belfast BT1 6BT ☏028/9031 5220. Offers medical advice before a trip and help afterwards in the event of a tropical disease.

Tropical Medical Bureau Grafton Buildings, 34 Grafton St, Dublin 2, and fourteen other centres across the Republic, ☏1850/487 674, ☜www .tmb.ie.

In Australia and New Zealand

Travellers' Medical and Vaccination Centres 27–29 Gilbert Place, Adelaide, SA 5000 ☏08/8212 7522, ☜www.tmvc.com.au;1/170 Queen St, Auckland ☏09/373 3531; 5/247 Adelaide St, Brisbane, Qld 4000 ☏07/3221 9066; 5/8–10 Hobart Place, Canberra, ACT 2600 ☏02/6257 7156; 270 Sandy Bay Rd, Sandy Bay Tas, Hobart 7005 ☏03/6223 7577; 2/393 Little Bourke St, Melbourne, Vic 3000 ☏03/9602 5788; Level 7, Dymocks Bldg, 428 George St, Sydney, NSW 2000 ☏02/9221 7133; Shop 15, Grand Arcade, 14–16 Willis St, Wellington ☏04/473 0991.

Costs, money and banks

Chile has a strong, stable economy with hardly any inflation (the rate has been in the low single figures for years now). For many goods and services, prices are closer to those in Europe and North America than in neighbouring Andean countries such as Peru and Bolivia, but road transport and eating out are still far less expensive.

Basic costs

On the whole, Chile is an expensive country compared to most of the rest of South America. Typical **accommodation** prices are usually around US$15 per night for a bottom-end double room, US$40 for a mid-range double with private bath, and anything from US$70 and up per room in a smart, attractive hotel. **Eating** out can be pricey in the evening, especially in big cities and more sophisticated restaurants, but a typical beef steak and French fries plus mineral water in an ordinary local restaurant still only costs around US$7. You can save money by having the set lunch time menus offered in most restaurants, usually at very reasonable prices, though this can get rather repetitive after a while. Another way to keep the costs down is to eat in the fast-food outlets you'll find in most towns and cities.

US dollars

We've given prices in **US dollars** below, to help you get an idea of basic costs before you're familiar with the local currency. Note, however, that you'll use Chilean pesos to pay for just about everything in Chile, with the exception of some hotels that also accept US dollars.

Thankfully **transport** is still relatively inexpensive, with long-distance buses offering particularly good value – for instance, the 2000-kilometre-journey from Santiago to Arica costs around US$40. In general, then, you'll need to allow at least US$200 a week to get by on a tight budget; at least US$350 a week to live a little more comfortably, staying in mid-range hotels and eating in restaurants most days; and from US$700 a week to live in luxury, staying in the more upmarket hotels and eating in the best restaurants. For details on **tipping**, see the "Directory" on p.82.

Hidden costs: IVA

The most widespread hidden cost in Chile is the **IVA** (*Impuesto al Valor Agregado*), a tax of eighteen percent added to most goods and services. Although most prices include IVA, there are many irritating exceptions – some tourist shops, for instance, quote prices without IVA, and even some restaurants have a discreet "prices do not include IVA" at the bottom of their menu. Hotel rates sometimes include IVA and sometimes don't; as a tourist, you're supposed to be exempt from IVA if you pay for your accommodation in US dollars, but it's quite a complicated system – see p.53 for more details. Car rental is almost always quoted without IVA, which really jacks the end price up. If in doubt, you should always clarify whether a price quoted to you, from souvenirs to room rates, includes IVA.

Youth and student discounts

Once obtained, various official and quasi-official **youth/student ID cards** soon pay for themselves in savings. Full-time students are eligible for the International Student ID Card (ISIC, Ⓦwww.isiccard.com), which entitles the bearer to special air, rail and bus fares and discounts at museums, theatres and other attractions. For Americans there's also a health benefit, providing up to $3000 in emergency medical coverage and $100 a day for 60 days in the hospital, plus a 24-hour hotline to call in the event of a medical, legal or financial emergency. The card costs $22 for Americans; Can$16 for Canadians; AUS$16.50 for Australians; NZ$21 for New Zealanders; and £7 in the UK.

You only have to be 26 or younger to qualify for the **International Youth Travel Card**, which costs US$22/£7 and carries the same benefits. Teachers qualify for the **International Teacher Card**, offering similar discounts and costing US$22, Can$16, AUS$16.50 and NZ$21. All these cards are available in the US from Council Travel, STA, and Travel CUTS; in Canada from Hostelling International; in Australia and New Zealand from STA or Campus Travel; and in the UK from usit Campus and STA. (See pp.29–34 for contact information.)

Several other travel organizations and accommodation groups also sell their own cards, good for various discounts. A university photo ID might open some doors, but is not easily recognizable, as are the ISIC cards. However, the latter are often not accepted as valid proof of age, for example in bars or liquor stores.

Currency

The basic unit of currency is the **peso**, usually represented by the $ sign (and by **CH$** in this book, for clarity). Notes come in 500 (currently being phased out of circulation and replaced by a coin), 1000, 5000, 10,000 and 20,000 (rare) denominations, while coins come in 1 (rare), 5, 10, 50, 100 and 500 peso denominations. There's a chronic shortage of change in Chile, and trying to pay for something small with a CH$10,000 note (sometimes even a CH$5000 note) invariably results in the shopkeeper scurrying around, desperately trying to beg change from his neighbours. It's a good idea to break up these larger notes whenever you can – in big supermarkets and post offices, for instance – and keep a stock of loose change and small notes on you at all times. Many hotels, particularly the more expensive ones, accept US dollars cash (and will give you a discount for paying this way; see p.53). Apart from this, however, it's more common to pay for everything in **local currency**, and most places, including the majority of restaurants and shops, won't accept anything else. You may, however, come across prices quoted in the mysterious "UF". This stands for *unidad de fomento* and is an index-linked monetary unit that is adjusted (every minute) on a daily basis to remain in line with inflation. It's normally reserved for dealing with large sums of money, and the only time you're likely to come across it is if you rent a vehicle (your liability, in the event of an accident, will probably be quoted in UFs on the rental contract). You'll find the **exchange rate** of the UF against the Chilean peso in the daily newspapers, along with the rates for all the other currencies.

Travellers' cheques

You should have a back-up source of funds, preferably **travellers' cheques**. These should always be in US dollars, and though most brands are accepted, it's best to be on the safe side and take one of the main brands such as American Express, Citibank or Thomas Cook. You can't use them like cash and will have to change them in a **casa de cambio** (exchange bureau), usually for a small commission. Most *casas de cambio* are open from Monday through Friday between 9am and 5.30pm, usually closing for a couple of hours at lunchtime; some also open Saturday mornings. However, while there are numerous *casas de cambio* in Santiago, and usually one or two in the larger provincial cities, they're by no means in all towns and cities, which is fairly limiting. Note that it's normally either impossible or prohibitively expensive to change cash and travellers' cheques at **banks**.

The usual fee for travellers' cheque sales is one or two percent, though this fee may be waived if you buy the cheques through a bank where you have an account. It pays to get a selection of denominations. Make sure to keep the purchase agreement and a record of cheque serial numbers safe and separate from the cheques themselves. In the event that cheques are lost or stolen, the issuing company will expect you to report the loss forthwith to their office; most companies claim to replace lost or stolen cheques within 24 hours.

Credit and debit cards and ATMs

Credit cards can be used either in ATMs or over the counter. Mastercard, Visa and American Express are accepted just about everywhere, but other cards may not be recognized. Remember that all cash advances are treated as loans, with interest accruing daily from the date of withdrawal; there may be a transaction fee on top of this. However, you may be able to make withdrawals from ATMs in Chile using your debit card, which is not liable to interest payments, and the flat transaction fee is usually quite small – your bank will able to advise on this. Make sure you have a personal identification number (PIN) that's designed to work overseas.

A compromise between travellers' cheques and plastic is Visa TravelMoney, a disposable pre-paid debit card with a PIN that works in all ATMs that take Visa cards. You load up your account with funds before leaving home, and when they run out, you simply throw the card away. You can buy up to nine cards to access the same funds – useful for couples or families travelling together – and it's a good idea to buy at least one extra as a back-up in case of loss or theft. There is also a 24-hour toll-free customer assistance number (℡1230-020-2136 from Chile). The card is available in most countries from branches of Thomas Cook and Citicorp. For more information, check the Visa Travel-Money website at ⊛http://international.visa.com/ps/products/vtravelmoney/

Wiring money

Having money wired from home using one of the companies listed below is never convenient or cheap, and should be considered a last resort. It's also possible to have money wired directly from a bank in your home country to a bank in Chile, although this is somewhat less reliable because it involves two separate institutions. If you go this route, your home bank will need the address of the branch bank where you want to pick up the money and the address and telex number of the Santiago head office, which will act as the clearing house; money wired this way normally takes two working days to arrive, and costs around £25/$40 per transaction.

Money-wiring companies

Travelers Express/MoneyGram US ☏ 1-800/926-9400, Canada ☏ 1-800/933-3278, UK ☏ 00-800/8971 8971, Ireland and New Zealand ☏ 00-800/666 3947, Australia ☏ 0011-800/666 3947, ⓦ www.moneygram.com.
Western Union US and Canada ☏ 1-800/325 6000, UK ☏ 0800/833 833, Republic of Ireland ☏ 1800/395 395, Australia ☏ 1800/173 833, New Zealand ☏ 0800/005 253, ⓦ www.westernunion .com.

Getting around

Travelling in Chile is easy, comfortable and, compared to Europe or North America, inexpensive. Most of the population travels by bus, and it's such a reliable, affordable option that you'll probably do likewise. However, internal airlines, catering primarily to business passengers, are handy for covering long distances in a hurry and last-minute flights can be quite reasonable. The country has a good road network with a low volume of traffic away from the major towns, which makes driving a fast and relatively stress-free way of getting around. In recent years Chile's rail network has fallen into decline and only an ever-shrinking service operates south of Santiago. South of Puerto Montt there are limited ferry services that provide a slow but scenic way of travelling as far as Puerto Natales.

By air

Chile is a country of almost unimaginable distances (it's more than 5000km by road from Arica to Punta Arenas), which makes **flying** by far the quickest and most convenient way of taking in both its northern and southern regions in a single trip. Despite the limited competition between LAN and the other airlines that serve the country's numerous regional airports, scheduled fares are quite high, though you can find good promotions from time to time. In the past, travelling with airlines other than LAN was a bit risky, as they sometimes went bust unexpectedly, leaving thousands of passengers stranded – as happened in 2001 with AeroContinente.

Far and away the leading airline is **LAN/ Lan Express** (☏ 5262000, in regions ☏ 6005262000, in the US ☏ 1-800/735-5526; ⓦ www.lan.com), which besides offering the widest choice of domestic flights, is Chile's principal long-haul carrier and the only one with flights to Easter Island. The **special fares** for selected flights, available, with two- to three-days' notice through the LAN website, are exceptionally good value; a round-trip ticket from Santiago to Puerto Montt, for instance, can be as little as CH$35,000, compared to the normal fare of over CH$95,000 return. See p.27 for details of LAN's **Visit Chile air pass**, which can only be bought outside Chile.

With more limited routings but usually lower prices, reliable newcomers **Sky Airlines** and **Aerolíneas del Sur** (☏ 6006002828, US toll-free ☏ 1-866/501-4679; ⓦ www.internationalms.com/skyairline) offer welcome competition.

Air taxis and regional airlines operate regular services to smaller destinations between

Puerto Montt and Puerto Williams, but they are susceptible to weather delays and won't fly without a minimum number of passengers (usually six people). Two companies also fly out from Santiago to Isla Robinson Crusoe, 650km off the mainland – for more details, see p.579.

Main domestic airports

Antofagasta ℡ 55/269077
Arica ℡ 58/211116
Balmaceda ℡ 67/272104
Calama ℡ 55/342348
Copiapo ℡ 52/214080
Iquique ℡ 57/420037
La Serena ℡ 51/272652
Puerto Montt ℡ 65/252018
Punta Arenas ℡ 61/219131
Santiago ℡ 6019416
Temuco ℡ 45/337782
Isla de Pascua ℡ 32/100237

Getting into town

Getting between Chile's airports and its city centres is fast, hassle-free, and inexpensive. Most of the main airports have dedicated **bus services** into the centre, or **minibus transfers** that drop off passengers at their hotels (at a cost of around CH$4000). The smaller airports, without these services, are always well-stocked with taxis and tend to be only a few kilometres outside the city centre (with Puerto Montt being a notable exception), keeping the cost of a taxi ride down. Only Santiago has flights leaving and departing at really antisocial hours, served by 24-hour minibus transfers.

By bus

Chile's long-distance **buses** offer an excellent service, far better than their European or North American counterparts – thanks mainly to the enormous amount of legroom, frequent departures and flexible itineraries – you can stop a bus at nearly any point of the route. Facilities depend less on individual companies than on the class of bus you travel on, with prices rising according to comfort level. A **pullman** (not to be confused with the large bus company of the same name) or **clásico** contains standard semi-reclining seats; a **semicama** has seats with twice the amount of legroom and that recline

a good deal more; and a **salon cama**, at the top of the luxury range, has wide seats (just three to a row) that recline to an almost horizontal position à la first class on an airplane. Most companies offer a choice of all three types of bus, particularly on their longer journeys. All buses have chemical toilets and most supply food at the stops and soft drinks during the ride. Some overnight services include meals or snacks, while others stop at restaurants where set meals might be included in the ticket price. Videos, piped music and bingo games are also common in-transit attractions (or irritations). Check out the locations of video screens first and sit yourself appropriately.

Thanks to the intense competition and price wars waged between the multitude of bus companies, **fares** are extremely low. As a rule of thumb, reckon on CH$1000 per hour travelled on standard inter-city buses, CH$800 per hour on local routes and at least CH$1500 per hour in the luxury long-distance buses. It always pays to compare fares offered by the different companies serving your destination, as you'll almost certainly find one offering a special deal. This price comparing is easily done at the **central terminal** used by long-distance buses in most cities, where you'll find separate booking offices for each company (though Tur Bus and Pullman Bus, the two largest companies, often have their own separate terminals close to the main terminal). Some towns, however, don't have a central terminal, in which case buses leave from their company offices, which are normally clustered in the town centre.

Owing to the popularity of bus travel, you should try to buy your ticket at least a few hours in advance, and preferably the day before travelling, especially if you plan to travel on a Friday. An added advantage of buying ahead is that you'll be able to choose a seat away from the toilets, either by the aisle or window and, more importantly, the side of the bus you sit on. Even with air conditioning, seats on the sunny side can get extremely hot, and you may find yourself peeking at the scenery through a curtain. There is little reason to buy a round-trip ticket unless you are travelling at peak season. The price is rarely different, and even when you have a return portion, you should go to the bus counter to reconfirm your seat.

When it comes to **boarding**, make sure that the departure time written on your ticket corresponds exactly to the time indicated on the little clock on the bus's front window, as your ticket is valid only on the bus it was booked for. Your luggage will be safely stored in lockers under the bus and the conductor will issue you a numbered stub for each article. Soon after departure – and while Chilean buses do not always leave punctually, you should never bank on a late departure – the conductor will check your ticket and leave you with a stub that must be kept until the end of your journey.

Be warned that if you're travelling north of Santiago on a long-distance route, or crossing an international border, the bus and all luggage may be searched by Ministry of Agriculture officials at checkpoints (often at regional frontiers or major junctions), and all sandwiches, fresh fruit and vegetables will be destroyed – while you stand waiting, even in the cold night air.

Local buses, colectivos and taxis

Local buses, often called *micros*, connect city centres with residential outskirts, and with nearby villages. These buses are often packed, and travelling with a large rucksack can be a problem, particularly if your journey coincides with students going to or from college, or with market day. Buses sticking to the confines of the town or city usually drive up and down the principal thoroughfares, and around the central square – the main points of the route and final destination are displayed on the inside of the front window, but it always helps to carry a street map and be able to point to your intended destination. Buses that leave the city for the countryside normally depart from their own *terminal rural*, which is usually next door or close to the Mercado Municipal (market building).

For some journeys, a faster alternative is provided by **colectivos**, which are shared taxis operating along a set route with fixed fares, normally only slightly more expensive than the local buses. Most *colectivos* look exactly like normal taxis (apart from being all black, not black and yellow) and have their route or final destination marked on a board on the roof, but in some cities, *colectivo* services are operated by bright yellow cars, often without a roof-board.

Taxis are normally black with a yellow roof, and in the bigger cities can be flagged down quickly on the street. Alternatively, you can usually find them on or near the central square, as well as outside bus terminals and train stations. As Chilean taxi drivers are often eager to charge foreigners too much, it's worth checking to see that the meter has been turned on before you start a journey and, if possible in Spanish, get an estimate for the fare to the nearest 500 pesos. Fares are clearly shown in the windscreen – but there is no limit to what the driver can charge, as long as it corresponds to the advertised price. Nearly all taxis will have similar signs – one saying 150 pesos (which is the starting price) and another saying 80 or 90 pesos, the fee per 200 metre increments. At tourist hotels beware of taxis that put two signs for 150 in the window and thus charge double.

By car

While Chile's towns and cities are linked by plenty of buses, most visitors are here for the country's wilderness areas, which are often difficult, and sometimes impossible, to reach on public transport. Many remote attractions are visited by tour companies operating out of the nearest major city, but for more independence, your best bet is to **rent a vehicle.** To do this, you need to be at least 21 years old and have a major credit card so you can leave a blank voucher as a guarantee. You're allowed to use your national driver's licence, but you're strongly advised to bring, in addition, an **international licence.** Chile's *carabineros* (police officers), who frequently stop drivers to check their documents, are often suspicious of unfamiliar foreign licences and are always happier when dealing with international ones. Traffic regulations in Chile are rarely enforced, except for speeding on the highways. The **speed limit** is 50km per hour or less in urban areas and 100km per hour on highways, and radar speed traps are commonplace. If an oncoming vehicle flashes its headlights, you're being warned of *carabineros* lurking ahead. If you do get pulled over, exercise the utmost courtesy and patience, and under no circumstances do or say anything which could possibly be interpreted as bribery (see also p.81).

Rental outlets and costs

Several international car-rental companies have offices throughout Chile, including Hertz, Avis, Budget and First. In addition to these, you'll find an abundance of local outlets which are often, but by no means always, less expensive than the international firms. The cost of car rental is much higher in Chile than in North America, and more on a par with European prices. Rates can vary quite a lot from one company to another, and it's always worth phoning as many as possible to compare prices. Basic **saloon cars** go from around US$350 to US$450 per week, while a 4WD **jeep** or **pick-up** truck can cost anything from US$500 to US$800-plus per week (less for non-4WD). Most outlets have lower rates if you're renting for a month or longer. Make sure that the price they quote includes IVA (the 18-percent Chilean value added tax), insurance and unlimited mileage. Your rental contract will almost certainly be in (legal and convoluted) Spanish – get the company to take you through it and explain everything. In most cases your liability, in the event of an accident, is normally around the US$500 mark (it'll be quoted in UFs; see p.46) and costs over this amount will be covered in total by the company.

Car rental agencies abroad

In the US and Canada

Avis US ☎1-800/230-4898, Canada ☎1-800/272-5871, ⓦ www.avis.com.
Budget US ☎1-800/527-0700, Canada ☎1-800/472-3325, ⓦ www.budget.com.
Dollar US ☎1-800/800-3665, ⓦ www.dollar.com.
Hertz US ☎1-800/654-3001, Canada ☎1-800/263-0600, ⓦ www.hertz.com.
National ☎1-800/962-7070, ⓦ www.nationalcar.com.

In the UK

Avis ☎0870/606 0100, ⓦ www.avis.co.uk.
Budget ☎0800/973 159, ⓦ www.budget.co.uk.
Hertz ☎0870/844 8844, ⓦ www.hertz.co.uk.

In Ireland

Avis Northern Ireland ☎028/902 40404, Republic of Ireland ☎021/428 1111, ⓦ www.avis.ie.
Budget Republic of Ireland ☎09/0662 7711, ⓦ www.budget.ie.
Hertz Republic of Ireland ☎01/676 7476, ⓦ www.hertz.ie.

In Australia

Avis ☎13 63 33 or 02/9353 9000, ⓦ www.avis.com.au.
Hertz ☎13 30 39 or 03/9698 2555, ⓦ www.hertz.com.au.

In New Zealand

Avis ☎09/526 2847 or 0800/655 111, ⓦ www.avis.co.nz.
Hertz ☎0800/654 321, ⓦ www.hertz.co.nz.

Motoring organizations

In the US and Canada

AAA ☎1-800/AAA-HELP, ⓦ www.aaa.com. Each state has its own club – check the phone book for local address and phone number.
CAA ☎613/247-0117, ⓦ www.caa.ca. Each region has its own club – check the phone book for local address and phone number.

In the UK and Ireland

AA UK ☎0870/600 0371, ⓦ www.theaa.com.
AA Ireland Dublin ☎01/617 9999, ⓦ www.aaireland.ie.
RAC UK ☎0800/550 055, ⓦ www.rac.co.uk.

In Australia and New Zealand

AAA Australia ☎02/6247 7311, ⓦ www.aaa.asn.au.
New Zealand AA New Zealand ☎0800/500 444, ⓦ www.nzaa.co.nz.

Driving in towns

Just about all Chilean towns are laid out on a grid plan, which makes navigating them pretty easy. However, the country is obsessed with **one-way traffic** systems, and you'll find that many streets in even the smallest towns are one-way only, the direction of traffic alternating with each successive street. The direction is usually indicated by a white arrow above the street name on each corner; if in doubt, look at the direction of the parked cars. **Parking** is normally allowed on most downtown streets (but on one side only), and around the Plaza de Armas (central square). You'll invariably be guided into a space by a wildly gesticulating *cuidador de autos* – a boy or young man who will offer to look after your car (quite unnecessarily) in return for a tip, normally of a couple of hundred pesos or so. In larger towns there's a small half-hourly charge for parking on the street, administered by eagle-eyed traffic wardens who slip tickets under your wipers every thirty minutes then pounce on you to collect your money before you leave (a small tip is expected, too). If you can't find a space to park in, keep a look out for large *"estacionamiento"* signs by the pavement, indicating private car parks, normally at around CH$500–600 an hour.

Driving on highways

The Panamerican highway, which runs through Chile from the Peruvian border to the southern tip of Chiloé, is known alternately as *Ruta 5, la Panamericana*, or *el longitudinal*, with *sur* (south) or *norte* (north) often added on to indicate which side of Santiago it's on. Thanks to a multi-billion dollar modernization project, it is quickly becoming a divided highway, with two lanes in each direction and a toll booth every 30km. This is undoubtedly a major improvement over most single-lane highways in Chile, which are prone to head-on collisions involving buses and trucks.

Backcountry and altiplano driving

You'll probably find that many places you want to get to are reached by dirt road, for which it's essential to rent a suitable vehicle, namely a **jeep** or **pick-up truck.** On regular dirt roads you rarely need a 4WD vehicle. The 2WD Chevrolet Luv pick-up is manufactured in Chile, and there are thousands of these trucks for rent and parts are readily available. For **altiplano driving**, however, you should pay extra to have 4WD (with the sturdiest tyres and highest clearance), as you can come across some dreadful roads, hundreds of kilometres from the nearest town. Make sure, too, that you take two spare tyres, not one, and that you always carry a funnel or tube for siphoning, and more than enough petrol. (Work it out

yourself then add lots – don't rely on what they say in the rental shop). Also pick up several 5-litre water jugs for a driving trip in the altiplano – it may be necessary for either the passengers or the engine at some point. It can be difficult to navigate in the altiplano, with so much open space and so few landmarks – a good tip is to make a careful note of your kilometre reading as you go along, so you can chart your progress over long roads with few markers. A compass is also helpful. Despite this tone of caution, it has to be emphasized that altiplano driving is among the most rewarding adventures that Chile offers.

Finally, a general point on **tyre punctures.** This is such a common occurrence in Chile that even the smallest towns have special workshops (bearing signs with a tyre painted white) where they are quickly and cheaply repaired.

Hitching

While we don't recommend hitching as a safe way of getting about, there's no denying that it's widely practised by Chileans themselves. In the summer it seems as though all the students in Chile are sitting beside the road with their thumb out, and in rural areas it's not uncommon for entire families to hitch a lift whenever they need to get into town. For backpackers, the large number of pick-up trucks on the road means there's a better chance than normal of being given a lift, as these vehicles have plenty of room to ditch your packs (and yourselves) in the back. Overseas tourists are much more likely to be given a lift if they identify themselves as such, as nearly everyone in Chile can trace their ancestry back to one European country or another, and many are keen to share their heritage with visitors from the fatherland. In general, you'll have a much better chance of getting a lift on a quiet rural road than on the Panamericana, where no one wants to stop for fear of being overtaken by slow-moving lorries. On the Panamericana, your best bet is to get a lift from someone parked at a busy *servicentro* (fast-food/petrol station complex).

By ferry

South of Puerto Montt, where the mainland breaks up into an archipelago, a network of ferries operates through the fjords, inlets and channels of Chile's far south, providing a far more scenic and romantic alternative to flights and long-distance buses. Two ferries in particular are very popular with tourists: one from Puerto Montt to Chacabuco and the San Raphael glacier, the other between Puerto Montt and Puerto Natales. The two main ferry companies are **Navimag** and **CTP**, both privately run. Both companies' ships transport cargo, vehicles and passengers, and are functional rather than luxurious. In addition to these two main routes, there are ferry links with Quellón on Chiloé, and with Chaitén, on the Carretera Austral, as well as a number of shorter routes forming a bridge along various points of the Carretera Austral (full details given on pp.448–449). There's also a ferry trip across Lago Todos Los Santos, in the Lake District, connecting Petrohué with Peulla, near the Argentine border, operated by **Andina del Sud** (see below and p.401).

Ferry companies

Andina del Sud Varas 437, Puerto Montt ℡ 65/257797, ℻ 270035; Del Salvador 72, Puerto Varas ℡ 65/232811, ℻ 232511.
Navimag ⓦ www.australis.com. Angelmo 2187, Puerto Montt ℡ 65/432300, ℻ 276611; Puerto Montt 262, Puerto Natales ℡ 61/414300, ℻ 414361; Av Independencia 830, Punta Arenas ℡ 61/200200, ℻ 225804; Av El Bosque Norte 0440, 11th floor, Santiago ℡ 4423120, ℻ 2035025.
TransMarChilay ℡ 6006008687, ⓦ www .transmarchilay.cl. 21 de Mayo 417, 2nd floor, Coyhaique ℡ 67/231971, ℻ 232700; Angelmo 2187, Puerto Montt ℡ 65/270411, ℻ 270415; Av Providencia 2653 local 24, Santiago ℡ 6006008688.

Main ferry routes

Petrohué–Peulla, across Lago Todos Los Santos Five hours; daily crossings (year-round) with Andina del Sud. See p.401.
Puerto Montt–Chacabuco: Twenty-four hours; one sailing per week with Navimag (year-round) and TransMarChilay (year-round). See p.408 and p.470.
Puerto Montt–Chacabuco–Laguna San Rafael: Five days, four nights (returning to Puerto Montt); one sailing per week with Navimag (year-round) and two, three or four with TransMarChilay (year-round). See p.408 and p.471.
Puerto Montt–Chaitén: Ten hours; one sailing per week with Navimag (Jan–Feb); three or four per week with TransMarChilay (year-round). See p.408 and p.456.
Puerto Montt–Puerto Natales: Four days, three nights; one sailing per week with Navimag (year-round). See p.408 and p.507.
Quellon–Chaitén: Five hours; three sailings per week with Navimag (Jan–Feb). See p.440 and p.456.

By train

Some fifty years ago, Chile possessed a huge network of **railways**, particularly in the far north where hundreds of kilometres of lines transported the region's nitrate ore down to the ports to be shipped abroad. Now that the nitrate days are over, no national railway lines operate north of Santiago, and what lines are left south of the capital are in ramshackle condition, unable to compete with the speed, low fares and punctuality offered by buses. Today only three daily trains pull out of Santiago's grand Estación Central, heading for Chillàn, Concepción and Temuco. The daytime trains offer two standards of compartment – *economía* and *salón* – while the overnight trains to Temuco and Concepción offer the added choice of *cama* and *dormitorio*, the latter in two-berth cabins in a classic 1920s carriage.

Accommodation

On the whole, the standard of accommodation in Chile is not that great and many visitors feel that prices are high for what you get, especially in mid- and upper-range hotels. Bottom-end accommodation starts at around US$15 for a double room, while you'll have to pay around US$40 for a double room with private bath in a decent mid-range hotel, and anything from US$70 for a smart, upmarket hotel. There's usually a wide range to choose from in the major tourist centres and the cities on the Panamericana, but in more remote areas you'll invariably have to make do with basic hospedajes (modest rooms, often in family homes). Most places include a small breakfast – bread roll, jam and instant coffee – in the price of the room, but you shouldn't always count on this, as some will charge extra for breakfast, and others won't serve it at all.

Note that the price of accommodation in the main tourist centres increases dramatically in **high season** – January and February – particularly in seaside resorts, where it can as much as double. Outside high season it's always worth trying to negotiate a discount, wherever you are. A simple *"¿tiene algo un poco màs economico?"* ("do you have anything a little cheaper?") or *"¿me puede dar un discuento?"* ("could you give me a discount?") will often get you a lower price on the spot. It's rarely necessary to make **reservations**, unless you've got your heart set on a particular hotel or *residencial*, in which case it can be a good idea to phone a few days in advance – especially if you plan to stay at the weekend, even more so if it's within striking distance of Santiago.

Note that room rates are supposed to be quoted inclusive of IVA (a Chilean goods and services tax of 18 percent), but you should always check beforehand (*¿está incluido el iva?*). Many mid- and most upper-range hotels give you the opportunity to pay for your accommodation in US dollars (with credit card), which exempts you from paying IVA. However, hotels are not eager to offer this discount – they need to be reminded forcefully. Often, though, if they can't take off IVA, they'll offer you a discount of ten percent if you pay cash.

Hotels

Chilean hotels are given a one- to five-star rating by Sernatur (the national tourist board), but this only reflects facilities and not standards, which vary widely from hotel to hotel. In

---

Accommodation price codes

Prices are for the cheapest **double room** in high season. In lodging places at the lower end of the scale, **single travellers** can expect to pay half this rate, but mid- and upper-range hotels usually charge the same for a single as for a double. Note that the price of accommodation in many tourist centres drops significantly outside January and February. Rough US equivalents are given according to the exchange rates around the time of publication.

❶ less than CH$5000 (~less than US$9)
❷ CH$5000–10,000 (~US$9–18)
❸ CH$10,000–15,000 (~US$18–28)
❹ CH$15,000–25,000 (~US$28–46)
❺ CH$25,000–35,000 (~US$46–65)
❻ CH$35,000–50,000 (~US$65–93)
❼ CH$50,000–75,000 (~US$93–140)
❽ CH$75,000–150,000 (~US$140-280)
❾ CH$150,000 and up (~US$280 and up)

practice, then, a three-star hotel could be far more attractive and comfortable than a four-star and even a five-star hotel; the only way to tell is to go and have a look, as even the room rates aren't a reliable indication of quality.

In general, **mid-range hotels** fall into two main categories: large, old houses with spacious, but sometimes tired, rooms; and modern, purpose-built hotels, usually with smaller rooms, no common areas and better facilities. You'll always get a private bathroom with a shower (rarely a bath), hot water and towels, and either an ancient colour TV or cable TV with dozens of English-language channels. As the price creeps up there's usually an improvement in decor and space, and at the upper end of the price range you can expect room service, a mini bar (*frigobar*), a private safe, a hotel restaurant, private parking and sometimes a swimming pool. The standards of **upmarket hotels** can still vary quite dramatically, however – ranging from stylish, contemporary city hotels or charming haciendas to grim, impersonal monoliths catering for businessmen. Finally, a word of note on **motels**, which are usually not economical roadside hotels, but places where couples go to have sex. Motel rooms are rented for three hours at very reasonable rates. Though you may get a few strange stares showing up with your backpack, they are a cheap and usually perfectly safe escape for a few hours.

Residenciales

Residenciales are the most widely available, and widely used, accommodation option in Chile. As with hotels, standards can vary enormously, but in general *residenciales* offer simple, modestly furnished rooms, usually off a corridor in the main house, or else in a row arranged around the backyard or patio. They usually contain little more than a bed (or up to four single beds), a rail for hanging clothes and a bedside table and lamp, though some provide additional furniture (perhaps a writing desk and chair) and a few more comforts such as a TV or a thermos for making tea or coffee. Most, but not all, have shared baths – note that you'll usually have to light the water heater (*calefon*) to get hot water each time you take a shower. Where places differ is in the upkeep or "freshness" of the rooms:

some of the really cheap rooms are dank and damp, with peeling paint and saggy beds, while others, though still very simple, have good bed linen, walls that are painted every summer, and a clean, swept, feel to them. Some of the slightly more expensive *residenciales* are very pleasant, particularly the large, nineteenth-century houses with waxed wooden floorboards and floor-to-ceiling windows that open onto balconies. While some *residenciales* cater exclusively to tourists, many, especially in the mining towns of the north, fill mainly with workmen, so you can't always expect to meet fellow travellers where you're staying.

Hospedajes and casas de familia

The distinction between a *residencial* and an *hospedaje* or *casa de familia* is often blurred. On the whole, the term **hospedaje** implies something rather modest, along the lines of the cheaper *residenciales*, while a **casa de familia** (or *casa familiar*) offers, as you'd expect, rooms inside a family home – sometimes just four or five rooms left vacant by grown-up children, other times in an extension added onto the main house. It's nothing like staying with a family, however, and the relationship between the guest and the owner is no different from that in a *residencial*. *Casas de familia* don't normally have a sign at the door, and if they do it usually just says "*Alojamiento*" ("lodging"); more commonly, members of the family might go and meet tourists at the bus station, handing out photocopied fliers or cards. These places are perfectly safe and you shouldn't worry about checking them out, though it's always wise to see a room before committing yourself to staying there. Sometimes you'll find details of *casas de familia* at tourist offices, as well; the one in Valparaíso hands out a long printed list of them.

Cabañas

Cabañas are very popular in Chile, and you'll find them in tourist spots up and down the country, particularly by the coast. They are basically holiday chalets and are geared towards families, usually with a fully equipped kitchen area, a sitting/dining area, one double bedroom and a second bedroom with bunks. They range from the very rustic to the distinctly grand, complete with daily maid service. They're often quite expensive at full rate (at least US$60) and the price is normally the same for two people as it is for four. That said, as they're used predominantly by Chileans, their popularity tends to be limited to January and February and sunny weekends, and outside these times demand is so low that you can normally get a very good discount. If there are just two of you, you have a particularly strong case for arguing the price down. Many *cabañas* are in superb locations, right by the ocean, and it can be wonderfully relaxing to self-cater for a few days in the off-season – cooking the fresh fish you bought in the local market and sipping your cabernet on the veranda looking out to sea.

Refugios

Many of the ranger stations in the national parks have a limited number of bunk beds available for tourists, at a charge of around US$8 per person. Known as **refugios**, these places are very rustic – often a small, wooden hut – but they usually have flushable toilets, hot running water, clean sheets and heavy woollen blankets. Some of them, such as those at the Salar de Surire and Lago Chungará, are in stunning locations; conditions in these places can be very inhospitable, however, and there's no doubt that a *refugio* offers a good deal more comfort and shelter than camping. Most *refugios* are open year-round, but if you're travelling in winter or other extreme weather conditions it's best to check with the regional forestry (Conaf) office in advance. While you're there, you can reserve beds in the *refugio*, as the Conaf staff will radio their colleagues and let them know when you're arriving. This is highly advisable if you're relying solely on the *refugio* for accommodation, but if you're travelling with a tent as a back-up, it's not really necessary to book ahead.

Hostels

Hostels are increasingly banding together to provide a link among Chile's major cities. What was until recently a score of isolated bargain spots is now starting to resemble a highly developed hostelling operation such as the one, for example, in New Zealand.

Unfortunately, news on the ground tends to be word of mouth, as new spots are being organized monthly – usually by Europeans who have travelled the world and are now seeing the business and personal opportunities in becoming a hostel owner in Chile. For the latest updates, the best information is found on the **Web**. Try one of the major search engines like Google, type in "hostelling and Chile", and then start sorting your way through the increasing number of options.

Hostels in Chile also tend to be among the best informal networks for information about **day-trips**. The hostels are often closely linked to local outdoor guides, horse trekking operations or local fishermen only too glad to rent their equipment for a modest fee.

Youth hostel associations

In the US

Hostelling International-American Youth Hostels ☎301/495-1240, ⊛www.hiayh.org. Annual membership for adults (18–55) is $28, for seniors (55 or over) is $18, and for under-18s and groups of ten or more, is free. Life memberships are $250.

In Canada

Hostelling International Canada ☎1-800/663 5777 or 613/237 7884, ⊛www.hihostels.ca. Rather than sell the traditional 1- or 2-year memberships, the association now sells one Individual Adult membership with a 28- to 16-month term. The length of the term depends on when the membership is sold, but a member can receive up to 28 months of membership for just $35+tax. Membership is free for under-18s and you can become a lifetime member for $175.

In England and Wales

Youth Hostel Association (YHA) ☎0870/770 8868, ⊛www.yha.org.uk. Annual membership £13.50; under-26s £10; lifetime £200.

In Scotland

Scottish Youth Hostel Association ☎01786/891 400. ⊛www.syha.org.uk. Annual membership £6, for under-18s £2.50; lifetime £60.

In Ireland

Irish Youth Hostel Association ☎01/830 4555, ⊛www.irelandyha.org. Annual membership €20; under-18s €10; family €40; lifetime €100.

In Northern Ireland

Hostelling International Northern Ireland
☎ 028/9032 4733, ⊛ www.hini.org.uk. Adult membership £13; under-18s £6; family £25; life £75.

In Australia

Australia Youth Hostels Association ☎ 02/9261 1111, ⊛ www.yha.com.au. Adult membership rate AUS$52 (under-18s, AUS$19) for the first twelve months and then AUS$37 each year after.

In New Zealand

Youth Hostelling Association New Zealand ☎ 0800/278 299 or 03/379 9970, ⊛ www.yha .co.nz. Adult membership NZ$40 for one year, NZ$60 for two and NZ$80 for three; under-18s free; lifetime NZ$300.

Camping

There are plenty of opportunities for **camping** in Chile, though it's not always the cheapest way to sleep. If you plan to do a lot of camping, equip yourself with the annual **camping guide** published by Turistel, which has details of every campsite in Chile. Published only in Spanish, this guide is titled *Turistel Rutero Camping* and has maps, prices and information. Even those who don't speak Spanish will find plenty of helpful information, ranging from trail maps to cabins. Official campsites range from plots of land with minimal facilities to swanky grounds with hot showers and private barbecue grills. The latter, often part of holiday complexes in seaside resorts, can be very expensive (around CH$15,000), and are usually only open between December and March.

It's also possible to camp **wild** in the countryside, but you'll really need your own transport if you plan to do this in remote areas. You should also bear in mind that most national parks don't allow camping outside designated areas, to protect the environment. Instead they tend to have either rustic camping areas administered by Conaf (very common in northern Chile), costing about CH$5,000 per tent, or else smart, expensive sites run by concessionaires (more common in the south) that charge about CH$20,000 for two to four people. As for **beaches**, some turn into informal, spontaneously erected campsites in the summer months; on others, camping is strictly forbidden and you'll be moved on by *carabineros* if you try. If you do end up camping wild on the beach or in the countryside, do bury or pack up your excrement, and take all your refuse with you when you leave. Note that butane gas and sometimes Camping Gaz are available in hardware shops in most towns and cities. If your stove takes white gas, you need to buy *bencina blanca*, which you'll find either in hardware stores or, more commonly, in pharmacies.

For details of **camping in Chiles's national parks**, see p.76.

Selecting a stove

If you plan to camp in Chile, an important consideration is the type of **stove** you bring. The best sort is probably the basic Camping Gaz model, as butane cylinders are widely available in hardware stores (*ferreterías*) and general stores in most Chilean cities, and there's less that can go wrong with them, though butane gas can fail or burn low at high altitudes. White gas (*bencina blanca*) is more difficult to come by, though it's often available in hardware shops and supermarkets. Stoves that take unleaded petrol are liable to clog up with impurities contained in Chilean petrol, so you should always carry spare parts with you. Multi-fuel stoves are a good alternative, though, again, always carry a couple of spare generators in case of clogging.

Eating and drinking

Chile boasts a vast range of quality raw produce, but many restaurants lack imagination, offering the same limited menu of fried chicken, boiled beef and fried fish, usually served with chips or mashed potatoes. That's not to say, however, that you can't eat well in Chile. One notable exception to the general dreariness of Chilean restaurant food is the country's superb fish and seafood. Other alternatives include the various traditional dishes, often called comida típica or comida criolla, still served in old-fashioned, family-oriented restaurants known as picadas. Furthermore, most cities have a couple of upmarket "international" restaurants, where the staple meats and fishes are prepared more elaborately and imaginatively, with varying degrees of success.

On the whole, eating out in Chile tends to be very inexpensive. In simple, local restaurants you can expect to pay around CH$3000–5000 for standard main courses. If you're aiming to keep costs way down, you can resort to the many **fast-food outlets** spread throughout the country, specializing in hot dogs, burgers and cheap pizzas. You could also head for the **municipal markets** found in most towns; besides offering an abundance of cheap, fresh produce, they are usually dotted with stalls selling basic bargain meals of soup or fried meat and rice. The best trick is to join the Chileans and make your main meal of the day **lunch**, when many restaurants offer a fixed-price menú del día. It is always much better value than the à la carte options. Many travellers only figure this out after several weeks of over-spending. Learn how to ask for the "menu", and the same food is instantly available for half price.

As for the other meals of the day, **breakfast** at most residenciales and hotels is usually a disappointing affair of toasted rolls, jam and tea or coffee, though if your hosts are inclined to pamper you, this will be accompanied by ham, cheese and cake. The great tradition of **onces** – literally "elevenses" but served, like afternoon tea, around 5 o'clock – is a light snack consisting of bread, ham, cheese and biscuits when taken at home, or huge fruit tarts and cakes when out in a salon de té. Except during annual holidays or at weekends, relatively few Chileans go out to dinner, which leaves most restaurants very quiet through the week.

Note, also, that most places don't open before 8 or 9pm for dinner.

Fish and seafood

Chile's **fish** and **seafood** rank among the best in the world. To sample the freshest offerings, head to one of the many **marisquerías** (fish restaurants), particularly those along the coasts of the Litoral Central and Norte Chico. For more on Chile's wide impressive variety of seafood, see the "Food and drink specialities" colour insert.

A note of caution: you should never collect shellfish from the beach to eat unless you know for sure that the area is free of red tide, an alga that makes shellfish toxic, causing death within a few hours of consumption (see p.41). There is little danger of eating shellfish contaminated by red tide in restaurants.

Meat dishes

Chileans are also tremendous carnivores, with **beef** featuring prominently on most restaurant menus and family dinner tables. The summertime **asado** (barbecue) is a national institution, giving Chilean men, who normally never lift a fork in the kitchen, the chance to roll up their sleeves and demonstrate their culinary prowess. Always slow, leisurely affairs, accompanied by lots of Chilean wine, asados take place not only in back gardens, but also in specially equipped picnic areas that fill to bursting on summer weekends. In the south, where the weather is less reliable, large covered grills known as *quinchos* provide an alternative venue for grilling; animals such as goats are often sliced in half and cooked in *quinchos* on long skewers, Brazilian-style. The restaurant equivalent of an *asado* is the **parrillada** – a mixture of grilled steaks, chops and sausages (in the best places cooked over charcoal), sometimes served on a hot grill by your table. Following beef in the popularity stakes is **chicken**, which is usually served fried, but can also be enjoyed oven- or spit-roasted. Chilean chickens are nearly all corn-fed and are delicious when well cooked. Succulent, spit-roasted chicken is widely available and inexpensive in Arica, in the far north, owing to the locally based chicken breeding industries. In central Chile, *pollo al coñac* is a popular, and very tasty, chicken casserole, served in large clay pots with brandy and cream. **Pork chops** also feature on many restaurant menus, but lamb (*cordero*) is hardly ever available, except in the Lake District, where it's a local speciality.

Traditional food

There's a wide range of older, traditional dishes – usually a fusion of indigenous and Hispanic influences – that are still very much a part of Chilean home cooking and can, with a little luck and effort, be found in the small, old-fashioned restaurants that survive in the hidden corners of town or out in the countryside. Though recipes vary from region to region, depending on the local produce available, there are a few core staples, including sweetcorn and potatoes. **Sweetcorn** forms the basis of two of the most traditional Chilean dishes: **humitas** – mashed corn, wrapped in corn husks and steamed – and **pastel de choclo**, a pie made of mince or chicken topped by pureed sweetcorn and sugar and then baked in the oven. The **potato**, meanwhile, is such an important staple in the Chilean diet that it has acquired its own mythology and folklore (see box opposite).

Another great traditional dish (or snack) is the **empanada**, as symbolic as the national flag, although it was introduced by the Spanish and is popular throughout South America. Baked or fried, large or small, sweet or savoury, *empanadas* (which are not unlike Cornish pasties) can be filled with almost anything, but the most traditional filling is *pino*, a mixture of minced beef, loads of onions, a slice of hard-boiled egg, and an olive, with the pit. (Beware, as this is a good way to leave a tooth in Chile!)

Also very typical are **soups** and **broths.** There are numerous varieties, of which the most famous, cropping up as a starter on many a set meal, is *cazuela*. Named after large Spanish saucepans, *cazuela* is celebrated as much for its appearance as for its taste, with ingredients carefully chosen and cooked to retain their colour and texture: pale yellow potato, orange pumpkin, split rice, green beans, peas and deep yellow sweetcorn swimming in stock, served in a large soup plate with a piece of meat on the bone surrounded by a layer of animal fat, and sprinkled with parsley and coriander. Other favourite one-pot broths include **caldillo**, very similar to *cazuela* but with fish instead of meat, and **escabechado**, a stew made with fish steaks that have been fried then soaked in vinegar. Doubtless because it is so economical, **offal** enjoys a long (though waning) history in Chilean cookery – slaughtermen in Santiago's original Matadero Municipal were given all the offal from the results of their daily labour, which formed the basis of a traditional stew, *caldo de Matadero*, while further south, the area around Rancagua is still famous for its roadside vendors with their bowls of cold pigs' trotters and knuckles.

Fast food

All of Chile's towns are well endowed with greasy-spoon cafés and snack bars – usually known as *fuentes de soda* or *schoperías* – serving draught beer and cheap fast food. This usually consists of **sandwiches**, which are consumed voraciously by Chileans of all ages and social standing – indeed, one variety, the **Barros Luco** (beef and melted cheese) is named after a former president who is said to have devised the combination. **Barros Jarpa** (ham and cheese) is another dietary staple. Chilean sandwiches are dauntingly large, and the layers of ingredients that ooze out from a roll make them impossible to eat with any degree of delicacy. The choice of fillings is firmly meat-based, with most options revolving around **churrasco**

– a thin cut of griddle-fried beef, rather like a minute steak. Sandwiches are served with a variety of toppings, including mayonnaise, tomato, mashed avocado, runner beans, lettuce, cheese, fried egg and chopped chillies. (Club sandwiches will probably contain them all.)

Chile is also the unlikely home of a variety of **hot dogs**. Sitting all by itself in a bun, the hot dog is simply called a *vienesa*, but it's called an *especial* when mayonnaise is squeezed along the top, and the addition of tomato, sauerkraut and avocado makes it a *dinámico*. The most popular version is the *italiano* – tomato, mayonnaise and avocado, which together resemble the colours of the Italian flag. It is not until the sausage is buried under extra sauerkraut and chopped tomato that it becomes completely *completo*.

Drinking

Soft **fizzy drinks** (*bebidas*) can be found everywhere in Chile, particularly Coca Cola, Sprite and Fanta. Bottled **mineral water**, too, is widely available, both with fizz (*con gas*) and without (*sin gas*). **Coffee**, in Chile, is usually instant Nescafé, although in the upmarket restaurants and city cafés it's increasingly easy to find good, real coffee (ask for *café de grano*). Chileans just haven't gotten the hang of making **tea**, which is nearly always served lukewarm and weak.

Potatoes

The **potato**, a staple in the Chilean diet, has long been the subject of numerous traditions and superstitions. Nowhere is this truer than in Chiloé, where potatoes must be sown during a waning moon in August or September, unless large *macho* specimens are required for seeds, in which case they are sown at the full moon. Neighbours help each other in every aspect of cultivation, a communal labouring tradition known as a **minga**. There are three main *mingas*: *quechatún*, the turning of the earth; *siembra de papa*, the planting; and *cosecha* or *sacadura*, the harvest.

Amongst the mythology and traditional customs associated with the potato are "magic stones" (*piedras cupucas*), which are found on Cerro Chepu, a hill near Ancud in Chiloé. Believed to have been hidden by witches (*brujos*), these porous silicone stones are carefully guarded until the potato plants bloom, and then the flowers are placed on them and burnt as a sacrifice.

Another potato myth holds that a small silver lizard, *el Lluhay*, feeds on potato flowers, and anyone who can catch one is guaranteed good fortune. Still another maintains that a maggot, *la co–ipone*, that lives in the potato root ball will prevent babies from crying when placed under their pillows.

Popular and traditional ways of eating potatoes

Chuchoca Mashed potato mixed with flour and pig fat, plastered onto a long, thick wooden pole (*chuchoquero*) and cooked over an open fire.

Colao Small cakes made from potato, wheat, pork fat and cracklings, cooked in hot embers.

Mallo de papas Potato stew.

Mayo de papas Peeled, boiled potatoes mashed with onions, chillies, pepper and pig fat.

Mayocan A potato, seaweed and dried-shellfish stew traditionally eaten for breakfast.

Milcao Small cakes of grated and mashed potato that are steamed like dumplings, baked or deep fried.

Pan de papas Baked flat round cakes of mashed potato mixed with flour, eggs and pig fat.

Papas rellenas Sausage-shaped rolls of mashed potato mixed with flour and filled with meat or shellfish.

Pastel de papas A baked dish with alternating layers of mashed potato and meat or shellfish topped with more potato.

If you take your tea with milk, beware of asking for *té con leche*, as this will simply be a cup of hot milk and a teabag. Similarly, if you ask for tea with *un poco de leche*, you'll probably get half milk and half water. For just a dash of milk, English-style, it's best not to say anything until your (milkless) tea has been brought to you, and then ask, as an afterthought, for a little milk. **Herbal teas** are widely available and come in countless flavours, some of which are internationally recognizable, while others are made from native plants. The most popular varieties are *manzanilla* (camomile), *menta* (mint) and *boldo* (a fragrant native plant). Where Chile really comes into its own, though, is with the delicious, freshly squeezed **fruit juices** (*jugos naturales*) available in many bars, restaurants and roadside stalls, especially in the fruit-producing regions of the Central Valley, and a few northern oases like Pica. Another home-grown drink is **mote con huesillo**, sold at numerous roadsides throughout the Central Valley and Lake District in summer. *Mote* is boiled or soaked barley grain, and *huesillos* are sun-dried peaches, though this sweet, gooey drink can be made with any fresh soft fruit.

Chilean **beer** doesn't come in many varieties, with Cristal and Escudo dominating the choice of bottled lagers, and Kunstman the only speciality brand to make a national mark.

There's always a good selection of **wine**, on the other hand though the choice on restaurant lists is usually limited to a handful of producers and in no way reflects the vast range of wines produced for export. Regarded as the Chilean national drink, **pisco sour** is a tangy, refreshing aperitif made from pisco (a white brandy created from distilled Moscatel grapes – freshly squeezed lemon juice and sugar. You may also come across a number of **regional specialities**, including *chicha de manzana* (apple cider), made at home by every *huaso* in the Central Valley. Further south, in the Lake District, a traditional element of many drinks is *harina tostada* (toasted maize flour), used by the Mapuches since pre-Spanish days. Today it's still common to see Mapuches sitting around a table with a large jug of frothy coffee-coloured liquid, which is dark beer mixed with *harina tostada*. The flour is also mixed with cheap wine made from dessert grapes, among other drinks, and is usually stocked by the sackful at local Lake District bars.

Communications

Chile's postal service, Correos de Chile, is fairly dependable and efficient, and overseas mail sent even from remote areas generally reaches its destination within a couple of weeks. Do not send any gifts to Chile using regular post; theft is extremely common for incoming shipments. For important shipping to Chile try express services such as Fed Ex and DHL. You'll also find it easy to make international phone calls and send faxes and emails from most Chilean towns. Internet access is very common throughout Chile.

Email

One of the best (and cheapest) ways to keep in touch while travelling is to sign up for a free Internet email address – if you haven't already done so – that can be accessed from anywhere, for example Yahoo! (@mail.yahoo .com) or Hotmail (@www.hotmail.com). Once you've set up your account, you'll be able to pick up and send mail from any

Internet café, web kiosk or hostel or hotel with Internet access.

@www.kropla.com is a useful website giving details of how to plug your laptop in when abroad, phone country codes around the world, and information about electrical systems in different countries.

Internet services

Chile is one of the most wired Latin American nations, surpassed perhaps only by Argentina. **Cybercafés** are everywhere, though many are haunts for adolescents playing nasty games. Broadband (*banda ancha*) access is quite common in cities, much less so in more remote places. **Internet access** typically costs about CH$250 for 15 minutes, but ranges from lightning fast to so slow you will use up the first quarter of an hour just getting a connection; demand your money back and try somewhere else.

Post

The Chilean **postal service** is very reliable for international mailings, but can be surprisingly erratic for domestic mailings. A letter from Santiago takes about five days to reach Europe, a little less time to reach North America. Allow a few extra days for letters mailed from other towns and cities in Chile. Post offices are marked by a blue Correos sign, and are usually on or near the Plaza de Armas of any town; postboxes are blue, and bear the blue Correos symbol. You can have letters mailed to you at the central post office of any town, using the poste restante system, known as **Lista de Correos** in Chile. The letters should be addressed: Sr/Sra/Srta FULL NAME (last name in capitals), Lista de Correos, Correo Central, CITY OR TOWN, Chile. The names of recipients are typed out in alphabetical order, sorted by last name, and posted up on a board. There are separate lists for men and women, which is why it helps to have a Sr or Sra/Srta in front of your name – otherwise, you should check both lists carefully. Also bear in mind that if a middle name is included, this is often taken to be the first part of your surname (Chileans have two last names, one taken from the father and another from the mother) so a letter addressed to George Thomas Marrs would probably be filed under T, and not M.

Once you've located your name, jot down the number next to it and present it, along with your passport, to the staff at the counter, along with a small fee (about US50¢ per letter). Unclaimed letters are kept for thirty days and then returned to the sender – it's a good idea to ask the sender to put *your* home address on the back of the envelope instead of theirs, so you'll end up with the letter eventually, even if you miss it in Chile.

An alternative to the Lista de Correos is to use the **American Express mail collection** service, though this is limited to Santiago, and the office (c/o Viajes Blanco, General Holley 148, ☎2336164) is far less convenient than the Correos Central. Letters should be addressed with your full name, followed by Cliente de American Express (just to avoid confusion); in theory, you're supposed to be an American Express customer to use this service, but no one seems to check.

Telephones

Chilean phone services are the best on the continent, with excellent lines and cheap rates that include calls to the US for as little as 10 cents a minute. But the system is also bewildering to the newcomer. In Chile, there's no single national telecommunications company, but roughly a dozen telecom companies, known as carriers (*portadores*). Stiff competition among the companies means that prices are low and constantly changing.

Each carrier has its own access code (see box). This will be the first three digits of the call from cell phones, private lines and public telephones. In nearly all cases, dial your chosen carrier's code, add "0", then the number. For example, to call England

Carrier codes
One Telcom (119)
Entel (123)
Telefónica Mundo (188; this one is the best overall)
BellSouth (181)
VTR (120)
Carrier 155 (155)
Telefónica del Sur (121)
Transam (113)
Manquehue (122)

you would dial 119 (or another company's code), then 0, then 44 and the number. For calls within Chile the "0" is dropped. To call Valparaíso from Santiago, for example, you would dial carrier code 119 (or whichever you choose), then 32 (for Valparaíso area), and the six- or seven-digit number.

You'll find a huge variety of public phones, but look for the more reliable blue phones owned by CTC or the stainless steel outlets owned by Entel. While theoretically all pay phones accept coins, most coins get jammed, so it's better to use prepaid **phone cards** (*tarjetas telefonicas*), which you can buy in denominations of CH\$3000, CH\$5000, and CH\$10,000 from news kiosks, in the metro and at a few corner shops. Using phonecards is a very practical way to phone abroad, and it's worth stocking up on them in major cities, as you can't always buy them in small towns and villages. Be careful to ask for a card for international calls (*llamadas internacionales*) or you may end up with a Chilean card for cellular phones. You can use a phone card multiple times, until its value runs out.

Besides calling from public phone booths, you can also use call centres, or **centros de llamadas.** There are dozens of these in most cities, and some of them offer cheap rates – particularly the small private ones which are more likely to have promotions and special offers. The catch, however, is that in most *centros de llamadas* you can't set a time limit for the call, so you have to be really careful about not talking too long, as you can quickly run up a huge bill. Note that you can normally send and receive **faxes** in these *centros*, as well as in many small shops, which advertise the service with signs on the window. But foreign faxes can easily run to US\$3 a page or more.

A final option is to take along an **international calling card**. Generally billed to your home phone account or credit card, these are very handy and easy to use, but are usually two or three times more expensive than buying a Chilean phonecard or using a *centro de llamadas*.

International calling cards

One of the most convenient ways of phoning home from abroad is via a **telephone charge card** from your phone company back home. Using a PIN number, you can make calls from most hotel, public and private phones that will be charged to your account. Since most major charge cards are free to obtain, it's certainly worth getting one at least for emergencies; enquire first though whether Chile is covered.

In the **US and Canada**, AT&T, MCI, Sprint, Canada Direct and other North American long-distance companies all enable their customers to make credit card calls while overseas, billed to your home number. Call your company's customer service line to find out if they provide service from Chile, and if so, what the toll-free access code is.

In **the UK and Ireland**, British Telecom (☎0800/345144, ⓦwww.chargecard.bt.com) will issue free to all BT customers the BT Charge Card, which can be used in 116 countries; AT&T also has the Global Calling Card; while NTL (☎0500/100 505) issues its own Global Calling Card, valid in more than sixty countries abroad, though the fees cannot be charged to a normal phone bill.

To call **Australia and New Zealand** from overseas, you can use telephone charge cards such as Telstra Telecard or Optus Calling Card in Australia, and Telecom NZ's Calling Card, which are charged back to a domestic account or credit card. Apply to Telstra (☎1800/038000), Optus (☎1300/300937) or Telecom NZ (☎04/8019000).

Calling home from overseas

Australia international access code + 61 + city code.
New Zealand international access code + 64 + city code.
Republic of Ireland international access code + 353 + city code.
UK and Northern Ireland international access code + 44 + city code.
USA and Canada international access code + 1 + area code.

Mobile phones

If you want to use your cell phone in Chile, you'll need to ask your service provider whether it will work abroad, and the rate per minute. Despite promises of reliable service, many travellers to Chile are disappointed with their cell phone service. For many reasons, the use of a foreign cell in Chile is often unreliable. In some cases, for example, you can't access messages while in Chile – a potentially debilitating problem on the road. If you truly need a cell phone and are visiting Chile for more than three weeks – buy one. They are sold at the airport and cost less than US$100. Minutes can then be bought as necessary.

If your phone provider at home offers Chile coverage, you may get charged extra for this depending on your existing package. You are also likely to be charged exorbitantly for incoming calls when abroad (these calls are free when you have a cell phone from Chile). If you want to retrieve messages while you're away, you'll have to ask your provider for a new access code, as your home one is unlikely to work abroad. For further information about using your phone abroad, check out ⓦwww.telecomsadvice.org.uk/features/using_your_mobile_abroad.htm.

The media

Chile's print media is of a very shoddy quality. The five major dailies include just a tiny amount of international news. TV is even worse, dominated by dreadful soaps, half-naked adolescent dance shows and game shows – though the daily weather slot is an unexpected highlight, as it zooms down the length of Chile, with excellent graphics representing the different geographical features. The radio is even worse than the television, though some of the very rural stations provide a fascinating insight into local communities.

The press

The Chilean **press**, resistant to government interference, has managed to uphold a strong tradition of editorial freedom ever since the country's first newspaper, *La Aurora*, was put together by an anti-royalist friar on an imported printing press in 1812, during the early days of the independence movement. One year before *La Aurora* folded in 1827, new newspaper, *El Mercurio*, went to Valparaíso. It has been in continuous circulation ever since, making it the minimal newspaper. The other news, which tends to be these two main newspapers produces a plethora of racy such as *La Segunda* (also part of the Edwards empire), as well as *¡Hola!*-style clones, including *Cosas* and *Vanidades*. For a more edifying read, try the selection of *Private Eye*-style satirical papers, such as *The Clinic* and the weekly examples of *más 7*, which provide a wide range of Chile's free press. In another Edwards product) news, as well as useful listings of national festivals and events. All these newspapers and magazines are sold at **pavement kiosks** found on the street corners of most towns, where they hang together like a patchwork curtain, clipped together with clothes pegs.

Television

Almost every household in Chile owns a television, which tends to be permanently switched on. The cult of the television is also very much in evidence in bars, cafés and the less expensive restaurants, which are often dominated by screens in the corner of the room. Cable TV is widespread, offering around 80 channels that frequently show US films and popular series like *Friends* and *Cheers* in English with Spanish subtitles, most commonly on the Cinecanal, Cinemax and Sony channels. CNN is always on offer (as is the omnipresent MTV) and BBC World is widely available.

Of the five terrestrial channels (curiously numbered 4, 7, 9, 11 and 13), top choice is Channel 7, the state-owned Televisión Nacional, which makes the best programmes in Chile, including decent documentaries. Among the others are the Universidad Católica (good documentaries from the BBC) and Megavisión (lots of talk shows and Mexican soaps) and Red Televisión (mainly dubbed American movies). Lunch time and evening **news coverage** – shown on Channels 7, 9, 11 and 13 – invariably starts with football highlights followed by bloody road accidents no matter what earth-shattering events have occurred in the rest of the world. Otherwise, soap operas, game shows and talent contests predominate, reaching an excruciating climax with *Sábado Gigante*, a truly dreadful talent contest where Chileans compete against one another. Popping up in endless commercials, peering down from advertising billboards and plastered over food packaging, the show's portiqable and larger-than-life compere, whose ~co. is an international institution other Dec~ reaches its zenith every ~e hosts the *Teletón*

event, which raises money for disabled children. If you happen to be in Chile during this event, you will see flocks of people at midnight rushing to donate pesos at the supermarkets. It is a rare demonstration of national solidarity, and the Chileans take the *Teletón* very seriously.

Radio

There is a compulsive Chilean habit, particularly prevalent amongst the owners of the country's quietest rural bars, of turning the **radio** on as soon as you walk through the door. Outside towns and cities, radio reception is quite poor. News stations are very rare, and when the reception is good you can hear the pages of newspapers being turned as a monotone voice reads one article after another, interrupted periodically by voiced-over jingles promoting democracy or government institutions.

An old-fashioned Chilean institution in this age of instant worldwide communications is the radio station which provides remote rural communities with their sole **message service.** Sitting in a quiet backwoods bar, locals bend an ear for news of family and friends and catch up on the latest developments of ongoing sagas that could easily be scripts for a soap opera.

To find local frequencies for English-language news on either the BBC or VOA, check out their websites, which offer local radio information and list all the service frequencies around the world: **BBC** ⓦ www.bbc.co.uk /worldservice; **Radio Canada** ⓦ www.rcinet .ca; **Voice of America** ⓦ www.voa.gov.

Opening hours and holidays

Most shops and services are open Monday through Friday from 9am to 1pm and 3pm to 6 or 7pm, and on Saturday from 10 or 11am until 2pm. Supermarkets stay open at lunchtime and may close as late as 11pm on weekdays and Saturdays in big cities. Large shopping malls are often open all day on Sundays. Banks have more limited hours, generally Monday through Friday from 9am to 2pm, but casas de cambio tend to use the same opening hours as shops.

Museums are nearly always shut on Mondays, and are often free on Sundays. Many **tourist offices** only open Monday through Friday throughout the year, with a break for lunch, but in summer (usually between December 15 and March 15) some increase their weekday hours and open on Saturday and sometimes Sunday; note that their hours are subject to frequent change. **Post offices** don't close at lunch time on weekdays and are open on Saturdays from 9am to 1pm.

February is the main holiday month in Chile, when there's an exodus from the big cities to the beaches or the Lake District, leaving some shops and restaurants closed. February is also an easy time to get around in Santiago, as the city appears half abandoned.

Public holidays

Apart from the statutory public holidays recognized nationwide, shops and offices may be closed for certain local festivals and on national and local election days, when the country comes to an almost complete standstill for 24 hours from midnight to midnight.

Major holidays

January 1 New Year's Day (Año nuevo)

Easter with national holidays on Good Friday, Easter Saturday and Easter Sunday are the climax to Holy Week (**Semana Santa**)

May 1 Labour Day (**Día del Trabajo**)

May 21 Combate Naval de Iquique. A Remembrance Day celebrating the end of the War of the Pacific after the naval victory at Iquique

June 15 Corpus Christi

June, last Monday San Pedro and San Pablo

August 15 Assumption of the Virgin

September 18 National Independence Day (**Fiestas Patrias**), in celebration of the first provisional government of 1810

September 19 Armed Forces Day (**Día del Ejército**)

October 12 Columbus Day (**Día de la Raza**), marking the discovery of America

November 1 All Saints' Day (**Todos los Santos**)

December 8 Immaculate Conception

December 25 Christmas Day (**Navidad**)

Spectator sports and festivals

The Chileans are not a particularly exuberant people (especially compared to their Argentine neighbours) and the country's entertainment scene sits firmly on the tame side of the fence. That said, passions are roused by several national enthusiasms – chiefly football and rodeo, which at their best are performed with electrifying skill and theatricality. Local and national fiestas provide other opportunities for the Chileans to let their hair down, and usually include a good deal of flag-waving, dancing, singing, drinking and eating of empanadas. If your Spanish is good, you'll also be entertained by the characteristic fast-thinking humour evident throughout Chilean culture, from the teasing jokes of young waiters and bar staff to the sophisticated word play that peppers the country's theatre, music and literature.

Football

El fútbol reigns supreme as Chile's favourite sport, and the top *futbolistas* are modern-day folk heroes whose exploits are frequently splashed across the front pages of the newspapers.

Introduced by British immigrants in the early 1800s, football in Chile can trace its history back to the playing fields of the Mackay School, one of the first English schools founded in Valparaíso, and its heritage is reflected in the names of the first clubs: Wanderers, Everton, Badminton, Morning Star and Green Cross.

Everton and Wanderers are still going strong, but the sport is now dominated by the Santiago teams of Colo Colo, Universidad Católica and Universidad de Chile. Matches featuring any of these teams are guaranteed a good turn out and a great atmosphere. There's rarely any trouble, with whole families coming along to enjoy the fun. In Santiago (unquestionably the best place to watch a match), tickets to see the main teams cost around CH$3000–6000 (US$5–10) at the bottom end, going up to CH$40,000 (US$60) for the most expensive seats. If you can't make it to a match, you'll still see plenty of football on the huge TVs that dominate most cafés and bars, including European games shown on cable channels (you may notice, too, that widespread exposure to English football has led many young Chileans to refer to an Englishman as a *húligan* rather than a *gringo*).

Football hardly has a **season** in Chile. In addition to the league games played between March and December, there are numerous other competitions of which the Copa de Libertadores is the most important. So you'll be able to catch the action whatever time of year you visit.

Horse racing

There are two very different types of **horse racing** in Chile: conventional track racing, known as *hípica*, and the much rougher and wilder *carreras a la chilena*. **Hípica** is a sport for rich Santiaguinos, who don their tweeds and posh frocks to go and watch it at the capital's Club Hípico and Hipódromo Chile, which have races throughout the year. The most important of these are the *St Leger* at the Hipódromo Chile on December 14, and the *Ensayo* at the Club Hípico on the first Sunday in November.

Carreras a la chilena are held anywhere in the country where two horses can be found to race against each other. Apart from the organized events which take place at village fiestas, these races are normally a result of one *huaso* betting another that his horse is faster. Held in any suitable field, well away from the prying eyes of the *carabineros*, the two-horse race can attract large crowds (who bet heavily on the outcome) and enterprising local families (who set up food and drink stalls). After a track is marked out with a piece of string, both horses and riders mill around, giving each other the evil eye for an hour or more. When the race begins, the tension is palpable as the two men and their beasts pit their strength and skill against each other, and the crowd is frozen in silence until the winner crosses the finishing post, whereupon it breaks out into loud, raucous whooping.

Rodeo

Rodeos evolved from the early colonial days when the cattle on the large *estancias* had to be rounded up and branded or slaughtered by *huasos* (Chilean "cowboys" or horsemen). The feats of horsemanship required to do so soon took on a competitive element, which eventually found an expression in the form of rodeos. Even though ranching has long declined in Chile, organized rodeos remain wildly popular, with many free competitions taking place in local stadiums (known as **medialunas**) throughout the season, which runs from

The Chilean huaso

"Of the many cowboys of the Americas, none remains as shrouded in mystery and contradiction as Chile's *huaso*", says Richard Slatta in *Cowboys of the Americas*. Certainly the *huaso* holds a special place in Chile's perception of its national identity and has become a potent symbolic figure over the years. But the definition and identity of the *huaso* is somewhat confused and subject to multiple, wildly differing interpretations. The one you're most likely to come across as a traveller is that of the "gentleman rider", the middle-class horseman who, while not a part of the landed elite, is a good few social rungs up from the landless labourer. This is the *huaso* you'll see in *cueca* performances (see p.68) and at rodeos, mounted on a fine-blooded steed and dressed in richly woven ponchos, silk sashes, high-heeled Cordova-leather boots and large silver spurs. This version of the *huaso* has evolved from a Spanish archetype – the dignified country gentleman and his horse – imported, along with cattle and horses, by the conquistadors. While not exactly a fiction, these gentlemen riders (labelled "postcard huasos" by Slatta) are, nonetheless, part of a romanticized image of the Chilean countryside and a far cry from the much larger and perhaps more authentic group of *huasos* who carried out the real horse-work on the land. More akin to the Argentine gaucho and the Mexican *vaquero*, this other type of *huaso* was a landless, badly paid, poorly dressed ranch-hand who worked on the large haciendas during the cattle round-up season. His prototype developed during the early years of the colony with the creation of the immense landed estates and the introduction of livestock-breeding, and by the eighteenth century was a fundamental cog in the rural economy. Despite the harsh reality of his lifestyle, the lower-class *huaso* is also the victim of myth-making, frequently depicted as a paragon of virtue and happiness – loyal to his master, honest, hard-working and at one with the land.

All types of *huasos*, whatever their social status, were renowned for outstanding **horsemanship**. One visiting Englishman in the nineteenth century described, with astonishment, the skilful Chilean cowboys who could "throw their lasso at full speed and entangle and secure the wildest animal". They were also marvelled at for their practice of training their horses to stop dead in their tracks at a single command, a technique known as *la sentada*. A skill mastered by *huasos* in the southern Central Valley (and borrowed from Argentine gauchos) was that of the *bolas* – three stones or metal balls attached to long leather straps, that were hurled at animals and wrapped around their legs, bringing them to the ground. *Huasos* also developed a whole host of equestrian games and contests including the *juego de cañas* (jousting with canes), the *tiro al gallo* (a mounted tug-of-war) and *topeadura* (a side-by-side pushing contest). Today these displays have a formal outlet in the regular **rodeos** (see p.287) that take place throughout the Central Valley. As for the working *huaso*, you'll still come across him in the back roads of rural central Chile, herding livestock, often wearing a broad-rimmed *huaso* hat and occasionally a bright poncho.

September to April. Taking in a rodeo not only allows you to watch the most dazzling equestrian skills inside the arena, but also to see the *huasos* decked out in all their traditional gear: ponchos, silver spurs and all. Added to this, the atmosphere is invariably loads of fun, with lots of whooping families and excited kids, and plenty of food and drink afterwards. For a fuller account of rodeos, see the box on p.287.

Cueca

Huasos are also the chief performers of **cueca**, Chile's national dance – a curious cross between thigh-slapping English morris dancing and smouldering *Sevillanas*. Its history can, in fact, be traced to the African slave dances, which were also the basis of the Brazilian samba and Peruvian *zamacueca*, and were introduced to Chile by a battalion of black soldiers in 1824. During the War of Independence, Chileans adopted their own forms of these dances known as *la Chilena*, *la Marinera* and *el Minero*, which eventually became a national victory dance known simply as the *cueca*. Although there are regional variations, the basic elements remain unchanged, consisting of couples strutting around each other in a courtship ritual, spurs jingling and handkerchiefs waving over their heads. The men are decked out in their finest *huaso* gear, while the women wear wide skirts and shawls. In the background, guitar-strumming musicians sing romantic ballads full of patriotic sentiments. If you are going to a fiesta and want to take part in a *cueca*, remember to take along a clean white handkerchief.

Festivals

Most of Chile's **festivals** are held to mark religious occasions, or to honour saints or the Virgin Mary. What's fascinating about them is the strong influence of pre-Spanish, pre-Christian rites, particularly in the Aymara communities of the Far North and the Mapuches of the south. Added to this is the influence of colourful folk traditions rooted in the Spanish expeditions of exploration and conquest, colonization and evangelism, slavery and revolution.

In the altiplano of the **Far North**, Aymara herdsmen celebrate Catholic holy days and the feasts of ancient cults along with ritual dancing and the offering of sacrificial llamas.

In **central Chile**, you'll witness the influence of colonial traditions. In the days of the conquest, an important ingredient of any fiesta was the verbal sparring between itinerant bards called *payadores*, who would compose and then try to resolve each other's impromptu rhyming riddles. The custom is kept alive at many fiestas in the Central Valley, where young poets spontaneously improvise *lolismos* and *locuciones*, forms of jocular verse that are quite unintelligible to an outsider. These rural fiestas always culminate in an energetic display of *cueca* dancing, washed down with plenty of wine and *chicha* – reminiscent of the entertainment organized by indulgent *hacienda*-owners for their peons.

In the **south**, the solemn Mapuche festivals are closely linked to mythology, magic and faith healing, agricultural rituals, and supplications to gods and spirits. Group dances (*purrún*) are performed with gentle movements; participants either move round in a circle or advance and retreat in lines. Most ceremonies are accompanied by mounted horn players whose four-metre-long bamboo instruments, *trutrucas*, require enormous lung power to produce a note. Other types of traditional wind instruments include a small pipe (*lolkiñ*), flute (*pinkulwe*), cow's horn (*kullkull*) and whistle (*pifilka*). Of all Mapuche musical instruments, the most important is the sacred drum (*kultrún*), which is only used by faith healers (*machis*).

Major festivals

For more on altiplano fiestas and ceremonies, see p.263.

January

20 *San Sebastián* Spaniards brought the first wooden image of San Sebastián to Chile in the seventeenth century. After a Mapuche raid on Chillán, the image was buried in a nearby field, and no one was able to raise it. The saint's feast day has become an important Mapuche festival, especially in Lonquimay, where it's celebrated with horse racing, feasting and drinking.

February

1–3 La Candelaria This has been celebrated throughout Chile since 1780, when a group of miners and muleteers discovered a stone image of the Virgin and Child while sheltering from an inexplicable thunderstorm in the Atacama. Typical festivities include religious processions and traditional dances.

End of the month Festival Internacional de la Canción This glitzy and wildly popular five-day festival is held in Viña del Mar's open-air amphitheatre, featuring performers from all over Latin America and broadcast to most Spanish-speaking countries in the world.

April

Easter Semana Santa (Holy Week) Among the nationwide Easter celebrations, look out for Santiago's solemn procession of penitents dressed in black habits, carrying crosses through the streets, and La Ligua's parade of mounted *huasos* followed by a giant penguin.

First Sunday after Easter Fiesta del Cuasimodo In many parts of central Chile, *huasos* parade through the streets on their horses, often accompanied by a priest sitting on a float covered in white lilies.

May

3 Santa Cruz de Mayo Throughout the altiplano, villages celebrate the cult of the Holy Cross, inspired in the seventeenth century by the Spaniards' obsession with crosses, which they carried everywhere, erected on hillsides and even carved in the air with their fingers. The festivities have strong pre-Christian elements, often including the sacrifice of a llama.

13 Procesión del Cristo de Mayo A huge parade through the streets of Santiago bearing the *Cristo de Mayo* – a sixteenth-century carving of Christ whose crown of thorns slipped to its neck during an earthquake, and which is said to have shed tears of blood when attempts were made to put the crown back in place.

June

13 Noche de San Juan Bautista An important feast night, celebrated by families up and down the country with a giant stew, known as the *Estofado de San Juan*. In Chiloé, an integral part of the feast are roasted potato balls called *tropones*, which burn the fingers and make people "dance the *tropón*" as they jig up and down, juggling them from hand to hand.

29 Fiesta de San Pedro Along the length of Chile's coast, fishermen decorate their boats and take the image of their patron saint out to sea – often at night with candles and flares burning – to pray for good weather and large catches.

July

12–18 Virgen de la Tirana The largest religious festival in Chile, held in La Tirana in the Far North, and attended by over 80,000 pilgrims and hundreds of costumed dancers (see p.257).

16 Virgen del Carmen Military parades throughout Chile honour the patron saint of the armed forces; the largest are in Maipú, on the southern outskirts of Santiago, where San Martín and Bernardo O'Higgins defeated Spanish Royalists in 1818.

August

21–31 Jesús Nazareno de Caguach Thousands of Chilotes flock to the archipelago's tiny island of Caguach to worship at a two-metre-high figure of Christ, donated by the Jesuits in the eighteenth century.

September

18 Fiestas Patrias Chile's Independence Day is celebrated throughout the country with street parties, music and dancing.

October

First Sunday Virgen de las Peñas Each year, numerous dance groups and more than 10,000 pilgrims from Chile, Peru, Bolivia and Argentina make their way along a tortuous cliff path to visit a rock carving of the Virgin in the Azapa valley, near Arica. There are many smaller festivals in other parts of Chile, too.

November

1 Todos los Santos (All Saints' Day) Traditionally, this is the day when Chileans tend their family graves. In the north, where

Aymara customs have become entwined with Christian ones, crosses are often removed from graves and left on the former bed of the deceased overnight. Candles are kept burning in the room, and a feast is served for family members, past and present.

2 Día de los Muertos (All Souls Day) A second vigil to the dead is held in cemeteries, with offerings of food and wine sprinkled on the graves. In some Far North villages, there's a tradition of reading a liturgy, always in Latin.

December

8 La Purísima Celebrated in many parts of Chile, the festival of the Immaculate Conception is at its liveliest in San Pedro de Atacama, where it's accompanied by traditional Aymara music and dancing.

23–27 Fiesta Grande de la Virgen de Andacollo More than 100,000 pilgrims from all over the north come to Andacollo, in Norte Chico to worship its Virgin and watch the famous masked dancers (see p.189).

Outdoor activities

Chile offers an enormous range of outdoor activities, including volcano-climbing, skiing, surfing, whitewater rafting, fly-fishing and horse-riding. Although Chile's tourism industry was traditionally geared towards Argentine holiday-makers who come to lie on the beaches, an increasing number of operators and outfitters are wising up to the potential of organized adventure tourism, offering one- or multi-day guided excursions.

Many of these companies are based in Pucón, in the Lake District, with a good sprinkling of other outfitters spread throughout the south. There are fewer opportunities for outdoor activities in the harsh deserts of the north, where altiplano jeep trips and mountain biking are the main options. If you plan to do any adventurous activities, be sure to check that you're covered by your **travel insurance**, or take out specialist insurance where necessary. For more information on outdoor activities, see also the "Adventure sports" colour insert.

Rafting and kayaking

Chile's many frothy rivers and streams afford incomparable rafting opportunities. Indeed, the country's top destinations, the mighty **Río Bío Bío** and the **Río Futaleufú** entice visitors from around the globe. Rafting trips generally range in length from one to eight days and, in the case of the Bío Bío, sometimes include the option of climbing 3160-metre Volcán Callaquén. **Prices** are normally around US$100 for a day's rafting, US$350 for a three-day trip (with all camping equipment and food provided), going up to US$1500–2000 for all-inclusive ten-day packages, with added excursions. In addition to these challenging rivers, gentler alternatives exist on the **Río Maipo** close to Santiago, the **Río Trancura** near Pucón, and the **Río Petrohue** near Puerto Varas. The Maipo makes a good day-trip from Santiago, while excursions on the last two are just half-day affairs and can usually be arranged on the spot, without advance reservations. In general, all rafting trips are extremely well organized, but you should always take great care in choosing your outfitter – this activity can be very dangerous in the hands of an inexperienced guide.

Chile's white-water rapids also offer excellent **kayaking**, though this is less developed as an organized activity – your best bet is probably to contact one of the US-based outfitters that have camps on the Bío Bío and Futaleufú (see p.76 for contacts). **Sea kayaking** is becoming increasingly popular in Chile, generally in the calm, flat waters of Chile's southern fjords, though people have been known to kayak around Cape Horn. Note that the Chilean navy is very sensitive about any foreign vessels (even kayaks) cruising in their waters, and if you're planning a trip through military waters, you'd be wise to inform the Chilean consulate or embassy in your country beforehand.

Hiking

For the most part, Chile is a very empty country with vast swaths of wilderness offering potential for fantastic hiking (and concealing no dangerous animals or snakes). Chileans, moreover, are often reluctant to stray far from their parked cars when they visit the countryside, so you'll find that most trails without vehicle access are blissfully quiet. However, the absence of a national enthusiasm for hiking also means that, compared to places of similar scenic beauty like California, British Columbia and New Zealand, Chile isn't particularly geared up to the hiking scene, with relatively few long-distance trails (given the total area) and a shortage of decent trekking maps. That said, what *is* on offer is superb, and ranks among the country's most rewarding attractions.

The **north** of Chile, with its harsh climate and landscape, isn't really suitable for hiking, and most walkers head for the lush native forests of Chile's **south**, peppered with waterfalls, lakes, hot springs and volcanoes. The best trails are nearly always inside **national parks** or reserves, where the *guardaparques* are a good source of advice on finding and following the paths. They should *always* be informed if you plan to do an overnight hike (so that if you don't come back, they'll know where to search for you). The majority of trails are for half-day or day hikes, though some parks offer a few long-distance hikes, sometimes linking up with trails in adjoining parks. The level of path maintenance and signing varies greatly from one park to another, and many of the more remote trails are indistinct and difficult to follow. Hardly any parks allow wild **camping**, while the few others that now allow it have a series of rustic camping areas that you're required to stick to – check with the *guardaparque*. If you do camp (and this is the best way to experience the Chilean wilderness) note that **forest and bush fires** are a very real hazard. Take great care when making a campfire (having checked beforehand that they're allowed). Also, never chop or break down vegetation for fuel, as most of Chile's native flora is endangered.

By far the most popular destination for hiking is **Torres del Paine** in the far south, which offers magnificent scenery but fairly crowded trails, especially in January and February. Many quieter, less well-known alternatives are scattered between Santiago and Tierra del Fuego, ranging from narrow

Where to hike

For those who want to plan a trip around a few hikes, we refer you to the following accounts in the *Guide*:

paths in the towering, snow-streaked central Andes, to hikes up to glaciers off the Carretera Austral.

If you go hiking, it's essential to be well-prepared – always carry plenty of water, wear a hat and sun block for protection against the sun and carry extra layers of warm clothing to guard against the sharp drop of temperatures after sundown. Even on day hikes, take enough supplies to provide for the eventuality of getting lost, and always carry a map and **compass** (brújula), preferably one bought in the southern hemisphere or adjusted for southern latitudes. Also, make a conscious effort to help preserve Chile's environment – where there's no toilet, bury human waste at least 20cm under the ground and 30m from the nearest river or lake; take away or burn all your **rubbish**; and use specially designed eco-friendly **detergents** for use in lakes and streams.

Climbing

The massive Andean cordillera offers a wide range of climbing possibilities. In the **Far North** of Chile, you can trek up several volcanoes over 6000m, including Volcán Parinacota (6330m), Volcán Llullaillaco (6700m) and Volcán Ojos del Salado (6950m). Although ropes and crampons aren't always needed, these ascents are suitable only for experienced climbers, and need a fair amount of independent planning, with only a few companies offering guided excursions.

In the **central Andes**, exciting climbs include Volcán Marmolejo (6100m) and Volcán Tupungato (6750m), while in the **south**, climbers head for Volcán Villarica (2840m) and Volcán Osorno (2652m), both of which you can tackle even with little mountaineering experience.

Throughout Chile there's a lot of tedious bureaucracy to get through before you can climb. To go up any mountain straddling an international border (which means most of the high Andean peaks), you need advance **permission** from the **Dirección de Fronteras y Límites** (DIFROL), Fourth Floor, Bandera 52, Santiago (☎2/6714110, ℻697 1909). To get this, write to or fax DIFROL with the planned dates and itinerary of the climb, listing full details (name,

nationality, date of birth, occupation, passport number, address) of each member of the climbing team, and your dates of entry and exit from Chile. Authorization will then be sent or faxed to you on a piece of paper that you must present to Conaf before ascending (if the peak is not within a national park, you must take the authorization to the nearest carabineros station). If your plans change while you're in Chile, you can usually amend the authorization or get a new one at the Gobernación of each provincial capital. You can also apply through a Chilean embassy in advance of your departure, or print and send a form from their website. There's further information on climbing in Chile on the Web at ⓦwww .escalando.cl or ⓦwww.trekkingchile.com.

Fly-fishing

Chile has an international, and well-deserved, reputation as one of the finest fly-fishing destinations in the world, counting Robert Redford, Jane Fonda, Ted Turner, Michael Douglas, Jimmy Carter and George Bush Sr among those to have fished its pristine waters, which are teeming with rainbow, brown and brook **trout**, and silver and Atlantic **salmon**. These fish are

Useful climbing contacts

American Alpine Club 710 Tenth St, Suite 100, Golden, CO 80401, USA ☎303/384-0110, ℻384-0111. A good source of pre-trip advice.

British Mountaineering Council 177–179 Burton Rd, Manchester M20 2BB, UK ☎0161/445 4747, ℻445 4500. Produces a very useful information sheet on mountaineering, and also provides specialist insurance for members.

Federación de Andinismo Almirante Simpson 77, Providencia, Santiago ☎2/2220799, ℻6359089. This friendly organization runs mountaineering courses, sells equipment, can put you in touch with guides and offers knowledgeable, helpful advice. It also helps out foreigners trying to arrange climbing authorization.

not native, but were introduced for sport in the late nineteenth century; since then, the wild population has flourished and multiplied, and is also supplemented by generous numbers of escapees from local fish farms. The fishing **season** varies slightly from region to region, but in general runs from November to May.

Traditionally, the best sport-fishing was considered to be in the Lake District, but while this region still offers great possibilities, attention has shifted to the more remote, pristine waters of **Aisén**, where a number of classy fishing lodges have sprung up, catering mainly to wealthy North American clients. Fishing in the Lake District is frequently done from river boats, while a typical day's fishing in Aisén begins with a ride in a motor dinghy through fjords, channels and islets towards an isolated river. You'll then wade upstream to shallower waters, usually equipped with a light six or seven weight rod, dry flies and brightly coloured streamers. Catches weigh in between 1 and 3kg – but note that many outfitters operate only on a catch and release basis, so don't count on being able to cook them for your supper.

Costs range from a reasonable US$70 per person for a day in the more visited waters of the Lake District (including full equipment hire and boat transport), to around US$400 per day to fish the scarcely touched waters of Aisén with top-notch guides. You may also need to get yourself a **licence** (CH$6300 for the whole country), widely available at town halls and specialist fishing shops, though many outfitters supply this as part of the package. To find out more about fly-fishing in Chile, contact the government agency **Servicio Nacional de Pesca** at Yungay 1737, Fourth Floor, Valparaíso, Chile (℡32/214371, ℻259564), or consult the excellent website Ⓦwww.flyfishchile.com.

Skiing

Chile offers the finest and most challenging **skiing** in South America. Many of the country's top slopes and resorts lie within very easy reach of Santiago, including **El Colorado**, **La Parva**, **Valle Nevado** and world-renowned **Portillo**. A bit further south, but no less impressive, stands the popular **Termas de Chillán**.

Horse trekking

Exploring Chile's dramatic landscapes on horseback is a highly memorable experience, though organized treks for tourists are only slowly taking off. The best possibilities are **around Santiago**, and in the **Central Valley**, where riding has been a way of life for centuries, and horses are sleek, fit and strong. Here, groups of riders make their way up to remote mountain passes, framed by soaring, jagged peaks, sloping pastures, and clear rivers. In addition to the spectacular scenery, you can also expect to see condors and other birds of prey circling around the peaks. Trips are usually from three to seven days, guided by local *arrieros*, who herd cattle up to high pastures in springtime and know the mountain paths intimately. You normally spend about five or six hours in the saddle each day; a lingering *asado* (barbecue), cooked over an open fire and accompanied by plenty of Chilean wine, will be part of the pleasure. At night, you sleep in tents transported by mules, and you'll be treated to the most breathtaking display of stars.

The only disadvantage of riding treks in the central Andes is that, due to the terrain, you're unlikely to get beyond a walk, and cantering is usually out of the question. If you want a faster pace, opt for the treks offered by some companies in Patagonia, where rolling grasslands provide plenty of opportunity for gallops – though the weather can often put a dampener on your trip.

Most outfitters only offer a few multi-day trips between December and March, and these need to be booked well in advance, as demand often exceeds supply. Casual, one-day riding trips, however, can be arranged on the spot in many Central Valley mountain villages for around CH$20,000 a day. Conaf rangers can often help you find an *arriero* for the day, especially in Monumento Nacional El Morado, Reserva Nacional Río de los Cipreses and Reserva Nacional Altos del Lircay.

Surfing

Chile does not spring to mind as a major surfing destination, but its beaches are pulling in an increasing number of in-the-know enthusiasts from North America, who come to ride the year-round breaks that pound the Pacific shore. By unanimous consent, the **best breaks** – mainly long left-handers – are concentrated around **Pichilemu**, near Rancagua, which is the site of the annual National Surfing Championships (quite a small affair). However, apart from the relatively small community of hard-core Chilean surfers, there's not much of a home-grown surfing "scene", and renting boards can be quite problematic. (Your best bet is Pichilemu's Surf Shop at Aníbal Pinto, esquina Ortúzar; ☎72/841236.) Another slight deterrent is the temperature of the water, cooled by the Humboldt Current to around 14°C, making at least a 3mm wetsuit essential. Further north, the warmer seas around Iquique and Arica are also increasingly popular with visiting surfers.

Mountain biking

For most of Chile's length there are extremely good and little-used dirt roads perfect for **cycling** – although the numerous potholes mean it's only worth attempting them on a **mountain bike**. For a serious trip, you should bring your own bike or buy one in Santiago – **renting** something of the quality required can be difficult to arrange. An alternative is to go on an organized biking excursion, where all equipment, including tents, will be provided. Note that during the summer, cycling in Patagonia and Tierra del Fuego is made almost impossible by incessant and ferociously strong winds. For information on popular mountain bike routes, see the "Adventure sports" section.

Your major problem will be getting hold of spare parts when you need them. Chileans are not great cyclists, so bike shops tend to be found only in Santiago and a few major cities. Your best bet is to visit such a shop, befriend the owner, and if you get into difficulty, call for parts to be sent as cargo on a long-distance bus. When on the road, bear in mind that long stretches are bereft of accommodation options and even the most basic services, so you must be completely self-sufficient and prepared for a long wait if you require assistance.

Some bus companies will not transport bicycles unless you wrap frame and wheels separately in cardboard. When you enter the country, you may well find that customs officials enter details of your bicycle in your passport to prevent you from selling it.

Adventure tourism operators and outfitters

Below is a selection of operators and outfitters for various outdoor activities. The list is by no means comprehensive, and new companies are constantly springing up to add to it – you can get more details from the relevant regional Sernatur office.

All-rounders

Altue Expediciones Encomenderos 83, Las Condes, Santiago ☎2/2321103, ☏2336799. Reliable, slick operation whose options include rafting the Río Maipo, Aconcagua and Ojos del Salado expeditions, and three- to seven-day horse treks.

Azimut 360 Arzobispo Casanova 3, Providencia, Santiago ☎62/7358034. Franco-Chilean outfit with a young, dynamic team of guides and a wide range of programmes, including mountain biking in the altiplano, Aconcagua expeditions, and climbs up Chile's highest volcanoes.

Cascada Expediciones, Orrego Luco 054, Providencia, Santiago ☎2/2342274, ☏2339768, ✉cascada@ibm.net. One of the early pioneers of adventure tourism in Chile, with a particular emphasis on activities in the Andes close to Santiago, where it has a permanent base in the Cajón del Maipo. Programmes include rafting and kayaking the Río Maipo, horse treks in the high cordillera, hiking and one-day mountain biking excursions

Sportstour Moneda 970, 14th floor, Santiago ☎2/6963100, ☏2/6982981. This well-run operation offers balloon rides and flights, among other tours.

Climbing

See also Azimut 360 and Altue Expediciones in "All-rounders" above for details of tours up Volcán Osorno, see p.393, and Volcán Villarica, p.361.

Concepto Indigo Ladrilleros 105, Puerto Natales ☎61/410678, ☏410169, ✉indigo@entelchile.net, 🖿www.conceptoindigo.com. A range of mountaineering and ice-climbing programmes in the Torres del Paine region, plus mountaineering courses. A very good company.

Mountain Service Paseo Las Palmas 2209, Providencia, Santiago ☎2/2330913, ☏2343438. An experienced, specialist company, dedicated to climbing Aconcagua, the major volcanoes and Torres del Paine.

Fly-fishing

For a list of guides and lodges on and around the Carretera Austral, see p.464.

Bahía Escocia Fly Fishing Lago Rupanco ⊤64/371515. Small, beautifully located lodge with fly-fishing excursions run by a US–Chilean couple. Can also book with English-run Travellers in Puerto Montt ⊤65/262099, Ⓕ258555, Ⓔgochile@entelchile.net.

Cumilahue Lodge PO Box 2, Llifen ⊤63/481015, Ⓕ481360. Very expensive packages at a luxury Lake District lodge run by Adrian Dufflocq, something of a legend on the Chilean fly-fishing scene.

Off Limits Adventures Fresia 273, Pucón ⊤45/441210, Ⓕ441604, Ⓔofflimitspucon@hotmail.com. Half-day and full-day excursions, plus fly-fishing lessons. One of the more affordable options.

Patagonia Adventure Lodges 445 Milan Dr, Suite 220, San José, CA 95134, USA ⊤408/432-8600, Ⓕ432-1190; Hube 418, El Bolson, RN 8430, Argentina ⊤9/449 3280. US-based company offering all-inclusive packages (seven days minimum), with accommodation in a range of luxury lodges in Chilean and Argentine Patagonia.

Turismo Aventur J Nogueira 1255, Punta Arenas ⊤61/243354, Ⓕ241197. A relative newcomer, offering fishing packages in almost untouched Patagonian waters, based at an attractive, rustic lodge.

Horse trekking

See also Altue Expediciones and Cascada Expediciones in "All-rounders", opposite.

Chile Nativo ⊤61/414367, Ⓕ61/415474, Ⓔinfo@chilenativo.com, Ⓦwww.chilenativo.com. Dynamic young outfit based in Puerto Natales, specializing in five- to twelve–day horse-trekking tours of the region, visiting out-of-the-way locations in addition to the Parque Nacional Torres del Paine.

Hacienda de los Andes Río Hurtado, near Ovalle ⊤53/691822, Ⓔinfo@haciendalosandes.com, Ⓦwww.haciendalosandes.com. Beautiful newly built ranch in a fantastic location in the Hurtado valley, between La Serena and Ovalle, offering exciting one- to four-day mountain treks on some of the finest mounts in the country.

La Posada Expediciones 1 Norte 2280, Talca ⊤71/243833, Ⓕ243822. Local outfit offering three-day horse treks in Reserva Nacional Altos del Lircay, through native forests and up to high mountains.

Pared Sur Juan Esteban Montero 5497, Las Condes, Santiago ⊤2/2073525, Ⓕ2073159, Ⓔparedsur@chilnet.cl. In addition to its extensive mountain biking programme, Pared Sur offers a one-week horse trek through the virgin landscape of Aisén, off the Carretera Austral.

Rancho de Caballos Lake District, near Pucón ⊤45/441575, Ⓕ441604. Ranch offering a range of treks from three to nine days.

Ride World Wide 58 Fentiman Rd, London SW8 1LF ⊤020/7735 1144, Ⓕ735 3179, Ⓦwww.rideworldwide.co.uk. UK-based company that hooks up with local riding outfitters around the world. In Chile, it offers a range of horseback treks from eight days to two weeks in the central cordillera, the Lake District and Patagonia. Groups are limited to six or eight people.

Terracotta Excursions Agustinas 1547, departamento 705, Santiago ⊤2/6988121, Ⓕ696 1097, Ⓔterracot@intercity.cl. Run and guided by a Santiago woman, this young company is an alternative to the more traditional, slightly macho *huaso* outfits. It offers a range of treks from one to eight days in the Andes and coastal mountains near Santiago.

Kayaking

Al Sur Expediciones Del Salvador 100, Puerto Varas ⊤ & Ⓕ65/232300, Ⓔalsur@telsur.cl, Ⓦwww.alsurexpeditions.com. One of the foremost adventure tour companies in the Lake District, and the first one to introduce sea kayaking in the fjords south of Puerto Montt.

Bío Bío Expeditions (see White-water rafting, p.76). This rafting outfitter also rents out kayaks to experienced kayakers, who accompany the rafting party down the Bío Bío or Futaleufú.

¡ecole! Urrutia 592, Pucón ⊤ & Ⓕ45/441675, Ⓔtrek@ecole.cl, Ⓦwww.ecole.cl. Ecologically focused tour company offering, among other activities, sea kayaking classes and day outings in the fjords south of Puerto Montt, and around Parque Pumalín, from its Puerto Montt branch.

Expediciones Chile 333 Earl's Rd, Bryson City, NY 12404, USA ⊤704/488-9082, Ⓕ488-2112, Ⓔoffice@kayakChile.com. River kayaking outfitter catering to all levels of experience, especially seasoned paddlers. Operated by former Olympic kayaker Chris Spelius.

Onas Patagonia Blanco Encalada 599, Casilla 78, Puerto Natales ⊤61/412707, Ⓔonas@chileaustral.com, Ⓦwww.chileaustral.com/onas. Sea kayaking excursions in the remote, bleak waters of Patagonia.

Mountain biking

See also Azimut 360 and Cascada Expediciones in "All-rounders" opposite.

Pared Sur Juan Esteban Montero 5497, Las Condes, Santiago ☎ 2/2073525, ℻ 2073159, ℮ paredsur@chilnet.cl. Pared Sur has been running mountain bike trips in Chile for longer than anyone else (over twelve years). It offers a wide range of programmes throughout the whole country.

Skiing

Full details of the resorts near Santiago are given on p.138.

Sportstour Moneda 970, 14th Floor, Santiago ☎ 2/6963100, ℻ 6982981, ℮ sportstour@chilnet .cl. Among a wide-ranging national programme, including hot-air balloon rides and flights on cockpit biplanes and gliders, this travel agent offers fully inclusive ski packages at the resorts near Santiago, and the Termas de Chillán ski centre.

White-water rafting

See also Cascada Expediciones and Altue Expediciones, listed on p.74.

Bío Bío Expeditions, PO Box 2028, Truckee, CA 96160, US ☎ 562/246-7238, ℻ 582-6865, ℡ www .bbxrafting.com. Headed by Laurence Alvarez, the captain of the US's World Championships rafting team, this experienced and friendly outfit offers ten-day packages on the Bío Bío and Futaleufú, plus one- to three-day excursions down the latter. Trips can be booked in Chile by Aquamotion, Imperial 0699, Puerto Varas (☎ 65/232747), in the UK by Adrift at 140–142 High St, Wandsworth, London SW18 4JJ (☎ 020/8874 4969) and in New Zealand by Adrift, PO Box 310, Queenstown (☎ 03/442 1615).

Grado Diez Huelén 222, oficina 31, Providencia, Santiago ☎ 2/2344130, ℻ 2344138, ℮ gradodie .z001@chilnet.cl. Long-established Chilean rafting company offering trips down the Río Maipo plus three- and five-day trips down the Bío Bío and Futaleufú.

Trancura O'Higgins 211-C, Pucón ☎ 45/441189, ℡ www.trancura.com. Major southern operator with high standards and friendly guides, offering rafting excursions down the Río Trancura (one day) and the Bío Bío (three days).

National parks and reserves

Some eighteen percent of Chile's mainland territory is protected by the state under the extensive Sistema Nacional de Areas Silvestres Protegidas (National Protected Wildlife Areas System), which is made up of thirty national parks, thirty-eight national reserves and eleven natural monuments. These inevitably include the country's most outstanding scenic attractions, but while there are provisions for tourism, the main aim is always to protect and manage native fauna and flora. Given Chile's great biodiversity, these vary tremendously from one region to another, and park objectives are as varied as protecting the flamingo populations of the altiplano lakes to monitoring glaciers off the southern fjords. Other important functions include preventing poaching (for instance of vicuñas in the altiplano) and guarding against forest fires. All protected areas are managed by the Corporación Nacional Forestal (better known as Conaf), established in 1972 as part of the Ministry of Agriculture.

Definitions and terms

National parks (*parques nacionales*) are generally large areas of unspoilt wilderness, usually featuring fragile endemic ecosystems. They include the most touristy and scenically beautiful of the protected areas, and often offer walking trails and, less frequently, camping areas. **National** reserves (*reservas nacionales*) are areas of ecological importance which have suffered some degree of natural degradation; there are fewer regulations to protect these areas, and "sustainable" commercial exploitation (such as mineral extraction) is allowed to take place. **Natural monuments** (*monumentos naturales*) tend to be important or endangered geological formations, or small areas of biological, anthropological or archeological significance. In 1976, two tree species, the araucaria and alerce, were awarded the status of natural monument. In addition to these three main categories, there are a small number of **nature sanctuaries** (*sanctuarios de la naturaleza*) and **protected Areas** (*areas de protección*), usually earmarked for their scientific or scenic interest. It is not difficult for the government to change the status of these areas, and national parks have been known to be downgraded so that their resources could be commercially exploited. In addition to these state-owned parks, there are several important private initiatives, including **Parque Pumalín** (see p.453), just south of Puerto Montt, with some of the most luxuriant native forest in the country, and the **Cañi Reserve** (see p.353), just outside Pucón.

Park administration

The administration of Chile's protected areas is highly centralized, with all important decisions coming from **Conaf's head office** in Santiago. This is a good place to visit before heading out of the capital (for the address, see p.95), as you can pick up brochures and basic maps of all the parks and buy several publications on native flora and fauna. In addition, each regional capital has a Conaf headquarters, which is useful for more practical pre-visit information, such as road conditions and hiking possibilities. The parks and reserves are staffed by Conaf **guardaparques** (park wardens), who live in rustic ranger stations (called *guarderías*); they're easily identifiable by their green uniforms and green peaked caps bearing the Conaf symbol. Chilean *guardaparques* are almost always friendly, enthusiastic and dedicated to their job, despite working extremely long hours under difficult conditions for little pay. They're often out of their stations all day, patrolling the park for poachers or other hazards or monitoring the various programmes set up to recuperate declining wildlife populations

MAJOR PARKS & RESERVES

or flora with conservation problems. Most parks are divided into several areas, known as "sectors" (*sectores*), and the larger ones have a small *guardería* in each *sector*.

Visiting the parks

No **permit** is needed to visit any of Chile's national parks; you simply turn up and pay your **entrance fee**, which is usually between CH$1000 and CH$3000, though some parks are free. Ease of **access** differs wildly

77

from one park to the next – a few have paved highways running through them, while others are served by appalling dirt tracks that are only passable for a few months of the year. Typically, though, parks are reached by rough, bumpy dirt roads. Getting to them often involves renting a vehicle or booking transport through a local tour company, as around two-thirds of Chile's national parks can't be reached by public transport.

Arriving at the park boundary, you'll normally pass a small hut (called the Conaf control) where you pay your entrance fee and pick up a basic map (usually photocopied and of poor quality). Some of the larger parks have more than one entrance point, served by different access roads. The main ranger station is always separate from the hut, sometimes just a few hundred metres away, and at times several kilometres. The station contains the rangers' living quarters and administrative office, and often a large map or scale model of the park, marking all the trails. The more

popular parks also have a **Centro de Información Ambiental** attached to the station, with displays on the park's flora and fauna and, in high season, slide shows and talks (*charlas*). A few parks now have **camping** areas. These are often rustic sites with basic facilities, run by Conaf, which charges around CH$5000–10,000 per tent. In other parks, particularly in the south, Conaf gives licences to **concessionaires**, who operate campsites and *cabañas*, which tend to be very expensive. Some of the more remote national parks, especially in the north, have small **refugios** attached to the ranger stations – these are usually rustic, stone-built huts (from CH$5000 per person) containing around eight to ten bunk beds, hot showers and gas stoves. Some of these are in stunning locations, such as the *refugios* overlooking the Salar de Surire (see p.277), and the ones with views across Lago Chungará to Volcán Parinacota (see p.276), though sadly the *refugios* are increasingly unreliable (closed, overbooked or dirty).

Shopping

While the handicrafts (artesanía) produced in Chile are nowhere near as diverse or colourful as in neighbouring Peru or Bolivia, you can still find a range of beautiful souvenirs that vary from region to region, usually sold in ferias artesanales (crafts markets) on or near the central squares of the main towns. As for day-to-day essentials, you'll be able to locate just about everything you need, from sun block to contact lens solution, in the main towns up and down the country.

Artesanía and other souvenirs

The finest and arguably most beautiful goods you can buy in Chile are the items – mainly jewellery – made of **lapis lazuli**, the deep-blue semi-precious stone found only in Chile and Afghanistan. The best place to buy these is in the Bellavista area of Santiago (see p.113); note that the deeper the colour of the stone, the better its quality. Though certainly less expensive than lapis exports sold abroad, they're still pricey, with

a reasonable-quality choker, for instance, costing anything from CH$30,000 (US$55).

Most *artesanía* is considerably less expensive. In the **Norte Grande**, the most common articles are hand-knitted alpaca sweaters, gloves and scarves, which you'll find in altiplano villages like Parinacota, or down in Arica and Iquique. The quality is usually fairly low, but they're inexpensive and very attractive all the same. In the **Norte Chico**, you can pick up some beautiful leather goods, particularly in the crafts markets of La Serena. You might also be tempted to buy a bottle of pisco there, so that you can re-create that pisco sour experience back home – though you're probably better off getting it at a supermarket in Santiago before you leave, to save yourself carting it about. The **Central Valley**, as the agricultural heartland of Chile, is famous for its *huaso* gear, and you'll find brightly coloured ponchos and stiff straw hats in the numerous working *huaso* shops. The highlight in the **Lake District** is the traditional Mapuche silver jewellery, while the **far south** is a good place to buy chunky, colourful knitwear.

A range of these goods can also be bought in the major crafts markets in **Santiago**, notably Los Dominicos market. Also worth checking out are Santiago's little **flea markets** (see p.129), where you can pick up wonderful objects like old South American stirrups and spurs, pre-War of the Pacific maps and English bric-a-brac left over from the nitrate era.

Essential goods

Chile is well-stocked in just about all of the essential day-to-day goods you may need to replenish while travelling. Pharmacies are particularly well supplied, and you'll have no difficulty buying things like tampons, condoms, contact lens supplies and toiletries, as well as an astonishing range of over-the-counter medicines. Slide film can be more difficult to come by outside Santiago and the major cities, so it's worth bringing a decent stock along with you. Ordinary film is widely available in most cities and not so expensive. English-language books aren't widely available, even in Santiago, and there are very few travellers' book-exchanges around – so bring enough reading material to keep you going. There's also a surprisingly poor selection of outdoor gear and camping equipment in Chile, so try to bring everything you need for the weather conditions you'll be travelling in.

Gay and lesbian travellers

Although Chile has moved on a long way in terms of attitudes to sexual and gender issues since the return to democracy, society remains extremely conservative, and homosexuality is still a taboo subject for most Chileans. One example is the fact that the country's only travel agency for gays and lesbians opted not to be advertised or even mentioned in this guide book, "in the interest of its customers who prefer to remain totally anonymous".

Outside Santiago – with the minor exceptions of some northern cities such as La Serena and Antofagasta – there are no gay venues, and it is advisable for same-sex couples to do as the locals do and remain discreet, especially in public. Machismo is deeply ingrained and mostly unchallenged by women, despite a growing feminist movement. That said, gay-bashing and other homophobic acts are rare and the government has passed anti-discrimination legislation. It has also been considering legalizing civil unions (without full marriage status or adoption rights) for

homosexuals, the front runner for the presidency has lent her support to this stance. While gays are open and prominent in the arts and entertainment, with gay TV soap characters and the like, the Church remains a strong force in Chilean society, and vows to fight any policies that "undermine the family as an institution". The courts have also been accused by gay rights groups of passing homophobic judgments, such as depriving lesbians of the custody of their children, while a judge outed in a national scandal was removed from a totally unrelated case.

Contacts for gay and lesbian travellers

Below is a short list of websites offering a range of information about gay travel in general and about Chile in particular.

In Chile

Gay Chile Ⓦ www.gaychile.com. By far and away the leading gay site in Chile, with national and international news, information about events and venues, mainly in the capital, contacts and chat services.

In the US and Canada

Damron ☎ 1-800/462-6654 or 415/255-0404, Ⓦ www.damron.com. Publisher of the **Men's Travel Guide**, a pocket-sized yearbook full of listings of hotels, bars, clubs and resources for gay men; the **Women's Traveler**, which provides similar listings for lesbians; the **Road Atlas**, which shows lodging and entertainment in major US cities; and **Damron Accommodations**, which provides detailed listings of over 1000 accommodations for gays and lesbians worldwide. All of these titles are offered at a discount on the website. No specific city guides – everything is incorporated in the yearbooks.

gaytravel.com ☎ 1-800/GAY-TRAVEL, Ⓦ www.gaytravel.com. The premier site for trip planning, bookings, and general information about international gay and lesbian travel.

International Gay & Lesbian Travel Association ☎ 1-800/448-8550 or 954/776-2626, Ⓦ www.iglta.org. Trade group that can provide a list of gay- and lesbian-owned or -friendly travel agents, accommodation and other travel businesses.

In the UK

Ⓦ www.gaytravel.co.uk Online gay and lesbian travel agent, offering good deals on all types of holiday. Also lists gay- and lesbian-friendly hotels around the world.

Dream Waves Holidays ☎ 0870/042 2475, Ⓦ www.gayholidaysdirect.com. Specializes in exclusively gay holidays, including skiing trips and summer sun packages.

Madison Travel ☎ 01273/202 532, Ⓦ www.madisontravel.co.uk. Established travel agents specializing in packages to gay- and lesbian-friendly mainstream destinations, and also to gay/lesbian destinations.

Respect Holidays ☎ 0870/770 0169, Ⓦ www.respect-holidays.co.uk. Offers exclusively gay packages to all popular European resorts. Also check out adverts in the weekly papers **Boyz** and **Pink Paper**, handed out free in gay venues.

In Australia and New Zealand

Gay and Lesbian Tourism Australia Ⓦ www.galta.com.au. Directory and links for gay and lesbian travel in Australia and worldwide.

New Zealand Gay and Lesbian Tourism Association ☎ 0800/123 429, Ⓦ www.nzglta.org.nz. Organization devoted to enhancing the New Zealand travel experience for gay, lesbian and bisexual visitors.

Parkside Travel ☎ 08/8274 1222, Ⓔ parkside@herveyworld.com.au. Gay travel agent associated with local branch of Hervey World Travel; all aspects of gay and lesbian travel worldwide.

Silke's Travel ☎ 1800/807 860 or 02/8347 2000, Ⓦ www.silkes.com.au. Long-established gay and lesbian specialist, with the emphasis on women's travel.

Tearaway Travel ☎ 1800/664 440 or 03/9510 6644, Ⓦ www.tearaway.com. Gay-specific business dealing with international and domestic travel.

Crime and personal safety

Chile is one the safest South American countries to travel in, and violent crime against tourists is rare. The kind of sophisticated tactics used by thieves in neighbouring Peru and Bolivia are extremely uncommon in Chile, and the fact that you can walk around without being gripped by paranoia is one of the country's major bonuses.

That's not to say, of course, that you don't need to be careful. On the contrary, opportunistic pickpocketing and petty thieving is rife in Santiago and major cities such as Valparaíso, Arica and Puerto Montt, and you should take all the normal precautions to safeguard your money and valuables, paying special attention in bus terminals and markets – wear a money belt, and keep it tucked inside the waistband of your trousers or skirt, out of sight, and don't wear flashy jewellery, flaunt expensive cameras or carry a handbag. It's also a good idea to keep photocopies of your passport, tourist card, driving licence, air tickets and credit card details separate from the originals – whether it's safer to carry the originals with you or leave them in your hotel is debatable, but whatever you do, you should always have some form of ID on you, even if this is just a photocopy of your passport.

Out of the cities, there's no fear of banditry or general lawlessness, as there is in many parts of South America. Chile's police force, the **carabineros**, have the whole country covered, with stations in even the most remote areas, particularly in border regions. In general, the *carabineros* are helpful, reliable and scrupulously courteous to foreign travellers, with an extremely low level of corruption – *never* offer a bribe to a policeman, as you will cause offence and make the situation worse. If you're robbed and need a police report for an insurance claim, you should go to the nearest *retén* (police station), where details of the theft will be entered in a logbook. You'll be issued a slip of paper with the record number of the entry, but in most cases a full report won't be typed out until your insurance company requests it. *Carabineros* rarely speak English, which can be used to your advantage to avoid paying speeding fines – which incidentally have become far more frequent on main highways since radar controls were stepped up.

Street demonstrations, which were a way of life in Chile in the 1980s, still erupt when students or human rights activists protest. Demonstrations can get out of control, and the police invariably respond with a choreographed battle plan that includes the use of massive amounts of tear gas and batons – you'd be wise to steer well clear of the local Plaza de Armas (and also at the Plaza Italia in Santiago) if you're in town when one's taking place.

Avoid taking photographs of **naval vessels** and **military areas**, including prisons – this is illegal, and you could have your film confiscated. Certain sensitive international border areas also have photographic restrictions, particularly between Arica and the Peruvian frontier, which is full of mine fields and tank emplacements.

Emergency telephone numbers

Air rescue 138 (for mountaineering accidents)
Ambulance 131
Carabineros 133
Coast Guard 137
Fire 132
Investigaciones 134 (for serious crimes)

Directory

Addresses These are nearly always written with just the street name (and often just the surname, if the street is named after a person) followed by the number; for example, Prat 135. In the case of avenues, however, the address usually starts with the word *avenida*, e.g. Avenida 21 de Mayo 553. Buildings without a street number are suffixed by s/n, short for *sin número* ("without a number").

Bargaining Hard haggling is neither commonly practiced nor expected in Chile, though a bit of bargaining is in order at many markets, particularly when buying *artesanía*. It's also worth trying to bargain down the price of hotel rooms (of whatever category), especially outside the peak months of January and February.

Disabled travellers Chile makes very few provisions for people with disabilities, and travellers with mobility problems will have to contend with a lack of lifts, high curbs, dangerous potholes on pavements and worse.

Earthquakes You can expect to experience a few mild tremors during your stay in Chile. If you feel the ground move slightly, don't be alarmed – it's highly unlikely to be a fully fledged earthquake. If, however, you're unlucky enough to be caught in one, don't panic (remember that buildings in this country are designed to withstand earthquakes). Whatever you do, don't run out into the street, as this is how most injuries and fatalities are caused. Instead, stand under a doorway, which is the strongest part of a building. Note that lights will automatically go off if the quake is over 5 on the Richter scale.

Electricity 220V/50Hz is the standard throughout Chile. The sockets are two-pronged, with round pins (as opposed to the flat pins common in neighbouring countries).

Laundry Towns with a lot of students or itinerant workers have plenty of laundries, but otherwise they can be few and far between. Chilean laundries are not self-service and charge by the kilo – usually a very low rate. Your clothes are not always sent back terribly clean, however, as many laundries are loath to use hot water.

Telephone jacks Chile uses international standard telephone jacks (the same as those in the USA), compatible with all standard fax and email connections.

Time differences From the end of October to late March, Chile observes Daylight Saving Time and is three hours behind GMT (Greenwich Mean Time). The country is four hours behind GMT the rest of the year.

Tipping It's customary to leave a ten percent tip in restaurants – service is rarely included in the bill. You are not, however, expected to tip taxi drivers.

Toilets You'll find few public toilets (*baños*) in Chilean squares or on street corners; instead, every bar and café has one which, unless a sign proclaims it *exclusivo por clientes*, passers-by can use on payment of fifty pesos. In bus stations, large shops and most busy commercial premises, there is an attendant who collects a fee and dispenses toilet paper (*papel higiénico*), normally referred to by the brand name Confort. Be warned that Chileans have a rather unpleasant custom of leaving used toilet paper in an open box or bucket next to the toilet, to prevent the flushing system from blocking up.

Women Chilean men – especially groups of young workmen on the street – take great pleasure in making revolting kissing noises at unaccompanied young women as they walk past. Faced with the same woman accompanied by a man, however, they wouldn't make a sound. Fair-haired or obviously gringo-looking women are most vulnerable, but even *Chilenas* find themselves the focus of this unwanted attention. Most of them just walk past and ignore them, and you'll probably find it easiest to do likewise. Apart from this irritating but essentially harmless habit, you're unlikely to find Chile a threatening place as a single woman traveller, and if you stray from the main tourist circuits you'll find yourself continually befriended by local families who feel dreadfully sorry for you, having to take a holiday alone.

Guide

Guide

1

Santiago and around

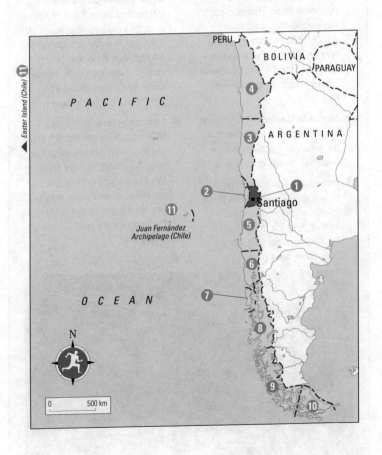

CHAPTER 1 # Highlights

✳ **Plaza de Armas** Gaze at the colonial architecture surrounding Santiago's lively central plaza – or sit on a park bench and just take in the hustle and bustle. **See p.101**

✳ **Museo Chileno de Arte Precolombino** This compact but exquisite collection of artefacts from dozens of pre-Hispanic civilizations features fine tapestries, intricate ceramics and dazzling gold jewels. **See p.105**

✳ **Mercado Central** At lunchtime the city's busy marketplace is an excellent place to sample fresh fish or seafood. **See p.112**

✳ **Bellavista** The traditional bohemian quarter offers great theatres and restaurants, and one of poet Pablo Neruda's homes, with its eclectic art collection. **See p.113**

✳ **Cerro San Cristóbal** Ride the elevator to the top of this steep hill where, on a clear day, you can see the snow-capped Andes towering over the city. **See p.113**

✳ **Cajón de Maipo** Blessed with sunny skies most of the year, this canyon southeast of Santiago is a prime location for Andean camping and hiking, plus you can go on multi-day horse treks that snake into Argentina and back. **See p.133**

✳ **Andean skiing** Skiers and snowboarders will delight in the four world-class ski areas near Santiago; for day-trips the slopes just east of the city are great while longer stays are best spent at the world-famous Portillo resort. **See p.138**

△ Plaza de Armas

Santiago and around

Set on a wide plain near the foot of the Andes, **Santiago** boasts one of the most dazzling backdrops of any capital city in the world. The views onto the towering cordillera after a rainstorm clears the air are magnificent, especially in winter, when the snow-covered peaks rise behind the city like a giant white rampart against the blue sky. Unfortunately, such vistas are few and far between, as these same mountains prevent winds from shifting the air trapped over the plain, leaving it thickly polluted with diesel fumes and dust. As a result, Santiago is frequently covered by a dense blanket of **smog** through which the Andes can be only dimly perceived – a smudged, tantalizing shadow of their real selves. The worst months for smog are between May and July.

The city itself is a great, sprawling metropolis of five million people – a third of the population of Chile. It's divided into 32 autonomous *comunas*, most of them squat, flat suburbs stretching from the centre ever further out. The historic centre of Santiago, in contrast, is compact and manageable, and, while not exactly beautiful, has a pleasant, enjoyable atmosphere. Part of its appeal comes from the fact that it's so green: tall, luxuriant trees fill the main square and line the riverbank, and there are many meticulously landscaped parks. Above all, though, it's the all-pervading sense of energy that makes the place so alluring, with crowds of Santiaguinos constantly milling through narrow streets packed with shoe-shiners, fruit barrows, news kiosks and sellers of everything from coat hangers to pirated CDs.

Architecturally, the city is a bit of a hotchpotch, thanks to a succession of earthquakes and a spate of undisciplined rebuilding in the 1960s and 1970s. Ugly office blocks and dingy *galerías* compete for space with beautifully maintained colonial buildings, while east of the centre Santiago's economic boom is reflected in the glittering new office buildings and international hotels of the *comunas* of Vitacura, Providencia and Las Condes. These different faces are part of a wider set of contrasts – between the gleaming, modern metro, for example, and the screeching, fume-belching buses; between the American-style shopping malls in the barrios altos and the shabby, old-fashioned shops in the historic centre; and, most significantly, between the well-heeled, briefcase-clutching professionals and the scores of pirate CD hustlers scrambling to make a living. It's not a place of excesses, however: homelessness is minimal compared to many other cities of this size, and there's no tension in the air or threat of violence. On the whole the capital is a good introduction to the country and its people, offering a pleasing choice of museums, markets, restaurants and nightspots, wrapped up in a friendly, if noisy, environment.

Most travellers stay here for just a few days before launching into far-flung trips to the north or south, but if you've time to spare you'd do well to use Santiago as a base while exploring the surrounding region. Some destinations

make easy day-trips, while others demand a couple of days or so. With the **Andes** so close and so accessible, you can be right in the mountains in an hour or two. In winter people go **skiing** for the day, with special buses laid on to and from the resorts; in warmer months the **Cajón del Maipo** (a deep canyon cutting into the high cordillera) offers fantastic trekking, horseback riding and whitewater rafting. Heading west towards Valparaíso (see p.147) you'll also find good hiking opportunities in the arid coastal mountains of **Parque Nacional La Campana**, where you can easily do a day's walking without seeing another soul. Nearby villages can provide a relaxing antidote to Santiago's constant din, like **Los Andes** to the north, or **Pomaire** to the west, famous for its incredibly cheap pottery. Still more tempting are the many **vineyards** within easy reach of Santiago, increasing numbers of which now offer tours and tastings. Finally, there are many excellent **beaches** less than two hours away by bus – for more on these, see Chapter Two.

Santiago

How much time you spend in **SANTIAGO** depends on the length of your stay in the country. It's by no means the highlight of Chile, and if time is really short a couple of days should suffice before you head off to the spectacular landscapes north or south of the city. That said, Santiago is the cultural, economic and educational hub of Chile, and the best place to come to grips with the country's identity. Dipping into Santiago's vibrant theatre and music scene, getting a sense of its history in the city's museums, checking out its varied restaurants, and striking up conversations with the wide variety of people you'll meet here will really help you scratch beneath the surface and get the most out of your time in this kaleidoscopic country.

Some history

Some seven years after Francisco Pizarro conquered Cuzco in Peru, he dispatched **Pedro de Valdivia** southwards to claim and settle more territory for the Spanish Crown. After eleven months of travelling, Valdivia and his 150 men reached what he considered to be a suitable site for a new city, and, on February 12, 1541, officially founded "Santiago de la Nueva Extremadura", wedged into a triangle of land bounded by the Río Mapocho to the north, its southern branch to the south and the rocky Santa Lucía hill to the east. A native population of **Picunches** was scattered around the region, but this didn't deter Valdivia from getting down to business: with great alacrity the main square was established and the surrounding streets were marked out with a string and ruler, a fort was built in the square (thus named "Plaza de Armas") and several other buildings were erected. Six months later they were all razed in a Picunche raid.

The town was doggedly rebuilt to the same plans, and Santiago began to take on the shape of a new colonial capital. But nine years after founding it, the Spaniards, in search of gold, shifted their attention to Arauco in the south, and Santiago became something of a backwater. Following the violent Mapuche uprising in 1553, however, the Spaniards were forced to abandon their towns south of the Bío Bío, and many returned to Santiago. Nonetheless, growth continued to be very slow: there were no easy riches to be had from gold or silver, so settlers were never large in number, and what opportunities the land offered were thwarted by strict trade restrictions imposed by Spain. Moreover, expansion was repeatedly knocked back by **earthquakes**, which shook the city at alarmingly regular intervals.

Santiago started to look like a real capital during the course of the eighteenth century, as trade restrictions were eased, more wealth was created, and the population increased. However, it wasn't until after independence in 1818 that expansion really got going, as the rich clamoured to build themselves glamorous mansions and the state erected beautiful public buildings such as the Teatro Municipal and the congress building; a visitor who returned to Santiago after a nine-year absence commented, "What a transformation! So many palaces! What architectural majesty and beauty!"

As the city entered the twentieth century it began to push eastwards into the new barrio alto and north into Bellavista. The horizontal spread has gone well beyond these limits since then, gobbling up outlying towns and villages at great speed; Gran Santiago now stretches 40km by 40km. Its central zones have shot up vertically, too, particularly in Providencia and Las Condes, where the showy high-rise buildings reflect the country's rapid economic growth over the past decade. Despite this dramatic transformation, however, the city's

The **telephone code** for Santiago is ☎2. Telephone numbers that begin with 9 are mobile phones. When calling from a fixed line to a mobile, dial "09" plus the number. For mobile to mobile calls, begin with just "9". For more telephone information see p.61.

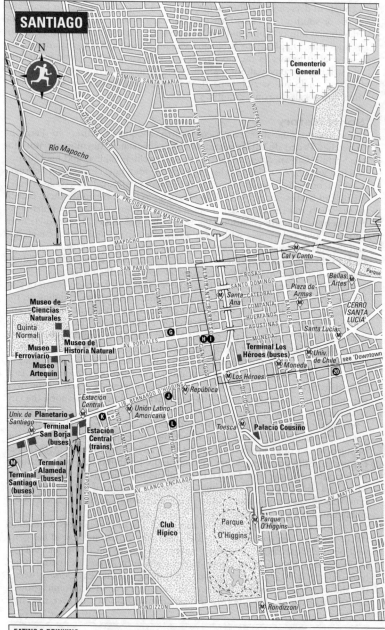

EATING & DRINKING

Akarana	**3**	Brannigan's	**4**	De Cangrego		El Huerto	**8**	Ozono	**13**	La Tecla	**24**
Astrid y Gastón	**10**	Café Melba	**2**	a Conejo	**18**	Infante 51	**15**	Roll's Bar	**11**	La Terraza	**21**
Barandaraián	**17**	Café del Patio	**12**	Club de Jazz	**23**	Liguria	**14**	Santo Remedio	**16**	Tomm	**6**
La Batuta	**22**	Caffeto	**9**	La Habana Vieja	**20**	Mister Ed	**5**	El Taller	**19**		

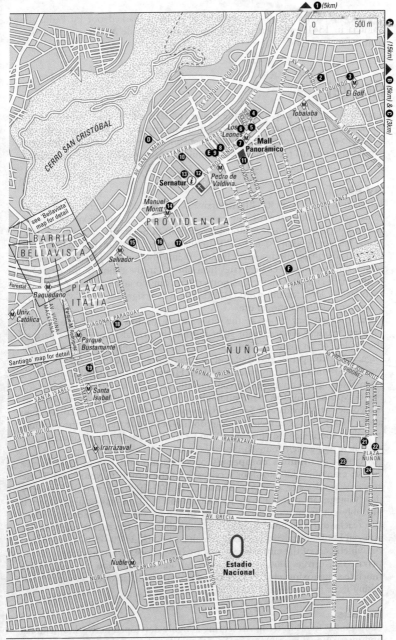

ACCOMMODATION

Urbano	**7**	La Casa Roja	**G**	Hotel Lyon	**F**	La Posada del Inglés	**A**
Zanzíbar	**1**	Dacarlo	**M**	Hotel Orly	**E**	Regal Pacific	**C**
		HI youth hostel	**H**	Hotel Tokyo	**I**	Residencial Alemaña	**L**
		Hotel Imperio	**K**	Hyatt Regency Santiago	**B**	Residencial Mery	**J**

Sheraton Santiago &
San Cristóbal Tower **D**

central core still sticks to the same street pattern marked out by Pedro de Valdivia in 1541, and its first public space, the Plaza de Armas, is still at the heart of its street life.

Arrival

Santiago is undoubtedly one of the easiest and least intimidating South American capitals to **arrive** in. Connections from the airport, bus terminals and train station to the centre of the city are frequent and straightforward, and while you should take normal precautions, you're unlikely to be hassled or feel threatened while you're finding your feet.

By air

International and domestic **flights** arrive at Arturo Merino Benítez airport in Pudahuel (the commune it is sometimes referred to as), some 26km northwest of Santiago. The smart international terminal has a **Sernatur** information desk (daily 8.45am–9.30pm; ☎6019320) in the baggage reclaim hall, where staff give out free maps and booklets. Nearby there's also a **casa de cambio**, Afex, which offers poorer exchange rates than options in the centre of the city. Out in the main arrivals hall, there's another Afex cambio and multiple **ATMs** on each level – look for the word "RedBanc", which signifies an ATM machine connected for international use.

The cheapest way to get to the city centre is by **bus**, with two companies offering frequent services from right outside the arrivals gate – buses park at the far left or far right ends of the curb. The blue Centropuerto bus has the edge, being cheaper (CH$1100) and running more frequently (7am–11.30pm; every 10–30min); it drops you off at **Los Héroes** on the Alameda (the city's main thoroughfare), where you can join the metro, catch numerous buses, or flag down a taxi. Tur Bus (6am–midnight; every 30min; CH$1300) takes you to the corner of Moneda and San Martín, a couple of blocks east of Los Héroes, and a walk to Moneda metro station. Both buses call at the domestic terminal as well as the international terminal, and each will usually drop passengers off anywhere along their route to the city centre.

A couple of **minibus companies**, operating from the row of desks by the airport exit, offer door-to-door services from the airport to your hotel. These are very good value, charging around CH$3700–5000 per person. The only disadvantages are that you have to wait around until the bus is full, and you'll probably get an unwanted city tour as they drop off other passengers before you reach your own hotel. Alongside the minibus counters there's a desk where you can book official airport **taxis**, which cost CH$12,000–15,000, depending on which part of the city you're going to. If you bargain (in Spanish) with the private taxi drivers touting for business outside the exit, you can usually pay much less, approximately CH$8,000 to any centrally located part of the city, but taking these taxis is at your own risk.

By bus

Santiago has four bus terminals serving a highly developed network of national and international buses. Most **international buses,** and those from **southern Chile,** arrive at the **Terminal de Buses Santiago** (also known as the **Terminal de Buses Sur** or **Estación Central**) on the Alameda, a few blocks west of the train station. Next door, the **Terminal de Buses Alameda** is the terminal for all Pullman Bus and Tur Bus journeys. From here, you can get to the centre by metro (Universidad de Santiago), or catch any of the numerous local buses and taxis hurtling east down the Alameda.

Most **buses from the north** arrive at the **Terminal San Borja**, right next to the train station and again handy for the metro (Estación Central) and buses to the centre. The much smaller **Terminal los Héroes** serves a mixture of buses from the north and south, and a few international ones; it's just north of the Alameda (near Los Héroes metro station) and is a short and cheap taxi ride from most central accommodation. For more details, see "Moving on from Santiago", p.131.

By train
The only train services in Chile are between Santiago and the south, with all trains arriving at and departing from the grand **Estación Central** on the Alameda, west of the centre. You can take the metro or numerous buses and taxis into the centre from right outside the station.

Information

The two main sources of tourist information are **Sernatur**, the national tourist board, and the **Oficina de Turismo** run by the Municipalidad de Santiago. **Conaf**, the national parks administration, also has an information centre in Santiago.

Sernatur
The **Sernatur** office is east of the city centre at Av Providencia 1550, between Manuel Montt and Pedro de Valdivia metro stations (Dec–March, Mon–Fri 9am–6.30pm, Sat 9am–2pm; ☎7318336 ⓦwww.sernatur.cl). It offers a range of free booklets on Santiago's attractions, accommodation and restaurants, and the staff, usually English-speaking, can answer most questions about services and facilities in the city. It's also a good place to stock up on information on the rest of Chile, with lists of accommodation in all the other regions, as well as some themed booklets such as *Wine Circuits, National Parks, Ski Centres, Beaches, the North, the South* and *Camping*; you have to ask for them, though, as they're usually kept out of sight. Be persistent in your information requests, as the staff tends to palm off the nearest brochure instead of the most appropriate.

Oficina de Turismo
Far more conveniently located – in the Casa Colorada, just off the Plaza de Armas at Merced 860 – the Municipalidad de Santiago's **Oficina de Turismo** (Mon–Fri, 10am–6pm; ☎6327783) has free maps, a range of booklets (including the excellent, and free, *Historical Heritage of Santiago*) and a friendly, competent staff. Free walking tours are available nearly every day, but you must ask for the *Walking around Santiago* brochure, which has the details.

Conaf
For information on Chile's national parks, visit **Conaf** at Av Presidente Bulnes 291 (Mon–Fri 9.30am–5.30pm; ☎3900125), where you can buy detailed information sheets (CH$100) on all the national parks and reserves, as well as books on native flora and fauna, and other mementos.

City transport

You'll probably spend most time in the city centre, which is entirely walk-able, but for journeys further afield you'll find public transport cheap, safe and abundant. For trips along the main east–west axis formed by the Alameda and its extensions, the **metro** is quickest. The city and suburbs are also served by thousands of **buses**, while **colectivos** offer a quick way out of the centre into surrounding districts. Regular **taxis** are numerous and inexpensive, and are in many cases the most convenient way to get about.

The metro

Santiago's spotless **metro** system (daily 6.30am–10.30pm, Ⓦ www.metro-chile .cl) is modern, efficient and safe, though packed solid at rush hour. Of the three (soon to be four) lines, #1 is the most useful (and crowded) running east–west under the Alameda and Avenida Providencia. Line #2 runs north–south from

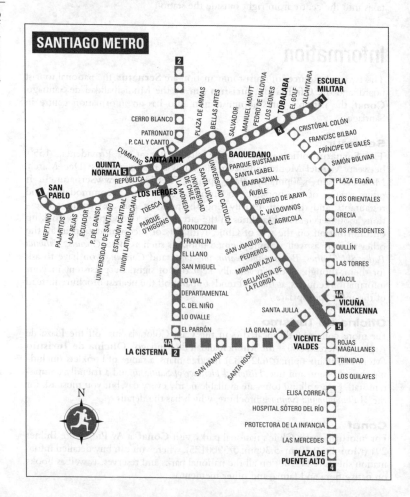

SANTIAGO METRO

Puente Cal y Canto, by the Río Mapocho, down to Lo Ovalle, crossing Line #1 at Los Héroes, and is useful for visiting Palacio Cousiño, Parque O'Higgins and the Franklin market. The most recently constructed Line #5 (which beat Lines #3 and #4 from the drawing board to reality) runs from the Quinta Normal station in a southeasterly direction, via Plaza de Armas and Bellas Artes stations, to outlying Bellavista de La Florida – not to be confused with the hip Bellavista neighbourhood in central Santiago. Lines #4 and #4A will link the eastern and southern parts of the city to Lines #1 and #2. The map shown here shows the newest additions as dotted lines.

Fares are the same for any length of journey, but fall into two different price brackets according to the time of day: the normal rate (7.15–9am & 6–7.30pm) is CH$430 while the lower fare, *rebajado* (6.30–7.15am, 9am–6pm & 7.30–10.30pm) is CH$340. For cheaper rates (CH$410 and CH$320, respectively) and less waiting, buy a Multivía card (costing CH$1000 plus however much you want to add on to it), a rechargeable multi-trip ticket from which each journey's fare is deducted until it runs out. (Note that because of the CH$1000 cost for the ticket, it's only worthwhile if you are staying in the city for quite some time).

Buses

Santiago has one of the highest densities of buses in the world, with more than 8000 of them choking the streets. City buses are called **micros**, and most are yellow. The most widely used form of transport in Santiago, they're very cheap – CH$320 a ride – and run from 5am until well past midnight. They're also very noisy, belch out smoke and are bewildering to the uninitiated – there's no bus route map available, and it was only recently that proper bus stops were introduced in the city.

However, buses do at least stick to fixed routes, and the destination and main points of the route are displayed on the front window. Beware, though, as buses hurtle along at breakneck speed, rarely braking for pedestrians, and fatalities are so common that a huge consumer backlash is finally forcing the government to do something about it. They're most useful for going east or west, along the Alameda – as a general rule, buses displaying Estación Central will take you west, while those displaying Providencia or Apoquindo are going east. If you're not sure where to get off, ask the driver ("*¿me puede avisar cuando lleguemos a . . .?*") and you'll no doubt find everyone else on the bus keeping an eye out for you. Santiago recently integrated a system so that you can use the same tickets for buses and metros.

Taxis

Santiago has more **taxis** than New York City, and in the centre you'll have no trouble flagging one down. Sometimes you'll have to track down a taxi rank and, away from commercial areas, you will have to call for one. Taxis are black with yellow roofs and have a small light in the top right-hand corner of the windscreen that's lit to show the cab is available. Fares are low by North American and European standards and are displayed on the window – usually CH$150 when the meter's started and CH$80 every 200m; you're not expected to add a tip. Drivers are allowed to charge much more at night, so first check the rate on the window before you begin the journey and try to verbally confirm an estimate to your location. **Scams** are frequent in taxis, including drivers taking extra-long routes, and rip-offs on large bills (the driver takes your CH$10,000 bill, switches it for a CH$1000 note, and asks for more). Be firm and pay with exact change (you supply the small bills), and most drivers will be more honest. Note that taxi drivers aren't tested on their knowledge of the city's streets in order to get a licence; if you're going somewhere out of the way, it's best to check where it is beforehand (there's a good A–Z in the back of the yellow pages).

Colectivos

Santiago's **colectivos** (collective taxis) look like ordinary taxis except they're black all over and cram in as many as four passengers at a time. They travel along fixed routes, mostly from the centre out to the suburbs; a sign on the roof indicates the destination. Plaza Baquedano (usually called Plaza Italia) is the starting point for many *colectivo* routes. Price varies along the route, but *colectivos* generally cost about the same as a bus.

Accommodation

There's plenty of **accommodation** in Santiago to suit most budgets, though *really* cheap places are scarce and tend to be rather squalid. Most of the city's low-price rooms are small, simple and sparsely furnished, often without a window but usually fairly clean. Moving up a notch or two you'll find more comfort in many of the small, moderately priced hotels, though you need to choose carefully as some of them can be dismal. Up-market hotels are abundant, especially in Providencia, ranging from good-value independent outfits to luxurious international chains. Prices in Santiago don't usually fluctuate much during the course of the year, although a few hotels charge more in summer (Nov–Feb). The prices listed are for the cheapest double room in high season. At the lower end of the scale, single travellers can expect to pay half this rate, but mid- and upper-range hotels usually charge the same rate for a single as for a double. Non-resident foreigners are exempt from the 19 percent tax on hotel rooms.

Central Santiago

From the Plaza de Armas east is the tidier, better-restored section of the historic centre, with the easiest walking access to most of the central attractions: the art museums, folk art markets, Cerro Santa Lucía, Bellavista, Parque Forestal and Cerro San Cristóbal. There are some good inexpensive lodgings and many middle- and upper-range options offering a wide variety of services.

Che Lagarto Hostel Tucapel Jiméniz 24 ☎6991493 ⊛www.chelagarto.com. Opposite Los Héroes bus terminal, this brand new hostel is bright and shiny, offering doubles with bath in addition to spacious dorms. Los Héroes metro. CH$6000 in dorm, doubles CH$15000. **❶**

City Hotel Compañía 1063 ☎6954526, Ⓕ6956775. Despite its location in the heart of the historic centre, right next to the Plaza de Armas, *City* is very quiet and pleasant. The rooms, some small, are clean and well kept. Some have a view of an airshaft, others of the street and the Cathedral. Best feature (by far) is the central location. Near Plaza de Armas metro station; free parking. **❸**

Crowne Plaza Santiago Alameda 136 ☎6381042, Ⓕ6336015, ⊛www.santiago .crowneplaza.com. Another of Santiago's top luxury hotels, with all the requisite services and amenities, including tennis courts and a gym. A great location for those who want easy access to the Bellavista neighbourhood. Rooms are spacious; upper floors on the eastern side have unobstructed views of the Andes. There's an excellent Italian restaurant. Baquedano metro. **❽**

Dacarlo Manuel Thompson 3940 ☎7764523 or 7787329, ⊛www.hoteldacarlo.cl. Newly built hotel is very clean but slightly kitsch, with funny paintings everywhere. Rooms are small, bathrooms even smaller. Astride the Alameda and Santiago bus terminals, Dacarlo is very handy for early morning departures or late night arrivals. The airport is just 20 minutes away. There's a nondescript restaurant and a bar. Free parking. Pila del Ganso metro. ❹

HI youth hostel Cienfuegos 151 ☎6718532. Highly recommended hostel, only a five-minute walk from Los Héroes metro, offers single dorm beds and four-person rooms. The English-speaking staff are very helpful. CH$6000 dorm.

Hotel Carrera Teatinos 180 ☎6982011, ℉6721083, ⓦwww.carrera.cl. Chile's oldest hotel and one of its most luxurious. On the Plaza de la Constitución, it offers privileged views of La Moneda, the presidential palace and several ministries. There's an outdoor pool on the roof. One of the three exclusive hotel restaurants, the *Jardín Secreto*, is a favourite among Santiago's elite. Stop in at the bar (open to non-guests) for fantastic sunset views. Moneda metro. ❽

Hotel Libertador Av Lib Bernardo O'Higgins 853 ☎6394211, ℉6337128. Large 1970s-style hotel opposite the Iglesia San Francisco. Spacious, comfortable rooms, all with TV and bath. A rooftop terrace has sun lounges and a plunge pool. Santa Lucía metro. ❺

Hotel Montecarlo Victoria Subercaseaux 209 ☎6381176, ℉6335577, ⓦwww.hotelmontecarlo .cl. A quiet hideaway, it's a mere two blocks from Alameda and near the art museums and the lively Barrio Lastarria neighbourhood. The small hotel has modernist architecture and unusual interior design. Ask for a room with a view of the hill. Rates include breakfast and parking. Universidad Católica metro. ❻

Hotel Nuevo Valparaíso Morandé 791 ☎6715698. The rooms are so cheap here that many gringos (especially language teachers) rent them by the month. They're not bad for the price, and there's a kitchen, though you need to bring your own utensils. Good place to meet other travellers. Puente Cal y Canto metro. ❸

Hotel París París 813 ☎ & ℉6394037. Popular budget hotel, tucked behind the Iglesia San Francisco. Most rooms have private bath, and there's a little interior patio where you can take breakfast. The friendly and trustworthy dueña runs a discreet "by the hour" business in some of her rooms. Another good place to meet other travellers. Universidad de Chile metro. ❸

Hotel París Nuevo París 813 ☎ & ℉6394037. Newer addition to the original hotel next door, with smart, comfortable rooms and immaculate bathrooms. Best-value hotel in Santiago in this price range, and a good choice for a couple of nights' comfort at the start or end of your trip. Universidad de Chile metro. ❹

Residencial Londres Londres 54 ☎6382215, ℉6323493, ⓔunico54 @ctcinternet.cl. The ideal place for travellers on a shoestring budget. It's an ancient, comfortable house in the quiet Londres neighbourhood, just a block from Alameda. Breakfast is included, but the one TV is in a common room and there's one phone per floor. No restaurant, bar, or parking. Reservations recommended. Universidad de Chile metro. ❸

Residencial Santo Domingo Santo Domingo 735 ☎ & ℉6396733, ⓔsantodomingoinn@hotmail .com. A fine and safe option for budget travellers, located just three blocks from the Plaza de Armas. The restored mansion has a marble entryway, hardwood floors, high ceilings and two interior patios, but some second-floor rooms are a bit shabby. Other deficits are the dingy neighborhood and ferocious traffic noise. Plaza de Armas metro. ❷

Vegas Hotel Londres 49 ☎6322498, ℉6325084, ⓦwww.hotelvegas.net. A national monument, in the quiet Londres neighbourhood, the Vegas is quaint, clean and cosy. Rooms have small reading areas set in lovely hexagonal alcoves. A small terrace is out back. There's also a café and a bar; breakfast is not included. Universidad de Chile metro. ❺

West of the historic centre: Barrio Brasil and Barrio República

From the Plaza de Armas west all the way to Santiago's bus terminals is the seedier part of central Santiago. But it's very up-and-coming, especially among students, thanks to its university campuses and ever-increasing numbers of cafés and bars.

West of the Norte-Sur highway, both north and south of Alameda, is Santiago's original upper-class neighbourhood, and it still has beautiful, old architecture. These barrios, Brasil to the north and República to the south, are mainly residential and are convenient to the bus terminals and the airport. For hotels in these barrios, the centre is just a metro or bus ride away.

La Casa Roja Agustinas 2113, Barrio Brasil ⊕6964241. Opened in 2002, this Aussie-owned place has made a name for itself as a backpackers' nexus. Huge remodelled mansion accommodates eighty in its various refurbished bunks and suites; there's also often live music played in the large backyard. República metro.**❷**

Hotel Imperio Av Lib Bernardo O'Higgins 2876 ⊕6897774, ⑤6892916. Comfortable, well-equipped hotel offering eighty rooms on the Alameda; rather dated but well cared for and good value. Estación Central metro. **❺**

Hotel Majestic Santo Domingo 1526 ⊕6958366, ⑤6974051, ⓦwww.hotel-majestic.co.cl. The *Majestic* is an eyesore from the outside, but the lobby takes you back to 1950s India. Rooms are tiny, and some don't have an outside view. The garden has a pool, palm trees and a small terrace. There's an excellent Indian restaurant, rare in Santiago. A fifteen-minute walk from Plaza de Armas. Santa Ana metro. **❻**

Hotel Tokyo Almirante Barroso 160 ⊕6714516, ⓦwww.hoteltokyo.cl. Tucked away on a little side street just west of the Pan-American high-way, the *Tokyo* is a gem of a hotel, decorated with antique furniture and Japanese artwork and collectables. Rooms are large, if a bit rundown. Enjoy breakfast in the flower garden. The heart of Barrio Brasil is very accessible from this hotel. Los Héroes metro. **❹**

Residencial Alemaña República 220 ⊕6713668. Immaculately clean budget accommodation on an attractive, tree-lined avenue. All meals available. There's no sign at the door. República metro. **❹**

Residencial Mery Pasaje República 36 ⊕ & ⑤6968883. Spotless rooms in a pleasant, cheerfully decorated *residencial* on a quiet alley round the corner from República metro. **❹**

Providencia

The glitzy commercial centre of Santiago, Providencia has a number of pricey lodging places, but a few off the beaten path are quiet and offer good value. As far as a place to base yourself, it does offer a good number of restaurants and bars, plus some interesting architecture, but the Suecia section, a common gringo hangout, is filled with rowdy dancehalls and occasionally bothersome drunks.

Apart Hotel Monteverde Pio Nono 193 ⊕7773607, ⑤7370341, ⓔaparthotelmonteverde@terra.cl. For visitors who like to be in the centre of everything, this is the place, right on Bellavista's main drag, which fills with partygoers and vendors on Friday and Saturday nights; surprisingly, though, no bar or restaurant inside. Rooms are clean and ample, with kitchenette and colour TVs, but no cable. This is the closest hotel to Pablo Neruda's Santiago house and to the entrance to Cerro San Cristóbal. Breakfast and parking included. Baquedano metro. **❹**

Hotel Lyon Av Ricardo Lyon 1525 ⊕2257732, ⑤2258697, ⓦwww.hotellyon.cl. Off the beaten path, this is a small, quiet and peaceful hotel. The fourteen rooms are large and comfortable; there's also a small living room and a nice yard. About fifteen blocks south of Av Providencia, not on any metro line. Free parking. **❺**

Hotel Orly Pedro de Valdivia 027 ⊕2318947, ⓦwww.orlyhotel.com. Immaculate and highly recommendable, *Orly* feels like a small-town bed and breakfast. Warm and cosy, it seems almost out of place in the heart of Providencia. The hotel has a bar and a fun little Internet café. Breakfast and parking are included. Pedro de Valdivia metro. **❻**

Hyatt Regency Santiago Av Kennedy 4601 ⊕2181234, ⑤2182513, ⓦwww.santiago.hyatt .com. Impeccable service, top restaurants and beautiful views of the Andes, along with a gym, sauna and clay tennis courts. The drawback is that it's stuck in a very sterile residential neigh-bourhood, within walking distance to nothing but the Parque Arauco shopping mall. Approxi-mately seven long blocks north of Escuela Militar metro. **❽**

Sheraton Santiago and San Cristóbal Tower Av Santa María 1742 ⊕7071000, ⑤7071010, ⓦwww.sheraton.cl. Santiago's *Sheraton* is two hotels in one: the original *Sheraton* built in 1970 and the luxurious *San Cristóbal Tower,* which opened in 1998. Nestled right into the side of Cerro San Cristóbal, the property offers impressive views, spacious rooms, ample green areas, a huge pool and a patio. It's all a bit removed from everything, though. **❽**

Las Condes and east

By far the most accessible to Santiago's three major ski centres and easy to reach from the airport as well, Las Condes has become Santiago's up-and-coming hotel neighbourhood. The city's two largest shopping centres and most of its art galleries are nearby, but central attractions are not within walking distance and most of these hotels are far from the metro line.

La Posada del Inglés Camino a Farellones 15201 ⊤ & ⑲ 2174105, ⑩ www.chile-hotels.com/laposada. An excellent choice for tourists who want to spend all day on the mountain and hit the town at night – but don't want to pay for slopeside lodging. On the road that winds up to the ski slope, but still 30km away, this is a British-run, lovely old house with great views of El Arrayán valley and the mountains. It has an outdoor terrace with two pools, and a lounge with a stone fireplace. Trendy El Arrayán neighbourhood, with bars, restaurants and three discos, is within walking distance. The kitchen serves plates of the day; there is no menu. Follow Av Las Condes to the edge of town; at the YPF petrol station just before Plaza San Enrique, follow signs to Farellones, a right turn. ❺

Regal Pacific Av Apoquindo 5680 ⊤ 3776304, ⑲ 3776318, ⑩ www.regal-pacific.com. A handsome, small five-star hotel just opposite the Manquehue shopping centre, frequented by skiers from Latin American countries and Asian businessmen. Rooms are quiet and have excellent views of the Andes. There's an indoor Jacuzzi, while the restaurant serves typical Chilean food and has an acclaimed chef. ❽

The City

Santiago isn't a city that demands major sightseeing, and you can get round many of its attractions on foot in two or three days. A tour of the compact core, centred on the bustling **Plaza de Armas**, should include visits to the **Palacio de la Moneda**, the excellent **Museo Chileno de Arte Precolombino**, and the evocative **Museo Colonial**, followed by a climb up **Cerro Santa Lucía**. Less strenuous options would be lunch at the intriguing **Mercado Central**, or just sitting in the plaza with an ice cream and a book.

North of downtown, on the other side of the Río Mapocho, it's an easy funicular ride up **Cerro San Cristóbal**, whose summit provides unrivalled views for miles around. At its foot, **Barrio Bellavista** is Santiago's "Latin Quarter", replete with small cafés, *salsatecas* and restaurants. This is where you'll find the house where **poet Pablo Neruda** lived, now a wonderful museum filled with objects he collected around the world. West of the centre, the once glamorous barrios that housed Santiago's moneyed classes at the beginning of the twentieth century make for rewarding, romantic wanders, and contain some splendid old mansions, including the sumptuous **Palacio Cousiño**. Moving east into the barrios altos of Providencia and Las Condes, the tone is newer and flasher. Apart from shiny malls, there's less to draw you out here, with the notable exception of the highly enjoyable arts and crafts market at **Los Dominicos**.

Plaza de Armas

The **Plaza de Armas** is the centre of Santiago and the country, both literally – all distances to the rest of Chile are measured from here – and symbolically. It was the first public space laid out by Pedro de Valdivia when he founded the city in 1541 and quickly became the nucleus of Santiago's administrative, commercial and social life. This is where the young capital's most important seats of power – the law courts, the governor's palace, and the cathedral – were built, and where its markets, bullfights (no longer allowed), festivals and other

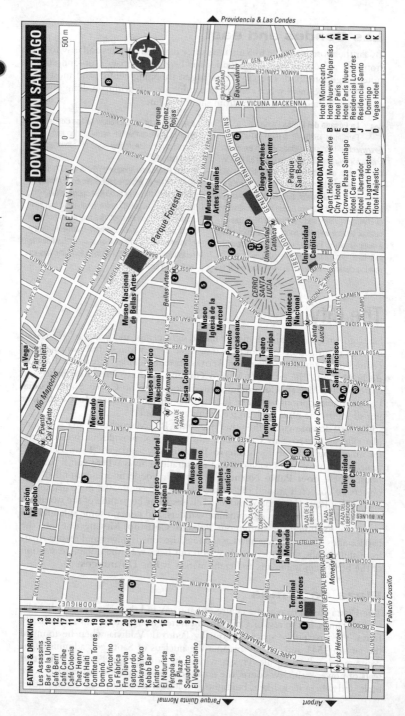

DOWNTOWN SANTIAGO

▲ Providencia & Las Condes

N

0   500 m

EATING & DRINKING

Les Assassins	3
Bar de la Unión	18
Café Berri	12
Café Caribe	17
Café Colonia	11
Chaz Henry	4
Café Haiti	9
Confitería Torres	19
Dominó	10
Don Victorino	14
La Fábrica	1
Fra Diavola	20
Gatopardo	13
Izakaya Yoko	5
Kebab Bar	16
Kintaro	2
El Naturista	8
Pérgola de la Plaza	15
Squadritto	6
El Vegetariano	7

ACCOMMODATION

Apart Hotel Montcarlo	F
Hotel Montverde	B
Hotel Nuevo Valparaíso	A
City Hotel	E
Hotel Paris	M
Crowne Plaza Santiago	G
Hotel Paris Nuevo	L
Hotel Carrera	H
Residencial Londres	C
Hotel Libertador	J
Residencial Santo	K
Che Lagarto Hostel	I
Domingo	
Hotel Majestic	D
Vegas Hotel	

Parque Quinta Normal ▲

Airport ▲

Palacio Cousiño ▲

public activities took place. Four and a half centuries later, this is still where the city's pulse beats loudest. Half an hour's people watching here is perhaps a visitor's best introduction to Santiago.

These days the open market space has been replaced by flower gardens and numerous trees; palms, poplars and eucalyptus tower over benches packed with Peruvian job hunters, giggling schoolchildren, gossiping old men, lovers, tourists, indulgent grandmothers and packs of uniformed shop girls on their lunch break. Forlorn photographers stand about with their old box cameras and mangy props – a toy lion to sit reluctant toddlers on, and a llama that looks asleep. Thirsty dogs hang around the fountain; shoe-shiners polish the feet of dour businessmen clutching *El Mercurio*; and ancient-looking chess players hold sombre tournaments inside the bandstand. All this against a backdrop of constant noise supplied by street performers, singers and howling evangelical preachers. Meanwhile, a constant ebb and flow of people march in and out of the great civic and religious buildings enclosing the square.

Correo Central and Municipalidad

On the northwest corner of the Plaza de Armas stands the candyfloss-coloured **Correo Central**, whose interior, with its tiered galleries crowned by a beautiful glass roof, is every bit as impressive as its elaborate facade. It was built in 1882 on the foundations of what had been the Palacio de los Gobernadores (governors' palace) during colonial times, and the Palacio de los Presidentes de Chile (presidential palace) after independence. Now given over to more mundane affairs, this is where you'll come to send postcards home and where you can pick up poste restante (see p.61).

In the same block, on the northeast corner of the square, is the pale, Neoclassical edifice of Santiago's **Municipalidad**. The first *cabildo* (town hall) was erected on this site back in the early seventeenth century and also contained the city's prison. Several reconstructions and restorations have taken place since then, most recently in 1895. A curious feature is that the basement is still divided into the original cells of the old prison, now used as offices. Note the city's coat of arms on the central pediment above the flags; it was donated by King Carlos V in 1552 to consolidate Santiago's status as a city.

Museo Histórico Nacional

Wedged between the Correo and the Municipalidad is the splendid **Palacio de la Real Audiencia**, an immaculately preserved colonial building that's borne witness to some of Santiago's most important turns of history. Built by the Spanish Crown between 1804 and 1807 to house the royal courts of justice, it had served this purpose for just two years when Chile's first government junta assembled here to replace the Spanish governor with its own elected leader. Eight years later it was the meeting place of Chile's first Congress, and the building was the seat of government until 1846, when President Bulnes moved to La Moneda. The Palacio's grand old rooms, arranged around a large central courtyard, today house the **Museo Histórico Nacional** (Tues–Sat 10am–5.30pm, Sun 10am–2pm; CH$600, free on Sun), crammed with eclectic and often fascinating relics of the past, including furniture, sewing machines and ladies' clothes – all of it fun to look at, but too chaotic to be really illuminating.

Cathedral and Museo de Arte Sagrado

The west side of the square is dominated by the grandiose stone bulk of the **Catedral Metropolitana** (Mon–Sat 9am–7pm, Sun 9am–noon). A combination of Neoclassical and Baroque styles, with its orderly columns and pediment

△ Correo Central

and its ornate bell towers, the cathedral bears the mark of **Joaquín Toesca,** who was brought over from Italy in 1780 to oversee its completion. Toesca went on to become the most important architect of colonial Chile, designing many of Santiago's public buildings, including La Moneda. This is actually the fifth church to be built on this site; the first was burnt down by Picunches just months after Valdivia had it built, and the others were destroyed by earthquakes in 1552, 1647 and 1730. Inside, take a look at the main altar, carved out of marble and richly embellished with bronze and lapis lazuli. Note also the intricately crafted silver frontal, the work of Bavarian Jesuits in the sixteenth century.

You'll find more examples of the Jesuits' exquisite silverwork in the **Museo de Arte Sagrado** (Mon 10.30am–1.30pm & 3.30–6pm; free) tucked away behind the main body of the cathedral. To find the entrance, go down the passage belonging to the bookshop next door to the cathedral. A gate at the bottom takes you back into the cathedral grounds and into one of Santiago's most evocative courtyards, where languid palm trees brush against crumbling colonial architecture. From here, signs point to the three rooms containing the museum's collection of religious paintings, sculpture, furniture and silverwork, including a finely crafted silver lectern and tabernacle. These pieces aside, none of it is as impressive as the stuff in the Museo Colonial in the Iglesia San Francisco (see p.110), but still makes for a rewarding browse.

Casa Colorada – Museo de Santiago

Just off the southeast corner of the plaza, at Merced 860, you'll find the **Casa Colorada,** built in 1769 and generally considered to be Santiago's best-preserved colonial house. With its clay-tiled roof, its row of balconied windows giving onto the street and its distinctive, deep-red walls, the two-storey mansion certainly provides a striking example of an eighteenth-century town residence. The house is built around two large patios, one of which you walk through to get to the **Museo de Santiago** (Tues–Fri 10am–6pm, Sat 10am–5pm, Sun 11am–2pm; CH$500, free on Sun; ☎6336700), which occupies five of the Casa Colorada's rooms. This rather humble museum is dedicated to the history of the city from pre-Columbian to modern times, which is illustrated mainly by scale models, maps and paintings. None of it's very slick, and there's no English commentary, but each room has a detailed information panel in Spanish which, if you're able or can be bothered to plough through, provides an excellent account of the various stages of Santiago's development.

Museo Chileno de Arte Precolombino

A stone's throw from the southwest corner of the Plaza de Armas, on the corner of Compañía and Bandera, stands the beautifully restored 1807 Real Casa de la Aduana (the old royal customs house) which now houses the **Museo Chileno de Arte Precolombino** (Tues–Sun 10am–6pm, closed all holidays; CH$2000, Sun free; ☎6887348). Unquestionably Chile's best museum, it brings together over three thousand pieces representing some one hundred pre-Columbian peoples of Latin America. The collection spans a period of about ten thousand years and covers regions from present-day Mexico down to southern Chile, brilliantly illustrating the artistic wealth and diversity of Latin America's many cultures. Good layout and lighting set off the delicate beauty of the exhibits, and the whole thing is a very manageable size. The permanent collection is displayed in seven rooms arranged around two courtyards, each room dedicated to a different cultural area. One of the keys to understanding the beauty of this collection is that the items were selected primarily on the basis of their artistic merit, rather than on their scientific or anthropological significance.

The museum's rooms take you on a north to south geographical tour of different areas of Latin America, starting with **Mesoamérica,** corresponding to present-day Mexico, Guatemala, Honduras, El Salvador and parts of Nicaragua; moving on to the **Area Intermedia**, covering what is now Ecuador, Colombia, Panama, Costa Rica and Nicaragua; followed by the **Andes Centrales**, or central Andean region (today's Peru and western Bolivia); and ending in the **Andes del Sur** (Chile itself and parts of Argentina).

Area Mesoamérica

Walking through the large double doors off the hall, you'll find yourself in the room devoted to items from **Mesoamérica**. Right in front of you is one of the most startling pieces in the museum: a statue of **Xipé-Totec,** the god of Spring, represented as a man covered in the skin of a monkey, exposing both male and female genitalia. At the time of the Spanish conquest, the cult of Xipé-Totec was widespread throughout most of Mesoamerica, and was celebrated in a bizarre ritual in which a young man would cover himself with the skin of a sacrificial victim and wear it until it rotted off, revealing his young, fresh skin and symbolizing the growth of new vegetation from the earth.

Another eye-catching object, further up the room on the left, is the elaborately ornamented **incense burner**, used by the Teotihuacán culture (300–600 AD) to pray for rain and good harvests. The face carved in the middle represents a rain god, and when the incense was burning, the smoke would escape from his eyes. Standing at the far end of the room, by the exit, a huge slab of stone features **bas-relief carvings** depict a hulking, armed warrior with two small figures at his feet. It originally formed part of an immense Maya structure, built between 600 and 900 AD. This hall also includes important Maya stone pieces, Aztec goldwork and Olmeca ceramics from 900 AD.

Area Intermedia

In this region the continent's oldest pottery was produced, along with some exquisite goldwork. Pottery made its first appearance in the Americas around 3000 BC on the coast of Ecuador, where it was created by the agricultural and fishing communities of the Valdivia culture. Among the museum's best examples of **Valdivia pottery** is the gorgeous little female figurine with a big, round belly and childlike face, thought to have been used for fertility rites carried out at harvest time. Other female representations include the Tumaco-La Tolita carving of a woman with her head thrown back, laughing, and the Jama-Coaque carving of a mother suckling her child at her breast – both images date from 500 BC to 500 AD, and both are touchingly naturalistic. Note also the wonderful **coca-leaf-chewing figures** known as *coqueros*, carved with a telltale lump in their mouth by the Capulí culture (500 BC–500 AD). As well as pottery, this *sala* contains some beautiful **gold objects,** such as the miniature, finely worked carvings produced by the Veraguas and Diquís cultures (700–1550 AD) featuring images of frightening monsters and open-jawed, long-fanged felines.

Area Andes Centrales

The next room is distinguished by its **masks** and **copper figurines**, many of which were retrieved from ancient graves. Among the collection are examples of the highly expressive work of the Moche culture (100 BC–800 AD), including copper figurines and masks, now a gorgeous jade-green colour, and a series of polished ceremonial pots decorated with images of animals, faces and houses. The room also features some noteworthy **textiles**. Hanging by the door as you go in is a fragment of painted cloth depicting three human figures with fanged jaws – this is the oldest textile in the museum, produced by the Chavín culture almost 3000 years ago, and still in astonishingly good condition. At the opposite end of the room is the striking Chimú tapestry (1100–1470 AD), densely illustrated with repeating geometric motifs in stunning, vividly preserved colours.

Area Andes del Sur

The final room contains treasures from modern Chile and northwest Argentina. Among the most striking pieces on display are the huge **ceramic urns** of the Aguada culture (600–900 AD), painted with bold geometric designs incorporating fantastic, often feline, images. Look out too for the wooden and stone **snuff trays**, carved by the San Pedro people of northern Chile between 300 and 1000 AD, and used with small tubes to inhale hallucinogenic substances. The curious thing on the wall that looks like a grass skirt is a relic from the Incas, who made it all the way down to central Chile during their expansion in the fifteenth century. Known as a **quipú**, it consists of many strands of wool attached to a single cord, and was used to keep various records – such as of taxes collected – by means of a complex system of knots tied in the strands. This hall also includes stunning examples of the native Chilean Mapuche art, including distinctive **silverware** and **wooden sculptures.** Similar items are still produced today in the Lake District.

Ahumada, Huérfanos and around

The southeast corner of downtown Santiago contains the city's busiest pedestrian thoroughfares, Ahumada and Huérfanos, and a miscellany of attractions. Running south from the west side of the Plaza de Armas to the Alameda, **Paseo Ahumada** is a seething mass of people at every moment of the day. Walking down, you'll pass sombre doorways leading into labyrinthine shopping arcades, *confiterías* serving preposterously large cream cakes and, between Agustinas and Moneda, the famous **Café Caribe** and **Café Haiti** (see p.119), where drearily dressed old businessmen enjoy the thrill of being served their *cortados* and *espresos* by scantily-clad waitresses. Take a moment to pop into the **Banco de Chile**, between Huérfanos and Agustinas; its vast hall, polished counters and beautiful old clock have changed little since the bank opened in 1925.

Paseo Huérfanos crosses Ahumada at right angles, one block south of the plaza, and is lined with numerous banks and cinemas. Several places of interest are dotted amongst the shops, office blocks and *galerías* of the surrounding streets. You could start with the **Basilica de la Merced**, a towering, Neo-Renaissance structure on the corner of Merced and Mac Iver, with a beautifully carved eighteenth-century pulpit. Attached to the church is a small **museum** (Tues–Fri 10am–1pm & 3–6pm; CH$500) where, among the usual crucifixes and other religious paraphernalia, you'll find a collection of Easter Island artefacts, including a wooden **rongorongo tablet**, carved in the undeciphered Easter Island script – one of just 29 left in the world (see p.562).

From here, head south for two blocks and turn right at Agustinas, where you'll find the dazzling white facade of the **Teatro Municipal**, a splendid French-style Neoclassical building, all arches and columns and perfect symmetry. This has been the capital's most prestigious venue for ballet, opera and classical music since it was inaugurated in 1857. It's worth asking to have a look around inside; the main auditorium is quite a sight, with its sumptuous red upholstery and crystal chandeliers. See p.127 for ticket information. Standing opposite the theatre, and mirroring its cool, smooth whiteness, is the **Mansión Subercaseaux**, built at the turn of the century for one of Santiago's wealthiest families, and now occupied by a bank. A little further along, at the corner of Agustinas and Estado, loom the green walls and yellow columns of the **Templo de San Agustín**, dating from 1608 but extensively rebuilt since then. The chief interest within its highly decorative interior is the wooden carving of Christ, just left of the main altar as you face it. Known as the *Cristo de Mayo,* it's the subject of an intriguing local legend. The story goes that the crown of thorns around the figure's head slipped down to its neck during the 1647 earthquake, and that when someone tried to move the crown back up to its head, the carved face of Christ began to bleed, and the ground started to shake. For this reason, the crown has remained untouched ever since, still hanging around the neck.

La Moneda, the Ex Congreso Nacional and the Tribunales de Justicia

The best approach to the **Palacio de la Moneda** is from the northern side of the vast, paved Plaza de la Constitución, three blocks east and south of the Plaza de Armas. From here you can appreciate the perfect symmetry and compact elegance of this low-lying Neoclassical building, spread across the entire block. The inner courtyards are open to the public; approach from the north side (away from Alameda) and stroll through.

△ Palacio de la Moneda

It was built between 1784 and 1805 by the celebrated Italian architect Joaquín Toesca for the purpose of housing the royal mint. This role was to be short-lived, however, and after some forty years it became the residential palace for the presidents of Chile, starting with Manuel Bulnes in 1848 and ending with Carlos Ibáñez del Campo in 1958. At this point it stopped being used as the president's home, but it continues to be the official seat of government. One ceremony worth watching is the **changing of the guard**, held in front of the palace at 10am on alternate days. Dozens of green-uniformed police officers, all remarkably similar in height, march around the square to the rather jolly Chilean national anthem. In front of the Justice Ministry is one of Chile's few monuments to President Salvador Allende, with his arm outstretched. This controversial work of public art pays homage to the man who died in La Moneda during the artillery and rocket siege that led to the installation of the military government in 1973.

North of the Plaza de la Constitución, at the corner of Morandé and Compañía, are another couple of impressive public buildings. The most beautiful, from the outside, is the white, temple-like Ex Congreso Nacional, set amidst lush gardens. This is where Congress used to meet, until it was dissolved on September 11, 1973, the day of the coup d'état (see p.602). In 1990, following the end of the military regime, a new congress building was erected in Valparaíso; since this one currently houses the Cancillería (foreign ministry), unfortunately public access to the inside is extremely limited.

On the southern side of Compañía, spanning the whole block, is the Tribunales de Justicia, an imposing Neoclassical building housing the highest court in Chile, the Corte Suprema. You'd never guess it from the outside, but this austere building conceals one of the most beautiful interiors in the city. To enter, just flash an ID at the guards, leave your knapsack and explore the long, narrow hall running the length of the building. Topped by a stunning glass-and-metal vault three floors above, the hall is flooded with natural light. If you want to take photos, you need to get permission from the *secretaría* on the first floor.

Along the Alameda

Officially the Avenida del Libertador Bernardo O'Higgins, Santiago's most vital east–west artery is universally known as the **Alameda**, a poplar-lined avenue used for strolling and recreation, and found in many Latin American cities. This one began life as *La Cañada* (or "channel"), when a branch of the Mapocho was sealed off shortly before independence, and a roadway was created over the old riverbed. A few years later, when the Supreme Director Bernardo O'Higgins decided that Santiago required an alameda, La Cañada was deemed the best place to put it: "There is no public boulevard where people may get together for honest relief and amusement during the resting hours, since the one known as Tajamar, because of its narrowness and irregularity, far from being cheerful, inspires sadness. La Cañada, because of its condition, extension, abundance of water and other circumstances, is the most apparent place for an alameda." Three rows of poplars were promptly planted along each side, and the Alameda was born, soon to become *the* place to take the evening promenade.

Since those quieter times the boulevard has evolved into the city's biggest, busiest, noisiest and most polluted thoroughfare, made up of a sea of yellow *micros* moving as one organic mass, all screeching brakes, frenetic horns and choking fumes. Still, it's an unavoidable axis and you'll probably spend a fair bit of time on it or under it: the main metro line runs beneath it, and some of Santiago's most interesting landmarks stand along it.

Cerro Santa Lucía and Barrio Lastarria

The lushly forested **Cerro Santa Lucía** is the most imaginative and exuberant piece of landscaping in Santiago. Looking at it now, it's hard to believe that for the first three centuries of the city's development this was nothing more than a barren, rocky outcrop, completely ignored despite its historical importance – it was at the foot of this hill that Santiago was officially founded by Valdivia, on February 12, 1541. It wasn't until 1872 that the city turned its attention to Santa Lucía once more, when the mayor of Santiago, Vicuña Mackenna, enlisted the labour of 150 prisoners to transform it into a grand public park.

Quasi-Gaudíesque in appearance, with its swirling pathways and Baroque terraces and turrets, this is a great place to come for panoramic views across the city, even when they're veiled behind a layer of smog. If slogging up the steps doesn't appeal, there's a free lift on the western side of the park, by the junction with Huérfanos. Up on the terrace is another branch of the Municipalidad de Santiago's **Oficina de Turismo** (Mon–Fri 10am–6pm; ☎6327783, ⓦwww .ciudad.cl/turismo), which offers free maps and free walking tours every Thursday at 11am as well as friendly, competent staff. While it's always busy and safe by day, several muggings have been reported in the Cerro Santa Lucía after dark, so hanging around to watch the sun go down, though tempting, isn't advisable.

Immediately west of the hill stands the massive **Biblioteca Nacional**, one of the largest libraries in Latin America (and handy for its free loos inside), while to the east, set back from the Alameda, is the quiet, arty **Barrio Lastarria** neighbourhood centred on **Plaza Mulato Gil** (Mon–Sat 11am–midnight), at the corner of Merced and Lastarria. This small cobbled square is enclosed by old buildings housing artists' workshops, galleries, an antiquarian bookshop, a café-restaurant and the **Museo de Artes Visuales** Jose Victorino Lastarria 307 (Tues–Sun 10.30am-6.30pm, CH$1000) which features some of the best new sculptures, painting and photography by Chile's emerging artists. The rest of the neighbourhood is well known for an up-and-coming restaurant scene (see p.120) that includes a more intimate, quiet side to the usual ruckus of Santiago.

Iglesia San Francisco and Barrio París-Londres

Looking west from the Biblioteca Nacional, you can't miss the **Iglesia San Francisco**, with its towering red walls jutting out into the street. This is the oldest building in Santiago, erected between 1586 and 1628 and the survivor of three great earthquakes. Take a look inside at the **Virgen del Socorro**, a small polychrome carving (rather lost in the vast main altar) brought to Chile on the saddle of Pedro de Valdivia in 1540 and credited with guiding him on his way, as well as fending off Indian attackers by throwing sand in their eyes. For all its age and beauty, the most remarkable feature of this church is its deep, hushed silence; you're just metres from the din of the Alameda but those buses seem a million miles away.

The monastery adjacent to the church houses the **Museo Colonial** (Tues–Sat 10am–1.30pm & 3–6.30pm, Sun 10am–2pm; CH$700), where you'll find a highly evocative collection of paintings, sculpture, furniture, keys and other objects dating from the colonial period, most of it religious and a good deal of it created in Peru, the seat of colonial government. Note the immense eighteenth-century **cedar door** of the first room you come to off the cloisters; carved into hundreds of intricately designed squares, this is one of the museum's most beautiful possessions. Inside the room, you'll find another arresting sight: a gigantic painting of the **genealogical tree of the Franciscan Order** consisting of 644 miniature portraits. Other highlights to look out for include the **Cristo Chilote**, a small wooden image of Christ on the cross, bearing unmistakeably South American features, carved in Chiloé in 1780; a roomful of delicately crafted **locks**; and, squeezed into the Gran Sala, a collection of 54 paintings depicting the life and miracles of **St Francis of Assisi**, quite overwhelming in their sheer size and number.

If you turn left as you leave the museum, you'll find yourself on Calle Londres, which intersects Calle París to form the **Barrio París-Londres**, tucked behind the Iglesia San Francisco on what used to be the monastery's orchards. These sinuous, cobbled streets lined with refurbished mansions and stylish hotels, look like a tiny piece of Paris's Latin Quarter. Created in 1923 by a team of architects, the barrio is undeniably attractive but feels incongruous to its surroundings; it's also odd the way it's made up of just two streets, and simply stops at the end of them.

From Universidad de Chile to Los Héroes

Back on the Alameda, walking west, you'll come to the yellow-washed walls of the **Universidad de Chile**, a fine French Neoclassical building dating from 1863. Opposite is the **Bolsa de Comercio**, Santiago's stock exchange, housed in a flamboyant, French Renaissance–style building that tapers to a thin wedge at the main entrance. One block further along you reach Plaza Bulnes, flanked by the **tomb** and massive **equestrian statue of Bernardo O'Higgins** to the south (often chained off to keep the public away), and to the north by the grey stone outline of the **Palacio de la Moneda** (see p.107), sitting with its back to the Alameda.

As you continue west past the 128-metre-high telecommunications tower known as the **Torre Entel,** the focus of New Year's Eve fireworks displays, you enter what was once the preserve of Santiago's moneyed elite, with several glorious mansions built around 1900 serving as reminders. The first to look out for is the French-style **Palacio Irarrázaval**, on the south side of the Alameda between San Ignacio and Dieciocho; built in 1906 by Cruz Montt, it now belongs to the Círculo Español and houses an old-fashioned restaurant. Adjoining it at the corner of Dieciocho, the slightly later and more ornate **Edificio Iñiguez**, by the same architect in league with Larraín Bravo, houses the institutional Confitería Torres (see p.120) – its original home was demolished to make way for the new edifice – said to be where the "national" sandwich, the Barros Luco (see p.58), was invented in honour of a leading politician. Then check out the 1917 **Palacio Ariztía**, headquarters in Santiago for the nation's deputies, a little further on in the next block; a fine copy of an Art Nouveau French mansion, again by Cruz Montt, it is set off by an iron-and-glass door canopy. Next door, the late-nineteenth-century **Palacio Errázuriz**, the oldest and finest of these Alameda mansions, is now the Brazilian Embassy. Built for Maximiano Errázuriz, mining mogul and leading socialite, it is a soberly elegant two-storey building in a Neoclassical style – the architect was Italian Eusebio Chelli. You're now standing opposite the triumphant **Monumento a los Héroes de la Concepción**, an imposing statue which borders the junction of the Alameda with the Avenida Norte Sur (the Panamericana); this is where metro Lines #1 and #2 intersect at Los Héroes station.

A detour to Palacio Cousiño

Take Line #2 to Toesca, one stop south of Los Héroes for a highly recommended detour to the **Palacio Cousiño** (Tues–Fri 9.30am–1.30pm & 2.30–5pm, Sat & Sun 9.30am–1.30pm; CH$1500) at Dieciocho 438 (turn left out of Toesca station). This was and remains the most magnificent of the historic palaces, the one that dazzled Santiago's high society by the sheer scale of its luxury and opulence. It was built between 1870 and 1878 for doña Isidora Goyenechea, the widow of Luis Cousiño, who'd amassed a fortune with his Lota coal mines and Chañarcillo silver mines. All the furnishings and decoration were shipped over from Europe, especially France, and top European craftsmen were brought here to work on the house. The first floor was burnt to ashes in 1968, but the ground floor remains totally intact, and provides a wonderful close-up view of turn-of-the-century craftsmanship at its best: Italian hand-painted tiles; Bohemian crystal chandeliers; mahogany, walnut and ebony parquet floors; a mosaic marble staircase; and French brocade and silk furnishings are just a few of the splendours of the palace. Visitors must take the 45-minute guided **tour**, available in Spanish or English.

West to Estación Central

West of Los Héroes, the Alameda continues its path through the once-wealthy neighbourhoods that were abandoned by Santiago's well-heeled a few decades ago, when the moneyed classes shifted to the more fashionable east side of town. After falling into serious decline, these areas are finally coming into their own again, as a younger generation has started renovating decaying mansions, opening up trendy cafés and bookshops and injecting a new vigour into the streets. One of the most beautiful of these neighbourhoods, on the northern side of the Alameda, between Avenida Brasil and Avenida Ricardo Cumming, is **Barrio Concha y Toro**, a jumble of twisting cobbled streets leading to a tiny round plaza with a fountain in the middle. Further north you'll find **Barrio Brasil**, one of the liveliest of the newly revived neighbourhoods, centred on the large, grand Plaza Brasil, full of children playing at the amusing cement sculpture playground and among the old silk-cotton and lime trees.

A few blocks west stands one of the Alameda's great landmarks: the stately **Estación Central**, featuring a colossal metal roof that was cast in the

Schneider-Creuzot foundry in France in 1896. It's the only functioning train station left in the city, with regular services to the south of Chile. Right opposite is the **Planetarium** Av O'Higgins 3349 (shows Fri 7pm, Sat & Sun 11am, noon, 3.30pm, 5pm; CH$2000; ☎7781325, ⓦwww.planetariochile.cl), which puts on high-tech audiovisual shows with astronomical themes.

Along the Río Mapocho

Besides the Alameda, the other major axis binding the old city is the **Río Mapocho**, filled with the muddy brown waters from the melted snow of the Andes. There are few historic buildings along here, as frequent flooding deterred riverside development until the Mapocho was canalized in 1891. Nonetheless, several city landmarks stand out, including the flamboyant **Mercado Central**, the **Estación Mapocho** and the elegant **Palacio de Bellas Artes**. Construction of a highway that will run under the riverbed began in 2002.

Mercado Central and Feria Municipal La Vega

If you follow Calle Puente north from the Plaza de Armas you'll reach the **Mercado Central** (daily 6am–4pm), close to the river's southern bank. This huge metal structure, prefabricated in England and erected in Santiago in 1868, contains a very picturesque fruit, vegetable and fish market that warrants a place on everyone's itinerary. The highlight is the fish stalls, packed with glistening eels, sharks and salmon, buckets of salt-crusted oysters, mussels and clams, and unidentifiable shells out of which live things with tentacles make occasional appearances. Overhead, rows of pink and grey fish hang from hooks, and white-coated fishmongers turn gutting and filleting into an art form. The best time to come here is at lunchtime, when you can feast at one of the many **fish restaurants** dotted around the market; the cheapest are those on the outer edge, but it's worth paying the extra to sit amongst the colour and atmosphere of the central hall.

True market addicts should cross the river and, by way of the sweetly perfumed **Mercado de Flores**, head for the gargantuan **Feria Municipal La Vega**, set a couple of blocks back from the riverbank opposite the Mercado Central. There's no pretty architecture here, and no tourists either; just serious shoppers and hundreds of stalls selling the whole gamut of Central Valley produce, from cows' innards and pigs' bellies to mountains of potatoes and onions, at a fraction of the price charged in the Mercado Central. Work your way to the back of the building and out into the maze of canopied stalls behind. La Vega is mainly wholesale, and the quantities of fresh fruit on display here are simply breathtaking: table after table piled high with raspberries, grapes, pears, apples, kiwis, plums, nectarines and peaches – all dappled by the sunlight poking through the awnings.

Estación Mapocho

Just west of the Mercado Central, right by the river, is the immense stone and metal **Estación Mapocho**, built in 1912 to house the terminal of the Valparaíso–Santiago railway line. With train service long discontinued, the station is now used as a cultural centre, housing exhibitions, plays and throbbing concerts by the likes of the Red Hot Chili Peppers and other popular performers. You can walk in and have a look inside, worth it if only for the view of its great copper, glass and marble roof. You'll also find a craft shop, restaurant and bookshop off the main hall. One of the continent's most important book fairs is also held here during the last week of November. This **Feria Nacional del**

Libro features appearances by authors such as Isabel Allende, Salvador's bestselling niece, and other world-class writers.

Parque Forestal neighbourhood

The **Parque Forestal**, stretching along the southern bank of the Mapocho between Puente Recoleta and Puente Pío Nono, was created at the turn of the century on land that was reclaimed from the river after it was channelled. Lined with long rows of trees and lampposts, it provides a picturesque setting for the **Palacio de Bellas Artes** (Tues–Sun 10am–7pm; CH$600), built to commemorate the centenary of Chilean independence. The palacio houses the **Museo de Bellas Artes,** featuring predominantly Chilean works from the beginning of the colonial period onwards, and the **Museo de Arte Contemporáneo**. The quality of the work is mixed, and none of the paintings equals the beauty of the building's vast white hall with its marble statues bathing in the natural light pouring in from the glass-and-iron ceiling. Some of the temporary exhibitions, however, are excellent.

Barrio Bellavista and Cerro San Cristóbal

Originally – and sometimes still - known as *La Chimba*, which means "the other side of the river" in Quichoa (the language of the Incas), **Barrio Bellavista** grew into first a residential area when Santiago's population started spilling across the river in the nineteenth century. Head across the Pío Nono bridge at the eastern end of the Parque Forestal and you'll find yourself on Calle Pío Nono, the main street of Bellavista. Nestling between the northern bank of the Mapocho and the steep slopes of Cerro San Cristóbal, Bellavista is a warren of quiet, leafy streets lined with idiosyncratic restaurants, steeped in a village-like atmosphere. Now a centre for restaurants, pubs, dancing and lofts, it has a reputation for being the capital's bohemian quarter, thanks in part to the fact that Pablo Neruda lived here, along with several other artists, writers and intellectuals. Many of the restaurants are small and atmospheric, and on Thursday, Friday and Saturday nights the district becomes one of Santiago's main dining (see p.120 for restaurants) and dancing centres. Another attraction is the evening handicraft market that spreads along the length of Pío Nono at weekends and is a good place to come for gifts or souvenirs. You might also be tempted by the dozens of lapis lazuli outlets running along Avenida Bellavista, between Puente Pío Nono and Puente del Arzobispo, but be warned that this semi-precious stone is not cheap, and there are few bargains to be found. There's no metro in Bellavista itself, but it's a short walk from Baquedano metro. While the neighbourhood is safe during the day, roaming drunks, especially after 2am on weekends, require a good deal of leeway and attention.

La Chascona

Tucked away in a tiny street at the foot of Cerro San Cristóbal – at Marquéz de la Plata 0192 – you'll find **La Chascona**, the house that the poet Pablo Neruda shared with his third wife, Matilde Urrutia, from 1955 until his death in 1973 (guided tours Tues–Sun 10am–1pm & 3–6pm; CH$1500 in Spanish, CH$2500 in English). It was named *La Chascona* ("tangle-haired woman") by Neruda, as a tribute to his wife's thick red hair. Today it's the headquarters of the Fundación Neruda, which has painstakingly restored this and the poet's two other houses – La Sebastiana in Valparaíso (see p.156) and Isla Negra, about 90km down the coast (see p.161) – to their original condition, opening them to the public.

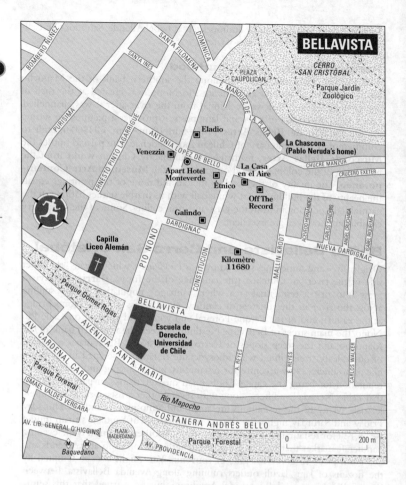

This house, split into three separate sections that climb up the hillside, is packed to the rafters with objects collected by Neruda, illuminating his loves, enthusiasms and obsessions. Beautiful African carvings jostle for space with Victorian dolls, music boxes, paperweights and coloured glasses; the floors are littered with old armchairs, stools, a rocking horse, exotic rugs and a sleeping toy lion. There are numerous references to Neruda's and Matilde's love for each other, such as the bars on the windows, in which their initials are entwined and lapped by breaking waves, and the portrait of Matilde by Diego Rivera, which has the profile of Neruda hidden in her hair. The third and highest level houses Neruda's library, containing more than nine thousand books, as well as the diploma he was given when awarded the Nobel Prize for Literature in 1971, and a replica of the medal.

Cerro San Cristóbal

A trip up to the summit of **Cerro San Cristóbal** is one of the highlights of a stay in Santiago, particularly on clear, sunny days when the views over the city and to the Andes are quite stunning. The hill is, in fact, a spur of the

Andes, jutting into the heart of the capital and rising to a peak of 860m, a point that's marked by a giant 22-metre-high statue of the *Virgen de la Inmaculada*. The easiest way to get up is to take the **funicular** from the station at the north end of Pío Nono in Bellavista (Tues–Sun 10am–8.30pm; CH$1000 return, CH$2500 return including cable-car trip, see below). It stops first at the dismal **zoo** and then continues up to the Terraza Bellavista, where you get out. From here it's a short but steep walk up to the huge white Virgin, where you'll be rewarded with fine views over Santiago's suburbs vanishing into hazy mountains. If you are fortunate enough to be in Santiago after a rain in the winter months, this view includes rows of snowy mountain peaks. Back down at Terraza Bellavista, a path leads west to the **teleférico** (cable car) station known as Estación Cumbre (joint ticket with funic-

△ Cerro San Cristóbal

ular; see above). This mini-gondola contraption provides hair-raising ski-lift-style rides to Estación Tupahue, then descends to Estación Oasis at the foot of the hill (and a long walk from anywhere).

For an afternoon picnic and swimming in the summer months, there is no better place in Santiago than the two huge pools atop the hill. The jointly run Piscina Tupahue and Piscina Antilén (Nov 15–March 15, Tues–Sun 10am–6pm; CH$5000) offer cool, clean swimming and, at 736m above the city, wonderful views. They are not cheap, but are a great escape, fun for families and romantic for couples. Many locals can't afford the entrance fee and peer down from stone walls surrounding the complex. A *colectivo* from the bottom of the hill costs just CH$300 one way.

Parque Quinta Normal and its museums

About 1km north of the Estación Central, the **Parque Quinta Normal** is perhaps the most elegant and peaceful of Santiago's parks. It was created in 1830 as a place to introduce and acclimatize foreign trees and plants to the city – Chileans from the nineteenth century onwards have been very fond of filling their public squares with a variety of different trees, many of them imported from abroad. Today the park is packed with some beautifully mature examples: Babylonian willows, Monterey pine, cypress, Douglas fir and poplars, to name just a few. Additional attractions include a pond with rowing boats for hire, and four **museums**. The best way to get here is to take the metro to Estación Central, then a bus or taxi up Avenida Matucana. Often deserted during the week, the park is packed on summer weekends.

Museo Nacional de Historia Natural

The grand, Neoclassical building near the park entrance on Matucana houses the **Museo Nacional de Historia Natural** (Tues–Sat 10am–5.30pm, Sun April–Aug noon–5.30pm, Sept–Mar 11am–6.30pm; CH$600; ☏6804600, ⓦwww.mnhn.cl). Founded in 1830 and occupying its present building since 1875, this is the oldest natural history museum in Latin America and still one of the most important. It's worth a visit for the colossal skeleton of a blue whale mounted in the vast entrance hall, and for the notable Easter Island collection on the second level, featuring a *moai*, an upturned topknot or hat, and the famous Santiago Staff, inscribed with the mysterious, undeciphered *rongo rongo* script (see p.562). Otherwise, a lack of funds has forced the museum to concentrate more on its role as an academic centre than as a place to inform and entertain the public, and the remaining displays amount to moth-eaten dioramas of Chilean landscapes and a roomful of stuffed birds.

Museo de Ciencia y Tecnología

A short distance west of the natural history museum is the **Museo de Ciencia y Tecnología** (Tues–Fri 10am–5pm, Sat & Sun 11am–6pm; CH$700). Far more modern and high-tech in feel than the natural history museum, it's geared primarily towards kids, demonstrating the basic principles of physics with entertaining, hands-on gadgets and displays.

Museo Ferroviario

Follow the road down towards the southern park gate, on Avenida Portales, and you'll reach the shiny black steam engines belonging to the outdoor **Museo Ferroviario** (Tues–Fri 10am–5.30pm, Sat & Sun 11am–5.30pm, guided tours available Sat & Sun mornings; CH$750; ☏6814627). The museum consists of fourteen pristine locomotives dating from 1893 to 1940, including a splendid Kitson-Meyer, manufactured in England in 1909 and shipped over to Chile, where it served the famous trans-Andean service from Los Andes to Mendoza in Argentina until 1971. Another highlight is the luxurious wood-panelled presidential train, built in 1911 for Ramón Barros Luco – if you ask nicely you'll be allowed to climb on board.

Museo Artequín

The wildly colourful glass and metal building standing opposite the park's Avenida Portales entrance was originally the Chilean pavilion in the Universal Exhibition in Paris, 1889. It now contains the engaging **Museo Artequín** (Tues–Fri 9am–5pm, Sat & Sun 11am-6pm; voluntary fee; ☏6818687) – short for Arte en la Quinta – which aims to bring people, especially schoolchildren, closer to art by exposing them to reproductions of the world's greatest paintings in a relaxed, less intimidating environment. They're all here, from El Greco and Delacroix through to Andy Warhol and Jackson Pollock, and copious plastic information cards tell you all about the artists and their work.

Parque O'Higgins

Perhaps the best reason to come to the spacious **Parque Bernardo O'Higgins**, a couple of kilometres or so southeast of the Quinta Normal, is to soak up the Chilean family atmosphere, as it's one of the most popular green spaces in the city. It was originally the Parque Cousiño, commissioned by Luis Cousiño, the entrepreneurial millionaire, in 1869, and *the* place to take your carriage rides in the late nineteenth century. These days working-class families and groups of kids flock here on summer weekends to enjoy the picnic areas, outdoor pools (very crowded), roller rink, basketball court and the gut-churning rides of **Fantasilandia**, an outdoor amusement park (April–Nov, Sat & Sun 11am–8pm; Dec–March, Tues–Fri 2–8pm, Sat & Sun 11am–8pm, closed when raining; CH\$4000). It's easy to reach via public transport; take Line #2 to the Parque O'Higgins station, then walk three blocks. The park also features **El Pueblito**, a collection of adobe buildings typical of the Chilean countryside and housing several cheap restaurants, some craft stalls and a handful of small museums. The best of these is the **Museo del Huaso** (Tues–Fri 10am–5pm, Sat & Sun 10am–2pm; free), dedicated to the Chilean cowboy, or horseman, with displays of spurs, saddles, ponchos and hats, and a big photo of Pope John Paul II decked out in a poncho when he visited the museum in April 1987 (he came to offer Mass at the chapel next door). There's also a tiny shell museum, an insect museum and a not very exciting aquarium. See p.67 for more on Chile's *huasos*.

Los barrios altos: Providencia, Las Condes and beyond

The barrios east of the city centre spreading into the foothills of the Andes are home to Santiago's moneyed elite; the farther you go and higher you get, the richer the people, bigger the houses and higher the gates. It's hard to believe that up until the beginning of this century there was virtually no one here; it was for its isolation and tranquillity that the Sisters of Providencia chose to build their convent on what is now Avenida Providencia in 1853. (By the way, the parallel street running in the other direction, Avenida 11 de Septiembre, takes its name from the date of the 1973 military coup, not the 2001 terrorist attacks in the United States.) Later, following a slow trickle of eastbound movement, there was a great exodus of wealthy families from their traditional preserves west of the city over to the new barrio alto in the 1920s, where they've been entrenched ever since.

The barrio you're most likely to visit is Providencia, as it's home to Sernatur, various adventure tourism and skiing outfits and a thriving nightlife scene. Further east in Las Condes the atmosphere is more residential, and apart from a few notable exceptions such as Los Dominicos market, there's less to pull you out here. If you've access to a car, however, or meet some Chileans who offer to give you a sightseeing tour (not uncommon), it can be quite fun to drive around the fabulously wealthy uptown barrios like El Arrayán and La Dehesa. You could even just sit on a bus to the end of Avenida Las Condes to watch the Andes get closer and closer and feel the city creep higher and higher.

Providencia

You can walk east along the Alameda to the centre of **Providencia** in about twenty or thirty minutes from the Universidad Católica, or else you could take the metro (to Manuel Montt, Pedro de Valdivia or Los Leones, depending on which stretch you want to get to), or hop on a *micro*. Providencia takes its name from its oldest building, the yellow-washed **Iglesia de Nuestra Señora de la Divina Providencia**, founded in 1853 – the interior is disappointingly dull. Opposite, occupying a former fruit and vegetable market, is **Sernatur** (see p.95), and a few blocks east of here you're into the commercial heart of the barrio, with its stylish stores and elegant cafés. Bland and faceless for some, Providencia is nonetheless convenient for its modern retail, buzzing nightlife and compact size.

Las Condes

As you move east to **Las Condes**, the shops and office blocks gradually thin out into a more residential district, punctuated with the occasional giant shopping mall, such as **Alto Las Condes**, Av Kennedy 901 (daily 10am–10pm). This proudly promotes itself as *"el Shopping Center más moderno de Latinoamérica"*, and with its 240 shops and pristine, antiseptic interior, it may be right. If this appeals, note that a free shuttle bus runs twice daily from most major hotels to the mall and back (℡2291383 for times). In addition, most of the buses running along the Alameda displaying "Las Condes" in the front window will stop near the mall.

The best overall collection of arts and crafts is found at **Pueblito de los Dominicos** market, Apoquindo 9085 (Tues–Sun 11am–7.30pm), a large, lively and expensive craft fair held in a mock village. It's a bit off the normal tourist trek: follow Avenida Apoquindo 4km past the Escuela Militar metro stop to the end. Bus Lines #327 and #326 go right by. It's well worth the trip, especially as a place for last-minute gifts and souvenirs. You'll find a wide range of beautiful handicrafts – made in workshops on site and sold at the stalls – as well as antiques, books, fossil shark teeth, a decent restaurant, and a quiet respite from the noise and grime of the city. Chilean sculptor Elias Rivera (in Stand 81) offers a fascinating collection of stone carvings. Next door is the **Iglesia Los Dominicos**, built by Toesca in the late eighteenth century; the church is usually locked, but you can admire its attractive colonial architecture from the gardens between 4pm and 8pm on weekdays. Buses marked "Apoquindo" come here from all along the Alameda, or you can take the metro out to Estación Militar then get a *colectivo* (under the bridge next to the station).

Eating

Santiago could make a serious bid for the title of fast-food capital of the world, with a proliferation of uninviting international and domestic **chains** spread around the city. Even so, those are often more inviting than the hundreds of tacky **fuentes de soda** offering beer, TV and high-cholesterol snacks – such as the *completo*, a blanket of mayonnaise atop a hot dog or the more basic grilled horse-meat sandwiches. Add to these the numerous stand-up **snack bars** on the south side of the Plaza de Armas, and you've got a comprehensive picture of the budget food scene in Santiago. For not much more you can eat more heartily and healthily in some of the old-fashioned **bars** or local **picadas** (inexpensive traditional canteens), which serve typical Chilean basics like *pastel de choclo*, *humitas* and *cazuela*.

Nonetheless, there's also an enormous choice of **restaurants**, from the humble to the outstanding, offering many different types of cuisine including Asian, Middle Eastern, Spanish, Peruvian, French and Italian. Some of these are modestly priced but the majority are expensive, although at **lunchtime** many places offer a good-value fixed-price **menú del día** or **menú ejecutivo**. For this reason a lot of restaurants, particularly downtown, tend to be packed at lunchtime but fairly quiet (sometimes empty) in the evening, at least during the week. In most places there's no need to **book ahead**; where it's advisable, we've included a phone number.

Santiago is not a café city, but there are a number of **coffee shops** catering to the great tradition of *onces* (afternoon tea). The influence of Chile's German immigrants is very much in evidence here, with many places serving delicious *küchen* and strudel.

Cafés and budget food

You don't have to resort to the ubiquitous, multinational burger chains to eat without spending too much in Santiago. This list includes a couple of **sandwich bars** and a **deli**, ideal for a low-cost snack or to buy ingredients for a picnic, plus a trio of **Japanese** eateries (often good budget options in Santiago unlike elsewhere).

You'll also find a curious and eclectic range of **cafés**, from homely coffee shops full of weary housewives to trendy, US-owned chains serving Seattle-style coffee and baguette sandwiches. An unusual (and not particularly politically correct) feature of the city is the tradition of **stand-up coffee bars**, known as *café con piernas,* of which there are dozens; they're staffed by micro-skirted or lingerie-clad waitresses serving inexpensive and generally decent cups of coffee. While mainly patronized by bored men from the offices, there is no taboo against women entering, and plenty of people do go just for the coffee, which is often better than anywhere else.

Bar de la Unión Nueva York 11, near the Bolsa, historic centre. Old wooden floors, shelves of dusty wine bottles and animated, garrulous old men make this an atmospheric place to pop in for a cheapo glass of wine served in cafeteria glasses or for a leisurely lunch. The food's tasty (lots of fish) and good value, and the servings are generous. Closed Sun.

Café Caribe Ahumada 120, historic centre. Traditional *café con piernas* where members of Chile's ageing business class stand around for what seems like hours, ogling the waitresses and talking on their mobile phones.

Café Colonia Mac Iver 161, between Moneda and Agustinas, historic centre. Matronly waitresses in German costume serve the best cakes, tarts, *küchen* and strudel in Santiago. The large café has been going for some fifty years and remains a perennial favourite with Santiago's housewives.

Café Haiti Ahumada 140, historic centre. One of a chain of *café con piernas*, casual, stand-up cafés serviced by scantily-clad waitresses. You may disapprove of the ethic, but the coffee is not to be sniffed at.

Chez Henry South side of Plaza de Armas, historic centre. Large delicatessen serving good ready-made hot and cold meals to take away, as well as fresh fruit, ice cream and other goodies. Great place to stock up before a road trip or picnic.

Café Público Pío Nono 389. Attractive and quiet Bellavista bar-café that also serves delicious home-made pastas and other light meals.

Caffeto Pedro de Valdivia 029, at Av Providencia. Good coffee shop with standard food, an Internet café next door, and a raised, glassed-in terrace perfect for people watching. Good place to arrange informal meetings, as it is on a very easy-to-find corner just a block from the metro.

Dominó 1016 Agustinas, historic centre. The most popular sandwich bar in Santiago, distinguished by its fresh, quality fillings. Closed Sun.

Fra Diavola París 836, near *Residencial Londres*, historic centre. Busy bustling sort of place offering superb-value fixed-price lunches with a daily changing menu (usually Italian-influenced). No dinner; closed Sat & Sun.

Galindo Corner of Constitución and Dardignac. Cheap food and strong drinks until all hours. In summer the tables spill out onto the street – something that has invited many nearby copycats – but the young bohemian crowd remains loyal to this classic Bellavista hang out.

Izakaya Yoko Merced 456, historic centre. Attractive Japanese canteen offering good, authentic food at unbeatable prices. Try one of the enormous bowls of soup with noodles, or the superb sushi that melts in your mouth. Closed Sun.

Kebab Bar La Bolsa 67, historic centre. This tiny restaurant serves up excellent Greek salads, fresh fruit juices, and thick meat sandwiches with Middle Eastern flavours. Blues music, too. Open until 8.30pm Mon–Fri; closed Sat & Sun.

Kintaro Monjitas 460, historic centre. A Japanese gem with great-value fixed-price lunches. They've got a book-like menu full of photos to help you choose your dishes. Closed Sun.

Las Lanzas Humberto Trucco 25, Plaza Ñuñoa. This traditional bar-restaurant, with tables spilling onto the pavement, is *the* classic drinking spot in Ñuñoa. They also offer a range of fish dishes at amazingly low prices.

Libro-Café Mediterráneo Purísima 161. Laid-back Bellavista café next door to its sister restaurant, *La Tasca Mediterráneo*. Soft music and lighting, books scattered about for your perusal, and a relaxed clientele. Hugely popular at weekends.

🏃 **Pérgola de la Plaza** Plaza Mulato Gil de Castro, off Lastarria, historic centre. Laid-back, arty café-restaurant on a lovely cobbled courtyard – one of the nicest corners in the city to unwind over a cup of coffee.

🏃 **Roll's Bar** Guardia Vieja 208, Providencia. Excellent sushi bar, with a small terrace, where they offer a large selection for under CH$5000.
El Siete (777) Alameda 777, across from Iglesia San Francisco, historic centre. Huge old rooms

covered in graffiti and packed with grungy students. Serves cheap beer and very interesting snacks like pigs' trotters sandwiches.
La Tecla Doctor Johow 320, south side of Plaza Ñuñoa. In the evening live jazz music and cocktails accompany the (vaguely) French and Spanish fare. The city's best pancakes, sweet and savoury, are served sizzling hot in clay-dishes, in this intimate, attractive restaurant; another speciality is the chocolate and caramel gateau. Closed Sun evening.
Urbano Av Ricardo Lyon 45, Providencia. Tucked into a tiny passageway, this stylish bar and restaurant serves tasty sushi and other reasonably priced Asian dishes.

Restaurants

Most of Santiago's **restaurants** are concentrated in five areas of town: Old Downtown, Barrio Lastarria, Bellavista, Providencia and El Bosque Norte. The first three areas more or less comprise Central Santiago, and thus are most accessible, but the others are conveniently on the metro line and not too terrible a trek. There are also some imaginative places springing up around Plaza Ñuñoa in the southeast part of town, and Vitacura (see p.122).

Perhaps the most memorable place for lunch in all of Santiago is the Mercado Central (see p.112), whose central hall is lined with *marisquerías*, the most famous and expensive being *Donde Augusto*; less pricey and perhaps more authentic are *Rincón Marino* and *Pailas Blancas*. Note that nearly all restaurants serve dinner until midnight from Tuesday to Saturday, but some are closed on Monday, and even more on Sunday.

Historic centre

Confitería Torres Corner of Alameda and Dieciocho, near Los Héroes. Open since 1879, this is the oldest restaurant in Santiago; don't come here for the food (overpriced meat and fish) but for the dark, wood-panelled walls, the old, tarnished mirrors, the sagging chairs and the fabulous atmosphere. At weekends there's live music from around 10.30pm. Closed Sun.

La Habana Vieja Tarapaca 755, between Santa Rosa and San Francisco. Large hall containing a restaurant, a small dance floor and a stage, best at the weekend when there's live salsa music with dancing. The mid-priced menu includes Cuban staples like cassava, yellow rice and black beans, and fried plantains. Closed Sun.

Barrio Lastarria

Reservations are recommended here, as many of the restaurants have fewer than ten tables. Parking is easy, and the barrio is just a two-minute walk from Universidad Católica metro stop. This neighbourhood generally is safe, but the Santa Lucia park around the hill is not a good place to go after midnight.

Don Victorino Lastarria 138 ☎6395263. The food (pastas, fish and meat) is not the best on this street, but it's one of the prettiest and most intimate places to dine, especially at the tables next to the little fountain on the terrace. Closed Sat lunch and Sun dinner.

🏃 **Gatopardo** Lastarria 192, just two blocks off the Alameda ☎6336420. Very classy restaurant with a beautiful interior featuring lots of modern art and an atrium supported by eight tree trunks from the south of Chile. Good, imaginatively prepared food, including a range of Mediterranean

Chilean specialities
Seafood, wine and pisco

Chile may not be considered much of a foodie destination, but what it does well it does extremely well. Start your evening with a beguiling pisco sour – zingy lemon juice spiked with distilled brandy – and then feast on some of the world's best clams and mussels, followed by a succulent hake or sole, served with roast potatoes and a simple salad of onions and tomatoes. Crack open a bottle of crisp Sauvignon Blanc produced in one of the country's lush vineyards and you have the perfect Chilean meal. ¡Buen provecho!

Fruits of the sea

Chile's long coastline stretches for a staggering 3700 kilometres, so it's no surprise that fish and seafood hold pride of place on the national menu. Indeed, Pablo Neruda was inspired to immortalize a fish stew – *caldillo de congrio* – in a poem. The range and quality of the shellfish in particular equals anything found in Brittany, Galicia or Newfoundland. For the widest choice, head to the coasts of the Litoral Central and Norte Chico, where a string of fishing villages serve the day's catch – so fresh it's practically flopping on your plate – in pungent *marisquerías*, or seafood taverns, clustered around the quay.

Chile abounds with traditional dishes, including the delectable *zarzuela*, a robust seafood stew enveloped in a piquant sauce, and *chupe*, a rich fish soup with butter, cheese, and breadcrumbs. Albacora (albacore tuna) and congrio (a firm-fleshed white fish – *not* conger eel, as it is often mistranslated) grace menus throughout the country. Opt for simplicity and enjoy them *a la plancha*, or grilled, which enhances their natural juices and flavours.

Shellfish lovers are spoiled for choice: Indulge in *paila marina*, a fragrant shellfish broth seasoned with fresh coriander, graze on platters of fresh almejas (clams), ostras (oysters) and pulpo (octopus) sprinkled with lemon, or try the more unusual erizos (sea urchins), also used to enrich sauces, braised locos (abalone) and picorocos, huge

Pulpo (octopus)

barnacles with crab-like tentacles poking out their shells.

Even if you're not normally adventurous with seafood, you should experiment. A delicious dish to start with is *machas a la parmesana* – pink razor clams, lightly baked in their shells and covered with grated parmesan cheese. Another tasty speciality, also very popular in Peru, is *ceviche*, or raw fish marinated in lemon juice. Look out, too, for *cancato*, a fillet of fish topped with cheese, tomato and sausage, pizza-fashion, and grilled over an open fire. The lobster-sized centolla (king crab) is a Patagonian delicacy, well worth sampling if you're in Chile's far south.

Steaming curanto

Around Puerto Montt and on the island of Chiloé, tuck into the local speciality of **curanto** – a fish and shellfish broth, sometimes studded with chicken and sausage, served out of huge, steaming cauldrons. If you're lucky you might even get to savour a traditional pit-cooked curanto: the shellfish is cooked over red-hot embers, together with whole potatoes and different kinds of potato cake in a hole in the ground. The pit is then covered with a lid of wild-rhubarb leaves, left to simmer away for ages, before being unearthed and served to the whole village.

The wines of Chile

Though Chile's international prominence as a wine-producing nation has come rather recently, wine has been made here ever since the 1540s, when the first Catholic missionaries planted vines so they could partake of the drink during Mass. The Spanish colonists, who had less spiritual motives in following the missionaries' lead, began small-scale production throughout Chile's Central Valley. It wasn't until 1851, though, that the first proper winery was established, when Silvestre Ochagavía imported a range of vine cuttings from France. His timing was spot on – just a few years later the dreaded phylloxera, a tiny aphid-like pest, began to devastate vine stocks across Europe. Chile is the only major wine-growing country in the world to have remained totally free from phylloxera, thanks to the formidable natural barriers that surround the country and, more recently, to rigorous import controls.

Ochagavía's trend-setting winery set in motion a spate of vineyard-planting in central Chile, mostly by old moneyed families, who erected fine mansions and parks next to their vines. The most prestigious and beautiful of these were in the Maipo Valley, southeast of Santiago, where the well-drained, lime-rich soils and temperate climate present perfect

Wine barrels

conditions for grape-growing. Many of the established wineries in the lush vineyards around Santiago offer tours and tastings (see box, p.135); if you visit during the harvesting month of March, you're rewarded with the fragrant, colourful spectacle of grapes being sorted and pressed.

The industry grew steadily throughout the twentieth century, but undemanding domestic tastes ensured that producers never had to try too hard, a fact reflected in the run-of-the-mill wines that dominated the Chilean market. Things changed fast, however, when Spain's leading producer Miguel Torres arrived on Chile's wine scene in

Grape harvest

Pisco, Chile's beloved brandy

Despite wine's popularity, the fruity, aromatic brandy known as **pisco** is Chile's undisputed national drink. Made from the distilled wine of muscatel grapes, it's produced in the transverse valleys of northern Chile, particularly the **Elqui Valley**, where consistently high temperatures, light, alkaline soil, and brilliant sunshine combine to produce grapes with a high sugar content and low acidity, perfect for distillation. Some believe its name derives from the Quechua word "Pisku", which means "flying bird"; others say that the drink was named for the small Peruvian port from which it was shipped, illegally, during colonial times. Even if you cannot visit a pisco distillery, be sure to sample a **pisco sour**, Chile's favourite cocktail made by adding lemon juice, a little sugar and sometimes a touch of frothy egg-white. A pisco sour, often on the house, is a ubiquitous welcoming gesture up and down the country.

Pisco sour

the 1980s, ushering in an era of modernization. Suddenly, wineries invested in state-of-the-art stainless-steel vats and incorporated cutting-edge methods of ageing, leading to sharp improvements in quality. These days, Chilean wines are among the most exciting in the New World, regularly winning medals and prizes at international wine fairs, rather than just thought of as cheap alternatives to bigger name brands – though many are an excellent value for the money.

In 1995 the Chilean government introduced an official appellation system, with five demarcated regions: Atacama, Coquimbo, Aconcagua, Central Valley and Southern Region. Most of the finest quality wines are produced in the Central Valley, which is subdivided into the four lateral valleys of Maipo (including the Santiago area), Rapel, Curicó and Maule. The principal grapes grown in this region are Cabernet Sauvignon, Merlot, Chardonnay, Sauvignon Blanc and Carmenère, the latest variety to splash onto Chile's wine scene.

The rediscovered Carmenère, a grape originally brought over from Bordeaux in the late nineteenth century, yields juicy reds with a firm structure, and has become the country's signature grape, as few other wine regions produce it. Chile's Cabernet Sauvignons emit a fruity bouquet with earthy, spicy hints. Maipo Valley Cabs are uniquely smoky, while those from Colchagua tend towards mineral tones. West of Santiago, the Casablanca area, part of the Aconcagua region, is producing excellent Chardonnays, considered by many to be the best whites in the country.

Chile's premier vintners include Casa Lapostolle, a joint venture between the French Marnier-Lapostolle and Chilean Rabat families, which is known for its superb Merlot; Concha y Toro, makers of award-winning Cabernet Sauvignons and co-producers of the top-notch label Almaviva; and the historic Viña Errázuriz, who have also formed a partnership with California winemaker Robert Mondavi to create the excellent Seña brand.

specialities and an excellent lunch time salad bar. Closed Sat lunch and Sun.

Les Assassins Merced 297B, near corner of Lastarria ☎6384280. Small, informal, very popular restaurant with lots of charm, serving traditional French food at reasonable prices. Closed Sun.

Squadritto Rosal 332, on east side of Cerro Santa Lucía ☎6322121. Superb and pricey Italian food in a stylish, slightly formal restaurant. Closed Sat lunch and Sun.

Bellavista

Calle Constitución, while just three blocks long, has become the epicentre of Chile's ethnic restaurants. It runs parallel and one block east of the main Bellavista drag, Pío Nono. Reservations are rarely necessary for parties of fewer than four.

Eladio Pío Nono 241. One of the best places in the city for a hearty Argentine steak. A good variety of reasonably priced meats, plus very expensive seafood specialties, including lobsters from the Robinson Crusoe Islands. Friendly, relaxed and eternally popular. Closed Sun dinner.

Étnico Constitución 172, at Lopez de Bello ☎7320119. Chic restaurant specializing in fresh Chilean seafood bound into sushi and sashimi packets at moderate prices. It attracts the beautiful people and gets buzzing most every night around 11pm. Great stop for pisco sours, a sushi platter and people watching. Closed Sun.

Kilomètre 11680 Dardignac 0145 ☎7770410. This large and cheerful French restaurant has one of Santiago's best-stocked wine cellars. As good for light snacks (try the excellent *tabla de quesos*)

as for the more exquisite and expensive dishes, like scallops in cream sauce.

Off the Record Antonia López de Bello 0155 ☎7777710. The moderately priced food served in an informal setting is mostly Chilean fare; if you come on a Monday evening, you'll have to fight for a seat: local authors and artists give talks or performances that attract a lively crowd. Closed Sun.

Venezzia Pío Nono 200. Said to be the oldest restaurant in the city (founded in the 1870s) and a former haunt of Pablo Neruda, this old-fashioned bar/*picada* has been around for decades and with its family atmosphere has more charm than many of its smarter, newer rivals. The food is mainly grills, sandwiches and other traditional snacks at reasonable prices. Closed Sun.

Providencia and Ñuñoa

Conveniently located on the metro, Providencia offers many bargain lunch spots and fewer, but still plentiful, dinner options. Nearby, though less accessible, Nuñoa has trendier eateries, often with good music thrown in.

Astrid y Gastón Antonio Bellet 201 ☎6509125. One of the best (and most expensive) fusion restaurants in Santiago. Service and presentation are impeccable; the duck salad and Catalan-inspired tuna in a honey sauce with black bean puree look and taste great. Alternatively you could kick off with crispy octopus with a passion-fruit and sesame sauce. Your dessert order – the souf-flés are irresistible – is taken first, so it can be specially prepared. Book a table at least two weeks in advance.

Barandaraián Manuel Montt 315 ☎2366854. Some of the best Peruvian food in Santiago is served here. Superb dishes include fish soup and *ceviche*. Dinners are in the middle price range, with good deals at lunch. Three blocks from the Manuel Montt metro stop.

De Cangrejo a Conejo Av Italia 805 ☎6344041. Although there's no sign on the door, there's still a queue, and word-of-mouth keeps this low-key place packed. The somewhat expensive, very innovative menu includes rabbit dishes and Chilean seafood. A bit off the beaten track, but basically a five- to ten-minute drive south of central Providencia; parking is easy. Reservations recommended.

Infante 51 J.M. Infante 51 ☎2643357, Providencia. Truly outstanding restaurant where simple but refined dishes of fish, seafood and lamb are served with a smile in a wonder-ful converted villa, with a quiet patio at the back. The Basque chef brings a touch of San Sebastián sophistication to fish from Juan Fernández or even as far away as Rapa Nui.

Liguria Av Providencia 1373. One of the most popular and packed restaurant bars in Santiago. Open nearly all night, this is the place for a 3am steak or Greek salad, or for the last drinking stop of the evening. Always crowded, thanks to the mid-range prices, but there is usually a table available in one of the back rooms.

Ozono Santa Beatriz 83 ☎ 2640361. Moderately priced restaurant in a beautifully restored house. In summer there's an outdoor barbeque and dining on patios. Specials include grilled tuna, and lamb dishes. Note the abundance of offerings from the restaurant's sponsor: Absolut vodka. Live jazz at lunch is a nice touch.

Santo Remedio, Roman Diaz 152 ☎ 2350984. *The* place for a Sunday night out, but also a good stopover for drinks any night of the week. Unique menu defies any category except delicious. Meals,

including breaded seafood and pasta with a choice of sauces, are accurately billed as "an aphrodisiacal experience". Medium price range.

El Taller Marin 0285 ☎ 2223016. Born from a catering company that developed a reputation for some of Chile's best banquets, this small, cosy and centrally located restaurant has a fanatical following among the city's gourmet elite. Superb fusion dishes incorporate great Chilean wines and seafood, while maintaining reasonable prices. This is among the best little finds in town. Reservations recommended.

La Terraza Jorge Washington 58, Plaza Ñuñoa. Lovely, mellow restaurant with a large terrace, serving typical meat and fish dishes and snacks. It fills with a young, trendy crowd, especially at weekends. Closed Sun dinner.

El Bosque Norte and Vitacura

These two exclusive neighbourhoods lie beyond the end of the metro line. As you'd expect, restaurants here tend to be more about money than taste, but the restaurants listed below are worth the extra outlay (including the taxi fare).

Akarana Reyes Lavalle 3310 ☎ 2319667. This hugely popular New Zealand restaurant offers everything from hearty lamb dishes to creations made with Chile's wealth of seafood, including squid and tuna. Friendly owner Nell serves tables

herself, bringing a homely touch to this charming spot. Not too far from El Golf metro.

Cafe Melba Don Carlos 2898 ☎ 2324546. Brunch, complete with eggs Benedict and fresh coffee, is a Sunday ritual for many expats. *Melba* also

Santiago's vegetarian restaurants

Chilean food revolves firmly around meat and fish, and vegetarians will quickly tire of the few meat-free staples such as *humitas* (corn mash in corn husk) and *empanadas de queso* (boiled dough with a chunk of flavourless cheese in the middle). Santiago does, however, offer a handful of good **vegetarian restaurants** serving modern, imaginative veggie food at low prices. Don't be surprised to find these places packed at lunch time, as they're popular with office workers.

Café del Patio Providencia 1670, at the back of the courtyard behind *Phone Box Pub*. Mainly sandwiches, salads and stir-fries served by bohemian waitresses dressed in black. There's a pretty outdoor patio. Closed Sat dinner and Sun.

El Huerto Orrego Luco 054, Providencia. The best veggie restaurant in Santiago, with a mouthwatering range of seasonal dishes; its Greek salad and gazpacho are especially recommended in summer. Note that the main restaurant is indoors, next door to the café section, which doesn't offer the full menu. Closed Sun.

El Naturista Moneda 846, near Estado, in the historic centre. The original pioneer of vegetarian food in Santiago, this large, inexpensive restaurant attracts a huge, frenetic crowd at lunch time; if there's no room, try the stand-up bar on the ground floor.

El Vegetariano Huérfanos 827, in *galería* (arcade) near corner of San Antonio, historic centre. An extensive, good-value menu, including excellent milkshakes and desserts (the apple pancakes are especially delicious). Upstairs is very pleasant, with stained-glass windows and overhead sunlight. Closed Sat dinner and Sun.

offers free Internet access and English-language message boards.

Risotto Vitacura 3809 ℗ 2281445. Three dozen varieties of the Italian rice dish, no less, all using the best arborio rice and delicious ingredients such as Ecuadorian prawns, shiitake and king crab, served in gleaming copper pans. Copious salads and well-prepared lamb or fish dishes accompanied by rice can be followed by sharp sorbets or fresh pineapple carpaccio. Smart, minimalist decor and efficient service. A tot of bitter lemoncello is served on the house. Reserve at weekends.

Zanzibar Monseñor Escriva de Balaguer 6400 ℗ 2180118. Inside the Borde del Río complex, this is one of the most beautiful restaurants in Santiago, with a host of different dining rooms, including a rooftop Moroccan-style lounge that is a great brunch spot. Astride the Río Mapocho and a glider port, the restaurant offers plenty of sights from its rooftop. Monthly full-moon parties feature belly dancers, body painting and a collection of fine dishes. Highly recommended, even if does take a 25-minute taxi ride to get here. Reservations necessary.

Drinking, music and nightlife

Santiago is no Buenos Aires or Rio. It is not a seven-nights-a-week party town, and compared to other Latin capitals can seem rather tame. That said, Thursdays, Fridays and Saturdays get quite lively, and huge, buzzing crowds pour into the streets and bars of the nightlife *zonas*. These fall into three main areas – Bellavista, Providencia and Ñuñoa – each with a distinct flavour and clientele. In addition, **the historic centre of Santiago** is seeing a renaissance, as young people turn apartments into lofts and old bars into trendy hangouts.

Bellavista, a short walk from Baquedano metro stop, is the most picturesque of the nightlife zones, with its colourful night-time market running the length of the main street. Though a number of loud discos are on Pío Nono, the area is characterized by its small, informal restaurants, many of them putting on live music after 11pm, usually guitar music, *boleros* or Latin (see the restaurant listings on p.121). Here you can feast, drink and dance in the same evening – everything is compact and you rarely will have to walk more than four or five blocks in any direction. It is generally a safe area except from about 2am to 6am on Saturday and Sunday mornings, when the alcohol-induced buzz can turn a bit ugly.

Providencia, particularly around the junction of Suecia and Holley, is packed with slick, American-style bars that pull in a huge crowd of professional types, including lots of expats and foreign visitors. It tends to be fairly lively through the week as well, filled with the after-work crowd. Drinks are much more expensive here, although most places offer happy hours; many of them also have live music at weekends, typically cover bands playing pop or rock favourites.

Ñuñoa is very different again. It's a residential neighbourhood popular with artists and families. The restaurants are centred on the Plaza Ñuñoa, but there are some spectacular exceptions that are worth hauling the map out for. This is where you'll find Santiago's "underground" scene; the bars and cafés lining the main square are filled with nonchalant students in ripped black jeans and leather jackets. Ñuñoa also has a couple of good live music venues, including Santiago's only jazz club. Take a blue Metrobus from Salvador metro station to the Plaza Ñuñoa. About 10 minutes drive south of the main drag, Ñuñoa is often overlooked by travellers and this is a mistake; once you find it, coming back is easy either by bus or a CH$3000–4000 cab ride from most central parts of Santiago.

These are the main areas for drinking and listening to music, though you'll find a number of other places scattered around the city – around Plaza Brasil, for example, or in Las Condes. When it comes to dancing, Santiago's **discotheques** are more widely dispersed, some of them quite a drive away.

The ones we've listed below are all reasonably central, easily reached by taxi (and some of them on foot). The club scene is notoriously difficult to pin down – places drift in and out of fashion, and open up and close down in an apparently random manner. The ones below should be reliable, but it's a good idea to seek advice from locals (bar staff are usually helpful). Prices at the most fashionable clubs are high, up to CH$10,000 per person, affordable only to the most affluent young Chileans.

When mega-famous bands or singers play in Santiago, they usually perform in the Estadio Nacional or Estación Mapocho. This is quite rare, however, and most South American and national bands play in smaller **venues** that offer a much more intimate atmosphere. For details of who's playing where and when, check the listings section (under "*Recitales*") of Friday's *El Mercurio* or *La Tercera del Día*, or visit *la Feria del Disco* at Ahumada 286, where performances are advertised and tickets are sold at the Ticketmaster counter. Excellent national bands to see live are classics Inti Illimani and Las Jaivas. Newer acts worth catching include La Floripondio, La Ley and Pozze Latina.

As you make your plans for the night, bear in mind that at the weekend things don't liven up until quite late in Santiago – from around 10 or 11pm in restaurants, and from about midnight to 1am in clubs.

Also be aware that the English word **"nightclub"** in Chile means "brothel". Prostitution is very common here: at least a dozen highly publicized brothels thrive throughout Santiago, and newspapers run pages of advertisements for "saunas".

Bars and live music venues

Santiago's **bars** range from dusty, mahogany-panelled corner bars full of ancient regulars to ultra-trendy, spaces selling designer beers. They are often good places to catch up on some musical entertainment too. **Live music** in Santiago ranges from romantic folk songs to Britpop covers, and you'll find venues everywhere from the historic centre to bohemian Ñuñoa, in bars, jazz clubs and special concert venues. The historic **Estación Mapocho** (see p.112) occasionally hosts concerts by international stars such as Joan Manuel Serrat and David Byrne; check www.estacionmapocho.cl for details.

La Batuta Jorge Washington 52, Plaza Ñuñoa. Dark room with a bar and a dance floor; no trendy decor but a great, grungy atmosphere. Hosts established and new bands (usually Fridays). It's a disco on Saturday. Don't dress smart. CH$3000.

Brannigan's Suecia 035. One of the more restrained bars in Providencia, where the music's rarely loud enough to rule out conversation. Good atmosphere.

Café-Berri Rosal 321. Small, old-fashioned bar-café hidden away on a little street east of Santa Lucía, in the historic centre. Friendly Basque staff and a young crowd give this place a great atmosphere, even midweek. Well worth seeking out.

La Casa en el Aire Antonia López de Bello 0125. Named after Neruda's poem *Voy a hacerte una casa en el aire*, this bar-café is one of the nicest places in Bellavista to enjoy a drink and live folk music, with occasional poetry recitals thrown in.

Club de Jazz Av José Pedro Alessandri 85, a block south of Plaza Ñuñoa. Comfortable, relaxed and friendly, with loads of atmosphere and an invariably excellent line-up of Chilean and international jazz musicians. Live music Thursday, Friday and Saturday. CH$3000.

La Fábrica Asunción 426. Trendy, centrally located pub, with a small dance floor and regular live music – everything from metal to folk. About CH$7500 for concerts.

Mister Ed Suecia 0152, Providencia. Noted for good live performances at weekends, often by well-known national bands. Get here before 10pm or there'll be no room left. Midweek it's a relaxing place to come for a drink.

Tomm General Holley 2366, Providencia. Popular place with students, for its cheap beer and good live music, mostly home-grown rock.

Discos

Santiago's nightclubs tend to be the preserve of the city's more affluent teenagers, and are well out of most young people's price range. In addition to the clubs listed below, *La Batuta* and *Tomm* (listed under "Live music venues", opposite) are popular places to go dancing.

Blondie Alameda 2879, north side, near ULA metro. Popular student hangout close to the university; loud music and dancing, with lots of techno. CH$3000.

Boomerang Holley 2285, Providencia. Chile's top beer joint is owned by an Australian who mixes moderately priced drinks, tasty bar food and rocking weekend parties. Popular with foreigners and young Chilenos, this is a good place to drink and dance until the wee hours of the morning.

Laberinto Vicuña Mackenna 915, near Irarrázaval. Very stylish, very contemporary club spread over various levels, galleries and passages of an old converted warehouse. Plays a mixture of house, indie and rock to cool young things in jeans. CH$8000.

La Maestra Vida Pío Nono 380, Bellavista. Small, crowded *salsateca* with a friendly atmosphere – no need to feel shy about practising your salsa here. All-age crowd, including plenty of ageing Latin American revolutionaries. Cover is CH$3000.

OZ Bilbao 477, Providencia. This expensive techno club is frequented by chic Chilean yuppies. Cover is CH$13,000.

Tantra Lounge Ernesto Pinto Lagarrigue 154, Bellavista. Great place to gawk at Chile's jet set trying to be fashionable and dancing away the evening. Expensive and probably not worth it except for voyeurs.

Gay Santiago

Santiago is the only city in Chile with anything resembling an organized gay community. The more progressive social background and the political sea change of the past few years have resulted in a far more relaxed attitude towards gay and lesbian issues than was found after the restoration of democracy. The gay scene, such as it is (do not expect San Francisco or London's Soho), centres on **Bellavista**, and consists of a couple of bars, a restaurant, several discos and some saunas; up-to-date information about these can be found on ⓦwww.chilegay.com. Chile's highly politicized Gay Pride Parade takes place in September, and there is a gay and lesbian film festival every January or February at the Cine Alameda (see p.127).

Bunker Bombero Nuñez 159. Somewhat gloomy nightclub that lives up to its name at times but nonetheless attracts a large crowd at weekends, thanks mainly to its varied music and cavernous back room, and on Thursdays when there is no entrance charge. Closed Sun and Mon. CH$5000.

Bokhara Pío Nono 430. Fun disco open every evening, with shows featuring drag artists and Brazilian dance troupes.

Capricho Español Purísima 65. Spanish and international cuisine in an atmospheric, neo-colonial building. Very gay friendly.

Farinelli Bombero Nuñez 68. This gay version of *café con piernas* (the waiters wear nothing but sequin waistcoats and revealing G-strings), lays on shows every evening, some of them hilarious comic drag acts requiring a decent level of Spanish for full appreciation. Reasonably priced drinks and ice creams, inevitably including a suggestive banana split.

Fausto Santa María 0382, Providencia. Popular gay disco, with strippers and drag shows. Open Wed–Sun. CH$4000, free before 11pm.

Friend's Bombero Nuñez 365. This aptly named friendly pub offers cabaret shows and strippers from 9pm onwards. Open Tues–Sat.

The arts and entertainment

Chile is noted in Latin America for the quality and range of its **theatre**, and Santiago is of course the best place to see it. Performances are staged in the many theatres and cultural centres dotted about the city, and take in everything from time-honoured classics to contemporary and experimental works. **Classical music** is performed in a number of venues, including theatres, cultural centres and churches; check out the cheap midday concerts held from around June to December at the Teatro Municipal. This is the most prestigious venue in Santiago for music, **dance** and **opera**, and although it tends to be fairly conservative in its repertoire, it occasionally puts on innovative new productions, usually from abroad. **Cinema** is very popular in Santiago, with a concentration of movie theatres on Huérfanos, in the historic centre, and several newer, modern ones in Providencia, Las Condes and Ñuñoa. Most films shown are mainstream US imports, usually in the original version with Spanish subtitles, but there are a number of **arts cinemas** showing non-commercial films and old movies. Nearly all cinemas have a half-price policy on Wednesdays that attracts huge crowds – get there early to queue, or buy your ticket earlier in the day.

Although all the Friday newspapers include comprehensive details of **what's on** at the weekend, none gives descriptions or synopses to help you work out what you're interested in (especially crucial when it comes to theatre). The best is probably *La Tercera*'s Friday supplement, though many Santiaguinos prefer the "*Wikén*" section that comes with Friday's *El Mercurio*. Increasingly, websites have current movie schedules (try ⓦ www.hoyts.cl). If you aren't able to buy one of the Friday papers, the tourist kiosk on Ahumada keeps a copy of *La Tercera*, and the daily papers give cinema listings for that day.

Finally, a word on **prices**: most entertainment in Santiago is quite affordable, with theatre and concert tickets commonly going for CH$3000 to CH$5000. Even the Teatro Municipal offers inexpensive ballet and opera (from CH$2000 for national productions and from CH$15,000 for international productions) though the better seats are considerably more expensive (as much as CH$60,000 for international opera).

Cinemas

Over the past five years, the number of movie screens in Chile has grown drastically. Instead of seedy old sticky-floor movie houses, the new cinemas offer Dolby sound, comfortable chairs and modern projection systems. Most of the best cinemas are in the eastern portion of the city.

Huérfanos is the main cinema street in the historic centre of Santiago. You will find latest Hollywood features in the modern facility at Hoyts (Huérfanos 735) and Chilefilms Grand Palace (Huérfanos 1176).

Mainstream

Chilefilms Grand Palace Huérfanos 1176. This cinema stays open late, offers big discounts on Wednesdays, and is very popular for ducking in for a midday movie while downtown.

Cinemark 12 Av Kennedy 9001, Mall Alto Las Condes. Twelve-screen, modern facility offering Hollywood's latest.

Cine Hoyts Huérfanos 735 ☎ 600 5000 400 (toll free). The most modern and comfortable theatre in central Santiago.

Cine Hoyts La Reina Av Ossa 655/Simon Bolivar 5840 ☎ 600 5000 400 (toll free), ⓦ www .cinehoyts.cl. Chile's largest movie complex, with sixteen screens, including two or three reserved for non-commercial art films or recent Chilean releases. The best overall cinema in Chile, but way out in La Reina, an eastern suburb. You'll probably require a taxi or car to get here.

Arts cinemas

For art house films – known as *cine arte* – try the following:

AIEP Miguel Claro 177 ☎ 2649698 Univeroity cinema screens off-beat European documentaries and art films.

Centro de Extensión de la Universidad Católica Alameda 390 ☎ 6866516. Especially good for older films, often presented as part of themed programmes such as "Fifty Years of the Cannes Festival" or "Spanish Film Week". Many free showings for students with ID.

Cine Alameda Alameda 139, near Plaza Baquedano ☎ 6648842. Comfy, well-arranged seats and a fast-changing, wide-ranging choice of foreign films. Accessible to all public transport.

Cine El Biógrafo Lastarria 181 ☎ 6334435. Old favourite on this trendy, restaurant-lined street. Shows mainly current European and non-Hollywood US films.

Cine Normandie Tarapacá 1181, in the historic centre ☎ 6972979. Has a reputation for showing obscure contemporary European films.

Theatre

We've listed some of the main theatres below, but quality performances are staged in many different venues, including various multipurpose cultural centres and sometimes in the open-air amphitheatre of the Palacio de Bellas Artes. Ask in the Sernatur kiosk on Ahumada for recommendations, check the weekend listings (and keep an eye out for anything involving Paz Bascuñan, Cristián Campos, Willy Semler or Lillian Ross as director). The best time to experience Chilean theatre is in January, when Santiago hosts "*Santiago a Mil*" (ⓦ www .stgoamil.cl) an enormous international **festival of theatre** (plus dance and other arts). During the rest of the year, many theatres are only open from Thursday to Saturday. Ticket prices are usually very reasonable, from CH$3500 to CH$6000. Very entertaining children's theatre is widely available on Saturday and Sunday afternoons.

Sala Galpón 7 Chucre Manzur 7, just around the corner from Etniko ☎ 7355484. This reputable venue has a consistently strong line-up of edgy Chilean performances featuring both top actors and up-and-comers.

Teatro Alcalá Bellavista 97 ☎ 7327161. Bellavista theatre with top actors and great performances practically guaranteed. Some of Chile's top performances are shown here.

Teatro Bellavista Dardignac 0110 ☎ 7352395. This long-established and reliable Bellavista theatre usually stages modern foreign plays, often comedies.

Teatro Providencia Manuel Montt 032 ☎ 3720535. Stages a variety of theatre, live music and comedy performances, usually top acts. Worth getting schedule.

Teatro San Gines Mallinkrodt 76 ☎ 7382159. Top Chilean productions are staged here, as are fine children's shows on weekend afternoons. Tickets are expensive.

Teatro de la Universidad Católica Jorge Washington 26 ☎ 2055652. Operated by the university, this venue offers classic shows and Chilean adaptations of international works. Located in the heart of Plaza Ñuñoa.

Classical music, dance and opera

In addition to the three main venues listed below, classical music concerts are also performed in many churches (often for free) and cultural centres – look under "*música selecta*" in the listings papers. Traditionally, the season lasts from March to December.

Teatro Municipal Agustinas 749 ☎ 6390282, ⓦ www.municipal.cl. Santiago's most prestigious performing arts venue, offering a menu of classical concerts, ballet and opera in a splendid old building.

Teatro Oriente Pedro de Valdivia, between Costanera and Providencia ☎2515321. Here you can enjoy classical music performed by Fundación Beethoven and visiting theatre and musical groups. Information and tickets at 11 de Septiembre 2214, oficina 66.

Teatro Universidad de Chile Providencia 043 ☎6344746. Another established venue for ballet and classical music, featuring both national groups (principally the Orquésta Sinfónica de Chile) and foreign artists on tour.

Shopping and markets

Santiago is a curious place to go **shopping**. The historic centre is packed with small, old-fashioned shops dedicated to weird and wonderful things like panty girdles and industrial-sized food processors, as well as an astonishing number of pharmacies. One of the first things that strikes you about these shops is that everything's kept behind the counter, with no opportunity for browsing or touching. Managing to buy something can be quite a challenge: you first have to convey what you want to one of the assistants, who'll give you a ticket showing the amount you need to pay; you then go to the cash desk where you pay for the goods and get your ticket stamped; finally, you take the stamped ticket to another desk where you exchange it for (hopefully) what you asked for.

Another oddity about shopping in the centre of the city is the warren of arcades, or *galerías*, most of them gloomy and uninviting, that seem to lurk behind every other doorway. Providencia and Las Condes, on the other hand, sport a slick array of fashionable boutiques and modern, American-style malls – better shopping, perhaps, but far less interesting.

Don't miss the fish stalls at the Mercado Central (see p.112) – where you can often sample produce on the spot – and the enormous variety of fruit at the Feria Municipal La Vega (see p.112), also a great place to people watch.

For the best selections of **wine** in Santiago, try *The Wine House*, Av Vitacura 2904 (☎2327257) and *Vinoteca*, Av Isidora Goynachea 2966 (☎3352349). *Vinos CyT*, Alonso de Córdova 2391, Vitacura (☎4269730, ⓦwww.vinoscyt.cl), a new shop opened by the Concha y Toro vineyard, offers books on Chilean wine, tastings and special sales.

Crafts, knitwear and lapis lazuli

Avenida Bellavista between Puente Pío Nono and Puente del Arzobispo. A string of workshops and salesrooms selling jewellery and other objects made of lapis lazuli.

Los Dominicos market next to Iglesia Los Dominicos in Las Condes. Excellent market with over two hundred stalls selling knitwear, ceramics, glass objects, books, antiques and lots more; see p.118 for details on how to get here. Tues–Sun 11am–7.30pm.

Feria Santa Lucía opposite Cerro Santa Lucía. Fairly large market selling crafts, clothes and lapis lazuli.

Books, magazines, records and CDs

Books Providencia 1652, in courtyard next to *Phone Box Pub*, near Sernatur. Secondhand English books, mainly best sellers and good selection of locally published, English-language travel books. In general, English-language books are expensive and hard to come by in Chile.

Feria del Disco Ahumada 286. The best place to buy Chilean and world music. The Ticketmaster counter is a good place to check about upcoming concerts.

Feria del Libro Huérfanos 623 ☎6396621. Largest bookshop in Santiago, with an excellent choice of Spanish-language novels, reference books and maps. Very little English-language material.

Librería Inglesa Huérfanos 669, local 11. Fairly good choice of Penguin paperbacks and other English-language books; very expensive.

Libro's San Antonio 236, local 815, and Pedro de Valdivia 039, Providencia. A small range of English-language paperbacks and a truly impressive selection of magazines, including *The Face*, *Wired*, *GQ* and *Gramophone* (plus a few bizarre titles, including *Tattoo Magazine*).

Shopping malls

Alto Las Condes Av Kennedy 9001, Las Condes. Huge, modern shopping mall with 245 shops. Connected to central Santiago by a free shuttle bus (℗ 2291383 for times). Daily 10am–10pm.

Arauco Outlet Mall Américo Vespucio 399. Low-cost clothes direct from the manufacturer. Shuttle buses from Ecuador metro station. Daily 10am–10pm.

La Dehesa El Rodeo, at La Dehesa. Small, very upmarket shopping centre. From the Alameda, take Bus #200, #201 or #202. Daily 10am–10pm.

Parque Arauco Av Kennedy 5413, Las Condes. Gets insanely busy at weekends as this is regarded as the best mall in town. Frequent shuttle buses from Estación Militar metro. Mon–Sat 10am–9pm, Sun 11am–9pm.

Flea markets and antiques

Anfiteatro Lo Castillo Candelería Goyenechea 3820, Vitacura. About twenty serious antiques dealers on the ground floor. Expensive. Mon–Fri 10am–2pm & 4–8pm, Sat 10am–2pm.

Anticuarios de Mapocho in the red warehouse at Brasil and Matucana, near Parque de los Reyes.

Lots of antique furniture, musical instruments, books and bric-a-brac. A wonderful place to browse. Sat & Sun 9am–late afternoon.

Franklin Market near Franklin metro. Enormous and very lively market running the length of two parallel streets, Franklin and Bío Bío. There's a lot of rubbish at the bottom end, near the metro, but if you walk about five blocks up to the junction with Victor Manual, there's a great flea market on the Franklin side, and lots of antiques stalls off Bío Bío. Sat & Sun 9am–afternoon.

Food and drink

Comercial San Agustín Puente 828. This huge liquor store stocks all kinds of wines and spirits at bargain prices. A good place for Chilean wine and pisco if you know what you want.

Confites Larbos Estado 26. A beautiful, old-fashioned shop selling fine wines, spirits and fancy foodstuffs (including small packets of Earl Grey teabags, very useful if you're sick of the Chilean variety).

The Wine House Av Vitacura 2904 ℗ 2327257. This constantly improving store offers good service and advice on quality wines, both Chilean and European.

Listings

Airlines Aerolíneas Argentinas, Moneda 756 ℗ 6393922; Air France, 6th floor, Alcantara 44 ℗ 2909300; Alitalia, Office 21, Av El Bosque Norte 0107 ℗ 3788230; American Airlines, Huérfanos 1199 ℗ 6790000; Avianca, Office 101-106, Santa Magdalena 116 ℗ 2706600; British Airways, 3rd floor, Isidora Goyenechea 2934 ℗ 3308600; Copa Airlines, Office 703, Fidel Oteiza 1921 ℗ 2002100; Iberia, 8th floor, Bandera 206 ℗ 8701070; Lacsa, 2nd floor, Dr Barros Borgoño 105 ℗ 2355500; LAN, Agustinas 640 ℗ 5262000; Lloyd Aero Boliviano ℗ 600/2002015; Lufthansa, 16th floor, Moneda 970 ℗ 6301655; Pluna, 9th floor, Av El Bosque Norte 0177 ℗ 7078000; Swiss, Office 810, Av Barros Errázuriz 1954 ℗ 2442888; United Airlines, Tenderini 171 ℗ 3370000; Varig, 9th floor, Av El Bosque Norte 0177 ℗ 7078000.

Airport information ℗ 6019709.

American Express To change travellers' cheques and cash, collect mail, get emergency cash and travel advice, including bookings and confirmations, go to Blanco Viajes, General Holley 148 ℗ 6369110 or 6369100. For card replacements and renewals, go to American Express, 10th floor, Isidora Goyenechea 3621 ℗ 3506700.

Banks, cambios and ATMs ATM machines can be found all over the historic centre, especially along Moneda, on Huérfanos between Ahumada and Mac Iver, on Miraflores and along Alameda itself. Note that banks are open only from 9am to 2pm. Many commercial establishments all over the city also have ATMs in the entryway; look for the maroon Redbanc sign. The best place to change cash and travellers' cheques is the cluster of change houses on Agustinas between Ahumada and Bandera. A good few to try are: Bombero, Ossa 1053 ℗ 6981703 (charges a commission for changing travellers' cheques; closed Sat); Afex, 9th floor, Moneda 1160 ℗ 6369000 or Pedro de Valdivia 044 or Agustinas 1148 (the last two branches are open Sat); Transpacific, Agustinas 1028 ℗ 6968763 or General Holley ℗ 2321176 (cheques in US dollars only, no commission; closed Sat). There is also a cluster of change houses on Pedro de Valdivia Norte, including Mojakar S.A., Pedro de Valdivia 059 ℗ 3789900 (charges a commission for changing travellers' cheques; closed Sat). Few Chilean banks are useful for changing dollars, but Citibank (many branches, including Huérfanos 770, Ahumada 40, Teatinos 180 and La Bolsa 64) charges no commission for changing US dollars into pesos.

Bike rental Lys, Miraflores 537 (ⓣ 6337300), also runs guided excursions into the Andes on mountain bikes. Pared Sur (ⓣ 2073525) offers bike rental and information.

Car rental Automóvil Club de Chile ⓣ 4311106 or 4311107; Avis, airport and San Pablo 9900 ⓣ 600/6019966; Budget, Francisco Bilbao 1439 ⓣ 3623200; Chilean Rent a Car, Bellavista 0183 ⓣ & ⓕ 7379650; Diamond, airport ⓣ 2112682 and Manquehue Sur 841 ⓣ 2121523; Dollar, Av Kennedy 8292 ⓣ 2025510; Just, Helvecia 228 ⓣ 2320900; Lacroce, Office 68, Av Apoquindo 6415 ⓣ 8214243; Lys, Miraflores 537 ⓣ 6337600.

Embassies Argentina, Miraflores 285 ⓣ 6331076; Australia, Gertrudis Echenique 420 ⓣ 5503500; Austria, 3rd floor, Barros Errázuriz 1968 ⓣ 2234774; Belgium, Office 1103, Providencia 2653 ⓣ 2321070; Brazil, Alonso Ovalle 1665 ⓣ 6982486; Canada, 12th floor, World Trade Centre, Nueva Tajamar 481 ⓣ 3629660; France, Condell 65 ⓣ 2251030; Germany, Office 302, Av Apoquindo 4445 ⓣ 4632500; Israel, San Sebastián 2812 ⓣ 7500500; Italy, Clemente Fabrés 1050 ⓣ 4708400; Netherlands, Las Violetas 2368 ⓣ 2236825; New Zealand, Office 703, El Golf 99 ⓣ 2909802; Peru, Av Andrés Bello 1751 ⓣ 2356451; South Africa, 16th floor, Av 11 de Septiembre 2353 ⓣ 2312862; Spain, Av Andrés Bello 1895 ⓣ 2352755; UK, Av El Bosque Norte 0125 ⓣ 3704100; USA, Av Andrés Bello 2800 ⓣ 2322600.

Emergencies Ambulance ⓣ 131; fire department (*bomberos*) ⓣ 132; police (*carabineros*) ⓣ 133.

Football matches Safe, albeit rowdy, matches held Mar–Dec, most games are on Saturday and Sunday. The National Stadium, Campo de Deportes, Av Grecia, is in Ñuñoa. Don't hang around after matches, as hooliganism is on the increase. The main Santiago teams are Colo Colo, Universidad Católica, Universidad de Chile, Unión Española and Palestino.

Hospitals Clínica Las Condes, Lo Fontecilla 441 ⓣ 2104000; Clínica Indisa, Av Santa María 01810 ⓣ 3625555; Clínica Las Lilas, Eleodoro Yánez 2887 ⓣ 4106666; Clínica Santa María, Av Santa María 0410 ⓣ 4102000; Clínica Universidad Católica, Lira 40, in the historic centre of the city ⓣ 3696000.

Internet access Internet cafés have boomed all over Santiago, so it's never very hard to find one, especially in commercial areas. Some well-known places are: *Café.com*, Alameda 143; *Ciber Librería Internacional*, Merced 324 ⓣ 6386245; *Cyber Café Internet*, Pedro de Valdivia 037 ⓣ 2333083; *Easy@net*, Las Palmas 2213 ⓣ 3337112;

Sicosis Pub basement, José Miguel de la Barra 544 ⓣ 6324462; *Sonnets Internet Café*, Londres 43.

LAN Pedro de Valdivia, at Av Providencia ⓣ 5262000, ⓦ www.lan.com. This central office for the LAN airline offers tours as well as dealing with seat assignments, itinerary changes and lost luggage. Or take care of these issues by logging on to the website in English.

Language courses Recommended places offering Spanish-language courses include: Centro Chileno Canadiense, Office 601, Av Luis Thayer Ojeda 0191 ⓣ & ⓕ 3341089; Instituto Chileno Británico, Santa Lucía 124 ⓣ 6382156, ⓕ 6326637; Instituto Chileno Norteamericano, Moneda 1467 ⓣ 6777000; Instituto de Idiomas Polyglot, Office 102, Villavicencio 361 ⓣ 6398078, ⓕ 6322485; Linguatec Language Center, Av Los Leones 439 ⓣ 2334356, ⓕ 2341380.

Laundry These laundry chains have branches all over town, the most central being: Sandrico, local 2B, Huérfanos 632, *galería* La Merced ⓣ 5574243, ⓕ 5574255 (Mon–Fri 8.30am–2pm & 3–7pm); Astra, Av Providencia 1604 ⓣ 2641946 (Mon–Fri 9.30am–8pm, Sat 9am–2pm).

Maps Topographical maps on all parts of Chile are available at the Instituto Geográfico, Militar Calle Dieciocho 369, near Toesca metro (ⓣ 69682221). You'll also find a good section of road maps for sale at the Fería del Libro, Huérfanos 623 (ⓣ 6396621). For tourist and walking maps, go to Sernatur, Av Providencia 1550 (ⓣ 7318310).

Newspapers There are numerous newspaper kiosks around town; those at the corner of Huérfanos and Ahumada sell a breathtaking range of foreign newspapers, including *Die Welt*, the *Financial Times*, *The New York Times*, the *Miami Herald* and a good selection of other European and Latin American newspapers.

Mountain climbing and outdoor equipment Several outdoor equipment stores have opened in the Avenida El Bosque Norte neighbourhood, especially on Encomenderos. Also try Patagonia Sport, Helvecia 210 (ⓣ 3351796), and Federación de Andinismo de Chile, Almirante Simpson 77 (ⓣ 2229140), which has a range of mountaineering and camping equipment. The highly recommended La Cumbre, Av Apoquindo 5258 (ⓣ 2209907, www .lacumbreonline.cl), run by friendly Ivo and Katja, has world-class boots, eyewear and climbing accessories as well as a small library of books about exploring the Andes. Basic fishing equipment available at Escamas, Av Brasil 121, just off Alameda (ⓣ 6710285). Fly-fishing equipment and information available at ⓦ www.flyshop.cl.

Pharmacies There's an abundance of pharmacies all over the historic centre, and smaller commercial

Moving on from Santiago

Sitting in the middle of the country, Santiago is the unrivalled **transportation hub** of Chile. All national transport networks lead to and from the capital, and most journeys between the north and south of Chile, including those by **air**, involve a change or at least a stop here. There are plenty of flights out of Santiago's **Aeropuerto Arturo Merino Benítez** (☏6901900) to all the major cities in the country. It's best to reserve your seat as far in advance as possible, as the cheaper fares tend to get booked up long before the flight; a travel agent should be able to give you a rundown of all the different options.

There are limited **train** services to the south. You'll find just five daily services from Santiago, including three to Chillán (two fast trains and one normal), a night train to Temuco and another night train to Concepción. All trains leave from the **Estación Central** on Alameda (☏3768500), next to the metro stop of the same name.

By far the greatest majority of transport services are provided by **buses**, run by a bewildering number of private companies. These operate out of **four terminals**.

The **Terminal de Buses Santiago**, more often known as **Terminal de Estación Central** (☏7791385), just west of the Universidad de Santiago metro station, is the largest (and most chaotic) of the terminals, with more than a hundred bus companies operating out of here. Services **south** down the Panamericana from this terminal are provided by all the major companies, including Andimar (☏7793810), Cóndor Bus (☏6806900), Ega (☏7645231), Inter Sur (☏7796312) and Tas Choapa (☏7794694). Buses to the **coastal resorts** of the *Litoral Central* (including Valpo) are run by Cóndor Bus (☏6806900) and Pullman Bus (☏7792026), though you can also get to these destinations from the Alameda and San Borja terminals (less frequent services).

Terminal de Buses Alameda (☏7780808) is used only by Tur Bus (☏2707500) and Pullman Bus (☏5603781), Chile's two largest and most comprehensive bus companies.

Terminal San Borja (☏7760645), a modern, well-organized station, is set at the back of a shopping mall behind the Estación Central (from the metro, follow the signs carefully to exit at the terminal). This is the main departure point for buses to the **north** of Chile, particularly for long-distance buses going right up to Iquique and Arica. There are several regional buses, as well, and some services to the coastal resorts. Bus companies going north include Elqui Bus (☏7787045), Pullman Bus (☏5603821) and Tas Choapa (☏7786827). Tur Bus (☏7787338) also runs services to the *Litoral*.

The fourth terminal **Los Héroes** (☏6974178; metro Los Héroes), is located on Tucapel Jiménez, just north of the Plaza de Los Héroes; the most **central** of the bus terminals, it hosts a mixture of northbound, southbound and international buses. It is used by eight companies: Buses Ahumada (☏6969798), Cruz del Sur (☏6969324), Fenix (☏6969321), Flota Barrios (☏6969311), Los Héroes (☏4410343), Libac (☏6985974), Pullman del Sur (☏6731967) and Tas Choapa (☏6969326).

The main bus companies serving **international destinations**, mostly out of **Estación Central** and **Los Héroes**, are Ahumada (☏7782703), Cata (☏7793660), Chilebus (☏7792429), El Rápido (☏7790316), Ormeño (☏7793443), Pluma (☏7796054), Pullman del Sur (☏7795243) and Tas Choapa (☏7794925). The most frequent services are to Mendoza (7hr) and Buenos Aires (22hr) in **Argentina**, but there are also direct buses to Lima (48hr) in **Peru** (Ormeño), São Paulo (62hr) and Rio (65hr) in **Brazil** (Chilebus and Pluma), Montevideo (28hr) in **Uruguay** (Ega and El Rápido) and Asunción in **Paraguay** (Pluma).

While you can normally turn up and buy a **ticket** for travelling the same day, it's better to buy it a day or more in advance, especially at weekends. For travel on the days around Christmas, New Year's Eve and Easter, you should buy your ticket at least a week ahead.

areas always have at least one. Farmacias Ahumada (τ 2224000) has a number of 24-hour branches, including Av Portugal 155, in the historic centre, and Av El Bosque 164, Providencia; they'll deliver to your hotel for a small charge.

Post offices Correo Central, Plaza de Armas 559 (Mon–Fri 8.30am–7pm, Sat 8.30am–1pm). Other branches at Moneda 1155, near Morandé; Local 17, Exposición 57 Paseo Estación; Av 11 de Septiembre 2092. Federal Express, Av Providencia 1951 τ 2315250, and San Camilo 190 τ 3616000, $\circledf$ 3616111; $\circledw$ www.FedEx.com; DHL, Suecia 072 τ 2327539; UPS, Unión Americana 221 τ 6890203, $\circledf$ 6850797, $\circledw$ www.ups.com.

Swimming pools Tupahue, near the Tupahue *teleférico* station on Cerro San Cristóbal (mid-Nov to mid-Mar, Tues–Sun 10am–7pm; CH$5000; τ 7766666 annex 150), is large and beautiful, but expensive. Piscina Antilén, also on Cerro San Cristóbal (Nov–Mar Wed–Mon 10am–7pm; CH$6000; τ 2326617), is in the same mould but harder to reach by public transport. Parque O'Higgins (Nov–Mar, Tue–Sat 1.30–6.30pm, Sun and public holidays 10.30am–6.30pm; CH$2000; τ 5569612) has a large outdoor pool that is much more affordable but gets quite crowded. There is also an Olympic-size pool in Parque Araucano, behind Parque Arauco shopping centre near Escuela Militar metro (τ 2124376). For an indoor pool, try Centro de Natación Patricia Thompson, Bilbao 2342 (CH$3500; τ 2044096), but call first to find out when it's open for free swimming.

Telephone centres Entel's biggest branch is at Morandé, between Huérfanos and Compañía (τ & $\circledf$ 3609447); it's air-conditioned, quiet, has plenty of phones and Internet access. You can also send and receive faxes here; they'll keep them for a month. Smaller Entel offices are at Huérfanos 1141, near corner of Morandé, and Mall del Centro Puente 689, near Mercado Central. Telefónica CTC Chile has *centros de llamadas* at Local 15, Universidad de Chile metro; Local 10 and 12, Moneda metro; and Local 145B and 167B, Mall Panorámico Av 11 de Septiembre 2155.

Train information τ 3768500.

Travel agents There are countless travel agents in the historic centre, among them: Andina del Sud, 2nd floor, Av El Golf 99 (τ 3880101), very friendly and professional, good for international flights and package holidays inside and outside Chile; Andy Tour, Agustinas 1056 (τ 6716592), for good-value packages in South America, especially to Peru and Argentina; ATM, Viajes Andrés de Fuenzalida 22, Office 1104 (τ 2444666, $\circled{e}$ atmviajes@entelchile .net), ask for Faride Alegría; Rapa Nui, 9th floor, Huérfanos 1160 (τ 6721050), mainly for international flights (not Easter Island specialists as the name suggests). There are plenty in Providencia as well, including: Chilean Travel Service, 1st floor, Antonio Bellet 77 (τ 2510400), professional all-rounders; Turismo Cocha, Av El Bosque Norte 0430 (τ 4641000), Chile's largest and most prestigious chain; Turismo Tajamar, Orrego Luco 023 (τ 3368000), national and international packages, member of the Chilean Association of Travel Agencies. All the above offer city tours and regional excursions; for adventure tourism in the region, see p.74.

Around Santiago

Santiago is close to some fine, and frequently overlooked, attractions, from national parks and thermal springs to sleepy villages and lush vineyards.

The obvious main attraction is the **Andes**, with the **Cajón del Maipo** providing good access into the cordillera, leading to the small but spectacular **Monumento Nacional El Morado**. In winter, **skiing** is a terrific possibility, the several excellent resorts are just a ninety-minute drive from the capital and increasingly offer year-round activities like hiking and mountain biking. **Wineries** are another of the area's highlights, with some of Chile's oldest and most famous vineyards within easy striking distance, often offering tours and tastings.

Towards the coast, **Parque Nacional La Campana** offers good hiking and requires a couple of days to be fully enjoyed, while **Pomaire**, to the east of the capital, is a picturesque village known for its inexpensive ceramics, country cooking and small town ambience. North of Santiago, head for the colonial town of **Los Andes**, surrounded by picturesque villages and mountain scenery. All these destinations are served by frequent buses; details are given in the text and in "Travel Details" on p.141.

Cajón del Maipo

The **CAJÓN DEL MAIPO** is a beautiful river valley carved out of the Andes by the Río Maipo. Served by a good paved road (for 48km of its 70km length) and punctuated by a string of hamlets offering tourist facilities, it's one of the most popular weekend escapes from the capital. The potential for outdoor adventures is enormous. Only a fraction of that potential has been realized, but organized **hiking**, **rafting**, and **mountain biking trips** are plentiful.

Start at the mouth of the *cajón,* just 25km southeast of Santiago, at Las Vizcachas. Here the scenery is lush and gentle, and as you climb into the valley you'll pass vineyards, orchards, roadside stalls selling locally produced fruit, and signs advertising homemade *küchen, miel* (honey) *pan amasado* (fresh oven-baked bread) and *chicha* (cider). Twenty-five kilometres on, you reach the administrative centre of the valley, **SAN JOSE DE MAIPO**, a small town that was founded in 1791 following the discovery of nearby silver deposits. It's quite attractive, with single-storey adobe houses and an old, colonial church. If you want to **stay**, try *Residencial Inesita*, Comercio 19321 (☎8611012; ❹). Drivers should note that this is the last place along the road where you can fill up with petrol. There are no banks or ATM machines in the valley, so bring cash.

Getting to Cajón del Maipo is easy from Santiago: blue and white Cajón del Maipo **buses** leave from a small terminal outside Parque O'Higgins, near the metro, with four buses daily going as far as El Volcán, and less frequent services to Baños Morales (daily Jan & Feb; weekends only Oct–March). From Plaza Italia, Tursmontaña (☎8500555) runs **minivans** to Baños Morales; call ahead for reservations. Most departures are early morning. For private vehicles the road is fine until San Gabriel, where it may be filled with rocks and landslides. Weekend traffic can be horrendous, with two- to three-hour backups. To avoid the traffic, make an early day of it, entering the *cajón* well before 10am and leaving before 3pm (or, if necessary, late at night).

San Alfonso

Some 15km beyond San José is **SAN ALFONSO** (1100m altitude), a lovely place to head if you just want to unwind for a few hours in beautiful mountain scenery. For longer

△ Cajón del Maipo

133

stays, it offers a good choice of **accommodation**: *Hostería Los Ciervos*, by the roadside (℡8611581; ❺) has a gorgeous, flower-filled terrace and a little swimming pool, while *Residencial España*, next door (℡8611543; ❸) is simpler, but very clean, with an excellent restaurant. Down by the river, the highly recommended *Cascada de las Animas* (℡8611303, ⓦwww.cascadadelasanimas .cl; CH$40,000 for a four-person cabin), set in a park, has log cabins and camping areas as well as a fabulous outdoor pool, a restaurant overlooking the steep river gorge and a good **bar**, La Tribú. Open year-round, it also offers **horse-riding** trips into the Andes, **kayak lessons** and **whitewater rafting** down the Maipo. You can also arrange rafting through Altué Expeditions in Santiago (℡2321103). There's a good ninety-minute walk from here up to the 20-metre **waterfall** (called the *Cascada de las Animas*) on the other side of the river; ask at the complex's reception for permission to cross the bridge.

Towards Baños Morales

Moving on from San Alfonso, the scenery becomes increasingly rugged and wild as you climb higher into the Andes. By the time you reach **San Gabriel**, 50km from the start of the valley road at Las Vizcachas, the steep walls of the valley are dried-out reds and browns – you are at 1300m. This uninteresting village marks the end of the asphalt road, which continues as a very poor dirt track for another 20km to Lo Valdés. To carry on, you have to go through a *carabineros* (police) checkpoint, so make sure you've got all your driving documents and passport with you. Unless you're in a 4WD you should expect to go *very* slowly from this point onwards. **EL VOLCÁN**, at km 56, is as far as the telephone lines go up the valley – it has a public phone, but little else, as the village was practically wiped out by a landslide some years ago. By now the scenery is really dramatic as you snake between 4000-metre-high mountains coloured with jagged mineral-patterns of violet, cream and blue.

About 12km on, a short track branches left across a rudimentary bridge to **BAÑOS MORALES**, the site of an uninviting thermal pool that's reputed to be good for rheumatism and arthritis. Despite its spectacular location, this is quite a grim little village, with lukewarm pools and a half-finished, slightly derelict feel to it. It is, however, the closest base to the beautiful, jagged-peaked **Monumento Nacional El Morado** and offers a number of **residenciales**, although none of them is that great: the just commendable *Pensión Díaz* (℡8611496; ❷) is the only one that stays open all year; the equally basic *Los Chicos Malos* (℡2/2885380; ❸) and slightly more comfortable *Hostería Baños Morales* (℡2269826; ❹) are open only in January, February and at Easter. There's also an unofficial **camping** area along the road by the river. If your budget allows it, head instead for the secluded and very comfortable *Refugio Alemán* (℡ & ℻2173519; ❻), at Lo Valdés, about 1km beyond the fork to Baños Morales. From here the road deteriorates into an even poorer track, but continues for another 11km to **Baños de Colina**, a series of natural thermal pools carved into the mountainside; for all their remoteness they can get horribly crowded in summer weekends, but otherwise are blissfully empty. This is also the embarkation for multi-day **horse treks** into the Andes. Up to week-long excursions often leave in packed caravans that snake into the mountains. For less arduous trips, many locals rent horses by the hour or afternoon (CH$5000 an hour).

Monumento Nacional El Morado and the Cajón del Morado

A path from the bus stop in Baños Morales crosses a bridge and leads to the Conaf hut at the entrance to **MONUMENTO NACIONAL EL MORADO**

Wine tours near Santiago

Santiago is within easy reach of some of the oldest **wineries** in Chile, several of which offer tours and tastings. Those by the Río Maipo, in particular, are beautifully located, with large swaths of emerald-green vines framed by the snow-capped cordillera and bright-blue skies. Harvesting takes place in March, and if you visit during this month you'll see the grapes being sorted and pressed – a real extravaganza of colours and smells. If you want to visit a vineyard you should book the day before; check websites or call. We've listed five, relatively easily reached wineries below; most are accessible by public transport.

Vinoteca De Martino 229 Manuel Rodríguez, Isla de Maipo ⓣ8192062, ⓦwww .demartino.cl. Mon–Fri 10am–1.30pm & 3–6.30pm, Sat 10am–1.30pm. An hour south of Santiago in the suburb of Isla de Maipo, this very friendly Italian winery offers free informal tours and "specialized" tours for a fee. Reservations are required for the specialized tours. To get here, take a bus from the San Borja bus station to Isla de Maipo and tell the driver to drop you at the winery Santa Inés. Driving, take the Carretera del Sol, exit at Talagante, take a left towards Isla de Maipo and follow the signs.

Viña Concha y Toro Virginia Subercaseaux 210, Pirque ⓣ8217000, ⓦwww.conchaytoro .com. Tours in English Mon–Sat 10am, 11.30am, noon & 3pm. This handsome vineyard was founded in 1883 by Don Melchor Concha y Toro, and in 1994 became the first ever winery to trade on the New York Stock Exchange. The tours take you around the original bodega, with its countless oak barrels and huge stainless steel vats, and end up at the salesroom, where you taste ordinary wines and must "buy your glass" for US$6. Take the Bellavista metro line (green) south to Avenida Vicuña Mackenna, Paradero 14. Get off the train and go to the bus stop and catch a southbound blue bus Line #74. This goes to Pirque; ask the driver to let you off at the winery. A decent map is online.

Viña Cousiño Macul 7100 Av Quilin ⓣ3514175, ⓦwww.cousinomacul.cl. Chile's oldest winery dates from 1550, when wine was shipped to Peru. Today the family produces wine at a number of vineyards. Much of this winery was ripped up in 2003 to make way for a US$2 billion housing development, and new vineyards were planted near the town of Buin, but the main estate and park still make a nice quick trip from central Santiago. Tours in English and Spanish Monday to Friday at 11am; reservations required at least three days in advance; US$6. Driving directions: take Americo Vespuccio south to the Quilin roundabout, head towards the mountains on Avenida Quilin and look for the sign at 7100. Otherwise, take bus line #390 east, towards the mountains; you can catch this on the Alameda, in the centre of the city. Bus Line #391 headed east also goes by the vineyard.

Viña Santa Carolina 2228 Av Tiltil, Macul ⓣ23609883. Two-hour tour (US$10 per person) includes tastings; reservations required two days in advance. Just twenty minutes from the centre, this vineyard has a remarkable old wine-processing plant that has been declared a national monument. Take metro Line #5 (green) south to the Rodrigo de Araya stop and walk west, towards the mountains, about three to five minutes. If you are driving, take Avenida Vicuna Mackenna south, then turn right on Rodrigo de Araya, and the vineyard is about 200 yards along, on the left.

Viña Undurraga, old road to Melpilla, km 34 ⓣ8172346, ⓦwww.undurraga.cl. Mon–Fri 10am, 11am, 2pm & 3.30pm; Sat 10am, 11.30am & 1pm; Sundays 10.30am, 11.45am & 1pm; reservations recommended; CH$4000. Still run by the Undurraga family, the vineyard was established in 1885, complete with mansion and park. It's a large, modern winery, and you're likely to be shown around not by a smiling public relations guide, but by someone who's directly involved in the wine-making, which makes it a whole lot more engaging. There is one free tasting at the end. The winery's a thirty-minute bus ride from Santiago – take a bus to Talagante from Terminal San Borja (every 15min), and ask the driver to drop you off at the vineyard.

(Oct–April daily 8.30am–6pm; CH$1300); here you should get the latest hiking and climbing information as landslides, snowmelts and the glaciers change the terrain from year to year. For more good trekking and hiking information, check in at **Lo Valdés Mountain Centre**, in the little town of Lo Valdés by the side of the road (☎2463113, ☎9/3378647, @info@lovaldes.com). The park's single eight-kilometre trail follows the Río Morales through a narrow valley that ends at the glacier that feeds the river. Towering above the glacier, and visible from almost all points along the trail, is the magnificent silhouette of El Mirador del Morado (4320m) and, just behind, El Morado itself (5060m). Apart from the first half-hour, the path is fairly level and not hard going, though you may find yourself feeling breathless as you gradually climb in altitude. About 5km beyond the Conaf hut – after roughly two to three hours of hiking – you reach a small **lake**, Laguna de Morado, where there is free camping, a toilet and water pump. Once past the lake, the path is less defined, but it's easy enough to pick your way through the stones to the black, slimy-looking **glacier** 3km beyond, at an altitude of 2500m. Don't enter the tempting ice caves – they are not stable. If you are not camping, this is a good place for day-trekkers to turn around and head back.

An alternative way to arrive is on **horseback**; guided rides (CH$12,000) depart from Baños Morales or outside the Conaf hut. There are also guided riding treks up the neighbouring **CAJÓN DEL MORADO**, which runs parallel to the Río Morales, a few kilometres east, and leads to a huge glacier towering over a chocolate-coloured lake full of great chunks of ice. It takes three hours to get there on horseback (CH$12,000) and about eight hours to walk, though you may be able to hitch a lift with a 4WD, which can get within half an hour's walk of the lake. If you plan to walk, make sure you have a good map and a compass, and have a word with the Conaf ranger first, as the route isn't obvious. For information on other guided trips to the park, contact Turismo Arpue (☎2117165), Manzur Expeditions (☎64356519) or Terra Incógnita (☎2028761, @www.terraincognita.cl).

Pomaire

Back in the other direction, some 50km southwest of Santiago, the dusty, quaint village of **POMAIRE** was one of the *pueblos de indios* created by the Spanish in the eighteenth century in an attempt to control the native population. Its inhabitants quickly built up a reputation for their **pottery**, and to this day Pomaire devotes itself almost exclusively to this craft. The village consists of one long street packed with dozens of workshops selling a vast range of pots, bowls and Chilean kitchenware that the English vocabulary has no words for. It's nearly all made from the same brown clay that the area's so rich in, though a few potters have started to work in white clay. Most of the shops create the same designs, but this doesn't make a browse any less appealing. Another draw is the chance to see the potters at work (except on Mondays, their day off), as they shape the clay by hand at the wheel.

Pomaire has also built up a reputation for its good, traditional **restaurants** (some of them specializing in giant 1.5-kilo *empanadas*); *Los Naranjos*, on main drag Roberto Bravo, near the signposted Casa Colorada, and *San Antonio*, on the street of the same name, are especially recommended. To get here from Santiago, take any of the **Melpilla buses** (every 15min) from the Terminal San Borja, behind the Estación Central, and ask to be set off at the side road to Pomaire (one hour from Santiago along Ruta 78, one and a half hours via Talagante). From here, *colectivos* run into the village, or you can walk it in about half an hour.

Los Andes

There's nothing wildly exciting about **LOS ANDES**, but this old colonial town, with its narrow streets and lively main square, is an agreeable place to while away an afternoon and makes a convenient base for day-trips to the ski resort of Portillo (see p.138). Eighty kilometres north of Santiago, on the international road to Mendoza, Argentina, it's set in the beautiful Aconcagua valley; the first ridge rises to 3500m and then soars to 6959m Aconcagua, the highest peak outside the Himalayas, just across the border in Argentina. The surrounding region is very fertile, and as you approach Los Andes from Santiago you'll pass vineyards and numerous peach and lemon orchards. About 10km short of the town, the **Santuario de Santa Teresa de los Andes** is a huge, modern church built in 1987 to house the remains of **Santa Teresa**, who became Chile's first saint when she was canonized in 1993. Her shrine attracts thousands of pilgrims each year, especially on July 13, her feast day.

You can find out more about the saint in the **Monasterio del Espíritu Santo**, a simple brick building on Avenida Santa Teresa in Los Andes, where she lived until her death in 1920, at the age of nineteen. A small museum upstairs (Tues–Sun 10am–6.30pm; CH$600) exhibits an assortment of memorabilia, including photos and clothes. Almost opposite, the **Museo Arqueológico** (Tues–Sun 10am–6.30pm; CH$600) has an impressive collection of pre-Columbian pottery, petroglyphs and skulls, and an astonishing mummy from the Atacama Desert. Almost everything's labelled in Spanish and English, and the enthusiastic curator (who speaks good English) will give you a free guided tour if you ask. Six blocks east, on the corner of Freire and Rancagua, **Cerámica Cala** is worth a stop. This family-run business sells pretty, hand-painted ceramics to retailers throughout Chile. Ask to see the artisans at work in their factory, and visit the small salesroom.

Other than this, the best thing to do in Los Andes is hang out in one of the cafés lining the square and watch the world go by or, if you're feeling energetic, climb **Cerro de la Virgen**, the hill rising behind the town. It takes about an hour to reach the top following the path from the picnic site on Independencia. The views are wonderful, especially just before sunset, when the whole valley is bathed in a clear, golden light.

Practicalities

Frequent **buses** for Los Andes run out of Terminal Los Héroes in Santiago, dropping you at the bus station on Membrillar, one block east of the main square; most of them stop at the Santuario de Santa Teresa en route. There's a helpful **Oficina de Turismo** (Mon–Fri 9am–2pm & 3–5pm) next door to the Municipalidad at Esmeralda 526; if it's closed, try the **Sernatur** kiosk (daily 10am–6pm) round the corner on Avenida Santa Teresa, next to the Esso station. If you want to **stay**, options include *Residencia Italiana* at Rodríguez 76 (℡34/423544; ❹), an attractive old house with pleasant rooms (but shared bath), and *Hotel Plaza,* at Esmeralda 367 (℡34/421169, ℱ426029; ❺) with well-equipped, but dowdy, rooms off the square, and its own pool. For **eating**, the French-owned *Comédie Française,* at Papudo 375, serves good-value French food, with live music at weekends; the restaurant in *Hotel Plaza* is more traditional, and very popular. For snacks, or **drinking**, there are a cluster of bars and cafés on the square and down Esmeralda.

Parque Nacional La Campana

Set in the dry, dusty mountains of the coastal range, **PARQUE NACIONAL LA CAMPANA** (June–Aug daily 8am–7pm; Sept–May daily 8am–6pm; CH$1500) is a wonderful place to go hiking and offers some of the best views in Chile. From the 1880-metre-high summit of Cerro La Campana you can see the Andes on one side and the Pacific Ocean on the other – in the words of Charles Darwin, who climbed the mountain in 1834, Chile is seen "as in a map". Another draw is the chance to see a profusion of **Chilean palms** in their natural habitat; this native tree was all but wiped out in the nineteenth century, and the Palmar de Ocoa, a grove in the northern section of the park, is one of just two remaining places in the country where you can find wild palms.

Skiing near Santiago

Santiago is only ninety minutes from some of the best **skiing** in South America. You don't need equipment to take advantage of this – rental skis, clothes and transport to the slopes are easily arranged – and the runs are close enough to the capital to make day-trips perfectly feasible. Sunshine is abundant and queues for lifts are practically nonexistent during weekdays. The season normally lasts from mid-June to early-October, with snow virtually guaranteed from mid-July to the first week in September. The most expensive and crowded periods of the year are the Chilean winter vacation, during the last weeks of July, and the national holidays the week of September 18. There are various options for day-trips from Santiago: either the two-hour highway drive to Portillo near the Argentine border, or the ninety-minute serpentine road to the service village of **Farellones**, where three resorts are increasingly linked together.

Farellones itself, sitting high in the Andes at the foot of Cero Colorado, is a straggling collection of hotels and apartments. It's connected by paved roads to the ski resorts of El Colorado (4km north), La Parva (2km further on), and chic resort Valle Nevado (a winding 14km east). **El Colorado** – also reached from Farellones by ski lift – has fifteen lifts and twenty-two runs, covering a wide range of levels. Elevations range from 2430m to 3333m. The resort's base is known as Villa El Colorado, and includes several apart-hotels, restaurants and pubs. Neighbouring **La Parva** has moderate terrain, huge swaths of backcountry skiing and an aged but classy feel. The skiing here is excellent, with some very long intermediate cruising runs and a vertical drop of nearly 1000m. The resort has thirty pistes and fourteen lifts, but limited accommodation facilities, as most people who come here have their own chalet or rent one. **Valle Nevado**, connected to both El Colorado and La Parva by ski runs, is a luxury resort with three first-class hotels and some very good restaurants. It has twenty-seven runs, eight lifts and is the clear favourite for snowboarders.

Set just off the international road from Los Andes, 7km short of the border with Argentina, **Portillo** is a classy place, with no condominiums and just one hotel – the restored 1940's *Hotel Portillo* (☎2630606, ⓦwww.skiportillo.com; ❻–❽), perched by the shores of the Laguna del Inca. This all-inclusive resort offers the most relaxing, hip ski scene in South America. Sun, snow and sex seem to be the themes at this southern winter home to the US, Austrian and Spanish national ski teams. Being farther from Santiago (149km), the hotel is designed for weekend or week-long bookings, with an extensive range of package deals. While most rooms are expensive, there are a wide variety of options, including bunks. The rate includes four meals a day and use of the outdoor heated pool and disco. Expect an eclectic crowd of Brazilians, Argentines and famous actors and business leaders. The ski runs at Portillo are world-class, and off-piste options are endless. Elevation ranges from 2510m to 3350m. There are twelve lifts, as well as extensive snow-making

You can also expect to see eagles and giant hummingbirds and, if you're lucky, mountain cats and foxes.

The park is located 110km northwest of Santiago, and about 60km east of Valparaíso. It's divided into three "sectors" – Ocoa, Granizo and Cajón Grande – each with its own entrance and Conaf control. **Sector Ocoa**, on the northern side of the Park, is where you'll find the palm trees – literally thousands of them. **Sector Granizo** and **Sector Cajón Grande** are both in the south of the park, close to the village of **Olmué**; this is the part to head for if you want to follow Darwin's footsteps and climb **Cerro La Campana**. While it's possible to get to Parque Nacional La Campana on a day-trip from Valparaíso, Viña or even, at a push, from Santiago, you should count on spending a couple of nights here to get the most out of a visit.

equipment. Portillo is avidly kid friendly and its ski school is routinely ranked one of the world's best.

All of the resorts described above have ski schools with English-speaking instructors, and equipment rental outlets.

Practicalities

The least expensive way to go skiing is to stay in Santiago and go up for the day. A number of **minibus** companies offer daily services to the resorts during the ski season, including Ski Total (☎2460156, ⓦwww.skitotal.cl), which also rents out equipment, goggles and clothes. It's based at Office 46 in the lower-ground level of the Omnium shopping mall at Av Apoquindo 4900, four blocks east of Estación Militar metro (any *micro* to Las Condes or Apoquindo will drop you there). Buses leave at 8.15am daily for El Colorado, La Parva and Valle Nevado, returning to Santiago at 7.30pm; advance reservations are essential. A return ticket costs around CH$6000, hotel pickup CH$12,000, full equipment rental an additional CH$13,000.

If you intend to drive up yourself, note that traffic is only allowed up the road to Farellones until noon, and back down to Santiago from 2pm onwards; tyre chains are often required but seldom used; they can be rented on the way up. Each resort has its own **lift ticket**, the price of which ranges from CH$10,000 on weekdays to CH$20,000 at weekends.

If you want to stay, you've got several **accommodation** options. At Farellones you could try cosy *Hotel Tupungato* (☎3211033; ❼) or the *Refugio Club Andino* (☎2425453, ❺). The choices in El Colorado include upmarket *Hotel Posada Farellones* (☎2013704; ❼) and *Edificio Villa Palomar* (☎3621111; ❻). The only commercial place to stay in La Parva is at the *Condominio Nueva La Parva* (☎2641574; ❼). For **rentals by the week** it is much more economical to negotiate with private owners – one broker is Cecilia Wilson Propiedades, Apoquindo 5555, Office 905 (☎2073700) who has a full roster of pricey ski chalets available year-round. Valle Nevado's hotels are all very upscale, and include the grand *Hotel Valle Nevado* (☎2060027, ⓦwww.vallenevado.com; ❼); heliskiing is on offer. Ski Total (see above) can give advice on accommodation, and make bookings for you. Your only lodging option in Portillo is the *Hotel Portillo* (see opposite).

All of the ski resorts have their **administrative offices in Santiago**: El Colorado is at the Omnium, Office 47, Av Apoquindo 4900, Las Condes (☎2463344, ⓦwww.elcolorado.cl); La Parva is at La Concepción 266, Office 301, Providencia (☎2641466. ⓦwww.skilaparva.cl); Valle Nevado is at Gertrudis Echeñique 441, Las Condes (☎6980103, ⓦwww.vallenevado.com); and Portillo is at Renato Sanchez 4270, Vitacura (☎2630595, ⓦ www.skiportillo.com).

There are **camping** areas in all three sectors, and plenty of **accommodation** in Olmué (see opposite).

Getting to the park

To get to **Sector Granizo** and **Sector Cajón Grande** you should aim for the gateway village of **Olmué**, reached via a long, roundabout route from Santiago, but far more directly from Valparaíso. There are direct **buses** from both directions: from Santiago, Buses Golondrina run every thirty minutes out of terminal San Borja; from Valparaíso's Playa Ancha, Ciferal Express run six times a day almost to the park entrance. If you're coming from Santiago **by car**, the quickest route is via Casablanca, Villa Alemana and Limache. Don't be tempted

Hiking in Parque Nacional La Campana

There are about a dozen very scenic **walks** in the park, most of them along good, well-maintained trails and many of them interconnected. The *Guía Ecoturismo* maps given away at the Conaf hut are excellent. If you plan to do some serious walking, try to get hold of a **map** from Sernatur before you come. This park is a model for all of Chile's national parks so there is plenty of English-language guide material, and a **website** (🌐 www.parquelacampana.cl). If you're on a day-hike you must get back to the Conaf control before it closes (7pm in winter, 6pm in summer); if you plan to camp in the park, inform the *guardaparque* when you sign in. Finally, there aren't many water sources along the trails so bring plenty of **water** with you. Also bring **sunblock**, the summer sun combined with the high altitude make it easy to get burned.

Sector Granizo

The well-marked 9km **Sendero el Andinista** up Cerro La Campana is the most popular, and possibly the most rewarding, trek in the park. It's quite hard going, especially the last ninety minutes, when it gets very steep, but the views from the top are breathtaking – and this is where Darwin climbed. Allow at least four and a half hours to get up and three to get down. **Sendero Los Peumos** is a pretty, four-kilometre walk (about three hours) up to the Portezuelo Ocoa, through gentle woodland for the first half, followed by a fairly steep climb. Three paths converge at the Portezuelo; you can either go back the way you came; take the right-hand path (Sendero Portezuelo Ocoa; see below) down through the Cajón Grande to that sector's Conaf control (about three hours); or follow the left-hand path (Sendero El Amasijo) through Sector Ocoa to the northernmost park entrance (another four hours; best if you're camping as there's no accommodation at the other end).

Sector Cajón Grande

The **Sendero Portezuelo Ocoa**, also known as **Sendero Los Robles**, is a seven-kilometre trail (about three hours) through beautiful woods with natural *miradores* giving views down to the Cuesta La Dormida. From the Portezuelo Ocoa, at the end of the path, you can link up with other paths as described above.

Sector Ocoa

Sendero La Cascada makes a lovely day-hike through lush palm groves to a 35-metre high waterfall, most impressive in early spring. The eight-kilometre path is mainly flat; allow about seven hours there and back. It has eight well-marked *estaciones* that describe local flora. **Sendero El Amasijo** is a seven-kilometre trail (3hrs) following the Estero Rabuco (a stream) through a scenic canyon before climbing steeply to the Portezuelo Ocoa. Most walkers make this a cross-park trek, continuing to Granizo or Cajón Grande (see above). Fast, fit walkers should be able to do it in a day, but it's more relaxing if you camp overnight.

to take the short route from Tiltil to Olmué across the Cuesta La Dormida – this is very scenic but unsuitable unless you're in a 4WD. From Olmué it's a further 9km to the park; regular buses (every 15min) run from the main square to **Granizo**; the last bus stop is a fifteen minute walk from the Conaf hut in Sector Granizo, and a forty-minute walk from Sector Cajón Grande.

Sector Ocoa is approached on a gravel road branching south from the Panamericana about halfway between Llaillay and Hijuelas; coming from Llaillay, it's the left turn just before the bridge across the Río Aconcagua. Any northbound bus along the Panamericana will drop you at the turn-off, but from here it's a twelve-kilometre hike to the park entrance, with minimal hitching opportunities.

Accommodation in Olmué

An agreeable village in a fertile valley, **Olmué** has a good choice of **places to stay**, many of them with pools. Cheapest is *Residencial Sarmiento,* Blanco Encalada 4647 (T 33/441263; ❸), with clean, simple rooms, most with bath, in a traditional adobe building. *Hostería El Copihué,* Portales 2203 (T & F 33/441544; ❺) has a nice pool, beautiful gardens full of vines and flowers and a good restaurant. About halfway along the road to the park, *Hostería Aire Puro,* Av Granizo 7672 (T 33/441381; ❻) has well-equipped *cabañas*, great views from its **restaurant**, and the obligatory pool.

Travel details

Buses (Domestic)

Santiago to: Ancud (4 daily; 18hr 30min); Antofagasta (hourly; 19hr); Arica (hourly; 30hr); Calama (hourly; 22hr); Caldera (10 daily; 12hr 30min); Castro (4 daily; 11hr 50min); Chañaral (every 2hr; 13hr 30min); Chillán (every 30min; 6hr); Concepción (every 30min; 8hr); Concón (every 30min; 2hr); Copiapó (hourly; 11hr 15min); Coquimbo (hourly; 6hr 10min); Curicó (every 30min; 2hr 45min); Iquique (hourly; 24hr); Isla Negra (every 30min; 1hr 50min); La Ligua (every 2hr; 2hr 30min); La Serena (every 6hr 30min); Los Andes (every 15min; 1hr 20min); Los Angeles (every 30min; 8hr); Los Lagos (3 daily; 12hr 30min); Los Vilos (hourly; 3hr 15min); Maitencillo (4 daily; 2hr 45min); Osorno (hourly; 13hr); Ovalle (hourly; 5hr 30min); Papudo (4 daily; 3hr); Pucón (8 daily; 12hr); Puerto Montt (hourly; 14hr); Puerto Varas (every 2hr; 13hr 30min); Rancagua (every 15min; 1hr 30min); San Fernando (every 15min; 2hr); Talca (every 20-30min; 3hr 30min); Talcahuano (hourly; 8hr); Taltal (1 daily; 18hr 30min); Temuco (hourly; 10hr); Valdivia (every 2hr; 12hr); Vallenar (hourly; 9hr 30min); Valparaíso (every 15min; 1hr 45min); Vicuña (3 daily; 8hr); Villarrica (8 daily; 11hr 30min); Viña del Mar (every 15min; 2hr); Zapallar (3 daily; 3hr 30min).

Buses (International)

Santiago to: Asunción (3 weekly; 30hr); Bariloche (1 daily; 16hr); Buenos Aires (1-2 daily; 20hr); Córdoba (1-2 daily; 16hr); Lima (2 weekly; 50hr); Mendoza (10 daily; 6hr); Montevideo (1 weekly; 28hr); Rio de Janeiro (4 weekly; 56hr); São Paulo (4 weekly; 50hr).

Flights

Santiago to: Antofagasta (15 daily; 3hr); Arica (8 daily; 3hr 30min); Balmaceda [Coyhaique] (7 daily; 3hr 45min); Calama (3 daily; 3hr 45min); Concepción (12 daily; 45min); Copiapó (8 daily; 3hr 20min); Iquique (10 daily; 3hr); La Serena (8 daily; 45min); Osorno (1 daily; 2hr 30min); Puerto Montt (4 daily; 2hr); Punta Arenas (7 daily; 4hr 30min); Temuco (3 daily; 1hr 45min).

Trains

Santiago to: Chillán (3 daily; 4-6hr); Concepción (1 daily; 9hr); Curicó (5 daily; 2hr 30min); Linares (5 daily; 4hr); Parral (5 daily; 4hr 30min); Rancagua (5 daily; 1hr); San Fernando (5 daily; 2hr); Talca (5 daily; 3hr); Temuco (1 daily; 13hr); Victoria (1 daily; 11hr).

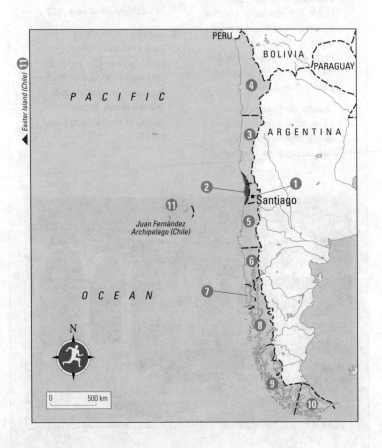

2

Valparaíso, Viña and the Central Coast

PERU

BOLIVIA

PARAGUAY

PACIFIC

④

③

ARGENTINA

②

①

•Santiago

⑪

Juan Fernández
Archipelago (Chile)

⑤

⑥

⑦

OCEAN

N

⑧

⑨

⑩

0   500 km

CHAPTER 2   # Highlights

* **Valparaíso** Chile's most remarkable city sits precariously on a dozen hills above a huge bay, with a quirky set of antique elevators that haul you up to panoramic lookouts. See p.147

* **Isla Negra** Chilean poet Pablo Neruda came here for inspiration and he penned many of his Nobel Prize-winning poems while gazing out at his favourite beach. See p.161

* **Quinta Vergara** A taste of exotic nature amidst all the beaches, this Viña park features all manner of subtropical trees and rare plants, plus a museum of fine art. See p.167

* **Reñaca** Enjoy daytime sunning or night-time clubbing at this leading seaside resort, packed full in summer with the younger set of vacationers. See p.172

* **Zapallar** With some of the best seafood in the region, soothingly empty beaches and opulently stylish houses, this eternally fashionable coastal resort is one of the pearls of the Riviera. See p.174

△ Quinta Vergara

Valparaíso, Viña and the Central Coast

O f Chile's 4000-kilometre-plus **coastline**, the brief central strip between Santo Domingo and Los Vilos is the most visited and most developed. Known as the *Litoral Central* by Chileans and rather optimistically promoted as the "Chilean Riviera" in many tourist brochures, this 250-kilometre stretch boasts bay after bay lined with gorgeous, white-sand beaches, and a string of coastal resort towns of varying size and character.

Valparaíso ("Valpo" for short) and **Viña del Mar** (or "Viña") sit next to each other near the middle of the strip. They are geographical neighbours but totally unlike in look and feel. Viña is Chile's largest beach resort and one of the ritziest. With its high-rise condominiums, casino, and seafront pizzerias, along with the northern beaches in nearby Reñaca where bronzed sunbathers laze until sunset and then go clubbing all night, Viña typifies modern hedonism. Valparaíso, on the other hand, has a much more natural, old-fashioned style, with ramshackle, brightly painted houses spilling chaotically down the hills to the sea, but no decent beaches. For beaches, you'll need to head south or, preferably, north to find anything from disco-packed pleasure grounds to tiny, secluded coves – if you know where to go (and where to avoid).

Closest to Santiago, via the toll highway ("Autopista del Sol" or, officially, Ruta 78), are the resorts **south of Valparaíso**, which are busier and more developed – especially Algarrobo and Cartagena, once quiet havens for holiday-makers, now horrific clusters of high-rise towers. Further south towards **Rocas de Santo Domingo**, there's an almost uninterrupted string of *cabañas*, villas and small, rather unpleasant resorts. Even so, along this section the development tends to be more low-key and low-scale, and it's still possible to find places with charm and a soul, especially where Pablo Neruda found them, such as **Isla Negra** – though it, too, is fast being swallowed up by rampant development. **San Antonio**, Chile's second port and the only place on the Litoral south of Valparaíso that doesn't rely on tourism for its livelihood, is nonetheless another nasty blot on the horizon, with its polluting industry and ugly buildings, that's best avoided.

Heading **north of Viña** is quite a different story; you leave most of the concrete behind at **Concón**, and from **Horcón** up, the coast begins to look more rugged and feels distinctly wild and windswept by the time you reach **Maitencillo**, where brown, sandstone cliffs tower above a huge, white beach. The stretch from here to **Papudo** is easily the most beautiful of the Litoral, as the road clings to the cliff edge, giving views down to empty coves and thundering surf. Not even the new villas and second-home complexes that have sprung up along here in the last few years have managed to spoil **Zapallar**, the most architecturally graceful of all the resorts, or Papudo, a small fishing town dramatically hemmed in by steep, green hills. Two more popular resorts lie further to the north, off the Panamericana as it thrusts into the deserts of the Norte Chico: **Los Vilos**, where a fish market and a seal colony provide alternative entertainment to sunbathing, and **Pichidangui**, whose handsome strand is backed by shady eucalyptus trees.

Note that most Chileans take their annual holiday in February, during which time all the resort towns, large and small, are unbearably crowded. They also get busy on weekends in December and January, but outside these times are remarkably quiet. November and March are probably the **best months** to be here, as the weather is usually agreeable and the beaches virtually deserted, especially midweek; in winter the resorts wear a forlorn, abandoned look but you can go for bracing walks along the empty, blustery beaches. This coast is prone to **fog** or cloudy weather even in the summer; temperatures in Valpo can be considerably lower than in Santiago when it is sunny in the capital but a cool, moist breeze is blowing in from the Pacific. From April to October **accommodation rates** are considerably lower, sometimes half of what is listed in our price guide, and even in November, December and March you should be able to negotiate a discount midweek. Some, but not all, beaches are safe for **swimming**, though you should definitely stay out of the water if a red flag is displayed; you might also be put off by the frigid **Humboldt current** that sweeps up the Pacific from the Antarctic coast, leaving the water chilly even in the height of summer.

Don't miss out on the exquisite **seafood** available all along the coast; look out for the *picoroco* inside its rock shell, which resembles something out of a sci-fi movie. Head for the little restaurants by the *caleta* where the local fishermen bring in their catch or, if you're renting a *cabaña* with its own kitchen, be adventurous and buy your supper from the market to cook for yourself. Finally a word on **transport**: there are numerous daily buses from Santiago to Valparaíso and Viña, and several direct services from the capital to most of the other resort towns (see p.178). From Valpo or Viña you can catch buses to all the resort towns in the Litoral. The stretch between Algarrobo and San Antonio is also served by frequent local buses which are much quicker if you go direct on Ruta 78 rather than via Viña and then heading south. From Horcón to Papudo there are fewer daily local connections – except during summer when buses run fairly frequently. On nearly all routes you can ask your driver to stop anywhere along the coast or highway so you can hop off at some isolated cove.

Valparaíso

Valparaíso es un montón, un racimo
de casas locas

Pablo Neruda

Spread over an amphitheatre of hills encircling a wide bay, **VALPARAÍSO** is perhaps the most memorable city in Chile. Its most striking feature is the array of houses – a mad, colourful tangle of them tumbling down the hills to a narrow shelf of land below. Few roads make it up these gradients and most people get up and down on the city's fifteen "lifts" or *ascensores*, a collection of ancient-looking funiculars that slowly haul you up to incredible viewpoints. The lower town, known as *El Plan*, named after Pedro Montt's reconstruction plan after the 1906 earthquake, is a series of narrow, traffic-choked streets packed with shops, banks, offices and abandoned warehouses, crowded round the quays and port that once made Valparaíso's fortune.

Some history

The bay was chosen as the site of the new colony's port as early as 1542, when Pedro de Valdivia decided it would "serve the trade of these lands and of Santiago". Growth was slow, however, owing to trading restrictions imposed by the Spanish Crown, but when Latin American trade was liberalized in the 1820s, following independence, Valparaíso started to come into its own. Located as it was on the shipping route from Europe to America's Pacific Coast, it became the main port of call and resupply centre for ships after they crossed the Straits of Magellan. As Chile's own foreign trade expanded with the silver and copper booms of the 1830s, the port became ever more active, but it was the government's innovative creation of public warehouses where merchants could store goods at low prices that really launched Valparaíso into its economic ascent.

Foreign businessmen, particularly British ones, flocked to the city where they ran trading empires built on copper, silver and nitrate. The wealth and influence of these men extended well beyond mining exports: they financed railways, trams and canals as well as electricity, telephone and gas networks, and by the late nineteenth century had turned Valparaíso into the foremost financial and commercial centre of Chile. The city outstripped Santiago in most urban developments, producing its own daily newspaper, banks and stock exchange long before the capital. Even as it prospered, though, Valparaíso continued to be dogged by the kind of violent setbacks that had always punctuated its history, from looting pirates and buccaneers to earthquakes and fires. On March 31, 1866, following Chile's entanglement in a dispute between Spain and Peru, the Spanish admiralty bombarded Valparaíso from its harbour for three hours, wreaking devastation on the city. It took a long time to rebuild it, but worse was still to come. On August 16, 1906, a colossal **earthquake** practically razed the city to the ground, killing over 2000 people, the majority by gas explosions. The disaster took a heavy toll on Valparaíso's fortunes, which never really recovered. Eight years later, the opening of the Panama Canal signalled the city's inexorable decline.

Today, Valparaíso's heyday is long gone, and the city wears a rundown, moth-eaten air. Crime and poverty are worse than elsewhere in Chile and at night the town can be dangerous. Note, too, that it has the highest rate of AIDS in the country as a result of the still rampant sex trade. That said, it's still a vital **working port** – one of the biggest in Chile – moving thousands of containers

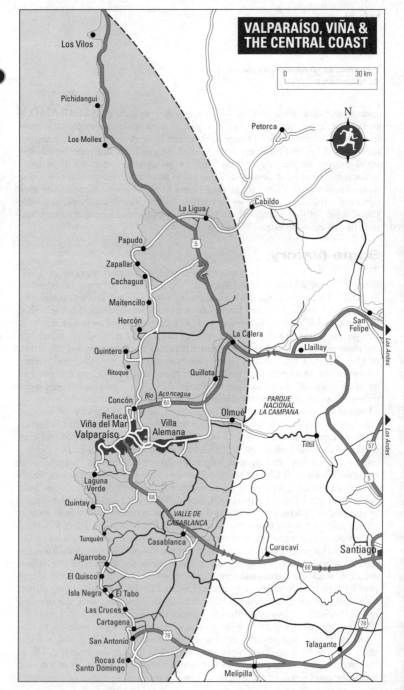

VALPARAÍSO, VIÑA &
THE CENTRAL COAST

0   30 km

N

Los Vilos

Pichidangui

Los Molles

Petorca

Cabildo

La Ligua

Papudo

Zapallar

Cachagua

Maitencillo

Horcón

La Calera

San
Felipe

Quintero

Quillota

Llaillay

Ritoque

Río Aconcagua

Concón

PARQUE
NACIONAL
LA CAMPANA

Reñaca

Olmué

Viña del Mar

Villa
Alemana

Valparaíso

Tiltil

Laguna
Verde

Quintay

VALLE DE
CASABLANCA

Tunquén

Casablanca

Curacaví

Santiago

Algarrobo

El Quisco

Isla Negra   El Tabo

Las Cruces

Cartagena

San Antonio

Talagante

Rocas de
Santo Domingo

Melipilla

Los Andes

Los Andes

annually, and has been the seat of Congress since the return to democracy in 1990. The port underwent a mini-economic boom in the early years of the new millennium, though the city's inhabitants, known as Porteños, do not seem to have benefited enormously. As the capital of Region V, it also has its share of galleries and museums, but the city's chief attractions lie in its crumbling, romantic atmosphere and stunning setting.

Arrival, information and getting around

Buses from Santiago (leaving every 10min from the Terminal Alameda) and other major cities pull in at the Terminal Rodoviario on the eastern end of Avenida Pedro Montt, opposite the Congreso Nacional building; there are **left luggage** lockers (buy a token from the adjacent news kiosk), though your bus company will probably store bags in its office. From here, it's about a twenty-minute walk west to the old town centre; plenty of **micros** and **colectivos** also go into the centre from right outside the station. A local **train** service travels to Valparaíso from Viña del Mar, dropping you next door to the port.

Information

The well-run municipal **oficina de turismo** hands out lists of accommodation and will sometimes ring to see if there are vacancies. There's a helpful branch with English-speaking attendants at the **bus station** (Dec 15–March 15, daily 10am–2pm & 3–7pm; March 16–Dec 14 Tues–Sun 10am–6pm; no phone). In the centre, the main branch is at the **town hall**, Condell 1490 (Mon–Fri 9am–2pm & 3.30–6pm; ☎32/939108), with additional kiosks at **Muelle Prat** by the port (daily: Dec 15–March 15 10am–7pm; March 16–Dec 14 10am–2pm & 3-6pm). Two good **websites** provide useful information about Valparaíso: ⓦwww.valparaisochile.cl is a bilingual site with good maps and photos, and ⓦwww.granvalparaiso.cl is a Spanish-language site with plenty of Valpo and Chilean history and current events.

Tours

Sernatur, the Chilean government's tourism bureau, has recently organized and modernized Valparaíso **tour companies**. Below you will find a select group of operators, most with offices in town, which offer tours that run the gamut from the five-hour "bohemia tour" (where you can drink and party and still find your way home) to day-trips to the beaches all the way up to Zapallar. Per-person prices range from CH$15,000 for a half day to CH$25,000 for a full day.

Andekat Chile Prat 725, Office 105
☎32/593834. City tours ranging from a three-hour excursion, which includes a visit to Pablo Neruda's home and several great hilltop views, to full-day wine tours in neighbouring valleys. Also good for trips to nearby coastal resorts.
Enlace Turistico ☎ & ⒻFcode 32/232313 or
☎9/8145855, Ⓔenlaceturistico@hotmail.com. Customized tours with options for families and elderly tourists, including historic, artistic and archaeological explorations of Valpo.

Marin Tour Pasaje Ross no. 149, Office 511
☎32/214534 or 9/4337575. Helpful tour agency that can arrange city tours focusing on Pablo Neruda or evening pub tours as well as airport shuttles and car rental.
Ruta Valparaíso ☎ & Ⓕ32/911972 or
☎9/8443958 (mobile), ⒺerutaValparaíso @terra.cl, ⓦwww.rutaValparaíso.cl. Guided bilingual city tours for groups or individuals. Trips on offer include a full-day tour to Isla Negra or a five-hour evening bar-hopping tour.

Orientation and getting around

Countless **micros** run east and west through the city: those displaying "Aduana" on the window will take you west through the centre, past the port, while those marked "P. Montt" will take you back to the bus station. To climb the hills to the neighbourhoods of the upper town, it's easiest to use the **ascensores**; some bus routes also take you to the upper town, and you can catch **colectivos** at Plazuela Ecuador, at the bottom of Calle Ecuador. **Taxis** are numerous (but more expensive than in Santiago) and can be flagged down on the street.

Accommodation

There's no shortage of **accommodation** in Valparaíso, the bulk of it simple and inexpensive. If you're on a short visit it's probably easiest to stay near the bus terminal and get buses in and out of the centre. If not, it's worth seeking out a room with a view up on the hills; several **bed and breakfasts** will pick you up at the bus station if you call ahead. It's a good idea to check out vacancies by phone or on the web, as accommodation isn't concentrated in a single area, but spread all over the city.

Alojamiento Mónica Venegas Av Argentina 322B ☏ 32/215673. Basic, immaculate rooms with the smell of fresh bread wafting in from the bakery next door. Those on the top floor are very quiet. Handy for the bus station. ❸

Alojamiento "Villa Kunterbunt" Quebrada Verde 192, Playa Ancha ☏ 32/288873, ✉ villakunterbuntvalpo@yahoo .de. Outside of the centre, but the reward is the friendliest welcome in town and a truly beautiful house – its attic room has windows on all sides and splendid views of the entire city. Take bus #1, #2, #5, #6 or #17 from the bus terminal and ask to be dropped at "Colegio María Auxiliadora", opposite the house. ❷

Brighton Bed & Breakfast Pasaje Atkinson 151, Cerro Concepción ☏ & ☏ 32/223513, ✉ brighton-valpo@entelchile.net. Stylish decor and fantastic views, but sagging beds, at this small British-run hotel in one of the prettiest parts of town, with an outdoor terrace looking onto the bay. Take Ascensor Concepción and head for the bright yellow building. ❺

Casa de Familia Costa Azul Aguirre Cerda 1079, Cerro Playa Ancha ☏ 9/8898641 or 32/494601, ⊛ www.casadefamiliacostaazul .com. This small bed and breakfast has an English-speaking staff, a pool and spectacular views of the bay from the bedrooms and dining room. Pick-ups can be arranged from anywhere in Valpo. ❹

Casa Juan Carrasco Abtao 668, Cerro Concepción ☏ 32/210737. Big old house next to the Lutheran church in a lovely, hilltop location just a short walk from Ascensor Concepción. Spotless rooms (a couple with great views, others with no outside windows) and the use of a kitchen. ❸

Casa Latina Papudo 462, Cerro Concepción ☏ 32/494622, ✉ clatina@vtr.net. This tiny bed and breakfast within walking distance of many attractions features nineteenth-century architecture smartly mixed with modern furnishings. Shared bathroom. ❹

The Grand House Federico Varela 27, Cerro La Cruz ☏ 32/212376, ⊛ www .thegrandhouse.cl. From this hilltop mansion, the entire bay stretches out below. English is spoken, and the friendly and hospitable home has shared baths, Internet connection and a library – but it's the view that will dazzle you. ❺

Hostal Kolping Francisco Valdés Vergara 622, in front of the Parque Italia ☏ & ☏ 32/216306. Very central but relatively quiet, with clean and pleasant rooms; some less expensive options for groups of four. ❹

Hotel Puerto Valparaíso Chacabuco 2362 ☏ & ☏ 32/217391, ⊛ www.comac.cl. This hotel dates from 1902 and has bathtubs, bronze beds and historic black-and-white photographs on the walls. The front rooms are bright and spacious, with small balconies, while the rear ones have no outside windows. ❹

Hotel Ultramar Tomás Pérez 173, Cerro Cárcel ☏ 32/210000, ⊛ www.hotelultramar .cl. Stylishly refurbished 1907 Italianate townhouse on three storeys, way up on one of the *cerros*. The fun decor features lots of black-and-white chequered tile floors. Rooms with a view are worth the extra cost. Check the website for promotions. ❼–❽

The City

Draped languidly but decorously over three dozen hills and arranged around a natural amphitheatre that plunges into the bay, Valparaíso isn't really about museums and sights but about exploring the labyrinthine streets and taking in magnificent panoramas. The eastern end of town near the bus terminal is of limited interest; best head west to the **old town** which stretches along a narrow strip of land between Plaza Victoria and Plaza Aduana, at the city's historic core. The port district, with its British-style banks and insurance offices, dingy bars blaring out tango and old-fashioned shops, is the most idiosyncratic part of the

△ Valparaíso ascensor

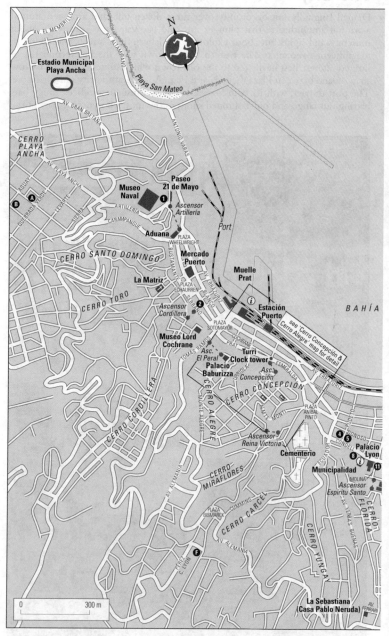

Estadio Municipal
Playa Ancha

AV. EL MEMBRILLO

AV. ALTAMIRANO

Playa San Mateo

AV. ANTONIO VARAS

CERRO
PLAYA
ANCHA

AV. GRAN BRETAÑA

AGUAY

QUEBRADA VERDE

AV. PLAYA ANCHA

SUBIDA

LEVARTE

B **A**

Museo
Naval **1**

Paseo
21 de Mayo

*Ascensor
Artillería*

ARTILLERÍA

CARAMPANGUE

BUSTAMANTE

Aduana

PLAZA
WHEELWRIGHT

Port

Mercado
Puerto

La Matriz

PLAZA
ECHAURREN

CERRO SANTO DOMINGO

CERRO TORO

*Ascensor
Cordillera* **2**

Muelle
Prat

Estación
Puerto

i

BAHÍA

AV. ERRÁZURIZ

CERRO CORDILLERA

Museo Lord
Cochrane

PLAZA
SOTOMAYOR

COCHRANE

PRAT

*Asc.
El Peral*

TOMAS RAMOS

Turri
Clock tower

Palacio
Baburizza

*Asc.
Concepción*

ESMERALDA

URIOLA

see Cerro Concepción &
Cerro Alegre map for detail

CERRO CONCEPCIÓN

CERRO ALEGRE

MONTE ALEGRE

ALMTE

MONTT

PLAZA
ANIBAL
PINTO

*Ascensor
Reina Victoria*

Cementerio

CERRO
MIRAFLORES

AV. ALEMANIA

CONDELL

EDWARDS

PLAZA
BISMARCK

CUMMING

AV. ALEMANIA

CERRO CARCEL

4 **5**

Palacio
Lyon

8 *i*

Municipalidad

MOLINA

*Ascensor
Espíritu Santo*

AV. FRANCIA

CERRO
YUNGAY

AV. TENÁS BUENAS

CERRO
FLORIDA

11

F

PEREZ

C. LYON

La Sebastiana
(Casa Pablo Neruda)

AV.
FERRARI

0   300 m

152

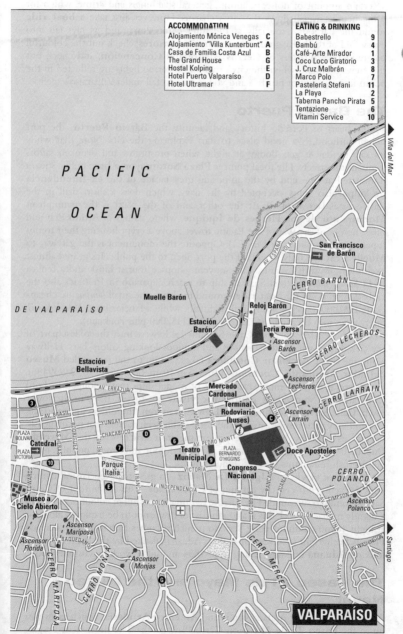

ACCOMMODATION

Alojamiento Mónica Venegas	C
Alojamiento "Villa Kunterbunt"	A
Casa de Familia Costa Azul	B
The Grand House	G
Hostal Kolping	E
Hotel Puerto Valparaíso	D
Hotel Ultramar	F

EATING & DRINKING

Babestrello	9
Bambú	4
Café-Arte Mirador	1
Coco Loco Giratorio	3
J. Cruz Malbrán	8
Marco Polo	7
Pastelería Stefani	11
La Playa	2
Taberna Pancho Pirata	5
Tentazione	6
Vitamin Service	10

PACIFIC

OCEAN

DE VALPARAÍSO

Viña del Mar ▶

Santiago ▶

San Francisco
de Barón

CERRO BARÓN

Muelle Barón

Reloj Barón

AV. ESPAÑA

CERRO LÉCHEROS

Estación
Barón

Feria Persa

Ascensor
Barón

Estación
Bellavista

Ascensor
Lecheros

AV. ERRÁZURIZ

Mercado
Cardonal

CERRO LARRAÍN

Terminal
Rodoviario
(buses)

Ascensor
Larraín

AV. BRASIL

YUNGAY

CHACABUCO

S. BOLIVAR

MORRIS

URUGUAY

SAN IGNACIO

AV. ARGENTINA

RODRIGUEZ

LAS HERAS

FREIRE

PLAZA
BOLÍVAR

Catedral

PLAZA
VICTORIA

AV. PEDRO MONTT

Doce Apóstoles

Teatro
Municipal

PLAZA
BERNARDO
O'HIGGINS

Parque
Italia

VICTORIA

Congreso
Nacional

JUANA ROSS

CERRO
POLANCO

EDWARDS

Museo a
Cielo Abierto

AV. FRANCIA

AV. INDEPENDENCIA

RETAMO

BARROS

RANCAGUA

AV. ARGENTINA

Ascensor
Polanco

SIMPSON

AV. COLÓN

AV. COLÓN

AV. WASHINGTON

Ascensor
Mariposa

Ascensor
Florida

BAQUEDANO

CERRO MONJA

Ascensor
Monjas

CERRO MERCED

CERRO
MARIPOSA

AV. ALEMANIA

SANTA ELENA

VALPARAÍSO

city and should not be missed. Unfortunately you'll also have to contend with a certain amount of noise, pollution, general shabbiness and crime, which for some people overshadows the city's charms. However, just take a **boat ride** round the harbour (especially as the sun's going down and its rays fall into every fold of the hills); go up two or three **ascensores**; check out the colourful old residential quarters of **Cerros Alegre** and **Concepción**, and check out the views by night, when the city's million flickering lights are reflected in the ocean like a basket of pearls – and you're sure to fall under Valparaíso's spell.

The Barrio Puerto

At the heart of Porteño history and identity, the **Barrio Puerto**, the port neighbourhood, is a good place to start exploring the city. Note that while it's safe by day, it gets dodgy at night, when prostitutes and drunken sailors frequent the streets. The focal point is **Plaza Sotomayor**, a large public square dominated at one end by the imposing grey facade of the **ex-Intendencia de Valparaíso** (now occupied by the navy, which does a short drill in the square weekdays at 6pm). At the other end of the plaza is the triumphant **Monumento de los Héroes de Iquique**, where statues of Arturo Prat and other heroes of the War of the Pacific tower above a crypt housing their tombs (open to the public each May 21). Opposite the monument is the gateway to **Muelle Prat**, the only stretch of the port open to the public. It's geared almost exclusively towards tourists, with souvenir shops, a tourist kiosk and a replica of *El Santiaguillo*, the first Spanish ship to reach Valparaíso in 1536. It's also the embarkation point for **boat rides** around the bay – the small *lanchas* are cheapest (CH$1000, every 20min until nightfall), while a fancier boat, *Yate Edén II*, offers rides into the night (℡32/691112; CH$2000 plus cocktails).

From the ex-Intendencia, Calle Serrano leads west into the oldest part of the city, dotted with battered shops and dubious-looking sailors' bars. Halfway along the street, **Ascensor Cordillera** takes you up to the red-walled **Museo del Mar Almirante Cochrane** (Tues–Sat 10am–6pm; free; ℡32/939486), where you'll find an impressive display of model ships that belonged to Lord Cochrane, and stupendous **panoramic vistas** out to sea. Back in the lower town, Calle Serrano continues to **Plaza Echaurren**, the oldest square in the city and very picturesque save for the wine-swilling characters that permanently occupy its benches. Just off the square, the iron structure of the **Mercado Puerto** houses a bustling market on its ground floor and several popular, inexpensive fish restaurants upstairs (lunch only).

A couple of blocks east, **Iglesia La Matriz** – a graceful, Neoclassical church with a seventeenth-century carving of Christ inside – sits at the foot of Cerro Santo Domingo surrounded by narrow, twisting streets full of colour, activity and a slightly menacing feel; this is a rough part of town, not to be explored alone or at night. If you continue along Serrano (which becomes Bustamante) you reach Plaza Wheelwright (also known as Plaza Aduana), flanked by the large, colonial-looking **Aduana** building, dating from 1854 and still a working customs house.

The Paseo 21 de Mayo and the Museo Naval

A few steps from the Aduana you'll find **Ascensor Artillería**, which takes you up to the **Paseo 21 de Mayo** on Cerro Playa Ancha. The most visited esplanade in the city, the paseo sports a row of uninspiring souvenir stalls and a fairly constant stream of tourists. Of all the city's viewpoints, this one provides the most spectacular panorama, taking in the whole bay of Valparaíso and sweeping 20km north to the Punta de Concón; on very clear days you can even see the smokestacks at the oil refinery of Ventanas, 45km away. The paseo curves around the luxuriant gardens of a former naval school, an impressive whitewashed building that now houses the excellent **Museo Naval y Marítimo** (Tues–Sun 10am–5.30pm; CH$500). The beautifully presented displays – which include paintings, photographs, weapons, uniforms, nautical instruments and personal objects – bring to life some of the figures so central to Chile's history, such as Ambrosio O'Higgins, Lord Cochrane and Arturo Prat. The museum also presents an interesting history of adventure travel as documented by sailors who battled to navigate the tip of South America in the era before the Panama Canal.

Plaza Sotomayor to Plaza Victoria

Valparaíso's **city centre** is formed by the narrow strip stretching from Plaza Sotomayor in the west and Plaza Victoria in the east. Almost completely devastated by the 1906 earthquake (see p.147), it has evolved into a mixture of ugly, modern blocks and many elegant buildings left over from the early twentieth century which were built to house banks and other financial institutions. Calle Prat, which runs east from Plaza Sotomayor, has some good examples – take a look inside the **Banco Santander** opposite the Turri clock tower, originally the Banco de Londres and dripping with bronze and marble brought over from England. Next door to the bank, **Ascensor Concepción** (also known as Ascensor Turri) provides access to Cerro Concepción, a pretty residential area that was once the preserve of English businessmen. Further east, **Plaza Aníbal Pinto** is a lovely cobbled square overlooked by a couple of the city's oldest restaurants, including *El Cinzano* (see p.160).

From here, the main drag continues along Calle Condell, where you'll find the **Palacio Lyon**, a splendid mansion dating from 1881 (one of the few to survive the earthquake) and now housing the **Museo de Historia Natural** (Tues–Sat 10am–1pm & 2–6pm, Sun 10am–2pm; CH$600, Wed free). This cash-starved museum tries hard to inform and entertain but its displays look dowdy and outdated. The central theme is *el mar de Chile*, covering the chemical, physical and biological aspects of the sea, marine flora and fauna (look for the case of stuffed penguins) and the influence of the sea on pre-Hispanic cultures. The cellars of the building have been converted into the **Galería Municipal de Arte** (Mon–Sat 10am–7pm; free), which puts on temporary art exhibitions with excellent oil paintings of the area; the entrance is on Condell, separate from the museum's.

Calle Condell ends at **Plaza Victoria**, a large tree-filled square where most of Valparaíso seems to come to chat and sit in the sunshine. It's flanked, on its eastern side, by the Gothic-looking **Iglesia Catedral de Valparaíso**, whose simply decorated interior includes a delicate ivory carving of Christ, and most intriguingly, a marble urn (in the crypt) containing the heart of the famous Chilean statesman Diego Portales. If you want to visit the cathedral, ask in the administrative office at the north side of the building, on Chacabuco (Mon–Fri 10am–1pm & 4–6.30pm). From the square, Calles Molina and Edwards lead to the **Museo a Cielo Abierto**, a circuit of narrow streets and passageways painted with seventeen colourful, bold, abstract murals by students and leading local artists, the most memorable being the enormous paintings by Chilean Roberto Matta. The increased graffiti destruction of the murals is the most obvious sign, however, that it's best not to linger around here.

Valparaíso's antiquated lifts

Most of Valparaíso's fifteen **ascensores**, or funicular "lifts", were built between 1883 and 1916 to provide a link between the lower town and the new residential quarters that were spreading up the hillsides. Appearances would suggest that they've scarcely been modernized since, but despite their rickety frames and alarming noises they've so far proved safe and reliable. What's more, nearly all drop off passengers at a panoramic viewpoint, usually atop their namesake hillside. The *ascensores* operate every few minutes from 7am to 11pm, and cost CH$70 to $120 one-way, usually less going down than up. Here are a few of the best, listed from east to west:

Ascensor Barón This *ascensor* has windows on all sides, so you get good views as you go up. Inaugurated in 1906, it was the first to be powered by an electric motor, still in perfect working order. The entrance is hidden away at the back of a clothes market, Feria Persa el Barón, off the seaward end of Avenida Argentina. At the top, you're allowed into the machinery room where you can watch the giant cogs go round as they haul the lift up and down. There's also a display of photos of all of Valpo's *ascensores*. Don't miss the magnificent view of the house-packed hills from the mirador.

Ascensor Polanco The most picturesque *ascensor*, and the only one that's totally vertical. It's approached through a cavernous, underground tunnel and rises 80m through a yellow wooden tower to a balcony that gives some of the best views in the city. A narrow bridge connects the tower to Cerro Polanco with its flaking, pastel houses in varying states of repair. Ascensor Polanco is on Calle Simpson, off Avenida Argentina (opposite Independencia).

Ascensor Concepción (also known as Ascensor Turri) Hidden in a small passage opposite the Turri clock tower, at the corner of Prat and Almirante Carreño, this was the first *ascensor* to be built, in 1883, and was originally powered by steam. It takes you up to the beautiful residential area of Cerro Concepción, well worth a visit (see opposite); just by the upper entrance you'll find *Café Turri* (see p.159) on Calle Prat, a great place to admire the views over a coffee or a meal.

Ascensor El Peral Next door to the Tribunales de Justicio, just off Plaza Sotomayor, this *ascensor* leads to one of the most romantic corners of the city: Paseo Yugoslavo, a little esplanade looking west onto some of Valparaíso's most beautiful houses, and backed by a flamboyant mansion housing the Museo de Bellas Artes. It's worth walking from here to Ascensor Concepción – see map opposite.

Ascensor Artillería Always busy with tourists, but highly recommended for the stunning vistas at the top, from the Paseo 21 de Mayo. It was built in 1893 to transport cadets to and from the naval school at the top of the hill, now the site of the very impressive *Museo Naval y Marítimo* (see p.155).

La Sebastiana – Neruda's house

Of Pablo Neruda's three houses open to the public (the others being La Chascona, p.113, and Isla Negra, p.161), **La Sebastiana** (Jan–Feb 10am–6.50pm; March–Dec Tues–Sun 10.30am–6pm; CH$2000), offers the most informal look at the poet, not least because it attracts the fewest crowds, and you aren't forced to take a guided tour so you can amble around at your own pace, armed with informative sheets in Spanish and English. Neruda moved into this house in 1961 with Matilde Urrutia, his third wife. Perched high on the aptly named Bellavista hill, giving dramatic views over the bay, it was his *casa en el aire* ("House in the Air") and although he spent less time here than in his other homes, he imprinted his style and enthusiasms on every corner of the house. After the 1973 coup it was repeatedly vandalized by the military but has been meticulously restored by the Fundación Neruda, which opened it as a museum in 1992. Its narrow, sinuous passages and bright colours seem to mirror the spirit of Valparaíso, and the countless bizarre objects brought here by the poet are simply astonishing, from the embalmed Venezuelan Coro-Coro bird hanging from the ceiling of the dining room to the wooden horse in the living room, taken from a merry-go-round in Paris. The house is located at Ferrari 692, off Avenida Alemania; to get there, take a three-minute ride in a #39 *colectivo* (CH$200) from Ecuador and Condell.

Cerros Alegre and Concepción

The hilltop residential quarter spread over **Cerros Alegre** and **Concepción** is a rambling maze of steep streets and small alleys lined with elegant, brightly painted houses and aristocratic mansions clinging precipitously to the hillside. It grew up as the enclave of Valparaíso's immigrant businessmen, particularly the English, who left their legacy in street names like Leighton, Templeman and Atkinson, and the Germans, whose influence can be seen in the many half-timbered, shuttered houses dotted about the area. There are two points of access from the lower town; **Ascensor Concepción** (see opposite), near the Turri clock tower in Calle Prat, takes you up to **Paseo Gervasoni** on Cerro Concepción, while **Ascensor El Peral** (see opposite), next to the Tribunales de Justicia just off Plaza Sotomayor, ascends to Cerro Alegre's **Paseo Yugoslavo**, one of the most attractive and peaceful parts of town. A good way to explore the area is to walk between the two *ascensores*: the Oficina de Turismo has produced a leaflet with a suggested **walking tour**, which takes you through some narrow alleys and hidden passageways – see map below, for the route.

Arriving at Paseo Yugoslavo you'll see an extravagant, four-storey mansion right behind the esplanade. This is **Palacio Baburizza**, built in 1916 for a

CERRO CONCEPCIÓN & CERRO ALEGRE

EATING & DRINKING
El Bar Inglés	5
Barparaíso	2
El Cinzano	8
La Piedra Feliz	1
Café Riquet	6
Café Turri	7
La Pérgola	9
La Tertulia	4
Valparaíso Eterno	3

Train Station

ERRÁZURIZ

GÓMEZ CARREÑO

URRIOLA

BLANCO

ESMERALDA

COCHRANE

Turri Clock tower

Ascensor Concepción

PRAT

GERVASONI

PASEO ATKINSON

PLAZA ANÍBAL PINTO

PAPUDO

PASEO YUGOSLAVO

CERRO CONCEPCIÓN

Lutheran Church

Ascensor El Peral

ABTAO

CONCEPCIÓN

Palacio Baburizza

TEMPLEMAN

PILCOMAYO

Palacio de Justicia

MONTE ALEGRE

URRIOLA

St Paul's Anglican Church

CERRO ALEGRE

LEIGHTON

PASAJE GÁLVEZ

PASAJE TEMPLEMAN

CUMMING

ALMIRANTE MONTT

Ascensor Reina Victoria

ELÍAS

MIRAMAR

ÁLVARO

PASEO DIMALOW

---- Walking Tour

0   100 m

N

ACCOMMODATION
Casa Latina	B
Brighton Bed & Breakfast	A
Casa Juan Carrasco	C

nitrate baron and now the home of the **Museo de Bellas Artes de Valparaíso** (Tues–Sun 10am–6pm; free), a hushed, scarcely visited museum with a collection of nineteenth- and twentieth-century Chilean and European art. It's a mixed bag, but worth a visit for the evocative paintings of an earlier Valparaíso by artists such as Juan Mauricio Rugendas, Alfred Helsby, Thomas Somerscales and, most notably, Juan Francisco González. Less highbrow in tone, and in some ways more rewarding, the **Casa Mirador de Lukas** (Tues–Sun 10.30am–2pm & 3.30–6pm; CH$500) sits just a few steps from the Ascensor Concepción, at Paseo Gervasoni 448. This little museum pays homage to *El Mercurio*'s great satirist and cartoonist, known simply as Lukas, who possessed a sharp talent for capturing the spirit of his country in the hilarious drawings he produced for the newspaper between 1958 and 1988, many of which are displayed here.

As you're walking around Cerro Concepción, don't miss the **Paseo Atkinson**, an esplanade affording great panoramas and lined with pretty houses whose tiny front gardens and window boxes recall their original English owners. From here you can see the tall tower of the **Lutheran church**, a distinctive, green-walled structure built in 1897; a block or so farther away you'll find the towerless **St Paul's Anglican Church** (built in 1858) whose solemn interior contains a huge organ donated by Queen Victoria in 1903.

Around the Congreso Nacional

If you arrive in Valparaíso by bus the first thing that hits you as you emerge from the station is the imposing **Congreso Nacional**, described by Collier and Sater in their *History of Chile* as "half neo-Babylonian, half post-modernist atrocity". It was one of Pinochet's projects, which perhaps explains its heavy-handed style, but the dictator relinquished power before it was completed. Its life began on March 11, 1990, when Patricio Aylwin was sworn in as president and Congress resumed its activities after a sixteen-year absence – away from the capital for the first time. It's not, in fact, as impregnable as it looks, and members of the public are allowed to go in and watch Congress in session (Senate Tues & Wed 4pm, Thurs 10am; Deputies Tues, Wed & Thurs 10.30am; closed last week of each month and Feb; passport required). Given the inconvenience of its distance from the capital, politicians have repeatedly discussed a plan to return Congress to Santiago and convert the building into a gigantic hotel, but so far no decision has been made. There's little else to hold your interest in this part of town, though one of Chile's best **antique/flea markets** is held every Saturday and Sunday at Plaza O'Higgins. It offers a great collection of books, clothes, nautical gear and cameras, though the prices are fairly high. The lively **flower, fruit and vegetable market** that runs along Avenida Argentina on Wednesday and Saturday is also worth a visit. While you're here, seek out **Ascensor Polanco** (see p.156), the most fascinating of the funiculars, reached by a long, underground tunnel and taking you up to a fine look-out tower. It's located on Calle Simpson, off the southern end of Avenida Argentina.

Eating, drinking and entertainment

Valparaíso's eating and drinking scene is one of the city's highlights, especially if you catch it in full swing on a Thursday, Friday or Saturday night. With one or two exceptions, its **restaurants** aren't notable for their food, but rather for their old-fashioned charm and warm, informal atmosphere. The city's speciality is its unpretentious **bar-restaurants** serving *comida típica* to local families, who turn out in their dozens to join in the singing and dancing on weekends, when many places have live *boleros, tangos,* or *música folklórica*. There's also a range of younger, hipper **bars**, some with live music and dancing (and usually a cover charge, which includes first drink). These are concentrated in one main area: the relatively safe **subida Ecuador**, climbing up from Plazuela Ecuador, and lined with cheap bars, pubs and restaurants, where the partying lasts all night. The pubs vanish and are rebaptized with different names practically on a monthly basis, so rather than searching out a particular locale, just head to the area and follow the crowds.

A second option is the **Barrio Puerto**, mainly along Errázuriz. Keep alert – even during the weekend when there are usually plenty of people going from bar to bar until the early hours of the morning. Most places are closed on Sunday night and tend to be very quiet Monday to Wednesday; at the weekend, bars and restaurants don't start to fill up until after 10pm, and many stay open until 5am or later. If you want to go **clubbing**, your best bet is to catch a bus out to Reñaca, effectively a suburb of Viña that has something of a monopoly on the local nightclub scene (see p.172).

Note that Valpo is *the place* to go in Chile to ring in the **New Year**, with huge parties and fireworks extravaganzas; be sure arrive by midday on the 30th or you'll get stuck in horrible traffic.

For an evening of culture, check out the programme at the **Teatro Municipal**, on the corner of Pedro Montt and Plaza O'Higgins, which features regular theatre, music and dance performances. As for **cinema**, the Hoyts, Pedro Montt 2111 (T32/594709), shows mainstream releases. You can find art movies at various cultural centres about town; check the back of the newspaper *El Mercurio de Valparaíso* for details.

Cafés and snacks

Babestrello Av Uruguay 426, on Plaza O'Higgins, opposite the bus terminal. Spacious coffee shop serving sticky cakes and coffee, and hot toast and jam – a good place for breakfast.

Café-Arte Mirador Paseo 21 de Mayo (top exit of ascensor Artillería). Small, arty café with sweeping views across the bay and a changing display of paintings by local artists. Closed Tuesday mornings.

Café Riquet Plaza Aníbal Pinto. Old-fashioned café-restaurant that's apparently frozen in time – it's been going for decades and the chef's been here seemingly forever. Come for tasty coffee, snacks and breakfast.

Marco Polo Pedro Montt 2199, opposite Parque Italia. Large, inexpensive Italian cafeteria not far from the bus terminal, serving hearty pasta lunches and snacks.

Pastelería Stefani Condell 1608, Plaza Victoria. Exquisite strawberry tarts and other delights, as well as a small stand-up bar where you can wash down your inexpensive cake with a coffee.

La Pérgola Almirante Montt 51. Utterly charming café-cum-tearoom-cum-snack bar where the freshly cut sandwiches have a deconstructionist twist, the cakes are irresistible and the coffee is up to Milan standards; jazz and

Latin music, and local artwork and jewellery for sale, are added bonuses, as is the smiling service.

Tentazione Pedro Montt 2484. Typical, TV-dominated *fuente de soda* (soda fountain) serving filling, cheap Chilean fare; handy for the bus station.

Vitamin Service Pedro Montt 1746, off Plaza Victoria. Delicious fruit juices and sandwiches – perfect for replenishing your energy.

Restaurants

Bambú Pudeto 450, off west end of Condell. Good-value vegetarian food – mainly omelettes, salads and soups – in a central location.

Café Turri Paseo Gervasoni, by upper exit of ascensor Concepción T32/252091. Classic restaurant with an outdoor terrace and panoramic views, especially magical at night. Excellent traditional meat and fish dishes (main courses around CH$8000); also operates as a café throughout the day. It has become very touristy of late, with a drop in quality and higher prices, but still warrants a visit.

Coco Loco Giratorio Blanco 1781, 21st and 22nd floors T32/227614. The superior – and higher – sister of the namesake restaurant in Santiago is a classic. Superb pisco sours followed by marinated fish, seafood, exquisitely prepared meat dishes and a faultless wine list, plus a revolving view of the entire city; if it sounds kitsch, that's because it is, right down to the lift-style Muzak, but the service is impeccable, the food delicious and the vistas unforgettable.

J. Cruz Malbrán Condell 1466, in side alley next to Municipalidad ☏ 32/211225. An extraordinary place, more like a museum than a restaurant, packed to the gills with china, old clocks, musical instruments, crucifixes and more. Famous for its filling, inexpensive *pan con carne mechada* (steak sandwiches) – not to be missed on any account.

Bars and pubs

El Bar Inglés Cochrane 851 (rear entrance at Blanco 870). Long-standing favourite since the early 1900s, and very popular for lunch though more expensive than its old-fashioned, crumbling decor might suggest. Check out wall map with listings of incoming boats, which come from all over.

Barparaíso Errázuriz 1041. Funky bar with a dance area downstairs overlooked by a dimly lit balcony where you can hang out and drink. Plays a mixture of rock, Latin and dance music; popular with students. Cover CH$4000

El Cinzano Plaza Aníbal Pinto 1182. Hugely popular place with a fantastic weekend atmosphere when it fills with locals and ageing crooners singing sentimental ballads.

La Piedra Feliz Errázuriz 1054, near junction with Blanco. Really mellow place with creaky wooden floors and plenty of tables to sit at and chat. There's live jazz on Tues, *boleros* on Wed, and various types of music on the weekends. Cover CH$3000.

La Playa Serrano 567. A sociable spot with a long, mahogany bar, dark wood-panelled walls and big old mirrors. Has live music and holds a crowd until 7am Sat and Sun.

Taberna Pancho Pirata Pudeto 489, off west end of Condell. Lively cellar-pub with stone walls and an intriguing, pirate-themed decor. One of the most popular drinking holes in town, it's open Thurs–Sat.

La Tertulia Esmeralda 1083, near Turri clock tower. Stylish restaurant-bar-café with polished floors, bright yellow walls and high ceilings. Serves Spanish food and generously filled hot sandwiches (*bocas calientes*); quite frantic at lunch time but very low-key by night.

Valparaíso Eterno corner of Blanco and A Señoret, one block east of Plaza Sotomayor. Dark rooms decorated with graffiti and wooden collages of the city's *ascensores* and houses. Live music on weekends until late and a *salsateca* in the basement; very popular with people of all ages.

Listings

Airlines LAN Esmeralda 1048 ☏ 32/251441, United, Urriola 87 piso 3 ☏ 32/216569.

Banks and exchange The main financial street is Prat, where you'll find plenty of banks with ATMs and *cambios*, including Exprinter at no. 895 and New York at no. 659. Of the banks, the Banco de Santiago is the best for currency exchange. There is an ATM machine at the bus station.

Car rental Mach Viña, Las Heras 428 ☏ 32/217762; Unión Rent a Car, Esmeralda 940 ☏ 32/226570; Bert Rent a Car, Victoria 2682 ☏ 32/212885.

Consulate United Kingdom, Blanco 1199, 5th floor ☏ 32/213063. Germany, Blanco 1215, Office 1102 ☏ 32/256749.

Department Stores Falabella and Ripley, both on Plaza Victoria, offer everything from digital cameras to socks.

Football Santiago Wanderers, the oldest club in the country, holds regular division one matches in the Estadio Municipal at Playa Ancha; see newspaper for dates and times.

Hospital Van Buren, Colón and San Ignacio ☏ 32/254074.

Instituto Chileno-Norteamericano Esmeralda 1069. Free films and cultural guides.

Internet *Ciber Internet*, Pedro Montt and General Cruz.

Laundry *Nuovolav*, Las Heras 554, two blocks west of Plaza Victoria.

Post office Prat 856.

Telephone offices Entel, Pedro Montt 1940 and Condell 149, opposite the Municipalidad; Telefónica, Plaza Victoria (daily 8.30am–midnight) and Sotomayor 55. Also cheap call centres around the bus station.

❷

Moving on from Valparaíso

Intercity (every 10min **to Santiago**) and **international buses** leave from the Terminal Rodoviario (℡32/939646). You can also get buses **up and down the coast** from the terminal, mainly with Sol del Pacífico (℡32/281026), Pullman Bus Costa (℡32/253125) and Mirasol (℡32/235985). To get **to Viña del Mar**, pick up a *micro* anywhere along Pedro Montt; they're very frequent and take about fifteen minutes, twice that time in bad traffic; alternatively take a train from the station next to Muelle Prat, off Plaza Sotomayor (every 15–30min), or even a boat from Muelle Prat (CH$1000). The Oficina de Turismo at the Municipalidad keeps timetables of all bus, train and boat services. For more information see "Travel Details" on p.178.

South of Valparaíso

Given that the coastal resorts **south of Valparaíso** are closer to, and more easily reached from, Santiago than those further north, it's not surprising that they're among the busiest and most developed of the *Litoral Central*. A trail of seaside towns, packed full of busy hotels, *cabañas* and *marisquerías*, are linked by numerous *micros* and *colectivos* all along this coast. Most of the towns sit on long, overcrowded beaches – in the summer, that is; in the winter they are just forlorn and abandoned, often lost in marine fog. The majority of the main resorts, such as the sprawling Algarrobo, El Tabo and Cartagena, are overrun with ugly apartment blocks and jam-packed with noisy vacationers. If you're looking for a more peaceful beach holiday, head instead to the exclusive and better preserved **Rocas de Santo Domingo**, 75km south of Valpo. By far the major attraction along the whole seaboard, however, is the fabulous **Isla Negra**, site of Pablo Neruda's extraordinary house, now a museum dedicated to the great poet.

Isla Negra

Since 1939, poet **Pablo Neruda** spent on and off forty years of his life here, enlarging his house and filling it with the strange and beautiful objects he ceaselessly gathered from far-flung corners of the world. The Fundación Neruda, acting on the wishes of the poet's widow, Matilde Urrutia, has transferred Neruda's and Matilde's graves to its garden and operates the house as a **museum** (guided tours in English or Spanish, Jan–Feb Tues–Sun 10am–8pm; March–Dec 10am–2pm & 3pm–6pm; CH$2400, CH$3000 for English guide; ℡35/461284, ℱ35/461582, ℯmuseodeisalnegra@hotmail.com). Inside, its winding passages and odd-shaped rooms are crammed full of exotic objects like ships' figureheads, Hindu carvings, African and Japanese masks, ships in bottles, seashells, butterflies, coloured bottles, Victorian postcards and a good deal more. It's an extraordinary place, spoiled only by the hurried, regimented pace of the tours.

There's little else to Isla Negra save a small, pretty beach that makes for a great picnic spot, and a couple of handicraft stalls in the main square, just under a kilometre from Neruda's home. If you want to stay – and the temptation is frequent – you'll find **rooms** at the historic *Hostería La Candela*, C de La

Pablo Neruda

The tiny village of **Isla Negra** was put firmly on the map when **Pablo Neruda** moved into a half-built house on the beach in 1939. Born **Neftalí Reyes** in 1904, this son of a local railwayman grew into a tall, pale and impoverished young man who wandered the streets of Santiago dressed in a swirling cape and a wide sombrero, where he made his name in the world of poetry under the pseudonym of Pablo Neruda, going on to become a **Nobel Laureate** in 1971. He published his first collection of poems, *Crepusculario*, in 1923 at his own expense, selling his furniture and pawning the watch given to him by his father to cover the costs. Success came quickly and when, the following year, he published a slim volume of sensual, tormented verses under the title of *Veinte Poemas de Amor y una Canción Desesperada* ("Twenty love poems and a song of despair") he suddenly found himself, at the age of twenty, with one of the fastest-growing readerships on the continent.

Despite the success of *Veinte Poemas*, Neruda still needed to earn a living to fund his writing, and so, aged twenty-four, he began his career as **Chilean consul** in Rangoon, the first of many posts. It seems ironic that this most "Chilean" of poets, whose verses are imprinted with the forests, rain, sea, lakes and volcanoes of southern Chile, and whose countrymen love him as a man of their soil, should have spent so much of his adult life far from his native land. His years in Rangoon, Colombo, Jakarta and Singapore were often intensely lonely, but also coloured with vivid episodes, not least the many sexual adventures he fondly recalls in his autobiography *Memoirs*. The most dramatic of these was his love affair with a woman in Rangoon who called herself **Josie Bliss**. Described by Neruda as his "Burmese panther . . . a love-smitten terrorist capable of anything", she was a jealous and possessive lover who would sometimes terrorize him with her silver dagger. When he was transferred to Ceylon, he left secretly, without telling her, but she turned up on his doorstep several months later, carrying a bag of rice (believing it grew only in Rangoon) and a selection of their favourite records. Neruda's outright rejection of her was to haunt him for many years, and Josie Bliss makes several appearances in his poems.

During his time in Asia, Neruda's poetry (published in the collection *Residencia en la Tierra*) was inward-looking, reflecting his experience of dislocation and solitude. His posts in Barcelona (1934) and Madrid (1935–36), however, marked a major turning point in his life and his work: with the outbreak of the **Spanish Civil War**, and the assassination of his close friend, Federico García Lorca, Neruda became intensely

Hostería 67 (☎32/461254, ⓦwwww.candela.cl; ❺); here you can soak in the ambience of a cosy hotel where Neruda himself once stayed. At no. 4160 on the same street, *La Flor de Isla Negra* (☎35/461043; ❸) offers less expensive and comfortable *cabañas*.

Rocas de Santo Domingo

Marking the end of the coast road and the southern extreme of the *Litoral Central*, **ROCAS DE SANTO DOMINGO** is less a holiday resort town and more an upscale residential area by the sea. Formerly an empty wasteland on the southern bank of the Río Maipo, it was designed and built from scratch in the 1940s following a nationwide architectural competition. Sixty years on, it still feels slightly artificial, its gardens too manicured, its streets too tidy. The beach however, is superb, stretching 20km south of the town, backed by nothing but sand dunes; even in the height of summer you don't have to walk far to committed to active politics. As consul for emigration, he threw himself into the task of providing Spanish refugees with a safe passage to Chile, and at the same time sought to give his poetry a meaningful "place in man's struggle", with *España en el Corazón*. On returning to Chile he became a member of the Communist Party, and was **elected senator** for the Antofagasta and Tarapacá regions, a role he took very seriously, tirelessly touring the desert pampas to talk to the workers. His politics were to land him in serious trouble, however, when newly elected president González Videla, who had enlisted Neruda's help in managing his presidential campaign, switched sides from left to right, and outlawed Communism. When Neruda publicly attacked González Videla, the president issued a warrant for his arrest, and he was forced into hiding. In 1949 the poet was smuggled across a southern pass in the Andes on horseback, and spent the next three years in exile, mainly in Europe.

It was during his years of **exile** that Neruda met the woman who was to inspire some of his most beautiful love poetry: Matilde Urrutia, whom he was later to marry. Neruda had been married twice before: first, briefly, to a Dutch woman he'd met as a young consul in Rangoon; and then for eighteen years to the Argentinian painter, Delia del Carril. The poet's writings scarcely mention his first wife, nor their daughter – his only child – who died when she was just eight years old, but Delia is described as "sweetest of consorts, thread of steel and honey. . . my perfect mate for eighteen years". It was so as not to wound Delia that *Los Versos del Capitán* – a book of passionate love poems written for Matilde on their secret hideaway in Capri – was published anonymously. Nonetheless, when the order for his arrest was revoked three years after his return to Santiago, Neruda divorced Delia and moved into **La Chascona**, in Santiago, and then to **Isla Negra** with Matilde. Based in Chile from then on, Neruda devoted himself to politics and poetry almost in equal measure. His dedication to both causes found its reward at the same time: in 1970, Salvador Allende, whose presidential campaign Neruda had tirelessly participated in, was elected president at the head of the socialist Unidad Popular. Then, the following year, Neruda was awarded the Nobel Prize for Literature, the second Chilean to attain the honour after Gabriela Mistral (see box, p.203). His happiness was to be short-lived, however. Diagnosed with cancer, and already bedridden, the poet was unable to withstand the shock brought on by the 1973 military coup, which left his dear friend Allende dead. Less than two weeks later, on September 23, Neruda died in Santiago with Matilde at his side.

escape the crowds. It's a very popular spot for **windsurfing**, but rentals are only sporadically available at the southern end of the beach near Estero Yali. There is just one **hotel** in Santo Domingo, the expensive *Hotel Rocas de Santo Domingo*, La Ronda 130 (☎35/444356, ℱ35/444494; ❺). The sand dunes further south are a perfect place for unofficial **camping**.

Viña del Mar and around

A fifteen-minute bus ride north of Valparaíso is all it takes to exchange the colourful and chaotic alleys of Valpo for the tree-lined avenues and ostentatious apartment high-rises of **VIÑA DEL MAR**. This is Chile's largest and best-known beach resort, drawing tens of thousands of mostly Chilean vacationers to its sands each summer. In many ways, it's indistinguishable from beach resorts elsewhere in the world, with its oceanfront condominiums, scores of bars and restaurants and centrally located casino, but lurking in the older corners of town are reminders of a graceful and dignified past, in the form of extravagant palaces, elegant villas and sumptuous gardens. Many of these date from the late nineteenth century when Viña del Mar – at that time a large hacienda – was subdivided into plots that were sold or rented to the wealthy families of Valparaíso and Santiago who came to spend their summers by the sea, emulating the fashion in Europe. The early decades of the twentieth century saw the arrival of many more visitors: hotels were built, restaurants opened, a casino was installed – and Viña's fate was sealed. Devoted as it is to tourism, Viña has plenty of accommodation, restaurants and the best shops and services in the region. The city also has a pair of **beautiful botanical gardens** with species from around the world and a museum with an important collection of art from Easter Island.

In February, Viña is packed for a week-long **International Music Festival**, showcasing mainly rising pop stars from Latin America (see p.167). In the past five years, Viña has been eclipsed by the host of new restaurants in Santiago and the beaches of La Serena (see p.192) but it's a comfortable, modern beachside city that offers a relaxing escape from the capital, perfect for bumming around for a couple of days at the beginning or end of your holiday.

Arrival, information and getting around

Intercity buses from Santiago (every 10min from Terminal de Buses Alameda) and elsewhere arrive at the **bus terminal** at the eastern end of Avenida Valparaíso in the southern part of town; best take a taxi to wherever you're staying, or a *micro* from the back of the terminal along Arlegui towards the centre and the sea. **From Valparaíso** you can get here by boat, train or *micro*: **boats** drop you off at Muelle Vergara; the centrally located **train station** is one block south of Plaza Vergara; and **micros** come down Calle Viana, parallel to the railway tracks, and turn into Plaza Vergara.

Information

The most convenient place to go for tourist **information** is the **Oficina de Turismo**, just off the northwest corner of Plaza Vergara, in front of the *Hotel O'Higgins* on Av Marina (Jan–Feb Mon–Fri 9am–9pm, Sat & Sun 10am–9pm; March–Dec Mon–Fri 9am–2pm & 3–7pm; ℡800800830, @www.visitevinadelmarchile.cl); it has many maps and comprehensive lists of hotels and *residenciales*. The **Sernatur** office (Mon–Fri 8.30am–2pm & 3–5.30pm; ℡32/882285, Ⓕ32/684117) is also helpful and well-stocked with maps and pamphlets, but very difficult to find. It's at Av Valparaíso 507, on the third floor (#302) of an office block set back from the main street, next door to an amusement arcade, on the corner of Valparaíso and Echevers. There's also a **Conaf** information office (Mon–Fri 9am–2pm; ℡32/441342 or 32/320210) at Pasaje 3 Norte 541, which has maps of Chilean national parks. For **cultural information**, try the **Chileno-Británico** institute, 3 Norte 824 (℡32/971061), and **Chileno-Norteamericano**, 2 Oriente 385 (℡32/686191). They provide listings and details about lectures, free movies, language courses and English-language libraries.

Getting around

Viña is an easy and compact city to get around. The grid-patterned streets here are named simply North, East or West: those parallel to the Marga Marga are 1 Norte, 2 Norte and so on, ascending in number the further away they are from the river. Streets intersecting them at right angles, running parallel to the coast are known as Oriente (East) or Poniente (West) depending on which side of Avenida Libertad they're on; the first street east of Libertad is 1 Oriente, the second is 2 Oriente, and so on, the same system applying on the other side.

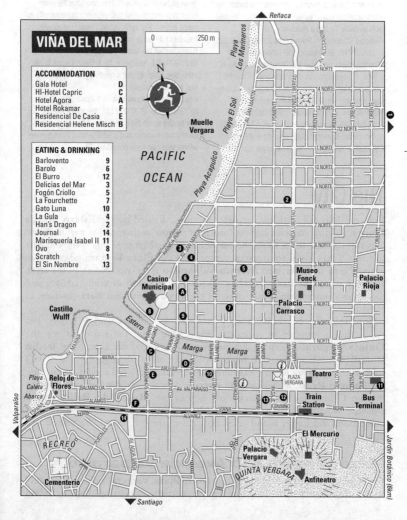

VIÑA DEL MAR

0   250 m

N

ACCOMMODATION
Gala Hotel	D
HI-Hotel Capric	C
Hotel Agora	A
Hotel Rokamar	F
Residencial De Casia	E
Residencial Helene Misch	B

EATING & DRINKING
Barlovento	9
Barolo	6
El Burro	12
Delicias del Mar	3
Fogón Criollo	5
La Fourchette	7
Gato Luna	10
La Gula	4
Han's Dragon	2
Journal	14
Marisquería Isabel II	11
Ovo	8
Scratch	1
El Sin Nombre	13

PACIFIC OCEAN

Reñaca

Muelle Vergara

Casino Municipal

Castillo Wulff

Museo Fonck

Palacio Rioja

Palacio Carrasco

Estero

Marga   Marga

Playa Caleta Abarca   Reloj de Flores

Teatro

Train Station

Bus Terminal

El Mercurio

Palacio Vergara

RECREO

Cementerio

QUINTA VERGARA   Anfiteatro

Valparaíso

Jardín Botánico (6km)

Santiago

165

Accommodation

Viña offers all manner of places to stay, from dingy hovels to five-star hotels, but most options are disappointing and overpriced. All the **budget accommodation** is in the southern part of town, particularly on Agua Santa and Von Schroeders, and the side streets off Avenida Valparaíso. **Smarter options**, though spread all over town, are especially abundant on the northern side. Only a few places offer sea views, as the oceanfront is taken up by residential condominiums. Prices drop significantly outside January and February. If you are coming in high season, book well in advance.

Gala Hotel Arlegui 273, local 10 ☎ 32/321500, ⓕ 689568, ⓔ galahotel@webhost.cl. Large, luxurious high-rise featuring modern art, contemporary decor and spacious rooms. It sits near the beach, and offers excellent ocean views and high-end amenities such as cable TV and a swimming pool. ❽

HI-Hotel Capric Von Schroeders 39 ☎ 32/978295, ⓕ 32/697718, ⓔ hotelcapric@yahoo.com. This HI hostel offers probably the cheapest clean beds in Viña, in simple rooms off a courtyard. Smarter rooms with private bath are in the adjacent *Hotel Capric*, where you'll also find the reception. ❹

Hotel Agora 51/2 Poniente 253 ☎ 32/694669, ⓕ 32/695165, ⓦ www.hotelagora.cl. A fabulously stylish pastel-coloured hotel offering eight impeccable rooms in an Art Deco style that seems right out of Miami. On a quiet street close to the sea. ❹

Hotel Rokamar Viana 107 ☎ & ⓕ 32/690019, ⓦ www.hotelrokamar.cl. This spacious 28-room hotel in a refurbished 100-year-old mansion offers many extras, like customized meals, not usually found in this price range. ❹

Residencial De Casia Von Schroeders 151 ☎ 32/971861. Adequate, fairly clean rooms in an attractive building that's relatively handy for the bus and rail stations. ❹

Residencial Helene Misch 1 Poniente 239 ☎ 32/971565, ⓕ 32/972135. Attractive *residencial*, run by the same family for over fifty years; quiet, comfortable rooms and a well-tended front garden where you can have breakfast. ❹

The City

Viña del Mar falls into two separate sections, divided by the **Estero Marga Marga**, a filthy, stagnant lagoon (much of it now reclaimed for parking) that cuts through the town to the ocean. South of the Marga Marga is the old part of town, Viña's lively commercial centre with the **Plaza Vergara** (also known as the **Plaza de Viña**) and **Avenida Valparaíso** at its core. North of the river, you can access the main **beaches** – Viña boasts 3.5km of sandy coast – and this is also where you'll find most of the **restaurants** and **bars** catering to tourists.

Note that the beaches get very crowded in January and February, but you'll find a number of appealing distractions from the sand and sea: the **Quinta Vergara**, an extravagant subtropical park, and the Conaf-run **Jardín Botánico**, a short bus ride from the centre, more than justify the town's sobriquet of *Ciudad Jardín* ("Garden City"). Handsome old residences include the **Palacio Rioja**, whose opulent interior is intact, and the **Palacio Vergara** (in the Quinta Vergara) which now houses the **Museo de Bellas Artes**. Another worthwhile museum is the **Museo Fonck**, which has a top-notch indigenous and Easter Island collection. All of these can easily be visited in a couple of days.

Plaza Vergara and Avenida Valparaíso

Viña's centre is marked by the large, green **Plaza Vergara**, full of tall, stately trees and surrounded by some fine, early twentieth-century buildings including the **Teatro Municipal** (the imposing Neoclassical building with a sweeping flight of steps leading to a grand entrance), the stately **Hotel O'Higgins**, and the Italian Renaissance-style **Club de Viña**, an exclusive gentlemen's dining club (opposite department store Fallabella). You'll also find a string of ponies and traps hanging around the square, on which you can take tours of the town (CH$8000 for 30min). The south side of the square borders **Avenida Valparaíso**, Viña's main commercial street, lined with shops, malls and fast-food outlets, and constantly bustling with people. Much of the activity occurs in the five blocks between the plaza and Calle Ecuador, boasting modern, attractive shops and *galerías* far better than those in downtown Santiago. There's also a good **feria artesanal** in Pasaje Cousiño, a narrow passage off the south side of the avenue, just west of Plaza Vergara where you can find inexpensive silver jewellery, T-shirts and hand-carved wooden bowls.

Quinta Vergara and the Museo de Bellas Artes

The exceptionally beautiful park **Quinta Vergara** (daily 7am–6pm; closed on rainy days), filled with exotic, subtropical trees and surrounded by wooded hills, sits two blocks south of Plaza Vergara, across the railway tracks. Designed in the early days of the colony, this was the site of the *casa patronal* (main estate) of the Hacienda Las Siete Hermanas, owned by the prominent Carrera family. Around 1840, the hacienda was bought by a rich Portuguese businessman, Francisco Alvarez, whose wife – an amateur botanist – set out to fill her gardens with rare plants and trees. Their son, Salvador Alvarez, was a seaman and brought back species from his voyages to the Far East, many of which still survive in the immaculately maintained gardens. Besides exploring the groves, you can follow paths up the hillsides, or walk round to the amphitheatre where concerts are performed regularly, including the hugely hyped **Festival Internacional de la Canción** (International Music Festival). This kitsch pop music extravaganza locks millions of Chileans to their TV sets for one week straight every February, and is by far the area's biggest annual event. During this time, the traffic and the crowds are out of hand, and booking accommodation ahead is essential. Tickets for performances can be purchased at Ticketmaster booths inside the Feria del Disco – a chain of music stores. The festival is mainly thousands of teeny boppers screaming at their idols, and anyone over twenty will feel old, but it is also a great way to see Chileans celebrating.

In the centre of the Quinta Vergara, near the huge and unattractive new offices of the *Mercurio* newspaper, sits the **Palacio Vergara**, a dazzling, whitewashed Venetian-style palace built in 1906 for Blanca Vergara de Errázuriz – granddaughter of the above-mentioned Salvador, and daughter of José Francisco Vergara, who officially founded Viña in 1874. The palace is now home to the **Museo de Bellas Artes** (Tues–Sun 10am–2pm & 3–6pm; CH$600), which has a decent collection of Chilean and European paintings from the fifteenth to nineteenth centuries, including works by **Rubens**, **Poussin** and a portrait by **Tintoretto** of a Venetian gentleman whose startling blue eyes and delicately lit face really stand apart from the other works.

Palacio Rioja and Palacio Carrasco

North of the Marga Marga at Quillota 214 you'll find the **Palacio Rioja**, built in the style of an eighteenth-century French chateau and surrounded by a sumptuous park, all that remains of the once extensive vineyards that gave the town its name. It was built in 1906 for Don Fernando Rioja Medel, a Spanish millionaire who owned the Banco Español among other enterprises. His family lived here until 1956, when the building was acquired by the Municipalidad which now runs it as a reception centre and a **museum** (Tues–Sun 10am–1.30m & 3–5.30pm; CH$600). The entire ground floor is perfectly preserved and provides a fascinating close-up view of early twentieth-century luxury, with its belle epoque furniture and glittering ballroom; the four daily guided tours are informative but in Spanish only. In the summer, the *Conservatorio de Música* (which occupies the former servants' quarters in the basement) gives concerts in the palace – check in the Oficina de Turismo (see p.164) for details.

Nearby, at Libertad 250, is the **Palacio Carrasco** (Mon–Fri 9.30am–1pm & 2–7pm, Sat & Sun 9.30am–1pm), an elegant, three-storey building designed in a French Neoclassical style by Alfredo Azancot Lei, the same architect responsible for the Palacio Rioja. It's owned by the Municipalidad, which runs it as the **Centro Cultural de Viña del Mar**, hosting a lively programme of exhibitions, plays and talks. The building also houses the municipal library and the city's historical archives.

Museo Francisco Fonck

The excellent **Museo Francisco Fonck**, just around the corner from the Palacio Carrasco at 4 Norte 784 (Tues–Sat 10am–6pm, Sun 10am–2pm; CH$1000), has one of the most important **Easter Island collections** in Chile, plus some fascinating pre-Hispanic exhibits and a modest natural history collection – the

refurbished ground floor is beautifully presented with an English-language explanation. The museum takes its name from the Prussian medic Franz Fonck (1830–1912) who studied botanical and archeological sites in central Chile and left his collections to the state. One of the museum's best pieces stands in the garden, by the entrance: a giant stone *moai*, brought to Chile from Easter Island by the Sociedad Fonck in 1950, and one of just six that exist outside the island. Inside, the three ground-floor rooms dedicated to Easter Island include wooden and stone carvings of those long, stylized faces (some of them around 500 years old), as well as jewellery, weapons, household and fishing utensils, and ceremonial objects. The rest of the ground floor

△ Museo Francisco Fonck

contains the pre-Hispanic collections, including some delicate Mapuche silver-work such as head and breast ornaments, musical instruments and bearded masks, and the 2000-year-old mummy of a small, huddled child found in an ancient burial site south of Arica. Upstairs, the dowdy and musty natural history section has some rather unsettling displays, among them a caseful of scorpions and photos of limbs deformed by their venom and an embalmed two-headed lamb, born in Casablanca in 1950. The museum shops sells good postcards and fine artwork inspired by Rapa Nui crafts.

The beaches and around

Viña's most central beach, and the only one south of the Marga Marga, is the **Playa Caleta Abarca**, a sheltered, sandy bay at the eastern end of Calle Viana. Just off the beach, at the foot of Cerro Castillo, you'll find the much-photographed **Reloj de Flores**, a large clock composed of colourful bedding plants and working dials. From here, the promenade continues north past the neo-Gothic **Castillo Wulff**, its spire and turrets jutting into the sea. Built in 1906 for a nitrate and coal baron, the house features a glass-floored passage with waves breaking below. For many years this was a museum, and though it is now closed to the public, you can always ask for an informal look around.

Just beyond the Castillo Wulff is the **Estero Marga Marga** – follow it inland a couple of blocks to reach the bridge that crosses it. On the other side, the **Casino Municipal** offers the usual slot machines, card games and top perform-ances by Chilean singers and performers – but it's also useful for its loos, air-conditioned restaurant and the all-night disco in the basement. The Casino sits in the middle of finely landscaped gardens, skirted by the coast road, **Avenida Perú**, which (once past the casino gardens) is lined by high-rise condominiums, ice-cream parlours and restaurants. A pedestrian promenade runs alongside the ocean but there's no sand here, just a stretch of rocks. A few blocks north, Avenida Perú swerves inland to make way for the long unbroken strip of sand stretching for over 3km towards Reñaca (see p.172). Though effec-tively one single beach, the different sections are each given their own name: just north of Avenida Perú is **Playa Acapulco**, a 200-metre-long beach that is very popular with locals but a bit hemmed in by high-rises, followed by **Playa El Sol** and **Playa Los Marineros**, which are often too rough for much swim-ming but packed thanks to easy parking. Finally there is **Playa Larga**, which has restaurants, showers and parking – all making it very crowded in summer. To get to the beaches, take any of the Reñaca or Concón buses from Puente Libertad (the bridge over the lagoon just north of Plaza Vergara), and get off at 10 or 12 Norte for Playas Acapulco and El Sol or ask the driver to let you off on the coast road for the beaches further north.

Eating, drinking and entertainment

Viña's **restaurants** are among the most varied outside the capital, and while many are geared towards tourists, the quality is usually good, and they offer some welcome alternatives to the *comida típica* you're restricted to in many other towns. Most, however, are fairly expensive, and if you're on a tight budget you'll have to make do with the fast-food outlets on Avenidas Valparaíso and San Martín.

Nightlife tends to be seasonal, reaching a heady peak in January and Febru-ary when everyone flocks to the clubs and bars of **Reñaca**, a suburb further up the coast (see p.172). During the summer months, *micros* run to and from Reñaca right through the night. In winter, the partying dies out, and the focus shifts back to Viña.

The grand **Teatro Municipal** (℡32/681739) puts on theatre, classical music and dance performances, and there's an excellent arts **cinema**, the Cine Arte on the Plaza Vergara (through the passage off the west side of the square). For mainstream movies, check out the Olimpo at Quinta 294 and Cinemark at the Mall Marina Arauco, on Libertad and 15 Norte.

Restaurants

Delicias del Mar San Martín 459. Smart Basque-influenced *marisquería* with a loyal clientele, mellow atmosphere and lots of fabulous chardonnays and semillons to choose from to accompany the crab lasagne or paella.

Fogón Criollo 5 Norte 476, near corner with 2 Poniente. Upmarket replica of a rural Chilean country restaurant. The *comida típica Chilena* is outstanding – try the spicy pork *arollados*, or the *conejo escabechado* (a rabbit casserole).

Han's Dragon Libertad and 8 Norte. Excellent Chinese restaurant specializing in sizzling *platos estilo Hong Kong*. Affordable fixed-price meals begin at CH$1600.

La Gula 5 Norte 147. Great pizzeria serving crispy ham and Roquefort pies on wooden boards; it's a shame about the noisy TV.

La Fourchette 3 Norte 370. Chic, pricey bistro where the menu reads like the culinary wish list of a Frenchman abroad: onion soup, snails and foie gras as starters, followed by fish in saffron sauce and other cordon bleu wonders.

Marisquería Isabel II C Mercado, opposite the Mercado Municipal. Local restaurant serving authentic, inexpensive fish dishes. Try the huge fish stew known as *paila marina*.

El Sin Nombre Pasaje Cousiño 12, off Av Valparaíso. Inexpensive bar-restaurant that specializes in cheap grills and fried fish, with live music or comedy at weekends.

Bars and clubs

Barlovento 2 Norte 145. Upmarket drinking spot.

Barolo 4 Norte 147. Posh pub catering to a moneyed casino crowd.

El Burro Pasaje Cousiño, off Av Valparaíso. Large, dark bar that turns into a disco after midnight on Friday and Saturday. Hugely popular with a mixed crowd of foreigners and local students. Cheap beer.

Gato Luna Arlegui 396. Local, sociable bar with Latin jazz and dancing at weekends.

Journal Agua Santa and Alvarez. Viña's university hangout, serving pitchers of beer around the clock (or until the wee hours, anyway).

Ovo Casino Municipal. *The* place to be seen sipping a pisco sour and showing off your fashionable attire; without a doubt, Viña's swishest nightclub.

Scratch Quillota and 12 Norte. This long-time favourite for dancing, in a new location, draws a university and older crowd; it's packed until sunrise most weekends.

Listings

Airlines LAN, Ecuador 80 (℡32/690365).

Banks and exchange Most banks and *cambios* are on Arlegui: of the *cambios*, try Afex at no. 641, Cambio Andino at no. 644. Banks on Arlegui (all with ATMs) include Banco Bhif at no. 665; Scotiabank, Plaza Vergara 103; BCI, Valparaíso 193; and Citibank, 1 Norte 633.

Bookshops Eurotex, in Galería Paseo del Mar, Valparaíso 554, for English-language fiction. Second-hand English novels (mostly best-seller types) available in Contactolibros, Von Schroeders 181.

Car rental Hertz, Quillota 766 ℡32/689918; March Rent a Car, Libertad 1080 ℡32/381080.

Internet *Cyber Blues Café*, Av. Valparaíso 196.

Laundry Lavarapido, Arlegui 440, three blocks west of Plaza Vergara.

Post office Next to the Oficina de Turismo, between Plaza Vergara and Puente Libertad.

Telephone offices Several offices near one another: at Valparaíso 628, near Pasaje Cousiño; at the corner of Valparaíso and Villanelo; at Valparaíso 510; and at 14 Norte 1184.

Tours Aguitur, Galeriá Fontana, Arlegui 364 Office 223 (℡32/711052) is the mainstay Viña tour association. They can arrange tours up and down the coast by day or by night. Prices range from half-day (CH$20,000 per person) to full-day (CH$35,000 per person).

Moving on from Viña

Buses that go **up the coast** (Central Placeres or Sol del Pacífico) don't stop at the bus terminal, but at Avenida Libertad (just north of Puente Libertad), with frequent services to Reñaca and Concón, and several daily to Horcón, Maitencillo, Zapallar and Papudo. *Colectivos* also pass this way en route to Reñaca and Concón. To go **down the coast**, your best bet is to catch a bus from **Valparaíso** (see p.147), reached by any *micro* (every 10min) marked "Puerto" or "Aduana" from Plaza Vergara or Arlegui. You can also get to Valparaíso by train (every 15–30min) from the station at the corner of Bohn and Sucre, just south of Plaza Vergara, or by boat from Muelle Vergara. **Intercity buses** leave from the bus terminal on Avenida Valparaíso, two blocks east of Plaza Vergara (**to Santiago** every 15min, 6am–9.30pm), along with buses **to Mendoza** in Argentina (daily 8.30am). For more information see "Travel Details" on p.178.

Jardín Botánico Nacional

Set in a sheltered valley surrounded by sun-baked hills, the Conaf-run **Jardín Botánico Nacional** (Tues–Sun 10am–6.30pm; CH$700; ☎35/672566) contains 3000 plant species from Chile and other Latin American countries, as well as Europe and Asia. It's just 6km from the centre of Viña but feels far more remote – take a short walk along its quiet paths and you'll feel you're right out in the countryside. The jardín is a ten-minute bus ride (#20, eastbound) from Calle Bohn.

North of Viña

North of Viña, the coast road meanders to the small fishing village of **Papudo**, about 75km away, and beyond to the farming town of **La Ligua** from where, via the Panamericana, you'll reach the family resort of **Los Vilos**. Hugging the oceanside in some stretches, darting inland in others, the northern coast road is far quieter than its southern counterpart, and very beautiful in some parts, particularly the northern reaches towards Papudo as you approach the parched hills and rugged outlines of the Norte Chico. **Cachagua** and **Zapallar** are the most exclusive resorts along this coast, catering mostly to wealthy visitors from Santiago who have their holiday residences here. Countless local buses head to **Reñaca** and neighbouring **Concón**, but services to the other resorts further north are less frequent; most can also be reached directly from Santiago (see "Travel details" on p.141). Unless you have your own vehicle, your best option is to pick one or two places and head for these, rather than resort-hopping up the coast, which is slow and tiresome on public transport, and doesn't offer enough variety to be worth the effort.

Reñaca

Lively **REÑACA**, just 6km north of central Viña, is a 1.5-kilometre stretch of coast swamped by bars, restaurants and terraced apartment blocks stacked up the hillside. It's among the country's cleanest beaches and the favoured resort of Chile's beautiful young things, who flock to its long beach by day and its bars and discos by night. Many people make day-trips from Santiago or stay further north and come in for an evening of dancing and drinking.

Accommodation here is expensive, with the exception of a pleasant camp-site on Santa Luisa 401 (☎32/832830; $15,000 per site); it's quite a steep walk from the beach but you can take the Concón bus up and down the hill. Otherwise, you're better off staying in Valparaíso or Viña and travelling here by *micro*. Reñaca's **discos** are also pricey (average cover about CH$10,000) but remain resolutely popular throughout the summer season; the most fashionable include *Kamikaze*, in from the coast at Vicuña Mackenna 1106. Every summer a host of new clubs appears, and others disappear, so ask around for the latest – there are always a slew of options for dancing on Thursday, Friday and Saturday nights.

Concón

CONCÓN, 10km north of Reñaca, is a funny sort of place: part concrete terraced apartment blocks, part elegant villas with flower-filled gardens, and part rundown, working-class fishing village, with six beaches spread out along the bay. When the wind is blowing south, nasty fumes from the nearby oil refinery may chase you away. From Reñaca, two roads head up here, one clinging to the scenic rocky coastline (passing a small sea lion colony off *El Mirador de los Lobos Marinos*), the other – followed by most buses – running inland, on the other side of the immense sand dunes rising steeply from the sea.

The most interesting bit of town is **La Boca**, the ramshackle commercial centre at the mouth of the Río Aconcagua. The *caleta* here was used to export the produce of the haciendas of the Aconcagua valley in the nineteenth century and is now a bustling fish quay, lined with modest, down-to-earth **marisquerías**, many with freshly caught fish hanging up for sale over the counter. They all serve first-rate seafood, particularly *La Perla del Pacífico*, Borgoño 25007, which stands out for its cooking, using the freshest crustaceans, if not for its ambience, which is positively ramshackle. You can also **rent horses** for beach trips from the men standing about the cluster of horses; the fee should be about US$5 an hour.

The most developed and popular beaches are **Playa Amarilla** and **Playa Negra**, south of La Boca, both of which see lots of bodyboarding. Concón makes an easy day-trip from Viña, but if you want **to stay** over, try *Mantagua* (☎32/811415, ⓦ www.mantagua.cl, ❻), which has expensive but well-furnished cabins as well as a well-maintained **campsite** (CH$17,000 per site). The camp-site is 3km north of the bridge over the Río Aconcagua and is wonderfully isolated outside of high season - and heavy discounts are usually available.

Horcón

The charming and picturesque – if slightly tatty – fishing village of **HORCÓN**, about 30km north of Concón, is a chaotic tumble of houses straggling down

△ Horcón

the hill to a rocky bay. (En route, you'll pass Quintero, a scruffy, forbidding town with filthy beaches, to be avoided at all costs.) In the summer, Horcón is taken over by artisans on the beach selling jewellery made from seashells and leather goods, and unfeasible numbers of young Chileans who come to chill out for the weekend. This is the alternative to Reñaca, catering to the sizeable hippy element of Chile's youth. Outside the heady summer months, Horcón takes on a quieter air: old men sit around the decaying fishing centre and talk about the weather, and not a great deal seems to happen.

The **beach** in front of the village is narrow, crowded and uninviting, but a short walk up the main street and then along Avenida Cau-Cau takes you down a steep, rickety staircase (watch out for protruding nails) to the remote **Playa Cau-Cau**, a pleasantly sheltered beach surrounded by wooded hills. The much respected *Caballo de Mar* **restaurant** – try the grilled fish – has been carefully built into the cliffs but a hideous condominium now mars the beauty of the area. In town, try the excellent, good-value *marisquerías* clustered around the fishermen's stalls. You'll find comfortable **rooms** at the relatively tasteful *Hostería Arancibia,* down by the waterfront (☎32/796169; ❹).

Maitencillo

Stretching 4km along one main street, **MAITENCILLO** is little more than a long, narrow strip of holiday homes, *cabañas* and hotels along the shoreline, catering to families from the capital who want to get away from it all. The chief reason for coming here is **Playa Aguas Blancas**, a superb white-sand beach sweeping 5km south of the village, backed by steep sandstone cliffs. For something a little different, **paragliding** professionals *Parapente Aventura* (☎32/770019 or 9/3322426, ❿www.parapente-aventura.cl) offer half-hour flights above the dunes for CH$25,000. To find them, head to the southern exit of Maitencillo and halfway up the hill on the right you'll see the sign; a short dirt road takes you to the hilltop launch site.

The best **accommodation** at Playa Aguas Blancas is *Cabañas Donde Julián*, Av Del Mar 78 (☎ & ⑤ 32/771091; ⑤) offering a handful of spacious cabins looking right onto the ocean; bargain hard outside high season for a discount. The highly recommended *Cabañas Hermansen*, Av del Mar 0592 (☎ 32/771026, ⑤), sit a five-minute drive north of Aguas Blancas and offer great views of the beach, nicely crafted cabins, bike rental and plenty of helpful tourist information. One block from the cabins is the only decent **bar** in the area, *La Canasta*, which attracts surfers from surrounding towns and builds up a rowdy crowd during the summer. Towards the northern end of the shore, *Residencial Abanico*, at Av del Mar 664 (☎ 32/771141; ④), has comfortable rooms and private bath. You'll find excellent, imaginatively prepared **seafood** at *El Tubo* (aka *La Pajarera*), ⚔ a wacky building with great vistas; it's towards the southern end of Avenida del Mar (and linked by funicular to *Marbella Resort*, an exclusive Club Med-type complex on top of the cliff.) *Restaurant La Caleta*, just off Playa La Caleta, is more homespun and less expensive. In between the two is the excellent *Tasca*, ⚔ where the service is extremely welcoming and the fish is fabulous – and make sure to leave room for the tasty desserts. If you're staying in a *cabaña* with a kitchen, choose your supper from the hooks of fish and buckets of clams, oysters and mussels at the morning market by the *caleta* and cook it yourself.

Cachagua

CACHAGUA, a short way north of Maitencillo, is home to a stunning beach, with a wide expanse of pale sand curling round the bay, backed by gentle hills. It is also synonymous with the Chilean upper crust, who parade about the unmade roads in their leather loafers and wool sweaters regardless of the temperature, then rush back to Santiago to see if they made the society pages. Cachagua is blessed by a relative lack of holiday homes and *cabañas* on the land off the beach, which is instead given over to a golf course. Ask for directions to the long staircase from Avenida del Mar down to **Playa Las Cujas**, a tiny beach that is spectacular – and often empty. Just off the coast, the Isla de los Pingüinos is a **penguin sanctuary**. Local fishermen sometimes offer boat rides to the island for CH$6000 per person – accept at your peril, for the smell of hundreds of Humboldt penguins can be nauseating.

What little **accommodation** Cachagua offers is up in the village, back from the beach: simple, adequate rooms are rented by Sra Albertina Sepúlveda, at Cachagua 658 (☎ 33/771044; ④), and by Sra Juana Ormeño, at Nemesio Vicuña 250 (☎ 33/771034; ④). To **eat**, you'll have to make do with the uninspiring fries and grills dished up at *Donde Juanito*, Cachagua 264, and *El Pollo con Chaleco*, nearby on the other side of the road.

Zapallar

Arguably the classiest and most attractive of all the Litoral's resorts, **ZAPALLAR** is set on a sheltered, horseshoe bay backed by lushly wooded hills where luxurious holiday homes and handsome old mansions nestle between the pine trees; the overall effect is not unlike one of the exclusive resorts on the Italian Riviera. Relaxing on the beach is the principal attraction, but you can also stroll along the coastal path around the bay, or walk up Avenida Zapallar, admiring the early-twentieth-century mansions A more strenuous possibility would be to hire a sea-kayak in the tiny harbour, where pelicans and gulls dive into the crystal-clear waters, or to climb the 692-metre-high **Cerro Higuera** that rises sharply between Zapallar and Papudo: the path, starting across the main road behind the tennis club, is very difficult to find, but the views from the top are superb. Go down the other side, to Papudo, where you can catch a *micro* back to Zapallar; allow about three hours up, and a couple of hours to get down.

If you feel like splashing out, the stylish *Hotel Isla Seca* ✠ (☎33/741224, ℱ33/741226; ●) up by the main road, at the northern end of the bay, offers quality **rooms**, its own pool and magnificent views, while *Residencial Villa Alicia*, Moisés Chacón 280 (☎33/741176; ●), is a good deal simpler but comfortable enough. Also, the woman in the shop next to the bus stop might be able to let you know who's renting private rooms in town. For **dining**, there's the excellent and pricey restaurant at the *Hotel Isla Seca*, which now has a beautiful rooftop terrace where you can feast on their special crab cakes. *El Chiringuito* (☎33/741024), ✠ down by the *caleta* at the southern tip of the bay, serves up legendary seafood – the scallops are absolutely divine – at marginally better prices. Note that it closes a few days of the week in the off season.

Papudo

The development in **PAPUDO**, just 10km around the headland, hasn't been as graceful as in neighbouring Zapallar, and several ugly buildings mar the seafront. That said, the steep hills looming dramatically behind the town are undeniably beautiful, and the place has a friendly, local atmosphere, particularly outside high season. The best beach is the long **Playa Grande**, which boasts dunes and sheltered sunbathing on the northern part. In fine weather, you can hire horses here and go for exhilarating rides across the sands.

Papudo has a wealth of **accommodation** centred mainly around the town square and on Fernández Concha, branching off from it. All the following offer clean rooms with private bath: *Residencial Armandini* at Fernández Concha 525 (☎33/791139; ●), *Hotel Moderno* at Fernández Concha 150 (☎33/791114, ℱ33/790165; ●; the rooms in main building are best), and *La Abeja*, at Chorrillos 3036 (☎ & ℱ33/791116; ●), near the beach. Papudo also has the most offbeat **restaurant** along the entire coast: *El Barco Rojo* (☎33/791488) on Playa Grande, owned by a hip young Parisian who arranges funky jazz and Latin concerts in his restaurant by night. The famous seafood menu is inexpensive and fantastic, and there's an excellent wine list.

La Ligua

The chief appeal of **LA LIGUA**, a bustling agricultural town, is its setting, enfolded by undulating hills that take on a rich honey glow in the early evening sunlight. La Ligua is also known for its confectionery, and all along the Panamericana Santiago-Arica highway near the crossroads leading to Papudo, to

The infamous La Quintrala of La Ligua

La Ligua was once notorious throughout the colony as the home of one of Chile's darkest figures: Doña Catalina de Los Ríos y Lispergeuer, or **La Quintrala**. Descended from one of the soldiers who formed Pedro de Valdivia's original band of colonizers, she was born in 1600 and inherited the large Hacienda de La Ligua. The female Lispergeuers were already known for their violent natures: Catalina's grandmother had murdered her husband by pouring mercury into his ears as he slept, and her mother had whipped one of her stepdaughters to death and attempted to poison the governor of Chile. Catalina proved herself to be more than their equal when, at 23, she murdered her father by serving him a poisoned chicken. The following year she killed a Knight of the Order of St John (after seducing him), and forced one of her servants to "confess" to the crime, for which he was hanged. Curiously, her bloody tendencies seemed to vanish during her twenty-four-year-marriage to Captain Alonso Campofrío Carvajal – only to return with added fervour when she became a widow at the age of fifty. It was at this point that she embarked on her most brutal period, regularly whipping and torturing her numerous slaves, often to the point of death. In 1660, the Bishop of Santiago appealed to the Real Audiencia (Royal Court) to intervene and investigate her behaviour. The enquiry concluded that she had murdered 39 people on her estate, without counting the murders committed before her marriage. La Quintrala evaded justice to the end, however, by dying before the charges could be brought against her. Today, in rural areas near La Ligua, her name still strikes fear in the hearts of children, warned by their mothers that if they are naughty La Quintrala will come to get them.

the west, and La Ligua, to the east, you'll see groups of energetic white-coated women waving at you to sell their *dulces de La Ligua* – sweet, sugary cakes famous throughout Chile.

In town, the limited attractions include the **Museo Arqueológico** at Pedro Polanco 698 (Tues–Fri 9.30am–1pm & 3.30–6.30pm, Sat 10am–2pm; CH$500), with displays including the skeleton and reconstructed burial site of a thirty-year-old Diaguita woman, ritually burned in the late sixteenth century. As for shopping, you'll find a *huaso* shop on the corner of Esmeralda and Condell, with a vast range of cowboy goods, from ponchos and hats to belts, spurs and saddles. La Ligua has also built a reputation for its knitwear; an artisans' market on the main square and countless nearby shops sell the handmade woollen clothes, though many are of questionable taste. There's not much choice in the way of **restaurants** – try *Montemar* at Portales 699, or *Antares* at Portales 404, for basic meat dishes and pizzas.

Pichidangui

North of the Papudo-La Ligua crossroads, the Panamericana follows the coast for some 200km before dipping inland again, towards Ovalle (see p.183). This stretch of highway takes you past a succession of gorgeous, white-sand **beaches** dotted with a few fishing villages and small resorts. Most of the time the beaches are completely deserted but, in January and February, rows of tents are spontaneously erected along the coast, forming huge, improvised campsites. Along the road, you'll also spot vendors waving grotesque goat's carcasses at passing cars, and stalls selling homemade cheeses, a regional speciality.

Set 4km back from the Panamericana, 50km beyond the Papudo-La Ligua interchange, is **PICHIDANGUI**, with a lovely beach that's up there with Chile's finest. The sudden sight of it as you reach the coastal avenue is quite stunning – 7km of white, powdery sand fringed by deep-green eucalyptus trees. There's little beachfront development to spoil the view, and the small town holds back from the shoreline, clinging to the rocky peninsula south of the bay. You'll find some decent **accommodation** should you choose to make a halt: *Residencial Lucero*, at the corner of Albacora and Dorado (☎53/531106; ❷–❸), has rather basic rooms with and without bath, while *La Rosa Náutica*, at El Dorado 120 (☎53/531133; ❹), offers more luxury and a good **restaurant**. Down in the eucalyptus woods backing onto the beach are some rustic but comfortable *cabañas* – try *Bahía Marina* (☎53/531120; ❻) – and an excellent **campsite**, *Camping El Bosque* (☎53/531030; CH$4500 per person).

Buses head to Los Molles and Pichidangui from the capital's Terminal de Buses Santiago (Condor Bus; ☎2/7793721) and from Valparaíso (Buses La Porteña, which leave from the company's office at Molina 366; ☎32/216568); the journey takes around three hours.

Los Vilos

Local legend has it that **LOS VILOS**, 30km north of Pichidangui, takes its name from the Hispanic corruption of "Lord Willow", a British pirate who was shipwrecked on the coast and decided to stay. It later became notorious as a danger spot where highway robbers held up horse-drawn carriages travelling between Santiago and La Serena, relieving their occupants of all their belongings and sometimes murdering them for good measure. These days it's a lively, cheerful seaside town that makes a great place to spend a couple of days by the sea without paying over the odds, with a wide choice of inexpensive *residenciales* and restaurants. The flip side to its affordability, however, is that it gets incredibly packed in January and February. The town's chief attraction is its long golden **beach**, but you could also pass an hour or two taking a boat trip around the harbour, wandering through the **fish market** on the *caleta*, or walking out to the **Isla de los Lobos**, a 1500-strong seal colony 200m off the coast, reached by a five-kilometre jeep track just south of the bay.

On the town's main street, *Residencial Central,* Av Caupolicán 693 (no phone; ❷), offers decent budget **rooms**, some with sea views. The clean, antique-filled *Residencial Vienesa* is at Av Los Vilos 11 (☎53/541143; ❷). *Hostería Lord Willow*, overlooking the beach at Av Los Vilos 1444 (☎53/541037; ❹), offers rooms with private bath that are more pleasant but overpriced. For reliable **seafood**, try *Costanera*, overlooking the bay at Purén 080 or the little *marisquerías* opposite the fish market. *Casa de Piedra* on the Panamericana, near the Shell station, is a more upmarket alternative, offering fish and seafood in elaborately prepared sauces.

From the capital, **buses** to Los Vilos leave from Terminal de Buses Santiago (Condor Bus; ☎2/7793721) or Terminal San Borja (Tacc Via Choapa ☎2/7787570, Combarbalá ☎2/7787362 and TurBus ☎2/2707500), taking just over three hours. From La Serena, several companies travel to Los Vilos, including Tas Choapa (☎51/225959), Tacc Expreso Norte (☎51/224857) and Pullman (☎51/225152); this trip also takes about three hours.

Travel details

Buses

Valparaíso to: Arica (15 daily; 26hr); Copiapó (6 daily, 11hr); Coquimbo (10 daily; 6hr); Isla Negra (every 15min; 1hr 30min); La Serena (16 daily, 6hr); Maitencillo (4 daily; 1hr 40min); Papudo (4 daily; 2hr); Puerto Montt (4 daily; 16hr); Santiago (every 15min; 1hr 30min); Temuco (3 daily, 9hr 30min); Viña del Mar (every 10min; 15min); Zapallar (hourly; 1hr 40min).

Viña del Mar to: Arica (2 daily; 26hr); Concón (every 15min; 15min); Copiapó (10 daily, 11hr); Horcón (hourly; 1hr); La Serena (12 daily; 6hrs); Maitencillo (hourly; 1hr 20min); Papudo (3 daily; 1hr 45min); Puerto Montt (4 daily; 16hr); Reñaca (every 15min; 25min); Santiago (every 15min; 1hr 30min); Zapallar (hourly; 1hr 30min).

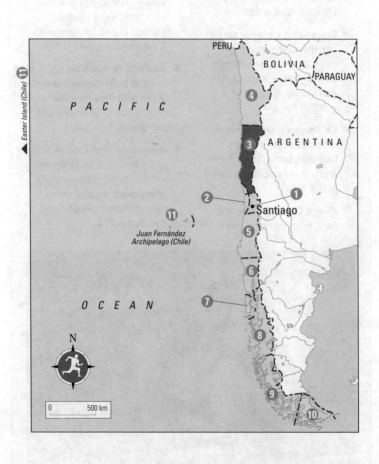

3

El Norte Chico

PERU

BOLIVIA

PARAGUAY

PACIFIC

ARGENTINA

4

3

2

1

Santiago

5

Juan Fernández
Archipelago (Chile)

11

6

7

OCEAN

8

N

9

10

0   500 km

CHAPTER 3 # Highlights

✱ **Feria Modelo de Ovalle** Wander this food market and fill your bags with plump olives, giant pumpkins, ripe tomatoes and very smelly cheeses. See p.185

✱ **Stargazing** Observe the unbelievably limpid night skies at two public-friendly observatories, at Andacollo and Vicuña. See p.189 & p.202

✱ **La Serena** Chile's second-oldest city offers long beaches, beautiful churches and a lively ambience. See p.192

✱ **Planta Capel** Sample the fiery, fruity brandy, Chile's national drink, straight from the barrel at the Elqui Valley's largest distillery. See p.201

✱ **Horse-riding in the Elqui Valley** Pretend you're in the Wild West as you gallop through Chile's untrammeled northern plains. See p.204

✱ **Desierto florido** If you're lucky to be in the right place at the right time, see the desert around Vallenar burst into bloom. See p.208

✱ **Nevado de Tres Cruces** One of the country's least-known national parks, with emerald-green lakes, snow-capped volcanoes and plentiful wild-life. See p.214

△ Horse-riding in El Norte Chico

El Norte Chico

A land of rolling, sun-baked hills streaked with sudden river valleys that cut across the earth in a flash of green, the **NORTE CHICO**, or "Little North", of Chile is what geographers call a "transitional zone". Its semi-arid scrubland and sparse vegetation mark the transformation from the country's fertile heartland to the barren deserts bordering Peru and Bolivia. From the Santiago perspective, the region is dubbed Norte Chico to distinguish it from the Norte Grande, or Great North (see next chapter). Starting somewhere around the Río Aconcagua, just north of Santiago, it stretches all the way to Taltal, and the southernmost reaches of the Atacama, more than 800km further north.

In between, a series of **rivers** – notably the Choapa, the Limarí, the Elqui, the Huasco and the Copiapó – flow year-round from the Andes to the coast, allowing the surrounding land to be irrigated and cultivated. The result is spectacular: lush, vibrant green terraces laden with olives, apricots and vines snake between the brown, parched walls of the valleys, forming a sensational visual contrast. The most famous product of these valleys is **pisco**, the pale, aromatic brandy distilled from sun-dried grapes and treasured by Chileans as their national drink (a claim vigorously contested by the Peruvians, who consider it their own).

Far more than agriculture, though, it's **mining** that has really shaped the region's growth, giving birth to towns, ports, railways and roads, and drawing large numbers of settlers to seek their fortune here. **Gold** was mined first by the Incas for ritual offerings, and then intensively, to exhaustion, by the Spaniards until the end of the eighteenth century. Next came the great **silver** bonanza of the nineteenth century, when a series of dramatic silver strikes – some of them accidental – set a frenzy of mining and prospecting in motion, propelling the region into its heyday. Further riches and glory came when the discovery of huge **copper** deposits turned the region into the world's largest copper producer from the 1840s to 1870s. Mining is still the most important regional industry, its presence most visible up in the cordillera, where huge mining trucks hurtle around the mountain roads, enveloped in clouds of dust.

The largest population centre – and one of the country's most fashionable seaside resorts – is **La Serena**, its pleasing, colonial-style architecture and lively atmosphere making it one of the few northern cities worth visiting for its own sake. It's also an ideal base for exploring the beautiful **Elqui Valley**, immortalized in the verses of the Nobel laureate Gabriela Mistral, and home to luxuriant vines and idyllic riverside hamlets. Less well-known but even more dramatic, the **Hurtado Valley**, to the south, features virgin trekking territory which can be reached from the unassuming market town of **Ovalle**. Just down the coast from La Serena lies the **Parque Nacional Fray Jorge**, with a microclimate that

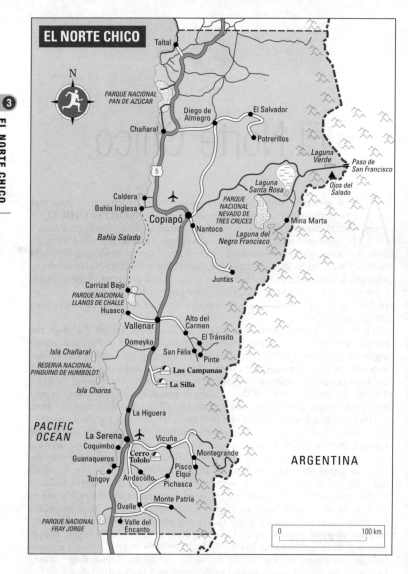

EL NORTE CHICO

Taltal

N

PARQUE NACIONAL PAN DE AZÚCAR

Diego de Almagro

El Salvador

Chañaral

Potrerillos

Laguna Verde

Paso de San Francisco

Caldera

Bahía Inglesa

Copiapó

Ojos del Salado

PARQUE NACIONAL NEVADO DE TRES CRUCES

Laguna Santa Rosa

Nantoco

Bahía Salado

Mina Marta

Laguna del Negro Francisco

Juntas

Carrizal Bajo

PARQUE NACIONAL LLANOS DE CHALLE

Huasco

Vallenar

Alto del Carmen

El Tránsito

Isla Chañaral

Domeyko

San Félix

Pinte

Las Campanas

RESERVA NACIONAL PINGUINO DE HUMBOLDT

La Silla

Isla Choros

La Higuera

PACIFIC OCEAN

La Serena

Vicuña

Coquimbo

Cerro Tololo

Montegrande

Guanaqueros

Pisco Elqui

ARGENTINA

Tongoy

Andacollo

Pichasca

Monte Patria

Ovalle

PARQUE NACIONAL FRAY JORGE

Valle del Encanto

0   100 km

supports a small, damp cloudforest – rather mangy compared to the great forests of the south but quite extraordinary in this landscape of brittle shrubs and cactus plants. Another botanical wonder is the famous *desierto florido* or **flowering desert**. Occasionally, after heavy winter rains, the normally dry earth sprouts vast expanses of vibrantly coloured flowers. This rare, unpredictable phenomenon, centred on **Vallenar**, occurs on average once every four to eight years.

Skies that are guaranteed cloudless almost year-round and very little air pollution have made the region the obvious choice for some of the world's major

astronomical observatories. They range from the state-of-the art facility at dazzling-white **Tololo** to the modest municipal installation at **Mamalluca**, near the picturesque village of **Vicuña**, where you don't have to be an expert reserving months in advance to look through the telescope. One of the newest and most accessible is at **Andacollo**.

The Norte Chico also boasts a string of superb **beaches**, some totally deserted and many of them tantalizingly visible from the Panamericana as you enter the region, to the north of Santiago. **Bahía Inglesa** is famous throughout Chile for its turquoise waters, though increasingly prolific algae is turning the bay greener.

Copiapó, the northernmost major city in the region, serves as a useful spring-board for excursions into the nearby **desert** or, farther afield, up into the high cordillera. Here the **Parque Nacional Nevado de Tres Cruces**, the **Volcán Ojos de Salado** and **Laguna Verde** present some of Chile's most magnificent yet least-visited landscapes: snow-topped volcanoes, bleached-white salt flats and azure lakes. A couple of hours to the north, near the towering cliffs and empty beaches of **Parque Nacional Pan de Azúcar**, a small island is home to colonies of seals, countless pelicans and thousands of penguins.

Bear in mind that, whereas the Norte Grande, Chile's northernmost region, can be visited all year-round – with the possible exception of the Bolivian winter, December to February – the Norte Chico is at its best in the **summer months** (October–March) when the valleys are at their greenest, the coast is likelier to be free of fog and the ocean and sky are pure blue. On the downside, resorts like La Serena and Bahía Inglesa can be horribly overcrowded and over-priced in the high season, especially January.

Ovalle and around

North of Los Vilos, the Panamericana follows a trail of lonely *caletas* before straying inland, weaving its way through valleys that gradually take on the characteristic sunburnt, semi-arid tones of northern Chile. Evidence of farm-ing and habitation peters out, and soon you're in wild, open country where the only signs of life are the numerous goats that roam the hills. Almost 380km north of Santiago – some 140km beyond Los Vilos – a lone sign points to the little-visited **OVALLE**.

The town's main claim to fame is as the birthplace of one of the country's outstanding contemporary writers, Luis Sepúlveda (see p.629). It's also a good base for exploring the deeply rural **Limarí Valley**, home to a few low-key but worthwhile attractions. To the northeast, a scenic road – an alternative route to Vicuña and the Elqui Valley (see p.200) – winds slowly up into the moun-tains, passing ancient petrified wood stumps at **Pichasca** and the delightful oasis village of **Hurtado**, which is the main settlement along the dramatic but seldom visited **Hurtado Valley**. If you head west, you'll find a concentration of rock carvings in the **Valle del Encanto**, a hot springs resort at the **Termas de Socos** and the impressive cloudforest reserve of **Parque Nacional Fray Jorge**, attracting an increasing number of visitors.

The Town

The lively **Plaza de Armas**, with expansive lawns, nineteenth-century Phoenix palms and rows of jacaranda, marks Ovalle's centre. Dominating the east side of the square is the white-and-mustard 1849 **Iglesia San Vicente Ferrer**, a large, colonial-style church, with thick adobe walls and a diminutive tower.

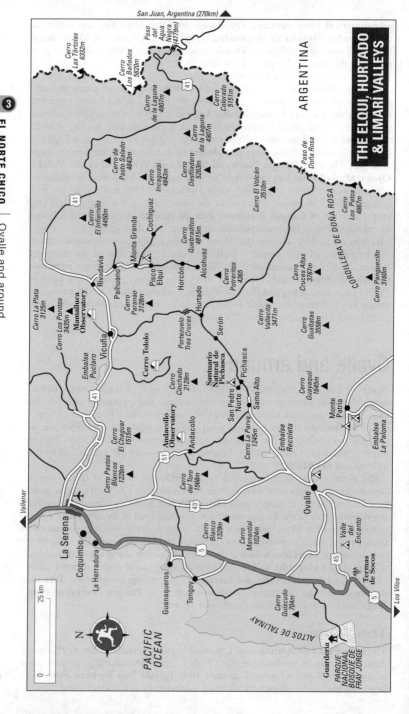

San Juan, Argentina (270km) ▲

Paso del Agua Negra (4779m)

Cerro Las Tórtolas 6332m

Cerro Los Bañados 5820m

ARGENTINA

41

Cerro Colorado 5151m

Cerro de Pasto Salado 4843m

Cerro de la Laguna 4907m

Cerro Incaguasi 4843m

Cerro Destilladero 5263m

Cerro de la Laguna 4907m

Paso de Doña Rosa

Cerro El Infiernillo 4450m

Monte Grande

Cochiguaz

Cerro Quebraditos 4815m

Cerro El Volcán 3510m

Cerro Los Patos 4867m

41

Rivadavia

Pisco Elqui

Horcón

Alcohuaz

Paihuano

Cerro Paranao 3128m

Hurtado

Cerro Potreritos 4365

CORDILLERA DE DOÑA ROSA

Cerro Panguecillo 3160m

Cerro La Plata 3125m

Cerro Los Porotos 3435m

Mamalluca Observatory

Vicuña

Serón

Cerro Vallecito 3471m

Cerro Cruces Altas 3787m

Embalse Puclaro

Cerro Tololo

Portezuelo Tres Cruces

Pichasca

Cerro Guaitatas 3558m

Cerro Cinchado 2129m

Santuario Natural de Pichasca

Samo Alto

Cerro Guayaquil 1645m

San Pedro Norte

THE ELQUI, HURTADO & LIMARÍ VALLEYS

Andacollo Observatory

Andacollo

Cerro La Parva 1245m

Embalse Recoleta

Monte Patria

Cerro Pastos Blancos 1228m

Cerro El Chaguar 1515m

51

Cerro del Toro 1568m

Embalse La Paloma

Vallenar ▲

La Serena

43

Ovalle

Cerro Blanco 1329m

Cerro Manantial 1024m

45

Valle del Encanto

Coquimbo

La Herradura

5

Guanaqueros

Tongoy

Termas de Socos

Cerro Quiscudo 704m

5

Los Vilos ▶

PACIFIC OCEAN

ALTOS DE TALINAY

PARQUE NACIONAL BOSQUE DE FRAY JORGE

Guardería

N

0   25 km

The streets around the square are narrow, traffic-choked and flanked by typical single-storey adobe houses. One of these streets, Libertad, has a couple of good traditional **leather shops** (opposite *Hotel Roxy*), where you'll find finely crafted belts, wallets, bags and *huaso* (cowboy) gear.

Ovalle's excellent **Museo del Limarí** (Tues–Fri 9am–6pm, Sat & Sun 10am–1pm; CH$600, free Sun) stands on the northeast edge of town in the grand old building that once housed the train station. About a third of the museum's 1800-piece collection of **Diaguita pottery** was damaged, some of it severely, in the 1997 earthquake, but the small amount on display is beautifully restored and shown to great effect in modern cases. Famed for its exquisite geometric designs painted in black, white and red onto terracotta surfaces, the pottery was produced by the Diaguita people who inhabited this part of Chile from 1000 AD until the Inca invasions in the sixteenth century.

Not far from the museum, about ten blocks east of the plaza (take an east-bound *micro* along Vicuña Mackenna), you'll find a huge, ramshackle iron hangar that houses the colourful **Feria Modelo de Ovalle** (Mon, Wed, Fri & Sat 6am–6pm), the largest fresh-produce market in the north of Chile and definitely worth a visit; you can pick up fantastic home-made cheeses (including some alarmingly pungent goat cheeses) as well as delicious dried figs and a vast range of fruit and vegetables.

Practicalities

If you arrive by **bus**, you'll be dropped at either the northern terminal, Terra-puerto Limarí, at Maestranza 443; or at the southern terminal, Medialuna, at Ariztia Oriente 769 (☎53/626612). In general, Tur Bus, Pullman, Tal and Flota Barrios buses stop at the former, while Pullman Carmelito, Covalle and Tas Choapa buses at the latter; some stop at both. Most also have offices and stops on the central Avenida Ariztía (known locally as the "Alameda"), three blocks east of the Plaza de Armas.

Much of the **accommodation** has seen better days; a few notable exceptions include the spruce *Hotel El Turismo*, Victoria 295 (☎ & ⓕ53/623536; ❺), offering spacious, well-kept rooms in a handsome old building with its own restaurant and parking; and the very similar *Gran Hotel*, at Vicuña Mackenna 210 (☎53/621084, ⓕ53/624122; ❹), albeit minus the restaurant and car park. For something more economical, try *Hotel Roxy*, Libertad 155 (☎53/620080; ❸), with comfortable if dated rooms ranged around a large, brightly painted patio filled with flowers, chairs and a cage of blackbirds.

Ovalle's **restaurants** tend to limit themselves to the standard dishes you find everywhere else in Chile – which is frustrating, considering this is the fresh-produce capital of the North. However, you will find a few worthwhile spots: sample the local river prawns and other carefully prepared dishes at *El Castillo*, ⚑ Av Romeral 10 (☎53/630584; closed Sun), in a handsome Art Nouveau villa in an otherwise rundown part of town not far from the Feria Modelo. Second best is *Los Braseros de Angello*, at the corner of Vicuña Mackenna and Santiago, serving delicious if unoriginal fare, including juicy *parrillas*, in pleasant surroundings marred only by the giant TV screen. Otherwise, the *Club Social de Ovalle*, on Vicuña Mackenna at no. 400, has decent fish and seafood. *Palmeiras*, Independencia 606, doles out traditional meat and fish in a large hall that fills with live music and dancing at weekends, while *El Quijote*, Arauco 294, is an intimate, bohemian sort of restaurant, with political graffiti and poetry on the walls, and an inexpensive menu featuring simple staples like *cazuela* and *lomo*. For snacks, drinks or a meal on Sunday, when everything else is closed, you can

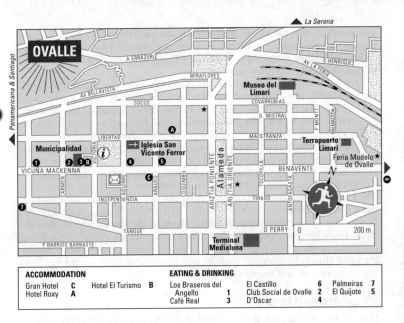

ACCOMMODATION			EATING & DRINKING			
Gran Hotel	**C**	Hotel El Turismo **B**	Los Braseros del		El Castillo	**6**	Palmeiras	**7**
Hotel Roxy	**A**		Angello	**1**	Club Social de Ovalle	**2**	El Quijote	**5**
			Café Real	**3**	D'Oscar	**4**	

do worse than *D'Oscar*, a café-bar on the southeast corner of the Plaza. If in need of real coffee, head to the appropriately named *Café Real*, Vicuña Mackenna 419, round the corner from *Hotel El Turismo*. You'll find several **ATMs** around the plaza.

Monumento Natural Pichasca and Hurtado

Northeast of Ovalle, a first-rate newly paved road climbs through the fertile Hurtado Valley, skirting – 12km out of town – the deep-blue expanse of water formed by the **Recoleta Dam**, one of three that irrigate the Limarí Valley. About 50km up the road, past a string of tiny villages, a side road to San Pedro de Pichasca dips down across the river leading, just beyond the village, to the Conaf-run **MONUMENTO NATURAL PICHASCA** (daily 9am–6pm; CH$1500), the site of a petrified wood, 70 million years old. As you arrive at the parking area, two paths diverge: the right-hand path leads north to a hillside scattered with stumps of **fossilized tree trunks**, some of them imprinted with the shape of leaves; the left-hand, or southern, path leads down to an enormous **cave** formed by an 80-metre gash in the hillside topped by a massive overhanging rock. Archeological discoveries inside the cave point to human habitation some 10,000 years ago. On market days it's possible to get to the turn-off to San Pedro de Pichasca on a rickety **bus** from Ovalle's Feria Modelo (see p.185), but this involves walking 3km from the main road to the site entrance, and then a further 2km to the cave and fossil remains.

Just under 30km further northeast of Pichasca, set amid dramatic mountain scenery, is the traditional oasis village of **HURTADO**, where the main draw, a couple of kilometres outside the village, is a Mexican-style ranch, the *Hacienda Los Andes* (☎53/1982106, ⓦ www.haciendalosandes.com; ⓖ). Run by an Austro-German couple, the hacienda's main focus is equestrian, offering three-night "horseback adventures", with treks and all meals included, plus transfers to and from La Serena or Ovalle, from US$370 per person. The spacious, comfortable rooms have appealing bathrooms and mesmerizing views across the verdant valley. They also serve excellent meals. Added to that, the horses are top quality – they're safe mounts even for inexperienced riders – and the rugged trails make for exciting explorations. But if you prefer to travel on your own two feet, the hacienda has a well-marked and mostly unchallenging path up the valley to a disused gold mine, a perfect picnic spot. You can also swim in the river and check out the Chilean rodeos in nearby villages. A couple of buses a week link Hurtado to Ovalle.

If you're **driving**, you can visit Pichasca and Hurtado as part of a longer tour through the valley, continuing to Vicuña (see p.200) via a difficult but doable road that fords several mountain streams and crosses several breathtaking mountain passes. You are rewarded by staggering views all the way. A dirt road leading northwards from Samo Alto, about 10km west of Pichasca, leads to Andacollo (see p.188), again through wonderful scenery.

Valle del Encanto and Termas de Socos

The dry, dusty **VALLE DEL ENCANTO** (daily 9am–4.30pm; CH$300) boasts one of Chile's densest collections of **petroglyphs** – images engraved on the surface of rocks – carved mainly by people of the El Molle culture (see p.589) between 100 and 600 AD. Most of the images are geometric motifs or stylized human outlines, including faces with large, wide eyes and elaborate headdresses. There are about thirty petroglyphs in total, concentrated in two separate areas: one near the picnic tables as you enter the site, and another reached by following the right-hand (western) path for about 1km. A few of the images are very striking, while others are faint and difficult to make out; the best time to visit is around 2–3pm, when the outlines are at their sharpest, unobscured by shadows. There's an erratically available free guide service, arranged on the spot when you turn up – if you can, it's worth taking advantage of this so as not to miss the most impressive petroglyphs. Note that you're not allowed to camp in the area. To get here from Ovalle, head 19km west to a heavily potholed dirt road that leads 5km south of Ruta 45 into the ravine.

When you're back on the Panamericana, look for a track just south of the turn-off to Ovalle, which leads 2km to the thermal baths complex of **TERMAS DE SOCOS**, noted for the 22°C (72°F) outdoor pool, surrounded by palm and eucalyptus trees, wicker armchairs and huge potted ferns, and the cubicles containing private bathtubs where you can soak in warm spring water, supposedly rich in medicinal properties. These are free if you're staying at the resort's studiously rustic **hotel** (T53/1982505, Santiago T & F2/2363336, Wwww.termasocos.cl; ⑧); otherwise, there's a charge of CH$3500 for the pool and CH$3500 for the baths. You'll also find a good **campsite** (Sept–April; T094180293; CH$2500 per person) with its own outdoor pool.

Parque Nacional Fray Jorge

A UNESCO world biosphere reserve since 1977, **PARQUE NACIONAL FRAY JORGE** (daily 9am–4.30pm; CH$1600) sits on the Altos de Talinay, a range of steep coastal hills plunging into the Pacific some 80km west of Ovalle and 110km south of La Serena. It extends over 100 square kilometres, but its focal point, and what visitors come to see, is the small **cloudforest** perched on the highest part of the sierra, about 600m above sea level.

The extraordinary thing about this forest is how sharply it contrasts with its surroundings, indeed with everywhere else in the area. Approaching it, you follow a dusty road through a charred landscape of cactus plants and brittle shrubs, and then, as you get closer to the coast, you'll notice patches of grey hovering over the sky. Suddenly you're on what looks and feels like a Scottish hill, enfolded by cold, damp cloud and swirling mist. This is the **camanchaca**, the thick coastal fog that rises from the ocean and condenses as it meets the land, supporting a cover of dense vegetation – fern, bracken and myrtle trees – normally found only in the south of Chile. Close to the parking area, a one-kilometre path dotted with information panels guides you through a poorly labelled range of plants and trees on the crest of the hill. Look down to where the ocean is and, if you're patient, you'll catch sudden glimpses of the crashing waves and little islets below as the mist temporarily clears. At the end of the path lies the **forest** proper, where a slippery, wooden boardwalk takes you through tall trees dripping with moisture. The whole trail takes less than half an hour to walk.

Practicalities

There's no public transport to the park, so unless you've got a rental car, your best bet is to arrange a trip by **taxi** (try Abel Olivares in Ovalle, ☎53/620352, or Transervice in La Serena, ☎51/212021) or take a **tour** from La Serena (see p.192). If you're **driving** here, allow about one and a half hours from Ovalle, a little more from La Serena. The park is reached by a dirt road that branches west from the Panamericana 14km north of the junction with Ruta 45 to Ovalle. From the turn-off, it's 18km to the park entrance, where you pay your fee and register your visit, and then another further 10km to the wood itself along a road that gets rough and extremely steep in some places. Three kilometres beyond the Conaf control there's a **picnic** area, but note that camping is no longer allowed anywhere in the park.

From Ovalle to La Serena

Ovalle is separated from the busy city of La Serena, some 90km north, by a series of gentle valleys and dried-out rivers, punctuated with the occasional abandoned mine or colonial mansion. The most direct, and most scenic, route between the two towns is along Ruta 43, from which a side road branches east to the charming pilgrimage centre of **Andacollo** – a worthwhile detour, especially now that it's home to one of the country's newest observatories, open to the public for evening stargazing. West of Ovalle, the Panamericana turns towards the ocean and skirts a string of small resorts that make a calmer and more attractive beach setting than the built-up coast at La Serena.

Andacollo and around

Enfolded by sun-bleached, rolling hills midway between Ovalle and La Serena, **ANDACOLLO** is a tidy little town of small adobe houses grouped around a long main street. It's been an important gold- and copper-mining centre ever since the Incas mined its hills in the sixteenth century, but is best known as the home of the **Virgen de Andacollo**, a small wooden carving that draws over 100,000 pilgrims to the town each year. Most of them arrive between December 23 and 26 to participate in the Fiesta Grande de la Virgen: four days of music and riotous dancing performed by costumed groups from all over Chile. Many of these dances have their roots in pre-Columbian rituals, such as the *bailes chinos*, recorded in Spanish chronicles around 1580 and thought to have been introduced by the Incas during their occupation in the late fifteenth

The Virgin of Andacollo

The true facts of the story of the **Virgin of Andacollo** – a 90-centimetre carving of the Virgin Mary considered to have miraculous powers – have long been lost in mythology and legend. One popular version has it that the whereabouts of the carving was revealed to an Indian named Collo by a heavenly apparition who urged him to go and seek it crying "¡Anda, Collo, Anda!" ("Go, Collo, Go!"). A more credible theory is that the image was taken from La Serena by priests fleeing the city when it was attacked and destroyed by Indians in 1549. They buried the carving in the hills near Andacollo, where it was accidentally discovered by an Indian some time later. Old chronicles tell of a rudimentary chapel erected in Andacollo around 1580, presumably to house the image, and of worship dances held there.

In any event it seems that the image went missing some time in the seventeenth century, prompting Andacollo's parish priest, Don Bernardino Alvarez del Tobar, to organize a collection to pay for a new one to be made. The sum of 24 pesos was duly raised and dispatched to Lima, Peru, where a new image of the Virgin was carved and returned to Andacollo, receiving its inaugural blessing on the first Sunday of October, 1676. The loss of the original image was providential, for the new one turned out to have far greater miracle-working powers than its predecessor. The Virgin's fame spread far and wide, and an intense cult of devotion sprang up. In 1901 the image was recognized as officially "miraculous" by the Vatican, and the Virgin was crowned in a dazzling ceremony attended by five bishops and 10,000 pilgrims.

century. Quieter, less frenetic celebrations take place during the Fiesta Chica on the first Sunday in October.

Even if you miss the fiestas it's still worth coming to check out the two temples erected in honour of the Virgin. Largest and grandest is the **Basílica**, which towers over Plaza Pedro Nolasco Videla, the main square, in breathtaking contrast to the small, simple scale of the rest of the town. Built 1873–93, almost entirely of wood in a Roman–Byzantine style, its pale, cream-coloured walls are topped by two colossal 50-metre towers and a stunning 45-metre dome. Inside, sunlight floods through the dome, falling onto huge wooden pillars painted to look like marble. On the other side of the square stands the smaller, stone-built **Templo Antiguo**, dating from 1789. This is where the image of the Virgin stands for most of the year, perched on the main altar, awaiting the great festival when it's transported to the Basílica to receive the petitions and prayers of the pilgrims. Devotees of the Virgin de Andacollo have left an astonishing quantity of gifts here over the years, ranging from artificial limbs and wooden crutches to jewellery, badges, china vases, model boats and exam certificates, all displayed in the crypt of the Templo Antiguo as part of the **Museo del Pelegrino** (ⓦ www.santuarioandacollo.cl; daily 10am–7pm; donation expected). You can reach Andacollo by bus or *colectivo* from Ovalle (1hr 30min) or La Serena (50min; see p.192).

For a more celestial experience, head to the brand new **Collowara Observatory** (named after the Aymara term for "land of the stars"), some 15km northeast of Andacollo, atop the 1300-metre Cerro Churqui. Built specifically for public use, like that run by the Municipalidad de Vicuña (see p.200), this observatory also features a top-quality Smith-Cassegrain telescope. The two-hour **evening tours** (CH\$3500) start with a high-tech audiovisual talk (in Spanish and English) about the galaxy and other astronomical matters, followed by the opportunity to observe the heavens through one of the telescopes – unless, of course, you're unlucky enough to be here on a cloudy night. You should be at the observatory ticket office at Urmeneta 599 (Mon–Sat 9am–10pm, Sun 10am–10pm;

△ Fiesta Grande de la Virgen

☎51/432964, ⓦwww.collowara.cl) half an hour before the scheduled visit (9pm, 10.30pm & 11.30pm). It's best to make a reservation in advance; minivan transport is provided to and from the observatory.

Tongoy

Some 60km north of the turn-off for Ovalle, a toll-paying side road branches off the Panamericana for **TONGOY**, a popular family resort spread over a hilly peninsula. It has two attractive sandy **beaches**, the Playa Socos, north of the peninsula, and the enormous Playa Grande, stretching 14km south. While there are plenty of hotels, *cabañas* and restaurants, development has been low-key, and the place remains pretty and relatively unspoiled. There's a good choice of **accommodation**. At *Linda Vista*, entrance at Costanera Sur 48 (☎51/391697; ⑤), artist Paula Hernández has a few wooden and glass *cabañas* dotted up a hillside overlooking the bay, each one decorated with her own canvases. The *Hotel Panorámico*, Av Mirador 455 (☎51/391944; ⑤), is crammed with 1950s items including a great TV set and a stand-up hairdryer. On the beachfront at Serena 460, *Yacolen* (☎51/391772; ③), offers basic but clean rooms off the yard behind the restaurant, with the two end rooms overlooking the beach, while 500m down Playa Grande, *Ripipal* (☎51/391226; CH$10,000 per site) is a quiet, year-round **campsite**. Also on the beach, next to the *caleta*, you'll find a row of excellent little **restaurants** serving delicious seafood – try *Negro Cerro* or *El Veguita*.

There's frequent **transport** to Tongoy from Coquimbo (Colectivos Alfamar; ☎51/323719) and from La Serena (Buses Serenamar; ☎51/296524).

Coquimbo and La Herradura

Spread over a rocky peninsula studded with colourful houses, the busy port of **COQUIMBO** was established during colonial times to serve neighbouring La Serena and became Chile's main copper exporter during the nineteenth century. Despite its undeniably impressive setting, the town has a slightly rough-edged, down-at-heel air, but is useful as an inexpensive base from which to enjoy La Serena's beaches, or for taking public transport to the nearby resorts of Guanaqueros and Tongoy.

Coquimbo's main street, Aldunate, runs parallel to the northern shore of the peninsula, at the foot of the steep hills that form the **upper town**, or *Parte Alta*. Several stairways lead from Aldunate up to lookout points with sweeping views down to the port and across the bay; if you can't face the climb, take any *micro* marked "*Parte Alta*". The peak is now crowned with a hideous, concrete "Third Millennium Cross", ablaze at night, which claims to be the only major spiritual monument in the world built at the turn of the millennium (which is just as well if they all looked like this one). The only conceivably redeeming feature is that you can enjoy superb panoramic views of the coast from up here.

Below, the central **Plaza de Armas**, halfway along Aldunate, is slowly being redesigned, with an odd domed structure taking up most of it. North of the square, mostly on Aldunate, you'll find the **Barrio Inglés**, a district with the city's finest houses, many of them carved in wood by English craftsmen during the prosperous mining era. The restored buildings are beautifully lit at night and often double as bars, restaurants or music venues. A couple of blocks north of Aldunate, Avenida Costanera runs along the shore, past the large **port**, the **terminal pesquero**, and along to the lively **fish market**. This area has been smartened up recently, and makes for a pleasant stroll along the ocean, provided you don't mind the strong whiff of fish.

The southern shore of the peninsula, known as **Guayacán**, has a sandy beach, dominated at one end by a huge mechanized port used for exporting iron. While you're here, take a look at the tall steeple of the nearby **Iglesia de Guayacán**, a prefabricated steel church designed and built in 1888 by Alexandre-Gustave Eiffel, of tower fame, and the **British cemetery**, built in 1860 at the behest of the British Admiralty and full of the graves of young sailors etched with heart-rending inscriptions like "*died falling from aloft*". (If the cemetery gates are locked, ask in the caretaker's house.)

Guayacán's beach curves south to that of **LA HERRADURA**, which although long, golden and sandy is marred by its proximity to the Panamericana. That said, the night-time views across the bay to the tip of Coquimbo are superb, and if you want to spend a night or two at the seaside, La Herradura makes a convenient, cheaper alternative to La Serena's Avenida del Mar.

Practicalities

Coquimbo's busy **bus terminal** is on the main road into town, near the junction of Videla with Balmaceda. Nearly all the main north–south inter-city buses stop here, as do local buses to coastal resorts like Tongoy and Guanaqueros. You can also get to the resorts, and to Guayacán and La Herradura, by **colectivo** - they pick up behind the bus terminal and throughout the centre of town. There's a *casa de cambio*, Afex, at Melgarejo 1355, plus a couple of **ATMs** on Plaza Prat, on the Plaza de Armas and at Aldunate 822. There's a fair choice of **accommodation** in town, the best being *Hotel Lig*, at Aldunate 1577 (T51/311171, F51/313717; ❹), with bright, comfortable rooms and private parking. *Hotel Iberia*, just off Aldunate at Lastra 400 (T51/312141, F51/326307; ❸), has spacious rooms, with and without bath, in an attractive old building. For **eating**, go to the little *marisquerías* by the fish market for simple, cheap seafood lunches, or try *Pastissima* at Aldunate 927 for filling, reasonably priced Italian and Chilean food fare. Further along you'll find the bizarre but not unattractive pub-restaurant *De Costa a Costa* (named for its 360-degree views enjoyed from the clumsy looking attic), Aldunate 501, 🍴 serving large helpings of meat and fish with draft beer and live music at weekends. The *Jazz Club*, 🍴, one of the best jazz venues in Chile and certainly outside Santiago, showcases home-grown musicians in a fabulous 1920s Barrio Inglés mansion at Aldunate 739.

In **La Herradura**, *Hotel La Herradura*, just off the beach at Av La Marina 200 (☎ & ⓕ 51/261647; ❹) offers decent rooms at reasonable prices. If you want the best views of the bay, head for *Hotel El Bucanero*, Av La Marina 201 (☎ 51/265153, ⓕ 51/260842; ❺), perched on a jetty projecting into the ocean; here you'll also find La Herradura's plushest **restaurant**, offering good but overpriced seafood and great views across to Coquimbo (best at night). Also looking out to sea, but with more modest prices, is the *Club de Yates*, a little further west along the beach.

La Serena and around

Sitting by the mouth of the Río Elqui, 11km north of Coquimbo, **LA SERENA** is for many visitors their first taste of northern Chile, after whizzing straight up from Santiago by road or air. The city centre is an attractive mix of pale colonial-style houses, carefully restored churches, craft markets tucked away on hidden squares and bustling crowds. Three kilometres away lies Avenida del Mar, a rather charmless esplanade lined with oceanfront aparthotels and *cabañas* that are packed in the summer and gloomily empty out of season.

La Serena is Chile's second-oldest city, with a history chequered by violence and drama. Founded by Pedro de Valdivia in 1544 as a staging post on the way to Peru, it got off to an unpromising start when it was completely destroyed in an **Indian attack** four years later. Undeterred, Valdivia refounded the city in a new location the following year, but La Serena continued to lead a precarious existence, subjected to frequent and often violent raids by pirates, many of them British (see box opposite). Happier times arrived in the nineteenth century, when the discovery of large silver deposits at Arqueros, just north of La Serena, marked the beginning of the region's great **silver boom**. These heady days saw the erection of some of the city's finest mansions and churches, as the mining magnates competed in their efforts to dazzle with their wealth.

It was in the 1940s, when **Gabriela González Videla**, president of Chile and local Serenense, instituted his "**Plan Serena**", that La Serena developed its signature architectural style. One of the key elements of Videla's urban remodelling scheme was the vigorous promotion of the Spanish colonial style, with facades restored or rebuilt on existing structures and strict stylistic controls imposed on new ones. Unimaginative and inflexible though some claimed these measures to be, the results are undeniably pleasing, and La Serena boasts an architectural harmony and beauty noticeably lacking in most Chilean cities. It's also surrounded by some rewarding places to visit. Close at hand, and with good bus and *colectivo* connections, are the fine beaches at Tongoy (see p.190) and, above all, the glorious **Elqui Valley**, one of the must-sees of the region. Further afield, the cloudforest reserve of **Parque Nacional Fray Jorge** and the penguin and dolphin sanctuary at **Parque Nacional Pinguino de Humboldt** are not served by public transport, but can be visited with several **tour companies** if you don't have your own wheels.

The Pacific buccaneers

La Serena was one of a string of ports on South America's Pacific seaboard regularly attacked and plundered by bands of buccaneers, out to loot the Spanish colonies of their gold, silver and other riches. The marauders - mainly British, but also French and Dutch - were positively encouraged by their own governments, who were intensely jealous of Spain's overseas possessions and eager to undermine their rival's glory. The English were particularly dreaded from their first arrival on the scene in 1578, when **Sir Francis Drake** sailed the *Golden Hind* through the Magellan Strait and up the coast of Chile. Drake's first port of call was Valparaíso where, besides ransacking the church for its silverware, he captured a Spanish ship containing 60,000 gold pesos and vast quantities of Chilean wine. Further north, he attempted to repeat his success at La Serena, but was thwarted by the fierce armed resistance mounted by its inhabitants. Peru yielded greater prizes, and when he returned to England, his ship heavy with booty, he was knighted by a jubilant Queen Elizabeth, who called him her "little pirate".

It wasn't until the second half of the sixteenth century, however, that the heyday of the Pacific buccaneers began in earnest. Among the most ruthless of the leaders was **Captain Bartholomew Sharp**, who in 1680 attacked and captured La Serena, where his hungry crew feasted on "strawberries as large as walnuts". Silver, on the other hand, was almost nowhere to be found, and when the inhabitants refused to pay a ransom, the embittered Sharp set fire to the town, almost burning it to the ground. That night, by way of revenge, one of the Spaniards sent a servant to float out to Sharp's boat on an inflated horsehide and set fire to the stern, but the blaze was extinguished before any real damage could be done. Also known for his cruelty was **Edward Davis**, who arrived in La Serena in 1685. Unable to capture the town, he retreated to the Iglesia Santo Domingo, which he looted and set on fire before fleeing the town.

As Britain and France established a more peaceful relationship with Spain towards the end of the seventeenth century, the plunderers no longer served their governments' ends, and the days of buccaneering drew to a close. Vivid memories of the terror they caused lived on for many years, however, and as late as 1835, Charles Darwin, while visiting La Serena, told of an old lady "who remarked how wonderfully strange it was that she should live to dine in the same room as an Englishman; for she remembered that twice as a girl, at the cry of "*Los Ingleses*", every soul, carrying what valuables they could, had taken to the mountains."

Arrival and information

La Serena's **bus terminal** is a half-hour walk south of the centre. There's no direct bus from the terminal into town, but there are plenty of taxis, charging about CH$1000; alternatively, you can flag down a *micro* from the Panamericana, a five-minute walk west. If you've flown in, you'll land at the **Aeropuerto La Florida**, some 5km to the east of town and served by taxis and transfers plus *micros* on the main road (ranging from CH$300–3500).

Sernatur has a well-stocked tourist office on the west side of the Plaza de Armas at Matta 461 (Jan & Feb Mon–Fri 8.45am–8pm, Sat 10am–2pm & 4–8pm, Sun 10am–2pm; March–Dec Mon–Fri 8.45am–5pm; ℡51/225199, ℻51/213956, ✉infocoquimbo@sernatur.cl). There's also a municipal **Oficina de Turismo** at the bus terminal (Tues–Sat 9.30am–1pm & 3.30–9pm), especially useful for accommodation, and a **kiosk** on the corner of Prat and Balmaceda (Mon–Sat 11am–2pm & 4–7pm). For detailed information on Parque Nacional Fray Jorge, Monumento Natural Pichasca and Parque

Nacional Pinguino de Humboldt, visit **Conaf** at Cordovez 281 (Mon–Fri 9am–1pm; ☎51/272798).

Accommodation

You'll find a large choice of budget accommodation and mid- to upmarket options in the **centre**. Avenida del Mar, 3km from town, offers only overpriced *cabañas* and hotels.

Hostal Family Home Av El Santo 1056 ☎51/212099, ⊛www.familyhome.cl. Delightful house that lives up to its name and is conveniently located between the bus terminal and the central plaza; single, double and triple rooms, some en-suite, plus use of kitchen.❷

Hostal del Mar Cuatro Esquinas at Av del Mar ☎51/225559, ℱ51/225816. Pleasant, well-furnished *cabañas* with a mid-sized pool, a short walk from the beach.❼

Hotel Los Balcones de Aragón Cienfuegos 289 ☎51/225724, ℱ51/211800 ⊛www .losbalconesdearagon.cl. Smart, upmarket rooms in a fine building with private parking. ❺

Hotel del Cid O'Higgins 138 ☎51/212692, ℱ51/222289, wwww.hoteldelcid.cl. Great hotel run by a Scots-Chilean couple, with a few comfortable rooms around a flower-filled terrace. ❺

Hotel Francisco de Aguirre Cordovez 210 ☎ & ℱ51/222991, ℮reservas@fransiscodeaguirre.tie .cl. La Serena's plushest hotel, with stylish rooms in a handsome old building, and a poolside restaurant open in summer. ❻

Hotel Londres Cordovez 550 ☎ & ℱ51/219066, ⊛www.hotellondres.cl. Clean and tidy rooms,

some with private bath and others with just a washbasin. ❺

Hotel Pacífico Av de la Barra 252 ☎51/225674. Ancient, rambling hotel with clean, basic rooms (some with bath, some without) and friendly staff. ❹

Hotel Pucará Balmaceda 319 ☎51/211966, ℱ51/11933. Efficiently run hotel with spacious, comfortable but drab rooms, and private parking. ❹

Residencial Suiza Cienfuegos 250 ☎51/216092, ℮residencial.suiza@terra.cl. Spotless, well-kept, highly recommended *residencial* with a fresh, modern feel.❹

Camping

Antares Calle Los Pescadores ☎51/243753, ℱ51/245207. Outrageously expensive campsite (CH$18,000 per site) with a sandy area to pitch your tents and a few tired *cabañas* for hire. (❻)

Sol di Mare Parcela 66 ☎51/312531. Lovely, grassy campsite down at the quieter end of the beach. Good facilities and lots of shade. CH$10,000 per site.

The City

La Serena, 2km inland from the northern sweep of the Bahía de Coquimbo, follows the usual grid pattern, with the leafy Plaza de Armas in the centre. It features the noteworthy **Museo Arqueológico**, but the city's main appeal lies in just strolling the streets and squares, admiring the grand old houses, browsing through the numerous crafts markets, wandering in and out of its many stone churches and hanging out in the plaza. In the warmer months, hordes of Chilean tourists head for the six-kilometre **beach**, along the Avenida del Mar.

Plaza de Armas

The grand **Iglesia Catedral** dominates the east side of the Plaza de Armas. Its pale walls date from 1844, when the previous church on the site was finally pulled down because of the damage wrought by the 1796 earthquake. Inside, among its more curious features are the wooden pillars, disguised to look like stone. Just off the opposite side of the square, on Cordovez, the pretty **Iglesia Santo Domingo** was first built in 1673 and then again in 1755, after it was sacked by the pirate Sharp (see p.193). Attached to it is a convent and a little *plazuela* containing a stone fountain, originally used by priests to wash their hands and said to be the oldest monument in the city.

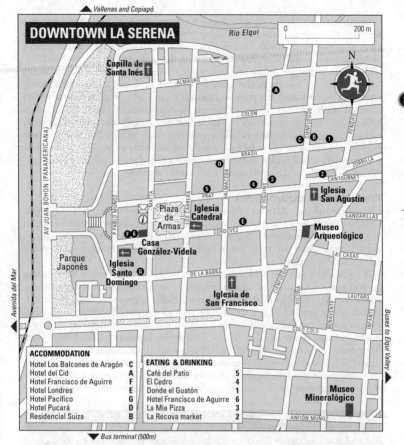

DOWNTOWN LA SERENA

Vallenas and Copiapó

Río Elqui

0   200 m

N

ACCOMMODATION

Hotel Los Balcones de Aragón	C
Hotel del Cid	A
Hotel Francisco de Aguirre	F
Hotel Londres	E
Hotel Pacífico	G
Hotel Pucará	D
Residencial Suiza	B

EATING & DRINKING

Café del Patio	5
El Cedro	4
Donde el Guatón	1
Hotel Francisco de Aguirre	6
La Mía Pizza	3
La Recova market	2

Bus terminal (500m)

The two-storey adobe house sitting on the southwest corner of the plaza was, from 1927 to 1977, home to Chile's erstwhile president, Gabriel González Videla, best known for outlawing the Communist party after using its support to gain power in 1946. Inside, a small and rather dull **museum** (Mon–Fri 10am–6pm, Sat 10am–1pm; CH$600) has an eclectic display of photos, objects, documents and paintings relating to the president's life and works, along with a section on regional history; the temporary art exhibitions, occasionally held here, are often better than the permanent display.

Museo Arqueológico

Entered through an imposing nineteenth-century portico on the corner of Cordovez and Cienfuegos, La Serena's **Museo Arqueológico** (Tues–Fri 9.30am–5.30pm, Sat 10am–1pm & 4–7pm, Sun 10am–1pm; CH$600, Sun free) boasts two outstanding treasures, though most of the displays could do with improving.

First is its large collection of **Diaguita pottery**, considered by many to be among the most beautiful pre-Columbian ceramics in South America. The terracotta pieces, dating from around 1000 to 1500 AD, are covered in intricate geometric designs painted in black and white and, in the later phases, red.

Starting with simple bowls and dishes made for domestic use, the Diaguitas went on to produce elaborately shaped ceremonial pots and jars, often in the form of humans or animals, or sometimes both, such as the famous *jarros patos*, or "duck jars", moulded in the form of a duck's body with a human head.

The museum's other gem is the giant stone statue, or **moai**, from Easter Island, "donated" to La Serena at the behest of President González Videla in 1952. Until recently it stood in a park on Avenida Colo Colo, covered in graffiti and urinated on by drunks. Then, as part of an exhibition of Easter Island art in 1996, it travelled to Barcelona, where it was accidentally decapitated. Tragedy turned to good fortune, however, when the insurance money from the accident paid for a brand-new *sala* to be built for the statue in the archeological museum. This is where you'll find it today, standing on a raised platform against a flattering azure backdrop, the joins at the neck hardly showing.

The rest of downtown

The eye-catching **Museo Mineralógico** (Mon–Fri 9.30am–12.30pm; CH$500), near the university, on Muñoz with Infante, displays a large selection of glittering mineral rocks, many of them mined in the region. Though it's worth a visit while you're in town, note that the similar museum in Copiapó is considerably better.

Of La Serena's numerous **crafts markets**, the biggest and best is the bustling **La Recova**, occupying two large patios inside an arcaded building opposite the Iglesia San Agustín. The quality of the merchandise is generally high, and goods include finely worked objects in *combabalita* (a locally mined marble), lapis lazuli jewellery, alpaca sweaters and candied papaya. Backing onto the Panamericana, two blocks west of the Plaza de Armas, the **Parque Japonés Kokoro No Niwa** (Tues–Sun 10am–6pm; CH$600), whose Japanese name means "Garden of the Heart", is an oasis of perfectly manicured lawns, ponds awash with water lilies, ice-white geese and little Japanese bridges and pagodas. Unfortunately, the sense of peace and tranquillity it creates is undermined by the din of the highway.

La Serena's churches

Including Iglesia Catedral and Iglesia Santo Domingo on the Plaza de Armas, a remarkable twenty-nine **churches** dot La Serena, lending an almost fairy-tale look to the city. This proliferation of places of worship dates from the earliest days of the city, when all the religious orders established bases to provide shelter for their clergy's frequent journeys between Santiago and Lima (the viceregal capital). Nearly all the churches are built of stone, which is unusual for Chile, and all are in mint condition. Standing at the corner of Balmaceda and de la Barra, the **Iglesia San Francisco** is one of La Serena's oldest churches, though the date of its construction is unknown, as the city archives were burnt in Sharp's raid of 1680. Its huge walls are one metre thick, covered in a stone facade carved in fanciful Baroque designs. Inside, the recently restored **Museo de Arte Religioso** contains a small but impressive collection of religious sculpture and paintings from the colonial period. Beautiful for its very plainness, the 1755 **Iglesia San Agustín**, on the corner of Cienfuegos and Cantournet, was originally the Jesuit church but was taken over by the Augustinians after the Jesuits were expelled from Chile in 1767. Its honey-toned stone walls were badly damaged in the 1975 earthquake, but have been skillfully restored. On the northern edge of town, overlooking the banks of the Río Elqui, the seventeenth-century **Capilla de Santa Inés** was constructed on the site of a rudimentary chapel erected by the first colonists and its thick white adobe walls recall the Andean churches of the northern *altiplano*.

△ Cerro Tololo observatory

Avenida del Mar

Stretching 6km round the rim of a wide, horseshoe bay just west of the city, the **Avenida del Mar** is a staid collection of glitzy hotels, tourist complexes and *cabañas* that bulge with visitors for two months of the year and are otherwise empty. In January and February hundreds of cars inch their way up and down the avenue, bumper to bumper, and mostly Chilean tourists pile onto the sandy beaches, which are clean but spoiled by the horrific high-rise backdrop. The southernmost end, linked to Coquimbo by a new bridge, offers views of the neighbouring harbour town, marred by the criminally ugly Third Millennium Cross. While there's no bus or *colectivo* service along the Avenida del Mar, you can take a *micro* headed for Coquimbo from just about any street corner (if in doubt, go to Avenida Francisco de Aguirre) and get off on the Panamericana either at Cuatro Esquinas or Peñuelas, both a short walk from the beach.

Eating, drinking and entertainment

You'll find a wide choice of **places to eat** in downtown La Serena, most of them unpretentious, unexceptional and not too expensive; **cafés** seem to congregate along Balmaceda while **bars** are mostly on O'Higgins. The Avenida del Mar restaurants, on the other hand, tend to be overpriced, though some offer fine views and a lively holiday atmosphere. **Nightlife** downtown is surprisingly quiet, while the pubs and discos by the beach are more seasonal, reaching their heady zenith in January and February – *Brooklyn's Corner Pub*, *Kamikaze*, *Scratch*, *Sundance* and *Quinta Ola* are current faves. There's a six-screen Cinemark **cinema** at Mall Plaza, next to the bus terminal. The La Recova **market**, at the corner of Cienfuegos and Cantournet, has dozens of good-value *marisquerías* (seafood) on the upper gallery of the handicrafts market, making it a perfect place for lunch.

Café del Patio Prat 470. La Serena's mellowest café-bar, with tables dotting a little patio and live jazz beneath a huge palm. A mellow place to spend an evening.

El Cedro Prat 572. Delicious Lebanese food, plus the usual Chilean dishes, are served in a pleasant, airy dining room with a patio.

Donde el Guatón Brazil 750. Lively, friendly and intimate, this colonial-style restaurant serves the best *parrilladas* in La Serena. Romantic *boleros*, the Latin answer to the waltz, at weekends.

Hotel Francisco de Aguirre Cordovez 210. If you're around in summer and fancy a splurge, this is the place to come, principally for its glamorous poolside setting. The French-influenced food is toothsome and well-presented.

La Mía Pizza O'Higgins 360. Come to this attractive café-style spot for decent, inexpensive pizzas and also breakfast. At Av del Mar 2100, you'll find an upmarket, seaview branch with outdoor summer seating that draws the crowds with fish and seafood in addition to the tasty pizzas and pasta dishes.

Observatories around La Serena

Thanks to the exceptional transparency of its skies, northern Chile is home to the largest concentration of astronomical **observatories** in the world. The region around La Serena, in particular, has been chosen by a number of international astronomical research institutions as the site of their telescopes, housed in white, futuristic domes that loom over the valleys from their hilltop locations. Among the research organizations that own the observatories are North American and European groups that need a base in the southern hemisphere (about a third of the sky seen here is never visible in the northern hemisphere).

Some of the observatories offer guided tours, including the impressive **Cerro Tololo** Inter-American Observatory, whose four-metre telescope was the strongest in the southern hemisphere until it was overtaken by Cerro Paranal's Very Large Telescope, the most powerful in the world, located near Antofagasta (see p.232).

Cerro Tololo is 70km east of La Serena, reached by a side road branching south of the Elqui Valley road. Tours take place every Saturday (9.30am–noon & 1–4pm) and need to be booked several days in advance (Ⓣ51/205200, Ⓕ51/205212, Ⓦwww.ctio.noao.edu, Ⓔkflores@ctio.noao.edu); quote the registration number of the vehicle you'll be arriving in. You'll be told to collect your visitor's permit from the observatory's offices in La Serena (up the hill behind the university, at Colina El Pino) the day before the tour, but ask to pick it up directly at the observatory gates; alternatively, take a pre-booked tour from La Serena (see box opposite), which takes care of all the details.

Some 150km northeast of La Serena, reached by a side road branching east from the Panamericana, **La Silla** is the site of the European Southern Observatory's fourteen telescopes, including two 3.6-metre optical reflectors; they are open to the public every Saturday from September to June, with advance bookings through the observatory's Santiago offices (Ⓣ2/2285006, Ⓦwww.eso.org); you can also contact the observatory directly (Ⓣ51/224932, Ⓕ51/224527). The observatory's La Serena office is at El Santo 1538 (Ⓣ51/225387, Ⓕ51/215175).

Thirty kilometres north of La Silla, the Carnegie Institute's observatory at **Las Campanas** contains four telescopes, with two 6.5-metre telescopes under construction as part of its Magellan Project. You can visit on Saturdays (2.30–5.30pm). Contact the observatory's offices in La Serena to make reservations (Ⓣ51/207301, Ⓕ51/227817, Ⓦwww.lco.cl, Ⓔpaty@lco.cl); they're located next to Cerro Tololo's offices on Colina El Pino.

All of these tours take place during the day and are free of charge but are strictly no-touching; a more hands-on night-time experience is provided by the Municipalidad de Vicuña's small but user-friendly observatory on **Cerro Mamalluca** (see p.202), 5km north of Vicuña and by the newer **Collowara** observatory outside Andacollo (see p.189).

Tours from La Serena

The two most popular day tours from La Serena are to the **Elqui Valley** (see p.200), taking in Vicuña, Montegrande and Pisco Elqui (also easily reached on public transport), and to the cloudforest reserve at **Parque Nacional Fray Jorge** (see p.187), about two hours' south of the city and not served by public transport. Other favourite destinations include nearby **beaches** such as Guanaqueros and Tongoy; **Andacollo**, an important pilgrimage centre 54km southeast of La Serena (see p.192); the ancient petroglyph site of the **Valle del Encanto**, near Ovalle (see p.183); **Monumento Natural Pichasca**, where you'll find the remains of a "fossilized wood" (see p.186); and, increasingly, the **Reserva Nacional Pinguino de Humboldt**, a penguin and dolphin sanctuary 120km north of La Serena. On Saturdays you can take tours to the international astronomical observatory of **Cerro Tololo** in the Elqui Valley (see box opposite). The **cost** of most tours ranges from CH\$20,000 to CH\$25,000 per person and a selection of reliable operators is given in the listings below.

Listings

Airlines LAN, Balmaceda 406 ☏51/221531.
Airport information ☏51/200900
Banks and exchange There are plenty of ATMs on or near the Plaza de Armas and the corner of Cordovez and Cienfuegos. For currency exchange, try Cambios La Portada, Prat 515 (daily 9am–11pm); Cambios Fides, Balmaceda 460, Office 7; Casa de Cambio Maya, Portales 305; and Gira Tour, Prat 689.
Car rental In addition to the airport, there are many outlets on Av Francisco de Aguirre, including Avis at no. 68 (☏ & ℱ51/227171); Bert at no. 312 (☏51/211475); Dollar at no. 58 (☏51/225714 ℱ51/211688); Econo-rent at no. 135 (☏51/220113); Hertz at no. 225 (☏51/225471, ℱ51/212166); and Oceanic at no. 62

(☏ & ℱ51/214007). Budget is at Balmaceda 3850 (☏ & ℱ51/297916) and Daire at Balmaceda 3856 (☏ & ℱ51/293140).
Internet *Talinay*, Prat 470.
Laundry Ro-Ma at Los Carrera 654.
Post office On the west side of Plaza de Armas, on the corner of Prat and Matta.
Taxis 24-hour radio taxis ☏51/211455.
Telephone offices Many in the centre, including at Cienfuegos 498, Cordovez 446 and O'Higgins 536.
Tour operators Best of a mixed bunch are Ingservitur, Matta 611 ☏ & ℱ51/220165 & 220167, ⓦwww.ingservtur.cl; and Talinay, Prat 470 ☏ & ℱ51/218658, ⓦwww.talinaychile.4mg.com.
Travel agencies For airline tickets, try Viajes Torremolinos at Prat 464 ☏51/226043.

Moving on from La Serena

Inter-city buses operate from La Serena's large, modern bus terminal on El Santo, southwest of the central plaza. From here, there are frequent services to Santiago and all the main cities and towns of the north, plus a few services to regional destinations. Buses for the **Elqui Valley** leave from the Plaza de Abastos on Esmeralda, just south of Colo Colo, about every 30 minutes. To get to **Tongoy**, take a Serenamar bus from the terminal (☏51/211707); the other **coastal resorts** are more easily reached from Coquimbo – to get there, take a *micro* (marked "Coquimbo", of course) from Av Francisco de Aguirre or any main south- or westbound street. Two **colectivo** services from La Serena operate from Calle Domeyko, one block south of Iglesia San Francisco: Anserco, at no. 524 (☏51/217567) goes to Andacollo, Vicuña and Ovalle; Tasco, at no. 575 (☏51/224517) goes to Vicuña, Montegrande and Pisco Elqui. From La Florida airport there are regular **flights** to Santiago and northern cities.

The Elqui Valley

Quiet, rural and extremely beautiful, the **ELQUI VALLEY** unfolds east from La Serena and into the Andes. Irrigated by canals fed by the Puclara and La Laguna dams, the valley floor is given over entirely to cultivation – of papayas, custard apples (*chirimoyas*), oranges, avocados and, most famously, the vast expanses of grape vines grown to produce **pisco**. It's the fluorescent green of these vines that makes the valley so stunning, forming a spectacular contrast with the charred, brown hills that rise on either side. Unfortunately, as the result of climate change – apparently brought about by the construction of the dams – fierce winds often blow along the valley off the reservoir, leading to the introduction of unsightly nylon windbreakers and protective netting to safeguard the delicate fruit from damage. Nonetheless, it's a lovely place. To get the full visual impact of the valley you need to visit between September and March, but this is a gorgeous region to spend a couple of days at any time of year.

Some 60km east of La Serena, appealing little **Vicuña** is the main town and transport hub of the Elqui Valley. Moving east from here, the valley gets higher and narrower and is dotted with tiny villages like **Montegrande** and the odd pisco distillery. The road from La Serena is paved for 105km as far as **Pisco Elqui**, a very pretty village that makes a great place to unwind for a couple of days. If you really want to get away from it all, head for one of the rustic *cabañas* dotted along the banks of the **Río Cochiguaz**, which forks east of the main valley at Montegrande, or delve beyond Pisco Elqui into the farthest reaches of the Elqui Valley itself. Buses will get you all the way to Horcón but not to the farthest village of all, **Alcohuaz**.

Vicuña and around

VICUÑA, an hour by bus inland from La Serena, is a neat and tidy agricultural town laid out around a large, luxuriantly landscaped square. It's a pleasant, easygoing place with a few low-key attractions, a good choice of places to stay and eat, and a visitor-friendly observatory on its doorstep.

Life revolves firmly around the central **plaza**, which has at its centre a huge stone replica of the **death mask** of Nobel Prize-winning poet **Gabriela Mistral**, the Elqui Valley's most famous daughter. On the square's northwest corner stands the **Iglesia de la Inmaculada Concepción**, topped by an

---

Getting around the Elqui Valley

Many tour companies in La Serena offer trips to the Elqui Valley, but it's hardly worth taking a tour, as public transport up and down the valley is so frequent and cheap. The two main **bus** companies are Frontera Elqui and Via Elqui (⊕51/211707). In **La Serena** they generally use a terminal southeast of the centre at the Plaza de Abastos, on Calle Esmeralda (just south of Colo Colo). But some buses depart from the main terminal, useful if you want to take off for the valley directly – just ask. Daily buses depart every half-hour for **Vicuña**, with about six of these continuing to **Montegrande** and **Pisco Elqui**; one or two a day forge all the way to Horcón. It might be worth investing in a **day pass**, which costs CH$4000 and is valid for 24 hours, so that you can hop on and off any bus plying the valley as many times as you choose. Tasco **colectivos** (Domeyko 575, ⊕51/224517) head from La Serena every half-hour for Vicuña, Montegrande and Pisco Elqui. A *colectivo* is even cheaper than a bus when two or three people are travelling together, but it's not necessarily a more comfortable option.

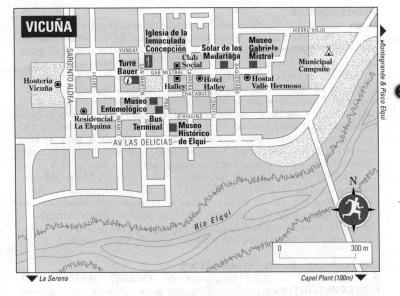

VICUÑA

Iglesia de la Inmaculada Concepción
Solar de los Madariaga
Museo Gabriela Mistral
Hierro Viejo
YUNGAY
Turre Bauer
Club Social
Municipal Campsite
Hostería Vicuña
SARGENTO ALDEA
FREIRE
SAN MARTÍN
GAB MISTRAL
Halley
CARRERA
Hotel Halley
BAQUEDANO
Hostal Valle Hermoso
Museo Entomológico
CHACABUCO
CONDELL
Residencial La Elquina
INFANTE
PRAT
Bus Terminal
O'HIGGINS
Museo Histórico de Elqui
AV LAS DELICIAS
Río Elqui
N
0   300 m
La Serena
Capel Plant (100m)
Montegrande & Pisco Elqui

impressive wooden tower built in 1909 – take a look inside at its vaulted polychrome ceiling, painted with delicate religious images and supported by immense wooden columns. Right next door, the eccentric **Torre Bauer** is a bright-red, mock-medieval tower prefabricated in Germany in 1905 and brought to Vicuña on the instructions of the town's German-born mayor, Adolfo Bauer; the adobe building supporting it houses the Municipalidad. Standing on the southern side of the square, the **Museo Entomológico** (Jan–March daily 10am–10pm; April–Dec Mon–Fri 10.30am–1.30pm & 3.30–7pm, Sat & Sun 10.30am–7pm; CH$600) hoards a fascinating collection of horror-movie creepie crawlies, such as hairy spiders and vicious-looking millipedes, plus exotic butterflies and shells.

Four blocks east of the square, at the end of Calle Gabriela Mistral, the **Museo Gabriela Mistral** (Jan & Feb Mon–Sat 10am–7pm, Sun 10am–6pm; March–Sept Mon–Fri 10am–1pm & 2.30–6.30pm, Sat 10am–1pm & 3–6pm, Sun 10am–1pm; Oct–Dec Mon–Fri 10am–1pm & 3–7pm, Sat 10am–1pm & 3–6pm, Sun 10am–1pm; CH$300) displays photos, prizes, articles and personal objects bequeathed to the city by the poet, along with panels giving an account of her life and works. A few doors down, at no. 683, is the **Solar de los Madariaga** (Jan & Feb daily 10am–7pm; rest of year erratic opening hours; CH$500), an old, colonial-style house preserved as a museum, displaying a modest collection of nineteenth-century furniture and clothes. Another unassuming little museum is the **Museo Histórico de Elqui** at Prat 90 (daily: March–Nov 10am–6pm; Dec–Feb 9am–8pm; CH$400), which houses a curious jumble of pre-Columbian ceramics and nineteenth-century paraphernalia. Just out of town, across the bridge by the filling station, you'll find the **Planta Capel**, the largest pisco distillery in the Elqui Valley. It offers free and very slick guided tours in English and Spanish every half hour (daily 10am–12.30pm & 2.30–6pm; also during lunch time in summer and on winter holidays and long weekends), with free tastings and the chance to buy bottles and souvenirs at the end.

Practicalities

Buses drop off at the small terminal at the corner of O'Higgins and Prat, one block south of the Plaza de Armas. Vicuña's **Oficina de Turismo** (Mon–Fri 9am–1pm & 2–5.30pm; ☏51/411359) is on the northwest corner of the plaza, beneath the Torre Bauer.

There's plenty of **accommodation**. The friendly *Residencial La Elquina*, at O'Higgins 65 (☏51/209125; ❸), offers rooms with and without bath around a flower-filled patio. The slightly more expensive *Hostal Valle Hermoso*, a handsome old building at Gabriela Mistral 706 (☏ & ℱ51/411206; ❸), has clean, spacious rooms (although some have no windows) with private bath and parking. The more upmarket *Hotel Halley* at Gabriela Mistral 404 (☏ & ℱ51/412070, ⓦ www.hotelhalley.cl; ❺) comes highly recommended, with large, impeccably decorated rooms in a colonial-style building, and access to a pool. Vicuña's top hotel, the *Hostería Vicuña*, at the western end of Gabriela Mistral (ⓦ www .hosteriavicuna.cl, ☏51/411301, ℱ51/411144; ❻), is overpriced but has a fabulous pool and one of Vicuña's better **restaurants**, with unadventurous but good-quality meat and fish dishes. The *Club Social* at Gabriela Mistral 445, serves basic, typical Chilean dishes, while *Halley*, across the road at no. 404, has a large, attractive dining room and is a good place for Sunday lunch.

Cerro Mamalluca observatory

Nine kilometres northeast of Vicuña, the **CERRO MAMALLUCA OBSERVATORY**, built specifically for public use, is run by the Municipalidad de Vicuña and features a 30-centimetre Smith-Cassegrain telescope donated by the Cerro Tololo team. The two-hour **evening tours** (CH$3500) start with a high-tech audiovisual talk on the history of the universe, and end with the chance to look through the telescope. If you're lucky, you might see a dazzling display of stars, planets, galaxies, nebulas and clusters, including Jupiter, Saturn's rings, the Orion nebula, the Andromeda galaxy and Sirius. These tours are aimed at utter beginners, but serious astronomers can arrange in-depth, small-group sessions (US$100) with two months' notice. The observatory also runs less scientific, alternative tours known as "*cosmovisión*", complete with Andean music – ask at the offices for more details. Assemble half an hour before the scheduled slot (Oct–April 8.30pm, 10.30pm & half past midnight; May–Sept 6.30pm & 8.30pm) at the observatory's administrative office in Vicuña, at Gabriela Mistral 260 (Mon–Sat 9am–10pm, Sun 10am–10pm; ☏51/411352, ℱ411255, ⓦ www.mamalluca.org, ⓔ observatorio@mamalluca.org), from where transport is provided to Cerro Mamalluca (CH$1500 return); reservations are essential, either by phone, fax, email or in person at the office. If you have your own transport you must still report to the offices, to confirm and pay for your reservation and to follow the minibus in a convoy.

Montegrande

The picturesque village of **MONTEGRANDE**, 34km east of Vicuña (if you're driving, take the right turn for Paihuano at Rivadavia), features a pretty church whose late-nineteenth-century wooden belfry looms over a surprisingly large square. The childhood home of Gabriela Mistral, Montegrande assiduously devotes itself to preserving her memory: her profile has been outlined in white stones on the valley wall opposite the plaza, and the school where she lived with and was taught by her sister has been turned into a **museum** (Dec–Feb Tues–Sun 10am–1pm & 3–7pm; March–Nov Tues–Sun 10am–1pm & 3–6pm; CH$300), displaying some of her furniture and belongings. Just south of the village, her **tomb** rests on a hillside, opposite the small **Capel plant** (tours Jan & Feb daily 10am–6pm; March–Dec Mon–Fri 10am–12.30pm & 2.30–6pm, Sat & Sun 2.30–6pm; free). Close by is the wacky **Galería de Arte Zen**, where you can admire esoteric art and have a tarot card reading.

Gabriela Mistral

Possibly even more than its pisco, the Elqui Valley's greatest source of pride is **Gabriela Mistral**, born in Vicuña in 1889 and, in 1945, the first Latin American to be awarded the **Nobel Prize for Literature**. A schoolmistress, a confirmed spinster and a deeply religious woman, Mistral is perceived by Chileans as an austere, distant and even intolerant figure, and yet her poetry reveals an aching sensitivity and passion, and her much romanticized life was punctuated with tragedy and grief.

Lucila Godoy de Alcayaga, as she was christened, was just 3 years old when her father abandoned the family, the first of several experiences of loss in her life. It was left to her older sister, Emiliana, to support her and her mother, and for the next eight years the three of them lived in the schoolhouse in the village of **Montegrande**, where Emiliana worked as a teacher. At the age of 14, she started work herself as an assistant schoolteacher, in a village close to La Serena, where she taught children by day and workmen learning to read by night. It was here, also, that she took her first steps into the world of literature, publishing several pieces in the local newspaper under the pseudonyms "Alguien" ("Someone"), "Soledad" ("Solitude") and "Alma" ("Soul"). When she was 20 years old, a railway worker, Romelio Ureta, who for three years had been asking her to marry him, committed suicide; in his pocket, a card was found bearing her name.

Although it would seem that his love for her was unrequited, the intense grief caused by Ureta's suicide was to inform much of Mistral's intensely morbid poetry, to which she devoted her time with increasing dedication while supporting herself with a series of teaching posts. In 1914 she won first prize in an important national poetry competition with *Los Sonetos de la Muerte* (Sonnets of Death), and in 1922 her first collection of verse was published under the title of *Desolación* (Desolation), followed a couple of years later by a second collection, *Ternura* (Tenderness). Her work received international acclaim, and in recognition, the Chilean Government offered Gabriela Mistral a position in the consular service, allowing her to concentrate almost exclusively on her poetry; here the parallel with Pablo Neruda (see p.162) is at its strongest. As consul, she spent many years abroad, particularly in the US, but her poems continued to look back to Chile, particularly her beloved **Elqui Valley,** which she described as "a cry of nature rising amidst the opaque mountains and intense blue sky". Her most frequently recurring themes, however, were her love of children and her perceived sorrow at her childlessness.

Though she never gave birth to a child, Gabriela Mistral did serve as a surrogate mother for her adored nephew, **Juan Miguel** or "Yin Yin", who had been placed in her care when he was just 9 months old; some say she never really loved anyone else, though she had some very close female friends, including her secretary (it was reported that they had an affair). Once again, though, tragedy struck: at the age of 17, Yin Yin committed suicide in Brazil, where she was serving as consul; it has been claimed that he swallowed arsenic because his aunt and adoptive mother was sexually abusing him. In any case, it was a loss from which she never recovered, and for which her Nobel prize, awarded two years later, could do little to console her. Gabriela Mistral outlived her nephew by twelve years, during which she continued to be regaled with international prizes, honorary degrees and other tributes, including the French Legion of Honour. In 1957, she died in New York of cancer of the pancreas at the age of 67, leaving the proceeds of all her works published in South America to the children of Montegrande.

If you need somewhere to eat, *El Mesón del Fraile*, serving predictable fare, beckons opposite the museum. For accommodation – there is none in Montegrande itself – either take the turn-off (from the fork by the Capel plant) for Cochiguaz (see opposite), or continue along the main road to Pisco Elqui, 4km away. Halfway between Montegrande and Pisco Elqui, in a wonderful quiet location with mountain views, is one of the area's best places **to stay**. Stylishly built *El Galpón*, at La Jarilla (☎51/1982587, ✉elgalponelqui@hotmail.com; ⑥), is owned by a friendly Chilean who lived for many years in the United States. Each of the rooms has a huge bathroom, TV and a minibar; two- and five-person *cabañas* are also available. The well-kept grounds have an eye-catching swimming pool.

Pisco Elqui and around

PISCO ELQUI was known as La Unión until 1939, when Gabriel González Videla – later President of Chile – cunningly renamed it to thwart Peru's efforts to gain exclusive rights to the name "Pisco". An idyllic village with fewer than 500 inhabitants, it boasts a beautiful square filled with lush palm trees and flowers, overlooked by a colourful church with a tall, wooden tower. Locals sell homemade jam and marmalade in the square, and its abundant shade provides a welcome relief from the sun. During **Carnaval**, in the second half of February, the town resounds with folk concerts and other entertainment; on the down side, accommodation gets fully booked then, the campsite bursts at the seams and a generally rowdy ambience pervades, with too many drunken revellers for many people's taste. Down by the main road, the **Solar de Pisco Elqui** is Chile's oldest pisco distillery, which today (considerably modernized) produces the famous Tres Erres brand. There are free **guided tours** (daily 10am–7pm) around the old part of the plant, with tastings at the end. You can also visit the 130-year-old private distillery at **Los Nichos**, 4km on from Pisco Elqui (daily 11am–1pm & 3–6pm); if there's no one there, ask in the red house next door.

Pisco Elqui has plenty of good **places to stay**. The *Hotel Elqui*, on O'Higgins, the main street (☎51/1982523; ④), offers eight immaculate rooms, some with balconies, in a charming old building with a pool. The friendly, German-run *El Tesoro de Elqui*, on Prat (☎51/1982609, ☏51/451958; ④), offers attractive, spotless *cabañas* and a gorgeous pool. For a real treat, stay up at *Los Misterios de Elqui* ☆ (☎51/1982544; ⑦), 800m out of town on the road to Alcohuaz. Designer-magazine *cabañas* with fabulous views are spaced comfortably apart among landscaped gardens leading down to a stunning swimming pool; a gourmet chef prepares delicious food in a tastefully decorated restaurant; and horse rides up the valley can be arranged. Pisco Elqui also has three **campsites**, the best being *El Olivo*, just off the main road (☎51/411338; CH$3000 per person), with shade and a small swimming pool. Apart from the one at *Los Misterios*, Pisco Elqui's best **restaurants** are in *Hotel Elqui*, which serves typical Chilean meat dishes on a large, vine-covered patio, and *El Tesoro de Elqui*, where you can tuck into excellent roast meats. On the plaza, try the adobe-walled *Mandarino* ☆ for great pizzas and snacks served around an open fire in the cooler months; next door in a rustic patio you can enjoy real coffee (not instant) or sip a delicious fresh fruit juice or shake.

Alcohuaz

Some 15km beyond Pisco Elqui, reached by a narrow road that leads through increasingly unspoiled countryside, ever deeper into the valley and past the sleepy village of **Horcón** (the end of the road for buses from La Serena), is the tiny community of **ALCOHUAZ**. Apart from a handsome terracotta-hued church (in sharp contrast to Horcón's, which is sky blue), this remote settlement has little to offer in the way of standard attractions. But it is home to a popular curiosity, the **bee cure centre** known as Colmenares Alcohuaz, or "Alcohuaz Hives" (℡51/97815331, Ⓔnelsoncorreacl@yahoo.cl). People come from throughout the country to treat all kinds of ills by means of apitherapy (bee stings) – after being tested for allergies, of course. You can also buy a variety of excellent bee products such as honey, royal jelly, propolis and creams to treat skin ailments. If you want **to stay** in Alcohuaz, you can choose between two new, unobtrusive *cabaña* complexes: *Refugios La Frontera* (℡09/2798109; ❺) and *Valle Hermoso* (℡51/270641; ❹).

Along the Río Cochiguaz

Back in Montegrande, a rough, unpaved road branches off the main route, dips down the valley and follows the northern bank of the **RÍO COCHIGUAZ**, a tributary of the Elqui. Rustic *cabañas* dot the river bank; many offer holistic therapies and meditation classes. The small community of **Cochiguaz**, 12km along the valley, was founded in the 1960s by a group of hippies in the belief that the Age of Aquarius had shifted the earth's magnetic centre from the Himalayas to the Elqui Valley. But don't let this put you off – the multicoloured highland scenery is fabulous and the remoteness and tranquillity of the valley irresistible. If you're walking from the turn-off, you can easily reach the first set of *cabañas*, called *Spa Naturista* (℡51/451067; ❻), 2km from the paved road. A further 3km along, friendly *El Albaricoque* (℡090153075, Ⓔcarmenhurtado74@yahoo .com; ❹) offers rustic *cabañas* in a wood by the river, and tasty vegetarian food.

EL NORTE CHICO | The Elqui Valley

Pisco

Pisco has been enjoyed by Chileans for more than four centuries, but it wasn't until the 1930s that it was organized into an effective commercial industry, starting with the official creation, of a pisco *denominación de origen*. Shortly afterwards, a large number of growers, who'd always been at the mercy of the private distilleries for the price they got for their grapes, joined together to form co-operatives to produce their own pisco. The largest were the tongue-twisting *Sociedad Cooperativa Control Pisquero de Elqui y Vitiviniculo de Norte Ltda* (known as "Pisco Control") and the *Cooperativa Agrícola y Pisquera del Elqui Ltda* (known as "Pisco Capel"), today the two most important producers in Chile, accounting for over ninety percent of all pisco to hit the shops.

The basic **distillation technique** is the same one that's been used since colonial times: in short, the fermented wine is boiled in copper stills, at 90°C, releasing vapours that are condensed, then kept in oak vats for three to six months. The alcohol – of 55° to 65° – is then diluted with water, according to the type of pisco it's being sold as: 30° or 32° for *Selección*; 35° for *Reservado*; 40° for *Especial*; and 43°, 46° and 50° for *Gran Pisco*. It's most commonly consumed as a tangy, refreshing aperitif known as **Pisco Sour**, an ice-cold mix of pisco, lemon juice and sugar – sometimes with whisked egg white for a frothy head and angostura bitters for an extra zing.

Note that the Peruvians also produce pisco and consider their own to be the only authentic sort, maintaining that the Chilean stuff is nothing short of counterfeit. The Chileans, of course, pass this off as jealousy, insisting that their pisco is far superior (it is certainly grapier) and proudly claiming that pisco is a Chilean, not Peruvian, drink. Whoever produced it first, there's no denying that the pisco lovingly distilled in the Elqui Valley is absolutely delicious, drunk neat or in a cocktail. A visit to one of the distilleries in the region is not to be missed – if only for the free tasting at the end.

About 13km from Montegrande you'll find luxurious *cabañas* at *Casa del Agua* (☎ & ℱ51/321371; ➎) set in fifteen acres of private land spanning both sides of the river. French-run *Camping Parque Ecológico Río Mágico* at Fundo Victoria (☎08/9711254; CH$4000 per person) is a great option for campers while at the very end of the road, 18km from Montegrande, *Camping Cochiguaz* (☎51/1982558; CH$2500 per person) has 24 sites with picnic tables and offers **horse-riding** tours of the valley.

Ruta 41 to Argentina

After Rivadavia – where the right fork leads to Pisco Elqui – **Ruta 41** from La Serena follows first the Río Turbio and then the Río de la Laguna all the way to the **Paso del Agua Negra** (4779m) and the Argentine border, nearly 170km away. Only partly tarmacked, often narrow and hemmed in by imposing mountains, many of them over 4000m high, this road is one of the most dramatic linking the two countries, and is open only from October or November to April. Seventy-five kilometres on from Rivadavia you'll come to the **Complejo Aduanero Junta del Toro**, the Chilean customs post (Dec–Apr daily 8am–6pm). The **Argentine border** lies some 95km from the customs post. On the other side of the frontier, the RN 150 winds down to the easygoing market town of Rodeo and hits the adobe-built town of Jachal, from where the RN 40 strikes south to the laid-back provincial capital of San Juan, nearly 270km on from the border post. For more details of these places consult the *Rough Guide to Argentina*.

Vallenar and around

North of La Serena, the Panamericana turns inland and heads via a couple of winding passes (Cuesta Buenos Aires and Cuesta Pajonales) towards the modest town of **VALLENAR**, 190km up the road. There are only a few sporadic signs of habitation in between, and nothing to tempt you off the highway save a detour down a 76-kilometre dirt track (opposite Domeyko) to the **Reserva Nacional Pinguino de Humboldt**, where you can take boat trips (CH$40,000 per boat) to Isla Chañaral, surrounded by bottle-nosed dolphins, and to nearby colonies of Humboldt penguins. Pushing on to Vallenar, you'll find a busy but somewhat run-down little town that acts as a service centre for local mining and agricultural industries. Founded in 1789 by Governor Ambrosio O'Higgins, who named the city after his native Ballinagh in Ireland, it makes a convenient base for an excursion east into the fertile **upper Huasco Valley**, laced with green vines and small pisco plants, or northwest towards the coast and, in the spring, the wildflowers of the **Parque Nacional Llanos de Challe**. The self-appointed "*capital del desierto florido*" (and vigorously promoted as such by the tourist authorities), Vallenar is indeed the best base for forays into the **flowering desert** (see box p.208), if you're here at the right time. In the town itself, the **Museo del Huasco** at Ramírez 1001 (Mon–Fri 9am–1pm & 3–6pm; CH$450) has some moderately diverting displays on indigenous cultures and photos of the flowering desert.

Practicalities

Vallenar's two main **bus terminals** are on either side of Prat, some six blocks west of the main square. The official tourist office (unfixed hours; ☎51/619215), however, is inconveniently located just off the Panamericana,

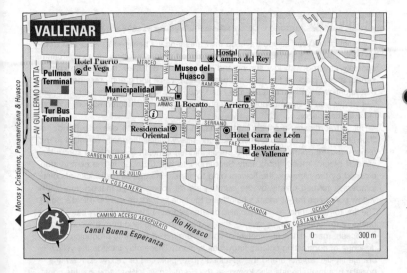

on the side road into town; a far better source of **tourist information** (Jan & Feb 9.30am–1.30pm & 4–7.30pm; March–Dec 9.30am–1.30pm & 3–6.30pm ☎51/611672, ⓦwww.elhuascodeatacama.cl) is the privately run, Dutch-supervised kiosk at the southwestern corner (no.30A) of the Plaza de Armas, also known as the Plaza Ambrosio O'Higgins.

Accommodation in Vallenar is on the whole overpriced but there are a few exceptions, including the budget rooms with private bath, set around a quiet patio, at *Residencial Oriental*, Serrano 720 (☎51/613889; ❷). *Hostal Camino del Rey* at Merced 943 (☎51/613184; ❹) has neat, box-like rooms with shared or private bath and its own parking, while the *Hotel Garra de León*, at Serrano 1052 (☎ & ⓕ51/613753; ❺), offers smart, spacious rooms with air conditioning, cable TV and pristine bathrooms, plus its own car park. Far and away superior, though, is the conveniently located *Hotel Puerto de Vega*, 🍴 right next to the bus terminal at Ramírez 201 (☎51/613870 ⓕ51/342955, ⓦwww.puertodevega.cl; ❺). It is the only boutique hotel in the whole region, with beautifully decorated rooms and suites, covered parking, a small swimming pool in a tidy garden, an Internet connection and huge, delicious breakfasts.

Of Vallenar's **restaurants**, the best is *Moros y Cristianos* (☎51/614600), a stylish place out on the Panamericana by the Huasco turn-off, run by a Leba-nese Chilean and serving slightly more interesting meat and fish dishes than the norm. The surprisingly good *Hostería de Vallenar*, at Alonso de Ercilla 848, offers well-cooked Chilean cuisine with imaginative sauces. The tastefully decorated, Chilean-Canadian-run *Arriero* 🍴, Prat 1061, dishes up huge *picadas* and juicy Argentine steaks. For pizzas and fast food, try *Il Boccato*, on the east side of the main square. There are no *cambios* in Vallenar, but several **ATMs** on Prat, between Brasil and Alonso de Ercilla.

The upper Huasco Valley

From Vallenar, a paved road follows the Río Huasco through a deep, attrac-tive valley that climbs towards the mountains. The road weaves back and

The flowering desert

For most of the year, as you travel up the Panamericana between Vallenar and Copiapó you'll cross a seemingly endless, semi-desert plain, stretching for nearly 100km, sparsely covered with low shrubs and *copao* cacti. But take the same journey in spring, and in place of the parched, brown earth, you'll find green grass dotted with beautiful flowers. If you're really lucky and you know where to go after a particularly wet winter, you'll happen upon fluorescent carpets of multicoloured flowers, stretching into the horizon.

This extraordinarily dramatic transformation is known as the **desierto florido**, or "flowering desert"; it occurs when unusually heavy rainfall (normally very light in this region) causes dormant bulbs and seeds, hidden beneath the earth, to sprout into sudden bloom, mostly from early September to late October. In the central strip, crossed by the highway, the flowers tend to appear in huge single blocks of colour (*praderas*), formed chiefly by the purple *pata de guanaco* ("guanaco's hoof"), the yellow *corona de fraile* ("monk's halo") and the blue *suspiro de campo* ("field's sigh"). The tiny forget-me-not-like *azulillo* also creates delicate blankets of baby blue. On the banks of the *quebradas*, or ravines, that snake across the land from the cordillera to the ocean, many different varieties of flowers are mixed together, producing a kaleidoscope of contrasting colours known as *jardines*. These may include the yellow or orange lily-like *añañuca* and the speckled white, pink, red or yellow *alstroemeria*, a popular plant with florists also known as the "Peruvian lily". West, towards the coast, you'll also find large crimson swaths of the endangered *garra de león* ("lion's claw"), particularly in the Parque Nacional Llanos de Challe, near Carrizal Bajo, created especially to protect them. Of course, removing any plant, whole or in part, is strictly forbidden by law.

There's no predicting the *desierto florido*, which is relatively rare – the frequency and intensity varies enormously, but the general phenomenon seems to occur every four to five years. According to local experts, 1997 and 2002 saw particularly memorable displays and some claim that 2004 was also a good year, but spring rainfall has undoubtedly been diminishing. The best **guide** in Vallenar, and a veritable gold mine of information about the dozens of flower varieties, is Roberto Alegría (☏51/613908 or 086044727).

forth across the river, taking you through dry, mauve-coloured hills and green orchards and vineyards. About 20km from the town, you pass the enormous **Santa Juana dam** which, after a season of heavy rainfall, overflows into a magnificent waterfall that can be viewed close-up from an observation deck. Thirty-eight kilometres from Vallenar, the valley forks at the confluence of the El Carmen and El Tránsito rivers. The right-hand road takes you up the **El Carmen Valley** where, just beyond the fork, you'll find **Alto del Carmen**, a pretty village that produces one of the best-known brands of pisco in Chile; you can visit the Planta Pisquera Alto del Carmen for a free tour and tastings (Feb–May Mon–Fri 9am–noon & 2–6pm, Sat 9am–noon). **Buses** leave Vallenar for Alto del Carmen five times a day, taking one hour. A further 26km up the now unpaved road, **San Félix** has a beautiful setting and a hundred-year-old **pisco plant** that produces high-quality, traditionally made pisco called Horcón Quemado. Guided tours (daily 8am–8pm; free) include a look at the old copper machinery and tastings at the end. There are two rustic **places to stay** in San Félix: *Pensión San Félix* (no phone; ❷), which has a restaurant, and *Pensión La Fortuna* (no phone; ❷).

The **El Tránsito Valley** (reached by taking the left-hand, unpaved road just before Alto del Carmen) was ignored by the Spaniards when they farmed the El

Carmen Valley during colonial times, and became one of the region's last enclaves of indigenous people. Narrower than the El Carmen Valley, the El Tránsito Valley is enclosed by white- and red-streaked hills that are the richest source of marble in Chile. About 30km along the road you reach **El Tránsito**, the largest village in the valley, with a fragrant, tree-filled plaza and a handsome old church. Seven kilometres on from here, a rough road branches south down the **quebrada de Pinte**, a gorge full of curious geological formations and marine fossils. At the end of the gorge, 5km from the turn-off, **Pinte** is a tiny oasis village with a beautiful white church surrounded by orange, lemon and lime trees; you can hire a guide here, Gabriel Rivera, to show you the geological features.

Parque Nacional Llanos de Challe and the northern beaches

If you have the good luck to be around while the desert's in bloom, head for the **PARQUE NACIONAL LLANOS DE CHALLE** (CH$3500), north-west of Vallenar, for the full impact . This 450-square kilometre swath of coastal plain has been singled out for national park status because of the abundance of **garra de león** – an exquisite, deep-red flower in danger of extinction – that grows here during the years of the *desierto florido*. The park is crossed by an 82-two-kilometre dirt road branching east from the Panamericana, 17km north of Vallenar, ending at **Carrizal Bajo**, a once-important mining port now home to a tiny fishing community made up of sixteen families. Three buses a week leave Vallenar for Carrizal Bajo (for details, check with Vallenar's Oficina de Turismo ☎51/619215). If you have a 4WD, a tent and a taste for wilderness, follow the very rough track north of Carrizal Bajo up to Puerto Viejo, near Caldera and Copiapó. The deserted **beaches** along this stretch, particularly the northern half, are breathtaking, with white sands and clear, turquoise waters.

Copiapó

Overlooked by rippling mountains, the prosperous city of **COPIAPÓ** sits in the flat basin of the **Río Copiapó**, some 60km from the coast and 145km north of Vallenar. The valley to the east is the most northerly of Chile's "transverse valleys" and – with the exception of the Río Loa which empties into the ocean near Iquique – the Copiapó is Chile's northernmost river to flow all the way from the Andes to the Pacific. Beyond this valley the transformation from semi-desert to serious desert is complete, and the bare, barren Atacama stretches a staggering 1000km north towards the Peruvian border. Just to the north of the city, Arabian–style dunes await exploration.

When Diego de Almagro made his long trek south from Cuzco in 1536, following the Inca Royal Road down the spine of the Andes, it was into this valley that he descended, recuperating from the gruelling journey at the *tambo*, or resting place, where Copiapó now stands. The valley had been occupied and cultivated by the Diaguita people starting around 1000 AD and then was inhabited, beginning around 1470, by the Incas, who mined gold and copper here. Although Spanish *encomenderos* (see p.592) occupied the valley from the beginning of the conquest, it wasn't until 1744 that the city of Copiapó was founded, initially as "San Francisco de la Selva". A series of random silver strikes in the nineteenth century, most notably at Chañarcillo, threw the region into a frenzied boom.

Following a period of decline at the beginning of the twentieth century, Copiapó is once more at the centre of a rich mining industry, revolving around copper, iron and gold. A lively, busy city of some 100,000 inhabitants, it has a fairly compact downtown composed of typical adobe houses, some churches and the odd mansion, with a large, tree-filled square at its centre.

There isn't a great deal to do here, however, and Copiapó's main use to travellers is as a springboard for excursions into the surrounding region – primarily up to the lakes and volcanoes of **Parque Nacional Nevado de Tres Cruces** and nearby **Volcán Ojos de Salado** and **Laguna Verde**, all sitting high in the Andes, or west into the famously beautiful seaside resort of **Bahía Inglesa**, or north to the marine wildlife and coastal scenery of **Parque Nacional Pan de Azúcar**. Closer at hand, the **Río Copiapó Valley** is a popular day-trip and one of the most stunning examples of desert irrigation in Chile. Unlike the more famous Elqui Valley, it's not marred by the nylon windbreakers and protective netting used to protect grape vines from wind damage.

Arrival and information

Copiapó's main **bus terminal**, served by most inter-city buses, is centrally located on the corner of Freire and Chacabuco, three blocks south of Plaza Prat. Next door, also on Chacabuco, is the **Tur Bus terminal**, while one block east, at Freire and Colipí, sits the **Pullman Bus terminal**. The new Desierto de Atacama **international airport** is just over 50km west of the city, at Chamomate, not far from Caldera. There are no buses from the airport into the centre, but there's usually a Manuel Flores Salinas **minibus** there to meet arriving planes; it will take you into town for CH$4000, whereas the other companies charge CH$7000 and a taxi will set you back CH$15,000-21,000.

A well-organized, helpful **Sernatur** office sits on the north side of Plaza Prat, at Los Carrera 691 (mid-Dec–Feb Mon–Fri 8.30am–6.30pm, Sat 10am–2pm;

March–mid-Dec Mon–Fri 8.30am–5.30pm; ☎52/212838). **Conaf**, at Juan Martínez 56 (Mon–Fri 9am–1pm & 2.30–5.30pm; ☎52/213404), will give you information on protected areas in this region, including Pan de Azúcar and Nevado de Tres Cruces national parks; it's also a good source of information on road conditions in the altiplano.

Accommodation

Copiapó has an excellent choice of upmarket **hotels** offering the levels of comfort and service you would expect, but rarely get, for the price. Decent mid-priced options, on the other hand, are thin on the ground, but there are plenty of adequate budget rooms.

Hotel La Casona O'Higgins 150 ☎52/217277, ℱ52/217278. This small, charming and impeccably decorated hotel has an English-speaking owner and serves excellent breakfasts, included in the rate. ❺

Hotel Chagall O'Higgins 760 ☎52/213775, ℱ52/211527. Modern hotel with an attractive lobby and bar, spacious, new-looking rooms, smart baths, a good restaurant and private parking. ❻

Hotel Diego de Almeida O'Higgins 656 ☎52/212075, ℱ52/212076. Large, stylish hotel with contemporary decor, pool, sauna and parking. ❻

Hotel Montecatini I Infante 766 ☎52/211363, ℱ52/217021. Bright, spacious rooms falling into two classes: smart, new *ejecutivo* and older but cheaper *turista*, both with private bath. Has its own parking. ❺

Hotel Palace Atacama 741 ☎52/212852. Reasonable but overpriced rooms with private bath around an attractive patio; try bargaining the rate down. ❹

Residencial Ben Bow Rodriguez 541 ☎52/217634. Cramped but perfectly fine little rooms, among the cheapest in town. ❷

Residencial Chacabuco O'Higgins 921 ☎52/213428. Simple but cared-for rooms off a tidy patio. ❸

The City

The nucleus of Copiapó is the large, green **Plaza Prat**, lined with 84 towering old pepper trees planted in 1880. On the southwest corner of the square stands the mid-nineteenth-century **Iglesia Catedral**, designed by the English architect William Rogers, sporting a Neoclassical three-door portico and topped by an unusual tiered wooden steeple. Just off the northeast corner of the square, at the corner of Colipí and Rodriguez, the University of Atacama's **Museo Mineralógico** (Mon–Fri 10am–1pm & 3.30–7pm, Sat 10am–1pm; CH$500) displays a glittering collection of over two thousand mineral samples from around the world, including huge chunks of malachite, amethyst, quartz, marble and onyx; it's a real pity that the museum is so poorly presented, with virtually no explanations or guides of any kind. Five blocks west of the square, at Atacama and Rancagua, the **Museo Regional** (Dec–Feb Mon–Fri 9am–7.30pm, Sat 11am–2pm & 4–7pm, Sun 11am–2pm; March–Nov Mon 2–5.45pm, Tues–Fri 9am–5.45pm, Sat 10am–1pm & 3–5.45pm, Sun 10am–1pm; CH$600) repays a visit, not least for the handsome mansion that houses it, the **Casa Matta**, built in the 1840s for one of Copiapó's wealthy mining barons. The museum's well-presented displays cover the exploration of the desert, the development of mining, the War of the Pacific, pre-Columbian peoples of the region and the Inca road system.

Towering over a tiny square that is the site of a busy Friday market selling fresh produce and household items, the imposing, red-walled 1872 **Iglesia San Francisco** sits one block south and west of the museum. The square's centre is marked by a statue of a rough-clad miner, tools in hand – none other than **Juan Godoy**, the goatherd who accidentally discovered the enormous silver deposits of nearby Chañarcillo in 1832, now honoured in Copiapó as a local legend. Just off the square, Avenida Matta leads north to the former **railway workers' residence**, a rather grand building with a large pediment supported by tall wooden columns. Round the corner, a couple of blocks down Martínez (the extension of Calle Atacama), the former **railway station**, built in 1854, displays photos and memorabilia of the Caldera–Copiapó railway, the first in Chile and third in South America (British Guiana, now Guyana, and Peru saw the first and second). Not close to anything in particular, out at the corner of Yerbas Buenas and Infante, the **Iglesia de Belén** – built by the Jesuits during the colonial period and restored in 1856 by a wealthy local family – also deserves a visit for its delicate structure and dainty wooden tower.

Eating, drinking and entertainment

Copiapó's **restaurants** are extremely uninspiring, but most of them are moderately priced. For cheap snacks, head for the row of cafés on Chacabuco, opposite the bus terminal – the least insalubrious is *Don Elías*. The **nightlife** scene is not what you'd call swinging, but if you're set on dancing you could try one of the city's **discos**: *Splash* at Juan Martínez 46 is a perennial favourite. There's a fairly large **cinema** with decent sound at Atacama 455.

Restaurants

Bavaria West side of Plaza Prat. Conveniently located branch of the ubiquitous chain serving sandwiches, snacks and meat dishes.

El Corsario Atacama 245. Old-fashioned restaurant with tables around the interior patio of an old adobe house. Offers basic Chilean dishes such as *pastel de choclo* and *humitas*.

Guajiro Pub Atacama, between Rancagua and Talcahuano. Large, dark restaurant specializing in hearty *parrilladas*.

Hotel Miramonti Ramón Freire 731, opposite Pullman Bus terminal. This elegant hotel restaurant serves decent but quite expensive Italian food– then spoils it all with appalling music.

Tours from Copiapó

A handful of companies and individuals offer tours out of Copiapó. Operators come and go, the best providing professional guides, others offering little more than glorified drivers. The main full-day destinations are east into the cordillera, taking in **Parque Nacional Nevado de Tres Cruces** and sometimes **Laguna Verde** and **Ojos de Salado** (see p.215); and north to **Parque Nacional Pan de Azúcar** (see p.218). Half-day trips go north into the **Atacama dunes**, west to the **beaches** around **Bahía Inglesa** (see p.217), or east up the **Copiapó River Valley** (see opposite). Ask at Sernatur in Copiapó for a list of guides.

Maximiliano Martínez of Aventurismo, at Colipí 844, Mall Plaza Real 212 (☎52/235340, www.aventurismo.cl) has been taking tourists up to Ojos de Salado, Laguna Verde and around for longer than anyone else in the business; trips to Laguna Verde and Laguna Santa Rosa cost around US$65 per person, minimum four. An excellent newcomer is Gran Atacama at Colipí 844, Mall Plaza Real 122 (☎52/21927, wwww.granatacama.cl); this highly professional outfit with enthusiastic, informed guides, offers half-day excursions or trips lasting a day, several days, a week or more, covering the whole region with a blend of adventure, culture and luxury. A three-night tour of the parks and coast costs around CH$400,000 per person.

Moving on from Copiapó

Copiapó has daily **bus services** to Santiago and Arica and all the major cities in between, as well as to local and regional destinations. **Inter-city** services are offered by all the main companies, including Flota Barrios (☎52/213645), Pullman Bus (☎52/218676), Tas Choapa (☎52/213793) and Tur Bus (☎52/212150). For **Caldera** and **Bahía Inglesa**, Recabarren has the most frequent service (about every 30min) from the side street opposite the main terminal. Casther (☎52/218889) has around seven daily buses up the **Copiapó River Valley**, which is also served by Abarán buses.

Listings

Airlines LAN, Los Carrera and Colipí, on the north-east corner of the main square ☎52/213512.
Airport information ☎52/235170.
Banks and exchange There are several ATMs on the main square, including Corp Banca at Chacabuco 481 and BCI at Chacabuco 449. Casa de Cambio Fides is at Atacama 541, on the 2nd floor of Galería Coimba.
Camping gear *Bencina blanca* (white gas) and butane gas are available at Ferretería El Herrerito, Atacama 699. Dolomiti at Chacabuco and Chañar-cillo, has a wide range of Camping Gaz appliances and other outdoor stuff.
Car rental Rodaggio, Colipí 127 (☎52/212153, ✉rodaggio@entelchile.net), has good-value 4x4

jeeps. Other firms include Carmona, R. Freire 466 ☎ & ☏52/216030; Hertz, Copayapú 173 ☎52/213522; and Retablo, Los Carrera 955 ☎ & ☏52/219384.
Internet *Zonavirtual* at Maipu 450, 2nd floor.
Laundry Good, cheap service at Lavasuper, Mackenna 430, between O'Higgins and Carrera.
Post office North side of Plaza Prat at Los Carrera 691.
Swimming Olympic-size swimming pool on Av Luis Flores.
Telephone centres Telefónica, corner of Los Carrera and Chacabuco; Entell, on the main square at Colipí 500.

Around Copiapó

The region around Copiapó features some of the most striking and varied landscapes in Chile. To the east, the **Río Copiapó Valley** offers the extraordinary spectacle of emerald-green vines growing in desert-dry hills, while high up in the Andes, you'll ascend a world of salt flats, volcanoes and lakes, encompassed by the **Parque Nacional Nevado de Tres Cruces**, the **Volcán Ojos de Salado** and the blue-green **Laguna Verde**. To the west, **Bahía Inglesa**, near the port of **Caldera**, could be a little chunk of the Mediterranean, with its pristine sands and odd-shaped rocks rising out of the sea. Further south, reached only in a 4x4, the coast is lined with wild, deserted **beaches** lapped by turquoise waters.

Río Copiapó Valley

Despite an acute shortage of rainfall, the **RÍO COPIAPÓ VALLEY** is one of the most important grape-growing areas of Chile. This is thanks mainly to new irrigation techniques that have been developed over the past fifteen years, tapping into the valley's abundance of underground flowing water. The combination of computer-controlled irrigation and a hot, dry climate ensures an early harvest, with the grapes on US supermarket shelves by October. While the Copiapó Valley is not quite as pastoral or picturesque as the Elqui Valley, its cultivated areas provide, more than anywhere else in the north, the most stunning contrast between deep-green produce and parched, dry earth – from September to May, in particular, it really is a sight to behold.

The first stretch from Copiapó is quite dull, though you do pass some note-worthy landmarks, like the large country mansion and church at **Nantoco** (23km from the city), built in 1878 for one of Copiapó's rich mining magnates and now in a lamentable state of disrepair. At kilometre 34, hidden behind a dense covering of palm trees on the right-hand side, the **Casa de Jotabeche** is another grand nineteenth-century residence, this one belonging to the promi-nent essayist José Joaquín Vallejo, known as "Jotabeche", who lived here until his death in 1858. By the time you reach Los Loros, 64km from Copiapó, the valley has become narrower, greener and prettier. Los Loros makes a good place to stop for **lunch** – try Sra Herrera at no. 62 of the main street, Martínez (knock on the big yellow door), for good, simple food served on a terrace overlooking the valley. Around 17km further on, a small track leads from the paved road up to **Viña del Cerro**, the heavily restored remains of a fifteenth-century Diaguita-Inca copper foundry. They include the low stone walls of what was once the control centre, the workers' quarters and 26 circular smelting ovens that were powered by wind and carbon fuel. The site is in a dramatic location, commanding panoramic views over the surrounding vineyards.

Parque Nacional Nevado de Tres Cruces and around

East of Copiapó, the Andes divide into two separate ranges – the Cordillera de Domeyko and the Cordillera de Claudio Gay – joined by a high basin, or plateau, that stretches all the way north to Bolivia. The waters trapped in this basin form vast salt flats and lakes towered over by enormous, snow-capped volcanoes, and wild vicuña and guanaco roam the sparsely vegetated hills. This is a truly awe-inspiring landscape, conveying an acute sense of wilderness and space. It's easier to fully appreciate it here than around San Pedro de Atacama, for instance, thanks to the general absence of tourists. The number of visitors has started to increase, however, following the creation in 1994 of the new **Parque Nacional Nevado de Tres Cruces**, which takes in a dazzling white salt flat, the **Salar de Maricunga**; two beautiful lakes, the **Laguna Santa Rosa** and **Laguna del Negro Francisco**; and the 6753-metre volcano, **Tres Cruces**.

Close to but not part of the park, by the border with Argentina, the stunning, blue-green **Laguna Verde** lies at the foot of the highest active volcano in the world, the 6893-metre **Volcán Ojos de Salado**. From Copiapó, it's about a three-hour drive to Laguna Santa Rosa, and a six-hour drive to Laguna Verde. Temperatures are low at all times of year, so take plenty of warm gear. There is no public transport to this area – for information on **tours** here see p.212.

Parque Nacional Nevado de Tres Cruces

The bumpy road up to **PARQUE NACIONAL NEVADO DE TRES CRUCES** (CH$3500 entrance fee) takes you through a brief stretch of desert before twisting up narrow canyons flanked by mineral-stained rocks. As you climb higher, the colours of the scoured, bare mountains become increasingly vibrant, ranging from oranges and golds to greens and violets. Some 165km from Copiapó, at an altitude of around 3700m, the road (following the signs to Mina Marta) reaches the first sector of the park, skirting the pale-blue **Laguna Santa Rosa**, home to dozens of pink flamingos. A track branching north of the road leads to a tiny wooden **refugio** maintained by Conaf on the western shore of the lake. It's a basic but convenient place to camp (no bunk beds, floor space only), with its own private views of the lake backed by the snow-capped **Volcán Tres Cruces**.

Immediately adjacent, the gleaming white **Salar de Maricunga** is Chile's most southerly salt flat, covering an area of over 80 square kilometres. A two- to three-hour drive south from here, past Mina Marta, the park's second sector is based around the large, deep-blue **Laguna del Negro Francisco**, some 4200m above sea level and home to abundant birdlife, including wild ducks and flamingos. Towering over the lake, the 6080-metre **Volcán Copiapó** was the site of an Inca sacrificial altar. Conaf has its park headquarters and a large, comfortable **refugio** (❸) about 4km from the lake; the *guardaparques* are very friendly and take visitors on educational excursions to the lake and around, but if you want to stay over check with Conaf in Copiapó first.

Laguna Verde and Volcán Ojos de Salado

The first, sudden sight of **LAGUNA VERDE** is stupendous. The intense colour of its waters – green or turquoise, depending on the time of day – almost leaps out at you from the muted browns and ochres of the surrounding land-scape. The lake lies at an altitude of 4500m, about 250km from Copiapó on the international road to Argentina (follow the signs to Paso San Francisco or Tinogasta). At the western end of the lake, a small shack contains a fabulous **hot-spring bath**, where you can soak and take blissful refuge from the biting wind outdoors. The best place to camp is just outside the bath, where a stone wall offers some protection from the wind, and hot streams provide useful washing-up water. At the lake's eastern end there's a *carabineros* checkpoint, where you should make yourself known if you plan to camp.

Laguna Verde is surrounded by huge volcanoes: Mulas Muertas, Incahuasi and the monumental **OJOS DE SALADO**. At 6893m, this is the highest peak in Chile and the highest active volcano in the world; its last two eruptions were in 1937 and 1956. A popular climb (between October and May), it's not techni-cally difficult, apart from the last 50m that border the crater. The base of the volcano is a twelve-kilometre walk from the abandoned *carabineros* checkpoint on the main road, and there are two *refugios* on the way up, one at 5100m and another at 5750m. If you need to arrange transport to the base, or a guide for the ascent, contact Maximiliano Martínez or his son Sebastián at Aventurismo (see p.212). As the volcano sits on the border with Argentina, climbers need to present written permission from the Dirección de Fronteras y Límites (see p.72) plus a Permiso Regional, obtained from the tourist office, to the *carabineros* before climbing up.

Caldera

Just over 70km west from Copiapó, **CALDERA** is a small, easygoing seaside town with a smattering of nineteenth-century buildings, a beach, a pier and a few good fish restaurants. Chosen as the terminus of Chile's first railway by mining and railway pioneer William Wheelwright, it became the country's second-largest port in the last decades of the nineteenth century, when it exported all the silver extracted in the region's dramatic silver boom. Caldera's two ports are still busy – one exporting table grapes, the other exporting copper – but they don't totally dominate the bay, which remains fairly attractive and clean. The town's only landmarks are the Gothic-towered **Iglesia de San Vicente** on the main square, built by English carpenters in 1862, and the former **train station** at the pier, dating from 1850 and looking a little sorry for itself these days. The

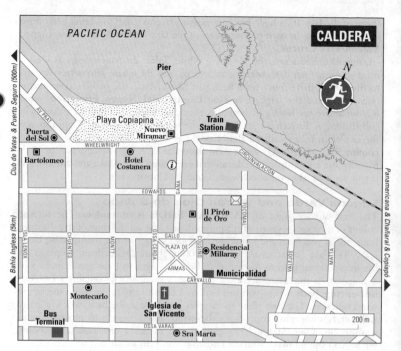

pier, down by the beach, makes for a pleasant stroll and is the starting point for **boat rides** around the bay in summer. Caldera's main **beach** is the sheltered, mid-sized Copiapina, while to the west of the pier, the large, windswept Playa Brava stretches towards the desert sands of the Norte Grande.

Practicalities

Caldera is a one-hour **bus** ride from Copiapó. The most frequent service is provided by Recabarren and Casther; buses depart from the side street opposite Copiapó's main bus terminal, arriving in Caldera at a small terminal at the corner of Cifuentes and Ossa Varas. **Sernatur** has a summertime kiosk (unfixed hours) on Calle Gana, by the seafront; otherwise, try the Municipalidad on the plaza.

The town has a reasonable spread of **accommodation**. The cheapest rooms – basic but clean and quiet – are at *Sra Marta's*, at Ossa Varas 461 (☏52/315222; ❷), while the nicest budget choice is probably *Residencial Millaray*, on the plaza at Cousiño 331 (☏52/315528; ❸), which has simple, airy rooms (some without bath) looking onto a leafy patio. For a step up in comfort, try *Montecarlo*, at Carvallo 627 (☏52/315388; ❹), offering *cabaña*-type rooms with bath, TV, fridge and private parking. The similarly priced *Hotel Costanera*, on the seafront at Wheelwright 543 (☏ & ℗ 52/316007; ❹) has spacious, clean rooms, some with sea views, and its own parking. Caldera's best hotel, the *Puerta del Sol*, at Wheelwright 750 (☏52/31505, ℗315507; ❺), features a mix of smart and dowdy rooms, and an attractive outdoor restaurant and pool area.

Many of Caldera's **restaurants** specialize in fish and shellfish. The best in town is the down-to-earth *Il Pirón de Oro*, Cousiño 218, which serves imaginatively prepared dishes, including exquisite dressed crab. *Nuevo Miramar* isn't quite as good (locals claim, disapprovingly, that they use frozen fish), but has a better location, right on the beach, with wonderful ocean views. *Puerto Seguro*, right at the other end of the beach and part of the *Club de Yates*, is a smart, stylish place with great views but not much atmosphere. Finish off your evening at *Bartolomeo*, a mellow **pub-café** at Wheelwright 747, which often has live jazz, folk or blues at the weekend.

There's a **phone office** at Edwards 360, while the **post office** is up the road at no. 339. The BCI **bank** opposite the *Nuevo Miramar* has an ATM.

Bahía Inglesa and the southern coast

The **beaches** of **BAHÍA INGLESA** are probably the most photographed in Chile, adorning wall calendars up and down the country. More than their white, powdery sands – which, after all, you can find the length of Chile's coast – it's the exquisite clarity of the turquoise sea, and the curious rock formations that rise out of it, that sets these beaches apart; unfortunately, green algae have invaded the bay, probably owing to fertilizer run-off from nearby farms, and the turquoise waters have gradually turned a murky green instead.

Several beaches are strung along the bay to the north of Caldera, separated by rocky outcrops: the long Playa Machas is the southernmost beach, followed by Playa La Piscina, then by Playa El Chuncho and finally Playa Blanca. Surprisingly, this resort area has not been swamped by the kind of ugly, large-scale construction that mars Viña del Mar and La Serena, and Bahía Inglesa remains a fairly compact collection of *cabañas* and a few hotels. While the place gets hideously crowded in the height of summer, at most other times it's peaceful and relaxing.

Practicalities

The problem with staying here is that **accommodation** tends to be ridiculously overpriced, but you should be able to bargain the rates down outside summer. *Cabañas Villa Alegre*, at the corner of Avenida El Morro and Valparaíso

△ Bahía Inglesa

(☎52/315074; ⑥), offers humble but well-equipped cabins – and discounts of up to fifty percent outside high season. Neighbouring *El Coral* (☎52/315331; ⑤) has comfortable rooms, two of them with good sea views, and an excellent, unpretentious fish restaurant. Further along Avenida El Morro, *Apart-Hotel Rocas de Bahía* (☎52/316005, ℱ52/316032, ⓦwww.petris.cl/rocasdebahia; ⑦) is a whitewashed apartment block overlooking the ocean, with a pleasant pool and a good restaurant. Back from the beachfront, three blocks behind *El Coral* at Copiapó 100, *Los Jardines de Bahía Inglesa* (☎52/315359; ⑤) has smart *cabañas* and a decent restaurant serving Italian-influenced fare. *Camping Bahía Inglesa* (☎ & ℱ 52/315424; CH$16,000 per site) is an expensive **campsite** just off Playa Las Machas.

Two **eateries** of note along the seafront are *El Plateado*, favoured by hippies and serving international cuisine including curries, outside, weather permitting; and, at the end of the promenade, *El Domo*, a futuristic tent-like cupola, inside which you can try some adventurous cuisine, or just linger over a real coffee or a drink.

You can also simply visit Bahía Inglesa for the day from Caldera, just 6km away; plenty of **buses** and **colectivos** (leaving from Caldera's central square) connect the two resorts, and also Copiapó. The best place to catch a *colectivo* back to Caldera is at the crossroads by *Los Jardines de Bahía Inglesa*; be aware that these are few and far between in the off-season.

The southern coast

South of Bahía Inglesa, beyond the little fishing village of Puerto Viejo that marks the end of the paved road, the coast is studded with a string of **superb beaches** lapped with crystal-clear water and backed by immense sand dunes. The scenery is particularly striking around **Bahía Salada**, a deserted bay indented with tiny coves some 130km south of Bahía Inglesa. You might be able to find a tour operator (see p.212) that arranges excursions to these beaches, but if you really want to appreciate the solitude and wilderness of this stretch of coast, you're better off renting a jeep and doing it yourself.

Parque Nacional Pan de Azúcar and around

North of Copiapó and Caldera, the first stop on the Panamericana is **Chañaral**, a drab, uninviting town useful principally as a base for visiting **Parque Nacional Pan de Azúcar**, 30km up the coast, with towering cliffs, unspoilt wildlife and fine beaches. Back on the highway, four hundred empty kilometres stretch north to the city of Antofagasta (see p.226), broken only by the small, neglected fishing town of **Taltal**, 135km on from Chañaral.

Chañaral

Sitting by a wide, white bay and the Panamericana, **CHAÑARAL**, 167km north of Copiapó, is a rather sorry-looking town of houses staggered up a hillside, with more than its fair share of stray dogs. Originally a small *caleta* used for shipping out the produce of an inland desert oasis, it still serves chiefly as an export centre, these days for the giant El Salvador copper mine, 130km east in the cordillera. Despite efforts to clean it up, Chañaral's huge beach remains contaminated by the toxic wastes deposited by the mine.

You can visit the **Parque Nacional Pan de Azúcar** from Chañaral, although it is preferable to visit the park as a day trip from Copiapó. Many north–south buses make a stop in the town; those that don't will drop you off if you ask. **Accommodation** choices are quite limited, such as the basic but clean and light *Hotel La Marina* on the main street at Merino Jarpa 562 (T52/480942; ❷; no hot water or private bath), and the marginally better-value *Residencial Sutivan* at Comercio 365 (T52/489123; ❸), with comfortable rooms at the back looking down to the ocean. Options for **eating** are little better: try *Nuria* on the main square, opposite the church, or the busy *El Rincón Porteño* at Merino Jarpa 567; both serve basic Chilean staples like fried fish and *lomo con papas* (steak and chips). There is an ATM at the BCI **bank**, Maipú 319.

Parque Nacional Pan de Azúcar

Home to two dozen varieties of cactus, guanacos and foxes, and countless birds, **PARQUE NACIONAL PAN DE AZÚCAR** is a 40-kilometre strip of desert containing the most stunning coastal scenery in the north of Chile. Steep hills and cliffs rise abruptly from the shore, which is lined with a series of pristine sandy beaches, some of them of the purest white imaginable. Though bare and stark, these hills make an unforgettable sight as they catch the late afternoon sun, when the whole coastline is bathed in rich shades of gold, pink and yellow. The only inhabited part of the park is **Caleta Pan de Azúcar**, 30km north of Chañaral, where you'll find a cluster of twenty or so fishermen's shacks as well as the Conaf information centre and a campsite (see p.220). Opposite the village, 2km off the shore, the **Isla Pan de Azúcar** is a small island sheltering a huge collection of marine wildlife, including seals, sea otters, plovers, cormorants, pelicans and more than three thousand Humboldt penguins; you can (and should – it's well worth it) take a boat trip out to get a close look at the wildlife. The island's distinctive conical silhouette gives the park its name "sugarloaf". For fabulous panoramic views up and down the coast, head to **Mirador Pan de Azúcar**, a well-signposted lookout point 10km north of the village; the different varieties of cactus are fascinating and you may have the place all to yourself – unless you're joined by a curious grey fox or guanaco. More difficult to reach, and less rewarding, **Las Lomitas** is a 700-metre-high clifftop about 30km north of the village; it's almost permanently shrouded in mist and is the site of a large black net, or "fog catcher", that condenses fog into water and collects it below.

Practicalities

There are two **access roads** to the park, both branching off the Panamericana: approaching from the south, the turn-off is at the north end of Chañaral, just past the cemetery; from the north, take the turn-off at Las Bombas, 45km north of Chañaral. Both roads are bumpy but passable in a car. There is no **public transport** to the park, but Chango Turismo (T52/480668 or 480484) runs a twice-daily **bus** (CH\$2000) to Caleta Pan de Azúcar from Chañaral; it leaves at 8am and 3pm from opposite the Pullman Bus terminal, at Freire 493, and returns from the park at 10am and 5pm (phone to confirm times). Chango Turismo also runs **jeep tours** to the Mirador Pan de Azúcar (CH\$7000) and Las Lomitas (CH\$15,000). Alternatively you could get a **taxi** (CH\$6000 each way from Chañaral; worth it if there are several in your group), or you can also come on a **day-trip** from Copiapó.

The **Conaf information centre** (daily 8.30am–12.30pm & 2–6pm), near the village, offers maps, leaflets and souvenirs. This is where you pay your park fee (CH\$3500). A single concessionaire (☏ & ☏52/480539) provides **camping** areas (CH\$10,000 per site) on the beaches around the village and at Playa Piqueros, further south, as well as two beautifully located *cabañas* (**⑤**) on a secluded beach north of the village. Rough camping is not allowed in the park. You can buy fish and water in the village, otherwise you need to bring everything yourself. **Boat trips** to the island depart from the *caleta* and cost CH\$4000 per person (minimum six people) or CH\$24,000 per boat trip. It takes about 1 hour 30 minutes to do the circuit; the best times are around 7 or 8am and 6pm, when the penguins come out to eat. Ask for Rodrigo Carvajal Robles of Pingüi Tours (✉ carvajalrodrigo@hotmail.com) at Las Conchas 7.

Taltal

There's only a single town beyond Chañaral until you get to Antofagasta, 400km of desert to the north – **TALTAL**. Strung along a narrow shelf of land at the foot of the coastal mountains, Taltal was once an important nitrate port used for exporting the *caliche* (nitrate ore) brought down from the pampas by the Taltal Railway Company, but now is just a small, marginal fishing town. If you are driving, it can make a convenient place to break your long desert journey– take the (signed) 25-kilometre side road branching west off the Panamericana about 120km north of Chañaral. Wander down to the **old railway terminus** and port to take a look at the former houses and offices of the Taltal Railway Company, clearly fine buildings in their heyday and now gently decaying. Also down here, in a small square at the corner of O'Higgins and Prat, stands one of the old **locomotives**, a shiny green "Kitson Meyer no. 59" containing a display of black and white photographs of Taltal during the nitrate era. Take a look, too, at the **Museo de Taltal** on Prat (Mon–Fri 9am–noon & 3–7.30pm; free), just north of the plaza, where you'll find an interesting but poorly presented collection of archeological finds from the region, including ancient arrowheads and tools, and a tiny Chinchorro mummy (see p.271).

The best **restaurants** in town, both serving fresh seafood, are the *Club Social de Taltal* in a large old building opposite the Municipalidad, off the plaza, and *Las Anclas*, by the sea at the corner of Martínez and Esmeralda. Several **bus companies**, including Tur Bus (☏55/611426), have offices in Taltal.

Travel details

Buses

Chañaral to: Antofagasta (15 daily; 5hr); Arica (5 daily; 15hr); Calama (10 daily; 8hr); Chuquicamata (2 daily; 8hr 20min); Copiapó (10 daily; 2hr); Iquique (8 daily; 11hr); La Serena (10 daily; 6hr); Mejillones (2 daily; 5hr 40min); Ovalle (10 daily; 9hr); Santiago (16 daily; 14hr); Taltal (2 daily; 2hr 30min); Tocopilla (2 daily; 8hr); Vallenar (14 daily; 4hr).

Copiapó to: Antofagasta (15 daily; 7hr); Arica (11 daily; 16hr); Calama (12 daily; 9hr 30min); Caldera (every 30min; 1hr); Chañaral (10 daily; 2hr); Iquique (12 daily; 13hr); La Serena (20 daily; 4hr); Ovalle (6 daily; 5hr 30min); Santiago (22 daily;

12hr); Vallenar (10 daily; 1hr 45min); Valparaíso (6 daily; 12hr).

La Serena to: Antofagasta (15 daily; 11hr); Arica (8 daily; 18hr); Calama (14 daily; 12hr 30min); Chañaral (7 daily; 6hr); Copiapó (20 daily; 4hr); Iquique (9 daily; 16hr); Montegrande (6 daily; 2hr 20min); Ovalle (18 daily; 1hr); Pisco Elqui (6 daily; 2hr 30min); Santiago (every 30min; 7hr); Vallenar (15 daily; 2hr 20min); Valparaíso (8 daily; 7hr); Vicuña (every 30min; 1hr 30min).

Ovalle to: Andacollo (4 daily; 2hr); Antofagasta (10 daily; 11hr); Arica (1 daily; 19hr); Calama (13hr); Chañaral (10 daily; 7hr); Copiapó (10 daily; 5hr); Iquique (2 daily; 19hr); La Serena

(18 daily; 1hr); Los Vilos (6 daily; 2hr); Santiago (15 daily; 6hr); Vallenar (5 daily; 4hr).

Vallenar to: Alto del Carmen (5 daily; 1hr); Antofagasta (10 daily; 9hr); Calama (10 daily; 11hr); Caldera (3 daily; 3hr); Chañaral (10 daily; 3hr 30min); Copiapó (10 daily; 1hr 45min); Iquique (2 daily; 14hr); La Serena (15 daily; 2hr 20min); Ovalle (5 daily; 4hr); Santiago (26 daily; 9hr 30min).

Flights

Note that some of these routes require stopovers; the travel times listed include stopovers.

Copiapó to: La Serena (3 daily; 45min); Santiago (3 daily; 2hr).

La Serena to: Antofagasta (3 daily; 2hr); Arica (1 daily; 4hr); Calama (2 daily; 3hr); Copiapó (3 daily; 45min); Iquique (3 daily; 3hr 30min); Santiago (5 daily; 50min).

El Norte Grande

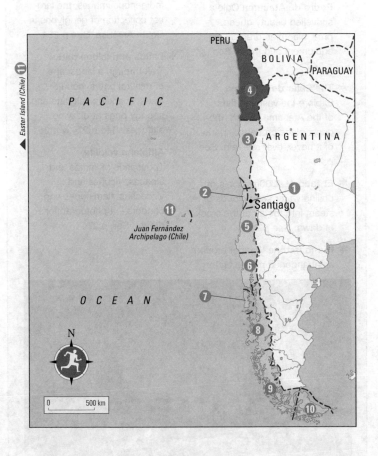

CHAPTER 4 Highlights

* **Chuquicamata** Visit one of the world's biggest open-pit copper mines near Calama. See p.237

* **Museo Arqueológico, San Pedro de Atacama** Ogle a shrivelled beauty queen, pre-Columbian drug-taking equipment and more. See p.240

* **The Salar de Atacama** Explore the vast salt flats of the Atacama Desert, the driest place on Earth – parts of it never, ever see rain. See p.244

* **El Tatio** At 4300m, pools of boiling water send clouds of steam into the air at the crack of dawn. See p.245

* **Humberstone** Wander around an abandoned nitrate factory – an eerily well-preserved ghost town stranded in the desert. See p.254

* **The Pintados geoglyphs** Discover these mysterious, indigenous images, the largest collection of geoglyphs in South America. See p.254

* **Lauca and Isluga parks** Trek through a landscape of mineral baths, cobalt lakes, sparkling salt flats and spongy bogs at dizzying altitudes. See p.274 & p.261

* **Altiplano wildlife** Thousands of llamas and alpacas, vicuñas and vizcachas, flamingoes and condors – a photographer's dream. See p.274

△ Valle de la Luna

El Norte Grande

Stretching away between the ocean and the great wall of the Andes, a seemingly endless belt of tawny sand, rock and mountain unfurls itself, more absolute and terrifying in its uncompromising aridity than the Sahara. The first glimpse of a strange land usually elates; but the sight of this grim desert oppresses the mind with a sense of singular desolation . . . It is only when the rays of the rising or setting sun kindle its sombre surface into the most gorgeous and improbable pink, purple, blue, crimson and orange that we feel the compelling fascination which all deserts exert.

Stephen Clissold, *Chilean Scrapbook*

Austerely beautiful, inhospitably arid and overwhelmingly vast, the **NORTE GRANDE** of Chile – sometimes referred to as the "Far North" – occupies almost a quarter of the country's mainland terri-tory but contains barely five percent of its population. Its single most outstanding feature is the **Atacama Desert**, stretching all the way down from the Peruvian border for over 1000km; the driest desert in the world, it contains areas where no rainfall has ever been recorded – ever. With a few exceptions the landscape of this desert is not one of Arabian golden sand dunes, but rather of bare rock and gravel spread over a wide *pampa* or plain, almost shockingly barren – alleviated only by crinkly mountains that glow bronze at twilight. To the west, the plain is lined by a range of coastal hills that drop abruptly to a narrow shelf of land where most of the region's towns and cities – chiefly prosperous **Antofagasta**, lively **Iquique** and colourful **Arica** – are scattered, hundreds of kilometres apart. East, the desert climbs towards the altiplano, which rises to the **altiplano**: a high, windswept plateau comprising salt flats ringed with snow-capped volcanoes, forming the heart of indigenous peoples life, but the oases that nestle that such a hostile has left countless

It seems almost inconceivable that such a host climate has left countless for thousands of years El Norte Grande ha desert coast near Arica some who've wrested a living either from the nineteenth century that Chile's in the Andean foothills. The excebecame apparent that the desert was relics of these people almed at great commercial value. So lucra-**chorro mummies** (sone in fact belonged to Bolivia and Peru. The seven thousand against Bolivia and Peru between 1878 and 1883, more recently red prize, and the desert pampas went on to yield their ... ri ... ti ...

enormous revenues for the next three decades. With the German invention of synthetic nitrates at the end of World War I, Chile's industry entered a rapid decline, but a financial crisis was averted when new mining techniques enabled low-grade **copper**, of which there are huge quantities in the region, to be profitably extracted. Today, this mineral continues to play the most important role in the country's economy, accounting for forty percent of Chile's exports and making it the world's leading copper supplier.

Formidable and desolate as it is, the region contains a wealth of superb attractions, and for many constitutes the highlight of a trip to Chile – particularly European travellers, who will find nothing remotely like it back home. The Pacific seaboard is lined by vast tracts of stunning **coastal scenery**, while inland the **desert pampa** itself impresses not only with its otherworldly geography, but also with a number of fascinating testimonies left by man. One of these is the trail of decaying nitrate **ghost towns**, including **Humberstone** and **Santa Laura**, easily reached from Iquique. Another are the immense images known as **geoglyphs** left by indigenous peoples on the hillsides and ravines of the desert – you'll find impressive examples at **Cerro Pintados**, south of Iquique, **Cerro Unitas**, east of Huara, and **Tiliviche**, between Huara and Arica.

As you journey towards and up into the cordillera, you'll come across attractive **oasis villages**, some – such as **Pica** and **Mamiña** – with **hot springs**. Up in the Andes, the altiplano is undoubtedly one of the country's highlights, with its dazzling **lakes**, **salt flats and volcanoes**, its abundance of **wildlife** and its tiny, whitewashed villages inhabited by native Aymaras. The main altiplano touring base – and, indeed, one of the most popular destinations in the whole country, for Chileans and foreigners alike – is **San Pedro de Atacama**, a pleasant oasis 315km northeast of Antofagasta, where numerous operators offer excursions to the famous **El Tatio geysers** and the haunting moonscapes of the **Valle de la Luna**. Further north, the stretch of altiplano within reach of Iquique and Arica boasts wild vicuña and spectacular scenery, preserved in **Parque Nacional Lauca** and several adjoining parks and reserves. The towns and cities of the Far North tend to be dreary and uninviting, but serve as unavoidable departure points for excursions into the hinterland.

Many of the region's attractions can be reached by **public transport**, though in order to explore the region in depth you'll need to book some tours or, better still, rent a 4WD vehicle. Whatever your mode of transport, don't underestimate the distances involved in getting to most points of interest, particularly to suʼiplano. It makes sense to isolate a few chosen highlights rather than try to ʼplano, which would be interminably time-consuming.

You ʼʼbing, which would be interminably time-consuming.

northern hᵉhe Far North at any time of year, but be aware that tour when sporadⁱ. busiest in July and August when most visitors from the can wash roadᵗⁱⁿe and visit. Also bear in mind the **Bolivian Winter**, Moreover, despiteⁿᵗ ʼʼʼetween December and February in the altiplano for Chileans. ʼⁱously disrupt communications and access. ʼᵉriod because it's the prime vacation time

Antofagasta aⁿ

Many tourists bypass the decidedʼʼ altogether, but as the regional caʼʼ – including banks, *cambios* and car-reʼʼ

TOFAGASTA
ʼʼful facilities
ʼʼrt hub.

EL NORTE GRANDE

PERU

Visviri

Tacna

PARQUE NACIONAL
LAUCA

Putre

Parinacota

Socoroma

Tambo Quemado

Arica

San Miguel
de Azapa

RESERVA NATURAL
LAS VICUÑAS

Salar de Surire

Enquelga

Colchane

Isluga

PARQUE NACIONAL
VOLCAN ISLUGA

Pisagua

Tiliviche

Cerro
Unitas

Chusmisa

Huara

Mamiña

Humberstone

Pozo
Almonte

La Tirana

Hot
Springs

BOLIVIA

Iquique

Cerro
Pintados

Pica

RESERVA NACIONAL
PAMPA DEL
TAMARUGAL

PACIFIC
OCEAN

Ollagüe

Tocopilla

Chuquicamata

Ayquina

Caspana

Maria
Elena

Calama

Chiu Chiu

Gatico
Cobija

Pedro de
Valdivia

Valle de
La Luna

San Pedro
Atac...

Mejillones

Chacabuco

Salar d...
Atac...

Socaire

Peine

Baquedano

ATACAMA

Antofagasta

DES...

ARGENTINA

Cerro
Paranal

227

0   100 km

N

A Bolivian town until 1879, when it was annexed by Chile in the War of the Pacific, Antofagasta is now Chile's fifth-largest city. It's also one of the most prosperous, serving as an export centre for the region's great mines, most notably Chuquicamata (see p.237). Sitting on a flat shelf between the ocean and the hills, Antofagasta has a compact downtown core, made up of dingy, traffic-choked streets that sport a few handsome old public buildings, and a modern stretch along the coastal avenue. On the way north, or as you head out to the airport, stop off at **La Portada**, an iconic natural arch of rock looming out of the sea.

South of the city centre the busy coastal avenue runs past a couple of tiny, coarse-sand **beaches**, first at the Balneario Municipal, then, much further south, at the Playa Huascar – take *micro* #3 from Washington, near the square. In this direction lie one of the city's most curious sights, the **Ruinas de Huanchaca**, vestiges of a disused silver refinery.

Arrival and information

If you're arriving by **bus**, you'll be dropped at one of several terminals, most within easy walking distance of downtown accommodation. The two main stations, where Tur Bus and Pullman operate, sit at opposite corners of Bolívar and Latorre. Coming in by **air**, you'll arrive at the Aeropuerto Cerro Moreno, 25km north of the city, right on the Tropic of Capricorn. From here, regular *colectivos* and infrequent *micros* head to the centre or you can take a minibus directly to your accommodation (they await every arrival).

For **tourist information**, head for the **Sernatur** office at Prat 384, on the ground floor of the Intendencia at the corner of the central plaza (Mon–Fri 8.30am–5.30pm; ☎ & ⓕ 55/451818–20, infoantofagasta@sernatur.net). For details on the protected areas around San Pedro de Atacama, which lies within this region, visit the regional **Conaf office** at Avenida Argentina 2510 (Mon–Fri 9am–1pm & 2.30–5.30pm; ☎55/222250).

Accommodation

You'll find an abundance of **accommodation** in Antofagasta, but the range tends to jump from cheap and basic to expensive (and not necessarily good-quality), with very few mid-priced options in between. Most places are in the downtown core, with the mostly expensive hotels, catering primarily to business travelers, on the coastal avenue.

Fr... mid-... ...tel Bolívar 558 ☎55/281219. Best with priv... ...offering spotless, modern rooms be noisy... cable TV. Some rooms can **Holiday In**... the centre ☎... super-clean Am... ...ia 1490, south of parking – a good... ...28888. Modern, desert is getting to... ...h pool and by plenty of *micros*. **Hotel Antofagasta Ba**... ...f if the ☎55/268259, ⓕ55/26... ...entre hotel overlooking the ocea... but overpriced rooms. **❼** **Hotel Ciudad de Ávila** Cond... ☎55/221040. Simple, no-frills ...

228

most rooms have private bath and external windows. **❸**
Hotel Colón San Martín 2434 ☎55/261851, ⓕ55/260872. Clean, fairly comfortable rooms with private bath. **❹**
Marzal Hotel Prat 867 ☎55/268063, ⓕ55/221733. Modern hotel offering spacious rooms with private bath and parking. **❹**
Residencial El Cobre Prat 749 ☎55/225162. Huge *residencial* with 58 rooms, some airy and ...ght, others dark and dingy. **❸**
...dencial Washington Washington 2480 ...592. Basic, cleanish rooms in a large old ...e main square. **❷**

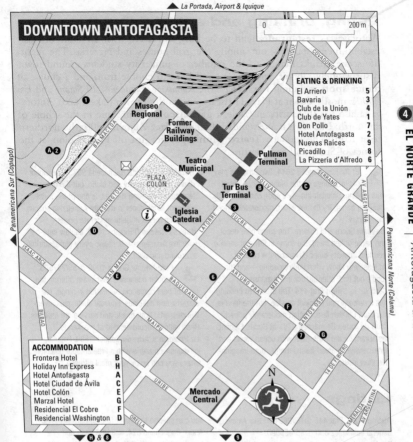

DOWNTOWN ANTOFAGASTA

La Portada, Airport & Iquique

0   200 m

Museo Regional

Former Railway Buildings

Teatro Municipal

Pullman Terminal

PLAZA COLÓN

Tur Bus Terminal

Iglesia Catedral

Mercado Central

Panamericana Sur (Copiapó)

Panamericana Norte (Calama)

EATING & DRINKING

El Arriero	5
Bavaria	3
Club de la Unión	4
Club de Yates	1
Don Pollo	7
Hotel Antofagasta	2
Nuevas Raíces	9
Picadillo	8
La Pizzería d'Alfredo	6

ACCOMMODATION

Frontera Hotel	B
Holiday Inn Express	H
Hotel Antofagasta	A
Hotel Ciudad de Ávila	C
Hotel Colón	E
Marzal Hotel	G
Residencial El Cobre	F
Residencial Washington	D

The City

In Antofagasta's centre sprawls the large, green **Plaza Colón**, dominated by a tall clock tower whose face is supposedly a replica of London's Big Ben – one of many tangible signs of the role played by the British in Antofagasta's commercial development. The city's administrative and public buildings, including the Neo-Gothic Iglesia Catedral, built between 1906 and 1917, surround the square. A couple of blocks northwest towards the port, along Bolívar, you'll find the magnificently restored nineteenth-century offices and railway terminus of the former Antofagasta and Bolivia Railway Company, complete with polished wooden verandahs and dark-green stucco walls (but with no public access). Opposite, at the corner of Bolívar and Balmaceda, sits the 1866 customs house, or **Aduana**, the oldest building in the city. Inside, the Museo Regional (Tues–Sat 9am–5pm, Sun 11am–2pm; CH$600, free Sun; www.dibam.cl) houses an impressive mineral display downstairs and, upstairs, a collection of clothes, furniture and general paraphernalia dating from the nitrate era. At the opposite end of town, at the corner of Ossa and Maipú, the huge, pink-and-cream Mercado Central sells fresh food and *artesanía*.

Eating, drinking and entertainment

Antofagasta's **restaurants** tend to be busy and lively, with a couple of classy establishments standing out among the grill houses and pizzerias. The nightlife scene, thanks mainly to the number of university students around town, is surprisingly vibrant, with some good **bars** to choose from and a choice of **dance spots** including *Vagón Habanero, Kamikaze, Bucanero's, El Sotano* and *Era 2000's*, mostly down at Playa Huascar, way south of town (take a taxi). Antofagasta also has that rarity in Chile, a **gay disco**, the only one in the whole of the north: *Underboys* is at Avenida Edmundo Pérez Zujovic 4800 (the northern coast road). The modern **Teatro Municipal** lies just off Plaza Colón, at the corner of Sucre and San Martín.

El Arriero Condell 2644. Two brothers play old jazz tunes on the piano every night at this inviting, Spanish-inn-style spot, complete with hanging hams. Try the excellent, moderately priced *parrilladas*.

Bavaria Sucre and Latorre. The same pine decor, the same grilled meat, the same indifferent service you find in every other *Bavaria* in the country. At least you know what you're getting – and the food's not bad, after all, nor is it expensive.

Club de la Unión Prat 474. The attractive building has a balcony and efficient service, but the food is standard Chilean fare, though moderately priced.

Club de Yates Balmaceda 2701 at Sucre. Elegant restaurant on the waterfront with ocean views and an expensive seafood-based menu, more imaginative than most.

Hotel Antofagasta Balmaceda 2575. The indoor dining room is empty and bland, but the outdoor terrace, overlooking the sea, is one of the most pleasant lunch spots in the city. Appetizing snacks and main meals at quite moderate prices.

Nuevas Raíces O'Higgins 1892. Mellow café-bar with live Andean or folk music every night, starting at around midnight.

Picadillo Av Grecia 1000 ☎55/247503. Popular oceanside restaurant offering the likes of beef carpaccio marinated in ginger for starters, and delicious, unusual sushi, plus inventive desserts; both music and service are faultless. Reservations recommended at weekends.

La Pizzería d'Alfredo Condell 2539. Popular, inexpensive pizzeria with a little outdoor balcony where you can enjoy your meal alfresco.

Listings

Airlines LAN, Prat 445 ☎55/265151; Sky Airlines, General Velásquez 890 ☎55/459090.

Banks and exchange There are several ATMs on the central square and the main commercial streets, including Prat, Washington and San Martín.

You can change the major foreign currencies at Ancla, Baquedano 524, and US$ cash and travellers' cheques at Nortour, Baquedano 474.

Camping gas White gas (*bencina blanca*) and butane gas available at Casa del Aseo, Matta 2578.

Moving on from Antofagasta

All the main **bus** companies offer services from Antofagasta up and down the **Panamericana**, and to **Calama**. There's a municipal central terminal at Argentina 1155, from where several companies operate, including Carmelita, Libac and Ramos Cholele, but many companies operate instead out of their own separate terminal, including: Camus, Riquelme 513 ☎55/267424; Fenix, San Martín 2717 ☎55/268896; Fepstur, Riquelme 513 ☎55/222982; Flota Barrios, Condell 2682 ☎55/351460; Géminis, Latorre 3055 ☎55/263968; Kenny Bus, Arauco 4270 ☎55/262216; Los Corsarios, Latorre 2805 ☎55/282187; Pullman Bus, Latorre 2805 ☎55/262591; Tur Bus, Latorre 2751 ☎55/220240. Direct **flights** go from Antofagasta to Calama, Iquique, Arica, La Serena and Santiago (see "Listings", above, for airlines). To get to the airport from downtown, take a taxi (CH$6000), or call Aerobus (☎55/262727) to order a minibus transfer (CH$2500) to pick you up from your hotel or wherever.

Car rental Avis, Balmaceda 2556 ☎ & ℱ55/226153; Budget, P.A. Cerda ☎55/214445; First, Bolívar 623 ☎55/225777.
Internet *ADSL*, at Pasaje López (Prat 482), has good prices and connections; English is spoken. Several other Internet outlets are along Latorre, near the plaza.
Laundry Laverap, 14 de Febrero 1802.
Post office On the central square, at Washington 2613.
Telephone offices Chilesat, Uribe 645; Chilexpress, Plaza Colón, Prat and Washington;

CTC, Uribe 746; Entel, Baquedano 751; Startel, Baquedano 1984; Telex Chile, Washington 260; VTR, Prat 288.
Travel agencies You'll find many travel agencies downtown, including Australian-run Inti Tour, Baquedano 460 ☎55/266185, ℱ55/260882; Rutas de Sal, José Miguel Carrera ☎55/386828, ℮info@rutasdesal.com, ⓦwww.rutasdesal.com; Tatio Travel Service, Washington 2513; and North Gate Tour, Baquedano 498.

Ruinas de Huanchaca and La Portada

These remains of an old Bolivian silver refinery sit on a hilltop a short distance inland, 3km south of the city centre by the Universidad del Norte. The **RUINAS DE HUANCHACA** were built to process the silver brought down from the Potosí mine (at that time the most important silver mine in South America), before being shipped out of Antofagasta. Looking at the square and circular walls of the complex from below, you'd be forgiven for thinking they were ruins of a pre-Columbian fortress. Sadly, access to the site is limited, so you may have to make do with viewing it from the outside. To get there, take *micro* #2, #4 or #10 from Prat.

A huge eroded arch looming out of the ocean, **La Portada** sits 16km north of Antofagasta along the coast road. Declared a national monument in 1990, the arch has become something of a regional symbol, and its picture graces postcards and wall calendars all over Chile. The upkeep of the site, however, is a disgrace: makeshift signs quite rightly warn you not to approach the crumbling cliffs or descend the rickety steps to the unsafe beach, while the nearby

△ La Portada

bar-restaurant and shops are often closed, even in high season, lending the place a sadly abandoned air.

To get there, take *micro* #15 from the Terminal Pesquero, or take one of the Mejillones-bound minibuses leaving from Bazar Acuario, at Latorre 2733, Bazar Mariela, at Latorre 2727, or Bazar Mejillones, Latorre 2715 – all near the Tur Bus terminal. If you're driving, follow the coast road north and take the turn-off to Juan López, from where La Portada is well signed.

Cerro Paranal observatory

A little under two hours south of Antofagasta, perched on **Cerro Paranal** at 2644m above sea level, is the latest result of international space-watching one-upmanship, the **European Southern Observatory** (ESO). While you have to be a recognized researcher to stand any chance of looking through its **Very Large Telescope** (VLT), currently the world's strongest, on certain weekends you can visit the dazzling site, set among suitably lunar, and even Mars-like, landscapes of reddish rock. In fact, NASA tested the Mars Pathfinder rover in the nearby Atacama Desert. To get here, head south from Antofagasta on the Panamericana (Ruta 5); the unpaved turn-off 24km south of the Mina Escondida crossroads leads due south over a mountain pass to the observatory.

The European Southern Observatory

The ESO belongs to a multinational European space research agency and, rivalling US counterparts such as the CTIO at Cerro Tololo near Vicuña, currently holds the record for the **world's most powerful telescope**. Meanwhile the VLT – strictly speaking a set of four 8.2-metre telescopes, each weighing 430 tonnes, whose combined might enables observers to see objects as small as humans on the Moon – has been fully operational since 2001. It's housed in a futuristic-looking set of four trapezoidal cylinders dramatically located on the barren Cerro Paranal, which averages 330 clear nights a year. A luxurious 120-room residence (for scientists only), complete with a cafeteria and an indoor garden (both open to the public), stands nearby.

The observatory is open to the public the latter two weekends of every month except December. Visits last a couple of hours and should be booked well in advance, as numbers are limited (Jan–Nov last two weekends of the month, Sat & Sun 2pm; free; ℡55/435395, ℻55/435995, ⓦwww.eso.org); the observatory receives some 5000 visitors annually. Remember to take warm clothing, as it is very cold inside the observatory. If you do not have your own transport, you can join an **organized tour** from Antofagasta; Agencia Rutas de Sal (see listings, p.231) runs occasional day-trips (CH$15,000 per person, including lunch).

Plans are afoot for another extremely powerful observatory in the region, the Atacama Large Millimeter Array (ALMA), a joint US-European venture that may involve Japan at a later date. The ALMA will comprise 64 radio-telescopes using millimetre radio waves rather than the VLT's optical-infrared and will likely be positioned 5000m above sea level at a site east of San Pedro de Atacama.

The ESO is also planning a so-called "Overwhelmingly Large Telescope" (an ironic reference to the names "Very Large" and "Extremely Large" already applied to telescopes and with the appropriate acronym of OWL), possibly in the same site as the ALMA. If funded, the 100-metre optical near-infrared telescope would be operational around 2015.

The northern coast road

Heading north out of Antofagasta you've got the choice of two routes: the coast road (Ruta 1) to Iquique, 492km away via Tocopilla, or the slightly longer Panamericana, which takes you across the arid nitrate pampa. The **coast road**, used by most buses in preference to the Panamericana, is shorter, more scenic but busier. Much of this coastline is heavily eroded, and the road twists around weird rock formations, home to bird colonies at the foot of huge cliffs. There are a couple of intriguing abandoned ports on the way, and two fair-sized towns, the hellishly ghoulish port of Mejillones (best avoided) and the impressively located but grim **Tocopilla**, neither of them terribly interesting but useful for filling up with petrol, if you're driving.

Cobija and Gatico

Scattered by the main road, 115km north of Antofagasta and 70km south of Tocopilla, are the half-decayed ruins of **COBIJA**. Looking at the crumbling shells that once were houses, it's hard to believe that this was Bolivia's first port, founded by the decree of Simón Bolívar in 1825, when there was nothing else on this coast. By 1860 it was a flourishing little town with over a thousand inhabitants, but was almost destroyed by a tidal wave in 1868 and a yellow fever epidemic the following year. With the emergence of Antofagasta as the region's main port, the last drops of lifeblood drained out of Cobija, and in 1907 its church was moved to Gatico and the town was abandoned. In addition to the ruins, there's a ransacked cemetery up by the road, full of body-shaped mounds of earth and a few open, empty coffins.

Ten kilometres north of Cobija the road passes more ruins, this time of **GATICO**, a former port that operated until 1930. An evocative reminder of the town's past, the huge *Casa de Huéspedes*, a grand, decaying hotel overlooks the sea – you can climb up the front entrance, wander around the empty rooms and admire the views from its verandah. Not far from the hotel are the rusty remains of the former railway terminus. Two kilometres north of Gatico, another abandoned **cemetery** stands right by the road, full of iron and wooden crosses bearing no names.

Tocopilla

A busy industrial town with 25,000 inhabitants, **TOCOPILLA**, 185km north of Antofagasta and 369km south of Iquique, has two thermoelectric plants, a mechanized nitrate port and a railway terminus serving the two nitrate workings at María Elena and Pedro de Valdivia. It's a cheerless sort of place, although the setting, at the foot of steep ochre hills looming over the town, is undeniably impressive. There is no reason to make a special trip here, but it's a handy place to stop over if you're driving along Ruta 1. It's also connected to Calama by a good 160-kilometre paved road, and some people like to head down here to fill their lungs with less rarefied air after a spell in the altiplano around San Pedro. The only monument to speak of is the wooden **Torre del Reloj**, a multi-coloured nineteenth-century clock tower near the pier at the corner of Prat and Baquedano. You'll find plenty of **restaurants** on 21 de Mayo, including a *Bavaria* and *Lucciano's Pizza*, four blocks north of the plaza; the nicest place to eat, though, is the *Club de la Unión*, an attractive wooden building opposite the clock tower at the corner of Baquedano and Prat.

The 370 or so kilometres that separate Tocopilla and Iquique are virtually uninhabited, with just a handful of tiny fishing *caletas* (coves) breaking the emptiness. Ruta 1 clings to the shore, taking you past sporadic beaches that increase in number the further north you go. For the most part, though, there's no access from the highway down to the ocean. If you're driving this route, remember that Tocopilla is the last petrol stop before Iquique. You should also note that there's a customs checkpoint 154km south of Iquique, where all vehicles must be registered including buses, even at night, and where items brought south from the Zona Franca are checked.

The nitrate pampa

Northeast of Antofagasta, the vast *pampa salitrera*, or **NITRATE PAMPA**, pans across the desert towards the cordillera – it's not the prettiest landscape in the world, a mass of scruffy plains that look as though they have been ploughed, fertilized and then left for fallow. If you take this road towards Iquique, you can either branch off for Calama and San Pedro de Atacama, or continue north, passing close to the last remaining nitrate *oficinas* (or plants) at Pedro de Valdivia and María Elena. Between 1890 and 1925 there were over 80 *oficinas*, here, extracting the nitrate ore and sending it down to the ports by railroad. Some of them are still standing, abandoned and in ruins, including Chacabuco, crumbling in the desert heat. Two highways cross the pampa: the Panamericana, heading due north, and Ruta 25, branching off northeast to the mining city of Calama. The former skirts **Pedro de Valdivia** and **María Elena**, both of which can be reached on public transport. Although you can find basic accommodation if you look hard enough (mainly in María Elena), you may as well forge on if you can; these are desperately soulless places to spend the night.

Baquedano and Chacabuco

Seventy kilometres northeast of Antofagasta, the Panamericana passes through **BAQUEDANO**, once an important railway junction, now a down-at-heel village. The rail tracks are still used by a few freight trains, but a large part of the station and workshops have been turned into an open-air **Museo Ferroviario** (daily 8am–12.30pm & 2–7pm; free) displaying many beautiful old locomotives, a couple of which you can climb aboard. If you want to stop for **lunch**, you'll find a couple of canteens on the main road, opposite the railtracks.

Thirty kilometres on from Baquedano, you reach the Carmen Alto junction. To the right, Ruta 25 goes to Calama, passing more than twenty abandoned nitrate *oficinas*, many of them reduced to a few stone walls and a pile of rubble. To the left, the Panamericana continues north, passing **CHACABUCO**, just beyond the junction on the right-hand side. Built in 1922 and abandoned in 1940, this former nitrate town is now a national monument and a fascinating relic of the pampa's past. The rows of tiny terraced workers' houses are still standing, along with the remains of the church, market and theatre. It's usually completely empty and is a decidedly eerie, even sinister, place to wander through, despite the blue sky and glare of the sun – especially when you consider that it was used as a concentration camp by the Pinochet regime.

Pedro de Valdivia

The newest "ghost town" on the pampa, abandoned only in 1996, **PEDRO DE VALDIVIA** lies 69km kilometres past the Carmen Alto junction, off a threadbare side road. It was created in 1931 by the Guggenheim brothers as their second large-scale nitrate plant, following the success of neighbouring María Elena (see below), established five years earlier. The plant itself is still working, and the huge chimneys belching out smoke form a dramatic backdrop to the deserted town. But it was too expensive to maintain two company towns, so the residents of Pedro de Valdivia were moved to María Elena, 36km further north. The architecture and layout are just like all the other ghost towns – small, whitewashed terraced houses, a plaza with a church, school and theatre – but the fact that it's so recently abandoned makes it, if anything, even more haunting. As you're wandering around the streets, you might happen upon old shoes, a teddy bear left behind in the move, a forsaken bicycle or an empty children's playground.

María Elena

After driving past so many decaying, abandoned nitrate towns, it's a relief to find one that's still alive and full of people. **MARÍA ELENA**, created in 1926, is the only inhabited nitrate town left in Chile, with a population of 7600. The tell-tale clouds of smoke and dust thrown high into the air from the plants are visible for miles around and while María Elena has the same houses and buildings as the ghost towns, here they're inhabited, and the dusty main square with its shrivelled palms bustles with locals. It's also home to an interesting little **archeological museum**, on the square (Mon–Sat 9am–1pm & 4–7pm, Sun 10am–1pm & 5–8pm; free). If he's there, get the director, Don Claudio, to guide you through the displays, most of which he amassed himself. They range from tombs, arrowheads and ceramics to memorabilia from the local nitrate towns.

The Chug Chug geoglyphs

The Panamericana is crossed by a lateral road, Ruta 24, 107km north of the Carmen Alto junction. This is connected to Tocopilla, 60km west, and Chuquicamata, 66km east. Just short of 50km along the road for Chuquicamata, a sign points north to the **CHUG CHUG GEOGLYPHS**, reached by a thirteen-kilometre dirt road that's just about passable in a car. These consist of some three hundred images spread over several hills, many of them clearly visible from below, including circles, zoomorphic figures, human faces and geometric designs. It's an impressive site, and certainly deserves a visit if you're driving in the area.

Calama and Chuquicamata

Sitting on the banks of the Río Loa, at an altitude of 2250m, **CALAMA** is a modern and rather bland town, whose chief role is as a service centre and residential base for **Chuquicamata**, the massive copper mine 16km north. It's a convenient place for sorting out money or doing laundry, and many visitors end up spending at least a night here on their way to or from San Pedro de Atacama, the famous oasis village and tourist centre 100km east.

Calama began life as a *tambo*, or resting place, at the intersection of two Inca roads – one running down the Andes, the other connecting the altiplano with the Pacific – and both Diego de Almagro and Pedro de Valdivia visited on their journeys into Chile. It was never heavily populated by pre-Hispanic peoples, who preferred nearby Chiu Chiu, with its less saline water supply. The town took on a new importance, however, as the stop on the Oruro–Antofagasta railway in 1892, and its future was sealed with the creation of the Chuquicamata

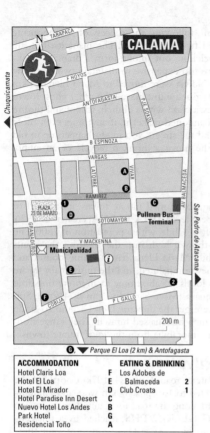

Parque El Loa (2 km) & Antofagasta

ACCOMMODATION		EATING & DRINKING	
Hotel Claris Loa	F	Los Adobes de	
Hotel El Loa	E	Balmaceda	2
Hotel El Mirador	D	Club Croata	1
Hotel Paradise Inn Desert	C		
Nuevo Hotel Los Andes	B		
Park Hotel	G		
Residencial Toño	A		

copper mine in 1911. Today its busy streets are built around a surprisingly small and laid-back central core.

Check out the **Parque El Loa**, where you'll find the **Museo Arqueológico** (Tues–Fri 10am–1pm & 3–7.30pm, Sat & Sun 3–7pm; CH$500), with a mini reconstruction of Chiu Chiu's church and displays on local pre-Columbian history. To get to the park, take a *colectivo* – #5 or #18 – on Vicuña Mackenna at the corner of Latorre, or *micros* #1b, #1c or #1d from Vivar at Mackenna.

Practicalities

Arriving by **bus** you'll be dropped at your bus company's office, generally near the city centre; there's no single terminal. Tur Bus has a brand-new terminal of its own, inconveniently more than a kilometre north of town – a taxi will charge CH$1500–2000 to the city centre. Some companies drop off at the shopping mall, also north of the centre.

If you're **flying** to Calama you'll land at the Aeropuerto El Loa, 5km south of the centre – the only way into town from here is by taxi (CH$5000). **Trains** from Bolivia pull in at the conveniently located station, three blocks east of the plaza. At the municipal **Oficina de Turismo** opposite the Municipalidad, Latorre and Vicuña Mackenna (Mon–Fri 9am–1pm & 3–7pm, Sat 9am–1pm; ☎55/345345), you can get maps and other basic information, but not much else.

Calama has a wide range of **accommodation**, but many places are overpriced owing to the mining clientele. Nonetheless, local hotels can get fully booked during the San Pedro tourist seasons. Beware of overbooking and always send a fax to confirm if possible. Good budget choices include *Residencial Toño*, at Vivar 1970 (☎55/341185; **❸**), offering very simple rooms, some with bath, and *Hotel El Loa*, Abaroa 1617 (☎55/341963; **❸**), with lots of basic but comfortable singles out the back, and a few doubles and triples in the main house. *Hotel El Mirador*, at Sotomayor 2064 (☎ & ☎ 55/340329; **❻**), is a lovely, small hotel with spacious rooms – including one with a Victorian cast-iron bath – and attractive furnishings. At the top end of the scale, the overpriced *Park Hotel*, at Camino al Aeropuerto 1392 (☎55/319900, ☎55/319901, ☎www.parkplaza.cl; **❻**), boasts elegant decor, a good restaurant and a swimming pool.

Most of Calama's **restaurants** offer reasonably priced, but not particularly inspiring fare. Open until late, the *Club Croata*, on the plaza, serves up decent if predictable food and a pleasant enough atmosphere while on the edge of town, at Balmaceda 1504, *Los Adobes de Balmaceda* features good-value *parrilladas* in a large, attractive old house that really fills up for Sunday lunch.

You'll find plenty of **ATMs** on Sotomayor, as well as a *cambio* at Tokori Tour, Latorre 2018, on the second floor. A number of companies **rent cars**: Avis, Pedro León Gallo 1985 (☎55/319757); Budget, Granaderos 2925 (☎55/341076); First, Felix Hoyos 2146 (☎55/315453); and Hertz, Latorre 1510 (☎55/341380).

Chuquicamata

One of the world's largest open-pit copper mines, **CHUQUICAMATA** (16km north of Calama) produces 600,000 tonnes per year – outstripped only by Mina Escondida, 200km southeast of Antofagasta, whose capacity exceeds 800,000 tonnes. Carved out of the ground like a giant, sunken amphitheatre, the massive mine dwarfs everything within it, making the huge trucks carrying the ore up from the crater floor – whose wheels alone are an incredible 4m high – look like tiny, crawling ants. Its size is the result of some ninety years of excavation, and its reserves are predicted to last at least until the middle of the twenty-first century. Along with all of Chile's large-scale copper mines, or *"grandes minerías"* as they're called, Chuquicamata belongs to Codelco, the government-owned copper corporation. Codelco also maintains the adjacent company town, complete with its own school, hospital, cinema and football stadium, but plans are under way to move the nine thousand workers and their families to Calama to make way for further excavation.

Regular yellow *colectivos* (20 min; CH$800) leave for Chuquicamata from Calle Abaroa, on Calama's main plaza; **guided tours** (Mon–Fri 2pm; CH$1000 donation to a children's charity supported by the mine) leave from the office next to the Banco del Estado. Book ahead at the tourist information office in Calama or by telephone (☎55/326469 or 322122). The tours last 1 hour 30 minutes and take place almost entirely on a bus, though you're allowed to get out at the viewpoint looking down to the pit – wear sensible shoes and clothing that covers most of your body. The rest of the tour takes you round the machinery yards and buildings of the plant, which you see from the outside only.

Moving on from Calama

Most visitors are in Calama on their way to San Pedro, with regular bus connections (around ten a day) provided by several companies, including Tur Bus at Balmaceda 1852 (☎55/341472), Buses Frontera, at Antofagasta 2041 (☎55/318543), with the most frequent service, and Buses Atacama, Abaroa 2105-B (☎55/314757). Note that the first bus is at 8.30am and the last around 9pm. The inter-city bus companies (for Tur Bus, see opposite) are spread around town, with Flota Barrios at Ramírez 2298 (☎55/341497); Géminis at Antofagasta 2239 (☎55/341993); and Pullman Bus at Sotomayor 1808 (☎55/319665). LAN, Latorre 1726 (☎55/341477), offers regular flights out of Calama to Santiago and the main northern cities.

Finally, there's the famously no-frills 20-hour **train** to Uyuni in Bolivia, base for the spectacular Salar de Uyuni; it leaves on Wednesdays at 11pm. You can buy tickets (around CH$7000) the same day from 3.30pm onwards at Balmaceda 1777. Alternatively try the quicker, slightly more comfortable bus to Uyuni – it takes about 12 hours and leaves every Wednesday and Sunday, weather permitting. You can buy tickets (CH$7000) from the offices of Buses Frontera (Tues, Wed, Sat & Sun; ☎55/316612).

San Pedro de Atacama and around

The little oasis village of **SAN PEDRO DE ATACAMA** (100km southeast of Calama), with its narrow dirt streets and adobe houses, has transformed itself, since the 1990s, into *the* tourism centre of Chile. Sitting at an altitude of 2400m between the desert and the altiplano, or *puna* (the high basin connecting the two branches of the cordillera), this has been an important settlement since pre-Hispanic times, originally as a major stop on the trading route connecting the llama herders of these highlands with the fishing communities of the Pacific. Later, during the nitrate era, it was the main rest stop on the cattle trail from Salta in Argentina to the nitrate *oficinas*, where the cattle were driven to supply the workers with fresh meat.

The large numbers of Chilean tourists and hordes of gringos here can come as quite a shock if you have just arrived from more remote parts of northern Chile. San Pedro has recently begun to lose some of its charm and is lined with overpriced, trendy-looking hotels with questionable cleanliness and poor service. Luckily, you will find exceptions (see reviews, opposite).

Arrival, information and orientation

Several **bus** companies have regular services from Calama to San Pedro (for details see box, p.237); they all have different drop-off points, all of which sit a couple of blocks off the main square, mostly along Licancábur. Head to the

SAN PEDRO DE ATACAMA

Museo Arqueológico

Artesanía

Municipalidad

Casa Incaica

Iglesia de San Pedro

EATING & DRINKING
Adobe	6
Café Etnico	2
Café Export	3
Café Sonchek	1
Hostería San Pedro de Atacama	10
La Casona	5
La Estaka	8
Milagro	7
Paacha	4
Tierra	9

ACCOMMODATION
Casa de Don Tomás	K
Explora	J
Hostal Katarpe	F
Hostal Takha Takha	G
Hostería San Pedro	I
Hotel Altiplánico	A
Hotel Kimal	H
Hotel Tambillo	C
Lodge Andino Terrantai	E
Residencial Chiloé	B
Residencial La Florida	D

0   100 m

plaza for the **post office** or the **Oficina de Turismo** (Jan–March Fri–Wed, 10am–2pm & 3–7pm; rest of the year, shorter hours but no lunch break; ☎55/851126, ⓦwww.sanpedroatacama.com); if it's closed, try the Municipalidad, also on the square, but do not expect very much help.

San Pedro's main street is **Caracoles**, which is where you'll find the biggest concentration of accommodation, eating places and services. Early in the new millennium, Calle Antofagasta was renamed Gustavo Le Paige and all houses in the village were given a number, but the changes have not quite sunk in. Note that there are **no banks or ATMs** in the village, though you can change money at a couple of *cambios*; many but by no means all restaurants and hotels accept credit cards, so check first.

Accommodation

There are loads of places offering **rooms** in San Pedro, including a number of comfortable *residenciales* plus some classy, upmarket places for those on a far more generous budget. Recently, more and more of the latter have sprung up, often with a now hackneyed pseudo-native architectural style – lots of adobe, stone walls and thatched roofs – but mercifully there have been no high-rises. A wonderful alternative, especially for those on a smaller budget, is provided by a new scheme of *albergues turísticos*, rural guesthouses in the villages of Peine and Socaire. Most have double rooms, some with private bath (❷–❹), and they usually serve breakfast and occasionally other meals. For details and bookings contact Red Licanhuasi at Caracoles 349 (☎55/851593, ⓦwww.lichanhuasi .com).

You'll also find several **campsites** within easy reach of the village centre; the two best are listed on p.240. If you're travelling alone and arrive at a busy time, you may have difficulty finding a **single room** in many *residenciales* and will probably be asked to share with another traveller. Many places will do your **laundry**, a boon since San Pedro lacks a commendable *lavandería*.

Hotels

Casa de Don Tomás Tocopilla s/n ☎55/851055, ⓕ55/851175, ⓦwww.dontomas.cl. Rustic, well-established hotel with spacious rooms, a pool, good breakfasts and a friendly welcome. Located away from the buzz of central San Pedro, 300m south of the crossroads with Caracoles. ❽

Hostal Katarpe Domingo Atienza ☎55/851033, ⓦwww.katarpe.cl. Excellent-value, comfortable rooms, most with private bath and fluffy towels. ❺

Hostería San Pedro Solcor ☎55/851011, ⓕ55/851048, ⓦwww.diegodealmagrohoteles .cl. Well-maintained, comfortable accommodation – mostly in little bungalows – and a fantastic swimming pool. The restaurant is very good, too. ❽

Hostal Takha Takha Caracoles ☎55/851038. Small but tidy and quiet rooms giving onto a pleasant garden. A good bet for singles. Also has spaces for camping. ❹

Hotel Altiplánico Domingo Atienza 282, ☎55/851212, ⓦwww.altiplanico.cl. Gorgeous hotel complex in typical San Pedro adobe-style, with fantastic views, tasteful decor, comfortable en-suite rooms, a swimming pool (albeit odd-looking), Internet access, a café-bar and bicycle rental. Located in a calm spot 250m from the centre, on the way to the Pukará de Quitor. ❽

Hotel Explora Ayllu de Larache ☎2/2066060, ⓦwww.explora.com. Located outside the village, in a world of its own, this Chilean chain resort offers its usual high standards of comfort, gastronomy and professional service in a beautiful setting. Mostly packages of at least three nights. ❾

Hotel Kimal Domingo Atienza ☎ & ⓕ55/851030, ⓦwww.kimal.cl. Spacious, light and very attractive rooms, combining contemporary, spartan architecture with plants and warm rugs. ❽

Hotel Tambillo Gustavo Le Paige s/n ☎ & ⓕ55/851078, ⓦwww.hoteltambillo.cl. Reasonably priced hotel offering fresh, clean rooms around a grim patio, and a dependable water supply. ❺

Lodge Andino Terrantai Tocopilla 411 ☎55/851045, ⓕ55/851037, ⓦwww.terrantai .com. Modern, stylish but slightly snobbish hotel

with bare stone walls and minimalist wooden furniture. For most of the year it offers only packages of two or three nights with all meals and excursions included. ❽
Residencial Chiloé Domingo Atienza ℡55/851017. Simple rooms kept very clean by the friendly owner. ❸
Residencial La Florida Tocopilla ℡55/851021. Basic but adequate rooms around a courtyard. No singles. ❷

Camping

Camping Cunza Gustavo Le Paige s/n (no phone). A fairly hard-ground campsite, along the main street, with shade provided by a straw roof over each site; around CH$2000 per person.
Edén Atacameño Tocanao ℡55/851154. Best campsite in San Pedro (around CH$2000 per person), a short distance south of the plaza, with lots of trees, water and an outdoor kitchen. Also has a few basic rooms (❶).

The Village

The focus of San Pedro is the little **plaza** at its centre, dotted with pepper trees and wooden benches. On its western side stands the squat white **Iglesia de San Pedro**, one of the largest Andean churches in the region. It's actually San Pedro's second church, built in 1744, just over 100 years after the original church was erected near the present site of the archeological museum. The bell tower was added towards the end of the nineteenth century, and the thick adobe walls surrounding the church rebuilt in 1978. Inside, religious icons look down from the brightly painted altar, among them a stern-looking Saint Peter, the village's patron saint. Overhead, the sloping roof is made of rough-hewn planks of cactus wood and gnarled rafters of reddish algarrobo timber, bound together with leather straps.

Opposite the church, on the other side of the square, sits San Pedro's oldest building, the lopsided **Casa Incaica**, now a souvenir store, dating from the earliest days of the colony; the roof seems to be in imminent danger of collapse. A narrow alley full of **artesanía** stalls, where you can buy alpaca knitwear and other souvenirs, links the square to the main bus stops to the north.

△ Prehistoric mummy

Don't miss the outstanding **Museo Arqueológico Gustavo Le Paige** (Mon–Fri 9am–noon & 2–6pm, Sat & Sun 10am–noon & 2–6pm; CH$2000), just off the northeast corner of the square. Named after the Belgian missionary-cum-archeologist who founded it in 1955, the museum houses more than 380,000 artefacts gathered from the region around San Pedro, of which the best examples are displayed in eight "naves" arranged around a central hall. Charting the development, step by step, of local pre-Columbian peoples, the displays range from Neolithic tools to sophisticated ceramics, taking in delicately carved wooden tablets and tubes used for inhaling hallucinogenic substances, and a number of gold and silver **ritual masks** worn by village elders during religious ceremonies. The most compelling exhibits are the prehistoric mummies, most famously that of a young woman sitting with her knees huddled up to her chest, her skin all withered and leathery, but her hair still thick and black. She is known affectionately as "Miss Chile".

Eating, drinking and entertainment

Thanks to the steady flow of young travellers passing through town, San Pedro boasts a lively **eating and drinking** scene. Just about every restaurant offers a fixed-price evening meal, with several choices of main course, usually including a vegetarian option; because of fierce competition, prices are not as high as you might expect. As with the accommodation, you'll see a definite "San Pedro look" among local restaurants, with a predilection for "native-style" adobe walls, wooden tables with benches, faux rock-paintings and other wacky decorations, and trendy staff. Many eating places double up as bars, sometimes with live music, while a couple of places also have **dancing**. Partying in San Pedro reaches a climax on **June 29**, when the village celebrates its saint's day with exuberant dancing and feasting.

Adobe Caracoles 211. Bustling outdoor restaurant with a roaring fire lit every night. Uncomfortable seats and pricey food but warm atmosphere, and the village's best Internet connection by far.
Café Etnico Tocopilla s/n. Excellent place for breakfast, a quick lunch, or afternoon tea, complete with tasty cakes, fruit juices, Internet connection and a funky ambience.
Café Export Caracoles and Tocanao. Real (not instant) coffee, snacks and sandwiches in a building and patio with striking décor, including Valle de la Luna–inspired tables, hand-crafted using adobe.
Café Sonchek Calama s/n. Quiet restaurant serving delicious, reasonably priced soups and pastas on a lovely patio behind the main building. Closed in evening and on Sundays.
La Casona Caracoles s/n. Informal and inexpensive, but arguably the best restaurant in San Pedro. The dining room is very elegant,

inside a large, colonial-style house, and the menu is fairly imaginative, with llama stew and some great puddings.
La Estaka Caracoles 259. Rustic restaurant-bar with young waiters and waitresses and loud music, open from breakfast-time until 1am. Very popular, though not cheap.
Milagro Caracoles and Tocopilla. Trendy, off-beat place, with an original menu including fondues and moderately priced pizzas and pasta.
Paacha Domingo Atienza s/n, in *Hotel Kimal*. Large, moderately priced restaurant with an attractive interior, good food and regular performances by Andean folk bands.
Tierra Caracoles 46. Tiny café specializing in low-priced home-made vegetarian food, including wholemeal bread, empanadas, fruit pancakes, yoghurt, salads and cakes.

Listings

Banks and exchange There are no banks, but two *casas de cambio*, one at Toconao, opposite Planeta, and the other on Caracoles.
Bicycles You can rent mountain bikes at Suri Expediciones, corner of Tocopilla and Gustavo Le Paige, for CH$1000/hour or CH$6000/day.
Internet Best connection is at Adobe's cybercafé on Caracoles (see above).

Post office Opposite the archeological museum.
Swimming pool There's a swimming pool (permanently open) at Pozo Tres, a three-kilometre walk east of the museum.
Telephone offices On the south side of the plaza; also has an Internet connection (and long queues).
Tour companies See box on p.243.

Around San Pedro

The spectacular landscape around San Pedro includes vast, desolate plains cradling numerous **volcanoes** of the most delicate colours imaginable, and beautiful **lakes** speckled pink with flamingoes. You'll also find the largest **salt flat** in Chile, the **Salar de Atacama**, a whole field full of fuming **geysers**

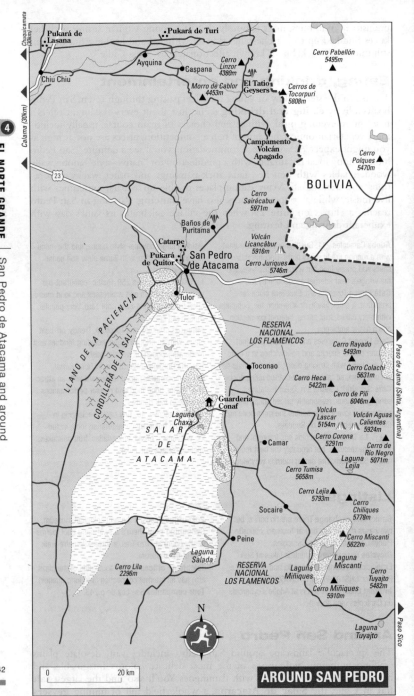

Chuquicamata (30km)

Calama (30km)

Pukará de Lasana

Pukará de Turi

Ayquina

Caspana

Chiu Chiu

Cerro Linzor 4380m

Morro de Cablor 4453m

El Tatio Geysers

Cerro Pabellón 5495m

Cerros de Tocorpuri 5808m

Cerro Polques 5470m

Campamento Volcán Apagado

BOLIVIA

23

Cerro Sairécabur 5971m

Baños de Puritama

Catarpe

Pukará de Quitor

San Pedro de Atacama

Volcán Licancábur 5916m

Cerro Juriques 5746m

Tulor

LLANO DE LA PACIENCIA

CORDILLERA DE LA SAL

RESERVA NACIONAL LOS FLAMENCOS

Toconao

Cerro Rayado 5493m

Paso de Jama (Salta Argentina)

Cerro Heca 5422m

Cerro Colachi 5631m

Cerro de Pili 6046m

Guardería Conaf

Laguna Chaxa

SALAR DE ATACAMA

Volcán Lascar 5154m

Volcán Aguas Calientes 5924m

Camar

Cerro Corona 5291m

Cerro de Río Negro 5071m

Laguna Lejía

Cerro Tumisa 5658m

Cerro Lejía 5793m

Socaire

Cerro Chiliques 5778m

Peine

Laguna Salada

Cerro Miscanti 5622m

RESERVA NACIONAL LOS FLAMENCOS

Laguna Miñiques

Laguna Miscanti

Cerro Tuyajto 5482m

Cerro Lila 2296m

Cerro Miñiques 5910m

Laguna Tuyajto

Paso Sico

N

0   20 km

AROUND SAN PEDRO

at El Tatio, a scattering of fertile **oasis villages**, and several fascinating **pre-Columbian ruins**.

Tours from San Pedro

San Pedro has a high concentration of **tour operators** offering similar excursions into the surrounding altiplano at pretty much the same prices. This can, of course, be a curse as well as a blessing, for it increases tourist traffic in the region to the point where it can be difficult to visit the awe-inspiring landscape of the puna in the kind of silence and isolation it really ought to be experienced in. Some of the tours are responsibly managed but many are not; the astounding environmental damage of late has finally, if belatedly, forced local communities (but not the national authorities) to take action; they now charge entrance fees to each site and do their best to clean up after visits. The **tourist office** keeps volumes of complaints registered by tourists and they are worth consulting to find out which operators to avoid.

Tours usually take place in minibuses, though smaller groups may travel in jeeps. Competition keeps prices relatively low – you can expect to pay from around CH$4000 to visit the Valle de la Luna, CH$12,000 for a tour to the Tatio geysers, and around CH$20,000 for a full-day tour of the local lakes and oases. Don't necessarily choose the cheapest tour, as some companies cram passengers in and offer below-par services, so it may be worth paying a couple of thousand pesos more. Do visit several companies – or their websites, where available – to get a feel for how they operate and to work out which one you prefer. If you don't speak Spanish, check that they can offer guides who speak your language (French, German and English being the most common on offer).

You will probably be touted by tour company employees as you walk along the streets. While this can be annoying, it is not necessarily a bad sign; many companies do it, and they might just be trying to make up a quorum for a particular tour. A selection of tour companies is given below with their specialization, if any. If a company does not appear on this list, it doesn't mean it's not worth checking out, it may just be new on the block. Check ⓦ www.sanpedroatacama.com for more information and links. We have not listed any companies about which we, or the local tourist office, have received a large number of complaints (usually concerning reliability of vehicles or lack of professionalism).

Tour operators

Atacama Connection Caracoles and Toconao ⓣ55/851548, ⓔatacamaconnection@entelchile.net. Long-established operator offering standard tours.

Atacama Desert Expeditions Tocopilla 411 (see *Lodge Andino Terrantai*, p.239). Pricier than most, but good reputation.

Azimut 360 Caracoles 195 ⓣ55/851469, ⓔbase-spa@netline.cl. The best operator for mountain ascents (plus the usual tours).

Cactus Domingo Atienza 419 ⓣ55/332837, ⓔcactustour@hotmail.com.

Cunza Ecoturismo Caracoles 205 ⓣ55/851183. The standard tours, with an ecological slant.

Desert Adventure Caracoles s/n ⓣ & ⓕ 55/851067, and also Latorre 1815, Calama ⓣ55/344894, ⓦwww.desertadventure.cl. Professional and reliable outfit; highly recommended.

Planeta Aventura Caracoles s/n ⓣ55/851023, ⓕ55/851156, ⓔchagomarq@yahoo.com.

Turismo Colque at Caracoles s/n ⓣ55/851109. The only company in San Pedro regularly offering trips across the border into Bolivia, to see the fabulous Salar de Uyuni (covered in the *Rough Guide to Bolivia*); the company has a very mixed reputation.

Turismo Ochoa Caracoles s/n ⓣ55/342479.

The otherworldliness of this region is reflected in the poetic names of its geographical features – Valle de la Luna (Valley of the Moon), Llano de la Paciencia (Plain of Patience), Garganta del Diablo (Devil's Throat) and Valle de la Muerte (Valley of the Dead), to mention but a few. You might prefer to explore these marvels by yourself, but several companies in San Pedro trip over themselves to take you on guided tours, often a more convenient option – see box on p.243.

Pukará de Quitor

Just 3km north of San Pedro (head up Calle Tocopilla then follow the river), the **PUKARÁ DE QUITOR** (CH$1200) is a ruined twelfth-century fortress built into a steep hillside on the west bank of the Río San Pedro. It has been partially restored, and you can make out the defence wall encircling a group of stone buildings huddled inside. According to Spanish chronicles, this *pukará* was stormed and taken by Francisco de Aguirre and thirty men as part of Pedro de Valdivia's conquest in 1540. Another 4km up the road you'll find the ruins of what used to be an Inca administrative centre at **Catarpe**, but there's little to see in comparison with the ruins of Quitor.

Valle de la Luna

The **VALLE DE LA LUNA** (CH$1500), or Valley of the Moon (about 14km west of San Pedro on the old road to Calama) really lives up to its name, presenting a dramatic lunar landscape of wind-eroded hills surrounding a crust-like valley floor, once the bottom of a lake. An immense sand dune sweeps across the valley, easy enough to climb and a great place to sit and survey the scenery. If you're prepared to battle your way through the flying sand, you can even walk along the dune's crest.

The valley is at its best at sunset, when it's transformed into a spellbinding palette of golds and reds, but you'll have to share this view with a multitude of fellow visitors, as all San Pedro tour operators offer daily sunset trips here. A more memorable (but more demanding) experience would be to get up before day breaks and cycle to the valley, arriving at sunrise for rental info). The way here is straightforward: take Caracoles west out of San Pedro and at the end take the left-hand turn, following the old road to Calama directly to the valley. Remember to bring plenty of water and sunscreen. Note that the valley is part of the Conaf-run Reserva Nacional Los Flamencos, and camping is not permitted.

Tulor

The site of the earliest example of settled habitation in the region, **TULOR**, 9km southwest of San Pedro, (CH$1500), dates from around 800 BC. Buried beneath a sand dune for hundreds of years, this settlement has remained remarkably intact. It was discovered only in the mid-twentieth century by Padre Le Paige, founder of the Museo Arqueológico in San Pedro. Today, the uppermost parts of the walls are exposed, protruding from the earth, while the rest remains buried under the sand. Two reconstructions of these igloo-like houses stand alongside the site.

The Salar de Atacama

The northern edge of this 3000-square-kilometre basin covered by a vast crust of saline minerals lies some 10km south of San Pedro. The largest salt flat in Chile, **SALAR DE ATACAMA** (CH$2000) is formed by waters flowing down from the Andes which, unable to escape from the basin, are forced to evaporate, leaving salt deposits on the earth. It's not a dazzling white like the Salar de Surire (see p.277), or Bolivia's Salar de Uyuni, but it's fascinating all the same – especially when you get out and take a close look at the crust, which looks like coral reef, or ice shards, and clanks when you walk on it. The *salar* contains several small lakes, including **Laguna Chaxa**, home to dozens of flamingoes, and the beautiful **Laguna Salada**, whose waters are covered with floating plates of salt. Many tour companies include a stop at the salt flat as part of a visit to the oases and lakes south of San Pedro.

The southern oases and lakes

Heading south from San Pedro, on the eastern side of the Salar de Atacama, you enter a region of beautiful lakes and tiny oasis villages. The first oasis, 38km south, is **Toconao**, whose softwater stream enters the village through the **Quebrada de Jérez** (CH$1000), a steep, narrow gorge with figs and quinces growing on its southern banks. Though not as pretty as some of the other villages, Toconao does possess a handsome whitewashed 1750 bell tower, set apart from the main church. Some 35km further south you reach **Camar**, a tiny hamlet with just sixty inhabitants, set amidst lush green terraces. **Socaire**, 15km beyond, is less picturesque, save for its little church set by a field of sunflowers. **Peine**, off a track branching west from the "main road" between Camar and Socaire, has a mid-eighteenth-century church and a large swimming pool, invariably full of squealing children. It is possible **to stay** in Peine and Socaire under the Red Licanhuasi rural guesthouse scheme run from San Pedro (see p.239).

One of the most stunning lakes in the region, **Laguna Miscanti** (near Socaire, 4350m above sea level; CH$2000), boasts brilliant blue waters. Adjacent lies the much smaller **Laguna Miñeques**, whose waters are a deep, dark blue; both lakes are protected areas, part of the Reserva Nacional Los Flamencos. Further south, pastel-coloured **Laguna Tuyajto** is home to dozens of flamingoes and is set against a fabulous backdrop of mineral-streaked mountains, while **Laguna Lejía**, further north, is filled with emerald-green waters tinged white with salt deposits floating on the surface; it, too, is home to large numbers of flamingoes.

The Tatio geysers

Getting to the **TATIO GEYSERS**, 95km north of San Pedro, is quite an ordeal: first, you drag yourself out of bed in the dead of night, with no electric lights to see by; you then stand shivering in the street while you wait for your tour company to come and pick you up at around 4am; and finally, you embark on a three-hour journey across a rough, bumpy road. Added to this is the some-what surreal experience of finding yourself in a pre-dawn rush hour, part of a caravan of minibuses following each other's lights across the desert.

But hardly anyone who makes the trip regrets it. At 4300m above sea level, El Tatio is the highest **geothermal** field in the world. It's essentially a large, flat field containing countless blowholes full of bubbling water that, between around 6 and 8am, send billowing clouds of steam high into the air (strictly speaking, though, geysers spurt water, not steam). At the same time, the spray forms pools of water on the ground, streaked with silver reflections as they catch the first rays of the sun. It's really a magnificent spectacle. Take great care, however, when walking around the field; the crust of earth is very thin in some parts, and serious accidents can happen. You should also remember that it will be freezing cold when you arrive, though once the sun's out the place warms up quite quickly.

There's a swimming pool near the geysers, visited by most tour companies, so remember to take your bathing suit. On the way back, some tour companies also pay a visit to the **Baños de Puritama** (CH$5000), a rocky pool filled with warm thermal water, 60km south of the geysers and run by a local community but owned and maintained by the Hotel Explora (see p.239).

From El Tatio to Calama

Spread between El Tatio and Calama is a series of charming oases and pre-Columbian remains, visited by several tour companies after a morning at the geysers. This is an excursion to take on your final day in San Pedro, as you can store your luggage in the minibus and get dropped off at Calama, before the tour returns to San Pedro. About 45km west of El Tatio (by road) and one of the most beautiful oases in Chile, **Caspana** sits in a fertile valley at the foot of a steep cliff. A small river runs through the valley, crossed by a little stone bridge that leads to the school and museum (Tues–Sun 9.30am–5.30pm; CH$500), where you'll find displays on Caspana's pre-Columbian origins. Across the river from the main village, perched high on a hill, the *pueblo viejo* is the site of the old church, dating from 1641, with steps leading up the bell tower. Not far from Caspana sits **Ayquina**, another picture-postcard village but almost deserted, coming to life only for its fiesta on September 8. Its houses, made entirely of stone, are clustered around the church, which has a distinctive five-tiered bell tower. The village's main street leads to a *mirador* overlooking the deep canyon through which the Río Salado runs, lined by dark-green terraces – a truly gorgeous view.

North of Ayquina lies the twelfth-century **Pukará de Turi**, the largest fortified village ever built in the region, and used as an administrative centre by the Incas towards the end of the fifteenth century. Today, you can still make out the outline of its streets and squares, and there are some half-standing circular towers. Heading west, towards Calama, you'll reach the twelfth-century **Pukará de Lasana** (CH$800), now partially restored and conserved as a national monument. It's fascinating to wander the narrow, maze-like streets laid out in a zigzag pattern.

One of the most beautiful Andean churches in Chile, the **Iglesia de San Francisco**, sits in **Chiu Chiu**, 8km south of Lasana, a tidy, well-maintained village built in 1674. A wide, squat whitewashed building, the church's adobe walls are over a metre thick, topped by a rough thatched roof. Perhaps most impressive are its massive doors, lined with cactus boards and decorated with leather cross-stitching. If you walk around the outside, within the thick white walls enclosing it, you'll find a tiny cemetery out the back. Chiu Chiu is just 33km east of Calama, so it can also be visited as part of a tour from there.

Iquique

Dramatically situated at the foot of the 800-metre coastal cordillera, with an enormous sand dune looming precariously above one of its barrios, **IQUIQUE**, 390km north of Calama, is a sprawling, busy and surprisingly cosmopolitan city. Iquique rivals Arica as the best place to base yourself for a tour of the extreme northern tip of the country. From here, you can easily arrange excursions into the interior, whose attractions include the famous nitrate ghost towns of **Humberstone** and **Santa Laura**, the beautiful hot-springs oases of **Pica** and **Matilla**, and the stunning altiplano scenery of **Parque Nacional Volcán Isluga**.

Some history

Iquique started out as a small settlement of indigenous fishing communities, and during the colonial period became a base for extracting guano deposits from the

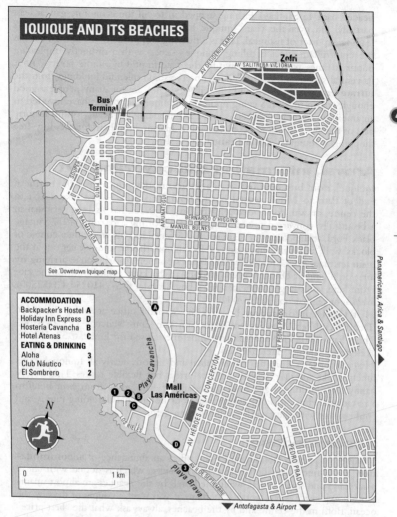

IQUIQUE AND ITS BEACHES

Zofri

AV DESIDERIO GARCÍA
AV SALITRERA VICTORIA

Bus Terminal

AV BALMACEDA
ANÍBAL PINTO
SOTOMAYOR

AMUNÁTEGUI
BERNARDO O'HIGGINS
MANUEL BULNES

See 'Downtown Iquique' map

AV PEDRO PRADO

ACCOMMODATION
Backpacker's Hostel **A**
Holiday Inn Express **D**
Hostería Cavancha **B**
Hotel Atenas **C**
EATING & DRINKING
Aloha **3**
Club Náutico **1**
El Sombrero **2**

Playa Cavancha

Mall Las Américas

AV HÉROES DE LA CONCEPCIÓN

LOS RIELES

PEDRO PRADO

N

Playa Brava

AV 21 DE SEPTIEMBRE

0   1 km

▼ **Antofagasta & Airport** ▼

coast. It continued to grow with the opening of a nearby silver mine in 1730, but its population never exceeded one hundred in the eighteenth century, and it wasn't until the great nineteenth-century nitrate boom that it really took off as a city.

Following its transferral to Chilean hands during the War of the Pacific (1878–83), Iquique became the **nitrate capital** of Chile – where the largest quantities of ore were shipped from, and where the wealthy nitrate barons based themselves, building opulent mansions all over the rapidly expanding city. By the end of the nineteenth century, Iquique was the wealthiest and most hedonistic city in Chile – it was said that more champagne was consumed here, per head, than in any other city in the world.

With the abrupt end of the nitrate era after World War I, Iquique's boom was over, and the grand mansions were left to fade and crumble as the industrialists headed back to Santiago. Fishing stepped in to fill the economic gap, at least partially, and over the years Iquique has transformed itself into the world's leading exporter of fishmeal. This is a thriving and prosperous industry, but has the unfortunate effect of filling Iquique's streets with a distinctly unpleasant odour at times, particularly down by the waterfront. On a more positive note, its central square and main avenue conserve some splendid buildings from the **nitrate era**, which, along with the city's beaches, are for many people a good enough reason to visit. Seizing upon this, Iquique authorities have invested in an ambitious restoration scheme aimed at enhancing the beauty of this historic part of the city. Still more people, mainly Chileans, head here for the duty-free shopping at Iquique's **Zona Franca**, or "Zofri".

Arrival, information and city transport

Iquique's main **bus terminal** is in a rather run-down quarter at the northern end of Patricio Lynch, several blocks from the centre – best take a taxi to the centre, or wait for a *colectivo*. **Tur Bus**, however, has its own terminal in a beautifully converted townhouse, proudly sporting a dazzling 1917 vintage black Ford, at the corner of Ramírez and Esmeralda. This saves you a couple of blocks' walk and is in a more agreeable neighbourhood, so don't get out at the main terminal even though Tur Bus buses stop there, too. If you're arriving **by air**, you'll land at Diego Arecena airport, a whacking 40km south of the city. From here, you can get to the centre by bus (Transfer ☎ 57/410250; CH$2500), *colectivo* or regular taxi (CH$7000).

For **tourist information**, head for the Sernatur office at Aníbal Pinto 436 (Dec 15–end Feb Mon–Sat 9am–8pm, Sun 9am–2pm; March 1–Dec 14 Mon–Thurs 9am–5pm, Fri 9am–4.30pm; sometimes closed for lunch; ☎ 57/312238, ℮ esernatur iquiq@entelchile.net).

Except for fares from the bus terminal and airport, nearly all Iquique's **taxis** function like *colectivos*, with fixed, low prices but flexible routes. This is very handy for shuttling to and from the beach, or even going from your hotel to a restaurant. Find out from Sernatur or your hotel what the going rate is, and confirm this with the taxi driver before you get in.

Accommodation

Iquique is a popular holiday resort and offers an abundance of **accommodation**. You'll find the widest choice in the centre, which is dotted with cheap *residenciales* and smart hotels, while the hotels by the beaches are almost unanimously expensive – but worth it, perhaps, if you want a couple of days by the ocean. Both in the centre and by the beaches, always ask what the "best price" is, as many places will give discounts when pushed. One thing to bear in mind is that, owing to the region's severe water shortage, water supplies are occasionally cut in the busy summer months, sometimes without warning.

Downtown Iquique

Hostal Pleamar Latorre 1036 ☎ 57/411840. Small but clean, quiet rooms with private bath and TV, giving onto a covered terrace with tables and chairs. ❸

Hostal Sol del Norte Juan Martínez 852 ☎ 57/421546. Simple but well-maintained rooms (with shared bath) off a long corridor, run by a very friendly *señora*. ❷

Hotel Arturo Prat Aníbal Pinto 695 ☎ 57/411067, Ⓕ 57/423309. Plush city-centre hotel with an elegant period front area containing the reception and restaurant, and modern rooms in tall blocks behind. Also has a small rooftop pool. ❺

Hotel Carlos Condell Baquedano 964 ☎ 57/424467, Ⓕ 57/422920. Beautiful old timber building on the historic stretch of Calle Baquedano.

The rooms at the front are looking worse for wear but open onto a wonderful verandah; those at the back are small and dark. ❹
Hotel Intillanka Obispo Labbé 825 ☎57/311104, ℱ57/311105. Friendly and efficiently run hotel offering 30 spacious, light rooms with private bath. Showing its age a little, but very clean. ❹
Hotel Riorsa Vivar 1542 ☎ & ℱ 57/423823. Good-quality, neat rooms with private bath and cable TV. The very helpful owner is also a plus. On the southern edge of town, an easy walk from the beach. ❹
Residencial Casa Grande Barros Arana 1071 ☎ & ℱ57/426846. Decent budget rooms in the main house, with high ceilings and wooden floors, but those out back are cramped and dingy. ❸
Residencial José Luis Ramírez 402. Bright, airy and fairly large rooms with shared bath – a good budget choice. ❷

The beaches

Backpacker's Hostel Amunategui 2075 ☎57/320223, evinko@terra.cl. Excellent, new HI-affiliated hostel offering weekly barbecues, surfboard and wetsuit rental and clean rooms and facilities. CH$5000 per person.
Holiday Inn Express 11 Septiembre 1690 ☎57/433300. Impersonal but immaculate US chain hotel, with a pool, air conditioning and spacious rooms with ocean views (at the front). Special discounts Fri–Sun. ❼
Hostería Cavancha Los Rieles 250 ☎ & ℱ 57/434800. Modern, 80-room hotel with tennis courts, swimming pool, a dining room overlooking the ocean and direct access to the beach. Rooms not as fresh as they could be. ❼
Hotel Atenas Los Rieles 738 ☎ & ℱ57/431100. Grand nitrate-era house with lots of character and beautifully furnished rooms with verandahs. A modern annexe out the back has plainer, less expensive rooms. ❺–❻

The City

Iquique falls into two quite distinct areas: **downtown**, lined with shops, services, and old historic buildings, and the modern stretch along the **oceanfront**, given over almost entirely to tourism. The **Zofri** duty-free zone is just north of the centre, in an industrial area.

Downtown

The focus of town is the large, partly pedestrianized **Plaza Prat**, dominated by the gleaming white **Teatro Municipal**, whose magnificent facade features Corinthian columns and statues representing the four seasons – spoiled at night by criminally hideous fairy lights. It was built in 1890 as an opera house and showcased some of the most distinguished divas of its time. These days, productions aren't quite so grand, featuring everything from national ballet to local school concerts. If the programme doesn't appeal, it's still worth taking a look inside (daily 9am–9pm; CH$500) to admire the lavish, if slightly faded, furnishings and the grand proportions of the auditorium. Opposite the theatre, in the centre of the square, the **Torre Reloj** is a tall white clock tower with Moorish arches, adopted by Iquique as the city's symbol. On the northeast corner of the square, the **Casino Español** – formerly a gentlemen's club, now a restaurant – features an extravagant interior with oil paintings depicting scenes from *Don Quijote*; it's definitely worth a visit.

Leading south, **Calle Baquedano** is lined with an extraordinary collection of turn-of-the-century timber houses, all with porches and balconies and fine wooden balustrades, and many undergoing loving restoration. This is the showcase of Iquique's nitrate architecture and has been designated a national monument. The street is pedestrianized from the plaza all the way down to the seafront, using noble materials such as fine stone for the paving and polished timber for the sidewalks. A ridiculously slow wooden **tram** chugs up and down, more a photo opportunity than a means of transport. Three buildings are open

△ Teatro Municipal

to the public: the **Sala de Artes Collahuasi** at no. 930 (open every evening till late; free), an impeccably restored building used for temporary art exhibitions, usually of outstanding quality; the **Museo Regional** at no. 951 (Mon–Fri 9am–5.30pm, Sat & Sun 10am–5pm; free), which houses an eclectic collection of pre-Hispanic and natural history artefacts, including deformed skulls and a pickled two-headed shark; and the **Palacio Astoreca** (Tues–Fri 10am–1pm & 4–7pm, Sat & Sun 11am–2pm; CH$400; entrance on O'Higgins), a glorious, though deteriorating, mansion featuring a massive wood-panelled entrance hall with a painted glass Art Nouveau ceiling.

The **Museo Naval**, one block south (Mon–Sat 4–7pm, Tues–Fri also 10am–1pm; CH$200), displays letters, maps and photos relating to Arturo Prat, hero of the War of the Pacific (see p.597), and, just behind, the **Caleta Pesquera**, or fishermen's wharfs, where the huge, yawning pelicans strutting around the pier make compelling viewing. You can take **boat tours** around the harbour from here, worth it for the views onto the steep desert mountains, rising like huge slabs of chocolate cake behind the city.

The beaches

Two beaches lie within striking distance of the city centre: **Playa Cavancha**, the nearest, most popular, and more sheltered, and **Playa Brava**, larger, less crowded and more windswept, but only suitable for daring surfers. You can just about walk to Playa Cavancha, which begins at the southern end of Amunategui, but it's far easier, and very cheap, to take one of the numerous taxis constantly travelling between the plaza and the beach; many continue to Playa Brava, as well, for a slightly higher fare. Both beaches, particularly Cavancha, are lined with modern hotels and apartment blocks, but the construction is fairly low-level, and not too ugly. Further south, between Playa Brava and the airport, there's a series of attractive sandy beaches including **Playa Blanca**, 13km south of the centre, **Playa Lobito**, at km 22, and the fishing cove of **Los Verdes**, at km 24. You can get to these on the airport bus or *colectivo*.

The Zofri

About 3km north of the centre, located in a large industrial compound, the duty-free shopping complex known as the **Zofri** (Mon–Fri 10am–1.30pm & 4.30–9pm, Sat 10am–2pm & 5–9pm) is widely touted as one of the great attractions of the north. Thousands of Chileans flock here from up and down the country to spend their money at what turns out, at close quarters, to be a big, ugly mall crammed full of small shops selling electronic items like cameras, watches and domestic gadgets. There's a curious mixture of the upmarket and the tacky, with the latter tending to dominate. The building itself is shabby and old-fashioned, and the bargains aren't really good enough to deserve a special trip. If you do want to check it out, take any *colectivo* marked "Zofri" heading north out of town – the east side of the Plaza or Calle Armunategui are both good bets for catching one.

Eating, drinking and entertainment

While there's a reasonable choice of **restaurants** in the centre, it's worth coming out to have at least one evening meal by the beach, to see the ocean lit up with coloured lights projected from the promenade. As for entertainment, you'll find several **discotheques** that get very crowded in summer and maintain a gentle buzz during low season. They are nearly all down on the Costanera Sur; leading names to look out for include *Kamikaze*, *Pharos*, *Nitro* and *Club*

Mex. Iquique's main **cinema** is at Mall Las Américas on Avenida Héroes de la Concepción (see "Iquique and its Beaches" map).

Downtown Iquique restaurants

Barracuda Gorostiaga 601, at Ramírez. Very popular wood-panelled pub serving wine by the glass, pisco sour, foreign beers, tea, coffee, milkshakes and delicious snacks, plus reasonably priced full-blown meals in the evening. Soft jazz music, lovely mellow atmosphere and top-notch service.

Bavaria Aníbal Pinto 926. Downstairs café and upstairs restaurant that are part of a nationwide chain specializing in mid-price meat dishes.

🏃 **Boulevard** Baquedano 790. Beautiful French-style (and French-owned) bistro with a stylish terrace offers a wonderful change from Chilean fare, if you are prepared to pay a little extra. The chef rustles up fantastic fish and seafood dishes, salads, crêpes, pasta, pizzas and even *tagines* (a Moroccan speciality of meat or fish cooked with herbs and spices in an earthenware pot). Excellent wines and delicious desserts, too.

Casino de Bomberos Serrano 520. Friendly firemen's canteen (open to the public), serving filling, tasty and inexpensive lunches.

Casino Español Plaza Prat 584. Huge, fabulous dining room decorated like a mock Moorish palace. The food is unexceptional, and a little overpriced, but this is a must-visit.

Club de la Unión Plaza Prat 278. Uninspired food (typical meat and fish dishes), but the building is spacious and rather grand, with views onto the Teatro Municipal. A good place for an inexpensive lunch.

Mercado Centenario Barros Arana, between Latorre and Sargento Aldea. Cheap fish lunches available upstairs at the ten or so bustling *marisquerías*.

El Rincón Mexicano Patricio Lynch 754. Cosy Mexican restaurant owned by football-mad Mario, with regular showings of Mexican games on the TV.

The food is not that great but nor is it expensive.

Taco Tequilla Thompson 123. Funky, colourful decor, good Mexican food and great tequilas. Very lively at weekends, when they have live *mariachis*. Watch out for overcharging; otherwise prices are alright.

Restaurants by the beach

Aloha 11 de Septiembre near *Holiday Inn Express*. Excellent but very expensive food served in a faux-rustic hut overlooking the beach. Good service and lovely views.

Club Náutico Los Rieles 110. First-rate, reasonably priced restaurant with great views from its outdoor terrace, especially at night.

El Sombrero Los Rieles 704. Rather formal, expensive restaurant specializing in seafood – invariably served up in rich, roux-based sauces. It's right by the sea, with floor-to-ceiling windows giving great views.

Bars

Golosita Baquedano 696. Little place serving pricey but deliciously thirst-quenching juices made with fruit from the oasis towns.

Mascarrieles Off Plaza Prat, by *Hotel Arturo Prat*. Friendly bar-restaurant with lots of dark wood panelling; popular with locals at lunch time or after work.

Split/Hrvatski Dom Plaza Prat, next to Casino Español. A little piece of Croatia on the Pacific, with its cosy interior lifted straight from the Dalmatian city it's named for, this friendly place does decent snacks and serves the best espresso around.

Timber House Bolívar 553. New pub, similar to the *Barracuda* (see above), in an old timber building, serving beers, cocktails and Mediterranean snacks.

Tours from Iquique

A number of Iquique tour companies offer one-day circular tours – from around CH$15,000 per person – taking in the nitrate ghost towns of **Humberstone** and **Santa Laura** (see p.254); the geoglyphs of Pintados (see p.254); the oases villages of **Matilla** and **Pica**, with a plunge in Pica's hot springs (see p.256); and the basilica and nitrate museum of **La Tirana** (see p.256). Another standard tour offered by some companies is the highly memorable route up into the cordillera, continuing north across the altiplano and descending in Arica; these excursions take in the geysers of **Puchildiza** (see p.261), **Parque Nacional Volcán Isluga** (see p.261), the **Salar de Surire** (see p.277) and **Parque Nacional Lauca** (see p.274). The tour entails three overnight stays, with prices starting around CH$100,000 per person. Recommended companies are given in the Listings section, opposite, under "Tour operators."

Moving on from Iquique

Most **long-distance buses** (including Tur Bus) depart from the Terminal Rodoviario, at the north end of Lynch, but many bus companies also have offices around the Mercado Centenario, including: Buses Carmelita, Barros Arana 841 (☏57/412337); Flota Barrios, Sargento Aldea 987 (☏57/426941); Ramos Cholele, Barros Arana 851 (☏57/411650); and Tur Bus, Barros Arana 825 (☏57/413028). Remember that Tur Bus also has its own impressive terminal at the corner of Ramírez and Esmeralda. There are regular daily buses to **Pica** (with stops at **Matilla** and **La Tirana**) with San Andrés, on the corner of Barros Arana and Sargento Aldea (☏57/413953), and Buses Tamarugal, Sargento Aldea 781 (☏57/412981). The latter also has daily services to **Mamiña** (Mon–Sat 8am & 4pm, Sun 8am only). Yellow *colectivos* for **Pozo Almonte** leave from the side of the market and will drop passengers at **Humberstone**. Buses Géminis, Obispo Labbé 151 (☏57/413315), goes to Salta in Argentina (erratic service), and Oruro and La Paz, in Bolivia. You can **fly** out of Iquique to most of the main cities of northern Chile, plus Santiago de Chile and Santa Cruz in Bolivia.

Airlines LAN, Tarapacá 465 ☏57/427600; Sky Airlines, Ramírez 411 ☏57/415013; TAM, Tarapacá 451 ☏57/390600.

Banks and exchange Iquique has numerous ATMs, including those at: Banco Santander, Plaza Prat; BCI, Tarapacá 404; Banco Sudamericano, Uribe 530; Corp-Banca, Serrano 343. There are fewer *casas de cambio*, but you could try Afex, on the corner of Serrano and Lynch, downtown, or Fides Ltda, at the Zofri Plaza de Servicios.

Car rental Best value may well be at Jofamar, Libertad 1156 ☏57/411639, or Stop, at Bulnes 168 ☏57/416382. You could also try: Budget, O'Higgins 1361 ☏57/422527; Continental, 18 de Septiembre 1054 ☏57/411426; Econorent, Obispo Labbé 1089 ☏57/423723, ⓦwwwreservas@econorent.net; Hertz, Souper 650 ☏57/420213; J. Reategui, Serrano 1058 ☏57/429490; Rocar, Cerro Dragón 2789 ☏57/435233; Senort, Souper 796 ☏57/413480.

Internet *Travel Web*, at Baquedano 770, is by far the best connection in town, with reasonable rates.

Laundry Lavamatic, Orella 756, near corner with Barros Arana; Lavalindo, O'Higgins 618, between Vivar and Ramírez; Autoservicio, San Martín 490.

Post office The main office is at Bolívar 485, a few blocks northeast of Plaza Prat.

Swimming pool There's a fantastic outdoor pool (☏57/411573) overlooking the Pacific at Avenida Costanera with Riquelme, opposite the Copec station.

Taxis Taxi Aeropuerto Plaza Prat ☏57/413368; Iquique ☏57/413848.

Telephone offices CTC, Serrano 620; Entel, Gorostiaga 287; Chilexpress, Tarapacá 580.

Tour operators Avitours, Baquedano 997 ☏57/473775, ⓔreservas@avitour.cl; Coki (Geotour), Baquedano 982 ☏ 57/428984, ⓔcokitouriqq@terra.cl; Jaws, Latorre 324 ☏ & ⓕ57/418336, ⓔtransjaws81@hotmail .com; Las Dunas, San Martín 829 ☏57/425124, ⓕ57/517068, ⓔhotellasdunas@entelchile.com; Surire Tours, Baquedano 1035 ☏ & ⓕ57/445440. Longest on the scene is Turismo Lirima, at Orella 548 (☏57/390404 & 390272, ⓕ57/390403, ⓔturismolirima@hotmail.com). For information on tours into the cordillera, see box opposite.

Travel agencies There are numerous travel agents in town, including Atlantic, at San Martín 421; and Aries 1, at Thompson 112.

Inland from Iquique

Iquique lies within easy reach of many inland sights. Just half an hour away, **Humberstone** and **Santa Laura** are perhaps the most haunting of all the nitrate ghost towns. South of here, close to the Panamericana, **Cerro Pintados** features a dense collection of geoglyphs, among the most impressive in Chile. East of Pintados sits the pretty oasis village of **Pica**, with a lovely thermal pool, while **Mamiña**, further north, is the Norte Grande's hot-springs town *par excellence*. You can also visit **La Tirana**, an important pilgrimage centre, famous for its colourful festival in July. Public transport around this area is sporadic but manageable.

Humberstone and Santa Laura

The best-preserved ghost town in Chile, **HUMBERSTONE** (daily 9am–7pm; CH$1000) is a nitrate *oficina* that was abandoned in 1960 and today appeals especially to lovers of industrial architecture. It sits some 45km inland from Iquique, by Ruta 16 just before it meets the Panamericana.

The town began life in 1862 as Oficina La Palma, but was renamed in 1925 in honour of its British manager, James "Santiago" Humberstone, an important nitrate entrepreneur famous for introducing the "Shanks" ore-refining system to the industry. In its time it was one of the busiest *oficinas* on the pampas; today it is an eerie, empty ghost town, slowly crumbling beneath the desert sun. What sets Humberstone apart from the other ghost towns is that just about all of it is still standing – from the white, terraced workers' houses (now in total disrepair) and the plaza with its bandstand, to the theatre, church and company store. The **theatre**, in particular, is highly evocative, with its rows of dusty seats staring at the stage. You should also seek out the **hotel**, and walk through to the back where you'll find a huge, empty **swimming pool** with a diving board – curiously the pool is made from the sections of a ship's iron hull. Located a short distance from the town are the sheds and workshops, with old tools and bits of machinery lying around, and invoices and order forms littering the floors.

At **SANTA LAURA**, about 2km down the road and clearly visible from Humberstone, you'll see only a couple of remaining houses, but the processing plant is quite amazing, seeming to loom into the air like a rusty old dinosaur. As you walk around the site, listening to the endless clanging of machinery banging in the wind, the sense of abandonment is nearly overwhelming.

Pampa del Tamarugal and Cerro Pintados geoglyphs

About 20km south of the junction between Ruta 16 and the Panamericana, the latter passes through the **RESERVA NACIONAL PAMPA DEL TAMARUGAL**, an extensive plantation of wispy, bush-like *tamarugo* trees. These are native to the region and are especially adapted to saline soils, with roots that are long enough to tap underground water supplies. There's a Conaf-run **campsite** here, exactly 24km south of Pozo Almonte, on the west side of the Panamericana. While the *tamarugos* aren't really interesting enough to merit a special trip, you can take a look at them on your way to the far more impressive **CERRO PINTADOS** (daily 9.30am–6.30pm; CH$1000), with the largest collection of **geoglyphs** in South America, situated within the reserve's boundaries. Extending 4km along a hillside, the site features four hundred images (not all of them visible from the ground) of animals, birds, humans and geometric patterns, etched on the surface or formed by a mosaic of little stones around the year 1000 AD. The felines, birds, snakes and flocks of llamas and vicuñas scratched into the rock are thought to have been indicators for livestock farmers. The circles, squares, dotted lines and human figures are more enigmatic, however, and may have had something to do with rituals, perhaps even sacrifices.

There's a picnic area near the biggest concentration of images, but it pays to explore the rest of the site as well. Cerro Pintados begins 5km west of the Panamericana, reached by a gravel road that branches off the highway 45km south of Pozo Almonte, almost opposite the turn-off to Pica. There's a Conaf control point 2km along the road, where you pay your entrance fee. If it's shut when you arrive, you can continue with your car as far as the barrier, which is just a short walk from the geoglyphs. If you haven't got your own transport,

The nitrate boom

Looking around the desert pampa, it's hard to believe that this scorched, lifeless wasteland was once so highly prized that a war was fought over it – and still more difficult to imagine it alive with smoking chimneys, grinding machinery, offices, houses and a massive workforce. But less than a century ago, the Far North of Chile was the scene of a thriving industry built on its vast **nitrate deposits**, heavily in demand in Europe and North America as a fertilizer. Nitrates were first exploited in the Atacama Desert in the 1860s, when the region still belonged to Bolivia (around Antofagasta) and Peru (around Iquique and Arica). From the early stages, however, the Chilean presence was very strong, both in terms of capital and labour – in the 1870s Chileans made up over fifty percent of the workforce in Iquique, and some eighty percent in Antofagasta, and the largest nitrate company, the **Compañía de Salitres y Ferrocarril de Antofagasta**, was a Chilean enterprise.

When in 1878 the Bolivian government violated an official agreement by raising export taxes on nitrate (hitting Chilean shareholders, including several prominent politicians), Chile protested by sending troops into Antofagasta. Two weeks later, Chile and Bolivia were at war, with Peru joining in (on the Bolivian side) within a couple of months. The War of the Pacific (see p.597) went on for five years, and resulted in Chile, the undisputed victor, extending its territory by 900km, taking in all of the nitrate grounds. With the return of political stability after the war, the nitrate industry began to boom in earnest, bringing in enormous export revenues for Chile. Foreign – particularly British – investors poured money into companies like the Liverpool Nitrate Company, and a trail of processing plants, known as **oficinas**, sprang up all over the pampa, connected to the seaports by an extensive railroad network.

Each *oficina* sat in the centre of its prescribed land, from where the raw nitrate ore – found just beneath the surface of the earth – was blasted using gunpowder. The chunks of ore, known as *caliche*, were then boiled in large copper vats, releasing a nitrate solution which was crystallized in the sun before being sent down to the ports to be shipped abroad. The plants themselves were grimy, noisy places. William Russell, a British journalist who toured the pampa in 1889, wrote: "The external aspect of the *oficina* was not unlike that of a north country coal or iron mine – tall chimneys and machinery, corrugated iron buildings, offices and houses, the shanties of workmen, a high bank of refuse." It was a hard life for the labourers, who worked long hours in dangerous conditions, and were housed in squalid shacks, often without running water and sewerage. The (mostly British) managers, meanwhile, lived in grand residences, dined on imported delicacies and enjoyed a whirl of social activities – Russell wrote of "picnics, nightly dances and even balls to which the neighbours came from the *oficinas* around, from Iquique and Pisagua below by special train, which conveyed bands of music and armies of cooks, confectioners and waiters". Nitrate provided more than half of the Chilean government's revenues until 1920, by which time the boom was over and the industry in decline.

It was World War I that dealt the first serious blow to the nitrate companies, when the suspension of sales to Germany – Chile's major European buyer – forced almost half the *oficinas* to close down. The final death knell was sounded when Germany, forced to seek alternative fertilizers, developed cheap synthetic nitrates which quickly displaced Chile's natural nitrates from their dominant role in the world market. Most of what was left of the industry was killed off by the World Depression in the 1930s, and today just two *oficinas* – María Elena and Pedro de Valdivia (see p.234) – remain in operation.

you should be able to arrange a lift there and back with a *colectivo* from the stand outside Iquique's Mercado Centenario – it's probably not a good idea to hitch and then try walking to the site from the Panamericana, owing to the relentless heat and lack of shade.

Pica and Matilla

As you cross the vast, desert pampa, the neighbouring oases of Pica and Matilla first appear as an improbable green smudge on the hazy horizon. As you get nearer, it becomes apparent that this is not a mirage and you are, indeed, approaching cultivated fields and trees. It's a remarkable sight, and anyone who has not seen a desert oasis should make a special effort to visit. By far the larger of the two oases, **PICA** is a sleepy little town overflowing with lemon and lime trees, bougainvilleas and jasmine. It's the largest supplier of fruits to Iquique – *limas de Pica* are famous throughout the country – and one of the treats of visiting is drinking the delicious *jugos naturales* – orange, mango, pear, guava and grapefruit juices – freshly squeezed in front of you in the little streetside kiosks. The tidy plaza, by the entrance to town, is overlooked by a beautiful pale-coloured **church** dedicated to St Andrew. It has a grand Neoclassical facade and was built in 1880. Pica's real selling point, however, is the **Cocha Resbaladero** (daily 8am–9pm; CH$1000), a gorgeous **hot-springs pool** carved into a rocky hollow with two caves at one end. It's at the far end of Calle Presidente Ibañez, quite a walk from the main part of town, but there are several places to stay up here if you want to be close to the waters.

The tiny, pretty village of **MATILLA**, about 5km away, has a beautiful church, albeit more humble than Pica's. You'll also see an eighteenth-century wine press, just off the plaza, used by the Spaniards to produce wine; the roots of grapevines were brought over by the conquistadors. While you're here, try the wonderful *jugos* in the café opposite the church.

Practicalities

The town has a rudimentary **Oficina de Turismo** in the Municipalidad on the main square (Mon–Fri 8.30am–1pm & 3–7pm), as well as several *centros de llamados* and a post office on Avenida O'Higgins, the main street. The nicest **place to stay** in the centre is *Hotel Los Emilios*, at Lord Cochrane 213, the first right from the plaza as you come into town (℡57/741126; ❸). It offers comfortable rooms with private bath in a handsome old house with a plunge pool in the back garden. Up by the hot springs, you'll find basic but clean rooms in *Residencial El Tambo*, at Ibañez 68 (℡57/741041; ❷), and a few attractive wooden *cabañas* overlooking the pool at Ibañez 57 (Sr Medina, ℡ & ℻ 57/741316; ❹). There's a **campsite**, *Camping Miraflores* (℡57/741338; CH$1200 per site), just round the corner on Calle Miraflores. As for **eating**, try *La Viña*, at Ibañez 79, up by the hot springs, or *Mía Pappa*, down in the centre at Balmaceda 118, where passable food is served in a quiet patio under the shade of fragrant citrus trees. The best **fruit juice stalls** are on Ibañez, towards the hot springs, and there's a wonderful **shop** selling home-made jams and conserves a little further along from the campsite.

La Tirana

Driving back to the Panamericana from Pica, if you take the right-hand (north-bound) road, rather than the left-hand one, you'll pass through the little town of **LA TIRANA**, 10km before you get back to the highway. It's a rather cheerless place, made up of dusty streets and neglected adobe houses, which makes it all the more surprising when you come upon the immense, paved square stretching out before the imposing **Santuario de la Tirana**. This curious church, at once grand and shabby, is made of wood covered in cream-coloured corrugated iron. It's the home of the **Virgen del Carmen**, a polychrome carving that is the object of a fervent cult of devotion. Every year, from July 12 to 18, up to eighty thousand pilgrims come to honour the Virgin and take part in the riotous **fiesta** in which dozens of masked, costumed dancers perform *bailes*

The Legend of La Tirana

La Tirana is named after an Inca princess whose story is vividly recorded in twelve large panels inside the town's church. It all began in 1535 when **Diego de Almagro** marched south from Cuzco to conquer Chile. He took with him some five hundred Spaniards and ten thousand locals, including Paullo Tupac, an Inca prince, and Huillac Huma, high priest of the cult of the Sun God, who was accompanied by his beautiful 23-year-old daughter, **la ñusta** (the princess). Unknown to Almagro, the party also included a number of **Wilkas**, or high-ranking warriors from the Inca Royal Army. When the party reached Atacama la Grande, the high priest took the opportunity to slip away from the group and flee to Charcas, where he planned to stir up rebellion against the Spaniards. Later, while the group was resting for several days in the oasis of **Pica**, the princess followed her father's lead and escaped from the Spaniards – with a hundred Wilkas and followers – and fled to the *tamarugo* forests which at that time covered much of the pampa. She lost no time in organizing her followers into a fierce and sophisticated army that, for the next four years, waged a relentless war against their oppressors, the Spaniards. Her mission was clear: death to all Spaniards, and to all Indians who had been baptized by them. Before long, this indomitable woman became known far and wide as La Tirana del Tamarugal – the Tyrant of the Tamarugal.

One day, in 1544, La Tirana's army attacked an enemy group and returned to their leader with a prisoner – a certain **Don Vasco de Almeyda**, one of the Portuguese miners established in Huantajaya. Don Vasco was clearly a man of exceptional qualities for, according to the legend, *"Mirarle y enamorarse fue una sola cosa"* – simply to look at him was to fall in love with him. La Tirana, hitherto immovable, fell passionately in love with the foreigner. But according to everything she stood and fought for, he must be sentenced to death. In desperation, she devised a ruse to prolong the prisoner's life: she consulted the stars and her tribe's gods, and claimed that they had ordered her to keep him alive until four moons had passed. For the next four months, La Tirana and her prisoner spent day after day talking to one another in the shade of the *tamarugos*, and a tender love grew up between them. The princess neglected her people and her duties, arousing the suspicion of the Wilkas, who began to keep a secret watch on her. As the fourth month was coming to an end, La Tirana asked her loved one if they would be reunited for eternity in heaven if she too were a Christian. On his affirmative reply, she begged him to baptize her, and bent down on her knees with her arms crossed against her breast. Pouring water over her head, Almeyda began to do so, but before he could finish, the couple were showered with arrows from the bows of the betrayed Wilkas. As she lay dying in the wood, the princess cried, "I am dying happy, sure as I am that my immortal soul will ascend to God's throne. All I ask is that after my death, you will bury me next to my lover and place a cross over our grave." Ten years later, when Padre Antonio Rondon arrived in these parts to evangelize the Indians, it was with astonishment and joy that he discovered a simple cross in a clearing of the wood. The priest erected a humble chapel on the site, which was later replaced by a larger building, and became, in time, the centre of worship in a town that took its name from the beautiful princess who had died there.

religiosos. These dances have their roots in pre-Spanish, pre-Christian times, with an exuberant, carnival feel wholly out of keeping with traditional Catholic celebrations. If you're not around to see them in action, you should at least visit the small **museum** in a wing of the church (Sat & Sun 10am–8pm; CH$100 donation) where many of the costumes and masks are displayed. (Try asking the caretaker to let you in if it's shut.)

The unique, family-run **Museo del Salitre**, standing opposite the church (entrance through the store next door; Mon–Sat 8am–1pm & 3–8pm: free) bursts with oddments left over from the nitrate era. These include old ice-cream makers, a film projector (with a reel of Hitchcock inside), typewriters, workers' clothes and boots, sewing machines, photos and, most bizarrely, a stuffed condor. All **buses** between Iquique and Pica make a stop in La Tirana (see p.256).

Mamiña

A paved road branches east from the Panamericana at Pozo Almonte and climbs gently through the desert to **MAMIÑA**, 74km away. First impressions of Mamiña are not encouraging; huddled on a hillside overlooking a valley, its narrow streets and crumbling stone houses seem to belong to a forgotten town, left to the mercy of the heat and dust. Continue down the valley, however, and its charms become more apparent as you come upon the fertile terraces emerald with alfalfa, and the little stream running through the gorge (*quebrada*). The real lure here, though, are the **hot springs** for which Mamiña is famous throughout Chile; the delicious bottled mineral water from here is on sale in the region only, as production is small. Unlike Pica, Mamiña doesn't have just one hot spring, but many, and their waters are piped to every house in the village. Furthermore, these waters are not merely hot, but are reputed to cure all manner of afflictions, from eczema and psoriasis to respiratory problems and anxiety. Whatever their medicinal value, there's no doubt that the waters are supremely relaxing to bathe in. This you can do in any of the village's hotels or *residenciales*, usually in your own private *tina*, or bathtub.

There are also a number of public springs, including the **Baños Ipla** (daily 8am–1.30pm & 3–9pm; CH$1000), down in the valley, whose four large *tinas* are filled with hot sulphurous water (45°C/115°F) bubbling up from underground. Nearby, the **Vertiente del Radium** is a little fountain whose radioactive waters are supposed to cure eye infections and, according to legend, restored the sight of an Inca princess. A short walk from here, behind the water-bottling plant, you'll find the mud baths of **Barros Chino** (daily 9am–4pm; CH$1000) where you plaster yourself in mud (don't let the caretaker do it for you), lie on a wooden rack while it dries, then wash it off in a small thermal pool.

When you're not wallowing in the waters, you can go walking in the outskirts of Mamiña. It's worth seeking out local sculptor Giuliano Pavez (ask in *Residencial Inti Raimi;* see opposite), who'll take you on guided walks into the nearby *cerros* and archeological sites. He always carries his flute with him, and listening to him play Andean melodies high up in the hills is a memorable experience. In the village, you should also take a look at the unusual two-towered church, built in 1632.

Practicalities

Mamiña is 125km – a two-and-a-half-hour drive – from Iquique. **Accommodation** is centred in two quite separate areas, one on the ridge overlooking the valley, and the other down in the valley, by the Baños Ipla. All are run on a **full-board basis**. Of the first lot, head for *Refugio del Salitrero*

(℡57/751203, ℻57/420330; ❻), Mamiña's oldest spa hotel, offering upmarket rooms in its new section and fairly basic ones in the old building. Down in "Sector Ipla", you'll find modest rooms at *Inti Raimi* (℡57/413218; ❸), run by a friendly young couple, and *El Tamarugal* (℡57/414663; ❸), whose dining room has lovely views. If you can afford to pamper yourself, try Austrian-run *Los Cardenales* (℡57/517000; ❺), which offers comfortable rooms in a large family house, fabulous *tinas* and a pool; or the *Llama Inn* (℡57/419893; ❹), with a bright, sunny dining room, a pool and a beautiful lounge with floor-to-ceiling windows giving stunning views. For a small fee you can **camp** in the yard behind *El Basian*, or in the land belonging to *Inti Raimi*; a better place, however, is by the pool on the track out to Cerro del Inca, about a 30-minute walk from the Ipla baths.

Up to Parque Nacional Volcán Isluga

At the one-horse-town of **Huara**, 33km up the Panamericana from the turn-off to Iquique, a good road branches east into the desert, then climbs high into the mountains, continuing all the way to Oruro in Bolivia. It's paved as far as **Colchane**, on the Chilean side of the border, but the main appeal lies in getting off the tarmac once you're up into the cordillera and heading for the deserted wilderness in and around **Parque Nacional Volcán Isluga**. Here you'll find a remote, isolated landscape of wide plains, dramatic, snow-capped volcanoes and semi-abandoned villages, home to indigenous Aymara herding communities that have been a part of this windswept land for thousands of years. Unlike Parque Nacional Lauca, further north, this region hasn't yet been "discovered", and it's unlikely you'll come across many other tourists. There are a number of attractions on the way up, as well, in particular the weird desert geoglyph known as the **Gigante de Atacama**, in the pampa, and the frozen geysers

La Ruta Altiplánica

In April 1998, regional municipalities from Chile, Bolivia and Peru pledged their commitment to the proposed **Ruta Altiplánica de Integración** – a paved highway stretching 1500km across the altiplano, from San Pedro de Atacama in Chile to Cuzco, Peru. The "altiplano summit" optimistically set the year 2000 as its goal for getting work started, but the multimillion-dollar costs of the project haven't even been calculated yet, let alone raised. Nonetheless, given that it has support from all three governments, the highway is a realistic prospect for the coming decade. If it's built, the road will certainly open up what's currently a remote and largely inaccessible area, and is likely to give an economic boost to the whole altiplano region.

In the meantime, crossing the altiplano's pothole-riddled dirt tracks by jeep is still the road adventure of a lifetime – and should be enjoyed to the full before the arrival of tarmac and increased traffic. Probably the best starting point is Iquique (the ascent in altitude is more gradual in this direction), heading into the cordillera as far as Parque Nacional Volcán Isluga, continuing north across the altiplano to Parque Nacional Lauca, and finally descending in Arica. It's a **700-kilometre journey**, and takes about four to five days at an easy pace. If you do the trip, remember that there's no petrol station once you're off the Panamericana, which means taking it all with you in jerry cans (*bidones*, available in most ironmongers). Always take far, far more than you think you need. Another essential precaution is to take two spare tyres, not just one. For more on 4WD driving, see Basics, p.51.

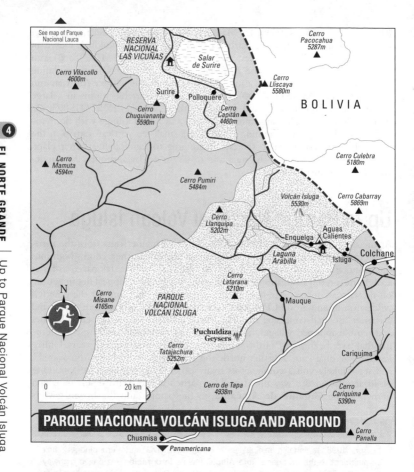

See map of Parque Nacional Lauca

RESERVA NACIONAL LAS VICUÑAS

Salar de Surire

Cerro Pacocahua 5287m

Cerro Vilacollo 4600m

Surire   Polloquère

Cerro Chuquiananta 5590m

Cerro Capitán 4460m

Cerro Lliscaya 5580m

BOLIVIA

Cerro Mamuta 4594m

Cerro Pumiri 5484m

Cerro Culebra 5180m

Volcán Isluga 5530m

Cerro Cabarray 5869m

Cerro Llanquipa 5202m

Enquelga   Aguas Calientes

Laguna Arabilla   Isluga   Colchane

N

Cerro Misane 4165m

PARQUE NACIONAL VOLCÁN ISLUGA

Cerro Latarana 5210m

Mauque

Puchuldiza Geysers

Cerro Tatajachura 5252m

Cariquima

0   20 km

Cerro de Tapa 4938m

Cerro Cariquima 5390m

PARQUE NACIONAL VOLCÁN ISLUGA AND AROUND

Chusmisa

Cerro Panalla

▼ *Panamericana*

of **Puchuldiza**, on the lower slopes of the Andes. There's no public transport around this region, so to explore it you must either take an organized tour from Iquique (see p.252), or rent a high-clearance vehicle, preferably 4WD.

Cerro Unitas and the Gigante de Atacama

The road starts out as a thin, solitary line trailing through the flat desert pampa – an endless expanse of dull yellow and brown. Thirteen kilometres from the turn-off at Huara, you pass an isolated hill, **CERRO UNITAS**, whose southern slope is adorned with the largest geoglyph in the world, the **GIGANTE DE ATACAMA**. This stylized anthropomorphic image is a full 86m long and looks like a giant alien, its head, eyes, mouth and torso represented by thick rectangular shapes. Its arms are outstretched, bent at the elbows, and a dozen rays project from its head, further adding to its extraterrestrial appearance. In his right hand he is holding a pair of scales, thought to represent justice, while the lizard-like reptile in his left hand is harder to interpret – possibly human power over nature. Cerro Unitas is set about 1km back from the main road; the image is best viewed around 200m from the foot of the hill.

Chusmisa and the Puchuldiza geysers

As the road continues east it starts to climb, gently, into the foothills of the Andes. Before long, you're twisting up the brown, dry slopes. The temperature drops noticeably as you leave the intense heat of the desert behind. Around 70km from Huara, a steep, rough track branches off the main road and crawls 5km down to the tiny, picturesque village of **CHUSMISA**, set at the bottom of a narrow, rocky canyon among terraced fields of onions, garlic and oregano. Farther along the road to Colchane, make the highly recommended detour to **PUCHULDIZA**, a geothermic field containing several **geysers** and dozens of bubbling water holes. Framed by a backdrop of distant volcanoes, the geysers shoot tall, strong jets of water high into the air, right next to a small lake tinged white with salt. The scene is particularly dramatic in mid-winter (June and July, sometimes as late as September), as the geysers' spray often freezes, forming a giant, blue-white ice block as big as a two-storey house and dripping all over with icicles.

While nowhere near as numerous as their counterparts at El Tatio, near San Pedro de Atacama (see p.245), the geysers here have two big advantages: first, they are full-fledged geysers and spurt water 24 hours a day, so there's no need to get up at the crack of dawn to visit; second, hardly anyone seems to come here, so you'll probably have the spectacle all to yourself. Take great care when inspecting the water holes, as the crust around them is thin in parts, and some of them hold water as hot as 85°C (185°F). Puchuldiza is reached at the end of a signed nineteen-kilometre dirt road branching north of the paved road, some 60km beyond the turn-off to Chusmisa. After visiting the geysers you could come back to the paved road and continue to Colchane, but a far more interesting option if you are not in a hurry is to retrace your route for part of the way then follow the signed turn-off to Mauque (a twenty-house village) and keep on going to Enquelga, about 15km away.

Parque Nacional Volcán Isluga

Lying in the heart of the altiplano, **PARQUE NACIONAL VOLCÁN ISLUGA** is named after the towering, snow-capped volcano whose 5500-metre peak dominates the park's landscape. Its administrative centre is in **Enquelga**, a dusty, tumbledown hamlet – 3850m above sea level – home to a small Aymara community. Many of its inhabitants, particularly the women, still dress in traditional, brightly coloured clothes, and live from tending llamas and cultivating potatoes and barley. There's a Conaf refugio in the village, with **accommodation** for five people (CH$5500 per person); it's supposed to be open year-round, but sometimes isn't. Two kilometres on from Enquelga, **Aguas Calientes** is a long, spring-fed pool containing warm (but not hot) waters, set in an idyllic location with terrific views of the volcano. The pool is surrounded by pea-green *bofedal* – a spongy grass, typical of the altiplano – and drains into a little stream, crossed every morning and evening by herds of llamas driven to and from the sierra by Aymara shepherdesses. There's a stone changing-hut next to it, and a few **camping** spaces and picnic areas, protected from the evening wind by thick stone walls.

Six kilometres east of Enquelga, still within the park's boundaries, **Isluga** is composed of a hundred or so stone and adobe houses huddled around one of the most beautiful churches of the altiplano. Built some time in the seventeenth century (it's not known when, exactly), it's a humble little church made of thick, whitewashed adobe that flashes like snow in the constant glare of the sun. The main building, containing a single nave, is enclosed by a low wall trimmed with delicate arches; just outside the wall sits the two-tier bell tower with steps leading up to the top, where you can sit and survey the scenery or watch the hummingbirds that fly in and out. The church, along with the entire village, remains locked up and abandoned for most of the year – Isluga is a "**ceremonial village**", whose inhabitants come back only for festivals, important religious ceremonies and funerals; the principal fiestas are held February 2 and 3, March 10, Easter week, and December 8, 12 and 21 through 25.

Colchane and Cariquima

Ten kilometres from Isluga, at the end of the paved road from Huara, at 3730 metres above sea level, **COLCHANE** is a small, grim border town of grid-laid streets and truckers' canteens. Most days, the only reason you might want to come here is for **accommodation** (very basic rooms in *Pensión Gómez*, opposite the telephone office; no phone; ❷); emergency **petrol** (*bencina verde*, or leadless petrol, may be available in Andrés García's backyard, in the street opposite the school, but don't bank on it); or to cross over into **Bolivia** (border control open daily 8am–7pm, sometimes closed at lunch time). Twice a month, however, on alternate Saturdays, Colchane takes on a bit of life and colour as the neighbouring altiplano villagers bring their fresh produce, weavings and knitwear to sell at the **market**.

A far more charming place to stay is **CARIQUIMA**, just 17km south of Colchane. It has picturesque, cleanly swept streets and an old altiplano-style church with a painted interior. Seek out the **crafts cooperative**, housed in a beautifully decorated building along one of the village's few streets; high-quality woollens are sold. Cariquima sits in the lee of the dramatic Nevado Cariquima, while, 5km to the north, is the minute hamlet of **Ancovinto**. There you'll see a forest of giant cacti that sway in the breeze and enjoy fantastic views across the altiplano to Bolivia and the Salar de Coipasa. The unnamed *hostería* (no phone; ❷) has no hot water and you cannot book ahead.

△ Aymara *fiesta*

The Aymara people are the second-largest indigenous linguistic group of South America (after the Quichoa). The culture flourished around **Lake Titicaca** and spread throughout the high-plain region, known as the altiplano, of what is now Bolivia, Peru and Chile. Today there are around three million Aymara scattered through these three countries, with the Chilean Aymara forming the smallest group, totalling some forty thousand people. Following the big migrations from the highlands to the coast that took place in the 1960s, most of the Aymara people of Chile now live and work in the coastal cities of **Arica** and **Iquique**. At least thirteen thousand Aymara, however, remain in the altiplano of northern Chile, where their lifestyle is still firmly rooted in the traditions of the past thousand years. The main economic activity is llama and sheep herding – which provides wool, milk, cheese, meat, leather and fertilizer – and the cultivation of crops such as potatoes and barley.

Traditionally, the Aymara live in **small communities**, called *ayllu*, based on extended family kinship; there are usually about a hundred people in each village. Their houses are made of stone and mud with rough thatched roofs, and most villages have a square and a small whitewashed church with a separate bell tower – often dating from the seventeenth century when Spanish missionaries evangelized the region.

Nowadays many of the smaller villages, such as Isluga, are left abandoned for most of the year, the houses securely locked up while their owners make their living down in the city or in the larger cordillera towns like Putre. Known as "ceremonial villages," they're shaken from their slumber and burst into life when all their people return for important religious festivals or funerals, usually two or three times a year. Andean **fiestas** are based on a fascinating blend of Catholic and indigenous rites. For instance, the aim of the fiestas is usually to worship the Virgin Mary, but sometimes a llama or lamb will be offered as a sacrificial victim – in some cases after the Virgin herself has put this request to the village *yatiri*, or elder. At the centre of Aymara culture is respect for the life-giving Mother Earth, known as *pachamama*, and traditional ceremonies – involving singing and dancing – are still carried out in some communities at sowing and harvest time.

The Aymara also believed that the tallest mountains looming over their villages contained spirits, or *mallku*, that guarded over them, protecting their animals and crops. Once a year, on **May 3** – Cruz de Mayo – the most traditional communities climb up the sacred mountains, where a village elder speaks to the *mallku*, which appears in the form of a condor. It's hard to assess to what extent these long-held beliefs survive only as habit and superstition, and to what extent they remain a fundamental part of the Aymara world view. Today's young Aymara go to local state schools and speak Spanish as their main language, and while traditional lifestyles continue in the altiplano, it's with increasingly closer links with mainstream Chilean life.

The Panamericana between Iquique and Arica

Some three hundred long, dusty kilometres spread out between Iquique and Arica in a continuous stretch of brown desert hills and dried-up rivers. Most people whizz up here in about four hours without stopping, but there are a couple of interesting places to visit on the way: **Tiliviche**'s nineteenth-century graveyard and pre-Columbian geoglyphs can be explored in an hour or so, while **Pisagua** – a crumbling, evocative nitrate port about an hour's drive west to the coast – is more suitable as a night's stopover.

Pisagua

Eighty kilometres north of the turn-off to Iquique, a poorly paved side road leads 52km down to the once-important, now forgotten town of **PISAGUA**. The final stretch is very steep, giving dramatic views down to the little toy town cowering by the ocean, the only sign of life on this barren desert coast. Pisagua is a funny sort of place, part scruffy, ramshackle fishing town, part fascinating relic of the past. It was one of the busiest and wealthiest ports of the nitrate era, and is still dotted with many grand nineteenth-century buildings, some of them restored and repainted, others decaying at the same slow pace as the rest of the town (which has only about 150 inhabitants today). Most striking is the handsome, white-and-blue timber **clock tower**, built in 1887 and still standing watch from the hillside. The other great monument to the nitrate era is the old **theatre**, a fine wooden building erected in 1892, with a typical nineteenth-century facade featuring tall wooden pillars, a balcony and a balustrade. You can borrow the key from the *carabineros* and wander inside to take a look at the large, empty stage, the rows of polished wooden seats, and the high ceiling, lavishly painted with cherubs dancing on clouds. The ghostliness of the place is made all the more intense by the monotonous sound of the waves crashing against the building's rear wall, which plunges directly down to the sea.

At the far end of town, next to the *carabineros* station, the village's more recent history is the subject of a haunting **mural** dedicated to the memory of those executed here during the military dictatorship, when Pisagua was used as a concentration camp. A couple of kilometres north, on the edge of the cemetery, the former site of the mass graves is marked by an open pit bearing a simple cross, a scattering of wreaths and a block of stone inscribed with a single line by Pablo Neruda: "Even though a thousand years shall pass, this site will never be cleansed of the blood of those who fell here."

There's a free (and shadeless) **campsite** close to the *carabineros* station, but to really soak up the nitrate-era atmosphere **stay** at *Hotel Pisagua* ✦ (☎57/731509; ❹ full board), on Calle Videla in what was once the town prison. The guest rooms are in a beautiful wooden building – originally the warders' residence – built around a large patio filled with tall, lush banana plants and squawking parrots. The prison cells, in the adjacent building, are now filled with snooker and ping-pong tables that guests can use. The hotel is also about the only place **to eat** in Pisagua, serving excellent, fresh fish and good breakfasts. There is no public transport here.

Hacienda de Tiliviche

Ten kilometres north of the turn-off for Pisagua, just before the bridge across the Quebrada de Tiliviche, a short track branches left (west) to the **HACIENDA DE TILIVICHE**. At the end of the track you'll find the old *casa patronal*, a charmingly dilapidated house overlooking a yard full of clucking chickens and lethargic dogs. It was built in 1855 for a British nitrate family and remained in British hands until very recently; the current owners have plans to renovate it and turn it into a hotel. Set within the hacienda grounds, on the other side of the stream, stands a nostalgic testimony to the nitrate era: the old **British Cemetery**, enclosed by tall iron railings and a huge, rusty gate – you can borrow the key from the hacienda caretaker. Inside, about a hundred lonely graves stand in the shade of a few *tamarugo* trees at the foot of the desolate mountain that rises over the *quebrada*. This stark desert setting is strikingly at odds with the very English inscriptions on the tombstones ("Thy will be done" and the like). The graves read like a who's who of the erstwhile British

❹

business community, including people like Herbert Harrison, the manager of the Tarapacá Waterworks Company and, most famously, **James Humberstone**, the manager of several nitrate *oficinas* (see p.255).

The southern wall of the *quebrada* also features some of the most impressive **geoglyphs** in Chile. They're best viewed from the pull-in just off the Panamericana, a few hundred metres up from the bridge on the northern side of the *quebrada*. From this vantage point, you can see the images in all their splendour – a large crowd of llamas covering the hillside. All of the llamas are moving in the same direction, towards the sea, and it's thought that the drawings were designed to guide caravans descending from the mountains on their journey towards the coast.

Arica and around

ARICA likes to call itself "*la ciudad de la eterna primavera*" – "City of Everlasting Spring". Chile's northernmost city, only 19km south of the Peruvian border, is certainly blessed with a mild climate, which, along with its sandy beaches, makes it a popular holiday resort for Chileans and Bolivians. Although a lingering sea fog can dampen spirits, in the winter especially, just head a few kilometres inland, and you'll usually find blue skies.

The city's compact, tidy centre sits proudly at the foot of the Morro cliff, the site of a major Chilean victory in the War of the Pacific (and cherished as a symbol of national glory). It was this war that delivered Arica into Chilean hands, in 1883, and while the city is emphatically Chilean today, there's no denying the strong presence of mestizo and Quichoa-speaking Peruvians on the streets, trading their fresh produce and *artesanía*. This, added to its role as Bolivia's main export centre, makes Arica more colourful, ethnically diverse and vibrant than most northern Chilean cities, although the early years of the new millennium have seen an economic slump, largely due to unrest in Bolivia and difficulties in Peru. The liveliest streets are pedestrianized Calles 21 de Mayo and Bolognesi, the latter clogged with **artesanía stalls**. Far from beautiful, Arica does boast a couple of fine pieces of nineteenth-century architecture, pretty squares filled with flowers and palm trees and a young, lively atmosphere. It's a pleasant enough place to spend a couple of days – or longer, if you feel like kicking back on the beach. A short taxi ride out of town, in the Azapa Valley, the marvellous **Museo Arqueológico** is one of Chile's best and certainly deserves a visit. A few hours east, up in the cordillera, **Parque Nacional Lauca** has become one of the most popular attractions in the north of Chile. A couple of Arica's tour operators will get you there if you don't relish the idea of driving yourself.

Arrival and information

Coming in **by bus**, you'll arrive at Arica's Terminal Rodoviario, which uniquely charges a CH$100 platform fee for all **departures**; make sure to pay this fee at your bus company desk, even if you already have a bus ticket. The terminal is quite a distance from town on Avenida Diego Portales, but you can easily catch a *colectivo* or *micro* into the centre. Arica's Chacalluta **airport** lies 18km north of the city and is connected to the centre by reasonably priced airport taxis (CH$5000). For tourist information, head for the **Sernatur** office in a sadly dilapidated old building at San Marcos 101 (Mon–Fri 8.30am–1pm & 3–7pm; ☎58/252054, ⓦ www.sernatur.cl). The regional **Conaf** office, at Vicuña

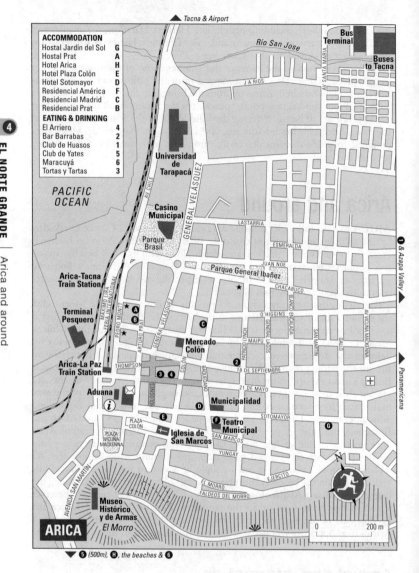

ACCOMMODATION
Hostal Jardín del Sol	G
Hostal Prat	A
Hotel Arica	H
Hotel Plaza Colón	E
Hotel Sotomayor	D
Residencial América	F
Residencial Madrid	C
Residencial Prat	B

EATING & DRINKING
El Arriero	4
Bar Barrabas	2
Club de Huasos	1
Club de Yates	5
Maracuyá	6
Tortas y Tartas	3

Tacna & Airport

Río San Jose

Bus Terminal

Buses to Tacna

PACIFIC OCEAN

Universidad de Tarapacá

Casino Municipal

Parque Brasil

Arica-Tacna Train Station

Terminal Pesquero

Arica-La Paz Train Station

Aduana

Parque General Ibañez

Mercado Colón

Municipalidad

Teatro Municipal

Iglesia de San Marcos

Museo Histórico y de Armas
El Morro

ARICA

0   200 m

⑤ (500m), ⓗ, the beaches & ⑥

Mackenna 820 (Mon–Fri 8.30am–5pm; ℡58/250750, ℻58/247467), has basic maps and information on Parque Nacional Lauca and adjoining protected areas. You can also reserve beds at the Conaf *refugíos* in these areas, if you know exactly when you'll be arriving (see box p.273).

Accommodation

Unlike Iquique, Arica has very little seafront accommodation, and what there is tends to be upmarket and overpriced. In the centre, there's no shortage of *residenciales*, ranging from the dirt-cheap to the polished and comfortable.

Typically for these parts, however, there's a lack of decent mid-range accommodation. **Camping** options are limited to *El Refugio* (☏58/227545; CH$8000 per site), a shady, grassy campsite with a pool, 1.5km up the Azapa Valley, reached by frequent *colectivos*. The valley is a welcome refuge from the hectic downtown but you won't find much accommodation – try the *Azapa Inn* (see p.270).

Hostal Jardín del Sol Sotomayor 848 ☏58/232795, ℻58/231462. Small, tidy rooms with private bath off a flower-filled courtyard with tables, chairs and a swing-sofa. Very friendly, too – great for the price. ❸

Hostal Prat Prat 555 ☏58/252138. Spartan but spotless little rooms with white walls, tiled floors and clean baths. A good bet in this price range – do not confuse with the *residencial* of the same name. ❸

Hotel Arica Av San Martín 599 ☏58/254540, ℻231133. Upmarket but rather dated and overpriced hotel overlooking the ocean, with pleasant rooms, *cabañas* and a pool. Mediocre food is served at its expensive *Península* restaurant. ❻

Hotel Plaza Colón San Marcos 261 ☏58/254424, ℻58/231244, ✉hotelplazacolon@entelchile.net. Cheerful pink-and-blue building with small, clean, modern rooms with balconies that offer good views of the plaza. ❺

Hotel Sotomayor Sotomayor 367 ☏58/232970, ℻58/251815, hotelsmarcos@entelchile.net. Formerly the Hotel San Marcos, it features clean, airy 1970s-style rooms (disappointing after the beautiful old Spanish tiles in the lobby) with private bath and parking. ❹

Residencial América Sotomayor 340 ☏58/254148. Good-value budget rooms with an encouraging odour of furniture polish. Some rooms have private bath. ❷

Residencial Madrid Baquedano 685 ☏58/231479, ℻58/255043. Humble little place offering clean rooms looking onto a pretty patio. ❷

Residencial Prat Prat 545 ☏58/251292. Thirteen spruce and simple rooms. ❸

The City

In the centre you'll find the small, tree-filled **Plaza Colón**, dominated by the **Iglesia de San Marcos**, a pretty white church with a high, Gothic spire and many tall, arched windows. Designed by Gustave Eiffel, this curious church, made entirely of iron, was prefabricated in France before being erected in Arica in 1876. The riveting key used to assemble the structure was kept in a display case inside the church, but when Chilean troops attacked, it was thrown into the sea to prevent the invaders from dismantling the church and stealing it as a war trophy (instead, they took the whole city).

Two blocks west, towards the port, rises another Eiffel-designed building – the 1874 **Aduana** (customs house) with an attractive stone facade of pink and white horizontal stripes. These days it's used as a cultural centre and puts on regular photographic and art exhibitions. It looks onto **Parque Baquedano**, a little square full of palm trees and shady benches, flanked to the south by the coastal avenue, and on its northern side by the Arica–La Paz **train station**. Wander inside this large wooden 1913 building and you'll find a couple of shiny black locomotives displayed in an interior patio, and a roomful of turn-of-the-century railway paraphernalia (ask a guard to let you in). There's another old locomotive in front of the station, a 1924 German model, formerly used on the Arica–La Paz line. Nearby lies the smelly but colourful **terminal pesquero**, where inquisitive pelicans wander around the fish stalls.

Arica's most visible feature is the 110-metre-high cliff known as **El Morro**, which signals the end of the coastal cordillera. Steps starting at the southern end of Calle Colón lead you to the top, where sweeping, panoramic views (especially impressive at night) and the **Museo Histórico y de Armas** (daily: March–Nov 8am–8pm; Dec–Feb 8am–10pm; CH$400) await. Built on top of a former Peruvian fortification, this museum is owned by the army, rather than the government, and has clearly had more money spent on it than most Chilean museums. The exhibits – primarily nineteenth-century guns and military uniforms – are very well displayed, but the theme is rather chauvinistic in tone, the main thrust being the superiority of the Chileans and the inferiority of the Peruvians in the Battle of the Morro, when Chilean forces stormed and took possession of the hilltop defence post.

The beaches

The closest beach to the centre is the popular **Playa El Laucho**, a curved, sandy cove about a twenty-minute walk down Avenida San Martín, south of El Morro. You can also get *micros* down the avenue, which continue to several other beaches, including **Playa La Lisera** and **Playa Brava**, both attractive, and the usually deserted **Playa Arenillas Negras**, a wide expanse of dark sand backed by low sand dunes, with a fish-processing factory at its southern end. Two kilometres north of the centre, **Playa Chinchorro** is a large, clean beach where you can rent jet skis in high season (Dec–March; CH$12,000 for 30min). This is also where you'll find Arica's Olympic-size **swimming pool** (Tues–Sun: Jan & Feb 3–6.30pm; March–Dec 9am–2pm; CH$1000), just back from the beach, enclosed by a large white wall. Further north, **Playa Las Machas** is quieter but more exposed to the wind. To get to **Playa Chinchorro**, take bus #5-A from General Velásquez with Chacabuco.

Tours from Arica

Three or four companies in Arica regularly offer **tours** up to **Parque Nacional Lauca** (see p.274). The problem, however, is that the most commonly available tour takes place in a single day, which means rushing from sea level to up to 4500m and down again in a short space of time – really not a good idea, and very likely to cause some ill effects, ranging from tiredness and mild headaches to acute dizziness and nausea. In very rare cases the effects can be more serious, and you should always check that the company carries a supply of oxygen and has a staff member trained to deal with emergencies. Altitude aside, the amount of time you spend inside a minibus is very tiring, which can spoil your experience of what is one of the most beautiful parts of Chile. Therefore it's really worth paying extra and taking a tour that includes at least one overnight stop in Putre; better still is one continuing south to the Salar de Surire (see p.277) and Parque Nacional Isluga (see p.261). One-day trips cost around CH$20,000 per person, while you can expect to pay around CH$45–70,000 for a one- or two-night tour, overnighting in Putre, and around CH$100,000 for a three-night tour, sleeping in Putre and Colchane.

Geotours Bolognesi 421 ☎58/253927, ℻58/251675, ✉yeotur@entelchile.net. Slick, professional but fairly impersonal company offering mostly one-day tours.

Latinorizons Bolognesi 449 & Thompson 236 ☎ & ℻58/250007, ⓦwww.latinorizons .com, ✉latinor@entelchile.net. Friendly Belgian-run company offering a wide range of altiplano tours, including overnight, with a more adventurous feel than most of the others on offer. They have their own *hostal* in Putre (see p.273). Extremely reliable and French and English spoken.

Parinacota Expediciones Prat 430, ☎ & ℻58/256227. Well-established company offering several options for visiting Parque Nacional Lauca and around, including the usual day-trip, an overnight stop in Putre and a two-night tour taking in the Salar de Surire.

Eating, drinking and entertainment

You'll find the biggest concentration of **restaurants, cafés** and **bars** on the pedestrianized section of 21 de Mayo, the city's main thoroughfare. Arica seems to be the national capital of the **roasted-chicken-on-a-spit** industry – low-cost places serving it dot Maipú, between Baquedano and Colón. The **disco** scene can get quite lively in high season, and even in low season there are a couple of locales where you'll always find a crowd on a Friday and Saturday night – the trendy *Bar Barrabas*, 18 de Septiembre 520, at the corner with Lynch, is decorated with wrought iron and odd architectural salvage pieces and offers good music and drinks. Otherwise head out to the Azapa Valley (see p.270) to places like *Sunset* or *Swing*.

El Arriero 21 de Mayo 385. Mid-price grill house serving tasty fillet steaks and other meat dishes; often has live folk music at weekends.

Club de Yates Ex Isla Alacrán. Privileged location, on a spur (once an island) projecting into the ocean, with outdoor seating and great views (especially at night). Serves reasonably priced omelettes, salads and meat and fish dishes. Closed to non-members Sat & Sun.

Maracuyá Av San Martín 0321, Playa La Lisera ☎58/227600. At this smart restaurant (one of Arica's best), sitting dramatically right over the ocean's edge, you're treated to a spectacle of breaking waves as you sample the boldly prepared fish and seafood.

Tortas y Tartas 21 de Mayo 233. With a terrace strategically located on the main drag and a bright, stylish decor, this godsend serves real coffee; excellent breakfasts; a range of sandwiches, snacks and crisp salads; some hot dishes; and delicious cakes (such as raspberry cheesecake). It offers a good selection of beers, wines and cocktails, too.

Listings

Airlines LAN, 21 de Mayo 345 ☎58/251641; Lloyd Aereo Boliviano, 21 de Mayo 423 ☎58/251919; Sky Airlines, Edificio Parque Colón, Chacabuco between Colón and Baquedano ☎58/251816 or 290768 at airport.

Banks and exchange Arica has many ATMs – mostly on 21 de Mayo – but only two *casas de cambio*: Yanulaque, at 21 de Mayo 175, will change most major currencies in cash (no travellers' cheques), though euros haven't quite caught on yet; Marta Daguer, 18 de Septiembre 330, deals only in US dollars. There are also several money changers on the street, at the corner of 21 de Mayo and Colón.

Car rental American Rent-a-Car, General Lagos 559 ☎58/252234; Budget, Avenida San Martín 599 ☎58/258911; Hertz, Baquedano 999 ☎58/231487; Klasse, Velásquez 760 ☎58/254498.

Moving on from Arica

You have many different options to head out of Arica. To get up to the **altiplano**, you can take a bus to **Putre** with Buses La Paloma, Germán Riesco 2071 (☎58/222710); to **Parinacota** with Buses Humire (☎58/253497); or to **Lago Chungará** on any bus to La Paz; you sometimes are asked to pay full fare to La Paz – refuse). From the main bus terminal there are plenty of **inter-city buses** heading south down the Panamericana, as far as Santiago. You can also catch buses at the main terminal to **La Paz**, in Bolivia (CH$7000–10,000; 7–8hr), with Tas Choapa (☎58/222817) and Géminis (☎58/241647); or alternatively you can depart from Galería San José, Av Santa María 2010, with Buses Litoral (58/254702) or Buses Trans Salvador (☎58/246064). **Tacna**, 55km north in Peru, can be reached easily by **colectivo** from Calle Chacabuco, between Baquedano and Colón. Tur Bus runs a daily "direct" service to **San Pedro de Atacama**, leaving around 10pm and arriving in time for breakfast the following day. There are regular **flights** from Arica to Iquique, Antofagasta, La Serena and Santiago, plus La Paz in Bolivia, and Arequipa and Lima in Peru.

Internet Net Ciber, Sotomayor 538, charges CH$400 an hour and offers an excellent connection and a student reduction.
Laundry Good-value washing and ironing at Lavandería La Moderna, 18 de Septiembre 457.
Post office Arturo Prat 305.
Taxis Radiotaxi Chacalluta, Prat 528 ☎58/250340; Taxi Turismo Pucarani ☎58/244997.
Tour operators See box p.268.

Telephone offices Entel, 21 de Mayo 388; CTC, Colón 476; Telex Chile, 21 de Mayo 372. Many more around town.
Travel agencies Among the numerous travel agencies in town are Mega Tour, Bolognesi 391 ☎58/254701; Tacora, 21 de Mayo 171 ☎58/232786; and Globo Tour, 21 de Mayo 260 ☎58/232909; all of these are good for air tickets, etc. For tours to Parque Nacional Lauca, see box p.268.

The Azapa Valley

Avenida Diego Portales extends out of Arica's city centre into the green **AZAPA VALLEY**. The far western end of the valley is, for all intents and purposes, a suburb of Arica, crammed as it is with condos and villas, some of which have been converted into trendy discos, along with a couple of good restaurants.

On your way out towards the Azapa Valley, on Calle Hualles, just south of the river, the **Poblado Artesanal** is a replica of an altiplano village, where twelve white houses serve as workshops for artisans selling handicrafts ranging from ceramics and glass to knitwear and leather items; its hours of operation are erratic.

Thirteen kilometres along the road, the outstanding **Museo Arqueológico** (daily: Jan & Feb 9am–8pm; March–Dec 10am–6pm; CH$1000), part of the University of Tarapacá, houses an excellent collection of regional pre-Columbian artefacts, including four extraordinary Chinchorro mummies (see box opposite) – of a man, a woman and two children – buried over 4000 years ago. Other exhibits include finely decorated Tiwanaku ceramics, ancient Andean musical instruments and snuff trays, and many beautifully-embroidered tapestries – look out for the one in Case 11, decorated with images of smiling women – and displays on contemporary Aymara culture. All the pieces are extremely well presented, and there are unusually explanatory leaflets available in several languages, including English, French and German.

In the nearby village of **San Miguel de Azapa**, the only place of interest is the fabulously multicoloured desert **cemetery**, which climbs like a mini-Valparaíso for the deceased towards a dune-like cliff. The colour comes from the artificial flowers laid on the graves. By the entrance sits the morbidly named **restaurant**, La Picá del Muertito (the "Little Dead Man's Snack-Bar"), famous for miles around for its first-rate pastel de choclo, a sugar-glazed corn-bake containing meat, egg and olives.

The Azapa Valley is also the site of several **geoglyphs**. The most impressive example is **Alto Ramírez**, a large, stylized human figure surrounded by geometric shapes; you can see it, at a distance, from the main road on the way to the museum (ask your colectivo driver to point it out to you) or take a detour to get a closer look.

Practicalities

If you want to get away from the pollution of downtown Arica, the Azapa Valley is a pleasant place to **stay**, though options are pretty much limited to the Azapa Inn at Guillermo Sánchez 660 (☎58/244517 or 58/225191, ⓦ www.azapainn .cl; ❻), at the beginning of the valley. Its spacious rooms, many with balconies, are in two-storey blocks spread around luxuriant sub-tropical grounds with a large swimming-pool; the restaurant serves imaginatively prepared dishes at reasonable prices. The **Club de Huasos** (km 3.5) is one of several country restaurants, all very popular with families, offering hearty, moderately priced Sunday lunches in the green Azapa Valley.

Colectivos for the Azapa Valley, including the Museo Arqueológico and the nearby geoglyphs, leave from the corner of Lynch and Chacabuco in Arica's centre.

Chinchorro mummies

In 1983, while laying a new pipeline near the foot of El Morro, the Arica water company came across a hoard of withered corpses buried a couple of metres beneath the sand. Work immediately ceased and archeologists from the University of Tarapacá were rushed in to assess the scene, which turned out to be a seven-thousand-year-old burial site containing 96 bodies – the largest and best-preserved find, to date, of **Chinchorro mummies**.

The ancient practice of mummification in this region – the oldest known in the world – was first identified in 1917 when **Max Uhle**, a German archeologist working in Arica, discovered a series of highly unusual human remains. The Atacama had already yielded prehistoric bodies naturally mummified by the heat and dryness of the desert, but Uhle realized that these bodies were different – they were, in fact, the result of an elaborate and highly skilled form of **artificial mummification** that had kept them intact for thousands of years. Further excavations revealed similar findings spread along the coast, concentrated between Arica and Camerones, 65km south, and it became apparent that they were relics of an ancient society that archeologists have named the Chinchorro culture. Uhle originally estimated that the Chinchorro people started mummifying their dead some 2000 years ago, but modern radiocarbon dating has established that the practice was well under way by 5000 BC – more than two millennia before the Egyptians began practising mummification.

No one knows exactly where the Chinchorro people came from; some archeologists speculate that they moved down from the north, others that they came from the Andean highlands. What's clear, however, is that by 7000 BC scattered groups of people – possibly extended families – were spread along the coast of Chile's Far North, where they lived on the abundant crabs, clams, mussels, seaweed, pelicans, sea lions and other marine life of the region, supplementing their diet with guanaco and wild berries.

The great simplicity of their hunter-gatherer lifestyle makes the sophisticated techniques they developed to **preserve the dead** all the more extraordinary. The practice involved removing the brain through a hole at the base of the skull, and removing all internal organs, which were probably discarded. After this, the cavities were dried with hot stones or fire and then refilled with straw and ashes. The bones of the arms and legs were replaced with sticks bound into place with reeds, and the skeleton was given extra padding before the body was stitched up. The face was then coated in paste that dried into a hard mask with a sculpted nose and incisions marking the eyes and mouth. The finishing touch was provided by a wig made of human hair that was attached to the skull.

One of the most curious aspects of the Chinchorro mummies is that they probably weren't buried immediately – signs of repeated "repair jobs" on many of them suggest they were kept on display and venerated before being wrapped in their reed shrouds and buried with their funerary offerings. Whether or not this was the case, there's no doubt that the cult of mummification was based on a complex approach to the dead and the afterlife. The Chinchorro culture performed this elaborate process for over three thousand years until, for unknown reasons, the practice died out around 1500 BC, and the era of the oldest known form of artificial mummification came to an end.

Up to Parque Nacional Lauca

Some 160km east of Arica, **Parque Nacional Lauca** is the perfect micro-cosm of the Chilean altiplano, offering snow-capped volcanoes, pristine lakes, whitewashed villages and wild vicuña – all conveniently located at the end of a paved highway, just four hours' drive from the city. The journey there takes you through some beautiful and varied scenery, ranging from deep-green vegeta-tion to rippling desert hills. There are several opportunities for overnighting en route to the park, which is strongly recommended to avoid the risk of altitude sickness. Once you're up there, you can head south across the altiplano to neighbouring **Parque Nacional Las Vicuñas** and the **Salar de Surire**, and if you're feeling really adventurous, continue to **Parque Nacional Volcán Isluga**, descending in Iquique. Remember to take warm clothing with you, as temperatures can drop as low as -20°C (-4°F) at night.

Lluta Valley

The first stretch of the journey along the Ruta 11 follows the saline Río Lluta through the fertile **LLUTA VALLEY**, an astonishingly green strip of land threading its way through brown, sterile hills. Around 15km northeast of Arica you'll notice a set of **geoglyphs** etched on the southern cliffs, representing a frog-like creature, an eagle and a giant human figure. As the road climbs up from the valley floor, the views down to the narrow cultivated belt are spectacular, especially when the early morning mist hovers over the hills, punctured by shafts of sunlight. As you climb to heights of around 2000–3000m you leave all traces of greenery behind, and the hillsides, now arid and dusty, are suddenly filled with hundreds of **candelabra cactus** plants (*Browningia candelaris*) – huge things up to 4m high but growing only a few millimetres a year, starkly silhouetted against the sky. About 90km up the road, you'll pass a brightly painted railway carriage and a wooden building by the roadside – this is **Posada Taki**, a café, inn, campsite and alternative tour agency run by a multilingual, hippie couple. At just over 3000m above sea level, it's a good place to stay to get acclimatized to the altitude, and the owners offer guided walks and jeep tours to local archeological sites, as well as home-made bread and *mate de coca*. About 10km on from here, look out for the sign on the right pointing to the **Pukará de Copaquilla**, the ruins of an Inca fortress standing on a promontory just off the road. Here you'll find the remains of several large circular stone walls built between 1350 and 950 BC, and sweeping views down to a steep, narrow canyon backed by endless rolling hills.

Socoroma

Sixteen kilometres beyond the *pukará*, a steep track branches left from the main road, leading treacherously down the hillside to the pre-Hispanic hamlet of **SOCOROMA**. It appears, from a distance, as a dark-green pocket of trees and fields lying at the bottom of a scrub-covered valley; close-up, it's a charming village with a jumble of cobbled streets and a restored sixteenth-century church. From behind the church you get fabulous, panoramic views onto the ancient green terraces staggered down the wall of the *quebrada* – they're used princi-pally for growing oregano, and during the spring and autumn harvest (roughly November and April) the whole village is filled with its aroma. Socoroma, at 3060m above sea level, also makes a quieter alternative to Putre for acclima-tizing overnight – basic **rooms** and **meals** are provided by the very friendly Emilia Humire (no phone; ❷), who also runs a shop selling home-made jams and other products.

Putre

The busy little mountain town of **PUTRE**, surrounded by a patchwork of green fields and Inca terraces, lies 24km on from Socoroma. At 3500m above sea level, it's a popular overnight stop en route to the higher altitudes of Parque Nacional Lauca – climbers, in particular, like to spend a few days walking in the hills here before attempting the volcanoes in the park. Putre's rustic houses are clustered around a large, green square, overlooked by the Municipalidad, which provides basic **tourist information** (Mon–Fri 8.30am–12.30pm & 3–6pm). Nearby, off the northeast corner of the square, you'll find the **church**, built in 1670 after an earthquake destroyed the original one, which, according to old Spanish chronicles, was clad in gold and silver. The current building, heavily restored in 1871, is considerably more modest, consisting of a small stone chapel and a whitewashed, straw-roofed bell tower. The village observes the Feast of the Assumption, August 15, with a week-long celebration that features much singing and dancing; accommodation is hard to find during this time.

Putre has several options for eating and sleeping. On Calle Baquedano, you'll find small, tidy **rooms** off a sunny backyard at *Residencial Cali* (no phone; ❷), and basic but reasonable rooms in a large, covered yard at *Residencial La Paloma* (no phone; ❷), where breakfasts are frugal. Across the bridge and up the track, *Hostería Las Vicuñas* (☏58/228564; ❻) is the smartest, and most expensive, place to stay, offering slightly faded-looking en-suite bungalow rooms. The new, comfortable *Chez Charlie* (❷) at Baquedano 590 is owned and run by Turismo Latinorizons in Arica (see p.268). Most of Putre's few **restaurants** are dire, with the exception of *Kuchu Marka* ⌁ on Baquedano, where you can get alpaca stew and other hearty mountain dishes like *picante de conejo* (a sort of rabbit curry) along with an excellent vegetarian option, in a cosy setting reminiscent of restaurants in San Pedro de Atacama. Otherwise you'll have to fall back on the spartan restaurant at *Residencial La Paloma*; *Rosamel*, on the plaza; and *Oasis*, on Cochrane – all equally basic. Alto Andino Nature Tours, along Baquedano (☏58/300013, ☒58/222735, ⊛www.birdingaltoandino .com, ✉beknapton@hotmail.com), is run by an Alaskan naturalist who offers wildlife-viewing excursions, specializing in ornithology and marine mammals, in Parque Nacional Lauca and coastal areas; consult the website for more details. She also has a few simple, clean rooms (❹), with heating, cooking and laundry facilities. Local guide Valentina Alave offers walks to interesting cave paintings 7km away – ask at the Municipalidad for more information. Buses La Paloma, Germán Riesco 2071 (☏58/222710; CH$1500), runs regular **buses** to Putre from Arica.

Conaf refugios

If you are travelling under your own steam but do not fancy camping in the open wilds of the cold, high altiplano, the various **Conaf refugios** dotted around the Parque Nacional Lauca, Parque Nacional Isluga and in between make for excellent places to stay. They have proper beds, some have decent facilities, and they are nearly all located in amazing spots, with views to linger over. The only problem is that in recent years their upkeep has been shoddy and they are sometimes left in a pitiful state by previous visitors. Worst of all, even if you book ahead through the Conaf offices in Arica or Iquique, reservations are not always respected and you might turn up to find no room at the inn.

Parque Nacional Lauca

As you continue up the main road, about 4km past the turn-off to Putre a little dirt road on the right leads 3km to the **Termas de Jurasi** – a beautifully situated tin shack containing two large baths of hot thermal water plus a large open-air, concrete pool, along with toilets and changing rooms (open daylight hours, CH$500–1000). Back on the paved road, a steep 7km up from the turn-off to the springs, at a 4400-metre-high mountain pass, you cross the boundary into **PARQUE NACIONAL LAUCA**. By now the air is thin and cold, and the road is flanked by light-green *bofedal* (highland pasture) where herds of wild vicuña come to feed in the mornings. Ten kilometres into the park, you reach the Conaf hut at **Las Cuevas**, a good place to stop to check on weather and road conditions and observe the comical antics of vizcachas, cuddly chinchilla-like rodents with curly tails and a spring-like leap. From here the road continues through a wide, green plain filled with grazing llamas and alpacas, passing the turn-off for Parinacota, 19km on from the Conaf hut, and Lago Chungará, a further 18km along the road.

Parinacota

The park's headquarters are in **PARINACOTA** (the name means "flamingo lake" in Aymara), an idyllic *pueblo altiplánico* composed of fifty or so crumbling,whitewashed houses huddled around a beautiful little **church**.

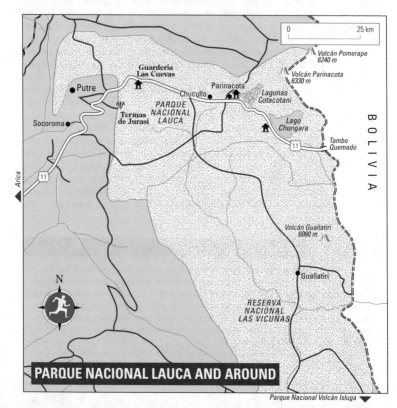

PARQUE NACIONAL LAUCA AND AROUND

Parque Nacional Volcán Isluga ▼

Built in 1789, this is one of Chile's most assiduously maintained Andean churches, sporting brilliant white walls and a bright-blue wooden door, trimmed with yellow and green. Like most churches of the altiplano, it has thick stone and adobe walls and a sloping straw roof, and is enclosed within a little white wall incorporating the bell tower into one of its corners. It's usually open in the morning (if not, you can borrow the key from the caretaker – ask at the *artesanía* stalls). Inside, you'll find a series of faded, centuries-old friezes depicting the Stations of the Cross and vivid scenes of sinners suffering in hell. There's also an unusual collection of skulls belonging to former priests, and a magical "walking" table that's kept chained to the wall, for fear it will wander off in the night.

△ Parinacota village

4

EL NORTE GRANDE | Up to Parque Nacional Lauca

Opposite the church, in the plaza, local women sell alpaca knitwear and other **artesanía** – a sign of life returning to Parinacota, which until recently was virtually depopulated. Many of its houses are still under lock and key for much of the year, their owners returning only for important fiestas and funerals (see box on p.263). The nearby **Conaf** administration centre, housed in a large, chalet-style building, makes a valiant attempt at informing the public about the park and its wildlife, and sometimes offers **camping** space out the back. Some villagers offer very basic **rooms** without hot water (❶–❷); ask around. You can reach Parinacota by **bus** from Arica with Buses Martínez, Pedro Montt 620 (Thurs & Sat; ☎58/232265), and, a few doors along at no. 662, Buses Humire (Tues & Fri; ☎58/253497).

Lagunas de Cotacotani

A collection of small, interconnected lakes lying in a dark lava field, filled with exquisite jade-green water, the **LAGUNAS DE COTACOTANI** lie about 8km east of Parinacota, clearly visible from the paved highway to Bolivia. The lakes were formed by volcanic eruptions and are surrounded by fine dust and cinder cones, further adding to their lunar appearance. The waters are filtered down from Lago Chungará and then continue to the *bofedal de Parinacota*, which is the source of the Río Lauca. On closer inspection the lakes aren't as lifeless

Walks and climbs in Parque Nacional Lauca

Lauca doesn't offer a great many hiking possibilities, and most people are content to just admire the scenery and the wildlife. There are, however, at least three half-day or day **walks** you can do, and many more possibilities for **climbing**. Remember to respect the altitude, and to allow yourself more time to cover distances that you could walk quite easily at lower elevations.

Cerro Choquelimpie No technical experience or equipment are necessary to climb this 5288-metre-high peak, reached in about four hours from the *refugio* at Lago Chungará. From the top, you get views down to the gold mine behind the mountain, and onto Lago Chungará and Volcán Parinacota.

Cerro Guane Guane A slow but straightforward climb up this 5096-metre peak is rewarded by panoramic views over the park. It's suitable for any fit person used to hill-climbing and takes around four hours to the top from the Conaf centre at Parinacota, and two to three hours back down.

Lago Chungará to Parinacota (or reverse) This 18-kilometre walk from the *refugio* at Lago Chungará to Parinacota takes about six hours. Follow the paved highway as far as the *mirador de Lagunas Cotacotani*, then climb down to the lakes, from where a jeep track continues to Parinacota.

Parinacota to Lagunas de Cotacotani A rewarding, not-too-difficult walk, taking about three hours (one way) from Parinacota; ask the Conaf *guardaparque* to point you in the direction of the jeep track you need to follow.

Sendero de excursión de Parinacota An easy, six-kilometre circular walk, marked by blue stones starting behind the Conaf centre, taking you past the *bofedal de Parinacota*, where you can observe numerous grazing alpaca. Good views onto surrounding mountains. Allow two to three hours.

Volcán Parinacota Suitable only for experienced climbers carrying crampons and ropes (though it's not always necessary to use them). Allow two days to get up and down from the base camp (a day's hike from Parinacota), including one night camping on the volcano. Avoid this climb between mid-December and February, because of the weather conditions.

as they first appear; many wild Andean geese flock here, while plentiful herds of alpaca graze the soggy marshland. This area is definitely worth exploring as a day hike from Parinacota, but if you are pressed for time take a good look from the *mirador* on the highway, marked by a giant multicoloured *zampoña* (Andean panpipes).

Lago Chungará

Eighteen kilometres on from Parinacota, at an altitude of 4600m, you'll see **LAGO CHUNGARÁ**, a wide blue lake spectacularly positioned at the foot of a snow-capped volcano that rises over its rim like a giant Christmas pudding covered in cream. This is 6330-metre-high **Volcán Parinacota**, one of the highest peaks in Chile and the park's most challenging climb. When the lake is mill-pond calm, in other words when there is no wind, the reflection of the volcano is the most memorable view in the entire region. On the southern shore of the lake, right by the highway, you'll find a small stone **Conaf refugio** with five beds (CH$5500 per person), a kitchen, **camping** spaces (CH$5000 per site) and unbeatable views. This is unquestionably the best place to stay in the park, allowing you to observe the changing colours of the lake and volcano at different times of day, from the transparent pinks of early morning to the deep blues and gleaming whites of the afternoon. From the *refugio* you can clamber down to the shore (much further away than it looks) and get closer views of the pink flamingoes, ducks and giant coots that live on the lake.

Reserva Nacional las Vicuñas and the Salar de Suriro

Directly south of Parque Nacional Lauca, the **RESERVA NACIONAL LAS VICUÑAS** stretches over 100km south across spectacular altiplano wilderness filled with wild vicuña, green *bofedales*, abandoned Aymara villages, groves of *queñoa* – spindly, rickety-looking trees belonging to a species that miraculously defies the treeline – and sweeping vistas of volcanoes. It's far less accessible than Lauca, with no public transport, which means hiring a high-clearance 4WD vehicle or taking an organized tour. Note that the drive into the reserve involves fording several streams, which are usually very low but can swell dangerously with heavy summer rains – check with Conaf before setting out. You will also have to contend with the huge borax trucks carrying heavy loads and generating bothersome clouds of dust, spoiling your enjoyment of the scenery. The reserve's administrative centre is about a 90-minute drive from Putre, in **Guallatire** (4428m altitude), a pretty hamlet with a traditional seventeenth-century Andean church. There's also an obligatory *carabineros* checkpoint here, and a Conaf *refugio* that is seldom in service. Looming over the village, snow-capped **Volcán Guallatire** puffs wispy plumes of smoke from its 6060-metre peak, while a grassy-banked stream snakes at its foot.

Following the road south of Guallatire, you'll be rewarded, about 40km on, with sudden, dramatic views of the **SALAR DE SURIRE**, a dazzling white salt flat containing several lakes with nesting colonies of three species of flamingo. Originally part of Parque Nacional Lauca, its status was changed to that of national monument in 1983 to allow borax to be mined from its surface. The mining is still going on today, and you can see the mine's enormous trucks driving over the *salar*, dwarfed by its massive dimensions but a nuisance nonetheless. On the west shore of the *salar* there's a Conaf **refugio** with four beds (CH$6000 per person), hot water and a kitchen. It's in a wonderful location with terrific views onto the salt flat, but it is often closed or bookings are not always respected, so do not rely on staying here. Sixteen kilometres from here, skirting the southern edge of the salt flat, **Polloquere** (also known as Aguas Calientes) is the site of several pale-blue pools filled with hot thermal water and with a muddy bottom reminiscent of the Dead Sea, an absolutely stunning place to take a bath, despite the lack of facilities – though be sure to get here in the morning, before the bone-chilling afternoon wind picks up. There are a couple of picnic areas and **camping** spaces here, too, but it's a treacherously exposed site.

Travel details

Buses

Antofagasta to: Arica (4 daily; 10hr); Calama (every hour; 3hr); Caldera (every hour; 6hr); Chañaral (16 daily; 5hr); Chuquicamata (5 daily; 3hr); Copiapó (every hour; 7hr); La Serena (16 daily; 11hr); María Elena (2 daily; 3hr); Mejillones (every 30min; 40min); Santiago (every hour; 20hr); Tocopilla (2hr 40min).

Arica to: Antofagasta (4 daily; 10hr); Calama (6 daily; 10hr); Chañaral (5 daily; 15hr); Copiapó (18 daily; 16hr); Iquique (every 30min; 4hr 30min); La Serena (18 daily; 18hr); Putre (1 daily; 3hr); San Pedro de Atacama (1 daily; 10hr); Santiago (18 daily; 29hr); Vallenar (18 daily; 20hr).

Calama to: Antofagasta (6 daily; 3hr); Arica (6 daily; 10hr); Chañaral (10 daily; 8hr); Chuquicamata (every 30min; 30min);

Copiapó (12 daily; 9hr 30min); Iquique (4 daily; 7hr); La Serena (14 daily; 12hr 30min); San Pedro de Atacama (1 hourly; 1hr 30min); Santiago (10 daily; 22hr 30min); Toconao (1 daily; 2hr 30min). **Iquique** to: Antofagasta (8 daily; 7hr); Arica (every 30min; 4hr 30min); Calama (4 daily; 7hr); Caldera (12 daily; 12hr); Chañaral (8 daily; 11hr); Chuquicamata (2 daily; 6hr 30min); Copiapó (12 daily; 13hr); La Serena (every hour; 16hr); La Tirana (7 daily; 1hr 40min); Mamiña (2 daily; 2hr 30min); María Elena (2 daily; 5hr); Mejillones (2 daily; 5hr); Pica (7 daily; 2hr); Santiago (every hour; 25hr); Tocopilla (7 daily; 3hr).

Flights

Antofagasta to: Arica (3 daily; 1hr 30min); Calama (3 daily; 35min); Iquique (6 daily; 45min); La Serena (3 daily; 2hr); Santiago (11 daily; 2hr).
Arica to: Antofagasta (3 daily; 1hr 30min); Calama (2 daily; 35min); Iquique (5 daily; 35min); La Serena (1 daily; 4hr); Santiago (8 daily; 3hr 30min).
Calama to: Antofagasta (3 daily; 35min); Arica (2 daily; 35min); Iquique (5 daily; 30min); La Serena (2 daily; 3hr); Santiago (5 daily; 2hr direct, 3hr via Antofagasta).
Iquique to: Antofagasta (6 daily; 45min); Arica (5 daily; 35min); Calama (5 daily; 30min); La Serena (3 daily; 3hr 30min); Santiago (11 daily; 2hr 20min).

The Central Valley

CHAPTER 5   # Highlights

✳ **Santa Cruz** Visit classic Chilean haciendas in this rustic wine valley town, then taste your way through the "Ruta del Vino", offering some of the world's best red wines. **See p.292**

✳ **Pichilemu and the beaches** Relax at this haven for water sports, which also doubles as an inexpensive launch pad for visiting the area's deserted beaches and nearby lakes. **See p.295**

✳ **Reserva Nacional Siete Tazas** This stunning park features lush forests, abundant waterfalls and natural swimming pools. **See p.300**

✳ **Altos del Lircay** Hiking trails, spectacular views and relatively easy access make one of Chile's few Andean parks perfect for camping trips. **See p.303**

✳ **Termas de Chillán** Legendary hot springs sit atop the side of a volcano; in the winter, the skiing is excellent, while the rest of the year you can hike, swim and embark on horse treks. **See p.312**

✳ **Salto del Laja** Marvel at these thundering waterfalls. **See p.323**

△ Salto del Laja

The Central Valley

Extending south from Santiago as far as the Río Bío Bío, Chile's **CENTRAL VALLEY** is a long, narrow plain hemmed in by the Andes to the east and the coastal range to the west, with a series of gentle ridges and lateral river valleys running between the two. This is the most fertile land in Chile, and the immense orchards, vineyards and pastures that cover the valley floor form a dazzling patchwork of greenery. Even in urban zones, country ways hold sway, and the Central Valley is perhaps the only part of Chile where it is not uncommon to see horse-drawn carts plodding down the Panamericana Highway, the main artery that runs south from Santiago, through Rancagua to Los Angeles in the southern section of the region and beyond. The kernel of the Central Valley lies between the capital and the city of **Chillán**, some 400km south – a region that for over two hundred years constituted the bulk of colonial Chile. It was here that the vast private estates known as *estancias*, or haciendas, were established, and where the country's most powerful families exercised an almost feudal rule over the countryside, a situation that persisted well into the twentieth century. These days most of the land is controlled by commercial food producers rather than old, moneyed families, but signs of the colonial way of life are still very much in evidence, with grand *casas patronales* lurking behind the adobe walls of the region's back lanes, and endless rows of poplars marking the divisions between the former estates. The people, too, have held on to many of their rural traditions: most farm workers still prefer to get around by horse, and the cult of the *huaso*, or "cowboy", is as strong as ever, as can be witnessed at the frequent **rodeos** held in stadiums known as *medialunas*.

Further south, the busy city of **Concepción** guards the mouth of the **Bío Bío**, the mighty river that for over three hundred years was the boundary between conquered, colonial Chile and unconquered **Mapuche territory**, whose occupants withstood domination until 1883. Until recently the river was more famous as a **whitewater rafting** destination, but hydroelectric dams tamed the raging torrent. Despite its rich soils having long been incorporated into the production belt of the Central Valley, traces of the frontier still linger, visible in the ruins of colonial Spanish forts, the proliferation of Mapuche place names and the tin-roof pioneer architecture. Beyond the Bío Bío, towards the Lake District, the landscape alters, too, the gently sloping plains giving way to verdant native forests and remote, Andean lakes.

Many visitors bypass the Central Valley altogether, whizzing south towards the more dramatic landscapes of the Lake District and beyond. Certainly the agricultural towns dotted along the highway – **Rancagua**, **San Fernando**, **Curicó**, **Talca** and **Los Angeles** – are, on the whole, rather dull, offering little

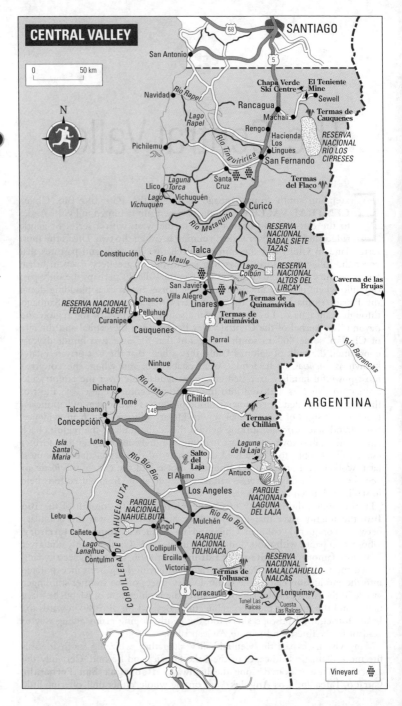

to tempt tourists off the bus or out of their car. But stray a few kilometres off the Panamericana and you'll catch a glimpse of an older Chile impossible to find elsewhere, abounding with pastoral charms, Chief among these are the splendid **haciendas**, the best of which lie near **Santa Cruz**. The region's small, **colonial villages**, with their colourful adobe houses topped by overhanging, clay-tiled roofs are another Central Valley highlight – among the prettiest examples are **Vichuquén**, west of Curicó, and **Villa Alegre**, south of Talca in the Maule Valley, where you can also visit a trail of lush, emerald **vineyards**.

Away from the valley floor, you'll find attractions of a very different nature. To the west, up in the coastal hills, a couple of lakes offer great **water sports** facilities, notably **Lago Rapel**, while further west a number of inviting **beaches** and cheerful seaside towns are scattered down the coast, among them the popular surfer hangout **Pichilemu**. East of the valley, the dry, dusty slopes of the Andes offer excellent **horse-riding** and **hiking** opportunities, particularly along the trails of protected areas such as **Reserva Nacional Los Cipreses**, near Rancagua, and **Reserva Nacional Altos del Lircay**, near Talca. After a strenuous day in the mountains, relax in one of the many **hot springs** in the area: the **Termas de Chillán** are at the base of a booming ski and adventure resort. Also rewarding are the beautiful **Termas de Cauquenes**, near San Fernando. The rustic **Termas de Tolhuaca**, southwest of Los Angeles, sit on the edge of the beautifully forested **Parque Nacional Tolhuaca**, and are also handy to one of Chile's more unusual natural sights: the **Túnel las Raíces**, cutting 4.5km through the cordillera, and the longest tunnel in South America. Built between 1929 and 1939, the 4,528-metre tunnel was designed to be part of a coast-to-coast railway project that was later shelved, and instead now enables the surfaced road from Curacautín to pass under the mountains on its way to the small logging town of Lonquimay.

Getting down the Central Valley by **public transport** is easy, with hundreds of **buses** ploughing down the Panamericana. Branching off into the cordillera and to the coast normally requires catching a "rural bus" from one of the cities dotted down the highway, though some of the more remote places can only be reached with your own transport. The **train** from Santiago stops at Rancagua, San Fernando, Curicó, Talca, Chillán and Concepción – much slower than the buses, but more leisurely and scenic. The amount of annual rainfall picks up steadily as you head south; by the time you reach the Bío Bío there is a significant amount of rain every month. While winter is never too cold and snowfall is plentiful in the foothills, most visitors come here between October and March.

Rancagua and the Rapel Valley

Zipping down the Panamericana from Santiago, you can reach the prosperous agricultural town of **Rancagua**, 87km south, in less than an hour. With a little time and your own transport, however, the old road from Santiago (signed

Alto Jahuel, running east along the highway) makes a far more appealing route, winding its way past swaths of vines, fruit trees and old haciendas, half-hidden behind their great adobe walls.

Once in town, you'll find little to hold your interest for more than a few hours – unless your arrival coincides with a **rodeo** – but Rancagua makes for a useful jumping-off point for several attractions in the adjacent **Rapel Valley**, including the 40-kilometre-long **Lago Rapel**, the largest artificial lake in Chile. In the opposite direction, a paved highway known as the Carretera del Cobre heads 60km east into the cordillera to the copper mine of **El Teniente** and the **Chapa Verde ski resort**, while a southern fork takes you to the charming **Termas de Cauquenes** and the nearby **Reserva Nacional Río los Cipreses**.

Rancagua

RANCAGUA presents a picture that is to repeat itself in most of the Central Valley towns – large, well-tended plaza; single-story adobe houses; a few colonial buildings; sprawling, faceless outskirts. It is, however, a particularly affluent version of the model, evident in the modern malls and department stores found in its centre, and in the care the municipality has lavished on the town's historic buildings. Unusually, its square is known not as the Plaza de Armas, but as the **Plaza de los Héroes**. Honouring the patriot soldiers, headed by Bernardo O'Higgins, who defended the city against Royalist forces in 1814, only to be crushed in what has gone down in Chilean history as the "Disaster of Rancagua". In the centre of the square, a rearing equestrian statue celebrates O'Higgins' triumphant return to the city, four years after he had left it in ruins, to present it with a coat of arms depicting a phoenix rising from the ashes. The square's other major monument is the towering, yellow-walled **Iglesia Catedral**; it dates originally from 1775 but, after sustaining heavy damage in the battle, was rebuilt in 1861 by an Italian architect who added the Doric columns and double tower.

One block north of the square, at the corner of Cuevas and Estado, the **Iglesia de la Merced** suffered fewer battle scars, despite being used as O'Higgins' headquarters, and its plain white walls and tower are the same that stood when the church was first built in the mid-eighteenth century. Another well-preserved colonial building is the eighteenth-century house occupied by the **Museo Regional de Rancagua** at Estado 685 (Tues–Fri 10am–6pm, Sat & Sun 9am–1pm; CH$600, free Sun and Tues; ☎72/221524, ⓦwww .museorancagua.cl) Built of thick white adobe walls around a large interior patio, this handsome, single-storey house is typical of the urban colonial style. Inside, three of its rooms maintain the decor and furnishings of that era, while another is crammed with objects and documents relating to the independence movement. Opposite the museum, at Estado 682, the 1812 **Casa del Pilar de Esquina** is a splendid two-storey late-colonial house, recently restored and open to visitors (with a bit of persistence). It's full of ceramics, textiles and leather goods as well as mementos of various industries, including salt mining and farming. One block south, on the corner of Cachapoal and Millán, the **Casa de Cultura** (Mon–Fri 8.30am–1pm & 3–6pm; free) is more accessible, hosting regular photographic and art exhibits – though the main draw is its rural colonial architecture, including thick foundations made of river boulders mortared with mud. Finally, no account of Rancagua could fail to mention its fame as Chile's **rodeo** capital, hosting the national rodeo championships during the last week of March or the first week of April in its *medialuna* on

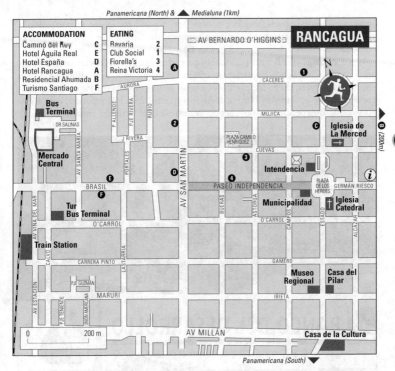

ACCOMMODATION
Camino del Rey   C
Hotel Águila Real   E
Hotel España   D
Hotel Rancagua   A
Residencial Ahumada   B
Turismo Santiago   F

EATING
Bavaria   2
Club Social   1
Fiorella's   3
Reina Victoria   4

the northern edge of town (on the corner of Av España and Germán Ibarra). The rodeo season runs from mid-September until the championships; for ticket information, see box on p.287.

Practicalities

Arriving by **bus**, you'll be dropped at the terminal at Salinas 1165 (☎72/225425); a couple of blocks south, the **train station** (☎72/230361) is served by half-hourly trains from Santiago. Trains north to the capital take just over an hour and cost CH$1100. There's an extremely helpful **Sernatur** office one block east of the plaza at Germán Riesco 277 (Mon–Fri 8.30am–5.15pm; ☎ & ℻72/230413, ℮inforancagua@sernatur.cl). Conaf's regional office, Cuevas 480 (☎72/204600), has basic maps and information on the area's national parks. **Accommodation** is basic and cheap at *Hotel España*, San Martín 367 (☎72/230141; ❹), which offers quiet, pleasant (if slightly neglected) rooms around an interior patio in an old, colonial-style building. *Hotel Rancagua*, a few blocks north at San Martín 85 (☎72/232663, ℮hotelrancagua@chile.com, ℗www.hotelrancagua.galeon .com/; ❺), has reasonably comfortable rooms upstairs in the main house, but better ones in an extension out the back. Two other hotels, face-to-face on Brasil, offer basic, if not exactly enchanting, facilities: *Turismo Santiago*, Brasil 1036 (☎72/230860, ℻72/230822, ℮hsantiago@entelchile.net; ❺–❻) and the *Águila Real*, across the street at Brasil 1045 (☎72/222047, ℻72/223002, ℮hsamour@ctcinternet.cl; ❺). In both cases, request a room away from the street for quieter mornings. The rather more stylish *Hotel Camino del Rey* at Estado 275 (☎72/239765, ℻72/232314, ℮hotelcaminodelrey@terra.cl; ❻) boasts an

attractive colonial facade, modern rooms, and a good restaurant. If you're looking for somewhere cheaper, your best option is the simple but secure *Residencial
Ahumada*, at Mujica 125 (☎72/225892; ❷).

As for **eating**, you'll find reasonably priced if unexciting dishes such as *pollo
asado* at the *Club Social*, an attractive cream-and-pink adobe building at Cáceres
486. Alternatively, there are plenty of cheap *fuentes de soda* on Paseo Independencia, plus the ubiquitous *Bavaria* at Av San Martín 255. The informal café *Reina
Victoria*, at Independencia 667, serves traditional, set lunches and other snacks.

△ Rancagua rodeo championships

Rodeos

The Central Valley is the birthplace and heartland of Chilean **rodeo**, whose season kicks off on Independence Day, September 18. Over the following six months, regional competitions eliminate all but the finest horses and *huasos* in the country, who go on to take part in the national championships in Rancagua in late March or early April. Rodeos are performed in *medialunas* (literally "half moons"), which are circular arenas divided by a curved wall, forming a crescent-shaped stadium and a smaller oval pen called an *apiñadero*. The participants are **huasos** – Chilean "cowboys", or horsemen – who cut a dashing figure with their bright, finely woven ponchos, broad-rimmed hats, carved wooden stirrups and shining silver spurs. *Huasos* are normally inseparable from their horses, but the mounts they ride in the rodeo are specially bred and trained *corraleros* that are far too valuable for day-to-day work.

A rodeo begins with an inspection of the horses and their riders by judges, who award points for appearance. This is followed by individual displays of horsemanship that make ordinary dressage look tame. In the main part of a rodeo, pairs of *huasos* have to drive a young cow, or *novillo*, around the edge of the arena and pin it up against a padded section of the wall. The teamwork between horses and riders is impressive to watch, with one riding as close to the rear of the *novillo* as possible while the other gallops sideways, keeping his horse's chest close to the cow's front shoulders. When they reach the cushion, the object is to bring the cow to a sudden stop and hold it up against the wall until the judges have awarded points for style.

Rodeos are as much about eating and drinking as anything else, and the canteen and foodstalls by a *medialuna* are a good place to sample **regional food**, gourmet wine and sweet fruity wines known as *chicha*. Rodeo events are spread over the course of a weekend and end with music and dancing. This is where you can see the **cueca** (see p.67) being danced at its flirtatious best. For the dates of official rodeos, contact the **Federación de Rodeos** in Santiago (T & F 2/6990115) or visit W www.rodeochileno.cl.

For a range of ice cream flavours, head to *Fiorella's* on the corner of Astorga and Cuevas.

LAN airlines has an office at Astorga 233-B (T 72/235573); SKY are at Bueras 393 (T 72/230781). You'll find multiple **banks** with ATMs on Paseo Independencia. **Car rental** is available at Weber Rentacar, Membrillar 40, Oficina 2 (T & F 72/226005) and Comercial O'Carrol 1120 (T 72/230041). Another alternative for getting into the hinterland is to book a **tour** with Turismo Dakota, Mujica 605 (T & F 72/228165, E turismodakota@atnchile.com). For a **casa de cambio**, there's AFEX, at Astorga 365 and Campos 363, Local 4, while Ciber Space, Alcázar 376, has **Internet**. Hipermercado Independencia, Av Miguel Ramirez 665, is a well-stocked **supermarket**. The local **travel agency** Cobretour, Astorga 409 (T 72/232532, F 72/239898), will arrange local tours, especially treks and horse-riding.

El Teniente copper mine and the Chapa Verde ski centre

Sixty kilometres east of Rancagua, up in the cordillera, **El Teniente** is the largest underground mine in the world, with more than 1500km of tunnels.

Local legend has it that its name – "the lieutenant" – refers to a disgraced Spanish officer who, while heading to Argentina to escape his creditors, discovered enormous copper deposits, thus making a fortune and saving himself from bankruptcy. Today the mine belongs to Codelco, the government-owned copper corporation, which also owns the famous Chuquicamata mine in the Far North.

You aren't allowed to just turn up and visit (a barrier blocks the access road), but group tours can be arranged by getting in touch with the owners of the mine, Codelco, Millán 220 in Rancagua (☎72/292000, ☎2/7877710 or ☎2/6903000 in Santiago) in advance. The five-hour tours – which cost from CH\$12,000, including bilingual guides and transport from Rancagua – kick off with a video on the copper industry and the mine, followed by a visit to the now abandoned company town of **Sewell** (⊛www.sewell .cl), staggered in dramatic tiers up the mountainside. After this, you don protective overalls, boots and a miner's lamp and go down the shafts to the gloomy underground tunnels, where you're shown all the different stages of the mining process. Children under 14 are not permitted and women are requested to wear trousers.

A few kilometres north of the mine, and ranging from 2300m to 3100m, is the Codelco-owned **Chapa Verde ski centre** (☎ & ⓕ72/217651, ⊛www .chapaverde.cl), initially built for the company's miners but now open to the public between July and September. It offers more than seven square kilometres of terrain, with 22 pistes, from beginner to advanced levels, served by three chairlifts and several drag lifts. You can rent all equipment at the ski centre, and with advance booking arrange ski lessons. There are no hotels or other accommodation, but check with ski area administration for information on private homes for rent. A simple **restaurant** offers reasonably priced snacks, drinks, meals and toilet facilities. You can drive up in your own vehicle (4WD is advisable) as long as you call the Ski Club (☎72/217651 or ☎72/294255) for a permit in advance. Otherwise, take Codelco's own bus service, Buses El Teniente, at Av Miguel Ramírez 665, Rancagua, next to the Lider Vecino supermarket (departures June–Sept weekdays at 9am, weekends at 8am and 9.30am, return trip daily at 4.30pm; CH\$4500). Lift tickets (CH\$16,000 adult, CH\$8500 children) are sold at Miguel Ramírez 655, the central offices of the ski centre. Full ski equipment rental costs CH\$14,000, full snowboard rental CH\$15,000.

Termas de Cauquenes

A couple of kilometres on from the turn-off to El Teniente, you'll come to a southern fork that branches towards **TERMAS DE CAUQUENES**, 6km beyond. Sitting high above the Río Cachapoal, surrounded by the steep foothills of the Andes, this is one of the most beautiful hot springs resorts in Chile. The centrepiece is the nineteenth-century *sala de baños*, a huge wooden hall with an extremely high ceiling, painted wooden beams, stained-glass windows and marble floor tiles. From the entrance, steps lead down to 24 cubicles containing the *tinas* – the original Carrara marble bathtubs that were installed in 1856, where guests take their hot thermal baths. The water, at a temperature between 42° and 48°C (107° and 118°F), contains magnesium, potassium and lithium among other minerals. It has been revered for its curative properties from the earliest days of the colony when, according to old chronicles, ailing

Jesuits were sent here to be cured of their "gout, syphilis, anaemia and many other problems". Over the years, the fame of the springs increased, and they were visited by a number of important figures, including Bernardo O'Higgins and the great Argentinean Liberator José de San Martín, who spent a month here after bringing his "Army of the Andes" across to liberate Chile from the Royalists. Charles Darwin also soaked his bones here during his voyage to South America.

As well as the *sala de baños*, there's an old, colonial-style chapel, an outdoor swimming pool and comfortable but unremarkable **rooms** (T & F72/899010, W www.termasdecauquenes.cl; ❽), some arranged around a pleasant patio, others looking down to the river. The **food**, however – served in an immense dining room with fine river views – is exceptional, prepared by the Swiss chefs who own the resort. You don't have to stay overnight in order to use the baths; day guests are charged CH$3500 for half an hour in the marble *tinas*, CH$3000 to use the outdoor pool. Buses Termas de Cauquenes runs a **bus** to the *termas*; it leaves at 11am and 5pm from Rancagua's Mercado Municipal, returning to Rancagua at 8.30am and 2pm (to confirm times, call the hotel).

Reserva Nacional Río de los Cipreses

Beyond the Termas de Cauquenes, the road continues for another 14km to the **RESERVA NACIONAL RÍO LOS CIPRESES** (daily 8.30am–6pm; CH$1700, camping CH$4,500; T72/297505). A little-visited gem of the Central Valley, the reserve encompasses 36 square kilometres of protected land stretched along the narrow canyon of the Río de los Cipreses, with altitudes ranging from 900m to 4900m. It's a great spot for multi-day **hiking** or **horse-riding**, and you may spot rare burrowing parrots, foxes, eagles and condors. Given the time necessary to get here, a trip to this park is best for travellers who want to spend at least three days.

At the entrance, a Conaf office provides maps and a diorama of the park, including trails up into the glaciers. Ask about the trails that offer a look at the parakeets nesting in the cliffs. From the office, a jeep track leads 6km to **Sector El Ranchillo**, a camping and picnic area. This is the end of the jeep track, and vehicles must be parked. From here, take the left fork just before El Ranchillo, continue past a second gate (locked) and after another 6km you'll reach **Sector Maitenes**, with a few camping areas and running water. Beyond, a trail follows the river along the canyon, passing through forests of towering cordillera cypress and other native trees, and with occasional views of high Andean peaks like Cerro El Indio and Cerro El Cotón. Lateral ravines regularly branch out from the river, leading to waterfalls, lakes and "hanging" valleys carved out of the hills by glaciers. These aren't signed, however, so unless you're with an *arriero* (horseman), it's safest to stick to the main path. Twenty kilometres on from Sector Maitenes, the path reaches **Sector Urriola**, where there's a rustic refugio (1500m) and a few camping areas; count on taking around six or seven hours to get here on foot from Maitenes, and about four or five on horseback. Beyond Urriola, the path continues for a further ten or so kilometres, giving great views onto the 4900-metre-high Volcán Palomo, looming ahead at the end of the valley. If you want to hire a **horse** call the reserve's administration number. Failing that, there are usually horses for hire in the corral a couple of kilometres before the reserve entrance.

Lago Rapel

Forty-kilometre-long **LAGO RAPEL** nestles in the low coastal hills southwest of Rancagua. It is, in fact, an artificial lake, formed in 1968 by the damming of the Cachapoal and Tinguiririca rivers, whose waters drain from the western tip of the lake into Río Rapel. The massive, concrete wall of the dam is an impressive sight, particularly when the floodgates are opened after heavy rain and the overflow spills out in a thunderous, foaming waterfall. The lake's main attractions, however, are its excellent **water sports facilities**, with speed boats, windsurfers and jet skis available for rent from several hotels and campsites.

Accommodation is often informal, with numerous *residenciales* between Puente El Durazano and El Manzano. The *Club Náutico Rapel* (T72/6381680 or T72/1982414), with camping for CH$15,000 per site, lies conveniently near the village of **El Manzano**, on the lake's western shore, and is easy to reach by public transport. Other places offering water sports and camping include *Camping Alemán*, along the lakeshore 8km west of El Manzano (T09/8833397), with camping (CH$4000 per person) and rustic *cabañas* (❹), and *Camping Bosque Hermoso*, set amid pine and eucalyptus trees 3km north of the village, just across the bridge (T72/512179; CH$5000 per site). *Hotel Jardín del Lago* (T & F2/2746784; ❺), a couple of kilometres further north, offers smart accommodation and water sports facilities as well. For longer stays, see the "*propiedades*" section in the Sunday edition of the newspaper *El Mercurio*, where house rentals are frequently listed. Buses Galgo (T72/511055) runs a **bus** to El Manzano from Rancagua's regional terminal every twenty minutes, and Buses Sextur (T72/231342) has service every hour.

San Fernando and the Colchagua Valley

Fifty-five kilometres south of Rancagua, **San Fernando** is a busy little town sitting in the 120-kilometre-long valley of the Río Tinguiririca, known locally as the **Colchagua Valley** after the province through which it runs. This is serious fruit-production territory, as signalled by the numerous fruit stalls and large Del Monte factories lining the highway on the approach to San Fernando. The town itself is emphatically agricultural and known throughout the region as *the* place to get your tractor repaired. Forty-one kilometres west is **Santa Cruz**, which boasts the **Hotel Santa Cruz Plaza**, a starting point for several popular excursions and site of a superb restaurant. **Hacienda Los Lingues**, a splendid, privately owned hacienda which operates as a hotel and is open for visits, lies 32km south of Rancagua. Still further east, high in the cordillera, the **Termas del Flaco** is an inexpensive option for soaking in hot springs. Around San Fernando, the **Ruta del Vino del Valle de Colchagua** takes in a trail of local vineyards as well as the excellent **Museo de Colchagua**, with historical regional artefacts, and **Hacienda El Huique**, while if you continue to the coast, you'll get to the hip, budget seaside town of **Pichilemu**, popular with surfers.

San Fernando

Surrounded by low, rippling hills washed golden in the sunlight, **SAN FERNANDO** makes for a pleasant amble along its narrow streets. The main commercial artery is Manuel Rodríguez, lined with shops, snack bars and – on the corner with Valdivia – the huge bulk of the nineteenth-century **Iglesia de San Francisco**, a Neo-Gothic church with a 32-metre-high tower. Clearly fond of its Gothic religious architecture, the town boasts another similar monument, the **Capilla San Juan de Dios**, eight blocks north of Manuel Rodríguez, on the corner of Negrete and Avenida Manso de Velasco. Built in 1884 as an attachment to the adjacent Hospital San Juan de Dios, it consists of a very high and narrow single nave containing a massive Baroque altar carved from dark, heavy wood.

Close by, at the corner of Avenida Manso de Velasco and Jiménez, the **Museo Casa Patronal de Lircunlauta** is a good deal less flamboyant – the oldest building in San Fernando, it was originally the *casa patronal* of the eighteenth-century Hacienda Lircunlauta, whose owner donated 450 "blocks" of land to San Fernando when the town was founded in 1742. It's a large, single-storey

building resting on thick stone foundations, with white adobe walls, an imposing entrance, and a sloping roof still covered with its original handmade clay tiles and supported by oak rafters and pillars. The house belongs to the Municipalidad and is occasionally used for art and photographic exhibitions; you can wander in to take a look around during office hours (Tues–Fri 9am–1pm & 3–7pm, Sat & Sun 10am–1pm & 4–6pm; CH$200).

Practicalities

Buses pull in at the **bus terminal** (⊤72/713912) on the corner of Avenida Manso de Velasco and Rancagua. There's no Oficina de Turismo, but the Municipalidad on the plaza at Carampangue and Argomedo has basic **information**. Of San Fernando's few **hotels**, three are on Manuel Rodríguez: at no. 770, second floor, friendly *Hotel Imperio* (⊤72/714595; ❸–❹) has comfortable rooms and a pleasant dining area; a couple of blocks west at no. 968, *Hotel Marcano* (⊤72/714759, ⨍713943; ❹) is darker and gloomier although rooms in the back extension are roomier and a bit brighter; while opposite, at no. 959, *Hotel Español* (⊤72/711098; ❺) offers bland, functional rooms with TV and phone. Slightly cheaper than the others, *Residencial Rahue* (❷) on Urriola is in an old house with high ceilings and a faded decor. *Hotel Diego Portales*, one block north at Av Bernardo O'Higgins 701 (⊤72/714696; ❹), has comfortable enough rooms and a decent **restaurant**, popular with locals. Other places to eat include the *Club Social*, Manuel Rodríguez 787, where you'll find typical, filling meat dishes such as *pollo asado* and *lomo*, while nearby *Café Roma*, at Manuel Rodríguez 815, serves sandwiches and other light snacks. There are two supermarkets to the west of the station. You can arrange **car rental** with Alvaro Asenjo at España 911, Office 3 (⊤ & ⨍72/712105). For **tours** and excursions, try Andes Sur Expediciones (⊤72/513620, ⓦwww.andes-sur.cl) or Mundo Aventura Rafting, Manuel Rodríguez 430 (⊤72/721733).

Hacienda Los Lingues

One of the oldest and best-preserved haciendas in Chile, **Hacienda Los Lingues** (ⓦwww.loslingues.com, ⊜informaciones@loslingues.com; bookings through office in Santiago at Av Providencia 1100, Torres de Tajamar C, oficina 205 ⊤2/2355446 or ⊤2/4310510, ⨍2/2357604), lies 20km northeast of San Fernando. It dates from 1599, when King Felipe III of Spain presented it as a gift to the first mayor of Santiago. Since then, the hacienda has remained in the same family and is today presided over by the elderly and redoubtable don Germán Claro-Lira. The main house dates from the seventeenth and early eighteenth century and bears all the hallmarks of the colonial *casa patronal*, including thick adobe walls and an overhanging clay-tiled roof supported by oak pillars that form a "corridor", or covered veranda, around its interior patio.

Inside, the European tastes of Chile's old moneyed families are reflected in the decoration and antique furniture of rooms such as the *"salón francés"* and the *"salón inglés"* – in the English Room, look out for the framed letter from Buckingham Palace, confirming that don Germán's wife is, in all likelihood, a very distant relative of the Queen of England. Although it now functions as a hotel – one of just four South American hotels to be a part of the exclusive Relais et Châteaux group – the hacienda is still, unquestionably, a family home: don Germán and his various relatives attend mass in the hacienda's chapel every evening, and the grand drawing rooms and library are in regular use. Even the guest bedrooms bear little resemblance to hotel rooms; they're liberally deco-rated with family portraits, old pictures and religious iconography. Outside are sumptuous, mature gardens, a *medialuna* and the stables where thoroughbred Aculeo horses are bred, reputed to be among the finest in South America. The high rates – double room in the main house (**⑨**) and in the guest house (**❺**) – deter most people from staying overnight, but you can visit the hacienda for the day on a cultural tour (US$80), which includes lunch, cocktails and the chance to watch a horse show. Buses for Los Lingues depart from the regional terminal in San Fernando.

Termas del Flaco

Some 107km east of San Fernando, sitting high in the cordillera 1700m above sea level, the **TERMAS DEL FLACO** (Dec–April; CH$700) are among the cheapest and consequently the most-visited thermal baths in the Central Valley. They're reached by a serpentine dirt road that follows the Río Tinguiririca through a beautiful gorge, so narrow in parts that *carabineros* allow traffic to go in only one direction at a time. On Monday through Saturday, traffic can start the trip down between 6am and 2pm, and traffic can start going up between 4pm and midnight; Sunday is variable, so ask the *carabineros* in San Fernando (☏72/711219). You'll need to stay at the baths overnight if you visit during the week. The wild beauty of the cordillera and the feeling of remoteness and solitude are, upon arriving, suddenly interrupted with the appearance of numer-ous shack-like, tin-roofed houses – almost all of them *residenciales* – crowded around the thermal baths. Nor are these baths particularly attractive, consisting of several rectangular concrete, open-air pools. The waters, however – which reach up to 57°C (135°F) in some pools – are just bliss. If you manage to get here mid week, when there are no crowds (except during high season, January and February), you can lie back, close your eyes and just relax, without another soul around. You'll find several short treks around the *termas*, including one that leads to a set of dinosaur footprints preserved in the rock.

Accommodation is abundant, with little to distinguish one place from the next, and most operating on a **full-board** basis. *Posada Amistad* (☏72/817227; **❹**) is right next to the bus stop, and offers small, basic rooms around a garden patio; overlooking the baths, *Posada La Ponderosa* (☏72/721477; **❹**) has good views, though some of the partition walls are very thin. Both are open only in season, December through February. You'll find more comfort in the roomy wooden *cabañas* at *Hotel Las Vegas* (office at Cillero 34, Rancagua ☏ & ⓕ 72/222478, Ⓦwww.termasdelflacohotellasvegas.cl; **❻**), which has a large dining room with floor-to-ceiling windows looking down to the valley and its own small thermal pool or the *Hotel Termas del Flaco* (office at O'Higgins 696, San Fernando ☏72/711832; **❻**), which has good-sized rooms with private baths, cable TV and an outdoor pool. Buses Amistad (☏72/452007) provides **transport** to the *termas*, with one departure daily from Rancagua and three daily from San Fernando.

Santa Cruz and around

West of San Fernando, the paved road running through the Colchagua Valley to the coast takes you past a couple of glorious **haciendas**, converted into muse-ums, as well as a trail of **wineries** (see box, p.295). The small, well-preserved

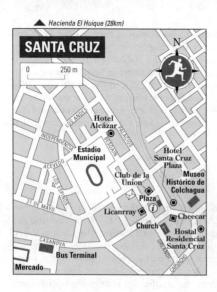

▲ Hacienda El Huique (28km)

SANTA CRUZ

N

0   250 m

Hotel
Alcázar

Estadio
Municipal

Hotel
Santa Cruz
Plaza

Club de la
Union

Museo
Histórico de
Colchagua

Plaza

Licanrray   *i*

Cheecar

Church   Hostal
Residencial
Santa Cruz

Bus Terminal

Mercado

town of **SANTA CRUZ**, 40km from San Fernando, sits in the heart of this renowned wine-making district. On the eastern corner of Plaza de Armas, you'll find the **Museo de Colchagua**, Errázuriz 145 (summer Tues–Sun 10am–7pm, winter Tues–Sun 10am–6pm; CH\$3000;   72/821050, museocol@entelchile.net, www.museocolchagua.cl), housed in a splendid, plum-coloured colonial hacienda, flanked by ancient palm trees. Displayed inside is a well designed if eclectic collection, including fossils, a huge amount of amber, pre-Columbian pottery, relics from the War of the Pacific and memorabilia from the Chilean Independence movement. Among the most evocative exhibits are the shiny black nineteenth-century carriages, steered by ghostly mannequins wearing Victorian capes, and the beautiful old saddles, carved wooden stirrups and silver spurs in the *huaso* display.

On the edge of the Plaza de Armas sits the impeccable *Hotel Santa Cruz Plaza*, Armas 286 (72/822529, reservas@hscp.cl, www.hotelsantacruzplaza.cl; ❽). Given that this is far and away the best hotel in the area, reservations are definitely necessary. The wine-tasting room (*enoteca*) features more than two hundred local varieties. Built by international arms dealer Carlos Cardoen ("the king of cluster bombs"), the restaurant, wines and service are all top-class. You'll find cheaper accommodation at the nicely decorated *Hotel Alcázar,* north of the plaza at Díaz Besoaín 285 (72/822465; ❹), or at the smart *Hostal Residencial Santa Cruz* (72/823125; ❸) opposite the petrol station on Carvacho. A handful of inexpensive traditional restaurants dot the west side of the plaza, including the basic but wholesome *Licanrray*, Plaza de Armas 130-A. The *Club Social* at Plaza de Armas 178, on the north side of the plaza, serves traditional Chilean staples such as *lomo de pobre*, whilst *Cheecar* on the southern side of the plaza offers tasty cakes and coffee.

Twenty-four kilometres beyond Santa Cruz, along the road towards the coast, and 6km past the Los Errázuriz bridge, sits the superb **Hacienda El Huique** (Tues–Sun 11am–5.30pm; Ch\$1000; 72/933083, www.elhuique.com). One of the Central Valley's loveliest haciendas, it is perfectly preserved, along with all its furniture and outbuildings, and open to the public as a museum. The hacienda's history dates from the seventeenth century, in the colonial period, but the current *casa patronal* was built in the early years of independence, in 1829. The main house is built around a beautiful large patio, filled with palm trees, flowers and climbing, sweet-smelling jasmine. Standing alongside, and entered through a huge doorway, is the **chapel**, sporting a 23-metre-high bell tower (Sunday Mass at 11.30am). Arranged around a series of patios behind the house are the various outbuildings, including store rooms, the dairy, the wine shed, the stables and the tack room, giving a clear picture of how life was organized on these almost totally self-supporting haciendas. Inside, the rooms are crammed

La Ruta del Vino del Valle de Colchagua

The Valle de Colchagua lies in the heart of one of Chile's finest wine-making districts, where many of the country's world-class wines originate. Fourteen wineries in the Valle have launched a wine tour called **La Ruta del Vino del Valle de Colchagua**. The tour operates out of Santa Cruz (see opposite). Wine tours (CH$58,000 per person for two people, CH$45,000 per person for up to five) run daily except for Sunday and include visits to three wineries with multilingual guides and the chance to sample two wines at each. Lunch is taken in some of the best restaurants in the valley. Information and reservations must be made 48 hours in advance at Plaza de Armas 298 in Santa Cruz (☎72/823199, ✉info@rutadelvino.cl, ⊛www.colchaguavalley .cl). Tours can also include a visit to either the Museo de Colchagua or the Hacienda El Huique (see opposite). The best time to take the tour is in late March, when the wineries organize their own Fiesta de la Vendima (grape-harvest festival), with demonstrations of the sorting, crushing and filtering processes, plus extra tastings. The following are some of the best wineries to visit directly. The family estate of **Viña Bisquertt** (☎72/821792, ✉bodega@bisquertt.cl, ⊛www.bisquertt.cl) has attractive colonial buildings and antique carriages in its tasting rooms; they began producing wines in 1991 and have won numerous awards, especially for their Merlot. The compact boutique winery at **Viña Santa Laura** (☎72/823179, ✉vslaura@entelchile .net, ⊛www.laurahartwig.cl) first planted vines in 1979, while the historic **Viu Manent** (☎72/858751, ✉winery@viumanent.cl, ⊛www.viumanent.cl) dates from 1935. **Viña Mont Gras** (☎72/822845, ✉info@montgras.cl, ⊛www.montgras.cl) produces, amongst others, the rare Carménère wine, largely for export.

with old furniture and family heirlooms – dark old oil paintings, crucifixes, fans, sepia photographs and personal objects belonging to the Echeñique family, who owned the hacienda for over two hundred years before donating it to the army in 1976. All these old-fashioned artefacts, combined with the remoteness and tranquillity of the setting, bolster the illusion of time standing still, with no intrusions from the outside world.

Pichilemu

If you continue west towards the coast you'll end up, 87km on from Santa Cruz, at the bustling seaside surfer town of **PICHILEMU** (3hr 30min from Santiago), built around a wide, sandy bay at the foot of a steep hill. The town dates from the second half of the nineteenth century, when Agustín Ross Edwards set out to create a European-style seaside resort connected to Santiago by railway. Today Pichilemu wears the charming, melancholy air of a faded Victorian seaside town. Elegant promenades and terraces overlook the bay, lined with distinctive balustrades painted cherry-pink and white; from the seafront, a broad flight of identically coloured steps sweeps up the hillside to the splendid **Parque Ross**, planted with century-old Phoenix palms and extravagant topiary. On the edge of the park, jutting out over the hillside, the grand old **casino** – the first in Chile – is perhaps the most evocative of Ross's legacies. It's now in disuse, with broken windows and its imposing nineteenth-century architecture in a sorry state of disrepair. In contrast to this faded elegance, Pichilemu's central streets are crammed with snack bars and *schoperías* catering to the crowds of young surfers who come to ride the waves – among the best in all of Chile. The most challenging surf is at Punta de Lobos, 6km south, where Chile's national surfing championships are held each summer. Look for the sea lions in the beach's peculiar escarpments.

Frequent **bus** services to Pichilemu are provided by Buses Andimar (⊤72/711817) and Buses Nilahue (⊤ & ⨍72/229358) from San Fernando and Rancagua. **Arriving** in town by bus, you'll be dropped a couple of blocks north of the main street, Calle Ortúzar. Nearby you'll find the Municipalidad de Pichilemu, at Angel Gaete 365 (Mon–Fri 8.30am–5.30pm; ⊤72/841017), where you can pick up a map of the town and a list of activities. For a local, insider's guide to town, try the Spanish-language website ⊛www .pichilemunews.cl. Cheap **accommodation**, whether camping or cabins, is abundant. Close to the beach and popular with surfers is *Residencial Mary Pily* on Washington Saldeas 30 (no phone; ❷–❹ depending on the season).

To escape the crowds, 3km south of town are the *DunaMar* condos, Avenida Comercio (⊤ & ⨍ 72/841676; ❻), a modern resort on the beach that boasts balconies with great views and an excellent seafood restaurant. Back in town, another good choice is the *Hotel Chile-España*, down towards the sea at Ortúzar 255 (⊤ & ⨍72/841314, ⊜hotelchileespana@terra.cl; ❸), where you'll find simple but neat rooms off a sunny glass-walled corridor dotted with plants and deck chairs. *Hotel Rex*, Av Ortúzar 124 (⊤72/841003; ❸) is under the same management and provides similar rooms. Some of the best value *residenciales* and *cabañas* catering to the surfers include the welcoming, well-kept *Residencial Antmalal* at Joaquín Aguirre 64 (⊤72/841004; ❷–❸) and the clean and secure *Cabañas Hecmar* at Av Comercio 614 (⊤72/841357; ❷). The popular *Hostería La Gloria* (⊤72/841052; ❸), ten blocks south of the seafront at J.J. Prieto 980, is worth the walk for its excellent and inexpensive seafood, including tasty *machas a la parmesana* and dressed crab. You'll find many cheap eats on Avenida Ross and Avenida Ortúzar.

For a tiny town, Pichilemu has plenty of **nightlife** – though most of it tends to be surf parties organized at the last minute. For dancing and drinking try *Disco 127* at Angel Gaete 127. Along Avenida Ortúzar there are a number of bars, including *Gigi Bar* and *El Toqui*, that get lively during the summer months.

Curicó and the Mataquito Valley

The Teno and Lontué rivers converge to form the broad Río Mataquito, which meanders West through Chilean wine country towards the Pacific. The manicured town of **Curicó** (54km south of San Fernando) sits in the Mataquito Valley and makes for an appealing place to break your journey – en route, perhaps, to the **wineries**, or further west to the **Lago Vichuquén**, near the coast, or the **Siete Tazas waterfalls**, southwest towards the mountains.

Curicó

Prosperous **CURICÓ** is built around one of the most beautiful central **plazas** in Chile, luxuriantly planted with sixty giant Canary Island palms. Standing in their shade, on the northern side of the square, is a highly ornate, dark-green wrought-iron **bandstand**, constructed in a New Orleans style in 1904, while close by an elaborate fountain featuring a cast-iron replica of *The Three Graces* spouts water into a small pond full of water lilies and black-necked swans. In contrast to these rather fanciful civic commissions, the memorial to **Toqui Lautaro** – the Mapuche chief at whose hands Spanish conquistador Pedro de Valdivia came to a grisly end – is a raw and powerful work, carved out of an ancient tree trunk by the Mapuche sculptor Heraclio "Kako" Calquín. Standing on the northwest corner of the square, the **Iglesia La Matriz** makes a curious sight, its grand Neoclassical facade giving onto an empty shell ever since the great 1985 earthquake. Next door, the dignified **Club de la Unión** escaped unscathed, its fine white pillars and balconies still perfectly intact. Beyond the plaza, there's little to do except wander around the town's lively streets (look out for the old cinema on the corner of Yungay and Merced, whose Art Deco facade features two malevolent-looking gargoyles).

Climb **Cerro Carlos Condell**, the little hill on the eastern edge of town, and survey the scene from its 99-metre-high summit or take a dip in its public swimming pool. While you're in town, it's worth making the easy excursion 5km south to the **winery** of Miguel Torres (Mon–Fri 9am–3pm & 4–5pm, Sat 10am–2pm; free; ☎75/310455, ⓦwww.torreswines.com), the innovative Spanish vintner who revolutionized the Chilean wine industry in the 1980s. You'll be given an informal tour, ending up, of course, at the *sala de ventas* (salesroom). There's also a fine restaurant here, the *Restaurant Viña Torres*, which

△ Curicó central plaza

ACCOMMODATION		EATING	
Hotel Comercio	A	Bavaria	3
Hotel Prat	C	Club de la Unión	4
Hotel Turismo	B	Salchipap's	2
Residencial Rahue	D	Whay Hau	1

serves Catalan dishes from 12.30 to 3.30pm. To get there, take a bus heading to Molina (every 10min) from the terminal and ask to be let off outside the *bodega*, which is right next to the Panamericana. Other wine tours, lasting half, one or two days, are arranged by an organization called Ruta del Vino Valles de Curicó, who have an office in front of the Plaza de Armas at Merced 341, second floor (℡75/328972, ⓔinfo@rvvc.cl, ⓦwww.rvvc.cl). This route, south of Curicó, is less well developed than the one in the Colchagua area, but cheaper because of this.

Practicalities

Arriving in Curicó by bus, you'll pull in at the **bus terminal** (℡75/328575) on the corner of Avenida Camilo Henríquez and Carmen, three blocks north of the plaza. The **train station** (℡75/310028) is on Prat, four blocks west of the Plaza de Armas. You can pick up a map of the town and other **tourist information** in the Municipalidad, opposite the Plaza de Armas. Reasonably priced **accommodation** is available at *Hotel Prat*, a large *residencial* at Peña 427 (℡75/311069; ❸) offering dark but spotless rooms. Similarly priced, *Residencial Rahue* at Peña 410 (℡75/312194; ❸) has brightly painted, comfortable rooms. One of the nicest spots in town is the ✵ *Hotel Turismo* at Carmen 727 (℡75/310552, Ⓕ75/312378, ⓔhturismo@tnet.cl, ⓦwww.hotelturismocurico.cl; ❺–❻), an uncharacter-istically chic modern hotel with a manicured courtyard, large lounge area complete with giant fireplace, bar and fine **restaurant**. The handsome old ✵ *Club de la Unión* right on the plaza serves filling Chilean staples. *Salchipap's*, on the corner of Montt and Rodríguez, has simple, standard dishes at reasonable rates, while *Whay Hau* at Yungay 853 doles out decent Cantonese dishes. *Bar Deportivo*, Montt 46, and *Molka's Bar*, Merced 447, are frequently lively places to have a drink. From March 15 to 20, the **wine festival** (*vendimia*) in the Plaza de Armas is a celebration of the grape harvest, complete with dances and beauty pageants.

Banks with ATM machines are on Calle Merced, near the plaza. Change money at **Casa de Cambio**, Merced 255, Local 106 or Forex at Carmen 497 and Yungay 649. The best **supermarket** in town is Unimarc, at Estado 43. For **car rental**, head to Rent a Car Curicó, Manso de Velasco 520 (℡75/312297).

Lago Vichuquén and around

West of Curicó, a scenic road follows the northern bank of the Río Mataquito through the fertile river valley, covered with wheat fields and fruit trees. Eighty-five kilometres along the paved road, just beyond the village of Hualañé, take the right fork and follow the signs for a further 25km along a dirt road to tiny

VICHUQUÉN. This is one of the best-preserved villages in the Central Valley, its narrow streets packed with flowers and orange trees and lined with brightly painted adobe houses. Most of these date from the mid-nineteenth century, but Vichuquén's history goes back much further: there was a settlement here long before the arrival of the Spaniards, and it was chosen by the Incas, during their expansion in the sixteenth century, as a site for one of their *mitimaes* – agricultural colonies populated by Quechua farmers brought down from Peru. You'll find relics of the Inca occupation in the village's small but interesting **Museo Colonial**, on Calle Rodríguez (daily 10.30am–1.30pm & 4–6pm; CH$550). The museum also features a 3000-year-old mummy, and displays on the conquest and the independence movement.

Four kilometres beyond you'll reach the southern tip of **Lago Vichuquén**, a long, narrow lake enclosed by deep-green, pine-covered hills. Considerably more upmarket than Lago Rapel, further north, this is a popular holiday destination with Santiago's upper classes, whose beautiful villas line the lakeshore, their lush, manicured gardens giving onto private beaches. There are several **places to stay** and **eat**. On the southern shore, in the village of **Aquelarre**, you'll find fine food and accommodation at both the unpretentious *Playa Aquelarre* (☎75/400030; ❻) and the luxurious *Marina Vichuquén* (☎75/400265, ⓕ75/400274, ⓦwww.marinavichuquen.cl; ❼), which also has excellent **water sports facilities**, as well as mountain bikes and horse-riding (all available for non-guests, too). Other options are dotted along the winding road that follows the lake's western shore: *Camping Vichuquén*, just beyond Aquelarre (☎75/400062, ⓦwww.campingvichuquen.cl) charges CH$3000–5000 per person depending on proximity to the lakeshore; *Cabañas Rincón Suizo*, a few kilometres further on (☎75/400012; ❹), has reasonably priced if past-their-best rooms and *cabañas*; while poorly signed *Cabañas del Tío Omar*, approaching the northern shore (☎75/400198; ❻), offers smart, secluded *cabañas* overlooking the lake.

Laguna Torca and Llico

Beyond the northern tip of the lake, the road comes to a junction. The right fork takes you across the rickety Puente de Llico to **RESERVA NACIONAL LAGUNA TORCA** (CH$1300), a marshy man-made lake a couple of kilometres away, preserved by Conaf as a breeding sanctuary for 106 species of birds, including hundreds of black-necked swans and other marine birds, which can be viewed from several wooden observation platforms. You can get more information from the Conaf office (just beyond the bridge, hiding behind the large house with the veranda) and there's a hard-to-find camping area (Sept–April; CH$8000 for up to six people) in a eucalyptus grove (turn right immediately after the bridge, then first left). Back at the junction, the left fork leads to nearby **LLICO**, a rugged little seaside town perched on the edge of an exposed sandy beach whose turbulent waves attract many surfers – during January and February numerous surf tournaments bring a buzz to this usually quiet beach.

Accommodation here is much cheaper than along the Lago Vichuquén. You'll find rooms right on the beachfront at *Residencial Miramar*, Carrera Pinto 48 (☎75/400032; ❸); the en-suite rooms are cramped, but they have balconies and good sea views. The *Miramar* also has an excellent seafood **restaurant** that pulls in a good crowd in summer, when brisk, efficient waiters tear around with steaming bowls of *paila marina* or plates piled high with fresh crabs, mussels or clams.

Reserva Nacional Radal Siete Tazas

Of all the natural phenomena in Chile, the **Siete Tazas**, 73km southeast of Curicó, must be one of the most extraordinary. In the depths of the native forest, a crystal-clear mountain river drops down a series of seven waterfalls, each of which has carved a sparkling *taza* – literally, a "teacup" – out of the rock. The falls are set within the Conaf-administered **RESERVA NACIONAL RADAL SIETE TAZAS** (April–Nov 8.30am–6pm; Dec–March 8.30am–8pm; CH$1500, camping CH$7500 for up to six), reached by a poor dirt road from the village of Molina, 18km southwest of Curicó – be sure to fill up with petrol there. Busy on summer weekends, this park is practically empty the rest of the year. Also within the reserve are forests, several hiking trails and the **Velo de Novia** ("Bride's Veil"), a 50-metre waterfall spilling out of a narrow gorge. Conaf has a small hut on the road towards the Siete Tazas, but for more information (about the geology of the area and the native trees in the surrounding forest), you need to go to the administrative office at **Parque Inglés**, 9km further east, at the end of the dirt road.

Hostería La Flor de la Canela (☎75/491613; ❹) offers small but adequate **rooms** with either private or shared facilities, near the administrative office, and they also serve tasty breakfasts and food. You can also camp in the area, including at *Radal Eco Adventure*, 1km before the town of Radal, on the right (☎9/3338719; CH$12,000 for up to five people); they also offer **treks** and a wealth of local information. For privacy, great swimming, horse rides and accommodation ranging from camping (CH$11,000 for up to six people) to cabins (CH$30,000 for up to six people), try *Valle de Las Catas*, a private ranch located inside the park (☎2/5353649, ✉vallelascatas@entelchile.net, ⓦwww.sietetazas.cl); it's halfway between Parque Inglés and the Siete Tazas, close to the Puente de Frutillar. You can get to the Siete Tazas on **public transport** from Curicó with Buses Hernández (☎75/522346), which has two services daily throughout the year. The best time of year to visit this park is from December through March, as the winter months are frequently snowy. In summer, the area is quite hot and, given the altitude, an easy place to get sunburnt.

Talca and the Maule Valley

The fairly unmemorable town of **Talca**, 67km south on the Panamericana from Curicó, is mainly used as a jumping-off point for several rewarding excursions spread along the valley of the **Río Maule**, which flows into the sea almost 250km west, at the industrial port of **Constitución**. The river has been dammed to the east of Talca, resulting in Lago Colbún. It's also of interest to **history** buffs, as this is where the Chilean declaration of independence was signed. Just east of town, the **Villa Cultural Huilquilemu** is a handsome nineteenth-century hacienda, open as a museum, while further east, high in the cordillera, the **Reserva Nacional Altos del Lircay** provides trails through dramatic mountain scenery. Further south, you'll find the neighbouring hot springs resorts of **Termas de Panimávida** and **Quinamávida** and, down on the valley floor, a proliferation of **vineyards**, many of them conveniently located between the town of **Villa Alegre** and village of **San Javier** on a route served by plenty of local buses from Talca. South from Constitución, a coast road leads to the seaside villages of **Chanco**, **Pelluhue** and **Curanipe**.

Talca

As the capital of Region VII, **TALCA** boasts its fair share of services and commercial activity, most of it centred on the main shopping street, **Calle 1 Sur**. Away from the frantic bustle of this thoroughfare, however, the rest of Talca seems to move at a snail's pace, not least the tranquil **Plaza de Armas**, shaded by graceful bougainvilleas, jacarandas and magnolias. Half-hidden beneath their foliage is a handsome 1904 iron bandstand and a number of stone statues plundered from Peru by the Talca Regiment in 1881, following their victories in the War of the Pacific. Standing on the northwest corner of the square, the Neo-Gothic **Cathedral**, built in 1954, is a pale grey church with a long, thin spire and a series of turrets running along each side. It's worth popping inside to look at the delicately coloured stained-glass Belgian windows and the sombre main altar under which a couple of long-dead bishops lie buried.

One block east of the square, on the corner of 1 Norte and 2 Oriente, the **Museo O'Higginiano** (Tues–Fri 10am–1pm & 3–7pm, Sat & Sun 10am–2pm; free) occupies a handsome colonial house that hosted some of the most important developments of the independence movement. It was here that Bernardo O'Higgins, future "Liberator" of Chile, lived as a child; where the Carrera brothers established the first *Junta de Gobierno* in 1813; and where in 1818, O'Higgins signed the declaration of Chilean independence. Today the museum houses copious (and rather dull) historical documents relating to Chilean independence, along with an eclectic assortment of oil paintings, sculpture, nineteenth-century furniture, pre-Columbian spearheads, old coins and more. A few blocks southwest at 2 Sur 1772 (near the corner with 5 Oriente),

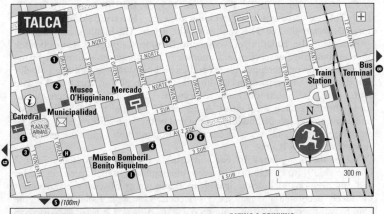

ACCOMMODATION				EATING & DRINKING	
Casa Chueca **B**	Hostal Victoria **I**	Hotel Napoli **D**		La Casa de la Esquina **5**	Picada José
Hostal del Puente **G**	Hotel Amalfi **C**	Hotel Plaza **F**		El Alero de Gastón **2**	Barrera **3**
Hostal Doña Maria **A**	Hotel Cordillera **E**	Marcos Gamero **H**		Casino de Bomberos **4**	Rubén Tapia **1**

the **Museo Bomberil Benito Riquelme** (Mon–Fri 8.30am–11pm; free) is crammed full of shiny red antique fire engines, hoses and other firefighting equipment, and makes for an enjoyable browse.

Practicalities

Buses to Talca pull in at the **Terminal de Buses** (T71/243270) on 2 Sur and 12 Oriente, ten blocks east of the Plaza de Armas. The **train station** is one block east of the bus terminal, at 11 Oriente 1150, on the other side of the tracks (T71/226254); it's served by trains from Santiago, Temuco and the nearby port of Constitución (while you're here, check out the funky murals on the walls of the ticket office). To get into the centre, take any *colectivo* or *micro* along 1 Sur (and to get back to the terminals, along 1 Norte). LAN has an office at 1 Sur 1030. There's a friendly and helpful **Sernatur** office just north of the Plaza at 1 Poniente 1281 (Mon–Fri 8.30am–5.30pm; T71/233669, F226940, Einfomaule@sernatur.cl), while **Conaf** is on the corner of 2 Poniente 1180 and 3 Sur (T71/228029).

You'll find a cluster of **places to stay** on 2 Sur, a few blocks west of the bus terminal. The stand-outs in town are the lovely *Hostal del Puente* beside the river at 1 Sur 411 (T71/220930, Ehostaldelpuente@terra.cl; ❹), with a patio and attractive gardens, the cheerful *Hotel Amalfi* at 2 Sur 1265 (T & F71/239292; ❹), which has rooms around a flower-filled patio with a little fountain, and *Hostal Victoria*, near the train station on 3 Sur 1078 (T71/232962; ❸), with basic rooms, shared baths and lots of fellow travellers. The *Hotel Cordillera*, at 2 Sur 1360 (T71/221817, F233078, Ehotelcordilleratalca@entelchile.net; ❹), has polished wooden floors and simple, whitewashed rooms (the best ones are those with shared bath). *Hotel Napoli* at 2 Sur 1314 (T71/227373; ❺) is a slightly more expensive option with a pleasant patio, as is the similarly priced, antique-filled *Hotel Marcos Gamero* at 1 Oriente 1070 (T71/223388; ❺). Another good choice is *Hostal Doña María*, 6 Oriente 1340, at 2 Norte (T71/225583; ❸), where you'll find clean rooms with private bath in an old house with a very pretty garden.

The German-Austrian guesthouse ⚡ *Casa Chueca*, 4km down the road to Las Ratras (office in Talca at Casilla 143, T71/1970096 or 9/8371440, F71/214226, Ecasachueca@trekkingchile.com, Wwww.trekkingchile.com; dorm ❷, private double ❺) is well worth the detour. The highly knowledgeable owners, who also run the tour company Turismo Caminante (see opposite), offer an abundance of services and amenities – including a pool, intensive Spanish lessons, salsa or merengue classes and a climbing wall – as well as a polyglot staff that will even prepare special dinners. They also plan to start a bird rescue centre here. The guesthouse is closed from June to August. To get here, phone ahead and then catch the Taxutal 'A' bus on 13 Oriente to the El Toro Bayo restaurant, an old colonial building at the end of the route, from where you'll be picked up. Alternatively, it's a 1.5-kilometre stroll northwest from the restaurant, along Camino Las Rastras.

One of the best **places to eat** and drink wine in Talca is *Rubén Tapia*, 2 Oriente 1339 (T71/215991, Wwww.rubentapia.cl), which prepares rabbit and other regional delicacies. Spanish food and plenty of wine are available at the nicely decorated and reasonably priced *La Casa de la Esquina*, 1 Poniente 896. Expensive but tasty dishes are served at *El Alero de Gastón* at 2 Norte 858 (T71/233785), where the usual fish and meat offerings are enlivened by a range of French-style sauces. For better-value and equally filling staples, head for the firemen's canteen, *Casino de Bomberos*, behind the **Museo Bomberil Benito**

Riquelme (see opposite). For drinks, try *El Barril* **pub**, 1 Norte 1352, which has live music on weekends.

Talca has several **casas de cambio** – AFEX Moneygram at 1 Sur 898, Oficina 15, and FOREX at 2 Oriente 1133 – and several **ATMs** on 1 Sur, around the plaza. Several **banks**, including Banco Santander, are at 1 Sur and 4 Oriente. You'll find several **car rental** outlets, including Comaba, San Miguel 2710 (☏71/263486), which is also a travel agency; Kovaks, 1 Norte 2183 (☏71/241868); Ballart, 9 Norte 1251 (☏71/226489); Rent a Car Quelle, 9 Norte 1040 (☏71/235754); and Rent a Car Rosselot at the corner of San Miguel and Varoli (☏71/247979). For **Internet access** head to *Cyberplanet Café*, 1 Poniente 1282, *Cybertec*, 6 Oriente 1467 and *Zona Cinco*, Oriente 1180. Talca area **climbing** information is available from Leonardo Cáceres Rencores (☏9/8923625), and **kayakers** will find plenty of equipment and help from Turismo 7 Rios, 1 Norte (☏71/210611, ✉turismo7rios@mixmail.com). A more general **adventure tour operator** in Talca is Turismo Caminante, Casilla 143 (☏71/1970097 or 09/8371440, ✉turismocaminante@hotmail .com, ⊛www.trekkingchile.com), which can provide travellers with bountiful information about trails, trekking, horse rides and Chile in general.

Villa Cultural Huilquilemu

Ten kilometres along the San Clemente Highway, the paved road that heads east out of Talca towards the Argentinian border, is the **VILLA CULTURAL HUILQUILEMU** (Tues–Fri 9am–1pm & 3–6.30pm, Sat noon–6pm; CH$500; ☏71/242474, ✉huilquilemu@huala.ucm.cl). A beautifully restored *casa patronal* built in 1850, it's now open to the public as a museum, administered by the Universidad Católica del Maule. Inside, three long rooms off a series of colonnaded courtyards are devoted to religious art, housing paintings, statues, cassocks, furniture and two vivid, life-sized tableaux carved out of wood depicting the Last Supper and the appearance of the Angel Gabriel to the Virgin Mary. Another room displays examples of regional *artesanía*, including pottery, woven baskets, wooden carvings, textiles and delicately woven horsehair miniatures. Wander out the back and you'll find a machinery shed full of wonderful old nineteenth-century farming and wine-making contraptions, whose precise function can only be guessed at.

There's also an *enoteca*, where several Maule Valley wineries offer tastings of their products; or, buy wine to wash down a meal in the excellent **restaurant**, open on weekends. Finally, you can take a stroll around the mature gardens, where a collection of abstract sculptures by young local artists are arranged in the shade of century-old native and exotic trees. The Villa Cultural Huilquilemu is an easy, fifteen-minute **bus ride** from Talca on any *micro* heading to San Clemente from the terminal (every 10min, CH$350).

Reserva Nacional Altos del Lircay

As you continue east along the road, a left fork onto a poor dirt road some 30km on from Villa Huilquilemu leads 27km to the mountain village of **Vilches** and from there to the entrance of the **RESERVA NACIONAL ALTOS DEL LIRCAY**, 6km beyond (daily Mar–Nov 9am–5pm; Dec–Feb 9am–8pm; CH$1000, camping $8000). This is an extremely beautiful part of the central cordillera, with a covering of ancient native forest and fantastic views onto surrounding mountain peaks and volcanoes streaked with snow. The road is complicated in winter months, so the best time to visit is October through May. There is plenty of free camping, and the **hiking trails** here are among the best in the region. Given the paucity of marked trails, maps and hiking opportunities in most Chilean parks, this is an ideal area to see the Andes on the way to or from Santiago. Close to the entrance, an **information centre** has displays on the flora and fauna within the park, and on the area's indigenous inhabitants, whose traces survive in the **piedras tacitas** (bowls used for grinding corn) carved out of a flat rock face a few hundred metres from the information centre along a signed path.

Of the various **trails** inside the reserve, the most popular is to a hilltop viewpoint at 2300m known as **El Ladrillero**. From the reserve entrance (get more detailed directions from the *guardaparque*), follow the steep track up the hillside for about 2.5km, then follow the signed turn-off, from where it's a stiff uphill walk of about five hours; count on eight hours round-trip. Water is available along the way. The views from the top are exhilarating, down to the canopy of native *coigües* and *lenga* forests covering the valley beneath, and across to the towering **Volcán Descabezado** and surrounding peaks, made famous by the book and film *Alive*, which told the story of the Uruguayan rugby team whose plane crashed here in October 1972. Sixteen of the forty-five players on board survived the crash and endured 72 days in the mountains, eating the corpses of their teammates, until they were eventually rescued. Up here you'll also find areas of exposed volcanic rock resembling giant crazy paving, giving the spot its name, which translates roughly as "brick paving". The hike from the campsite to **Laguna del Alto**, a lagoon inside a volcanic crater, is eight hours round-trip, with great lookout spots along the way. Other paths in the reserve lead through forested ravines, past small lakes and up to *miradores* (viewpoints), but they're unsigned, and difficult to find with the rudimentary map available from Conaf.

If you want to explore further, try it on **horse-back**. In Vilches, contact don Eladio (℡09/3418064), who offers rides into the park. Turismo La Posada, based at 1 Norte 2280 in Talca (℡09/7456471), offers three-day rides through the reserve, with good-quality horses, guides and camping equipment, for about US$250 per person (transport from and back to Talca, and all food included). You can make your own way with Buses Vilches (℡71/246128), which runs two daily **buses** up to Vilches Alto, continuing to the reserve entrance in summer.

There's no **accommodation** within the park, but you're allowed to camp wild. But because of wildfire dangers, no campfires are allowed; stoves are recommended. In Vilches Alto, 7km east of the park, you will find a growing number of places to stay and eat, including the comfortable *Cabañas Campo Lindo* (℡71/226765; ❹); *Hostería de Vilches* (℡71/621463; ❸), with kitchen facilities, *cabañas* for four people and a pool; and *Hostal Alto Vilches* (℡71/235442; ❸), with a swimming pool, lots of information on local hikes and excursions and three meals a day included in the rate.

Lago Colbún, the Termas de Panimávida, and Quinamávida

There are various approaches to **LAGO COLBÚN**, Chile's largest artificial reservoir, stretching 40km from east to west. From Talca, drive east and carefully follow signs to stay on Ruta 115, which is a scenic mountain road to the northern shore of the lake. Lago Colbún was created between 1980 and 1985 when the Río Maule was dammed as part of a huge hydroelectricity project, and it wasn't long before its shores, framed by undulating hills, were dotted with holiday chalets, wooden cabins and mini-markets. The town of Colbún is not actually on the lake, but just west of it.

Accommodation options include *Hotel Casas El Colorado*, on the north shore, at km 46 (T71/221750; ❹), a huge, restored colonial home with a park. In the town of Colbún is *Hotel Parador de Colbún*, about 2km from the lake at Novoa 419 (T73/351058, F73/351027, Wwww.paradorcolbun.cl; ❹), with simple rooms and a bar. *Cabañas Lago Colbún* (T71/242446 or 9/8956401, Wwww.cabanaslagocolbun.cl; ❺) has sheltered cabins in the woods for up to six people; it's open year-round. *Complejo Turístico Valshi*, several kilometres further on (T71/211565, Evalshi220@hotmail.com, Wwww.maulecordillera.cl; ❹), offers full amenities amid pleasant, tranquil surroundings. There are several **campsites**, too, but these are along the **southern shore**, which can be a pain to get to – though two bridges span the lake, access to them is often barred by the hydroelectricity company, which means going back to the Panamericana and driving instead along the southern bank of the Río Maule. This route provides access to **Colbún Alto**, a small village on the southwest shore of the lake, with several well-equipped campsites, including *Camping Pehuenche*, on the lakeshore (T73/217070 or 9/3489720; ❸). The village is served year-round by taxis from Linares.

The Río Maule road also leads to a couple of neighbouring hot-springs resorts, 5km south of the town of Colbún. The first one you reach is the **TERMAS DE PANIMAVIDA** (T73/211743, F73/351108; ❼), a nineteenth-century hacienda-style building built around numerous courtyards and patios. These are filled with immaculate gardens overflowing with rose bushes, flowering trees and ornamental fountains, and form a sharp contrast to the rambling old building, which has rather gone to seed, its grand ballrooms no longer in use. It is, however, full of character, especially the distinctly Victorian-looking wing housing the long row of cubicles where guests soak in the thermal waters (not especially hot at 33°C/91°F), mud baths and steam rooms. There are also a couple of outdoor pools, backed by lovely views onto the foothills of the cordillera. Five kilometres further south, the **Termas de Quinamávida** (T73/213887, Ereservas@termasdequinamavida.cl, Wwww.termasdequinamavida.cl; ❻) is another labyrinthine hotel, this one featuring a huge indoor thermal pool (like a massive hot bath) in addition to the usual *tinas*, mud baths, massage and Turkish baths. Attempts have been made, though not altogether successfully, to keep the building up-to-date, leaving a curious mixture of smart modern wings and dated, 1970s areas. Moreover, the guests here all seem 80 if they're a day, and the set dinner is carefully chosen with dentures in mind. Both *termas* can be visited for the day, with use of the waters costing from CH$4000–6000. You can get there from Santiago on **public transport** with Buses Villa Prat, but the bus service from Talca has been suspended. The bus leaves Santiago at 8.15am from the Terminal de Buses Sur (T2/3761758 for reservations).

San Javier, Villa Alegre and the wineries

Twenty kilometres south of Talca is a massive iron bridge over the Río Maule, followed by the turn-off to **SAN JAVIER**, a bustling little town sitting in the heart of the Maule Valley's wine country. It was clearly an important commercial centre in its day, as testified by the stately nineteenth-century mansions surrounding its wide plaza, which sports a finely carved statue of Bernardo O'Higgins in its centre. Today the town's main interest lies in its proximity to two dozen local **vineyards**, spread between and around San Javier and the village of **Villa Alegre**, 9km further south, all of which are marked on a map distributed by Sernatur in Talca. Tours of what is now called the **Ruta del Vino Valle del Maule** are becoming increasingly organized and include some fifteen wineries that are open to the public. Half-day or full-day bilingual tours can be arranged through the Ruta del Vino Valle del Maule Enoteca at Villa Cultural Huilquilemu (Mon–Fri 9am–6.30pm, Sat–Sun midday–7pm; ☎71/246460, ✆ wineroute@entelchile.net, Ⓦ www.chilewineroute.com, Ⓦ www .valledemaule.cl); 48 hours' notice is recommended. Half-day tours lasting four hours and visiting two wineries cost US$22 each for groups of four (US$10 if use your own transport). Full-day tours lasting seven hours visit three vineyards and cost US$60 per person for groups of four (US$46 with own transport). Each tour includes wine tastings. Two-day tours cost US$98 and include a visit to Altos del Lircay or trips to Vista Alegre and Yerbas Buenas. Be warned, however, that this is not Napa or Sonoma. Most of these wineries seem scarcely aware of tourists, and while none object to visitors having a look round, few offer formal tours and tastings.

One notable exception is **Viña Balduzzi** at Av Balmaceda 1189 in San Javier (Mon–Sat 9am–6pm; ☎73/322138, Ⓦwww.balduzziwines.com), which offers half-hour tours (CH$1000) of its *bodegas* that take you through the wine-making process, followed by free tastings and the chance to buy its wines, most of which are produced exclusively for export. With 200 acres of vineyards and beautiful grounds featuring an old *casa patronal*, a chapel and a *parque centenario* full of 100-year-old trees, this is a very picturesque example of a Central Valley winery. Others in the vicinity of San Javier include **Viña Vinos del Sur** (☎73/1972188, Ⓦwww.vinosdelsur.cl) to the northwest, **Viña Gillmore** (☎73/1975539, Ⓦwww.gillmore.cl), one of the oldest vineyards in Chile, and the family enterprise of **Viña J Bouchón** (☎73/1972708, Ⓦwww .jbouchon.cl), founded in 1892, and located on the road west from San Javier to Constitución.

Continuing south from San Javier you approach **VILLA ALEGRE** through a stunning avenue of trees whose branches meet overhead to form a dense green canopy. This is one of the most beautifully preserved villages in the Central Valley, and a stroll down its main street, lined with fragrant orange trees, will take you past grand *casas patronales* set in luxuriant grounds, and an almost uninterrupted stretch of nineteenth-century adobe houses topped by overhanging clay-tiled roofs leaning on thick wooden pillars. Vineyards here include **Viña El Aromo**, just off the avenue of trees (☎71/242438, Ⓦwww.elaromo.cl), whose modern, busy *bodegas* can be toured with a bit of advance notice. Also open to the public is one of Chile's oldest vineyards: founded in 1825, **Viña Carta Vieja**, Encina 231 Villa Alegre (☎73/381612, ✆info@cartavieja.cl, Ⓦwww.cartavieja.com), is on the access road to the Panamericana (right on the bus route), with impressive grounds and a lobby plastered with wine awards. It's mainly geared to showing potential clients around, but will arrange a tour if you ring the day before and is also open to the public daily from 5 to 6pm.

This circuit makes an excellent day-trip from Talca, and is, moreover, very easy to do on **public transport**, with Interbus, 13 Oriente 880 (☎71/242930) and Pullman del Sur, 2 Sur s/n (☎71/244039) providing frequent services down the Panamericana, into Villa Alegre, up to San Javier and back to Talca. There are few **places to stay** in Villa Alegre; try the tranquil *Villa Alegre Hotel* on Cancha de Carrera s/n (☎73/381214; ❸), set in a colonial house. There are also a couple of choices in San Javier, including *Residencial y Restaurante El Aromo*, Cancha de Carreras 2348 (☎73/322797; ❸).

Constitución and the coast

Halfway between San Javier and Villa Alegre, at the mouth of the Río Maule, sits the busy port of **CONSTITUCIÓN**. Now a popular holiday resort, the occasional foul stench of the local cellulose plant can permeate every corner of town, making it unlikely that you'll want to spend a lot of time here. While passing through, however, you could stop off for a drink and a snack at one of the cafés lining the shady Plaza de Armas, dominated by the rose-pink **Templo Parroquial**, built in 1860 and sporting a grand Palladian facade with three massive doors, topped by a long, pointy spire. Other possible diversions include a stroll along the wooded banks of the **Río Maule**, where you can poke your head in the shipyards to see the traditional, twenty-metre-long wooden boats being built, or a walk out to the town's grey-sand **beaches**, where huge and weird rock formations loom out of the sea. Among these is the impressive **Piedra de la Iglesia**, which does indeed resemble a towering stone church, and the fancifully named **Arco de los Enamorados** ("Lovers' Arch") and **Piedra Calabocillos** ("The Snail"). Otherwise, the main reason you might want to come here is to move on to the 60km of quiet beaches and small fishing towns stretching to the south.

From Talca, Constitución is served by plenty of **buses** and a daily **train**, which pull in opposite each other on the riverside, a few blocks northeast of the plaza. Should you need to **stay** here, head for the good-value *Residencial Anita* at Prieto 357 (☎71/673700; ❷), a small, clean, family house; *Hotel Avendaño* at O'Higgins 681 (☎71/672958; ❹), in an 1840 house with antique furniture and a pleasant patio; or the fairly smart *Hostería Constitución*, Echeverría 460 (☎71/671450, ℱ673735; ❺), perched on the banks of the Maule, with good river views and a decent restaurant. There are also a couple of beachside **campsites** on the coast road out of town – *Calabocillos* is 2km south (☎71/673988; ❷) – while *Hotel Posada Colonial*, Portales 85 (☎71/672887; ❹), offers basic furnishings. A little further afield, 12km south of Constitución on the road to Chanco, is the *Casa del Bosque Ruta Verde* (☎71/674824, ℮tours@rutaverde.cl, ⓦwww.rutaverde .cl; ❸), a pleasant wooden house surrounded by forest; they use solar power and offer horse-riding and boat trips. Besides the *Hostería Constitución*, good places to **eat** include the string of rustic fish restaurants lining the beach, near the pier – though the fumes wafting from the cellulose plant are enough to put many a diner off their food.

Chanco and the Reserva Nacional Federico Albert

From Constitución, a paved road follows the coast as far as the little seaside resort of **Curanipe**, 80km south. The first 40km takes you past extensive pine plantations bordered by grey, empty beaches and sand dunes. At km 72 there are signs for **Area Silvestre Laguna Reloca** (Mon–Fri 3–6pm, Sat & Sun 9am–6pm; free); this private park is home to flamingoes, swans and plenty of other aquatic birds. Eight kilometres past the reserve, you reach **CHANCO**, a tiny village almost fossilized in the nineteenth century, populated by ageing farmers who transport their wheat, beans and potatoes to market on creaky, ox-drawn carts. Its narrow streets are lined by colourful old adobe houses, fronted by wooden verandas, large oak doors and long, thin windows. The village's wonderful sky-blue **church** has images of various saints covering its interior.

On the northern edge of the village, the **RESERVA NACIONAL FEDER-ICO ALBERT** (daily 8am–6pm; CH$1000; ☎71/242474) is a dense pine and eucalyptus forest planted in the late nineteenth century in an attempt to hold back the advance of the coastal sand dunes – which by then had already usurped much valuable farmland. Within the forest there's an attractive **camping** area (CH$7500 per site), while a three-kilometre **path** skirts the edge of the reserve, leading to an enormous sandy **beach** with small kiosks, picnic tables and running water. Amongst the large sand dunes, planted with tall reeds to stop them from drifting, you'll find vast stretches of sheltered sites to pitch a tent. Camping aside, the only places to **stay** in Chanco are the rudimentary *Hostal Mohor* at Av Fuentealba 135 (☎73/551026), which also serves traditional dishes in its restaurant; the rather plain but functional *Residencial Lucy* at Errázuriz 2671 (☎73/1971145); and the hospitable, nameless *hospedaje* at Errázuriz 141 (☎71/551052; ❷), one block from the reserve entrance. It also provides **meals**, although a better option is *Restaurante Yugo* at Freire 292. Chanco is served by several daily **buses** from Constitución and Talca, run by Buses Contimar, 2 Sur s/n (☎71/244197).

Pelluhue and Curanipe

The pleasant summer seaside resort of **PELLUHUE** (11km south of Chanco) is composed of an undisciplined collection of houses strung around a long, curving black-sand beach. The consistent waves make it a popular destination with surfers. You'll find stacks of places to **stay**, including *Hostería Las Palmeras* at Condell 837 (☎73/541051; ❷), an old and slightly run-down building with a small garden on the edge of a cliff and access to a secluded cove. About 3km south of town, near the top of a steep hill, is *Cabañas Campomar* (☎73/541000, ⓔcampomar@ctcinternet.cl, ⓦwww.campomar.tuportal.com), which offers log cabins with an ocean view and a swimming pool for CH$31,000 for up to four people. *Hostería Blanca Reyes*, Prat 615 (☎ & ⓕ73/541061, ⓔblancareyes@123mail.cl; ❹), has clean, simple rooms, ocean views and serves terrific local seafood dishes. The town has an untidy, slightly ramshackle feel to it, however, that doesn't encourage you to stay long, and you'd be better off continuing another 7km south to the prettier village of **CURANIPE**. With a backdrop of rolling hills, wheat fields and meadows, Curanipe's dark-sand **beach**, with colourful wooden fishing boats pulled onto the sands, is a lovely place to hang out   though that's just about all there is do here. You'll find neat, simple **rooms** at the *Hostería Pacífico*, on Comercio 509 (☎73/556016; ❹). There's also an attractive **campsite**, *Los Pinos*, set in pine and eucalyptus woods right by the beach. For fresh, locally caught fish, try the **restaurant** in the *Hostería Pacífico*, or the two little beachside *picadas* down the track from the *Hostería*. Buses Amigo (☎73/511992) has **bus** service to Pelluhue and Curanipe from Constitución and Chanco. Buses Pullman del Sur (☎71/244039) and Buses Bonanza (☎71/242498) run buses from Talca (along the southern route, via the town of Cauquenes).

Chillán and the Itata Valley

Back on the Panamericana, a hundred and fifty kilometres – punctuated by the nondescript towns of **Linares** and **Parral** – separate Talca from the busy city of **Chillán**, sitting in the middle of the **Itata Valley**. Though lush and very beautiful, the broad valley is short on specific attractions, which amount to a **naval museum** in the village of Ninhue, 50km northwest of Chillán, and the hot-springs resort and ski centre of the **Termas de Chillán**, 80km east, high in the cordillera.

Chillán

Lively **CHILLÁN** is famous throughout Chile as the birthplace of Bernardo O'Higgins, the founding father of the republic. Unlike most of the towns staggered down the highway, it is, moreover, a place worth visiting in its own

right – principally for its vast **handicrafts market** and fascinating **Mexican murals** – and not just as a staging post to arrange transport to neighbouring attractions.

Arrival and information

Nearly all **long-distance buses** use the Terminal María Teresa at Av O'Higgins 010 (☎42/272149), on the northern edge of town. Buses Lit, Buses Nilahue, Cóndor Bus, InterSur, JAC, Tas Choapa and Tur Bus all operate from here. **Local** and **regional buses** operate out of the centrally located Terminal Rural, Maipón 890, a few blocks southeast of the plaza (☎42/223606). **Trains** from Santiago, Temuco and Concepción pull in opposite the old bus terminal on Avenida Brasil (☎42/222424), five blocks west of the plaza. You can pick up tourist information at **Sernatur**, 18 de Septiembre 455 (Mon–Fri 8.30am–7.30pm; ☎ & ℱ71/223272, ✉infochillan@sernatur.cl) and at the **Oficina de Turismo** in the Municipalidad on the Plaza de Armas at 18 de Septiembre 590 (Mon–Fri 9am–1pm & 3–7pm, sporadic hours May–Aug; ☎42/214117). **Conaf** has an office at Arrau 738 (☎42/221085).

Accommodation

Chillán offers a wide range of accommodation, although the upper- and mid-range hotels cater primarily to business travellers and tend to be functional rather than intimate. Budget accommodation is plentiful, but not of a great standard. Thanks to a recent influx of hip, young travellers from Chile and abroad, conveniences like private baths, constant hot water and Internet access are becoming more common in lower-priced lodging.

Casa Sonia Segui Itata 288 ☎42/214879. A popular, boisterous family house offering excellent-value rooms and kitchen facilities. Note that solo travellers might have to share rooms when it gets busy. **❷**

Gran Hotel Isabel Riquelme Arauco 600 ☎42/213663, ℱ42/211541, ✉hotelir@termaschillan.cl, ⊛www.termaschillan.cl or ⊛www.hotelisabelriquelme.cl. Old-fashioned hotel with large en-suite rooms and a restaurant with a good international menu and cheaper set meals. **❻**

Hostal Canadá Libertad 269, second floor ☎42/234515, ✉hostalcanada@hotmail.com. Small and clean, with bright, airy rooms and a rooftop terrace. **❷**

Hostal Rukalaf Arauco 740 ☎ & ℱ42/230393. Centrally located hotel with affable owners, offering decent rooms with private bathrooms and breakfast as well as secure parking. **❹**

Hotel Floresta 18 de Septiembre 278 ☎ & ℱ42/222253. Traditional, clean and pleasant house on a quiet tree-lined street. **❸**

Hotel Javiera Carrera Carrera 481 ☎ & ℱ42/221175, ✉hotel.javiera.carrera@terra.cl. Neat and comfortable, with good facilities and fair-size rooms. **❹**

Hotel Las Terrazas Constitución 664 ☎42/227000, ℱ42/227001, ✉hotel@lasterrazas.cl, ⊛www.lasterrazas.cl. On the fifth floor of a modern office block, this is an attractively decorated hotel with bright, comfortable, well-equipped rooms. **❺–❻**

Residencial 18 18 de Septiembre 317 ☎42/211102. An immaculate *residencial* complete with pool table and games room. Simple, inexpensive but filling meals are available. **❷**

The Town

Thanks to periodic earthquakes and regular Mapuche attacks, Chillán has repeatedly been rebuilt since its founding in 1550. The last major earthquake was in 1939, and most of Chillán's present architecture dates from the reconstruction of the city during the 1940s. Despite its lack of historic buildings, however, it's not an unattractive place, with wide avenues and no fewer than five open squares (that's more than any other Chilean city of its size). The focal square is the **Plaza Bernardo O'Higgins**, dominated by a giant, 36-metre concrete cross, erected to commemorate the thirty thousand inhabitants who died in the 1939 earthquake, and the futuristic, earthquake-resistant **cathedral**, built between 1941 and 1961 in the form of nine tall arches.

A few blocks northwest, the **Escuela México**, a school built with money donated by the Mexican government following the 1939 disaster, looks out over the leafy **Plaza de los Héroes de Iquique**. On Pablo Neruda's initiative, two renowned Mexican artists, David Alfaro Siqueiros and Xavier Guerrero, decorated the school's main staircase and library with fabulous murals (now a little worse for the wear) depicting pivotal figures of Mexican and Chilean history. The Mexican images, entitled *Muerte al Invasor* ("Death to the Invader"), feature lots of barely clothed native heroes and evil-looking, heavily armed Europeans engaged in various acts of cruelty. The Chilean tableau is even more gruesome, dominated by the lacerated, bleeding body of the Mapuche *toqui*, Galvarino, and his bloodthirsty Spanish captors. Joining them is a diverse group of figures that includes Luís Emilio Recabarren, the radical left-wing politician, Francisco Bilbao, the polemical essayist, and, of course, Bernardo O'Higgins, the Liberator. The school allows visitors access to the murals (Mon–Fri 10am–1pm & 3–6.30pm) in return for a small donation.

Seven blocks east, on Plaza General Lagos, the **Convento San Francisco**, dating from 1906, is one of the few buildings to have survived the 1939 earthquake, albeit in a lamentable state of repair. Inside, the **Museo Franciscano** (Tues–Sun 9am–1pm & 3–6pm; CH$500) contains a collection of colonial furniture, religious objects and military items brought to the region by members of the Franciscan order. The Franciscan clergy arrived in 1585 to convert the Mapuches, establishing fifteen missions between Chillán and Río Bueno, some 500km south. Their main targets were the sons of local Mapuche chiefs, whom they instructed in theology, philosophy, rhetoric and Latin. Five blocks south of here, filling the Plaza de la Merced, the daily **Feria de Chillán** is an exuberant open-air market selling a vast range of fresh produce and *artesanía*, ranging from knitwear and leather items to jewellery, paintings and ceramics. A souvenir-hunter's paradise, the market is especially lively on Saturdays, when it bulges out of the square and spreads into the surrounding streets. Three blocks south, tucked away in the Naval Club at Isabel Riquelme 1173, the **Museo Naval Arturo Prat** (Mon–Fri 10am–noon & 3–5pm; free) contains a small and rather disappointing collection of model ships (naval fans will be better off skipping this and heading straight for the museum at Ninhue – see p.314). Wrapping up Chillán's attractions is the **Parque Monumental Bernardo O'Higgins** (daily: April–Nov 8am–6pm; Dec–March 8am–8pm; free), a short bus ride south along Avenida O'Higgins. It's a handsomely landscaped park featuring a 60-metre wall covered with a badly faded mosaic depicting the life of the city's most famous son. In a small chapel nearby, O'Higgins' mother, Isabel Riquelme, and his sister, Rosita, are both buried, not far from the site where Bernardo was born.

Eating

For a cheap bite and a great, buzzing atmosphere, head one block north of the Feria de Chillán to the hectic **Mercado Cubierto**, crammed with butchers' stands and busy food stalls, and the slightly more restrained **Mercado Modelo**, with good-value restaurants and lines of communal tables. Next door, the **Roble Mall** has plenty of fast-food outlets that are another inexpensive option.

La Abuelita Constitución 635. The best place in Chillán for cakes and coffee, served in an attractive pastelería with wood furnishings.

Casino de Bomberos El Roble and 18 de Septiembre. Cheap Chilean cuisine served in the simple fire station canteen.

Centro Español Arauco 555. A bright, cheerful restaurant serving all the usual Chilean staples plus a range of Spanish specialities, including paella.

Club Comercial Arauco 745. Down-to-earth, inexpensive restaurant specializing in Chilean meats – especially great steaks, simply prepared. The airy dining room looks out onto a large patio.

Club Nuble 18 de Septiembre 224. With its exceptionally attentive staff and formal dining room, this place has the atmosphere of an old-fashioned gentlemen's club. The tasty menu includes meat dishes in a wide variety of sauces.

Fuente Alemana Arauco 661. Good coffee, rich cakes and hot meat sandwiches are served in a slightly disappointing, standard café.

Jai Yang Libertad 250. Reliable Chinese restaurant on a bustling main road provides standard fare.

Paraíso Oriental Constitucion 715. Reasonably priced Chinese dishes served swiftly and efficiently in calm surroundings.

Restaurante Vegetariano Arcoiris El Roble 525. Good-value vegetarian lunches, including delicious omelettes and salads.

Listings

Banks and exchange There are plenty of ATMs around the plaza on Arauco and Constitución. To change travellers' cheques or cash, try AFEX Cambios Schuler, Constitución 608 (Mon–Fri 9am–2pm & 3.30–7pm).

Car rental First, 18 de Septiembre 380 ☎42/211218; Rent a Car Chillán, 18 de Septiembre 380 ☎42/212243.

Hospital Herminia Martin (☎42/212345) is five blocks east of the Plaza de Armas, at the corner of Argentina and Francisco Ramírez.

Internet *Planet*, Arauco 683, 2nd floor; *Cybercom*, Constitución 664, Office 113.

Laundry There's a reasonably priced *lavandería*, Lavamatic, on Arturo Prat, between Claudio Arrau and Carrera. Fast Clean, at Bulnes 723, is another option.

Post Office The main *correo* is at Av Libertad 505, on the Plaza de Armas.

Telephone offices Entel is at 18 de Septiembre 746. CTC is at Arauco 625.

Travel Agencies Alas Tour, Libertad 485, Office 403 ☎42/238301 and Munditur, Libertad 692-A, ☎42/231248, ✉munditur@entelchile.net.

Termas de Chillán

The most famous and most developed mountain resort south of Santiago is the **Termas de Chillán** (information in Santiago at Pío X 2460, Office 508, ☎ & ☎2/2331313, ✉ventanas@termaschillan.cl, ⓦwww.termaschillan.cl; information in Chillán at Panamericana Norte 3651, ☎42/434200), an all-season tourist complex 80km east of Chillán, nestled at the foot of the 3122-metre **Volcán Chillán**. Surrounded by glorious alpine scenery, it possesses nine open-air **thermal pools** (whose high content of sulphur and iron is alleged to cure numerous illnesses), **steam baths** inside dripping caves, hot **mud baths**, and a state-of-the-art **spa** centre, offering massages, facials, hydro-massages and a range of other treatments applied with frightening-looking contraptions. If you're travelling with small children, this is a great spot to bring them to – it's often packed with kids and is very child-friendly. The hot baths and spa function year-round, but in winter the emphasis shifts to the resort's excellent **skiing** facilities, which include nine lifts, 28 runs, one of which is 2500m, the longest in South America, and a snowboard park. A full variety of ski packages and pricing options are available. Prices soar during certain weeks in July, when Chilean schools have a break. Other winter activities include heli-skiing, snow-biking, snowboarding and sleigh-rides pulled by Alaskan malamutes. Summer activities also abound, from hiking and mountain biking to tennis.

Adventure **sports**

If you're looking to experience an adrenaline rush in the great outdoors, you've come to the right place. Chile boasts vast tracts of unspoilt wilderness – much of it preserved within thirty-one national parks – so it's no surprise that *turismo de aventura* has long been a main lure for visitors. The country's highly varied landscape, from soaring peaks to flat altiplano, lends itself to a wide range of adventure activities: scale mighty volcanoes, mountain bike across shimmering salt flats, shoot down frothy rapids, ski glistening peaks, all without crowds trailing you.

Skiing Volcán Villarrica

Kayaking the southern fjords

Mountain biking in the Far North

Snow **sports**

Chile features some of the best skiing in the southern hemisphere and the scenery to match. Whether you're carving through fragrant alpine forest or traversing the remote back-country, you can enjoy some of the finest vistas in South America, from dramatic backdrops of the harsh, jagged Andes and smouldering volcanoes to the vast, tumultuous ocean extending into the distance. On high-altitude slopes, the very dry powder snow – known as "champagne snow" – is of a quality found nowhere else.

Conveniently, the finest resorts lie just 40km from Santiago: you can easily ski neighbouring El Colorado, La Parva and Valle Nevado on a day-trip from the capital, while classy Portillo, 149km north, lies within comfortable striking distance for a weekend visit. Top ski teams frequently train on Portillo's slopes, where many speed records have been broken. Nowhere else in Chile can match these spots, but the Termas de Chillán ski centre, 480km south, isn't too far behind, offering the longest run in South America and steaming thermal pools for après-ski relaxation.

For a fun and much cheaper alternative to the main resorts, head to the fledgling, rustic ski centres dotted along the Andes south of Santiago. These include Chapa Verde, near Rancagua; Antuco, near Concepción; and El Fraile, near Coyhaique. The Centro de Ski Pucón, on the slopes of Volcán Villarrica, is ideal for families and less experienced skiers, while Cerro Mirador's exciting slopes, near Punta Arenas, draw avid thrill-seekers. Numerous resorts also offer other activities for snow-addicts, including snowboarding, tobogganing, snow-shoe walking and skidooing.

Volcano **vertigo**

Volcanoes are as defining a feature of Chile's geography as the altiplano plateau in the north or broken coastline in the south. The Andean cordillera, running the entire length of Chile, is loaded with possibilities to scale their slopes, from relatively easy day climbs for novices to challenging peaks for experts. In the Far North rise a series of huge, isolated behemoths over 6000m high that experienced climbers can tackle, including Volcán Parinacota, Volcán Llullaillaco and Volcán Ojos del Salado, Chile's highest peak and the tallest active volcano in the world.

You'll also find several challenging, technical climbs in the central Andes, from Volcán Marmolejo

White-water rafting on Río Futaleufú

to Volcán Tupungato. In the south lie the relatively diminutive volcanoes of Osorno and Villarrica – ideal for climbers with little or no experience; you can ascend these perfectly conical volcanoes on day-trips with several companies. Further south, the most popular ascents are the giant, vertiginous granite towers – Torre Central (2600m) and Cerro Paine Grande (3248m) – at the heart of Torres del Paine National Park. The Chilean climbing season extends from October to May, but the best months are January to March.

River **rush**

Countless world-class rivers cascade down the Andes, providing unforgettable white-water rafting. The once great Bío Bío, on the southern edge of the Central Valley, has been controversially tamed by a hydroelectric dam, so now the Futaleufú – venue of the Rafting World Championships in 2000 – by the Carretera Austral, and the nearby Río Baker, have risen to prominence as Chile's most challenging rivers. Both feature class III to V rapids (out of a grading system of I to VI, with VI being commercially unraftable), as well as splendid vistas of colossal volcanoes, thundering waterfalls and teeming native forest.

In the Lake District, rivers tumbling from the mountains also make for hair-raising thrills, including the roiling Río Trancura and Río Petrohue, with a seventeen-kilometre run through

Biplane over the Andes

The **Andes**
from the sky

For dizzying, birds-eye vistas of the Andean peaks, climb aboard a **hot-air balloon** or take flight in a cockpit **biplane** or **glider**, offered by various tour companies in and around Santiago. You can usually sail the skies throughout the year, due to Chile's relatively stable weather. **Paragliding** offers the chance to soar above a rolling countryside flanked by magnificent mountains. The mild conditions along the coast near Valparaíso are perfect for newbies, while those with more experience can embark on longer flights from around Santiago, the ski slopes further south and Iquique in the north.

thirteen III+ rapids. Closer to Santiago snakes the popular Río Maipo, which has exciting waters still accessible for beginners.

You can also kayak the country's waterways and lakes, although this sector of the industry is less well developed. The rivers represent a range of challenges, but because trickier sections can be easily portaged, novices are able to go along with experts. Perhaps the greatest potential for visitors lies in the burgeoning sport of sea kayaking, most often in the calm, protected waters of the southern fjords, amidst the archipelago on the eastern side of Chiloé or in the Gulf of Ancud near Hornopirén and Parque Pumalín.

Mountain **biking**

Chile's vast number of dirt tracks make for exciting mountain biking. These little-used roads criss-cross the untrammelled wilderness and provide access to breathtaking natural areas that many people miss. Favourite routes include descents from the Andes or from start-points high on the sides of volcanoes. Many cyclists pedal the popular Carretera Austral from Puerto Montt to Cochrane, which rambles through sheer cliffs and lush forest – but be prepared for spells of dismal weather along the way.

Cycling around the relatively flat altiplano in the Far North offers an incredible way to experience the region's solitude and beauty, though it's definitely more suited to an organized trip with a support vehicle, as it can be difficult to arrange any additional transport on your own (though mining lorries will sometimes pick up cyclists). Note, too, that the total absence of drinking water along the way and extreme fluctuations of temperature may mean you have to carry a very heavy load.

Trekking through Parque Nacional Torres del Paine

Sendero de Chile

To mark the 2010 bicentenary of the founding of the Chilean republic, President Lagos decided to create a monumental icon that united and symbolized the entire country, and in 2001, the hugely ambitious **Sendero de Chile** (Path of Chile) was born. The idea seems somewhat far-fetched at a glance: to thread a footpath the entire 4320-kilometre-length of the country, from the Peruvian border to Cape Horn, along the foothills of the Andes, with branches on Easter Island and the Juan Fernández Archipelago. To trek the whole of it would be the equivalent of walking from the Scottish borders to Timbuktu.

The **first section** opened in the Conguillío National Park, snaking for 17km across steep slopes blanketed in monkey-puzzle trees. Since then, stretches have been created in the central and southern parts of the country, showcasing the diverse countryside to great effect, from the eerie volcanic landscape of Parque Nacional Laguna del Laja to the dewy forests around Cerro Castillo and Parque Nacional Torres del Paine.

No one is betting on when it will be completed, but the achievement as it stands, some 805km of track in individual sections of up to 67km, is still stunning. More paths are added every year by volunteers, the armed forces and local works projects, though completion is not projected until at least 2010.

Each part of the trail has an office that provides details on where you can stay along the route, either in tents or more formal accommodation. For further information, check out the helpful ⊛www.senderodechile.cl.

△ Termas de Chillán

There are three types of **accommodation** within the resort itself, all of it top-range and very expensive. The large ✕ *Gran Hotel Termas de Chillán* (☎2/3668800 in Santiago, ☎42/434200 in Chillan; ❾) is the plushest, with first-class hotel rooms. The *Hotel Pirigallo* has both regular hotel rooms (❽) and condominium apartments that sleep up to six people (❾). From the end of June to mid-October, the resort offers week-long packages, which include half-board, complimentary use of the hot springs, saunas and health club, a seven-day lift pass and a one-hour daily group ski lesson. Prices vary but at their most expensive, the two weeks in the middle of July, double room rates for a week start at CH$840,000 (US$1400). If you're put off by the high accommodation rates, during the summer you might consider visiting for the day: use of the hot sulphur pools costs CH$12,000, while the steam baths are CH$20,000; during the ski season (normally June–Sept), **lift tickets** cost from CH$17,500. If you don't mind being 7km from the slopes, try the plush *Hotel Pirimahuida* (❽), whose room rate includes the use of a daily shuttle service to the slopes. As for eating, there are five **restaurants** scattered around the complex, serving a range of food from simple snacks to fine cuisine.

On the way up to the resort you'll pass several **campsites** along the road between km 50 and km 57. Crowded on summer weekends, these pleasant sites sit near the riverbank and offer basic facilities. Further along, between km 68 and km 75, a growing number of **lodgings** have sprung up, including *Cabañas Los Nirres* at km 71 (☎42/1973898, ✉nirres@123.cl, ⓦwww.losnirres.cl; dorm ❸, apartments for two ❹, for six ❼), which has a pool, sauna, games room and can organize bike hire; *Cabañas Blanche Neige* (☎42/242044, ✉blancheneige@vallelastrancas.cl; ❼ for up to six people), with wood-panelled cabañas and well-equipped kitchens and *Hosteling Las Trancas*, at km 73, next to the police station (☎42/213764, ⓕ 42/243211, ⓦwww.hostellinglastrancas.com; dorm ❷, *cabañas* for up to six people ❺–❻), which is the best value option in the area. The various accommodation options here are between a ten- to fifteen-minute drive from the *termas*.

Additionally, you'll find plenty of well-equipped cabins available for rent; among the best is the excellent *Parador Jamón, Pan y Vino*, at km 74

(☎42/242316, ⓕ42/211054, ⓦwww.nevadosdechillan.cl; ❼), a mountain chalet that offers the additional perk of great home-cooking, including many Spanish dishes. It's a worthwhile, though scarcely cheaper, alternative to the resort's own accommodation. A good listing of cabins is available on the Web at ⓦwww .vallelastrancas.cl and ⓦwww.nevadosdechillan.cl. Linea Azul (☎42/211192) runs a year-round bus service to Valle Las Trancas and on to the Termas, departing from Chillán at 8am and returning at 6pm (☎42/211192; CH$1800).

Santuario Cuna de Prat

Naval enthusiasts who were disappointed with Chillán's Museo Prat will not be let down by the splendidly preserved colonial **Hacienda San Agustín de Puñal** (Tues–Sun 10am–6pm; CH$1000) just outside the small village of **Ninhue**, 50km northwest of Chillán. Arturo Prat was born here in 1848, and the area is now a shrine to the naval hero, who died in 1879 in the Battle of Iquique while trying to capture a Peruvian ironclad gunship armed only with a sword. Inside the hacienda is a museum devoted to the hero, the **SANTU-ARIO CUNA DE PRAT**. While the national obsession with the young officer – who has a thousand Chilean plazas and streets named after him – continues to mystify outsiders, the museum's collection of polished, lovingly cared-for naval memorabilia and colonial furniture are worth a visit in their own right, and the building they're housed in, with its large interior patio and elegant verandas, is a beautiful example of colonial rural architecture.

Concepción and the Bío Bío Valley

South of Chillán and the Itata Valley, Chile is intersected by the great **Río Bío Bío**, generally considered to mark the southern limit of the Central Valley. One of Chile's longest rivers, it cuts a 380-kilometre diagonal slash across the country, emptying into the ocean by the large city of **Concepción**, over 200km north of its source in the Andean mountains. Recently, the river has enjoyed fame as a world-class **whitewater rafting** destination, although it is now being tamed and brought under control by hydroelectric projects and man-made dams. However, for more than three hundred years the Bío Bío was simply "La Frontera", forming the border beyond which Spanish colonization was unable to spread, fiercely repulsed by the native **Mapuche** population.

Today, the Bío Bío Valley, which stretches 400km southwest from the mouth of the Río Bío Bío near Concepción, still feels like a border, or transition zone, between the gentle pastures and meadows of central Chile, and the lakes and volcanoes of the south. While the valley floor is still covered in the characteristic blanket of cultivation, dotted with typical Central Valley towns such as **Los**

Angeles and **Angol**, the landscape on either side is clearly different. To the west, the **coastal range** – little more than gentle hills further north – takes on the abrupt outlines of real mountains, densely covered with the commercial pine forests' neat rows of trees and, further south, native araucaria trees in their hundreds, protected within the **Parque Nacional Nahuelbuta**. Cut off by these mountains, the towns strung down the coast road south of Concepción – such as **Lota**, **Arauco**, **Lebu** and **Cañete** – feel like isolated outposts, an impression enhanced by the ruins of old **forts** left over from the Spanish–Mapuche wars. To the east, the Andes take on a different appearance, too: wetter and greener, with several outstandingly beautiful wilderness areas like **Parque Nacional Laguna del Laja**, with its volcanic landscape and stunning lake, and **Parque Nacional Tolhuaca**, which also boasts the beautiful araucaria trees.

Concepción

The sprawling, fast-paced metropolis of **CONCEPCIÓN** is the region's administrative capital and economic powerhouse, and Chile's second-largest city. It sits at the mouth of the Bío Bío, 112km southwest of Chillán. A toll road connects the city to the Panamericana with turn-offs well marked near the cities of Chillán, from the north, and Collipulli, from the south. The commercial nucleus of the local forestry, agricultural, hydroelectric and coal industries, the city is surrounded by some of the ugliest industrial suburbs in the country. Nor can its centre be considered attractive, with its spread of dreary, anonymous buildings, few of them over sixty years old.

This lack of civic splendour reflects the long series of catastrophes that have punctuated Concepción's growth – from the incessant Mapuche raids during the city's days as a Spanish garrison, guarding La Frontera, to the devastating earthquakes that have razed it to the ground dozens of times since its founding in 1551. It does, however, have the energy and buzz of a thriving commercial centre, and the large number of students here at the Universidad Austral de Chile gives the place a young, lively feel and an excellent nightlife. By day, Concepción's chief attractions are its **Galería de la Historia**, depicting the city's turbulent history, and the striking Mexican mural inside the **Casa del Arte**. Sixteen kilometres north, moored in the harbour of neighbouring **Talcahuano**, the historic ironclad **gunship** *Huáscar* is another popular tourist attraction, easily reached from Concepción.

Arrival and information

Most **buses** arrive at the Terminal Collao, northeast of the centre at Tegualda 860, just off the Autopista General Bonilla (☏41/316666); from here, plenty of *colectivos* and taxis will take you into town. If you arrive with Tur Bus or Linea Azul, you may be dropped at the smaller Terminal Chillancito, also called the Terminal Henríquez, off the Autopista General Bonilla at Av Henríquez 2565 (☏41/315036). Most bus companies have their offices in the Collao terminal. However, Tur Bus also has offices at Tucapel 530 (☏41/232895), Cruz del Sur at Barros Arana 935 (☏41/240917) and Tas Choapa at Carrera 387. **Trains** from Santiago and Chillán arrive at the train station on Av Arturo Prat 501, six blocks west of the plaza (☏41/226925). If you're **flying** to Concepción, you'll land at Aeropuerto Carriel Sur, 5km northwest of town, from where you can get a taxi or minibus directly to your hotel. Airport Service (☏41/239371) runs shuttles from the airport to hotels.

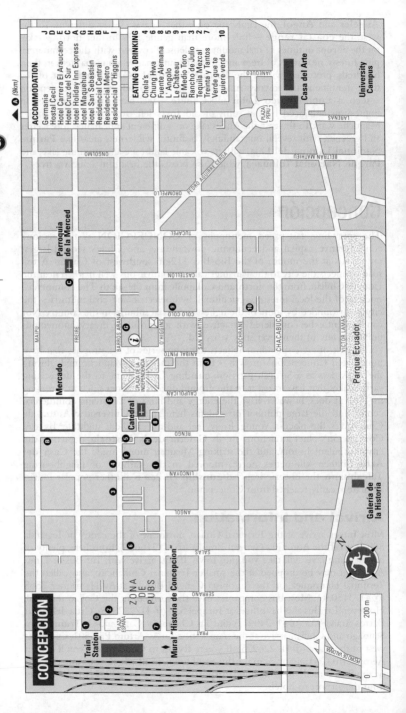

CONCEPCIÓN

ACCOMMODATION

Germania	J
Hostal Cecil	D
Hotel Carrera El Araucano	E
Hotel Cruz del Sur	C
Hotel Holiday Inn Express	A
Hotel Maquehue	G
Hotel San Sebastián	H
Residencia Central	B
Residencia Metro	F
Residencia O'Higgins	I

EATING & DRINKING

Chela's	4
Chung Hwa	6
Fuente Alemana	8
L' Angolo	5
Le Château	9
El Medio Toro	1
Rancho de Julio	3
Tequila Mezcal	2
Treinta y Tantos	7
Verde que te quiere verde	10

Casa del Arte

University Campus

Plaza Perú

Parroquia de la Merced

Mercado

Catedral

Plaza de la Independencia

Parque Ecuador

Galería de la Historia

Zona de Pubs

Plaza España

Train Station

Mural "Historia de Concepción"

200 m

You can pick up maps, brochures and other tourist information at **Sernatur** on the central square at Aníbal Pinto 460 (April–Nov Mon–Fri 8.30am–1pm & 3–5.30pm; Dec–March Mon–Fri 8.30am–8pm, Sat 9am–2pm; ☎41/227976, ✉infobiobio@sernatur.cl). **Conaf** has an office at Barros Arana 215, second floor (☎41/248048).

Accommodation

Concepción is well-endowed with upmarket **hotels** catering to business travellers, but budget accommodation is very hard to find, with no rock-bottom options at all.

Germania Aníbal Pinto 295 ☎41/747000, ✇www .hotelgermania.cl. Modern rooms with most amenities, either in the main house or in an attached apartment. ❻

Hostal Cecil Barros Arana 9 ☎ & ℻41/226603. Opposite the train station, this clean hostel may have seen better days but is welcoming, well-situated and has a decent café. ❹

🏃 **Hotel Carrera El Araucano** Caupolicán 521 ☎41/740606, ℻740690, ✉guests .concepcion@carrera.cl. Top-notch luxury hotel with an indoor pool and an excellent restaurant with a terrace over the Plaza de Armas. ❽

Hotel Cruz del Sur Freire 889 ☎41/230944, ℻41/233655, ✉hotelcruzdelsur@terra.cl. This comfortable, mid-range hotel has large shared rooms for up to five people. ❺

Hotel Holiday Inn Express Av San Andrés 38 ☎ & ℻41/481484, ✉reservas.chile@talbot.cl, ✇www.hiexpress.com. All the comforts of a North American chain hotel, including pool, Jacuzzi, cable TV, immaculate rooms, fluffy white towels and your own coffee percolator. The downside is that it's way out of the centre. ❻

Hotel Manquehue Aníbal Pinto 14 ☎41/954984, ✉reservas@hotelmanquehue.cl, ✇www .hotelmanquehue.co.cl. A quiet hotel on the 7th floor with pleasant en-suite rooms, some of which command fine views over the city. ❹

Hotel San Sebastián Rengo 463 ☎42/910270, ℻41/243412. Small hotel with its own parking and bright, spotless, slightly old-fashioned rooms with private bath. ❹

Residencial Central Rengo 673, 2nd floor ☎41/227309. An old building with lots of character and large, slightly shabby rooms, a few with outside windows. ❸

Residencial Metro Barros Arana 464 ☎41/225305. Attracts a large backpacker crowd and serves a big breakfast. Close to the Mercado Central and the plaza. ❸

Residencial O'Higgins O'Higgins 457 ☎41/228303. A small B&B with basic but adequate rooms off a long corridor; it's among the cheapest places in town. ❸

The Town

The focal point of Concepción is its busy **Plaza de la Independencia**, where Bernardo O'Higgins read the Chilean declaration of independence in January 1818. In the centre, a classical column rises above the main fountain, atop which stands a gold-painted statue symbolizing the region's agricultural wealth. On the western side of the plaza rises the Romanesque-Byzantine **Catedral de la Santísima Concepción**, built between 1940 and 1950 and adorned with faded mosaics by Alejandro Rubio Dalmati. Adjacent to the cathedral is the **Museo de Arte Sagrado** (Caupolicán 441; Tue–Fri 10am–2pm & 4–8pm, Sat–Sun 11am–2pm; CH\$400), featuring colonial artwork, marble statues gold-embroidered vestments and religious artefacts.

For a more in-depth introduction to the city, head for the **Galería de la Historia** (Tues–Fri 10am–1.30pm & 3–6.30pm, Sat–Sun 10am–2pm & 3–7pm; free) at the southern end of Lincoyán, in Parque Ecuador, where you'll find a series of impressive dioramas, some with sound and light effects, depicting the long and troubled history of Concepción. All the models and figures are beautifully made and give a good idea of the trials and tribulations suffered by the early inhabitants of this frontier town. Walk up to the far end of the park and on to Calle Larenas, where you'll reach the **Universidad Austral de Chile**, set in splendid, landscaped gardens surrounded by thickly wooded hills. This is Chile's third-largest university and has the curious distinction of being funded by the local lottery. It houses one of Chile's largest national art collections, displayed in the **Casa del Arte** (Tues–Fri 10am–6pm, Sat 10am–4pm, Sun 10am–1pm; free). The bulk of the collection consists of nineteenth-century landscapes and portraits by Chilean artists, but the showpiece is the magnificent mural in the entrance hall, *Presencia de América Latina*, painted by the Mexican artist Jorge González Camarena in 1964. Dominating the mural is the giant visage of an *indígena*, representing all the indigenous peoples of the continent, while the many faces of different nationalities superimposed on it indicate the intrusion of outside cultures and fusion of races that characterize Latin America. Woven into the densely packed images are the flags of every Latin American country, and several national icons such as Chile's condor and the feathered serpent, Quetzalcoatl, the Mexican symbol of culture. You'll find another mural, though not quite in the same league, inside the **railway station**. Over 6m long and 4m tall, this massive *Historia de Concepción*, painted by the Chilean artist Gregorio de la Fuente in 1964, depicts Concepción's history from its pre-Spanish days of smiling, contented Mapuches, through the violent Arauco war, and into the modern era of economic strength.

At the western end of the Bío Bío estuary, a fifteen-minute taxi ride from the city centre, a large park with several kilometres of footpaths and an extensive collection of native and exotic trees surrounds the **Museo Hualpén** (Tues–Sun 10am–1pm & 2–6pm; free, CH$1500 for parking). The traditional single-storey hacienda building houses an eclectic collection of souvenirs from every corner of the globe, picked up by the millionaire industrialist Pedro del Río over three world trips in the nineteenth century. Oriental furniture, Egyptian art, a collection of smoking pipes, and Hindu and Mapuche silver body ornaments, alongside fossils and mineral specimens, fill the rooms.

Sixteen kilometres northeast of Concepción is the industrial city and naval base Talcahuano, where the historic ironclad gunship **Huáscar** is moored. From Calle Chacabuco in Concepción, white buses marked "Base Naval" go from Avenida Collao and O'Higgins right to the entrance of the base, where you need to ask the guard for permission to visit the ship (Tues–Sun 9.30am–noon & 2–5.30pm; CH$1000). The *Huáscar* was built for the Peruvian navy at Birkenhead in 1866 and controlled the naval engagements during the War of the Pacific until 1879, when it was trapped off Cape Angamos, near Antofagasta, and forced to surrender. Kept in an immaculate state of preservation, the *Huáscar* is one of only two vessels of its type still afloat today. Note that you'll need to present your passport at the gate, and, although cameras are allowed, you should take care not to photograph the base installations or naval ships.

Eating, drinking and nightlife

Concepción has a good range of **eating** places to suit all pockets, and boasts the liveliest **nightlife** in the Central Valley, fuelled by the large student population. The **Barrio Estación** has a buzzing night scene, concentrated on Calle Prat, that revolves mainly around a string of small, intimate restaurants that double up as bars on Friday and Saturday night; *Tequilla Mexcal*, at Prat 532, is one such place. You'll also find plenty of drinking holes on Calle Prat, including the lively *Comanche Pub*, at no. 442. If you want to go **clubbing**, head for the steamy *Hot House* at O'Higgins 2002, a short taxi ride out of town. Note that few of the places in the Barrio Estación are open for lunch, but you can enjoy a good, inexpensive meal at one of the dozens of little *picadas* in the **Mercado Central**, on the corner of Freire and Caupolicán.

Chung Hwa Barros Arana 262. Good cheap Chinese food available in this unpretentious spot.

Fuente Alemana O'Higgins 513. Reliable Chilean staples sold alongside German cakes and beers.

L'Angolo Barros Arana 494. Large, moderately priced and very popular café, full of young couples, families and frantic waiters serving delicious light meals and beer.

Le Château Colo-Colo 340 ☎41/229977. Easily the city's best restaurant, with an expensive, French-based menu of imaginative seafood and meat dishes.

El Medio Toro Prat 594. A friendly *picada* serving authentic *criollo* food like *pastel de choclo* and *humitas*. A good place for a quiet drink and a chat.

El Naturista Barros Arana 244. For inexpensive veggie lunches, this is the place – though they seem to include green beans and corn on every dish. Lunch only.

El Rancho de Julio Barros Arana 337. Head here for excellent steaks and generous *parilladas*, at decent prices, served by waiters wearing slightly comical Argentine gaucho outfits.

Tequila Mezcal Prat 532. Colourfully decorated Mexican restaurant, serving tasty fajitas and burritos, accompanied by lots of raucous margarita and tequila drinking at the weekend. Moderately priced.

Treinta y Tantos Prat 404. The longest-standing student haunt in the Barrio Estación, serving more than thirty varieties of inexpensive empanadas in a cosy setting with mellow music. Dinner only.

Verde que te quiere verde Colo Colo 170. Organic, vegetarian restaurant offering fresh juices, salads and more hearty fare in a chic, dapper dining room adjacent to an artists' gallery.

Listings

Airlines Aerolineas Argentinas, Aníbal Pinto 509, Oficina 201 ☎41/747060; American Airlines, Barros Arana 340, Local 2 ☎521616, ⒻP521611; LAN, Barros Arana 600 ☎41/248824 and Colo-Colo 550.

Banks and exchange There are many banks with ATMs, most of them on O'Higgins, by the plaza. To change money, try Cambio Fides and AFEX inside the small shopping centre at Barros Arana 565. Another is Varex, at O'Higgins 537.

Bicycle repairs Martínez, Maipu 297.

Car rental Avis, Chacabuco 726 ☎41/235837, ⒻP254551 and at the airport ☎41/180089; Budget,

Chacabuco 175 ☎41/12438, ⒻP211315 and at the airport ☎41/732070; Econorent, Castel-lón 134 ☎41/225377, ⒻP41/245550 and at the airport ☎41/732121; First, Cochrane 862 ☎ & ⒻP42/223121 and at the airport ☎41/732050; Full Famas, O'Higgins 320 ☎41/248300; Hertz, Prat 248 ☎41/230341.

Cinema Theatre Cine Concepción, O'Higgins 650 ☎42/227193.

Consulates Argentina, O'Higgins 420 Oficina 82 ☎41/230257; Canada, Caupolicán 245 ☎41/367553; UK, Galvarino 692 ☎41/225655; Italy, Barros Arana 245 ☎41/229506.

Moving on from Concepción

There are direct **buses** to most towns and cities between Santiago and Puerto Montt, with the majority of companies leaving from the Terminal Puchucay (Collao). A notable exception is Tur Bus, whose downtown office is Tucapel 530 (☎41/316989), and which leaves from both the Terminal Puchucay and the Terminal Chillancito-Henríquez (see "Arrival and Information" p.315). If you're heading up the coast to **Tomé**, take a Costa Azul bus from Chacabuco street (☎41/651267). The coastal route south of Concepción to **Cañete, Arauco, Lebu** and **Contulmo** is served by Los Alces, Salas 1444 (☎41/240855) and Buses J. Ewert, Lincoyán 1425 (☎41/229212); both companies leave from Prat, near the train station. Moving on **by train**, there's a daily service to Santiago, and three per day to Chillán. There are regular **flights** from Concepción to most major cities between Arica and Punta Arenas. Several minibus companies offer inexpensive door-to-door transfers to the airport, including Airport Service (☎41/239371).

Internet *Double Click*, Chacabuco 707; *@internet*, Barros Arana 439.
Hospital San Martín and Lautaro ☎41/208500 or 41/224280.
Laundry Laverap, Caupolicán 334; Lavalimp, Freire 1360.
Post office Corner of O'Higgins and Colo-Colo.
Shipping Navimag, San Martín 553 ☎41/911910.
Telephone centres Entel, Barros Arana 541 and Colo-Colo 487.

Train information ☎41/226925 (often busy).
Travel agents There's a cluster of travel agents in an office block at O'Higgins 630, including Turismo Cocha, Oficina 309 ☎41/237303 and Aventuratur, Ejército 599 ☎41/819634. Elsewhere, you could try Chile Travel, Rengo 465 ☎41/226112, © chiletravel@entelchile.net or Gestur, Rengo 484 ☎ & ⑤ 41/225975.

The northern beaches

North of Concepción, a series of small towns and golden, sandy bays stretches up the coastline as far as the mouth of the Río Itata, 60km beyond. The first 44km, past Dichato, is paved and served by regular **buses** and **colectivos**. Heading up the road, 12km out of the city centre, you pass through the suburb of **Penco**, where the remains of a Spanish fort, **Fuerte La Planchada**, recall the area's turbulent history. Built in 1687, the fort was destroyed and rebuilt many times before becoming a prison to hold patriot soldiers during the War of Independence. Today it has been efficiently reconstructed, and retains the original long stone wall from where Spanish soldiers fired at raiding Mapuches and the occasional British pirate ship. On the fort's edge, *Casino Oriente* restaurant has steaks and fresh seafood delicacies.

A couple of gentle hills separate Penco from **Lirquén**, a small industrial harbour used for exporting timber. Its beach is nothing special, but the nearby tangle of narrow streets known as the **Barrio Chino** is full of first-class, excellent-value seafood restaurants, famous throughout the region for their clam dishes and the *paila marina* – a collection of largely unidentifiable sea creatures boiled into a salty, thick soup. Beyond Lirquén, the road runs inland for 30km through tree plantations, and the only access to the ocean along here is controlled by *Punta de Parra* (☎ & ⑤ 41/739669, ⓦ www.puntadeparra.cl). It has cabins that accommodate up to four (CH$26,000 per night) and charges CH$5000 per vehicle for admittance to the powdery white sands. There's a restaurant here, too, as well as a beautiful coastal walk along the old rail tracks that skirt this beach and several even more secluded ones.

Twenty-eight kilometres out of Concepción, the thriving timber centre, textile town and port of **Tomé** is squeezed into a small flat-bottomed valley, its suburbs pushed up the slopes of surrounding hills. Hidden from the drab town by a rocky point is the long, white-sand **Playa El Morro**, with several places to **stay** including *Cabañas Broadway*, Av Werner 1210 (☎41/658475; ❹) and *Hotel Althome*, Sotomayor 669 (☎41/650807; ❹). The beach, while very attractive, gets dreadfully crowded on summer weekends; a quieter alternative is **Playa Cocholgue**, a fine white beach studded with rocky outcrops, reached by taking the four-kilometre side road off the main coast road as you head out of Tomé. Eight kilometres north, **Dichato** – free of factories and commercial wharfs – is the most popular beach resort along this part of the coast, with a handful of **accommodation** options spread along the crescent-shaped, coastal avenue, Pedro Aguirre Cerda. *Cabañas Asturias*, at no. 734 (☎41/683000; ❹), offers inviting, fully furnished rooms and a seafood restaurant with excellent views; another good choice, at no. 760, is *Bahía Velero* (☎41/683014; ❹), a small beachside hotel with a patio where the owners like to lay on barbecues or let guests organize their own. At the southern end of the avenue, at no. 201, is the smart *Manantial* (T & F 41/681003, E consultas@hotelmanantial.cl, W www .hotelmanantial.cl; 5), boasting bright rooms with balconies and sea views, and a good, though expensive, **restaurant** serving exquisite seafood, including ceviche and a dish of salmon and conger eel in a shrimp, crab and margarita sauce. Other places to enjoy quality fish and shellfish include *Costa Bella*, Pedro Aguirre Cerda 774, and *Montecarlo*, Pedro Aguirre Ceda 665. Four kilometres north of Dichato, towards the Río Itata, there's a woodsy and restful **campsite**, *El Encanto* (T 41/650462 or 09/4400578; CH$10,000 per tent), with picnic tables, swimming, fishing and barbecue grills. Beyond here, the road turns to dirt and passes through dense forests with tracks leading off to a series of isolated, yellow-sand **beaches**, pounded by strong waves. Among the most beautiful of these are **Playa Purda**, 8km north of Dichato, and tiny **Playa Merquiche**, a further 2km north.

The southern coast road and beyond

South of Concepción, a decent road skirts the ocean, passing through the towns of Coronel, **Lota** and Arauco. This area was deserted until the mid-nineteenth century, when the Santiago industrialist Matías Cousiño discovered the enormous submarine coal seam – the **Costa del Carbón** – running off the coast.

About 150km south of Concepción, **Lebu** has great beaches, while nearby **Cañete**'s Mapuche museum is worth a visit en route to pretty **Lago Lanalhue**, 51km from Lebu. Rural areas along the coast all the way to Temuco are hotly contested battlegrounds. Intentional forest fires set by Mapuche groups asserting ancestral land claims were once frequent, and travellers were warned to avoid conflict areas where *tomas* (land seizures) were taking place, as bloody confrontations with police occurred quite frequently. Although the issue remains unresolved, there have been no recently confirmed fires or seizures. Locals can be coaxed into explaining the skirmishes in this mini-uprising, which was part of a 500-year Mapuche effort to resist assimilation by modern Chile. Los Alces and Buses J. Ewert have regular **bus** services along this route from Concepción. For coastal trips of any length, lists of cabins and housing options are maintained by the **Lanalhue Tourism Board** (T 41/613317, E info@lanalhueturismo.cl, W www.lanalhueturismo.cl).

Lota

Squeezed into a small valley on the edge of the sea, the soot-streaked town of **LOTA** was the site of Chile's first and largest coal mine, opened by Matías Cousiño in 1849. Production finally ceased in 1997, and today the ex-colliery is turning its attention to tourism, with newly installed hotels, swimming pools and a casino. The town centre, in the lower part of town known as Lota Bajo, does not inspire enthusiasm, though while you're here you should check out the curious **statue of the Virgin**, carved out of coal, in the church on the plaza. Spread up the hillside west of the centre is Lota Alto, containing the former miners' residences and administrative buildings, as well as the impressive **Iglesia San Matías**, where the coal baron lies buried. From here it's a short walk to the attractive **Parque de Lota** (daily: April–Oct 10am–6pm; Nov–March 10am–8pm; CH$1600), a formal garden laid out by an English landscape gardener in 1862 under the direction of Cousiño's wife, doña Isidora Goyenechea. The park also has colonial homes, a museum containing a motley collection of photographs and colonial possessions (free for visitors to the Parque de Lota, CH$600 just to visit the museum) and actors who dress and speak like characters from the last century. An earthquake destroyed the Cousiño family palace in 1960, but the ponds, fountains and Neoclassical allegorical statues have survived, interlaced with a confusing maze of narrow footpaths, which lead to a viewpoint and lighthouse on the end of the promontory. You can visit the **coal mine** on **tours** (daily 10am–5pm; ☎41/870682) guided by ex-miners, with the choice of going down the 820-metre shaft of the **Chiflón del Diablo** (CH$4000) or to the much deeper **Pique Carlos**, 1500m below ground (CH$6000) – a fascinating experience, involving a ride on a mine train through tunnels under the sea. You'll also find an above-ground museum housing old tools and mining equipment and a shop selling curios made from coal. Lota makes an easy daytrip from Concepción, with regular **bus services** provided by Buses J. Ewert, leaving from Los Carrera and Tucapel, near the train station.

Isla Santa María

From Lota's pier you can take a two-hour boat ride (departures Tues, Thur and Sat at 11am; CH$5000 return; ☎41/871322 or 09/5657253) to **ISLA SANTA MARÍA**, a small, lush island with steep cliffs, rolling hills and a population of about three thousand farmers and fishermen. El Club Aéreo Concepción (☎9/4654593) flies to the island for CH$60,000 per person. The island's mild climate and fertile soil have supported small Mapuche communities for hundreds of years. There are several secluded bays scattered around the island, with good beaches, sea lion colonies and excellent fishing for hake, bass and *congrio*. Other activities include boat trips and tractor rides with Juan Carlos Vargas (☎9/7423228) and **horse rides** with René Guzmán. Basic **accommodation** is available at *Residencial Roma*, Galvarino 223 (☎41/876257; ❷). A slightly better bet is *Hotel Angel de Peredo* at Carlos Cousino 149 (☎41/876824; ❸). Since boats **return** to Lota on Mondays, Wednesdays and Fridays at 7.30am, you will need to stay on the island overnight, unless you opt to take the more expensive option and fly back and forth.

Lebu

Seventy-six kilometres south of Lota, past a number of nondescript forestry and fishing towns, a 31-kilometre side road shoots off the highway to the small coastal town of **LEBU**, one of the few places still mining coal in this region. The main reason you might want to come here is for its huge, unspoiled **beaches**, including **Playa Millaneco**, 3km north, where you'll find several massive caves overgrown with ferns and lichen. Lebu's only other attraction is its pair of bronze cannon on display in the plaza, which were cast in Lima in 1778 and bear the Spanish coat of arms. No one is quite sure how they arrived in Lebu, but they were probably part of the booty brought back from Peru at the end of the War of the Pacific by Maximiliano Errázuriz, the owner of the local coal mines. The best place to **stay** is at *Hotel Central*, Pérez 183 (☎ & ℱ41/511904; ❹), a 110-year-old building with comfortable, excellently maintained rooms and a good **restaurant** that often serves the local speciality – king crab.

Cañete

Back on the highway, 16km south of the turn-off for Lebu, **CAÑETE** is a busy agricultural town perched on a small rise above a bend in the Río Tucapel. Just off the northern end of the main street, commanding fine views over the river valley, the historic **Fuerte Tucapel** was founded by Spanish conquistador

Pedro de Valdivia in 1552 and the site of his gruesome death at the hands of the Mapuche chief Lautaro two years later. The ruins – which amount to little more than a bit of stone terracing and four rusty cannon – actually date from the nineteenth-century reconstruction of the fort, when it was used in the later phases of the war against the Mapuche. Just south of town, 1km down the highway, the **Mapuche Museum** (Mon–Fri 9.30am–6pm, Sat 10.30am–6pm, Sun 1–6pm; CH$600; ☎41/611093) houses a fine collection of indigenous artefacts, including textiles, silver jewellery, musical instruments and weapons. Perhaps the most striking exhibit is the *ruca* in the museum's garden – a traditional Mapuche dwelling made of wood and straw. In sedate contrast, the museum's upstairs room is given over to ceramics manufactured in Lota during the late nineteenth and early twentieth century, providing a good look at middle-class tastes of the time.

If you want to **stay** in Cañete, head for the 100-year-old *Hotel Gajardo* at Séptimo de Línea 817 (☎41/611218; ❷), a family-run hotel in a charming building overlooking the valley, which only has rooms with shared bathroom facilities. For private bath, try the *Hotel Alonso de Ercilla*, at Villagrán 641 (☎41/611974; ❸) or *Hotel Nahuelbuta* at Villagrán 644 (☎41/611073; ❸). The best place to **eat** is at the *Club Social* on the plaza, in an unprepossessing building but serving well-cooked meat and fish dishes. From Cañete, a dirt road climbs 46km to Parque Nacional Nahuelbuta (see p.327), while the highway curves south through a lower pass in the Cordillera de Nahuelbuta.

Lago Lanalhue

Ten kilometres out of Cañete, the road reaches the northern shore of **LAGO LANALHUE**, nestled amongst dense pine forests on the western slopes of the coastal range. Its waters are crystal clear and warmer than the Pacific, and its heavily indented shores form numerous peninsulas and bays, some of them containing fine white sand. There are many **campsites** and **hotels** around the lake, including the *Posada Camping Playa Tranquila* (☎41/618016; ❺), a creaky old German farmhouse almost standing in the lake by the beach on its eastern shore. Close by is another fine old farmhouse, the *Cabañas Licahue* (☎09/8702822; ❺), with a swimming pool, access to several forest walks, and good home cooking. On the southern shore, upscale *Hosteriá Lanalhue* (☎41/247542; ❺) has quiet rooms on the edge of the lake with a small beach; it's open from December through March. You can buy basic provisions in the village of **Contulmo**, about 5km along the highway – while you're there, carry on a couple of kilometres around the south shore of the lake to visit the **Molino Grollmus** (Jan–April Mon–Sat 10–11am & 6–7pm, but probably more sporadic; CH$500), an early twentieth-century wooden mill whose gardens contain an impressive collection of *copihues* (Chile's national flower, the one featured on the boxes of the most common brand of matches) in the country. Some 44km east of Contulmo, the highway forks, with one branch heading to the town of Angol (see p.326), and the other continuing south to the Panamericana.

Down the Panamericana to the Salto del Laja and Los Angeles

From Concepción, the southern coastal route makes an appealing diversion, but if you're in a hurry you'll want to take the direct 85km trunk road back to the Panamericana. Heading south from there, the first major town you reach is **Los Angeles**, some 50km down the highway; halfway along this route, the Panamericana crosses the Río Laja. Until recently the highway passed directly by the **Salto del Laja**, which ranks among the most impressive waterfalls in Chile. It's still a good break spot on the long drive from Santiago, but beware of old maps that show the highway cruising by the falls. To actually get to the Salto del Laja, you'll need to follow the turn off-signs for the "Salto", which lead to the old highway. From there you will see the falls – cascading almost 50m from two crescent-shaped cliffs down to a rocky canyon, they appear as a broad white curtain of foam, almost like a miniature Niagara Falls.

There are parking spaces around the bridge (surrounded by tacky souvenir stalls), and a short path passes through the cabins and campground of the *Complejo Turístico Los Manantiales* (T & F 43/314275; ❹) to a closer viewpoint. Other options include the rooms at *Hotel Salto del Laja*, Panamericana km 480, about 30km north of Los Angeles (T 43/321706, F 43/313996, E saltodellaja@entelchile.net, W www.saltodellaja.cl; ❺), which has 60 acres of parks, delightful swimming holes, Jacuzzis and waterfall views. For low-budget camping, you'll find numerous places convenient to public transport. One kilometre south of the falls, the road east (by the church) holds two year-round campsites, jointly run. The first, *Salta Chica* (T 43/314772 or 43/318220; ❷), lies 800m from the highway and has beautiful but noisy campsites. Up the road 1.5km is *Playa Caliboro* (T 43/318220; ❷) with a mini beach and swimming natural pool. Both are CH$8000 for up to five people, including hot water all day. Further south at km 495, the year-round hotel, *El Rincon* (T 09/4415019, F 43/317168, E elrincon@cvmail.cl, W www.contactchile.cl/elrincon; ❺), has cheap single rooms (❷) in addition to regular doubles, as well as pricey campsites (CH$15,000) in lovely surroundings. It also offers excursions into the practically uninhabited foothills. If you're relying on **public transport**, your best bet is to visit the falls on a short trip from Los Angeles on one of the frequent Buses Bío Bío services to Chillán – they run every fifteen minutes in both directions, so when you're ready to come back you can just flag one down without having to wait too long.

Los Angeles

LOS ANGELES itself is an easy-going agricultural town, pleasant enough with its leafy Plaza de Armas and bustling commercial core, but without any great attractions to grab your interest. Housed in the library on the southeast corner of the plaza is the town's single museum, the **Museo de la Alta Frontera** (Mon–Fri 8am–1.45pm & 2.45–6.45pm; free) where, amongst the stash of colonial rifles left over from the Arauco war, you'll find a collection of gleaming Mapuche silver ornaments and jewellery – best appreciated in January and February, when some of the items are worn and displayed to stunning effect by a local Mapuche model. While you're here, wander up to the north end of Colón, eight blocks from the plaza, to take a look at the colonial **Parroquia Perpetuo Socorro**, a church whose handsome colonnaded cloisters enclose a flower-filled garden. Otherwise, the town's main attraction for travellers is as a jumping-off point for the beautiful scenery of the **Parque Nacional Laguna del Laja** (see opposite).

Practicalities

Arriving in Los Angeles by bus, you'll be dropped at the terminal on Av Sor Vicenta 2051 (T 43/318730), the northern access road from the Panamericana;

from here, plenty of *colectivos* go into the centre. You can get **tourist informa tion** from the Oficina de Turismo in the Municipalidad, on the southeast corner of the Plaza de Armas (Mon–Fri 8.30am–1pm & 3–5.30pm; ☎43/409400), and from Cayaqui Turismo, Lautaro 252 (☎ & ⓕ43/322248). Conaf has an office at Manso de Velasco 275 (☎43/322126).

Los Angeles is short on inexpensive **accommodation**, but you'll find a few adequate spots including *Hotel Central* at Almagro 377 (☎43/323381; ❷) for basic rooms off a courtyard, or *Residencial Almagro*, Caupolicán 651 (☎43/322782; ❷), a family home with slightly gloomy rooms. Moving up the scale, *Gran Hotel Muso*, Valdivia 222 (☎43/313183, ⓦwww.hotelmuso.cl; ❻) has a bizarre decor of mismatched purple curtains, paisley quilts and abstract paint- ings, and rather faded rooms, while *Hotel Mariscal Alcázar*, Lautaro 385 (☎ & ⓕ43/311725, ehalcazar@entelchile.net; ❻) is modern and well-equipped. One of the best **restaurants** in town is at the *Club de la Union*, at Colón 261 – next door to the tourist office – which serves appetizing Chilean fare and a tasty set lunch menu. *Julio's Pizza*, Colón 452, serves generously topped home-made pizzas and pasta, and *Centro Español*, on the corner of Colon and Rengo, offers an inexpensive fixed-price menu of typical Chilean dishes such as *pastel del choclo*. *Café Suizo* at Lautaro 346 serves good coffee and *kuchen*. Local **laundry** services include Lavajet Suprema at Valdivia 516 and Lavandería Wash House at Baquedano 121. LAN has an office at Lautaro 196 (☎43/319847). You can rent cars with First, Néstor del Río 402 (☎43/369119), and Interbruna, Caupolicán 350 (☎ & ⓕ 43/313812).

Parque Nacional Laguna del Laja

Set in an otherworldly volcanic landscape of lava flows and honeycombed rock, the **Parque Nacional Laguna del Laja** (daily: April–Nov 8am–6pm; Dec–March 8am–9pm; CH$750; ☎43/321086) takes its name from the great green lake formed by the 1752 eruption of **Volcán Antuco** (2985m). The road from Los Angeles, 93km from the park, is paved for the first 66km to **Antuco**; after that, the road surface is gravel but in decent condition (4WD not neces- sary) for the 30km to the park entrance.

The park boundary is 4km east of the village of **EL ABANICO**, but the Conaf hut, where you pay your entrance fee, is 12km on from the village (though they're thinking of moving it closer to the park boundary), and the administrative and environmental **Centro de Informaciones** at Chacay, which offers talks and videos about the park, lies another kilometre beyond the hut. From here, an easy path leads a couple of kilometres to a pair of large, thundering waterfalls, **Salto las Chilcas** and **Salto del Torbellino**, fed by underground channels from the lake, which emerge here to form the source of the Río Laja. Hikes to the summit are not particularly difficult, but allow four to five hours for the trip up and three hours for the hike down, and wear strong boots as the volcanic rocks will shred light footwear. Ask at the Conaf hut for seasonal conditions and other information.

The road through the park continues east from the information centre towards the lake, passing a small **ski centre** (5km along the road) that operates from June through October on the slopes of the volcano. There's a small restaurant and simple refuge here. At this point, the road deteriorates into a terrible dirt track that skirts the southern shore of the lake for 22km, continuing to the Paso Pichachén and the Argentine border. Few vehicles make it along here, so the road serves as

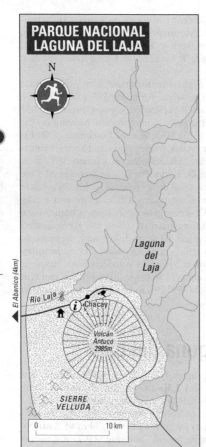

PARQUE NACIONAL
LAGUNA DEL LAJA

N

Laguna
del
Laja

El Abanico (4km)

Río Laja

Chacay

Volcán
Antuco
2985m

SIERRE
VELLUDA

0   10 km

an excellent walking trail through
the sterile landscape, with changing views of the lake and of the
mountains of **Sierra Velluda** in the
southwest, which are studded with
hanging glaciers. From the administrative centre of Chacay, short trails
lead to the Salto Las Chilcas and
Salto de Torbellino.

Getting to the park by **public
transport** is difficult: from
Los Angeles' Terminal Rural,
at Villagrán 501, Buses ERS
(☎ 43/322356) has five daily
services to El Abanico (three
on Sunday), but from there it's
a twelve-kilometre hike to the
Conaf office, and another 5km
to the lake. The only **accommodation** in the park is *Cabañas y
Camping Lagunillas* (☎ 43/321086),
which has secluded camping areas
(CH$7000 per site), four spacious
cabañas (**⑥**) and a **restaurant** by
the banks of the Río Laja, on the
way to the Conaf administration.

Angol

Sixty-four kilometres southwest of
Los Angeles, **ANGOL** is the final
major town before Temuco, the
gateway to the Lake District, and
serves as a useful base for visiting the nearby **Parque Nacional
Nahuelbuta**. The town's Plaza de Armas is one of the liveliest and most attractive in the region, full of kids on roller skates, toddlers on pedal cars and watchful
grandparents sitting beneath the shade of the numerous elms, cypresses and cedars.
In the centre of the square, the corners of a large, rectangular pool are guarded
by four finely carved marble statues of women representing the continents of
Asia, Africa, Europe and America. Dating from 1895, the statues are dated and
slightly comical; stereotypical props used to identify the continents include
a feather headdress and skirt for Miss America and a ridiculous fez for Miss
Asia. Standing on the southern side of the square is the **Cathedral**, an unexceptional red-brick church with a large tower, but there's a far prettier church
five blocks northwest, on the corner of Vergara and Covadonga – the adobe,
square-fronted **Iglesia de San Buenaventura**, painted cream and pink, and
topped by a yellow wooden tower. Founded by the Franciscan order in 1863,
this was the first Spanish church built south of the Bío Bío and functioned as
the centre of missionary work amongst the Mapuches carried out by Franciscans
after the Jesuits were expelled from Chile. Angol's **Museo de Historia**, on

Sepulveda 371 (Mon–Sat 9am–7pm; donation), displays the town's historical memorabilia, including interesting photos from the late 1880s. Better, though, is the **Museo Dillman Bullock** (Mon–Fri 9am–1pm & 3–7pm, Sat–Sun 10am–7pm; CH$450; ☎45/711142) out in the suburbs, 5km south down Avenida Bernardo O'Higgins, reached by *colectivo* from the Plaza de Armas. It's set within an agricultural college known as **El Vergel** and contains a strange assortment of archeology including pre-Columbian funeral urns, a moth-eaten mummy, Mapuche artefacts and malformed foetuses all collected by Dr Dillman Bullock, the college's first director. It's worth visiting for the grounds alone, which are beautifully landscaped with an exuberant spread of flowers and shrubs, as well as sequoias and oaks.

Practicalities

On the museum grounds is the *Hostal El Vergel* (☎45/712103 or 712403; ❹), Angol's best **place to stay**, with large rooms in an old wooden house, and a good restaurant. You'll find a few decent places in town. *Hotel Millaray* at Prat 420 (☎45/711570; ❸–❹) is a decent, good-value spot and therefore very popular; *Residencial Olimpia*, at Caupolicán 625 (☎45/711162; ❸), has reasonable rooms in a family home; a couple of blocks along at no. 498, the *Hotel Club Social* (☎ & ☎ 45/711103; ❹) offers light, airy rooms, an outdoor pool, a wood-panelled games room with fine old billiards tables, and a decent **restaurant**. At *Josánh Paecha*, Caupolicán 579, you can eat both snacks and more substantial meals in the attractive garden in nice weather. Angol's long-distance **bus terminal** is conveniently located on the corner of Caupolicán 200 and Chorillos (☎45/711100), one block north of the plaza, while rural services operate from the far end of Lautaro, three blocks east of the plaza. There's a very helpful **Oficina de Turismo** at the fork of O'Higgins and Bonilla (Mon–Fri 8.30am–1pm & 2.30–6pm; ☎45/201556), just over the river from the town centre. You can get information on Parque Nacional Nahuelbuta at Conaf's office at Prat 191 (Mon–Fri 9am–2pm; ☎45/711870).

Parque Nacional Nahuelbuta

From Angol, a dirt road (difficult to pass after rain) climbs 35km west to the entrance of **PARQUE NACIONAL NAHUELBUTA** (daily: April–Nov 8am–6pm; Dec–March 8am–9pm; CH$2000), spread over the highest part of the Cordillera de Nahuelbuta. The park was created in 1939 to protect the last remaining **araucaria trees** in the coastal mountains, after the surrounding native forest had been wiped out and replaced with thousands of radiata pines for the pulp and paper industry. Today it's a 68-square-kilometre enclave of mixed evergreen and deciduous forest, providing the coastal cordillera's only major refuge for wildlife such as foxes, pumas and *pudús* (pygmy deer). You're unlikely to catch sight of any of these shy animals, though if you look up amongst the tree trunks you may well see large black woodpeckers hammering away. Of the park's trees, star billing goes to the towering araucarias, with their thick umbrellas of curved, overlapping branches covered in stiff pine needles. Some of these trees are over 40m high, and the most mature ones in the park are more than a 1000 years old. In addition to these, you'll see giant coigües; smaller lenga, whose leaves turn dark red in autumn; and a dense undergrowth of ferns, shrubs and lichens. Many of these trees are draped in a stringy green lichen, adding a mysterious touch to the forest.

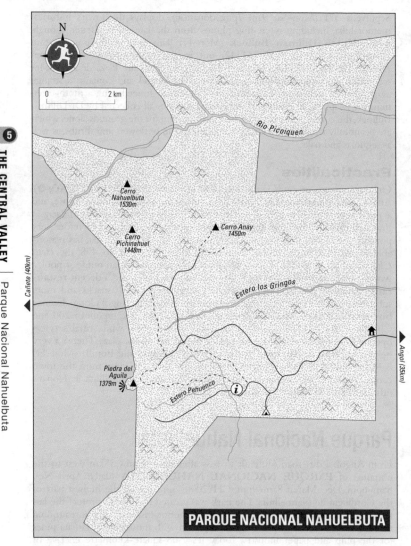

Cañete (40km)

Angol (35km)

PARQUE NACIONAL NAHUELBUTA

You can find out more about the park's flora and fauna at the **Centro de Informaciones**, 5km west along the road from the entrance. From here there are two treks: an interesting, 700-metre interpretative loop through the forest and an easy one-hour, four-kilometre hike (look out for the giant araucaria about five minutes' walk along the path, estimated to be 1800 years old) up to the **Piedra del Aguila**. This craggy rock, at 1450m, offers superb views that on clear days take in the whole width of Chile, from the Andes to the Pacific. At a slightly lower, flatter rock a few metres west, you can enjoy even better views onto the smoking volcanoes of the northern Lake District. To get here by car, take the road through the park to the signed car park, from where it's a twenty-minute walk up to the viewpoint past a series of information panels on the trees. Another rewarding trek leads up the gentle slopes of **Cerro Anay**, 4km north of the information centre, reached by a jeep track followed by a short path. Its 1400-metre peak is the best place to take in the whole of the park, with the distribution of the different types of tree clearly standing out.

Practicalities

There's no regular **public transport** to Parque Nacional Nahuelbuta for some of the year but in the summer Buses Angol and Buses Nahuelbuta come from Angol's rural terminal and from a stop on the corner of Ilabaca and Caupolicán respectively to Vegas Blancas (25km to the west of Angol) and stop at El Cruce, an hour's walk from the entrance. The park is open year-round, but expect snow and 4WD conditions June through September. There are two **camping** areas (CH$5500 per site), *Pehuenco* next to the information centre, with showers and toilets, and the more rustic *Coimallín*, with no facilities, about a twenty-minute walk away in Sector Coimallín. Bring all food, as there's nowhere to buy supplies in the park.

Parque Nacional Tolhuaca

Back on the Panamericana, 40km south of the turn-off to Angol, a detour into the Andean foothills will take you to another area of protected native forest, **PARQUE NACIONAL TOLHUACA** (daily: May–Nov 8am–6pm; Dec–April 8am–9pm; CH$1700), a pristine landscape offering some of the finest hiking in the region. The park covers a long and relatively narrow strip of land stretching through the valley of the Río Malleco, hemmed in by steep, thickly wooded hills. Dominating the bottom of the valley is the wide and shallow **Laguna Malleco**, bordered by tall reeds rich in birdlife, while other attractions include waterfalls, small lakes and hundreds of araucaria trees.

The best **approach** to the park is along the 57-kilometre dirt road (via the village of Inspector Fernández) branching east from the Panamericana, a couple of kilometres north of **Victoria** (a small, ramshackle town of no interest). This leads directly to the Conaf administration on the southeastern shore of Laguna Malleco, where you'll also find **camping** (CH$8000 per site) and picnic areas. From here, a footpath follows the northern shore of the lake for about 3km, through lush evergreen forest

△ Araucaria trees

▼ Inspector Fernández (57km) & Victoria Curacautín (33km) ▼

to the **Salto Malleco**, where the lake's waters spill down into the Río Malleco, forming a spectacular 50-metre waterfall. About halfway along this path, another trail branches north, climbing steeply up the hillside before forking in two. The left fork follows the twelve-kilometre **Sendero Prados de Mesacura** across a gentle plain before climbing steeply again through dense forest. The right fork follows the **Sendero Lagunillas** (also 12km), climbing moderately to a group of small lakes near the summit of Cerro Amarillo, from where you get fabulous panoramic views onto the surrounding peaks, including the 2800-metre Volcán Tolhuaca. Both of these are full-day hikes, requiring an early start. Following the flat path along the northern bank of the Río Malleco eastwards, after about 5km you'll reach the trailhead of the eight-kilometre **Sendero Laguna Verde**, which climbs up and around a steep hill to the small, emerald-green Laguna Verde, 1300m above sea level and surrounded by soaring peaks. This makes a good camping spot, allowing you to spread the walk over two days.

Termas de Tolhuaca

From the Conaf office, a bouncy nine-kilometre dirt road leads to the **TERMAS DE TOLHUACA** (daily 8.30am–6pm; CH$1700; ☎45/881164, ℱ55/881211, ℮tolhuaca@ctcreuna.cl, ☀www.termasdetolhuaca.co.cl), just outside the park's boundaries. You can also access the thermal pools from the south – leaving Curacautín, drive 34km north. The source of the *termas* is at the bottom of a narrow, rocky canyon, inside a large cave, where bubbling, sulphurous water seeps out of the rocks, and steam vents fill the cave with fumaroles, forming a kind of stone-age sauna. The small pools around the cave are too hot to paddle in, but a little further down the canyon, where the thermal water has mixed with cold stream water, there's a gorgeous natural pool that you can bathe in. The hot springs have been commercially exploited since 1898, shortly after they were discovered by a Russian surveyor who'd been hired to map the state's lands.

The current administration operates two **hotels** (❺–❻), one down in the canyon, close to the cave, the other higher up, near a large swimming pool filled with thermal water. The rooms are very simple for the price, but the location (particularly of the lower hotel) is stunning. You can also visit the *termas* for the day; CH$5500 buys access to the swimming pool, river and "cave sauna". It can get very busy here in January and February, especially at weekends, but outside these months the place is blissfully quiet.

The road to Lonquimay

At the dreary little town of **Victoria**, a paved road branches west from the Panamericana to the small agricultural town of **Lonquimay**, 115km away, passing the entrance to the **Reserva Nacional Malcahuello-Nalcas** en route. There's nothing especially appealing about Lonquimay itself, but the road there – running through a narrow valley overlooked by towering volcanoes – is spectacular, particularly the stretch across the **Cuesta de las Raíces**. Fifty-six kilometres out of Victoria, the road passes through the logging town of **Curacautín**, from where a 40-kilometre dirt road branches south to Lago Conguillío, in **Parque Nacional Conguillío** (see p.345). As the northern gateway to the park, Curacautín has its fair share of hotels, including the staid but well-run *Hotel Plaza*, at Yungay 157 on the Plaza de Armas (☎45/881256; ❹), and the *Hotel Turismo*, Tarapacá 140 (☎45/881116; ❷), a clean, spacious old building that also offers tasty set meals. There's little to make you want to stay in town, however, but a better option is to carry on to the more dramatic scenery further along the road – including the 60-metre waterfall, **Salto del Indio**, just off the road, 14km out of Curacautín, and, 7km beyond, the 50-metre **Saltos de la Princesa**. Three kilometres past the falls is the smart **Termas de Manzanar** hotel (☎45/881200, ✉termasmanzanar@indecom.cl, ⊛www.termasmanzanar.cl; ❼), where a number of the rooms have private spa tubs. A full 27km east of town sits the well-furnished and very popular youth hostel *La Suiza Andina* (☎9/9849541 or 45/1973725, ☏45/881892, ⊛www.suizaandina.com; ❷–❸), which provides up-to-date hiking information, horse and bike rentals, camping and laundry facilities.

Reserva Nacional Malalcahuello-Nalcas

Some 30km west of Curacautín, you'll pass the entrance to the **RESERVA NACIONAL MALALCAHUELLO-NALCAS** (daily: May–Nov 8am–6pm; Dec–April 8am–8pm; free), with the administrative office just a few hundred metres from the road. The Conaf staff are extremely helpful and friendly, and while there's no official **camping** in the reserve, they often let people camp for free in the gardens by the wardens' house. The attractions here are hiking, fly fishing and horse treks. Hiking trips on the Lonquimay Volcano take about four hours up, one down, and an ice axe and crampons are required. Ask for information at Conaf or the *Suiza Andina* hostel. Local teacher José Córdoba serves as a guide; you can ask for him in Malalcahuello, where the ascent begins. Another popular walk is the seven-kilometre **Sendero Piedra Santa**, a trail through different types of vegetation that, with an accompanying leaflet, illustrate the techniques used by Conaf to protect and manage native forest. The trail passes through quite separate areas of evergreen tepa (similar to the laurel, with strongly perfumed leaves), raulí (featuring a long, thin, cylindrical trunk), coigüe (up to 40m high, with branches only on the upper part of their trunks), lenga (home to the black woodpecker) and the famous araucaria. As well as being a good place to learn about Chile's native trees, parts of the path give excellent views onto 3125-metre **Volcán Llaima**, and 2890-metre **Volcán Lonquimay**. Count on around five hours to complete the trail.

Cuesta de Las Raíces

A couple of kilometres further along the main road from the administration, a gravel road (signed Volcán Lonquimay) branches north, and then forks in two. The left fork leads 4km to a small **Los Arenales ski centre** (☎09/8930435,

@ esquilosarenales@hotmail.com; ski ticket CH$7500, equipment rental CH$8000, half-day group ski school CH$15,000), which has eight runs on the slopes of the volcano. Open year-round, it offers overnight accommodation in the form of bunk beds (❹), and there's also a café. From here, the track continues up to a lookout point over **Cráter Navidad**, the gaping hole produced when the volcano last erupted, on Christmas Day 1988. The right fork leads 26km to the village of Lonquimay, across the **CUESTA DE LAS RAÍCES**, part of the volcanic chain that forms the highest peaks in this section of the Andes. This is a beautiful drive, through lush araucaria forests, with birds of prey, such as buzzards, swooping around the tree branches. From the pass at the top, you get an extraordinary view down over the araucarias (which normally tower above you), spread out below like a vast green carpet.

An alternative route to Lonquimay is through the **Túnel de Las Raíces** (open 24hrs; CH$1000 each way), reached by continuing along the paved road. Built in 1930 as a railway tunnel, in an abortive attempt to connect the Pacific and Atlantic by railroad, this four-and-a-half-kilometre tunnel is the longest in South America, but only wide enough for traffic to pass through in one direction at a time; be prepared to wait up to an hour for the traffic direction to reverse. Driving through is quite an adventure, as it's constantly dripping with water and littered with potholes and puddles. In winter it's even more dramatic – huge, metre-long icicles hang from the roof, transforming the tunnel into a sort of frozen Gothic cathedral.

Lonquimay

After the excitement of driving through the tunnel or crossing the Cuesta de Las Raíces, the rather sedate little town of **LONQUIMAY**, sitting at the end of the paved road, is something of a let-down. A quiet collection of small wooden houses and corner shops, the town boasts only one interesting feature – a bizarre street plan. It's laid out in the shape of a rugby ball, with an elliptical Plaza de Armas. Lonquimay is, however, beautifully located on a flat, fertile plain, to the east of the Andes. The only part of the country to cross the cordillera, it was claimed by Chile because the Bío Bío rises here, fed by numerous meandering rivers that flow through a 100-kilometre stretch of pampa. There are several places to **stay** in Lonquimay, including *Hostal Follil Pewenche*, Carrera Pinto 110 (☎45/891110; ❸), with good en-suite rooms; *Hostería Don Juancho*, O'Higgins 1130 (☎45/891140; ❸), a simple, unassuming homestay; *Hotel de Turismo*, Caupolicán 925 (☎45/891087; ❸), offering neat, sunny rooms with flowery curtains; and *Hostería El Pehuén*, O'Higgins 945 (☎45/891071; ❹), with pleasant en-suite rooms and a good-value **restaurant**.

Travel details

Buses

Chillán to: Concepción (every 15min; 1hr 15min); Curicó (8 daily; 2hr 30min); Los Angeles (every half hour; 1hr 15min); Puerto Montt (10 daily; 9hr); Rancagua (10 daily; 3hr 30min); San Fernando (10 daily; 3hr); Santiago (20 daily; 5hr); Talca (12 daily; 2hr); Temuco (10 daily; 3hr).

Concepción to: Cañete (every 30min; 3hr); Chillán (every 15min; 1hr 15min); Contulmo (5 daily; 4hr); Lebu (every 15min; 2hr 20min); Los Angeles (every 30min; 1hr 15min); Puerto Montt (15 daily; 10hr); Santiago (every half hour; 6hr); Talca (11 daily; 3hr 30min); Temuco (every hour; 4hr); Tomé (every 20min; 40min); Valdivia (11 daily; 7hr).
Curicó to: Chillán (8 daily; 2hr 30min); San Fernando (every 15min; 40min).

Los Angeles to: Angol (every 30min; 45min); Chillán (every half hour; 1hr 15min); Concepción (every half-hour; 1hr 15min); El Abanico (7 daily; 1hr 30min); Puerto Montt (10 daily; 8hr); Rancagua (5 daily; 4hr 30min); San Fernando (5 daily; 4hr); Talca (15 daily; 3hr); Temuco (20 daily; 2hr).

Rancagua to: Chillán (10 daily; 3hr 30min); Concepción (5 daily; 5hr); Lago Rapel-El Manzano (every 15min until 6.15pm; 2hr); Los Angeles (5 daily; 4hr 30min); Pichilemu (18 daily; 2hr 30min); Puerto Montt (10 daily; 13hr); San Fernando (every 15min; 40min); Santa Cruz (15 daily; 1hr 30min); Santiago (every 15min; 1hr); Talca (every 30min; 2hr); Temuco (10 daily; 7hr); Termas de Cauquenes (2 daily; 1hr 15min).

San Fernando to: Angol (2 daily; 7hr); Chillán (10 daily; 3hr); Concepción (5 daily; 5hr 30min); Curicó (every 15min; 40min); Lago Rapel-El Manzano (every 15min; 2hr 45min); Los Angeles (5 daily; 4hr); Pichilemu (every 30min; 1hr 40min); Puerto Montt (10 daily; 12hr 30min); Rancagua (every 15min; 40min); Santa Cruz (every hour; 45min); Santiago (every 15min; 1hr 30min); Talca (every 30min; 1hr 30min); Temuco (10 daily; 6hr 30min); Valdivia (5 daily; 9hr).

Talca to: Chanco (6 daily; 3hr 30min); Chillán (12 daily; 2hr); Concepción (11 daily; 3hr 30min); Constitución (summer: every 20min, winter 4 daily; 1hr 20min); Curanipe (summer: every hour; winter: 3 daily; 1hr 30min); Los Angeles (15 daily; 3hr); Pelluhue (summer: every hour; winter 3 daily; 1hr 20min); Puerto Montt (9 daily; 11hr 30min); Radal Siete Tazas (2 daily; 1hr 45min); Rancagua (every 30min; 2hr); San Fernando (every 30min; 1hr 30min); San Javier (every 15min; 30min); Santiago (20 daily; 3hr 30min); Temuco (15 daily; 5hr 30min); Vilches Alto (summer: 6 daily; winter 2 daily; 1hr 30min); Villa Alegre (every 15min; 20min).

Trains

Chillán to: Concepción (1 daily, 3hr 30min); Curicó (5 daily; 2hr 30min); Rancagua (5 daily; 3hr 30min); San Fernando (5 daily; 3hr); Santiago (5 daily; 4hr 15min); Talca (5 daily; 1hr 30min).

Curicó to: Chillán (5 daily; 2hr 30min); Rancagua (5 daily; 1hr); San Fernando (5 daily; 30min); Santiago (5 daily; 1 hr 45min); Talca (5 daily; 1hr).

Rancagua to: Chillán (5 daily; 3hr 30min); Curicó (5 daily; 1hr); San Fernando (13 daily; 30min–1hr); Santiago (metrotrén, 21 daily; 1hr); Talca (5 daily; 2hr).

San Fernando to: Chillán (5 daily; 3hr); Curicó (5 daily; 30min); Rancagua (18 daily; 30min–1hr); Santiago (metrotrén, 13 daily; 1hr 45min); Talca (5 daily; 1hr 30min).

Talca to: Chillán (5 daily; 1hr 30min); Curicó (5 daily; 1hr); Rancagua (5 daily; 2hr); San Fernando (5 daily; 1hr 30min); Santiago (5 daily; 2hr 45min).

Flights

Concepción to: Puerto Montt (6 daily; 1hr 45min); Santiago (10 daily; 1hr).

The Lake District

CHAPTER 6

Highlights

* **Parque Nacional Conguillío** Hiking is spectacular in this Andean park, where fresh volcano fields mix with ancient araucaria forests. **See p.345**

* **Lago Villarrica** At the capital of adventure tourism for Southern Chile, you can climb smoking Volcán Villarrica, raft the rapids of the Trancura or disappear into the hills on mountain bike trails. **See p.348**

* **Siete Lagos** Get away from the crowds by exploring Andean lakes that have only recently been opened to tourists. **See p.363**

* **Valdivia** Find a surprising mix of European history at this lively coastal city, where German breweries and old Spanish forts are surrounded by rivers and bays. **See p.369**

* **Lago Todos Los Santos** Its emerald green waters run up to the Argentine border, and are surrounded by Parque Nacional Vicente Pérez Rosales, Chile's largest park. **See p.394**

* **Estuario de Reloncaví** A top spot for hiking, kayaking or horse-trekking into the oldest forests of the Americas, including the Cochamó Valley, known as "Chile's Yosemite". **See p.396**

* **Puerto Varas** The introduction to Patagonia, where you can embark on rafting and fishing expeditions after gorging on the best food in the region. **See p.397**

△ Puerto Montt

The Lake District

The landscape gradually softens as you travel south along the Panamericana. Beyond the Central Valley, the road is bordered by undulating parkland, where herds of Aberdeen Angus graze under ancient oaks and beeches. This is the **LAKE DISTRICT**, which stretches 339km from **Temuco** in the north to **Puerto Montt** in the south, a region of lush farmland, dense forest, snow-capped volcanoes and deep, clear lakes, hidden for the most part in the mountains. As you drive, you can see far off to the east the occasional pyramid of a distant volcano, emitting clouds of ominous smoke, beneath which lie some of the two dozen lakes that give the region its name.

Until the 1880s, when small farm settlements arrived, the entire lakes region was blanketed in thick forests: to the north, the high, spindly araucaria; on the coast, dense *selva valdiviana*; and to the very south, 2000-year-old alerces. These forests were inhabited by the tenacious **Mapuche** (literally "people of the land"), who fought off the Inca and resisted Spanish attempts at colonization for 350 years before finally falling to the Chilean Army in the 1880s. This heritage is a badge of honour in today's Chile, and at least half a million of the region's population claims this ancestry. Throughout the Lake District there are extensive indigenous *reducciones* (reservations), and many of the museums in the area have impressive displays on Mapuche history, the centrepieces of which are collections of beautiful **silverware**.

In little over a century since the subjugation of the Mapuche, the sweat of German, Austrian and Swiss settlers has transformed this region into some of the finest **dairy farmland** in Chile: much of the primeval forest has been grubbed up (though patches remain); pines and eucalyptus trees have been planted with Prussian precision; and rolling meadowland is laid out like a blanket.

The efforts of the European settlers opened the area up to travellers, and tourists have been coming here for a hundred years. The traditional centre of tourism is the adventure sports capital **Pucón**, on the shores of **Lago Villarrica**. Here you can climb the 2840-metre **Volcán Villarrica** (and slide down the side, with an ice axe for a break) or descend into its bowels through long-cooled lava tubes. You can also hike, fish or swim in and around Lago Villarrica itself. Further south, the town of **Puerto Varas** on **Lago Llanquihue** steadily mounts a challenge to Pucón. It offers the chance to climb the Mount Fuji-like **Volcán Osorno** (2652m), horse-trek to the oldest forests in the Americas, take a boat to Argentina across the emerald-coloured **Lago Todos Los Santos**, or hike in the wilderness of the **Parque Nacional Vicente Pérez Rosales**. The serenity of the sleeping volcanoes, and the blackened earth scorched by active ones, characterize this unique corner of

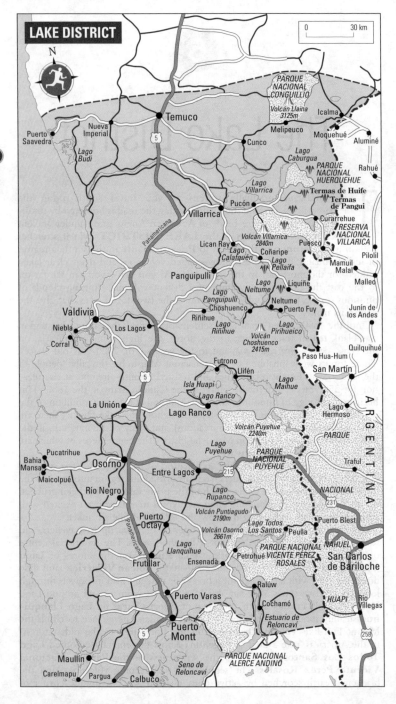

the world. In some places, such as **Parque Nacional Conguillío**, you can see the force of volcanic destruction; there, in the space of a couple of kilometres, a field of lava has torched a forest and buried it under molten rock. In other places you can feel a more benevolent side of this volcanic power – for example, in the **thermal springs** near **Puyehue** or **Liquiñe**, where you can soak your bones in steaming hot mineral waters.

But the Lake District isn't all developed for tourists by any means. For those who have the time and energy to travel to more remote areas, this region offers places that seem completely untouched by humanity. One such spot is the hardly visited **Lago Riñihue** in the **Siete Lagos**, where you can simply sit and fish and forget about the 21st century.

Travelling around the main resorts of the Lake District is fast improving as the Panamericana is now a divided highway with tolls every hour or so. Buses run regularly north and south along here, and east and west from the main transport hubs of Temuco, Osorno and Puerto Montt. Getting to more remote areas, however, can be a challenge, as the roads are bad and only served by the occasional local truck or by striking up a deal with the taxi fleets found in the main cities and towns.

Temuco and around

Once a Mapuche stronghold, **TEMUCO**, 677km south of Santiago, is the largest city in southern Chile, a commercial centre filled with jostling crowds and horn-honking traffic. Most visitors use it solely as a transport hub (the gateway to the Lake District, it's home to countless **bus services**) or as a base for exploring **Parque Nacional Conguillío** and the western mountains. But the city itself has a certain charm, due in great part to its rich **Mapuche heritage**. This is particularly evident in and around the colourful **markets**, which are among the best places in the country to hear the Mapuche language spoken. And if you don't visit another museum in the Lake District, you should at least pop into Temuco's **Museo Regional de la Araucanía**, where you'll see examples of some beautiful Mapuche silver treasure. Temuco is also proud of its connections with Chile's Nobel laureates, **Pablo Neruda** and **Gabriela Mistral** (Neruda went to school, and Mistral taught here), although the links aren't exploited as well as they could be.

Temuco was founded in 1881, and it was only when the railway from Santiago arrived in 1893 that the city began to prosper. An influx of seven thousand European immigrants from seven different countries formed the farming and commercial nucleus that soon transformed the forested valleys and plains. Delicatessen shelves in the ultramodern supermarkets reflect the cosmopolitan origins of these people, where locally made Camembert and cheddar are lined up behind dangling chorizos and *cotechini*.

Arrival and information

The **train station** (☎45/233416) is eight blocks east of the town centre at Barros Arana and Lautaro. If you're coming from a nearby town by **bus**, you'll be dropped at the rural bus terminal on Pinto and Balmaceda (☎54/210494), seven blocks north and seven east of the main Plaza Aníbal Pinto. The main long-distance bus terminal is at Vicente Pérez Rosales 01609, Sector Pueblo Nuevo (☎45/225005). Temuco's **airport**, Maquehue, lies 6km southwest of town (☎45/377718, ☎45/337782), although there are plans to build a new

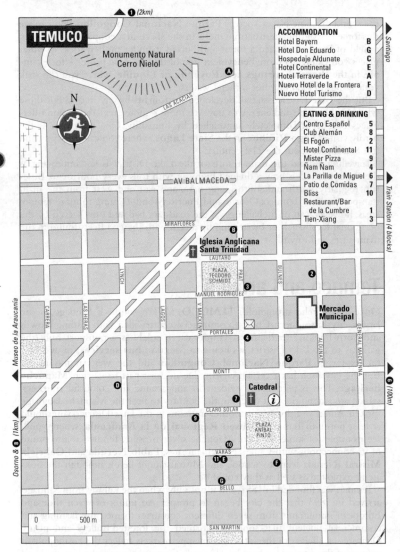

TEMUCO

Monumento Natural
Cerro Ñielol

ACCOMMODATION

Hotel Bayern	B
Hotel Don Eduardo	G
Hospedaje Aldunate	C
Hotel Continental	E
Hotel Terraverde	A
Nuevo Hotel de la Frontera	F
Nuevo Hotel Turismo	D

EATING & DRINKING

Centro Español	5
Club Alemán	8
El Fogón	2
Hotel Continental	11
Mister Pizza	9
Ñam Ñam	4
La Parilla de Miguel	6
Patio de Comidas	7
Bliss	10
Restaurant/Bar de la Cumbre	1
Tien-Xiang	3

airport in response to the continual increase in visitors. There are no buses to downtown, though Gira Tours (☎ & ℱ45/406494) can arrange transfers if you call in advance, and there are plenty of cabs outside.

For general **tourist information**, visit the Sernatur office on the north-east corner of Plaza Aníbal Pinto at Claro Solar 899 (Jan–Feb Mon–Sat 8.30am–8.30pm, Sun 8.30am–2pm; March–Dec Mon–Thurs 9am–2pm & 3–5.30pm, Fri 9am–2pm & 3–4.30pm; ☎45/211969, ℱ45/215509, ⓔinfoaraucania@sernatur.cl). There's also a tourist kiosk by the entrance to the Mercado Municipal (☎45/216360). The city's website, ⓦwww.temucochile.com,

Copihue

Chile's national flower is the rare **copihue**, a climbing plant found in the temperate rainforests of both the coastal and Andean cordilleras and most common between Concepción and Temuco. Reaching heights of up to four metres, the plant is extremely delicate and difficult to see. Only when it blooms between March and May does it stand out amongst other creepers, displaying conical, bell-shaped flowers five to ten centimetres long, ranging in colour from red and pink to almost pure white. Don't confuse it with the coicopihue, a much more widespread plant that grows between Valdivia and the Magallanes. The **coicopihue** looks much more plastic, and has reddish flowers that bloom from November to April.

Traditionally, the Mapuche have used most of the copihue plant: the flowers are edible, tasting quite sweet, and the stems and roots are used for making fine baskets, as well as being ground up and used to treat gout, rheumatism and venereal disease.

has helpful information, though it's largely in Spanish. For **maps** and information about the region's **national parks**, including Parque Nacional Conguillío, visit Conaf at Bilbao 931, second floor (Mon–Fri 8.30am–2pm; ⓣ45/298114, ⓔtemuco@conaf.cl); the staff is helpful if you can get past the secretaries.

Accommodation

Temuco is filled with **hotels**, ranging from luxury to well below basic. Most of the reasonable places to stay are near the centrally located Plaza Aníbal Pinto while the cheapest dives are around the rural bus terminal and open-air market; both these areas are not safe to wander around after dark.

Hospedaje Aldunate Aldunate 187 ⓣ45/213548. A clean, basic house with a pleasant communal sitting room and use of kitchen facilities. Ask to look at your room before you agree to a price, as some are rather drab and have no windows. Dorm accommodations also available. ❷

Hotel Bayern Prat 146 ⓣ45/276000, ⓕ45/212291, ⓔreservas@hotelbayern.cl, ⓦwww.hotelbayern.cl. This smart hotel has smallish rooms with modern amenities and slightly larger, better *ejecutivo* rooms, some with attractive exposed wooden beams and fireplaces. ❹–❺

Hotel Continental Antonio Varas 708 ⓣ45/238973, ⓕ45/233830, ⓔcontinental@ifrance.com. Hardly a cobweb has been touched in this old building, constructed in 1890. It's long been a popular haunt of Chile's political and literary elite: room nine was favoured by Pablo Neruda, room ten (joined to room nine by a connecting door) by Gabriela Mistral, and presidents Cerda and Allende preferred room eleven. It's worth reserving one of the better en-suite rooms in advance, but they cost an extra US$14. ❸–❹

Hotel Don Eduardo Bello 755 ⓣ & ⓕ45/214133, ⓔdeduardo@ctc.internet.cl. Although modern and well-furnished, this aparthotel doesn't seem to attract many customers so you can often get a good deal. Parking and kitchen facilities included. ❹

Hotel Terraverde Av Prat 0220 ⓣ45/239999, ⓕ45/239455, ⓦwww.panamericanahoteles.cl. Part of the Hotelera Pan Americana chain, this is the most luxurious hotel in the city and is located in the quiet outskirts. Facilities include a swimming pool and an international restaurant. ❼

Nuevo Hotel de la Frontera Bulnes 726 ⓣ & ⓕ45/200400, ⓦwww.hotelfrontera.cl. Facing each other across the street are two hotels, the *Clásico* and the *Nuevo*, that share many facilities. The *Nuevo* has the edge, as it's slightly more modern and has a decent restaurant and piano bar. ❺

Nuevo Hotel Turismo Lynch 563 ⓣ & ⓕ45/232902, ⓦwww.nuevohotelturismo.cl. This central three-story, thirty-room business hotel, with large and comfortable rooms, is wired with Internet and cable TV. ❹

The Town

Temuco is divided by **Avenida Caupolicán**, once part of the Panamericana, until the highway was rerouted around the town. To the west of Caupolicán are the city's quiet and exclusive residential districts, while to the east is an unattractive maze of shops and offices, rebuilt twice following a devastating fire in 1928 and a massive earthquake in 1960. The main commercial centre runs north from Plaza Aníbal Pinto along Bulnes and Prat – the cheaper shops and supermarkets are on Portales, between Bulnes and the train station.

Plaza Aníbal Pinto and Mercado Municipal

Temuco's centre is the **Plaza Aníbal Pinto**, luxuriant with fine native and imported trees, set off by a large monument depicting the struggle between the Spanish and the Mapuche Indians. The square is a relaxing place to sit and watch the world go by, but there's not much of interest around it, save, at a push, for the **Cathedral** on the northwest corner, next to a tower block adorned with an enormous cross. A modern church, it's bright and airy inside, but the yellow stained glass casts a strangely discomforting light and clashes terribly with the burgundy carpet.

A few blocks northeast of the Plaza, at the corner of Portales and Aldunate, the sprawling **Mercado Municipal** (Mon–Sat 8am–8pm & Sun 8.30am–4pm; ☎45/210964), built in 1929, is one of the best covered markets in the country. Festooned with strings of sausages and salamis, the stalls around the edge, all occupied by butchers and fishmongers, are loud with the din of whirring band saws meeting bone. In contrast, the centre of the market is a pleasant, peaceful retreat with benches and gurgling fountains, a choice of restaurants and countless craft stalls selling silver Mapuche jewellery, baskets, musical instruments, woven ponchos and more. At the entrance on Aldunate, a traditional hat stall sells inexpensive sombreros.

Plaza Teodoro Schmidt and around

Northwest of the market is **Plaza Teodoro Schmidt**, an attractive square planted with lime trees and European oaks, which in summer is filled with students selling their handiwork at small craft stalls. On the corner of the square by Lautaro and Mackenna, the clapboard **Iglesia Anglicana Santa Trinidad**, constructed in 1906, is one of the few remaining old buildings in the city centre.

Five blocks north of the Plaza Teodoro Schmidt lies the **Monumento Natural Cerro Ñielol** (daily: April–Nov 8.30am–6pm; Dec–March 8.30am–10pm; CH$700), a densely forested hill with some enjoyable walking trails. From March through May, this a good place to see red pendant **copihues**, Chile's national flower (see box p.341), while on clear days, check out the impressive view from the hilltop **lookout point**: take a taxi or hike up and relax in the café near the summit. Some say that it was on this hill in February 1881 that a treaty was signed between the Mapuche and the Chilean Army for the peaceful foundation of the future city, an event commemorated by a plaque on a patagua tree. (Most historians, however, maintain that the treaty was signed outside of town.)

East to the train station and Parque Museo Ferroviario

Out to the east, opposite the train station, is Chile's liveliest and most colourful fruit and vegetable market, the **Feria Libre** (daily: summer 8.30am–5pm; winter 8.30am–4pm. Spread across the two blocks of Avenida Pinto between Barros Arana and Avenida Balmaceda, every inch is crammed with fresh produce from all over

Chile. This is a good place to savour typical local dishes in one of the numerous restaurants, or try one of the cold pig's trotters sold on every street corner. The star attractions for most visitors, though, are the Mapuche women in traditional dress, but be warned that they might take offence at having their photographs taken.

Train buffs should walk the six blocks north to **Parque Museo Ferroviario Pablo Neruda**, site of the old rail engine house, maintenance workshops and sidings (Tues–Sun 9am–6pm; free). Among the old rolling stock and machinery are a dozen steam engines built in the US and Europe between 1915 and 1953. These were last fired up in 1972 when Chile's road hauliers went on strike during Allende's presidency. A presidential coach, built in Germany in 1923, is also on display. It has two en-suite bedrooms and a kitchen–living room of walnut wood and dark leather furniture.

Museo Regional de la Araucanía

The important **Museo Regional de la Araucanía**, Av Alemania 084 (Mon–Fri 10am–5.30pm, Sat 11am–5.30pm, Sun 11am–2pm; CH$500, Sun free; ℡45/730062), sits ten blocks west of the centre; take bus #1 or *colectivo* #11 from Manuel Montt.

A fine 1920s house with a garden full of stately palms and totem poles of fat-faced people with buckteeth, its most striking exhibit is the collection of silver **Mapuche jewellery**. Still worn by the indigenous women today, this ornamentation was originally an overt display of wealth and a means of keeping treasure portable in times of crisis; it is now a distinct art form. The combination of functionality and exhibition is best represented in the *punzón*, a cloak-fastening pin with a large orb or disc at one end. Also stunning are the *trarilonko* (a necklace of discs and silver links) and a thick, three-stranded pendant called a *prendedor akuncha*. Sadly, the museum's display, while beautiful, is a bit short on detailed explanation.

Upstairs there's a room on the **War of Arauco** (the long, bitter war the Spanish fought with the Mapuche over three hundred years until the late nineteenth century), illustrated by reproductions of old engravings. There's also a display of arms, the Spanish breastplates and swords a stark contrast with the rocks and clubs of the Mapuche. The inequality of weapons makes it all the more impressive that the Mapuche held the Spanish off for as long as they did, a feat the mighty Incas in the north never achieved. In the light of this, the sad pictures of the nineteenth-century Mapuche forced into reservations (*reducciones*) are all the more depressing.

The adjacent room deals with the area's many colonizers. A picture of President Kruger, the Afrikaner hero who stood up to the British in South Africa, is the whiskery testament to sixty Boers who made their way out here at the turn of the century to found the now defunct town of "Transvaal".

Eating and drinking

Temuco is not short of good places to eat, but it *is* a bit lacking on things to do afterwards. You'll find the cheapest set meals at the Mercado Municipal (see opposite), where a number of restaurants offering basic but filling Chilean dishes, including tasty stews, tout aggressively for business.

Bliss Antonio Varas 755. This atypical fast-food restaurant has the unique combination of loud zebra stripes and soft natural woods. It's a great place for vegetarians, with a large self-service counter and a salad bar.

Centro Español Bulnes 483. Enormous two-storey restaurant more suited to grand functions than quiet dining, though the downstairs bar has a charming, tiny garden. Ask for a plate of sliced *jamón Serrano*, a traditional Spanish ham made locally. All the meals are quite reasonably priced and large. On Fri and Sat, there's a special *Mesón de Sancho*, a dinner-dance with *parilladas*.

Club Alemán Senador Estébanez 772. Although a little way from the city centre, this Tyrolean chalet is a good place to come for very typical, moderately priced German food.

El Fogón Aldunate 288. A lively, colourful restaurant with attention to detail right down to the jaunty hand-painted plates. Offal, meat and shellfish *parilladas* are a speciality and cost CH\$11,000 for two. If you're brave, try the knockout *chuponao*, a punch made with *aguardiente* (grain alcohol).

Hotel Continental Antonio Varas 708. Both the wall clock and time itself seem to have stopped in this traditional old hotel bar. At midday there is a clubby atmosphere with regulars sipping aperitifs and playing dice games on well-scarred wooden tables underneath deer antlers. A giant, rattling Kelvinator refrigerator adds to the charm.

Mister Pizza Claro Solar and Vicuña Mackenna. Cheap pizzas and friendly service in a place filled

with students drinking *Kuntsmann* beer. Try the pizza with *merkén*, the traditional Mapuche hot sauce.

Ñam Ñam Portales 802, on the corner of Prat. A lively and inexpensive sandwich bar that also serves basic and very cheap pizzas and main meals.

La Parilla de Miguel Montt 1095. Rustic restaurant with a great wine list complemented by top-rated steaks – none of it cheap, though.

Patio de Comidas Falabella, fourth floor, in front of Plaza Aníbal Pinto. Take a break from the road at this handy spot with several fast-food eateries serving hotdogs, burgers and empanadas.

Restaurant/Bar de la Cumbre Cerro Ñielol. In the glare of daylight, the restaurant doesn't look too inviting, but it's worth a visit to enjoy a drink and the excellent views over the city from the terrace. The dinner-dances on Fri and Sat nights are also fun.

Tien-Xiang Prat, on the corner of Rodríguez. A comfortable, typically decorated Chinese restaurant with efficient service and good-value menu.

Listings

Airlines Iberia (Spain), Prat 350, Oficina 809 ☎45/215321; KLM, Claro Solar 727 ☎45/232326; LAN, Bulnes 687 ☎45/272138; Sky Airlines, Bulnes 655, Oficina 4 ☎45/747300; United, Claro Solar 727 ☎45/232326; Varig, Bello 870 ☎45/213120.

Banks and exchange Cambio Christopher, Bulnes 667, Local 202 ☎45/211680; Cambio Global, Bulnes 655, Local 1 ☎45/213699; Cambio Inter, Claro Solar 780, Local 5 ☎45/23660; Comex, Prat 427 ☎45/64880 and Prat 529 ☎45/641815.

Buses Bío Bío, Lautaro 853 ☎45/210599; Cóndor Bus, Claro Solar 598 ☎45/230979; Flota Erbuc, Miraflores 1149 ☎45/233958; Igi Llaima, Miraflores 1535 ☎45/257074; JAC, Claro Solar 598 ☎45/230979; Nar Bus, Miraflores 1535 ☎45/257074; Tur Bus, Claro Solar 598

☎45/258361; Cruz del Sur and Pullman Sur, Claro Solar 599 ☎45/730310.

Car rental Automóvil Club de Chile, San Martín 0278 ☎45/248903; Avis, V. Mackenna 448 ☎45/237575; Budget, at the airport ☎45/338836; Turismo Christopher, Antonio Varas 522 ☎ & ☎45/215988; First Rentacar, Antonio Varas 1036 ☎45/233890; Hertz, Las Heras 999 ☎45/318585; Econo-rent, Lynch 471 ☎45/215997. Many companies also have kiosks at the airport.

Consulates France, Varas 708 ☎45/238973; Germany, Caupolicán 648, 2nd floor ☎45/212387; Netherlands, España 494 ☎45/247292; Italy, Caupolicán 110, Oficina 202 ☎45/212300; Spain, M. Montt 816, Oficina 31 ☎45/210976.

Moving on from Temuco

Temuco is served by dozens of buses going up and down the Panamericana, and there's also a regular service to the coast at Puerto Saavedra and up into the mountains at Curacautín, Melipeuco and Parque Nacional Conguillío. A frequent service travels to Pucón, Villarrica and the Siete Lagos. Most of the long-distance buses now leave from the new terminal (taxis to town available for CH\$1,200), and local buses use the rural bus terminal on Pinto and Balmaceda.

Day and night train services go to Santiago, a journey that takes eleven hours (starting at CH\$7000). There are also proposals for a line to start running again between Temuco and Puerto Montt. Temuco's airport has eight daily flights to Santiago as well as service to most other major cities in Chile.

Hospital Hospital Regional, M.Montt 115 ☎45/296100; Clínica Alemana, Senador Estébanez 645 ☎45/201201.

Internet *Kafé.com*, Bulnes 314, Local 8.

Laundry Marva, M. Montt 415 and 1099; Ni-Zu, Aldunate 842.

Shopping For local crafts, try Casa de la Mujer Mapuche, Matta 283 (☎45/233886). Also try the Plaza Teodoro Schmidt, the Mercado Municipal and the Feria Libre.

Telephone centres Telefónica del Sur, Bulnes 537; Entel, Lautaro 1051 and 1311; Global, Bulnes 361, Local 102.

Tour operators Turismo Gira, M. Montt 1027, Oficina 204 (☎45/406494), is a highly respected local operator and can arrange tours to Mapuche *reducciones*, the coast and the national parks. Turismo Christopher, Bulnes 667, Local 202 (☎45/211680), is the Temuco office of a countrywide chain.

Parque Zoológico Ti-Koyam

For an interesting diversion north of Temuco, head to the **PARQUE ZOOLÓG-ICO TI-KOYAM** (Tues–Sun 10.30am–8pm; CH$1000; ☎45/531987), 18km north at km 653, where rare native animals such as puma and pudú roam the thickly forested 25-acre grounds alongside more common creatures including llamas and foxes and a number of other species from Central and South America. Several interpretative trails wind through native woods, offering the opportunity to view these rare and elusive animals relatively close-up. You'll also find designated children's play areas.

Parque Nacional Conguillío

The grey peak of Volcán Llaima (3125m) looms over the horizon about 80km east of Temuco. Wrapped around its neck is **PARQUE NACIONAL CONGUILLÍO** (daily 8am–9pm; CH$2800), a park the volcano has been doing its best to destroy with belch after belch of foul black lava. The latest noticeable eruptions here were in March 1996, and a massive fire in 2002 only added to the sense of constant evolution. It's a fascinating sight – the northern sector is lush, high forest, with steep cliffs covered in spindly armed araucaria trees often draped in furry lime-green moss. In the south, however, the volcano has wreaked havoc. The road from Temuco passes over a wide lava flow, consisting of either rolling plains of thin dust or walls of recently congealed spiked rock, and across the valley you can see two isolated hillocks of green in a sea of black – all that was missed by the unstoppable burning rivers.

The volcano dominates the park, a malevolent smouldering presence, biding its time before its next eruption. It's one of the three most active volcanoes on the continent (Chile can claim another, in Villarrica near Pucón); its last serious eruption was in 1957, though as recently as 1994 a lake, Lago Arco Iris, was formed by a fresh lava flow that blocked a river. You pass this lake on the road to the park administration office from the south; it's now as clear as ice, pierced only by the silver trunks of massive dead trees.

The northern route into the park is through the village of **Curacautín** (97km from Temuco), entering the park at sector Laguna Captrén, while the southern road from **Melipeuco** enters at sector Truful-Truful. The park administration office sits midway between the two, to the northeast of Volcán Llaima, near the wide Lago Conguillío, where you'll also find an excellent visitor centre (daily 9am–1pm & 3–7pm; ◎www.parquenacionalconguillio.cl).

Exploring the park

The park splits neatly into two main sectors, formed by the volcano's western and eastern slopes. Each has its own seasonal appeal. The **western slopes**, otherwise known as Sector Los Paraguas, shine in winter, boasting a small ski centre, the Centro de Esquí Las Araucarias (T 45/562313), with breathtaking views, two drag lifts, three runs and a refuge near the tree line. There's no hiking on the western slopes so in summer the focus shifts to the **eastern slopes**, which form the bulk of the park and are further subdivided around the two entry points (see p.345).

Those with sufficient experience, an ice axe and crampons can make the difficult five- to seven-hour **ascent of Volcán Llaima**, but you need permission from Conaf (who will want evidence of your climbing ability). You also must be prepared to deal with crevasses and fumaroles – beware of sulphur fumes at the summit. Aside from this, the best trek in the park is the several-day-long **Sierra Nevada hike**, which starts from Playa Linda on the eastern shore of Lago Conguillío, and heads up through the forest towards the mountains before plummeting down to the sedimenting, evaporating Lago Captrén, west of your starting point. The other long trail in the park, **Los Carpinteros**, is a pretty easy eight-kilometre, five-hour round-trip that starts from Lago Captrén. The highlight is an araucaria that's estimated to be 1500 years old. For a full list of trails, visit the Conaf administration office in Temuco.

Less strenuous activities are available in summer, with details posted on the visitor notice board. These include guided hikes along the trails, excursions to other parts of the park, and talks on native birds and mammals. You can go boating on the lake – boats cost CH$1500 an hour from the shop that doubles as the reception for the *cabañas* (see opposite) – or take one of the hour-long self-guided nature rambles through the beautiful forest in sector Truful-Truful. The visitor centre also has excellent displays – the best in Chile – on the geology, flora and fauna of the park. The exhibition on volcanism is particularly fascinating, especially with the brooding presence of Volcán Llaima looming on the other side of the window. Look out for the pyroclastic rock (a piece of material thrown out from the volcano when it erupted), a nugget of which has been sculpted by the air through which it flew into a smooth bomb-shape.

Park practicalities

Getting to the park without your own transport is difficult, though buses will take you as far as the gateway towns. The southern gateway to the eastern section is the tiny village of **Melipeuco**, 91km east of Temuco and 30km south of the park administration. Nar Bus (T 45/257074) runs seven **buses** a day from Temuco (four on Sun). If you get stuck in Melipeuco, there's a surprisingly good *hostería* called *Huetelén* (T 45/581005), which has wood-stove-heated *cabañas* (❹) and a basic double room (❸).

The northern route into the park is through the village of **Curacautín**, 75km from Temuco and 30km from the administration. Buses Flota Erbuc (T 45/233958) and Buses Bío Bío, Lautaro 853 (T 45/210599) run about twenty services daily from Temuco. From Curacautín you can get a taxi (CH$20,000) to the park. In winter, buses go the 106km from Temuco to the western ski slopes, but off-season, rural buses stop 20km short at the village of **Cherquenco**.

The best trekking and housing outpost is the well-marked Swiss-run hostel ⚲ *La Suizandina*, at km 83 from Temuco (T 45/1973725, ✉ lasuizandina@gmx .net, ⊛ www.suizandina.com; ❺). Open year-round, it has cabins and a small hostel from which park treks are organized, including a not-difficult ascent of the stunning volcano Volcán Lonquimay, 30km east, northeast of Curacautín.

There are plenty of **places to stay** in the park, all pretty pricey. On the edge of a dense wood, 6km in from the Melipeuco entrance, is a complex of expensive five-person *cabañas* called *La Baita Conguillío* (T & F 45/730138,

ⓔ labaita@entelchile.net, ⓦ www.labaita.co.cl; ⓞ). It's also an **activity contre**, co-ordinating trekking and eco-tourism in the summer, and skiing and snow-walking in the winter, with other programmes run year-round. There are similarly priced *cabañas* (ⓣ 45/298213; ⓺–⓻) near the park administration office – ask in the well-stocked shop on the shores of Lago Conguillío. The lower-priced *cabañas* are circular huts strapped to trees and quite a novelty, though the bedding provided is useless, so consider bringing a sleeping bag for additional comfort. *Cabañas Santa Elvira de Tracura,* 18km from Melipeuco (ⓣ 45/230227; ⓹), offers three fully furnished, comfortable *cabañas* here.

Camping in the park is extraordinarily expensive. There are about one hundred sites, mainly at Lago Conguillío and Lago Captrén, all run by concessionaires charging CH$15,000 a pitch. They're only open from November through April. Wild camping is not allowed.

From Temuco to the coast

With two national parks in the cordillera east of Temuco, it's understandable that very few visitors turn their attention westwards towards the **coast**. However, if you have time to spare or if you'd like a change from mountains and lakes, the seaside here is a refreshing change, with pretty beaches and Lago Budi, Chile's only saltwater lake, abundant in Pacific Ocean birdlife. The trip out here is interesting too, as the road passes through Mapuche communities where you'll see people living in traditional *rucas* (large communal thatched houses). A fantastic art collective, the Cholchol Foundation (Mon–Fri 9am–6pm; ⓦ www .cholchol.org), offers a top selection of Mapuche weavings in the town of **Labranza**, 16km west of Temuco on the road to Nueva Imperial and Puerto Saavedra. Though finding it requires a bit of luck, tell the driver of the Temuco to Nueva Imperial bus to stop at "Vivero San Miguel."

Puerto Saavedra

Dull as ditchwater, **PUERTO SAAVEDRA**, at the mouth of the Imperio River, 85km west of Temuco, is redeemed by its pleasant, nearby beaches and excellent fishing and birdwatching. Once a thriving port, it was hit by a tidal wave in 1960 that not only flattened all its houses but also completely changed the course of the river near its mouth. Luckily, the inhabitants realized the wave was coming and headed for higher ground in time.

You can easily reach the village by regular bus from Temuco. As for food, it boasts several worthwhile little restaurants, all of which have clean, basic **rooms**: the hospitable *Hostería Rucaleufú,* Alessandri 22 (ⓣ 45/687794; ⓷) also provides tasty meals. Five kilometres south of Puerto Saavedra is the extremely popular *Hostería Boca Budi* (ⓣ 45/1972989; ⓸), beautifully sited on the coast.

Lago Budi and the coast road south

LAGO BUDI, Chile's only saltwater lake, lies 22km south of Puerto Saavedra. It's not that impressive to look at, but offers a rare treat for birdwatchers: the lake's an extremely important breeding ground for an estimated one hundred and thirty species and a haven for a multitude of birdlife, especially black-necked swans. The surrounding countryside of gently undulating farmland is interesting too, as it's part of a large Mapuche *reducción.* a little in from the coast.

It's difficult to get down here using public transport, but Temuco's tour operators organize day-trips that cost around CH$15,000 (minimum of four people). Those with a car should consider driving the hundred kilometres south to Valdivia, via a beautiful and almost unused road along a very remote, uninhabited coast.

Lago Villarrica and around

LAGO VILLARRICA, tucked in the mountains some 86km to the southeast of Temuco, is Chile's most visited lake. The reason for its popularity lies not in its size – at only 173 square kilometres, this isn't one of the Andes' biggest lakes – nor even in the beauty lent by the lush forests along its northern shore and the symmetrical cone of Volcán Villarrica (2840m) to the east. Rather, the draw is **Pucón**, 25km along its eastern shore, a town that has made full use of its natural bounty – including two national parks, thundering rivers and a clutch of accessible hot springs – to become one of Patagonia's prime outdoor adventure centres. At the other end of the lake from Pucón is **Villarrica**, a less aesthetically pleasing but functional town with cheap rooms for rent and a beautiful view.

The area around Lago Villarrica was first settled by the Spanish in the late sixteenth century, but they didn't have much time to enjoy their new territory, as their towns were sacked by the Mapuche in 1602. Recolonization didn't take place until the Mapuche were destroyed 250 years later. With the arrival of the railroad from Santiago in 1933, the area became one of Chile's prime holiday destinations.

Villarrica

Despite sitting on the southwestern edge of the lake with a beautiful view of the volcano, **VILLARRICA** the town has a distinct lack of holiday atmosphere, and most people drive straight through it on their way to Pucón. It's pleasant enough, though, and it does have the merit of being cheaper and less crowded than its illustrious neighbour. The tourist office is particularly useful for an overview of the area.

The Town

Those interested in the Mapuche will leap at Villarrica's sole attraction, the municipal **Museo Histórico y Arqueológico**, on the main drag, adjacent to the tourist office, at Pedro de Valdivia 1050 (Jan–March Mon–Sat 9am–1pm & 6–10pm; April–Dec Mon–Fri 9am–1.30pm & 3.30–7.30pm; CH$100). It features some good displays of silver jewellery and musical instruments, and an exclusive collection of unusual Mapuche masks, while in the garden a traditional thatched *ruca* has been constructed employing thatching and wattling techniques unchanged for centuries. You'll learn even more about the Mapuche culture if you're here during the annual **festival** (late Jan to early Feb), which features traditional crafts, music and dance. You can pick up crafts year-round at the **Feria Artesanal**, around the corner from the museum on Pedro de Valdivia and Acevedo.

And that's pretty much all there is to do, other than wander down General Körner – named after the architect of the Chilean Army, the man who introduced the goosestep to the country – to the small dock on the waterfront, where you can rent a boat or just sit in the small café watching windsurfers and dinghy sailors get into trouble when El Puelche, a fierce wind that bedevils the lake, picks up.

Practicalities

Regular **buses** from Temuco, Santiago and Argentina drop passengers on Pedro de Valdivia, four blocks south and one west of the central plaza. Rural buses, meanwhile, pull in at the terminal on the corner of Manuel Antonio Matta and

LAGO VILLARRICA AND AROUND

Map labels:

Río Blanco
Termas de Río Blanco
PARQUE NACIONAL HUERQUEHUE
CERROS PICOS DEL CABURGUA
Termas Los Pozones
Termas de Quimey-Co
Termas de Huife
Cerro Redondo 1554m
RESERVA FORESTAL CAÑI
Estero Cunco
Lago Verde
Refugio Tinquilco
Lago Toro
Lago Tinquilco
Tinquilco
Paillaco
Llentane
Estero Coinuaco
Playa Negra
Lago Caburgua
Playa Negra
Pichares
Puerto Trafampulli
Río Trafampulli
Cerro La Teta
Caburgua
Ojos del Caburgua
Carileufu Falls
Río Pucón
Lago Colico
Cerro Chaquilcura 1621m
Reducción Quelhue
Río Plata
Río Liucura
Río Trancura
Río Turbio
Río Claro
Estero Totoral
El Pastal
La Leonera
Quelhue
Pucón
Río Longlong
Laguna Las Ranas
Los Raulíes
Trarileufu
Amulén
Lago Huilipilun
Santa Filomena
Bellavista
Lago Villarrica
Villa Julia
Molco
Cerro La Plaza 734m
Pedregoso
Turingia
Loncovaca
Puerto Pinar
María Luisa
Pichilafquén
Lago Pichilafquén
Villarrica
Edelweis

Directional references:
Lican Ray (30km)
Volcán Villarrica (15km), & Parque Nacional Villarrica, Sector Rucapillán (7km)
Termas de Panqui (27km) & Termas de Palguin (19km)
Termas de Parque (35km), Parque Nacional Villarrica, Sectors Quetrupillán (26km) & Puesco (60km), Argentina (87km)
Curarrehue (35km), Parque Nacional Villarrica, Sectors Quetrupillán (26km) & Puesco (60km), Argentina (87km)
Temuco (82km)
Valdivia (104km)

N
0   10 km

Vicente Reyes, three blocks south of the plaza. Small shuttle buses connect the town with Pucón, leaving almost every five minutes around the corner from the long-distance bus terminal, on Bilbao. The excellent **Oficina de Turismo** is at Pedro de Valdivia 1070 (mid-March to mid-Dec Mon–Sat 8.30am–1pm & 2.30–6.30pm; mid-Dec to mid-March daily 8.30am–11pm; ☎45/206618, ℻45/206640, ✉turis@entelchile.com, ⓦwww.villarrica-chile.net).

Villarrica isn't short of **accommodation**, and if you don't mind a half-hour ride every time you need to visit Pucón, you could save a hefty bit of money by staying here. At the cheaper end of the scale there's ⚲ *La Torre Suiza*, Bilbao 969 (☎45/411213, ✉info@torresuiza.com, ⓦwww.torresuiza. com; ❸), run by two world cyclists who've finally hung up their pedals. It offers double rooms, dorm rooms or tents, plus an open kitchen, bike rental, broadband Internet access and a book exchange. Alternatively, try the spotless *Hotel Kolping* at Riquelme 399 (☎45/411388; ❹), which also provides an excellent breakfast. Mid-range, there's *Hostería de la Colina*, Las Colinas 115 (☎ & ℻45/411503, ⓦwww.hosteriadelacolina.com; ❺–❼), run by two US teachers who have developed a fabulous hilltop inn featuring a beautiful lake view, large breakfasts (not included in the room rate), home-made ice cream and a very helpful website. The rooms are either in the main building or one of two cottages with lots of wood panelling and great views. At the more expensive end of the market you'll find *Hotel El Ciervo*, General Körner 241 (☎45/411215, ✉elciervo@villaricanet.com, ⓦwww .hotelelciervo.cl; ❺–❼), a converted family house owned by descendants of early German immigrants, with an attractive garden, a swimming pool and a terrace overlooking the lake.

Camping is also an option; buy your supplies in Villarrica where prices are cheaper. The lakeside sites on Playa Lopez near the eastern end of town are exposed to the wind. *Du Lac* (Dec–March; ☎45/210466, ℻45/214495; ❷) is the better option, planted with shrubs that offer some shelter, and with a good café in which to take refuge. You'll find six to eight camping options along the road to Pucón, but they are pricey – CH$12,000–18,000 per site and many are part of larger complexes that include minimarkets and big crowds in the summer. Huimpalay-Lemu, at km 12 out of Villarica (☎45/450075, ⓦwww .interpatagonia.com/huimpalaylemu; campsite CH$22,000) has nice, comfort-able beachfront camping open year-round.

Villarrica's **restaurants** are reasonably priced, many with far superior views to any in Pucón. You're guaranteed a pricey but fantastic Chilean meal of meat or seafood at *El Tabor*, Epulef 1187. *Las Brasas*, Pedro de Valdivia 529, which specializes in reasonably priced char-grilled meat, is a carnivore's delight. Meat-eaters will also enjoy *La Cava de Roble*, Letelier 658, where you can carve into superb steaks and wild boar on a pleasant upstairs terrace and choose from a large range of wines. *El Rey del Marisco*, Valentín Letelier 1030, has moderately priced and highly recommended seafood. The most popular lunch spot in town is *Club Social Treffpunkt*, Pedro de Valdivia 640, which has good-value set meals as well as *pastel de choclo* and other typical Chilean dishes. For a quiet **drink** on rare calm sunny days, visit *Parque Náutico*, Arturo Prat 880, a bar-restaurant that has a bright but exposed balcony right on the edge of the lake. Gringos tend to congregate at the ⚲ *Travellers Pub-Restaurant* at Letelier 753, lured by the diverse range of dishes drawn from India, China and Southeast Asia. Decent vegetarian food is also available, as are pancakes, fruit salads and milkshakes. Though there is an overabundance of facilities in town, for overall tourist services, you'll see bigger crowds and better choices in Pucón.

Pucón

Nature smiled on **PUCÓN**, 25 slow kilometres (radar traps) further along the lake from Villarrica, and helped turn it into one of Patagonia's great tourist destinations. Every year, thousands flock here to climb Volcán Villarrica, ride horses on the volcanoe's slopes in Parque Nacional Villarrica, raft the Río Trancura rapids, hike in the remote forested corners of Parque Nacional Huerquehue, fish in the crystal-clear rivers or soak their bones in the many thermal spas surrounding the town: the *termas* de Menetúe, Huife, Panqui, San Luis, Quimey-Co, Los Pozones and Palguin.

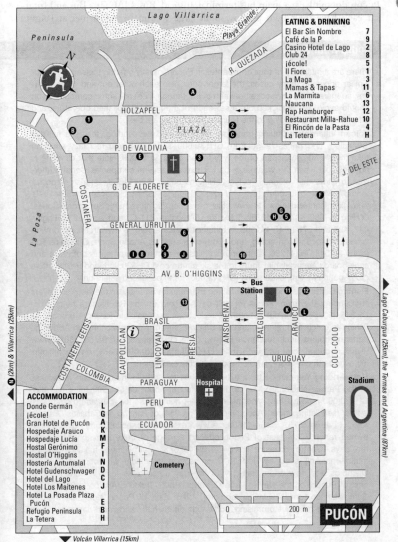

EATING & DRINKING

El Bar Sin Nombre	7
Café de la P	9
Casino Hotel de Lago	2
Club 24	8
¡école!	5
Il Fiore	1
La Maga	3
Mamas & Tapas	11
La Marmita	6
Naucana	13
Rap Hamburger	12
Restaurant Milla-Rahue	10
El Rincón de la Pasta	4
La Tetera	H

ACCOMMODATION

Donde Germán	L
¡école!	G
Gran Hotel de Pucón	A
Hospedaje Arauco	K
Hospedaje Lucía	M
Hostal Gerónimo	F
Hostal O'Higgins	I
Hostería Antumalal	N
Hotel Gudenschwager	D
Hotel del Lago	C
Hotel Los Maitenes	J
Hotel La Posada Plaza Pucón	E
Refugio Peninsula	B
La Tetera	H

Lago Villarrica

Playa Grande

R. QUEZADA

Peninsula

N

HOLZAPFEL

PLAZA

P. DE VALDIVIA

G. DE ALDERETE

J. DEL ESTE

La Poza

GENERAL URRUTIA

AV. B. O'HIGGINS

Bus Station

BRASIL

ANSORENA

PALGUIN

ARAUCO

COLO-COLO

CAUPOLICAN

LINCOYAN

FRESIA

URUGUAY

COLOMBIA

PARAGUAY

Hospital

Stadium

PERU

ECUADOR

Cemetery

COSTANERA

COSTANERA GEISS

(2km) & Villarrica (25km)

Lago Caburgua (25km), the *Termas* and Argentina (87km)

0   200 m

PUCÓN

Volcán Villarrica (15km)

But while there is undoubtedly lots to do around Pucón and plenty of places to eat and drink when you return, the town somehow lacks charm – Pucón has none of the authenticity of say, San Pedro de Atacama or Valparaíso. Everything is set up to help you sample the accessible side of Chilean wilderness, but you wouldn't want to live here: it rains seven months a year, and masses of tourists descend on the town between December 15 and March 1. Still, this probably won't stop you from enjoying yourself in Pucón, whether you arrive at the height of the crowded high season or during the more peaceful swing seasons (Sept–Nov and March–April).

Arrival and information

Pucón doesn't have a main bus terminal. Instead, Buses JAC, Tur Bus and Intersur each have their own purpose-built large terminals, the former at Palguin

Tours from Pucón

There are a multitude of **tour companies** in Pucón, mostly offering the same trips for similar prices. In many cases, the larger ones help each other out and share punters, so there's little to choose between them, though there are some companies you should avoid. We've picked out a selection of the more established operators, and arranged them according to the tours at which they are best.

Volcán Villarrica Including transport, climbing and descending, this is a full-day excursion, and prices range from CH$30,000–$35,000; if you feel lazy you can take the ski lift up for part of the way for an extra CH$4000. Note that climbing is not possible when the weather is bad. There are several companies Conaf authorizes to climb the volcano: Politur, O'Higgins 635 (T45/441373, ©turismo@politur.com, W www.politur.com); Sol y Nieve, O'Higgins 192 at Lincoyán (T45/441070, ©solnieve@entelchile.net, W www.chile-travel.com/solnieve.htm); Sur Expediciones, O'Higgins 660 (T45/444030); Trancura, O'Higgins 211-C, and also at O'Higgins 447, 498 and 575 (T45/441189, ©turismo@trancura.com, W www.trancura.com). In winter, the focus is on skiing, and companies such as Andén Sport, O'Higgins 535 (T45/441048, F441236, ©andentur@chilesat.net) rent equipment – both skis and snowboards are available. Tours to the ski centre cost CH$20,000, and Politur offers cross-country skiing excursions (CH$42,000) for experienced skiers only.

Fishing Both fly-fishing and boat fishing trips can be arranged in the lakes and rivers surrounding the town. Prices for half-day's fishing on the Río Liucura range from CH$45,000–$65,000, but substantial reductions are available for large groups. All fishing is catch and release, and the season is from November through April. The better companies include Mario's Fishing Zone, O'Higgins 590 (T9/7607280, W www.flyfishingpucon.com) and Off Limits, O'Higgins 560 (T45/442681, W www.offlimits.cl), who both offer half-, whole- and multi-day expeditions.

Horse-riding You can go for a full-day or half-day ride in the mountain wilderness of the Parque Nacional Villarrica. Prices start at about CH$15,000 for a half-day, CH$30,000 for a full-day. Most agencies offer riding tours, or you can go directly to ¡école! (see listing under "Accommodation", p.354) or Rancho de Caballos "Palguin Alto" (T45/441575, F45/441604, W www.rancho-de-caballos.com), a German-owned ranch 32km east of Pucón offering a range of treks from three hours to ten days. Centro Ecuestre Huepil (T9/6432673, ©info@huepil-malal.cl, W www.huepil-malal.cl) is run by Rodolfo Coombs, a master rider who competed in the Olympics and now offers half-day to five-day horse treks leaving from the hills east of Pucón, on the way to Lago Caburga. Horse Trekking Antilco (T9/7139758, ©info@antilco.com, W www.antilco.com), 12km east of Pucón alongside the Río Liucura is a new but promising outfit that offers half- and multi-day excursions

605 (☎45/443963; buses to Temuco every 20min, to Villarrica every 15min), the latter two sharing a terminal on O'Higgins 910 on the outskirts of town (☎45/443328). Other buses stop at a terminal on O'Higgins and Palguín.

The **Cámara de Turismo** has a well-stocked kiosk on the corner of Caupolicán and Brazil, where the road from Villarrica enters town (daily 10am–2pm & 3–7pm; ☎45/441671, ℮info@puconturismo.cl, ⓦwww .puconturismo.cl or ⓦwww.puconline.cl). The well-stocked **Oficina de Turismo Municipal** is at O'Higgins 488 (Mon–Fri 8.30am–7pm, Sat & Sun 9am–7pm; ☎45/293002, ⒻLake/293003). For information about national parks, head to Conaf at Lincoyán 336 (Mon–Fri 8.30am–noon & 2–6.30pm; ☎45/443781). The better *hospedajes* also have first-hand experience of what foreign travellers enjoy doing, and most can share detailed maps, photographs and videos, as well as up-to-date knowledge of the tour companies.

tailored to suit abilities in the Liucura Valley and surrounding countryside. They also arrange kayaking and provide camping or indoor accommodation. English and German spoken.

Rafting There are three basic runs. The upper (alto) Trancura is a fourteen-kilometre run with eight rapids, some grade 3 to 4; the lower (bajo) Trancura is tamer, though still grade 2 to 3, so its description in some of the flyers as a "family outing" is a misnomer. Both of these trips are half- or full-day excursions. The three-day trip to the mighty Bío Bío, a grade 4 to 5 river, includes food and accommodation in tents. Sol y Nieve and Trancura (see Volcán Villarrica, opposite) have the latest equipment or try the kayaking and rafting specialists Aguaventura Expediciones at Palguín 336 (☎45/444246, ℮info@aguaventura.com, ⓦwww.aguaventura.com). Prices for two-three hours rafting range from CH$18,000 for the lower Trancura to CH$22,000 for the upper Trancura. The trip to the Bío Bío costs CH$150,000. The season for rafting – depending on the amount of rainfall – is September/October (December for the upper Trancura) to March/April. Often the rafts all go down the river together, and the river can be very crowded in high season, so don't expect to experience the isolation of wilderness.

Flying and parachuting For tandem paragliding, contact Fabrice Pini, Colo Colo 830 (☎9/4111072); a half-hour is CH$38,000. Off Limits (see p.356) offers tandem sky dives for CH$180,000, and Aguaventura (see above) charges CH$140,000 for a one-hour tandem jump.

Tours of the area A sedate tour of the area in a minibus is run by every company in town, and will generally take in the Ojos de Caburgua, some waterfalls and any or all of the thermal springs at Huife, Palguín, Menetúe and Pozones (see p.358). Prices range from around CH$10,000–15,000. Going farther afield, there are guided hiking trips in the Parque Nacional Huerquehue that include the lakes Tinquilco, Toro, Verde and Chico and cost CH$12,000.

Eco-tours One Pucón company runs slightly different tours from the ones listed above. The helpful *¡école!* (see p.354) is a great resource. In association with the Lahuen Foundation, it owns and operates a pristine araucaria forest sanctuary called Cañi about 30km east of Pucón on the road to the Termas de Huife, where it runs ecologically sensitive tours from around CH$10,000. The sanctuary was created as a sustainable resource for the local Pichares community. Pudú, puma and other wildlife, as well as a wealth of birds, frequent the 1185 acres of protected hills, forest and lakes, through which a stiff nine-kilometre trail climbs to provide stunning views of Volcán Villarrica, Quetrupillán, Lanín and Llaima. A refuge inside the reserve offers accommodation for those on overnight trips.

Accommodation

One of the advantages in Pucón's rise in popularity is that competition at the lower end of the market has kept hotel costs relatively stable. At the upper end, though, prices double from Christmas to the end of February, and you need to book in advance. If you are looking to escape the crowds, head 23km east from Pucón towards Curarrehue, to the welcoming ✗ *Kila Leufu* (☎9/7118064, ⓔinfo@kilaleufu.cl, ⓦwww.kilaleufu.cl; ❸), a Mapuche farmhouse with a warm family environment where you can relax and enjoy the lovely surrounding countryside or enjoy activities such as kayaking, mountain biking and horse-riding.

Donde Germán Brasil 640 ☎45/442444, ⓔdondegerman@latinmail.com, ⓦwww .dondegerman.cl. Run by a knowledgeable local rafting guide, this charming wooden chalet has a spacious garden and terrace and offers use of its kitchen, laundry service and free Internet access to its guests. ❷

✗ **¡ecole!** Urrutia 592 ☎ & ⓕ45/441675, ⓔecole@entelchile.net, ⓦwww.ecole.cl. With owners who are deeply involved in conservation projects throughout Patagonia, including the Cañi reserve (see p.353), this excellent *residencial* offers a wealth of fantastic traveller information through its onsite agency (ⓦwww.outdoorexperience.org). The rooms are comfortable, well-furnished and often booked, so reserve well in advance. There are also some dorm beds available (❷). Many travellers come for the fine vegetarian restaurant with a charming trellised courtyard covered in vines. ❹

Gran Hotel de Pucón Holzapfel 190 ☎45/441001, ⓔreservas@granhotelpucon.com, ⓦwww.granhotelpucon. Right on the most popular part of the beach, the *Gran Hotel* is probably the most famous hotel in Chile, and in the summer both it and its beach get very busy. It rested on its laurels for years until a major fire forced the owners to bring it into the twentieth century.❾

Hospedaje Arauco Arauco 272 ☎45/442223. A friendly family-run house, with good clean rooms – the garden ones are particularly nice. Guests may use the kitchen. ❷

Hospedaje Lucía Lincoyán 565 ☎45/441721. A private house run by a warm landlady who lets guests use the kitchen and will rent out mountain bikes and a fishing boat. ❷

Hostal Gerónimo Alderete 665 ☎45/443762, ⓔjohana@geronimo.cl, ⓦwww.geronimo.cl. Pleasant, quiet upper-end hostel set slightly away from the main streets, with a restaurant serving delicious home-made pasta. ❹

Hostal O'Higgins O'Higgins 136-A ☎45/441153, ⓕ441334. Although this is right on the main avenue above an ice cream parlour, the rooms are very quiet, light and airy.❹

Hotel Antumalal 2km outside Pucón, on the road to Villarrica ☎45/441011, ⓕ45/441013, ⓔhotel@antumalal.com, ⓦwww.antumalal.com. A quiet refuge, this architectural gem was designed by a student of Frank Lloyd Wright, and it looks characteristically low-slung and unashamedly 1960s – the original decor and furnishings have been preserved. It is a hotel with class: the service is excellent, the views over the lake are picturesque, and both Queen Elizabeth II and Jimmy Stewart have stayed here. ❽

Hotel Gudenschwager Valdivia 12 ☎ & ⓕ45/441156, ⓔgudens@cepri.cl. In 1930, the descendants of one of Villarrica's 1880s settlers opened this hotel as a remote lodge catering for fly-fishermen. The shingle-sided old wooden building retains its traditional charm, but it isn't the tranquil lake hideaway it once was. ❻

Hotel del Lago Ansorena 23 on the corner of Valdivia ☎ & ⓕ45/291000, ⓔreservas@hoteldellago.com, ⓦwww .hoteldellago.com. A luxury hotel right above the casino, and one block away from the beach. Its facilities include both indoor and outdoor swimming pools, a gym and a sauna. ❼–❽

Hotel Los Maitenes Fresia 354 ☎45/441820, ⓔinfo@hotelmaitenes.cl, ⓦwww.hotelmaitenes .cl. A clean, central hotel with parquet floors, helpful staff and plentiful breakfasts. Reservations recommended in high season. ❻

Hotel La Posada Plaza Pucón Valdivia 191 ☎45/441088, ⓔlaposada@unete.com, ⓦwww .hotelplazapucon.cl. A large, smart hotel with a dining room that overlooks the plaza. A handful of spacious *cabañas* are also available. ❻

Refugio Peninsula Holzapfel 11 ☎45/443398, ⓔalvaro@refugiopeninsula.cl, ⓦwww .refugiopeninsula.cl. This traditional old house, exuding a cosy atmosphere, boasts an ideal location in the quieter part of town, close to the beach. You can stay in comfortable rooms (❸) or well-maintained cabins (❺).

✗ **La Tetera** Urrutia 580 ☎45/441462, ⓔinfo@tetera.cl, ⓦwww.tetera.cl. This small, charming guesthouse provides a soothing escape from the crowds. Stay in comfy rooms and hang out with others in the communal lounges and inviting sun terrace. A library offers a book swap service and Spanish courses are available.

The deservedly popular café offers afternoon tea, *küchen* and decent meals, including pasta and omelettes. **4**

The Town

Your first sight of Pucón will probably be the bright carved wooden flowers for sale, stuck into bushes by the side of the road – not real, but freshly carved from local woods, rather like Pucón itself. The town resembles a postcard, set in the shadow of a fuming volcano and by the shore of a deep-blue lake, whose waters are often cut by slashing lines of white foam churned up by water-skiers. The streets are wide and regular, and the whole town gives off a feeling of affluence and youth, bustling as it does with tourist agencies, Internet cafés and hostels.

The main street, Avenida O'Higgins, cuts the town in two. A wide boulevard crammed with expensive cars and busy shops, its pavements throng with healthy bronzed Californians and multilingual Europeans passing out flyers to passers-by. Take a stroll to the sandy beach of **Playa Grande**, packed with oiled and sweating sunbathers lying in the shadow of the *Gran Hotel*, where in high season you can rent jet skis. Move on to **La Poza**, Pucón's other beach, and gaze at the boats in the marina. After this, there isn't much more to take in, but around town there's plenty to do and see: the mighty river **Trancura** with its rapids; the iced cone of the volcano **Villarrica**; the deep-green of the **Parque Nacional Huerquehue**, dotted with forest lakes; and the steaming waters of the many **hot springs** that are scattered throughout the region's hills.

Eating

When metropolitan Chile decided to come to Pucón, the unfashionable *cazuelas* and plates of fried *empanadas* were cast out and replaced with crepes presented on wooden platters, among other novelties. An oasis of variety in a

△ Forest lakes around Pucón

country that tends to lack a sense of culinary adventure, Pucón is a prime place to eat well.

Café de la P Lincoyán 395 at O'Higgins. Pucón's best *chocolatería*, serving delicious cakes and tarts in a laid-back, cosy venue that also doubles as a relaxed bar.

Casino Hotel de Lago Ansorena at Valdivia. Unless you are an inveterate gambler, the drawback of the *Casino*'s excellent restaurant is the sight and sound of people playing one-armed bandits just outside its windows. The food, though, is high-quality French and Italian and only moderately expensive.

Club 24 O'Higgins 192. A fast(ish)-food café for insomniacs, and one of the cheapest places to eat giant sandwiches and burgers in Pucón.

¡école! Urrutia 592. Tasty, inexpensive and imaginative vegetarian dishes – moussaka, burritos and large, large salads – served in peace and quiet in a vine-covered courtyard or an attractive dining room.

Il Fiore Holzapfel 83. There's a bewildering choice of home-made pastas and sauces on this upscale menu, including three different types of lasagne. If it's busy the service can be very slow.

La Maga Fresia 125. This Uruguayan *parillada* specializes in excellent meat dishes, most of which are prepared on the enormous fires outside the entrance. Wash it all down with a robust wine.

La Marmita Fresia 300. A rare example in Pucón of a restaurant with candlelit tables and an intimate ambience. Two-person fondues (CH$18,000) are the speciality; indulge your sweet tooth and wallow in a chocolate one.

Rap Hamburger O'Higgins at Arauco. A lively joint popular with the younger set for its super-size sandwiches and late-night burgers.

Restaurant Milla-Rahue O'Higgins 460. A popular, mid-range fish and seafood restaurant on the main avenue. Dishes feature some interesting sauces.

El Rincón de la Pasta Fresia 284. The extensive menu includes home-made pasta topped with tasty, fresh sauces, served in a warm, inviting dining room, complete with fireplace.

La Tetera Urrutia 580. A refreshing selection of teas, including the otherwise unobtainable lapsang souchong, properly made in a pot. They also serve fine, home-made cakes, not just confections of whipped cream.

Drinking

As you might expect from a town with so many young travellers, Pucón has a great nightlife scene, where the pisco flows and the music (a mixture of western and salsa) plays until the early hours.

Bar Bazul Lincoyán 361. Tables outside in the road let you take a breather from the pulsating salsa and disco music. It only really gets going here after 11pm.

El Bar Sin Nombre Lincoyán 361. A dark, intimate hang-out that also serves sushi.

Kamikaze Camino International. This lively spot, 2.5km out of town towards Argentina, is one of a chain of bars from the north. Look for the aeroplane sticking out of the roof.

Mamas and Tapas O'Higgins 597. In a large, dimly lit, wooden and glass building, a young, drinking crowd knocks back seriously strong pisco sours late into the night.

Listings

Airlines LAN, Gral. Urrutia 102 (☎45/443516) has flights from December to March only.

Banks and money There are ATMs on O'Higgins (Banco Estado del Chile) and on Fresia between Gral Alderete and Gral. Urrutia (Banco de Chile). *Cambios* include Cambio Cash, O'Higgins 255 (☎45/449582) and Turismo Christopher, O'Higgins 335 (☎45/449013), opposite the enormous supermarket, which also has an ATM inside.

Bicycle Rental Trancura, O'Higgins 261.

Book Exchange La Tetera, Urrutia 580.

Buses Buses Power, Palguin 550 ☎45/441055; Cóndor Bus, Colo Colo 430 ☎45/443023; Igi Llaima, Colo Colo 465 ☎45/442061; Intersur, O'Higgins 910 ☎45/443963; JAC, Palguin 605 ☎45/443963; Tur Bus, O'Higgins 910 ☎45/443963.

Camping and fishing equipment Mario's Fishing Zone, O'Higgins 590 ☎9/7607280; Off Limits, Fresia 273 ☎45/442681.

Car rental Turismo Christopher, O'Higgins 335-C ☎45/449013; Hertz, Fresia 220 ☎45/441664; Pucón Rent A Car, Colo Colo 340 ☎45/443052.

Hospital San Francisco, Uruguay 325 ☎45/441177.

Internet *Bar Brinkhouse*, Ansorena 243; *Beni Internet*, O'Higgins 555; *Sur Expediciones*, O'Higgins 660.
Laundry Elena, Gral. Urrutia 520; Laundry Express, O'Higgins 660 ; Lavandería La Esperanza, Colo Colo 475.

Post Office Fresia 183, **Telephone centre** Entel, at Ansorena 299 and Ansorena 425.
Water sports The marina on La Poza will often rent out jet skis in summer, or contact one of the tour operators in the box on p.352.

Lago Caburgua and around

If you want to escape the noise of town for awhile, make for the tranquil **LAGO CABURGUA**. Take the international road towards Argentina for 8km, then turn at the signed left, heading northeast. After 17km, hang a left and 500m later you will come to the **Ojos de Caburgua** (Eyes of Caburgua), a pair of waterfalls in the forest plunging into a deep pool of crystal-clear water. Thousands of years ago, an eruption blocked this southern end of the valley, drowning it, and the water from the lake now flows out through subterranean streams and porous rock until it reappears here. You can drive (parking CH$1000), or request that the bus to Caburga stop (walking in is free). In the middle of the day, it's usually overrun with tourists – and the unpaved car park turns into a dust bowl – so if you'd like some solitude, visit early in the morning, before the hordes arrive. Six kilometres further, the road arrives at the southern end of Lago Caburgua on a broad sandy beach, looking onto a long lake bordered by scrub- and forest-covered craggy peaks. The southern shore of the lake is densely developed with *cabañas* and campsites, but they're mostly hidden behind the trees. Just to the southwest unfolds **Playa Blanca**, a beach composed of fine, pale rock crystals known locally as *ala de mosca* – literally, as thin as a fly's wing. You can rent paddle boats at Playa Negra, which is about ten minutes southeast of Playa Blanca.

Practicalities

There's no cheap **accommodation** here; out of the mid-range spots, the picturesque *Cabanas Pehuén*, on Playa Blanca (☎2732228; six-person cabin for CH$35,000) is the nicest, but it can get noisy outside. A well-appointed, friendly guest house, *Landhaus San Sebastian* (☎45/1972360, ✉info@landhaus-chile .com, ⓦwww.landhaus-chile.com; ❺), sits adjacent to the Ojos de Caburga. For **camping**, try *Playa Blanca* (CH$10,000), a large park with plenty of isolated places to pitch a tent and private access to a small, secluded white-sand cove. It's a bit far back along the road to the restaurants and larger beaches, but it's possible to rock-hop or wade round the edge of the lake.

Many minibuses and *colectivos* come to the lake area from Pucón, leaving from both the rural bus terminal and the JAC terminal, though the service drops off somewhat in winter.

Parque Nacional Huerquehue

Rising up almost 2000m from the eastern shore of Lago Caburgua are the forest-clad hills and peaks that form the 125-square-kilometre **PARQUE NACIONAL HUERQUEHUE** (daily: summer 8.30am–9pm; winter 8.30am–6pm; CH$2200). Crowned by araucaria forests, the horseshoe-shaped **Cerros Picos de Caburgua** (Caburgua Mountains) enclose a dozen breathtakingly beautiful lakes of which the largest four – Tinquilco, Chico, Toro and Verde – are easily accessible.

Although volcanic in origin, Huerquehue's peaks have been dormant for thousands of years, and consequently it has a much richer biodiversity than neighbouring Parque Nacional Villarrica. At lower altitudes there are mixed forests of coigüe, one of the southern beeches, and the attractive conifer *mañío de hojas cortas*. Where areas of forest have been affected by fire you'll find impenetrable undergrowth of *colihue* and *quila*, types of native Chilean bamboo, incredibly irritating when you're trying to bushwhack.

Over eighty **bird** species have been sighted in the park, including two woodpeckers (the Magellanic and its smaller striped cousin), the delightful white-crested *diucón* or *fío-fío* and the seldom seen but often heard red-chested *chucao*. Trout swim in the park's numerous lakes and rivers, introduced by European immigrants and now attracting the large heron (*garza cuca*) and great grebes. The fascinating little Darwin's frog is also found here.

The park entrance, 35km from Pucón, is called **El Nido del Aguila** (named after a nearby waterfall, the Eagle's Nest). From the entrance, a trail leads into

Termas around Pucón

The combination of volcanic activity and a deep pool of tourist dollars means that there are more commercialized **hot springs** around Pucón than in any other town in Chile. The facilities on offer are varied, ranging from very basic to luxurious, but the alleged health-giving properties of the waters are just about the same: bathing in or drinking from them can benefit arthritis, nervous ailments and mental fatigue. There are some more extravagant claims, however, and the waters at Palguín, for example, are apparently good for respiratory ailments, kidney problems, nerves, rheumatism, problems of the heart and the digestion, gastrointestinal disorders, joint pain, skin problems, ulcers, gout, sciatica, asthma and arthritis. Whether this is true or not, there's nothing quite as relaxing as lying in a pool of steaming, volcanically heated water, especially when it's cold, dark, raining or even snowing all around you.

The *termas* are mainly divided into two river valleys, the Río Liucura and the Río Trancura. We've arranged them in order of proximity to Pucón. Getting to the *termas* without your own car is difficult, though occasional *colectivos* pass by. Your best bet is to hop on a **minibus**; JAC, at Miguel Ansornea 299 in Pucón, runs a local service to Huife for CH$1500. Other alternatives are to charter a cab for the day (about CH$20,000) or to hire a **colectivo**, which costs from CH$2000 per person each way (minimum of 4 people) and ask the driver to wait for you. Your hotel should be able to help with the arrangements (*¡école!* – see p.354 – has negotiated special rates with several taxi firms).

Liucura Valley

Termas Quimey-Co ☎45/441903; CH$5000 a day. Two relatively simple but good swimming pools have been dug out of the rock right beside the Río Liucura, in an attractive spot with native forest coming right down to the river's edge. From Pucón, drive towards Lago Caburgua and turn right at km 15, then continue for another 10km.

Termas de Huife 4km further on ☎ & ℱ45/1975666, ℮info@termashuife.cl, ℗www.termashuife.cl; CH$7500 a day or CH$4000 for just the outdoor pools. A well-designed complex with varied temperature pools, a tranquil atmosphere and a first-class swimming pool. It gets busy and entry is restricted, so you'll need to book in high season. Bus transfers from Pucón cost CH$13,000. In addition to the hot springs there is a canopy tour (CH$8000), where you explore the forest while in harnesses hung from cables suspended high above the ground. There's a good restaurant, and luxurious double-bed cabañas (office in Pucón at Alderete 324 ☎45/449570, ℮oficina@termashuife.cl; CH$99,000 for two) should you wish to stay.

Termas Los Pozones 2km beyond Huife; no phone; CH$3500 before 9pm, CH$4500 after. Simple, shallow pools dug out beside the river and dammed up with stones. It's the forest: you can make it to the lakes Chico, Toro and Verde in two to three hours from here, but the path's a little steep. If you're going to hike further in, keep to the well-signed trails, as the forest can be dense and it's easy to lose your bearings: in 1997, two backpackers got so thoroughly lost that it took the Chilean Army two weeks to dig them out. You'll find the *JLM Pucón Trekking Map* useful – it's readily available in Santiago and Pucón. There's a two-day hike that continues on beyond the closer lakes, heading north of Lake Tinquilco towards the dense central forest and a Conaf campsite, *Renalue*, where you can spend the night (CH$6000 per site). The trail then continues 8km (about 3hr) further, to the remote Centro Termal San Sebastian, a thermal spring outside the park's northeastern boundaries, where you'll find a refuge (CH$3000) and a couple of houses.

open all night, though there is a three-hour time limit so that people don't just use it for the cheap accommodation.

Río Trancura Valley

Termas de Menetúe 5km west of San Luis bridge ℡ & ℱ 45/441877, ℮ info@menetue .com; ฀ www.menetue.com; CH$6500 a day, double cabins CH$57,000. There's an office in Pucón at Lincoyán 243 ℡ 45/443124. Set in beautiful gardens near the river, with naturally heated rock pools, a small restaurant and *cabañas*. The swimming pools are open December through April, while the *termas* operate year-round. To get here, head out of Pucón towards Argentina on the international road for 27km then turn left across the Puente (bridge) San Luis and continue west for 5km.

Termas de San Luis 2km to the east of the San Luis bridge ℡ & ℱ 45/412880, ℮ termasdesanluis@entelchile.net, ฀ www.termasdesanluis.cl; CH$5000. Also known as the "Kerpen Centro Vacacional", this modern but sensitively built complex blends in well with the wooded surroundings. It has a covered thermal pool, an open-air swimming pool and a sauna as well as a bar and restaurant. *Cabañas* with private tubs and full board cost from CH$70,000 (office in Pucón at Pedro de Valdivia 0500 ℡ 45/412800).

Termas de Panqui 15km further east of Termas de San Luis ℡ 45/442039, ℱ 45/442040; CH$7000. A North American reinterpretation of the Andean forest, Panqui concentrates on the more mystical side of the hot springs, and calls itself a "Healing Retreat Centre". There are two thermal pools, a swimming pool, a mud bath, a medicine wheel, and also massages, Reiki and aquatic Shiatsu. You can camp here (CH$6000 per person), or stay in tepees (CH$10,000 per person) or the small hotel (CH$13,000 per person). The vegetarian restaurant serves hearty, healthy meals.

Parque Nacional Villarrica

Termas de Palguín ℡ 45/441968, ℮ info@termasdepalguin.cl, ฀ www .termasdepalguin.cl. The most remote *termas* from Pucón are deep in the Quetrupillán sector of the Parque Nacional Villarrica. The gloriously rustic old hotel here burnt down in 1998 and has been replaced by a more modern, conventional place to stay (℡ 45/441968; ❼) that is nonetheless comfortable and equipped with all the amenities. Entrance to the all-curing waters costs CH$4000 per person. To get here by car, drive 18km along the Camino International towards Argentina, then turn right after a bridge near the village of Llafenco Alto, and drive 13km south down the dirt road.

Practicalities

Campsites fringe the park entrance. Conaf has its own site near the entrance (CH$8800) or try Olga's or El Rincón Tinquilco (both CH$7000). However, the most acclaimed accommodation is the *Refugio Tinquilco*, on the northeastern shores of Lake Tinquilco (Ⓣ2/7777673, Ⓕ2/7323079, Ⓔpatriciolanfranco @entelchle.net, Ⓦwww.tinquilco.cl; ❸). Run by two of the authors of the *Insight Guide to Chile*, this airy, welcoming hostel offers both en-suite doubles and bunks; pluses include a sauna, use of a kitchen and loads of good advice on exploring the park.

Buses JAC run twice daily from Pucón to a village called **Paillaco**, 7km down the road from El Nido del Aguila and then on to the *guardería* on the east side of Lago Tinquilco (CH$1500). A taxi to the park entrance costs around CH$10,000. Alternatively, *¡ecole!* (see p.354) can arrange transportation to the park for you (CH$14,000, minimum four people). If you're driving, take the road to Lago Caburgua and turn right at km 14, from where it's 16km to the park entrance.

Parque Nacional Villarrica

The centrepiece of the **PARQUE NACIONAL VILLARRICA** (daily: May–Sept 8am–6pm; Oct–April 8am–9pm; CH$2000) is, of course, the **Volcán Villarrica**, just 15km south of Pucón, in all its smoking, snow-capped glory.

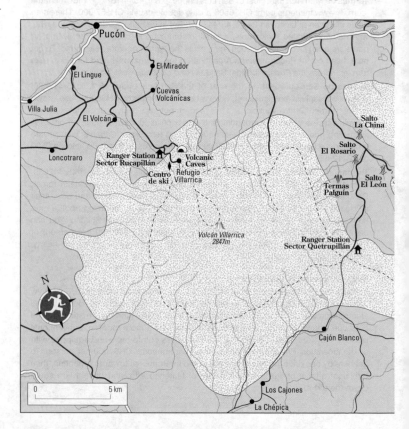

The vast majority of visitors do no more than trek up, have a look at the crater, then wildly body-slide down. But the park is much more than its most celebrated feature: it stretches 40km to the Argentine border (74km by road), contains two other volcanoes, and is one of the few national parks in the Lake District in which you can camp wild and hike for long distances.

The park divides into three sections: **Rucapillán**, nearest to Pucón and containing Volcán Villarrica; **Quetrupillán**, next along, entered 9km beyond the turning-point to the Termas de Palguín on the dirt track that leads from the international road to Coñaripe; and **Puesco**, near the border with Argentina. This region was inhabited long before the arrival of the Spanish, and the names of its peaks reflect this: Volcán Villarrica's original Mapuche name, Rucapillán, means "house of the devil", because of its frequent eruptions, while Quetrupillán, the dormant volcano next-door, means "mute devil". Another peak towards the border with Argentina is called Quinquili, or "devil's fang".

Sector Rucapillán
SECTOR RUCAPILLÁN, home to the magnificent **Volcán Villarrica** (2840m), presents a visual contradiction: below the tree line it's a lush forest, home to a wide variety of bird and plant life; above it's a black waste of lava, dotted with snow and encrusted with an ice-cap. The volcano forms the

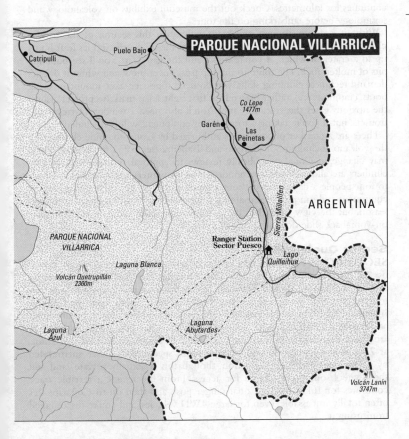

obvious focal point, standing sentinel over the park, and it's very active – there were sixteen recorded eruptions in the twentieth century. It most recently blew its top in 1984, though there were underground explosions in 1992, and part of the crater fell inside itself in 1996. Despite this, it's quite safe to visit, as considerable warning is given before serious activity.

A good road branches off the Pucón–Villarrica road, running up the northern slopes of the volcano. After 7km you reach the **park entrance**, and almost halfway up, 12km from Pucón, is the **ski centre**, run by the *Gran Hotel de Pucón* (see p.354; late June–mid-Oct; full-day lift ticket CH$16,000) with a café and restaurant. You can hire equipment here, but it's much more expensive than from the agencies in Pucón (see p.352). The volcano has nine lifts and twenty pistes, comprising six black runs, and a complicated web of six red runs, three blue runs and around half a dozen green runs.

Just under a kilometre after the entrance, a signpost points you to the **Volcanic Caves** (daily: Jan–Feb 9am–9pm; March–Dec 10am–6pm; CH$6000, one-hour Spanish-language tour). A large lava tube, the main cave is big enough at its opening to drive a tank into and looks rather like a dragon's lair: the rock walls and ceiling could almost be made of scales. It's dank and wet, but there's a dry path for almost 350m, and electric bulbs so you can see the multicoloured minerals on the walls. The tube hasn't been fully explored and apparently continues for kilometres. Check out the museum exhibits on volcanology and seismology before embarking on the tour.

Without a doubt, though, the main activity in this section of the park is **climbing the volcano**. The path leaves from the ski centre, and it's four hours up to a crater in which, if you're lucky and the gas clears, you'll see bubbling pits of molten rock. The route to the top passes over snow, and whilst it doesn't demand technical climbing skills, you do need ropes, ice-axes, mountaineering boots, crampons and, rather bizarrely at first sight, a gas mask (to protect against the noxious gases the volcano emits). You'll also need a windproof jacket and trousers, but if you're taking a tour, all this equipment will be included.

There are a number of companies authorized by Conaf to guide climbers up the volcano, including Sol y Nieve and Trancura (see p.352 for details). These may change, as Conaf periodically reviews its approval. A maximum of nine climbers are allowed with one guide (fewer in winter), but Conaf will let up to four people a day climb without a guide if they've got the experience and equipment and can prove their ability. It all gets very crowded up there in high season, but the view on a clear day is stupendous, followed by a rollicking sit-on-your-back slide down the side of a volcano.

Sector Quetrupillán

SECTOR QUETRUPILLÁN, the middle section of the park, is dominated by the rarely visited majesty of Volcán Quetrupillán (2009m). It's a remote area of wilderness, tucked between two volcanoes and accessible only on foot, by horse or down a rough side road that turns south from the Camino International 18km out of Pucón. Here you can find the contemporary hotel at **Termas de Palguín**, with its all-curing waters (see box, p.359). Here there are also four **waterfalls** – Palguín, la China, El León and Turbina. La China, at 73m, is the highest, but El León is more spectacular; all are surrounded by native trees and lush vegetation, though this is actually private land and the owners sometimes charge for access. From the *termas*, a terrible track continues for 10km to the Conaf ranger post, and then on to Coñaripe. It's often totally impassable, even for large 4WD vehicles, and you're discouraged from using it.

Sector Puesco

East of Quetrupillán, close by the border with Argentina, the third part of the park, **SECTOR PUESCO** is very beautiful, and rather like the Canadian Rockies, with pine forests and craggy mountainsides. The Conaf station is at the settlement of Puesco, where there's nothing else except a customs post and a *hostería*. From here it's a seven-hour walk west to **Laguna Abutardes**, tucked in the side of dormant **Volcán Quetrupillán** (2360m), a haven for birds, with ancient araucaria trees sweeping almost to its shore. On your way here from Pucón, 10km out of the village of Curarrehue, keep an eye out on the left (east) for the **Cordón de las Peinetas**, a rock formation that looks a little like a small version of the Torres del Paine, the famous rock towers in the south of Chile. Note that you can also walk to Puesco from Rupacillá, on a trail that winds through virgin forest, including the most southerly stands of araucaria in Chile. The journey takes seven days – longer if you're tempted by the numerous side trails to waterfalls, precipices and springs. You need to carry lots of water, as the seasonal streams can't be relied on, and should take the *JLM Pucón Trekking Map*, widely available in Pucón. Wild camping is allowed.

Right on the border with Argentina (the border runs right through the summit) is **Volcán Lanín**, the least-visited volcano in the park and with no trails. If you intend to trek or climb it, you'll need to get permission from Conaf and DIFROL and you must be *very* careful not to cross into Argentina.

Park practicalities

Hostería Trancura at Puesco has decent *cabañas* (❹) and a campsite (CH$3000). There are also **campsites** near the entrance to Rucapillán (CH$4000), but the only campsite actually in the park is near the Quetrupillán Conaf station (CH$8800).

There's no **public transport** to Sector Rucapillán, though there are dozens of tour buses, and a taxi from Pucón will cost around CH$10,000. In the winter, most tour agencies will take you to the park for CH$5000 per person, leaving Pucón at 9.30am and returning at 4.30pm (see p.352 for a list of companies). To get to Quetrupillán and Puesco, either take one of the local buses that ply the international road, or get on an international bus heading to Junín de los Andes in Argentina and ask to be dropped off. Although you should be able to get off at the Puesco customs post and Conaf station, the nearest you'll get to Quetrupillán will be the hamlet of **Palguín Bajo**, 9km away down a dirt track. If you've got permission, take the same bus to get to Volcán Lanín.

The Siete Lagos

Overshadowed by the sexier resort of Pucón, the region known as **SIETE LAGOS** – Seven Lakes – is the next one south of Villarrica. Six of the lakes are in Chile, one (Lago Lacar) in Argentina, and all are linked by rivers in one hydrological system. They offer a mixture of attractive small villages with good tourist facilities, and countless tracks that plunge deep into remote parts of the cordillera.

The Siete Lagos' relative tranquillity owes itself to the area having been largely ignored by the Spanish. Pedro de Valdivia was the first European to visit it in 1551, but apart from a short-lived silver mining enterprise, the Spanish kept away. The Siete Lagos' first settlement, Lican Ray, was a small trading post

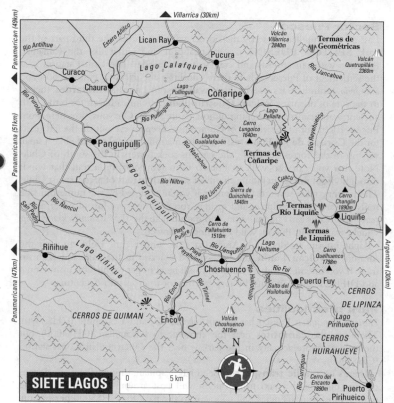

founded in the late nineteenth century to serve the Pehuenche and Mapuche Indians driven from the pampas by Argentine clearances.

Today the busiest lakes are the largest ones, the relatively warm **Lago Calafquén**, 30km south of Villarrica along a tarred road, and **Lago Panguipulli**, 17km on. The next valley down contains the slightly smaller **Lago Riñihue**, hardly visited and perfect for nature lovers and fishermen. To the east of Calafquén, beside a little-used road into Argentina, lies **Lago Pellaifa**, near a concentration of good *termas*. To the east of Lagos Panguipulli and Riñihue, nestling deep in the pre-cordillera and surrounded by 2000-metre peaks, are the most remote of the Siete Lagos, **Lago Neltume** and **Lago Pirihueico**, neither of which was accessible by road until thirty years ago and today are rapidly making their way onto the map.

Lago Calafquén and around

The most developed of the seven lakes, **Lago Calafquén** features a driveable road for the 30km along its northern shore between the settlements of **Lican Ray** and **Coñaripe**, and a decent dirt road around most of the rest. In a pattern that's typical of the Lake District, the western end is surrounded by rich farmland that stretches all the way to the coastal mountains, while the northern and southern shores are steep forested hillsides with only occasional pockets of fertile land and isolated farmsteads. To the east is tiny **Lago Pellaifa**, created by an earthquake in 1960 that altered the water flow in the region. It's bordered by an international road to Argentina that passes a clutch of thermal springs around the mountain hamlet of **Liquiñe**.

Lican Ray

LICAN RAY, a slightly scruffy holiday town with a shady plaza bordered by loud video-game arcades, lies 30km south of Villarrica, on the northernmost point of Lago Calafquén. Most of the town's roads are narrow dirt tracks that throw up dust in summer and become quagmires in the rain. The town has two pleasant **beaches**, Playa Chica, with a small forested promontory, and Playa Grande, a strip of dark sand framed by the surrounding hills and exposed to frequent freezing winds, but given the shallowness, the water is far warmer than other lakes in the area. In the summer you can rent boats at both beaches, but it's cheaper at Playa Chica.

From March through November, the town is pretty much dead, but during the first weekend of January, Lican Ray becomes famous. The whole length of the main street, General Urrutia, is transformed into Chile's **largest outdoor barbecue** (*asado*) in which some three hundred lambs meet their bitter, spicy ends. The origins of the feast aren't clear, but the excuse given is that it's to celebrate the beginning of summer, and each year's is bigger than the last as the town attempts to break its own world record.

The helpful and friendly **Oficina de Turismo** is on the plaza at Urrutia 310 (daily: Jan–Feb 9am–11pm; March–Dec Mon–Sat 9am–1pm & 3–6pm; ☎45/431516). There's no shortage of **places to stay** in Lican Ray. One of the best is *Hostería Inaltulafquén*, on Playa Grande at Cacique Punulef 510 (☎ & ℱ45/431115; ❹), an attractive, slightly shabby house with pleasant rooms, owned by a helpful Canadian couple who organize local tours. *Hospedaje Los Nietos*, Manquel 125, on the road to Coñaripe (☎45/431078; ❸), has decent rooms, but the lakefront cabins with kitchen and room for six people are a better deal. *Hotel Becker*, Manquel 105 (☎45/431553; ❺), offers rooms with balconies overlooking Playa Chica and the lake. Two kilometres out of town on the road to Coñaripe is *Cabañas and Camping Foresta* (☎ & ℱ45/431480), an expensive shady campsite in the woods, with sites for six people (CH$10,000) and *cabañas* for four (CH$50,000).

Lican Ray is well-connected to the rest of the Lake District and beyond: Buses JAC runs hourly services from a terminal east of the plaza at Cacique Marichanquín 240 to Villarrica, Pucón, Valdivia, Temuco and Santiago as well as to Lago Calafquén and Panguipulli. Cóndor Bus and Igi Llaima travel to Villarrica.

Coñaripe and Liquiñe

Laid-back **COÑARIPE**, a 21-kilometre drive along the northern shore of Lago Calafquén, has just a couple of good black-sand beaches and a sleepy air that's occasionally disturbed by erupting volcanoes. The small image of Christ on the lakeshore by the entrance to town is a memorial to two lava-engulfed victims and a testament to the uncertainty of living in this volcanically unstable area.

The municipal **Oficina de Turismo** is in a kiosk on the main street, Avenida Guido Beck de Ramberga, at the entrance to town from Lican Ray (daily: Dec–March 9am–9pm; ☎63/317378). As for **accommodation**, try the *Hotel Entre Montañas*, Guido Beck de Ramberga 496 (☎63/317298, ℱ45/408300; ❸), a modern pine-and-plastic building with a cheerful restaurant and small en-suite rooms.

After Coñaripe there's a junction; the road to the right (south) follows the shore of Lago Calafquén to the town of Panguipulli (see opposite), while the main road in front (east) climbs through native forest – with superb views of Lago Pellaifa, Volcán Villarrica and Choshuenco – for 22km to the tiny village of **LIQUIÑE**. Overlooked by a church and on the banks of the deep, wide Río Liquiñe, this pretty hamlet is surrounded by mountains and has a climate all of its own: in the summer the 2000-metre peaks trap the heat and it's difficult

Liquine and the termas

East of Coñaripe, deep in the mountainous forest either side of the little-used international road to Argentina, you'll find numerous **thermal springs**, less well known than those around Pucón, but every bit as good. They are listed here in order of proximity to Coñaripe.

Termas Geométricas 15km northeast of Canaripe ☎45/431407, ⓦwww .termasgeometricas.cl. The latest and most exclusive set of thermal springs in the region, with seventeen smart, slate-covered pools, which cost CH$10,000 to use, linked by a series of wooden walkways strung along a half-mile mountain stream amid lush vegetation. Grass-roofed shelters blend into the surroundings but there is no overnight accommodation here.

Termas de Coñaripe 15km southeast from Coñaripe ☎ & Ⓕ45/411111 or 63/317330, ⒺInfo@termasconaripe.cl, ⓦwww.termasconaripe.cl. This popular holiday complex, built from glass and wood, has a good restaurant, serving locally-sourced food including trout from the on-site farm, and first-class accommodation, with full-board double rooms (❽). The termas from which the place gets its name have been diverted into four swimming pools of varying temperatures, which cost CH$5500 to use.

Eco Termas Pellaifa Road to Liquiñe, km 16 ☎ & Ⓕ45/411973 or ☎9/8942584, ⓦwww.panguipulli.cl. Simple open-air pools; entrance CH$2000.

Termas Manquecura 2km up a bad track marked with a painted condor at the entrance to Liquiñe ☎63/311060 (messages). Rustic open-air pools sit among the fields, along with mud baths, a small restaurant and some basic *cabañas* (❹). Entry to the termas costs CH$1500, and they can become surprisingly busy, with coach parties staying for several days.

Termas Río Liquiñe On the river bank in the centre of the village ☎ & Ⓕ63/317377. The *cabañas* (❺) have thermal water piped into private baths, and there's a big, square thermal swimming pool, access to which costs CH$4000.

Termas Liquiñe 100m from Rio Liquiñe ☎ & Ⓕ63/311060. Owned by the Chilean Navy and slightly run-down, but at the foot of a steep, forested hill and with a peaceful, secluded swimming pool and good *cabañas* (❹). Access costs CH$1500; closed to the public during the summer.

Termas Trafipán Just below the tree line from Termas Liquiñe ☎63/311060 (messages). A simple pool and rustic private baths, fed by a spring 600m above. The water is pleasantly unsulphurous, and the cost is CH$1500.

Termas Punulaf A 15-minute walk from the town of Liquiñe across open fields (local children will take you for a tip) ☎63/311060 (messages). A large indoor pool, plus an open-air pool fringed by trees, mud baths and private tubs that cost CH$1500 to use. If you want to use the pools early in the morning or late at night you can camp (CH$5000) or stay in cabins (❹–❺).

Termas Hipólito Muñoz 8km from Liquiñe (towards Argentina) ☎63/311060 (messages). A campsite (CH$5000) and a few rustic *cabañas* in a beautiful, thickly forested riverside setting. There is a charge of CH$1500 to use the pools, which have been dug out beside the river, and there are mud baths, too.

to believe that you're deep in the southern Andes. The hills around the village are strewn with **thermal springs** (see box opposite). Many of these have been developed and offer **accommodation**, but if you're looking for something a bit more comfortable, try *Termas Río Liquiñe*, in Liquiñe on the international road (☎63/311060; ❺); cabins have private thermal baths, and the rate includes three meals a day.

Coñaripe is served by frequent **buses** from Villarrica, operated by Buses JAC, Buses Estrella del Sur and Igi Llaima; two buses continue on to Liquiñe. There are also buses from both Coñaripe and Liquiñe to Panguipulli, operated by Buses San Pedro and Buses Pirehueico. Ask at the local tourism office for the latest bus schedules – they tend to change yearly.

Lago Panguipulli and around

Ten kilometres south of Lago Calafquén is the northern snout of long, thin **Lago Panguipulli**, a lake that stretches 26km southeast into the cordillera. Its western edge is a shore of little bays and hills, its east is cleared forest, the trees long since felled and taken by boat to the neat little town of Panguipulli on the lake's northwesternmost tip. Thirty years ago, a road was built around the uninhabited eastern shore to the remote Lagos **Neltume** and **Pirehueico**. These beautiful lakes are hardly touched by humanity and difficult to visit, as much of the lakefront is private property; one great view can be had from the ferry that crosses Lago Pirehueico, carrying cars and passengers towards Argentina.

Panguipulli

The attractive village of **PANGUIPULLI**, bright with colourful roses, dark copper beech trees and manicured lawns, sits amid rolling fields, forests and peaks of grey and purple. You can get here following the southern shore road from Coñaripe (37km), but it's more easily reached via one of two 50- to 60-kilometre spurs from the Panamericana.

Founded in 1885, Panguipulli started life as a trading post for Pehuenche and Mapuche Indians driven off the Argentine pampas. It grew beyond these humble origins in 1903 when a Capuchin mission was established here, and when the railway arrived in 1937, the town became an important timber centre. The trees are gone now, and the boom is over, but Panguipulli remains the administrative hub for the Siete Lagos, with bustling shops, services and accommodation. It's best known today as the **town of roses**, with an estimated 14,000 closely pruned rose bushes lining the streets, and a crowd-pulling folk festival, *Semana de las Rosas*, the last week of January, when the city hosts art exhibits and concerts.

There's not much to do in Panguipulli except sit on the beach, smell the roses and check out the famous **church** (unpredictable opening hours), around the corner from Plaza Arturo Prat. Built by the Capuchins and envied and copied throughout the Lake District, the church was modelled on traditional chapels around Berne in Switzerland. It's an unexpected sight – a twin-towered latticed confection of yellow, red, brown and white, looking like a massive iced chocolate cake. Down on the lakefront are a group of **wooden statues** – two Indians, a missionary and a pioneer – each carved from a single block of wood.

Practicalities

Near the church, on Plaza Arturo Prat, you'll find the helpful **Oficina de Turismo** (Jan–Feb daily 9am–9pm; March–Dec Mon–Sat 9am–6pm; ☎63/312202, ℻63/311334, ✉turmpangui@telsur.cl, ◍www.panguipulli.cl).

There's plenty of accommodation here, dating back to the heyday of rail transport and lake steamers, and for the most part all with wobbly wooden beds. Try the *Hostal Familiar* at Los Ulmos 62 (☎63/311483; ❷), which has a multilingual staff (German, English), big breakfasts and lots of local tourism information. About the same standard is *Hospedaje Monserrat*, O'Higgins 1112 (☎63/311443; ❷), a very popular place with young Chileans who enjoy the lively atmosphere and don't seem to mind queuing for the solitary bathroom. If you want a bit more luxury, try the friendly *Hostal España*, O'Higgins 790 (☎ & ⒻXX63/311166, Ⓔhostal-espana@elsitio.cl; ❹–❺), more like a family house than a hotel, with large, comfortable en-suite rooms. The nearest **campsite** is *Camping El Bosque*, just off the Plaza de Armas and close to the beach (☎63/311489).

Panguipulli's no town for gourmets, but it does have a **cookery school** – *Restaurant La Escuela*, Freire 394 – which, in January and February, opens its doors to the paying public. Apart from this, at the recommended *Café Central*, Martínez de Rozas 880, you can enjoy a meal of *pollo asado* (grilled chicken) or *pescado frito* (fried fish) on a secluded patio with a small garden. *Restaurant Girasol* at Martínez de Rozas 663 also serves Chilean specialities such as *pollo asado* and *pastel de choclo*, whilst *Gardylafquen* at Martínez de Rozas 722 offers slightly more sophisticated, western fare such as stuffed aubergines.

Panguipulli is very well-connected to the rest of the Lake District. The **bus terminal** is at Gabriela Mistral 1000, and there are local and long-distance services heading as far afield as Santiago. The major bus companies are Pirehueico (☎63/311497), Igi Llaima (☎63/3111647), Tur Bus (☎63/311377) and Inter Sur (☎63/311647). As for banks, you'll find a branch of BCI with an ATM.

Southeast towards the border

Turning right from the shore road at the southern end of Lago Panguipulli, 42km from Panguipulli town, you'll pass along a magnificent avenue of trees, which forms an incongruous entrance to tiny **Choshuenco**. A steamer port in the days when boats plied the waters of Lago Panguipulli, Choshuenco is now a small village with just over five hundred human inhabitants, and the remains of an old dead steamer rusting on the beach. It's a base for fishermen in the summer and for wild boar hunters in the winter, who tend to stay in *Hostería Pulmahue*, Av Alemania s/n, at the end of the beach just outside the village (☎63/318224; ❹). The hostería has a commanding view of the lake, the atmosphere of a mountain hunting lodge, a roaring log fire and hearty home cooking. *Hostería Rucapillán*, San Martín 85 (63/318220; ❹) offers heated wooden cabins, a good restaurant and fishing, rafting and boating excursions.

Fifteen kilometres along a dirt road southwest of Choshuenco is **Enco**, a tiny logging camp at the end of Lago Riñihue, the next lake south of Lago Panguipulli. From Enco, a nine-kilometre track leads up through the Reserva Nacional Mocho Choshuenco to a ski refuge, just above the tree line, which can be used as a base for climbing **Volcán Choshuenco** (2415m). Another 30-kilometre logging track leads to the town of **Riñihue** on the southern shore of the lake, passing through thick forest and along the edges of high cliffs to reveal constantly changing views across the lake. Walkers or cyclists who use it are unlikely to meet another soul. Be warned, though, that temporary bridges cross countless streams which, after even moderate rainstorms, turn long sections of the track into one great sticky bog.

Lago Neltume and Lago Pirehueico

Back on what was the shore road, 5km after the turn for Choshuenco, a gravel road branches left to smallish **LAGO NELTUME**, depositing you on its eastern shore, where much of the waterfront is effectively closed to the public. The other side of the lake is a mountain: the densely forested side of the impressive Cerro Paillahuinte, which rises 1435m straight up from the water. In Neltume town, *Pensión Gortari*, Los Castaños, in front of the firehouse (☎63/1973707; ❸), offers basic beds. Heading once more towards Argentina, after another 7km you'll reach the waterfalls **Saltos del Huilo Huilo**, a powerful torrent forced through a ten-metre-wide green cleft in the rock to deafening effect.

Six kilometres further on lies **LAGO PIREHUEICO**. Pirehueico means "worm of water" in the local Mapuche language, and there couldn't be a better name for this curving, twisting, snake-like lake, bordered by forest-clad mountains. It's crossed by a **ferry**, from Puerto Fuy in the north to Puerto Pirehueico in the south (April–Nov one daily, departing 12.30pm and returning at 4pm; 1.5hr; Dec–March twice daily, departing Puerto Fuy at 8am and 3pm, returning at 10.30am and 7pm; CH$10,000 for cars, CH$1000 for passengers; ☎63/311334). There isn't much in either village: **Puerto Fuy** has one general store and some basic accommodation, usually occupied by temporary workers; **Puerto Pirehueico** has just the one lodging, a *residencial* that serves lunch and snacks. Hardly anyone stops in either place, but because of their remoteness, the surrounding lakes and forests are home to more wildlife than most of the national parks. Eleven kilometres further is the **border**, where there is a café and a customs post, open 8am to 8pm, year-round. If you're planning to cross the border in a rental car, bring written authorization from the rental company and ask the rental shop for full paperwork details – many travellers are barred from crossing because of documentation problems.

If you don't have a car, getting to these lakes is a problem, as public transport doesn't go beyond Choshuenco and there isn't enough traffic to make hitching anything more than a long, boring wait.

Lago Riñihue

LAGO RIÑIHUE, the beautiful flooded valley to the south of Lago Panguipulli and the last of the Siete Lagos, has been almost completely untouched by tourism. There is no apparent reason why: the tiny village of **Riñihue** on the western shore of the lake was the first to be connected to the railway in 1910; there's a good tar road linking it with the Panamericana, 50km to the west; and the area is well-known by Chileans for producing famous Swiss- and German-style hard cheeses.

The village itself is merely a collection of houses built on the slight rise pushed up by an old, long-melted glacier, with a small village store, a disco and a small bar. You'll find few facilities, but one alluring spot to experience the gorgeous outdoors is at the mouth of the Río San Pedro, on the northern shore of the lake, where *Hotel Riñimapu* and its seventeen **rooms** are quietly tucked away (☎ & ☎63/311388, ⦿www.rinimapu.cl; ❻–❼). It has no TV or Internet access, but boasts fifty acres of fields, a tennis court and a prime launch pad for kayakers and rafters. The owner speaks French and English.

Valdivia and around

Apart from a very minor private road from Puerto Fuy round the far side of Volcán Choshuenco, the only way south from the Siete Lagos is to head back to the Panamericana, via Panguipulli (60km) or Riñihue (47km). Both routes end up at **Los Lagos**, a town that used to be an important river port, but these days is little more than a petrol station with history. From here the Panamericana stretches off into the distance, though a major road (known simply as "the road to Valdivia") shoots west to **VALDIVIA** and the coast, well worth the diversion for a quick blast of sea air.

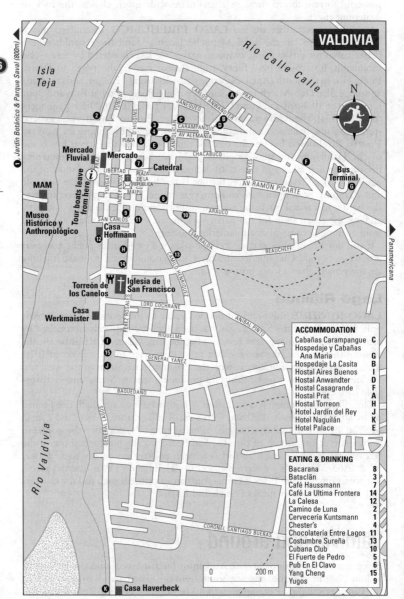

VALDIVIA

Río Calle Calle

Isla Teja

1 Jardín Botánico & Parque Saval (800m)

Panamericana

MAM

Museo Histórico y Anthropológico

Mercado Fluvial

Mercado

Catedral

Tour boats leave from here

Casa Hoffmann

Torreón de los Canelos

Iglesia de San Francisco

Casa Werkmaister

Casa Haverbeck

ACCOMMODATION

Cabañas Carampangue	C
Hospedaje y Cabañas Ana Maria	G
Hospedaje La Casita	B
Hostal Aires Buenos	I
Hostal Anwandter	D
Hostal Casagrande	F
Hostal Prat	A
Hostal Torreon	H
Hotel Jardín del Rey	J
Hotel Naguilán	K
Hotel Palace	E

EATING & DRINKING

Bacarana	8
Bataclän	3
Café Haussmann	7
Café La Ultima Frontera	14
La Calesa	12
Camino de Luna	2
Cervecería Kuntsmann	1
Chester's	4
Chocolatería Entre Lagos	11
Costumbre Sureña	13
Cubana Club	10
El Fuerte de Pedro	5
Pub En El Clavo	15
Yang Cheng	9
Yugos	9

0   200 m

Valdivia is a vibrant, cosmopolitan mixture of the colonial and the contemporary, with concrete apartment buildings and weathered mansions. In some intangible way it still feels like a colonial city even though many of its old buildings are gone – lost to earthquakes, fires and floods throughout the last century. The 1960 earthquake, the largest in recent memory, triggered a massive tidal wave that swamped all Chile's coast from here down to the island of Chiloé (see p.415) and altered the courses of numerous rivers.

Today Valdivia is focused on water. The centre of town is a little soulless, difficult to tell apart from many others in Chile, but it's by the river that you'll find the city's heart, bustling with a lively market, the **Mercado Fluvial**. Tours leave from the quay near the market for the seventeenth-century **Spanish coastal forts** of **Niebla** and **Corral**. Across the river is the island of **Teja**, a place of quiet and calm, where you can find Valdivia's excellent **Museo Histórico y Antropológico Maurice van de Maele**.

Some history

Pedro de Valdivia founded his city as a supply halt on the route to Lima, six days' sail from the Magellan Strait. He chose the confluence of the rivers Calle Calle and Cruces as a suitable location because it was defensible and had access to both the sea and the inland plains, but it wasn't strategic enough a spot and had to be abandoned in 1599 after the Mapuche uprisings. The site was almost immediately pounced on by the Dutch, who wanted to create an enclave on the coast of South America, but was reoccupied by the Spanish in 1645, who realized that such actions threatened the Spanish Empire. To counter the threat, the Viceroy in Peru ordered a string of forts – including Corral and Niebla – to be built. These were strengthened when Britain threatened in 1770, and by the time of the wars of Chilean independence, Valdivia was a formidable redoubt.

After independence there was a great influx of German settlers, who founded shipyards, breweries and mills, industrializing the area quickly and building Chile's first blast furnace in 1913. They have left their mark on the town, and despite the earthquakes' destruction and the subsequent ugly concrete reconstruction, enough remains on Calle General Lagos to give an impression of what the city looked like in its days of nineteenth-century Teutonic splendour.

Arrival and information

Although Valdivia is 50km from the Panamericana, so many long-distance buses pass through the city that it's almost impossible not to come here. The highly efficient **bus terminal** (☏63/212212), surrounded by *hospedajes*, is on the corner of Anwandter and Muñoz, five blocks from the city centre. It has a superb information kiosk (daily 8am–10pm), which maintains a current listing of approved accommodation. Coastal buses to Niebla and beyond operate from the city end of Puente Pedro de Valdivia. If you're driving from the Panamericana, an alternative and very scenic way to reach the city is along the 50-kilometre dirt road from Los Lagos, which follows the majestic Río Calle Calle. There's very little traffic along this route.

Valdivia's **airport** lies 32km northeast of town in the village of Pichoy. There are several flights a day between Valdivia and Santiago as well as weekday services from Temuco and Concepción. Taxis (CH$7000) meet flights and Transfer Valdivia (CH$1500 per person) runs a minibus into town.

Sernatur, with the usual full complement of leaflets and **information**, is at Prat 555, next to the river between the cruise boats and the Mercado Fluvial (Mon–Thur 8.30am–5.30pm, Fri 8.30am–4.30pm; ☏63/342300,

ⓕ63/344046, ⓔinfovaldivia@sernatur.cl). More helpful and motivated are the staff at the municipal **Oficina de Turismo**, in the indoor market across from the Mercado Fluvial (Dec–March Mon–Sat 9am–9pm, Sat & Sun 9am–noon & 4–8pm; ⓣ63/233156). You can also find useful information at ⓦwww .valdiviachile.cl and ⓦwww.valdivia.cl. For information on parks and treks, contact Conaf at Ismael Valdés 431 (Mon–Fri 9am–1pm & 3–5pm; ⓣ63/245200).

Accommodation

In January and February, when Valdivia's student population is on holiday the city has some of the cheapest accommodation in the Lake District. In the mid-range are beautiful old private homes with excellent services and at the top end, several luxury hotels. You'll find decent campsites at *Camping Isla Teja*, Los Cipreses 1125 (ⓣ & ⓕ63/225855, ⓔcislateja@telsur.cl; CH$10,000), with a beach along the river that offers a pleasant escape from downtown Valdivia – a 40-minute walk away via Pedro de Valdivia bridge.

Cabañas Carampangue Carampangue 458 ⓣ63/216910. Comfortable, well-maintained cabins in the heart of the city. **④**

Hopsedaje y Cabañas Ana María José Martí 11 ⓣ63/222468. Very close to the bus station, this is a good place for small groups to stay, with five-bed *cabañas* as well as rooms, some of which have bunk beds. **③**

Hospedaje La Casita Anwandter 607 ⓣ63/218405. A small, spotless *hospedaje* with just a handful of rooms; guests can use the kitchen facilities. **②**

Hostal Aires Buenos General Lagos 1036 ⓣ & ⓕ63/206304, ⓦwww.airesbuenos.cl. This HI hostel is housed in an attractively restored building dating from 1890. Guests have access to the kitchen and to the Internet, and can take Spanish or tango lessons. Dorm rooms CH$5000 per person; private rooms (**③**) also available.

Hostal Anwandter Anwandter 601 ⓣ63/218587. This family home, in a quiet locale just off the river, features independent mini apartments with private bath and kitchens, and also cable TV and central heating. **④**

Hostal Casagrande Anwandter 880 ⓣ & ⓕ63/202035. Enormous, well-maintained mansion near the bus terminal, but with a view of the river.

Rooms have cable TV – and good laundry facilities are a big plus. **④**

Hostal Prat Av Prat 595 ⓣ63/222020. Overlooking the river, this smart, refurbished hotel with en-suite rooms and cable TV is run by a small, energetic woman who's eager to please. **④**

Hostal Torreón Pérez Rosales 783 ⓣ63/212622, ⓔhostorreon@telsur.cl. Opposite the Torreón del Barro towers, this large, elegant building has a pleasant atmosphere and comfortable rooms. **⑤**

Hotel Jardín del Rey General Lagos 1190 ⓣ & ⓕ63/218562, ⓔinfo@hoteljardindelrey.cl, ⓦwww .hoteljardindelrey.cl. A building oozing colonial charm and retaining the dignified bearing of a prosperous family home. The en-suite rooms are very large and comfortable. **④**

Hotel Naguilán General Lagos 1927 ⓣ63/212851, ⓕ63/222740, ⓔreservas@hotelnaguilan.com, ⓦwww.hotelnaguilan.com. Part of the Best Western chain and right on the edge of the Río Valdivia, this modern hotel with a swimming pool has rooms overlooking a reed-covered island and facing the setting sun – which gives the place its Mapuche name. **⑦**

Hotel Palace Chacabuco 308 ⓣ63/213319, ⓔhotelpalace@surnet.cl, ⓦwww.valdiviachile.cl /hotelpalace. Comfortable hotel that's very central, and suffers slightly from street noise as a result. **④**

The Town

Unlike most Chilean towns, Valdivia's social centre is not its plaza but its **waterfront**, where the Río Calle Calle and the Río Cau Cau meet the Río Valdivia. The rivers bend sharply to form a "U" shape; the *costanera* road travels along the south and east banks. Inland from the rivers, to the east, lies the modern concrete town centre. Avenida Ramón Picarte serves as the main east-to-west street and Yungay as the main north-to-south street, with the name changing to General Lagos three blocks south of the indoor market. Opposite the town centre, across the Pedro de Valdivia bridge, sits **Isla Teja**. A haven of tranquillity, the island is home to the **Museo Histórico y Antropológico Maurice van de Maele** and has beautiful views back across the river to the Mercado Fluvial. It's also the site of the large and prestigious Universidad Austral de Chile.

Just south of the bridge to Isla Teja is the **Mercado Fluvial** and Valdivia's fish quay on the riverfront, with wizened fishermen gutting and selling rows of *congrio* (a cod-like white fish) and *merluza* (hake) and setting out battalions of monstrous red spider crabs, some the size of a small child, on concrete slabs covered with striped awnings. Giant sea lions congregate behind the stands, waiting for scraps. Opposite, on the other side of the path, vendors sell all types of bright fruit, vegetables and strings of smoked shellfish. Across the road, the **indoor market**, probably the cleanest and most orderly in Chile, features good crafts stalls and restaurants. The *marisquerías* (seafood restaurants) inside this modern arcade are great places to stop for lunch. Just to the south of the Mercado Fluvial, touts offer ferry tours (see box below).

The centre of town holds fewer attractions. You'll see a couple of squat, grubby defensive towers that date from 1774 – **Torreón del Barro** on Avenida Picarte and **Torreón de los Canelos** on the corner of Yerbas Buenas and General Lagos. However most visitors go to **Calle General Lagos**, which heads south out of town parallel with the river. This old street is filled with Valdivia's gems, a series of nobly proportioned nineteenth-century buildings. Take a stroll down the road and peek through the railings at the austere, double-staircased **Casa Werkmaister** (between Cochrane and Riquelme) and at the crinkly gabled

Ferry tours

Just down from the Mercado Fluvial there are the kiosks and touts of the ferry tour companies, offering to take you down to the **coastal forts**, or upriver to the **wetlands**. The tours on offer vary greatly. One of the most important factors in choosing a boat is the weather – the amount of deck space varies considerably from one vessel to another and you don't want to be sitting out in the rain all afternoon. Lunch is an optional extra on several boats and policy varies as to whether you can consume your own food and drink on board. Above all, it's worth checking what languages the running commentary is going to be in, if there is one, and if you can escape it by going out on deck. Remember to shop around, as one tout may be offering a trip at twice the price of his neighbour. Group discounts (for more than four people) are easily negotiable with a bit of Spanish.

Among the best tours is aboard the 160-person catamaran *Extasis* (T & F63/340093; CH$15,000, including lunch, wine and liqueurs); this pricey, comfortable excursion visits two islands and leaves at 1.30pm and returns at 7.30pm. For trips to the Santuario de la Naturaleza Río Cruces (see p.378), try private operator *Isla del Río* (T63/225244), also leaving at 1.30pm and returning at 7.30pm. The 250-person *Neptuno* (T & F63/218952) runs a large loop behind Isla del Rey, with hour-long stops at several forts. Daily tours (Sept–March) begin at 1.30pm and return at 7.30pm. The CH$14,000 fee includes bilingual guides, veggie or steak lunch and live music; the tour is much cheaper without lunch, or in the off-season. *Bahia* (T63/224680) has a fleet of four boats with a capacity of 50 each and runs hour-long trips around Isla Teja for CH$3000 per person or to Santuario de la Naturaleza Río Cruces for CH$6000 per person. *Orion III* (T63/210533, F210522, E hetours@telsur .cl) is a 108-person boat offering trips that include a stop for lunch on an island. After the break, the tour continues to one of the nearby forts. Between December 15 and March 15 daily trips depart at 1.30pm, return at 8pm and include lunch on the island and a snack.

Conjunto Haverbeck on the way out of town, or the many others between the two. The only one you can actually visit is **Casa Hoffmann**, at Yungay 733 (Tues–Sun 10am–1pm & 4–7pm; free), also known as the Centro Cultural "El Austral". It was constructed in 1870 as a private residence by Alberto Thater, a German who came to Valdivia in 1857, and has been lovingly restored and furnished in the style favoured by successful merchants during Valdivia's golden years: bright, strong decoration which looks almost Regency-style, with *trompe l'oeil* wall hangings and mismatched, passed-down furniture. Temporary art exhibitions are mounted in the upstairs rooms. On February 9, the city celebrates the founding of Valdivia, and between the second and third Saturday of February all of Valdivia comes out to celebrate "Valdivia Week": the river lights up with a **parade of boats**, and Conaf, at Ismael Valdés 431 (℡63/218822), puts on a memorable fireworks show.

Isla Teja

Your first sight of **Isla Teja** will probably be from the Mercado Fluvial, as you look beyond the fishmongers' stalls at the banks across the river. Only the easternmost part of the island is developed, the rest is low-lying reed beds and wetland. It's a quiet place, and the part of Isla Teja that Valdivia has stretched onto has a low-key, suburban atmosphere.

The island is reached via the concrete bridge to the north of the Mercado Fluvial. Heading south from the bridge is Isla Teja's main attraction, the splendidly sited **Museo Histórico y Antropológico Maurice van de Maele** (April–Nov Tues–Sun 10am–1pm & 2–6pm; Dec–March daily 10am–1pm & 2–8pm; CH$1200; ℡63/221972), in an old colonial house surrounded by a veranda. It was once owned by Karl Anwandter, founder of Chile's first

brewery, and like the Casa Hoffman (see above), it's still furnished with the trappings of nineteenth-century European society, including a double piano, an ornate red-marble fireplace and a magic lantern. Also on display is a fascinating collection of old sepia prints of the first German settlers.

The highlight of the museum is the collection of **Mapuche artefacts**, mainly silverwork and cloth. The latter resembles the patterns of the Aymara and Quechua, indigenous peoples from the north of Chile and Peru. The display of Mapuche silver is good too, and, if you haven't visited a museum in the Lake District yet, you should come and see examples of their heavy, intricate, yet strangely contemporary-looking jewellery. There's also a collection of reproductions of old photographs that show the silver's

△ Mapuche girl

original owners and how it would have been worn. The museum contains other bits and bobs: some lovely old maps of South America on the wall of the stairway, and a room of memorabilia pertaining to Lord Cochrane (see box below) and his staff.

Next door to the Museo Histórico, housed in Valdivia's old brewery, is the **Museo de Arte Contemporaneo**, or "MAC", as it's known (open Sept–April

---

Lord Cochrane

South America's struggle for independence is a colourful blend of farce and heroism, performed by a polyglot band of brigands and adventurers, most of whom were seasoned veterans of the Peninsular War and knew little but the art of warfare. **Lord Thomas Cochrane**, tenth Earl of Dundonald, was one such man.

Cochrane was born into an impoverished family in Annsfield, Lanarkshire, in 1775. At the age of seventeen he entered the Royal Navy as a midshipman, and over the next twelve years wreaked more havoc on the Spanish and French forces than Nelson, prompting Napoleon to dub him **Le Loup de Mer** (the Seawolf). In 1818, however, when he was approached by Chile's political agent in Britain to be the first Vice Admiral of Chile's three-ship navy, Cochrane was in trouble: he'd just been imprisoned for taking part in successfully defrauding the London Stock Exchange of half a million pounds. Cochrane accepted the Chileans' offer with alacrity – he needed the money. For their part, the Chileans – desperate for a naval commander with bravado to take on the Spanish Navy, the key to the ultimate defeat of the Spanish in South America – were happy to overlook his shady past. José de San Martín, commander-in-chief of the Chilean Army, described him as "a great child who will give a lot of trouble but his services may prove invaluable".

Valdivia was the key to the Spanish supply routes, and was so well-fortified by the Spanish that it was called the "Gibraltar of South America". **General Ramón Freire**, the Chilean general waging a bitter war against the Spanish-backed Mapuche Indians, considered that "cold calculation would make it appear that the attempt to take Valdivia is madness". However, late one summer evening in 1820, Cochrane sailed into the mouth of the Río Valdivia on board a captured fifty-gun barque, right under the noses of the Spaniards and their 118 bronze cannon. There he broke out the Spanish colours and requested a pilot, whom he promptly clapped in irons, then sailed back out to sea. Convinced that such a ruse could work again he went north to Concepción and persuaded a reluctant General Freire to lend him men and ships to undertake a seemingly impossible attack on Spain's most impregnable Pacific port. Freire offered Cochrane as much as he could because, he said, "the Spaniards will hardly believe us in earnest even when we commence".

Cochrane sailed south, anchored under the guns of Fuerte Aguada del Inglés, and attempted, once more, to pass off his ships as Spanish. The attempt failed, and the garrison opened fire on the ships' landing party of forty marines. But with the defenders distracted, a small group of soldiers led by a young Chilean ensign called Vidal were able to storm the fort from the rear. The Spaniards retreated in utter confusion, and the main Chilean force drove them out of one fort after another before finally taking Corral. The remaining forts were cleared of Spanish, and Valdivia was taken. Over seven hundred Spaniards had been defeated with the loss of seven Chileans.

When Cochrane left South America seven years later, he had played a decisive role in securing independence for not only Chile, but Peru and Brazil as well, and at the ripe old age of seventy he was helping drive the Turks from Greece. After his peaceful death in 1860 he was buried in Westminster Abbey, and *The London Times* wrote: "there have been greater heroes because there have been heroes with greater opportunities". On the corners of his tombstone are the coats-of-arms of Chile, Peru, Brazil and Greece.

Tues–Fri 10am–1pm & 3–6pm, Sat & Sun 3–7pm; CH$800; ☏63/221968, ⓦwww.macvaldivia.uach.cl). The attractive modern building is quite bare inside, with a raw, unfinished feel – white partition walls, a rough concrete ceiling and giant panoramic windows overlooking the river. MAC doesn't have a permanent collection, but features visiting modern art exhibitions and installations as well as more standard works.

North of the MAC and the Museo Histórico, at the end of Avenida Los Lingues, are two parks. The **Jardín Botánico**, east of the road in the grounds of the Universidad Austral de Chile (daily: April–Nov 8am–7pm; Dec–March 8am–8pm; donation), sits peacefully on the banks of Ríos Cau Cau and Calle Calle, with a large collection of trees and shrubs from around the world. By the river end of Avenida Los Lingues, to the west of the university campus, is the entrance to the much larger **Parque Saval** (daily 8am–6pm; CH$300), where waterfowl thrive on the attractive Laguna de los Lotus.

Eating and drinking

Valdivia has a couple of excellent restaurants, serving Chilean food with a Germanic twist, as well as the usual *lomo con papas fritas* outlets. Like most university towns, it also has a number of lively bars and discotheques that thrive during term time.

Restaurants and cafés

Bacarana Arauco 379. Student hang-out that serves up hearty sandwiches and local brew at low prices.

Café Haussmann O'Higgins 394. A small, old-fashioned bar where businessmen chat over beer and plates of raw mince tartar on toast or sip coffee and savour the excellent home-made cakes.

Café La Ultima Frontera Pérez Rosales 787. A slightly scruffy building conceals this fashionable, bohemian café that serves tasty sandwiches, vegetarian dishes and real coffee.

La Calesa Yungay 735 ☏63/225467. Peruvian-owned, expensive international restaurant in a well-preserved colonial building. The menu includes steak Diane and chocolate fudge cake, and while some of the foreign dishes work well, the best ones are Peruvian. Closed Sat evenings & Sun.

Camino de Luna Costanera Arturo Prat. Moored on a boat just upstream from the bridge to Isla Teja, this is the best restaurant in Valdivia. It's expensive, but the German-Chilean cusine is worth it and includes such hybrid concoctions as the *strudel de mariscos*.

Chester's C Henríquez 314. A small, cheerful café serving good-value fast food such as *empanadas* and hot dogs.

🏃 **Chocolatería Entre Lagos** Vicente Pérez Rosales 622–640. A famous chocolate shop, known for its rich cakes, and connected to a *salón de té* that sells giant veggie sandwiches, a wide range of ice creams and fresh-squeezed natural fruit juices.

Costumbre Sureña Camilo Henríquez 746. Tasty homestyle Chilean cooking that is particularly popular with locals, who gather here for *pastel de choclo* and *pollo asado a lo olla*.

Yang Cheng General Lagos 1118. Typical Cantonese cuisine at reasonable prices in a restaurant set behind a small oriental garden.

Yugos Pérez Rosales 649. Attentive waiters deliver delicious Chilean fusion food, including *parilladas* and *jabali* (wild boar) at this inviting restaurant with a wooden interior and tables decked out in green check.

Bars and clubs

Bataclän C Henríquez 326. Open from midnight until 5am, this music bar has live bands at weekends. The dance floor is inky dark and intimate.

Cervecería Kuntsmann On the road to Niebla ☏63/292969, ⓦwww.cerveza-kuntsmann.cl. Chile's premiere local brewery offers guided tours of this plant, with tastings followed by a lunch of German food.

Cubana Club Esmeralda 680. Salsa and merengue tunes tempt people onto the dance floor in this lively venue.

El Fuerte de Pedro Caupolicán and Alemania. Designed in the style of a Spanish fort, this bar attracts a student crowd with music and dancing until dawn.

Pub En El Clavo Camilo Henriquez 361. Large, rather nondescript bar that hosts live music, mostly rock and pop, at the weekends.

Tragobar Beauchef 620. Very popular, recommended bar with wide selection of drinks and a friendly staff.

Listings

Airlines LAN, Maipú 271, in front of Plaza de la Republica ☎63/258844; Iberia-American Airlines, Arauco 417 ☎63/212421.

Banks and exchange There are various banks with ATMs in the centre of town, including Banco de Chile, at C Henríquez and Letelier. For *cambios*, try AFEX Cambio La Reconquista, Galería Arauco 331, Local 24; Turismo Cochrane. Arauco 435; and Money Exchange, Carampangue 325.

Buses Most companies have offices at the bus terminal, at Muñoz 360, ☎63/212212. Buses JAC ☎63/212925, and at Arauco 241 ☎63/224307; Cruz del Sur ☎63/213842; Igi Llaima ☎63/213842; Pirehueico ☎63/213834 and at Baquedano 143; Tur Bus ☎63/226010, and at O'Higgins 460 ☎63/342563.

Car rental Assef y Méndez, General Lagos 1335 ☎ & ⑤63/213205, ⑥eassef@telsur.cl, ⑩www.assefymendez.com and at the airport ☎63/272245; Autovald, Pérez Rosales 660, ☎63/212786, ⑥autovald@telsur.cl; Budget, Pedro Aguirre Cerda 1154 and at the airport ☎63/340060; First Rentacar, Los Laureles 365 ☎63/225060; Hertz, Ramón Picarte 640 ☎ & ⑤63/218316.

Hospital Clinica Alemana, Beaucheff 765 ☎63/246100.

Internet *Club Internet*, Esmeralda 614; *Atec*, Esmeralda 579, Local 17; *Café Phonet*, Libertad 127.

Laundry Lavamatic, Walter Schmidt 305, Local 6; Lavaseco Au Chic, Arauco 436; Laverap, Arauco 697, Local 2.

Telephone centres Telefónica del Sur, Yungay and San Carlos; *Café Phonet*, Libertad 127; Chilexpress, C. Henríquez 458.

Tour operators Anticura Expediciones, Anfión Muñoz 327 ☎63/212630, ⑥expediciones@anticura.com, ⑩www .anticura.com; Avytour, Libertad 12, second floor ☎63/530271; Los Notros, O'Higgins 189 ☎63/211030, ⑥lnotros@telsur.cl, ⑩www .turismolosnotros.cl; Outdoors Chile, Arica 2263 ☎63/253377, ⑩www.outdoors-chile.com; Turismo Conosur, Yungay 129 ☎63/212757, ⑥conosur@telsur.cl; and Turismo Cochrane, Arauco 435 ☎63/212213, ⑥cochrane@telsur.cl, ⑩www.surdechile.cl. La Isla Turismo Náutico, Arica 2233 (☎63/227909, ⑥islote@uol.cl) runs trips to Haaverbeck Island, across from Valdivia, which was destroyed by the 1960 earthquake and rebuilt for tourists.

Shopping Arts and crafts at Feria, A. Prat and Arauco, in front of the river market.

Niebla and Corral

At the mouth of the Río Valdivia, 18km from Valdivia by boat or car, is **NIEBLA** and its fort (April–Oct Tues–Sun 10am–5.30pm; Nov–March Tues–Sun 10am–7pm; CH$600, free on Wed). Niebla itself is a motley string of *cabañas* and restaurants half-hidden from the road, often grey with mist or rain (*niebla* means fog in Spanish), but the fort is a little jewel. The **Fuerte de Niebla** (or Castillo de la Pura y Limpia Concepción de Montfort de Lemus, to give the full name), was originally built by the Spanish from 1667 to 1672 as part of an extensive line of defences of this key position in their empire, and massively enlarged in the eighteenth century according to the design of the Royal Engineers in Madrid. Today it's been restored and houses a small museum, but the most interesting things are the old features: the powder room, double-walled and well below ground level, the crenulated curtain wall hacked out of the bare rock, and the twelve slightly rusting cannons. The view from up here, high above the sea, is inspiring, and you can appreciate how the fort dominated the mouth of the river far below. Boats arrive here from Valdivia, and *colectivos* run regularly from Yungay near the Mercado Fluvial and cost CH$500.

You'll find a few **accommodation** options in the Niebla area. *Hotel El Castillo*, Antonio Ducce 750 (☎ & ⑤63/282061, ⑩www.interpatagonia .com/elcastillo; **⑤**), is a huge mansion astride the fort, offering views of the river, central heating, bountiful breakfasts and horse rentals. *Hostería Riechers*, Antonio Ducce 795 (☎ & ⑤63/282043, ⑩www.niebla.co.cl; **④**), offers well-equipped cabins surrounded by native forests, plus a good restaurant. In front of Los Enamorados beach, *Cabañas del Abuelo*, Camino Valdivia-Niebla km 20 (℡ & ℻63/282321; ❹) has cabins surrounded by trees, and sportfishing and trekking opportunities.

On the other side of the estuary lies the little village of **CORRAL**; it used to be a thriving port until it was flattened by the 1960 tidal wave. Another Spanish fort, **Castillo de San Luis de Alba de Almargos**, is located here (daily: March–Dec 9am–6pm; mid-Dec–Feb 9am–8pm; CH$500). The only way across the river is by a half-hour ferry ride – boats leave from the pier at the entrance to town. Keep an eye open for seals and old men with rakes on the islands collecting *pelillo*, a tangled, hairy seaweed that is used for medicines and foods. For those who want to drive and have time to spare, there's an attractive 75-kilometre road from Niebla to Corral via Valdivia, which passes through thick forest along the banks of the rivers Valdivia, Angachilla, Futa and Tornagaleones. There is also a daily bus (except Sunday) from Valdivia to Corral.

Corral's fort is just above the waterline and was built to complement Niebla's height. It's more ornate than the fort at Niebla, with little, stone-roofed towers to protect those unfortunates who had to keep a look-out for the fall of the shells. From December 15 until the end of February, there's a twice daily re-enactment of an attack by corsairs at 3pm and 5pm. The show ranges from an impressive display of period uniforms and weapons to a wet, miserable performance by two men, a musket and a tired donkey. If you wish to **stay** in Corral, *Cabañas y Camping El Morrito*, km 48 on the road to Corral (℡ & ℻63/212092; ❸), has furnished cabins, hot water and pretty beaches. The small but welcoming *Hospedaje Mariel*, Tarapacá 56 (℡63/471290; ❸), offers simple but cosy rooms.

Santuario de la Naturaleza Río Cruces

After the 1960 earthquake, the 50km of low-lying land around the Río Cruces north of Valdivia was flooded, forming an extensive delta which has been protected as the **Santuario de la Naturaleza Río Cruces**. This marsh now forms an important breeding ground and resting place for more than ninety species of migrating birds. The importance of this wetland area was officially recognized by UNESCO in 1981, and 48 square kilometres became a protected nature reserve in 1982. You can catch glimpses of the area as you travel along the road between Temuco and Valdivia, but to fully appreciate it you need to take a boat tour from Valdivia.

Lago Ranco

Dozens of distant high and rugged mountains surround pretty **LAGO RANCO**, 91km east of Valdivia. The lake is big – the second largest in the region, covering over 400 square kilometres – and is bordered to the west by flat land, and to the east by the rising Andes. Around the lake's edge is a 121-kilometre dirt road, passing the village of **Futrono** – small and tidy but boring – and leading to **Llifén** on the eastern shore, a compact village with good fishing. Beyond Llifén, hidden away in the mountains, is **Lago Maihue**, untouched and almost unvisited, while on the southeast shore is the village of **Lago Ranco**, undeveloped and shabby. In the middle of the lake sits **Isla Huapi**, a Mapuche *reducción*, which you can visit from Futrono.

In any other country, Lago Ranco, because of its great size, would be a major tourist attraction, but in Chile's Lake District it suffers from lots of competition: it's not as rustic as the Siete Lagos to the north, nor as fashionable as Lago

Llanquihue to the south, and there's no way it can compare with Pucón's Lago Villarrica. Despite this, the lake is a pleasant place to come and fish, look at the scenery, and simply relax.

Futrono and Isla Huapi

FUTRONO, the village on the northern shore of Lago Ranco, is a one-street town with a well-stocked **Oficina de Turismo** on the corner of the plaza at Balmaceda and O'Higgins (Mon–Fri: mid-March–mid-Dec 9am–1pm & 2–5pm; mid-Dec–mid-March 9am–9pm; ☎63/482640) but nothing much else to offer. It's a ten-minute walk from the lake, has no decent beach, and as a result has seen minimal tourist development. The only draw is that the **boats for Isla Huapi**, the Mapuche reserve, leave from here twice daily in summer and during the rest of the year, on Mondays, Wednesdays, Fridays and Saturdays at 7am, returning at 5pm. The crossing costs CH$1000. Futrono is connected to Valdivia by one bus an hour, run by Buses Futrono (☎63/481279).

Futrono has a couple of **places to stay**: *Cabañas Lahuenco*, km 1, Sector Cun Cun (☎63/481326, ℗63/481236, ⓔcab_lahuenco@hotmail.com; ❹), is well-situated in front of the lake and guests may use the kitchen and laundry. Nearer the centre of the village, *Hospedaje Futrono*, Balmaceda 90 (☎63/481265; ❸), is a safe bet for its cosy ambience as is *Hostería El Rincón Arabe*, Manuel Montt and Monsalve (☎63/481406; ❸), with a small quiet garden, a swimming pool and a restaurant specializing in Arab food.

ISLA HUAPI, the largest island in the middle of Lago Ranco, is a Mapuche *reducción* and a haven of peace and quiet, with pocket-sized fields, scattered huts and winding tracks just wide enough for the teams of oxen that pull water carts up from the lakeshore. Visitors are made very welcome but you should be sensitive, especially with your camera. Note that there's no accommodation on the island.

Llifén and Lago Maihue

Tucked on a ledge between the forest and the lake, **LLIFÉN**, 22km along the northern shore from Futrono, is a remote little place, but it's been a famous **fishing destination** since the 1930s, when the logging companies moved in and discovered that its rivers and lakes were teeming with fish. There's plenty of **accommodation** here, most of it oriented towards fishermen, and quite expensive. Just outside the village on its own private beach is *Hostería Huequecura* (☎9/4256276; ❺), which has excellent views across the lake and an agreeable, informal air. *Cabañas y Hostería Licán*, with no formal address, but hard to miss

---

Isla Huapi festival

Two Mapuche communities live on the **Isla Huapi**, and they meet twice a year – at the full moon in January or February and again at the full moon in June. This great council, called **trapëmuwn**, lasts for twenty-four hours. With its origins in the ancient harvest ceremony, *lepún*, the council decides on all community matters. Held in the open, the proceedings are shrouded from the view of outside observers by a thick stockade of branches, which also serve to protect the participants from the elements, but there is enough to see and hear, including **traditional music** and **dancing.** The seemingly interminable debates are periodically broken by the beating of **drums** (*kultrún*) and blowing of **pipes** (*trutruca*). Take food and drink to sustain you throughout the day.

in this small town (℡63/1971917; ❸), offers basic rooms. Twelve kilometres east of town is the *Cumilahue Lodge* (℡ & Ⓕ 63/231027; ❽), one of Chile's leading fly-fishing lodges, set in native forest with exclusive river access.

Even more remote than Llifén, and hardly explored, is **Lago Maihue**, 12km to the east as the crow flies, but 33km by road. It's a beautiful, lonely lake, surrounded by forest and with the snow-capped peaks of the high Andes on the horizon. There's no accommodation here, not even a village, just the occasional farmer, so wild **camping** is the only option. There's no public transport either, so to get here you have to hitch or drive. The road north to Puerto Fuy is gated and not open to the public.

Lago Ranco village

Scruffy **LAGO RANCO** village, 47km south of Llifén, has a neglected charm – dogs doze against the streets' peeling weatherboard and the lakefront is hidden by a jungle of trees. There's a good beach, and a two-minute swim into the lake offers beautiful views of the cordillera. To get here from Llifén, take the rough but passable dirt road, dotted with the occasional campsite and *hostería*, that follows the southern edge of the lake. The **tourist office** (Dec–March Mon–Fri 10am–9pm; no phone), run by helpful, friendly volunteers, is on the western edge of town,

You can pitch a tent at *Camping Los Bandurrias*, Valparaíso 207 (℡63/491420; CH$2000 per person). Alternatively, on the lakefront are a couple of passable neighbouring *residenciales*: *Casona Italiana*, Viña del Mar 145 (℡63/491225; ❸), with cute, comfy *cabañas* that look like oversized dolls' houses; and *Hostería Phoenix*, Viña del Mar 359 (℡63/491226; ❹), a little hotel with a restaurant. For the best in natural surroundings, however, head to *Hotel Parque Thule* (℡63/491293; ❹), 2km out of town, a well-run hotel that sits amid verdant gardens sweeping down to the lake. *Ruca Ranco*, near the jetty, serves flavourful Chilean set meals.

Several **bus** companies service Lago Ranco: Inter Sur, Tur Bus, Pirehueico and Expresso Panguipulli travel from Valdivia hourly, and there are also regular services from Santiago and Osorno.

Osorno and around

As with the Siete Lagos, the only way of getting south from Lago Ranco is to head back to the Panamericana. The 50-kilometre road west of Lago Ranco village joins the highway at the unremarkable town of **Río Bueno**, 30km south of which is **OSORNO**.

Despite being founded in one of the best defensive positions of all the Spaniards' frontier forts, Osorno was regularly sacked by Mapuche Indians from 1553 until 1796, at which point Chile's governor, Ambrosio O'Higgins, ordered it to be resettled. From tentative beginnings, it has grown into a thriving city mainly due to the industry of European settlers who felled the forests and began to develop the great dairy herds that form the backbone of the local economy today.

Osorno is an agricultural city: it's almost easier to buy a tractor here than to cash a traveller's cheque, and it has little for the tourist – except **buses**. As the transport hub for the southern Lake District and starting point for the region's main road into Argentina, it has an abundance of public transport, making it a snap to visit Osorno's surrounding attractions – **Lago Puyehue** in the

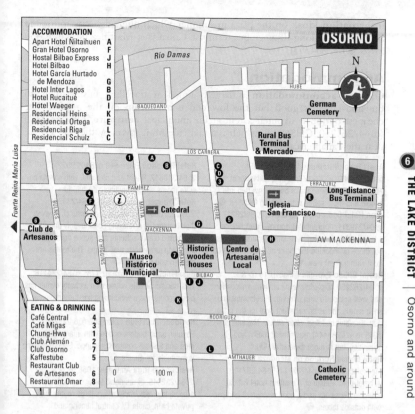

Within the map image:

OSORNO

N

ACCOMMODATION
Apart Hotel Ñiltaihuen	A
Gran Hotel Osorno	F
Hostal Bilbao Express	J
Hotel Bilbao	H
Hotel García Hurtado de Mendoza	G
Hotel Inter Lagos	B
Hotel Rucaitué	D
Hotel Waeger	I
Residencial Heins	K
Residencial Ortega	E
Residencial Riga	L
Residencial Schulz	C

EATING & DRINKING
Café Central	4
Café Migas	3
Chung-Hwa	1
Club Alemán	2
Club Osorno	7
Kaffestube	5
Restaurant Club de Artesanos	6
Restaurant Omar	8

Río Damas

German Cemetery

Rural Bus Terminal & Mercado

Long-distance Bus Terminal

Iglesia San Francisco

Catedral

Club de Artesanos

Museo Histórico Municipal

Historic wooden houses

Centro de Artesanía Local

AV MACKENNA

Fuerte Reina María Luisa

Catholic Cemetery

0   100 m

Street labels: Río Damas, HUBE, BAQUEDANO, LOS CARRERA, RAMIREZ, BULNES, MATTA, FREIRE, ERRAZURIZ, ANGOL, MACKENNA, O'HIGGINS, COCHRANE, BILBAO, PRAT, COLON, RODRIGUEZ, AMTHAUER

---

cordillera; **Parque Nacional Puyehue**, one of Chile's most-visited national parks; **Volcán Antillanca**, which boasts some of the best skiing south of Santiago; and quiet, little-visited **Lago Rupanco**. And if you've had enough of mountains and lakes for the moment, to the west there are the long sandy beaches on the Pacific coast around **Bahía Mansa**.

Arrival and information

Osorno's two **bus terminals** are less than a block from each other on Calle Errázuriz and close to the city centre. The long-distance terminal is at Errázuriz 1400 (☎64/234149), and the rural terminal is at Mercado Municipal, Errázuriz 1300 (☎64/232073). Rail services no longer run to Osorno.

Seven kilometres from the city, Osorno's **airport**, known as Cañal Bajo or Carlos Hott Siebert (☎64/232529 or 64/240540), is served by daily LAN flights from Temuco and Santiago. Taxis wait for incoming flights.

Sernatur's **information office**, O'Higgins 667 (Mon–Fri 8.30am–1pm & 2.30–6.30pm; ☎64/237575, ☎64/234104, ✉infosorno@sernatur.cl), is in the Gobernación building on the west side of the Plaza de Armas and has plenty of maps and leaflets. The municipal **Oficina de Turismo**, Mackenna 851, eighth floor (Dec–March Mon–Sun 10am–7pm; ☎64/264250, ☎64/256275) is in the Municipalid building, on the south side of the plaza. There's also an information kiosk on the plaza in summer, which offers free city tours, and another in the long-distance bus terminal. Conaf is at Martínez de Rozas 430 (T & F 64/234393).

Accommodation

Osorno's **accommodation** is largely aimed at travelling businessmen, so the mid-range is good but the low end is a bit thin on the ground. The cheapest option is to pitch a tent at the municipal **campsite**, *Olegario Mohr* (T 64/264250; CH$6000), which is a taxi ride from town, by the Río Damas near the Panamericana.

Apart Hotel Ñiltaihuen Los Carrera 951 T 64/234960, F 231177, E tnilque@telsur.cl. An old colonial house that's been converted into double and triple suites with cooking facilities. **⑤**

Gran Hotel Osorno O'Higgins 615 T 64/232171, F 64/239311, E granhotelosorno@entelchile.net. A large 1950s building, with small, spartan rooms, but those overlooking the Plaza de Armas make up for it with a great view. **⑤**

Hostal Bilbao Express Bilbao 1019 T & F 64/262200, E pazla@telsur.cl. Jolly, welcoming and well-equipped with parking, a restaurant and snug rooms, this is an excellent deal for the price (**③**). Its sister building, *Hotel Bilbao*, Mackenna 1205 (T 63/264444), has similar rooms and amenities, but is more expensive (**④**).

Hotel García Hurtado de Mendoza Juan Mackenna 1040 T 64/237111, F 64/237113, E hotel-ghm@telsur.cl. A modern hotel with a sauna, gymnasium and a good restaurant and bar with outside tables. **⑦**

Hotel Inter Lagos Cochrane 515 T & F 64/234695, E reservas@hotelinterlagos.cl, W www.hotelinterlagos.cl. Of all the similar hotels aimed at businessmen, the *Inter Lagos* has the most character, and the staff are very friendly. **⑥**

Hotel Rucaitué Freire 546 T 64/239922, F 64/310617. Bright and cheerful, with simple en-suite rooms and an inviting café-bar. **⑤**

Hotel Waeger Cochrane 816 T 64/233721, F 64/237080, E hotelwaeger@telsur.cl, W www .hotelwaeger.cl. A relaxing hotel, mainly due to the muted colour scheme and subtle lighting from intriguing junk-metal wall lamps. The rooms are modern and pleasant. **⑥**

Residencial Hein Errázuriz 1757 T 64/234116. This traditional little house with a chatty owner has clean rooms and a welcoming bar-turned-dining room. **③**

Residencial Ortega Colón 602 T 64/232592. Popular, basic budget option with a large dining area and a small communal lounge. Secure parking is available for guests. **②**

Residencial Riga Amthauer 1058 T & F 64/232945, E resiriga@telsur.cl. Much like a hotel, this *residencial* offers large rooms with private bath, cable TV, central heating and parking. **④**

Residencial Schulz Freire 530 T 64/237211, F 64/246466. Once past the overwhelming log cabin of a lobby, the rooms in this establishment are clean and cheerful. **④**

The City

What strikes you first about Osorno are its ghastly **churches**, the most obvious being the **Catedral San Mateo** on the Plaza de Armas. Topped with a large concrete lattice shaped like a two-dimensional, five-storey abstract of a bishop's mitre, this grim ferro-cement facade stamps an impression of uncompromising ugly modernity on everything around it. There's another horrible church, **Iglesia San Francisco**, whose untreated concrete exterior appears uncompleted, three blocks east.

The southern side of the Plaza is Calle Juan Mackenna, the east–west road on which the Municipalidad stands. If you walk two blocks east, you'll see a row of **wooden houses**, built between 1876 and 1923, that miraculously survived earthquake, fire and ruthless property developers and have been declared national monuments. The prettiest is the two-storey clapboard **Casa Schüller**, painted cream, with a grey roof, an ornate porch, and a hexagonal side tower that sports a weather vane. Unfortunately, you can't go inside most of them, except for the pink-and-green **Casa Stückrath**, at no. 1069, which is also a shop. One block southwest of Juan Mackenna is the **Museo Histórico Municipal**, Matta 809 at Bilbao (Jan–March Mon–Thurs 9.30am–5.30pm, Fri 9.30am–4.30pm, Sat 2–6pm; April–Dec Mon–Thurs 9.30am–5.30pm; free; ☎64/238615), housed in one of Osorno's earliest stone buildings, constructed in 1929, and a little disappointing. Osorno's history is depicted mainly in some old photographs, with a collection of daggers and swords from the colonial era, as well as the odd piece of Mapuche pottery and cloth. The gloomy ground-floor rooms grab the attention the most, as they contain the bones, teeth and tusks of a mastodon, one of the giant herbivores that roamed the central plain between the coastal range and the Andes twenty thousand years ago. Also here are artefacts belonging to the Atacameña, which thrived around Azapa near Arica in the Far North, including fragments of textiles, pottery shards and a mummified body thousands of years old.

The ancient world is also in evidence five blocks or so west of the plaza, south of the bridge over the Río Rahue. The reconstructed fort, **Fuerte Reina María Luisa**, sits on the site of the town's original foundations. From the low stone battlements, there is a good view down onto the river, lined with tall Lombardy poplars and weeping willows.

Eating and drinking

The food in Osorno has a strong Germanic flavour, a legacy of the nineteenth-century settlers. Don't miss out on the Germanic cakes (*küchen*), tarts (*tortas*) and chocolates.

Café Central O'Higgins 610. Come here for American breakfasts, hamburgers, sandwiches, real coffee and good service.

Café Migas Freire 584. This warm café serves up *empanadas*, Chilean lunch specials and *küchen*.

Chung-Hwa Matta 517. One of the oldest Chinese restaurants in the south, with a friendly family atmosphere but average food.

Club Alemán O'Higgins 563. An old-fashioned spot, with moderately priced local specialities made with trout, pork or venison, and a separate cosy bar with wood panelling and incongruous tartan decor.

Club Osorno Cochrane 759. From the outside, this club looks very uninviting, more like a Methodist meeting hall than a gaming den. Inside, however, you'll find a quiet bar serving a wide range of

appetizing nibbles (*picoteos*) to keep the local businessmen going during their games of *dudo* (liar's dice). Set lunches are served all afternoon during the week. Closed Sun.

Restaurant Club de Artesanos Mackenna 634. Inexpensive Chilean food, particularly fish and seafood, served in a hassle-free setting with a relaxed atmosphere, along with the locally produced beer, Märzen.

Kaffeestube Mackenna 1150. Busy café within the Supermercado Las Brisas serving hot drinks and sweets, as well as main meals, which makes for a good pit stop while exploring the town.

Restaurant Omar O'Higgins 827, second floor. This informal restaurant serves a mixture of Arab fare and cheap Chilean staples.

Listings

Airlines LAN, E. Ramírez 802 ☎ & ℻64/314909.

Banks and exchange There are banks and ATMs around the plaza. For *cambios*, try Cambio Tur, Juan Mackenna 1004; Turismo Frontera, E. Ramírez 959, Local 11; Cambio Mundial, E. Ramírez 949, Oficina 11.

Bus companies International buses (Terminal de Buses): Cruz del Sur ☎ & ℻64/232777,

ⓦwww.busescruzdelsur.cl; Tas Choapa Internacional ☎64/233933. Regional buses: Buses Pirehueico ☎64/233050; Igi Llaima ☎64/234371; Intersur ☎64/231325; Pullman Sur ☎64/232777; Tur Bus ☎ & ℻64/234170, ⓦwww.turbus.cl; Via Tur ☎64/230118. Local for the coast: Buses Maicolpué ☎64/234003; Buses Mar ☎64/236163. For Puyehue: Puyehue ☎64/245026; Expresos Lago Puyehue ☎64/243914.

Car rental Automóvil Club de Chile, Bulnes 463
☎63/232269; Econorent Car Rental, Freire 848
☎64/235303, ℗250743 and at the airport.
Consulates France, O'Higgins 517 ☎64/232647;
Germany, Matta 549 Oficina 406 ☎64/232151.
Hospital Hospital Base, off Guillermo Buhler 1765,
La Cantera ☎64/259200.
Internet *Gea.com*, J. Mackenna 1140, Local 1;
Cibercafé Diginet, Los Carrera 662; *PC Play*, E.
Ramírez 1107, Local 9; *Cyber @ Kafé*, Lynch 1334,
Local 6.
Shopping Alta Artesanía, Juan Mackenna 1069
(☎64/232446, ✉db@entelchile.net), is crammed

with every conceivable type of gift, from replica
Mapuche jewellery to flying ducks. You can pick up
very good leatherwork in the Mercado Municipal,
Errázuriz s/n.
Telephone centre Entel, Eleuterio Ramírez 1107,
Local 9.
Tour operators Tours to Parque Nacional
Puyehue cost CH$30,000 for a half-day and
CH$40,000 for a full day. Turismo Oasis, O'Higgins
779 (☎63/237297); Aventur, Zenteno 1203
(☎64/238632); and
Ñiltur, Mackenna 1069 (☎ 64/232446) are well-
respected local operators.

Bahía Mansa, Maicolpué and the coast

Until recently, the only occupant of **BAHÍA MANSA** and its neighbouring beaches was a small fishing fleet. The paving of the 64-kilometre tarred road west from Osorno changed that, and this small, sandy stretch of coast is now an increasingly popular summer holiday area. It's all a bit basic, though, and informal chalets without any proper services are springing up all over the vertiginous hillsides. Other development plans include an agreement to turn the area into a marine conservation park, taking advantage of the wealth and diversity of marine life, including dolphins and seabirds, found off the coast.

There's not much at Bahía Mansa itself, just a fish dock surrounded by high cliffs and simple accommodation at *Hospedaje Don Cheo* (☎63/1975330; ❷). Head 2km further south, however, and you'll come to the friendly village of **MAICOLPUÉ**, set on a large, beautiful bay and busy with bars, discos, good-value seafood restaurants and a couple of rustic but comfortable places to stay. The German/Chilean-owned *Hostería Miller* (☎64/1975360; ❹) has comfy *cabañas* and rooms with good views. A scruffy campsite by the beach (☎63/1975431) costs CH$3000 (cold showers are extra) per tent pitch or CH$12,000 for a *cabaña*, and there are some small secluded bays where wild camping is possible.

North of Bahía Mansa, a four-kilometre road follows the very beautiful Río Tarahuín to the pretty beach of **Pucatrihue**, which is free from crowds and provides a tranquil place to swim and unwind. You can easily visit the coast on a day-trip from Osorno: Buses Mar and Maicolpué come here twice daily, departing from the Mercado Municipal in the suburb of Rahue.

Lago Puyehue and thermal springs

The 47-kilometre road that shoots east from Osorno to **LAGO PUYEHUE** passes through some rich and fertile farmland. Every hundred metres or so you'll see roadside signs advertising *miel* (honey), *tomates* (tomatoes), *frambuesas* (raspberries), *frutillas* (strawberries) and, just occasionally, *toros* (bulls). It's a land of flat, lush meadows and trees, and of battered aluminium milk churns left by the road for collection. As the road nears the lake, you'll see rugged hills and mountains on the horizon, including the spiked pyramid of **Volcán Puntiagudo** (2490m). Reaching the village of **Entre Lagos**, you'll catch a glimpse of Lago Puyehue stretching away into the distance, enclosed in deep-green hills.

Entre Lagos is pleasant enough and can serve as a base from which to explore the thermal springs further up the road, but it has no real tourist facilities, save for a clutch of *residenciales*. The priciest night's sleep is at *Hostería Entre Lagos*,

Ramírez 65 (℗ & ℗64/371225; ❹), right on the edge of the lake, with modern en-suite rooms and a reasonable restaurant. But *Hostal Millaray*, Ramírez 333 (℗64/371251; ❸), is better – it's an excellent B&B, with a secluded balcony overlooking the water. The cheapest option is *Hospedaje y Cabañas Miraflores*, Ramírez 480 (℗64/371275; ❷). This lakeside hotel has four cabins (CH$25,000 for 6 people) as well as a bar and restaurant. *Chacrita*, on the edge of town by the main road, is a good place to **eat**, with enormous portions of meat.

As you drive east of Entre Lagos, the lake appears and disappears through the trees on your left, and the lakeshore is dotted with campsites, *hospedajes* and hotels. There's a fork after 32km: the left-hand road heads on to the Anticura section of the Parque Nacional Puyehue and the Argentine border, while the right-hand one leads to the Aguas Calientes section and the Antillanca skiing resort, passing the thermal springs of one of Chile's most famous and fashionable hotels (see below).

The thermal springs

Chile's finest hot spring accommodation, the ⚜ **Hotel Termas de Puyehue** (Ⓔreservas@hotelpuyehue.cl; Ⓦwww.puyehue.cl; reservations in Osorno at Matta 1216 ℗64/232881, Ⓔhotel@puyehue.cl; in Santiago at Vitacura 2898 ℗2/2342440, ℉2/2831010, Ⓔventas@puyehue.cl; ❽) features sprawling gardens and a plush resort with attractively furnished standard double rooms, surrounded by the main attractions of an Olympic-sized pool and tubs, spa facilities and treatment rooms. The verdant complex also boasts a fine restaurant serving international cuisine and occasionally hosts concerts. The indoor pools (CH$9000) are open daily 8am–9pm; outdoor pools (CH$6000) operate daily 9am–8pm. Bus transfers (around CH$50,000) from Osorno airport can be arranged with the hotel.

Other cheaper hot springs in the area include the pools and resort at *Aguas Calientes* (℗64/331710, Ⓔreservas@termasaguascalientes.com, Ⓦwww.puyehue.cl or Ⓦwww.termasaguascalientes.com), right at the entrance to the Parque Nacional Puyehue. It has *tinas* (personal bathtubs; CH$7000), double *tinas* (so you can bathe with a friend) and outdoor and indoor pools; use of the latter is included in the price of a *cabaña* in summer. These *cabañas* (❻–❼) are well-equipped (modern fridges, cookers, wood stoves and so on), but they are arranged in a military-style row that offers little privacy. For those who want to stay somewhere more private, try the two **campsites**: scenic, well-sited *Camping Chanleufú* (CH$12,000 for two) includes access to the outdoor pool; and the more informal *Camping Los Derrumbes* (CH$8000 for four people). Wild camping is also permitted in the national park.

For an adrenaline rush, explore the forest around the entrance to the national park on an hour-long canopy tour (℗64/331745, Ⓦwww.puyehue .cl, Ⓔcanopy@puyehue.cl; Mon–Sun daily 9am–8pm; CH$12,000 per person), where you're suspended from a harness and cables high above the forest floor and negotiate a circuit of eight platforms, over almost 800m, without having any impact on the flora.

Expresos Lago Puyehue and Buses Puyehue each run a daily **bus** from Osorno to the *termas*.

Parque Nacional Puyehue

PARQUE NACIONAL PUYEHUE (daily 8am–9pm; CH$1000; ℗64/236988 & 64/232881), 81km from Osorno, is one of Chile's busiest national parks, largely because of the traffic on the international road that

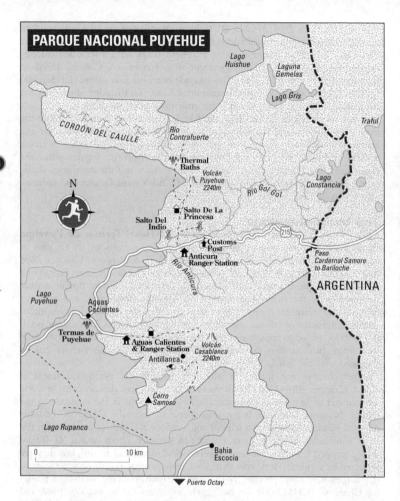

PARQUE NACIONAL PUYEHUE

Lago Huishue

Laguna Gemelas

Lago Gris

Traful

CORDÓN DEL CAULLE

Río Contrafuerte

Thermal Baths

Volcán Puyehue 2240m

Río Gol Gol

N

Lago Constancia

Salto De La Princesa

Salto Del Indio

Customs Post

215

Anticura Ranger Station

Paso Carderal Samore to Bariloche

Río Anticura

ARGENTINA

Lago Puyehue

Aguas Cacientes

Termas de Puyehue

Aguas Calientes & Ranger Station

Volcán Casablanca 2240m

Antillanca

Cerro Samoso

Lago Rupanco

0   10 km

Bahía Escocia

▼ Puerto Octay

runs through its middle. It's part of a massive, 15,000-square-kilometre area of protected wilderness, one of the largest in the Andes: it borders the Parque Nacional Vicente Pérez Rosales to the south, and some Argentine parks that stretch all the way to Pucón's Parque Nacional Villarrica in the north. The land is high temperate rainforest spread over two volcanoes, Volcán Puyehue (2240m) to the north, and Volcán Casablanca (1990m), on the west slope of which is the Antillanca ski resort.

The park's divided into three sectors: **Aguas Calientes** where the *termas* are, **Antillanca** and **Anticura**, straddling the international road.

Aguas Calientes

The Conaf station and information centre is at **AGUAS CALIENTES**, where there's a large, detailed **map of the park** on the wall, invaluable for orienting yourself, along with basic park maps that you can take with you. There are several **walks** in the area, mainly short, self-guided nature trails, such as the

Sendero Rápidos del Chanleufú, a 1250-metre track alongside the river rapids. There are also a couple of longer hikes, such as El Pionero, a steep 90-minute walk up a nearby hill, from where there's a good view of Volcán Casablanca, the Río Chanleufú and part of Lago Puyehue. A two-day trip, Lago Bertín y Antillanca (17km), follows the old road to Antillanca sector, through the dense forest along the banks of the Río Chanleufú. There's a six-bed **refugio** around the halfway point at Lago Bertín, deep in the heart of the park, and the next day you can continue on to Antillanca, 9km further on, returning to Aguas Calientes along the road (there's usually enough traffic to hitch).

Antillanca

The **ski centre** at **ANTILLANCA**, the *Centro Turístico De Ski Antillanca* (℡64/242010, ✉info@skiantillanca.com, ⊛www.skiantillanca.com, reservations in Osorno at the Club Andino Osorno at O'Higgins 1073 ℡64/238877), is 18km from Aguas Calientes by road. You can stay in the refuge (**⑥**) or in the hotel (**⑦**). The centre is open all year (ski season July–Aug) and has 9 lifts and 28 ski slopes for all skill levels. It also has a restaurant, open-air swimming pool, gymnasium, ski-rental shop and a few apartments that book up quickly in season. In summer it's relatively quiet, with excellent views along the cordillera, right across the central plain to the Pacific Ocean, and is a popular destination for mountain bikers. In winter, it gets so busy that traffic on the last 8km up to the ski centre is subject to time restrictions (up 8am–noon & 2–5.30pm; down noon–2pm & after 5.30pm).

Anticura

ANTICURA lies 22km from Aguas Calientes; to get here, head back to the junction by the *Hotel Termas de Puyehue* and then along the international road to Argentina, a pretty stretch with lakes on either side. You'll find a number of short **hikes** around the Conaf station, mostly designed for car drivers who just want to get out for a quick amble; the prettiest is the 850-metre walk to El Salto del Indio (CH$1000), a half-hour stroll through a forest of ancient coigüe to a broad waterfall. More adventurous is the 22-kilometre return trail to Volcán Puyehue, which starts 2km west of Anticura, opposite a church, where there's a small Conaf office. The beginning of the path passes over some private property, where you'll have to pay CH$6000 to cross the land either on foot or you can arrange for a guide and horses (El Caulle Expediciones, 1145 Los Carreras, Oficina 15, Osorno, ℡64/233233, ✉elcaulle@telsur.cl, ⊛www.elcaulle.com). The fee entitles you to use the basic refuge, which sleeps sixteen; it's a three-hour walk along the trail from the Conaf office. Shortly past the refuge, the trail forks: the right-hand route goes up the volcano for 6km (2hr; no special equipment needed), and from the crater there are views over Lagos Puyehue and Rupanco. The left-hand path leads to a thermal spring next to an icy stream, half a day's walk from the refuge. You can mix the waters and bathe – an amazing experience at night, cooking yourself gently in the waters underneath the stars. A 25-kilometre stretch of track, beginning in Anticura and linking the two sectors of the park whilst skirting the eastern flank of Volcán Casablanca, is slated to become part of the Sendero de Chile (see "Adventure sports" colour insert).

Park practicalities

The only places to stay or eat in the park are at the ski centre, the refuges, and the *Hotel Termas de Puyehue* and the Aguas Calientes complex. There are a number of **buses** a day to Aguas Calientes from Osorno, taking a little over an hour, run by Expresos Lago Puyehue (5 daily) and Flor Bus (12 daily). Some of the buses continue on to Anticura. There aren't any buses to Antillanca, but Agencia Aventur in Osorno (see p.384) arranges transport on request. The Chilean customs post, Pajaritos (daily: May–mid-Oct 9am–7pm; mid-Oct–April 8am–9pm) is 4km down the road from Anticura, and the Argentine border post, Paso Cardernal Samore, is 44km beyond it.

Lago Rupanco

LAGO RUPANCO, 13km south of Lago Puyehue, is a very pretty flat blue lake, delved into by fingers of pine-covered spurs and ringed by five volcanoes. To the west of the lake the land is flat pasture, lined with hedgerows and rows of stately poplars, and in the east it rises into forest, volcanoes and towering rock ridges. With no tar road it's still rural and undeveloped, and much of the traffic is made up of horsebound *huasos* and their dogs, driving herds of cattle in clouds of dust.

If you expect **to stay**, the eastern end of the lake is just about completely owned by *Hacienda Rupanco* (Ⓣ & Ⓕ64/203000, Ⓦwww.haciendarupanco .com; ❽), one of the largest dairy farms in Chile. It has recently diversified into upmarket tourism (ambassadors spend their holidays here) and offers a couple of well-furnished houses and a wide range of activities on its vast lands: horse-riding (from CH$9400 for a half-day), fishing (from CH$47,000 for a day) and "agrotourism" – generally helping out with the livestock and seeing how the farm works (CH$11,750 a day). If this is too rich for your blood, then head 23km along the south bank of the lake, where you'll hit the other end of the scale. The *Hostería Piedra Negra Rupanco* (no phone; ❷) looks like it's shut – dogs bark as you come in, the main building is locked and the locks are rusted – but up a hill by the chicken coop there's usually someone who will let you use the musty old *cabañas*. At the far east of the lake, 23km beyond the *hostería*, there's one of the most beautifully sited fishing lodges in the whole Lake District. *Bahía Escocia Fly Fishing* (Ⓣ64/1974731, Ⓔbahiaescocia@entelchile.net; ❼) 2km beyond the bus stop in the village of **Puerto Rico**, looks out over the rugged hills and down the lake towards the pastoral west. The lodge has all the atmosphere of a family home, and it's run by a Chilean-American couple, he a fly-fishing guide, and she a chef from Seattle. It's more a centre for fishing (three-day package from CH$565,000 per person) and horse trips than a backpacker's lodge, but even if you don't want to fish or ride horses it's worth staying here because it's so gorgeous and well-run.

Igi Llaima runs one **bus** a day (2hr) from Osorno to Puerto Rico, the village 2km west of the *Bahia Escocia* lodge. A boat often meets it and transfers passengers off to the trailhead of the Los Todos Santos hike (see p.394), charging CH$20,000 per boatload.

Lago Llanquihue and around

An immense inland sea of 870 square kilometres, **LAGO LLANQUIHUE** boasts a backdrop for one of the icons of the Lake District, the Mount Fuji-like **Volcán Osorno** (2661m), in all its stunning, symmetrical perfection. The sight of it is all the more extraordinary because the lake is not surrounded by the extreme country you normally associate with volcanoes, but by gently rolling pastures scattered with black and white Friesian cows and stalls selling German pastries and smoked trout. The easiest way here from Lago Rupanco is to travel back to Osorno and then down the Panamericana 55km – you'll spot the lake from the road.

The little villages around Lago Llanquihue differ greatly. **Frutillar Bajo**, on the lake's western shore, is a summer holiday resort beloved by Chileans; **Puerto Octay**, to the north, is a neat little Bavarian-looking town; and bustling **Puerto Varas**, in the south, is fast challenging Pucón as the Lake District's adventure tourism centre. One thing that unites them is their shared German heritage, a result of an influx of German and Swiss settlers in the mid-nineteenth century. Some people still speak German rather than Spanish at home and live in houses filled with portraits of flaxen-haired, pale-eyed European men in high-collared apparel.

By the time you come to the village of **Ensenada**, on the far eastern shore of the lake, forest has overtaken dairy fields and the land begins to rise as you enter the foothills of the Andes. This forest extends to the border, and is protected by the **Parque Nacional Vicente Pérez Rosales**. The national park is a favourite scenic route into Argentina, as it contains the magical green waters of **Lago Todos Los Santos**, which offers a spectacular trip to Argentina using a combination of ferries across the lake and buses leaving from Puerto Montt.

South of Ensenada the road winds its way down through isolated country to the placid calm of Chile's northernmost **fjord**, a branch of the Estuario de Reloncaví. Here, a hundred kilometres inland from the open sea, you can hire a plane or horse-trek into South America's oldest rainforest – the famous alerce groves found in the valleys above the village of **Cochamó**.

Frutillar Bajo

The Panamericana first approaches Lago Llanquihue at Frutillar Alto. This low-cost housing suburb sits just 4km west of **FRUTILLAR BAJO**, a little village of black-sand beaches, manicured landscaping and a magical view of Volcán Osorno, soaring above the shimmering surface of the lake. Because it's so popular it gets very crowded here in summer, especially during the last week of January to the first week of February, when the town hosts a **classical music festival** (ⓦ www.semanasmusicales.cl).

There are only two main streets in Frutillar Bajo: Vicente Pérez Rosales and Avenida Phillippi, which both run parallel to the coast. At the bottom of the hill leading from Frutillar Alto, near the junction with Vicente Pérez Rosales, is a beautifully tended garden, an old water mill and several other traditional wooden buildings that make up the **Museo Colonial Alemán** (daily: summer 10am–8pm; winter Tues–Sun 10am–2pm & 3–6pm; CH$1600). The museum houses a wide variety of household objects and farm machinery used by the earliest immigrants to Llanquihue, but most interesting is the barn outside. Circular barns *(campanarios)* like the one that houses a collection of early agricultural machinery here, were once a common sight in the coastal mountains. Inside, pairs of horses were tethered to the central pillar and driven round in circles, threshing sheaves of corn with their hoofs. But the barns have completely vanished. Further up the hill in the **Casa del Herrero**, the blacksmith's house, you can buy horseshoes with your name stamped on them, and higher up still is the reconstruction of a typical early farmhouse filled with period furniture.

If you cross over the main road by the museum and turn left at the end of Vicente Pérez Rosales, you'll come to a dirt road that leads to the **Reserva Forestal Edmundo Winkler** (Jan–Feb daily 9am–7pm; March–Dec Mon–Sat 9am–4pm; CH$1000). Hemmed in by low hills, in an area of perfectly preserved native forest, is an experimental forestry station set up by the Universidad Austral de Chile. In January and February students and staff conduct guided walks and help visitors to identify the sixty species of trees, flowers and shrubs that grow here. The station also sells native and exotic saplings.

Practicalities

You'll **arrive** in Frutillar Alto, not Frutillar Bajo, unless you've caught one of the summer minibuses that run directly here from Puerto Montt and Puerto Varas. From Frutillar Alto, you can walk the 4km down to the lakeshore or catch one of the *colectivos* that operate shuttle services (CH$300) from the Varmontt stop on the main street, Carlos Richter. In Frutillar Bajo there's a lakefront **tourist information office**, on Avenida Phillippi and O'Higgins (Dec–March daily 9am–9pm; ☎65/420198, ⓦ www.frutillarsur.cl).

Apart from the bank and town hall, every building in Frutillar seems to offer **accommodation** during the summer. Any place on Avenida Phillippi with rooms facing the lake charges a premium and gets booked up well in advance, though if you *must* have a lakeshore bed there are some excellent farmhouse B&Bs outside the village. In the centre, one of the cheapest options is *Hostería Trayén*, Phillippi 963 (☎65/421346; ❸). The rooms are good and have private bathrooms, and guests may use the communal kitchen; breakfast is included. *Hospedaje Nohelia*, Phillippi 615 (☎65/421310; ❸), offers rooms with private bath in a restored old wooden home in front of the lake. The friendly hostess serves a big German-style breakfast. The price is very negotiable in the off-season.

The HI hostel *Hostería Winkler*, Phillippi 1155 (☎65/421388, ⓦ www .hostelling.cl/frutillar.html; ❹), has well-maintained dorms (CH$6000 per person) and the private rooms here offer superb views of the lake. There is also a kitchen and a bathroom. *Hotel Klein Salzburg* at Phillippi 663 (☎65/421201, ⓕ65/421750; ❹) is an attractive colonial house overlooking the lake, with a restaurant that's a popular choice for snacks but also offers heartier meals of Chilean fare.

Just to the south of Frutillar is *Hotel Posada Campesina* (☎65/422396, ⓔ pcampesina@frutillarsur.cl; ❸). Set on a small peninsula adjacent to the beach, this large tourist complex provides all the amenities for family or group holidays within easy reach of the town. In addition to the hotel, you'll find a handful of *cabañas* that accommodate six (CH$30,000), and a number of tent pitches for camping (CH$10,000 per site). Six kilometres north, in a sheltered bay off the road to Puerto Octay, is the *Hostería y Camping Playa Maqui* (☎65/330000, ⓔ mwohlke@ditec.cl; ❹). This large, traditional house, built in 1880, sits amid native woods and offers a tranquil escape from the hubbub in town. You can also **camp** here (CH$10,000–12,000 for up to ten people).

There's no shortage of places to **eat** in Frutillar; *onces* (afternoon tea) is almost an obligatory ritual. You'll find several cafés along Phillippi where you can partake in this custom, all of which serve home-made *küchen*. *Salón de Té Trayén*, Phillippi 963, with large picture windows (and connected to the *Hostería* of the same name), is the best spot to sit and soak up the calories and the views. For reasonably priced set lunches, head for *Club de Bomberos*, Phillippi 1065, in the old Art Deco fire station. The quiet club room upstairs has a good view over the lake and an impressive mural of a fire, with caricatures of the local firemen. Frutillar's *Club Alemán*, at Phillippi 741, has excellent service and tasty set lunches as well as a traditional à la carte menu. *Café Restaurant Andes* at Phillippi 1057 serves a wide selection of reasonably priced fish and meat dishes as well as *onces*. *Selva Negra*, at Antonio Varas 24, offers a combination of traditional German food and local seafood dishes.

For **shopping**, try ACAF, at Phillippi and O'Higgins, with arts and crafts, weavings, wool, jams and sweets. There's not much in the way of other services in

Frutillar, and you're better off making the trip down to Puerto Varas for changing money and the like, but there is a **casa de cambio** at Phillippi 883, and also a telephone centre. You'll find an ATM at Banco Santander, Phillippi 555.

Buses leave Frutillar for Puerto Montt every ten minutes, operated by Thaebus (San Pedro 255 ☎65/420120), Full Express (Alessandri and Richter ☎65/421522) and Expresos Puerto Varas (Alessandri and Richter). Buses going further afield, such as to Temuco and Santiago, include Cruz del Sur, Alessandri and Portales, Tur Bus, Diego Portales 150, and Fierro, Alessandri and Richter. A small **travel agency**, *Agencia de Viaje Frutitur*, Diego Portales 150 (☎65/421810, Ⓔfrutitur@surnet.cl), can organize excursions, book hotels or rent you a car.

Puerto Octay and around

From Frutillar, a dirt road follows the shore of the lake, passing some attractive farmhouses and churches set in rolling meadowland punctuated with stately lines of tall poplars. This is a restrained countryside, contrasting with the dark shoulders of the plutonic Volcán Osorno further down the road. Thirty kilometres northeast of Frutillar, around Lago Llanquihue, lies **PUERTO OCTAY**, a friendly little town by the lakeshore, nestling in the crook of some hills. With its needle-steepled church and balconied houses with ornate eaves, it looks as though it's been transplanted to Chile from the Alps.

Puerto Octay was the first settlement on Lago Llanquihue and dates from 1852. The name (so the story goes) arose because of a village store that was opened here by one Cristino Ochs. It was the only shop for kilometres around, and people often used to ask each other "what's Ochs got?", which in Spanish became *"¿Ochs hay?"*, hence Octay. The town developed into an important port in the days of the lake steamer, and today it's the municipal centre for a vast territory stretching up to Lago Rupanco in the north. It is proud of its long history, and a little envious of Frutillar's success with the tourists, yet remains a charming, cheaper and more authentic alternative to some of the other towns in the region.

If you're interested in the history of the village, visit the small Museum "El Colono", on the second floor of the 1920 Casa Niklitschek, at Independencia 591 (Tues–Sun 10am–1pm & 3–7pm; CH$500; ☎64/391523). It focuses on German colonization and is filled with musical instruments, tableware and old photographs. There are plenty of old agricultural machines and stills for making the sweet alcoholic *chicha* drink, a local speciality.

Some of Puerto Octay's older buildings include the 1894 **Casa Haase** at Pedro Montt 344. The elderly owner will sometimes show visitors (especially if they're German) the interior, which still has the original hand-stencilled decorations. You'll find a couple of nice **beaches** nearby: the grey-sand **La Baja** is only 3km from Puerto Octay on Península Centinela (the headland to the south of the village). Peaceful **Maitén**, 9km to the east along the shore, features the settlement's original 1867 wooden church.

Practicalities

You can reach Puerto Octay from Osorno on Buses Vía Octay, which runs two services an hour. There are five buses a day from Frutillar and Puerto Montt. Puerto Octay's **Oficina de Turismo** (Dec–March Mon–Fri 9am–9pm; ☎64/391750, Ⓦwww.puertooctay.cl) is next door to the Municipalidad on the Plaza de Armas, and staffed by garrulous volunteers.

As for **accommodation**, Puerto Octay has a couple of little *residenciales* and the posh hotel *Hotel Centinela* (☎ & Ⓕ64/391326, Ⓦwww.hotelcentinela .cl; ❼) on the end of Península Centinela, 5km from Octay. Decorated in its original 1913 "High Bavarian" style, it looks as though it hasn't changed since King Edward VIII stayed here in 1931, when he was still the Prince of Wales. Ask for a room overlooking the lake which costs fractionally more than rooms with forest views. *Hostería La Baja*, at the base of the peninsula, 4km from Octay (Ⓣ64/391269; ❸), offers cheap accommodation in a quiet refuge; breakfast is included. ⚡ *Zapato Amarillo*, 2.5km north of Puerto Octay (Ⓣ64/391575, Ⓔshiela@telsur.cl, Ⓦwww.zapatoamarillo.8k.com; doubles ❹, dorm ❷) has a homely main lodge with grass roof and wooden interior, while an eight-bed dorm, kitchen and communal area are in a separate building. Meals served in the main house include a sumptuous cheese fondue. They also have canoe, bike, sailing boat and climbing gear rentals, Internet access (and their website is excellent) and free pick-up in town; the owners speak German and English and can organize a series of excursions to Vicente Pérez Rosales National Park or to Volcán Osorno. You can **camp** at *Camping El Molino*, on the *costanera* (Dec–Feb; Ⓣ64/391375; ❷ for up to five people).

For **eating**, the expensive and highly acclaimed restaurant at *Hotel Centinela* serves up fantastic steaks and seafood, plus an outdoor patio during the summer with a spectacular vista. Cheaper alternatives in town include the wholesome *Baviera* on the west side of the plaza at Germán Wulf 582, and *El Fogon de Anita*, on the northern edge of town, one kilometre along the road to Osorno, which serves *parrilladas*. Three kilometres out of Puerto Octay on the road to Frutillar is *Tante Valy*, a reasonably priced and very typical German style tea house with cakes (*küchen*) and tea.

The northern shore

The road continues around Lago Llanquihue, passing beaches, fields and the villages of **Puerto Fonk** (20km) and **Puerto Klocker** (29km). This was the part of the area that was first settled, and it was here in 1852 that 21 German families were allocated plots to farm. A plaque on the simple church at Playa Maitén commemorates the centenary of the settlers' arrival. (While you're there, note the weather vane of an angel blowing a trumpet on the top of the

△ Volcán Osorno

church steeple.) *Cabanas Los Guindos*, in Puerto Fonck (☎ & ⓕ64/391300; ❹) has three cabins in a forested setting, with a tiny beach and quiet surroundings, though it's sometimes very windy. Shortly after Puerto Klocker, there's a turning to the east that leads 20km up the northern slope of Volcán Osorno to an unserviced **refuge** called *La Picada*, but the main road continues around the lake for 36km to **Las Cascadas**, a quiet village with a beach, a couple of houses, a *hospedaje* and a *carabineros* checkpoint. Beyond here the scenery changes as the road – recently paved the whole way – narrows and ploughs into dense scrub and forest. The fields have gone, and through the trees you catch glimpses of the volcano towering above you, no longer picturesque but menacing. Beneath the volcano, 4km south of Las Cascades and 15km north of Ensenada, is **Canopy Lodge** (☎65/234020, ⓔ contacto@canopychile.cl, ⓦ www.canopychile.cl), with ten *cabañas*, a restaurant and a pub. Set amid native forest, this was the first company in Chile to set up a canopy tour for visitors to explore the forest suspended from wires, high above the ground. Tours last 2-3 hours and cost CH$25.000. Horse-riding and fishing excursions are also offered.

About 8km north of Puerto Octay in the town of Nochaco is the recommended **Agroturismo Fundo Merlín** (☎64/396245; ❷), which offers inexpensive camping (CH$4000) on two hundred acres of land, with plenty of opportunities to hike the canyons and river valleys, and free horseback riding.

Volcán Osorno and Ensenada

Nineteen kilometres after Las Cascadas, deep in the forest, there's a turning to the east heading up the slopes of **VOLCÁN OSORNO**. It's 14km up to the *La Burbuja* refuge and Conaf station, from where there's a spectacular view. To the west you can see across Lago Llanquihue, the central plain and across to the sea, and dominating the skyline to the south are the jagged peaks of Volcán Calbuco, which erupted spectacularly in 1893, ripping its summit apart and hurling rocks all the way to the coast. Up here, keeping Conaf company, are two ski centres: the renovated Centro de Esquí La Burbuja, owned by the *Hotel Vicente Pérez Rosales* in Puerto Montt (☎65/252571, ⓕ65/312572), and the *Refugio Teski Ski Club* (☎65/212012), a rustic hut pegged out with wires to prevent it from taking off, with bunkrooms (CH$6000 per person) and a cosy little café with vibrant photographs of Volcán Osorno's deep-blue ice caves. It has two chairlifts and seven runs open to skiers.

You can climb the volcano from *La Burbuja*. It's about five hours to the summit (two to the snowline, three more to the top), and there are many crevasses, so ice equipment is needed and a guide recommended. Conaf authorizes three companies to guide people up: AquaMotion, Al Sur and Tranco Expediciones (see Puerto Varas, p.401). In the Conaf station, you'll find a maudlin display of obituary photographs and emotional letters from friends and relatives of tourists who have died or vanished in the crevasses on this seemingly innocuous hillside. In Mapuche mythology, a spirit called *hueñauca* lives on the volcano and preys on humans.

Back down on Llanquihue's shore road, 2km further, is a local beauty spot. From a car park, a signpost directs visitors to a ten-minute walk through the trees to **Laguna Verde**, an attractive pond near the edge of a lake. Almost immediately after the Laguna Verde car park, the road breaks clear of the forest and you arrive in **ENSENADA**, a small village in a lovely location on the shores of the lake. It has basic services and is a good base from which to make excursions as it's at a staggered crossroads. There's a bit of **accommodation** here, starting with the campsite on the lakeshore, *Camping Trauco Playa Parque* (☎65/212033),

4km west of Ensenada, with a private beach and good facilities including tours and bike and boat rental; sites cost from CH$10,000. *Hospedaje Ruedas Viejas* (℡ & ℱ65/212050; ❹) is a B&B lost in a 1940s time warp, with an attractive old garden by the edge of the lake. *Cabanas Los Alamos* (℡65/212055, or 9/5197134, CH$20,000 per four-person cabin) is well-marked in Ensenada and offers four cabins with kitchens, plenty of privacy, friendly service and a great lake view. *Hotel Ensenada* (℡65/212028, ℱ65/212017, ✉info@hotelensenada .cl, ✇www.hotelensenada.cl; ❼), has been around for 100 years and looks like the kind of stylish place that Bonnie and Clyde might have settled down at, with lost of antiques and large, well-appointed rooms. For gourmet dining, try the smoked salmon and savoury Chilean barbeque at *Restaurant Las Tranqueras* on Route 225, km 41 (℡65/212056). The plush resort *Yan Kee Way Lodge* (℡65/212030, ✉reserve@southernchileexp.com, ✇www.yankeewaylodge .com; ❾), 1km south at km 42, specializes in fly-fishing excursions but also offers a number of other all-inclusive programmes. The excellent restaurant, *Latitud 42°*, features a comprehensive wine list of 200 labels from 30 Chilean vineyards; it's also open to non-guests.

To get to Ensenada, take a **bus** headed towards Petrohué from Puerto Montt via Puerto Varas.

Lago Todos Los Santos and Parque Nacional Vicente Pérez Rosales

The **Saltos de Petrohué** (daily: summer 8.30am–8.30pm; winter 9am–6pm; CH$1200), a series of impressive, boiling rapids formed by an extremely hard layer of lava that has been eroded into small channels, lie 10km from Ensenada, off a road that leads through incredibly dense forest. Wild flowers thrive in the humid conditions around the falls, and there are marked nature trails along the river bank. Unfortunately this area is plagued during hot, dry summers by two biting flies, the *petros (sandfly)* and *tábanos* (horsefly), whose persistent pestering has to be experienced to be believed. About the only advice local people can offer in dealing with these silent monsters is not to wear dark clothing, particularly blue. According to local legend, these rapids are the home of another monster, *cuchivilu*, which resembles a giant puma with a claw on the end of its tail.

The volcanic rock in the area was part of a tongue of lava sent this way by Volcán Osorno in 1850, an eruption that diverted the Petrohué River from its old course into Lago Llanquihue. As you drive alongside the river, areas of regenerating forest are clearly visible, and every Spring sections of the road are washed away when rain and snow-melt pour down the flanks of the volcano. At the end of the road lies **LAGO TODOS LOS SANTOS**, deep green and stunningly clear, one of the most beautiful in the Lake District – it's also known as Lago Esmeralda (Emerald Lake) because of the intense colour of its water. The lake and the forests that crowd its shores are protected by the Parque Nacional Vicente Pérez Rosales. On the other side of the lake is a road that leads to the Argentine border. This route was first used as a border crossing by Jesuit missionaries in the seventeenth century, in their attempts to convert the Tehuelche Indians on the pampas. The lake's now a twisting, turning, flooded valley, with forested banks and a sense of isolation in the jagged, pine-forested hills.

From Petrohué to Peulla

The hamlet of **PETROHUÉ** sits on the western shore of Lago Todos Los Santos. The settlement dates from the early twentieth century, when one

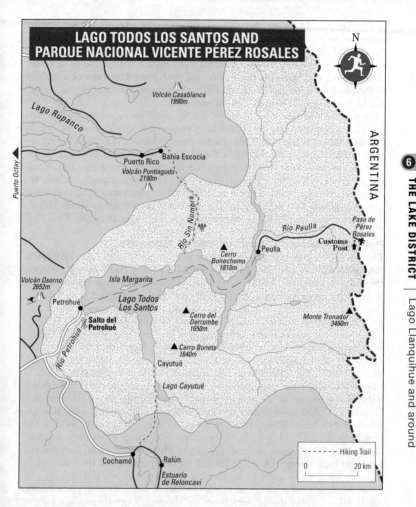

LAGO TODOS LOS SANTOS AND PARQUE NACIONAL VICENTE PÉREZ ROSALES

N

Lago Rupanco

Volcán Casablanca
1990m

Puerto Octay

Puerto Rico   Bahía Escocia

Volcán Puntiagudo
2190m

ARGENTINA

Río Sin Nombre

Río Peulla

Paso de
Pérez
Rosales

Peulla

Customs
Post

Cerro
Bonechemo
1810m

Volcán Osorno
2652m

Isla Margarita

Petrohué

Lago Todos
Los Santos

Salto del
Petrohué

Cerro del
Derrumbe
1650m

Monte Tronador
3460m

Río Petrohué

Cerro Bonete
1640m

Cayutué

Lago Cayutué

- - - - Hiking Trail

0   20 km

Cochamó   Ralún

Estuario
de Reloncaví

Ricardo Roth began taking tourists across the lakes between Puerto Varas and Bariloche, a venture that led to the construction of two hotels – *Petrohué* and *Peulla* (see below and p.396) and the foundation of Andina del Sud tour company. Roth is buried on the lake's Isla Margarita, and when tour boats pass they blow their horns in memory of him.

These days Petrohué is a bit of a hole, cursed in the summer by persistent biting insects, shouting children and libidinous adolescents. There's a post office here, some boats for rent on the lake and a couple of very expensive **places to stay**. In the forest near the falls is *Fundo El Salto Lodge* (no phone; ❾), a charming and well-established fly-fishing lodge. On the edge of the lake stands the *Hotel Petrohué* (☎65/212025, ✉reservas@petrohue.com, ⓦwww.petrohue.com; office in Puerto Varas at Casilla 850; ❽) which recently reopened after being badly damaged in a fire, and has four comfortable lakeside *cabañas* that sleep up to four people (❽) and a campsite on the beach (CH$7000 for up to four people). There are also a couple of alternative, cheaper options on the other side of the river – ask one of the boatmen to ferry you across. *Hospedaje Familia Kuschel* (℡65/277832; ❷) offers a basic room in the family home, or you can camp for CH$2500 per tent. Sra Rosa Burgos charges the same to stay in her house, *El Umakudau*. Both places sell fresh trout. Five **buses** travel daily to Petrohué from Puerto Montt via Puerto Varas, run by Buses JM year-round, and by Fierro and Buses Adriazola in summer.

Andina del Sud (see Puerto Montt, p.409) offers **tours** on the lake, which provide unsurpassed views of Volcán Osorno, the spiked peak of Volcán Puntiagudo, and highest of all, the glacier-covered Monte Tronador. Day excursions to **PEULLA**, at the far end of the lake, leave at 10.30am. At Peulla, there's little except the border post (daily: Jan–March 8am–9pm; April–Dec 8am–8pm) and the *Hotel Peulla* (℡65/258041, ⓦwww.chile-hotels.com/puellahot.htm; ❼), a large old wooden building that is functional rather than comfortable and seems to have capitalized on its proximity to a number of spectacular locations, including a picturesque waterfall. Argentine customs is 23km east, at Laguna Frias.

Parque Nacional Vicente Pérez Rosales

The whole forest around Lago Todos Los Santos is protected by the **PARQUE NACIONAL VICENTE PÉREZ ROSALES** (daily: April–Nov 9am–6pm; Dec–March 9am–8pm; CH$1200), Chile's oldest national park. It's covered by an excellent **map** published by JLM, *Ruta de los Jesuitas (No.15)*, available in Puerto Varas and Puerto Montt. The Conaf information centre in Petrohué also has trail maps and a model on which you can pick out the hikes.

There are some short **trails**, and two longer. The best shorter trail, Paso Desolación, a seven-hour, twelve-kilometre forest walk, leaves from Petrohué, and passes two *refugios*, *Winttner* and *Los Curas*. You can make a detour down to the lake, to Playa Larga, a three-hour trek through woods to a quiet little beach.

For the longer trails, you'll need to rent a **boat** from the dock at Petrohué (CH$35,000 for up to six people) to get to the starting point. The first trail, Termas de Callao, starts from the northern shores of the lake by the Río Sin Nombre (No-Name River). Head up the river – the path is reasonably clear but be sure to always head upwards to the source – and after about three hours of climbing you reach some thermal springs and a basic refuge. From here you can either go back down to Lago Todos Los Santos, having asked the boatman to pick you up again, or carry on up to the Laguna Los Quetros and over the pass – another two hours' hike – and then descend to Lago Rupanco (see p.388), which takes another three hours. From the shores of Lago Rupanco, it's about another hour (west) to Puerto Rico, from where there are buses to Osorno (see p.380). Sometimes there's a boat-taxi waiting at the point where the trail reaches Lago Ranco, to take you to the bus stop.

The second hike leaves from **Cayutué**, a village down a channel, on the south shore of the lake, and follows the missionaries' route south to Ralún on the Estuario de Reloncaví (see below). It's about a seventeen-kilometre hike, and is an easy walk along a heavily rutted logging road where fresh clear-cuts are encroaching the virgin stands.

Avoid wearing dark clothing when hiking, or else you risk attracting the local biting **horseflies** (*tábanos*).

The Estuario de Reloncaví

On the way back to Ensenada from Parque Nacional Vicente Pérez Rosales, a southern fork, 1km before the town of Ensenada, will take you 33km along a good road, fringed with large bushes of wild fuchsia and giant rhubarb plants, to the tranquil **ESTUARIO DE RELONCAVÍ**. The fjord, now packed with salmon farming operations, is a good place to escape and unwind or to horse-trek into the **Cochamó Valley**, home to the oldest standing trees in South America. Your first view of the bay comes as you descend to **Ralún**, a small town with a couple of stores and frequent buses to Puerto Montt. The bay is an amazing colour – bright green from one angle, deepest blue from another – and at the far end, standing sentinel over the fjord's exit, is Volcán Yate (2111m).

Ralún sits near the junction of two roads; the road west of the fjord leads to a hydroelectric project, passing the edge of the Parque Nacional Alerce Andino (see p.449). The other road, along the east side of the fjord, goes through wild, dramatic scenery, with waterfalls crashing underneath snow-capped mountains. This is the beginning of the landscape of the **Carretera Austral**, a pioneer-ing expansion into Southern Chile (see Chapter 8), and there are unmapped trails through virgin forests in these mountains ready to be explored by the adventurous. (Beware that the underbrush in many places makes bushwhacking practically impossible.) Many of these trails lead to Argentina, and throughout history the low passes in this area have been used by bandits, missionaries and merchants to crisscross the Andes. One of the most frequently trodden trails into Argentina starts at Puelo, the village at the end of this road, and eventually leads to El Bolsón on the other side of the cordillera.

After 14km, the road reaches **Cochamó** (see above), a beautiful little fishing village flanked with pine-clad hills. Sra Idita Moreno Paillán runs a *hospedaje* (T65/216256; ❸) in the top floor of the general store on the seafront. It's a bargain of a place, with new varnished wood everywhere, a balcony (if you can brave the fierce wind that whips down the fjord) and a steep staircase that would be easy to tumble down. There's also the small and rustic *Hotel Cochamó*, Catedral 19 (T65/216212; ❸), which is often full of salmon farmers. About 4km south is the adventure tourism complex *Campo Aventura* (Oct–May 15; T65/232910, Einfo@campo-aventura.com, Wwww.campo-aventura.com; ❸), specializing in horse-trekking, hiking and kayaking.

Buses Fierro has a regular service to Cochamó from Puerto Montt, with stops at Ralún and places along the way; **buses** leave Puerto Montt daily at 8.15am, noon and 5pm and return from Río Puelo (31km down the road) at 7am, 1pm and 4pm.

Puerto Varas

If you return to Ensenada and then take the road to the west, you'll pass along an excellent tarred road along Lago Llanquihue's southern shore, and the land once again becomes tamed, lush and pastoral. After 47km you'll reach **PUERTO VARAS**, a spruce little town with wide streets, grassy lawns and exquisite views of two volcanoes, Osorno and Calbuco. It's a bit like Pucón, and like Pucón there's not much to see in the town itself – the reason you come to Puerto Varas is for its tourist facilities. However, it does have some old buildings because, despite recent rapid growth, it's not a new settlement – tourism took off in Puerto Varas as long ago as 1903, when the trail between Lago Todos Los Santos and Argentina was first opened.

Arrival and information

The only way of reaching Puerto Varas these days is by **bus**, as the train no longer currently runs here. There are plans for a regular train service to begin again between Temuco and Puerto Montt, stopping at Puerto Varas. The bus companies

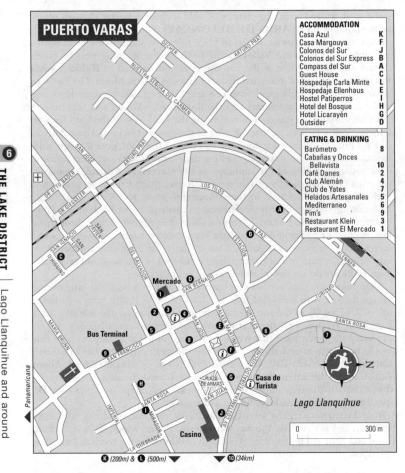

Panamericana

PUERTO VARAS

ACCOMMODATION	
Casa Azul	K
Casa Margouya	F
Colonos del Sur	J
Colonos del Sur Express	B
Compass del Sur	A
Guest House	C
Hospedaje Carla Minte	L
Hospedaje Ellenhaus	E
Hostel Patiperros	I
Hotel del Bosque	H
Hotel Licarayén	G
Outsider	D

EATING & DRINKING	
Barómetro	8
Cabañas y Onces Bellavista	10
Café Danes	2
Club Alemán	4
Club de Yates	7
Helados Artesanales	5
Mediterraneo	6
Pim's	9
Restaurant Klein	3
Restaurant El Mercado	1

Lago Llanquihue

0   300 m

K (200m) & **L** (500m) ▼   ▼ **10** (34km)

are scattered around town: many of the efficient minibuses that connect Puerto Varas to Ensenada and Petrohué stop at a bus shelter on San Bernardo opposite the Esso petrol station, and others use a shelter in Del Salvador between Santa Rosas and San Francisco. For tourist information, head to **Casa del Turista** on the wharf, Piedraplén s/n, Muelle de Puerto Varas (daily 9am–1.30pm & 3–7pm; ☎65/237956 or ☎65/237272, Ⓔcorporacion@puertovaras.org, Ⓦwww.puertovaras.org). The Agrupación de Hospedajes **Informatur**, on the Plaza de Armas, at San José and Santa Rosa (daily: Jan–March 8am–11pm; April–Dec Mon–Sat 9am–2pm & 4–8pm; ☎65/338542, Ⓦwww.informatur .com) offers basic info but is often closed in the off-season. Books El Libro del Capitán, Walker Martinez 417, Local 12, has a good selection of books on the area, some of which are available in English.

Accommodation

A number of private houses let **rooms** during the summer, particularly along San Francisco, and the tourist office will have an up-to-date list of them. They are often better value than some of the central *hospedajes*, which are severely overpriced, charging around CH$20,000 for bed and breakfast, a situation that gets worse in summer, when the town fills with people making the Todos Los Santos lake crossing to Argentina. Another option is to stay at one of the **farms** that offer "agrotourism" packages: a mixture of bed, breakfast and mucking out the horses. An organization called AGRHOSA, San José on the corner of Santa Rosa (℡65/338542) has the details.

Casa Azul Manzanal 66 at Rosario ℡65/232904, ℮casaazul@telsur.cl, ⓦwww.casaazul.net. Plenty of other travellers stay at this popular spot, with smallish rooms which can get noisy due to the thin walls and bare wooden floors. There's a reading room, free Internet access, a kitchen, garden and terrace. In addition to private rooms (**4**), you can also stay in dorm beds.

Casa Margouya Santa Rosa 318 ℡65/511648, ℮info@margouya.com, ⓦwww.margouya.com. Smack in the centre, this vibrant, 24-hour hostel is a great spot to meet other travellers. Dorm rooms cost CH$6500–7500, and you also get free use of the kitchen, a laundry service and a book exchange. The helpful owners speak English and French and can advise you on all sorts of activities around the area.

Colonos del Sur Del Salvador 24 ℡65/233039, ℱ65/233394, ℮reservas@colonosdelsur.cl, ⓦwww.colonosdelsur.cl. An exclusive beachfront hotel with lots of polished wood, an indoor swimming pool and a sauna. **7**–**8**

Colonos del Sur Express La Paz 507 ℡65/235555, ⓦwww.colonosdelsur.cl. A cheaper, sister hotel to the exclusive beachfront accommodation (see above); the spotless three-storey colonial house looms over the centre and has an outdoor pool with panoramic views. **6**

Compass del Sur Klenner 467 ℡65/232044, ℮info@compassdelsur.cl, ⓦwww.compassdelsur .cl. A traditional house, near the old railway station, with a large kitchen, shared or private rooms, Internet access and private parking. **3**–**4**

Guest House O'Higgins 608, at Purisima ℡65/231521, ℮guesthouse@vicki -johnson.com, ⓦwww.vicki-johnson.com.

Beautifully restored mansion, with big, sunny rooms, owned by a California transplant. Extras range from yoga and massage to Internet access. **5**

Hospedaje Carla Minte Maipo 1010 ℡ & ℱ65/232880, ℮bucarey@telsur.cl, ⓦwww .interpatagonia.com/carlaminte. Several blocks away from downtown, this quaint house offers clean rooms, cable TV and breakfast. **3**

Hospedaje Ellenhaus Walker Martínez 239 ℡ & ℱ65/233577, ⓦwww.ellenhaus.cl. A German woman rents out a small, clean, quiet upstairs apartment and maintains a travel agency, Internet centre and bike rental. **3**

Hostel Patiperros Mirador 135 at Santa Rosa ℡65/235050, ℮jardinsa@surnet.cl, ⓦwww .jardinsa.cl. Slightly anaemic-looking HI with basic dorm beds, Internet access, laundry service and safe locker storage.

Hotel del Bosque Santa Rosa 714 ℡65/232897. Sweeping views from this two-star hotel, where all eleven rooms have private baths and the staff can arrange local excursions, including rental cars. **5**

Hotel Licarayén San José 114 ℡65/232305, ℱ65/232955, ⓦwww.hotelicarayen.cl. An oversized Swiss chalet with lake vistas, clean rooms and excellent service. The Jacuzzi suites on the top floor boast the best views. **6**

Outsider San Bernardo 318 ℡65/232910, ℮outsider@telsur.cl, ⓦwww.campo-aventura .com. Excellent little bed and breakfast that offers simple rooms, strong showers and storage facilities, all atop the helpful Campo Aventura Tour Operator (see p.401) on the first floor. The multilingual staff know the area well. **5**

The Town

Puerto Varas is built on a long bay that curves from southeast to northwest, and the heart of town is clustered around a small pier to the northwest. Here you'll find the **Plaza de Armas**, an attractive little square, often filled with a **crafts market** selling woollens, lapis lazuli, imitation Mapuche jewellery and ceramics. The plaza holds some interest, but you'll be tempted down to the **waterfront** to view Volcán Osorno's conical perfection glimmering above the waves. (From the docks you can rent motorboats for any imaginable tour of the lake.)

Other attractions are few and far between. **Casa Kuschel**, on Klenner, was built in 1915 in the Baroque Bavarian style; it is now owned by eco-philanthropist

Doug Tompkins (see p.454) and sports a wonderful wooden onion-dome. On Calle San Francisco, the 1918 **Iglesia del Sagrado Corazón** sits atop a hill looking down on the town and lake and towards the volcanoes. Built of *roble*, a Chilean oak, the church is modelled on the Marienkirche in Germany's Black Forest.

The thin strip of sandy beach at **Puerto Chico**, at the southeast end of Puerto Varas' long bay, is the best in town and also the nightly hang-out spot, with a variety of pubs and discotheques. Nearby is the rebuilt and gaudy **Casino de Puerto Varas**, for those interested in gambling or some inexpensive drinks.

Eating and drinking

The food's good in Puerto Varas, and while most of the **restaurants** are in the centre there are other worthwhile ones out towards Puerto Chico and beyond.

Barómetro San Pedro 418. Small bar with draft beer, so-so food and a cheery crowd.

Cabañas y Onces Bellavista 34km along the road to Ensenada. A way out of town, this excellent café is known not only for its *onces* (afternoon tea), but also because a female puma lives here as a pet.

Café Danes Del Salvador 441. Old-fashioned tea room that serves superb cakes and tarts, and also main meals. Open late.

Club Alemán San José 415. One of the oldest German clubs in the country, with a suitably subdued atmosphere, moderate prices and a traditional menu to match.

Club de Yates Santa Rosa 161. One of the finest top-end restaurants in Puerto Varas, boasting an idyllic spot on a pier, with superb views of Volcán Osorno from the floor-to-ceiling panoramic windows. They serve a wide variety of international cuisine, specializing in fish dishes.

Helados Artesanales San Francisco 437. Excellent home-made ice cream is the attraction here.

Ibis Pérez Rosales 1117. Varied menu specializing in fresh seafood dishes served in inviting, contemporary surroundings.

Mediterraneo Santa Rosa 068. Enjoy Spanish tapas, pasta and tasty vegetarian dishes at this attractive lakefront restaurant with an outdoor deck.

Merlin Imperial 0605, south of the centre, Ⓦ www.merlinrestaurant.cl. The renowned *Merlin* is set in a restored colonial house and serves outstanding contemporary Chilean cuisine with a twist for reasonable prices.

Pim's San Francisco 712. In the summer this bar is packed with plenty of young adventure kayak types and their fans. You can chow on burgers and Tex Mex, but most come for the extensive list of potent drinks.

Restaurant Klein Del Salvador and San Francisco. Typical Chilean food, with delicious soups and meat dishes, and an inexpensive set menu.

Listings

Airlines LAN, Av Gramados 560 ☏ 65/234799.

Banks and exchange There are many banks with ATMs around the Plaza de Armas and along Del Salvador, including Banco de Chile, Del Salvador 210. For a *cambio*, try AFEX Exchange, Del Salvador 257, Local 11 (in the Galería Real), or across the street at Del Salvador 231, and Travel Sur, San Pedro 451 or San José 261.

Bus Buses JAC and Cóndor Bus, Walker Martínez 227-A; Cruz del Sur, Pullman Sur and Bus Norte, Walker Martínez 239-B ☏ & Ⓕ 65/236969; Tas Choapa, Walker Martínez 230 ☏ 65/233831; Tur Bus, San Pedro 210 ☏ 65/233787; Intersur, Walker Martínez 227-B ☏ & Ⓕ 65/236995.

Car rental Hunter Rent a Car, San José 130 ☏ & Ⓕ 65/237950, Ⓔ hunters@telsur.cl; Adriazola Turismo Expediciones, Santa Rosa 340 ☏ 65/233477.

Fishing Equipment Gray & Orvis, San Francisco 447. Ask for the latest details on required fishing licences.

Hospital Clínica Alemana, Otto Bader 810 ☏ 65/232336. This professional setup is fine for most minor needs.

Internet *Comell*, San Francisco 430, across from the Municipalidad, and also Del Salvador 264.

Laundry Lavandería Schnee, San Pedro 26-A.

Post Office San José 242 at San Pedro.

Shopping Vicki Johnson Fine Food & Gifts, Santa Rosa 318, Ⓦ www.vicki-johnson.com, specializes in home-made chocolates and also carries sweaters, jewellery and art; she's a good source for local tips on travel and eating, too. The Feria Artesanal, in the park across from the Plaza de Armas and the Casino, on Del Salvador, features

The main tours offered by the many companies in Puerto Varas are rafting on the Río Petrohué (grade 3 and 4; from CH$20,000 for a half-day); canyoning (climbing down precipices and waterfalls; CH$30,000 for a half-day); climbing Volcán Osorno (from CH$100,000); hiking in the Parque Nacional Vicente Pérez Rosales (from CH$95,000 for two days on the Termas de Callao trail – see p.394); and horse-riding, generally on the slopes of Volcán Calbuco, through old coigüe forest (from CH$35,000 for a half-day).

Adriazola Turismo Expediciones Santa Rosa 340 ⊤65/233472, ⓦwww.adriazolafly-fishing.com. Fly-fishing specialist that also offers rafting and trekking excursions.

Al Sur Expediciones Del Salvador 100 ⊤ & Ⓕ65/232300; Ⓔalsur@telsur.cl, ⓦwww.alsurexpeditions.com. A good company – one of those authorized by Conaf as guides on Volcán Osorno. In addition to the standard tours above, it offers sea-kayaking to Parque Pumalín on the Careterra Austral (CH$340,000 for a six-day trip; see p.453) and rafting trips on the Ríos Petrohué, Puelo and Futaleufú. Also has a branch in Puerto Montt.

Andina del Sud Del Salvador 72 ⊤65/232811, Ⓕ232511, Ⓔadspuerto.varas @andinadelsud.cl, ⓦwww.crucedelagos.cl. Distinguished Lake District war-horse of a tour company, owning a monopoly on crossings on Lago Todos Los Santos. Also has a branch in Puerto Montt.

AquaMotion San Francisco 328 ⊤65/232747; Ⓔinfo@aquamotion.cl, ⓦwww.aqua-motion.com. A well-respected agent with German- and English-speaking guides, authorized by Conaf to guide up Volcán Osorno. Great for fishing trips but also for canyoning, trekking, horse-riding, rafting, canoeing and canopy tours. Also has a branch in Puerto Montt.

Campo Aventura San Bernardo 318 ⊤ & Ⓕ65/232910, Ⓔinfo@campo-aventura.com, ⓦwww.campo-aventura.com. The place to go for horse-trekking, from one day to ten days into the foothills of Cochamó valley near the Estuario de Reloncaví (see p.396). Run by Lex Fautsch, who has developed a multilingual team. Customized options, like veggie meals, are available.

CTS San Francisco 320 ⊤65/237330, Ⓕ65/237329, Ⓔctsotv@telsur.cl, ⓦwww.ctsturismo.cl. Offers all the standard trips, plus one to Parque Pumalin (p.453), the million-acre private park near Chaiten.

Eco Travel Costanera s/n ⊤65/233222, Ⓔecotravel@entelchile.net. Ecological and cultural tours to Parque Alerce Andino (p.449) and other regions.

Grayfly San José 192 ⊤ & Ⓕ65/310734, Ⓔfishing@grayfly.com, ⓦwww.grayfly.com. Offers fishing trips on Lake Llanquihue or fly-fishing in Río Puelo with camping in the mountains. Custom trips are easily arranged.

Kokayak San José 320 ⊤65/346433, Ⓔinfo@kokayak.com, ⓦwww.kokayak.com. Rafting and kayaking specialist who run half- to fifteen-day trips throughout southern Chile.

Tranco Expediciones San Pedro 422 ⊤65/311311, ⓦwww.trancoexpediciones.cl. An agency authorized to guide up Volcán Osorno that also organizes rafting trips.

Travel Art Imperial 0661 ⊤65/232198, ⓦwww.travelart.cl. Custom-tailored trekking and mountain biking tours.

Tres Piedras San Pedro 465 ⊤65/346452, Ⓔinfotres@trespiedras.cl, ⓦwww.trespiedras.cl. Fly-fishing specialist organizing bespoke tours.

arts and crafts. La Picá de la Abeja, Camino a Ensenada km 28.5 (⊤9/8731582), is an entire store dedicated to honey, with different natural flavours from the flowering Ulmo tree of the region. It also sells pollen and honey products. Vinopolis, San José 128, sells Chilean wines.

Puerto Montt and around

After passing Puerto Varas, the Panamericana begins to run out of land. It approaches a large bay where the central plain, the valley which has run for thousands of kilometres down Chile between the Andes and the coast, slips

△ Puerto Montt ferry

gently under the sea. This is the Seno de Reloncaví, and on its edge is the city of **PUERTO MONTT**, 17km south of Puerto Varas.

Puerto Montt looks like a rundown port at the end of the road. It was exactly that for many years, when both the Panamericana and the railway from Santiago ended here. The Panamericana now carries on southwest to the island of Chiloé, and the railway has retreated north to Temuco, but the place still looks the same: collapsing wooden houses with rustic shingle roofs under a frequent cloud of fog and cold. But that doesn't mean that Puerto Montt is sleepy – in fact, it's a busy port, with a billion-dollar-a-year salmon farming industry fishing. For tourists it's an important, albeit ugly, launchpad: the gateway to the rugged isolation of the Careterra Austral, and the embarkation point for the long-distance ferry trips to the famous Laguna San Rafael (see p.471), with its floating glacier, or through the fjords to Puerto Natales in the far south (see p.507). Far nearer, but equally exotic is the world's largest privately owned nature reserve – the one million pristine acres known as Pumalin Park (see p.453).

Arrival and information

If you're arriving by **bus**, you'll pull in at the terminal, which is on the seafront (Av Portales s/n), six blocks west of the town centre. It's a short walk to downtown, or you can take one of the many cabs or *colectivos* that run in that direction. The **ferry terminal** is a further half-kilometre out of town, southwest towards the suburb of Angelmó. Again, taxis and *colectivos* run frequently into town. The **airport** (☎65/486200, ℻65/486226) is 16km northwest of Puerto Montt; flights are met by the ETM bus company, which will take you to the bus terminal for CH$1100. A taxi from the airport to town costs CH$12,000. The **railway** was badly damaged by a landslide and abandoned. Although some of the old tracks are still visible, the old train station has been demolished and a giant shopping mall built in its place. However, rail services are slated to resume in the future, with the introduction of a line between Temuco and Puerto Montt. When they do, trains will stop at the La Paloma station to the northeast of the town.

Puerto Montt has several **tourist information offices**. The most brusque is the main Oficina de Turismo, on the southeastern corner of the Plaza de Armas in a seafront park (daily: mid-March–mid-Dec Mon–Fri 9am–6.30pm & Sat 9am–1pm; mid-Dec–mid-March 9am–9pm; ☎65/261823). In summer, the Oficina de Turismo runs a friendlier kiosk in the bus station (daily 9am–9pm; ☎65/261848) and another at the point where the Panamericana enters the city's northern outskirts (same hours as kiosk; ☎65/261838). Sernatur's office is on the second floor of the Edificio Intendencia Regional, at Av Décima Región 480 (mid-Dec–mid-March Mon–Thurs 8.30am–5.30pm, Fri 8.30am–4.30pm; ☎65/256999, ℮infoloslagos@sernatur.cl). It's by far the best choice in town, with scores of maps and leaflets. The building is set on a hill behind the town and can be accessed via O'Higgins. There is also useful information available online at ⓦwww.puertomonttchile.cl. Conaf has an office at Amunategui 500 (☎65/486701). They have poor maps but a terrific overview for regional parks, changing trail maps and other useful information for visiting the Alerce Andino, Hornopiren and Vincente Pérez Rosales national parks. For more info on Parque Pumalin, try the office at Buin 356 (☎65/250079, ⓦwww.pumalinpark.org).

Accommodation

There's no shortage of cheap **accommodation** in Puerto Montt, and it's generally a buyer's market. Nor is it difficult to find, for although touting for

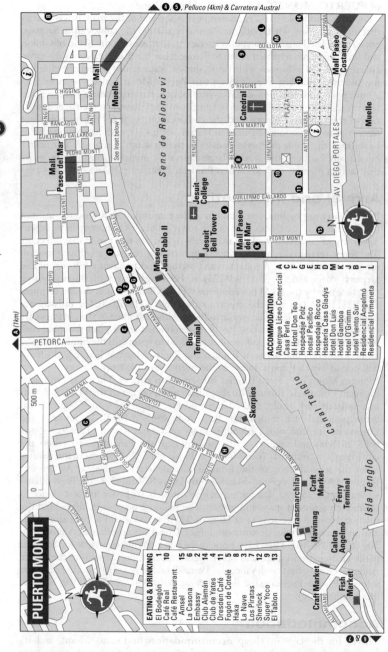

▲ 4, 5, Pelluco (4km) & Carretera Austral

Seno de Reloncaví

Muelle

See inset below

PUERTO MONTT

N

0   500 m

Bus Terminal

Skorpios

Museo Juan Pablo II

PETORCA

Craft Market

Transmarchilay

Navimag

Ferry Terminal

Caleta Angelmó

Fish Market

Craft Market

Isla Tenglo

Canal Tenglo

EATING & DRINKING

El Bodegón	1
Café Real	10
Café Restaurant	15
Amsel	6
La Casona	2
Embassy	14
Club Alemán	4
Club de Yates	11
Dresden Café	5
Fogón de Cotelé	3
Haka	8
La Nave	7
Los Piratas	12
Sherlock	9
Super Yoco	13
El Tablón	

Inset map

Quillota

O'Higgins

Catedral

PLAZA

San Martín

Jesuit College

Jesuit Bell Tower

Mall Paseo del Mar

Mall Paseo Costanera

Muelle

Av Diego Portales

N

ACCOMMODATION

Albergue Liceo Comercial	A
Casa Perla	C
HI Hotel Don Teo	F
Hospedaje Polz	G
Hostal Pacífico	E
Hospedaje Rocco	H
Hostería Casa Gladys	D
Hotel Don Luis	M
Hotel Gamboa	K
Hotel O'Grimm	J
Hotel Viento Sur	B
Residencial Angelmó	I
Residencial Urmeneta	L

accommodation is now illegal at Puerto Montt's bus station, you'll still have a couple of people sidle up to you and whisper an offer of somewhere to stay. Additionally, a conglomeration of hotel owners run a kiosk at the eastern end of the bus station, where you can get useful accommodation info. At the top end, you'll find a couple of good hotels, but prices rise dramatically in the summer. Camping is intermittently available at *El Ciervo*, 1km west of Angelmó on the road to Chinquihue, Pacheco Altamirano 3084 (☏65/253972), and more regularly at *Paredes*, 4km west of Angelmó on the same road (☏65/258394). At *Paredes*, a site with electricity and hot water costs from CH$10,000 per tent; buses and *colectivos* run here from the terminal. On the road to Chinquihue at km 15, you'll find *Camping Cabañas Los Alamos* (☏65/264666; ❹), a comfortable site with electricity, hot water and a beautiful view of the bay.

Albergue Liceo Comercial Buin 383 ☏65/258289. A school that turns into a hostel during the holidays, providing the cheapest lodging in town. There are about a hundred beds, living is communal and you have to supply your own sleeping bag. Open Jan–Feb only.

Casa Perla Trigal 312 ☏65/262104, ✉mail @casaperla.com, ⓦwww.casaperla.com. Simple rooms in a Chilean home packed with antiques and decorations. Pluses here include a garden, Internet access and an English-speaking staff. Spanish lessons are available and breakfast is included. ❷

Hospedaje Polz Juan José Mira 1002 ☏65/252851. A yappy dog and a spiral staircase, but basic, clean rooms and a reasonable location. ❷

Hospedaje Rocco Pudeto 233 ☏65/272897, ⓦwww.hospedajerocco.cl. Clean hostel offering dorm, double and quadruple rooms. Guests can use the kitchen and take advantage of the laundry service and Internet access. ❸

Hostal Pacifico Juan José Mira 1088 ☏ & ⒻÐ65/256229, ✉info@hostalpacifico.cl, ⓦwww .hostalpacifico.cl. This well-cared for, quiet property offers modern rooms with cable TV and private bath, friendly staff and parking. A short way uphill from the bus terminal. ❹

Hostería Casa Gladys Ancud 112 ☏65/260247. Ramshackle building with paper-thin walls (so it can be noisy in the rooms) but nonetheless friendly and welcoming. ❷

Hotel Don Luis Quillota 146 at Urmeneta ☏65/259001, ⒻÐ65/259005, ✉hdluis@entelchile .net, ⓦwww.hoteldonluis.cl. Part of the Best Western chain, this hotel is in a tall building, with treacherous marble tiles on the foyer floor. Meals

in the comfortable restaurant are limited to a daily CH$6000 fixed menu. ❼

Hotel Don Teo Andrés Bello 990, second floor ☏65/251625. This hotel has a friendly staff, a convivial atmosphere, private rooms and a good, albeit noisy, location next to the bus station; breakfast is included. ❹

Hotel Gamboa Pedro Montt 157 ☏65/252741. Lovely, central old place with creaking floorboards and the smell of fresh furniture polish. The showers can be weak. ❹

Hotel O'Grimm Guillermo Gallardo 211 at Benavente ☏65/252845, ⒻÐ65/258600, ✉hotel@ogrimm.cl, ⓦwww.ogrimm.cl. The stone-clad entrance might put some off, but this is a comfortable modern hotel with decent rooms and a good restaurant. ❻

Hotel Viento Sur Ejército 200 ☏65/258701, ⒻÐ65/314732, ✉reservas@hotelvientosur.cl, ⓦwww.hotelvientosur.cl. One of the best-positioned hotels in the city, on the hill overlooking the bay – although its excellent views have been partly obscured by the new shopping mall built on the waterfront. It's beautifully decorated with native woods, and there's a small restaurant that specializes in fish and home-made pasta. ❼

Residencial Angelmó Angelmó 2196 ☏65/257938. Bang opposite the ferry terminal, this hostel is a little spartan, but the owner is friendly and helpful, and there's a communal kitchen. ❸

Residencial Urmeneta Urmeneta 290 ☏65/253262. The heart of this old building is the kitchen, and guests have breakfast sitting among piles of clean laundry while an endless array of women bustle around vast cauldrons that bubble away on an enormous old hob. ❷

The City

Puerto Montt is strung out along the bay. To the east, around a headland, lie the beach and university district of Pelluco, and to the west, down past the port and opposite Isla Tenglo, you'll find the best local fishing district – Angelmó. Off to the south are the hills and fjords of the unbroken rainforest, often obscured by clouds and occasionally temptingly visible. Climb the hills on a clear day and to the north you can see Volcán Calbuco, and even Volcán Osorno.

Puerto Montt was founded by the same influx of German colonizers that settled Lago Llanquihue to the north, but very little is left of the old city. For example, the **cathedral** on the Plaza de Armas was flattened in the 1960 earthquake, and the building you see today doesn't bear much resemblance to the original. It's based on the Parthenon in Athens, not entirely successfully, but the inside is peaceful and lined with Grecian columns. Three blocks away, on Guillermo Gallardo, a much better job has been done in restoring the wooden 1872 **Jesuit church**, with an impressive blue vaulted ceiling.

Ten blocks west of the Plaza is Puerto Montt's museum, **Museo Juan Pablo II**, Portales 991, next to the bus terminal (Mon–Fri 9am–7pm, Sat 9am–1pm; Jan & Feb also open Sun 10am–6pm; CH$250). Built to commemorate the pope's visit in 1987, it's not the greatest museum in the country. But an upgrade in 2002 replaced the stuffy colonial exhibits with an examination of the oldest known human settlement of the Americas – **Monte Verde**, on the outskirts of Puerto Montt. Human tools found at Monte Verde date to 20,000 BC. This discovery in 1976 challenges the belief that human settlements started in the Bering Straits and migrated south. The rest of the museum now includes expanded exhibits on Pre-Columbian cultures and local Santería religious beliefs.

Angelmó

A kilometre further west sits the neighbourhood of **ANGELMÓ**, the most attractive side of Puerto Montt, where the *costanera* (coastal road) features a **feria artesanal**, or crafts market, its stalls crammed with wooden and copper souvenirs, woven baskets and furniture, fleece rugs, and woollen sweaters, socks, gloves, hats and ponchos. Jewellery stalls sell rings and bracelets made out of Chilean silver and semi-precious stones, particularly lapis lazuli, while other stalls have fine leather saddles and tack for horses, and glistening spurs for *huasos*. On the opposite side of the road are stalls selling country cheeses, honey, bottles of powerful *licor de oro* and dried sea produce: square bundles of tightly wrapped seaweed that looks like withered intestines, and smoked shellfish in long strings of red and grey, that hang from doorways, tempting scrawny cats onto their hind legs.

Angelmó was once a thriving small harbour, and the channel between it and the island offshore, **Isla Tenglo**, was filled with black-hulled sailing boats, then the only means of transport to the islands south of Puerto Montt and isolated communities now reached by road. Launches still go to the islands, and horse-drawn carts are used to unload cargoes of charcoal, seaweed and shellfish. These fleets are a common sight, particularly near the bus terminal, with small horses hauling their loads up Puerto Montt's steep hills.

Angelmó means fresh **seafood** in Chile. At the end of the road, a pleasant walk along the water from the centre of town, past the mountain of shredded native forests, leads to a thriving **fish market**. Angelmó is a combination of many fish retailers and various restaurants operated by ebullient mothers and daughters who crowd around the cauldrons, tempting punters by lifting the lids off steaming vats of *curanto* (a seafood extravaganza with sausages). There are few better places in Chile to get a feel for the country's rich diversity of marine life. Walk behind the stalls and down to the yellow boats and local fisherman are only too happy to explain their latest harvest of varied eels, crabs and deep-sea wonders.

Eating and drinking

In addition to Angelmó, which is known for (not inexpensive) seafood, other districts around Puerto Montt have become famous for their food. **Chinquihue**, seven kilometres west, has some good restaurants, as has **Pelluco**, the university district to the east. Western-style fast-food restaurants can be found on the top floor of the Paseo del Mar, the mall on Urmeneta between Pedro Montt and Cauquenes.

El Bodegón Antonio Varas 931. An old-fashioned workers' restaurant where set lunches of traditional, Chilean fare cost CH$2000.

Café Real Rancagua 137. Simple café that serves *empanadas*, cheap set lunches, ice cream and *Küchen*.

Café Restaurant Amsel Portales and O'Higgins. An ideal place to read or talk with friends, while enjoying delicious beef dishes and inexpensive sandwiches.

La Casona Chinquihue km 8 ☎65/255044. Facing the sea, this first-class restaurant serves fresh seafood with fine wines. It can get busy, so it's a good idea to book.

Club Alemán Antonio Varas 264. An excellent, mid-range restaurant with starched tablecloths. Attentive waiters serve tasty dishes, including the enormous seafood platter for two.

Club de Yates Juan Soler Manfredini 200, Pelluco ☎65/284000. On a pier sticking out into the ocean, with a bright neon light on top, the *Club de Yates* is hard to miss. It's less ostentatious on the inside, and is one of the best seafood restaurants in Puerto Montt – but expensive. Booking is advisable.

Dresden Café Antonio Varas 486 at Guillermo Gallardo. Attractive, pleasant coffee shop and deli, with sandwiches and generous wedges of cake, where you can watch the world go by.

Embassy Ancud 106. Fairly pricey, more formal restaurant serving standard Chilean dishes and top quality seafood.

Fogón de Cotelé Juan Soler Manfredini 1661, Pelluco ☎65/278000. A good view over the sea, and the best steak in Puerto Montt: the meat is charcoal-grilled in front of you. Booking is essential, meals are pricey, and the owner has been known to turn away tourists he doesn't like the look of.

Haka Rancagua 196 at Benavente. Lively pub-restaurant full of atmosphere that serves international grub and decent drinks, and also hosts live music.

Kalabaza Antonio Varas 629. Inviting, small venue popular with travellers where you can stop in for a beer and a snack as well as vegetarian dishes.

La Nave Ancud and Antonio Varas. Inexpensive fresh seafood in simple surroundings particularly popular with locals.

Los Piratas Angelmó beyond the fish market. Excellent seafood, Chilean dishes and French fare are the highlights here, making it a great budget alternative to the Angelmó market.

Sherlock Rancagua and Antonio Varas. Cheap Chilean staples including *lomito* and *barros jarpa* as well as good fish dishes are doled out in this decent café-bar, which fills with locals in the evening.

Super Yoco Quillota 259. The decor isn't wonder-ful, and the service can be slow, but this is the best place in town for traditional and reasonably priced meat dishes such as *parilladas*, huge mixed grills and *pichangas*, mountains of chips with spicy sausages, pickles and hard-boiled eggs. Closed Sun.

El Tablon Antonio Varas and O'Higgins. This infor-mal bar-restaurant has intimate booths and serves enormous, cheap sandwiches, burgers and main meals. You can also order a three-litre tower of *Küntsmann* beer that comes with its own tap.

Listings

Airlines LAN, O'Higgins 167 at Urmeneta ☎65/253002, ℻65/278172; SKY, San Martín 189 at Benavente ☎65/437555.

Banks and exchange AFEX, Av Diego Portales 516, and El Tepual airport; Exchange, Talca 84; La Moneda de Oro, Bus Terminal Oficina 37. There are many banks with ATMs along Antonio Varas and Urmeneta.

Bus The main bus terminal is on Diego Portales. All of the main companies have offices here, including

Bus Norte Internacional; Cruz del Sur and Pullman Bus Sur are at Antonio Varas 437 ☎65/254731 or 65/281717); Río de la Plata ☎65/253841; Tas Choapa ☎65/254826; Varmontt ☎800202092 or 65/254410; Cóndor Bus ☎65/312123; Igi Llaima ☎65/254519; Lit ☎65/254011; Tur Bus ☎65/253329, and also at Urmeneta 582 ☎65/271909.

Car rental The first four companies also have offices at the airport: Automóvil Club de Chile,

One of the main reasons people travel to Puerto Montt is to catch a **ferry** south. From Puerto Montt you can sail to Chaitén on the Carretera Austral, Quellón on the island of Chiloé, Puerto Chacabuco on the Carretera Austral, the Laguna San Rafael far south in the fjords of the southern coast, and Puerto Natales in Magallanes. These ferry trips are almost always fully booked in summer, and you must **reserve ahead** if you want to be certain of travelling.

The seas on these ferry rides are usually flat calm, because most of the time the ferries are sailing in fjords that protect them from bad weather. The wind on deck, however, can be ferocious. The exception is the trip to Puerto Natales, when the *Magallanes* heads out to the Pacific across the Golfo de Penas, where even travellers with the sturdiest sea legs have been known to lose their *empanadas*. The trips are long and can be boring, but the scenery is spectacular: wild forests, steep mountains and placid fjords. There are cafés and restaurants on most boats, but you should bring some extra food and alcohol, as the prices on board can be exorbitant.

There are several main companies operating ferries. Each has a range of accommodation and fares, which are reduced in low season. Unless otherwise noted, the prices below correspond to the cheapest accommodation for a single passenger during high season. Bear in mind that prices are variable and can fluctuate.

Aysén Express O'Higgins 167, Office 307 ☎65/437599, ⊛www.aysenexpress.cl. Relatively new company offering a swift catamaran service from Puerto Montt to Chaitén (CH\$23,000), Quellón (CH\$28,000), Puerto Chacabuco (CH\$40,000) and the Laguna San Rafael (CH\$99,000). Departures are usually on Friday, returning on Sunday.

Navimag Av Angelmó 2187 ☎65/270416, ℗65/270415, ⊛www.navimag.com. The busiest of Puerto Montt's ferry companies; it's recommended that you book ahead at least a month before travel. They hold reservations for up to fifteen days before the boat leaves, after which you must pay or lose your berth. Within two weeks before travel, you can't make a provisional reservation and must pay up front to secure a ticket. Students with ID get a ten percent discount. Navimag offers several standards of travel, from individual beds to cabins. If you only book a bed you will share with other passengers; you'll get a locker for storage and a curtain for privacy but no other private space, and complete bedding but no towels. Cabins are more private, and more expensive, may have a sea view and come with complete bedding and towels.

The short-distance *Alejandrina* serves Chaitén and Quellón; it costs CH\$10,000 from Puerto Montt to Chaitén (9hr). (For the Chaitén to Quellón leg, see p.457.) It

Esmeralda 70 ☎65/254776; Avis, Urmeneta 1037 ☎65/253307; Budget, Antonio Varas 162 ☎65/286277; Econorent, Ejercito 600 ☎65/254888; Egartur, Benavente 575, Local 3 ☎65/257336; Fama's Rent a Car, Diego Portales 506 ☎65/258060; Travi Rent a Car, Benavente 405, Oficina 404 ☎65/257137, ℗65/256438; Hertz, A. Varas 126 ☎ & ℗65/259585.
Consulates Argentina, Cauquenes 94, 2nd floor ☎65/253996; Germany, Antonio Varas 525, Oficina 306 ☎65/252828; Netherlands, Chorrillos 1582 ☎65/253003; Spain, Rancagua 113 ☎65/252729.
Hospital Hospital Regional, Seminario s/n ☎65/253992.

Internet *Mundosur*, San Martín 232. *Cybercafé*, Antonio Varas 161 and 930. Also several options on Av Angelmó.
Laundry Center, Antonio Varas 700; Yessilt, Urmeneta 300, Local 4.
Shopping The best crafts are in Angelmó, while across from the bus terminal is another market called Pueblito de Melipulli. Patagonia outdoor equipment is sold at Niklitschek y Morgado ltda, Antonio Varas 445. Arte Nativo, Av Angelmo 1860 (☎9/8173885), on the way to the Angelmó fish market, has a beautiful selection of Chilean art, wood carvings and jewellery, including many small gifts that travel well.
Taxi Settur ☎65/251515; Radiotaxi Alexander ☎ & ℗65/272559.

sails from Puerto Montt on Thursdays, Fridays, Saturdays and Sundays, returning on Fridays, Saturdays, Sundays and Mondays.

The middle-distance *Puerto Edén* serves Puerto Chacabuco and the Laguna San Rafael; it costs from CH$180,000 to CH$380,000 round-trip from Puerto Montt to Laguna San Rafael (5 days, 4 nights), and CH$30,000 (berth) or CH$120,000 (cabin) one-way to Puerto Chacabuco (24hr). (For details of the trip from Puerto Chacabuco to the Laguna, see p.472.) To take a car on the ferry from Puerto Montt to Puerto Chacabuco it costs an additional CH$95,000. It sails from Puerto Montt every Wednesday and Saturday and returns from Puerto Chacabuco on Fridays and Tuesdays.

The long-distance *Magallanes* heads all the way down to Puerto Natales; it costs from CH$195,000 to CH$1,014,000 to Puerto Natales (3 days, price includes full board, glacier excursions and informative lectures), sailing from Puerto Montt on Mondays and returning from Puerto Natales on Fridays. To transport a car it's CH$222,000.

Skorpios Av Angelmó 1660 ☎65/252619, ℻65/258315, ⓦwww.skorpios.cl. Upmarket company running expensive, luxury cruises. The *Skorpios I* sails every Monday from Puerto Chacabuco to the San Rafael Glacier over four days/three nights and every Friday over five days/four nights. Single cabins in high season cost CH$600,000. The *Skorpios II* Sails from Puerto Montt every Saturday on a seven-day/six-night journey to the San Rafael Glacier. Single cabins cost CH$1,080,000. The *Skorpios III* sails every Sunday from Puerto Natales on a five-day cruise through the fjords. Single cabins in high season cost CH$1,680,000.

TransMarChilay Av Angelmó 2187 ☎65/270430, ℻65/270415, ⓦwww .transmarchillay.cl. Generally less busy than Navimag, but again for the trip down to the Laguna you have to reserve in advance and pay up front to be sure of a ticket.

The short-distance *Barcaza Pincoya* travels to Chaitén and Quellón; it costs from CH$12,000 for the Chaitén trip (10hr), CH$65,000 per car. (For the Chaitén to Quellón leg, see p.457.) It sails from Puerto Montt to Chaitén on Mondays, Tuesdays, Thursdays and Fridays, and from Chaitén to Puerto Montt on Mondays, Wednesdays and Fridays.

The middle-distance *El Colono* serves Puerto Chacabuco and the Laguna San Rafael; it costs from CH$13,500 to Puerto Chacabuco (26hr one-way), and CH$133,000 for the round-trip to Laguna San Rafael (5 days, 4 nights). It sails from Puerto Montt on Fridays, and from Chacabuco on Saturdays. Sailings in summer only.

Telephone centre Entel, Pedro Montt 75, Pedro Montt 114 and Rosales 148.

Tour operators Tours offered from Puerto Montt are basically the same as those offered from Puerto Varas (see p.401). Travellers, General Bulnes 1009 (☎65/262099, ⓦwww.travellers.cl, ℮info @travellers.cl) is a thoroughly helpful company that provides general information as well as booking tours; it's owned by an Englishman who's become a fixture in the south of Chile. Other travel agents/tour operators in town are Eureka Turismo, Guillermo Gallardo 65 ☎65/255146, ⓦwww.chile-travel .com/eureka.htm; Ace Turismo, A. Varas 445 ☎65/257686; Andina del Sud, Antonio Varas 437 ☎65/257797, ℮adsmontt@chilesat.net; Kayak Austral, Trigal 312 ☎65/262104, ⓦwww .kayakaustral.com; Ríos Austral, Casilla 1229 ☎65/258663, ⓦwww.riosaustral.com.

The road to Chiloé

After Puerto Montt, the Panamericana heads off to the southwest, the only direction left to go. The road is at first full of pretty *cabañas*, then salmon oil plants, which give off faint smells, and then rolling hills and greenery.

Calbuco

The attractive, estuary town of **CALBUCO**, about 55km southwest of Puerto Montt, sits on mud flats with views onto small islands. It's reached by a causeway that links it to the mainland.

Built on an island hillock, Calbuco was originally a Spanish fort, Real Fuerte de San Miguel, founded in 1602, but grew during the days of the Mapuche revolt as Spaniards fled here, abandoning their farms and settlements. Ironically enough, it was close to this retreat that the Spaniards' Pacific Fleet suffered its final defeat in 1866 at the hands of Chilean and Peruvian ships commanded by Admirals Prat and Grau. Today Calbuco is a town with steep streets and a flaking-paint charm. Its central plaza is hemmed in by the sea on one side, and on the other by a yellow, German-style **church** with steeple, inside which is an image of the Archangel Michael, brought here by the Spanish. The interesting **Museo Histórico Municipal**, Goycolea and Errázuriz (daily 10.30am–1pm & 3–6.30pm; free) has a selection of photographs, colonial artefacts and archeological finds, including 6000-year-old carved stones. You can get tourist information at the **tourist office** on Errázuriz 371 and in the summer from a kiosk on Avenida Los Héroes.

There are a couple of **places to stay**. The *Gran Hotel Calbuco*, Av Los Héroes 502 (T & F 65/461833; ⑤), is above a popular restaurant on the seafront at the entrance to town and has good views. Just around the corner, *Hotel Colonial*, Eulogio Goycolea 16 (T & F 65/461546; ④) sits on a quiet street and has attractive en-suite rooms. You can tuck into good **seafood** in this fishing community, especially at the fine *Costa Azul*, Av Vicuña Mackenna 202. These hotels and restaurants also operate **tours** to the islands where the way of life remains little changed since the departure of the Spaniards. Intersur, Bohle, Full Express and Fierro run buses to Calbuco from Puerto Montt every ten minutes.

Maullín and Carelampu

If you ignore the left-hand turn for Calbuco some 30km southwest of Puerto Montt and instead continue southwest for a further 20km, there is a right-hand junction that leads 25km west to **MAULLÍN**. Set on the Pacific Coast, Maullín is a weather-beaten town, largely made of rusted corrugated iron and wood-tiled walls, the sort of place where the dogs are too lazy to get out of the way of an approaching car. This village was founded at an important crossing point of a sprawling estuary, on which shellfish are cultivated and sole thrive. Ferries still cross the river as they did in colonial times, but Maullín is no longer the gateway to Chiloé that it was a century ago.

Sixteen kilometres south of Maullín on the coastal road is **CARELAMPU**, another dying port town, and a favourite target of Dutch corsairs in the seventeenth century. The sleepy village comes alive on February 2, the **Fiesta de la Candelaria**, when brightly coloured boats pack the bay, and the single street is lined with food stalls selling every type of traditional dish. The fields around Carelampu are all turned over to car parking, and the air fills with smoke from hundreds of cooking fires. Buses ETM run a half-hourly service from Puerto Montt to Maullín and Carelampu on weekdays, and an hourly one at weekends.

Pargua and the ferry to Chiloé

The modern port for Chiloé is **PARGUA**, opposite the Chilote village of Chacao, 11km southwest of the turn-off to Maullín. There's nothing much here except the ferries operated by TransMarChilay, which are flat landing crafts that run in relays across the straits. During daylight, the most you'll have to wait is half an hour, and the crossing takes another half-hour. It costs CH$7200 for a car and CH$600 for foot passengers.

Travel details

Buses

Osorno to: Aguas Calientes, Puyehue (17 daily; 1hr); Bahía Mansa (4 daily; 2hr); Bariloche, Argentina (every 2hr; 5hr plus border formalities); Entre Lagos (10 daily; 40min); Panguipulli (5 daily; 2hr 30min); Puerto Montt (every 30min; 1hr 30min); Puerto Octay (every 30min; 1hr); Puerto Varas (every 30min; 1hr); Santiago (every hour; 10hr); Temuco (every 30min; 3hr); Valdivia (every 30min, 1hr 30min).

Puerto Montt to: Ancud (6 daily; 2hr); Bariloche, Argentina (1 daily; 7hr 30min plus border formalities); Calbuco (every 15min; 1hr 30min); Castro (every 30min; 3hr 30min); Frutillar (every 15min; 1hr); Maullín (every 30min; 1hr 40min); Osorno (every 30min; 1hr 30min); Pargua (every 30min; 1hr); Panguipulli (5 daily; 4hr); Puerto Varas (every 15min; 30min); Ralun (4 daily; 2hr 30min); Santiago (every 30min; 14hr); Temuco (every hour; 5hr); Valdivia (every 30min; 3hr).

Temuco to: Melipueco (8 daily; 2hr 30min); Osorno (every 30min; 3hr); Panguipulli (every hour; 2hr 30min); Pucon (every 30min; 2hr); Puerto Saavedra (every hour; 1hr 30min); Puerto Varas (every hour; 5hr 30min); Santiago (every 30min; 8hr 30min); Valdivia (every 30min; 2hr 30min); Villarica (every 30min; 1hr 45min).

Valdivia to: Futrono (every hour; 2hr 30min); Lago Ranco (every 30min; 3hr); Niebla (every 15min; 30min); Osorno (every 30min; 1hr 30min); Panguipulli (every hour; 2hr); Puerto Montt (every 30min; 3hr 30min); Puerto Varas (every 30min; 3hr); Santiago (every hour; 11hr); Temuco (every 30min; 2hr 15min).

Ferries

Puerto Montt to: Castro (2 weekly; 4hr); Chacabuco (4 weekly; 24hr); Chaitén (1–4 weekly; 10hr); Laguna San Rafael (4 weekly, Dec–March; 4–5 days return); Puerto Natales (1–2 weekly; 4 days); Quellón (1-2 weekly; 6hr).

Flights

Osorno to: Santiago (3 daily; 2hr); Temuco (2 daily; 30min).

Puerto Montt to: Bariloche, Argentina (1 weekly; 2hr); Balmaceda/Coihaique (3 daily; 1hr); Concepción (1 daily; 1hr 45min); Punta Arenas (6 daily; 2hr 10min); Santiago (10 daily; 1hr 30min); Temuco (1 daily; 45min).

Temuco to: Balmaceda (3 daily; 1hr); Osorno (2 daily; 30min); Puerto Montt (1 daily; 45min); Santiago (8 daily; 2hr); Valdivia (1 daily; 1hr 40min).

Valdivia to: Santiago (2 daily; 2hr); Temuco (1 daily; 45min).

7

Chiloé

PERU

BOLIVIA

PARAGUAY

PACIFIC

ARGENTINA

Santiago

Juan Fernández
Archipelago (Chile)

OCEAN

N

0   500 km

Easter Island (Chile)

CHAPTER 7

Highlights

* **Museo Regional** The seaside town of Ancud features this excellent museum with a stellar collection of Chilote artefacts. **See p.421**

* **Taste *curanto*** Dig into Chiloé's national dish, a savoury hotchpotch of meat, seafood and potatoes, traditionally cooked out in the open. **See p.422**

* **Palafitos in Castro** Slums or shrines? Insalubrious yet picturesque fishermen's houses on stilts, the last remaining in the country. **See p.425**

* **Isla Quinchao** A soothing spot to experience the slow pace of Chiloé's lesser isles. **See p.433**

* **Parque Nacional Chiloé** Explore the remains of the region's once vast forests by hiking its interior trails. **See p.435**

* **Chonchi** Chiloé's most attractive town is proud of its age-old customs celebrated in the Museo de las Tradiciones. **See p.438**

△ Castro palafitos

Chiloé

mmediately to the south of the Lake District, the already slim Chilean mainland narrows even further and the straight Pacific coastline splinters into a seemingly never-ending series of islands and inlets continuing all the way down to Cape Horn. The fascinating **CHILOÉ** archipelago is a haven of rural tranquillity. The main island, forming the bulk of its territory, is **Isla Grande**, South America's second largest (the biggest being the main island of Tierra del Fuego, shared with Argentina). Exposed to the ocean on its moist westward flank, Isla Grande is separated from Chaitén (see p.456) and its hinterland by the sheltered, but not always smooth, Golfo de Ancud, across which are scattered the lesser Chilote islands, some of them no bigger than rocks.

A verdant rectangle of rolling hills, 200km long by 70km wide, Isla Grande is sliced in half lengthways by the Panamericana as it tears past the two main towns, **Ancud** and **Castro**; the latter, the island's colourful capital, makes the best base for exploration, especially if you have no transport of your own. Regular buses trundle up and down the highway, and the lesser roads are generally served by at least one bus a day. However, the ideal way to explore is by going on an organized tour, or, better still, to drive or cycle along the islands' minor roads, which hold surprises at almost every turn. It's well worth heading west into the densely forested **Parque Nacional Chiloé**, the most accessible part of the almost pristine wilderness of the coastal rainforest, which can be visited on excursions from Castro.

To Isla Grande's east are dozens of tiny islands, most of them uninhabited and practically unreachable. Of the 35 that are inhabited, the two largest and simplest to visit are **Isla Quinchao** and **Isla Lemuy**, both easily accessible by bus and car. Along the winding dirt roads of these remote outposts, you're likely to see *huasos* driving cattle, ox-carts piled high with firewood or barrels of *chicha* (cider), and apparently ambulant hay-stacks that seem to move on a cushion of air – until you take a closer look and see they are being pulled on the typical Chilote *birloches* (sledges).

Famous throughout Chile for its myths and legends, missionaries and churches, countryfolk and farmers, Chiloé is a land where the pace of life is slow and little substantial has changed in the 450 years since the arrival of the Spaniards, who called it New Galicia. Small fishing villages still glean a slender living from the sea, while farmers tend cattle and harvest apples, potatoes, wheat and oats. More than 150 eighteenth- and nineteenth-century **wooden churches** and **chapels**, with their characteristic arched porticoes and towers, dot the land; sixteen of them are protected by UNESCO's world heritage status. Chiloé is also one of the few places in the country where you can still see **palafitos**, precarious but picturesque timber houses built on stilts on the edge of the sea or estuaries; these were once the traditional dwellings of most of the fisherfolk of southern Chile.

Things *have* moved on, of course. The locals no longer farm their animals in rude woven-branch corrals, iron and horses have replaced the primitive tools that were once used to till the ground, and people don't habitate shelters of thatch, hide or sealskin called *rucas*. Nor do canoes (*dalca*) ply the ocean in search of fish, and the people are no longer governed in small tribal groups or *caví*, as in the time of the indigenous Huilliches, Mapuche and Chonos. But much of the old culture has been preserved, assimilated into Hispanic tradition by a profound mixing of the Spanish and indigenous cultures that occurred here

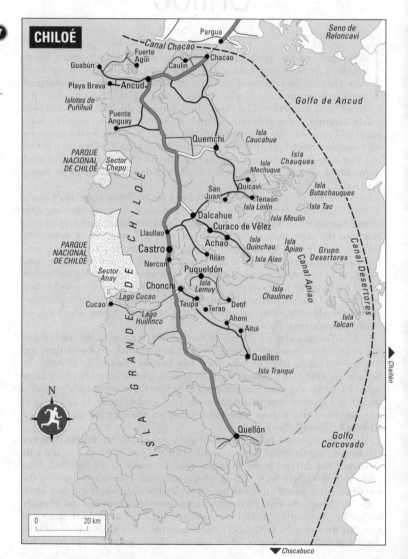

more than in other parts of South America. The settlers lived cheek-by-jowl with the indigenous Chilotes – everyone wore the same clothes, lived in the same villages and relied on the same subsistence crops for survival. This mixing of traditions has made today's Chiloé more "pagan Catholic" than Roman Catholic, and all sorts of **supernatural beings** are still believed to inhabit the archipelago. It wasn't only in a geographical sense that Chiloé was described by the visiting Charles Darwin in 1835 as "the end of Christendom".

Arriving in Chiloé

Although there are controversial plans to build a **bridge** across the narrow straits that separate Chiloé's Isla Grande from the mainland south of Puerto Montt – the project has suffered a number of delays due to soaring costs and is unlikely to be finished before 2011 – at present you must take one of the regular ferries to get to the island. Scheduled ferry and catamaran services also criss-cross the gulf, linking Puerto Montt, Chaitén, Castro and Quellón, making it relatively straightforward to combine a visit to both the island and the nearby mainland; Chaitén is the main northerly entry point to the dramatic Carretera Austral. The ferries, operated by TransMarChilay, from Pargua, 59km southwest of Puerto Montt on the mainland (daily every 30min; 35min; no reservation required; CH$600, cars CH$7200) arrive at **Chacao** on the Isla Grande's northern shore. There's not much here to detain you, except perhaps the excellent **tourist kiosk** half a kilometre along the road to Ancud (Jan–March daily 9am–9pm; ☎65/262811 ext 237). If you've no transport you can pick up one of the **buses** coming off the ferry, which run every fifteen minutes to Ancud (CH$1000) or Castro (CH$1500). Most people take one of the frequent buses from Puerto Montt; the fare includes the ferry ride, and your bus takes you on to your Chiloé destination.

Ancud and around

The Panamericana shoots west from Chacao, 33km to Ancud, Chiloé's main northern settlement and second biggest town. After nine kilometres, though, a turn-off to the right leads to the little village of **Caulín**, a handful of exposed houses on the edge of a windswept, kilometre-wide sandy beach. When the tide's in, the water comes right up to the houses' doorsteps and covers the road – the distance between high and low tide marks here is one of the greatest in the world. This makes collecting shellfish easy, and the village is famous for the **oyster beds** that lie just offshore. You can sample the delicacies at the fine *Ostras Caulín* restaurant (mobile ☎09/6437005, ✉ostrascaulin@terra.cl) and stay at the *Hotel Caulín* (☎09/3301220, ✉contacto@hotelcaulin.cl, ⊛www .hotelcaulin.cl; ❺–❻), with cosy rooms and five-person *cabañas*. Thanks to the views and feeling of isolation, it can be idyllic here if the weather is good, but it can also be a rain-lashed nightmare, in which case you're better off taking a bus (Buses Lorca; 4 daily) all the way down to Ancud.

Often overlooked by travellers on their way to Castro, **ANCUD** is a pretty little seaside town and a lively fishing port, with an excellent **museum**. Founded in 1769 as a Spanish stronghold, after Peruvian independence in 1824, it became the crown's last possession in South America – the pathetic remains of a once proud empire. Its forts resisted one attempt at capture, but finally fell in January 1826 when the lonely and demoralized Spanish garrison fled into the forest in the face of a small Chilean attack. The remains of these Spanish forts

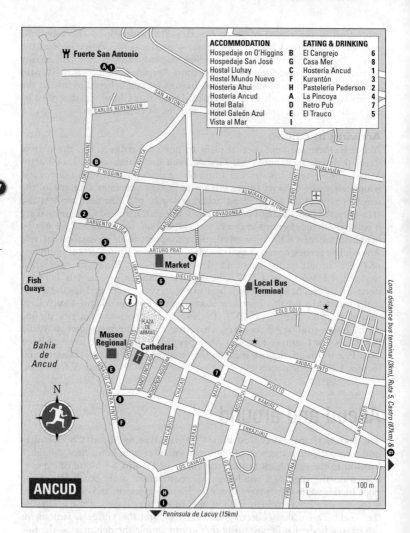

ACCOMMODATION

Hospedaje on O'Higgins	B
Hospedaje San José	G
Hostal Lluhay	C
Hostel Mundo Nuevo	F
Hostería Ahui	H
Hostería Ancud	A
Hotel Balai	D
Hotel Galeón Azul	E
Vista al Mar	I

EATING & DRINKING

El Cangrejo	6
Casa Mer	8
Hostería Ancud	1
Kurantón	3
Pastelería Pederson	2
La Pincoya	4
Retro Pub	7
El Trauco	5

ANCUD

Long distance bus terminal (3km), Ruta 5, Castro (87km) & G

Peninsula de Lacuy (15km)

– **Fuerte San Antonio** in the town and **Fuerte Agüi** on a peninsula to the northwest – can still be visited today and command wonderful views out over the bay. One of Chile's most important *pingüineras*, or **penguin colonies**, clings to **Islotes de Puñihuil**, a set of tiny islets just off the coast to the west of Ancud at Pumillahue. Intrepid hikers will head down the Pacific coast to visit Sector Chepu, the least accessible section of the **Parque Nacional Chiloé**.

Arrival and information

Long-distance buses **arrive** in the terminal on Calle Aníbal Pinto, a five-minute taxi ride (CH$1000) from the Plaza de Armas towards Ruta 5. The local bus terminal is on Pedro Montt, opposite Dieciocho. Ancud's tourist information office is **Sernatur**, on the Plaza de Armas at Libertad 665 (Jan–March Mon–Fri

8.30am–5.30pm, Fri 8.30am–4.30pm; ⊤65/622800, ⓔatuncud@hotmail.com).
It has information on the entire archipelago and is far better than the tourist
kiosk in Castro (see p.426).

Accommodation

There's much more **accommodation** in Ancud in the summer, when many
private houses open their doors to offer bed and breakfast, but there's enough
to go around even in winter. For rooms in private houses (❸–❹) in the nearby
countryside, contact the Oficina de Agroturismo (⊤65/628333, ⓕ65/622722)
or enquire at Sernatur.

Hospedaje O'Higgins 6 ⊤65/622266. Despite its
shabby exterior, this is the best budget accommodation in Ancud, with an almost life-size bronze
statue facing the front door and well-proportioned,
pale-wood-panelled bright rooms with views over
the bay. Closed April–Dec. ❷

Hospedaje San José Pudeto 619 ⊤65/622467.
Recommended family-run *hospedaje* whose owner
will take you to and from the bus terminal. Clean
and comfortable, with Internet access and a good
kitchen open to guests. ❶

Hostal Lluhay Lord Cochrane 458
⊤ & ⓕ65/622656, ⓔelluhay@entelchile.net. This
marvellous hostal looks modest from the outside,
but inside you'll discover a 200-year-old French
rosewood piano, a collection of antique gramo-
phones and one of the best-stocked bars in Ancud.
The rooms have private baths, and the friendly
owners will arrange private tours. Credit cards are
accepted. ❹

Hostal Mundo Nuevo Costanera
748 ⊤65/628383 or ⊤93508375,
ⓔhostal@newworld.cl, ⓦwww.newworld.cl.
Friendly, spotless hostal on the waterfront with a
large garden and a seaview terrace. Guests can
use the kitchen facilities. Breakfast is included and
they offer bike rental. The helpful Swiss owner
speaks English and German. ❹

Hostería Ahui Av Costanera 906 ⊤65/622415. A
three-storey beachfront building, with good views
from the comfortable en-suite rooms, making it a
popular mid-range choice. ❹

Hostería Ancud San Antonio 30 ⊤65/622340,
ⓕ65/622350, ⓦwww.hosteriaancud.com. Built up
on the peninsula just to the north, this is the best
hotel in town, with a luxurious log-cabin feel and
large picture windows overlooking the sea. ❼

Hotel Balai Pudeto 169 ⊤65/622966, ⓦwww
.hotelbalai.cl. Unusual local art and trinkets lend
this hotel plenty of character although some of its
rooms are dark. ❹

Hotel Galeón Azul Libertad 751
⊤ & ⓕ65/622543, ⓔgaleonazul@surnet.cl. The
views across the Golfo de Quetalmahue from this
vibrantly coloured hotel are staggering, but despite
high-quality, modern rooms, its exposed position
and rickety feel give the place a slightly desolate
air. ❻

Vista al Mar Av Costanera 918
⊤ & ⓕ65/622617, ⓔvistaalmar@123.cl,
ⓦwww.vistaalmar.cl. This clean and recently refurbished place is both a hotel and a youth hostel. If
you're the only ones staying in the hostel (three
rooms on the top floor), you'll get the cheapest
apartment in town with a bonus of great views. ❸

The Town

Ancud is built on a small, square promontory jutting into the Canal de Chacao
and the Golfo de Quetalmahue. The town is spread along two hilly sides of an
old river bed, and – unlike most Chilean cities – isn't laid out on a grid pattern,
but is a chaotic mass of streets and one-way systems. The centre is the **Plaza
de Armas**, a pretty little square which, in summer, is filled with the temporary
craft stalls that spill out of the colourful **Mercado Municipal**, one block to
the north.

There are some more stalls a block to the west, down near the hectic **fishing
harbour**, a great place to hang around and watch the catch being hauled in;
from here it's transferred to the large shed where it's sold to merchants. You can
watch whole families deftly baiting enormous coils of deep-water fishing lines.

Chilote mythology

The Chiloé islands have long been rife with myths and legends, especially in the remote rural regions, where tradition and superstition hold sway. Colourful creatures crop up in stories throughout the archipelago, most often born out of the region's isolation and the hardships endured living there. Many of these bewitching characters embody the islands' creation and its relationship to the forests and the sea.

Trauco A deformed and ugly troll with coarse swollen features, Trauco dresses in ragged clothes and a conical cap and carries a stone axe or wooden club, a *pahueldún*. He preys on women, usually with the intention of stealing their virginity.

Camahueto This young, agile bull sports a short golden horn, a *cacho*, and a silvery hide. He lives in watery grottoes or marshy lakes until adulthood, when he migrates to the sea, wreaking havoc on crops and vegetation along the way. To prevent this from happening, a farmer must summon a *machi*, or wizard, to lasso him with a length of kelp. If a wizard catches Camahueto during a full moon, they are able to pull out the horn, turning him into a docile calf.

Fiura An ugly, squat woman with halitosis, she lives in the woods, clothed in moss. The coquettish Fiura – who many believe is a she-devil - bathes in waterfalls, where she hopes to seduce young men before driving them insane.

Invunche Stolen at birth by a witch, Invunche was transformed into a deformed monster with one leg crooked behind his back so that he can never escape. He feeds on goats' flesh and stands guard at the entrance to the witch's cavern, grunting or emitting bloodcurdling screams. If you're unlucky enough to spot him, you'll be frozen to that spot forever.

Basilisco A giant snake with the head of a cockerel, Basilisco turns people to stone with its gaze. At night, Basilisco enters houses and sucks the breath from sleeping inhabitants, so that they waste away into shrivelled skeletons.

Caleuche This ghostly ship that glows in the fog showcases dancing and beautiful music onboard. Journeying through the archipelago, it's crewed by shipwrecked sailors and those who have been lured by the enchanting music. The Caleuche travels at great speeds both above and below the water, and can disappear in a trice, leaving only the echoes of captivating music.

Pincoya A goddess of extraordinary beauty, Pincoya personifies the spirit of the ocean and is responsible for the abundance or scarcity of fish in the sea. She dances half-naked, draped in kelp, on the beaches or tops of waves. If she's spotted facing the sea, the village will enjoy an ample supply of seafood. If she's looking towards the land, there will be a shortage.

Voladora A witch who changes into a bird to perform the duties of a sorcerer's messenger, Voladora travels under the cover of night and can only be detected by her terrible cries, like those of a wounded or distressed animal. If one hears her anguished screams, they're in for a spell of bad luck.

Brujo This is the general term for a witch. In Chiloé, the *brujos* hide out in a cave near the town of Quicavi. To become a witch, an individual must wash away baptism in a waterfall for forty days, assassinate a loved one, and sign a pact in their own blood with the devil, stating when the evil one can claim their soul. Witches are capable of great mischief and can cause illness and death, even from afar.

Caballo Marino An extraordinary horse used by the witches, this giant, unsightly creature can carry up to thirteen at a time as he transports his charges to and from the phantom ship Caleuche. Caballo Marino is often spotted around a rocky coastline, streaming with water as it rises from the waves, having just delivered the witches to the ship.

Just south, a crushed-shell promenade leads past half a dozen intriguing pieces of **sculpture**, including a Henry Moore-style piece of a woman giving birth.

The Museo Regional

Perched above the promenade is the **Museo Regional** (officially and more poetically known as the Museo Azul de las Islas de Chiloé), a fort-like building with a blue facade. Its entrance is on Libertad, one block south of the Plaza de Armas (Jan–Feb Mon–Fri 10.30am–7.30pm, Sat & Sun 10am–7.30pm; March–Dec Tues–Fri 10am–5.30pm, Sat & Sun, holidays 10am–2pm; CH$600, children CH$300). Outside, on an untidy patio, you can inspect a traditional **fogón**, a type of hut introduced into Chiloé by the first Spanish missionaries three hundred years ago. A fire would burn in the middle of the floor, filling the roof space with smoke and curing the fish and potatoes hanging there. These were the staples of the Chilote diet, but during festivals pigs would be slaughtered and Chilotes would eat hams (*jamones*), smoked ribs (*costillares*), crackling (*chicharrones*), blood sausages (*longanizas*) and brawn (*queso de cabeza*). Whilst the slaughtered pigs were being processed, Chilotes would quench their thirst with large quantities of cider (*chicha de manzana*). Also on the patio are the hollowed-out tree trunk where apples were pulped with long sticks; the flexible woven baskets where the pulp was strained; and an old wooden corkscrew where it was pressed.

The patio used to house an exact copy of the *Goleta Ancud*, a **schooner** revered throughout Chile (its photo adorns many a poster) because, in 1843, it carried the first Chilean settlers down to the Magellan Strait (see p.489). It was the culmination of a great tradition of Chilote boat-building, starting off with boats made from rough planks lashed together with vines and caulked with alerce bark (unfortunately, as stripping bark off alerces contributed to their demise). The replica failed to survive Ancud's harsh winters and the museum now displays photographs of the vessel.

Also outside are a collection of rustic **carved demons** from Chilote mythology (see box opposite). They may look funny, but the locals take them seriously. For example, the figure of a demon called a *trauco* – a hideous woodland troll still blamed in Chiloé for unwanted pregnancies – has actually been chained up, not against theft but to stop it from getting into mischief. Calling someone a *trauco* is a common insult in this region.

Inside the museum is an excellent, partly interactive exhibit, with explanations in Spanish only, covering various aspects of life in the archipelago, with an emphasis on domesticity and arts and crafts. Alongside beautiful photographs are fine examples of the traditional flat circular trays used for husking grain; the lightweight ones with a coarse weave for collecting shellfish; and distinctively fine-meshed liquid strainers. You'll also find **sledges**, a form of transport that evolved to deal with Chiloé's muddy tracks and small, steep fields.

North of the Plaza de Armas

Walking back down to the fishing harbour from the museum, you'll find yourself at the end of Calle Lord Cochrane, a road that follows the coast to the north and heads uphill. If you follow it, you'll come to the reconstructed walls of the Spanish **Fuerte de San Antonio**, which affords a sweeping view over the Golfo de Quetalmahue and out to the Pacific Ocean. By 1786, the Spanish had built an impressive chain of twelve such forts and gun batteries to control the passage of ships through the Canal de Chacao and protect the anchorage in the Bahía de Ancud, and the sixteen cannon in the Fuerte de San Antonio combined with the fifteen in Castillo de San Miguel de Agüi (on the peninsula across the water) could sink any ship entering the bay. Further round this windswept headland, past the *Hostería de Ancud*, is the **Balneario Arena Gruesa**, a popular swimming beach in summer, sheltered by high cliffs. Further still is the **Mirador Cerro Eluaihue**, from which there's a bird's-eye view of the great Río Pudeto estuary stretching away to the southwest, speckled with hundreds of tiny fishing boats lying at anchor.

Eating and drinking

Being a fishing town, Ancud has a sizeable collection of good **seafood restaurants**, albeit with similar menus. Most huddle around the sheltered courtyard in the Mercado Municipal, where it can get so busy that at times it's difficult to tell who's supposed to be serving you.

El Cangrejo Dieciocho 155. Basic, cheap café food, but with a particularly fine *empanada de mariscos*.

Casa Mer Costanera and Errázuriz. Reasonably priced, superbly cooked dishes including steak stuffed with prawns and mushrooms, and a wide range of seafood, all served in a large dining room with chunky wood furniture and large panoramic windows overlooking the sea.

Hostería Ancud San Antonio 30. The hostería has a good but expensive restaurant serving international food, and is the best place for a blowout meal.

Kurantón Prat 94. All kinds of excellent dishes, meat and fish, on offer in cosy surroundings, but the speciality is the eponymous *curanto*, a meat, fish and shellfish stew. Relatively high prices but service and quality to justify it

Pastelería Pederson Lord Cochrane 470. Enjoy unbeatable harbour views as you tuck into a delicious, reasonably priced lunch or *once*. The *küchen* are unforgettable, especially the raspberry cream cake (in season).

La Pincoya Prat 61. One of the best places to eat *curanto* and *ceviche*, with a family-run atmosphere, low prices and excellent service.

Retro Pub Maipú 615. Decent burgers and pasta as well as Tex-Mex dishes are served in this dark bar which turns into a lively nightspot.

El Trauco Blanco 515 at Prat. A tourist-oriented seafood restaurant near the market, with garrulous waiters and decent food, at slightly higher prices than similar places.

Listings

Banks and exchange There are ATMs at BCI and Banco de Chile, one block away from the inland side of the Plaza. There aren't any *cambios*, so you should change money before you come here.
Hospital Almirante Latore 301 ☏65/622355.
Internet Inside the gallery at Pudeto 276 or at the

Entel call centre at Allende 740; Internet access is CH$700 an hour.
Laundry Lavandería Clean Center, Pudeto 45, around the corner from Sernatur.
Telephone centres Several near the market.

Tours From Ancud

A number of trips and tours are offered around Ancud, including day-trips to Peninsula de Lacuy (see opposite), to the penguin colony near Pumillahue (see opposite), and multi-day boat trips of the archipelago. Most are run by reputable agencies with bilingual guides.

Recommended tour companies include **Patagon Chiloé**, Bellavista 491 (☏65/622128), **Excursiones Balai**, Pudeto 169 (☏65/622541), and **Travel Adventures**, Prat 176 (☏65/625977). For ambitious sailing trips across to the mainland via lesser Chilote islands, check out **Austral Adventures**, Cochrane 432 (☏65/625977, ✉tours@austral-adventures.com, ⊛www.australadventures.com), a US-run outfit with a beautiful boat, *Cahuella*, on which they offer multi-day tours of the archipelago that also visit Parque Nacional Pumalin; they're also the best operators for excursions to the penguin colony and land-based excursions within reach of Ancud (CH$30,000–40,000 per person).

Around Ancud

The road soon runs out of tar as you head **west** out of Ancud towards the Pacific Ocean. On the way you'll pass people laying out a stinking grey seaweed by the side of the road to dry. Called *pelillo* ("fine hair") because it resembles human hair, this alga has a dual purpose: agar-agar, a gelatinous substance used in the food industry, can be extracted from it, or the seaweed can be woven into a fibre.

After 14km, you reach the left-hand turning that leads to **Pumillahue**, 13km farther away, near which is the long, curving **Playa Brava**. Just off the coast lies the rocky outcrop of the **Islotes de Puñihuil**, a **penguin colony** monitored and protected by the Otway Foundation (Casilla 499, Puerto Montt ☎ & ℱ65/278500) which used to look after another important nesting site in southern Patagonia near Punta Arenas, until ousted by the site's owners. This thriving colony is unique to Chile in that it is visited by both Magallanic and Humboldt penguins in the breeding and rearing season, between December and March. The adults fish most of the day, so the optimum visiting time is early or late in the day. The Foundation runs well-explained trips in zodiac dinghies to see the penguins and other marine fauna, including the delightful *chungungos* or sea otters. The excursions, which depart from a jetty, cost around CH\$4000 per person. Local fishermen also offer trips to see the penguins, at a lower fee, but their lack of knowledge and respect for the wildlife – they get far too close to the penguins and their chicks – counteracts the small financial saving. Buses Mar Brava runs a couple of buses from Ancud every day except Sunday, but a better option, if you have no wheels, is to come on a day-trip with Austral Adventures (see box opposite), who throw in walking, kayaking and other activities, plus a picnic.

Just after the Pumillahue turn-off you reach the edge of the **Península de Lacuy**, a long arm of land that reaches out into the Pacific then bends back inland. Shortly afterwards, the road forks, with the left branch leading to the quiet white-sand beach of **Playa Guabún**, and ultimately to the northern tip of the peninsula and **Faro Corona**, an isolated lighthouse on a remote promontory. The right fork deposits you, after 21km, below **Fuerte Agüi** (always open; free) at the peninsula's easternmost edge, directly across the water from Ancud. The road worsens as you approach the fort, eventually petering out by a pleasant sandy beach, and you have to walk the final kilometre through a quiet forest, disturbed only by the sound of your feet, the buzzing of insects and the occasional put-put of a distant fishing boat. The fort was the last toehold of the Spanish Empire in South America, but today all that's left is a tranquil grassy lawn around a battery of rusting cannon. Standing on its ancient walls you can see right over the bay to Ancud and, on a clear day, all the way to Volcán Calbuco above Puerto Montt (see p.402).

You can get to the peninsula by boat or bus. The *Amadeus I* boat, Blanco Encalada 587 (☎65/623334; CH\$5000), leaves at noon daily from Ancud's port. Keep a lookout for seals and dolphins as you cross the bay. Buses Mar (CH\$2000) depart from Ancud's local bus terminal up to four times daily depending on the time of year.

Thirty kilometres **south** of Ancud is the northern section of the **Parque Nacional Chiloé**, called **sector Chepu** (Dec–March daylight hours; CH\$1000), noted for its **wetlands**. Created by the flooding following the 1960 earthquake, they are now rich in birdlife. The sector is remote and extremely difficult to get to, and unless you're a dedicated hiker with time to spare you'd be better off visiting the southern sector, **sector Anay**, accessible by public transport

from Castro (see below). Still, if you're determined, head south along the Panamericana, then turn right (west) 22km out of Ancud and continue to the tiny
settlement of **Puerto Anguay**. From here, hike west for ninety minutes along
the Río Chepu, cross the estuary – you can usually rent a fisherman's boat – and
finally, hike south. After four hours you'll reach the Conaf station at Río Lar.

From Ancud to Castro

The Panamericana heads southward, through a gently undulating landscape of
fertile farmland and copses hemmed in by hedgerows of wild fuchsia until, after
some 70km, it reaches **Castro**. It's a fast road but the scenery is a little humdrum;
if you have your own vehicle or a bit of time, it's worth taking things at a slower
pace and travelling along the coast instead: turn east off the highway 41km from
Ancud, and drive the 22km to **Quemchi**, before turning south. Here you'll get
a much richer flavour of Chiloé, passing through small maritime villages, such as
Tenaún and Quicaví (see p.432), with their characteristic wooden churches, and
travelling through the homelands of some of the islands' myths.

Quemchi is an attractive little town with narrow, irregular streets sloping down
to the water's edge. Beyond the fishing boats that lie beached on the sand is the
wooded, field-strewn island of Caucahue, across an often choppy sea. Quemchi
is a quiet place; once the centre of an important timber industry, it now relies
on salmon and shellfish farms for its existence. A couple of kilometres south,
there's a tiny wooded island, **Isla Aucar**, only accessible by a 500-metre-long
footbridge. Nestled on the island is a small wooden **church** with a duck-egg-
blue roof and white walls. If you have your own transport you can continue
towards Castro via Dalcahue and other seaside villages described later in the
chapter – by public transport these places are accessible only from Castro.

There's a helpful **tourist information** hut in Quemchi's plaza (Jan–March
10am–6pm) and several **places to stay**: the central, friendly *Hospedaje La
Tranquera*, almost overhanging the sea at Yungay 40 (T65/691250; ❸), with
clean, bare rooms and a picturesque view; the simple yet homely *Hospedaje
El Embrujo*, Pedro Montt 431 (T65/651262; ❷) and, 3km north of town, the
attractive *Hospedaje Tubildad* (T65/691305; ❸) with a garden and sea views. You
can get to Quemchi on one of five daily **buses** from Ancud, operated by Buses
el Río and Queilen Bus (T65/253468 for both).

Castro and around

Built on a small promontory at the head of a twenty-kilometre fjord, **CASTRO**
occupies an unusual position both physically and historically. Founded in 1567,
it's the third-oldest city in Chile, but it never became strategically important
because it's a terrible harbour for sailing ships. It only flourished because the
Jesuits chose to base their mission here, as a result of their efforts it became a
centre of evangelism, education and commerce.

Castro has had its fair share of difficulties. It was destroyed by earthquake in
1646, by fire in 1729, by earthquake again in 1739, by fire again in 1890, by fire
once more in 1936, and most recently by earthquake and tidal wave in 1960.
Anyone else would have given up and moved long ago, but the Chilotes keep
hanging on. Nor has nature been the only troublemaker – in the autumn of
1600 the town was sacked by the Dutch corsair Balthasar de Cordes, who killed

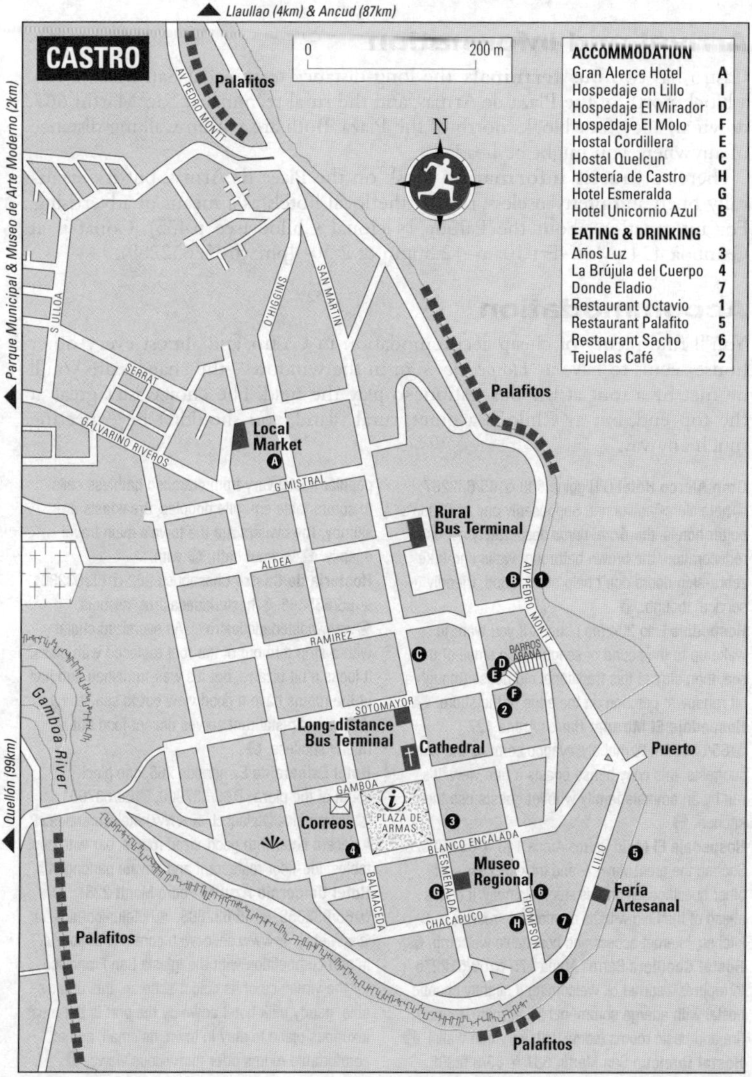
Llaullao (4km) & Ancud (87km)
CASTRO
0
200 m
ACCOMMODATION
Gran Alerce Hotel A
Hospedaje on Lillo I
Hospedaje El Mirador D
Hospedaje El Molo F
Hostal Cordillera E
Hostal Quelcun C
Hostería de Castro H
Hotel Esmeralda G
Hotel Unicornio Azul B
EATING & DRINKING
Años Luz 3
La Brújula del Cuerpo 4
Donde Eladio 7
Restaurant Octavio 1
Restaurant Palafito 5
Restaurant Sacho 6
Tejuelas Café 2
N
Parque Municipal & Museo de Arte Moderno (2km)
Quellón (99km)
Palafitos
AV PEDRO MONTT
S ULLOA
O'HIGGINS
SAN MARTIN
SERRAT
GALVARINO RIVEROS
Local Market
G MISTRAL
Rural Bus Terminal
ALDEA
RAMIREZ
BARROS ARANA
SOTOMAYOR
Long-distance Bus Terminal
Cathedral
Puerto
Gamboa River
GAMBOA
PLAZA DE ARMAS
Correos
BLANCO ENCALADA
LILLO
Museo Regional
Feria Artesanal
ESMERALDA
BALMACEDA
CHACABUCO
THOMPSON

all the Spanish men he found and enslaved all the women (except Doña Inés de Bazán, who has become a Chilean heroine because she spiked the corsairs' guns and wet their powder, allowing some of her compatriots to escape). Not satisfied, the Dutch sacked the place again in 1643.

Today most of these traumas have been forgotten, and life here is now placid and slow. The tumults have taken their toll, burning, shaking or washing away most of old Castro, though some buildings have miraculously survived, such as the garish **Iglesia San Francisco** on the Plaza de Armas, and the groups of brightly coloured **palafitos** (houses on stilts) on the waterfront to the north and south of town.

Arrival and information

Castro has two **bus terminals**, the long-distance terminal at San Martín 486, a block north of the Plaza de Armas, and the rural terminal at San Martín 667, down an alley four blocks north of the Plaza. Both are within walking distance of anywhere you might be headed.

There's a **tourist information** kiosk on the Plaza de Armas, but it's erratically open and pretty useless, run by the local hotels as a means of advertising. For information about the Parque Nacional Chiloé (see p.435), Conaf is at Gamboa 424 (Mon–Fri 10am–12.30pm & 2.30–4pm; ☎65/632289).

Accommodation

You'll find plenty of cheap accommodation in Castro, and almost every other house seems to have a "*Hospedaje*" sign in the window – the chances are you'll be met by a tout at the bus station, so play the field. The choice isn't great at the top end, but as Chiloé's a quiet, rural island, you shouldn't be expecting much anyway.

Gran Alerce Hotel O'Higgins 808 ☎65/632267, ✆hotelalerc@telsur.net. Supposedly one of Chiloé's better hotels, the *Gran Alerce* desperately needs redecoration: the brown bathroom walls and fake zebra-skin doors don't help at all. Good, friendly service, though. ❺

Hospedaje Lillo 204 (no phone). If you want to wake up to the sound of seagulls and smell of the sea, then stay at this traditional old house (though a bit rundown) perched on the edge of the shore. ❷

Hospedaje El Mirador Barros Arana 127 ☎65/633795, ✆maboly@yahoo.com. As the name suggests, this cosy house boasts a fine view. It's run by an amiable family who let guests use their kitchen. ❸

Hospedaje El Molo Barros Arana 140 ☎65/635026. Sharing the great views – and tricky access – of other guesthouses on this steep stairway, it edges ahead of the field with its comfortable rooms, kitchen, Internet access and hospitable welcome. ❸

Hostal Codillera Barros Arana 175 ☎09/5122767, ✆mpjtres@surnet.cl. Welcoming if slightly chaotic hostal with a large communal living room, roaring fire and basic rooms (some with very thin walls). ❸

Hostal Quelcun San Martín 581 ☎65/632396, ✆65/638717, ✆quelcun@telsur.cl. Rooms in this popular hostel vary from cramped bathless cells to comfortable en-suite doubles. Breakfasts are skimpy. The owners run the town's main travel agency. ❷ without bath, ❹ with.

Hostería de Castro Chacabuco 202 ☎65/632301, ✆65/635688, ✆hosteriadecastro@telsur.cl, ✇www.hosteriadecastro.cl. An oversized chalet with a strip torn out of the roof replaced with glass. It looks a bit bizarre, but it's well-furnished and half of the rooms have a good view out to sea. Its *Las Araucarias* restaurant serves decent food but is utterly soulless. ❻

Hotel Esmeralda Esmeralda 266, one block south of the plaza ☎65/637900, ✆65/637901, ✆hesmeralda@telsur.cl, ✇www.hotelesmeralda.cl. A decent hotel with good-sized rooms, bar with pool tables, top-floor restaurant and private parking. ❻

Hotel Unicornio Azul Av Pedro Montt 228 ☎65/632359, ✆65/632808, ✆hotelunicornioazul @surnet.cl, ✇www.chiloeweb.com/unicornioazul. In stiff competition with the Iglesia San Francisco for the virulence of its colour scheme, this unmissable, gaudy pink hotel down by the port is the most luxurious place to stay in town. Its small, quaint, comfortable rooms offer marvellous views. ❻

The Town

Somewhat on the scruffy side, but charming nonetheless, Castro has the feel of an isolated town on the edge of the modern mainstream, like the west coast of Ireland or the maritime provinces of Canada. The promontory on which it's centred is small, only five blocks wide and nine blocks long, and is fringed on the north and south by the town's **palafitos**, rickety shacks on stilts that the local government is torn between preserving as national monuments and condemning as unsanitary slums.

△ Castro fjord

The centre of town is the **Plaza de Armas**, a block and a half from the southern tip of the promontory. On the northeastern corner sits Castro's church, the **Iglesia San Francisco**. Painted bright orangey-pink and purple for Pope John Paul II's visit in 1987 and looking almost luminescent from afar, it's now a more muted yellow and lilac. It was designed in 1906 by an Italian, who originally wanted to build it using concrete; it's just as well he didn't, because it's unlikely that concrete would have survived the 1960 earthquake. As it is, the box-frame structure, sheathed in sheets of beaten tin moulded to resemble the wooden shingles characteristic of Chilote architecture, survived well. The impressive interior is a harmonious blend of the island's native hardwoods, lit with a soft light that brings out their warm hues.

Just off the southeast corner of the Plaza de Armas, on Calle Esmeralda, is the **Museo Regional** (Jan–Feb Mon–Sat 9.30am–7pm, Sun 10.30am–1pm; March–Dec Mon–Sat 9.30am–1pm & 3-6.30pm, Sun 10.30am–1pm; ☎65/635967; free), a small but well-laid-out museum containing artefacts from the various aboriginal tribes that inhabited the Chiloé archipelago before the arrival of the Spanish. Here you can find their stone tools, fish hooks and spear heads. Contemporary times are documented in a large collection of photographs, mostly taken before the earthquake, and there's also a bicycle made out of wood, a wonderful emblem of Chiloé's *cultura de madera* (wood-working culture).

The road **Blanco Encalada** runs south of the plaza. A few days before the catastrophic 1936 fire that just about burned Castro to the ground, several people living here reported seeing a giant sea-lion come out of the water and waddle up the street. In a community where superstition is second nature, this apparition was widely accepted as an evil omen. Perhaps it was, though you didn't really need an omen to foresee the danger: Castro of the 1930s was a fire waiting to happen, built as it was almost entirely of back-to-back wooden buildings. When the fire struck, the only thing the inhabitants could do was head for the sea, the one sanctuary available. They took to their boats and watched their homes burn from the waters of the icy fjord.

Two blocks east of the plaza, down by the water, is the **feria artesanal**, a large covered market where hand-knitted woollens vie for space with home-grown vegetables. Despite the day-trippers from mainland Chile, there is an almost religious peace inside the market, broken only by the clicking of sturdy women knitting the pullovers that the region is famous for. Next to the market there's a line of **palafitos** on the sea, used today as restaurants. They're a great place to come and eat, but they get packed at lunch time, so it's much more relaxing in the afternoon.

Beyond the promontory the town stretches out to the northwest, where modern low-cost houses have been erected for a rural population that doesn't have much hope of finding work in the fields. Out here is the **Parque Municipal** (accessible by buses and taxis from the centre of town) where you can enjoy excellent views over Castro, across the archipelago and out towards the Andes. Nearby is the **Museo de Arte Moderno**, or **MAM** (Jan–Feb daily 10am–7pm; Nov, Dec & March Mon–Fri 11am–2pm; rest of year by appointment only; donation), a group of restored wooden barns that is home to a collection of modern art, including works by local artists.

Every February – usually during the third week – the park hosts an enormous feast, the culmination of the **Festival Costumbrista**, a celebration of traditional Chilote life, when *curantos* (meat and seafood stews) are cooked in great cauldrons, meat is roasted over open fires, and balls of grated potato – *tropón* – are baked on hot embers. When the outer part is cooked, the *tropón* is removed from the fire and the crisp shell peeled off and eaten – the inevitable burnt fingers and resultant hot-potato juggling and hopping are known as *bailar el tropón* (dancing the *tropón*).

Eating and drinking

Castro's menus are dominated by seafood plucked fresh from the fjord by the town's fleet of fishermen. The *palafito* restaurants opposite the feria artesanal, by the waterfront, offer decent fish dishes at reasonable prices.

Años Luz San Martín 309. This modern, sophisticated café with a dazzling yellow façade is *the* place to be seen in Castro. Excellent coffee and drinks are served from a fishing-boat converted into a bar. The food, including delicious salads and cakes, is good too, if a little overpriced, as is the Internet access.

La Brújula del Cuerpo O'Higgins 308, on the corner of the plaza near the fire station. A bright café with a menu that's a bit laboured – dishes are given fire-related names – but it's inexpensive and lively, making it a pleasant spot for a drink and a sandwich.

Donde Eladio Lillo 97. This inviting restaurant overlooks the sea and specializes in large portions of fresh seafood that draws plenty of locals at lunch time.

Restaurant Don Octavio Av Pedro Montt 261. A smart family-run waterfront restaurant with a fine view over the sea, typical Chilean food and good service, though the prices are on the high side.

Restaurant Palafito Lillo 30. The main *palafito* restaurant by the market, serving standard Chilean seafood at reasonable prices in a beautiful setting over the placid waters of Castro's fjord.

Restaurant Sacho Thompson 213 ☏65/632079. The best restaurant in Castro. It's slightly dingy downstairs, but the upstairs dining area offers views across the fjord. The service can be a little frosty and the prices are higher than elsewhere, but even this cannot detract from the heavenly seafood, such as *carapacho* (crab). It's worth booking an upstairs table in the evening.

Tejuelas Café Serrano 469. Basic burgers, hot dogs and other inexpensive fare, but some of the dishes have more local colour, including the delicious smoked salmon.

Listings

Airlines LAN, Blanco Encalada 299
☎65/635254.

Banks and exchange There are ATMs around
the Plaza de Armas, and Sr Julio Barrientos at
Chacabuco 286 (☎65/625079) exchanges
money.

Bookshop El Tren Libros, Thompson 229, has a
small selection of second-hand books in English,
German and French as well as a good array of
Spanish books.

Car rental Automotriz del Sur, Esmeralda 260
(☎65/637777, ☞65/637373), and Salfa Sur,
Gabriela Mistral 499 (☎65/632704), are both
cheaper than outfits in Puerto Montt.

Internet access *Asesoft*, Galería Insular, O'Higgins
670/2, CH$700 an hour.

Laundry Clean Centre, Serano 440, or Lavoseco
Unico, Gamboa 594.

Post office Plaza de Armas, O'Higgins 388.

Telephone centres Several around the Plaza de
Armas or at Esmeralda 220, San Martín 581 and
Latorre 275.

Tour operators Pehuén Expediciones, Blanco
Encalada 299 (☎65/632361, ☞65/635254,
ⓔ pehuentr@entelchile.net) is an experienced outfit; its office is where you book
catamaran tickets for Chaitén. In summer
they run boat trips, lasting from a day to a
week, to the small, uninhabited islands of
the Chilote archipelago; they are also LAN
agents. Pehuén Expediciones offers city tours
(CH$7000), trips to Isla Quinchao (CH$20,000)
and excursions to the Parque Nacional Chiloé
(CH$18,500). Turismo Isla Grande, Thompson
241 (☎65/632384) takes bookings for Trans-
MarChilay and Navimag ferries, as well as
organizing tours to Dalcahue and Isla Quinchao
or the Parque Nacional Chiloé. Turismo Quelcun,
San Martín 581 (☎65/632396, ☞65/638717,
ⓔ quelcun@telsur.cl), associated with the hotel
(see p.426), runs reliable tours of the Chilote
archipelago at competitive prices (CH$12,000–
15,000 for day-long outings, often with food
included).

Chilote churches around Castro

Chiloé is famous for its **churches** (see box p.431), and the small villages around
Castro boast a wide variety of them. Four kilometres to the north of Castro
on the road to Ancud, a badly signed turn to the east leads to the small village
of **Llaullao** (the name of a golf-ball-sized fungus the locals once used to turn
into a type of moonshine). There's not much to the village, just a couple of
streets on a hillock dominated by its pretty **church**, a long squat building with
a tower and portico. The townspeople are very proud of the church because it
has been declared a national monument and is on UNESCO's World Heritage
list. Anyone inside when you visit will often offer to show you around, and you
can climb up into the tower to inspect the deep-blue barrelled roof. *Micros* and
colectivos run here from Castro, or you can take any bus to Ancud and ask to be
dropped at the crossroads.

Directly across the fjord from Castro, a nineteen-kilometre road cuts
through a peninsula of gently undulating farmland, ending at **Rilán**, a
small village that dates from 1658. Facing a plaza near the edge of a small
bay is a large church, **Iglesia Santa Maria**, with a five-arched portico and
three-storey bell tower, extensively renovated after it was badly damaged in
a fierce 1990 storm. There's nowhere to stay in Rilán, but you can always
camp on the beach. Three buses call in every weekday from Castro's local
bus terminal.

Four kilometres south of Castro, the church in the village of **NERCÓN**
is a variation on the theme. The **Iglesia de Nuestra Señora de Gracia
de Nercón** dates from 1734 and, a rarity on the island, has a little
churchyard. The interior is decorated with imitation marbling, and on
September 29 it's further festooned with foliage when the village celebrates
St Michael's day.

Dalcahue and Isla Quinchao

To the northeast of Castro are some of the archipelago's most attractive communities – including the endearing market town of **Dalcahue**, the sleepy fishing hamlets of **Tenaún** and **Quicaví** – and two contrasting islands: remote, little-visited **Isla Mechuque**, and the second-largest in the archipelago after Isla Grande, **Isla Quinchao**. The main town on Isla Quinchao, **Achao**, rewards a detour with some of the finest examples of Chilote carpentry. A number of these destinations can be reached from Ancud if you have your own means of transport, but if you're reliant on public transport or guided tours, it's easiest to access them from Castro.

△ Chilote church

Chilote churches

It is impossible to visit Chiloé and not be struck by the sight of the archipelago's **wooden churches**. In the early nineteenth century these impressively large buildings would have been the heart of a Chilote village, whereas nowadays many only have a couple of buildings nearby, and Mass is often only once a year. Several of the churches have been declared national monuments, an honour crowned in 2001 when UNESCO accepted sixteen of them on its prestigious World Heritage list.

The churches generally face the sea and are built near a beach or safe landing place with an open area, plaza or *explanada* in front of them. The outside of the churches is almost always bare, and the only thing that expresses anything but functionality is the three-tiered, **hexagonal bell tower** that rises up directly above an open-fronted portico. The facades, doors and windows are often brightly painted, and the walls clad with plain clapboard or wooden tiles, *tejuelas* (tiles or shingles), drawing on the island's strong *cultura de Madera* (woodworking culture). culture). Inside, the double-pitched roof creates a feeling of space and tranquillity. All the churches have three naves separated by columns, which in the larger buildings are highly decorated, supporting barrel-vaulted ceilings. The ceilings are often painted too, with allegorical panels or sometimes with golden constellations of stars painted on an electric blue background.

Only the *pueblos* with a priest had a main church, or *iglesia parroquial*. If there was no church, the missionaries used to visit once a year, as part of their so-called *misión circular*. Using only native canoes, they carried everything required to hold a mass with them, such as tables, sacraments and religious images carved out of wood. When the priest arrived, one of the eldest Chilotes would lead a procession carrying an image of Jesus, and behind him two youths would follow with depictions of San Juan and the Virgin. They would be followed by married men carrying a statue of San Isidro and married women carrying one of Santa Neoburga. If the *pueblo* was important enough there would be a small *capilla* (bell tower) with altars to receive the statues. The building where the missionaries stayed was known as a *residencia*, *villa*, *casa ermita* or *catecera*, and was looked after by a local trustee called a *Fiscal*, whose function was somewhere between that of a verger and lay preacher. This honorary position still exists and, in Chiloé's remoter areas, the *Fiscal* commands great respect in his community.

In 1996, Chiloé's churches were placed on the list of 100 endangered world monuments. The non-profit **Fundación Cultural Amigos de las Iglesias de Chiloé**, with European Union help, has been rescuing and restoring these fragile monuments through initiatives such as an association of young carpenters. The foundation has offices in Castro at San Martín 436, next to the Iglesia San Francisco, and accepts donations of all amounts. For more information on Chiloé's churches, check out the informative ⊛ www.interpatagonia.com/iglesiaschiloe.

On the way to Dalcahue, along the track from Llaullao, the photogenic little church of **Nuestra Señora de los Astilleros** stands in the middle of nowhere, just by the side road to Rilán (see p.429). It was grotesquely moved here by tractor from the village of Tey in May 2001 – as a media stunt. It's nearly always closed, but you might be lucky enough to find it open. You can also ask at a nearby house to try and track down the keys.

Dalcahue and around

The bustling, historical town of **DALCAHUE** lies 68km south of Ancud, and 20km from Castro via the turn-off at Llaullao. Along the busy waterfront there's a thriving traditional boat-building industry and a constant stream of landing craft loading and unloading supplies for salmon farms, including live fish brought here for processing. Moreover, a small car-ferry provides the only link with nearby **Isla Quinchao** (see opposite), the second largest in the Chiloé archipelago.

Until 1960, most of Dalcahue's inhabitants lived in *palafitos* along the edge of the sea, but that year's earthquake and tsunami destroyed them all. The town was rebuilt, and the *palafitos* were replaced by a coast road and an attractive little square that's very much the heart of town these days. On one side of the square stands an open-sided market building, constructed in the vain hope of retaining Dalcahue as the centre of Chiloé's handmade knitwear industry. Tour buses still come here from miles away on Sundays, but for the rest of the week the town's trade has been eclipsed by Castro. On the opposite corner of the square is an Aladdin's cave of a **museum** (Mon–Fri 9am–1pm & 2–6pm; free), filled with a chaotic but somehow beguiling mess of pre-Hispanic and colonial artefacts and stuffed birds. Also on the square, near the museum, is an imposing 1893 church with a unique nine-arched portico. It stands on the site of the original Jesuit mission and boasts wide, panoramic views of the channel.

Dalcahue straddles a river and is dominated by two east–west roads, Ramón Freire and the *costanera*, or coastal road, officially Calle Montt (confusingly also called Calle Ana Wagner), joined by a north–south road, O'Higgins. Buses and *colectivos* to Castro pull in at the little square where Ramón Freire meets O'Higgins, and the ferry for Isla Quinchao leaves from the western end of town. You'll find some reasonable **accommodation**, including a slew of *residenciales* clustered near the church. The most welcoming is *Hospedaje Dalcahue* (❷), on the south side of the plaza at Pedro Aguirre Cerda 003. Right in the centre of town sits *Pensión Putemun*, Freire 305 (☎65/651330; ❸), with comfortable rooms above a large busy restaurant. *Residencial La Playa*, Rodríguez 009 (☎65/641397; ❷), offers simple rooms with shared facilities, while *Hotel La Isla*, Mocopulli 113 (☎65/641241; ❹), features more modern amenities behind a traditional exterior. The line of small shops in the square includes some colourful fishermen's bars that do cheap **meals**. *Café Dalca*, Freire 502, also serves good quality, inexpensive seafood. For something a little more upmarket, try the *Restaurant Brisas Marinas* overlooking the sea to the east of Pedro Montt, which has a good seafood menu and serves excellent squid. The restaurant at *Residencial La Playa*, Rodríguez 009, serves generous portions of *curanto* on Sundays. Avoid the notoriously unfresh seafood on offer in and around the market.

Tenaún, Quicaví and Isla Mechuque

From Dalcahue, a pleasing rural road heads northeast towards Quemchi, following the coast. After about 20km, look for the sidetrack leading down to the tiny village of **San Juan**, the island's most famous **boat-building** centre. Keep your eyes peeled for the reed beds around here, which are home to one of the highest concentrations of black-necked swans. Note also the centuries-old stone corrals, artificial pools which the Chilotes used to trap fish when the tide went out. San Juan once had a graveyard, but when the 1960 tidal wave hit the village all the miniature wooden grave shelters floated out to sea.

A few kilometres further along, another small road heads to the somnolent village of **TENAÚN**, 8km away; it's nothing more than two rows of houses facing each other across a kind of elongated plaza, but the buildings are perfect examples of the island's vernacular architecture, a mixture of grand two-storey and quaint little fishermen's cottages. Smiling down at them is Chiloé's arguably most extraordinary **church**, painted white with two huge pale blue stars daubed onto the wall above the entrance and three vibrant blue and red towers. There's been a church in the village since 1734, but the present structure dates from 1861. It originally had twin towers at either side, but these were so poorly constructed that they had to be torn down two years later and replaced with the main tower and two small lateral ones you can see today. There's no public transport access here, nor any accommodation.

Six kilometres beyond Tenaún on the main road, a turn to the east leads, after 7km, to the scattered houses that make up the seafront village of **QUICAVÍ**, whose ostensible sleepiness belies its importance in Chilote mythology. It's said that the coast between here and the next settlement south, Tenaún, is pitted with **caves** inhabited by witches, wizards and *peúchos*, responsible for transmitting mysterious untreatable diseases, and beautiful sirens, who tempt fishermen to their deaths with stories of a wonderful underwater paradise (those who succumb are never seen again, except on the ghostly sailing ship of lost souls, *El Caleuche*). Perhaps because of this wealth of superstition, the missionaries built a larger than usual **church** in Quicaví. One of the most important in Chiloé, it's an imposing brown barn of a place with a graceful arched entrance, but as it's almost permanently locked you'll find it difficult to get a look inside. There's a daily **bus** to Quicaví from Castro (see p.424), leaving in the middle of the afternoon. There's no **accommodation** here, but you can ask one of the locals if you can camp on the beach.

Small launches depart from the jetties at Tenaún or Quicaví, depending on the tides, for the beautiful island of **ISLA MECHUQUE**, the largest and most easily accessible of the Chauques subgroup. Since the launches only sail when they have a quorum of passengers, the surest way of making this magical trip past unspoiled island scenery is to go on an organized excursion from Castro. The highlight of such trips to the "town" of Mechuque, the island's only settlement to speak of, is a genuine *curanto* prepared before your eyes in an outdoor pit. The tiny village huddles round a triangular plaza and its two parts, on either side of an inlet, are joined by an impressive wooden bridge.

Isla Quinchao

For some, **ISLA QUINCHAO**, a thin strip of land 30km long and for the most part not wider than 5km, is the cultural heart of the whole of Chiloé. Rich in traditional wooden architecture and pastoral calm, this island is a mere ten-minute ferry ride from Dalcahue (services every half-hour 7am–11pm; foot passengers free, cars Jan–March CH$3000 return, April–Dec CH$1000 return). The ferry arrives at a tiny quay, at the end of a dirt road that bisects the island.

Isla Quinchao only has two towns of any size, **Curaco de Vélez** and **Achao**, neither of which has more than a handful of buildings, but you'll get a better taste of traditional Chilote life from visiting either than you would from any museum.

Curaco de Vélez

Twelve kilometres from the ferry terminal, **Curaco de Vélez** comprises a couple of streets of weather-beaten shingled houses set around a beautiful bay and bordered by gently rolling hills. The Plaza de Armas features an unusual sight – some decapitated **church steeples**, docked from the tops of old churches, and a bust of local hero Almirante Riveros, who commanded the fleet that captured the Peruvian ironclad *Huáscar* during the War of the Pacific (see p.597). Riveros was not the only Chilean notable to be born here;

the town also boasts of its sons Contralmirante Manuel Oyarzun, who took part as well in the *Huáscar* engagement, and Piloto Carlos Miller Norton, who navigated the *Goleta Ancud* during its voyage to the Magellan Strait. The locals are very proud of this history – one of the town's nicknames is *Cuna de Héroes* (Birthplace of Heroes) – and celebrate it on October 8 every year, when hordes of smartly dressed schoolchildren march around the Plaza de Armas, accompanied by the discordant tones of the fire brigade band, which is decked out in tarnished old Kaiser helmets and ill-fitting uniforms. The parade was first held rather more impressively in 1931, when six thousand people watched the president of the Republic arrive on a battleship, accompanied by submarines and flying boats.

Nearly all visitors to the island call at Curaco de Vélez, but there are few places offering **accommodation**; the best option, with comfortable rooms in a pleasant timber building, is *Central*, Errázuriz 9 (☎65/667238; ❸). There are only a couple of places to **eat**, *Bahía*, an upmarket shellfish restaurant on the *costanera*, or coastal road, or *Nido del Jabalí*, Riveros 11, a downmarket café.

Achao

As you come over the hill and get your first view of **ACHAO**, resting in a fertile valley by the sea, 13km southeast of Curaco de Vélez, you could be forgiven for thinking you were arriving at an English seaside village. But the sight of the Chilote church, the snow-capped volcano peaks across the gulf in the distance, and the rows of single-storey houses faced with alerce shingles soon puts you straight. Just about every building is clad with these shingles, or *tejuelas*, coloured shades of soft pastels and silver not by faded paint but by colonies of yellow, green and grey lichens.

Achao is a living museum of Chiloé's *cultura de madera* (woodworking culture). The **church**, built in 1862 of many different types of wood, is a prime example of a typical Chilote church – a great solid, squat structure more than 40 metres long and totally devoid of exterior embellishment. The main framework is made from *ciprés de las Guaitecas*, a conifer that was once the most common tree species of the Chiloé archipelago, and *mañío*, a tree still common in southern Chile. Originally the exterior was clad with alerce shingles, but most of these have been replaced with *ciprés* boarding. In contrast to the plain outer shell, the interior is a riot of colour and architectural styles, with an intricately vaulted ceiling running the length of a broad central nave. Restoration work is a constant and expensive necessity – if you look around the *luma* wood floorboards, you can see the church's foundations, a rare glimpse into the way these old buildings were constructed. All the joints are fixed with wooden plugs and dowels, even the dozens of shingles on the building's outside, which had to be laboriously drilled and nailed in place with plugs made from *canelo*, another type of Chilean wood.

Achao's other defining feature is its hectic **boat ramp** at the end of Calle Serrano. It's one of the few places you can still see traditional sailing boats with whole families sleeping in large open cockpits and cooking on naked flames. All sorts of cargo is loaded and unloaded here, and there is a small market at the top of the ramp selling island produce. Launches go to the islands of the Chiloé archipelago and you might be able to hire a fisherman to take you out to visit one of them.

The town's not short of **places to stay**. The stand-out *Hostería La Nave*, one block north of the boat ramp at Calle Prat on the corner of Calle Aldea (☎ & Ⓕ65/661219; ❸), rises on stilts over the beach and is furnished with lots of bright, cheery natural wood. On the north side of the Plaza de Armas is

Hostal Plaza (☎65/661219; ❸), a reputable bed and breakfast in a very comfortable family house. The smart, modern *Hospedaje Sol y Lluvias*, ➍ Serrano and Jara (☎65/253996; ❸), offers comfortable rooms, while *Hospedaje São Paulo*, Serrano 52 (☎65/661245; ❷), is cheap, cheerful and located above a lively, inexpensive restaurant. The best **restaurant** in town is at the *Hostería La Nave*, but *Mar y Velas*, overlooking the busy boat ramp, is better for people watching – at lunchtime, half of Achao's population passes by.

Regular buses come to Achao each day from Castro via Dalcahue, run by San Cristóbal.

Ten kilometres south of Achao is Chiloé's largest church, the **Iglesia de Nuestra Señora de Gracia de Quinchao**, sitting rather incongruously near the edge of the sea, surrounded by half a dozen fishermen's cottages. From 1605, there's been a church here, and ever since construction on the existing 60-metre building was begun in 1869, its upkeep has sapped church funds; on several occasions the church has come close to collapsing on the congregation. Apart from its size, the church is unremarkable, save for an important religious festival on December 7 and 8, when pilgrims – and their sick horses – come to be healed by the Señora.

Parque Nacional Chiloé, sector Anay

Every summer, unperturbed by the infamously changeable weather along this particularly exposed stretch of seaboard, hordes of Chilean backpackers descend on **PARQUE NACIONAL CHILOÉ**, **SECTOR ANAY** (daily: Jan–Feb 9am–8pm; March–Dec 9am–1pm & 2–7pm; CH$1000; ⓦ www.parquechiloe .com), 45km southwest of Castro, keen to camp on its twenty kilometres of white-sand beach and to explore the dense forest. This section of the national park (the other is sector Chepu – see p.423) covers 350 square kilometres of the Cordillera de Piuchen (Piuchen Range), rising up to 800m above sea level. It's reached by a 25-kilometre road that shoots west from a junction on the Panamericana, 20km south of Castro.

At the end of the road is the gateway to the park, the picturesque but ramshackle village of **Cucao**, dominated by water. It straddles a sluggish, murky river and sits near the sea and two lakes, Lago Cucao and Lago Huillinco, which almost bisect the island at this point. Its few streets of tumbledown wooden huts are littered with whalebones, fishing floats and flotsam and jetsam from the Pacific. Clam-fishing and seaweed-gathering are big business, with wet-suited divers swimming out to sea to set their nets.

For many years, a traditional Chilote community of Huilliches lived off this narrow coastal plain, collecting shellfish and growing potatoes, *quinoa* (a South American grain) and strawberries. With the arrival of missionaries in 1734, **gold** was found, and from then on the area was inhabited by a couple of hundred prospectors who scratched a bare living from the small streams that trickled out of the impenetrable forest. This all changed on May 21, 1960, when a **tidal wave** swept two kilometres inland and then retreated, taking with it the church, the houses and an unlucky gold panner called Abraham Lincoln. The geography of the coast changed forever, as Lago Cucao became flooded and forced its way out to the sea, cutting a new river as it went. The fragile vegetation along the beach was torn away, and sand dunes quickly buried fields and farms.

Cucao has since recovered, although it's still a remote community: the village has only been reachable by road since 1983. Today buses drive along a new

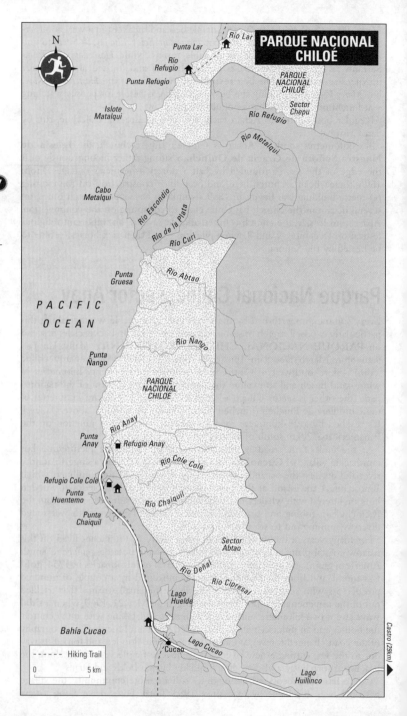

PARQUE NACIONAL
CHILOÉ

*PARQUE
NACIONAL
CHILOÉ
Sector
Chepu*

Río Lar

Punta Lar

Río
Refugio

Punta Refugio

Río Refugio

Río Metalqui

*Islote
Matalqui*

Río Escondio

Río de la Plata

*Cabo
Metalqui*

Río Curi

Río Abtao

*Punta
Gruesa*

PACIFIC
OCEAN

Río Ñango

*Punta
Ñango*

PARQUE
NACIONAL
CHILOÉ

Río Anay

*Punta
Anay*

Refugio Anay

Río Cole Cole

Refugio Cole Cole

*Punta
Huentemo*

Río Chaiquil

*Punta
Chaiquil*

Sector
Abtao

Río Deñal

Río Cipresal

Lago
Huelde

Bahía Cucao

Cucao

Lago Cucao

Lago
Huillinco

- - - - Hiking Trail

0   5 km

Castro (29km)

road carved out of the southern shore of the two lakes, and stop on the village football field by a suspension bridge that leads to the national park. Cucao's basic **accommodation** is in houses near the bridge: *La Paloma* (no phone; ❷) has floor space that you can sleep on, a garden in which you can camp, hot showers and a communal kitchen. Just across the river is the German-owned *Parador Darwin* ⚓ (closed June & July; messages ℡65/6333040, ⓦwww.cucao .cl; ❸) with attractive *cabaña* rooms and a small restaurant serving goulash, cakes, fish and clams. A little further up the road is *El Fogon de Cucao* (℡09/9465685, ⓔelfogondecucao@hotmail.com; ❹), a pleasant bed and breakfast that also organizes horse-riding and trekking expeditions. It has a separate restaurant, overlooking the waterfront, which is open to anyone. Out of season, the best place to stay is *Hospedaje Paraíso* (℡09/2965465; ❷), when the snug little kitchen provides respite from the wind and rain. A converted barn next door serves fried fish and boiled potatoes. You can camp in the gardens of most of these places, and there's also a spot for wild camping by the river mouth, with a freshwater spring nearby.

One of the best ways of getting around is by **horse**, and there are dozens that can be hired from the villagers, either with guides or without. On the whole they are scrawny, plodding old nags, well used to carrying novice passengers, though they don't come cheap – *Parador Darwin*, for example, rents out its horses for CH$2500 an hour or CH$12,000 a day.

Exploring the park

Across Cucao's suspension bridge and at the northern end of the wide, sandy beach is the Conaf **Cucao Ranger Post** (also known as the Chanquin Ranger Post), with cabañas (❺) that accommodate up to six people. There's also a **visitor centre** (daily: Jan–Feb 9am–8pm; March–Dec 9am–1pm & 2–7pm, ℡09/6442489, ⓔvidasur@telsur.cl) that explains the various environments you'll find in the park, and features a display of wonderful old Chilote wooden contraptions, including those used to wash gravel for gold. Close to the visitor centre (ask for directions) there are some short nature walks in the forest, but to fully experience the beauty of the park, you have to cross about 5km of beach. On a summer's day this can be tiresome, as the sand is very fine and hard to walk on, and biting flies called *tavanos* dog your every step.

There are a couple of short **hikes** that start from here. The first is the 770-metre Sendero Interpretivo "El Tepual" through an area of the Tepu forest, which thrives in this humid bogland; there are log walkways across the wetter sections. You'll enjoy fine views at the start of the walk, looking over the lake, the mountains and the village. The second hike is Sendero Dunas de Cucao, just short of a kilometre, through the regenerating scrub on the sand dunes. On parts of this walk you have to bend almost double as you walk through tunnels of dense vegetation, most of it clearly labelled, while on others you can stroll along the sands whilst looking out for the giant rhubarb-like *nalca* plants whose enormous parasol leaves are used as natural lids when making *curanto*. A little more taxing is the three-kilometre (one-way) walk along the beach to Lago Huelde, technically outside the park boundary, where you pick up a nine-kilometre trail known as Sendero Rancho Grande along the Río Cipresal up to the edge of the tree line, revealing beautiful views.

The park's longest hike, and its most popular, is the beautiful twenty-kilometre (4–6hr) walk north along the coast and through dense, native evergreen forest to the Conaf *refugio* at **Cole Cole**, just by Punta Huentemo, the second headland south of the Cucao ranger post. Call in at the houses along the first couple of kilometres, where people will sell bread, fish, clams and meat if they have any to spare. You can also continue another 5km north to the *Refugio Anay*, which is as far north and as remote as you can go.

There are at least two **buses** a day to Cucao from Castro, leaving from the rural bus station. Be warned that in high season they can be so packed that even standing room is short.

South of Castro

South of Castro, the Ruta 5 plunges down for almost another hundred kilo-metres to Chiloé's southernmost town, **Quellón**. Not only the farthest town in Chiloé, it's also the end of the Panamericana, a road that – save for the Darién gap in Colombia – extends all the way down from Alaska, thousands of kilometres to the north. Apart from the anecdotal significance of reaching the southern extremity of one of the world's longest roads, travelling down the highway's final stretch is rather prosaic – the scenery down here is easy on the eye and certainly not dramatic.

Quellón itself is a bustling commercial centre and busy fishing port, with no real sights. But its seafront is pleasant, and while you wait for your ferry, you can enjoy, weather permitting, some of the finest views in Chiloé, across the harbour and the gulf to the cordillera behind Chaitén. If possible, on your way down you might like to turn your attention away from the main road and explore the tongue of land that stretches to the southeast of Castro, leaving the Panamericana at a fork 17km to the south. Here, a minor road branches east to follow the coast, passing **Chonchi**, the best-preserved town in Chiloé, and the ferry to **Isla Lemuy**, an island refuge of traditional Chiloé, before winding up, after 46km, at the fishing village of **Queilen**.

Chonchi

Lined around the most sheltered harbour on the island are the beautiful old build-ings of **CHONCHI**, structures that have hardly changed since the eighteenth century. In those days, the town thrived on timber exports and was home to the wood baron Ciriaco Alvarez, who earned the name *El Rey de Ciprés* (The Cypress King) by stripping the archipelago of almost all of its native forest. Despite being Chiloé's first millionaire, he dressed in rags and would sweat alongside his workers as they loaded his ships with pit props for Europe and railway sleepers for Peru. There have been some changes in Chonchi since Alvarez's day – the *palafitos* that once lined the seafront were all destroyed by the 1960 earthquake – but Chonchi's steeply curving main street, Calle Centenario, still retains its beauty. Another disaster struck in early 2002, when a fire reduced a number of fine harbour-front timber buildings to ashes; a fund was set up to rebuild them and, rather belatedly, reconstruction has begun. Otherwise, the majority of Chonchi's splendid **timber buildings** have survived human and natural disasters, making it most people's favourite town in the entire archipelago.

The town's cheerfully painted **church** rewards a visit. While it's not original and has been rebuilt over the years, it has recently been restored to its full glory, and the Neoclassical facade is one of the island's finest. Inside, is an image of the Virgin Mary, *La Virgin de la Candelaria*, which the locals believe saved them from the marauding corsairs that sacked Castro; the Virgin is noisily honoured at a festival every February 2, when townspeople fire guns into the air to symbolize a pirate attack. A short way down the main street from the church is the informative **Museo de las Tradiciones Chonchinas**, Centenario 116, (summer Mon–Sat 9am–8pm; winter Mon–Sat 10am–1pm; donation), a beautifully restored old traditional house filled with furniture, fittings and a large collection of photographs from the tree-felling heyday of *El Rey de Ciprés*.

Practicalities

A couple of doors along from the museum at Centenario 102 is one of Chonchi's best **places to stay**, *Hotel Huildín* (T65/671388; ❹), quite a museum piece in itself. As is typical in large old Chilote houses, the upstairs bedrooms are large and high-ceilinged and face onto an enclosed veranda which runs around two sides of the building. Slightly tucked away on the eastern end of the seafront, *Esmeralda by the Sea* ⚓ (T & F65/671328, Eesmeraldachonchi @hotmail.com; ❷–❸) is a small *hospedaje* with a helpful English-speaking owner who organizes land and sea tours; it offers a book exchange, email facilities, a laundry and evening meals. Camping in the sheltered garden costs CH$2000 per person, and they even rent out equipment. You could also try *Posada El Antiguo Chalet*, on the western edge of town, just uphill from the harbour (T65/671221; ❺); it's a beautiful, natural-wood house built in 1934 by one of the timber kings and set in large, well-kept grounds.

Eating well in Chonchi can be tricky – for some reason, restaurants here come and go as quickly as the tides – but *El Trebol*, Irarrázaval 187, at the southern end of the waterfront above the local market, and *La Quilla*, Andrade 183, both of which serve decent enough seafood dishes, seem to be standing the test of time.

There are **buses**, run by such operators as Buses Regional Sur and Queilen Bus (T65/253468), every hour from Castro to Chonchi.

Isla Lemuy

On the coast 3km south of Chonchi at **Huicha**, a ferry (daily 8am–9.30pm; Mon–Sat every 30min, Sun every 1hr; 20min; CH$3000) heads to **ISLA LEMUY**, the third-largest island in the Chiloé archipelago, which, at 120 square kilometres, is only slightly smaller than Isla Quinchao. Seldom visited by tourists, Lemuy is wonderfully peaceful and quiet. If you're looking for bright lights and refinement, pass this island by – there's nothing in the way of even moderately sophisticated facilities for visitors. But if you're searching for traditional rural Chiloé, you'll more than find it in the tiny little villages that dot the island: **Ichuac**, 4km from the ferry terminal at Chulchuy; **Puqueldón**, the island's main settlement, 5km to Ichuac's east; and **Aldachido**, 9km from Puqueldón on the tip of the northern coast. Each boasts just a few houses and in some cases a fine old church. The most remote of all is **Detif**, on an isolated, bleak headland at the far eastern end of the island, about 20km from Puqueldón. There's not much more than a chapel, inside which fishermen hang model boats, but on a clear day you can sit on the grass outside the chapel and stare at a view – across the flat calm of the Gulf of Corcovado, studded with islands, to the mainland and the brooding Volcán Michinmahuida – that hasn't changed for thousands of years.

The only **place to stay** on the island is near the village of **Puchilco**, 4km northeast of the main road from Puqueldón to Detif. Here, there's a green and orange farmhouse where the Perez family takes in guests (no phone; ❸) – don't be surprised to see the occasional sheep wandering around their front garden. There's one **bus** daily to Isla Lemuy from Castro, run by Dalcahue Expresso; the bus crosses to the island on the ferry.

The road from Chonchi to Queilen

Back on the mainland, the dirt road to Queilen runs above a string of pretty little villages down by the sea – Tepua, Terao, Ahoni and Aituy. The roads down to these villages are steep, and old or weak cars can't make the gradient. You'll notice around some of these villages, **Tepua**, for example, graveyards filled with strange huts. These are *mausoleos*, traditional structures in this part of Chiloé, shelters that protect mourners from the elements when they visit the graves of the dead. Some can be simple and basic, but others are wonderfully ornate affairs, like miniature Chilote houses, the outsides clad in alerce shingle and the insides beautifully vaulted and protected by delicate screens. They stand in contrast to the stark graves themselves, normally just plain crosses painted with the family name.

Forty-six kilometres from Chonchi, the road pulls into **QUEILEN**, a little fishing town whose one main street, Alessandri, bisects the neck of a long, sandy peninsula. The western end of town is very pretty, lined with fishermen's houses built on a long beach sheltered by **Isla Tranqui**, which lies just off the coast. The only thing to do here is relax, although in February the town hosts a craft fair in which all types of local products are sold, from handicrafts and farming equipment to traditional medicines.

The town is short on **places to stay**, but try the *Hospedaje Laura Gonzalez*, O'Higgins 93 (☎65/258271 ext 305; ❷), or the church-run *Albergue Parroquial*, Calle 21 de Mayo 49 (☎65/258271, ext 237), with beds and floor space – they don't have a fixed charge but ask you to pay what you can afford. You can **eat** at *Restaurant Melinka*, upstairs at Alessandri 56, where there's friendly service, pleasant surroundings and fish, fish and more fish. Queilen Bus (☎65/253468) runs seven **buses** a day to Queilen from Castro.

Quellón

If, at the junction where the coast road heads southeast to Chonchi and Queilen, you stick on the Panamericana and head south, you'll speed along the last 80km of the Ruta 5 to **QUELLÓN**, a commercial fishing port. The main reason to come here is to catch a **ferry** across to Chaitén (see p.456) or down to Chacabuco (see p.470). The town has been by turns a Jesuit mission, a coaling depot for the Chilean navy, a meteorological centre and a messenger-pigeon station. This changed in 1906 when the Patagonian logging companies arrived and drove roads and narrow-gauge railways into the **Cordillera de Pirulil**, an otherwise uninhabited and unexplored mountain range to the west. There they stripped the mountains, and by 1950 when the plant closed and the company's employees returned to Patagonia, a forest that once covered a third of Chiloé had been chopped down.

Today Quellón is a small place, based around three scruffy streets that run roughly east–west, parallel to the coast: the seafront *costanera* (officially called Miramar and Pedro Montt); Ercilla, running north of the *costanera*; and Ladrilleros, farther north still. The central **Plaza de Armas** is on two small streets sandwiched between the Costanera and Ercilla. One thing to do while waiting for your ferry is visit the small but interesting **Museo Inchin Cuivi Ant**, Ladrilleros 225 (daily Jan–March 10am–1pm & 2–8pm; CH$500), with Chilote flour mills, looms and wooden apple-presses on display. The black-and-white historical photographs at the **Museo Municipal**, Gómez García (Mon–Fri 8.30am–1pm & 2.30–6.30pm; free) are interesting enough to merit a quick look.

Practicalities

Hourly **buses** from Castro (CH$1500) deposit you at the terminal a block west of the Plaza on Calle Cerda, while **ferries** from Puerto Chacabuco and Chaitén – operated by Navimag, Costanera (℡65/682207, ℻65/682601), and TransMarChilay (℡65/680511, ℻65/680513), both at Costanera Pedro Montt 457 – as well as the **catamaran** run by Aysén Express (℡65/680047), call at the harbour a block south. There's a good **Oficina de Turismo** on the corner of Gomez García and Santos Vargas, a block north of the Plaza de Armas (daily 9am–1pm & 2–6pm; no phone).

You'll find a wide choice of **places to stay** along the Costanera, none particularly luxurious – but they can bail you out if the ferry arrives too late to catch a bus to Castro. Plushest is the *Hotel Melimoyu*, Costanera Pedro Montt 369 (℡65/681310, ℻65/681250, ⓔhosteriaquellon@hotmail.com; ❹), with good en-suite rooms and a restaurant that looks across the bay. Failing that, try the shingle-clad *Tierra del Fuego*, closer to the ferry port at Costanera Pedro Montt 445 (℡65/682079, ℻65/681226; ❸–❹), where the airy en-suite doubles are a good deal, the stark bathless rooms less so. *Hotel Los Suizos*, Ladrilleros 399 (℡65/681787; ❹), is a comfortable and smart option to the north of the plaza. More basic but clean are *Hotel Playa*, Costanera Pedro Montt 427 (℡65/681278; ❷), and the comparable *Hotel Chico Leo*, Costanera Pedro Montt 325 (℡65/681567; ❸). The *Albergue Torino*, La Paz 24 (no phone; ❶), will let you lay your sleeping bag on the floor. The best place to **eat** by far is the restaurant at the *Hostería Quellón*, specializing in all forms of crab at reasonable prices, closely rivalled by the inexpensive restaurant at *Hotel Los Suizos*, Ladrilleros 399, which does a passable attempt at a Swiss fondue.

In January and February there are a three or four ferries a week for Chaitén (5hr; CH$10,000 per passenger, CH$12,000 for a reclining seat; reservations ℡65/432300), usually leaving in the afternoon or late at night. A ferry leaves once a week for Puerto Chacabuco, normally on Saturday evening. Note that the ferries may be subject to delays, and cancellations are not unheard of. Outside the peak season the service is much less frequent and even more erratic. The only **tour company** in town is Turismo Millaguén, Gomez García s/n (℡65/681431), offering two-hour boat trips around the harbour in January and February for CH$6000.

Travel details

Buses

Ancud to: Castro (every 15min; 1hr 15min); Caulín (4 daily; 30min); Chacao (every 15min; 30min); Península de Lacuy and Fuerte Agüi (1 daily; 45min); Puerto Montt (every 30min; 1hr 30min–2hr); Quemchi (5–6 daily; 1hr).

Castro to: Achao (3 daily; 1hr 50min); Ancud (every 15min; 1hr 15min); Chonchi (every 30min; 30min); Cucao and the Parque Nacional Chiloé, sector Anay (4 daily; 1hr 45min); Curaco de Vélez (3 daily; 1hr 30min); Dalcahue (every 30min; 30min); Llaullao (every 15min; 15min); Puerto Montt (every 30min; 3hr); Punta Arenas, via Argentina (2 weekly, 32hr); Puqueldón (at least 2 daily; 1hr 15min); Queilen (7 daily; 1hr 30min); Quellón (hourly; 2hr 15min).

Puerto Montt to: Ancud (every 30min; 1hr 30min–2hr); Pargua (every 30min; 30min).

Ferries and Catamarans

Castro to: Chaitén (2–3 weekly; 3hr); Puerto Montt (1–4 weekly; 9hr).

Chaitén to: Castro (2–3 weekly; 3hr); Puerto Montt (1–4 weekly; 10hr); Quellón (1–4 weekly; 5hr).

Pargua to: Chacao (2–4 hourly; 30min).

Puerto Montt to: Castro (1–4 weekly; 9hr).

Quellón to: Chaitén (1–4 weekly; 1.5hrs–5hr); Puerto Chacabuco (1 weekly in summer; 10–20hr).

8

The Carretera Austral

CHAPTER 8

Highlights

* **White-water rafting at Futaleufú** "Purgatory", "Hell" and "Terminator" are just three of the world-class rapids you can hurtle down on the "Fu". **See p.459**

* **Termas de Puyuhuapi** Soak your bones and gaze at the southern night skies at Chile's premier spa resort. **See p.462**

* **Ventisquero Colgante** Gawk at the suspended glaciers that seem to defy gravity along the Southern Highway in the Parque Nacional Queulat. **See p.466**

* **Laguna San Rafael glacier** Catch it while you can: this gigantic tongue of ice with its own lagoon may be gone by 2030. **See p.471**

* **Crossing Lago General Carrera** Bundle up before taking the ferry across the second-largest lake in South America. **See p.479**

* **Villa O'Higgins** If you want to say you went as far down the Carretera Austral as you could. **See p.485**

△ Fern fronds in Parque Pumalín

The Carretera Austral

From Puerto Montt, the **Carretera Austral**, or "Southern Highway", stretches over 1000km south through the wettest, greenest, wildest and narrowest part of Chile, ending its mammoth journey at the tiny settlement of Villa O'Higgins, a long, long way from anywhere. Carving its path through tracts of untouched wilderness, the route takes in soaring, snow-capped mountains, Ice Age glaciers, blue-green fjords, turquoise lakes and rivers, and one of the world's largest swaths of temperate rainforest. Most of it falls into **Aisén**, Chile's "last frontier", the final region to be opened up in the early twentieth century. A hundred years on, Aisén remains very sparsely populated, and still has the cut-off, marginal feel of a pioneer zone.

The original inhabitants of this rain-swept land were the nomadic, hunter-gatherer **Tehuelches** of the interior, and the canoe-faring **Alcalufes**, who fished the fjords and channels of the coast, but both peoples had become extinct by the late nineteenth century. In 1903, the government initiated a colonization programme that ultimately handed over thousands of hectares of land to three large livestock companies, on the condition that they promote settlement and export their produce from Chilean ports. Only one of them managed to meet the latter requirement, the other two depending entirely on Argentina for communications and transportation. At the same time, a wave of individual pioneers – known as **colonos** – came down from the north to try their luck. Some arrived by sea, settling on the shores of rivers and fjords where they chopped down trees, built sawmills and shipped their produce up the coast. Others crossed over from Argentina and farmed land near the border on the edge of the concessionaires' *estancias* (ranches), forming a handful of permanent settlements. Like the livestock companies, these were totally dependent on Argentina for trade and communications.

Faced with the encroaching influence of its bigger and more powerful neighbour, and mindful of Argentina's hankering for a claim on the Pacific, the government set out actively to "Chileanize" this new zone organizing rodeos, for instance, and funding patriotic fiestas. Over the years, the population grew, communities expanded and communications improved, but the perceived need for state control of the region did not diminish, and explains the rationale behind the construction of the Carretera Austral, initiated by **General Pinochet** in 1976. Building the road – also known as the "Camino Austral" or "Southern Way" – was a colossal undertaking, swallowing up hundreds of billions of pesos. The first section was finished in 1983, followed by two more stretches in 1988. Engineers completed the final 100km in 2000, from tiny Puerto Yungay to the frontier outpost of Villa O'Higgins, by the Argentine border. Further south, the mainland gives way to an impenetrable ice field bordered by a shredded mass

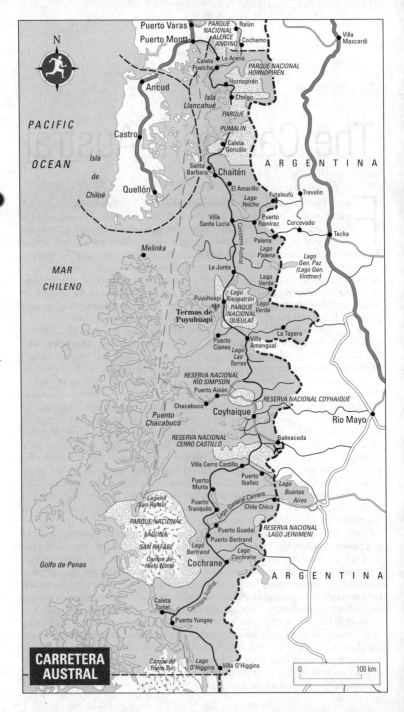

CARRETERA
AUSTRAL

of islets that thwart even the most ambitious of road-building schemes. And so, from the end of this road, the only options are to go back the way you came or to cross over into Argentina.

Whatever political agenda was behind it, the Carretera Austral has provided access to an area of outstanding natural beauty, enjoyed by increasing – but still small – numbers of Chilean and foreign visitors. The attractions kick in from the very beginning: less than 50km down the road from Puerto Montt, you're at the first national park – **Parque Nacional Alerce Andino**, home to ancient alerce trees – followed, some 70km beyond, by **Parque Nacional Hornopirén**, with its perfect, conical volcano. At privately owned **Parque Pumalín**, the Carretera cuts a passage through virgin temperate rainforest, on one of the loveliest stretches of the entire road. A couple of hours' drive beyond the small town and ferry terminal of **Chaitén**, a side road branches east to the border village of Futaleufú, a growing centre for **whitewater rafting** and other activities. Continuing down the Carretera Austral, you come to **Parque Nacional Queulat**, whose extraordinary hanging glacier and excellent trails make this one of the most rewarding places to get off the road and into the hinterland. After a couple of days hiking and camping, don't miss the chance to soak your bones in the secluded hot pools of the nearby **Termas de Puyuhuapi**, the most luxurious thermal resort in Chile.

The effects of settlement and land clearance become more apparent the nearer you get to the regional capital of **Coyhaique**, a thriving city of 40,000 inhabitants, with a wide range of useful services, including the region's main airport at Balmaceda. West of here, the little port of **Puerto Chacabuco** is the principal starting point for boat excursions to the sensational **Laguna San Rafael glacier**, a fifteen-kilometre tongue of ice spilling into a lagoon. South of Coyhaique, the road loops around South America's second largest lake, **Lago General Carrera**, blessed by a balmy microclimate supporting several lakeside farming villages, such as rough and ready **Chile Chico**.

The final stretch of the Carretera connects the little town of **Cochrane** to **Puerto Yungay**, a remote port huddled on the edge of a fjord between the northern and southern icefields, and, farther still, the even more isolated hamlet of **Villa O'Higgins**. The unusual settlement of **Caleta Tortel**, where wooden bridges link the houses and the aroma of cypress-timber fills the air, is also more easily accessible these days since a side road linked it to the main highway.

Getting around

"Doing" the Carretera Austral requires a certain amount of forward planning, and time should always be allowed for unexpected delays. A limited **bus** service does exist between the few main towns along the road (see box, p.448), but it's very sporadic and provides little opportunity for getting off along the way and exploring the backcountry. If you really want to get the most out of the region, you'll need your own transport, which for a growing number of visitors means a **mountain bike**, but for most others, a **rented vehicle**. The road has a hard dirt covering which even in heavy rainfall rarely turns muddy. The layer of loose gravel on top, however, can make the surface very slippery, and by far the best option is a sturdy pick-up truck which will hold the road well; 4WD is a bonus, but not essential. There are sufficient **petrol** stations along the way to get by without carrying your own fuel, but it's always worth keeping a spare supply in case you get caught out.

When you glance at a map, the choice of **routes** seems quite straightforward – down, and back up again – but a number of **ferry** services create extra possibilities albeit with certain restrictions. Crucially, the first part of the road, between Puerto Montt and Chaitén, is "bridged" by two ferry crossings, one of which (the six-hour crossing between Hornopirén and Caleta Gonzalo) operates *only* in January and February. Outside these months you can still take one of the year-round ferries from Puerto Montt or Quellón to Chaitén, 200km down the Carretera Austral, and to Puerto Chacabuco, a further 420km south. Alternatively, if you manage to get the paperwork sorted out, you could start or end the journey on the largely paved roads on the Argentine side of the border, with convenient border crossings at Futaleufú and Chile Chico. Another option is to **fly** to Coyhaique and use it as a base for exploring the southern part of the Carretera Austral, either in a rented vehicle or by public transport.

Carretera Austral transport and practicalities

Ferries

It's always a good idea to book your ticket at least a week in advance, particularly in January and February. For details on services to the Laguna San Rafael, see p.471, and for more information on the **ferry** companies, see p.51 in Basics.

La Arena–Caleta Puelche (see p.451): Thirty minutes. Nine crossings per day in each direction, operated year-round by TransMarChilay; CH$5000 per car, passengers free.

Hornopirén–Caleta Gonzalo (see p.453): Six hours. One daily in each direction, operated only in January and February by TransMarChilay; cars CH$56,000, passengers CH$9000.

Puerto Montt–Chaitén: Ten hours. TransMarChilay departs from Puerto Montt on Mondays, Tuesdays, Thursdays and Fridays, and from Chaitén on Mondays, Wednesdays and Fridays throughout the year. Between December and March Navimag runs three to four crossings per week in each direction. Fares are from CH$12,000 per person, plus CH$65,000 for a vehicle. Aysén Express undertakes five crossings per week. Each takes four hours and costs from CH$23,000.

Quellón–Chaitén: Six hours. Navimag does four crossings per week between December and March. Fares are from CH$10,000 per person and CH$50,000 per vehicle. Aysén Express operates a catamaran service up to five times weekly during the summer which takes two hours and costs around CH$10,000.

Castro–Chaitén: Seven hours. TransMarChilay makes three crossings per week in each direction, departing Chaitén on Wednesdays, Saturdays and Sundays and leaving Castro later on the same days. Fares are around CH$12,000 per person and CH$65,000 per vehicle.

Puerto Montt–Puerto Chacabuco: Twenty-four hours. Two crossings per week in each direction with Navimag, departing Puerto Montt on Wednesdays and Saturdays and leaving Puerto Chacabuco on Fridays and Tuesdays. Fares start from CH$30,000 for the most basic berth and rise to CH$40,000 for a bunk in a quadruple cabin or CH$80,000 in a double cabin. Vehicles cost around CH$95,000. Aysén Express operates a weekly catamaran service that takes eleven hours and costs around CH$40,000.

Quellón–Puerto Chacabuco: TransMarChilay departs from Quellón on Saturdays and from Puerto Chacabuco on Mondays; fares are around CH$10,000 per passenger and CH$55,000 per vehicle. Aysén Express operates a weekly service (CH$28,000).

Parque Nacional Alerce Andino and around

Heading out of Puerto Montt, the Carretera Austral hugs the shore of the Reloncaví fjord, skirting wide mud flats and empty beaches. Some 40km down the road – just beyond the Puente de Lenca – a signed track branches left and leads 7km to the southern entrance of **PARQUE NACIONAL ALERCE ANDINO** (daily 9am–noon & 1–5pm; CH$1500), where you'll find a small **Conaf** hut, a ranger station and a **camping** area (CH$4000 per site). The park was created in 1982 to protect the region's ancient and rapidly depleting alerce forests, threatened with extinction by intense logging activity. Almost 20,000 hectares – half the park's land area – are covered by the massive alerces, mixed in with other native species like coigüe and lenga. This dense covering is spread

Buses

The following is an outline of the main **bus links** down the Carretera Austral; fuller details are given in relevant parts of the chapter and in "Travel Details", p.486.

Puerto Montt–Hornopirén: 3 daily; 5hr (Buses Fierro ☎65/253600).

Caleta Gonzalo–Chaitén: buses meet ferry arrivals.

Chaitén–Futaleufú: 6 or 7 per week; 4hr.

Chaitén–Coyhaique: 1 or 2 daily; 12hr.

Coyhaique–Cochrane: 5 per week; 10hr.

Cochrane–Villa O'Higgins: 1 or 2 per week; 6–7hr.

Distances

Expect to drive slowly along most of the road, somewhere between 40kph and 55kph, rarely faster; always give yourself plenty of leeway (for example, six hours for Chaitén to Puyuhuapi), and allow for delays.

Puerto Montt–La Arena: 45km

Caleta Puelche–Hornopirén: 50km

Caleta Gonzalo–Chaitén: 56km

Chaitén–Puyuhuapi: 196km

Villa Santa Lucía–Futaleufú: 75km

Puyuhuapi–Coyhaique: 225km

Coyhaique–Cochrane: 350km

Cochrane–Chile Chico: 195km

Cochrane–Villa O'Higgins: 235km

Petrol stations

Reliable **petrol stations** are positioned at adequate intervals along the road at: Hornopirén; Chaitén; La Junta; Puyuhuapi; Puerto Cisnes; Puerto Aisén; Puerto Chacabuco; Coyhaique; Chile Chico; and Cochrane (the most southerly). In addition, you can *sometimes* buy petrol over the counter in small stores, but you shouldn't rely on this. Many travellers choose to carry a spare canister of petrol to avoid the risk of being caught short.

over a landscape of steep hills and narrow glacial valleys dotted with dozens of lakes.

Unfortunately, very little of this wilderness is accessible, as the badly under-funded park lacks the resources to maintain its footpaths. Maps still show what was once a fabulous three-day hiking trail from the park's southern entrance, off the Carretera Austral, to the northern entrance at Correntoso (connected to Puerto Montt by a 46-kilometre dirt road), but the central portion has become impenetrable. What's left still makes a good, long **day-hike**, though – from the Conaf hut (in the southern entrance), the path follows the Río Chaica for 5km as far as the pretty **Laguna Chaiquenes**, surrounded by steep, forested hills. On the way, about an hour from the hut, you pass some impressive waterfalls, and twenty minutes later, a huge, 3000-year-old alerce tree. From Laguna Chaiquenes, the now deteriorating path heads north for a further 4km, as far as the long, thin **Laguna Triángulo**, where it peters out. Count on taking around two and a half hours to get to Laguna Chaiquenes, and another three hours to get to Laguna Triángulo.

Parque Los Alerces de Lenca

Branching north from the access track to the national park, a steep and extremely rough jeep track (signed "Lodge") – best not attempted unless you have 4WD – zigzags up through the adjoining, privately owned **PARQUE LOS ALERCES DE LENCA**, extending over 2000 hectares of land. As you climb higher, you enter a dense covering of old-growth alerces, many of them looking grey and lifeless, towering like decrepit, elderly giants over the

Alerce trees

The famed **alerce** trees – accorded national monument status by the government in 1976 – are endemic to southern Chile and Argentina and grow in high, soggy soil, usually on mountainsides between 600m and 800m above sea level. Among the **largest trees in the world**, they can rise to a height of 45m, with a trunk diameter of up to 4m. After shooting up rapidly during their first hundred years, they slow down dramatically, their diameter increasing just 1mm every three years. As they grow, they lose their lower branches, keeping only their top crown of dark-green, broccoli-like leaves. The lighter, lower leaves belong to parasite trees, which often prove useful to the ancient alerces, supporting them when they topple and keeping them alive. When the surrounding forest – made up principally of coigüe, mañío and canelo – is cut down, the exposed alerces often have their tops blown off by the wind, leaving them shattered and dead-looking, with mangy side branches. The very old ones start rotting from the inside out, and it's not uncommon to find them lying on the forest floor, chopped down for their wood only to be abandoned when it was discovered that their insides had decayed.

The trees' grey, papery bark conceals a beautiful, reddish-brown and extremely **valuable wood**; a large tree is worth tens of thousands of dollars. In the late-nineteenth and early-twentieth centuries, the trees were chopped down at random by early colonizers – sometimes to be used for telegraph poles or shingles, but often just to clear land which was later found to be useless for agriculture. Today, it's illegal to chop down an alerce, but it's not forbidden to sell the wood of dead trees. This leaves a lot of room for getting round the protection laws, as landowners have been known to find clever ways of causing premature death to their trees.

younger and greener coigües, lengas and ñires. Some 7km up the track, look out for the small sign pointing to *El Tata* ("The Daddy") – a gnarled colossus, estimated to be a staggering 3500 years old. Five kilometres beyond, the track comes to a halt at the park's centrepiece, the **Alerce Mountain Lodge** (T & F 65/286969, W www.mountainlodge.cl), a sensitively designed timber lodge built around the alerces, with a 2000-year-old tree growing through the veranda. Set in a small depression by a romantic lake, this is one of the most peaceful, beautiful and isolated places to stay in Chile, and makes for a memorable experience of the country's wilderness without roughing it. Of course, you do pay dearly for the privilege – a three-night stay (the minimum) starts at CH$550,000 for a double room; this includes all meals and various excursions led by friendly guides, including short or long hikes through the forests, a stiff climb up to a panoramic viewpoint, and horseback treks. At day's end, you can relax in a sauna and Jacuzzi. Although the "park" operates more like a private estate, geared towards overnight guests, you may book a day-visit, including lunch and guided excursions, for CH$60,000 per person. If you don't have your own transport, the lodge's staff will pick you up and take you back to Puerto Montt.

Hornopirén and around

The sheltered, sandy cove of **La Arena** lies 13km south of the turn-off to Parque Nacional Alerce Andino, along an extremely narrow stretch of the road blasted out of a cliff. It's the departure point of a **ferry** (9 per day; CH$5000 per car, passengers free), which operates on a first-come, first-served basis. After the thirty-minute crossing, the ferry lands at tiny **Caleta Puelche**, from where the road winds through 58km of thickly forested hills, before arriving at the village of **HORNOPIRÉN** (also known as río Negro). Here you catch another **ferry** to Caleta Gonzalo, where the Carretera continues. TransMarChilay's *Mailén* (Jan & Feb only; 1 daily; 6hr; around CH$9000 for passengers, CH$56,000 for cars) usually leaves Hornopirén at 4pm (returning from Caleta Gonzalo at 9am). Plans are underway to build a ferry terminal at Pichicolo, 15km west of Hornopirén, which would cut sailing times to Caleta Gonzalo by almost an hour and ensure year-round service.

Perched on the northern shore of a wide fjord, at the foot of **Volcán Hornopirén**, the village enjoys a spectacular location, though low, grey clouds and mist frequently obscure the view. An important timber centre in the nineteenth century and hit hard by the decline of the industry in the early twentieth century, Hornopirén has been stirred back to life by an invasion of salmon farmers, who plod the streets in their distinctive white rubber boots. The village's new prosperity is reflected in the shiny, mock-Victorian street lamps on the plaza, and the immaculate, modern church, sporting bright-red alerce shingles and a green roof.

Thanks to the steady flow of summer visitors passing through to catch the ferry, there's no shortage of places to **stay** in Hornopirén. Sitting on the edge of the sea, the charming, wooden *Hotel Hornopirén*, Ignacio Carrera Pinto 388 (T 65/217256; ❸), boasts an antiquated sauna. A cheap option is the friendly *Hospedaje Chuchito* on O'Higgins (T 65/217210; ❶), while *Central Plaza's* timber *cabañas*, down from the square on Lago Pinto Concha (T 65/217247; ❺), offer good deals for groups. The attached **restaurant**, one of Hornopirén's best, features a huge *quincho* (a cement base topped with a grill), over which meat and fish are barbecued on skewers. Popular with locals, the inexpensive *Monteverde*, on O'Higgins, serves typical Chilean fried fish and meat.

Around Hornopirén

Because Hornopirén is so near the beginning of the Carretera Austral, most visitors are eager just to catch the ferry and push on down the road – which is a shame, as the village's surroundings really deserve a bit of exploration. Set aside a day to hike along the Río Blanco in **Parque Nacional Volcán Hornopirén**, or to visit the hot springs on **Isla Llancahué**. If you've only got a morning to spare, spend a couple of hours driving along the scenic **road to Cholgo** before getting back with plenty of time to catch the afternoon ferry.

Parque Nacional Volcán Hornopirén

To the east of Hornopirén unfold the 500 square kilometres of protected wilderness that make up **PARQUE NACIONAL VOLCÁN HORNOPIRÉN** (24hr; free). The park's namesake and centrepiece, 16km along a muddy track from the village, is the perfectly conical **Volcán Hornopirén**, whose steep slopes are densely forested, discouraging all but the most determined of hikers from reaching the 1500-metre summit. Five kilometres further along the track lies the seldom-visited **Lago General Pinto Concha**, with excellent fishing and stunning views onto the 2111-metre **Volcán Yate**.

Back towards the village, a turn-off from the track leads south around the end of the fjord to a modern bridge over the turbulent **Río Blanco**, filled with milky-white, freezing-cold water. A well-defined, eight-kilometre path follows the river upstream, passing through alternating patches of pastureland and forest before reaching a small farm. Although years of logging have stripped much of the native forest, you'll still encounter grand swaths of alerce, coigüe, tepa and lenga around here, and if you continue on above the tree line, you'll enter a landscape of ice-covered peaks and glaciers. This makes a great **day-hike**, and you're unlikely to see another soul all day. Other trails are currently being developed to link Parque Nacional Volcán Hornopirén with Parque Pumalín.

Isla Llancahué

One of the best excursions from Hornopirén is a boat trip to **ISLA LLANCA-HUÉ**, a small, forested island sitting at the head of the fjord, famous for its 50°C (122°F) **natural hot springs**. You'll find an old, timber-built **hotel** here, the *Termas de Llancahué* (☎09/642 4857; ❹), where for CH$5000 you can wallow in single or communal hot tubs and an open-air swimming pool overlooking a rocky bay. Or, enjoy the jets of hot water that emerge on the beach, cooled down by sea water but still hot enough for a good soaking, even in the grey, drizzly weather that so often plagues the area. It's a fifty-minute boat ride to the island from Hornopirén, costing around CH$40,000 return, per boat; the hotel runs a shuttle boat service from Hornopirén at 3pm daily during the summer, or you can arrange a ride in the village with Jorge Espinosa (☎65/217263). It's normally possible to pay less if you go from the village of Cholgo (see below), which is closer to the island. Most boatmen also offer trips to the remote, isolated thermal springs known as the **Termas de Cahuelmó** (see opposite), but at around CH$90,000 return, this is a very expensive trip.

The road to Cholgo

South of Hornopirén, the Carretera Austral continues a further 28km to the tiny hamlet of **CHOLGO**, running partly through Parque Nacional Volcán

Hornopirén, and then through land belonging to the Pumalín Project (see box, p.454). The breathtaking route crosses glacier-fed rivers framed by soaring, snow-capped peaks, before tracing its way along the edge of a cliff, squeezed between the ocean and the overhanging forest. Heading even a small way down is highly memorable, and the numerous ravines that branch off the road, cutting through the forest, make for great, scrambly **hiking**. Cholgo itself is nothing special – just a cluster of houses and black salmon-farming rafts bobbing in the bay. For the moment there's nowhere to stay, but they plan to install a visitor centre and camping areas as part of the northern section of Parque Pumalín, which currently can only be accessed by this road.

Parque Pumalín

After six hours of sailing through the island-studded channel between Chiloé and the mainland, the ferry from Hornopirén enters the steep-sided Reñihué fjord and unloads its passengers at **Caleta Gonzalo**, where the Carretera Austral resumes its course. Getting off the boat, you'll find yourself at the main arrival point of **PARQUE PUMALÍN**, the world's largest privately owned conservation area, covering 320,000 hectares (790,400 acres) of land. The Pumalín Project, founded by North American millionaire Douglas Tompkins to protect one of the world's last strongholds of temperate rainforest, has generated a considerable amount of controversy over the past five years. But, standing at Caleta Gonzalo, faced with the jungle-like vegetation covering every inch of visible land, few would deny that the park represents a magnificent environmental achievement. It's a place of overwhelming natural beauty, with hauntingly calm lakes reflecting stands of alerce trees, ferocious waterfalls gushing through chasms of dark rock, and high, snowy-peaked mountains off which glaciers dangle precariously. You'd do well to set aside at least a day to explore but, if you've no time to hang around, you can still enjoy the landscape as you follow the Carretera Austral through the park – squeezed between steep-sided hills covered in dense, dripping foliage, with wispy clouds frequently hovering over the mountains.

Exploring the park

Parque Pumalín falls into two sections, cut in half by a large chunk of land owned by ENDESA, the energy corporation (see box, p.454). The **northern section** boasts the gloriously isolated **Termas de Cahuelmó**: a series of natural hot pools, carved out of the rock at the end of a steep, narrow fjord, accessible only by boat. You'll find a rustic camping area nearby, from where a five-kilometre trail leads to the crystal-clear **Lago Abascal**, surrounded by dramatic scenery. Getting here is expensive, costing around CH$80,000 per boat trip, which is best arranged in Hornopirén (see p.451) or Cholgo (see opposite).

Park Pumalín advance information

To book accommodation or for any other information, contact Park Pumalín's Puerto Montt office at Buín 356 (☎65/250079, ⓕ65/255145, Ⓔpumalin@telsur.cl) or at O'Higgins 62 in Chaitén (☎65/731341). You can also get information from its US office at Building 1062, Fort Cronkhite, Sausalito, CA 94965 (☎415/2299339, ⓌWww .parquepumalin.cl).

Douglas Tompkins and the Pumalín Project

In 1995 it was publicly announced that a North American millionaire, **Douglas Tompkins**, had used intermediaries to buy a 3000-square-kilometre chunk of southern Chile – marking the beginning of a five-year national soap opera that transformed Tompkins into one of the most controversial public figures in the country. The beginning of the saga dates back to 1991 when the 49-year-old Californian, deeply disillusioned with the corporate world, and increasingly committed to environmental issues, sold his fifty percent share in the Esprit clothing empire, bought an abandoned ranch in Chile and moved there with his wife and kids. Their new home was stranded on the edge of the **Reñihué fjord**, 130km south of Puerto Montt, surrounded by one of the world's largest remaining tracts of virgin temperate rainforest. Inspired by the "deep ecology" movement pioneered by the Norwegian environmentalist **Arne Naess**, Tompkins set out to acquire more of the surrounding wilderness, with the aim of protecting it from the threat of commercial exploitation. As he did so, he was seized with the idea of creating a massive, privately funded national park, which would ensure permanent protection of the **ancient forest** while providing low-impact facilities for visitors.

Over the next four years Tompkins spent more than US$14 million buying up adjoining tracts of land, in most cases hiding his identity to prevent prices from shooting up. His initial secrecy was to have damaging repercussions, however, for once his land acquisitions became public knowledge, he was engulfed by a wave of suspicion and hostility, fuelled by several right-wing politicians and the press. The biggest cause for alarm, it seemed, was the fact that Tompkins' land stretched from the Argentine border to the Pacific Ocean, effectively "cutting Chile in two". His motives were questioned by everyone, with all sorts of wild accusations and conspiracy theories flying around: some claimed he planned to set up a new Jewish state, others that he would use the land as a dumping ground for North American nuclear waste, while many were simply unhappy with the way he was applying his corporate drive for acquisition of their native territory.

Tompkins attempted to quell the paranoia by appearing on national television, explaining his intentions to create **Parque Pumalín**, a nature sanctuary with free access. Slowly, the public – or some of it – was won over. But the long struggle to have his lands declared a Santuario de la Naturaleza by the government – a status frequently conferred on private land, and the first step that would enable Tompkins to transfer ownership to a conservation foundation – was continually thwarted. Another problem was Huinay, a 740,000-acre property owned by the Catholic University of Valparaíso, separating the two separate chunks of Tompkins' land. When the university announced its intentions to sell Huinay, it was natural that Tompkins should attempt to buy it, to join the gap in his proposed park. Obstructions came from all directions, including church leaders who protested that Tompkins' belief in family planning was an affront to Catholicism. Eventually, the government agreed to support Tompkins' aims to establish Parque Pumalín – on the condition that for one year he would not buy more than 7000 contiguous hectares (17,250 acres) of land in the south of Chile. Left with little choice other than to accept this deal, Tompkins looked on as Huinay was sold to ENDESA, Chile's largest energy corporation.

So, the park that caused so much fear by cutting through the width of Chile is itself severed through its middle. Ownership of Parque Pumalín was transferred to the US-based **Conservation Land Trust**, who in 2003 donated it to the Chilean Fundación Pumalín, whose board includes Tompkins and his wife. In the meantime, ENDESA has yet to release details of its plans for Huinay, and Tompkins, determined to save a little more unspoiled terrain from development, in 2001 purchased another chunk of land near the Termas del Amarillo, south of Chaitén.

The **southern section** has more infrastructure geared towards visitors. At Caleta Gonzalo, a wooden bridge across the river leads to a "**demonstration farm**", where visitors can get a close-up view of the kind of small-scale, ecologically friendly farming and animal husbandry that the project is promoting in the local community, with tours through the organic gardens, and demonstrations of cheese, jam and honey making. Nearby, close to the ferry ramp, the **Sendero Cascadas** is a steep twisty trail through a canopy of overhanging foliage up to a fifteen-metre waterfall (3hr round-trip).

Three other trails have been carved out of the forest, branching off from the Carretera Austral as it heads south through the park. Twelve kilometres down the road, **Sendero Tronador** is probably the most exciting, crossing a narrow gorge filled with a rushing, white-water stream, climbing up to a look-out point with fabulous views onto Volcán Michinmahuida, and ending at a pristine lake with a camping area alongside (1hr 30min to get there). One kilometre south, **Sendero Los Alerces** is a twenty-minute circular route, dotted with information panels, through a grove of ancient, colossal alerces. Another kilometre down the road, the **Sendero Cascadas Escondidas** (also with a camping area) is an easy, half-hour walk through the forest to several high, slender waterfalls. Exactly 15km down the road, right by the wooden distance marker, is a small, muddy **hot springs** pool, almost hidden by foliage, near the side of the road – a great place to dip your feet before moving on from the park.

Practicalities

Immediately beyond the ferry ramp, where you arrive, sits the park's **information centre** (daily 8am–8pm) – a rotunda-shaped timber building with a high, beamed roof and a huge copper-covered stove in its centre. Here, English-speaking staff hand out leaflets explaining the project's aims and detailing the trails in the park, and there's a range of locally produced *artesanía* for sale, including hand-knitted sweaters and hats. Opposite the information centre is a **café** (daily 7.30am–11pm), whose stylish interior features a large open fire, lots of pale, polished wood and black-and-white prints of alerce trees. It serves simple but delicious organic food, including home-made bread, locally caught fish and succulent roast lamb; if you plan to camp (see p.456) and cook your own stuff, call in here for a supply of firewood, fresh bread, vegetables and herbs.

△ Parque Pumalín rainforest

THE CARRETERA AUSTRAL | Parque Pumalín

455

You can also enquire here about available **accommodation** in the seven nearby four-person 🛖 *cabañas* (**⑤**–**⑥**) lining the edge of the shore. Designed by Douglas Tompkins himself, they're impeccably tasteful inside, with waxed wooden floors, good quality bed linen made of natural fabrics and bed frames constructed from reclaimed alerce wood. You'll also find several **camping** areas, the main one just a few hundred metres from the information centre, with basic sites (CH$1500) and covered areas with picnic tables (CH$5000). There are barbecue facilities here as well. Six other campsites lie to the south, dotted along 20km of very scenic road, some adjacent to trekking trails, and a further half dozen scattered sites to the east, in the southern sector of the park.

Chaitén

Just beyond the southern limit of Parque Pumalín, 25km south of Caleta Gonzalo, the Carretera Austral skirts the pale, calm expanse of **Lago Blanco**, which reflects Chile's most southerly stands of alerce trees in its smooth surface, before turning west towards the coast. Twenty kilometres beyond, it reaches the ocean at the tiny hamlet of **Santa Barbara**, where a short track leads to a gorgeous, crescent-shaped **beach** dominated by Cerro Vilcún, a sugarloaf mountain looming over the bay. The beach, fringed by deep-green forest, is filled with dark, volcanic sand, and makes a great place to camp, though there are no facilities – for these, continue 7km down the road to *Camping Los Arrayanes* (☎65/218242; CH$4000 per site), equipped with showers and picnic areas.

A further 4km south, you'll reach the little town of **CHAITÉN**, whose ferry terminal is the starting point for journeys south along the Carretera Austral outside January and February, when the Hornopirén–Caleta Gonzalo ferry doesn't function. Built on a flat stretch of land at the mouth of the Blanco and Yelcho rivers, and surrounded by densely forested mountains, Chaitén is beautifully located but rather charmless, made up of squat, modern houses and wide, grid-laid streets indented with potholes that are invariably filled with water. As the provincial capital and only commercial centre between Puerto Montt and Coyhaique, 420km south, it does, however, offer a number of extremely useful **services**, including supermarkets, a petrol station, car mechanics, a public telephone, tour companies, a pharmacy and plenty of places to stay and eat, prompting most people travelling down the Carretera to spend a night or two here. Unfortunately, the town's only **ATM**, in the Banco del Estado, on the corner of Libertad and

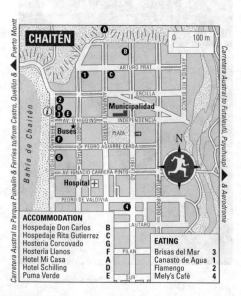

CHAITÉN

0   100 m

ARTURO PRAT

ERCILLA

AVENIDA RIO BLANCO

Municipalidad

AV. O'HIGGINS

INDEPENDENCIA

Buses

PLAZA

PEDRO AGUIRRE CERDA

B. O'HIGGINS

AV. IGNACIO CARRERA PINTO

Hospital ✚

PEDRO DE VALDIVIA

Carretera Austral to Futaleufú, Puyuhuapi ▶

& Aerodrome

Muelle Pardo

▲ Puerto Montt

Carretera Austral to/from Castro, Quellón &

Bahía de Chaitén

Carretera Austral to Parque Pumalín & Ferries to/from Castro, Quellón &

ACCOMMODATION

Hospedaje Don Carlos	B
Hospedaje Rita Gutierrez	C
Hosteria Corcovado	G
Hosteria Llanos	F
Hotel Mi Casa	A
Hotel Schilling	D
Puma Verde	E

LAUTARO

PILAN

SUR

EATING

Brisas del Mar	3
Canasto de Agua	1
Flamengo	2
Mely's Café	4

O'Higgins, is unreliable and prone to refusing cards; the next reliable ATM is way down at Puerto Aisén. The bank may also change US dollars, but gives very poor rates and usually won't exchange traveller's cheques.

Practicalities

There's a **tourist kiosk** (mid-Dec–mid-March 8.30am–9pm) on the corner of Costanera and O'Higgins but you'll find a better equipped **Sernatur** office on the plaza at O'Higgins 284 (T65/731082). Alternatively, try the Pumalín Park office at O'Higgins 62 (Mon–Sat 9am–1pm & 3–7pm, Sun 10am–4pm; T65/731341,) or the Chaitur Excursiones office (see below). The cheapest **accommodation** options include *Hospedaje Rita* (T65/731502; ②) on the corner of Almirante Riveros and Prat, where the jovial and eccentric Rita offers basic shared rooms and a large garden in which to pitch tents. You can also try the very friendly and welcoming, though quite cramped, *Hospedaje Don Carlos* at Almirante Riveros 53 (T65/731287 & 09/8095078; ②). The homely *Hosteria Corcovado* (T65/731221, Ecorcovado@chile.com; ②–③), on the corner of Corcovado and Pedro Aguirre Cerda, has four cabañas that accommodate up to four people and has an excellent restaurant attached. Best in the mid-range is well-run *Hostería Llanos*, down on the esplanade at Corcovado 378 (T65/731332; ④), where you can get decent meals, including breakfast. Perched on top of the hill north of town, commanding fine views over the bay, *Hotel Mi Casa*, Av Norte 206 (T & F65/731285, Ehmicasa@123.cl, Wwww .hotelmicasa.cl; ⑤), offers decent but overpriced rooms in a bungalow-style building that also boasts a gym and sauna. Better value in this price range is the *Hotel Schilling* on the seafront at Corcovado 230 (T65/731295; ⑤), with comfortable en-suite rooms often booked ahead by groups. The Pumalín Project runs a beautifully furnished *hostería*, the *Puma Verde*, offering delicious food, at O'Higgins 54 (T65/731184 & 65/232300, Ereservaspumaverde @surnet.cl, Wwww.parquepumalin.cl; ⑤); it's next door to the Project's Chaitén offices and shop.

8

Tours and transport from Chaitén

Run by the highly knowledgeable, infinitely helpful and slightly eccentric Nicholas La Penna, Chaitur Excursiones (T65/731429, Enchaitur@hotmail.com), at O'Higgins 67, offers a range of **tours** (in English and Spanish) around Chaitén, taking you north to Parque Pumalín, south to glaciers and lakes along the Carretera Austral, and to the Termas del Amarillo (see p.458). He can also arrange boat trips on the fjord and sea-kayaking. The office serves as the unofficial **bus terminal**, where you can buy tickets and catch buses to Coyhaique and Futaleufú (several times a week, Dec–March only); he can also sort out your follow-on transport and accommodation through contacts farther down the Carretera. Unfortunately the other staff are less knowledgeable and if the owner is away or busy, service varies.

There are regular **ferries** to and from Puerto Montt and Quellón with TransMarChilay, Corcovado 266 (T65/731272) and Navimag, Pinto 188 (T65/731570), as well as faster catamarans operated by Aysen Express, c/o Chaitur Excursiones, O'Higgins 67 (T65/731429) that also serve Puerto Chacabuco.

Flights to Puerto Montt (35min) are offered by a number of small airline companies that seem to come and go with bewildering regularity: most reliable are Aeromet at Corcovado 243 (T65/731844) and Aerosur on the corner of Carrera Pinto and Almirante Riveros (T65/731228) which both fly daily at around noon, charging CH$25,000–35,000 for a one-way ticket.

Places to **eat** include *Brisas del Mar* at Av Corcovado 278, with a sea view and basic fish and meat dishes, and the smarter *Canasto de Agua* at Prat 65, which does hearty *parrilladas*. Best of all is the *Flamengo* at Corcovado 218, with unbeatable seafood dishes served with more style than anywhere else in town. Travellers in desperate need of real coffee will find relief at *Mely's Café*, tucked away at Libertad 641 – they also serve mouthwatering *küchen*. The best supermarket is on the seafront, Avenida Corcovado, along with telephone centres and a petrol station.

South to Villa Santa Lucía

The stretch of road south of Chaitén reveals a series of heart-stopping views – as you cross the bridge into the village of **El Amarillo**, for example, 25km down the road, look left and you'll see a massive, gravity-defying glacier hanging off the edge of **Volcán Michinmahuida**, 9km north. There's no particular reason to stay overnight in El Amarillo, but should you need a break in your journey, there are several **accommodation** options, including simple *Hospedaje Marcela* (☎65/264422; ❹), which organizes multi-day horse rides to the volcano, and the smarter *Cabañas Los Galpones del Volcán* (☎65/731453; ❺), with sweeping views and a friendly owner who can advise on local trekking paths. The best of these is the challenging, three-day hike southeast through the Serranías Nevadas (or "Snowy Mountains") to Futaleufú (see opposite), along an unfinished track built in 1956 in a failed attempt to connect the two towns by road.

Just beyond the bridge into El Amarillo, a side road winds 5km up a wooded hillside to the **Termas del Amarillo** (daily: Jan & Feb 9am–9pm, March–Dec 9am–6pm; CH$1500), a couple of rustic open-air pools filled with thermal water, often over 50°C (122°F), set in a clearing in the wood and run by the Municipalidad. There are also mud baths and private tubs, as well as cold showers to cool off in and a few camping areas (CH$2000 per person). Near the pools sits the simple *Hospedaje Los Manios* (☎65/731210; ❷), with basic rooms and kitchen facilities in a rickety house or five *cabañas* for up to six people.

Continuing down the Carretera Austral about 20km, you cross the **Río Yelcho** on a modern suspension bridge that looks startlingly out of place in the wilderness. Just across it the road arrives at the tiny hamlet of Puerto Cárdenas on the northern tip of **Lago Yelcho**, a large, glacial lake famed for its abundant salmon and trout. You'll find basic **accommodation** at *Hospedaje Lulu* (☎65/264429; ❷). Several places along the lakeshore also offer accommodation and fishing excursions, including the upmarket *Hotel Yelcho in Patagonia* (reservations ☎ & ℱ65/731337 or in Santiago ☎2/632 6117, ℯhotel@yelcho .cl, ⓌWww.yelcho.cl; ❻), with *cabañas* for 4–6 people, camping areas and a decent restaurant. Before you cross Puente Ventisquero, the next bridge south, a well-trodden muddy path leads uphill from a parking area for about an hour-and-a-half, past some giant *nalca* plants, to **Ventisquero Yelcho**, a small but impressive glacier feeding a number of high waterfalls that tumble down the mountainside. Be careful at the end of the trail – frequent landslides can make the approach to the waterfalls and glacier itself extremely hazardous.

Twenty kilometres south you reach **Villa Santa Lucía**, a dull, modern settlement established in 1982, made up of regimented rows of prefabricated houses. There's a military base here, along with telephone services, shops selling basic provisions and a couple of *hospedajes*; however, few people stop here, preferring to head east towards the mountain village of Futaleufú (see opposite) – up the first major side road off the Carretera Austral – or south to Puerto Puyuhuapi (see p.462).

The Futaleufú Valley

The 80-kilometre side trip up the **FUTALEUFÚ VALLEY** is one of the most enjoyable diversions off the Carretera Austral. Heading east from Villa Santa Lucía, you first skirt the southern shore of Lago Yelcho for 30km, before arriving at Puerto Ramírez, where there is a fork in the road. The right turn goes to the quiet border village of **Palena**, while the left branch follows the turquoise **Río Futaleufú** for 17km through towering gorges, lush forests and snow-streaked mountain peaks. With its big "explosion waves" and massive "rodeo holes", Futaleufú is regarded by many professional rafters and kayakers as the most challenging whitewater river in the world. Though it's relatively undiscovered compared to big crowd-pullers like the Zambezi and the Colorado, a growing number of Chilean and US operators offer **rafting** trips down the river, which begins by passing through a basalt gorge, known as the "*Gates of Hell*", and boasts over 40 class IV–V rapids with alarming names like *Purgatorio* and *Terminador*; for details of operators, see p.76 in Basics.

Drifting away from the river, the road winds through forest and pastureland before skirting the edge of **Lago Lonconao**, a picturesque alpine lake whose deep-blue waters reflect the perfect symmetry of the surrounding mountains. Six kilometres beyond, a short track branches left to another beautiful lake, **Lago Espolón**, teeming with salmon and trout and bordered by sandy beaches.

Accommodation and camping in the Futaleufú Valley

A string of **campsites** and **hosterías** has sprung up along the road to Futaleufú since the 1990s, many of them in lovely spots overlooking the Futaleufú and Espolón rivers, or on the shores of neighbouring lakes. We've given a selection below, including their distance from the Carretera Austral as a reference.

Camping Cara del Indio km 54. One of the best campsites in the valley, on the side of a cliff perched over the river. CH\$3500 per person includes firewood and use of hot showers and a sauna.
Camping La Vega km 77. Attractive campground right by the Río Espolón, with shady sites under native coigüe trees and clean, modern sanitary facilities. CH\$4000 per site.
La Casa del Campo Lago Espolón, km 70 ☏65/311443, ⓦ www.lagoespolon.cl. A small lakeside farmhouse owned by a welcoming couple who give guests the run of the kitchen and let campers pitch tents in their garden. Meals, *asados* (barbecues), horse rides and fishing excursions are available. ❸
Hostal Alexis Puerto Piedra, km 25 ☏65/731505. Built on a wooden promontory on the shores of Lago Yelcho, this colonial farmhouse offers comfortable rooms, peace and quiet and fishing excursions. ❹
Hostería Verónica Puerto Ramírez, km 30 ☏65/731258. A small, clean and friendly place to stay, with simple rooms and fishing boats for rent. ❸

Futaleufú

The pretty, pastel-painted village of **FUTALEUFÚ**, 8km from Lago Espolón, was until fairly recently a remote frontier outpost and now serves as a popular summer base for rafting, kayaking, fishing and hiking.

Originally settled in the 1920s, the town completely depended on Argentina until a horse trail was built to connect it with the Chilean coast in the 1930s. Communications with the rest of Chile increased slightly in the 1950s with the arrival of an aerodrome and light plane services. Notoriously changeable weather, however, made flying an unreliable form of transport and in 1952 one plane had to make an emergency landing on one of the village's streets, which now bears the name of "Piloto Carmona" in honour of the unlucky pilot. Following the completion of the nearby stretch of the Carretera Austral in 1988, Futaleufú finally became connected to the rest of Chile by road – though it's easier to travel north and south by crossing the border into Argentina than plod along the bumpy Carretera. Twice-weekly buses (Mon & Fri) head to the **Argentine border** at Paso Futaleufú at 9am and 6pm (customs post open daily 8am–10pm), 10km east of Futaleufú.

Accommodation

For what used to be a sleepy backwater lost in the mountains, Futaleufú itself boasts a surprisingly good bunch of **places to stay**. As for camping, try the peaceful *Camping Puerto Espolón* (open Jan–Feb only; CH$2000 per person), with its own beach, on the southern edge of town adjacent to the Río Espolón.

Hospedaje Adolfo O'Higgins 302 ☎65/721256. One of the quieter places in Futa, with basic, comfortable rooms and a top-notch breakfast. ❷
Hospedaje Cañete Mistral 374 ☎65/721214. In a calm setting, this house provides basic cubicles separated by paper-thin partitions. ❷
🏃 **Hostería río Grande** O'Higgins 397 ☎65/721320, ⓦwww.hosteriariogrande .com. This modern, timber-built hotel is one of the best places to stay for miles around, with its chic-rustic decor, good quality en-suite rooms and fine restaurant and bar. The owners, who speak English, Dutch and German, also operate Centro Aventura Futaleufú (see opposite), out of the hotel. ❼
Hotel El Barranco O'Higgins 172 ☎65/721314, ⓔhotel@elbarrancochile.cl, ⓦwww .elbarrancochile.com. Modern hotel on outskirts of town with full amenities; they organize guided treks, boating trips and fishing expeditions as well as rent out mountain bikes. ❼
Hotel Continental Balmaceda 597 ☎65/721222. One of the village's oldest hotels, in a large, traditional *casa de familia* with polished wooden

floors, creaking beds, shared bathrooms and hearty meals. ❷
Lodge Frontera Patagónica 5km south of town ☎65/721320, ⓔfronterapatagonica@hotmail.com. This Dutch-Chilean-owned complex of handsome four-person cabins with wood-burning stoves is a good bet for groups. Breakfast is included and other meals available. They also organize fishing, kayaking and rafting trips. ❼
Posada Campesina La Gringa Aldea and Carrera ☎65/721260, ⓦwww.lagringahostal.homestead .com/f.html. Sitting in a beautiful garden, this charming house away from the bustle of the centre has the best view of the surrounding countryside. "La Gringa" (a.k.a. Lucia Harismendy de Witt) was the first person in Futaleufú to provide accommodation to visitors. ❻
Posada Ely Balmaceda 409 ☎65/721205. Genial bed and breakfast in a white-shingled house. ❹
Residencial Carahue O'Higgins 332 ☎65/721221. Very simple rooms in a basic house that also offers kitchen facilities. ❷

The village

Sitting on the Río Futaleufú, near its confluence with the Rio Espolón, and surrounded by forested, snowy peaks, Futaleufú (also known fondly as "Fu" or "Futa") more than earns the grandiose slogan – "A landscape painted by God" – coined by its inhabitants. The only shadow hanging over this heavenly picture is a plan by the energy corporation ENDESA to construct a dam and to build a hydroelectric plant on the river, which would ruin the river for rafting and have far-reaching environmental implications. The plan currently faces concerted opposition by locals, tourism operators and environmentalists. In the summer

8

Outdoor activities around Futaleufú

Most people come to Futaleufú for the slew of **outdoor activities**, including hiking, horse-trekking, mountain biking, fly-fishing, floating (drifting down a river on an inner tube), canyoning (abseiling down canyons) and canoeing, in addition to the obligatory rafting and kayaking trips. Various outfits offer these activities, including **Centro Aventura Futaleufú**, run by the American Olympic team kayaker Chris Spelius, which operates out of the *Hostería río Grande* (see opposite; ⓦwww.raftingchile .com). **Club de Rafting y Kayak** at Cerda 545 (☏65/721298), **Austral Excursiones**, on the corner of Hermanos Carrera and Rodriguéz (☏65/721239) and **Guias Nativos** at Cerda 697 (☏65/721281) also organize professional outings on the river. Expect to pay around CH$15,000 for a relatively simple run down the Río Epsolón, CH$35,000 for a half-day excursion on the Río Futaleufú and CH$60,000 for a full day on the Futa that includes tackling Class V rapids. For horse-riding contact **Rancho Las Ruedas** on Piloto Carmona 337 (☏65/721294, ⓔrancholasruedas@123.cl); horses cost around CH$3000 per hour or CH$12,000 per day. For more information on agencies and types of trip available, visit the **Oficina de Información Turística** (see below).

an **Oficina de Información Turística** operates on the south side of the Plaza de Armas at O'Higgins 536.

Eating and drinking

Most hotels and *hospedajes* in this area also offer **meals**; the best is the cosmopolitan *Hostería Río Grande*. As for **drinking**, the most popular spot with gringos is, again, *Hostería Río Grande* – for something a bit more local, with cheaper beer, try *El Campesino* on the corner of Balmaceda and Prat.

Hostería Río Grande O'Higgins 397. The top restaurant in town, with a European-influenced menu of meat and seafood dishes, stylish decor and young crowd.
Hotel El Barranco O'Higgins 172. A close second to *Hostería Río Grande*, with an attractive dining room offering a menu of tasty meat dishes.
Martín Pescador Balmaceda 603. Circular restaurant with large panoramic windows that

serves a wide selection of decent food and a good range of wines.
Restaurant Encuentro O'Higgins 653. Come here for cheap, simple lunches and sandwiches served all day.
Restaurant Futaleufú Cerda and Sargento Aldea. Bright and airy, with inexpensive but hearty meat and fish dishes.
Sur Andes Cerda 308. A good bet for snacks, and a great place for fruit juices and other drinks.

South to Puyuhuapi, Parque Nacional Queulat and Puerto Cisnes

Back on the Carretera Austral, heading south, the road follows the gleaming, jade-green waters of the Río Frío, where you can picnic on its pleasant banks. Some 70km south of Villa Santa Lucía you reach **La Junta**, a depressing collection of tin houses established in 1983 as one of General Pinochet's "new towns". You won't want to linger in La Junta, but it does offer several services, including a grocery shop, a petrol station, a phone and a few **places to stay** – if you're in need of emergency accommodation, try *Hostería Valderas* (☏67/314105; ❸) or *Residencial Copihué* (☏67/314184; ❷), both on Calle Varas and both rather basic. The smart *Hostal Espacio y Tiempo* (☏67/314141, info@espacioytiempo.cl, www.espacioytiempo.cl; ⑥), on the main road next to the service station, has decent rooms but is overpriced. Your best bet, however, is to press on for 45km to the charming village of **Puyuhuapi**, the departure point for excursions to the **Termas de Puyuhuapi**, and a convenient base for exploring **Parque Nacional Queulat**. On the way to the village, the Carretera enters the northern sector of the park, where you'll see a dramatic change in the landscape as the towering hills close in, forming a narrow valley streaked with waterfalls. The southwest edge of the park, some 90km on from Puyuhuapi, is bordered by the little town of **Puerto Cisnes**, a low-key, scenic detour from the Carretera Austral.

Puyuhuapi

Squatting at the head of the narrow Ventisquero fjord, surrounded by steep, wooded hills, quaint little **PUYUHUAPI** is a great place to break your journey along the Carretera Austral in either direction – not only for the wild beauty of its setting, but also for its proximity to the most compelling attractions in the whole region, the **Termas de Puyuhuapi** and the **Parque Queulat**. Puyuhuapi's rambling streets and old timber houses offer a pleasing contrast to the utilitarian "villages" installed along the Carretera in the 1980s after the completion of the road. You could easily while away an enjoyable hour or two just strolling around or hanging out by the old jetty, trying to spot dolphins in the green waters.

The village's history goes back to the 1930s when four young German immigrants from Sudetenland (now in the Czech Republic) settled here. Each of the four friends found a wife in Chile – some of them also of German descent – and established a family. Many of their descendants still live in Puyuhuapi, which has an unmistakably Teutonic look with its steep-roofed chalets and well-tended gardens. Although the settlers' activities were always commercial, dark rumours circulated during World War II that they were setting up a supply base for German submarines. In fact, their sole concern seems to have been a carpet manufacturing business that somehow flourished in this tiny

△ Puyuhaupi

colony in the middle of nowhere and acquired fame throughout the country. The Hopperdietzels' **carpet factory** (T67/325131, Wwww.puyuhuap1.com; Mon–Fri 8.30am-1pm & 3-7.30pm) – by the shore, opposite the landmark petrol station – is still going strong. They offer guided **tours** (every 30min, Mon–Fri 10.30am-4pm; CH$1000), where you can watch the dextrous women weavers, working in pairs, clunk away at ancient wooden looms in an old shed, while their husbands shave and beat the carpets into finished articles across the road.

The **tourist office** (see below) has pamphlets on two short trails in the town; one is a circuit through the centre past historical buildings, concluding in a steep half-hour climb to a panoramic viewpoint overlooking the head of the fjord and surrounding mountains. Another trail takes you through forest and scrub, often on boardwalks, to a lovely waterfall.

Practicalities

There is a small but helpful tourist office on Avenida Otto Uebel, in the centre of town that has erratic opening hours, but which stocks information leaflets about the town and can provide useful ideas for short excursions.

The best place to **stay** in Puyuhuapi is the *Casa Ludwig* at Av Otto Uebel s/n (T67/325220, El.ludwig@entelchile.net, Wwww.contactchile.cl /casaludwig; ❸ shared bath, ❺ en-suite), a delightful yellow chalet with comfortable rooms, polished wooden floors and great views, run by a charming lady who even lets people camp in the house or on the grounds. Or, head to the very Teutonic *Hostería Alemana* at Av Otto Uebel 450 (T & F67/325118, Ehosteria-alemana@entelchile.net; ❺), a large, elegant timber house set in a mature garden. Opposite, *Hospedaje Mercury* (T67/325102; ❷) is closer to the budget end but still pleasant and scrupulously clean, with small, neat rooms and pastel-coloured walls. The *Residencial Elizabeth*, Circunvalación s/n (T67/325106; ❷), offers simple rooms and filling home-cooked meals. Outside of town, try the fishing lodge *Cabañas El Pangue* (see box, p.464), with comfortable cabins or the *Termas de Puyuhuapi* lodge (see below).

In the village, you can tuck into excellent **meals** at the cute *Café Rossbach*, opposite the carpet factory, where wild berries are used in their mouthwatering *küchen*. Equally delicious *küchen* and other simple dishes are offered at *Kermes*, Circunvalación 14, in a cottage with a colourful garden – the CH$3000 full lunch is an unbeatable value. Best of all, though, is the excellent *Lluvia Marina*, next to *Casa Ludwig* on Avenida Otto Uebel, where you can get real coffee, home-made cakes and reasonably priced meals, including salmon *ceviche*, onion soup, pasta, pizza and meat dishes. It's only open in January and February.

Termas de Puyuhuapi

The luxurious thermal baths, lodge and spa at **TERMAS DE PUYUH-UAPI** (T67/325103 & 67/325117; in Santiago, Fidel Oteiza 1921, oficina 1006 T2/2256489, F2/2748111, Einfo@patagonia-connection.com, Wwww.patagoniaconnex.cl) enjoy a fantastic location, marooned on the edge of a peninsula on the opposite side of the fjord from the Carretera. Behind rises a steep jungle of rainforest, making the resort inaccessible by land and reachable only by boat. Four times a day from December to March (10am, 12.30pm, 3.30pm & 7pm), and less frequently off-season, a motor launch collects passengers from a signposted wooden jetty a few minutes beyond the village's rarely used airstrip, 15km south of Puyuhuapi, and whisks them across the water on a ten-minute ride to the lodge. It's hard to imagine a more romantic form of arrival, even in one of the frequent downpours that plague the region. Phone ahead of your arrival, especially during off-season, to ensure that you are met by the launch.

The thermal baths used to be a handful of ramshackle cabins that no one cared much about; in the late 1980s one Eberhard Kossman, an East German shipbuilding magnate who in his youth swam to the West in a wetsuit made out of inner tubes, took them over and transformed the baths into a series of low-lying, beautifully designed buildings made of reddish-brown alerce timber and lots of glass. Apart from its spectacular location, the main reason to come here is to soak in the steaming **hot springs**, channelled into three outdoor

Fly-fishing around the Carretera Austral

Traditionally, it was the waters in the Lake District that attracted most anglers. However, while there's still some great fishing to be had there, the growth in the region's population, and ease of access to the lakes and rivers have increased fishing pressure and prompted enthusiasts to turn their attention to the **fjords** south of Puerto Montt – now considered to be the most exciting fly-fishing region in Chile. Here, local boatmen whisk fishermen through the bewildering maze of channels and islets to remote, hidden rivers, as clear as glass and teeming with fish. Many people have achieved their personal record here. Acrobatic dolphins, sea lion colonies, snow-capped volcanoes and virgin forest all add to the magic of the scene.

The Carretera Austral has opened up the area to opportunities for anglers, and a number of first-class fishing lodges have sprung up around the region. If you plan to do some serious fishing, bring a 6 or 7 weight **rod** with a reliable reel capable of carrying at least 90m of 9kg backing. You'll need a forward floating line, as well as a fast sink-tip line or shooting head. Your fly box should include a wide range of brightly coloured streamers and a selection of nymphs and dry flies. As for clothing, both neoprene and breathable waders work here, and a rain jacket is a must. The **season** varies slightly according to the area, but in general lasts from October or November to May. You need a **licence** to fish, which costs around CH$5000 and is widely available in town halls and sport-fishing shops. To find out more about fly-fishing in Chile, contact the **Servicio Nacional de Pesca** (a government agency) at Victoria 2832, Valparaíso (T 32/819441, F 32//256311, W www.sernapesca.cl) or consult the excellent website of the professional fly-fishing tour operator **FlyfishChile**, based at San Francisco 328, Puerto Varas (T 65/232747, F 65/235938, E info@flyfishchile .com, W www.flyfishchile.com).

Lodges and operators along the Carretera Austral

Outlined below are a few of the more established lodges and operators, all of which have English- and Spanish-speaking guides. You can obtain a fuller list from **Sernatur** in Coyhaique, at Bulnes 35 (T & F 67/231752, E infoaisen@sernatur.cl). Most lodges are of an extremely high standard, and charge between US$2000–4500 per person for a seven-night package including accommodation, fishing guide, all food and an open bar.

Cabañas El Pangue Lago Risopatrón, 18km north of Puyuhuapi T 67/325128, E elpangue@entelchile.net, W www.elpangue.cl. Stay in comfortable *cabañas* and fish for trout in the lake itself or in the Queulat Fjord.

El Saltamontes Lodge Casilla 565, Coyhaique T & F 67/232779. Charming lodge on the banks of the Río Nireguao, about 100km northeast of Coyhaique, offering dry fly-fishing (strictly catch and release) for brown trout.

pools reached by a short walk through the forest. Two of the pools are large enough to swim in, and sit right on the edge of the fjord, while the third one, containing the hottest water, is a small pond enclosed by overhanging ferns and native trees. There's a large indoor pool, too, part of the new state-of-the-art **spa** centre (closed Mon) specializing in "thalassotherapy" (treatments involving heated seawater and seaweed) and massage.

You don't need to be an overnight guest to visit, though day visits are limited when the lodge is full, so you should phone ahead to book: a **day visit** costs CH$10,000 for the outdoor pools, CH$20,000 for the use of the indoor pool and CH$5000 for the round-trip boat ride (free to guests). The restaurant serves delicious three-course meals made with fresh local produce, and there's

Futaleufú Lodge near Futaleufú; information from Casilla 1238 ☏ & ℱ32/812659. North American Jim Repine spent many years guiding in Alaska before coming down to the Futaleufú river valley. With just a few guests per week, and excellent food and wine, this is an intimate, relaxing lodge, especially geared towards couples. Rainbow and brown trout are most prevalent, with wading right at the front door.

Heart of Patagonia Lodge Casilla 324, Coyhaique ☏ & ℱ67/233701, Ⓦwww
.heartofpatagonia.com, ℰinfo@heartofpatagonia.com. One of the more easily reached lodges, on the banks of the Río Simpson and connected to the city of Coyhaique by paved road. Up to six guests can stay in this intimate, homely lodge run by a welcoming family.

Hotel El Barranco O'Higgins 172, Futaleufú ☏65/721314, ℰhotel@elbarrancochile
.cl, Ⓦwww.elbarrancochile.cl. A readily accessible two-storey hotel made from native timber and boasting an outdoor pool that has a rustic, mountain feel. Its restaurant serves international and regional food whilst the bar specializes in Chilean wine.

Isla Monita Lodge information from Alvaro Casanova 287A, Santiago ☏2/2030023, ℰislamonita@entelchile.net, Ⓦwww.islamonita.cl. A remote, deluxe lodge sitting on a tiny island in the middle of Lago Yelcho, reached by a short flight from Chaitén. They offer dry and wet fly-fishing from wooden boats. The lake has abundant salmon and trout, and the national fly-fishing record was set here with a salmon of 17kg.

Patagonia Baker Lodge Puerto Bertrand ☏ & ℱ67/411903, Ⓦwww.pbl.cl, ℰinfolodge@pbl.cl. New complex alongside the world-renowned Río Baker, which is teeming with brown and rainbow trout as well as good-sized salmon. Deluxe rooms have electric heating and private bathrooms as well as a stunning view of the Río Baker. The lodge also boasts two halls with open fireplaces and a gourmet restaurant.

Patagonia Tours Service Colón 203 ☏ & ℱ67/232522. Long-established operator offering a range of camp-based fishing trips, including adventurous four-day excursions to Villa O'Higgins at the end of the Carretera Austral. The cost of US$1600 per person includes return flights from Santiago as well as food, accommodation and guides.

Ruca Chalhuafe Lodge Ensenada 50km from Puerto Varas on the shore of Lago Llanquihue, at the foot of Volcán Osorno ☏65/335376, Ⓦwww.rucachalhuafe.cl. An attractive lodge boasting more than twenty rivers, five lakes and a number of creeks within an 80-kilometre radius.

Termas de Puyuhuapi Puyuhuapi ☏67/325103, Ⓦwww.patagoniaconnex.cl. Luxury lodge (see p.463), combining a spectacular location and sensational thermal baths with top-notch guides who possess an intricate knowledge of the area's most hidden rivers and channels.

also a cheaper cafeteria by the hot pools. If you do decide to stay, you're richly rewarded, as you can indulge in the magical experience of lying in the steaming pools in the middle of the night, gazing at millions of stars overhead. It's worth paying the extra for one of the eight shoreside rooms whose floor-to-ceiling windows give fabulous views across the fjord. You can also visit the resort in conjunction with a cruise to the Laguna San Rafael glacier on board the resort's own catamaran – for more details, see box, p.472. The resort offers upmarket **fly-fishing** excursions (see box, p.464) through the maze of scarcely-visited channels and rivers to the west of Puyuhuapi, led by top-of-the-range English-speaking guides.

Parque Nacional Queulat

PARQUE NACIONAL QUEULAT features a vast expanse of virgin forest, towering granite peaks and rumbling glaciers. The Carretera Austral runs through or along the edge of the park for 70km, entering the northern boundary 15km north of Puyuhuapi and crossing the southern limit 55km south of the village. Along the way, a number of trails lead off from the road into the park. If you're not keen on straying far from the car, you can easily reach several scenic highlights from parking areas just off the highway. Twelve kilometres north of Puyuhuapi, a track pulls off the road to the **Conaf** *guardería* of Sector Angostura (daily 24hr; free), on the shores of the long, thin **Lago Risopatrón**. The lake, flanked by steep mountains jutting abruptly out of its deep-blue waters, is a lovely spot, and the **camping** area (CH$7000 per site) near the Conaf hut is one of the prettiest along the entire road.

By far the most popular sight, and the only port of call for the majority of the park's visitors, is the incredible **Ventisquero Colgante**, or "hanging glacier", 36km south of Puyuhuapi. Wedged between two peaks, forming a V-shaped mass of blue-white ice, the glacier indeed seems to hang suspended over a sheer rock face. Long fingers of ice feed two thundering waterfalls that plummet 150m down to Laguna Los Témpanos, below. Adding to the spectacle, large blocks of ice periodically calve off the glacier and crash down the rocks to the lake. The easiest way to get a look at the glacier is from the **viewpoint** at the end of a signed two-kilometre road branching off the Carretera Austral, about 24km south of Puyuhuapi; Conaf charges a CH$1500 fee to visit this sector of the park (daily: April–Nov 8.30am–5.30pm; Dec–March 8.30am–9pm), which you pay at the hut en route to the parking area adjacent to a rather rundown **information centre**, with faded photographs of the decline of the glacier. From the parking area, follow the signposted trail 250m to the viewpoint. Beneath the hanging glacier is the **Laguna Los Témpanos**, literally "Iceberg Lagoon" – referring to the large icebergs that floated on its surface until as recently as twenty years ago. Today, however, the Ventisquero Colgante has retreated too far to discharge icebergs, and the lake's emerald waters are covered with just a few bobbing blocks of ice. The lake is not visible from the viewpoint but if you cross the suspension bridge over the river and turn right, a 600-metre trail leads to the Laguna Los Témpanos through dense native forest, from where you get excellent views of the glacier. If you turn left from the bridge, a path climbs 3.3km to a higher viewpoint. A couple of more demanding **trails** through this sector are described in the box, opposite – you can get further information from the Conaf hut or the adjacent wardens' houses. There's also a **camping** area (CH$7000 per site) by the river, on a fairly hard ground with toilets and cold showers.

Continuing along the Carretera Austral, some 20km south of the Ventisquero Colgante, you pass another short, easy footpath (signed Sendero Padre

There are no long-distance **hikes** in the park, and no possibility of getting off the trails, due to the density of the forest. That said, the day- or half-day hikes listed below are among the finest in Chile, taking you through pristine, seldom-visited wilderness and rewarding you with superb views. The best times to hike here are from mid-November to February to see the forests carpeted with wild flowers, or in late-March to early-May, when the leaves of the ñire and lenga trees turn bright red and orange.

Sendero Laguna Los Pumos Starting at the *guardería* by Lago Risopatrón, this seven-kilometre trail (one-way) starts with a steep ascent, climbing from just above sea level to 1100m. From the plateau at the top, you get sweeping views onto surrounding mountains and out to the fjord. The trail then descends through a pass, leading to the shimmering Laguna Los Pumos, bordered by a sandy beach. Allow around 3hr up and 2hr down.

Sendero Río Cascada An easy but exhilarating hike, branching off from the Carretera Austral on the southern edge of the park, just beyond the Portezuelo de Queulat (look out for the sign on the right-hand side of the road as you travel south). The trail leads 1.7km through ancient trees covered in moss and threads of lichen, and ends at the Río Cascadas. From here, follow the river up the hill for another 800m, and you'll arrive at its source – a jade-green lake at the foot of a granite cliff, topped by a glacier and streaked by waterfalls. It takes around 1hr 30min to 2hr to get up, a little less to get back.

Sendero Río Ventisquero Starting close to the car park in Sector Ventisquero, this six-kilometre trail follows the southern bank of the Río Ventisquero Valley, first climbing steeply through woods, then flattening out over open land, close to the river. The views over the valley are magnificent, and you see several glaciers along the way (though *not* the Ventisquero Colgante). It's currently about a 5–6hr round trip, though Conaf has longstanding plans to extend the trail for a further 12km, leading to the foot of a glacier – check how far they've got before you set off.

García) leading 200m down to a viewpoint over the **Saltos Padre García**, a powerful waterfall dropping 30m into the Río Queulat. It's named after the Jesuit priest who, in 1766, was the first Spaniard to explore the Queulat river, while searching for the mythical "City of the Caesars" (a Chilean El Dorado) after hearing what he thought were church bells ringing from within the forest. Just beyond, the road narrows and starts zigzagging up the steep **Cuesta de Queulat**, through sheer-sided mountains crowned with glaciers. At the top, as you drive through the pass (known as the Portezuelo de Queulat), you're met with a fabulous view onto a massive glacier, directly ahead. Five kilometres beyond, as the road heads down again, you get a glimpse of another mighty waterfall, 40-metre-high **Saltos del Cóndor**, which you can make out through the forest on your right. Just beyond is the southern boundary of the park.

Puerto Cisnes

A small fishing village in a dramatic setting near the entrance to the Puyuhuapi fjord, **PUERTO CISNES** sits at the end of a 35-kilometre side road that branches west from the Carretera Austral, just beyond the southern limit of Parque Nacional Queulat. Colourful fishing boats line the beach in front of higgledy-piggledy wooden houses that seem to fight for a foothold on the tiny patch of land, overshadowed by brooding, vertical mountains. Though there's

△ Hiking in Parque Nacional Queulat

little actually to *do* in Puerto Cisnes, it's worth making this detour if only to witness the incredible feats of engineering it took to build and widen the road, blasted out of a cliff along the edge of the fjord.

Puerto Cisnes began life as a solitary sawmill, set up by a German pioneer in 1929. A few other settlers followed, and eventually a small community sprang up. The most influential player in Puerto Cisnes' fortunes was Eugenia Pircio-Biroli, a remarkable Italian woman who arrived in 1957 and devoted all her energies to improving conditions in the village. While construction of the Carretera Austral was underway, there were no plans to connect it to Puerto Cisnes – so the feisty Doña Eugenia, who by that time had been elected mayor, decamped to Santiago and so persistently and successfully pestered General Pinochet to give her village road access that she became a household name throughout the country.

Accommodation in the village is quite expensive for what you get, though you should be able to haggle prices down outside January and February. *Hospedaje Bellavista*, Séptimo de Línea 112 (☎67/346408; ❸) offers snug rooms. *Hostal Michay*, Gabriela Mistral 112 (☎67/346462; ❹), is an attractive old *casa de familia* with comfortable rooms and excellent breakfasts, while *Hostería Gaucho*, perched on the edge of a stream at Holmberg 140 (☎67/346514; ❸), has more facilities, with a restaurant and bar. *Cabañas Manzur*, by the entrance to the village at Ethel Dunn 75 (☎67/346453; ❺) features a few modern self-catering *cabañas* with a view across the Puyuhuapi fjord; backpackers are welcome to camp in the garden for around CH$5000 per tent. As for **eating**, besides the *Hostería Gaucho*'s simple but wholesome restaurant, try the decent meat and seafood dishes at *El Guairao*, near the bridge at Piloto Pardo 58, the tasty snacks at *Pub K-Co's* at 21 de Mayo 25 and the small fishermen's bars along the road by the sea. Sample the local speciality of *puyes*, similar to whitebait and absolutely delicious.

Puerto Aisén, Puerto Chacabuco and the Laguna San Rafael glacier

Heading south once again, the Carretera Austral follows the Río Cisnes along the foot of a massive granite outcrop known as the **Piedra del Gato**, where several simple crosses honour the workmen killed while blasting through the rock. Some 25km on from here, you pass **Villa Amengual**, another of Pinochet's tin towns, and, a few kilometres beyond, pretty **Lago Las Torres**, backed by craggy, pyramidal mountains. Gradually, the dense forest is replaced by rolling farmland and wide-open pastures, cleared by settlers in the 1940s. Their main clearance method was fire, which frequently got out of control and whose legacy can be seen in the hundreds of burned-out black and silver tree stumps that poke out of the hillsides. Just over 100km south of the turn-off to Puerto Cisnes, you reach a fork in the road: to the left, it leads to the regional capital of **Coyhaique**, while to the right, a paved section of the Carretera Austral heads west to the small town of **Puerto Aisén**, providing an oasis of tarmac after hours of constant jolting along the dirt highway. From Puerto Aisén, more paved roads link up with Coyhaique, and with the port and ferry terminal at **Puerto Chacabuco**, the departure point for day-cruises to the **Laguna San Rafael glacier**.

Puerto Aisén

Founded in 1914 as a port for shipping out cattle, **PUERTO AISÉN** literally became a backwater when its harbour silted up, forcing commercial vessels to use nearby Puerto Chacabuco from 1960. Most of its shops, houses and residents stayed put, however, and Puerto Aisén is still an important service centre and residential nucleus, with a long main street lined with supermarkets, bars and restaurants. The town serves as a useful overnight base before or after a journey to the San Rafael glacier. You can stock up on supplies here; you'll find reliable **ATMs** at the banks on the plaza; and **LAN** has an office at Sargento Aldea 1141.

The town itself has few sights, but *Turismo Rucaray*, an efficient travel agency on the plaza at Teniente Merino 668 (℡67/332862, ℻67/332725, ✉rucary@entelchile.net) offers a range of **fishing excursions** to the surrounding lakes, and can book cruise or ferry tickets for the Laguna San Rafael glacier – and possibly a wonderful boat ride down the narrow and spectacular **Aisén fjord**, taking in the natural hot springs of the **Termas del Chilconal**, about two hours downstream. You can also drive up the twelve-kilometre gravel road north of town to **Lago Los Palos** – a small, glass-like lake set in a wide valley. For other suggestions or more information, visit the **Oficina de Turismo** at the back of the Municipalidad, on the tree-lined plaza (daily in summer, 10.30am–9.30pm).

Practicalities

Residencial Serrano Montaner, Serrano Montaner 471 (℡67/332574; ❸), offers simple, clean **rooms** with shared bath. The agreeable *Hospedaje San Jorge*, Ramírez and Serrano Montaner (℡67/333587; ❸), also serves an inexpensive lunch and dinner. Modern *Hotel Caicahues*, Michimalonco 660 (℡67/336326, ✉caicahue@patagoniachile.cl; ❺), has en-suite rooms, a restaurant and a bar. *Hospedaje Marclara*, Caupolicán and Carrera (℡67/333030; ❺), offers respectable rooms at the top of a tight flight of stairs while the fractionally cheaper

Hotel Roxy at Sargento Aldea 550 (℗67/332704; ❹) is comfortable enough but rather bland.

The top spot for **eating** in town is the popular *Isla Verde*, Teniente Merino 710, specializing in fish and seafood. The busy *Restaurante El Muelle*, Eleuterio Ramírez 353, serves fresh fish dishes. You'll find sandwiches, pizzas and other snacks at many cafés that line the main street, Sargento Aldea, including *Café Entre Amigos* at no. 1077, *Dina's* at no. 382 and no. 1120, and *Rincón Chilote* at no. 353. Enjoy an evening drink at the cheerful *Eko Pub*, Teniente Merino 998. **Buses** for neighbouring Puerto Chacabuco leave every ten minutes from all along Sargento Aldea, and for Coyhaique every hour from no. 1090 of the same street.

Puerto Chacabuco

Fifteen kilometres west of Puerto Aisén, the busy port of **PUERTO CHACABUCO** sits dramatically on a natural harbour enclosed by craggy, jagged peaks brushed with snow. Scanning this panorama, it's almost impossible to distinguish any outlet to the sea, so you might think you were standing before a lake. Turn away from the ocean and you're greeted with a very different sight: rows of ugly fish processing factories stagger down the road to the shore, and the jetty is flanked by large, grim-looking warehouses often emitting a nauseating smell of fish. All in all, you won't want to linger for long.

It is, however, the embarkation point for day-trips to one of the most spectacular sights in Chile, the **Laguna San Rafael glacier** (see opposite). As the boats set out early in the morning, and get back late, you might want to spend a night here before and after the trip, although the more appealing Puerto Aisén lies only a short distance away. If you do happen to stay, the few sights around are associated with the *Hotel Loberías de Aisén* (see opposite), notably the **Parque Aiken del Sur** (ⓦwww.parqueaikendelsur.cl), an unspoilt area of woodland, meadows and marsh taking in a chunk of **Lago Riesgo**, just off the road between Puerto Chacabuco and Puerto Aisén, only 10km from the former. The informative **visitor centre** features interactive exhibitions on the region's flora, fauna and anthropology. It also has information on three interpretative nature **trails** that take you through varying landscapes up to panoramic views or to the **Barba del Viejo waterfalls**. The shortest is 600m (about an hour) and the longest covers just over 2km (three hours of gentle walking). Bilingual guides are available to help you navigate these trails if you wish. You can also go kayaking in the park's rivers and even plant a tree or a shrub. An **arboretum** preserves 32 species of native trees while at the *quincho*, a traditional dining area set around a giant fireplace, you can enjoy barbecued lamb after a pisco sour.

Puerto Chacabuco also serves as the terminal for ferries to and from Puerto Montt and Quellón, operated by TransMarChilay (℗ & ℗67/351144) whose office is on the road down to the ferry ramp, and Navimag (see p.472). If you've just disembarked from one of these ferries, you'll probably want to head out of town immediately – the ferries are usually met by minibuses to Puerto Aisén, from where you can catch buses to Coyhaique (with Buses Don Carlos, Sargento Aldea 1090; ℗67/332918).

Practicalities

A cluster of basic *residenciales* has sprung up on the road down towards the ferry terminal, opposite the blue-and-white Pesca Chile warehouse: *Residencial Moraleda*, O'Higgins 82 (℗67/351155; ❸), is the best of a motley bunch, with neat, spartan **rooms**, whitewashed wooden walls, decent showers and a

restaurant downstairs. The *Ofqui* (☎67/351150; ❸), just round the corner, has a cosy dining room with a huge open fire, but many of its rooms are in the dark, cramped basement. Both of these places lie a two-minute walk from the ferry ramp. Up on the hill, a ten-minute walk away at José Miguel Carrera 50, sits the far more attractive, and expensive, *Hotel Loberías de Aisén* (☎ & ⓕ67/351115, ⓦwww.hoteloberiasdelsur.cl; ❼), with beautifully renovated, tastefully furnished, en-suite rooms, a gym, a sauna and a renowned fish restaurant. The more basic, cheaper *Hostal La Estrella* (☎67/351127; ❸) lies a little further on at José Miguel Carrera 412.

San Rafael glacier

From Puerto Chacabuco, a 200-kilometre boat ride through the labyrinthine fjords of Aisén brings you to the dazzling **San Rafael glacier**, spilling into the broad Laguna San Rafael (you can fly, too, but travelling by water is far preferable; for details on how to visit the glacier, see box, p.472). The journey – four to sixteen hours, depending on type of craft – is a spectacle in itself, as boats edge their way through narrow channels hemmed in by precipitous cliffs dripping with vegetation. You get little sense of entering the Pacific, as the chain of islands that form the Chonos archipelago blends into one seething mass of mottled green, creating a natural barrier between the mainland and the open sea. After sailing down the long, thin Golfo de Elefantes, the boat enters the seemingly unnavigable Río Témpanos, or "Iceberg River", before emerging into the Laguna San Rafael. Floating in the lagoon are dozens of **icebergs**, fashioned by wind and rain into monumental Henry Moore-style sculptures, holes and all, with such a vibrant electric-blue colour that they appear to be lit from within. Their precarious balance is upset by the gentlest of wakes from a passing boat, whereupon, brought suddenly to life, they bob up and down in the water before finding a new equilibrium.

Sailing around these icy phantoms, you approach the giant **glacier** at the far end of the lagoon. Over 4km wide, and rearing out of the water to a height of 70m, it really is a dizzying sight. While the cruise boat keeps at a safe distance, to avoid being trapped by icebergs, you'll probably be given the chance to get a closer look on board an inflatable motor dinghy – but not too close, as the huge blocks of ice that, with a deafening roar, calve off into the water create dangerous, crashing waves. What you can see from the boat is in fact just the tip of the glacier's "tongue", which extends some 15km from its source. If you look at the rocks that encircle the lagoon, either side of this tongue, you'll see a series of white markers, painted by scientists since the 1980s to monitor the position of the glacier's edge. It is, unmistakeably, retreating fast, frequently by as much as 100m a year. Early explorers reported that, in 1800, the glacier filled three-quarters of the lagoon, and archive photographs from the beginning of the twentieth century show it as being far longer than it is today. It is estimated that by the year 2030, the glacier will be gone.

Stretching beyond the shores of the lagoon are the 4.2 million acres of land that make up **Parque Nacional Laguna San Rafael**, of which the eponymous laguna forms just a tiny fraction. Almost half this vast area is covered by the immense icefield known as the **Campo de Hielo Norte**; it feeds eighteen other glaciers on top of this one and contains over 250 lakes and lagoons. The 4058-metre **Monte San Valentín**, the highest peak in the southern Andes, towers over the frozen plateau. The Laguna San Rafael is the only accessible part of the park, though – to Conaf's continual frustration – the thousands of tourists who visit the glacier each summer by boat are exempt from the CH$3000 entrance fee, payable only if you land. A mere 500 or so per year do so, most of them on the light aeroplanes that fly tourists over the glacier and touch down for a couple of hours. A longer stay at the park is very difficult to arrange; for those who manage to, Conaf offers accommodation in a *refugio* with hot water and electricity (CH$60,000 for six people) or you can camp for CH$2000 per

Visiting the San Rafael glacier

The glacier is accessible *only* by boat or plane. **Flights** from Coyhaique in five-seater planes are offered by three companies (see below), last ninety minutes each way and cost CH$100,000–120,000 per person – usually requiring a full plane. Flying over the icefield is indeed an unforgettable experience, but the most sensational views of the glacier are from the small **dinghies** that thread through the icebergs towards its base, usually included as part of a visit to the laguna **by sea**. Scheduled departures leave from Puerto Chacabuco and Puerto Montt (via Puerto Chacabuco) throughout the warmer months. Cruises in slow **ships** from Puerto Montt and Puerto Chacabuco (from where San Rafael is a sixteen-hour voyage) require between one and five nights aboard and cost between CH$120,000 and CH$480,000 per person. These are run by **Navimag**, **TransMarChilay** and the far more luxurious **Skorpios** (see below).

Several companies, including Aysén Express (see below), now compete with modern **catamarans** out of Puerto Chacabuco (four or five hours each way). These day trips cost around CH$150,000 per person but include three meals and operate an open bar – it is now a tradition to drink a whisky or cocktail containing "thousand-year-old ice cubes" chipped from an iceberg. You usually get a couple of hours or more at the glacier, with passengers taking it in turns to get a close-up view in a zodiac. Some only operate in January and February, others run from September to March.

Catamarans

Aysén Express Santa Magdalena 75, Oficina 212, Providencia, Santiago ☏2/3350579, ⓦwww.aysenexpress.cl; O'Higgins 167, oficina 307, Puerto Montt ☏65/437599.

Catamaranes del Sur Isidora Goyenechea 3250, Oficina 802, Santiago ☏2/3337127, Ⓕance2/2329736, ⓦwww.catamaranesdelsur.cl; Av Diego Portales 510, Puerto Montt ☏65/267533.

Patagonia Connection Fidel Oteiza 1921, Oficina 1006, Santiago ☏2/2256489, Ⓕ2/2748111, ⓦwww.patagoniaconnex.cl. These excursions may be combined with a stay at the *Termas de Puyuhuapi* (see p.463) on multiple-day packages.

Cruise ships and ferries

Navimag (ferries) Av El Bosque Norte 0440, Santiago ☏2/2035030, Ⓕ2/2035025, ⓦwww.australis.com; Angelmó 2187, Puerto Montt ☏65/253318, Ⓕ65/258540.

Skorpios (cruise ships) Agusto Leguia Norte 118, Las Condes, Santiago ☏2/2311030, Ⓕ2/232 2269, Ⓔskorpios@tmm.cl; Angelmó 1660, Puerto Montt ☏65/256619, Ⓕ65/258315, ⓦwww.skorpios.cl. Cruise ships.

TransMarChilay (ferries) Av Providencia 2653, local 24, Santiago ☏ & Ⓕ2/633 5959; Angelmó 2187, Puerto Montt ☏65/270416, Ⓕ65/270415, ⓦwww.transmarchilay.cl; O'Higgins s/n, Puerto Chacabuco ☏ & Ⓕ67/351144.

Flight agents

Aero Don Carlos Subteniente Cruz 630 ☏67/232981, ⓦwww.doncarlos.cl.

Aerohein Baquedano 500, Coyhaique ☏ & Ⓕ67/232772, ⓦwww.aerohein.cl.

Transportes San Rafael 18 de Septiembre 469, Coyhaique 233408 ☏67/232048, Ⓕ67/233408.

person. The Conaf *guardería* is close to the glacier, by the shores of the laguna. From here, a seven-kilometre trail leads to a breathtaking viewpoint over the sprawling, icy tongue, taking around two hours up and slightly less coming down – too long to fit in if you only have a couple of hours between plane rides.

Coyhaique and around

From Puerto Chacabuco, a paved section of the Carretera heads 15km east to Puerto Aisén, continuing 67km to the city of **Coyhaique**. The scenic route holds fast to the Río Simpson as it rushes through the **Reserva Nacional Río Simpson**, sandwiched between tall, craggy cliffs. Thirty-two kilometres out of Puerto Aisén, a small wooden sign by the road (labeled "Museo") points to the reserve's administration office and attached **museum** (daily: April–Nov 8.30am–5.30pm, Dec–March 8.30am–9pm; CH$500) on local flora and fauna, of which the best exhibit is the huge stump of a 400-year-old lenga tree in the garden. The reserve's main attractions are conveniently located right by the road: 1km on from the museum, you'll pass the **Cascada de la Virgen**, a tall, graceful waterfall that drops in two stages, separated by a pool of water; a further 8km east thunders another waterfall, the **Velo de la Novia**, or "bride's veil", so named for its diaphanous spray. Shortly after, the road leaves the Río Simpson and turns south, giving sweeping panoramic views onto Coyhaique, sitting in a wide, golden valley at the foot of the towering basalt bluff known as Cerro McKay.

ACCOMMODATION
La Estancia   J
HI Albergue Las
  Salamandras   L
Hospedaje Lautaro   M
Hostal Bon   H
Hostería Coyhaique   D
Hotel Araucaria   G
Hotel Libanés   N
Hotel Los Ñires   B
Hotel Luis Loyola   K
Patagonia Hotel   C
El Reloj   E
Residencial Lo de Rocco   F
Residencial Puerto Varas   I
Sra Herminia Mansilla   A

COYHAIQUE

Museo Regional
de la Patagonia

Monumento
al Ovejero

Feria de Artesanos

Galería
Artesanal

Bus
Terminal

Piedra
del Indio

N

(1km)

0   200 m

EATING & DRINKING
Bar West   10
Café Oriente   4
Café Peña Quilantal   8
Cafetería Alemana   3
Casino de Bomberos   2
La Cassona   7
Entre Amigos Restaurant   C
Express   12
La Fiorentina   9
La Olla   5
Pub Zeta   1
El Reloj   6
Ricer   11

Coyhaique

After the smattering of half-dead villages scattered down the Carretera Austral, Aisén's thriving regional capital, **COYHAIQUE**, comes as a bit of a shock, with its smart boutiques, lively cafés and streets packed with traffic and pedestrians. The city's forty-five thousand inhabitants make up half the region's population, and it's the only place along the Carretera that offers a wide range of services, from pharmacies and banks to laundries and car-rental outlets. Although resolutely urban, it's also a good launch pad for some great **day-trips** that will give you a taste of the region's wilderness – for more details see p.476.

Arrival and information

Most **buses** pull in at the centrally located terminal on the corner of Lautaro and Magallanes, though a few arrive at and depart from their respective company offices, separate from the terminal. Coyhaique's nearest airport is Aerodromo Teniente Vidal, 5km west of town, but it's a small affair, used only by local small-plane companies flying in from regional aerodromes. All LAN flights land at the **Aeropuerto de Balmaceda**, 55km south, and are met by **minibuses** that take passengers to their hotels for around CH$2500.

You can pick up information on the city and the region at the very helpful **Sernatur** office, at Bulnes 35 (Mon–Fri 8.30am–5.30pm; ☎67/231752, ⓕ67/233949, ⓔinfoaisen@sernatur.cl), which produces printed lists of Coyhaique's accommodation (with prices), restaurants, transport facilities and tour operators. During summer you'll also find an **information** kiosk on the plaza. For more on Aisén's national parks and reserves, visit **Conaf**'s Oficina Patrimonio Silvestre at 12 de Octobre 382 (Mon–Fri 8.30am–noon & 3–5.30pm; ☎67/231065).

Accommodation

Coyhaique offers a wide choice of **places to stay**, from simple *hospedajes* to upmarket hotels. Prices are very reasonable at the lower end of the scale, but many mid- and upper-range hotels are decidedly overpriced. You can **camp** at *Camping Alborado*, 1km out of town on the road to Puerto Aisén, which has clean, sheltered sites (CH$5000 per site); at *Ogana*, on Avenida Ogana, Pasaje 8, set in a small orchard with a hut for cooking and hot showers (CH$2500 per person); and at *HI Albergue Las Salamandras* (listed below; CH$5000 per site). You'll also find camping facilities in Reserva Nacional Coyhaique.

La Estancia Colón 166 ☎67/250193, ⓔcabanaslaestancia@latinmail.com. This tiny house has three simple, tidy rooms, one with private bath. ❹

HI Albergue Las Salamandras Carretera Teniente Vidal, km 1.5 ☎ & ⓕ67/211865, ⓔsalamandras _cl@yahoo.com, ⓦwww.salamandras.cl. Set in a wood by a river 1.5km along the road to Teniente Vidal, this popular Spanish-run hostel offers the use of a kitchen, laundry facilities, mountain-bike rental and a range of excursions, including cross-country skiing during Coyhaique's long winter. ❸

Hospedaje Lautaro Lautaro 269 ☎ & ⓕ67/238116. An attractive old house in a quiet garden with single, double and triple rooms and a bunk dormitory. The helpful owners have their own minibus and organize local tours, including horse-trekking. ❸

Hostal Araucaria Vielmo 71 ☎67/232707. Quiet hostel, on the western edge of town, with good-sized rooms, some with superb views of the valley. The friendly owners also organize car hire. ❹

Hostal Bon Serrano 91 ☎ & ⓕ67/231189. Small hotel with thin partition walls and a mixture of shared baths and en-suite rooms; a few are a little cramped. It's a friendly place, though, with a good restaurant that specializes in hearty *parrilladas*. ❹

Hostería Coyhaique Magallanes 131 ☎67/231137, ⓔhotelsa@ctcinternet.cl. Imposing gates give way to ample gardens and a relatively low-key four-star hotel with modern amenities; it's favoured by large tour groups. **❼**

Hotel Libanés Simpson 367 ☎67/256262, ✉hlibanes@entelchile,net. Soulless newer hotel with bland but functional accommodation and a cafe-bar. **❺**

Hotel Luís Loyola Prat 455 ☎ & ℻67/234200. A modern hotel with eighteen en-suite rooms, all with cable TV and central heating. Probably the best choice in this price range. **❺**

Hotel Los Ñires Baquedano 315 ☎67/232261, ℻67/233372, ✉info@doncarlos.cl. One of the older hotels in town but a slightly dreary atmosphere and a large, good restaurant. **❻**

Patagonia Hotel General Para 551 ☎67/254960, ℻67/254962, ✉reservas@patagoniahotel.cl, ⊛www.patagoniahotel.cl. A modern establishment with well-furnished rooms and a good restaurant (see p.476). **❻**

El Reloj Baquedano 828 ☎ & ℻67/231108, ✉htlelreloj@patagoniachile.com. Better than ever in its new location (a tastefully converted lumberyard), El Reloj is spotlessly clean with comfortable en-suite rooms and Coyhaique's best restaurant (see p.476). **❼**

Residencial Lo de Rocco 21 de Mayo 668 ☎67/231285. A *casa familiar* with neat, basic rooms and comfortable beds; note that the upstairs rooms are inconveniently separated from the bathroom by a steep wooden staircase. **❸**

Residencial Puerto Varas Serrano 168 ☎67/233689, ℻67/235931. Clean, well-maintained *residencial* with spacious doubles and a few tiny singles, mostly with shared bath. The front en-suite room is a great deal if you want a private bathroom and don't mind not having any added frills. **❹**

Sra Herminia Mansilla 21 de Mayo 60 ☎67/231579. Neat and tidy *casa familiar*, slightly out of the centre, with light, airy rooms and a friendly owner who is very proud of the long list of foreign visitors in her guestbook. **❷**

The Town

After the rigid grid layout of most Chilean towns and cities, Coyhaique's infuriatingly irregular street plan tends to throw most visitors, who can be spotted wandering around, map in hand, hopelessly lost. At its centre – and to blame for the chaos – sprawls the large, five-sided **Plaza de Armas**, purportedly inspired by Paris' twelve-sided Place de l'Etoile, and from which the main streets radiate. Depending on the weather, the plaza's densely planted trees provide shade or shelter. On the southwest corner with Horn, the small **Feria de Artesanos** sells jewellery and leather goods, while just across the plaza on the corner with Montt, the **Galería Artesanal de Cema Chile** features a wide range of handicrafts, including knitwear, weavings, wooden carvings and ceramics.

Continue up Montt, walking away from the plaza, and you'll come to Baquedano, the city's main thoroughfare. Immediately to your right stands one of Coyhaique's quirkiest landmarks, the **Monumento al Ovejero**, a large sculpture of a shepherd and a flock of sheep; if you go to Punta Arenas (see p.491) you'll see virtually the same monument in handsome bronze, whereas this one, covered in whitewash, looks as though all concerned were caught in a blizzard. Almost opposite the monument, within the chalet-like Casa de Cultura, stands the **Museo Regional de la Patagonia** (Jan & Feb daily 9am–8pm; March–Dec Mon–Fri 9am–6pm; CH$400), where an informative collection of black-and-white photographs vividly captures the "Wild West" frontier atmosphere during the opening up of Aisén at the turn of the century. Other exhibits include archeological finds that prove that the Tehuelche people once roamed this far north, while Chonos fishing groups inhabited the coastal islands and channels. Finally, you can head on a half-hour walk out to the **Piedra del Indio**, a large rock outcrop weathered into the form of a profile – popularly believed to be that of a former Tehuelche chieftain. It sits next to the bridge over the Río Simpson, reached by following Avenida Simpson south out of town.

Eating and drinking

Although Coyhaique's **restaurants** are, on the whole, no more adventurous than those in most other Chilean cities, they're a real treat after the limited

Tours from Coyhaique

Adventure tour companies come and go quite frequently in Coyhaique – check with **Sernatur**, as they know which are good and what each offers. You can expect to pay around CH$20,000 for a day excursion, around CH$85,000 for two days and CH$200,000 for five-day trips. Andes Patagónicos, Horn 48 (T67/216711, ⓔap@patagoniachile.cl, ⓦwww.ap.cl), is a good bet for arranging half-day and full-day **tours** to the nearby **lakes** (see p.478), to see local **rock art** and to **Reserva Nacional Cerro Castillo** (see p.479), among other destinations. They also rent ski gear and organize shuttles to the Cerro El Fraile slopes, 29km south of the town. Aisén Tour, at Parra 97 (T67/237070), Geoturismo Patagonia, Eusébio Lillo 315 (T67/237456 & 67/238406, ⓦwww.geoturismopatagonia.cl) and Turaustralis, Moraleda 589 (T67/239696), offer similar trips at comparable prices. Aventura Turismo, 21 de Mayo 477 (T & F 67/234748), concentrates on places south along the Carretera Austral, including the marble caves at **Puerto Tranquilo** (see p.482) and five-day excursions to the **Campo de Hielo Norte** (see p.471).

Several operators are particularly strong on **fishing** excursions, including Expediciones Coyhaique, Portales 195 (T & F67/232300), Patagonia Tours, Colón 203 (T & F67/232522), and Patagonia Guias, Moraleda 540 (T67/670082, ⓦwww.patagoniaguias.cl); for more on fishing in the region, see p.464. If you're interested in **horse-trekking**, try 45° Latitud Sur Expediciones, Barroso 626 (T67/238036, F67/235294). A good choice for guided **mountaineering** in the region is Cochrane Patagonia at Teniente Merino 750 (T & F67/522197). Alternatively, try Espacio Vertical at Serrano 23 (T & F67/235836, ⓦwww.ze.cl/espaciovertical.html). For **kayaking** or **whitewater rafting** on the Río Simpson, Río Paloma or Río Mañihuales approach Patagonia Adventure Expeditions at Dussen 357 (T & F67/219894, ⓦwww.patagoniachile.com).

choice along the rest of the Carretera Austral. As for **drinking** and **nightlife**, you'll find several pub-discos to choose from, of which *Pub Zeta*, at Morelada 420, is probably the best. Or try the popular drinking hole *Bar West* at Bilbao 110, done up like a Wild West saloon. If you're after something more authentic, check out *Café Peña Quilantal* at Baquedano 791, for live *música folklórica* and *boleros*. Nightlife is quiet everywhere through the week, and at the weekend doesn't warm up until after midnight.

Café Alemana Condell 119. With its scrubbed pine tables and floral furnishings, this is an attractive place for a snack, though there's nothing remotely German about the menu, which offers the usual *lomos*, pizzas and sandwiches – plus above-average pancakes and home-made ice creams.

Café Oriente Condell 201. This small, basic café serves up reasonable snacks and sandwiches as well as *küchen*.

Casino de Bomberos General Parra 365. Slightly hidden away, Coyhaique's firemen's canteen - packed and lively - is one of the best places in town for lunch, with excellent-value set meals.

Entre Amigos Restaurant *Patagonia Hotel*, General Parra 551. This reasonably priced, formal restaurant, serves a large selection of vegetarian dishes.

La Cassona Vielmo 77. Come to this upmarket spot for both Chilean staples and more elaborate

meals; the fixed-price lunch is good value.

La Fiorentina Prat 230. Reliable Italian food – mostly pasta and pizza – served in pleasant surroundings makes this one of the most popular eateries in town.

Expresss Prat 402. Bustling with locals, particularly at lunch time when they flock here for the cheap set meals.

La Olla Prat 176 T67/234700. Run by a charming man from Extremadura, this cosy, old-fashioned restaurant does excellent paellas every Sunday (and through the week if you phone in advance) and first-class *estofado de cordero* (lamb stew) all at reasonable prices.

El Reloj Baquedano 828. Some of the tastiest (but pricey) food in town, such as lamb with rosemary, is served in this sophisticated dining room tended by the friendly hoteliers.

Ricer Horn 48. Just off the plaza, this bright and cheerful café attracts a lot of gringos, partly for its vegetarian dishes. There's a more upscale restaurant upstairs, decorated with evocative photographs of the early pioneers, and knick-knacks from the early 1900s.

Listings

Airlines Aero Don Carlos, Subteniente Cruz 63 ☎67/231981, ⓦwww.doncarlos.cl; Aerohein, Baquedano 500 ☎67/232772, ⓦwww.aerohein.cl; LAN, General Parra 402 ☎67/231188, ⓕ67/232197; SKY, Prat 203, at Dussen ☎67/240825.

Banks and exchange Banco Santander has an ATM at Condell 184, and there are several *cambios*, including Cambio Mendoza at Condell 140; Emperador at Bilbao 222; Lucia Saldivia at Condell 140; and Turismo Prado at 21 de Mayo 417.

Bike rental Figon at Simpson 888 ☎67/234616. Bike repairs at Bilbao 500 and Simpson 231.

Car rental AGS, Av Ogana 1298 ☎67/235354, ⓕ67/231511; Aisén, Bilbao 926 ☎67/231532; Andes Patagónicos, Horn 48 ☎67/216711, ⓕ67/216712; Automóvil Club de Chile, Bolívar 194 ☎ & ⓕ67/231649; Automundo, Bilbao 510 ☎67/231621, ⓕ67/231794; Budget, Errázuriz 454 ☎67/255171, ⓕ67/255172; Traeger-Hertz, Baquedano 457 ☎67/231648, ⓕ67/231946.

Ferry Aysén Express, who operate catamarans to Chacabuco and the San Rafael glacier, is at 149 Condell St ☎67/240956, ⓔviajes@aysenexpress.cl.

Hospital The regional hospital is on Calle Hospital 68 ☎67/233171.

Internet access *Ciber Patagonia*, at the corner of 21 de Mayo and Condell. Alternatively, try *Zona Sur* at Prat 347 or *Entel* immediately opposite.

Laundry All Clean is a reasonably priced laundromat at Parra 55. Alternatively, try Lavandería QL at Bilbao 160 or Lavamatic at Simpson 417.

Post Office Cochrane 202, near Plaza de Armas.

Outdoor equipment Patagonia Outdoors, at Horn 47, has a wide selection of camping and fishing gear, plus outdoor clothes.

Telephone centres There are *centro de llamados* at Horn 51, Parra 224 and Merino 848. Entel has a phone centre at Prat 340.

Around Coyhaique

You can do a number of rewarding day-trips from Coyhaique, dipping into Aisén's backcountry and getting back to a comfortable bed at night. The nearest target is **Reserva Nacional Coyhaique**, just north of the city, which has several good trails. To the south, side tracks lead both east and west off the paved road to a spread of lakes, of which **Lago Elizade** and **Lago Atravesado** are the most impressive. Slightly further afield, continuing south down the paved road, the **Reserva Nacional Cerro Castillo** encompasses the magnificent silhouette of its namesake mountain.

Reserva Nacional Coyhaique

Just 4km north of the city – about a 45-minute walk – the **RESERVA NACIONAL COYHAIQUE** (daily: April–Nov 8.30am–6.30pm, Dec–March 8.30am–9pm; CH$600), huddled at the foot of towering Cerro McKay is an easily accessible slice of wilderness, featuring areas of native forest, a couple of lakes and fantastic views down to the Coyhaique. Thanks partly to the efforts of locally based volunteers, a series of clear, well-maintained paths weaves through the reserve – they're displayed on a large map in the *guardería* by the entrance, alongside a scale model of the reserve. **Sendero Los Leñeros** leads almost 2km from the *guardería* through native lenga and ñire trees to a **camping** area (CH$3500 per site), from where the path continues for another 1.8km through pine trees to **Laguna Verde**, a small lake with a few picnic tables on its shore. From here, you pick up with a jeep track which, if you follow it north for a couple of hundred metres, will take you to the trailhead of **Sendero Las Piedras**, leading 13km up to and across a ridge, giving breathtaking views for miles around. This is by far the best

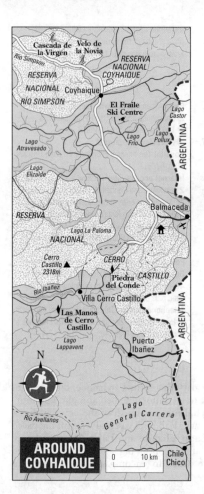

AROUND
COYHAIQUE

0   10 km

Chile
Chico

hike in the reserve, and, though steep in parts, isn't too difficult, taking roughly four hours to complete. After descending at the other end, a side path branches off to **Lago Venus**, an attractive lake 1km beyond, reached by walking through dense native forest. Alternatively, keep on going another couple of hundred metres and you'll join up with **Sendero El Chucao**, which leads 2.6km back to the *guardería*.

Lakes south of Coyhaique

South of Coyhaique, two separate round-trips of about 100km apiece take you through wild and totally contrasting scenery, via a series of picture-postcard lakes. Both boast superb fishing and great backdrops for a stroll, though there are no proper hiking trails. Note, too, that the roads are poor and almost totally unsigned, so take a good map if you'll be travelling in your own vehicle.

Heading southwest, if you cross the bridge out of town past the Piedra del Indio (see p.475) and keep going straight for 20km, you'll get to the remote and very beautiful **Lago Atravesado**, set among steeply forested hills whose deep-green shades are mirrored in the water. Double back on your tracks for 4km and take the first right turn to head through rolling farmland past the **Seis Lagunas** – a group of six little ponds, nestled in the fields. Carry on down the track and turn right for long, slender **Lago Elizalde**, spectacularly set amongst lush forest and mountains. From here, you can return to the paved road to Coyhaique via the rather rundown little village of **Villa Frei**.

The second route takes you through a very different landscape of flat Patagonian steppe, carpeted with golden *coirón* grass. Following the paved road south out of Coyhaique, the first left turn leads to little **Lago Frío**, tucked at the foot of the rustic El Fraile ski centre. A few kilometres further east is **Lago Pollux**, enclosed by dense reeds which provide a haven for nesting birds. Just beyond, **Lago Castor** stretches right to the Argentine border. From the lake's shore, the road turns north towards the international road to Argentina – take the left (west) turn to get back to Coyhaique.

Reserva Nacional Cerro Castillo

About an hour's drive south of Coyhaique, the Carretera Austral crosses the (unsigned) northern boundary of **RESERVA NACIONAL CERRO CASTILLO**. In stark contrast to the rich grazing land you've left behind, you're suddenly faced with a wild, windswept landscape. Spread out below you is a broad river valley flanked by densely forested lower slopes that rise to a breathtaking panorama of barren, rocky peaks. Dominating the skyline is the reserve's eponymous centrepiece, **Cerro Castillo**, whose needlepoint spires loom over the valley like the turrets of a Transylvanian castle. Further down the road, 64km from the city, you pass the *guardería* on your left (daily: April–Nov 8.30am–5.30pm, Dec–March 8.30am–9pm; CH$500), which has a basic **camping** area (CH$2500) with a covered grill for cooking. You can also pick up a map of the reserve here, showing the two **long-distance hiking trails** that branch off from the Carretera Austral.

The first, 36-kilometre **Sendero Río Blanco**, forks left (east) some 3km south of the *guardería*, and follows the Río Blanco up the fairly steep slopes of Cerro Pico Gancho, through forests of native lenga. It then loops back down, rejoining the Carretera Austral at the **Piedra del Conde**, a curious rock formation 16km from the *guardería*. This hike takes two days to complete. The second, more rewarding, route is the challenging three- to four-day **Sendero Valle La Lima**, which branches right (west) from the road 6km south of the *guardería*, and follows the Río La Lima towards the peak of Cerro Castillo. On the way, you pass the stunning **Laguna Cerro Castillo**, at the foot of a glacier suspended from the mountainside, before descending to the village of **Villa Cerro Castillo** (see p.481), where you can find comfortable accommodation and catch a bus back to Coyhaique. Note that both trails are very poorly marked, and not always easy to follow – you can get more detailed route advice from the *guardaparque*, who should be informed before you set off. You can get here on any of the **buses** from Coyhaique to Villa Cerro Castillo.

Across Lago General Carrera to Chile Chico

Just beyond the southern boundary of Reserva Nacional Cerro Castillo, a 31-kilometre side road shoots south from the Carretera Austral to the tiny village of **Puerto Ibáñez**, on the northern shore of **Lago General Carrera**. This

---

Ferries across Lago General Carrera

The **ferry** El Pilchero, operated by Sotramín, makes the crossing between Puerto Ibáñez and Chile Chico. Offices are in Coyhaique, at Baquedano 146A (℡67/233466 and 67/231255, ℻67/233367) and in Chile Chico (℡67/411864). The crossing takes 2hr 30min – be prepared for a rough ride as strong winds often whip up gigantic waves on this huge exposed lake – and costs CH$2100 for passengers, and CH$19,000 per vehicle. Ferries set off from Puerto Ibáñez at 9am on Monday, Wednesday, Thursday, Friday and Sunday and from Chile Chico at 4pm on the same days. Check these times well ahead because they are subject to change; reservations are a good idea as space is limited. When buying your ticket in Chile Chico you can also buy the onward minibus ticket to Coyhaique.

lake, encircled by rocky, sharp-peaked mountains, is the second largest in South America, and stretches east into Argentina, where it is known as Lago Buenos Aires. With its craggy, brush-covered shores, turquoise bays and balmy climate, comparisons with the Mediterranean are not out of place. Regular ferries connect Puerto Ibáñez with the small town of **Chile Chico**, on the opposite shore, making an attractive alternative to following the Carretera Austral around the lake. From Chile Chico, a 128-kilometre road skirts the lake's southern shore, joining the Carretera just beyond the village of Puerto Gaudal.

Puerto Ibáñez

Sitting in a green, fertile plain, divided up by rows of soldier-like poplars, in sharp contrast with the barren hills around it, **PUERTO IBÁÑEZ** is a shrinking and somewhat lifeless village, worth visiting only to catch the ferry across Lago General Carrera. Founded in 1908, it was once an important harbour for boats plying the lake with produce from the remote *estancias* at the eastern end, but it fell into decline when the construction of the Carretera Austral provided nearby villages with direct access to Coyhaique. These days it lives off agriculture, made possible by the warm microclimate that surrounds the entire lake. There's nothing much to do here, though you can check out the village's *artesanía* shops that offer a curious line in pottery clad in sheep and goat leather.

Puerto Ibáñez has several places to **stay**: at Bertrand Dickson 31, *Residencial Ibáñez* (☎67/423227; **②**) has simple but comfortable rooms looking out across the lake; at no. 282, *Residencial Vientos del Sur* (☎67/423208; **②**) is a clean, modern *casa familial*, offering decent set **meals**; María Turnena at no. 16 (☎67/423207; **②**) has five basic beds but no hot water; and *Cabañas Shehen Aike* at Risopatrón 55 (☎67/423284, ⓦwww.shehenaike.cl; **④**) offers a roomier alternative with better facilities. **Minibuses** travel from Coyhaique to Puerto Ibáñez; they leave from Calle Prat (opposite the shop Calaforte) or will collect passengers from their homes or hotels and get here in time for the ferry. Phone to book a place as far in advance as possible with Colectivos Sr Parra (☎67/251073) or Yamil Ali (☎67/250346).

Chile Chico

Sitting on the southern shore of Lago General Carrera, the small agricultural town of **CHILE CHICO** has a rather abandoned feel to it, an impression enhanced by the layer of ash deposited by the eruption of nearby Volcán Hudson in 1991 – ash that still fills the streets with grey clouds when the wind gets up (and it often does). The town was settled by farmers who crossed over from Argentina in 1909, causing a conflict known as the "Chile Chico war" when they refused to hand over land to the concessionaires given grants by the government. The new settlement depended entirely on Argentina until a road was built between Coyhaique and Puerto Ibáñez in 1952, after which Chile Chico's orchards became Coyhaique's main source of fresh fruit. While the fruit trees haven't really recovered from the volcanic eruption, the town's fortunes have been boosted slightly by the recent influx of mine workers and tourists.

You can pick up a town map at the **Oficina de Turismo** (Mon–Sat 10am–5pm; ☎67/411123) on main street O'Higgins, at the corner of Lautaro. Upstairs, a small **museum** (same hours) shows off a few Tehuelche artefacts and fossils of giant molluscs and other marine animals, including whales, reminders that thousands of years ago this area was covered by the sea. It is all exquisitely laid out but the exhibits range from the sublime to the ridiculous: alongside moving photographs of the after-effects of the volcanic explosion is a preserved beer bottle of the Araucana brand, a relic from the defunct neighbourhood brewery. Curiously the museum is joined by a footbridge to a disused British-built ferryboat, the *Andes*, that used to ply the lake until inclement conditions got the better of it. Another oddity, welcome in a town with so little to do, is the **fire station**, farther along the main drag, where an antiquated 1959 fire engine, proudly displayed, looks like something out of a Buster Keaton movie.

Practicalities

Accommodation includes a string of basic *hospedajes* and hotels on O'Higgins, the best of which are *Hospedaje Avenida* at no. 420 (no phone; ❷), *Hotel Turismo* at no. 750 (☎67/411031; ❸) and *Hotel Plaza* on the corner of O'Higgins and Balmaceda (☎67/411215; ❸). *Hotel Ventura*, Carrera 290 (☎67/411311; ❹), has compact, creaky rooms and a large communal area whilst *Residencial Don Luis* at Balmaceda 175 (☎67/411384; ❹) is clean and welcoming. Better though, is *Hostería de la Patagonia* at Chacra 3-A (☎ & ℻67/411337; ❹), a charming, old-fashioned house tucked away in a large garden on the eastern edge of town; opposite, *Casa Quinta No Me Olvides* (☎9/8338006; ❷) is popular with backpackers, with seven basic, good-value rooms and space to camp in the large orchard. Just off the main plaza, and much more central, at Rodríguez 252, is the comfortable *Residencial Aguas Azules* (☎67/411320; ❹), overlooking the lake.

Onward from Chile Chico

Moving on from Chile Chico, Transportes Ales, Rosa Amelia 820 (☎67/411739), operates a **bus** service west to the Carretera Austral and down to Cochrane (see p.483) on Tuesdays and Fridays; the road first follows a treacherously narrow corniche hugging the lake's southern shore, offering views across the blue and green water to the mountains on the other side. Acotrans at Prat 317 (☎67/411841) gets you to Los Antiguos across the Argentine border for CH$2000. Daily flights head to Coyhaique (CH$20,000) with Aero Don Carlos at O'Higgins 264 (☎67/231981).

If you've got your own transport, you can make a detour to the **Reserva Nacional Lago Jeinimeni** (daily: April–Nov 8.30am–6.30pm, Dec–March 8.30am–9pm; CH$800) before rejoining the Carretera Austral. Reached by a 60-kilometre rough road running parallel to the border with Argentina, the reserve is a wild, scarcely visited region of forests, glaciers and lakes, with a sizeable population of *huemul* (an endangered species of native deer). Its centrepiece is **Lago Jeinimeni**, a striking, indigo lake enclosed by thickly forested hills. You'll find a campsite (CH$2000) near the lake's outlet. Old farming trails to other lakes and small peaks are being upgraded for hikers and horse-riders.

Around Lago General Carrera

Crossing Lago General Carrera to Chile Chico is very scenic, but looping around the lake along the Carretera Austral offers equally spectacular, if not better, panoramas – in this case of the grey-and-pink mountains west of the road, plus a few glimpses of the Campo de Hielo Norte (northern icefield; see p.471). Nine kilometres on from the turn-off to Puerto Ibáñez, you pass **Villa Cerro Castillo**, a dreary, lifeless town whose sole draw is its dramatic views onto the jagged silhouette of Cerro Castillo (see p.479). You'll find a few grocery shops and **places to stay** here, including friendly *Residencial El Castillo* at O'Higgins 241 (no phone; **❷**) by the turn-off into town, run by a delightful woman offering wholesome home cooking. Just across the bridge outside the town, a signed two-kilometre track leads steeply uphill to **Las Manos de Cerro Castillo**, a dense collection of over 100 handprints, in three separate panels, at the foot of a sheer basalt rock face. The images, mostly negative prints against a red background, are thought to have been left by the Tehuelche people between 5000 and 8000 years ago. They're now preserved as a national monument; you don't have to pay a viewing fee, but most people leave a small donation with the guide in the wooden hut.

Farther along the Carretera Austral, the next sign of life – about 100km on from Villa Cerro Castillo – is the five-kilometre side road to **Puerto Murta**, a tiny cattle-farming community (and former logging centre) sitting on a long, thin arm of Lago General Carrera, with a couple of simple places to **stay** that share the public telephone (☎67/419600), including shoreside *Hostería General Carrera* at 5 de Abril 647 (**❸**), *Hospedaje La Bahía* at no. 653 (**❷**) and *Residencial Patagonia* at Pasaje España 64 (**❷**). *Cabañas Gato Negro* (☎67/419600; **❹**) at 10 de Julio 242 offers more comfortable *cabañas*. After bypassing Puerto Murta, shortly beyond the turn-off, the Carretera hits the shore of the lake and clings to it for the next 75km, giving striking views across the gleaming, emerald water.

Some 25km south of the turn for Puerto Murta you'll reach **Puerto Tranquilo**, a picturesque lakeside hamlet with basic services, including simple **rooms** at *Hospedaje Bellavista*, Arrayanes 300 (☎67/419500; **❷**), *Residencial Darka*, Arrayanes 330 (☎67/419500; **❷**), *Hostal Los Pinos*, 2 Oriente 41 (☎67/411637; **❹**) and *Residencial Carretera Austral*, 1 Sur 223 (☎67/419500; **❸**). The latter runs short boat rides (CH\$15,000 for 5 people) across the lake to the **Capilla de Mármol** ("Marble Chapel"), a heavily eroded limestone cliff looming out of the water, streaked with blue-and-white patterns and gashed with caves which can be entered by boat.

A new road has been cleared from Puerto Tranquilo, heading 85km west along the course of the Río Exploradores to Puerto Grosse on the coast at Bahía Exploradores. In the future Puerto Grosse will likely become a launch pad for trips to Laguna San Rafael glacier, which lies around 60km to the south. The road also provides access to the slopes of the 4058-metre **Monte San Valentín**, the highest peak in Chilean Patagonia.

Twenty kilometres south of Puerto Tranquilo, you'll cross a bridge over the Río Leones – look west for distant views onto the dazzling white glaciers of the Campo de Hielo Norte. Immediately after the bridge a rough track leads west for 28km to Lago Leones, at the foot of Cerro Nyades, from where there is good access to, and exceptional views of, the glaciers.

A further fifteen kilometres down the road lies the outlet of **Lago General Carrera**, that drains into the adjacent Lago Bertrand. Shortly afterwards, you'll reach **Cruce El Maitén**, a fork in the road; the left road leads northeast along the southern edge of Lago General Carrera to Puerto Guadal and Chile Chico. A cluster of upmarket timber *cabañas*, many catering to those on trout-fishing excursions, sit around Cruce El Maitén. The accommodation is generally of a high standard and most have good restaurants attached and offer activities such as horse-riding or trekking in addition to fishing trips. Choices include the comfortable *Pasarela Lodge 2* (☎67/411425; **❺**) and *Cabañas Bahía Catalina* (☎67/232920; **❺**), the well-furnished *Cabañas Bahía Escondida* (☎ & ℱ67/231872; **❼**), *Cabañas Mallín Colorado* (☎67/411443, ⓦ www.mallincolorado .cl; **❼**), with rustic cabins made of native timber that offer outstanding views of Lago General Carrera, and the luxurious *Hotel Hacienda Tres Lagos* (☎ & ℱ67/411323, ⓦ www.haciendatreslagos.cl, ⓔ ventas@haciendatreslagos.cl; **❼**), whose elegant white-walled rooms and library are filled with wooden furniture and boast panoramic windows that look out over a small beach. Two kilometres along the road to Chile Chico is the *Terra Luna Lodge* (T67/431263, W www .terra-luna.cl; **7**), with attractive bungalows and a Jacuzzi.

Pushing on from Cruce El Maitén, about 25km further south, you arrive at the charming little village of **Puerto Bertrand**, sitting near the head of the turquoise Río Baker. You'll find a highly recommended tour agency here, Patagonia Adventure Expeditions (T & F67/411330, E info@adventurepatagonia .com, W www.adventurepatagonia.com), offering whitewater rafting, fishing and horse-riding plus kayaking trips in the pristine wilderness around the village. Several stylish spots offer **accommodation**: *Cabañas Rápidos del Río Baker* (T67/411550, E info@rapidosdelriobaker.com; **8**), 3km south of the town, *Río Baker Lodge* (T67/411903; **6**), 1km south, and *Hostería Campo Baker* (T67/411447; **7**), in the village itself – plus the more affordable but perfectly serviceable *Residencial Quimey* (T67/419900; **3**).

From Cochrane to Villa O'Higgins

The last major stop on the Carretera Austral, and the first proper town since Coyhaique, **COCHRANE** lies 50km south of Puerto Bertrand. It's also the very final place where you can be sure of finding fuel. Founded by the government in 1930 in an attempt to create a southern urban centre in the newly opened region, it remained a backwater until it was designated the provincial capital in 1954 when it quickly filled up with civil servants and their families. There's not much to do here, but the paved, orderly streets spreading out from the neat Plaza de Armas, and array of efficient services, make this a prime spot to rest up after the wildness of the Carretera Austral. You'll find an **information** kiosk on the plaza during the summer months (Mon–Sat 9am–1pm & 2.30–8pm). To the north of the plaza, in the Centro Cultural, is a small **museum** (daily 9am–1pm & 3–7pm) with a paltry selection of pioneer artefacts.

The relatively new *Hostal Lago Esmeralda* at San Valentín 141 (T67/522621; **3**) has tastefully furnished **rooms** and one of the best **restaurants**, serving delicious, if uninventive, food. The pricier, inn-style *Hotel Ultimo Paraíso* at Lago Brown 455 (T67/522361; **6**) offers tastefully decorated rooms, while the older *Hotel Wellmann* at Las Golondrinas 36 (T67/522171; **5**) has rather faded accommodation. Simpler, less expensive options include *Residencial Sur Austral* at Prat 334 (T67/522150; **2**) and *Hospedaje Paola* at Lago Brown 150 (T67/522215; **2**), which also allows camping. *El Fogón*, San Valentín 651, serves up filling *parrilladas* and *Café El Farolito*, Teniente Merino 546, sells sandwiches and other light snacks. While in town, you can make a day-trip to the **Reserva Nacional Tamango** (daily: April–Nov 8.30am–6.30pm, Dec–March 8.30am–9pm; CH$1500), 9km east, set on the banks of **Lago Cochrane**, a skinny, twisting lake that straddles the Argentine border. The reserve is notable for its population of wild *huemul* (native deer); if you're lucky, you'll spot some on the five-hour guided walks with Conaf rangers (around CH$5000 per person). You can get more information from **Conaf** (T67/422164) in Cochrane on the northwest corner of the square.

Caleta Tortel

Just over 100km beyond Cochrane, you come to the embarcadero de Río Vagabundo. From here fifteen-passenger launches (*lanchas*) and eight-passenger motorboats (*chatas*) ferry residents and visitors to the tiny, remote hamlet of **CALETA TORTEL**, located at the mouth of the Río Baker and at the head of one of many fjords poking into a remote landmass between the northern and southern icefields. Besides flights from Coyhaique, these boats were the only means of getting to the town until 2002, when a twenty-kilometre road, following the course of the Río Baker, was opened. You can still go by water if you prefer – *lanchas* take three hours, and the smaller *chatas* half that time, and they cost CH$90,000 and CH$70,000 one way respectively, making them feasible only if you are in a group. You may, however, be allowed on the twice-weekly state-run boat for a fraction of the price; consult the tourist office in Coyhaique for the latest details. Aero Don Carlos (Subteniente Cruz 63, Coyhaique; ☏67/231981) also operates weekly flights (1hr 20min) from Coyhaique; book well in advance.

Caleta Tortel was first colonized in the early twentieth century by a lumber company interested in the dense forests of **ciprés de las Guaitecas**, an endemic tree appreciated for its long-lasting, aromatic wood. It soon grew into a scattered settlement of quaint wooden houses, each with its own jetty and linked by a network of plankways and bridges made of cypress, whose heady aroma fills the air especially after the rains which fall frequently here. Put on the map when Britain's Prince William worked on an Operation Raleigh project here before going to university, Tortel is also renowned for a mysterious incident that gave its name to a nearby island, the **Isla de los Muertos** (Island of the Dead). Dozens of employees involved in the original timber-felling scheme a century ago suddenly died in unexplained circumstances – officially the cause was an epidemic of some kind, possibly scurvy, but rumours suggested they were poisoned, maybe deliberately so that the company didn't have to pay their wages. You can visit this morbid but beautifully unspoiled place on a short boat-trip from Tortel. Also within easy reach by boat are two glaciers: Ventisquero Steffen, which originates from the northern ice-field, three hours north, and Ventisquero Jorge Montt, an enormous bluish ice-wall that comes from the south ice-field, three hours south, both best done if you can muster a group, as the trip is charged per vessel.

A handful of places in town offer basic but pleasant **accommodation**, as well as **meals**, including *Hospedaje Brunilda Landeros* (**2**) and *Sr Juan Nahuel's* (**2**) at Playa Ancha, and *Sra Luisa Escobar's home* (**2**) at Sector Base.

Puerto Yungay

The tiny, bleak settlement of **PUERTO YUNGAY** sits 20km beyond the turn-off to Caleta Tortel. En route, the Carretera winds past emerald lakes and fast-flowing rivers, offering sporadic but clear views onto the Campo de Hielo Norte. Puerto Yungay itself, which until the end of the twentieth century was the last stop on the highway, consists of little more than a military camp that housed the construction team extending the Carretera Austral to Villa O'Higgins (see opposite). There are no attractions here and no accommodation; for lodging you have to forge on to Villa O'Higgins, another 100km south.

To continue down the road beyond Puerto Yungay you must first cross the Estero Mitchell, the long estuary of the Río Bravo: two ferries, with room for two or three vehicles, make the 45-minute crossing, departing from Puerto Yungay at 10am, noon and 3pm and leaving Puerto Bravo at 11am, 1pm and 4pm (free). Just 4km beyond the ferry's arrival point, a side road follows the Estero Steele southwards and will eventually reach Ventisquero Montt, the first stage of an implausibly ambitious project to build a road around the western side of the ice cap all the way to Puerto Natales, a long, long way to the south, and thereby link almost the whole of Chile by road.

The end of the road: Villa O'Higgins

Tiny **VILLA O'HIGGINS** is reached via the very final – and particularly spectacular – 100-kilometre stretch of the Carretera beyond Puerto Yungay: the road seems to fly over the crags. The village sits at the head of a narrow arm of Lago O'Higgins, a beautiful Andean lake squeezed by mountainous peninsulas into something that on the map looks like an electrocuted spider. Half of the lake's spindly waterways lie in Argentine territory where it's called Lago San Martín, after Argentina's independence hero.

Most of the earliest settlers – who came at the beginning of the twentieth century, when it was most easily accessible from Argentina – were British. The first Chilean settlers did not arrive until the 1920s, and the town wasn't officially founded and given its present name until 1966.

Several glaciers, including Ventisquero O'Higgins, spill into Lago O'Higgins from the massive Campo de Hielo Sur – a titanic ice cap that blocks any further progress southwards of the Carretera. They can be visited by boat from the concrete jetty at **Bahía Bahamondez**, 7km south of town. From there, in the summer months (Dec–March), a cross-lake ferry travels biweekly to the Argentine side, from where there is an irregular bus service to Tres Lagos and on to El Calafate (see p.526). Check before setting out with the Sernatur office in Coyhaique (see p.474).

Villa O'Higgins, while growing rapidly, is still rather nondescript, visited if at all just to say you've completed the length of the Carretera journey. Immediately north is the entrance to the **Reserva Natural Shoën** (open during daylight hours for most of the year; free), which has a number of *miradores*, viewpoints affording magnificent views across the village and its surroundings, including the peaks of the Campo de Hielo. You'll be very lucky indeed to spot a *huemul* (a deer whose indigenous name gives the park its title) but on any of the many paths and walkways you'll likely see foxes and a decent variety of flora, including glens of lenga and ñire. The *guardaparque* at the park entrance can answer any questions (in Spanish) and provide information about **camping** facilities.

Practicalities

Given its remote location and harsh conditions, Villa O'Higgins is not a place to turn up on spec; call the Municipalidad on ☏67/211849 or check out these informative websites: ⓦwww.ohiggins.cl and ⓦwww.turismoohiggins .cl For trekking, mountain bike and horseback excursions, visit Villa O'Higgins Expediciones at Hernán Merino 367 (ⓔinfo@villaohiggins.com). The Comité Turistico Villa O'Higgins at Río Pascua 191, on the plaza, can also organize fishing guides and horses as well as set up trekking and other outdoor activities. You'll find an **information** kiosk on the plaza during the summer; they can provide trekking guides. There's only a shared public telephone and no places to change or withdraw money.

The reliable, oddly named *Hospedaje Apocalipsis 1:3*, Pasaje Lago El Salto 345 (☏67/234813; ❹), has pleasant **rooms**, as does the more impersonal *Hospedaje Patagonia* at Calle Río Pascua 1956 (☏67/234813; ❹). There are also a handful of *residencials* on Pasaje Lago El Salto that sometimes take in guests. Two **restaurants** prepare uninspired but inexpensive local fare: *Campo de Hielo Sur* and the *Patagonia*, both on Calle Lago Christie. **Bus** services run once or twice a week between Cochrane and Villa O'Higgins (at least 6 hours, CH\$8000), whilst Aéreos Don Carlos operates a twice weekly flight between Cochrane and Villa O'Higgins on Mondays and Thursdays (CH\$120,000 return).

Travel details

Buses

Chaitén to: Coyhaique (1–2 daily; 12hr); Futaleufú (6–7 weekly; 3hr 30min); La Junta (3 weekly; 6hr).
Coyhaique to: Chaitén (1–2 daily; 12hr); Cochrane (4 weekly; 10hr); La Junta (2 weekly; 6hr); Puerto Aisén (15 daily; 1hr); Puerto Cisnes (1 daily; 4hr); Puerto Ibáñez (1 daily; 2hr 30min); Punta Arenas, via Argentina (1 weekly Jan & Feb; 24hr).
Cochrane to: Villa O'Higgins (1–2 weekly; 6–7hr).

Ferries and catamarans

Caleta Gonzalo to: Hornopirén (Jan & Feb 1 daily; 6hr).
Caleta Puelche to: La Arena (7–10 daily; 30min).
Chaitén to: Castro (catamaran: 3 weekly in season, 2hr 40min; ferry: 3 weekly, 4hr); Puerto Montt (catamaran: 3 weekly in season, 4hr; ferry: 1–4 weekly, 10hr); Quellón (1–4 weekly; 5hr).
Hornopirén to: Caleta Gonzalo (Jan & Feb only, 1 daily; 5hr).

La Arena to: Caleta Puelche (7–10 daily; 30min).
Puerto Chacabuco to: Laguna San Rafael (Dec–March 2 weekly; 16hr; catamaran several weekly in season, 5hr); Puerto Montt (2–4 weekly; 24hr); Quellón (1–3 weekly; 20hr).
Puerto Ibáñez to: Chile Chico (4–7 weekly; 2hr 30min).

Flights

Balmaceda (for Coyhaique) to: Puerto Montt (4 daily; 1hr); Punta Arenas (4daily; 2hr); Santiago (4 daily; 3hr).
Chaitén to: Puerto Montt (1 daily; 1hr).
Cochrane to: Villa O'Higgins (2 weekly; 30min).
Coyhaique (aerodrome) to: Caleta Tortel (1 weekly; 1hr 20min); Chile Chico (4 weekly; 40min); Cochrane (2 weekly; 1hr); San Rafael glacier (daily in season; 1hr 30min); Villa O'Higgins (2 weekly; 1hr 30min).

9

Southern Patagonia

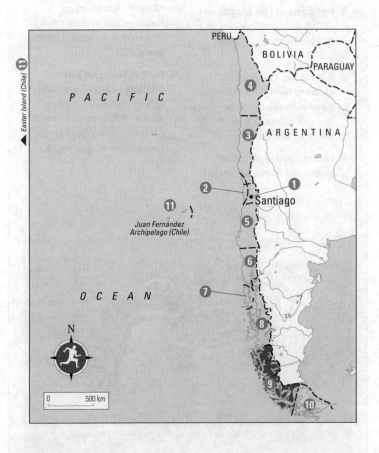

CHAPTER 9 **Highlights**

✳ **Cemetery at Punta Arenas**
Visit this moving – and beautiful – memorial to the pioneers from Britain and Spain, Croatia and Italy. **See p.498**

✳ **Penguins at Isla Magdalena**
Watch their comic antics on this island sanctuary. **See p.503**

✳ **A boat trip to exquisite glaciers** Sail up the fjord from Natales to see the frozen flows of Balmaceda and Serrano. **See p.512**

✳ **Hiking Parque Nacional Torres del Paine** Set aside at least a few days to trek through this spectacular park, an unforgettable experience. **See p.513**

✳ **The "Cuernos" and the "Torres"** Admire giant curlicues and vertical towers of granite in Torres del Paine. **See p.520**

✳ **Parque Nacional Los Glaciares** On the Argentine side of Patagonia, explore the Fitz Roy Sector or check out the mesmerizing Glaciar Perito Moreno. **See p.524**

△ Penguins at Monumento Natural Isla Magdalena

Southern Patagonia

P atagonia lies tucked away right at the southernmost tip of the Americas – indeed of the world's landmass, not counting Antarctica. Geographically ill-defined, "Patagonia" usually refers to the narrow triangle of land south of a line between Puerto Montt, in Chile, and Argentina's Península Valdés, while in Chile the term is usually reserved for **SOUTHERN PATAGONIA**. Much of this area is flat and dreary **pampa** – and nearly all of it across the border in Argentina – but in the western sliver of land shared by both countries, the Andes take a last, dramatic breath before plunging into the ocean.

Its very name holds a fascination for many travellers, including those of the armchair variety, but the reality can be harsh: Patagonia is cursed by a persistent wind (trees grow horizontally here, sculpted by the gales), winters are cold and summers short. It's still pretty much as described in the 1881 *Across Patagonia* by the eccentric nineteenth-century English traveller, Lady Florence Dixie: "Nowhere else are you so completely alone. Nowhere else is there an area of 100,000 square miles which you may gallop over, and where, whilst enjoying a healthy, bracing climate, you are safe from the persecution of fever, friends, savage tribes, obnoxious animals, telephones, letters and every other nuisance you are elsewhere liable to be exposed to."

These days large numbers of Chileans and non-Chilean visitors come to Patagonia principally to hike in the country's most famous and stunning national park, **Parque Nacional Torres del Paine**, a massif crowned with otherworldly granite towers. Others want to follow in the footsteps of the region's famous travellers, such as navigator Ferdinand Magellan, naturalist Charles Darwin, and author Bruce Chatwin. Others still come to gaze at the **glaciers** that calve icebergs into the sea, watch the **penguins**, and discover what it's like down here, at the very foot of the world.

This southern part of Chile was originally inhabited by the hunters of the bleak Patagonian desert and the seafaring canoeists of the hundreds of rainy islands, fjords and shores of the western coast. The first European to discover the area was **Ferdinand Magellan**, a Portuguese navigator in the service of the Spanish crown who came searching for a westerly sea route to the legendary Spice Islands and their untold wealth. The Spanish quickly colonized the area, and by 1584 there were two settlements, both of which failed catastrophically (see box p.502). No European tried to settle the place again for another two hundred and fifty years.

The voyages of the *Beagle*, from 1826 to 1834, renewed interest in the area. The British admiralty sent out the *Beagle* to explore the Magellan Strait, and onboard the second voyage was none other than the young Darwin. The foreign

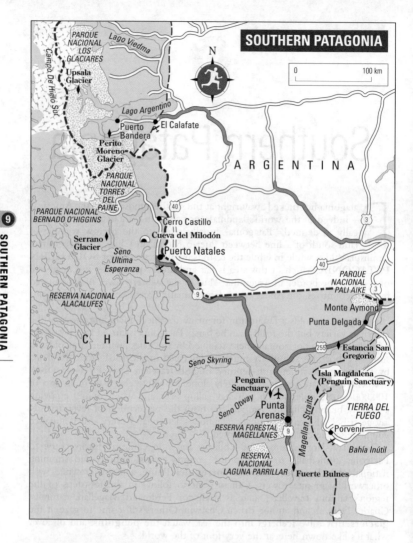

attention disturbed the Chileans, who had always considered this land theirs, and so in 1843 they sent their first settlers to the area. This in turn disturbed the Argentines, who had considered the area *theirs*, and in the 1870s the two narrowly avoided war over the territory, not for the last time. But it wasn't until the discovery of gold and the realization that the land was excellent for sheep farming that the settlements of either the Argentines or the Chileans amounted to much. The gold rush didn't last long, but sheep farming did, and the owners of ranches, or *estancias*, saw great wealth in the late nineteenth century.

Wool is no longer a big earner, and has been replaced by **oil** as the region's main resource. Argentina and Chile have nearly gone to war several times since independence over frontier disputes in the region but the territorial squabbles have for the most part settled down, and Chile now occupies all the land on either side of the Magellan Strait (giving the country a tiny but prized opening to the Atlantic Ocean) along with over half of Tierra del Fuego (see Chapter 10). The Chileans call the area the province of **Magallanes**, in the explorer's honour, and it's one of the least inhabited areas in Chile. The provincial capital is the lively city of **Punta Arenas**, and the only other town of any size is superbly located **Puerto Natales** in the northwest, gateway to Torres del Paine. Both settlements seem to huddle patiently with their backs against the elements.

Since the whole of this region is physically cut off from the rest of Chile by two vast ice caps, the only links with territory to the north are by air, water or through **Argentina**. The last option allows you to visit some of the finest landscapes in Chile's eastern neighbour, including the **Parque Nacional Los Glaciares**, where both the **Fitz Roy Massif**, near El Chaltén, and the **Glaciar Perito Moreno**, accessible from the town El Calafate, are rightly regarded among Argentina's biggest draws.

Chilean Patagonia

Chilean Patagonia can be divided up into four distinct areas: **Punta Arenas** and its surroundings; **Puerto Natales** and the unforgettable **Torres del Paine National Park**; the broad expanse of frigid grassland between the two towns, stretching to the Atlantic coast and taking in the rather less impressive **Parque Nacional Pali Aike**; and the remote, hardly visited **islands** of the Pacific coast. Punta Arenas and Puerto Natales are linked by an excellent and frequent **bus** service, and the area around Parque Nacional Pali Aike is served by the occasional bus. But there's just no way of getting to the islands without your own boat.

Punta Arenas and around

Seen from the air, **PUNTA ARENAS**, 3090km south of Santiago, seems lost in the flat barren plains and vast expanses of water that surround it, a sprawling patchwork of galvanized tin roofs struggling up from the shores of the Magellan Strait. On the ground, however, the city looks much more substantial and modern, especially in the centre where glass and concrete office buildings have replaced the ramshackle wooden houses, paid for in part by the oil that's been flowing into the city since the first wells started gushing in 1945.

Arenas started life 60km south of where it is now, at a place called **Fuerte Bulnes**, the first Chilean settlement along the Magellan Strait. Fuerte Bulnes was founded in 1843 by Captain John Williams, a seaman from Bristol in the service of the Chileans, to forestall any other country's attempts at colonization. In 1848 the new settlement moved to a more suitable location to the north, named by an English sailor "Sandy Point", loosely translated into "Punta Arenas" in Spanish. Originally envisaged as a penal colony, it ran into trouble just three years after the move when the prisoners revolted, executed the governor, captured two visiting ships (marooning their passengers), and attempted to escape to Brazil. It was only because of the courage of the American skipper of one of the captured boats, and the fact that the mutineers got blind-drunk on looted French cognac, that they were recaptured.

Punta Arenas blossomed in the nineteenth-century sheep boom, when thriving immigrant communities from Croatia, Germany and elsewhere sprang up and left their marks – the British built **St James' Church** and the **British School**, and immigrants of other nationalities constructed the magnificent houses around the central **Plaza Muñoz Gamero**. Today Punta Arenas is enjoying another boom of sorts, with oil revenues flowing into the town the **Zona Franca** ("duty free zone") attracting shoppers (and some disappointed tourists), and several very decent museums, especially the **Museo del Recuerdo**.

Despite these attractions, Punta Arenas is not the most scintillating of places – Lady Florence Dixie opined in 1881: "I suppose there may possibly be drearier places but I do not think it is probable". But as the only true city in the south, it's well-equipped with services, and a useful base for exploring both Chilean Patagonia and Tierra del Fuego. Nearby lie a couple of charming local sights – the **penguin sanctuary** of **Isla Magdalena** and, to the west, the **Reserva Forestal Magallanes**.

Arrival and information

Most travellers arrive at the user-friendly **airport**, housed in a very handsome modern building, 20km north of town. It's quite a busy little place, with a bustling café, ATMs, Internet access and car-rental desks. Taxis to the centre charge CH$6000, minibuses CH$2500 and buses – run by a company called Transfer (℡61/222241) – cost CH$1500; they all meet incoming flights. Many people make directly for **Puerto Natales** and **Torres del Paine**, a headlong rush partly catered to by the local bus companies, which sometimes stop at the airport in both directions, so that plenty of travellers never set foot in Arenas itself.

The town doesn't have a bus terminal as such, so different **bus companies** drop passengers at various points around town, though all within five blocks of the main Plaza Muñoz Gamero. You might also arrive at Punta Arenas by **ferry** from Porvenir, in Tierra del Fuego. The ferry terminal is a shortish taxi ride (CH$1000) from downtown, along the Natales road to the north.

Information

Punta Arenas has an excellent **Sernatur** office off the northeastern corner of the Plaza Muñoz Gamero, at Magallanes 960 (Mon–Fri 8.15am–7pm, Sat 9am–1pm & 3–7pm; ℡61/248790, ✉infomagallanes@sernatur.cl, ⓦwww
.puntaarenas.cl), with helpful staff and lots of information on both the city and the region. Should you find it closed, try the city tourist office, housed in a kiosk on the southern side of the plaza (April–Nov Mon–Fri 8am–5pm; Dec–March Mon–Fri 8am–8pm, Sat 9am–6.30pm, Sun 9am–2pm; ℡61/200610). **Conaf** sits at Avenida Bulnes 0309, fourth Floor (Mon–Thurs 8.30am–5.50pm, Fri 8.30am–4.50pm; ℡61/238875) – they offer lots of information on the area's national parks and reserves, though rather surprisingly don't have any maps.

Accommodation

Punta Arenas boasts a wide range of hotels, hostels and *residenciales* in all price ranges. However, the cheapest places fill up quickly and don't take bookings,

Zona Franca (3km), Ferry Terminal (5km) & Airport (20km) **A** ▲

PUNTA ARENAS

ANGAMOS

MAIPÚ

AV MANUEL BULNES

Museo Salesiano

Santuario María Auxiliadora

SARMIENTO DE GAMBOA

H DE MAGALLANES

CROACIA

MEJICANA

BORIES

SAMPAIO

JORGE MONT

CARRERA PINTO

Río de las Minas

AV COLÓN

AV ESPAÑA

A SANHUEZA

CHILOÉ

NAVARRO

O'HIGGINS

JOSÉ MENÉNDEZ

Charley Milward's House

St James'

Museo Regional Magallanes

WALDO SEGUEL

PEDRO MONTT

Museo Naval

21 DE MAYO

Catedral

FAGNANO

NOGUEIRA

PLAZA MUÑOZ GAMERO

ROCA

ERRÁZURIZ

BALMACEDA

Port

Magellan Straits

0   200 m

AV INDEPENDENCIA

▼ Fuerte Bulnes (51km)

9

SOUTHERN PATAGONIA | Punta Arenas and around

ACCOMMODATION

Backpackers' Paradise	G
Blue House	S
Cabo de Hornos	N
Dinka's House	C
Hostal al Fin del Mundo	R
Calafate I	J
Calafate II	L
Hostal de la Patagonia	E
Hostal Independencia	T
Hostal José Menéndez	K
Hostal La Estancia	H
Hotel Finis Terrae	I
Hotel Isla Rey Jorge	Q
Hotel José Nogueira	M
Huala	D
Lodging Manuel	F
Mercurio	O
Pink House	A
Plaza Hotel	P
Residencial Sonia Kuscevic	B

EATING & DRINKING

Hotel José Nogueira	6	La Luna	5	Pub Coral	4	Sotito's Bar	10	La Tasca	9
Lomit's	3	El Mercado	1	Pub Olijoe	11	La Taberna del Club			
		Pub 1900	2	El Quijote	8	de la Unión	7		

so to be sure of a budget room, arrive early in the day. During the low season, hotels often offer reduced rates to fill their rooms.

Backpackers' Paradise Ignacio Carrera Pinto 1022 ⓣ61/246325, ⓔbackpackersparadise @hotmail.com. The most popular backpackers' hostel in town, with 30 bunks (CH$3500 per person) in two open-plan rooms. Extras include cable TV, Internet access and use of the kitchen.

Blue House Balmaceda 545 ⓣ61/227006, ⓔcrigar73@hotmail.com. Half a dozen rooms with three to five bunks each (CH$3500 per person), several shared bathrooms and a kitchen make this a good bargain, despite the scruffy disorder.

Dinka's House Caupolicán 169 ⓣ61/226056. Run by a large, Croatian woman, this velvet-curtained family house overflows with people, who seem to spend most of their time eating. It's very welcoming, but can get noisy, plus it's eight blocks from the plaza. ❷

Hostal Al Fin del Mundo O'Higgins 1026 ⓣ61/710185. Roomy, centrally located hostel with laundry facilities, baggage storage and Internet access available. ❷

Hostal Calafate I Lautaro Navarro 850 ⓣ & ⓕ61/248415, ⓔhostal@calafate.tie.cl, ⓦwww .calafate.tie.cl. A pleasant, clean townhouse with a commodious living room and personable owners. Breakfast is included, English spoken and some rooms have their own bathroom. Often full, so book ahead. ❸–❹

Hostal Calafate II Magellanes 926 ⓣ & ⓕ61/241281, ⓔhostal@calafate.tie.cl, ⓦwww .calafate.tie.cl. The younger sister hostel, within a rambling old hotel, suffers somewhat from street noise. A cybercafé (offering a free half-hour for guests) and a travel outfit occupy the ground floor. ❹

🏃 **Hostal La Estancia** O'Higgins 765 ⓣ61/249130, ⓔreservas_laestancia @hotmail.com. Warm and hospitable, this *hostal* features high-ceilinged dorms on the ground floor and bright rooms set around a communal landing on the first floor. Breakfast is included and there's Internet access. ❸

Hostal Independencia Independencia 374 ⓣ61/227572. Relaxed accommodation with use of the kitchen and a generous breakfast for CH$1500. You can also camp in the grounds. ❷

Hostal José Menéndez José Menéndez 882, one block from Plaza de Armas ⓣ61/221279. Stay in fine, well-appointed rooms in a converted pioneer house with secure parking. ❹

Hostal de la Patagonia O'Higgins 730 ⓣ61/249970, ⓕ61/223670, ⓔhostalpatagonia @entelchile.com, ⓦwww.ecotourpatagonia.com. A snug, friendly home offering spruce accommodation with beds that have good mattresses. En-suite rooms cost more, but they offer hefty discounts off-season. Breakfast is included. ❹

Hotel Finis Terrae Av Cristóbal Colón 766 ⓣ61/228200, ⓕ61/248124, ⓔfinister@ctcreuna .cl, ⓦwww.hotelfinisterrae.com. An overpriced, bland, modern chalet-hotel with a penthouse restaurant that features views over the city. Large discounts are available out of season. ❽

Hotel Isla Rey Jorge 21 de Mayo 1243 ⓣ & ⓕ61/248220, ⓦwww.islareyjorge.com. Contemporary, comfortable hotel with rooms decorated in a traditional English style. A pub-restaurant downstairs specializes in regional dishes. ❼

🏃 **Hotel José Nogueira** Bories 959 ⓣ61/248840, ⓕ61/248832, ⓔrvanogueira@entelchile.net, ⓦwww .hotelnogueira.com. This lovely hotel boasts a prime location on the plaza, in the Palacio Sara Braun: the rooms are a little cramped because of the restrictions of converting the old building into a hotel, but it's still the most stylish place to stay in Punta Arenas. Don't miss the excellent restaurant (see p.498) in Sara Braun's winter garden. ❽

Hotel Panamericana Cabo de Hornos Plaza Muñoz Gamero 1025 ⓣ & ⓕ61/242134 or 229473, ⓔgciacabo@entelchile.net, ⓦwww .hch.co.cl. A monolithic edifice, dominating the city centre, contains this recently refurbished grand hotel. Smart rooms have cable TV, minibar, security boxes and telephones. Buffet breakfast is included. The hotel also boasts a sauna, a good restaurant serving national and international cuisine, and a first-class bar with a diverse but expensive selection of drinks. ❽

Huala Maipú 851 ⓣ61/244244. A very good little *hospedaje* – but perhaps a little far out at seven blocks from the centre – with a double room and a bunk room, kitchen for residents' use and a friendly English-speaking owner. ❷

Lodging Manuel O'Higgins 648 ⓣ61/220567, ⓕ61/221295. One of the cheapest places in town — basic, noisy and a bit squalid, but friendly. Cable TV, Internet access and use of the kitchen are nice pluses. ❷

Mercurio Fagnano 595 ⓣ & ⓕ61/242300, ⓔmercurio@chileaustral.com, ⓦwww.chileaustral .com/mercurio. Simple yet comfortable hotel in the downtown area, near the Plaza de Armas. Rooms have television and telephones and there is a decent restaurant on-site. ❺

Pink House Caupolicán 99 ⓣ61/222436, ⓔpinkhous@ctcinternet.cl. Quiet hostel away from

the centre, by the coast, which offers clean, simple rooms with shared or private bathrooms, use of the kitchen facilities and luggage storage. ❸
Plaza Hotel José Nogueira 116 ⓣ & ⓕ61/2248613. Smaller, more intimate hotel on the second floor of a traditional building on the Plaza de Armas. ❹–❺

Residencial Sonia Kuscevic Pasaje Darwin 175 ⓣ & ⓕ61/248543, ⓔhostalsk@entelchile.net. A compact, long-established *residencial* in a 1970s building with parking. Discount for Hostelling International members. ❸–❹

The City

Set on a bleak windy edge of the Magellan strait, Punta Arenas faces eastward to the ocean, an unusual orientation for a Chilean city. The city has four main streets, all designed to be wide enough to herd sheep through, though modern cars are a more frequent sight these days. The north–south axes are **Avenidas España and Bulnes**, the east–west are **Avenidas Independencia and Colón**. Contained within them, the centre of town is quite compact, and focused around the central **Plaza Muñoz Gamero**. The main shopping street, **Bories**, which runs north from the west of the plaza, bustles with people, especially when the sun's out, but the rest of town has a Sunday-afternoon feeling even midweek.

Around the Plaza

The tranquil **Plaza Muñoz Gamero**, featuring shady pathways under magnificent hundred-year-old Monterey cypresses, fills with strolling couples in the evening. In the middle rises an imposing **monument to Ferdinand Magellan**, donated by the sheep baron José Menéndez, who modestly ensured that his name was just about as big as Magellan's. You'll notice that the toe of one stylized Ona Indian has been polished to a shine – if you touch it (some say kiss it), tradition has it that you'll return to Punta Arenas.

Around the plaza rise several grand houses dating from the wool boom. The only one you can visit is the **Palacio Sara Braun** (Mon–Fri 10.30am– 1pm & 5–8.30pm; CH$1000), on the northwestern corner, now divided between the Club de la Unión and the *Hotel José Nogueira* (see "Accommodation", opposite). Designed by a French architect, Numa Mayer, for Sara Braun, widow of one of the great sheep barons, it originally rivalled the great houses of Santiago. It was built over the course of nine years with materials imported from Europe at great expense, and after forty years of renovation is once again full of marble fireplaces and crystal chandeliers.

△ Magellan monument

If you walk along the northern edge of the square to Calle Hernando de Magallanes and turn north, you'll find another glorious house: the **Palacio Braun Menéndez**. It's no longer a family residence, having been donated to the nation some years ago to become the home of the **Museo Regional Magallanes** (May–Sept Mon–Sun 10.30am–2pm; Oct–April Mon–Sat 10.30am–5pm & Sun 10.30am–2pm; CH$1000, free on Sun and holidays). Overshadowed by ancient evergreen trees, the exterior looks rather gloomy in contrast to the brilliance of the interior, which is naturally lit by a glass cupola in the roof. After donning soft overshoes to protect the polished wooden floors, you can visit the beautifully preserved private quarters, a time-capsule 1903 French family home. Lavishly decorated and filled with European furniture and paintings, the dining room, bedrooms and sitting rooms recall a wealthy middle-class lifestyle achieved by few who came to Patagonia in search of it. Standing in his gleaming snow-white bathroom, you can easily imagine the larger-than-life Russian

Magellan, pioneer of global exploration

Fernão Magalhães, known to English-speakers as **Ferdinand Magellan**, was born in about 1480 in northern **Portugal**, and had an adventurous early life: in his twenties he saw service with the Portuguese fleets in their wars against the Muslims of the Indian Ocean, and by 1515 he was a veteran of the campaigns in Morocco, where he was wounded, resulting in a limp that he would have for the rest of his life. In 1516, after being refused a rise in his pension by the king of Portugal, Magellan took his services to **Spain**.

These days were the beginning of European exploration, prompted mainly by the desire to seek out new routes to the East and its valuable Spice Islands (the Moluccas of Indonesia). The Portuguese had an early start, and managed to dominate the sea lanes around the coast of Africa, prompting other European powers to search for alternative routes. Magellan believed that the answer lay to the west, under or through the newly discovered American continents, and he asked the king of Spain, **Charles I**, to fund his search. Charles agreed, eager to prove that the Spice Islands lay in the half of the New World that the pope had just assigned to Spain.

On September 20, 1519, Magellan sailed west as admiral of a fleet of five ships. They crossed the Atlantic Ocean, entered the bay of Rio de Janeiro on December 13, and started to search the coast of South America for the elusive passage. It was a long and hard hunt, and not all Magellan's fleet believed there was a strait: on Easter Day 1520, Magellan had to quash a mutiny by his Spanish captains. But on October 21, 1520, his flagship, the **Trinidad**, finally rounded Cabo Virgenes and entered the strait that now bears his name. Thirty-six days later the open seas of an ocean were sighted, and Magellan wept for joy. They named the new ocean "the Pacific" for its calmness after the storms of the strait, and set out across it. They did not expect it to be so wide.

They sailed for four months without seeing land. Their food and water ran out: "We ate only old biscuit reduced to powder, which stank from rat droppings ... and we drank water that was yellow and stinking. We also ate the ox hides that were under the main yard ... and sawdust, and rats each of which cost a ducat." Then Magellan himself was killed in a fight with the natives of Mactán Island, but the fleet didn't turn back, petrified of attempting to go through the straits at the bottom of South America for a second time. Three years after they'd set out, just one of Magellan's original five ships finally limped back to Spain. It was loaded with spice (cloves and nutmeg) and manned by only eighteen of the original crew, men wasted and half-dead, "weaker than men have ever been before". The voyage's chronicler said he could not imagine the journey ever being repeated.

immigrant Braun Hamburguer enjoying a good hot soak after supervising the shearing of his two million sheep out on the desolate pampas.

Seven of the fourteen rooms in the museum are devoted to a permanent exhibition detailing the colonization of Patagonia and Tierra del Fuego. The rooms leading off the hall contain sepia photographs of the city, depicting its ramshackle and temporary appearance during the early years, while dusty old account books and documents reveal that the founding families controlled not only the sheep trade, but an immense range of other commercial activities. In effect, they *were* the city.

One and a half blocks east of the plaza sits the engaging **Museo Naval y Marítimo** at Pedro Montt 981 (Tues–Sat: June–Sept 9.30am–12.30pm & 2–5pm, Oct–May 9.30am–6pm; CH$700). It houses a collection of minutely detailed scale models of Chilean naval ships and, to emphasize the Chilean claim to the Antarctic, a glass freezer containing a blue lump of Antarctic ice.

Three blocks south of Pedro Montt is the shabby **port**. Dotted along the shore to the south, the remains of rusting wrecks are reminders of the treacherous southern waters and fierce winds that scourge Punta Arenas: the most impressive are the bare ribs of the *Lord Lonsdale*, beached here in 1942. There are, however, no remains of the most spectacular wrecking of a ship at Punta Arenas, that of the Royal Navy cruiser *HMS Dotterel*. On April 26, 1881, the *Dotterel* was anchored out in the bay when its ammunition exploded. The ship was blown into thousands of pieces, which were scattered over Punta Arenas, along with three hundred of the ship's company. Every window in Punta Arenas was broken by the blast. One of the five survivors was the ship's captain, who noticed a small detonation while relaxing in a hot bath in his cabin, and, realizing that something was amiss, squirmed out of his porthole and dived into the sea. When the mammoth secondary explosion struck, he'd swum some distance from the ship and escaped unharmed, apart from having all his hair singed off.

St James' Church and the British School

Three blocks west of the plaza, along Waldo Seguel, are two modest but finely proportioned buildings, **St James' Church** and the **British School**, which recall the era when the British influence in Punta Arenas was at its zenith. In those days, the town was still called Sandy Point, sterling widely accepted as currency, and a leading member of the community was one **Charley Milward**, great uncle of the author **Bruce Chatwin**. Chatwin wrote his travelogue *In Patagonia* about his trip here to learn more about Milward, ex-sea captain and adventurer, who helped discover a chunk of a deep-frozen prehistoric ground sloth in the Cueva del Milodón (see p.511). Around the corner at España 959 you can see Milward's old house (not open to the public), part Victorian parsonage, part castle. It was here, in 1914, that the famous explorer Sir Ernest Shackleton stayed and planned the rescue of his stranded crew after his ship, the *Endurance*, was crushed by ice in the Antarctic. (For a detailed account of Shackleton's expedition and rescue, consult Ⓦ www.south-pole.com.)

If you cross Avenida España and climb some steps up to the **Mirador Cerro la Cruz**, you can enjoy a pretty view over the city's multicoloured roofs.

Museo Salesiano Maggiorino Borgatello and around

Seven blocks north of the plaza, on the west side of the wide Avenida Manuel Bulnes, is the **Santuario María Auxiliadora**, a grimy Neo-Gothic church and convent. The bland interior of the church contains more than its fair share of grotesquely tormented statuary, complete with toupees made from human hair. To the right of the church is the **Museo Salesiano Maggiorino Borgatello**

(Tues–Sun 10am–12.30 & 3–6pm; CH$1500). Amongst the cases of geological samples, jars of pickled marine animals and trays of mounted insects, displays vividly depict the daily life of the extinct Fuegian Indians. The weapons used by these accomplished hunters varied amongst the different tribes: the Alacaluf and Yahgan Indians, who fished from canoes, made long spears with viciously barbed heads for catching fish, while the Ona (Selk'nam) and Haush were expert bowmen and used different types of arrows depending on their prey. The Europeans regarded the Tehuelches as the finest horsemen they had ever seen and marvelled at the skill with which they could bring down a guanaco or rhea (a type of ostrich, locally called a *ñandú*) using *bolas* (a throwing weapon of heavy balls linked with string). The museum has a large collection of these weapons and the stone tools used to make them.

One room of the museum is completely taken up by a full-size copy of the **Cave of Hands** (Cueva de las Manos) the original of which is near Chile Chico, 1600km north of Punta Arenas (see p.482). The 11,000-year-old rock paintings are typical of the nomadic art found throughout Patagonia. The hand images, which give most of these caves their name, were created in two ways: either by wetting the rock with blood and pressing a hand on it, or by blowing ground rock around a hand, creating a silhouette. Among the other paintings are geometric designs and delicate illustrations of guanacos and rheas.

Two blocks north of the Museo Salesiano, on the other side of Avenida Bulnes, lies the city's magnificent **cemetery** (daily: summer 7.30am–8pm, winter 8am–6pm; free), which covers four city blocks and is the most fascinating sight in Punta Arenas. Crisscrossed by a network of footpaths lined with immaculately clipped cypresses, this eclectic necropolis reflects the turbulent history of Patagonia in marble and stone. The simple statue of a solitary Fuegian Indian, and the solemn epitaphs on the headstones of the pioneers and sailors interred far from their native soil, are dwarfed by the ostentatious mausoleums constructed at the end of last century. In 1919, 25 years after the cemetery opened, Sara Braun commissioned the imposing Neoclassical entrance to the cemetery, but even this is but a modest attempt at immortality in comparison with José Menéndez's colossal replica of Victor Emmanuel II's wedding-cake tomb in Rome.

The Museo del Recuerdo and Zona Franca

Take one of the many buses or *colectivos* from the centre with "Zona Franca" written on the front and you'll arrive at Punta Arenas' duty-free shopping zone, 3km north of the centre of town. An industrial park with shops, the **Zona Franca** is southern Chile's temple to consumerism. You'll find a big shopping mall (Mon–Sat 10am–12.30pm & 3–8pm), mainly packed with electrical retailers, and a street of large shops with a quite bewildering array of whisky, including brands like Dunhill and Burberrys.

Outside the Zona, on the grass in the middle of Avenida Bulnes, sits a life-size bronze statue of a shepherd, his dog, a horse and some sheep, erected in 1943. Portrayed struggling into the teeth of a gale, these figures commemorate the first three hundred sheep brought to Punta Arenas in 1876. If you've been to Coyhaique (see p.474) you will have seen an albino version of the monument (in comparison, like Bo Peep, Arenas' shepherd appears to have lost a sheep or two). On the other side of the Avenida is the **Instituto Patagonia**, a centre for cultural and scientific research set in extensive grounds that also contain the **Museo del Recuerdo** (Mon–Fri 8.30–11.30am & 2.30–6.30pm, Sat 8am–12.30pm; CH$1000). This "museum of recollections" features an open-air display of horse-drawn vehicles, farm machinery, steam engines and cars used in the region at the turn of the twentieth century. You'll also find a small-scale

9

replica of the reconstructed Fuerte Bulnes (see p.503) and some timber-framed buildings from an old *estancia*, built between 1870 and 1930. These old pioneers' houses, originally sited 50km south of the city, were declared national monuments in 1974 and brought here ten years later. There's also a *trinero*, or sledge, a common form of transport in southern Chile because of the wet climate and steep terrain. Two of the other exhibits show the Chilean love of nicknames: the municipal refuse cart was also used to pick up stray dogs, and therefore became known as the *perrera* (dog-catcher's wagon), while the cumbersome steamroller was dubbed *la bicicleta del Alcalde* (the mayor's bicycle).

Eating and drinking

It's an affordable pleasure to eat out in Arenas, and the local speciality, king crab *(centolla)* makes for a tasty treat, either on its own or in a gratin or chowder *(chupe)*. Many of the country's excellent wines are widely available, and owing to the Zona Franca, imported lagers are easier to find in Punta Arenas than elsewhere, should you want a change from Chilean brews.

Hotel José Nogueira Carlos Bories 959 ☎61/248840. Relax with a pisco sour or enjoy a reasonably priced fillet steak with crab sauce in the hotel's restaurant housed in a beautiful vine-draped conservatory.

Lomit's José Menéndez 722. The usual range of Chilean-style fast food, without French fries. Coffee and drinks make this a popular meeting-place, especially since it stays open late.

La Luna O'Higgins 1017. One of Arenas' best eateries features fine fare, a bright blue and yellow decor, Latin rhythms and friendly service. After a perfect pisco sour, try the *chupe del día* or other well-cooked dishes (CH$4000). Don't forget to pin your place of origin on the maps decorating the walls.

El Mercado Mejicana 617, second floor. First-class seafood served 24 hours a day, including moderately priced lunch menus and more expensive dinner dishes. There's a full-size *centolla* mounted on the wall, so you can see just how big these crustacean monsters really are.

Pub Coral José Menéndez 848. Decent pizzas and absolutely huge sandwiches are served in functional surroundings; they occasionally host karaoke.

Pub Olijoe Errázuriz 970. A cosy pub, great for drinks and snacks, with wooden panelling and a no-smoking area. Open from 7pm until late, it is *the* place to be seen in Arenas.

El Quijote Lautaro Navarro 1087. Red neon in the window makes this place look seedier than it really is. The set lunches are good and cheap (CH$2500), and they also do shellfish.

Sotito's Bar O'Higgins 1138 ☎61/221061. The bare brick walls and starched linen tablecloths conjure up an elegant New York or London brasserie. Attentive waiters serve large portions of meat and seafood, including *milanesa de pollo*. During the high season, booking is recommended Friday through Sunday.

La Tasca Plaza Muñoz Gamero 771, second floor. Enjoy a lovely view over the plaza from the tables by the window in this attractive, wood-ceilinged building. Efficient (if brusque) waiters serve up standard Chilean fare and tasty seafood dishes.

Nightlife and entertainment

In summer it doesn't get dark before 10.30pm in Arenas, so the evening doesn't really begin until well past midnight. As a result, most places don't open their doors until around 1am.

Discotheque Kamikaze Bories 655. This is by far the best club in town to come and dance the night away.

Discotheque Torreones Km 5.5-Sur. Described by the tourist office as "a disco for adults", it plays more Latin and Seventies music than its rivals.

Pub 1900 Bories 793 at Colón, in the *Hotel Tierra del Fuego*. With tinted glass and thick carpets,

this laid-back café-bar is a chill spot for a couple of drinks.

La Taberna del Club de la Unión Plaza Muñoz Gamero 716. In the basement of the Palacio Sara Braun, this upmarket venue, decorated with black and white maritime photographs, is a pleasant choice for quiet drinks.

Listings

Airlines DAP, O'Higgins 891 ☎61/223340, ℻61/221693, ⓔ ventas@aeroviasdap.cl, ⓦ www.dap.cl; LAN, Lautaro Navarro 999, on the corner of Pedro Montt ☎61/241232 or 247079, ℻61/241536, ⓦ www.lanchile.cl; Vic's Servicios Aéros, O'Higgins 1055 ☎61/235837, ℻61/235835, ⓦ www.vics.co.cl.

Banks and exchange Most of the banks are clustered around the plaza especially on its eastern side. There are also plenty at the Zona Franca. *Cambios* include: La Hermanidad, Lautaro Navarro 1099; Scott, Lautaro Navarro and Roca; Stop, José Nogueira 1168 and Menéndez 556; Sur Cambios, Lautaro Navarro 1001; Tour América, Lautaro Navarro 1109.

Books There's a small shop in the Instituto Patagonia (see p.498), Av Bulnes, that sells recent issues of the institute's magazine and expensive, beautifully illustrated books. The institute's library is also open to visitors. Also try Southern Patagonia at Bories 404, and Local 122-A in the Zona Franca.

Bus companies Bus El Pingüino, Armando Sanhueza 745 (☎61/221812), for Río Gallegos in Argentina with connections to Buenos Aires and Los Antiguos; Bus Sur, José Menéndez 565 (☎61/227145, ⓦ www.bus-sur.cl), for tours to Seno Otway penguin colony, Fuerte Bulnes and Pali Aike, Puerto Natales, Coyhaique, Puerto Montt, and Castro on Chiloé; Buses Fernández, Armando Sanhueza 745 (☎61/242313, ⓦ www .busesfernandez.com), for tours to Seno Otway penguin colony and Puerto Natales; Buses Ghisoni, Lautaro Navarro 971 (☎61/223205, ℻61/222078), for Río Gallegos and Río Grande in Argentina; Buses Pacheco, Av Colón 900 (☎61/242174, ⓦ www .busespacheco.co.cl), for Osorno, Puerto Montt, Castro, Puerto Natales and Río Gallegos and Río Grande in Argentina; Queilén, Armando Sanhueza 745 (☎61/221812) and Lautaro Navarro 975, for Osorno, Puerto Montt and Castro; Transfer, Pedro Montt 966 (☎61/244475), for the airport, Puerto Natales and tours to the Seno Otway penguin colony; Buses Tecni Austral, Lautaro Navarro 975 (☎61/223205), for Ushuaia in Argentina; Turibus, Armando Sanhueza 745 (☎61/227970), for Osorno, Puerto Montt and Castro. Remember that buses for anywhere north of Puerto Natales travel through Argentina.

Car rental Automóvil Club de Chile, Bulnes 0658 ☎61/215544; Avis (Emsa), Roca 1044 ☎61/229049 and at the airport; Budget, O'Higgins 964 ☎61/241696, ⓦ www .budgetpatagonia.cl; Hertz, O'Higgins 987 ☎61/248742 and at the airport; International,

Waldo Seguel 443 ☎61/228323, ⓦ www .international-rac.com, and at the airport; Lotus, Mejicana 694 ☎ & ℻61/241697; Lubag, Magallanes 970 ☎61/242023; Magallanes, O'Higgins 949 ☎61/220780, ⓦ www.magallanesrentacar .cl; Paine Rent a Car, José Menéndez 631 ☎ & ℻61/240852. Because there are so many loose stones on Patagonian roads, you are almost guaranteed to get a shattered windscreen or headlight, so it's a good idea to ask how much you'll have to pay if the car's glass gets damaged. Some companies (for example, International) charge a fixed fee per crack and don't ask you to pay for a whole new windscreen.

Consulates Argentina, 21 de Mayo 1878 ☎61/261912 or 261532, ℻61/261264; Brazil, Arauco 769 ☎61/241093, ℻61/226290; Paraguay, Av Bulnes 0928, Dpto.14, 1st floor ☎61/211825; UK, Catarata de Niaguara 01325 ☎ & ℻61/211535; Uruguay, José Nogueira 1238 ☎61/241053, ℻61/226822.

Hospital Hospital Regional, Angamos 180, between Señoret and Zenteno ☎61/244040.

Internet Calafate II, Magallanes 926 – best rates and connection in town. Alternatively try Netsur on the corner of Mejicana and Bories.

Laundry Lavandería Record, O'Higgins 969; Laveseco Josseau, Carrera Pinto 766; Limpc, 21 de Mayo 1261.

Post office Bories 911.

Telephone offices There are phone centres at Bories 801A, Lautaro Navarro 931 and Nogueira 1116.

Tour operators To visit the Torres del Paine national park, you're better off travelling up to Puerto Natales and visiting a tour operator there (see p.512). To visit the penguin sanctuaries or any of the sights near Punta Arenas, it's cheaper to take one of the bus companies' tours or ask in your hotel – trips cost around CH\$5000 for a half-day. To arrange a boat trip to Antarctica or the Falkland Islands, contact Turismo Cabo de Hornos, Plaza Muñoz Gamero 1039 (☎61/241321), which also has an office in Santiago at Augustinas 814, Oficina 706 (☎2/6339119, ℻2/6338480; ⓔ hornos@chilepac.net); or COMAPA, Magallanes 990 (☎61/200200, ⓦ www.comapa.com), which also takes bookings for the Navimag ferry from Puerto Natales to Puerto Montt and runs the *Melinka*, the boat that visits the Isla Magdalena penguin sanctuary for CH\$15,000. Inhospita Patagonia, Lautaro Navarro 1013 (☎ & ℻61/224510) arranges tours to Antarctica as well as trips to Isla Navarino and Argentine

Patagonia. Larger, well-established general operators offering group and custom-tailored tours include Arka Patagonia, Magallanes 345 (☎61/248167, ✆info@arkapatagonia.com, ⓦwww.arkapatagonia.com), Aventour, España 872 (☎61/241197, ✆aventour@entelchile.net, ⓦwww.aventourpatagonia.com), Eco Tour Patagonia, O'Higgins 730 (☎61/249970, ✆61/223670, ✆ecotourpatagonia@entelchile.net, ⓦwww.ecotourpatagonia.com), Turismo Aónikenk, Magallanes 619 (☎ & ✆ 61/228332, ✆turismo@aonikenk.com, ⓦwww.aonikenk.com), Turismo Viento Sur, Fagnano 585 (☎61/226930, ✆61/229628, ✆agencia@vientosur.com, ⓦwww .vientosur.com), and Turismo Yamana, Errazuriz 932 (☎61/710567, ✆61/240056, ✆turismo@yamana .cl, ⓦwww.turismoyamana.cl).

South of Punta Arenas

Shortly after leaving Arenas' city limits, the road becomes dirt, and as you drive south you're treated to views out over the Strait of Magellan to Tierra del Fuego – if it's not raining, that is. After 26km you come to a *carabineros* checkpoint by an old, slightly rotting monument to Swiss settlers, where a signed road to the right (west) leads 16km past thousands of silver-black tree stumps to the **Reserva Nacional Laguna Parrillar** (mid-Oct–end-April Mon–Fri 8.30am–6pm, Sat–Sun 8.30am–8pm; CH$1000). A popular fishing and picnic spot, the wide, grey-black lake is surrounded by low bleak hills covered in a dense scrub and flanked by stubby, withered trees. You can see fishermen wading out in all weathers, attempting to catch salmon or trout as fierce winds whip up white horses across the water. You'll find a couple of *fogones*, or barbecue grills, which cost CH$5000 to use, and a fairly poor half-hour nature walk in a forest of scrubby lenga near the reserve's entrance. Camping sites cost CH$12,000. There's no public transport here.

If you return to the main road and continue south, the next settlement is **Punta Carrera**, just a couple of fishermen's shacks by the sea. It was here that

Moving on from Punta Arenas

The **ferry** for **Porvenir** in Tierra del Fuego is the *Melinka*, an old tub-like landing craft with a three-storey metal house stuck on the back. It leaves from the ferry terminal at Tres Puentes, 5km north of town, Tuesdays through Saturdays at 9am, and on Sundays at 9.30am to make the crossing (2.5hr) to Bahía Chilota, 5km west of Porvenir. It returns from Bahía Chilota from Tuesday to Saturday at 2pm, on Sundays from September to April at 5pm and from May to August at 3.30pm. The timetable can change due to the weather, so it's worth checking in advance. Book a space for a car with Transbordadora Austral Broom at Bulnes 05075 (☎61/218100, ✆61/212126, ⓦwww.tabsa.cl). One-way fares are CH$4000 for a foot passenger and CH$25,000 for a car.

Buses to **Ushuaia**, via Bahía Azul, take 12 hours and cost between CH$15,000 and CH$20,000 one-way. **Buses** to **Puerto Natales** (3hr) leave regularly throughout the day from Avenida Colón, two blocks north of the plaza, and cost CH$3000–4000 one-way, CH$6000 return. There are also buses to Río Gallegos and Río Grande in Argentina, Coyhaique, Puerto Montt and Chiloé – see "Listings".

Scheduled **flights** (see "Basics" p.47) leave Punta Arenas' airport for Balmaceda, Puerto Montt and Santiago. In summer, a small operator called **DAP** runs twice daily flights (except Sundays) to Porvenir (US$46 return), daily flights (except Sunday) to Puerto Williams (US$128 return), and twice weekly flights to Ushuaia (US$200 return). In winter, the flights are much less frequent, if they go at all. A charter airline, **Vic's Servicios Aéros**, flies twice weekly to Porvenir (US$35) and also to Isla Robinson Crusoe.

9

SOUTHERN PATAGONIA | Punta Arenas and around

some of the first *estancias* in the area were built; they have since been transported to Punta Arenas (see p.491). There's a tiny historical **graveyard** by the side of the road, which is so small – only an enclosed patch of turf with a couple of modern crosses – that you'd never notice it but for the massive signpost. Just

How Puerto Hambre got its name

In the sixteenth century, the **Magellan Strait** was one of the most important secrets in the world, guarded carefully by the Spanish, but by 1578 it had been discovered by Sir **Francis Drake**. The Viceroy of Peru, determined to close the strait to all but the Spanish, sent off his most skilled navigator, **Pedro Sarmiento de Gamboa**, to hunt Drake down and take him, dead or alive. Drake gave Sarmiento the slip, but Sarmiento realized that if the Spanish were to keep the strait for themselves, it had to be fortified and settled. He proposed to Charles I that the area be colonized, and in 1581 set sail from Spain with a massive expedition of 23 ships and 3000 people (the conquistador Pizarro had vanquished the Incas with a mere 168). Storms took some ships, others were sunk by English pirates, while yet more gave up and returned to Spain, but in 1583 Sarmiento made it to **Cabo Virgenes**, the Atlantic entrance to the strait, with a mere five ships and 500 men and women. However, as he was unloading his supplies a tempest blew up and forced four of his ships out to sea. For two weeks these ships attempted to sail back to the stranded colonists, before having to admit defeat and return to Spain, battered and almost wrecked.

Sarmiento was not disheartened, and started by founding a city half a league from Cabo Virgenes, calling it Nombre de Jesus. He continued on and founded another city, Rey Don Felipe, building a wooden curtain wall, a chapel, a town hall and a monastery. Land was cleared and seed sowed. In time, Sarmiento decided to visit his first colony, and in his sole remaining ship set sail for Nombre de Jesus. Another storm blew up and forced him out to sea, and despite all his efforts he could not return to the strait. "Seeing how desperate was their plight," he wrote, describing himself in the third person, "the Governor grieved more than at the loss of life itself, and could not contain his tears at the thought that he could not even take leave of his friends and companions."

He made for Brazil, intending to send the colonists help. He sent one ship, and it sank. He led another and it too sank – he himself only just survived by clinging to the wreckage. On the third attempt the crew mutinied, and he had to return to Brazil, from where he sent impassioned requests to the Spanish court that his colonists might be relieved or resupplied. These were refused. He resolved to travel to Spain and in 1585 embarked for Europe, but was captured by English pirates and taken to England. There he charmed Walter Raleigh into pleading his case, and Queen Elizabeth I released him. Sarmiento, still with his settlers in his heart, set off once more for Spain, and was promptly captured by French Huguenots. They didn't release him for two years. He finally secured his liberty, and in 1590 arrived at the Spanish court. No one listened to him. He died, old, scarred, worn by care, and not knowing what happened to his colonists.

What did happen is almost as sad as the fate of Sarmiento himself. By the end of 1586, only eighteen colonists were alive, the rest having starved. A year later they sighted a ship, and were aghast when they discovered that it wasn't a friendly Spanish galleon, but belonged to a squadron of corsairs under the English buccaneer Thomas Cavendish. Only one of the remaining colonists, a soldier called Tomé Hernández, trusted the Englishman enough to accept his offer of transport to Europe, and then the winds changed, and Cavendish sailed on. All the other settlers died. Cavendish, shocked by the wretched sight of the village, scored out the words "Rey Don Felipe" on his sea-chart and renamed it with the name it bears today: "Port Famine" ("Puerto Hambre" in Spanish).

south of here, 48km from Arenas, you'll see a large **white obelisk** around which the road forks. Vaingloriously, this is a monument to the geographical centre of Chile, right here by the toe of South America. It takes into account Chilean Antarctic territory right down to the South Pole, a segment of land approximately the same as that also claimed by Argentina and Britain.

The road to the left of the obelisk leads 2km south to **Puerto Hambre** ("Port Famine"). Puerto Hambre is the site of one of the first two Spanish colonies on the Magellan Strait and one of the saddest stories in the history of the Spanish empire (see box, opposite). All that's left is a plaque, a concrete dolmen, and the ruins of a church, sitting forlornly on a little promontory exposed to the elements. The road to the right of the obelisk leads to **Fuerte Bulnes** (no set opening hours; free), a 1940s reconstruction of the first Chilean settlement in the area. Fuerte Bulnes was founded in September 1843 by a boatload of sailors from Ancud in Chiloé, captained by one John Williams. They came to pre-empt colonization from Europe, and only just made it: a few hours after they arrived, a French warship, the *Phaeton*, turned up and planted the tricolour on the shore. After Williams protested, the French moved off and annexed Tahiti in the Pacific instead. There are a number of old cannon, sturdy but empty log cabins and a lookout tower, all with a decidedly neglected air, and the whole place looks more like a children's adventure playground than an important national monument. Standing slightly apart is a small wooden **chapel**, adorned inside with gifts and supplications left by visitors, giving it a shrine-like atmosphere. In good weather you can see across the strait from the fort, and behind Dawson Island rise the 2000-metre peaks of the snow- and ice-covered Cordillera Darwin (further south in Tierra del Fuego), dominated by the majestic, solitary peak of Mount Sarmiento.

There's no public transport down here, and to reach Fuerte Bulnes without your own car you have to take a tour from Punta Arenas.

The Reserva Forestal Magallanes

The pretty **RESERVA FORESTAL MAGALLANES** (Nov–mid-April Mon–Fri 8.30am–8pm; CH$1000), 196 square kilometres of protected Magellanic forest, lies just 10km west of Arenas. It's used mainly as a picnic centre, with dozens of *fogónes* hidden away in the trees or standing alone in the occasional glade (CH$5000 per site). There's no camping here, and no public transport. A taxi here from Punta Arenas costs around CH$4000. The forest has two entrances, both of which provide wonderful views back over the city, across the Magellan Strait and towards Tierra del Fuego.

A road to the north leads to the reserve's main entrance, at a dense forest of short, stubby trees. You can embark on a couple of hikes here, including the **Sendero Mirador** (1km, 30min) and the **Sendero de Chile Tramo Bocatoma–Las Minas** (3km, 1hr), both through native coigue and lenga trees, and the **Sendero Las Lengas** (3.5km, 1hr) to the **ski centre**, the site of the reserve's second entrance, also accessible from the road to the south. Known as **Club Andino** or the Centro de Esquí Cerro Mirador, the ski centre boasts a nature trail, with labels describing different tree species, and café that's open year-round (Tues–Sun). In winter, from June to August, it's a fabulous place to ski, with eleven runs through the forest, a 1200-metre chair-lift (CH$12,000 a day), a ski-school and equipment for rent (CH$10,000 per day).

Monumento Natural Isla Magdalena

One of the largest penguin colonies in southern Chile, **MONUMENTO NATURAL ISLA MAGDALENA** is home to more than 120,000 Magellanic penguins (also called jackass penguins because of the braying noise they make). The small island, just one square kilometre and topped by a pretty red lighthouse, lies 35km northeast of Arenas, two hours away by boat and easily visible from the city in clear weather. Fifteen-metre-high cliffs surround the island; they're covered in tufts of grass, under which the penguins dig their burrows. In September or October each year, the birds migrate back here and find their mate — they're monogamous and remain faithful to one partner all their lives. They start burrowing, and the female lays two eggs in the nest. When the chicks hatch, in November, both parents nurture the young, one adult remaining with the chick, the other going fishing. In late January the ground is covered with drifts of white down, blown about by the wind, as the chicks shed their baby feathers and get ready for their first trips into the ocean. By the end of March the penguins have returned to sea again.

You can get surprisingly close to the birds as they half hide in the waving grass, but if they start to cock their heads from side to side you're disturbing them; try not to upset the chicks in particular. The birds are well protected by Conaf *guardaparques*, and their nests are fenced off, so you can't get too close to the chicks in any case. The birds seem to feel that there's safety in numbers, and when in a group they appear blasé about any human presence. You can reach Isla Magdalena by the *Melinka*, a passenger ferry operated by Turismo COMAPA (see p.500). It departs at 4pm every Tuesday, Thursday and Saturday in season (Dec–Feb). The five-hour round-trip, which includes one hour viewing the penguin nesting area, costs CH$22,000, half-price for children, and is worth it for the ride alone. There's nowhere to stay on the island, though naturalists with a good reason and a special Conaf permit can overnight in the lighthouse.

North of Punta Arenas

To the north of Punta Arenas, just after the airport, you'll see a thin strip of pebbly beach, steep cliff and withered-tree forest, called **Parque Chabunco**, where locals come to picnic: the section by the road can get crowded, but down towards the beach it's more pleasant. Twenty-seven kilometres out of Punta Arenas you'll come across a *carabineros* checkpoint, at which the road forks and a good dirt road strikes out to the west across the open pampa towards Seno Otway. The road crosses flat, bleak plains of brown-green grass, where shy *ñandúes* (Patagonian ostriches) lurk, and passes the massive **Mina Pecket**, thought to be the world's largest surface coal reserve, an enormous complex of high, dark slag heaps and dirt and noise.

After 65km, a couple of shacks appear over the brow of a hill, marking the **Seno Otway penguin colony** (mid-Oct–end-March 8am–7pm; CH$2000). This nesting site of 5000 or so Magellanic penguins used to be looked after by a non-profit-making organization, staffed by knowledgeable volunteers from Chile and other countries, but the land recently changed hands and is now run as a potentially lucrative tourist attraction instead. The Seno Otway organization has moved up to Chiloé, to try and protect the penguin colonies near Ancud (see p.417), and the colony here has been left at the mercy of busloads of tourists, supervised only by the odd guard and the more scrupulous guides. The area is divided into two zones, with a rope fence to keep you away from the penguins and give them some privacy.

The best time to see the penguins is in the morning (before 10am) or evening (after 5pm), before or after they go fishing. You're not allowed on the beach itself, but ramshackle beachfront hides strung along an 1800-metre walkway let you watch the birds amble out of the water, particularly amusing when

Chilean
wildlife

Chile's diverse animal kingdom inhabits a landscape of extremes, covering mountains, lakes, desert, seacoast and glaciers. The country's formidable natural barriers – the immense Pacific, the lofty Andes and the desolate Atacama – have prevented contact between its species and their counterparts on the rest of the continent, resulting in an exceptional degree of endemism. Indeed, a full one third of Chile's mammals are not found anywhere else in the world; these include the nimble pudu, a miniature deer on the verge of extinction that darts though the woodlands of Chiloé. It's easy to build a trip – or multiple ones – around wildlife-spotting; what follows covers some of the more identifiable species you may see, from camelids, South American relatives of the camel and dromedary, to a slew of frisky, furry rodents that have narrowly escaped extinction despite being highly appreciated for their meat and pelts. Whether through binoculars or with the naked eye, you should also be able to spy a colourful array of birdlife, from tiny hummingbirds to giant condors, via raucous parrots, pink flamingoes and comical penguins.

Guanaco

Camelids of the altiplano

Camelids are prevalent throughout the highland regions of South America, and all four species of them can be found in Chile's barren altiplano (upland plateau). Best known is the shaggy **llama**, whose thick wool and remarkable strength as a beast of burden make it one of the continent's iconic animals, vital to the communities of northern Chile as well as all along the Andes. Its slightly smaller but even more hirsute cousin, the **alpaca** is uniquely adapted to clambering up and down

Llamas

in these high altitudes, as it can rapidly increase the number of red blood cells in its body to facilitate oxygenation.

Unlike the llama and alpaca, the frail-looking **vicuña**, which also roams the **altiplano**, resists domestication. It has attracted the attention of hunters since pre-colonial times because of the exceptional fineness of its coat; indeed, only Inca royalty was allowed to wear the animal's highly prized fur. Thought to be the common ancestor of the other three South American camelids, the wild **guanaco**, also fawn in colour but far bigger than the vicuña, survives today in isolated herds above Arica and Iquique and down in Patagonia. Lone males can often be spotted standing proudly on roadside viewpoints, while the smaller females and photogenic young follow in groups when the all-clear signal is given.

Pudu

Endangered furry rodents

An obvious target of predators, rodents abound in Chile's temperate grasslands and mountains. At the first sign of danger, the endemic mountain **vizcacha**, with its long furry ears and a curly tail, emits a high-pitched whistle to alert the rest of the colony who propel themselves to safety with their powerful hind legs. Its distant relative, the coastal or long-tailed **chinchilla** (looking like a cross between an overgrown hamster and a hare), used to be found in huge numbers – early explorers described rock faces teeming with the creatures. The chinchilla's downfall has been its exceptionally soft, thick coat, each follicle growing eighty hairs. Creating an impressive barrier against the cold and fleas alike, the fur was soon in worldwide demand, and chinchillas were trapped in their thousands. By the time an embargo was declared in 1918, the animal was all but extinct and remains extremely rare to this day.

Wildcats and their prey

You'll have a harder time getting close to the wildcats – not that you'd want to. In the southern pampas and low savannahs, the **mara**, or **Patagonian cavy**, which looks more like a hare than a feline, can break into a swift run, zigzagging at speeds of 45km per hour to escape humans and its habitual hunters such as the voracious **puma**. Other wildcats, from the **colo-colo** – the spitting image of a ginger tom – to the **guiña** also stalk these grasslands. The **grison**, a grey marten-like hunter with a black nose, leaves shelter at dusk and steams through the surrounding countryside in search of rodents, birds, eggs, reptiles and molluscs. When threatened, it squirts a foul-smelling vapour from its anal gland.

Birds

Newcomers to the southern hemisphere will encounter a curious mix of familiar and unknown birds, while even experienced ornithologists will swoon at Chile's many endemics and oddities. One such unmistakeable bird, the dandy-like **Inca**

Chinchillas

tern, sports scarlet legs and bill and a brilliant white forked moustache. Others are known more by their calls: the shrill sounds of the **chestnut-throated huet-huet** and the **chucao**, furtive woodland foragers, ring through Chile's temperate rainforest, while the gregarious **crested caracara**, found on the edges of southern forests, hollers its greetings so heartily that it arches its head all the way onto its back.

Sea birds – from penguins to pelicans

With such bountiful nutritive supplies in the chilly Humboldt Current, Chile enjoys one of the richest and most varied populations of sea birds in the world. The **Peruvian pelican**, a dapper species with its pronounced yellow crest, is found only around the current, as are the **Humboldt penguin** and four species of the gawky-looking **storm petrels**, who swarm behind fishing boats awaiting the ejection of galley waste. The southern giant petrel has been aptly described as "a pugnacious, ungainly and uncouth scavenger". Not so the striking **black skimmer**, whose masterly flight enables it to glide just above the water, tilling a perfect furrow with its longer lower beak as it goes. But perhaps the most eye-catching is the largest of all the sea birds, the **albatross**, eight species of which migrate through Chilean waters.

To see more of Chile's penguins you'll need to head south. **Rockhopper penguins**, named for their peculiar, stuttering gait, congregate around the fjords and islets of Patagonia. **Magellanic penguins**, also called jackass penguins because of the braying noise they make, are found in numerous breeding sites along the southern Chilean coast; sail from Punta Arenas to the noisy, smelly penguin colony of Monumento Natural Isla Magdalena (see p.503) and you'll find a steep-sided chunk of moorland stranded in the middle of the Magellan Straits, with nothing on it but a lighthouse and more than 120,000 of the waddling birds. Meanwhile, the **Emperor penguin** – the tallest, at over a metre – lives on the ice floes of Antarctica; able to withstand temperatures of -40°C (-40°F) and gale-force winds, it is the most southerly breeding of any bird.

Flamingoes at Salar de Atacama

Some of the more renowned species make their homes in the soaring mountains. One of the world's largest, the mighty **Andean condor**, with a wingspan of over three metres, wheels over Chile's magnificent peaks, buoyed by the upward thermals. High in the Andes near the Bolivian border, several species of **flamingo** gather at remote saltwater lakes, including the **Chilean flamingo**, recognizable for its grey-green feet with red joints, and the **James's flamingo**, which was thought to be extinct for fifty years until its rediscovery in the 1950s. The most magnificently hued of the flamingoes, it has a delicate pinkish tinge, bursting into crimson at the base of the neck that gradually fades over the wings. **Darwin's rhea** or **ñandú** also inhabits the highland regions and parts of the far south. Resembling the ostrich or emu, it hides its periscopic head and neck under its bushy feathers to blend in with the surrounding brush. If this doesn't work, it can run faster than a galloping horse, with its neck stretched out horizontally in front.

Magellanic penguins

they amble en masse. However, penguin traffic jams are developing at about 5pm — too many people come in the evening, and the penguins are reluctant to come ashore or go inland. They are forced to wait, sometimes for up to an hour, while the chicks get very hungry, so try to make it here in the morning. Better still, go and see the far larger, better-cared-for colony on Isla Magdalena (see p.503).

There's no public transport out here, and most of the traffic is made up of tours, who refuse lifts to hitchers. Cyclists will be punished by the persistent wind. The easiest way to get here, then, is to drive or join a tour, which takes three hours in all and costs CH$7000 to CH$10,000. Tours are run by any of the operators listed on p.500, by many of the bus companies and by most hotels.

Northeast to Chile's Atlantic coast

Heading northeast from Arenas, you pass through grassland that's desolate, barren and harsh, formed by an elemental wind that colours the sky with ever-changing clouds and blows with a persistence and ferocity that has to be felt to be believed. As you drive you can catch sight of grey, dowdy *ñandúes*, and large brown-and-white guanacos, and if you're very lucky you might see a hairy armadillo, which can only be closely approached from downwind because, although almost blind, it has a very acute sense of smell. When frightened it digs itself into the ground at incredible speed. In the past, hungry *huasos* would try and dig out these little animals, usually a fruitless task.

Sixteen kilometres after the turning to Seno Otway, you pass a semi-abandoned hotel called the *Hotel Cabeza del Mar*, wonderfully sited on a sheltered lagoon and looking like a French country *brasserie*. Shortly after this lies a crossroads (48km from Punta Arenas); the left (northwest) fork leads to Puerto Natales. The right-hand fork heads to the Atlantic, through miles and miles of Patagonian steppe, past dozens of little piles of blue glass that are the remains of shattered windscreens. The large oil terminal of San Gregorio looms on the right, and with it the only petrol station for miles around.

A short distance further is the **Estancia San Gregorio**, once owned by José Menéndez, and part of his Sociedad Explotadora de Tierra del Fuego, which controlled 13,500 square kilometres of grazing land and owned two million sheep. All that's left are the weathered ochre bricks and peeling paintwork of several imposing old buildings, dominated by the escarpment behind. Dating back to 1882, these storehouses, shearing sheds and *huasos'* sleeping quarters have survived vandalism and revolution, but are now slowly rotting, accompanied on the seashore by the ribs of the sailing barque *Ambassador* and the steamship *Amadeo*, skeletal reminders of the Menéndez fleet.

The only maintained buildings include a pretty church – visible from the road but locked – and an old *estancia* house, off the road, at the end of a kilometre-long avenue of gale-blasted trees that were once delicate topiary. At the end of the avenue is a gate flanked by pillars, crowned with a couple of eroded stone sheep. The gardens beyond are still prim and well-kept, surrounded by a high wooden fence for protection against the wind, and the house beyond is closed to the public.

Further down the main road is the plain but decent *Hotel Sanhueza* (no phone; ❷), a wonderful place to thaw out after wandering around the *estancia*. You can warm yourself by a large old cast-iron stove, meet the hotel's friendly hairy dog, and eat well-prepared food – a set lunch costs CH$2500. The only other accommodation in the area is the *Hostería El Tehuelche* (☎61/1983002; ❹), 30km further on, by the turning to the Primera Angostura (see p.506). The *hostería* was built in 1900 by an English *estancia* family and retains its atmosphere of colonial opulence, with high-ceilinged airy rooms, polished wood floors and a large conservatory.

The Primera Angostura ("First Narrows") is the narrowest point of the Magellan Strait, and it's here that the **ferries to Tierra del Fuego** cross from the mainland. The ferries leave from the port of Punta Delgada, 16km from the main road (not to be confused with the town of Punta Delgada, 11km up the road towards Monte Aymond). Two ferries, one slightly larger than the other, make the trip, departing from Punta Delgada (8.30am–10.15pm) and Bahía Azul (9.15am–11pm). They leave about every forty minutes in summer, and every ninety in winter, except at **low tide**, when they don't run at all. For schedule information, check with the ferry company, Transbordadora Austral Broom, Av Bulnes 05075, Punta Arenas (℡61/218100, ℱ61/212126, ⓦwww.tabsa.com), or at Sernatur in Punta Arenas. The crossing takes twenty minutes and costs CH$11,200 for a car, CH$1300 for foot passengers.

Parque Nacional Pali Aike

Eleven kilometres beyond the turning for the ferry is the small town of Punta Delgada and the road heading 18km north to Chilean Patagonia's minor national park, the seldom-visited **PARQUE NACIONAL PALI AIKE** (Oct–April daily 9am–6pm; CH$1000). The park's entrance looms up out of the barren rolling plains, green roof first, as if rising from the bowels of the earth; the sight explains its Aonikenk Indian name, meaning "desolate place". In sharp contrast to the rock castles of Torres del Paine in the west, this is an area of flat heath land, very like Dartmoor in England, with tussocks of beige grass and enormous skies. Strange volcanic formations, pimples and towers, dot the heath, and on either side of the road lies the occasional depression filled with evaporating water and ringed by white tidemarks, where you can occasionally spot flamingoes.

Almost half of the park, the eastern side nearer Argentina, is covered by fields of jagged black rock, the **Escorial del Diablo** ("Devil's slag heap"), surrounding a burst crater called the **Morada del Diablo** ("Dwelling of the devil"). To the south of the Escorial unfolds a ridge of congealed lava, ten metres high, covered in black, orange and lime-green lichen and so full of holes and air bubbles that it looks like a piece of Baroque carving, or a Japanese drawing of a wave, or a fractal. In this wall of rock, 8km from the park entrance, is **Pali Aike**, a cave excavated by the famous archeologist Junius Bird in 1937. He discovered a two-metre-deep sediment containing evidence of prehistoric inhabitation, including bones of the Milodón (a prehistoric ground sloth) and an extinct American horse, dating from 9000 years ago. There are four treks in the park, including a 1700m ascent to the Morada del Diablo crater rim. The best of these though is a nine-kilometre (2hr 45min) **walk** across flat, windy, exposed terrain (carry water) that leads from Pali Aike to remote, picturesque **Laguna Ana** to the northwest.

Wild camping is not permitted in the park and there's no public transport here – the nearest you'll get is the main road, 25km away, on buses heading towards Río Gallegos in Argentina or Tierra del Fuego.

Back on the main road, it's another 22km before the **border crossing** at **Monte Aymond** (daily: April–Nov 8am–10pm; Dec–March 24hr), which is also referred to as the Paso Integración Austral. You'll find a basic restaurant here.

Puerto Natales and around

Chilean Patagonia's second city, **PUERTO NATALES** (just under 250km north of Punta Arenas), enjoys a stunning location at the edge of the pampa, sitting by a body of water fringed by tall peaks. There's not much in the town itself except tour operators, restaurants and accommodation, but it's a useful base for visiting the **Parque Nacional Torres del Paine**, the nearby **Cueva del Milodón**, the glaciers of the **Parque Nacional Bernardo O'Higgins**, and, across the border in Argentina, the **Parque Nacional Los Glaciales**. Consequently, the town is flush with tourist dollars and filled with nylon-clad, Gore-tex-booted hikers. Natales (as it is generally called) is also a good transport hub, home to the terminal of the **Navimag** ferry from Puerto Montt in the Lake District, and linked to Punta Arenas by a regular bus service. Daily buses head up to Torres del Paine, and you'll also find regular services to Argentina and frequent tourist boats to the glaciers.

Arrival and information

The Navimag ferry terminal is on the coastal road, or *costanera*, five blocks west of the Plaza de Armas (℡61/411421, ℻61/411642). There's no bus terminal, so each bus pulls in outside its company's offices, all a couple of blocks from the Plaza de Armas (see "Listings" for addresses).

The helpful **Sernatur** office sits at Costanera Pedro Montt 19 at the junction with Phillipi (April–Nov Mon–Fri 8.30am–6pm, Sat & Sun 9.30am–12.30pm; Dec–March daily 8.30am–8pm; ℡61/412125, ✉infonatales@sernatur.cl). You can also pick up information at the **Officina Municipal** in the museum (see p.509) at Bulnes 285 (℡61/411263). The **Conaf** office, O'Higgins 584 (Mon–Fri 8.30am–6pm; ℡61/411438), is often woefully ill-equipped, so for information about Torres del Paine, visit Path@gone, the travel agent that runs the park's refuges (see box p.512).

Accommodation

Accommodation in Natales is not normally a problem, as many people let out rooms in their houses — you'll be offered half a dozen as you step off the bus. There's a good choice of more expensive hotels, too. Even so, it is wise to book ahead, especially for stays in January. **Camping Josmar 2** at Esmeralda 517 (℡61/414417; ❶) has rudimentary camping sites and a basic restaurant.

Albergue Path@gone Eberhard 595 ℡61/413291, ✉pathgone@entelchile.net. Bright, spotless Hostelling International (HI) affiliate above the Path@gone office, which has dorm rooms and a compact kitchenette, but suffers from its noisy location.
Café Melissa Blanco Encalada 258 ℡61/411944. Primarily a café, but with some snug rooms on the first floor. Beware the gold lamé bed-covers. ❸
🏃 **Casa Cecilia** Tomás Rogers 60 ℡ & ℻61/411797, ✉redcecilia@entelchile.net. A warm, cosy *hospedaje* kept to a Swiss standard of hygiene, with good beds, a decent breakfast and tasty, home-baked bread. Also runs tours and rents bikes. ❸

Casa Dickson Bulnes 307 ℡61/411871. A well-heated house, with a large kitchen open to guests, and decent bathrooms. They offer a minibus service to the park. ❸
🏃 **Concepto Indigo** Ladrill-eros 105 ℡61/413609, ℻61/410169, ✉indigo@entelchile.net, ⓦwww.conceptoindigo.com. A large wooden building right by the water, this hostel has large double and multi-bed top-floor rooms, some with their own bath and all with unparalleled views towards the mountains. There is also a climbing wall on the sheltered, inland side of the building. Closed in the winter. ❹
🏃 **Costaustralis** Av Pedro Montt 262 ℡61/412000, ✉reservas.hotel@terra.cl or

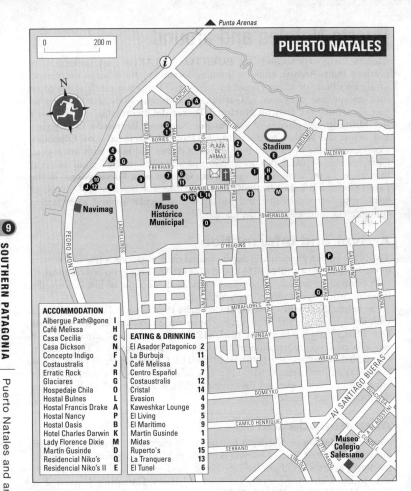

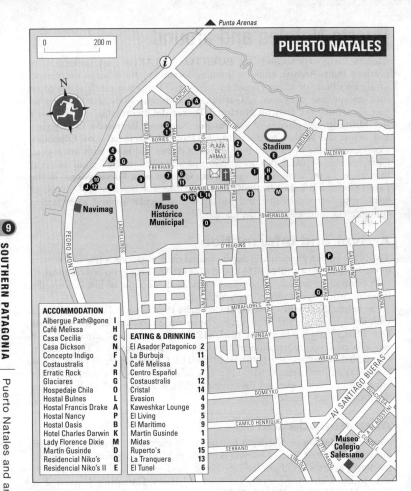

▲ *Punta Arenas*

PUERTO NATALES

0 — 200 m

N

Sánchez

B A

Phillip

C

Bories

Magallanes

Rogers

D

Baros Arana

Plaza de Armas

3

2 5

Stadium

E

Angamos

Valdivia

4
F G

Eberhard

7

6
11

Arturo Prat

I H
8

M

Manuel Bulnes

10
J 12

K

9

N 15 L 14

13

Navimag

Museo
Histórico
Municipal

O

Esmeralda

Pedro Montt

Ladrilleros

O'Higgins

Carrera Pinto

Blanco Encalada

Baquedano

P

Galvarino

Chorrillos

B Zamora

Q
Ramírez

Miraflores

R

Yungay

Arauco

Domeyko

Camilo Henríquez

Serrano

Av Santiago Bueras

Guacolda

Lincoln

Pedro Pardo

Museo
Colegio
Salesiano

ACCOMMODATION

Albergue Path@gone	I
Café Melissa	H
Casa Cecilia	C
Casa Dickson	N
Concepto Indigo	F
Costaustralis	J
Erratic Rock	R
Glaciares	G
Hospedaje Chila	O
Hostal Bulnes	L
Hostal Francis Drake	A
Hostal Nancy	P
Hostal Oasis	B
Hotel Charles Darwin	K
Lady Florence Dixie	M
Martín Gusinde	D
Residencial Niko's	Q
Residencial Niko's II	E

EATING & DRINKING

El Asador Patagonico	2
La Burbuja	11
Café Melissa	8
Centro Español	7
Costaustralis	12
Cristal	14
Evasion	4
Kaweshkar Lounge	9
El Living	5
El Marítimo	9
Martín Gusinde	1
Midas	3
Ruperto's	15
La Tranquera	13
El Tunel	6

costaus@ctcreuna.cl, ⓦ www.costaustralis
.com. The most luxurious hotel in town, right on
the waterfront, with modern rooms and all mod
cons. Rooms with a city view are cheaper than
those with a sea view. Off-season discounts
available. ❽

Erratic Rock Baquedano 719 ☏ 61/410355,
ⓔ info@erraticrock.com, ⓦ www.erraticrock
.com. Centrally located two-storey building popular
with trekkers and climbers. Free Internet access,
book exchange and luggage storage. Friendly,
experienced staff can arrange half-day, full-day and
multi-day trips. ❸–❹

Glaciares Eberhard 104 ☏ 61/411452,
ⓔ glaciares@entelchile.net, ⓦ www.hotelglaciares
.co.cl. Inside a building that can't make up its mind

whether it's faux-Tudor or Swiss chalet, there's a
clean, welcoming modern hotel. ❼

Hospedaje Chila Carrera Pinto 442 ☏ 61/413981.
Sociable lodging with a marvellously hospitable,
helpful family, a spacious kitchen that guests may
use, and clean shared bathrooms – but some
squeaky beds. ❷

Hostal Bulnes Bulnes 407 ☏ 61/411307,
ⓔ info@hostalbulnes.com, ⓦ www.hostalbulnes
.com. Cosy hostel with a family atmosphere and
well-informed, knowledgeable owners. ❹

Hostal Francis Drake Phillipi 383 ☏ 61/411533,
ⓦ www.chileaustral.com/francisdrake. This smart,
quiet place is a little removed from the centre
but has excellent views of the Ultima Esperanza
sound. ❺

Hostal Nancy Ramirez 540 ☎61/410022,
🄴 nancy@natleslodge.cl, 🅆 www.natleslodge
.cl. Helpful, backpacker-friendly place that can offer
advice and rent out equipment. **❸**

Hostal Oasis Señoret 332 ☎61/411675,
🄴 resoasis@hotmail.com. Friendly place offering
some quiet en-suite rooms, central heating and
good breakfasts. **❸**

Hotel Charles Darwin Bulnes 90 ☎61/412478.
Relatively new hotel just back from the
waterfront that has well-maintained rooms, a bar
and two reading rooms, each with panoramic
views. **❺**

Lady Florence Dixie Bulnes 659 ☎61/411158,
🄵 61/411943, 🄴 florence@chileanpatagonia
.com, 🅆 www.chileanpatagonia.com/florence.
A long-established place, with spacious rooms,
private baths and a slightly old-fashioned
ambience. **❼**

Martín Gusinde Bories 278 ☎61/412820,
🄵 61/225986, 🄴 hqrey@terra.cl, 🅆 www
.austrohoteles.cl. Extremely friendly, comfortable
hotel, with luxurious bathrooms and smart (though
busily decorated) rooms with TV. Also boasts
one of the best restaurants in town (see p.510).
Same owners as *Hostería Lago Grey* in Parque
Nacional Torres del Paine (see p.515); joint bookings possible. Substantial discounts available out
of season. **❼**

Residencial Niko's Ramirez 669 ☎61/412810,
🄴 residencialnikos@hotmail.com. A firm favourite
with backpackers, this is a good place to meet
other travellers, and a handy alternative if
Patagonia Adventure is full. **❷–❸**

Residencial Niko's II Phillipi 528 ☎61/411500.
Sister building of the original on Ramirez; offers
use of kitchen facilities, a laundry service and
Internet access to guests. **❸**

The Town

Puerto Natales sits on the lovely Seno Ultima Esperanza ("Last Hope Sound"),
a narrow turquoise channel that regularly gets whipped up frothy waves.
Grey mountains line the other side, coated with ice and snow, a contrast to
the flat pampa to the east of the town. The channel's name comes from the
1557 explorer, Juan Ladrilleros, who came upon it when he was at the end
of his tether while searching for the western entrance to the Magellan Strait.
He found the strait, but almost all his crew died in the attempt. Following in
his footsteps is a little easier these days, as boats sail three times a day to the
Balmaceda and **Serrano** glaciers, two rivers of ice that flow into the sea (see
box, p.512).

Natales centres on the **Plaza de Armas**, a pleasant spot to prepare for a trek
or unwind after it. The **church** looks a bit uninspiring from the outside, but
features a beautiful altarpiece that occupies one entire wall and depicts local
Indians, dignitaries, the Madonna and Child, and, behind their shoulders, a
delicate painting of the Torres del Paine.

A couple of blocks west of the plaza you'll find the small but well laid-out
Museo Histórico Municipal at Bulnes 285 (summer daily 9am–12.30pm
& 3–8pm; winter Mon–Fri 9am–12.30pm & 2.30–6pm, Sat-Sun 3–6pm;
CH$1000). A carved milodón (see p.511) with a silly smile guards the entrance
to a room full of photos of Aonikenk and Kaweshkar Indians, the area's
original inhabitants: some look unkempt and nervous, others quite noble, and
all wear thick, heavy cloaks, clasped at the groin. The next room holds a collection of memorabilia relating to the region's first settler, a rather fierce-looking
German called Herman Eberhard – look out for his ingenious collapsible boat.
Next door to this are some relics of the Bories sheep-packing plant (the ruins
of which can still be seen on the outskirts of town), which used to process
300,000 sheep a year; the collection includes a ceramic hot water bottle, a
couple of firemen's helmets and a partially squashed trumpet. In a shed out
the back there's the usual collection of stuffed animals: a black-necked swan,
a ñandú, a condor (note the chicken-like feet – the stories of condors carrying away sheep and small children are all myths). If you're still interested in
stuffed animals, then visit the one-room stuffed zoo of the **Museo Colegio**

Salesiano, at Padre Rossa 1456 (daily 9am–1pm & 3–6pm; free), in the southeast of town.

Eating and drinking

Natales has a number of **restaurants** catering to the thousands of tourists passing through each year, and the quality of food is for the most part better than in other similar-sized towns in Chile. For *empanadas* and other snacks, you can try one of the well-stocked **supermarkets**, such as *San Sebastián* at Baquedano 570. However, Natales isn't blessed with bars and clubs – exhausted trekkers seem to collapse into bed rather than drink and dance.

El Asador Patagonico Prat 158. On the eastern side of the plaza, this quality restaurant specializing in grilled meat and spit-roast lamb can easily be identified by the barbecue pit in the window.

La Burbuja Bulnes 300. Bright, lively café-restaurant serving reasonably priced fish and seafood dishes.

Café Melissa Blanco Encalada 258. A bit antiseptic, but with enormous windows that look out onto the main street, and giant sandwiches to match.

Centro Español Magallanes 247. Traditional Chilean restaurant that serves a wide range of fish and meat dishes.

Costaustralis Pedro Montt 262. The hotel has two restaurants, both with beautiful views out over the Sound. The cafeteria serves standard Chilean food and real coffee, while the upmarket restaurant features international food at international prices.

Cristal Bulnes 433–440. Pleasantly decorated in yellow, this fish restaurant offers, remarkably for Chile, fish prepared in other ways than frying. The salmon in butter is particularly good, and not that expensive.

Evasion Ladrilleros 105. Run by Concepto Indigo (see p.507), this trendy spot has sandwiches on wholemeal rolls as big as dinner plates, vegetarian dishes and good pizzas in the evening – though all at higher-than-average prices.

Kaweshkar Lounge Eberhard 161. This corrugated, lime-green shack hides a decent pub that serves a variety of filling meals including pizzas, tacos and salads.

El Living Prat 156 ⓦ www.el-living.com. Smart wooden tables, soothing decor and pleasant tunes create a perfect setting for a drink and a snack or light meal. Cocktails, selected wines, yoghurt drinks, real tea, coffee, cake, moderately priced salads and vegetarian dishes, and even banana sandwiches are available. Closed during the winter.

El Marítimo Pedro Montt 214. A prime spot to come and refuel after a long trek, with truly enormous *lomo a la pobre* (steak with a fried egg on top), excellent seafood spreads and a glorious view to stare at while you digest.

Martín Gusinde Bories 278. Chic restaurant serving conventional but well-prepared meat and seafood dishes, at a price, accompanied by a good selection of wines. Attentive service.

Midas Tomás Rogers 169. Cheerful café on the square, and the only place in these windswept parts that attempts to keep tables and umbrellas upright outside on the pavement despite the gales.

Ruperto's Bulnes s/n. An English-run pub with decent music (live at weekends), a well-stocked bar and a cybercorner.

La Tranquera Bulnes 579. Surly staff serve up standard, inexpensive Chilean fare at this casual restaurant where the walls are covered in photos. It's one of the few places in town that's open on Sundays in the off-season.

El Tunel Eberhard 301. The only nightclub in town – this dynamic spot comes alive late and stays open until 5am and has sumptuous sofas, swings and excellent cocktails.

Listings

Airlines DAP, Bulnes 100 ☏61/415100; LanChile, Rogers 78 ☏61/411236.

Banks and exchange There's an ATM in Banco Santiago, Bulnes 436, and a whole string of *cambios* on Blanco Encalada, including Andes Patagónicos at no. 226, Latino Americana at no. 189 and Omega at no. 238.

Bus companies Buses Cootra, Baquedano 244 ☏61/412785; Buses Fernandez, Eberhard 555 ☏61/411111; Buses Pacheco, Baquedano 244 ☏61/414513; Bus Sur, Baquedano 534 ☏61/411325; Buses Transfer, Baquedano 414 ☏61/410681; Turismo Zaahj, Arturo Prat 236 ☏61/412260, ⒻE61/411355.

Camping equipment Most of the tour operators rent equipment, but try Path@gone, Eberhard 212, which has a wide range of equipment, from stoves (CH$500 a day) to sleeping bags (CH$1500 a day). For butane cylinders, try the hardware shop Casa Pivcevic, Bulnes 613.

Car rental Agencia Andes, Fagnano 523 ☎61/411594; Andes Patagónicos, Blanco Encalada 266 ☎61/411728; EMSA (Avis agent), Bulnes 632 ☎61/410775; Motor Car Puerto Natales, Blanco Encalada 330 ☎61/413593, ⓦwww.motorcars.cl.

Hospital Hospital Puerto Natales, Ignacio Carrera Pinto 537 ☎61/411582 or 411581.

Internet *Concepto Indigo*, Ladrilleros 105 (6–11pm), plus lots of others such as *El Rincón del Tata*, Prat 236 and *Patagoni@net* at Blanco Encalada 330.

Laundry Milodón, Baquedano 642; Servilaundry, Bulnes 513.

Photographic processing Foto Austral, Bulnes 5.

Post office Eberhard 429

Tour operators See box, p.512.

From Puerto Natales to Torres del Paine

From Natales, a fast 150-kilometre road runs through flat Patagonian desert to the Torres del Paine national park. It's a dull drive, except for the **Cueva del Milodón** (summer daily 8am–9pm, winter daily 8.30am–6pm; CH$3000), a standard stop after 21km.

Marked by a large plastic monster at the end of a five-kilometre dirt road signposted left off the main route, the cave itself isn't much more than a hole in the ground, but it has an important history. In 1895 the German settler Herman Eberhard, who owned the land bordering the cave, discovered a human skull and a large piece of skin from an unidentifiable animal. Over the next few years explorers systematically excavated the cave, and dug up an assortment of bones and more fragments of skin, which they eventually traced to a giant sloth called a milodón. This creature was thought to be long extinct, but the excavated skin looked so fresh that rumours began to circulate that it might still be alive. In 1900 an expedition sponsored by London's *Daily Express* arrived to investigate, but no live creatures were found. The skin, it turned out, was so well preserved because it had been deep-frozen by the frigid Patagonian climate. However, the discovery of a stone wall across the cave, and of neatly cut grass stalks in the animal's faeces, led researchers to conclude that ten thousand years ago, a group of Tehuelche Indians had captured a giant sloth and kept it confined here. Modern scientists disagree and think that the Tehuelche herded guanacos here, not mylodons. Shortly after

Moving on from Puerto Natales

Buses to **Punta Arenas** (3hr) leave regularly throughout the day from the various companies' addresses (see "Listings", opposite) and cost CH$4000 one way. They usually stop at Punta Arenas airport on the way – check when you buy your ticket.

The Navimag **ferry** to Puerto Montt leaves once a week during summer, less often in winter. During high season, quadruple cabins start at US$390 per person, double cabins at US$720 per person and single cabins at US$1440. Prices include meals on board and glacier excursions. For more details, see p.507 and p.51.

Buses to the **Torres del Paine** (3hr; CH$7000–10,000 return) leave every morning from 7 to 8am, and every afternoon between 1 and 3pm. They stop anywhere along the road, within reason, but invariably make a halt at three places in the park itself – the park entrance at Laguna Amarga, the Lago Pehoé *guardería* and the park administration building. From October to April, various companies also operate buses from Puerto Natales to **El Calafate** (see p.526) in Argentina (CH$10,000 one way, CH$18,000 return; 5 hr). DAP (see "Listings", opposite) operates a summer air-bridge service between Natales and Calafate every weekday morning; the **flight** takes an hour and costs around CH$30,000 each way including tax.

Tour companies

There are a handful of standard tours run by every one of the dozens of tour operators in town: a half-day trip to the **Cueva del Milodón** (CH$3000), see p.511; a day-trip to the Argentine town of **El Calafate** and the **Parque Nacional Los Glaciares** (from CH$30,000, park entrance extra), mainly to witness the Glaciar Perito Moreno, see p.527; a day-trip to **Torres del Paine** (CH$15,000, park entrance extra), see below; and a boat trip up the Ultima Esperanza Sound to the **Balmaceda and Serrano glaciers**, see p.512. For this last trip, there are two types of boat running: the *21 de Mayo* (CH$25,000) is a slow single-hulled craft, and it also gives you the opportunity of travelling in small inflatable boats up the Serrano River to the Torres del Paine national park (see Turismo 21 de Mayo, opposite); and the two catamarans, (CH$30,000), which are pricier but get you to the glaciers faster and allow you an extra hour to explore and perhaps go for an ice hike (see Concepto Indigo, p.507).

As usual, many of the operators offering standard tours are pretty indistinguishable, but we've selected some of the more reliable names. However, just because a company's not listed here doesn't mean it's no good. There are also a few organizations in town offering slightly different options, taking in off-the-beaten-track destinations.

Aventour Bulnes 698 ⓣ & ⓕ61/410825. A Punta Arenas company that's recently expanded into Puerto Natales and is now running one of the catamarans to the glaciers.

Baqueano Zamora Baquedano 534 ⓣ & ⓕ61/412911, ⓔbaqueanoz@tie.cl, ⓦwww.baqueanozamora.com. This outfit arranges horse-trekking in Torres del Paine from a couple of hours (at around CH$30,000 an hour) as well as longer hikes of up to four days.

Big Foot Bories 206 ⓣ61/414611, ⓕ61/414276, ⓔexplore@bigfootpatagonia.com, ⓦwww.bigfootpatagonia.com. They specialize in climbing and kayaking, offering a day of ice-hiking on Glacier Grey (upward of CH$55,000) and one-, two-, and three-day ice-climbing seminars (CH$99,000–267,000.) They also run kayaking day-trips on the Eberhard Fjord from CH$50,000, three-day kayaking tours down the Río Serran (starting from CH$260,000) and a four-day journey to the Tyndall Glacier from CH$315,000.

Chile Nativo Barros Arana 176, casilla 42 ⓣ61/411835, ⓕ61/415474, ⓔinfo@chilenativo.com, ⓦwww.chilenativo.com. Dynamic young outfit specializing in top-end bespoke trips including three- to eight-day horse-trekking tours of the

the 1900 expedition an unscrupulous gold prospector and Charley Milward (see p.497) dynamited the cave's floor, uncovering and then selling the remaining skin and bones. Two pieces made their way to Britain: one to the Natural History Museum in London, and the other to Charley Milward's family.

To the northwest of the cave, the Seno Ultima Esperanza continues on for about 100km until it meets the Río Serrano, which, after 36km, arrives at the **Balmaceda** and **Serrano glaciers**. A boat trip here (run by most of the tour operators in Puerto Natales – see above) is one of the most beautiful in the entire area. It takes seven hours and you pass a colony of cormorants and a slippery mass of sea lions. The glaciers themselves make an impressive sight, especially when a chunk of ice the size of a small house breaks off and crashes into the water. They form the tip of the **Parque Nacional Bernardo O'Higgins**, the largest and (in terms of people per area) least visited national park in the whole of Chile. The east of the park is almost entirely made up of the Campo de Hielo Sur (the Southern Ice Field); the west is comprised of fjords, islands and untouched forest. The Navimag boat (see p.511) passes through, but the only way of exploring the park in any detail is to have your own boat.

region, visiting out-of-the-way locations, in addition to bird-spotting and photographic safaris.

Estancia Travel Casa 13-b, Puerto Bories ℡ & ℻61/412221, ⓔinfo@estanciatravel .com, ⓦwww.estanciatravel.com. British run top-end company based just outside Puerto Natales that specializes in multi-day horse-riding trips around southern Patagonia and the Torres del Paine. Also organizes kayaking and fly-fishing excursions.

Knudsen Blanco Encalada 284 ℡ & ℻61/411819, ⓔknudsen@pnet.cl. A friendly old company running conventional tours.

Patagonia Ice Blanco Encalada 183 ℡ & ℻61/410630. Runs the basic tours, changes money and makes flight arrangements.

Path@gone Eberhard 595 ℡61/413291, ℻61/413290, ⓔpathgone@entelchile.com, ⓦwww.pathgone.com. The shared office of three of the biggest companies in Puerto Natales. **Andescape** (℡61/412877, ℻61/412592, ⓔandescape@terra.cl, ⓦwww .andescapetour.cl) and **Fantastico Sur** (℡61/411572, ⓔinfo@lastorres.com, ⓦwww .lastorres.com/lodges) run the *refugios* in the Torres del Paine park and are the first stop if you want to book a bed there. The third company, **Onas Patagonia** (℡ & ℻61/412707, ⓔonas@chileaustral.com, ⓦwww.onaspatagonia.com), specializes in water-based activities, including trips up the Serrano River in a Zodiac inflatable boat (CH$60,000) and a two-day sea kayaking excursion (CH$150,000).

Servitur Arturo Prat 353 ℡61/411858, ℻61/411328, ⓔservitour@terra.cl, ⓦwww .servitour.cl. An established local company, specializing in tours to Torres del Paine.

Tour Express Bulnes 769 ℡61/410734, ℻61/411639, ⓔinfo@tourexpress.cl, ⓦwww .tourexpress.cl. Organizes decent tours to Torres del Paine as well as to the Perito Moreno Glacier.

Turismo 21 de Mayo Eberhard 554 ℡ & ℻61/411978 and Ladrilleros 171 ℡ & ℻61/411176, ⓔ21demayo@chileaustral.com, ⓦwww.turismo21demayo.cl. Organizes day trips and sailing excursions to Parque Nacional Bernardo O'Higgins on their private cutter, *21 de Mayo*, and yacht, *Alberto de Angostini*.

Turismo Río Natales Bulnes 100 ℡ & ℻61/415100. Small outfit offering a selection of standard tours to Torres del Paine and the Milodón Cave as well as kayaking and trips to the glaciers.

Back on the main road, you'll find accommodation at the simple but attractive *Hotel Posada Tres Pasos*, 38km north of Puerto Natales (℡61/225167 or 02/1969630, ⓦwww.hotel3pasos.cl; ❺). The border village of **Cerro Castillo** (border open Dec–March 8am–10pm), 58km north of Puerto Natales, has a basic cafeteria and the reasonable *Hospedaje Loreto Belén* (℡61/413063; ❹). The most that the tourist leaflet can boast of is a 1943 sheep-shearing shed. Around 10km north of Cerro Castillo, you'll come to the turn-off to the beautifully sited *Hostería El Pionero*, km 315, Ruta 9 (℡61/412911; ❼), owned and run by Baqueano Zamora, an agency that specializes in horse-trekking (see box, above).

Parque Nacional Torres del Paine

One of the world's stunning geographical features is the **Paine Massif** (56km northwest of Cerro Castillo), the unforgettable centrepiece of the **PARQUE NACIONAL TORRES DEL PAINE** (daily 8.30am–8pm;

△ Gaucho, Torres del Paine

summer CH$10,000 for foreigners, CH$4000 for Chileans; winter CH$5000 for foreigners, CH$3000 for Chileans). Rising above the flat brown pampa, the massif features a small range of mountains topped by weird twisted peaks and unfeasibly smooth towers. Wandering around the giants' castles and demons' lairs is one of the highlights of any trip to Chile. On the eastern side are the soaring, unnaturally elegant **Torres del Paine** ("Paine Towers"), the icon of the park, and further west, the dark-capped, sculpted **Cuernos del Paine** ("Paine Horns"), which rise above the moonscape of the **Valle del Francés** ("French Valley"). To the east of the park is the broad ice river of **Glaciar Grey**, and on the plains at the mountains' feet large herds of **guanacos** and the odd *ñandú* still run wild.

That said, if you're coming here to taste wilderness you may be disappointed, as the park is usually full of people and fully equipped with *refugios*, campsites and hotels. The compensation for this development, though, is that the park is well managed, there's hardly any litter on the trails, people generally camp only in designated sites and erosion is being kept to a minimum. And should you get lost, the *guardaparques* will come out to look for you, as all the campsites and refuges in the park are linked by radio.

Arrival and information

The only entrance to the park for those coming by bus is 117km from Natales at **Laguna Amarga**. The Conaf station (*guardería*) here isn't much more than a hut with a map on the wall where you pay your entrance fee and give your name, but a regular bus connects it with the *Hostería Las Torres* (CH$3500; entitles you to a free night of camping at the *Hostería Las Torres* or at *Los Cuernos*, see opposite and p.519), 7km to the west, the starting point of the two most important trails. If you don't want to take the bus, expect to walk for about 1.5hr before reaching the start point of the treks. The buses from Natales continue along to the south of the massif and Lago Nordenskjöld, to arrive at the **Lago Pehoé** *guardería* after another 19km, near the departure point for the ferry to

Refugio Pehoé and the impressive cataract of Salto Grande (Large Waterfalls). The road continues beyond here, past Hostería Pehoé, Camping Pehoé and Hotel Explora, opposite Salto Chico, to reach the **park administration** building (daily 8.30am–8pm) after 18km, around which there's a visitor centre, a refuge, a grocery store, a *hostería* and even a post office. On the map, it looks like you can continue on along this road, and eventually return to Puerto Natales, but you can't because the road's not open to the public. You can also enter the park on the **inflatable boats** that travel up the Río Serrano (see Onas Patagonia, under Path@gone, in box on p.513). These arrive opposite *Hostería Cabañas del Paine*, where they're met by a minibus that heads 9km north to the park administration building, where you catch a bus.

The best place for general **information** is the park administration building, although all the *guarderías* can provide information about the state of the trails. Most also have a large map of the park to help you get your bearings. You'll be given a basic overview map of the park and trails when you pay your entrance fee. Alternatively, *Torres del Paine*, number 13 in the JLM/ Entel series, covers the area in more detail and is widely available in Puerto Natales.

In January and February the park is crammed with holidaymakers, so the **best months to visit** are November and December or March and April. Although in winter (June to September) temperatures can fall to -10°C (14°F) or even lower, freezing lakes and icing over trails, and there's the possibility of snow (though it's surprisingly rare), the small numbers of visitors, lack of wind and often clear visibility can also make this another good time to come – just wrap up warmly.

Accommodation

You'll find several different types of accommodation in the park: unserviced (free) campsites, serviced campsites, *refugios*, and *hosterías*. Wild camping isn't permitted.

Hosterías

The park's **hosterías** are expensive in comparison with those in Puerto Natales or Punta Arenas – the rooms are mostly decent enough but unimaginative, and the same goes for the food in the restaurants.

Hostería Lago Grey ☏ & ℱ61/410172, ℮hgrey@terra.cl or ℮info@lagogrey.cl, ⓦwww .lagogrey.cl. This *hostería* has a beautiful view of Glaciar Grey, across a lake dotted with floating icebergs. They also run boat trips (CH$140,000 per person) and dinghy runs (CH$70,000) on Lago Grey as well as dinghy runs down the Ríos Pingo and Grey (CH$40,000 per person). The guides are excellent. ❽

Hostería Mirador del Payne ☏61/228712, ℱ61/410498, ℮hosteria@miradordelpayne.com, ⓦwww.miradordelpayne.com/. Formerly known as the *Estancia Lazo*, this is a colonial-style house with a veranda and eight *cabañas* beneath Laguna Verde, beneath the mirador Sierra del Toro, in a quiet corner of the park. ❽

Hostería Pehoé ☏61/411390 or ☏2/2350252, ℮gerencia@pehoe.com, ⓦwww.pehoe.cl. Beautifully sited on a small island in Lago Pehoé looking out to the highest peaks of the Paine Massif. There's a warm bar and restaurant. ❽

Hostería Las Torres ☏61/411572 and ☏61/710050, ℮info@lastorres.com, ⓦwww .lastorres.com. Spread out across a couple of fields and seemingly growing every year, *Las Torres* has the feel of an *estancia*, and good views up to the Torres del Paine. They sometimes arrange sheep-shearing exhibitions followed by barbecues, so you can shave your meal before you eat it. ❽

Hotel Explora ☏61/411247, ℮explora@torresdelpaine.com, ⓦwww.explora .com. Conceived as a base for expeditions, this is the most extravagant hotel in the park, set near the Salto Chico. Twenty-five tours are offered, from day treks to horse-riding. Fully inclusive eight-night packages cost upward of US$2740 and rise to US$4778 for suites with a view of Paine Grande; four-night packages start at US$1560. ❾

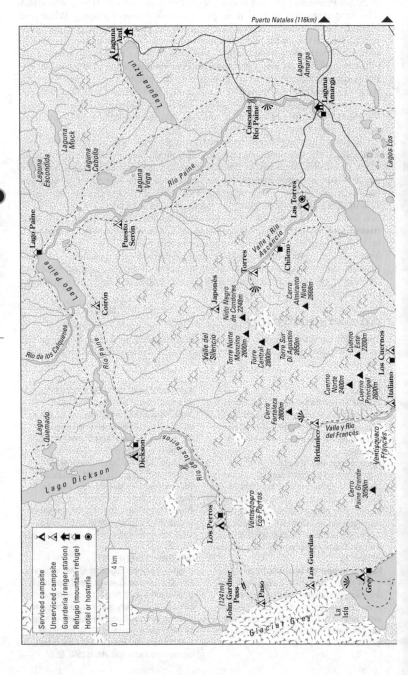

Serviced campsite
Unserviced campsite
Guardería (ranger station)
Refugio (mountain refuge)
Hotel or hostería

0   4 km

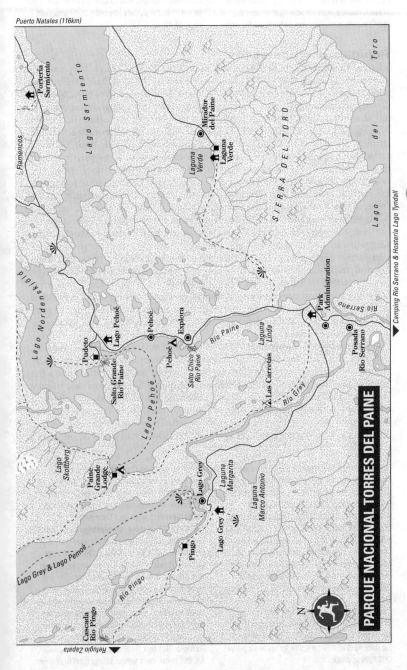

PARQUE NACIONAL TORRES DEL PAINE

Portería Sarmiento

Flamencos

Lago Sarmiento

Mirador del Paine

Laguna Verde

SIERRA DEL TORO

Lago del Toro

Lago Nordenskjöld

Pudeto

Lago Pehoé

Pehoé

Explora

Pehoé

Salto Grande Río Paine

Salto Chico Río Paine

Río Paine

Laguna Linda

Las Carretas

Río Grey

Park Administration

Río Serrano

Posada Río Serrano

▶ Camping Río Serrano & Hostería Lago Tyndall

Lago Skottberg

Paine Grande Lodge

Lago Pehoé

Lago Grey

Laguna Margarita

Laguna Marco Antonio

Lago Grey & Lago Pehoé

Lago Grey

Pingo

Río Pingo

Cascada Río Pingo

◀ Refugio Zapata

N

Posada Río Serrano ☎61/410684. Comfortable *hostería* housed in an attractive old structure near the park administration building, on the site : of the first *estancia*. Run by Baqueano Zamora (see p.512), the posada has been much improved recently. **❻–❼**

Refugios and campsites

The **refugios** in the park are usually open from September to May and are generally closed by the weather during the rest of the year. Most are run by two companies, Fantástico Sur (☎61/226054, ✉info@lastorres.com, ⊕www .lastorres.com/lodges) and Andescape (☎61/412877, ✉andescape@terra .cl, ⊕www.andescapetour.cl), who share the Path@gone office in Puerto Natales, at Eberhard 595 (☎61/413290 or 413291, ✉pathgone@entelchile .com; see box p.513). Buildings range from a bare hut with nothing but a wood-fired stove (usually free) to modern chalets with a restaurant, which charge around CH$19,000 per person for a bed. A slightly discounted rate is available if you book in advance and pay in US dollars, since foreigners are exempt from the sales tax levied on the charge. Cooked evening meals are available in the *refugios* for around CH$8500. You can also get breakfast (CH$4000–5000) and lunch boxes. None comes with bedding, although you can rent a sleeping bag (CH$3500–4500) at the flashier places. Much of the year you can just turn up and get a bunk, but from December to February everywhere gets very busy, so you'll need to book in advance. If you're camping and took the shuttle bus from Laguna Amarga to Hostería Las Torres, you're entitled to a free night's camping at either Camping Las Torres or at Los Cuernos upon presentation of the ticket. Conaf also operates a number of free *refugios* throughout the park (Zapata, Pingo, Laguna Verde, Laguna Amarga, Lago Paine and Pudeto) although these are very basic and frequently in poor states of repair.

The **unserviced campsites** (Campamento Las Torres, Japonés, Italiano, Británico, Los Guardos, Paso, Coirón and Puesto Seron on the Torres del Paine Circuit and Campamento Las Carretas to the south) are free and are just a flat patch of land and a *fogón*. All the **serviced campsites** listed below cost money (around CH$3500 per person, unless otherwise stated below), but they do have ablution blocks. There are sometimes even small shops connected to the *refugios* although these tend to charge vastly inflated prices for food and drink; for instance a gas canister will set you back CH$5000 and a can of soft drink CH$1200.

Campamento Los Perros (Andescape). Last campsite (CH$3500 per person) before the John Garner pass – there used to be a *refugio* here too, but it was burnt down by careless trekkers.
Campamento Serón (Fantástico Sur). At the end of the first normal day's hike on the "Circuit" (see p.521), a campsite at the bottom of the northeast corner of the massif (CH$3500 per person).
Camping Lago Pehoé ☎61/266910. Campsite on the eastern edge of Lago Pehoé beneath a couple of excellent miradors. CH$12,000 for up to six people.
Camping Laguna Azul ☎61/411157, ✉qulloa@laraucana.cl, ⊕www.laraucana.cl. On the shores of a little-visited lake to the northeast of the park. CH$10,000 for a site for up to six people, CH$3000 to picnic.

Camping Serrano ☎61/691931. Out of the way, south of the park administration building, this campsite is on a bend in the Río Serrano and accessible from the road. A site costs CH$8000.
Paine Grande Lodge and Camping ☎61/412742, ⊕www.verticepatagonia.cl (Andescape). This new, modern structure, also known as Refugio Pehoé or Vertice Lodge (CH$19,000 per person), stands alongside the old wooden *refugio* and is a firm favourite for its scenic location and modern comforts, even though the building itself is an eyesore. You can camp in the adjoining grassy fields (CH$3500 per person). There is a separate toilet and cooking block (with free gas) for campers, and also a small store within the lodge.
Refugio Dickson (Andescape). Quiet and peaceful, this is the most remote refuge (CH$13,000 per

person) in the park, on the shores of Lago Dickson on the northern part of the Circuit. Camping also possible (CH$3500 per person).

Refugio Lago del Toro (no phone). The Conaf-run *refugio* near the park administration building (ask there), just a hut with a wood stove. CH$5000 per bed.

Refugio y Camping Chileno (Fantástico Sur). It's halfway up the Valle Ascencio, at the foot of the Torres del Paine. CH$19,000 per person at the refuge, CH$3500 at the campsite.

Refugio y Camping Grey (Andescape). A popular *refugio* (CH$13,000 per person) and campsite (CH$3500 per person) thanks to its position by Glaciar Grey.

Refugio y Camping Las Torres (Fantástico Sur). Near the park entrance at the Laguna Amarga and the *Hostería Las Torres*, this place is a first-night stop for those who are taking it easy. CH$19,000 per person in the refuge, CH$3500 per person to camp.

Refugio y Camping Los Cuernos (Fantástico Sur). An isolated modern hut (CH$19,000 per person) in a forest beneath the Cuernos del Paine, on the northern shore of Lago Nordenskjöld, with a restaurant and campsite (CH$3500 per person). Campers may use a small stove in the *refugio* to cook for CH$1000.

Exploring the park

You'll have seen photographs of the park long before you visit, as the pristine-smooth rock towers that are the actual **Torres del Paine** grace just about every piece of tourist literature – not to mention calendars – produced in Chile. And yet nothing really prepares you for your first sight of it all. As you travel across the barren featureless expanses of Patagonia, your eye gets accustomed to dreary flatness, and then suddenly the **Paine Massif** rises up from the grasslands like a mirage. In your shock, it's easy to shoot off a roll of film before you even get a good view of these chiselled turrets, but it's best to wait until you're closer, as the finest views are from the south bank of Lago Nordenskjöld, whose waters act as a great reflecting mirror.

What you see is one very large mountain, or set of mountains, the main body of which is made up of the twin peaks of **Monte Almirante Nieto** (2668m and 2640m). The massif is essentially an enormous rectangle of rock, 22km long and 14km wide, cut into by two valleys – the **Valle Ascencio** in the east, and the **Valle del Francés** in the middle. From every angle the massif looks

△ Parque Nacional Torres del Paine

Fire in Torres del Paine

On February 17th 2005, during the peak tourist season, a ferocious **fire** broke out in the **Parque Nacional Torres del Paine**. A Czech trekker, camping in an unofficial spot usually used for grazing, accidentally knocked over a campstove, which ignited the tinder dry grass. Strong winds fanned the fire, which raged for over a month. In the end, 800 firefighters from both Chile and Argentina were able to bring the blaze under control, but only once the winds abated. According to preliminary reports by *Conaf*, the fire affected approximately seven percent of the park, damaging around 15,000 hectares making it the worst fire in the park for two decades. Although the principal features of the park and the main trekking routes escaped undamaged, the eastern reaches around Laguna Azul and Laguna Cebolla were badly affected. Experts consider that it will take the park twelve years to recover. Although a massive **restoration project**, including reforestation and the reintroduction of native species, is underway, it's still possible to see charred trees and vast, startling ashy scars on the approach to Hosteria Las Torres (see p.515) and throughout the fire-ravaged sectors. The trekker has acknowledged his responsibility, expressed great remorse and donated US$1000 to the fund.

Throughout the month of the fire, the park remained open and there has been no noticeable dip in visitors to Torres del Paine. The park authorities acted quickly to reassure nervous tour operators and to announce that the park remained a stunning, rugged wilderness that could be explored safely. Their only request is that visitors to the park abide by the regulations and respect the set of rules laid out to preserve and protect this natural treasure.

---

different and reveals hidden peaks, valleys and cliffs. The western edge is fringed by **Glaciar Grey**, which is more than 7km wide at its largest point and stretches back into the **Campo de Hielo Sur** ("Southern Ice Field"), over ten thousand square kilometres of ice cap and one of the largest ice fields outside the poles.

The best way to explore the massif is on foot, and there are two hikes (see below) that take in most of the main features; they are well marked with red or orange paint. Both start in the east, at the foot of the **Valle Ascencio**, up which hide the three **Torres del Paine** – Torre Monzino (2600m), **Torre Central** (2800m) and **Torre D'Agostini** (2850m). Further west, guarding the entrance to the Valle del Francés, are the **Cuernos del Paine**, a set of incredibly carved towers capped with dark rock peaks: **Cuerno Principal** (2600m), **Cuerno Este** (2200m) and **Cuerno Norte** (2400m). The **Valle del Francés** itself is one of the glories of the park, a high-altitude valley ringed by a rock curtain-wall, broken by peaks whose names describe them well: Catedral ("Cathedral",), Castillo ("Castle"), Espada ("Sword") and Aleta de Tiburon ("Shark's Fin"). Both hikes also visit the icy bastion of the **Glaciar Grey**.

Around the massif lie large pools and rivers of glacial melt water, which flow to the nearby fjords of the Seno Ultima Esperanza. The main river is the Río Serrano, a freezing torrent that plunges through uninhabited rainforest and leads to the glaciers **Serrano** and **Balmaceda** in Parque Nacional Bernardo O'Higgins (see p.512).

Hikes in the park

There are two extremely popular hikes. First is the traditional **"Circuit"**, for which you need a week at least. This is for the more leisurely hiker, though that doesn't mean it is all smooth sailing. Those with less time tend to opt for the shorter, more intense **"W" trail**, which takes you to the "stars" of the park, the Towers themselves. Anyone set on seeing more, or getting away from the madding crowds, especially in the January high season, can explore lesser known trails such as the walk to **Laguna Azul** and on to Lago Paine, or the climb to **Mirador Zapata**.

The Circuit

The most common way of seeing the park, the Circuit is a six- to seven-day walk around the whole of the massif, longer if you're tempted up the Valle del Francés or the Valle Ascencio along the way (see "The W", p.522). It's not as daunting as it sounds, as for the most part it's quite flat. That said, there's one stiff pass, the Paso John Gardner, where you have to climb 600m, and a couple of steep climbs if you're heading up either of the two valleys. Though you can tackle it in either direction, the counterclockwise route is easier and also means that your first sight of the Glaciar Grey will be more dramatic. Therefore the day-by-day description of the hike below takes that direction.

You should aim to be at the *Hostería Las Torres* at 11am (feasible if you catch the 7am bus from Puerto Natales). If the weather is promising you may want to see the **Torres** first (on the "W" trail, see p.522). If that's the case, start up the **Valle Ascencio** early in the afternoon, spend the night at *Hostería Las Torres*, and then hike the Circuit the next day. Otherwise head off northeast in the signposted direction of *Campamento Serón*. (Go back down the road along which the bus brought you to the *hostería* — the path strikes off to the north, or left, 1km from it.) The first day's hike takes four to five hours, through gentle meadows grazed by large herds of guanacos; you should spend the night at *Serón*.

The second day takes you to *Refugio Dickson*, a five- to six-hour slog along the Río Paine. This section of the trail tends to be boggy mud, especially later on, but it is for the most part shaded and you are treated to fabulous views of Cerro Stokes and other peaks; about halfway along is the unserviced *Coirón* campsite, set among trees at the western end of Lago Paine, useful if you want to break the journey. The modern *refugio* sits at the southern end of iceberg-flecked Lago Dickson. Fast trekkers can get here from *Hostería Las Torres* in ten hours, but that hardly leaves time to admire the scenery on the way.

Day three, keeping to the conventional schedule, will get you to *Campamento Los Perros*, through dense forest and past a pretty little waterfall, four hours on from *Dickson*. At *Los Perros*, where you can admire fantastic views of cascade-veiled mountains and a host of glaciers, you need to wait for the weather to be in your favour before starting on a three- to four-hour climb to the top of **Paso John Gardner** (1241m) following cairns and orange markings that are sometimes covered by snow. Make sure you are waterproofed, as there's no way of escaping most of the freezing streams and bogs through which you'll have to walk, though thankfully the Río de los Perros has been bridged. The reward for all this is the staggering view from the top of the pass over the icy pinnacles of **Glaciar Grey** and the vast immaculate expanse of the **Campo del Hielo Sur** (Southern Ice Field), and in any case the path becomes drier and rockier the higher up you climb. On the other side of the pass the path descends steeply, and is overgrown by beech forest or scourged by the wind, and it's easy to get lost here despite the cairns to show the way. Mud, scree-filled ravines and fallen tree trunks conspire to make this one of the toughest stretches of the whole circuit, but the views, weather permitting, are fabulous. Ideally you want to reach *Refugio y Camping Grey*, six or seven hours from the pass, by nightfall, but if the weather's foul that won't be possible. Don't worry if you're not going to make it, as there's a small unserviced campsite at the foot of the pass called

Campamento Paso, one to two hours from the high point of the trek; a stream nearby provides drinking water. Much better, but another three hours farther down, is *Campamento Las Guardas* (also free), which at least has toilets and an area for cooking.

Refugio y Camping Grey is beautifully sited at the foot of Glaciar Grey. A short side path leads to a mirador overlooking the snout of the glacier. It is possible to take the following day off and go for ice-hikes over the glacier (organized by Big Foot/Concepto Indigo in Puerto Natales, see p.512), undertake a mini trek on La Isla, in the centre of Lago Grey, in order to get a different perspective on the glacier or just admire the views across this fascinating mass of Ice Age ice. From here, it's a long day's trek along the northern shore of Lago Grey, around the southernmost corner of the massif and back along to the mouth of the **Valle del Francés**, via the *Paine Grande Lodge*. From there you can either head up the valley (see "The W"), or continue on for another two hours to *Refugio Los Cuernos* and *Camping Los Cuernos*, which nestle under the shadow of the strangely weathered ram's horns of the **Cuernos del Paine**. After *Los Cuernos* you've almost made it, with only a four-hour stroll along the northwest side of Lago Nordenskjöld to the circuit starting point at the *Hostería Las Torres*.

The "W"

The "W" is the current favourite hike, partly because it is quicker to do than the Circuit. It's called the "W" because the route you follow looks like a "W", up three valleys and along the bottom of the southern face of the massif. On average it takes four to five days to complete all three valleys.

From the *Hostería Las Torres*, you start by heading west along the foot of the massif. Just after a bridge you head uphill, up the Valle Ascencio, and it's possible to spend the first night in the *Refugio y Camping Chileno*, and leave your pack there if you want. It's a hard climb, but rest assured that the very worst bit is at the beginning and just about anyone can manage it if they pace themselves. If you find yourself at *Chileno* with time to burn, press on through lenga brush, fording a stream, to the *Campamento Torres*, a free, unserviced campsite by another stream, ninety minutes up the valley from *Chileno* at the foot of the track up to the **Torres** themselves. From *Campamento Torres* most people turn west and head up the small valley to the foot of the peaks, much of the route involving a thigh-aching clamber up uneven boulders. After around forty-five minutes you arrive: if the clouds clear you are treated to a stunning postcard view across Laguna Torres, a grey tarn, up to the three strange statuesque towers that give the massif and park their name and the sheer Cerro Nido de Condor down which waterfalls sometimes cascade. Give yourself some time, after the stiff climb, to take in the sheer majesty of them; they are at their most gorgeous in dawn or late afternoon light.

An alternative trek from *Campamento Torres* is to press on north for an hour or so, guided by cairns, to the *Campamento Japonés*, another free and unserviced site that is popular with climbers hoping to tackle the Torres. Along the way the path crosses a couple of icy brooks and some massive rock falls, so have your wits about you. At *Japonés* you'll find a hidden valley, aptly called the **Valle del Silencio**, that also heads west. It's much less visited than the Torres and a great place to escape the crowds.

For the middle arm of the W, the **Valle del Francés**, head downhill again towards the *Hostería Las Torres*, but, after you reach the bridge where you turned up the Valle Ascencio, turn right (west) and continue along the foot of the massif. After three hours of trekking along the northwest banks of deep-blue Lago Nordenskjöld, you'll reach the *Refugio y Camping Los Cuernos*, an excellent place to stay the night (see p.519). Alternatively you can press on another two hours to the free *Campamento Italiano* (unserviced except for toilets), which has two sections, one higher up the valley. Water has to be drawn from the Río del Frances. From *Italiano*, head due north up the Valle del Francés. It takes two and a half hours of hiking, some of it rather steep, but with great views of the **Glaciar Francés** along the way, to reach another campsite, *Campamento Británico* (free, with drinking water but no toilets). Allow another hour or two to trudge up granite scree and reach a viewpoint at the head of the valley, taking time if possible on the way to admire Paine Grande, the massif's highest peak at 3050m, to your west. You should also be able to see the fin-shaped Aleta del Tiburón (1850m) to the north, and the twisted Cuernos to the southeast, plus the castle-like Fortaleza ("Fortress"), peaking at 2800m, ahead of you. In truly clear weather you can also spy the backside of the Torres. Now turn around and head south again.

Back down at *Campamento Italiano*, cross the suspension bridge spanning the Río del Frances and carry on to the west via the eastern shore of Lago Skottsberg, and after two hours you'll cross a series of moraine ridges to reach the *Paine Grande Lodge and Camping*, where you should spend the night. From here, head northwest through ñire glens, up the northern side of **Lago Grey**, the third arm of the "W", to *Refugio Grey* and *Camping Grey*, relatively near Glaciar Grey, a four-hour walk away. About a third of the way up the aptly named **Quebrada de los Vientos** ("Windy Gorge"), is a marked viewpoint over Lago Grey, just after the much smaller **Laguna Roca**, home to duck colonies. The route up to the *refugio* and campsite, past waterfalls and striped cliffs, is not one steady climb, but a roller-coaster of valleys, streams and lenga copses. Once you're at the top, don't miss the nearby *mirador*, affording great views of the glacier.

From *Grey*, unless you are now tempted by the Circuit, you must go back the way you came, to *Paine Grande*. Here, apart from walking back to *Hostería Las Torres*, there are two options. One is to pick up a **boat** across Lago Pehoé (Nov & late-March daily at 12.30pm and 6.30pm; Dec–mid-March three times daily at 10am, 12.30pm and 6.30pm; rest of year daily at 12.30pm; CH$10,000 with one piece of luggage, tickets sold at the shop in the campsite or on board) to *Refugio Pudeto*, half a kilometre from the main road, from where you can catch a bus to Puerto Natales (they wait for the boat crossing). Note that if there's too much wind, the boat doesn't operate. In that case, the alternative way out is the four- to five-hour hike to the park administration building along the long, flat pampa to the south of Lago Pehoé. From the park administration there are regular buses to Puerto Natales, the last leaving at 6.30pm.

Other trails

The two most popular walks by no means exhaust the park. There's a three-and-a-half-hour signposted walk from Guardería Laguna Amarga to **Laguna Azul**, a secluded and little-visited lake in the northeast, on whose banks camping is usually possible. From Laguna Azul there's a four-hour trail past Laguna Cebolla to **Lago Paine**, where there's an unserviced refuge, with lots of wild berries nearby for extra sustenance, and thereafter it's another long four-hour trudge to *Refugio Dickson*, which you can reach only if you can arrange for someone to ferry you across the Río Paine.

Laguna Verde is another remote lake, five hours' walk through lenga forest; the trail starts to the east of the park administration building, which is also served by a spur from the Torres del Paine–Puerto Natales road. The fact that so few people come here encourages an abundance of wildlife (guanacos, foxes, hares, rheas and loads of birds), the main reason for doing this trail. Another seldom-trod path takes you up to **Mirador Zapata**, five to six hours from *Guardería Lago Grey* at the southern tip of Lago Grey, itself a four-and-a-half-hour walk from the park administration building. It's a steep but doable climb, rewarding you with views of all the park's lakes plus the ice cap and a magnificent glacier, Glaciar Pingo. You'll find unserviced campsites along the route at the basic *Refugio Pingo* and *Refugio Zapata*. There is also a steep, signposted one-hour trek up the hill behind the *guardería* to Mirador Ferrier, with excellent views.

Other ways of exploring the park

If you want to explore the park but don't want to walk, there are a few different options. You can hire **horses** from the *Hostería Las Torres* and trek to the Torres, the Cuernos, or along the shore of Lago Nordenskjöld — prices start at around CH\$20,000 for three hours. For a similar price, you can ride in a **four-wheel-drive vehicle** on the tracks to Lago Paine in the north, or Lago Azul in the south. The *Hostería Las Torres* can arrange this, too, as can Andescape (see p.513). Alternatively, Zodiac inflatable **boats** run up and down the Río Serrano (prices start around CH\$45,000; see Onas Patagonia, p.513), while a large, conventional boat run by *Hostería Lago Grey* makes a three-hour return trip (CH\$30,000) twice daily to Glaciar Grey at 9am and 3pm. The boat cannot make the run when the lake's blocked by ice.

To **climb** in the park, you'll need to get a permit from the Dirección de Fronteras y Limites (see "Basics", p.72, for details), and Conaf; the latter costs CH\$60,000 and covers any ascent.

Into Argentina: Parque Nacional Los Glaciares

Just over the easily crossed border in Argentina are two of the region's star attractions: the trekkers' and climbers' paradise of the **Fitz Roy Sector** in the north of the **Parque Nacional Los Glaciares**, accessed from relaxed **El Chaltén**; and, to the south, the craggy blue face of the **Glaciar Perito Moreno**, regularly cited as one of the world's natural wonders, situated near the touristy town of **El Calafate**, only five hours by bus from Puerto Natales.

The wild expanse of the **Parque Nacional Los Glaciares** encompasses several environments: the enormous sterile glaciers that flow down from the heights of the Southern Continental Ice Cap; thick, sub-Antarctic woodland of deciduous lenga and *ñire*, and evergreen *guindo* and *canelo*; savage unclimbed crags where 5000mm of precipitation falls in a year; and billiard-table Patagonian *meseta* with an annual rainfall of little more than 100mm. A southern chunk of the park was ceded to Chile in 1999 after the dispute over borders in the area of the ice cap, but it remains Argentina's largest. The vast majority of the park is off-limits to the public, and most travellers visit only the Fitz Roy Sector and the area around the Glaciar Perito Moreno. For more detailed information see the *Rough Guide to Argentina*.

The Fitz Roy Massif and El Chaltén

The northernmost section of Argentina's **Parque Nacional Los Glaciares** contains the **FITZ ROY MASSIF**, boasting some of the most breathtakingly beautiful mountain peaks on the planet. Two concentric jaws of jagged teeth puncture the Patagonian sky, with the 3445-metre incisor of **Monte Fitz Roy** at the centre.

The base for **trekking** in this area is **EL CHALTÉN**, which has expanded greatly since it was established in 1985 in a rather uncoordinated fashion, not always sympathetic to its natural surroundings. There's not much to do here, save gear up for hikes, but the atmosphere is pleasant and relaxed with a good mix of Argentines and foreign visitors.

Call in at the **national park information centre**, about 800 metres before the village (daily 8am–8pm; ℡ & ℻02962/493004), which offers all kinds of general information, plus specifics for climbers, who *must* register here, as should anyone planning to stay at the Lago Toro *refugio* and campsite to the south. Try to make one of the centre's highly informative, free slide shows in English on Thursdays at 8pm. The helpful tourist office is located in the Comisión de Fomento (May–Sept Mon–Fri 9am–3pm; Oct–April Mon–Fri 8am–8pm, Sat–Sun noon–7pm; ℡02962/493011), on the left of the main street just as you enter the town.

Stay at *La Base*, Lago del Desierto (℡02962/493031; ❹), which has some of the best-value rooms around, several with rare mountain views; the neat rooms with great beds or smart bungalows of *Casa de Piedra*, Lago del Desierto s/n (℡ & ℻02962/493015; ❻), whose knowledgeable geologist owner also works as a guide; or, more cheaply, at a hostel such as *Albergue Patagonia*, San Martín 493 (℡ & ℻02962/493019; AR$22 for HI members) or *Condor de los Andes*, Río de la Vuelta s/n (℡02962/493101; closed in winter) which has cosy double rooms for AR$90 and dorm beds for AR$22 . You can enjoy tasty fare, including venison ragout, at *Ruca Mahuida* on Lionel Terray, just off San Martín. Alternatively, try *Fuegi Bistro*, the restaurant of *Albergue Patagonia* (see above) or the cosy confitería *La Casita* opposite the Fitz Roy Inn on San Martín. Stock up on supplies at the *Stella Maris* **supermarket**, at the beginning of Avenida San Martín, and *El Gringuito*, a couple of blocks away on Calle Antonio Rojo.

Trekking in the park

The area's claim to be the trekking capital of Argentina is justified, and the closer you get to the mountains, the clearer their beauty becomes. Early mornings are the best time for views and photography. Adequate outdoor clothing is essential at all times of the year, as snowstorms are possible even in midsummer. Unlike in Torres del Paine, one of the beauties of this park is that those with limited time, or who don't consider themselves in peak fitness, can still make worthwhile **day walks**, using El Chaltén as a base, and thus not have to lug around heavy rucksacks. For those who enjoy camping, the quintessential **Monte Fitz Roy/Cerro Torre** loop at the centre of the park makes a good three-day option, given decent weather. You can head on the central loop in either direction but the advantage of going counterclockwise is that you avoid the steep climb up to Lagunas Madre y Hija from the valley, and you have the

Facts and figures about Argentina

The political and economic crisis that erupted in Argentina in late 2001 made for unfortunate headlines across the world. For the tourist, especially in the areas covered in this book, there is absolutely no cause for concern. The situation calmed down during 2002, and the new exchange rate of AR$3.60 to the US dollar (previously one peso was worth one dollar) has stabilized. Nonetheless, if the Argentine peso changes in value, the prices given here will inevitably be affected, so always check accommodation rates and so forth before booking. Some tourist outfits, including hotels, continue to charge at their old prices, but in US dollars, and the government seems unable or perhaps unwilling to outlaw such hyperinflationary moves. Other things remain unchanged: most countries' citizens need no visa to enter Argentina for ninety days or less. The international dialling code for Argentina is ☎0054.

wind at your back when returning down that valley to Chaltén. However, the biggest gamble is always what the weather will be like around Cerro Torre, so if this most unpredictable of peaks is visible on day one, you should probably head for it first.

El Calafate

EL CALAFATE is the centre of the tourist network in the deep south of mainland Argentine Patagonia. Since the 2001 devaluation (see box, above), El Calafate has been inundated with visitors. The town has expanded accordingly, but hotel and restaurant prices have gone up. Nonetheless, it does offer some decent budget hostel accommodation and a couple of well-stocked, reasonably priced supermarkets.

All **buses** stop at the terminal on Avenida Julio Roca, on the hillside one block above the main thoroughfare, Avenida Libertador to which it is connected by a flight of steps. The helpful **tourist office** is situated in the terminal (daily: April–Oct 8am–10pm; Nov–March 8am–11pm; ☎ & ℻02902/491090, ⓦwww.elcalafate.gov.ar) and can help track down accommodation. The **national park information office**, at Libertador 1302 (Mon–Fri 8am–9.30pm, Sat & Sun 10am–9.30pm, ☎02902/491545, ℯapnglaciares@cotecal .com.ar), has some useful maps, sells fishing licences, and will give you the latest information on campsites near the glacier.

Of the plentiful **accommodation**, *Los Alamos*, Gob Moyano and Bustillo (☎02902/491144, ℻02902/491186, ⓦwww.posadalosalamos.com; ❽) is the most luxurious, with wood-panelled rooms, an excellent restaurant, and even a Lilliputian golf course. You'll find cheaper rooms at *Hospedaje Familiar Lago Azul*, Perito Moreno 83 (☎02902/491419; ❷), in the family home of a charming Echeverría couple. For hostel accommodation, try the spacious *America del Sur*, Puerto Deseado s/n (☎02902/493525, ⓦwww.americahostel.com .ar), which has doubles (❹) and dorm rooms (AR$25 per person) overlooking the lake. *Hostel del Glaciar Pioneros*, Los Pioneros s/n (Oct–March ☎ & ℻02902/491243, closed off season, ⓦwww.glaciar.com; ❷–❹), is El Calafate's original hostel and boasts clean, four-bed rooms, plus kitchen, free shuttle to and from bus terminal, a good-value restaurant and travel services; more expensive private rooms with en-suite bathroom are available. A sister hostel, *Hostel del Glaciar Libertador*, Av Libertador s/n (☎ & ℻02902/491243, www.glaciar.com)

offers similar services but the dorm rooms (AR\$22 per person) have en-suite bathrooms and are set around a courtyard.

For **food**, try *La Posta*, on the grounds of the *Los Alamos* hotel (☏02902/491144), where an exotic international menu includes dishes such as excellent rolled lamb with rosehip sauce – prices are high by local standards. *La Tablita*, Coronel Rosales 28, by the bridge into town, is justifiably popular with locals for its serious-sized lamb or beef parillas and enormous steaks at reasonable rates, while *Pura Vida* at Libertador 1876 serves up traditional food with a modern touch as well as tasty vegetarian dishes in an A-frame cabin. For decent wood-oven pizzas, head to *La Lechuza* on the corner of Libertador and 1 de Mayo.

Glaciar Perito Moreno

The main sightseeing area of the **Parque Nacional Los Glaciares**, the part containing the glaciers that give it its name, is the southern sector within reach of El Calafate. Here you'll find one of Argentina's leading attractions, the **GLACIAR PERITO MORENO**; head a little more than 30km past the park's **main gate** (AR\$5 per person, AR\$3 per vehicle) to the series of **boardwalks** from where you can view the spectacle. The glacier sweeps down off the ice cap in a great motorway curve, a jagged mass of crevasses and towering, knife-edged obelisks of ice (seracs), almost unsullied by the streaks of dirty moraine that discolour many of its counterparts. When it collides with the southern arm of Lago Argentino, the show really begins. Vast blocks of ice, some weighing hundreds of tonnes, detonate off the face of the glacier with the report of a small cannon and come crashing down into the waters below. These frozen depth-charges then come surging back to the surface as icebergs, sending out a fairy ring of smaller lumps that form a protecting reef around the berg, which is left to float in a mirror-smooth pool of its own.

While these dramatic bombs or ruptures do happen from time to time, you'll usually have to content yourself with the thuds, cracks, creaks and grinding crunches that the glacier habitually makes, as well as the wonderful variety of colours of the ice: it's marbled in places with streaks of muddy grey and copper sulphate blue, whilst at the bottom the pressurized, de-oxygenated ice has a deep blue, waxy sheen. Many people can while away hours in thrall to it, with some spending the whole day and returning the next to see it in different lights. The glacier tends to be more active in sunny weather and in the afternoon.

Park practicalities

Guided day excursions to the glacier are offered by virtually all agencies in El Calafate allowing around four hours at the ice face, the minimum required to appreciate this spectacle. The excursions run by *Hostel del Glaciar* and *Hostel del Glaciar Libertador* (AR\$76) are highly recommended, as is their two-day Chaltén glacier trekking trip (AR\$399). *Chaltén Travel* at Libertador 1174 also offer good trips with knowledgeable guides. If you don't want to be restricted to a tour, you can catch a twice-daily shuttle bus service run by Caltur (AR\$20 each way) that departs El Calafate at 7am and 3.30pm, returning at 12.30pm and 6pm, rent a car (around AR\$200 per day), hire a *remise* taxi (AR\$180; be sure to negotiate the length of waiting time before setting out), or hitch. Remember that the glacier lies a long way from the park entrance itself (over 30km). Once at the glacier, it is worth taking the hour-long round boat trip to the face of the glacier (AR$25) to inspect the towering wall of ice close up.

Currently, the only **hotel** close to the Moreno glacier (and with views of its left flank) is *Los Notros* (℡011/4814-3934, ⓦwww.losnotros.com; ❾; open mid-Sept to May), 22km from the park entrance.

Boat trips to the Upsala and Spegazzini glaciers are run as a park's concession by Renée Fernández Campbell out of **Puerto Bandera** (a tiny harbour at the mouth of the Canal de los Témpanos, in the northern reaches of the Península de Magallanes), using a fleet of modern catamarans and launches. Prices are the same at all the agencies (AR$180 plus AR$20 park entrance) or you can buy direct from Fernandez Campbell at Libertador 867 (℡02902/491155). Trips run throughout the year, with daily departures on popular routes in high season.

Travel details

Buses

Puerto Natales to: Cerro Castillo (4 weekly; 1hr 30min); El Calafate, Argentina (2 daily; 5hr); Parque Nacional Torres del Paine (12 daily; 2hr 30min–3hr 30min); Punta Arenas (hourly; 3hr); Río Gallegos, Argentina (3 weekly; 5hr). Ushuaia, Argentina (3 weekly; 13hr).

Punta Arenas to: Estancia San Gregorio (1 daily; 3hr 30min); Monte Aymond (1 daily; 5hr, including formalities); Puerto Natales (every hour; 3hr); Río Gallegos, Argentina (1 daily; 7hr); Río Grande, Argentina (1 daily; 8hr 30min); Ushuaia, Argentina (Mon-Sat 1 daily; 12hr).

Río Turbio, Argentina to: El Calafate (2 daily; 4hr); Río Gallegos (4 daily; 5hr).

Ferries

Puerto Natales to: Puerto Montt (weekly; 66hr).
Punta Arenas to: Porvenir (1 daily except Mon; 2hr 30min-3hr); Puerto Williams (Nov-March 4 monthly; 36hr).
Punta Delgada to: Bahía Azul, Tierra del Fuego (every 1hr 30min, except at low tide; 30min).

Flights

Puerto Natales to: El Calafate, Argentina (5 weekly; 1hr).
Punta Arenas to: Balmaceda (2 daily; 1hr); Porvenir (Mon-Sat 1 daily; 15min); Puerto Montt (2 daily; 2hr); Puerto Williams (summer 6 weekly, winter 3 weekly; 1hr 30min); Santiago (several daily; 4hr); Ushuaia, Argentina (3 weekly; 1hr).

10

Tierra del Fuego

10

TIERRA DEL FUEGO | Highlights

* **Isla Navarino** Fly or sail to Puerto Williams, the most southerly town on Earth. See p.537

* **Cape Horn** Even if you don't kayak around it, consider rounding the tip in a ship or viewing its harsh beauty from the air. See p.539

* **Skiing at Ushuaia** Zip down the slopes of the winter sports resort dramatically located at the end of the world. See p.542

* **Boat trip along the Beagle Channel** Spot sea lions and skuas, cormorants and albatrosses, and maybe even killer whales. See p.546

* **Estancia Harberton** Sample home-made jam and cake at Fuego's most historic homestead. See p.547

* **Parque Nacional Tierra del Fuego** Explore this fascinating chunk of jagged mountains, beech forest, bogs, tundra and beautiful coast. See p.548

△ Candelaria Salesian Mission

10

Tierra del Fuego

At the bottom end of the South American continent, and split between Chile and Argentina, **TIERRA DEL FUEGO** ("Land of Fires") holds nearly as much fascination for travellers as Patagonia, from which it is separated by the Magellan Strait. Though comprising a number of islands, it's more or less the sum of its most developed part, the **Isla Grande**, the biggest island in South America. Its eastern section, roughly a third of the island, along with a few islets, belong to Argentina, and the rest is Chilean territory.

By far and away the leading tourist attraction is the well-known city of **Ushuaia**, a year-round resort on the south coast, and on **the Argentine side** of Tierra del Fuego. Beautifully located and backed by distinctive jagged mountains, it is *the* base for visiting the tremendous **Beagle Channel**, rich in **marine wildlife**, and the wild, forested peaks of the **Cordillera Darwin**. The lakes, forests and tundra of **Parque Nacional Tierra del Fuego** lie just 12km to the west of Ushuaia. Historic **Estancia Harberton**, home to descendants of Thomas Bridges, an Anglican missionary who settled here in 1871, is also an easy excursion from the city.

You won't miss much, on the other hand, if you leave the windswept plains and scrubby *coirón* grasslands in the north of the island to the sheep that thrive there. The main Argentine town up there is **Río Grande**, a bleak place but a useful overnight stop for travellers exploring the island's heartland or for those entering the region by ferry. It's especially popular with fly-fishermen who come here from all over the world hoping to outwit the seagoing **brown trout** of the Río Grande, regarded as the world's premier river for that species.

On **the Chilean side**, you'll find the main town of **Porvenir**, accessible from Punta Arenas by air and ferry, and a string of oil settlements. In fact, the importance of oil is evident throughout the region, from pipelines that follow the road to the remains of windscreens shattered by the flying stones kicked up by the wheels of enormous oil trucks thundering across the steppe.

Further south, hills appear and the countryside becomes less barren, with the thick woodland and clear brooks near little **Camerón** in Chile. To the southeast, a number of exquisite lakes, including the aptly named **Lago Blanco**, also in Chile, are principally favoured by anglers. In the far south, the densely forested 2000-metre peaks of the cordillera, the Andes' tail-end, make Chilean territory all but inaccessible, as do the remote Fuegian Channels, where the sea winds its way between hundreds of uninhabited islands. Beneath the mountains, glaciers meander through narrow valleys before breaking up in the Beagle Channel. South of Isla Grande, across the Beagle Channel, lies **Isla Navarino**, home to the surprisingly welcoming naval base of **Puerto Williams**, plus one of the best hiking trails in the archipelago, the **Los Dientes Circuit**. Beyond Navarino are the **Islas Wollaston**, whose southerly tip is **Cape Horn**, the land's end of the Americas, accessible only by sea or air.

Back in the Argentine sector, you'll find the scenic **Lago Fagnano**, and village of **Tolhuin** at its eastern end. From Tolhuin to the 2985-metre **Paso Garibaldi**, the gateway to Ushuaia by road, you'll travel through patches of low, transitional **Fuegian woodland**, where the lichen beards hanging from the gnarled branches make it look as though a tickertape parade had just passed by. Much of the area's beauty, together with its isolated *estancias*, are only really accessible to those with their own transport. Try the loop along the RCf and RCh roads or, better still, **RCa**, which winds through some wonderfully rugged scenery along the eastern coastline.

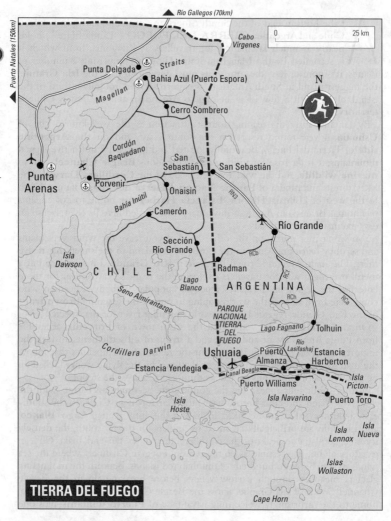

TIERRA DEL FUEGO

The triangular southeastern chunk of the island, Península Mitre, is one of the least accessible parts of the whole of Argentina: an intemperate, boggy wilderness for which a gaucho guide, waterproof clothing, loads of time and inexhaustible stamina are the requisites. Even harder to get to is **Isla de los Estados** (Staten Island), lying off the peninsula's extremity, Cabo San Diego. Almost perpetually swathed in mist and cloud, it is a land of deep fjords, swamps, scrubby sub-Antarctic forests and craggy peaks, surrounded by fierce currents. Plans are afoot to turn it into a provincial nature reserve, but you can only visit it currently via the extremely expensive chartered launch from Ushuaia.

People tend to visit Tierra del Fuego between December and February, when Ushuaia in particular gets very busy. However, in March and April the countryside is daubed with the spectacular autumnal colours of the southern beech, while springtime (October to mid-November), before the tourist season gets going, is also a great time to come, though it can be even windier than normal. In general, the climate is milder than you might expect given the latitude. Temperatures rarely plummet way below freezing as they can on the mainland, and in January temperatures over 20°C (68°F) are not uncommon. When the sea breezes drop, you can enjoy sunbathing, though sunscreen is vital as the ozone layer is treacherously thin here.

Travelling around Isla Grande without your own car is difficult, as public transport is infrequent. If at all possible introduce yourself to the island, or leave it behind, with the stunning aerial views afforded by a **flight** between Ushuaia and Punta Arenas, Río Gallegos or even Buenos Aires.

Chilean Tierra del Fuego

The nondescript settlement of **Porvenir** huddles on the Magellan Strait across from Punta Arenas. Flat plains cover much of northern and central Isla Grande, but the southern reaches, especially the virtually inaccessible Cordillera Darwin, are characterized by dramatic, snow-capped mountains. The dense forests and crystalline rivers southeast of **Camerón** stretch towards a series of lakes, including the beautiful **Lago Blanco**. There are plans to turn the highly photogenic landscape around **Bahía Yendegaia**, due west of Ushuaia, Argentina, into a destination aimed at adventure tourism, but at present it's extremely difficult to

Getting to Tierra del Fuego from the Chilean mainland

There are several **ferries** to **Isla Grande** from the Chilean mainland. The *Melinka* leaves from Punta Arenas (see p.501) and arrives at Porvenir, while the *Bahía Azul* and *Pionero* ferries cross the Primera Angostura (see p.506) and arrive at Puerto Espora, also known as Bahía Azul. Both are run by Transbordadora Austral Broom, Av Bulnes 5075, in Punta Arenas (℡61/218100, ⊛www.tabsa.cl). You can also **fly** from Punta Arenas to Porvenir with DAP (see p.501), or take the bus to Ushuaia via Bahía Azul and San Sebastián (see p.501). Getting to **Isla Navarino** is more difficult (see p.537).

visit. To the south of Isla Grande, across the Beagle Channel, is **Isla Navarino**, home to the quirky little **Puerto Williams**, the southernmost permanently inhabited place in the world, unless you count the bases on Antarctica. In the remote western areas of the archipelago lie the largely unexplored **Fuegian Channels**, where the sea winds its way between hundreds of uninhabited islands, all that's left of the mighty Andes as they slip gently under the sea. To the south of Isla Navarino are the **Islas Wollaston**, where you'll find **Cabo de Hornos**, known to English speakers as Cape Horn, the very end of the American continent.

Porvenir and around

A collection of brightly painted corrugated iron houses set in a narrow bay of the same name, **PORVENIR** (optimistically meaning "future"), lies 35km east of Punta Arenas across the Magellan Strait and 147km west of the border crossing at San Sebastián. The town gives off the impression of order stamped on nature, with neat topiary leading down the main street, Philippi, from an immaculate Plaza de Armas. On the seafront the Parque del Recuerdo sports a curve of flagpoles, the painted skeleton of a steam engine and the mounted stern of a boat.

The town started life in 1883 as a police outpost during the Fuegian gold rush and has since been settled by foreigners: first came the British managers of sheep farms, and then refugees from Croatia after World War II. You can read the history of the town in the names of the dead at the **cemetery** (daily 8am–6pm) four blocks north of the plaza: Mary Montgomery Mackenzie lies with Neil Morrison Morrison opposite Rosenda Manquemilla Muñoz, who is beside Juan Senkovic Restovich. At the far end of the trees, you'll find the tomb of the Mimica Scarpa family, resembling a miniature mosque, complete with a scaled-down minaret. The only other site of interest in Porvenir is the **Museo Provincial Fernando Cordero Rusque** on the north corner of the Plaza (Mon–Thurs 9am–5pm, Fri 9am–4pm, Sat & Sun 11am–2pm & 3–5pm; CH$500), with photographs of miners and machinery, a collection of cine cameras from the early days of Chilean film and the usual collection of stuffed animals. The museum also doubles as a tourist office of sorts (T61/580098).

Practicalities

Ferries from Punta Arenas arrive at Bahía Chilota, 5km to the west of Porvenir along the bay, where a taxi into town costs CH$2000, and a *colectivo* CH$500. You'll find some bright fishermen's houses, a restaurant staffed by a couple of taciturn women, and an absurd one-way traffic system (there are only two streets). The **bus** pulls in to the corner of Riobo and Sampaio, a couple of blocks northeast of the Plaza. The **aerodrome** sits 5km north of town, and flights are met by taxis that charge CH$2500 to take you into Porvenir.

There are a number of reasonable **places to stay**. The modern *Hostal Patagonia*, Jorge Schythe 230 (T61/580371; ❸) offers quality en-suite rooms, while the friendly *Residential Colón*, Riobo 198 (T61/580593; ❷–❸) has a large, bright dining room; guests may use the kitchen and you can also camp on a patch of ground outside (CH$2000). *Hotel España*, Croacia 698 (T61/580160; ❸–❹), a deceptively large old building run by a formidable woman, features both basic rooms with shared bathrooms and plush en-suite doubles. At the cosy ⚡ *Hotel Rosas*, Philippi 296 (T & F61/580088; ❹), the knowledgeable owner has lots of information on the region. At the high end of the market and the far western end of Teniente Merino, at no. 1253, the comfortable *Hostería Los Flamencos* (T & F61/580049; ❺) enjoys harbour views but is overpriced and somewhat neglected by its owners.

You won't find many **places to eat** in town, and the best is probably *Club Croata*, Señoret 542, serving well-prepared standard Chilean fare (but do check your bill). The restaurant in the *Hotel Rosas* (see opposite) offers generous seafood dishes and the *Puerto Montt*, Croacia 1169, near *Los Flamencos*, has moderately priced seafood. *Hotel España* does good sandwiches and set meals.

You can **change money** at the Banco del Estado, Philippi 265 and use the Internet at Philippi 375; there's a post office on the plaza.

Buses run regularly to Río Grande in Argentina (daily except Mon; CH$9000), where you can get a connection to Ushuaia or Punta Arenas. The schedule changes often, so it's a good idea to check before you travel, but generally depart around noon.

You can buy tickets for the **ferry** back to Punta Arenas from Tabsa in a kiosk on the *costanera* (Calle Señoret s/n, Sector Costero T61/580089; Mon–Fri 9am–noon & 2–6.30pm, Sat 9am–noon & 3–6pm). If that's shut, the restaurant at Bahía Chilota sells tickets for the ferry an hour before it leaves (departures Tues–Sat 2pm & Sun 5pm, but again, check times well ahead). The airline DAP, whose offices are in the same building as Tabsa on Calle Señoret (T61/580089), sells **plane** tickets to Punta Arenas (departures Mon–Sat, twice daily: US$25 with a maximum of 10kg luggage).

Northeast to Cerro Sombrero and Bahía Azul

The first 20km out of Porvenir heading north is lined with large shallow lakes, ranging in colour from turquoise to sapphire and often adorned with dazzling pink flamingoes. After that excitement, there's not much for the next 86km until you reach the turning to the right that leads to Chilean Tierra del Fuego's other town, **CERRO SOMBRERO**, a small oil town looming up out of the moonscape, snugly ensconced on the top of a small flat hill and bristling with TV aerials like something out of the *Mad Max* movies. It's not worth travelling to the ends of the earth to visit, but it's a helpful place to stop if you need petrol or just want a break. The Plaza de Armas is blessed with a plant-filled conservatory. Also, being an oil town, it's not short of heating. There are a couple of places to stay, the best of which is ♣ *Hostería Tunkelén*, which sits at the bottom of the hill (T61/212757; ❸). This pleasant truck stop, run by a hospitable family, has a quality en-suite room in the main house, and a large outside block of rooms with one shared bathroom. Best of all, they have an enormous, efficient water heating system. Such things become very important in Tierra del Fuego.

Forty-three kilometres north of Cerro Sombrero (139km from Porvenir), the **ferry** that crosses the Primera Angostura departs from a place known locally as **BAHÍA AZUL**, but usually marked "Puerto Espora" on maps. There's nothing at the ferry terminal except a telephone and a couple of buildings, one of them a café serving snacks.

East across the Baquedano Hills to the border

A little-used road heads east from Porvenir across the **BAQUEDANO HILLS**, where most of the region's gold was discovered. It starts with a beautiful view,

20km outside Porvenir, looking back down to the town and across the strait to Punta Arenas. All around, the landscape bears the reminders of the gold that was mined here — 41km from Porvenir you pass a gold washer, and then the road crosses the Río del Oro (Gold River), where you'll see the rusting remains of an original dredge. After a steep descent, you come to the main Porvenir–San Sebastián road, and after another 84km of numbingly dull, flat wilderness you reach the **San Sebastián frontier**. There are two San Sebastiáns – the Chilean border post and a fully-fledged village further on in Argentina. All there is on the Chilean side is a hotel, *Hostería La Frontera* (☎61/224731; ❺), where you are unlikely to want or need to stay, and the crossing post (daily: April–Oct 8am–10pm; Nov–March 24hr), where you can expect fairly lengthy delays.

South to Lago Blanco

While the north of Isla Grande is flat, bleak wasteland, in the south, around beautiful **LAGO BLANCO**, you'll find forest where you can trek, fish and camp. This area tends to be ignored by travellers who set their minds on only visiting the Argentine town of Ushuaia.

With little traffic down here, the only realistic means of travelling is in a rental car, though an erratic bus service does run between Porvenir and Camerón. The prettiest road is the one that follows the coast, starting along the northern shore of **Bahía Inutil**, a wide bay that got its curious name by being a useless anchorage for sailing ships. After 99km you reach a crossroads; turn south, and a little past the village of Onaisin you pass a little **English cemetery**. The gravestones have short inscriptions in English that hint at tragic stories: "killed by Indians", "accidentally drowned" and "died in a storm".

The coast road then skirts around the south of Bahía Inutil, giving beautiful views across to **Isla Dawson**. It passes the occasional small cluster of bare fishermen's huts – keep an eye out for the windlasses used to keep the small boats out of the reach of the furious sea, but be careful of taking photos here, as the whole area is a military zone. When the tide's out, you can see a more ancient way of catching fish – underwater stone *corrales* (pens) built by the Ona Indians to trap fish when the tide turned. Just before the village of **Camerón**, the road turns inland and leaves the bay. Camerón was once a Scottish settlement, hence the name, and is built on either side of the Río Shetland. Once it was a thriving town, the centre of the largest sheep farm on the island, but nowadays all that's left are some neat little workers' houses and a large shearing shed.

From here, the land begins to lose its Patagonian severity, and as you travel inland you'll see dense forest. Thirty-seven kilometres in, you pass another rusting reminder of the gold rush – a 1904 dredge, now preserved as a national monument. Some 20km later, the road forks north to San Sebastián, and south to a place called Sección Río Grande, where an iron bridge crosses the river. You are now surrounded by Magellanic forest, occasionally interspersed with open grassland, all of which resembles a well-tended park. If you're lucky you'll see guanacos.

Twenty-one kilometres further lies **Lago Blanco** itself, majestic and brooding, surrounded by steeply forested hills and snow-covered mountains. The lake is being developed, with *cabañas* springing up around its edge and a romantic fishing lodge on an island in the middle. In a few years' time it might resemble some of the over-developed resorts of the Lake District, but at the moment it's a place of isolation and escape. Arranging somewhere to stay is difficult, since there are no telephones down here, only radio phones. Two lodges share a contact number in Punta Arenas and charge similar high-end rates: *Tierra del Fuego Lodge*

Charles Darwin, the Beagle and Jemmy Button

In the early nineteenth century, the land around the **Magellan Strait** was all but unknown, so in 1826 the British Admiralty sent two ships, the **Adventure** and the **Beagle**, to explore it. The expedition's leader, **Robert Fitzroy**, was a liberal man, and for the most part encouraged his men to be friendly and careful in the way they dealt with the Fuegian Indians. However, when one of his ship's boats was stolen, Fitzroy retaliated by kidnapping four Indians and holding them hostage. The boat was never returned, so Fitzroy took the Indians back to England.

The sailors couldn't pronounce the Indians' names, and poetically rechristened them "Boat Memory", "York Minster", "Jemmy Button" and "Fuegia Basket". Boat Memory, described as an intelligent young man, died of smallpox on reaching London, but the others survived and were educated and accepted into English society. The only woman, Fuegia Basket, was presented at court and charmed the King and Queen, who gave her a lace cap and a golden ring. Jemmy Button became a dandy; Darwin described him as: "... short, thick and fat, but vain of his personal appearance; he used to wear gloves, his hair was neatly cut, and he was distressed if his well-polished shoes were dirtied. He was fond of admiring himself in a looking glass..."

Some years later, in 1831, Fitzroy returned to Tierra del Fuego on the *Beagle*, with the three Fuegian Indians on board, and **Charles Darwin** as his naturalist. Fitzroy intended to return the Indians to their homeland with a missionary, in an attempt to "civilize" and evangelize the rest of the Fuegians. The missionary didn't last more than three days before asking to be taken back onboard, but it was hoped that Jemmy Button, York Minster and Fuegia Basket might be a kernel of Britishness in this far-off corner of the world. Unsurprisingly, however, when the *Beagle* returned a year later, the natives had returned to their traditional lifestyles.

---

in Río Rassmusen and *Refugio Isla Victoria* in Lago Blanco itself (☏61/241197; open Sept–March; ❸).

Isla Navarino

Apart from tiny **Puerto Williams** and a few *estancias* along the northern coast, **ISLA NAVARINO**, the largish island to the south of Isla Grande, is an uninhabited wilderness studded with barren peaks and isolated valleys. Covering about 4000 square kilometres, virtually unspoilt and mostly inaccessible, Navarino is dominated by a dramatic range of peaks, the **Cordón Dientes del Perro** ("Dog's Teeth Rampart") through which weaves a 70-kilometre hiking trail called the **Los Dientes Circuit**. A sign of the remoteness of the island is the fact that this trail is more the result of wandering indigenous guanacos than of man. What has spoilt some of the landscape, especially the woodland, however, is the devastation brought about by feral **beavers**, originally introduced from Canada for fur-farming. Once protected but now hunted extensively – and sold for their meat and their pelts – these cuddly looking but destructive animals have gnawed through countless tree trunks, and their dams cause terrible flooding.

The quickest and most reliable way to get to Isla Navarino is to **fly** (CH\$38,000 one-way) with DAP from Punta Arenas to Puerto Williams (see p.501), a spectacular journey when the weather is good, and bumpy when it's bad. In summer, flights depart at 3pm Tuesday to Saturday. In winter, there are

△ Beaver dam

flights Tuesday, Thursday and Saturday. A **ferry** travels from Punta Arenas once a week; it departs Punta Arenas Wednesday at 6pm and returns from Puerto Williams on Saturday at 10pm; (around 36hr; fares start at US$120). COMAPA (see p.500) also runs a four-day luxury cruise on the *Terra Australis* (Ⓦwww.australis.com), from US$681 per person. You might be lucky and catch a ride on a private boat crossing from Ushuaia, but don't count on this. Also, with Chilean-Argentine relations continually thawing, long-promised scheduled crossings between the rival southernmost towns might soon be a reality, so check with the tourist information offices in Ushuaia and Punta Arenas.

Puerto Williams

PUERTO WILLIAMS sits nestled in a small bay on the north shore of Isla Navarino, 82km due east and ever so slightly south of Ushuaia along the Beagle Channel. "Williams" is something of a thorn in Argentina's toe, since despite all the publicity and hype about Ushuaia being the most southerly town in the world, that dubious privilege actually belongs to Puerto Williams instead. Founded as a military outpost and officially the capital of Chilean Antarctica, the town looks tranquil and idyllic on a fine day, colourful roofs surrounded by the jagged peaks of **Los Dientes** (also known as the Colmillos). Known as "Puerto Luisa" until 1956 and as "Uspashun" to the native Yámana, Puerto Williams is a tiny place, with a centre not much bigger than a single square kilometre. Although the first things you notice on your approach by sea or air are likely to be the Chilean Navy's sinister black gunboats, the town is extremely relaxed and welcoming. At the **Museo Martín Gusinde**, Comandante Aragay 1 (April–Sept Mon–Thurs 8am–1pm & 2.30–6.15pm, Sat–Sun 2.30–6.30pm; Oct–March Mon–Thurs 9am–1pm & 2.30–7pm, Sat–Sun 2.30–6.30pm; free), in the far western end of town, well-laid-out photographs and maps chart the history and exploration of the region, from the days of the Fuegian Indians, through the gold rush, to the commercial shipping of today. There's also a collection of knick-knacks donated by modern kayakers who've paddled

Having come this far south, many travellers like to go the whole hog and "round the Cape", erroneously translated into Spanish as Cabo de Hornos (which in fact means "Ovens Cape"). This is no easy feat, especially if you follow earlier madmen and try and do it in a kayak (not recommended). Ask around in Puerto Williams – SIM travel agency (see p.540) being a good place to start – about **boat trips** to the most southerly point of the world's land mass, barring Antarctica. Weather permitting you disembark on a shingle beach, climb a rickety ladder and visit the tiny Chilean naval base, lighthouse and chapel; there's not much to do otherwise and it's all quite desolate. DAP (see p.540) and the local flying clubs also run not-terribly-expensive 30-minute flights from both Punta Arenas and Puerto Williams that do a loop over the headland and return without landing. These air excursions treat you to incredible views of Isla Navarino and the Darwin peaks. As always, weather is a vital factor.

around Cape Horn, not far south of here, and an informative display of the island's flora and fauna illustrated by the usual array of stuffed creatures and dried vegetation. The true purpose of any visit to Williams, however, is to fulfil a desire to come this far south and away from "civilization".

Practicalities

On **arrival** at the midget airport, you'll be met by at least one private car acting as a makeshift taxi that will take you into town. The trip is farther than it looks, as the peninsula on which the airfield is built is separated from Puerto Williams by a long, narrow channel. Stop in at the **Oficina de Turismo**, not far from the museum at Ibáñez 130 (Dec–March Mon–Fri 10am–1pm & 3–6pm; ℡61/621011), for copies of maps, but note that not much else is available there.

   Accommodation, mostly basic but decent, is clustered in the centre. Try *Pensión Flor Cañuñán*, Lewaia 107 (℡61/621163; ❶), which has rooms in a rather basic but warm hut, with the bathroom in the main house; *Residencial Onashaga*, Uspashun 15, on the corner of Nueva (℡61/621081; ❸), for a family bed and breakfast; or the excellent *Refugio Coirón*, Maragaño 168 (℡ & ℻61/621150; ❸), which has shared rooms with bunks, a kitchen open to guests and space for camping. The *Camblor*, Subtenente Patricio Capdeville 4 (℡ & ℻61/621033; ❺), offers private bathrooms and boasts a fine restaurant. The welcoming *Pensión Temuco*, at Piloto Pardo 224 (℡ & ℻61/621113; ❸), has rooms with private bathroom and you can use the kitchen. Next door, at Piloto Pardo 222, is the similar Hostal Pusaki (℡61/621116; ❸).

   At the small, friendly *Los Dientes del Navarino*, in the centre, you'll probably have to settle for the Chilean *menú del día* or a sandwich. Better though are the restaurants at the *Camblor* (see above) and *Cabo de Hornos* at Maragaño 146, which serve *centolla*, lamb and beaver. Head to the excellent *Supermercado Simón y Simón* to buy delicious bread, *empanadas* and amazingly good wine, along with everything else you might need for a picnic. There is no **nightlife** as such here: to while away your evening visit the *Club de Yates Micalvi*, an ex-Navy supply ship with a markedly "old salt" atmosphere and a well-stocked bar where you can chat and drink until the early hours or try the *Pingüino Pub* in the Centro Comercial or the occasionally rowdy *Discoteca Extasis* at Colón 716.

   Banco de Chile, Yelcho s/n, gives cash advances on credit cards and changes money. You can also change money in the **bank** on the main plaza or the Centro Comercial, where you'll also find a **post office**. A CTC **telephone centre** is on the main plaza as well.

The main **tour agency** is SIM (Sea and Ice and Mountains Adventures) on the main plaza (ⓣ61/621150, ⓔcoiron@simltd.com, ⓦwww.simltd.com) – they also run the *Refugio Coirón*. Ask them for details of treks around the island and boat trips down to Cape Horn. Other agencies include Karanka Expeditions at Teniente Muñoz 241 (ⓣ61/621150) and Victory Adventure Expeditions at Teniente Muñoz 118 (ⓣ61/621010, ⓦwww.victory-cruises .com), who specialize in sailing trips to Ushuaia and voyages to Cape Horn. DAP has its offices in the Centro Comercial (ⓣ61/621114 or 621051) and Tabsa is at Costanera 435 (ⓣ61/621015).

Around Puerto Williams

The 70-kilometre **Los Dientes Circuit** leaves from the statue of the Virgin Mary, about one kilometre **west** of town on the road to the airport. There you'll find a turning uphill, which leads to a waterfall and a dammed stream, to the left of which is a marked trail. Allow at least four and as many as seven days to complete the circuit, taking plentiful supplies and decent outdoor gear and anticipating bad weather, even snow in summer; inform people in town before leaving, in case you need to be rescued. Near the start of the trail, 3km west of Puerto Williams, is the entrance to the experimental **Parque Etnobotánico Omora** (daylight hours; donation; ⓔwhitethroatedcaracara @yahoo.com, ⓦwww.cabodehornos.org), named for the world's southernmost hummingbird. A part-state, part-private enterprise, the park plays an educational and environmental role, protecting the *ñirre* and lenga forest by, among other things, encouraging locals to cull beavers for their meat. Native birds, including the red-headed Magellanic woodpecker (*lana*) and the ruffed-legged owl (*kujurf*), are monitored, along with other endangered species of flora and fauna. Omora also successfully campaigned to have UNESCO designate the Cape Horn Biosphere Reserve in June 2005. Find out more, as well as additional details about the park's interpretative trails, at the visitor's centre near the entrance.

Further along the coast, beyond the Virgin, lie numerous picturesque little bays and islands with an abundance of bird life, both along the shore and on the edge of the forest. Near **Bahía Virginia**, you'll find large middens of mussel and clam shells left by what must once have been a large settlement of Yámana. Twelve kilometres out of town, an *estancia* owned by the MacLean family has been developed into a *centolla*- and shellfish-processing factory, and there you can eat in the friendly workers' café. On the western tip of the island is Puerto Navarino, home to a handful of Chilean marines and their families. South of here is the site of an old missionary settlement, at Walaia, which is being developed by COMAPA into the Parque Arqueológico Caleta Walaia, dedicated to documenting the Yámana culture.

Border crossings

The only operative land border crossing between the Chilean and Argentine halves of Tierra del Fuego's Isla Grande is at **San Sebastián**, in the north of the island. The respective customs posts (April–Oct 8am–10pm; Nov–March open 24hr) are several hundred metres apart, some 15km west of the Argentine village of the same name. Formalities are straightforward if somewhat lengthy at times. You may not take any fresh fruit, meat or dairy products into Chile, and Argentine officers sometimes recip-rocate. Note that Argentina is one hour ahead of Chile from March to October.

An easy stroll 2km to the **east** of Puerto Williams is the straggly hamlet of **Ukika**, a small collection of houses where a dozen or so people of Yámana descent live. You can buy reed baskets and replica canoes, but do not take photographs unless invited to do so. Beyond, the road continues, giving beautiful views across the Beagle Channel before ducking into the forest and heading inland. It emerges once again at **Puerto Toro**, the end of the last road in South America, looking out at **Picton Island** and beyond, into the endless seas of the Atlantic Ocean.

Ushuaia and Argentine Tierra del Fuego

Argentina possesses the easternmost third of **Isla Grande**, plus Isla de los Estados and a smattering of tiny islets to the south. Also way down south, lies **Ushuaia**, meaning "westward-looking bay" in the indigenous Yámana tongue. It's Tierra del Fuego's main tourist destination, with winter skiing and summer trekking high on the list of activities. A colourful, if rather chaotic town, it occupies a stunning mountain-backed location on the **Beagle Channel**, along which you can observe all manner of **marine wildlife**, from skuas to sea lions. Ushuaia makes for an ideal base to explore the wilds of southern Isla Grande, including the **Parque Nacional Tierra del Fuego**, a very short distance to the west. Historic **Harberton**, one of the emblematic *estancias*, or ranches, of

△ Parque Nacional Tierra del Fuego

the archipelago, also lies within day-trip range. The biggest town in the sheep-rich north is drab **Río Grande**, whose namesake river teems with brown trout eagerly awaiting the angler's hook, but otherwise is only worth a stop to see the **Candelaria Salesian Mission**. Centrally located **Tolhuin**, at the eastern end of ribbon-shaped **Lago Fagnano**, doesn't offer much more than a break in your journey. For more detailed information see the *Rough Guide to Argentina;* also see "Facts and figures about Argentina" box on p.526.

Ushuaia and around

Dramatically located between the mountains and the sea, **USHUAIA** tumbles down the hillside to the wide, encircling arm of land that protects its bay from the southwesterly winds and occasional thrashing storms of the icy **Beagle Channel**. Not only does Ushuaia have a couple of its own sights of interest, but it is also a convenient base for discovering the rugged beauty of the lands that border this historically important sea channel, or for taking boat trips along the channel itself.

In 1869, Reverend Waite Stirling became Tierra del Fuego's first white settler when he founded his **Anglican mission** amongst the Yámana here. Stirling stayed for six months before being recalled to the Falklands Islands to be

appointed Anglican bishop for South America. Thomas Bridges, his assistant, returned to take over the mission in 1871, after which time Ushuaia began to figure on mariners' charts as a place of refuge in the event of shipwreck. In 1896, in order to consolidate its sovereignty and open up the region to wider colonization, the Argentine government used a popular nineteenth-century tactic and established a **penal colony** here, eventually closed by Perón in 1947.

Arrival and information

The international **airport**, Malvinas Argentinas, sits 4km southwest of town; a **taxi** to the centre costs about AR$6. **Buses** arrive and depart from their companies' respective offices (see "Listings", p.545).

Avenida San Martín is the main thoroughfare. At no. 674 you'll find the **tourist office** (Easter–Oct Mon–Fri 8am–10pm, Sat & Sun 9am–8pm; Nov–Easter Mon–Fri 8am–midnight, Sat & Sun 9am–11pm; ☏02901/432001 or 424500, free local information line ☏0800/3331476, Ⓕ2901/432000, Ⓦwww .e-ushuaia.com), with English-speaking staff and an excellent free illustrated guide to the region. For information on trekking and climbing, contact the **Club Andino Ushuaia**, Fadul 50 (daily 3–10pm; ☏ & Ⓕ02901/422335); register with them before you make any trek or climb.

Accommodation

Ushuaia offers a good range of hotels and hostels, most on the first four streets parallel to the bay. You'll find a couple of **refugios**, too: *Club Andino* (☏02901/1560-3001; ❶), next to the Martial ski centre, and *Refugio del Mochilero*, really more of a hostel, at 25 de Mayo 241 (☏02901/436129; Ⓔrefmoch@infovia.com.ar; ❷). **Campsites** include the well-equipped *Pista del Andino*, Alem 2873 (☏ & Ⓕ02901/435890; AR$8 per person); the *Ushuaia Rugby Club*, by the Río Pipo, 5km from town (☏02901/435796; AR$5 per person) and the *Camping Municipal*, 8km from the centre, which is basic but free. From December through February, you should book **accommodation** in advance, even for hostels. Many hotels charge a ten percent surcharge on credit cards and travellers' cheques.

Cap Polonio San Martín 746 ☏ & Ⓕ02901/422140, Ⓔcappolonio@tierradelfuego .org.ar. Comfortable hotel with spruce rooms and pleasant bathrooms. Also runs the *Marcopolo* restaurant next door. ❹

La Casa Gob. Paz 1380 ☏02901/423202, Ⓔcasalaga@satlink.com. A highly recommended, spotlessly clean B&B with great views from the breakfast nook. Rooms have shared bathrooms. English, French, German and Spanish are spoken. Worth reserving in advance. Often closed May–Aug. ❷

Cruz del Sur Gob. Deloqui 636 ☏02901/423110. Ⓔxdelsur@yahoo .com. Clean dorms, decent kitchen and a fun ambience.

Cumbres del Martial Luis Martial 3560 ☏02901/424779, Ⓦwww.cumbresdelmartial .ar. This fabulously sited hotel sits by the glacier chairlift and has excellent views of the city and the

channel. It combines enticing decor and tasteful charm with modern amenities. ❼

Las Hayas Resort Luis Martial 1650 ☏02901/430710, Ⓕ02901/430719, Ⓦwww .tierradelfuego.org.ar/lashayas. Five-star hotel: luxurious, quiet and high up, 4km from centre. Most of the stylish, commodious rooms enjoy sea views. Singles are almost the same price as doubles; there are no triples. Facilities include a health spa and indoor swimming pool. Shuttle bus to port and centre. ❽

Hotel Albatross Maipú 505 ☏02901/423206, Ⓔalbatross@tierradelfuego.org.ar. Well-appointed hotel with superb seafront location, although oddly none of the rooms have sea views. ❼

Hotel Cabo de Hornos San Martín and Rosas ☏ & Ⓕ 02901/422313, Ⓔcabodehornos@arnet .com.ar. A decent, very central mid-range hotel. Beds have firm matresses and some rooms offer sea views. ❺

Hotel del Glaciar Luis Martial 2355 ⓣ 02901/430604, ⓕ 02901/430636, ⓦ www .hoteldelglaciar.com. A large four-star hotel at the foot of the Glaciar Martial chair lift, 5km up the steep mountainside from the centre (free shuttle bus). Choose between a mountain or sea view. Single rooms cost only slightly less than doubles. **⓼**

🏃 **Residencial Linares** Gob. Deloqui 1522 ⓣ 02901/423594, ⓔ linaresd@infovia.com .ar. An excellent B&B in a cosy, split-level house with sterling views of the Beagle Channel. You can use the living room after 4pm. **❸**

Torre al Sur Hostel Gob. Paz 1437 ⓣ 02901/430745, ⓔ torrealsur@speedy.com .ar. A popular, friendly HI-affiliated hostel that gets extremely busy in summer, when it can be cramped and noisy. It has great views, a small kitchen, inexpensive meals and cheap Internet access. **❷**

Villa Brescia Hotel San Martín 1299 ⓣ & ⓕ 02901/433276, ⓔ info@villabrescia.com.ar. One of the best mid-range hotels, with bright rooms and panoramic views from the second floor. **❺**

The Town

Start your explorations by the pier, the Muelle Turístico, on the seafront avenue, Maipú, at the corner with Lasserre. The 1920s **Provincial Legislature** overlooking the sea is one of the town's most stately buildings. Northeast of here you'll find the small, edifying **Museo del Fin del Mundo**, at Maipú 175 (daily 9am–8pm; ⓣ 02901/421863; AR$10), with exhibits on the region's history and wildlife, including the serene polychrome figurehead of the *Duchess of Albany*, a ship wrecked on the eastern end of the island in 1893, and a rare example of the Selk'nam–Spanish dictionary written by the Salesian missionary, José María Beauvoir.

You can visit the former **prison** to see the **Museo del Presidio**, also called Museo Marítimo (daily 9am–8pm; ⓣ 02901/437481; AR$15), two blocks further along the seafront and two more inland, at Yaganes and Gobernador Paz. It houses a motley collection of exhibits, with the central draw being the sprawling prison building itself, whose wings radiate out like spokes from a half-wheel. The most celebrated prisoner to stay in the cells was the early twentieth-century anarchist Simón Radowitzsky, whose miserable stay and subsequent brief escape in 1918 are recounted by Bruce Chatwin in *In Patagonia*. The best exhibits are the painstakingly made scale models of famous **ships** from the island's history, and a much cruder, if equally fascinating, reconstruction of a Yámana canoe, complete with video of the archeologists' making it according to authentic techniques.

Head 7km behind the town to the hanging **Glaciar Martial**, with first-rate views of the Beagle Channel and the islands of Chile. To get there, walk or take one of several buses (four companies offering ten daily departures; AR$3–5) from the Muelle Turístico up to the *Hotel Del Glaciar*, and then climb or take the **chair lift** (AR$7) from behind the hotel. Bring sun protection: the ozone hole affects these latitudes and solar radiation can be fierce.

Winter sports

To **ski** at the end of the world, come some time from late May to early September and head to either the small Club Andino, 3km from town, or the ski run by Glaciar Martial (see above). Equipment rental costs between AR$20 and $60 a day. You'll also find excellent cross-country and several downhill skiing options in the Sierra Alvear (see p.546), including the modern Cerro Castor centre (ⓦ www.cerrocastor .com), 26km from town.

Eating and drinking

Ushuaia is crammed with eateries of all kinds plus tea rooms serving thick hot chocolate and Germanic cakes. Self-caterers will find all they need at one of two **supermarkets** in town: Mega Gonzalo at San Martín 131, and La Anónima on the corner of Gob. Paz and Rivadavia.

Restaurants and cafés

Bodegón Fueguino Laserre. Very central spot popular with young gringos, tempted by the home-brewed beer, melt-in-your-mouth lamb and a wide range of wine.

Café Central 25 de Mayo 50. This smart, bright coffee shop, with designer sofas and a fashion magazine decor, offers the city's best home-made ice cream by far.

Ideal San Martín 393. Housed in one of Ushuaia's more venerable buildings, the *Ideal* serves king crab thermidor at a price, while grilled trout and other dishes are less expensive. Out of season, it serves a value-for-money *tenedor libre*.

Kaupe Roca 470 ☏ 02901/422704. Hands down the best restaurant in Ushuaia, with friendly service, delicious food, including excellent shellfish and *centolla*, and unpretentious decor in what is essentially just a family home with a fabulous view. Moderate to expensive.

Marcopolo San Martín 748, in the *Cap Polonio* hotel. This bright restaurant serves breakfast, lunch, tea and dinner, including trout stuffed with crab, and juicy *parrillas*; it's on the expensive side.

El Nono Gob. Deloqui 429. Unfussy and amiable local diner serves giant hamburgers and snacks, and also a bargain *menú del día* that includes a soft drink.

La Rueda San Martín 193. One of the town's best options for carnivores, serving a full *parrillada* at knock-down prices.

Shelknam San Martín 273. A decent *confitería*-café on the main drag, with a lively buzz throughout the day.

Tía Elvira Maipú 349. Enjoy a fine selection of somewhat pricey fresh seafood, excellent mussels and a delicious *merluza negra a la Marquery* (black hake in a seafood sauce). They offer a good list of Argentine wines, too.

El Turco San Martín 1440. Sizeable, hearty portions of pizza, home-made pasta and meat dishes at low prices; excellent moderately priced lunch menu. Good-humoured service is another plus. Closed Sun lunch.

Bars and discos

Barny's Antártida Argentina 173. A disco that's popular in high season, if none too sophisticated in its decor or choice of hybrid pop tunes.

Náutico Maipú and Belgrano. A sit-down bar with fireplace and occasional live music for a more laid-back crowd who prefer chatting to dancing.

Sheik Gob. Paz and Roca. Club playing a standard mix of mainstream pop tunes to a mostly tourist crowd.

Listings

Airlines Aerolíneas Argentinas, Roca 116 ☏ 02901/421218; DAP, Deloqui 555 ☏ 02901/431110; LADE, San Martín 542 ☏ 02901/421123.

Banks and exchanges ATMs at most banks, most of which are along San Martín, as is the main *casa de cambio*, at no. 877. There's a Western Union office at Gob. Paz 921.

Bus companies Líder, Gob. Paz 921 ☏ 02901/436421; Tecni Austral, Roca 157 ☏ 02901/431408.

Car rental Arg Tagle, San Martín 1199 ☏ 02901/422744; Avis, airport ☏ 02901/433323; Cardos, San Martín 845 ☏ 02901/436388;

Europcar, Maipú 857 ☏ 02901/430786; Localiza, San Martín 1222 ☏ 02901/430739.

Telephone centres Several *locutorios* along San Martín or Locutorio del Sur at Laserre 124.

Travel agencies All Patagonia, Juana Fadul 26 ☏ 02901/433622, ⓦ www.allpatagonia .com; Compañía de Guías de Patagonia, Gob. Campos 795 ☏ 02901/437753; Canal Fun & Nature, Rivadavia 82 ☏ 02901/437395, ⓦ www.canalfun.com; Rumbo Sur, San Martín 342 ☏ 02901/421139, ⓦ www.rumbosur.com.ar; Tolkeyen, Maipú 237 ☏ 02901/437073; Turismo de Campo, 25 de Mayo 34 ☏ 02901/437329.

Beagle Channel

No visit to Ushuaia is complete without a journey on the **BEAGLE CHAN-NEL**, the majestic, mountain-fringed sea passage to the south of the city. Most **boat trips** start and finish in Ushuaia, and you can enjoy the best views of town looking back at it from the straits. The standard tours visit Les Eclaireurs Lighthouse – sometimes erroneously called the Lighthouse at the End of the World; Isla de los Pájaros; and Isla de los Lobos. The main draw of these excursions is the chance to spot the **marine wildlife** that lives along the channel, including albatrosses, giant petrels, skuas, cormorants, South American terns, Magellanic penguins and lots of gulls and ducks; resident sea mammals are sea lions, Peale's dolphins, minke whales and, if you're lucky, killer whales or southern right whales. Boats depart from the pier, **Muelle Turístico**, where you'll find a huddle of agents' booking huts. Try the *Barracuda*, offering three-hour tours (9.30am & 3pm; AR$60); or Héctor Monsalve's trips for small groups on the quiet motorized sailboat, *Tres Marías* (℡02901/421897; Nov–Easter 9.30am & 3pm; 4hr; AR$90), which includes a stop at Islas Bridges to see Yámana shell middens. Monsalve also arranges **diving** trips in the clear waters of the channel, as do Ushuaia Divers (℡02901/423159, ℻02901/444701; AR$100 a day).

Ushuaia to Paso Garibaldi, Sierra Valdivieso and Sierra Alvear

The road from Ushuaia to **PASO GARIBALDI** winds its way north and east through dramatic forested scenery, with great views of the valleys and savage mountain ranges that cross the southern part of the island, running diagonally northwest to southeast. The rugged, serrated peaks of the **SIERRA VALDIVIESO** and **SIERRA ALVEAR** make ideal bushwhacking territory, though do not underestimate the need for orienteering skills or the unpredictable nature of the weather: blizzards can hit at any time of year. You must also be prepared to get thoroughly soaked when crossing boggy ground and the ubiquitous streams, but you'll be rewarded by the sight of **beaver dams** up to two and a half metres high.

Heading northeast from Ushuaia, the RN-3 curls up around the foot of **Monte Olivia**, following the **Río Olivia** valley. To the right of the road, you can just catch a glimpse of the attractive **Velo de la Novia** (Bridal Veil Falls),

Moving on from Ushuaia

Ushuaia is linked **by air** to Río Grande (AR$25), Río Gallegos (AR$60) and El Calafate ($AR70–100), plus other destinations, including Buenos Aires; and by **bus** to Río Grande (AR$30) and Río Gallegos (AR$40), via Chile.

For anyone travelling on to **southern Chile**, you can choose between plane and bus/ferry, depending on the season – bear in mind that it's extremely costly, when permitted, to take a rented car across the border. Regular, but not terribly frequent, **buses** do the day-long trip from Ushuaia to Punta Arenas (AR$50–60), entailing a short **ferry** ride at Primera Angostura (see p.506), or more rarely the longer Porvenir crossing (see p.501). Departures are at around 6am, getting you into Arenas by evening (see "Listings" for bus companies). In the summer, DAP (see p.545) runs weekly **flights** to Punta Arenas (US$100 one way; book well ahead). An interesting, potentially faster alternative to the Ushuaia-Arenas bus is to fly to Río Gallegos with another company (see "Listings"), and take a bus either to Arenas or Natales (around 6hr; AR$20–25).

peeping through the trees. Further up the RN-3, you enter the **Valle de Tierra Mayor**, the valley of the Río Lasıfashaj. This is a popular area for winter sports, and one of the first centres you'll come across is *Altos del Valle*, 18km out of Ushuaia (T & F 02901/422234 for reservations). This breeding centre for baying huskies (husky rides available) offers rustic *refugio*-style **accommodation** (bring sleeping bags; AR$10 per person plus AR$5 for breakfast). For **trekking** (guided or otherwise), you'll find a relatively clear trail to Laguna Esmeralda, and a challenging hike to Glaciar Alvear. A kilometre beyond this centre is the highly recommended refuge, *Nunatak* (T 02901/423240, F 424108; E antartur@tierradelfuego.ml.org; bring a sleeping bag; AR$10 with basic breakfast), with tremendous views across the peat flatlands of the valley floor and up to the peaks of Cerro Bonete (1100m) and Cerro Alvear (1425m).

Estancia Harberton and the RCj

The unsealed **RCj** is one of the most interesting branch roads on the island, offering spectacular views of the Beagle Channel. The turn-off for the RCj is 40km south of Ushuaia on the RN-3; 25km from the turn-off, you emerge from the forested route near a delightful lagoon fringed by the skeletons of *Nothofagus* beeches, and you can look right across the Beagle Channel to the Chilean naval town of Puerto Williams (see p.538). A few hundred metres beyond here, the road splits: take the left-hand fork heading eastwards across rolling open country and past a famous clump of **banner trees**, swept back in exaggerated quiffs by the unremitting wind.

Ten kilometres beyond the turn-off and 85km east of Ushuaia is **ESTANCIA HARBERTON**, an ordered assortment of whitewashed buildings on the shores of a sheltered bay (daily 9am–7pm; T 02901/422742, F 02901/422743, W www.estanciaharberton.com). This farmstead served as a voluntary refuge for groups of Yámana, Selk'nam and Mannekenk – here, even the warlike Selk'nam refrained from hostilities. It was built by the Reverend Thomas Bridges, author of the Yámana–English dictionary, and is now run by his great-grandson, Tommy Goodall, and Goodall's wife, Nathalie, a renowned biologist who oversees the impressive marine mammal museum, **Museo Acatushún** (daily 9am–7pm, W www.acatushun.com; AR$5). The museum contains the bones and skeletons of more than 4000 specimens, including small cetaceans (dolphins, porpoises and beaked whales), seals and sea lions and more than 80 species of bird. You can take an informative tour to learn about the anatomy, ecology and behaviour of these southernmost animals. Entrance to the *estancia* proper at Haberton is by **guided tour** only (45min–1hr 30min; mid–Oct to mid–April 10am–7pm; last tour 5.30pm; AR$15). The *Mánacatush* **tearoom** is the only part of the main *estancia* building open to the public: you can enjoy afternoon tea, with large helpings of cake and delicious home-made jams, or – if you book two days in advance – a generous three-course lunch. If at all possible, spend a night here, either in the *Old Shepherd's House* (AR$240 per person, includes breakfast), the *Old Cook's House* (AR$210 per person), or at one of the *estancia's* three **campsites**: all are free, but you must first register at the tearoom and obtain a permit.

While at Haberton you can cross (twice daily in summer; 1hr 30min; AR$50) to the Reserva Yecapasela on Isla Martillo, also known as **Penguin Island**, home to two species of penguin and a large shag colony.

Beyond Harberton, the RCj runs for forty spectacular kilometres to **Estancia Moat**, past the uninhabited islands that guard the eastern mouth of the Beagle

Channel: **Picton**, **Nueva** and **Lennox**. They have a controversial past, since both Chile and Argentina long claimed sovereignty over them. Simmering tensions threatened to boil over between 1977 and 1979, when manoeuvres by the military regimes of both powers brought the two to the brink of war. Arbitration was left in the hands of the British Crown, which ruled in favour of Chile.

Five companies run buses from Ushuaia to Harberton, departing at 9.30am or 10am, with one daily service at 3pm, returning at 2pm, 4pm and 8pm. The return fare is AR$40-60; look for the latest schedules from the tourist office.

Parque Nacional Tierra Del Fuego

The **PARQUE NACIONAL TIERRA DEL FUEGO**, a mere 12km west of Ushuaia, protects 630 square kilometres of jagged mountains, intricate lakes, southern beech forest, swampy peat bog, sub-Antarctic tundra and verdant coastline. The park stretches along the frontier with Chile, from the Beagle Channel to the **Sierra de Injugoyen** north of Lago Fagnano, but only the southernmost quarter is open to the public, accessed by the RN-3 from Ushuaia. Fortunately, this area contains much of the park's most beautiful scenery, if also some of the wettest, so bring your rain gear. It's broken down into three main sectors: Bahía Ensenada and Río Pipo in the east; Lago Roca further to the west; and the Lapataia area to the south of Lago Roca, which includes Lago Verde and, at the end of RN-3, Bahía Lapataia on the Beagle Channel. While here you may see **birds** such as Magellanic woodpeckers, condors, torrent ducks, steamer ducks, upland geese and buff-necked ibises, and **mammals** such as guanacos, the rare

PARQUE NACIONAL TIERRA DEL FUEGO

Canal Beagle

sea otter, Patagonian grey foxes, and their larger, endangered cousin, the native Fuegian fox, once heavily hunted for its pelt. The park offers several relatively unchallenging though beautiful **trails**, many of which are completed in minutes rather than hours or days. The Senda Costera (Coastal Path) connects Bahía Ensenada with Lago Roca or Bahía Lapataia; and the comparatively tough Cerro Guanaco climbs from Lago Roca.

Practicalities

The most common (and cheapest) access to the park is along the good dirt road from Ushuaia (sometimes cut off briefly by snowfalls in late May to early October). You can also come via the rather expensive, gimmicky tourist railway of

△ Grey fox

El Tren del Fin del Mundo (AR$50 each way, ⓦ www.trendelfindelmundo .com.ar), which departs from a station 8km west of Ushuaia. The 4.5km trip to the park takes 40 minutes. You must pay an entrance fee of AR$12 at the main park gate, except in winter. Virtually all travel agencies in Ushuaia offer **tours** of the park (around AR$40); most last four hours and stop at the major places of interest – be sure to book on a minibus and try to avoid the big tour buses.

You'll find four main areas for **camping** in the park: Bahía Ensenada and Río Pipo are currently free, but you're better off heading to the paying sites of the Lago Roca and Lago Verde areas. The latter boasts the two most beautifully sited campsites in the park, right next door to each other and encircled by the Río Ovando: *Camping Lago Verde* (ⓣ02901/421433, ⓔlagunaverde@tierradelfuego .ml.org; AR$2 per person), with a tiny toilet block and sink, a shop, and tent rental (AR$10 a day, sleeping bags included); and *Camping Los Cauquenes* (pay at *Lago Verde*; AR$2 per person) just across the road.

Bahía Ensenada

The small **BAHÍA ENSENADA**, 2km south of the crossroads by the Tren del Fin del Mundo train station, is where you'll find the jetty for boats to Lapataia and the Isla Redonda. It's also the trailhead for one of the most pleasant walks in the park, the highly recommended **Senda Costera** (7km; 3hr). The not-too-strenuous route takes you through dense coastal forest of evergreen beech, Winter's bark, and lenga while affording spectacular views from the Beagle Channel shoreline. On the way, you'll pass grass-covered mounds that are the ancient campsite **middens** of the Yámana. These mounds are protected archeological sites and should not be disturbed.

Cerro Guanaco

Another recommended, if tiring trek, is the climb up **CERRO GUANACO** (8km; 3hr), the 970-metre-high mountain ridge on the north side of Lago Roca. Remember that, at any time of the year, the weather can be capricious, so bring adequate clothing even if you set out in glorious sunshine. Take the

Hito XXIV path from the car park at Lago Roca and after ten minutes you'll cross a small bridge over a stream. Immediately afterwards, the path forks: left to Hito XXIV and right up the slope to the Cerro. The path up the forested mountainside is not hazardous, but after rain you're sure to encounter some slippery tree roots and muddy patches.

The view from the crest to the south is memorable: the tangle of islands and rivers of the Archipiélago Cormoránes, Lapataia's sinuous curves, the Isla Redonda in the Beagle Channel, and across to the Chilean islands, Hoste and Navarino, separated by the Murray Narrows.

Río Grande and Tolhuin

The drab, sprawling city of **RÍO GRANDE** grew up on the river of the same name as a port for exporting sheep products, but lost its prominence due to the treacherous tides. Don't miss the lovely **Candelaria Salesian Mission**, 11km to the north on the RN-3, a smart collection of whitewashed buildings grouped around a modest but elegant chapel. To reach the mission from town, take the Línea B bus "Misión" from Avenida San Martín (hourly; 25min; AR$1).

The most comfortable **accommodation** is the restful ✹ *Posada de los Sauces*, El Cano 839 (☎ & ℱ02964/430672, ✉info@posadadelossauces.com, ⓦwww .posadadelossauces.com.ar; ❺), across the road from the bus terminal, with a relaxed lounge bar and a high-quality *à la carte* restaurant.

South of Río Grande, you pass the turn-off for the **RCb**, worth detouring for 1km to see the tiny village of **Estancia José Menéndez**, whose shearing shed is emblazoned by the tremendous stuffed head of a prize ewe, its face obscured by an over-effusive wig of curls. The *estancia* was founded as Estancia Primera Argentina in 1896 by Menéndez, a powerful sheep magnate. The RCb continues across the steppe for 70km to the Chilean frontier at **Radman**, where there's a little-used **border crossing** (Nov–March 8am–9pm), providing a route to Porvenir (see p.534).

Tolhuin and Lago Fagnano

TOLHUIN was built in the 1970s to provide a focus for the heartland of Isla Grande. It has an artificial commune-like feel, but makes a useful halfway point to break your journey if you're driving between Ushuaia and Río Grande. South from the village take the scenic old RN-3 route, which cuts across the eastern end – or *cabecera* – of **Lago Fagnano**, 3km to the southwest of the village, along a splendid causeway. This impressive lake is flanked by ranges of hills, and straddles the Chilean border at its westernmost extremity. Buses stop in Tolhuin at the *Panadería La Unión*, a bakery and restaurant that acts as the hub of village life. The *Hostal de la Cuesta*, at Angela Loij 696 in Tolhuin (☎02964/492037, ℱ492049; ❸, with breakfast), offers cosy, cabin-style **lodging** with views across to the mountains.

Travel details

Buses

Porvenir to: Río Grande (Tues–Sun 1 daily; 3hr 30min); Ushuaia, only via Río Grande (Tues–Sun 1 daily; 7hr).
Punta Arenas to: Ushuaia, Argentina (several weekly; 12hr).
Río Grande to: Tolhuin (11 daily; 1hr 30min); Ushuaia (7–8 daily; 4hr).
Tolhuin to: Río Grande (11 daily; 1hr 30min); Ushuaia (6 daily; 2hr).
Ushuaia to: El Calafate (Mon–Sat 1 daily; 14hr); Punta Arenas (Mon–Sat 1 daily; 12hr); Puerto Natales (3 weekly; 13hr); Río Gallegos (Mon–Sat 1 daily; 9hr); Río Grande (7–8 daily; 4hr); Tolhuin (6–8 daily; 2hr).

Ferries

Punta Arenas to: Porvenir (1 daily except Mon; 2hr 30min–3hr); Puerto Williams (4 monthly; 36hr).

Punta Delgada to: Bahía Azul (Puerto Espora), Tierra del Fuego (every 1hr 30min, tides permitting; 20–30min).

Flights

Punta Arenas to: Porvenir (6 weekly; 15min); Puerto Williams (4 weekly; 1hr 30min); Río Grande (summer: 1 weekly; 1hr); Ushuaia (summer: 1 weekly; 1hr).
Río Grande to: Punta Arenas (summer: 1 weekly 1hr); Río Gallegos (1 daily; 45min); Ushuaia (1 daily; 35min).
Ushuaia to: Buenos Aires (2–4 daily; 3hr 30min); El Calafate (1 daily; 2hr 15min, longer if stopover at Río Gallegos); Puerto Madryn, Argentina (6 weekly; 2hr); Punta Arenas (summer: 3 weekly; 1hr); Río Gallegos (6 weekly; 1hr); Río Grande (6 weekly; 35min); Trelew, Argentina (irregular; 2hr).

11

Easter Island and the Juan Fernández Archipelago

553

CHAPTER 11

Highlights

* **Tapati** If you are here late January–early February, discover the mysterious roots of Easter Island's ancient culture at its carnival, featuring everything from traditional dancing and singing to hurtling down volcanic slopes on banana trunks. **See p.559**

* **Ahu Tongariki** Fifteen impeccably restored moai (giant statues) line up to be admired against a backdrop of green cliffs and roaring waves. **See p.569**

* **Rano Raraku** This mighty mountain at the heart of Rapa Nui is where the moai were quarried – and some, too big to move, never left the rock where they were hewn. **See p.569**

* **Orongo** Imagine the mind-boggling rituals of the bird-man cult as you gaze out at craggy islets in a sapphire-blue ocean or inwards to a reed-filled crater at one of the island's most breathtaking natural sites. **See p.577**

* **Juan Fernández flora and fauna** Frolic with sea lions, watch the antics of hummingbirds and observe dozens of endemic species of plant on this treasure island of unique (and painfully fragile) wildlife. **See p.578**

△ Seals on San Juan Archipelago

Easter Island and the Juan Fernández Archipelago

C hile is the proud possessor of two remote island territories, mysterious **EASTER ISLAND** and the virtually unknown **JUAN FERNÁN-DEZ ARCHIPELAGO**, collectively referred to as the Islas Esporádicas (or "Far Flung Isles") as they are so far from the mainland, way, way out in the Pacific Ocean. Both are classified as national parks, and each has been singled out by UNESCO for special protection. Neither is easy to get to and most visitors to Chile never do, but those who make the journey will find their effort and expenditure richly rewarded with a set of tantalizingly enigmatic statues and one of the world's most precarious ecosystems, respectively.

Lost in the vastness of the ocean and mysteries of time, tiny **Easter Island** (Isla de Pascua or, in the native tongue, Rapa Nui) was annexed by Chile in 1888, but more than a century later it remains a world unto itself, surrounded on all sides by huge expanses of empty ocean. Its closest inhabited neighbour is Pitcairn Island, 2250km northwest, while to the east it's separated from the nearest point of the Chilean coast by 3878 kilometres of empty sea – about the distance between Spain and Newfoundland. Isolation on this scale is barely comprehensible, though you begin to feel something of the island's remoteness during the five hours it takes to fly here from Santiago or Tahiti (the closest international airports and only links with the outside world, barring the odd sailing boat or supplies vessel).

Once on Easter Island, you're faced with a windswept land of low, gently rolling hills and steep cliffs riddled with caves, pounded on all sides by crashing waves. Spanning just 23km at its longest stretch, the island is triangular in shape, with low-lying extinct volcanoes rising out of each corner. Scattered between these points, running parallel to the shore, are the unique monuments that have made this little island universally famous – the dozens of monolithic stone **statues** of squat torsos and long, brooding heads looming sombrely over the coast. These are the **moai**, among the most arresting and intriguing ancient sculptures in the world. Their fascination lies not only in their visual impact, but also in the many questions that surround them: Why were they made? When? What did they signify? And how on earth were they transported and erected? Such questions are indicative of the extent to which Easter Island's past remains unknown. The lack of information available to us about the society that created these statues lends the island its sense of mystery.

Much closer to the mainland, at a mere 675km due west of Valparaíso, but still relatively unknown, the **Juan Fernández Archipelago** is, ironically, far more difficult to reach. It is served only by a couple of tiny light aircraft, and extremely infrequent ships. With their sharp, jagged peaks soaring dramatically out of the ocean, coated in a thick tangle of lush, deep-green foliage, the islands boast a topography that counts among the most spectacular in the whole of Chile. On top of this comes a compelling history, spilling over with adventure and romance. The archipelago's largest and only inhabited island – **Isla Robinson Crusoe** – started out as a pirates' refuge. Notorious freebooters like Bartholomew Sharp and William Dampier used it as a watering spot during their raids on the Pacific seaboard in the seventeenth century. In 1709 the faraway island was brought to public attention when the Scottish seaman Alexander Selkirk was rescued from its shores after being marooned there for more than four years. Selkirk's story was to go down in literary history when Daniel Defoe used it as the basis for his classic novel, *The Adventures of Robinson Crusoe* (see p.579). These days, the island's small community (descended from Chilean and European colonizers) milks the Crusoe connections to death in an attempt to boost the tourist trade, but this remains very low-key, and the Juan Fernández Archipelago is still an adventurous destination, well off the beaten track.

Easter Island

We were surrounded, as in a hall of mirrors, by enormous faces circling about us, seen from in front, in profile and at every angle. . . We had them above us, beneath us and on both sides. We clambered over noses and chins and trod on mouths and gigantic fists, while huge bodies lay leaning over us on the ledges higher up. As our eyes gradually became trained to distinguish art from nature, we perceived that the whole mountain was one single swarm of bodies and heads.

Thor Heyerdahl, Aku Aku

One of the most remote places on earth, tiny **EASTER ISLAND**, or **Rapa Nui** as both the island and its inhabitants are known by its native people, is home to some 4000 islanders. Two thirds are indigenous (called *pascuenses* in Spanish), with the rest being mainly *continentales* (Chilean immigrants, known disparagingly to the natives as "Contis"). The Rapa Nui have fine-boned Polynesian features and speak their own Polynesian-based language (also called Rapa Nui) in addition to Spanish. Virtually the entire population lives in the island's single settlement, **Hanga Roa**, and just about all the islanders make their living from tourism, which has been growing steadily ever since an airstrip was built here in 1968. Before that, Easter Island's only contact with the outside world was a once-yearly visit by a Chilean warship, sent to bring provisions and mail.

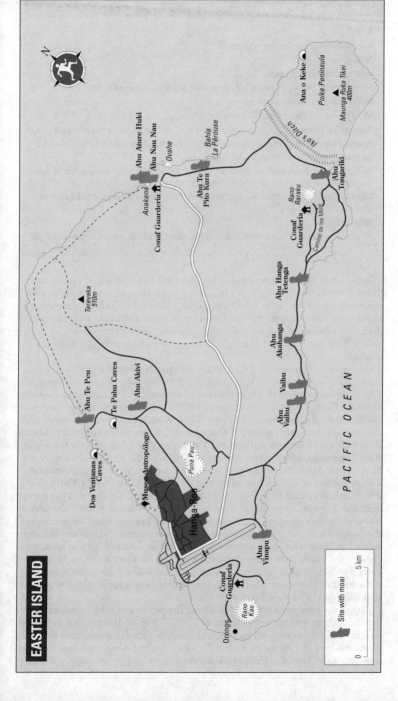

EASTER ISLAND

N

Terevaka 510m

Ahu Te Peu
Te Pahu Caves
Ahu Akivi

Dos Ventanas Caves

Museo Antropológico

Puna Pau

Hanga Roa

Rano Kau

Orongo
Conaf Guarderia

Ahu Vinapu

PACIFIC OCEAN

Ahu Vaihu
Vaihu

Ahu Akahanga

Ahu Hanga Tetenga

Conaf Guarderia
Rano Raraku
Camino de los Moai

Ahu Tongariki

Ahu Te Pito Kura
Bahia La Pérouse

Ovahe
Ahu Nau Nau
Ahu Ature Huki
Anakena
Conaf Guarderia

Iko's Ditch

Ana o Keke
Poike Peninsula
▲ *Maunga Puka Tikei 400m*

0 — 5 km

● Site with moai

Easter Island glossary

Ana Cave

Ahu Platform on which the moai stand

Ariki Chief

Ariki henua Highest leader

Hare Paenga House (dwelling place), shaped like an overturned boat

Mana Spiritual, supernatural power

Moai Carved stone images of heads and torsos

Pukao Cylindrical red stone "hats" or "topknots" placed on some moais' heads

Rongo rongo Undeciphered symbols resembling a script carved on tablets of wood

Tangata honui Elderly man of high status

Tangata manu Translated as "Birdman"; the victor of the annual competition to find the first egg of the sooty tern, part of a sacred ritual

Tapu Sacred, taboo, often referring to objects that may only be touched by certain people

Tatu Tattoo

Te pito o te henua The mystical name of the island meaning "navel of the world"

Today, LAN deposits a jet-load of tourists onto the little island two or three times a week, which sometimes leaves the impression that the most remote inhabited island on earth is swarming with visitors. This can be a serious fly in the ointment, though it's also true that the vast majority of tourists limit their exploration of the sites to quick, guided tours in minibuses, so with only a little patience and the right timing you can have the monuments to yourself.

Most points of interest are found within **Parque Nacional Rapa Nui**, which is formed by a wide strip of land running around the edge of most of the island. There's open access to all the park's land at all times, and the only place where a visitor's fee is charged is at Orongo (CH$5000). If you're pushed for time you should, as an absolute minimum, visit **Rano Kau**, a huge volcanic crater and site of the ceremonial village of **Orongo**; the **Rano Raraku** quarry, where almost all the moai were carved; and the largest ahu (platform) on the island, **Ahu Tongariki**, which boasts fifteen moai. With a little more time to spare, try to see **Ahu Akivi**, an inland ahu with seven well-preserved moai; **Anakena**, a palm-fringed beach and site of an ahu with seven moai; the **Te Pahu** caves, which are connected by a 150m lava tube; the beach of **Ovahe**; and the finely built ahu **Vinapu**. These suggestions are really just a starting point – the whole island is highly rewarding, and there are plenty of opportunities for getting off the beaten track and exploring the less obvious attractions such as the volcanic mound of **Terevaka**, with impressive views of the island. With a vehicle, you can see the major sites quite comfortably in two or three full days, but a few extra days would allow you to take your time and soak up the atmosphere. This is the kind of place most people only come to once in a lifetime. If you plan to visit most places on foot, leave yourself a week.

There's no ideal time to visit the island; the weather is fairly constant year-round, with an average temperature of 23°C (73°F) in January and February, and 18°C (64°F) in July and August, with moderate rainfall throughout the year. From the end of January to end of February is the busiest time and also the most exciting. The islanders put on an extravagant display of singing, dancing and feasting during their annual two-week **Tapati Rapa Nui festival**, held in late January or early February.

Getting to Easter Island is possible only with LAN, which flies here from Santiago's international airport two or three times a week. The standard fare is about CH$500,000 round-trip; lower fares are sometimes available, especially if you book from outside of Chile. Some flights from the mainland continue to Papeete, Tahiti. Make sure you arrive at Santiago airport at least three hours before departure as LAN notoriously overbooks these flights.

Post-contact history

Easter Island clearly enjoyed a long, rich history before it was "discovered" and named by Dutch naval commander **Jacob Roggeveen** on Easter Sunday, 1722. However, in the absence of any written records left by the islanders (or any that we can read), Roggeveen's **log** is the earliest written account we have of the island. In it, he colourfully describes the excited inhabitants who, visiting the ship, "were so bold that they took the hats and caps of the sailors from their heads and jumped with their plunder overboard". His party spent only a single day on land, long enough to observe the "particularly high erected stone images", which "caused us to be struck with astonishment, because we could not comprehend how it was possible that these people, who are devoid of heavy thick timber for making any machines, as well as strong ropes, nevertheless had been able to erect such images, which were fully thirty feet high and thick in proportion".

After their departure, it was another 48 years before Easter Island was revisited, this time by the Spanish commander **Felipe González**, who mapped the island and claimed it for King Carlos III of Spain during a six-day stay. Four years later, **Captain Cook** anchored here in the hope of restoring the health of his crew, who had developed scurvy during their long search for the "southern continent". As there were few provisions to be found, Cook stayed only four days, but he too observed with incredulity the "stupendous figures" erected on the island, though he noted that some lay strewn on the ground, toppled from their platforms. Later visitors reported an increasing number of **fallen statues**, and by 1825, all of the moai on Hanga Roa bay had been destroyed. When the English doctor Linton Palmer visited in 1868, he confirmed there wasn't a single statue left standing on the island.

The mass destruction of statues suggests serious internal strife, but the biggest threat to Easter Island's civilization was to come from outside. In 1805 the island was raided by the first of the **slave traders**, when an American schooner captured twelve men and ten women to be used as seal hunters on the Juan Fernández Islands. After three days at sea, the prisoners were released from captivity and allowed onto the deck, whereupon they promptly threw themselves overboard in a desperate attempt to swim back to the island. All of them drowned. Between 1862 and 1864, Peruvian sailors landed on the island and enticed the inhabitants onto the bay with a large display of gifts. They then attacked and captured over 2500 people, who were shipped off to work as slaves in the Peruvian guano mines and estates. After most of the islanders had died from disease and appalling work conditions in the mines, the Bishop of Tahiti, Tepano Jaussen, finally managed to persuade the Peruvian government to repatriate the remaining prisoners – most of whom died on the return voyage home. Tragically, the sixteen who made it back infected the rest of the islanders with smallpox and TB, reducing the population to near one hundred. Critically, the loss of life was accompanied by the loss of a crucial part of the island's culture and collective memory, for the last *ariki henua* (high chief), *moari*

The details of Easter Island's pre-contact history remain, now, and probably forever, outside our full knowledge. The island's centuries-long isolation, added to the absence of written historical records and the decimation of the indigenous population in the nineteenth century, conspire to leave few clues that might explain the settlement and development of this people. Instead, archeologists, scientists, linguists and anthropologists have had to painstakingly gather what evidence there is in an attempt to piece together the historical jigsaw puzzle and gain a clearer picture of the island's past. At the same time, the legends and chronicles passed orally from generation to generation over hundreds of years – and assiduously documented by several European investigators – provide their own versions of the island's history. Subject as oral history is to exaggeration, embellishment, confusion and reinvention over the years, it would be unwise to read these legends as pure facts, but they do, at the very least, provide us with a glimpse of how the Easter Islanders view their world and their ancestry.

What the islanders say: the arrival of Hotu Matu'a

The islanders claim that the original colonizer of Easter Island was **Hotu Matu'a**, a great *ariki henua*, or chief, who lived in a (now unknown) place called **Hiva**, possibly in Polynesia, perhaps the Marquesas. Hotu Matu'a was forced to flee Hiva when the sexual misdemeanours of his brother aroused the anger of a rival chief, who declared war on Hotu Matu'a's tribe. It had been revealed to Hotu Matu'a's tattooist in a dream, or "spirit voyage", that an island with craters and fine beaches awaited his master, so the chief dispatched a reconnaissance party to find this promised land, following on some time later with his family, servants and fellow colonists in a large double canoe. He arrived safely on Anakena beach, just as his wife was giving birth to their first son. Hotu Matu'a and his family lived in a cave on this beach while his servants built him a house; meanwhile, the colonists set to work planting the seeds and shoots they'd brought with them, living only from fish until the resultant taros, yams, bananas and sugarcane could be eaten. They had also brought chickens and rats, which survived and bred on the island.

As *ariki henua*, Hotu Matu'a's role was not that of political leader, but rather of a revered and important person in possession of great supernatural qualities, or *mana*. Accordingly, he and the place where he lived were *tapu*, or sacred and untouchable, and so Hotu Matu'a and his family lived at Anakena while the rest of his party dispersed around the island, where their families expanded and new communities began to spring up. Eventually these grew into eight separate kin-groups, each with its own *tangata honui*, or leader. As time passed and generation after generation was born, these groups became more sophisticated and stratified, made up of a diverse collection of priests, fishermen, farmers and craftsmen. It appears that everyone lived in close co-operation and relative harmony until conflict broke out between warring clans, leading to the toppling of the statues and the breakdown of society (see p.559).

What the experts say: east or west?

Central to any discussion of Easter Island's settlement are the controversial theories of **Thor Heyerdahl** (1906–2002), the Norwegian explorer-archeologist whose widely

(keepers of sacred knowledge), and *tangata rongo rongo* (specialist readers) were among those who perished.

A certain degree of stability came when the first missionary, **Eugène Eyraud**, arrived on the island in 1864 and set to converting its people to Christianity, a mission fully accomplished by the time of his death, four years later. The peace was disrupted, however, when the French plantation owner, **Jean-Baptiste Onésime Dutrou-Bornier**, bought up large tracts of land and proceeded to run the island publicized expeditions, best-selling books, and prolific TV series made him a household name in the 1960s, and, more importantly, generated an enormous amount of academic interest in the island's history. In 1936, while he was living in the Marquesas Islands, he heard a legend claiming that the first settlers of the Marquesas had arrived from an eastern land on the other side of the sea, under the leadership of a king called Tiki. Further investigations unearthed an old Peruvian legend of a ruler known as **Kon Tiki** who, following military defeat, fled to the Peruvian coast where he built a raft and sailed west with his supporters. Was this the same Tiki of the Marquesan story? Could such a voyage be possible? In 1948 Heyerdahl proved, quite spectacularly, that it was indeed possible when he and five companions successfully sailed a traditionally constructed balsa raft (the *Kon Tiki* from Peru to an island east of Tahiti in a 101-day voyage.

This was followed up, in 1955, with a ground-breaking **expedition to Easter Island** where Heyerdahl and a team of professional archeologists spent five months excavating the monuments, houses and other sites. Unlike the archeologists, Heyerdahl was convinced that Easter Island had been colonized by settlers from South America. He backed up his theory with some persuasive but highly selective details, concentrating on the fact that winds and currents in the Pacific move in a westward, not an eastward, direction; on the presence in Polynesia of the sweet potato, indisputably of South American origin; on the resemblance between the close-fitting stonework of some Easter Island platforms and some types of Inca masonry; and on the ancient Peruvian custom of artificially extending the ear lobes, just like the islanders at the time of European contact. He failed to explain, however, the total absence of South American pottery and textiles in Polynesia – pivotal elements of that continent's culture – and the fact that no trace of any indigenous South American language had been found there.

Seductive as Heyerdahl's theories were, they never really gained currency in the academic world. The view of most experts, then and now, is that Easter Island was colonized by Polynesians from the west – an opinion backed by linguistic evidence, physical anthropology, including bone analysis, and the proliferation on Easter Island of Polynesian plants such as taro, yam, bananas and sugarcane. Which precise part of Polynesia these settlers came from is still open to debate, though the **Marquesas** is thought to be the most likely point of departure (for the settlement not only of Easter Island, but also of Hawaii and New Zealand).

As for the date of the settlers' arrival, all we can be sure of is that they were constructing ahu (ceremonial platforms) by 800 AD. No one knows for sure if this culture developed in complete isolation, or if another wave of colonists arrived at a later date, as suggested in some of the oral traditions. Most scholars tend to think that Easter Island's archeological remains point towards an unbroken line of cultural development, interrupted only by European discovery. What they still can't satisfactorily explain, however, is the presence of the South American sweet potato, which remains a perplexing mystery – letting in a tiny chink of hope for Thor Heyerdahl's theory.

as his personal ranch, paying the islanders a pittance for their hard labour and resorting to violence when they wouldn't co-operate. When the missionaries opposed Doutrou-Bornier's exploitation of the islanders, he instigated armed attacks on their missions, forcing them to evacuate the island. He dealt a further blow to the island's slowly recovering population by sending all but a hundred islanders to Tahiti to work on his partner's plantation. His autocratic rule finally came to an end in 1877, when he was murdered by the oppressed islanders.

Rongo rongo

In 1864, in his account of his nine-month residence on Easter Island, the French missionary **Eugène Eyraud** wrote of an intriguing form of writing he'd come across in the islanders' homes:

In all the houses are encountered tablets or staffs of wood covered with hieroglyphics. These are figures of animals unknown in the island which the people inscribed with sharp stones. Each figure has its name but the little account that they take of these tablets inclines me to believe these signs, the remains of primitive writing, are for them today a usage which they preserved without enquiry into their meaning.

This was the first the outside world had heard of the **inscribed wooden tablets**, known by the Rapa Nui as *ko hau motu mo rongo rong*" or "lines of script for recitation". The revelation of this unheard-of script prompted a flurry of academic interest, but, predictably, the rongo rongo tablets remained firmly beyond the grasp of the scholars who came to study them, for none of the islanders knew how to read them, though a few had heard them recited in their childhood. Almost 140 years later, no one has succeeded in deciphering them.

The script consists of tiny, tightly packed symbols carved in straight lines across the wooden boards. The symbols, which include representations of people, animals, birds and plants, are upside down on each alternate line, requiring the reader to turn the board around at the end of each line. Late nineteenth-century oral testimonies suggest that the tablets contained records of genealogies, creation myths, wars and deaths, and religious hymns. They claim that the knowledge of reading and writing the script was in the hands of a few specialists, the last of whom were probably killed off with the slave raids and TB epidemics in the 1860s.

Of the numerous tablets noted by Father Eugène, the vast majority have disappeared. Many of them were destroyed by their owners for fear that the strictly *tapu* objects would pass into foreign hands, invoking the rage of the ancestors. Others were hidden in secret underground caves where they decomposed in the damp air. Today, only 29 rongo rongo tablets remain in existence, all of them spirited off to overseas museums. Modern scholars are scarcely any further on than they were when the tablets were first brought to light. Some believe that the script was developed after the first European contact, inspired by the written documents that the Spaniards made the island's chiefs sign in 1770; others dispute the fact that it is a script at all. The most widely accepted theory is that, rather than representing grammatical sentences, the symbols were **mnemonics** for use in recitals and chanting. While it seems unlikely that the rongo rongo code will ever be cracked, we are at least left with the outstanding craftsmanship of the exquisitely carved tablets, which deserve equal attention as works of art as of repositories of lost information. You can see rongo rongo tablets in Santiago's Museo de la Merced (see p.107) and at museums in Rome, London and Washington DC. Craftsmen on the island make often outstanding copies of the tablets, though the biggest and best will set you back US$400 or more, and, on ecological grounds, you should not encourage the use of precious rare wood.

The **Chilean government** acquired the lands that had belonged to Doutrou-Bornier, and went on to purchase most of the remaining land on the island, leaving only the village of **Hanga Roa** in the possession of the islanders. Then, on September 9, 1888, the Chilean Navy – apparently with the islanders' consent – officially **annexed** Easter Island, declaring it Chilean territory, primarily in order to control the huge sector of ocean between it and the mainland. Chile, however, took no real interest in the place and leased it off to Williamson Balfour, a British wool-trading company, which virtually governed the island according to its own needs and interests. Although the livestock caused irreparable erosion and destruction, the moai sites were protected and the island's population was revived thanks to food, work and efficient organization. In 1953, the company's lease was revoked and the Chilean Navy stepped in to resume command. The islanders were given no say in the running of their affairs, however, and seemed to be regarded more as property than as citizens.

It was not until 1964, eighty years after annexation, that they were allowed outside Hanga Roa (let alone off the island), and granted full citizenship and the right to vote. Since the return to democracy and especially since the election of President Lagos there has been a more enlightened approach on the part of the Chilean government, which has finally transferred the management of most local affairs, especially education, which is now bilingual, to the islanders.

△ Easter Island petroglyph

Hanga Roa

Nestling in the southwest corner of the island, the village of **HANGA ROA** is somewhat low on attractions (even the island's single **museum** is out of town – see p.576), but as it contains all the accommodation and other services, this is where you'll be based. Its long, sprawling streets, lined with single-storey houses and fragrant eucalyptus trees, are mostly unpaved, giving the place the unfinished feel of a recently settled frontier town.

Arrival and information

The **airport** is on the southern edge of Hanga Roa, about 1km from the centre. When you emerge from the aeroplane you'll be met by every single *residencial* owner on the island, each one trying to snap up your custom, and some eager to adorn you with hand-threaded garlands of flowers as a sign of welcome. It's possible to walk to any part of town in less than half an hour, but most of the *residenciales* are widely dispersed around the village, and it can be a drag traipsing from one to another, particularly as many owners don't return from the airport for some time as they wait to fill up their jeeps with guests. In any case, it's probably a good idea to arrange your accommodation by fax, telephone or (unreliably) by email ahead of time, especially during busy times such as Tapati, the Easter Island carnival, or as a last resort, while you're here at

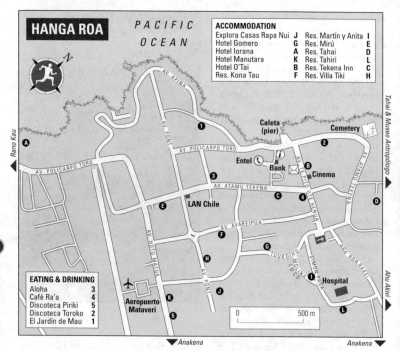

HANGA ROA

PACIFIC OCEAN

ACCOMMODATION

Explora Casas Rapa Nui	J	Res. Martín y Anita	I
Hotel Gomero	G	Res. Mirú	E
Hotel Iorana	A	Res. Tahai	D
Hotel Manutara	K	Res. Tahiri	L
Hotel O'Tai	B	Res. Tekena Inn	C
Res. Kona Tau	F	Res. Villa Tiki	H

Rano Kau

AV. APINA

Caleta (pier)

Cemetery

AV. POLICARPO TORO

Entel

Bank

Cinema

AV. ATAMU TEKENA

LAN Chile

AV. AVAREIPUA

AV. HOTU MATUA

AV. PONT

TUUKOIHU

SIMON PAOA

ARA ROA RAKI

Hospital

EATING & DRINKING

Aloha	3
Café Ra'a	4
Discoteca Piriki	5
Discoteca Toroko	2
El Jardín de Mau	1

Aeropuerto Mataveri

0   500 m

Anakena

Anakena

Tahai & Museo Antropológico

Ahu Akivi

the airport, thus securing a lift into town from the owner; make it clear, though, that you'll take the room only if you like it when you see it. There is a centralized **fax number** for many *residenciales*: ℱ 32/100105.

Sernatur has an all but useless office down towards the *caleta*, at Tu'u Maheke and Apina (Mon–Fri 8.30am–1pm & 2.30–6pm, Sat 8.30am–1pm; ℡ & ℱ 32/100255, ✉ sernatur_rapanui@entelchile.net). Very little of its printed information is on display, so you'll have to beg for the lists of the island's accommodation, restaurants and other services. **Conaf**'s administration centre is on Calle Atamu Tekena (Mon–Fri 8am–1pm & 2–5pm; ℡ 32/100236).

Accommodation

Accommodation on Easter Island is very expensive for what you get – a typical double room (almost always with private bath) in a *residencial* costs around US\$50–75 (usually credit cards not accepted), while a smart hotel room costs from US\$75–125 (here you can use plastic). This, plus the fact that just about everything else is pricey too, and the absence of a reliable ATM – the single machine at the bank only accepts Mastercard or equivalents – means you should bring a plentiful supply of cash, much of it in US currency. There are over thirty **residenciales** on the island – most of them family homes (invariably bungalows) with a few extra rooms added on – and about ten proper **hotels**, which tend to earn their living from package-tour block bookings. Most places offer evening **meals** at a set rate, usually around US\$15–20 in *residenciales* and US\$30–40 in hotels. Room rates are usually quoted in US dollars; Chilean pesos are usually but not always accepted. Always try **bargaining** the price down, but note that the Rapa Nui are astute negotiators and will generally try to charge you as much as they think you're prepared to pay. Finally, bear in mind that addresses are rarely used, so the best way to find a hotel or *residencial* listed below is by means of our map. For some establishments, it's usually better to give the owner's name when you're asking for directions (we've included this in each listing, where necessary).

Note that camping among or near the sites is illegal. Hanga Roa's only official **campsite**, run by Ana Rapu, is by the beach, close to her *residencial*. The fee (US$5 per person) includes hot water showers and the use of a kitchen. In addition, many *residencial* owners have allowed camping in their gardens for years, charging around US$10 per tent or per person, depending on their mood – *Tekena Inn* is a good bet.

Explora Casas Rapa Nui Reservations at Av Americo Vespucio Sur 80, Piso 5, Las Condes, Santiago de Chile ☏ 2/2066060, ⓦ www.explora .com. Comfortable guesthouses reflecting the *Explora* philosophy of "a good bed, a hot shower, a good meal, and a great bottle of wine". Each of the 9 rooms has the creature comforts you would expect from the luxury chain, including a Jacuzzi, a cosy dining area and bar, plus an outdoor barbecue area. ❽–❾

🏃 **Hotel Gomero** Calle Tu'u Koihu ☏ 32/100313, ⓦ www.hotelgomero.com. A lush garden-patio, with a pool, and a high standard of comfort and decor are found at this peaceful hotel, efficiently run by a *pascuense*-Austrian couple. Good food is served in a smart dining area with great views. ❼

Hotel Iorana off Av Atamu Tekena ☏ 32/100312, ⓕ 32/100444, ⓔ tokitour@entelchile.net. The rooms of this upmarket hotel aren't as smart as you'd expect for the price, but the secluded location, looking down to the ocean, is unbeatable. As well as a regular outdoor pool, there's a "natural" pool enclosed by rocks and filled with seawater. ❽

Hotel Manutara ☏ 32/100297, ⓕ 32/100768, ⓔ akuaku-stgo@entelchile.net. A short walk from the airport, this friendly, well-run place has spacious, comfortable rooms spread across extensive grounds, with a pool, filling breakfasts and lots of peace and quiet; visits of the main sites are on offer through Aku Aku Tours, one of the better agencies. ❼

Hotel O'Tai Av Te Pito Te Henua ☏ 32/100250, ⓕ 32/100560, ⓔ otairapanui@entelchile.net. Smart, well-furnished bungalow rooms with patio doors, set in a large, flower-filled garden. The centrally located hotel is owned by Rosita Cardinali. ❼

🏃 **Residencial Martín y Anita** Calle Simón Paoa ☏ & ⓕ 32/100593,

ⓔ hmanita@entelchile.net. Attractive house offering six pleasant, sun-filled rooms set in a lovely garden with a patio and garden chairs. ❻

Residencial Kona Tau Av Avareipua ☏ 32/100321, ⓕ 32/100105, ⓔ konatau@entelchile.net. Simple rooms in a friendly family home; close to the airport but inconvenient for the rest of town. ❸

Residencial Mirú Av Atamu Tekena ☏ 32/100365. Run by two cheerful sisters, Sandra and Janet, this *residencial* offers brightly coloured, fairly spacious rooms on Atamu Tekena. ❹

Residencial Tahai Sendero Tahai ☏ 32/100395, ⓕ 32/100105, ⓔ rapanui@entelchile.net. Owned by Maria Hey, this place offers spacious, slightly neglected, but very tranquil rooms about a 10min walk from the village. There's a large wooden veranda here, where you can sit and admire the garden, overflowing with flowers and banana trees. ❼

Residencial Tahiri Calle Ara Roa Rakei ☏ 32/100570, ⓕ 32/100105, ⓔ rpakomio@entelchile.net. Spotless bungalow rooms, with white walls and bright floral prints, looking onto a lush, green garden. The young owner, Tutti Pakomio, is very welcoming, too, making this a good choice. ❻

Residencial Tekena Inn Av Atamu Tekena ☏ 32/100289, ⓕ 32/100105. The rooms here, set well back from the main street, feel a little dated, but they're clean, with private bath, and better value than many others of a similar standard; Juan Nahoe Calderón is the owner. ❸

Residencial Villa Tiki Av Pont ☏ & ⓕ 32/100327, ⓔ tiki@entelchile.net. Georgina Paoa owns these spacious, neat rooms with sweeping views onto the hills. There's also a large, well-tended garden that's great to relax in. ❻

The Village

Hanga Roa been the island's main residential sector since the 1860s, when Catholic missionaries relocated the islanders here to facilitate their conversion. A relic of those early days is the small stone **church** in the northeast corner of town, where islanders still congregate every Sunday morning – join them, if you're around, for an unforgettable rhapsody of joyful Polynesian hymns. In addition to the church there are the other community staples, like the Gobernación (government building), the post office and the bank (**ATMs** for MasterCard only), all close to each other down towards the *caleta* (natural harbour). Also down here, overlooking the harbour, you'll find a couple of badly fractured **moai** erected on an ahu – quite exciting when you've just arrived, but nothing compared to what's ahead of you. The rest of town is made up principally of the very long main street, Atamu Tekena, lined with souvenir shops, small supermarkets, expensive **Internet** cafés and sundry eateries, plus the undisciplined, winding lanes that branch off it.

Eating, drinking and entertainment

Most people eat at their *residencial* or hotel, so demand for **places to eat** isn't that high. That said, what's on offer is pretty good, including a couple of excellent, though expensive, fish restaurants, and a number of cheaper outlets serving quick snacks like pizzas, *empanadas* and burgers. You should avoid the much-publicized restaurants around the *caleta*, however, as they are rip-off territory, combining high prices with rude service and overrated food. *El Jardín de Mau*, along Policarpo Toro, is an outstanding exception: beautifully situated, with great views across the ocean, it offers soothing decor, refined fish and seafood and professional service, though prices are above average. Two of the best places along commercial Atamu Tekena are: *Café Ra'a*, at the northern end, the only place on the island serving decent espressos, plus delicious cakes, pastries, sandwiches and snacks, making it ideal for breakfast, while the benefits some way to the south at *Aloha* are zingy pisco sours, ultra-fresh seafood and some more unusual fare at reasonable prices by Easter Island standards – payable by credit card.

The "**cinema**" at the *Hotel Manavai* on Avenida Te Pito Te Henua has screenings every Monday and Thursday at 9.30pm of the Hollywood view of *Rapa Nui*. There's a small but lively local **nightlife** scene, focused on a couple of **bars** and two **discos** – with established favourite *Piriki*, on Avenida Hotu Matu'a, near the airport, leading the way. Then there's *Toroko*, down near the *caleta*. These are good places to meet the islanders, as they're geared more towards young Rapa Nui than tourists, though the strong local feel can be slightly daunting when you first walk in – expect lots of turned heads. Less authentic, but more "exotic", entertainment is offered in the form of regular hula dances (beautiful women, grass skirts, swaying hips) held at various restaurants and hotels – keep your eye open for fliers.

These are tame, soulless offerings, however, compared to the genuine hulas you'll see for free at **Tapati Rapa Nui**, the annual two-week festival held in late January or early February. Famous for celebrating Rapa Nui culture, tradition and history, the festival, features dancing, body painting competitions, sculpture competitions, choral recitals, surfing displays, re-enactments of old legends and huge earth-oven feasts. If you plan to visit during the festival, make all reservations – for accommodation, car rental, tour guides, etc – several weeks in advance, as this is by far the busiest time of year on the island.

Listings

Airline LAN, midway along Atamu Tekena ☎32/100279.
Banks and exchange The best place to change travellers' cheques (US dollars only) is at the

Sunoco petrol station on Av Hotu Matu'a, which gives reasonable rates and charges no commission. The BancoEstado, down by the *caleta* (Mon–Fri 8am–noon), will change dollars but at rates about three percent worse than on mainland Chile; one ATM, accepting only MasterCard. Hotels may grant you a cash advance but at extortionate rates. Best bet is to bring both dollars and pesos from the mainland.

Camping As you can't bring fuel on the plane, you'll need to buy it on the island. White gas (bencina blanca) is hard to come by, but is usually stocked at Kai Nene supermarket on Atamu Tekena. Make sure your tent is ant-proof.

Car and motorbike rental In addition to the car-hire firms, many souvenir shops and even supermarkets on Atamu Tekena hire jeeps as a sideline, usually with just a couple of vehicles available. Outlets include Easter Island Rent a Car ☎32/100326; Hertz ☎32/100654; Comercial Insular ☎32/100480; Kia Koe ☎32/100282; Tekena Inn ☎32/100289; and Haunani Rent a

Car ☎32/100353, ⓔhaunani@rapanui.cl. Average daily rates range from US$40 to US$50. Beware: At night many people drive with the lights out.

Hospital The only clinic is just east of the church.

Laundry Best to ask at your residencial or hotel.

Mountain bikes Several shops on Atamu Tekena, including Kodak and Via Mona; compare state of bikes and prices.

Post Office Opposite *Hotel O'Tai*, the cost of postage is the same as from mainland Chile.

Scuba rental Mike Rapu at Caleta Hanga Roa (☎32/973857, ⓔmikerapudiving@entelchile.net) has equipment and offers local tours.

Telephone centre Near the bank; faxing facilities, cheap calls to mainland Chile, very expensive to rest of world.

Getting around Easter Island

The layout of the island's roads encourages you to visit the sites on several different trips: one taking in the south coast, Rano Raraku and Anakena on a long circular route; another going inland to Ahu Akivi, either returning along the west coast, via Tahai, or else covering the coastal path on foot in a separate trip; and finally climbing up to Rano Kau and Orongo.

It's worth putting some thought into how you want to **get around** the island, as the type of transport you choose can make a big difference to your experience of the place. The easiest, most hassle-free choice is to take an **organized tour**, but while this ensures you get to see a large number of sites, with guided commentary (and without getting lost), you can feel you're on a sightseeing conveyer belt – and it seems a shame to visit the most remote inhabited island in the world with a crowd of other tourists. Tours usually cost around US$50 for a full day, and US$30 for a half-day. Three recommended **tour companies** on the island are: Aku Aku Tours at Hotu Matu'a (☎32/100770, ⓔakuaku-stgo@entelchile.net), and Hanga Roa Travel at Avenida Tu'u Koihu (☎32/551158, ⓔhfritsch@entelchile.net), which provide a variety of extensive tours; and Mahinatur, at Hotu Matu'a with Atamu Tekena (☎ & ⓕ32/100220, ⓦwww.mahinatur.cl), one of the island's oldest tour operators with information on everything from scuba diving to bus rental. Both have comfortable vehicles and guides fluent in Spanish, English, French, Italian and German. In addition to these, numerous hotels, *residenciales* and local people offer jeep or minibus tours.

If you want more solitude and independence, you can hire a **jeep** or a **motorbike** (see "Listings", above), which can be quite an adventure as the roads can be bumpy. This is a very popular option, so you should book your vehicle as soon as you can after arrival (or even before), before the rest of your plane beats you to it. Another alternative is to visit the island on **horseback**. You'll find a lot of places offering horses, from *residenciales* to souvenir shops, but they're often wild, badly cared-for and rather mangy. For sleek, healthy beasts, contact Roberto (☎32/100474), French-born Patrice (☎32/100518), or Julio (☎32/100540) – or ask Sernatur for a recommendation. Finally, you could consider visiting some sites on a **mountain bike** (see "Listings", above) or **on foot**, though walking round the whole island would be quite a challenge. Walking from Hanga Roa, easy targets include Ahu Tahai (30min), Rano Kau (1hr) and Vinapu (1hr 30min).

The southeastern circuit

The loop formed by the sixteen-kilometre southern coast road and the thirty-kilometre paved road from Anakena to Hanga Roa lends itself to a convenient sightseeing route that takes in some of the island's most impressive sights – including **Vinapu**, **Ahu Tongariki**, **Rano Raraku** and **Anakena**. The road bypasses the **Poike Peninsula**, though it's possible (if not terribly rewarding) to explore this area on foot. Most visitors do this circuit with a rental vehicle or on a tour, and it's too far to do on horseback in a single day.

Vinapu

From Hanga Roa, follow Avenida Hotu Matu'a down to the southern coast road then turn right, just after the white oil containers, and you'll reach **VINAPU**, the site of two large ahus. Anyone who's seen Macchu Pichu or other Inca ruins will be amazed by the similarity of the masonry of Vinapu's main ahu, made of huge, mortarless blocks of stone vividly described by Thor Heyerdahl as "cut like cheese and fitted carefully to one another without a crack or a hole". It's easy to imagine the thrill Heyerdahl must have felt on seeing this stonework, given his conviction that Easter Island had been settled from South America, and it's not surprising he begged the question: "Could it be the master masons from Peru who had been busy out here too?" Close to this platform, known as Vinapu I, is another ahu, Vinapu II, whose stonework is vastly inferior to its neighbour, consisting of roughly hewn stones and boulders fitted loosely together.

The sequence of construction of the two ahus has been vigorously debated. The Norwegian expedition was the first to excavate the site and, with radiocarbon dating, concluded that the precisely carved Vinapu I (the famous stone that caused so much ink to flow) was among the earliest built on the island, and that Vinapu II was a much later construction. This supported Heyerdahl's theory that the island's first settlers imported the highly specialized stone-carving techniques of Peru, and that later platforms, after a period of degeneration, were built by "far less capable architects, who were no longer masters of the complicated Inca technique". Modern archeologists, however, believe that this impressive masonry is simply a perfected example of a style developed locally on Easter Island, and more recent radiocarbon tests have given Vinapu I a new date of 1516 AD, and Vinapu II a date of 857 AD – the reverse of Heyerdahl's sequence. Both ahus once supported moai, now lying in fragments behind the platforms, and another moai stands half-buried in the ground in front of Vinapu I, perhaps intended to be raised to the platform, which bears a pedestal that was never filled.

Along the southern coast

Back on the coast road, heading northeast towards Poike, you'll pass site after site of toppled moai, all knocked from their ahu and lying prostrate on the ground. Many lie flat on their faces in a position of humiliation, evoking, quite intensely, a sense of the violence, destruction and tragedy that marked the final phase of the island's pre-history, when warring clans desecrated and destroyed the sacred sites of their enemies. Above all, there's an acute impression of futility, and of wasted human effort.

The first site you pass is **Vaihu**, where eight tall statues lie face-down on the ground, their red stone topknots strewn along the coast. Three kilometres further along, **Ahu Akahanga** presents an equally mournful picture of a row of fallen moai; according to some oral traditions, it's also the burial place of Hotu Matu'a, the island's first settler and king. Further up the coast, **Ahu Hanga Tetenga** is the site of the largest moai – 9.94m – ever transported to a platform. It's not clear if the statue was successfully erected, as its eye sockets were never carved (usually the finishing touch). In any event, it now lies shattered at the foot of its ahu, leaving no clues as to whether it fell during erection or was toppled at a later date.

Just beyond Ahu Hanga Tetenga, the road forks. The left-hand branch, known as the **Camino de los Moai**, leads to the quarry of Rano Raraku (see below). It's thought to have been the main roadway along which the statues were transported from the quarry, and is still littered with abandoned statues, fallen by the wayside en route to their platforms. The right-hand branch continues up the coast to the magnificent Ahu Tongariki. Note that Rano Raraku can also be approached from Ahu Tongariki.

Ahu Tongariki

The fifteen colossal moai lined up on **AHU TONGARIKI** make a sensational sight. This was the largest number of moai ever erected on a single ahu, and the platform, some 200m long, was the largest built on the island. It was totally destroyed in 1960 when a massive tsunami, caused by an earthquake in Chile, swept across this corner of the island, dragging the platform blocks and the statues 90m inland – a remarkable distance, given that the statues weigh up to thirty tonnes each.

In November 1988, Sergio Rapu, former Governor of Easter Island, was being interviewed for a **Japanese television programme**, and said that if they had a crane they could save the moai; a Japanese man watching the show decided to act and a committee was set up in Japan. The whole site was restored by Chilean archeologists Claudio Cristino and Patricia Vargas of the **Easter Island Studies Institute**, **University of Chile**, in a five-year project; the project team included a group of forty islanders, specialists from the Nara Institute of Japan and recognized international experts in stone conservation. The restoration was completed in 1995 and today the statues stand tall and proud on their ahu, the very picture of dignity. One of them is wearing a red topknot, and several have holes in their earlobes, which perhaps had obsidian or coral disks inserted in them. The most curious feature, though, is the faint outline of **goatee beards** carved on some of these moai – among the very few on the island with such facial decoration.

Rano Raraku

North of Tongariki, **RANO RARAKU** rises from the land in a hulking mass of volcanic stone. This crag is where almost all of the island's statues were produced, carved directly from the "tuff" (compacted volcanic ash) of the crater's outer slopes. The first surprise, on approaching the crater from the car park, are the dozens of **giant heads** sprouting from the ground. Tall, thin and angular, with long noses and hollow cheeks, these are the island's most widely photographed statues and have become the classic image of Easter Island presented to the outside world. It was originally thought that these heads were bodiless, but when archeologists began digging earlier this century they discovered whole torsos and arms buried beneath the ground. They are, in fact, finished moai brought down from the quarry, and were probably placed in shallow pits (that gradually built up) until they could be transported to their ahu. Clearly these were the last of the moai to be completed, and one of them bears

The enduring symbol of Easter Island always has been, and doubtless always will be, the monolithic **statues** or moai that line its shores. That's not to say there's nothing else to command our attention on the island. On the contrary, its elaborate rock carvings, ceremonial platforms, intriguing architecture and spectacular volcanic geography are all compelling attractions in their own right. And yet, inevitably, they're overshadowed to the point of oblivion by the overwhelming presence of the moai, whose haughty features stare at us from every corner of the island. These moai astonish for a good many reasons, not least because they are utterly unique. A Neolithic statue cult on this scale would impress in any location, but the fact that it developed in total isolation on a tiny island in the middle of the Pacific almost defies belief. How did this Stone Age people, with no cross-cultural contact or outside influence, create such a specialized and advanced carving industry? And why did they take it to such extremes? There are some 400 finished statues scattered around the island, and almost as many in the statue quarry, in varying stages of completion. Clearly the people of Easter Island were in the grip of an extraordinary obsession – that led them, it would seem, to accomplish towering artistic achievements, but also, ultimately, to wreak devastation on their own society.

The Easter Island moai range in height from 2m to about 20m, and while no two statues are identical, all are carved in the same highly stylized manner. Each figure – probably male – is represented down to the level of the hips. Their bellies are gently rounded, their nipples clearly marked, and their arms are held tightly by their sides, with their strange, long-fingered hands placed across their abdomens. Their heads are long and rectangular, with pointed chins; prominent, angular noses; and thin, tight lips curled into an expression of disdain. According to the assertions of the islanders, which are consistent with widespread Polynesian tradition, these figures represented important **ancestors**, such as chiefs and priests, and were erected on the ancestral land of the kin-group these individuals belonged to, which they would watch over and protect with their *mana* (almost all the moai are looking inland, rather than gazing out to sea). It's possible, also, that some statues were commissioned during the lifetime of the people they commemorate, who presumably wanted their memorials to be as impressive as possible, perhaps leading to intense competition over their size and splendour. Almost all the statues were carved out of the quarry at **Rano Raraku**, one of the island's volcanic craters. It's impossible to establish exactly when the first were carved, as radiocarbon dating works only on organic material, but archeologists have proposed tentative dates of around 1000 AD for the early statues, and around the fifteenth century for the bulk of the statues, when production was at its peak. What we do know, however, is *how* they were carved, as the hundreds of abandoned tools and unfinished statues in Rano Raraku demonstrate quite clearly how their forms were chiselled out of the rock face until they were attached to it by only a thin keel running down their spine. When all was completed but their eye sockets, they were freed from their keel and slid down the slope of the quarry, then temporarily erected in a pit until they were transported to their ahus.

Transporting the moai

Just how they were **moved** across the island remains a mystery. Not only were the statues extremely heavy (weighing, on average, some 20-25 tonnes), but many were embellished with delicate carvings in bas relief representing tattoos or loin cloths. These were carved before transportation, and must have required very careful handling not to be damaged. The island's oral histories offer no clues as to how the moai were moved, claiming that the statues' *mana* enabled them to walk a short distance each day until they reached their platforms. More plausible modern theories have included horizontal swivelling and vertical swivelling, but since it was established in the 1980s that the island was once densely covered by two species of

EASTER ISLAND | The southeastern circuit

⑪

tree – the shrublike *toromiro* and a large palm closely related to *Jubae chilensis* – it's been assumed that they were dragged either on wooden sledges, or on top of rollers, probably heavily padded by palm fronds.

Raising the moai

How the statues were **erected** onto their platforms in the absence of any type of machinery is another enigma, though much light was thrown onto this in a now-famous experiment conducted by Thor Heyerdahl in 1955. Heyerdahl challenged the island's mayor to raise a fallen, 25-tonne statue at Anakena Beach and, under the mayor's supervision, twelve islanders raised the statue in eighteen days, using two levers and slipping layer after layer of stones underneath the horizontal statue. Little by little, it was raised on the bed of stones until it was level with its platform; at this point, the layers of pebbles were placed only under its head, until the statue was nearly vertical and could be slipped into place. Archeologists agree that this method is highly likely to have been used to raise the statues. In contrast, no one has been able to demonstrate how the large, heavy "topknots" were placed on the raised statues' heads – a monumental feat, achieved only with the use of a crane in modern times.

The statue-carvers

Quite clearly, the mass production, the transportation and the erection of these monoliths must have involved an enormous amount of work. Oral tradition and archeological records suggest that there was no central controlling power on Easter Island, and that its society was based around independent clans, or **kin-groups**, each with its own high-ranking members. Presumably, then, the statue-carvers were not forced to work by a central authority, but worked voluntarily for their kin-group – indeed, it seems they were highly revered members of a privileged class who were exempt from food production and were supported by farmers and fishermen on the island. Such a system must have involved a great deal of economic co-operation, which appears to have been successfully maintained for hundreds of years. Then, in the later stages of the island's pre-history, something went wrong and the system collapsed. Groups that had worked peacefully, if competitively, alongside each other at Rano Raraku withdrew from the quarry and exchanged their tools for weapons, as the island became engulfed by internal strife and warfare. The island's archeologi-cal record reveals a sudden, dramatic proliferation of obsidian **weapons** during the eighteenth century, as well as the remains of violently beaten skulls, and evidence of the widespread use of caves as refuges. In several locations archeologists have found possible evidence of cannibalism – something that features prominently in the island's oral traditions. The most dramatic testimony of this period of conflict, however, is provided by the hundreds of fallen statues littering the island, deliberately and systematically toppled from their platforms as enemy groups set out to dese-crate each other's sacred sites. The Spanish expedition, under González, reported no toppled statues in 1770 after a fairly thorough exploration of the island, but just four years later, Captain Cook saw many **overturned figures** lying next to their platforms. Almost a century later, in 1868, a visiting English doctor found that not a single statue remained standing on the island.

So what went wrong on Easter Island?

What caused this highly organized and productive civilization to self-destruct? Why was a culture of interdependence and collaboration exchanged for one of violence and conflict? It seems likely that the seeds of social collapse lay, paradoxically, in the statue cult – or rather the extremes it was taken to by the islanders. In the words of William Mulloy, a member of the Norwegian expedition: "[statue carving] came to take up so much of the force of the culture that such important activities as farming and fishing were neglected, and the people didn't have enough to eat. You can carry statue-making only so far". It seems that as the impulse to produce moai required more and more hands, the delicate balance between food distribution and statue-carving was destroyed. This situation was profoundly aggravated by the growing scarcity of food brought about possibly by overpopulation, and certainly by deforestation, following centuries of logging for boat-building, fuel consumption and statue-transportation. By the time the Europeans arrived in the eighteenth century, there was scarcely a tree left on the island, and the large palm, shown by pollen samples to have been once abundant, had become extinct. This must have had a catastrophic effect on the islanders' ability to feed themselves: deep-sea fishing became increasingly difficult, and eventually impossible, owing to the lack of wood available for new canoes, and even land cultivation was affected, as the deforestation caused soil erosion. In this climate of encroaching deprivation, it begins to be clear why the system broke down, why the farmers and fishermen were no longer willing or able to pool their spoils – and why the Easter Island civilization descended into anarchy, dragging its majestic monuments with it.

an image on its chest of a three-masted sailing ship, suggesting that they were carved after European contact.

As you move higher up Ranu Raraku's slopes, you gradually become aware that you are surrounded by hundreds of **unfinished statues** carved out of the rock. As you look carefully you will see that what looked like a mere ledge is an arm, and an overhanging rock is a nose. Make sure you stick to the worn paths and do not clamber on the rocks/statues; your guide can be severely punished for allowing anyone to do so.

Among this mass of shapes, still attached to the rock face, is **El Gigante**, the biggest moai ever carved, stretching over 20m from top to bottom. Experts

△ Rano Raraku Volcano

believe it would have been impossible to transport, let alone erect, this monster, and it's been suggested that it was never intended to be moved. A faint path leads up to the top of the crater rim where you'll find, on the other side, more buried moai, staggered down the green slopes of the interior. At the bottom, a large, murky lake is covered with floating reeds, adding to the strangeness of the scene. It is the scene of a "triathlon", one of the most impressive contests in the Tapati, the island carnival (see p.566).

The Poike Peninsula

East of Rano Raraku, the **POIKE PENINSULA** is a green, gently rounded plateau bound in by steep cliffs. Few people venture onto this part of the island, which is fenced off and used for cattle grazing. You can hop across the fence quite easily, and walk round the edge of the peninsula in about four hours, but there's no shade, no path and little to see but cows and ocean. Poike's main interest lies in the myths and legends associated with it. One tells of the **cave of the virgins**, *Ana o Keke*, where a number of young girls were confined for months on end so that their skin would remain as pale as possible. Another one, more famous, is of the battle of the **"Long Ears" and "Short Ears"** (see box below). This battle is supposed to have taken place in the 3.5-kilometre-long ditch separating the peninsula from the rest of the island, known as *Ko te Ava o Iko*, or "Iko's ditch".

The myth of the "Long Ears" and the "Short Ears"

An oft-repeated oral tradition has it that the island's population, in the time just before the toppling of the statues, was divided into two principal groups, **the "Short Ears" and the "Long Ears"**, so called because the latter pierced their ears and used wooden disks to extend their lobes right down to their shoulders – a practice still current at the time of the first European visitors. In fact all the islanders did this and the whole myth is based on a mistranslation. The word *epe* means "ear" in the Rapa Nui tongue, and it seems that the two clans were really the *Hanau eepe* ("short and stocky people") and the *Hanau momoko* ("tall and slim people"); the strange mix-up came from mistranslating *eepe* – short and stocky – as "ear".

Anyway, the story goes that the "Long Ears", who saw themselves as more aristocratic, were extremely domineering, and that the "Short Ears" resented them intensely. Things came to a head, as it were, when the "Long Ears" tried to force the "Short Ears" to clear the island of the many loose stones that covered its surface and throw them into the sea, to make more land available for agriculture. This was the final straw for the "Short Ears", who rebelled, forcing the "Long Ears" to retreat to the **Poike Peninsula** at the eastern end of the island. Here the "Long Ears" dug a series of deep ditches separating the peninsula from the rest of the island, and filled them with branches and grass, intending to force their enemies inside and set them alight. Their plans were thwarted, however, when a "Short Ears" woman who was married to one of the "Long Ears" alerted her people to this scheme, and, with a secret signal, allowed them to pass into the peninsula and surround their enemies while they were sleeping. When the "Short Ears" attacked, the "Long Ears" had nowhere to run but straight into their own ditch, which the "Short Ears" gleefully set fire to. The "Long Ears" roasted to death in the pits, but three of them escaped, and fled into hiding. Two of them were caught and executed, but one, a certain **Ororoina**, was allowed to live, and went on to father many children – whose descendants, to this day, are proud of their *Hanau momoko* heritage.

11 EASTER ISLAND | The southeastern circuit

573

Early investigators thought the ditch was a natural geographic feature and that the islanders had simply invented a myth to explain its presence, but the Norwegian expedition was able to prove that the trench was either an artificial extension of a natural feature, or else entirely man-made. Moreover, they discovered traces of intense burning which radiocarbon dating placed at 1676 AD, corresponding to estimates, based on oral traditions, of when this battle took place. Modern archeologists, however, are far from convinced, mainly because no weapons or mass human remains have been found in the ditch. They speculate that the evidence of burning could easily be associated with cooking (the islanders commonly cooked in holes in the ground), or even with slash-and-burn agriculture.

North to Anakena

From the southern coast, the road turns inland, cutting past the Poike Peninsula, and leads directly to Ovahe and Anakena. On the way, look out for **Ahu te Pito Kura**, down by Bahía La Perouse (signposted). This is the site of **Paro**, probably the largest moai successfully erected on a platform, at 9.8m tall (it's just a fraction smaller than the moai transported to Ahu Hanga Tetenga on the southern coast, which seems not to have been successfully erected). Paro is thought to have been one of the last moai to be moved and erected, and is estimated to weigh a staggering ninety tonnes. No one has attempted to restore and re-erect the giant, which still lies face down before its ahu, surrounded by rubble.

Further north, **Ovahe** is a tiny, secluded and exquisitely beautiful beach, its white sands lapped by crystal-clear waters at the foot of a large volcanic cliff. There's just about room to pitch a tent on the grassy patch next to the cliff – locals swear the tide never comes in this far, though it certainly gets unnervingly close. A little further up the coast, **Playa Anakena** is much larger, and presents a picture-postcard scene of powdery golden sands fringed by swaying palm trees, great for an afternoon of swimming or sunbathing. You can camp by the **Conaf** office across from the beach, which offers shade and limited water.

ANAKENA has a special place in Rapa Nui oral history, which holds it to be the landing site and dwelling place of Hotu Matu'a, the island's first colonizer (see p.560). It's also home to the splendid moai of **Ahu Nau Nau**, which were so deeply covered in sand until their restoration, led by local archeologist Sergio Rapu Haoa in 1978, that they were largely protected from the effects of weathering. Their haughty facial features are particularly fine, and some of them have delicate spiral designs carved in bas relief on their buttocks, perhaps representing tattoos. What makes these moai really striking, though, are the large, gleaming white eyes inserted into their eye sockets, fixed in a slightly upturned gaze towards the sky. Archeologists had always assumed that the statues' eye sockets had remained empty, but when fragments of white coral and a circular red pebble were discovered here in 1978, it was found that they fitted together to form an oval eye with a red iris. It's not known if all the statues on the island had such eyes, as the only other fragments found have been at Vinapu. The reproduction eyes of the Nau Nau moai completely transform their faces, seemingly bringing them to life.

Just up the hillside by the beach you'll find the squat and rather corpulent moai of **Ahu Ature Huki**. This was the first moai to be re-erected on the island in the experiment carried out by Thor Heyerdahl in 1955, when twelve strong islanders showed they could raise a 25-tonne statue in eighteen days (see box on p.570).

△ Moai statues

The northern circuit

Although the triangle formed by Vinapu, Tongariki and Anakena contains the densest concentration of sites, the western and northern parts of the island are also well worth exploring. Attractions include the impressive moai of **Tapai** and **Ahu Akivi**, plus a network of underground **caves**.

There are two roads serving this area: one runs inland to Aku Akivi, then continues to Ahu Te Peu on the coast; another follows the shoreline from Hanga Roa north to Ahu Te Peu, where it joins the inland road. You can cover both roads in a circular route, either on foot (about 6hr), on horseback, or in a vehicle; if you're driving, note that the coastal track is difficult to make out and extremely rough, and should only be attempted in a high-clearance 4WD. An alternative is to do two separate day-trips, perhaps driving up the inland road, and walking along the coast. The very northern corner of the island is scarcely visited by anyone, as there's no access for vehicles beyond Te Peu. You can, however, continue up the coast on foot, following it all the way round to Anakena – a long, hot hike (8hr from Hanga Roa) but immeasurably peaceful, and offering good views.

Tahai and around

To get to Tahai, a favourite spot for viewing colourful sunsets, walk north from the *caleta* past the cemetery, taking the path that hugs the coast. After about ten minutes you reach the ceremonial centre of **TAHAI**, composed of three ahus. The first, **Ahu Vai Uri**, supports four broad, squat moai, two of which have badly damaged heads, and the stump of a fifth statue. In front of the ahu is the outline of a flattened esplanade, presumed to have been used as a ceremonial site. Archeological remains suggest that some individuals – possibly chiefs and priests – used to live near these ceremonial sites, in several locations on the island, in stone, oval houses called *hare paenga* that looked like an upturned canoe. You can see the foundations of one of these houses near Ahu Vai Uri. The second platform is **Ahu Tahai** itself, topped by a lone, weathered moai. Finally, **Ahu Kote Riku** is the site of a well-preserved moai fitted with white, glinting eyes (added recently) and a red topknot. The ashes of the American William Mulloy (1917-1987), responsible for many of the archeological restorations on the island, are encased in a small monument overlooking Tahai, to the south of the complex.

About half a kilometre further north, set well back from the coastal path, the **Museo Antropológico "Sebastian Englert"** (Tues–Fri 9.30am–12.30pm & 2–5.30pm, Sat & Sun 9.30am–12.30pm; CH\$1000; ☏32/100296 ⓦwww .museorapanui.cl) is housed in a modern, rotunda-shaped building. Its contents focus on the daily life of the Rapa Nui and include a very evocative collection of black-and-white photographs of islanders from about 1915 onwards. In addition, there are several displays on language, crops and bones pointing to the Polynesian origin of the Rapa Nui people, as well as some examples of carvings and spearheads, and fragments of original moai eyes. It's not unmissable, but is worth a look-in if you're walking up the coast.

Dos Ventanas Caves and Ahu Te Peu

Back on the coast road, continue north for about 3km – until you reach the point where you're standing opposite two little islands out at sea – and look out for the stone cairn by the left-hand side of the road signalling a track down towards the cliffs. At the end of the track, a tiny opening in the ground is the entrance to a pitch-black passage (take a head or pocket torch), which continues 50m underground to the adjoining **DOS VENTANAS CAVES**. Both caves are flooded with light streaming in from the "windows", or gaping holes, that open out of the cliff wall. Prepare for a rush of adrenaline as you approach the edges, as both drop vertically down to a bed of sharp rocks and pounding waves many metres below. It's very easy to miss the path down to the cave, never mind find the opening, and your best hope is that a tour van is parked outside.

About 1km further up the coast you reach **AHU TE PEU**, a large platform made of big, well-fitted rocks. The moai that once stood on the ahu still lie flat on the ground, left as they were during the period of warfare. Scattered around the ahu are the remains of many boat-shaped *hare paenga*, including one that's sixty metres long. It's thought that this was the site of the village of the Miru clan, the direct descendants of Hotu Matu'a.

At Ahu Te Peu, most people join up with the inland road and head back to Hanga Roa via Ahu Akivi. You can, however, continue north, either heading up the gentle volcanic cone of **Terevaka**, where you'll be rewarded with fine views across the island from its 510-metre summit, the highest point of the island (no path; 1hr up), or else follow the coastline round to Playa Anakena (4–5hr). On the way, you'll pass many fallen moai, none of them restored, as well as the ruins of stone houses and chicken pens.

Inland to Puna Pau, Ahu Akivi and the Te Pahu Caves

From Hanga Roa, heading up the inland road to Ahu Akivi (first left from the paved road to Anakena) you'll pass a signed track branching left to **PUNA PAU**, a low volcanic crater made of rusty-coloured rock, known as "scoria".

It was out of this rock that the islanders carved the **pukao** – the cylindrical "topknots" worn by up to seventy of the moai standing on ahu. No one knows for sure what these cylinders represented, and suggestions have ranged from grass hats and turbans through to topknots (of hair) and feather headdresses. Up in the quarry, and along the track to the top, you can see thirty or so finished *pukao* lying on the ground.

Back on the road, continue north and you'll reach **AHU AKIVI**, whose seven moai are the only ones to have been erected inland, and the only ones that look towards the sea. In fact, it's been discovered that they are oriented directly towards the rising summer solstice, along with several other ahu, suggesting that solar positions were of significance to the islanders. These curious facts aside, Ahu Akivi is a great collection of statues, in excellent condition. They were raised in 1960 by William Mulloy and Gonzalo Figueroa, two of the archeologists recruited by Heyerdahl in 1955, both of whom went on to devote their entire careers to Easter Island.

From Ahu Akivi, the road turns towards the coast, where it meets Ahu Te Peu (see opposite). On the way, look out for the second path branching left from the main road, and follow it towards the thick, green leaves apparently sprouting from the ground. On closer inspection you'll find that they belong to tall bamboo trees growing in a magical underground garden at the bottom of a deep cave, along with sweet potatoes, taro, avocados, lemons and sugarcane. Clamber down and you'll find that the cave leads properly underground into a tunnel that you can follow without any fear of getting lost. About 150m further on, you'll emerge into another huge cave (once used as a dwelling place), where blinding shafts of sunlight announce the exit above ground. These are the **TE PAHU CAVES**, and the corridor connecting them is a lava tube created by volcanic activity millions of years ago, along with many other underground channels that riddle this part of the island.

Rano Kau and Orongo

The ceremonial village of **ORONGO** enjoys the most spectacular location on the island, perched high on the rim of the giant volcanic crater of **RANU KAU**. On one side, a steep slope descends to the bottom of the crater, which holds a vast lake covered in a bright-green mat of floating reeds. On the other side, a near-vertical drop plunges 300m down to the dark-blue ocean. Orongo is easily reached from Hanga Roa, either by car or taxi in ten minutes, or on foot in about an hour (follow the footpath branching right from the main road, just after the Conaf sign, continuing up the hill through the eucalyptus trees). Either way, you'll end up at the Conaf hut at the top, where you're supposed to pay your park fee (unfixed hours; CH$5000) but often don't have to, as it's frequently unstaffed. The village, a short distance beyond, consists of the partially restored remains of some 48 low-lying, oval-shaped huts made of thin stone slabs, each with a tiny entrance just large enough to crawl through (don't try). A few steps from the houses, on the face of some basalt outcrops looking out to sea, you'll find a dense group of exquisitely carved **petroglyphs** depicting curled-up human figures with birds' heads and long curved beaks. These bas-relief images honour an important annual ceremony dedicated to the **cult of the birdman**. Unlike much of the island's heritage, a great deal is known about this ceremony, as it was practised right up to 1878 (though no one knows when it began).

The birdman ceremony

The ritual of the birdman took place at the September **equinox**, when the chiefs of the various kin-groups on the island assembled at Orongo – the only time of year the village was occupied – to take part in a ritual competition. The object of this competition was to find the first egg laid by the sooty tern (a migratory bird) on Motu Nui, the largest of three islets sitting opposite Orongo (the name means "listen", referring to the listening out for the call of the man who found the egg), 2km out to sea. Each chief could either seek the egg himself or choose a servant to act as his representative. Most chiefs chose the latter option, which is no surprise, given the dangers the egg-hunter had to face – first scaling down the sheer cliff to the ocean, then swimming through shark-infested waters out to the islet. It could take several weeks for the egg to be found; meanwhile, the chiefs would remain in Orongo, where they participated in ritual dances, songs and prayers.

Once the sacred egg was finally found, its discoverer would bellow the name of his master across the sea, and then swim back to the island with the egg tucked into a headband. The victorious chief now became the new *tangata manu*, or **birdman**. The new birdman would first have all the hair shaved off his head, including eyebrows and eyelashes; he would then be taken off, with his egg, to a sacred house at the foot of Rano Raraku, where he would live in strict seclusion for a whole year. He was allowed to eat only certain foods prepared by a special servant, and was forbidden to bathe or cut his nails. His kin-group, meanwhile, was endowed with a special, high status, which was often taken as an excuse for members to dominate and bully their rival groups. At the end of the year, the sacred powers of the egg vanished, and the ritual would begin all over again.

The Juan Fernández Archipelago

The **JUAN FERNÁNDEZ ARCHIPELAGO** is formed by the peaks of a submerged volcanic mountain range rising from the sea bed. It's made up of two principal islands; a third, much smaller, island; and numerous rocky islets. The archipelago is named for **João Fernandes**, the Portuguese sailor who discovered it on November 22, 1574, while straying out to sea to avoid coastal winds and currents in an attempt to shorten the journey between Lima and Valparaíso. This day is observed with celebrations on the archipelago every year. The more easterly of the two main islands was called, quite simply, **Más a Tierra** ("Nearer Land"), while the other, 187km further west, was known as **Más Afuera** ("Farther Out"). Fernandes made a brief attempt to colonize the three uninhabited islands, introducing vegetables and goats, which multiplied in great numbers (the third, smallest, island was later known as Goat Island, officially as Isla Santa Clara). These were still flourishing when British buccaneers started making occasional calls here to stock up on water and fresh meat between their raids on the mainland.

Following Alexander Selkirk's much-publicized rescue (see box, opposite), more and more buccaneers began calling here, prompting the Spanish Crown to take official possession of the archipelago in 1742, building a series of forts around Más a Tierra. The island was then used as a **penal colony** for many years, and it wasn't until the mid-nineteenth century that a mixture of Chilean and European colonizers formed a permanent settlement here. In 1966, with an eye on the islands' potential as a tourist destination, the Chilean government changed Más a Tierra's name to **Isla Robinson Crusoe**, while Más Afuera became **Isla Alejandro Selkirk**, seasonal home to lobster fishermen. Today, only a few hundred tourists make it out here each year, most of them arriving between October and March, when the climate is warm and dry, and the seawater is perfect for bathing.

Isla Robinson Crusoe

Twenty-two kilometres long, and 7km at its widest point, **ISLA ROBINSON CRUSOE** is the archipelago's only permanently inhabited island. Most of the five hundred or so islanders – some of them descendants of the Swiss Baron de Rodt and his compatriots who settled the island at the end of the nineteenth century and exploited the native sandalwood forest to extinction – live in the little village of **San Juan Bautista**, on the sheltered Bahía Cumberland. The main economic activity is trapping **lobsters**, and one of the highlights of a stay here is accompanying a fisherman, for a small cost, out to haul in his catch – most trips include a fresh-as-it-comes lobster supper, prepared over a small stove on the boat. Lobsters aside, the island's two principal attractions are the sites associated with the famous castaway **Alexander Selkirk** – from the replica of his cave dwelling to his real-life lookout point – and the abundant **plant life** that covers the soaring peaks in a dense layer of vegetation. Of the 146 plant species that grow here, 101 are endemic or unique to the island (the second highest proportion in the world after Hawaii), which is both a national park and a UNESCO World Biosphere Reserve. Most prolific, and most stunning, is the luxuriant rainforest that covers the island's higher slopes, where the giant ferns and thick undergrowth are almost impenetrable.

Alexander Selkirk

Daniel Defoe's story of Robinson Crusoe, the world's most famous literary castaway, was inspired by the misadventures of the real-life Scottish mariner **Alexander Selkirk**, who was marooned on Isla Robinson Crusoe (then Más a Tierra) in 1704 while crossing the Pacific on a privateering expedition. Unlike Crusoe, who was shipwrecked, Selkirk actually asked to be put ashore following a series of quarrels with his captain. The irascible sailor regretted his decision as soon he was deposited on the beach with a few scanty supplies, but his cries from the shore begging to be taken back onboard were ignored. Selkirk spent four years and four months on the island, with only his Bible and dozens of wild goats for company. During that time he was transformed into an extraordinary athlete, as he hunted the goats on foot, and a devout Christian, addicted to his Bible. Following his rescue by a British ship in 1709, however, Selkirk lost no time in reverting to his buccaneering ways, joining in attacks on Spanish vessels all the way home. Back in Fife, the former castaway became something of a celebrity and threw himself into a life of drink and women. Fourteen years after his rescue, Selkirk finally met his end when he took up the seafaring life once more, set off on another privateering expedition, and died of fever in the tropics.

The legendary goats that ran wild here in Selkirk's day have had their numbers sharply reduced by Conaf, in an attempt to protect the rare endemic plant species they were devouring. **Mosquitoes**, however, abound, so be sure to bring plenty of repellent. Another thing to bear in mind is that food is very expensive, so it might be worth bringing a supply over from the mainland. The local specialities of lobster and fish are cheaper than on the continent but fresh fruit and vegetables are all but non-existent and regarded as a luxury. If you plan to camp, note that petrol is very difficult to come by (there are only a couple of cars on the island), and you'd be much better off with a butane gas stove.

Getting to Isla Robinson Crusoe

Getting to Isla Robinson Crusoe is an adventure in itself, involving a flight on a small plane – six to eighteen seats – that judders and wobbles for most of the two and a half hours it takes to get there. Two companies fly out to the island, both imposing a strict 10-kilo luggage allowance. Transportes Aéreos Isla Robinson Crusoe (or TAIRC), Avenida Pajaritos 3030, Oficina 604 Maipú, Santiago (℡2/5344650, ℻5313772, ✉tairc@cmet.net, ⌨www.tairc.cl), flies daily from December through February, and three or four times a week in October and November and from early March until Easter, departing from **Aerodromo Los Cerrillos**, 8km southwest of Santiago (℡2/5331424); the rest of the year island residents are given priority on a skeleton service. Línea de Aeroservicios SA (usually shortened to LASSA), based at **Aerodromo Tobalaba**, Avenida Larraín 7941, La Reina, Santiago (℡2/2731458, ℻2734309, ✉lassa@entelchile.net, ⌨www.robinsoncrusoetours.cl), runs a similar service to TAIRC, mostly departing from Tobalaba aerodrome. Both airlines charge about CH$300,000 return, half fare for children. TAIRC also offers four- to five-day **packages**, including accommodation and excursions, at around CH$400,000–600,000 per person. Note that both aerodromes are due to close, so their land can be used for development, and their future is uncertain. You could also try your luck with Naviera del Sur Limitada, Línea Naviera Blanco 1041, Oficina 18, Valparaíso (℡32/594304), which sometimes has a cabin to fill on its monthly or so cargo voyages to and from the archipelago.

The island's little **airstrip** is 13km from the village of San Juan Bautista; it's possible to hike it in nine hours or so, but most passengers sensibly opt for the fifty- to ninety-minute ride by **motor launch** (usually included in the price of your flight), often accompanied by numerous yelping sea lions. It can be a rough ride, coming after the bumpy plane journey, so motion sickness tablets are a sensible precaution for landlubbers.

San Juan Bautista

Huddled by the shores of Bahía Cumberland, at the foot of a green curtain of mountains, **SAN JUAN BAUTISTA** is the island's only village and home to some five hundred inhabitants. With only a few dirt streets lined with simple wooden houses, there's not a lot to do here, and for most people it's just a base from which to explore the island's interior and the coast. That said, there are several historical relics dotted about the place, and wandering round them makes a good introduction to the island. You could start with the **Fuerte Santa Barbara**, a small stone fort perched on a hillside just north of the plaza. Heavily restored in 1974, it was originally built by the Spanish in 1749 in an attempt to prevent buccaneers from using the island as a watering point. Right next to

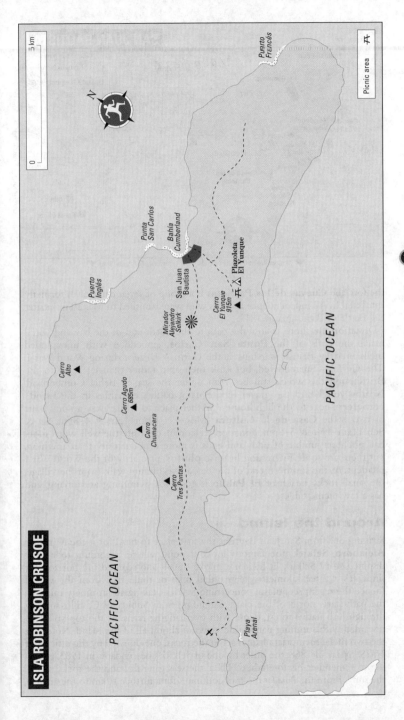

SAN JUAN BAUTISTA

Cemetery
Football Pitch
Gimnasio
Pier
Casa de la Cultura
Residencial Villa Green
Conaf
El Barón de Rodt
Municipalidad
Cueva de los Patriotas
Fuerte Santa Barbara
La Bahía
Clinic
Conaf Office
PACIFIC OCEAN
Bahía Cumberland
El Palillo
Refugio Naútico
Hostal Charpentier
PLAZA
LARRAIN ALCADE
LARRAIN ALCADE
DRESDEN
ROBINSON CRUSOE
DEL REY
LOS PATRICIOS
CALLE LA POLVORA
J. FERNANDEZ
EL CASTILLO
VICENTE GONZALEZ
LORD ANSON
SANDERO EL PANGAL
Hostería El Pangal (3km)

0   200 m

Mirador Alejandro Selkirk (3km)   Plazoleta El Yunque (3km)

the fort, the **Cuevas de los Patriotas** is a group of seven dank caves formerly inhabited by 42 independence fighters who were banished to Más a Tierra after the Battle of Rancagua in 1814.

Down on the shore, follow the path to the north end of the bay and you'll reach the cliffs of the **Punta San Carlos**, embedded with unexploded shells fired by British warships at the German *Dresden* during World War I. The Germans surrendered, but sank their ship rather than let it go to the British, and the wreck still lies 70m under the sea, in Bahía Cumberland. Nearby you'll find the graves of the naval battle's casualties in the island's **cemetery**, next to the lighthouse. Another place to while away a rainy hour or two is the **Casa de la Cultura** (Mon–Fri 10am–1pm & 4–8pm, Sat & Sun 11am–1pm & 5–8pm; donation welcome), opposite the well-worn football pitch; its jumble of odds and ends is more of a curiosity than anything, but there are some interesting historic **photos**, primarily of the World War I incident. At the southern end of the bay, a five-minute walk from the village, the small rocky beach of **El Palillo** is good for swimming and diving, and has a few picnic tables.

Around the island

Striking out from San Juan Bautista, the first place to head for is the **Mirador Alejandro Selkirk**, the famous lookout point where, according to a now disputed story, Selkirk lit his daily smoke signals and scoured the horizon for ships. It's a three-kilometre steep uphill hike or mule trek from the village (hence the recent scepticism concerning Selkirk), taking about ninety minutes; the path starts north of the plaza, extending from Subida El Castillo, snaking through lush native forest, dense with overhanging ferns. At the top you'll be rewarded with stunning panoramic views of almost all of the island. Note, too, the two metal memorial plaques set in the rocks, one donated by the officers of *HMS Topaze* in 1868, the other by one of Selkirk's descendants in 1983, pledging to remember his forefather "Till a' the seas gang dry and the rocks melt i' the sun". From the *mirador* the trail continues for a further 10km to the airstrip, at the southwestern tip of the island; allow about eight hours to get there, and take plenty of water.

Another often muddy three-kilometre trail leads from the village (continuing from Calle El Yunque; allow 45min) through native forest to **Plazoleta El Yunque**, a lookout point and picnic site at the foot of Cerro El Yunque, the island's tallest mountain at 915m. The stone ruins near the site are the remains of the house of Hugo Weber, the "German Robinson Crusoe", who spent twelve years living as a hermit here after escaping from the *Dresden* in 1915. Most other destinations are reached by **boat** with local fishermen, who will drop you off in the morning and pick you up at the end of their day's work, around 8pm – it's a good idea, as a precaution, not to pay for your return journey until *after* you've been picked up. At **Puerto Inglés**, a fifteen-minute boat ride from the village, you'll find a mock-up of the cave where Selkirk took refuge. The terrain is very rugged around here, and it makes a beautiful place to camp, though be sure to choose a reliable fisherman to come and pick you up the next day, or else you'll have to fight your way though dense overgrowth and up steep hillsides to get back to the village. Just south of the airstrip, **Playa Arenal** is the island's only sandy beach. It's a glorious place to spend a couple of days, with its warm, transparent waters. Two hours and thirty minutes by boat through islets and seal colonies, it can also be reached on foot near the end of the trail to the airstrip from the *mirador*.

Island practicalities

All services and accommodation are to be found in or just outside San Juan Bautista. The **Municipalidad** (Mon–Fri 8.30am–1pm; ℡32/701045 or 32/751067, ℱ751047, ℗www.comunajuanfernandez.cl), off the southwest corner of the plaza, hands out **tourist information**, including accommodation lists, maps and leaflets. A joint environmentalist project with the Dutch government (since abandoned by the European partners owing to bureaucratic hitches to put it euphemistically) led to the production of multilingual leaflets explaining the island's flora and fauna – including the endangered Juan Fernández hummingbird (Sephanoides fernandensis) – and how to protect it. To find out more about the island's trails and wildlife and, more importantly, to register and pay your park **entrance fee** (CH$3000 valid for a week), visit the **CONAF** kiosk on the main square (Mon–Fri 8.45am–12.30pm & 2–5.30pm) or the Conaf Information Centre at Sendero El Pangal 130 (℡32/751022), just south of the village. At the latter you can study an excellent display, explaining the salient aspects of the island's wildlife, and see a detailed model of the island itself, showing just how mountainous it is. The village "centre", with its expensive groceries and bakeries, is a good place to ask around for guides with mules or fishermen with boats; negotiate the price and time firmly but don't be surprised if you are stood up, especially on mornings following the many merry fiestas held to relieve the monotony of insular life.

Accommodation, which can be booked together with your flight, tends to be simple, but is expensive by Chilean standards. By far the best place to stay in terms of location, comfort, service and all other criteria, is the professionally run ⚓ *Refugio Naútico* (℡ & ℱ32/751077, ℗www.islarobinsoncrusoe.cl; ❼, half board), at Ignacio Carrera Pinto 280, along the shoreline, past El Palillo. With its own sea access, plus kayaks, boats and diving equipment, as the outfit's name suggests, this place is oriented towards, but not exclusively for, people interested in spending time on or under the water. Don't miss their half-day **trip to the sea lion colony** where you can get right up close to the friendly mammals and their cuddly pups. The food and pisco sours at the refugio are top notch, with expertly cooked fish straight from the ocean and even sushi once a week; credit cards are accepted. *Hostal Charpentier* next door at Ignacio Carrera Pinto 256 (T & F 32/751010; ❺, half board), has a few decent rooms with lovely views, mostly used as overspill for the refugio itself.

Other lodgings can be found on the west side of the plaza, where *Residencial Villa Green* (T 32/751039; ❺, half board) offers clean, comfortable doubles with private bath. A full three kilometres south of the village at Caleta El Pangal, the LASSA-run *Hostería El Pangal* (T & F in Santiago 2/2734354; ❻, half board) is the largest (with 24 rooms) option but is rather isolated, with limited electricity supplies, cramped rooms and slipping standards; note that passengers on LASSA flights are entitled to a discount and are ferried there by a separate launch. A far cheaper alternative is to **camp**, the only option being out at Plazoleta El Yunque, but the damp ground, prolific mosquitoes and chilly nights should be borne in mind.

For more information about rooms for rent and any other accommodation, plus general information about tourism on the island, contact the Municipalidad or, prior to travel, the **Viña del Mar Sernatur office** (see p.164), which is responsible for the archipelago. Apart from the Refugio Naútico, Endémica Expediciones, run by a Chilean couple (Sector Muelle, T 32/751003, W www .endemica.com), offers kayaking, snorkelling and diving, and angling excursions, at reasonable prices.

Most visitors **eat** at their hotel, but if you're camping, or fancy a change, try *La Bahía* on Larraín Alcalde for first-rate lobster and fish (it's a good idea to get your orders in a few hours before you plan to eat). An excellent alternative, a way up La Polvora, is the no-nonsense *El Barón de Rodt*, run by the Swiss baron's great-granddaughter, and renowned for its moreish lobster *empanadas* and chunky sandwiches filled with *vidriola* (a deliciously fleshy local fish).

There's a basic **clinic**, and a **post office** in a hut just off the plaza, next to the Municipalidad, with a direct-dial public **telephone**. Be sure to take plenty of cash with you as there are no **banks** or *cambios* on the island, and cheques and credit cards are not usually accepted.

Contexts

Contexts

A brief history of Chile

Enveloped by the Andes, the Atacama Desert and the Pacific Ocean, Chile has evolved almost as an island, relatively undisturbed by the turbulence that has raged through much of South America's history. Though inhabited by indigenous groups for millennia, the country's actual recorded history dates from the sixteenth-century arrival of the Spaniards. The colonial society that emerged and the ensuing struggle for independence resemble that of the whole continent, but, from its early days as a republic, Chile took on its own political shape, distinct from that of its neighbours. With its largely ordered, constitutional model of government, and a healthy respect for the law, Chile earned itself the sobriquet of "the England of South America" in the nineteenth century. More recently, however, it returned to the attention of the outside world with the repressive military regime of General Augusto Pinochet in the 1970s and 1980s. Today, with democracy firmly back in place, Chile is an outward-looking nation boasting political and economic stability, albeit with some serious social inequalities and unresolved political legacies lurking beneath the surface.

The beginnings

Chile's anthropological record, like that of all the Americas, began when the first groups of Asians crossed the land bridge connecting Siberia to Alaska before the end of the last Ice Age, when the sea level was 70–100m lower than it is today. Archeologists are unable to tell us exactly when this **first migration** occurred, but it's generally thought to have been between 25,000 and 40,000 years ago.

What *is* known is that by 12,000 BC the descendants of these people, supplemented by further waves of migration from Asia, had spread down the whole of North and South America as far as the southern tip of Patagonia. While some devoted themselves to fishing, the majority were probably nomadic hunters living off the animals that inhabited the region at the time – mastodons (prehistoric elephants), mammoths, giant armadillos and wild horses. When the last Ice Age came to an end around 11,000 BC, the climate changed abruptly and many of these animals became extinct. The hunters were forced to adapt, supplementing their diet by gathering fruits and seeds. Eventually this led to the deliberate cultivation of foodstuffs and the domestication of animals, and along with these incipient agricultural practices came more stable communities and important developments, such as pottery and burial customs. Slowly, distinct cultural groups emerged, shaped by their very different environments and the resources available to them.

The pre-Columbian cultures

In the absence of written records, archeologists have had to piece together information about Chile's **pre-Columbian cultures** from what these groups have left behind, principally funerary offerings found in burial sites and domestic objects left in former dwelling places. The strata in which the remains are buried (plus the use of radiocarbon dating) indicate the chronology in which these developments took place. However, variations in Chile's geography from north to south present unequal conditions for the preservation of artefacts and have led to a far greater knowledge of the cultures of the north than of the south.

El Norte Grande

More is known about the pre-Columbian cultures of Chile's Norte Grande – the Far North – than of any other part of the country. The extreme dryness of the Atacama Desert preserved archeological remains for thousands of years. One of the earliest groups of people to leave its mark was the **Chinchorro culture**, a collection of nomadic fishing communities that lived along the desert coast some 8000 years ago. By 5000 BC, the Chinchorro had developed the practice of **mummifying their dead** (see box, p.271) – 2000 years earlier than the Egyptians. Their technique, which involved removing internal organs and tissues and replacing them with vegetable fibres and mud, survived for 4000 years and is the oldest known in the world.

By around 500 BC, life in El Norte Grande was based largely on agriculture, supplemented by fishing in the coastal areas, and herding llamas and alpacas in the Andean highlands. Although vast tracts of the region are taken up by barren desert, a number of oases provided fertile land where agricultural communities were able to dedicate themselves to the cultivation of maize, beans, squash, chillies and potatoes. They lived in permanent dwellings, usually consisting of circular huts surrounding a shared patio, and often with a cemetery nearby.

Among the most important (and longest-lasting) of these early agricultural groups was the **San Pedro culture** (also known as the Atacameño culture), which settled along the salt-flat oases around San Pedro de Atacama around 500 BC. They produced ceramics, textiles, and objects in copper and stone, along with delicately carved wooden snuff tablets and tubes used for inhaling hallucinogenic substances – a custom probably introduced by the **Tihuanaco culture** around 300 AD. This latter was a powerful religious state based near the southern shores of Lake Titicaca in present-day Bolivia, and its influence extended over most of northern Chile and much of Peru for many centuries. The Tihuanaco impact was most visible in the spread of its ceramics and textiles, often decorated with images of cats, condors and snakes, which probably had religious significance. The Tihuanaco also fostered an active trading system, encouraging the exchange of goods between regions, bringing about increased social stratification, with those at the top controlling the commercial traffic.

Sometime between 900 and 1200 AD, the Tihuanaco culture declined and collapsed, for reasons unknown today. The regional cultures of the Norte Grande were then free to reassert their individual authority and identity, expressing their independence with a series of *pukarás* (fortresses) dotted around the altiplano. This period of *desarrollo regional* ("regional development"), as it is known, was halted only by the arrival of the Incas in the late fifteenth century (see p.590).

El Norte Chico

Around 300 AD, when the peoples of the Norte Grande had been living in fixed agricultural communities for several centuries, those of the Norte Chico were just beginning to abandon their lives of hunting and gathering, and turn to cattle herding and farming. The resulting **El Molle culture** was composed of communities that settled along the river valleys between Copiapó and Illapel, where they developed a system of artificial irrigation to cultivate maize, beans, squash and possibly cotton. They also herded llamas, a practice recorded in numerous petroglyphs, and produced the first ceramics of the Norte Chico. Between 700 and 800 AD the El Molle culture declined and was replaced by a new cultural group known as **Las Animas**, which probably originated in the Argentine highlands. The changes introduced by this culture included rapid developments in metalworking; new, more decorative, styles of pottery; and – most curiously – the custom of ritual sacrifice of llamas.

Towards 1000 AD an important **Diaguita culture** appeared in the Norte Chico, dominating the region over the next five centuries until the Spanish invasion. The Diaguitas tended to live in large villages along the river valleys, presided over by a chief and a shaman. Each valley was divided into two sections: a "lower" section, towards the coast, which was ruled by one chief, and a "higher" section, towards the mountains, ruled by another. Their economy was based on agriculture, herding, mining and metalworking, and was supplemented by fishing on the coast, aided by the invention of inflated sealskin rafts. The Diaguitas' greatest achievement, however, was their outstandingly fine pottery, characterized by intricate white, black and red geometric patterns.

Central Chile

The first agricultural groups to settle in central Chile were the **El Bato** and **Llolleo** peoples, from around 300 AD. The El Bato group occupied the zone between the Río Choapa (near Illapel) and the Río Maipo (south of Santiago); its highly polished monochrome pottery indicates that it was strongly influenced by the El Molle culture from the Norte Chico. The Llolleo settlements were spread along the coastal plains between the Río Aconcagua (just north of Santiago) and the Río Maule (near Talca). One of the most striking characteristics of this culture was their custom of burying their dead under their own houses, with small children buried in clay urns.

Later, around 900 AD, the Aconcagua emerged as the dominant culture in Central Chile; these people lived in houses made of branches and mud and dedicated themselves to growing beans, maize, squash and potatoes; they also developed far more specialized ceramics than had previously existed in the region.

Araucania

While relatively little is known about the development of the cultures of the south of Chile, owing to a paucity of archeological remains, it's generally agreed that the first group to adopt cultivation was the **Pitrén culture**, around 600 AD. This comprised small family groups spread between the Bío Bío and Lago Llanquihue, where they grew maize and potatoes on a small scale, as well as hunting and gathering. They also produced ceramics, often decorated with zoomorphic and anthropomorphic images, which they usually buried with their dead.

Around 1000 AD a new community, known as **El Vergel**, emerged in the region between Angol and Temuco. Its economy combined hunting and gathering with the cultivation of potatoes, maize, beans and squash, and it is likely that its people were the first to domesticate guanacos. Other practices these people brought to the region included burying their dead in ceramic urns, which they decorated with red and white paint. They also developed a very beautiful style of pottery, now known as Valdivia pottery, characterized by parallel zigzag lines and shaded triangles.

Sometime in the fourteenth century a group of nomadic hunters called the *moluche* ("people of war") arrived from Argentina and occupied the land between the Itata and Toltén rivers. They absorbed the existing Pitrén and El Vergel cultures to form a new entity called **Mapuche** ("people of the land"). While engaging in fishing, hunting and gathering, their lifestyle was based principally on herding and farming – labour was divided between the sexes, with men responsible for preparing the fields, and women for sowing and harvesting. The basic social unit was the family clan, or "lov", which were independent from each other and autonomous. Its isolation meant the Mapuche culture didn't develop any further until forced to unite in the face of the Spanish invasion.

The far south

The narrow channels, fjords, impenetrable jungles and wild steppes of the far south have never encouraged communities to settle in one place. Accordingly, the peoples that inhabited this region led a more primitive lifestyle than those further north – they could not adopt agriculture as their main economy, and so maintained their tradition of hunting and fishing in nomadic groups. Groups like the **Selk'nam** and the **Tehuelche** hunted guanaco and rhea on the Patagonian steppes, and lived in temporary wigwam-like structures covered in guanaco skins. The **Yámana** and **Chono** people hunted seals, otters, birds and gathered shellfish in their canoes, constantly moving from place to place. None of the Patagonian or Fuegian groups produced ceramics, manufacturing instead bows, arrows, lassos, baskets and warm skin capes. Their understanding of the world was rich in mythology and symbolism – the Selk'nam, for instance, believed that many birds and animals were spirits that had once been human; they also practised elaborate initiation rites marking the passage from boyhood into manhood, involving physical tests and secret ceremonies. Unlike the other native peoples of Chile, these groups were never incorporated into Spanish colonial society, and their lifestyles remained virtually unchanged until the twentieth century, when the clash with seal hunters and sheep farmers led to their disappearance.

The Inca conquest

While the native peoples of Chile were developing relatively simple communities based on agriculture, herding and fishing, a great civilization was emerging further to the north – that of the **Incas**. This people arrived in Cusco around 1200 AD and by the fifteenth century had developed a sophisticated and highly organized society that boasted palaces, temples and fortresses of great architectural sophistication. In 1463, the Inca emperor, Pachacuti, initiated a period of massive **expansion** that saw the conquest of lands stretching north to modern-day Quito and south as far as the Río Maule in Chile, where its progress was halted by the fierce resistance of the Mapuches.

The impact of the Incas in Chile was considerable: they constructed a breathtaking network of roads connecting the conquered lands to the capital of the empire in Cusco (later very useful to the Spanish conquistadors), and forced the subjugated peoples to pay tribute to the Inca ruler and to use **Quechua** as their official language. While the Incas tolerated indigenous cults, they required their subjects also to adopt the **cult of the sun**, a central tenet of the Inca religion. Sun worship usually took place at altars built on high mountain peaks where the sun's first rays were received; it sometimes involved human sacrifice, but more commonly animals or objects like silver figurines were offered as substitutes. Remains of Inca worship sites have been found on numerous mountains in Chile, the most famous being Cerro El Plomo, near Santiago, where the frozen body of a small child, undoubtedly offered as a sacrifice, was discovered in 1954. The Inca occupation of Chile spanned a relatively short period of time – about 70 years in the Norte Grande and perhaps just 30 in Central Chile. It was interrupted first by civil war in Cusco, caused by the struggle between two rivals over succession to the throne. Then, in 1532, the Spanish arrived in Peru, marking the beginning of the end of the Inca Empire.

The Spanish conquest

It was while seeking a westward route to Asia across the Atlantic that **Christopher Columbus** inadvertently "discovered" the Americas in 1492. His patron, Queen Isabella of Spain, supported him on two further expeditions, and sent settlers to colonize the Caribbean island of Hispaniola (site of today's Haiti and Dominican Republic). It gradually became apparent that the islands were not part of Asia, and that a giant landmass – indeed a whole continent – separated them from the East. After colonizing several other islands, the explorers and adventurers, backed by the Spanish Crown, turned their attention to the mainland, and the period of conquest began in earnest. In 1521 **Hernán Cortés** defeated the great **Aztec Empire** in Mexico and then in 1524 **Francisco Pizarro** and his partner **Diego de Almagro** set out to find the rich empire they had been told lay further south. After several failed attempts, they finally landed on the coast of **Peru** in 1532, where they found the great **Inca Empire** racked by civil war. Pizarro speedily conquered the empire, aided by advanced military weapons and tactics, the high morale of his men, their frenzied desire for gold and glory and, most significantly, the devastating effect of Old World diseases on the indigenous population. Within a few years, Peru was firmly in Spanish hands.

Diego de Almagro was entrusted with the mission of carrying the conquest further south to the region named **Chile**, spoken of by the Peruvian natives as a land rich in gold and silver. In 1535, Almagro and his four hundred men set off from Cusco and followed an Incan road down the spine of the Andes as far as the Aconcagua Valley, suffering extreme deprivation and hardship along the way. To make matters worse, the conquistador found none of the riches the Peruvians had spoken of. Bitterly disappointed, Almagro returned to Cusco, where his deteriorating relations with Pizarro led to armed combat and death at the hands of Pizarro's brothers.

Three years later, **Pedro de Valdivia** (one of Pizarro's most trusted officers) was granted license to colonize Chile. Owing to its lack of gold and the miseries of the first expedition, Chile was not an attractive destination, and so it was with just ten compatriots, a group of native porters and his mistress, Inés Suarez, that Valdivia set off from Cusco in 1540. Almost a year later, having picked up 150 extra men en route, Valdivia reached the Río Mapocho in the Aconcagua

Valley, where he founded **Santiago de la Nueva Extremadura** on February 12, 1541. The new "city" was hastily put together, with all the trappings of a colonial capital, including church, prison, court and *cabildo* (town council), which elected Valdivia as governor. It was a humble affair, regularly attacked and destroyed by local Picunches, but the new colonists were determined to stay and did not return to Peru.

Over the next decade, Valdivia attempted to expand the colony, founding the cities of **La Serena** in the north in 1544 and **Concepción** in the south in 1550, followed by a handful of other centres in the south. It was here that the Spaniards faced the fierce resistance of the **Mapuches** (known by the Spanish as the Araucanians), who successfully prevented the spread of colonization south of the Bío Bío River, which became known as **La Frontera**. It was in a confrontation with the Mapuches that Valdivia met his death in 1553, at the hands of the famous chief **Lautaro**. The details of Valdivia's execution are believed to be particularly grisly – some versions claim he was forced to swallow molten gold, others that he was lanced to death by a crowd of warriors, one of whom sliced through his breast and ripped out his heart.

In the panic caused by Valdivia's death, the southern colonists retreated to Santiago, leaving only Concepción as a garrison outpost, occupied mainly by soldiers guarding La Frontera. A new governor – Don García Hurtado de Mendoza – was dispatched from Peru, and by the time his term of office ended, in 1561, the natives in the central region had been subjugated and colonization was effectively complete.

Colonial society

The new colony was a marginal, isolated and unprofitable addition to Spain's empire in the Americas, which revolved around the viceroyalties of Mexico and Peru. The need to maintain a standing army to guard La Frontera, and the absence of large quantities of precious metals to fund it, meant that Chile ran at a deficit for most of the colonial period. Administratively, it was designated a "**captaincy-general**", ruled by a governor with the help of an *audiencia* (a high court, whose function included advising the governor). All high officials were sent from Spain as representatives of the king, whose authority was absolute, and whose instructions were communicated via the *Consejo de Indias* (Council of the Indies). Chile, however, received little attention and, enclosed within the mighty barriers of the Atacama Desert and Andean cordillera, was more or less left to its own devices.

Growth was very slow, amounting to no more than five thousand settlers by 1600. Most of these lived from the farming of land handed out by the governor in grants known as **mercedes de tierra**, spreading over the valleys near Santiago and in the Central Valley. At the same time, large "grants" of indigenous people were given to the colonists in what was known as the **encomienda** system – the *encomienda* being the group of natives allocated to an *encomendero*. In theory, the *encomenderos* were supposed to look after the wellbeing of their charges and convert them to Christianity in exchange for tribute (by means of work) offered to the Spanish Crown. In reality, the system simply provided the colonists with a large slave workforce that they could treat however they pleased, which was often appallingly. From the very beginning, then, the *mercedes de tierra* and *encomiendas* established a pattern that was to dominate Chile's rural society until modern times: namely, large estates owned by seigniorial landlords at the head of a dependent, disempowered workforce.

During the **seventeenth century** this pattern became more clearly defined with the emergence and economic dominance of the **hacienda**. Enclosed within thick, protective walls, haciendas were self-sufficient, self-contained entities, whose buildings – arranged around numerous courtyards – comprised workshops, wine *bodegas*, dairies, a chapel and the *casa patronal*, the landowner's home. Initially the workforce was provided by *encomiendas*, but, with tragic inevitability, the indigenous population rapidly decreased through exposure to Old World diseases. In its place there sprang up a new generation of **mestizos**, the result of miscegenation between the Spanish colonists (almost exclusively male in the early years) and indigenous women.

In time, a more or less homogeneous *mestizo* population came to make up the bulk of the Chilean workforce, presided over by a ruling, landowning elite made up of **peninsulares** (Spaniards born in Spain) and **criollos** (those of Spanish blood born in the colony). Most *mestizos* were incorporated into the haciendas either as peons or as **inquilinos** – labourers allowed to farm a small plot of land in return for year-round service (a practice that continued until the twentieth century). The main activities on the haciendas were livestock raising and the cultivation of cereals and fruit. Production was healthy but never reached particularly high levels, owing to Spanish trading restrictions, which prevented the colonies from trading freely with each other or with Spain.

Along with the haciendas, the other main shaping force in Chilean society was the **Catholic Church**. From the colony's earliest days, missionaries from most orders poured into Chile and embarked on a zealous programme of conversion in the farthest flung corners of the territory, erecting chapels and crosses wherever they went. Their success was rapid and set the seal on the "pacification" of the Indians, who were less likely to cause trouble if they could be incorporated into the Hispanic culture and their sense of separate identity diminished. The Catholicism that emerged wasn't an altogether orthodox version, as many indigenous elements of worship – such as ritual dancing and sacrificial offerings – were incorporated into this new religion, and even now survive in Chile's more remote communities, especially in the north. Nonetheless, both *indígenas* and *mestizos* embraced the symbolic elements of the Catholic faith with enthusiasm, and several cults sprang up around supposedly miraculous icons, such as the **Cristo de Mayo** in Santiago, believed to have bled real blood after an earthquake in 1647.

The most influential element of the Church was the **Jesuit order** (Compañía de Jesús), which arrived in Chile in 1593 and quickly established itself as one of the colony's largest landowners. In a paternalistic arrangement, the Jesuits gathered hundreds of indigenous families to their missions, where they were fed, clothed, converted, taught Spanish and instructed in many skills from weaving to glass manufacturing. As a result, the order's numerous workshops were the most productive and profitable in the country, as was the case throughout Spanish America – until the Jesuits were suddenly expelled from the Spanish Empire in 1767, when the Crown was persuaded that they had become too powerful to tolerate.

The first half of the **eighteenth century** saw little real advance in Chile's development. Patterns that had been established earlier on were simply reinforced: the *mestizo* population grew, and the dominance of the great landed estates (known as *latifundia*) was bolstered by the creation of **mayorazgos**, a system of entailment that allowed (at a price) the wealthiest landowners to pass on their property without having to divide it among their heirs. The bulk of the population was rural and attached to the estates, principally spread between the Aconcagua and the Maule valleys, with only a very limited urban population outside of Santiago.

Things did change noticeably, however, with the reign of **Charles III**, from 1759 to 1788. The most progressive of the Bourbon monarchs (who had replaced the Habsburg Dynasty in Spain in 1700), the king set about improving the management of the American colonies and increasing their productivity, so as to augment revenues. Among his reforms was the relaxation of the stifling trade restrictions that had hampered economic growth throughout much of Spanish America. Suddenly, the colonies were able to trade freely with each other and with Spain. There was no overnight miracle, but Chilean trade did expand considerably, particularly with neighbouring Río de la Plata (future Argentina).

At the same time, imports soared, and the need to pay for them in gold or silver stimulated a small **mining boom** in the Norte Chico. Settlements sprang up around the mining centres, and some, such as Copiapó, Vallenar and Illapel, were granted official city status. All in all, there was an emerging spirit of change and progress, which gave a sense of empowerment to Chile's *criollos*, who had always been barred from the highest colonial offices. But while Chile's commercial horizons were widening, the king's administrative shake-ups – which involved sending a number of *intendants* to the colonies to tighten up administration and eradicate abuses of local power – was experienced as unwanted interference. The resulting tension would soon find a more focused channel.

The struggle for independence

Chile entered the **nineteenth century** with a burgeoning sense of its own identity. The *criollo* elite, while fiercely loyal to the Spanish king, was becoming increasingly alienated from the *peninsulares* dispatched from Spain to administer the colony, and the gap between them was widening with each successive generation. *Criollo* aspirations of playing a more active role in government (and thus of looking after their own interests, not just the Crown's) were given a sudden, unexpected opportunity for fulfilment when Napoleon invaded Spain in 1808 and deposed Ferdinand VII. **Local juntas** sprang up in Spain's main cities to organize resistance to Napoleon, and they were soon followed by a number of locally elected juntas in the American colonies. In Chile, over four hundred leading citizens gathered in Santiago on September 18, 1810, and elected a six-man **junta**, made up of Chileans. It must be stressed that the junta's initial objective was to "preserve the sovereignty of Ferdinand VII" in the absence of legitimate authority, and few entertained thoughts of independence at this stage. The junta did, however, go on to implement several far-reaching reforms: trade was liberalized; a Congress was elected; and the *real audiencia* (royal court) was replaced by a tribunal with Chilean judges.

Soon, a minority of *criollos* began to seek a far greater degree of autonomy for the colony, and whispers of independence grew. This small tide was given dramatic impetus in November, 1811, when **José Miguel Carrera**, a member of one of the wealthiest and most influential *criollo* families in Chile, seized power, dissolving Congress and appointing himself head of a new, more radical, junta. His actions were swift and bold, and included the creation of a Chilean flag and the drafting of a provisional constitution that declared all rulings issued outside Chile to be illegitimate. Greatly alarmed, the viceroy of Peru – where the colonial machinery remained intact – sent troops in early 1813 down to the old-guard strongholds of Chiloé and Valdivia to prepare for an assault on Santiago. In response, Carrera charged down to confront them with Chilean troops (whose generals numbered one Bernardo O'Higgins, the son of a former viceroy of Peru), and war was effectively declared. Loyalties were now thrown sharply into focus with the **Royalists** on one side, made up of Spaniards and pro-Spanish Chileans, and the **Patriots** on the other, made up of *criollos* who supported some form of self-government.

Bernardo O'Higgins and José de San Martín

When Carrera's military leadership did not produce impressive results, the junta voted to replace him with **Bernardo O'Higgins**, who proved far more adept at holding off the Royalist forces. In July 1814, the power-hungry Carrera returned to Santiago and overthrew the government once more, reinstating himself at its head and causing considerable upheaval. In October of that year, Royalist troops, taking advantage of the chaos, began to advance on Santiago. O'Higgins mounted a desperate and heroic defence at Rancagua, attempting to hold them back, but Carrera's promised reinforcements never arrived, and the Patriots were overwhelmingly defeated. The "**Disaster of Rancagua**", as it is known, marked the end of La Patria Vieja (the name given to the fledgling independent nation) and its leaders fled across the Andean border to Mendoza in Argentina, as the Royalist troops marched triumphantly into Santiago.

The victory coincided with the defeat of Napoleon in Spain and the restoration of Ferdinand VII, who immediately set out to crack down on all insurgent elements in his American colonies. In Chile, some forty Patriot *criollos* were exiled to the Juan Fernández Islands, where they were to live in caves, and every reform instigated by the junta was reversed. The Spanish Crown's attempt to turn back the clock and revert to a centralized, interventionist colonial government was felt as repressive and authoritarian by *criollos* throughout the continent.

Just as the great general **Simón Bolívar** was preparing anti-Spanish campaigns in Venezuela that would liberate the northern half of the continent, **José de San Martín**, the Argentine general, was drawing plans for South American emancipation from his base in Mendoza, near the Chilean border. San Martín knew that independence could never be assured until the Spanish were ejected from their heartland in Peru, which he planned to achieve by first liberating Chile, from where he would launch a naval attack on Lima. To this end, San Martín was rigorously recruiting and training an army – known as the **Army of the Andes** – whose numbers were considerably increased by the Chilean Patriots who fled across the border after their defeat at Rancagua. With O'Higgins in command of the Chilean division, San Martín's army scaled the cordillera over four different passes in February 1817. On the twelfth, Patriot forces surprised the Spaniards and defeated them at the Battle of Chacabuco, just north of Santiago. The Royalists fled to the south, and the Patriots entered the capital in triumph. Fighting continued after Royalist reinforcements were sent from Peru, but when San Martín inflicted devastating losses on their army at the Battle of Maipú in April 1818, the Patriot victory was complete, setting the final seal on Chilean independence. Leadership of the new country was offered to San Martín, but he declined – instead, the job went to Bernardo O'Higgins, who was elected Supreme Director by an assembly of Chile's leading *criollos*.

O'Higgins' immediate task was to put together a national navy with which to clear the southern coast of remaining Royalist troublemakers and launch the seaborne attack on Peru. A flotilla was equipped and placed under the command of a British admiral, **Lord Thomas Cochrane**, who successfully captured Callao, the port of Lima, in 1820. With the colonial nerve centre effectively toppled, the days of the Spanish Empire in the Americas were numbered. Turning his attention from liberation to government, however, O'Higgins was confronted with a whole set of new problems, not least the near bankruptcy caused by crippling war costs. Resentment at the stiff taxes imposed to recoup these costs caused widespread discontent, and after five years of difficult rule O'Higgins was forced to step down. The former hero exiled himself in Peru, where he remained until his death in 1842, leaving the new republic of Chile with the challenge of building itself into a nation.

The early republic

The transition from colony to republic was not smooth. In its first thirteen years of independence, Chile got through five constitutions and eleven changes of government, marked by continual tussles between **Liberal** and **Conservative** factions. Then, in 1829, the Conservatives, with the support of the army, imposed an authoritarian-style government that ushered in a long period of political stability, making Chile the envy of Latin America. The chief architect of the regime was **Diego Portales**, who never stood for presidency, preferring to run the show from various cabinet posts. Convinced that Chile could only move forward under a strong, centralist government able to maintain rigorous order, Portales designed, in 1833, the **Constitution** that was to underpin Chilean government for 92 years. It granted enormous powers to the president, allowing him, for instance, to veto any legislation passed by Congress, and protecting him from impeachment until his term of office had expired (two five-year terms were allowed).

Portales was not, however, without his detractors, and in 1837, in protest at the government's invasion of Peru (which had been forcibly annexed by the Bolivian president), he was brutally gunned down by political opponents. This atrocity led to increased support for the government, which went on to defeat the Peru-Bolivia Confederation – to the great pride of Chilean citizens.

The growing self-confidence of the nation, added to the political and social stability within it, created conditions that were favourable to growth. Between the 1830s and 1870s international trade took off rapidly, with hugely increased wheat exports fuelled by the Californian and Australian gold rushes, and, more significantly, **a silver- and copper-mining boom** in the Norte Chico. At the same time, advances in technology and communications saw railways, roads, steamships and telegraphs opening up the country. Its populated territory expanded, too: a government programme encouraged Europeans to come over and settle the lakeland region of the south, which was duly cleared and farmed by some four thousand German immigrants. Meanwhile, Santiago and Valparaíso were being transformed – with avenues, parks, palaces and mansions, and an ever-expanding population. Only the countryside in the Central Valley heartland showed no real change, dominated as it was by haciendas whose owners frequently neglected their estates in favour of other business interests.

In time, the nation began to tire of the authoritarian model of government established by Portales, and the influence of Liberal politics began to gain ground. In 1871 the election of **Federico Errázuriz Zañartu** as president marked the beginning of twenty years of Liberal government. Many of the Liberals' reforms were aimed at reducing the undiminished power of the Church: they legalized free worship in private places; they introduced civil cemeteries, where persons of any faith could be buried; and they instituted civil marriages and registries. The Liberals also went some way towards reducing the individual power of the president, and giving Congress a stronger role in government. The breath of fresh air and sense of optimism produced by these reforms suffered a deathblow, however, when a world recession between 1876 and 1878 sent copper and silver prices tumbling and brought wheat exports to a virtual halt, plunging Chile into economic crisis.

The War of the Pacific

Rescue was at hand in what at first appeared to be yet another calamitous situation. Ever since the 1860s, when two enterprising Chileans started exploiting the vast nitrate deposits of the Atacama Desert, Chilean capital and labour had dominated the region's growing **nitrate** industry (see box, p.255). Most activity took place on the pampas around Antofagasta, which Chile had formally acknowledged as Bolivian territory in 1874 – following lengthy border disputes – in exchange for an assurance from Bolivia that export tariffs would not be raised for 25 years. Many of Chile's most prominent politicians had shares in the nitrate companies, so when Bolivia flouted its agreement by raising export taxes in 1878 – directly hitting shareholders' pockets – they were up in arms, and determined to take action.

With tension mounting, Chilean troops invaded Antofagasta in February 1879 and soon took control of the surrounding coastal strip. Within two weeks Chile and Bolivia were at war, with Peru drawn into the conflict on Bolivia's side within a couple of months. It soon became clear that success would depend on **naval supremacy** – Bolivia did not have a navy, leaving Peru and Chile pitted against each other, and fairly evenly matched. Following a series of early losses, Chile secured an overwhelming maritime victory in August 1879, when it captured Peru's principal warship, the *Huáscar*. The coast was now clear for the invasion of Peru's nitrate territories, and the emphasis shifted to land fighting. Casualties were heavy on both sides, but by June 1880 Chile had secured control of these areas with a resounding victory at El Morro, Arica.

With the nitrate fields theirs, the Chilean government would doubtless have been happy to bring the war to a close, but the public was clamouring for blood: it wanted Peru brought to its knees with the capture of Lima. In January 1881 Peru's humiliation was complete when Chilean troops occupied the capital. Peru was still not ready to give up, though, and the war dragged on for two more years, resulting in heavy human loss and exhausting both sides. Eventually, Peru accepted defeat, sealed by the **Treaty of Ancón** in October 1883 (an official truce with Bolivia was not signed until April the following year).

By the conclusion of the war, Chile had extended its territory by one-third, acquiring the Peruvian province of Tarapacá, and the Bolivian littoral (thus depriving Bolivia of sea access). Its new, nitrate-rich pampas yielded enormous, almost overnight wealth, refilling government coffers and restoring national confidence.

Arturo Prat

Nothing has captured the Chilean imagination like the heroic, and tragic, efforts of **Arturo Prat** in the Battle of Iquique. On the morning of May 21, 1879, the *Esmeralda* – an old wooden boat under Prat's command – found itself under attack from Peruvian artillery on one side, and from the ironclad warship, the *Huáscar*, on the other. The two vessels could not have been more unevenly matched: the *Huáscar* boasted 300lb cannon, while those of the *Esmeralda* were only 40lb. When the *Huáscar* rammed the *Esmeralda*, Prat refused to give in, instead leaping aboard the enemy's vessel, sword in hand, determined to fight to the end. The gesture was futile, and Prat was killed on the warship's deck, but the commander's dignity and self-sacrifice have made him Chile's favourite national hero, in whose honour a thousand avenues and squares have been named.

Civil War and the Parliamentary Republic

Unfettered by war, the nitrate industry began to boom in earnest, and by 1890 export taxes on nitrates were providing over 50 percent of government revenue. With national confidence running high and the economy in such good shape, the government's position looked unassailable. Within a short time, however, cracks began to appear in the constitutional framework, expressed by mounting tension between the legislature (Congress) and the executive branch (chiefly the president).

The conflict came to a dramatic head under the presidency of **José Manuel Balmaceda** (1886–1891), a Liberal but autocratic leader who believed passionately in the president's right to run a strong executive branch – an approach jarringly at odds with the political trend of the previous couple of decades. One of the unifying objectives of the various Liberal parties was the elimination of electoral intervention, and when Balmaceda was seen to influence Congressional elections in 1886, many Liberals were outraged and withdrew their support. Equally polarizing was the president's determination to insist on his right to pick and choose his cabinet, without the approval of Congress – whose response was to refuse to pass legislation authorizing the following year's budget until Balmaceda agreed to appoint a cabinet in which they had confidence.

Neither side would give way, and as the deadline for budget approval drew close, it became obvious that Balmaceda would either have to give in to Congress's demands, or act against the Constitution. When he chose the latter option, declaring that he would carry 1890's budget through to 1891, Congress revolted, propelling the two sides into war. Balmaceda held the army's support, while Congress secured the backing of the navy. Operating out of Iquique, where they established a junta, Congress was able to use nitrate funds to recruit and train an army. In August that year, its troops landed near Valparaíso, where they defeated Balmaceda's army in two long, bloody battles. The president, whose refusal to give in was absolute, fled to the Argentine embassy, where he wrote poignant farewell notes to his family and friends before shooting himself in the head.

The authoritarian model of government established by Diego Portales in the 1830s, already undermined over the previous two decades, had now collapsed.

Taking its place was a system – dubbed the **Parliamentary Republic** – based on an all-powerful legislature and an extremely weak executive. Now it was Congress who imposed cabinets on the president, not the other way round, with frequent clashes and constantly shifting allegiances seeing cabinets formed and dissolved with breathtaking frequency – between 1891 and 1915 the government got through more than sixty ministries. This chronic instability seriously hampered government action, although, ironically, the one arena where great progress was made was the public works programme vigorously promoted by Balmaceda, which saw rapid construction of state railways, roads, bridges, schools, hospitals, prisons and town halls.

The advent of industrialization

All this was taking place against a background of momentous social and economic change that the government, bound up with its continual infighting, seemed scarcely aware of. One of the by-products of the nitrate industry was increased **industrialization** elsewhere in Chile, as manufacturing stepped up to service increased production in the north. This, combined with the growth of railways, coal mining, education, construction and banking, saw a period of rapid **social diversification**. A new group of merchants, managers, bureaucrats and teachers formed an emerging middle class, while the increasingly urban workforce – usually living in dire poverty – formed a new working class more visible than its counterpart on the large rural estates.

It was in the nitrate fields of the north that an embryonic **labour movement** began to take root, as workers protested against the appalling conditions they were forced to live and work in. With no political representation to voice these grievances, **strikes** became the main form of protest, spreading from the mining cities of the north to the docks of Valparaíso. The government's heavy-handed attempts to suppress the strikes – reaching a peak of brutality when almost two hundred men, women and children were shot dead in Iquique, in 1907 – were symptomatic of its inability to deal with the social changes taking place in the country. When the nitrate industry entered a rapid decline with the outbreak of World War I in 1914, leaving thousands of workers unemployed and causing inflation to soar, Chile's domestic situation deteriorated further.

1920–1970

The first leader committed to dealing with the republic's mounting social problems was **Arturo Alessandri**, elected in 1920 on the strength of an ambitious reform programme. The weakness of his position, however, in the face of an all-powerful and obstructive Congress, prevented him from putting any of his plans into action, and after four years hardly anything had been achieved. Then, in 1924, a strange set of events was set in motion when an army junta – frustrated by the lack of government action – forced the cabinet to resign and had Alessandri appoint military men to key cabinet positions. The president appeared quite willing to accommodate the junta, which used its muscle to ensure that Congress swiftly passed a series of social reform laws, including legislation to protect workers' rights. After several months, however, the relationship between the president and his military cabinet began to unravel and Alessandri fled to Argentina in exile.

More drama was to follow when, on January 23, 1925, a rival junta led by Colonel **Carlos Ibañez** staged a coup, deposed the government and invited Alessandri to return to Chile to complete his term of office. With Ibañez's weight behind him, Alessandri set about redrafting the Constitution, with the aim of restoring authority to the president and reducing the power of Congress. This was achieved with the **Constitution of 1925**, which represented a radical departure from the one of 1833, incorporating protective welfare measures among other reforms. Despite this victory, however, tensions between Ibañez and Alessandri led to the president's resignation. The way was now clear for the military strongman, Ibañez, to get himself elected as president in May 1927.

Ibañez's presidency was a curious contradiction, at once highly autocratic, with severe restrictions on freedom of expression, and refreshingly progressive, ushering in a series of badly needed reforms promoting agriculture, industry and education. His early years were successful, bringing about improvements in living standards across all sections of society, and stimulating national prosperity. But when the Wall Street crash of 1929 sparked off a worldwide Depression, Chile's economy collapsed virtually overnight, producing deep social unrest. Faced with a wave of street demonstrations and strikes, Ibañez was forced to resign in July 1931. The task of restoring stability to the nation fell to the old populist, Alessandri, who was re-elected in 1932.

Military interference in government affairs was now at an end (for a few decades, at least), and the country settled down to a period of orderly political evolution, no longer held back by a weak executive. What emerged was a highly diverse multi-party system embracing a wide spectrum of political persuasions. After 1938, the government was dominated by the **Radical Party**, a centre-right group principally representing the middle classes. Radical presidents such as Pedro Aguirre Cerda, Juan Antonio Ríos and Gabriel Gonzalez Videla took an active role in regenerating Chile's economy, investing in state-sponsored steelworks, copper refineries, fisheries and power supplies. In the 1950s, left-wing groups gained considerable ground as the voting franchise widened, but old-guard landowners were able to counter this by controlling the votes of the thousands of peasants who depended on them for their survival, thus ensuring a firm swing back to the right. Nonetheless, it was by a very narrow margin that the socialist Salvador Allende was defeated by the Conservative Jorge Alessandri (son of Arturo) in the 1958 elections, causing widespread alarm among the wealthy elite. As the next election approached in 1964, the upper classes, with the discreet backing of the USA (still reeling from the shock of the Cuban missile crisis), threw all their efforts into securing the election of **Eduardo Frei**, the candidate of the rising young **Christian Democrat Party**.

In power, Frei turned out to be a good deal more progressive than his right-wing supporters could have imagined, initiating – to their horror – bold **agrarian reforms** that allowed the expropriation of all farms of more than 180 hectares. The other memorable achievement of the Frei administration was the "Chileanization" of the **copper industry**, which had replaced nitrates as the country's dominant source of revenue, and which was almost exclusively in the hands of North American corporations. Frei's policy gave the state a 51 percent stake in all the major copper mines, providing instant revenues to fund his social reform programme. These included the introduction of a minimum wage and impressive improvements in education, and made Frei's government popular with the working classes, though his reforms were unable to keep pace with the rush of expectations and demands. At the same time, Conservative groups became increasingly alarmed at the direction in which Frei was steering the country, prompting Liberals and Conservatives to join forces and form the new

National Party, aimed at putting a check on reform. As Chile approached the 1970s, its population grew sharply polarized between those who clamoured for further social reform and greater representation of the working class, and those to whom this was anathema and to be reversed at all costs.

Salvador Allende and the Unidad Popular

On September 4, 1970, **Salvador Allende** was elected as Chile's first social-ist president, heading a coalition of six left-wing parties, known as the **Unidad Popular** (UP). His majority, however, was tiny, and while half the country rejoiced, full of hopes for a better future, the other half feared a slide towards communism. Allende was passionately committed to improv-ing the lot of the poorest sectors of society, whose appalling living condi-tions had shocked him when he had encountered them in his training as a doctor. His government pledged, among other things, to nationalize Chilean industries, to redistribute the nation's wealth, to increase popular participa-tion in government, and to speed up agrarian reform, though there were disagreements as to how fast these changes should be made. Within a year, over eighty major companies had been nationalized, including the copper mines, which were expropriated without compensation. The following year, radical agrarian reform was enforced, with over 60 percent of irrigated land – including all haciendas with more than 80 hectares – taken into govern-ment hands for redistribution among the rural workforce. In one fell swoop, the *latifundia* system that had dominated rural Chile for more than 400 years was irrevocably dismantled.

In the short term, Allende's govern-ment was both successful and popu-lar, presiding as it did over a period of economic growth, rising wages and falling unemploy-ment. But it wasn't long before strains began to be felt. For a start, government expenditure soon exceeded income by a huge margin, creat-ing an enormous deficit. The looming economic crisis was dramatically acceler-ated when the world copper price fell by some 27 percent, cutting government

△ Salvador Allende

revenue still further. Inflation began to rise uncontrollably, with wages unable to keep pace, and before long food shortages became commonplace.

Part of the UP's failure stemmed from the sharp divisions within the coalition, particularly between those who, like Allende, were in favour of a measured pace of reform, and those pressing for rapid, revolutionary change. The internal disunity led to a lack of coordination in implementing policy, and an irreversible slide towards political chaos. Making matters worse were the extremist far-left groups outside the government – notably the Revolutionary Left Movement, or **MIR** – which urged the workers to take reform into their own hands by seizing possession of the haciendas and factories where they worked.

Opposition to the government rose sharply during 1972, both from political parties outside the coalition (such as the Christian Democrats, who had previously supported Allende) and from widening sectors of the public. Panic was fuelled by the right-wing press and reinforced behind the scenes by the CIA, who, it later emerged, had been given a US$8 million budget with which to destabilize the Allende government. Strikes broke out across the country, culminating in the truckers' stoppage of October 1972, which virtually paralysed the economy. By 1973, with the country rocked by civil disorder, it was clear to all that the government could not survive for much longer.

The military coup

On the morning of September 11, 1973, tanks rolled through the capital and surrounded the presidential palace, La Moneda, marking the beginning of the **military coup** that Chile had been expecting for months. La Moneda was evacuated and Salvador Allende was offered a safe passage to exile. He refused, and in an emotional speech broadcast live on radio from the palace, vowed that he would never give up, and that he was ready to repay the loyalty of the Chilean people with his life. In this unique moment of history, citizens heard their president declare "I have faith in Chile and in its destiny. Other men will overcome this dark and bitter moment . . . You must go on, safe in the knowledge that sooner rather than later, the great avenues will open once more, and free men will march along them to create a better society . . . These are my last words, but I am sure that my sacrifice will not be in vain." Shortly afterwards, the signals were cut short, and jets began to drop their bombs. At the end of the day, Allende was found dead in the ruins of the palace, clutching a submachine gun, with which, it is widely believed, he had killed himself.

The Pinochet years

The coup was headed by a four-man junta of whom **General Augusto Pinochet**, chief of the army, quickly emerged as the dominant figure. Although Chile had seen military intervention in government affairs on two occasions in the past, these had been the exception to a highly constitutional norm. Nothing in the country's political history prepared its people for the brutality of this operation. In the days and weeks following the takeover, at least seven thousand people – journalists, politicians, socialists, trade union organizers and so on – were herded into the national football stadium, where many were executed, and still more were tortured. Curfews were imposed, the press was placed under the strict control of the junta, and military officers were sent in to take charge of factories, universities and other seats of socialist support. Before long,

Congress had been dissolved, opposition parties and trade unions banned, and thousands of Chileans had fled the country.

General Pinochet saw his mission – and it was one in which he was supported by a sizeable portion of the population – as being that of rescuing Chile from the Left and, by extension, from the economic and political chaos into which it had undoubtedly fallen. To achieve this, he planned not to hand the country over to a right-wing political party of his approval, but to take it into his own hands and rule it himself. His key strategy was to be the adoption of a radical **free-market economy**, which involved a complete reversal of Allende's policies and a drastic restructuring of government and society. In this he was influenced by a group of Chilean economists known as "the Chicago boys", who had carried out postgraduate studies at the University of Chicago, where they'd come into contact with the monetarist theories of Milton Friedman. Almost immediately, price controls were abolished, government expenditure was slashed, most state-owned companies were privatized, import tariffs were reduced, and attempts were made to liberalize investment and attract foreign capital.

Such measures would take time to work, and called for a period of intense austerity. Sure enough, unemployment soared, wages plummeted, industrial output dropped, and the lower and middle classes became significantly poorer. At the same time, as Pinochet strove to reduce the role of the state in society, social welfare became increasingly neglected, particularly health and education. By the late 1970s, the economy was showing signs of growth and inflation was finally beginning to drop – from an annual rate of 900 percent in 1973 to 65 percent in 1977 and down to a respectable 9.5 percent in 1981. Soon, there was talk of the Chilean "economic miracle" in international circles. The boom did not last, however, and in 1982, Chile found itself, along with much of Latin America, in the grip of a serious **debt crisis** which swept away the previous advances: the country was plunged into recession, with hundreds of private enterprises going bankrupt and unemployment rising to over 30 percent. It wasn't until the late 1980s that the economy recovered and Pinochet's free-market policies achieved the results he sought, with sustained growth, controlled inflation, booming, diversified exports and reduced unemployment. This prosperity, however, did not benefit all Chileans, and 49 percent of Chile's private wealth remained in the hands of 10 percent of its population.

Pinochet's free-market experiment had only been possible with the tools of ruthless repression at his disposal. His chief instrument was the secret police known as the **DINA**, which carried out surveillance on civilian (and even military) society, brutally silencing all opposition. Although the wholesale repression that followed the coup diminished in scale after the first year, regular "disappearances", torture and executions continued throughout Pinochet's regime. The regime was actively, if clandestinely, supported by the US, through the CIA, which even helped with the elimination of dissidents. In the absence of any organized political opposition, only the Catholic Church spoke out against the government's human rights violations, providing assistance and sanctuary to those who suffered, and vigilantly documenting all reports of abuse. Pinochet held the country in such a tight, personal grip – famously claiming "there is not a leaf that stirs in Chile without my knowing it" – that it doubtless became difficult for him to conceive of an end to his authority. The Constitution that he had drawn up in 1980 – ratified by a tightly controlled **plebiscite** – guaranteed him power until 1988, at which point the public would be given the chance to either accept military rule for another eight years, or else call for elections.

From the mid-1980s, **public protest** against Pinochet's regime began to be voiced, both in regular street demonstrations and with the reformation of political opposition parties (still officially banned). Open repression was stepped down as international attention became increasingly focused on the Chilean government's behaviour, and the US (a major source of foreign investment) made clear that it favoured a return to democracy. In this climate, the opposition parties were able to develop a united strategy in their efforts to oust the dictator. As the referendum in which Chile would decide whether or not to reject military rule drew closer, the opposition forces banded together to lead a highly professional and convincing "no" campaign. Pinochet remained convinced of his own victory, and with control of all media, and the intimidation tactics of a powerful police state at his disposal, it is easy to see why. But when the plebiscite took place on **October 5, 1988**, 55 percent of the nation voted "no" to continued military rule.

After sixteen years in power, the writing was on the wall for Pinochet's dictatorship. Much to everyone's surprise, he accepted his defeat without resistance and prepared to step down. But the handover system gave him one more year in power before democratic elections would be held – a year in which he hastily prepared **amnesty laws** that would protect both himself and the military from facing any charges of human rights abuses levied by the new government, and that would make his constitutional model extremely difficult to amend. A year later, on December 14, 1989, the Christian Democrat Patricio Aylwin, at the head of a seventeen-party centre-ground coalition called the **Concertación de los Partidos por la Democracia**, became Chile's first democratically elected president in seventeen years.

Return to democracy

The handover of power was smooth and handled with cautious goodwill on all sides, including the military. **Patricio Aylwin** was in the fortunate position of inheriting a robust economy and an optimistic public. Yet he faced serious challenges, including the need to channel substantial funds into those areas neglected by the previous regime while sustaining economic growth, and to address human rights abuses without antagonizing the military and endangering the transition to democracy.

Pinochet's **economic** model was barely contested, and was vigorously applied in an effort to promote "growth with equity" (the Concertación's electoral slogan). Foreign investment poured into the country and exports continued to rise, keeping economic growth at high levels and allowing Aylwin to divert resources into health and education. He was also felt to be making genuine efforts to alleviate the problems faced by the poorest members of society.

On the matter of **human rights** issues, progress was more difficult. One of the new government's first actions was the establishment of a **National Commission for Truth and Reconciliation** to investigate and document the abuses committed by the military regime. The commission's 1991 report confirmed 2279 executions, disappearances, and deaths caused by torture, and listed a further 641 suspected cases. But although compensation was paid to the families of the victims, the few attempts made to bring the perpetrators to justice were unsuccessful, owing to the protective **amnesty laws** passed by Pinochet before he relinquished power.

After a successful four-year term, the Concertación was in 1993 once again elected to power, headed by the Christian Democrat **Eduardo Frei** (son of the 1964–70 president). Frei's policies were essentially a continuation of his predecessors', with a firmer emphasis on tackling human rights issues and eradicating severe poverty. His success was mixed. His National Programme for Overcoming Poverty, established in 1994, was seen as inconsistent and ineffective. More progress was made on **human rights**, with courts finally willing to find ways of getting round Pinochet's amnesty laws. In 1995, there were breakthrough convictions of six former *carabineros*, two former DINA (secret police) agents, and most significantly, of General Manuel Contreras and Brigadier Pedro Espinoza, these last sentenced to life imprisonment in "Punta Peuco", a jail built purposely for high-profile human rights criminals.

In its last couple of years, Frei's government ran into unexpected problems. Firstly, the Asian economic crisis of 1998 had serious repercussions on the Chilean economy, hitting exports, foreign investment (much of which came from Southeast Asia) and the value of the peso, which has been sliding gradually ever since. At the same time, the unresolved tensions over lack of justice for Pinochet erupted afresh when the general retired from his position of commander-in-chief of the army in early 1998 but immediately took up a seat in Congress as life senator. Pinochet was dramatically thrust into the spotlight once more when he was arrested in a London hospital on October 16, 1998, following a request for his **extradition** to Spain to face charges of murder and torture. The arrest provoked strong reactions in Chile: families of Pinochet's victims rejoiced euphorically; supporters of the general were outraged, burning British flags in the streets; while the government, in a difficult position, denounced the arrest as an affront to national sovereignty and demanded Pinochet's immediate return to Chile – whereupon, they claimed, his alleged crimes would be dealt with in the Chilean courts.

After a protracted and complex legal battle, during which the British judiciary ruled in Pinochet's favour and against him, in April 1999 Britain's Home Secretary, **Jack Straw**, announced that proceedings could go ahead. They again got bogged down, this time over whether the former dictator was fit to stand trial, with the British minister holding the final decision.

The Lagos years

In December 1999, the first round of presidential elections left two frontrunners neck and neck in the second round: the Concentación's candidate, aocialist **Ricardo Lagos**, a former education minister under Aylwin who had famously voiced criticism of Pinochet in the late 1980s, and **Joaquín Lavín**, who had served under the general and was standing on a firmly right-wing platform. Lagos pulled off an eleventh-hour victory on January 16, 2000, beating his opponent narrowly – 51 percent to 49.

The **Pinochet affair** dogged the newly elected president and has repeatedly reared its ugly head since. Britain finally decided to send Pinochet back to Chile in early March 2000, just before Lagos was sworn in at La Moneda. There was an international outcry when he was welcomed back with pomp and circumstance by the armed forces, and Congress granted all former heads of state **lifelong immunity** from prosecution. Even Lagos expressed support for such a move, to quell any stirrings in the military. Yet the former dictator was stripped of his immunity in June and faced charges for kidnapping opponents before Christmas 2000. At the beginning of 2001 he was judged mentally fit for trial, and, at the end of January Chilean judge **Juan Guzmán** ordered Pinochet's house arrest. But within months the case fizzled out yet again, and in July 2001 all charges against Pinochet were dropped after a Santiago court decided he was, after all, unfit to stand trial. Nevertheless, like the former tyrant himself, the case would not lie down and die. Further appeals and counter appeals meant that the affair dragged on for one more year. Finally the country's Supreme Court ruled, in early July 2002, that Pinochet was indeed prevented from standing for trial on mental-health grounds. He responded by resigning as life senator from Chile's Congress and was reported as saying that he did so "with a clear conscience", unleashing a furore among his opponents.

Spectre-like, Pinochet returned to the fore amid a **financial scandal** in 2005. Though the ex-dictator had always claimed that, unlike many of his peers, his only interest was the wellbeing of his country and not of his pocket, it transpired that he and/or his relatives had creamed off tens of millions of dollars in murky wheeling and dealing and carefully stashed the laundered booty in US bank accounts, one of them at Riggs; cooperation with the US financial authorities revealed the existence of the funds, a very generous nest egg for his family. In February 2005, the Riggs Bank donated $8 million to a pension fund set up for the families of 3000 victims of human rights abuses under the general's regime. In June 2005 the courts decided that he was fit to stand trial to answer the corruption charges.

Human rights and the military regime continued to haunt the political arena. Several more cases resulted in prison sentences for violators, but the government controversially approved measures aimed at imposing a time limit on human rights investigations, which some claimed were dragging on excessively. In spectacular circumstances, former secret police chief **Manuel Contreras**, who had already served part of an earlier life sentence, was arrested in early 2005 on fresh charges – he allegedly tried to shoot the officers who went to his house to detain him. Another former officer, under investigation, preferred to turn his gun on himself, and his suicide threatened to destabilize the delicate relationship between the government and the military.

In the meantime the highly popular Lagos implemented an ambitious programme based on reforming the State. Lagos was determined to continue with his predecessors' overhaul of two main areas of social policy: **health and education**. Universal free medical care is the eventual goal but hospitals and other services, mostly in a pitiful state after years of neglect, have been improved. After compulsory schooling, shortened to the bare minimum by Pinochet, was dramatically lengthened, plans to recruit more teachers, improve their training and raise their salaries have been implemented. **Divorce** was finally legalized in late 2004 (leaving only Malta and the Philippines divorce-free), despite opposition by the Church, which has said it will do all it can to obstruct the new, democratically enacted law – but abortion remains utterly taboo. Infrastructure has been improved, government has been modernized, pension schemes have become more efficient and **welfare benefits** increased substantially, though they remain low by developed-country standards. A stronger economy than in most South American countries has enabled these social reforms to take place, but there are concerns that its strength relies too much on a few primary industries, such as copper mining, salmon farming and the production of fresh fruit for export; manufacturing and service industries, with the exception of tourism, remain weak. **Economic growth** dropped to 5 percent in mid-2005, while unemployment rose to over 7 per cent of the active population.

Lagos also tried to tackle the thorny issue of **indigenous peoples' rights**, handing back large tracts of land to Mapuches and others early on in his presidency. This backfired somewhat, with emboldened *indígenas* demanding even more of their land back, resulting in some ugly clashes with the police in early 2002, when demonstrators tried to block the construction of a new road through land claimed by Mapuches; there have been several similar incidents in recent years.

The closely related issue of the **environment** has also proved a difficult dragon to slay. In a country where so much income is generated by mining and logging, it is not easy to reconcile ecological concerns – an issue raised by indigenous peoples, who feel their heritage is being destroyed – with the desire to produce and export, in the interest of economic prosperity. An environmentally disastrous **fire in the Torres del Paine** national park in early 2005 (see box, p.520), which devastated hundreds of hectares of fragile ecosystems, drew attention to the authorities' unpreparedness to deal with such catastrophes. An independent study by a US university published in early 2005 condemned Chile as one of the region's worst performers in the field of **environmental protection**, as an increasingly investigative media uncovered stories of irreversible pollution resulting from unrestricted economic activities, mostly mining and forestry.

International relations, in particular with the country's neighbours, were decidedly rocky as Lagos headed towards the end of his term of office. His dismissive remarks plus chauvinistic Chilean media coverage following the arrest of two young Chileans, accused of defacing an ancient wall in the Incan city of Cusco, did little to smooth relations with **Peru**, Chile's traditional rival to the north. Chile's refusal to negotiate a guaranteed ocean access for landlocked **Bolivia** further soured relations with another long-time foe. And **Argentina's** decision to prioritize its domestic gas demand, at the risk of cutting supplies to Chile, increased trans-Andean tensions. They had previously been fuelled by remarks made by Chilean Foreign Minister, Ignacio Walker, suggesting that Argentina's ruling Peronists were anti-democratic – he was given a book on the history of Perón by his Argentine opposite number during an official visit to Buenos Aires. In something of a foreign policy victory for Santiago, but by no means an easy one, **José Miguel Insulza**, a former Chilean Interior Minister, was elected Head of the 34-country Organization of American States (OAS) in May 2005, despite opposition from the United States, which had backed a more pro-Washington Mexican candidate for the post.

Chile today

Since March 2006, Chile has had a woman president, socialist **Michelle Bachelet,** elected by a comfortable margin in the second-round run-off on January 15 of that year. She initially beat Santiago mayor Joaquín Lavín – of the hard right Independent Democratic Union – and the marginal Communist candidate, in the first-round ballot at the end of 2005. Then she stood against charismatic businessman, Sebastián Piñera, of the centre right National Renewal Party, in the *balotaje* (decisive second round). Piñera, who is the billionaire owner of the TV channel Chilevisión, and president of LAN, the national airline, has been likened to Italy's Silvio Berlusconi – not least by Lavín supporters, furious at Piñera's decision to run and split the right-wing vote. Bachelet, a physician, went into exile in Australia and East Germany in the 1970s after her father, a moderate Air Force general, was assassinated under Pinochet. In her victory speech she said that a **feminine touch** was needed to smooth international relations and promised to work for greater friendship between Chile and its neighbours, particularly Argentina.

Her election as Chile's first female Head of State also makes her the first woman to be directly and democratically elected in South American history. Indeed, one of outgoing President Lagos' stated aims had been to reduce the acute **gender inequality** in the country, and he appointed Chile's first female ministers for defence (Bachelet herself) and foreign affairs (her erstwhile rival in the presidential race, Soledad Alvear). The number of women in the principal judicial bodies has also gone up while the House of Deputies had two woman Speakers at the beginning of the millennium, right-of-centre Adriana Muñoz, and left-winger Isabel Allende Bussi (not to be confused with her namesake, the famous novelist and niece of Salvador Allende).

Criticized during the campaign for her vague policies and indecision, Bachelet starts her presidency with a strong mandate, a supportive parliament and many expectations. The fact that she was detained and tortured, along with her mother, in the early Pinochet years before her family was allowed to leave the country, enhanced her popularity on the Left; but her **progressive stance** on delicate issues such as divorce, human rights and religion (she is a professed agnostic) and the fact that she is separated from her husband and did not marry the father of her third child put off many traditional voters even in her own camp. That said she is staunchly opposed to abortion and gay marriage (but not to some kind of official recognition of same-sex couples).

Chile is, after all, an undeniably conservative country and despite years of sustained economic growth, the social divide is wider than ever, with an impoverished working class, a precarious middle class and an embittered but ultra-wealthy entrepreneurial class. That a country with such traditional politics has elected a woman to its highest office may be a glimmer of hope for its future, and perhaps other countries will now look to it as a model.

Landscape and the environment

One of South America's smaller countries, Chile is roughly the same size as France and Britain combined – but stretched over the equivalent distance of Vancouver to Panama. This sliver of land, on average just 180km across, spans 4350km from the desert of the north to the subantarctic ice-fields in the south, and encompasses almost every kind of natural habitat along the way.

Geography

Geographically, Chile is divided into a number of latitudinal **zones**, each of which shows clear differences in terms of climate, vegetation and fauna. These zones only tell part of the story, though, with Chile's three principal landforms – the Andes, the central depression and the coastal range, running the length of the country – all having a significant impact on the local ecology. The **Andes**, in particular, straddles all of Chile's disparate regions. Characterized by precipitous slopes with ravines cut deep into the rock, at points the range acts as a great, impenetrable wall dividing Chile from neighbouring Argentina and Bolivia. Scores of **volcanoes**, many topping 6000m, line these borders, where episodic eruptions and seismic activity are everyday realities. The country's highest peak, Ojos de Salado (6893m), is also the world's highest active volcano; Aconcagua (6959m), the globe's tallest peak outside the Himalayas, lies a few kilometres over the Argentine border.

In the far north, the **Norte Grande** region stretches from the Peruvian border over 1000km south to the Copiapó river valley. Covering the central depression between the Andes and the coastal range lies the **Atacama Desert**, thought to be the driest place on earth. Surprisingly, the desert is unusually temperate, due to the moderating influence of the Humboldt Current, a cold-water sea current just off the coast. While thick fog banks, known as *camanchaca*, accumulate along the coast where the cold water meets the warm air, a high-pressure zone prevents the cloud from producing rain and moving inland.

A search for wildlife is a pretty fruitless activity in these barren northern wastes. The frustrated ornithologist A.W. Johnson remarked that the desert was "without doubt one of the most completely arid and utterly lifeless areas in the whole world". It's a very different story, however, up in the Andes bordering the Atacama, where a high plateau known as the **altiplano** is home to a diverse wildlife population and an otherworldly landscape of volcanoes, lakes and salt flats.

The semi-arid **Norte Chico**, bounded roughly by the Copiapó Valley and the Aconcagua Valley, just north of Santiago, forms a transitional zone, where the inhospitable northern desert gives way to scrubland and eventually forests further south, as precipitation levels increase. The heat of the sun here is tempered by air humidity, making the land suitable for irrigation farming. The crops of tobacco and cotton that predominated in the colonial era have since been replaced by more lucrative exotic fruits, such as papaya and *cherimoya*.

Throughout the north mining has also long been prevalent, thanks to the high levels of nitrates, copper, silver and other minerals in the soil.

Beyond Santiago, the region known as the **Central Valley** extends south to the Bío Bío River. Mineral-rich earth coupled with warm dry summers and short humid winters have provided ideal conditions here for growing grapes, peaches, pears, plums, mangoes, melons and apricots. As the country's primary agricultural zone, as well as a major centre of industry, it is no surprise that this region is home to around 80 percent of the country's population, almost half based in the capital.

Towards the southern end of the Central Valley, forests signal a marked increase in precipitation levels. Systematic **afforestation**, begun over a hundred years ago in Arauco province, has seen the introduction of a variety of foreign trees, such as eucalyptus and Australian myrrh. No species has flourished as well as the radiata pine, however, which far exceeded the rate of development normal in its native California; concern is mounting that its success is damaging Chile's fragile endemic forest habitats.

In the **Lake District**, between Temuco and Puerto Montt, precipitation reaches 2300mm a year, allowing luxuriant native forests to predominate over the rolling foothills of the coastal range. To the east, azure lakes, remnants of the last glacial age, are backed by conical, snowcapped **volcanoes**. Amongst the many volcanoes active, both Villarrica and Llaima have erupted ten times in the last hundred years.

Beyond Puerto Montt, the central depression submerges into the sea, while the tops of the coastal mountains nudge through the water in a mosaic of **islands** and **fjords**. It is here, in this splintered and remote region, that continental Chile finally runs out of dry land: the Carretera Austral, the highway that runs south from Puerto Montt, is cut short after 1000km by two massive ice fields, the largest in the southern hemisphere outside Antarctica. **Southern Patagonia** is a mostly inhospitable place, with continual westerly winds roaring off the sea and dumping up to seven metres of snow, sleet, hail and rain on the western slopes every year. Even so, the glaciated scenery, with its perfect U-shaped valleys and rugged mountains, has an indisputable grandeur. In stark contrast, the monotonous grasslands of the Patagonian pampa, which lies in the rain shadow on the eastern side of the Andes, describe the beginning of a quite different habitat.

Tierra del Fuego ("Land of Fire") is an archipelago separated from mainland Chile by the Magellan Strait. Mountains and forests dominate the south of the region, while the north hosts little more than windswept grasses. From Cape Horn, South America's southernmost point, Antarctica is a mere 1000km away.

Flora

Extraordinary diversity of altitude, latitude and precipitation inevitably leads to an extraordinary diversity of flora. Only humid tropical forest fails to feature in Chile's rich and varied ecology. The tropical area in the far north is stricken with aridity too severe to support most plant life, except at higher altitudes, where **xerophytes** ("dry growers"), such as **cacti**, begin to appear. Ninety percent of Chile's vascular plants are from the cactus family, many of them endemic and endangered. On the altiplano, **tough grasses** and **brush** associated with minimal rainfall support the herds of grazing alpaca.

△ Chilean palms

Moving south towards Central Chile, where the climate is more balanced and water less scarce, **sclerophyllous** ("rigid leaf") shrubs and trees feature leathery leaves that help them retain water. As rainfall increases towards the south, these plants begin to blend with **temperate rainforests**. In the heavily populated areas of this central region, such woodlands have suffered widespread deforestation as land has been cleared for farming and housing, and only patches remain. In Parque Nacional La Campana near Santiago, for example, stands the last forest of endangered **Chilean palm** (*Jubaea chilensis*), sole reminder of a time when millions of the trees covered the area, favoured as they were for the flavour of their sap.

Further south the **temperate rainforests** have fared a little better, constituting almost a quarter of this type of habitat worldwide. Over 95 percent of the fifty tree species found here are endemic, including the **araucaria** (*Araucaria araucana*), known in English as the **monkey puzzle**, Chile's national tree, and rare **southern beeches** (*Nothofagus*) – principally *coïgue*, *ñire*, *raulí* and *lenga* – which vie for sunlight, towering up to 40m into the air to break clear of the canopy. The **alerce**, or **Chilean false larch** (*Fitzroya cupressoides*), a relative of the North American sequoia, takes several hundred years to reach maturity and can live for 4000 years, providing the loggers don't get there first. The tree is best seen in the areas around Puerto Montt.

In Chilean Patagonia, **evergreen beeches** (*Nothofagus betuloides*) grow in the sheltered areas bordering the great fields of ice, while their **deciduous** cousins *Nothofagus pumilio* and *antarctica* prefer the drier eastern flanks of the Andes. Where the canopy is broken, dazzling scarlet *embothrium*, yellow *berberis* bedecked with mauve berries, and deep-red *Pernettya* emblazon the ground. Rare **orchids** and pink **oxalis** interweave in a tapestry of colour. Such brilliant displays are impossible on the coastal Magellanic **moorland**, where high levels of precipitation drown all but the sphagnum **bog** communities and **dwarf shrubs**. Here, the wind-beaten **Magellanic gunnera** grows only a few centimetres high, a tiny fraction of what its relatives are capable of in the Valdivian rainforest. Meanwhile, the rain shadow effect on the eastern Patagonian steppe supports little more than coarse tussocks of *festuca* grasses.

Environmental Issues

The slow destruction of Chile's environment was set in motion by the Spanish in the sixteenth century, though it wasn't until the early twentieth century, with widespread settlement and increased industrialization, that the scale reached damaging levels. Today, although Chile has suffered less environmental degradation than most other countries with comparable resources, there are few habitats that have not been affected in some way by human activity, and it's debatable whether the government is prepared to prioritize future protection over financial exploitation.

There was little interest in environmental issues in Chile until large-scale disruption caused by the appalling **smog in Santiago**, considered by Greenpeace to be the third most polluted city in Latin America, mobilized public concern. Most years the capital's schools are suspended for days on end and people are warned to stay indoors as a dense cloud of toxic gases hangs over the capital, caught between the two surrounding mountain ranges. The problem is worsened in dry weather, when the concentration of contaminated air is not dissolved by rain. Pressure from the urban middle class has forced the government to introduce (many say weak) measures to lessen air pollution in Santiago and has encouraged politicians to include environmental elements to their policies.

The most important new **environmental law**, following a guarantee in the 1980 Constitution that all Chileans have "the right to live in an environment free of pollution", is the Environmental Act of 1994, which has standardized procedures for assessing environmental damage, while encouraging public involvement by allowing citizens to bring charges against violators, even if they have not been directly affected by them. One successful application of this new law occurred in 1997, when the Chilean Supreme Court overturned a government-approved project involving the logging for woodchips of centuries-old, endangered forests of native lenga, a cherry-like beech found in the Tierra del Fuego.

Chile's precious **temperate rainforests** have been threatened for many years by intensive logging and the introduction of harmful foreign species, with large tracts razed in the free-for-all scramble to colonize remote areas. The worst damage occurred in the prewar years, but illegal clearance is still common today. The alerce, an evergreen with a life span of 4000 years, has been a target of international campaigning as it continues to be logged because of the high commercial value of its wood, despite a law passed in 1976 making it illegal to cut live alerces. Yet landowners burn the trees or strip their bark to kill them first, thus evading the hands of the law. Many thousands of hectares of alerce forest are wiped out in this manner every year.

Meanwhile in the central regions native trees have been wiped out to make space for the commercial planting of more profitable foreign species. In many areas the practice has left only islands of indigenous forest in an ocean of introduced eucalyptus and radiata pine. The result is genetic isolation of both flora and fauna, leaving many mammals with distinct ecological needs imprisoned in small pockets of native woodland. The few thin strips that connect such pockets are the only way for many species to maintain communication with the rest of their population. If these corridors are destroyed, countless endemic organisms face extinction.

In the north **mining** is a major cause of environmental concern. Chuquicamata, near Antofagasta, is the biggest open-pit copper mine in the world and

The El Niño effect

Nature's footnote to the end of the millennium, the **1997–98 El Niño** wreaked havoc with global climate patterns and brought chaos to the world. In parts of Chile, Peru and Ecuador, floods and landslides engulfed people and animals, houses, farms and factories, while torrents swept away bridges, roads and railways. Elsewhere, severe droughts scorched the earth, drying up forests and bushland and creating the tinderbox conditions that sparked off raging fires. Clouds of poisonous smoke billowed into the atmosphere, affecting 70 million people in Southeast Asia, while millions of others risked starvation following widespread crop failure. As the Pacific countries affected by El Niño picked up the pieces, conservative estimates of the cost of reparation put it at around US$20 billion.

In Chile, **flooding** was the worst it had been for a decade, as 80,000 people were made homeless in June 1998 alone. The warm coastal water associated with El Niño drove fish stocks to cooler places, crippling the fishing industry and killing millions of marine animals. But while some watched their crops and livestock drown, the rains also filled irrigation basins that had been at a critically low level for years, and water surges saved the hydroelectric companies from having to ration their power output. In the Atacama Desert, freak rainfall woke up the barren soil, causing it to burst into blossom.

The El Niño phenomenon is no new thing. Records document such events over 400 years ago, but it was only in the 1960s that the Norwegian meteorologist Jacob Bjerknes identified the processes that lead to such an event. He saw that the El Niño (meaning "the Little Boy" or "the Christ Child", a name given by Peruvian fishermen to the body of warm water that would arrive around Christmas) was intimately connected to extremes in the so-called **Southern Oscillation**, a feature where atmospheric pressure between the eastern equatorial Pacific and the Indo-Australian areas behaves as a seesaw, one rising as the other falls.

In "normal" years easterly trade winds blow west across the Pacific, pushing warm surface water towards Indonesia, Australia and the Philippines, where the water becomes about 8°C warmer and about 50cm higher than on the other side of the ocean. In the east, the displacement of the sea allows cold, nutrient-rich water, known as the Humboldt or Peru Current, to swell up from the depths along the coast of South America, providing food for countless marine and bird species.

An El Niño event occurs when the trade winds fall off and the layer of warm water in the west laps back across the ocean, warming up the east Pacific and cooling the west. Consequently, air temperatures across the Pacific begin to even out, tipping the balance of the atmospheric pressure seesaw, which further reduces the strength of the trade winds. Thus the process is enhanced, as warm water continues to build up in the eastern Pacific, bringing with it abnormal amounts of rainfall to coastal South America, while completely starving other areas of precipitation. The warm water also forces the cold Humboldt Current and its microorganisms to deeper levels, effectively removing a vital link in the marine food chain, killing innumerable fish, sea birds and mammals. Meanwhile, the upset in the Southern Oscillation disturbs weather systems all around the world, resulting in severe and unexpected weather.

Since 1980 or so, El Niño-Southern Oscillation (ENSO) events seem to have become stronger, longer and more frequent, leading many to suggest that human activity, such as the warming of the earth's atmosphere through the greenhouse effect, could well be having an influence. If this is true, failure to cut emissions of greenhouse gases may in the end cost the lives and livelihoods of millions of people across the world.

A relatively mild El Niño in early 2002 meant that while the ski season was one of the best in the last ten years, torrential rains in central Chile left 50,000 people homeless and killed nine.

C

continues to grow. Now visible from space, the giant pit threatens to swallow up the town that grew with it, as 600,000 tons of rock are dug up every day, spewing arsenic-rich dust into the air. Plans are underway to move all residents of Chuquicamata to Calama by the end of 2006. The plume from the smelting works carries 200km to San Pedro de Atacama, a pre-colonial village in the east. The country's mines consume vast quantities of water, often contaminating it in the process. In tandem with agricultural irrigation, reckless water usage is taking its toll on wildlife, as animals find the search for drinking places increasingly difficult. Even the human population has been put out, relying in some northern villages on an ingenious invention that turns fog into drinking water.

Overexploitation of the land and sea have brought further problems. Incompetent or negligent farming, either through overgrazing or the clearing of vegetation, has resulted in extensive **desertification**, particularly in the north. Meanwhile, careless practices in the fishing industry are upsetting the fragile balance of Chile's **marine life**. A leaked government report shows that some fish stocks were depleted by as much as 96 percent between 1985 and 1993.

On a global level, many believe human-induced climate change to be a leading cause of the **El Niño phenomenon**, which has badly damaged Chile's fisheries, agriculture and marine species (see box, p.613). Moreover, the expansion of the hole in the ozone layer over Antarctica has put many people, especially in Patagonia, on guard against the harmful ultraviolet rays that seep through it.

Chile has been more effective than most Latin American countries in its opposition to the damage brought about by the excesses of unfettered capitalism, and awareness of the delicacy of the country's habitats and its unique species is growing. The Lagos government seemed to take ecological issues very seriously. However, environmentalists continue to bemoan the lack of concerted pressure, claiming that many merely respond occasionally and emotionally to images churned out in the media rather than pushing consistently for action and reform.

Chilean music: Nueva Canción

Chile has produced a wide range of music genres, from cueca to bolero, but none has been so important and influential as Nueva Canción, the "New Song" movement that developed in Chile in the 1960s, along with parallel movements in Argentina, Uruguay and also Cuba. A music rooted in the guitar traditions of the troubadour, the songs could be love lyric or chronicle, lament or call to action, and, as such, they have played a part in Latin America's political and cultural struggles. In Chile, the great singer-songwriter Víctor Jara was murdered for his art by Pinochet's thugs, while groups like Inti Illimani were forced into exile. In an extract taken from the *Rough Guide to World Music*, Jan Fairley looks at the history and legacy of this music of "guitar as gun".

Latin America's revolutionary politics have found expression in many of the continent's musics, but never more directly than in **nueva canción**. This "new song" emerged in the 1960s in Argentina and Chile, and over the next three decades it fulfilled an important role in countries from Uruguay to Nicaragua, and (in a different relationship to government) across the Caribbean in Cuba. It was brought to international attention, above all, through the lyrical songs of Chilean theatre director and singer-songwriter Víctor Jara, who was murdered by the military in Chile during the 1973 coup d'etat.

Pity the singer . . .

Pity the singer who doesn't risk his guitar and himself ... who never knew that we were the seed that today is life.

Cuban **Pablo Milanés** *"Pobre del cantor"*

Nueva canción as a movement spans a period of over thirty years, from the early 1960s, when its musicians became part of the political struggle to bring about change and reform in their own countries. As a result of their activities, many of their number were arrested or forced into exile by dictatorships which through murder, torture and disappearance wiped out so much of a generation. The sense of a movement grew as the musicians involved met one another at festivals in Cuba, Nicaragua, Peru, Mexico, Argentina and Brazil, visited each others' countries, and occasionally sang each others' songs. At the end of the 1990s, with the return to democracy on the continent, the singers continued to pursue their careers in different ways, while maintaining long-term friendships and exchanges.

The 1960s was a time of politics and idealism in South America – far more so than in Europe or North America. There was a stark challenge presented by the continent's obvious inequalities, its inherited power and wealth, its corrupt regimes, and by the denial of literacy and education to much of the population. It is within this context that nueva canción singers and writers must be understood. With voice and guitar, they composed songs of their own hopes and experiences in places where many of those involved in struggles for change regularly met and socialized.

It is a music that is now, in some ways, out of date: the revolutionary past, the 1960s rhetoric of guitar as gun and song as bullet. Yet the songs – poems written to be performed – are classic expressions of the years of hope and struggle for change, their beauty and truth later nurturing those suffering under dictatorship, and those forced into exile. They are still known by heart by audiences throughout the continent and exile communities in Europe.

Nueva canción was an expression of politics in its widest sense. It was not "protest song" as such. The musicians involved were not card-carrying members of any international organization and were often independent of political parties – although in the early 1970s the Chilean musicians were closely linked with the Popular Unity government of Salvador Allende, the first socialist president and government to be legitimately elected through the ballot box.

What linked these and other musicians of the movement was an ethical stance – a commitment to improve conditions for the majority of people in Latin America. To that end they sang not only in concerts and clubs but in factories, in shanty towns, community centres and at political meetings and street demonstrations. People in protest the world over have joined in the Chilean street anthems *El Pueblo Unido Jamàs Sera Vencido* (The People United Will Never Be Defeated) and *Venceremos* (We Will Win).

Yupanqui and Violeta Parra

The roots of the nueva canción movement lie in the work of two key figures, whose music bridged rural and urban life and culture in the 1940s and 50s: the Argentine **Atahualpa Yupanqui** (1908–1992) and the Chilean **Violeta Parra** (1917–1967). Each had a passionate interest in his or her nation's rural musical traditions, which had both an Iberian and Amerindian sensibility. Their work was in some respects paralleled by the Cuban Carlos Puebla.

Atahualpa Yupanqui, spent much of his early life travelling around Argentina, collecting popular songs from itinerant *payadores* (improvising poets, Chile's indigenous rappers) and folk singers in rural areas. He also wrote his own songs, and during a long career introduced a new integrity to Argentine folk music – and an assertive political outlook which ultimately forced him into exile in Paris.

Violeta Parra's career in Chile mirrored that of Yupanqui. She travelled extensively, singing with and collecting songs from old *payadores* and preserved and popularized them through radio broadcasts and records. She also composed new material based on these rural song traditions, creating a model and repertoire for what became nueva canción. Her songs celebrated the rural and regional, the music of the peasant, the land-worker and the marginalized migrant.

Musically, Parra was also significant in her popularization of **Andean or Amerindian instruments** – the armadillo-shelled *charango*, the *quena* (bamboo flute) and panpipes, and in her enthusiasm for the **French chanson** tradition. She spent time in Paris in the 1960s with her children Angel and Isabel, where they met Yupanqui, Edith Piaf and the flautist Gilbert Favre, who was to found the influential Andean band, Los Jaivas, and with whom Violeta fell in love. Returning to Buenos Aires, she performed in a tent in the district of La Reina, which came to be called the Carpa de La Reina (The Queen's Tent). However, with a long history of depression, she committed suicide in 1967.

Parra left behind a legacy of exquisite songs, many of them with a wry sense of humour, including the unparalleled *Gracias a la vida* (Thanks to life), later covered by Joan Baez and a host of others. Even her love songs seem informed by an awareness of poverty and injustice, while direct pieces like *Qué dirà el Santo Padre?* (What does the Sainted Pope Say?) highlighted the Church's responsibility to take action. As Parra wrote (in the form she often used in her songs) in her autobiography:

I sing to the Chilean people
if I have something to say
I don't take up the guitar
to win applause
I sing of the difference there is
between what is certain
and what is false
otherwise I don't sing.

The movement takes off

Nueva canción emerged as a real force in the mid-1960s, when various governments on the continent were trying to effect democratic social change. The search for a Latin American cultural identity became a spontaneous part of this wider struggle for self-determination, and music was a part of the process.

The first crystallization of a nueva canción ideal in Chile emerged with the opening of a crucial new folk club. This was and is the legendary crucible of nueva canción, the **Peña de los Parra**, which **Angel and Isabel Parra**, inspired by the Paris *chanson* nightclubs, opened in downtown Santiago in 1965. Among the regular singer-songwriters who performed here were Víctor Jara and Patricio Manns. Their audiences, in the politically charged and optimistic period prior to the election of Allende's government, were enthusiastic activists and fellow musicians.

Víctor Jara

The great singer-songwriter and theatre director **Víctor Jara** took nueva canción onto a world stage. His songs, and his life, continue to reverberate, and he has been recorded by rock singers like Sting, Bruce Springsteen, Peter Gabriel and Jackson Brown, and (memorably) by the British singer Robert Wyatt. All have been moved by Jara's story and inspired by his example.

Jara was born into a rural family who came to live in a shanty-town on the barren outskirts of Santiago when Víctor's father died; he was just eleven. His mother sang as a *cantora* for births, marriages and deaths, keeping her family alive by running a food-stall in the main Santiago market. It was from his mother and her work that Jara gained his intuitive knowledge of Chilean guitar and singing styles.

He began performing his songs in the early 1960s and from the beginning caused a furore. During the government of Eduardo Frei, for example, his playful version of a traditional piece, *La Beata* – a send-up of the desires of a nun – was banned, as was his accusatory *Preguntas por Puerto Montt* (Questions for Puerto Montt), which accused the minister of the interior of the massacre of poor landless peasants in the south of Chile. Working with Isabel Parra and the group

△ Víctor Jarra

Huamari, Jara went on to create a sequence of songs called *La Población*, based on the history and life of Santiago's shanty-town communities. His great gift was a deceptively simple and direct style applied to whatever he did.

One of his best-loved songs, *Te recuerdo Amanda* (I remember you Amanda), is a good example of the simplicity of his craft. A hauntingly under-stated love song, it tells the story of a girl who goes to meet her man, Manuel, at the factory gates; he never appears because of an "accident", and Amanda waits in vain. In many of his songs, Jara subtly interwove allusions to his own life with the experiences of other ordinary people – Amanda and Manuel were the names of his parents.

Jara's influence was immense, both on nueva canción singers and the Andean-oriented groups like **Inti Illimani** and **Quilapayún** (see p.620), whom he worked with often, encouraging them to forge their own new performance styles. Enormously popular and fun-loving, he was nevertheless clear about his role as a singer: "The authentic revolutionary should be behind the guitar, so that the guitar becomes an instrument of struggle, so that it can also shoot like a gun." As he sang in 1972 in his song *Manifiesto*, a tender serenade which with hindsight has been seen as his testimony, "I don't sing just for love of singing, but for the statements made by my guitar, honest, its heart of earth, like the dove it goes flying. . . Song sung by a man who will die singing, truthfully singing his song".

Like many Chilean musicians, Jara was deeply involved with the Unidad Popular government of Salvador Allende, who in 1970, following his election, had appeared on an open-air stage in Santiago surrounded by musicians under a banner saying "There can be no revolution without song". Three years later, on September 11, 1973 – along with hundreds of others who had legitimately supported the government – Jara was arrested by the military and taken to the same downtown stadium in which he had won the First Festival of New Chilean Song in 1969. Tortured, his hands and wrists broken, his body was found with five others, riddled with machine-gun bullets, dumped alongside a wall of the Metropolitan Cemetery; his face was later recognized amongst a pile of uniden-tified bodies in one of the Santiago mortuaries by a worker. He was just 35.

Jara left behind a song composed during the final hours of his life, written down and remembered by those who were with him at the end, called as a

Plegaria un Labrador (Prayer to a Labourer)

Stand up and look at the mountain
From where the wind comes, the sun and the water
You who direct the courses of the rivers
You who have sown the flight of your soul
Stand up and look at your hands
So as to grow
Clasp your brother's, in your own
Together we will move united by blood
Today is the time that can become tomorrow

Deliver us from the one who dominates us
through misery
Bring to us your reign of justice and equality
Blow like the wind the flower of the canyon
Clean like fire the barrel of my gun
Let your will at last come about here on earth
Give to us your strength and valour so as to fight
Blow like the wind the flower of the canyon
Clean like fire the barrel of my gun

Stand up and look at your hands
So as to grow
Clasp your brother's, in your own
Together we will move united by blood
Now and in the hour of our death
Amen.

Víctor Jara

poem of testimony *Estadio Chile* (Chile Stadium). It was later set a cappella to music as *Ay canto, que mal me sales*, by his friend and colleague Isabel Parra.

Exiles and Andean sounds

After Pinochet's coup d'état anything remotely associated with the Allende government and its values came under censorship, including books and records, whose possession could be cause for arrest. The junta issued warnings to musicians and folklorists that it would be unwise for them to play nueva canción, or indeed any of the Andean instruments associated with its sound – *charangos*, panpipes and *quenas*.

It was not exactly a ban but it was menacing enough to force the scene well underground – and abroad, where many Chilean musicians lived out the junta years in exile. Their numbers included the groups Inti Illimani and Quilapayún and later Illapu (see p.622), Sergio Ortega, Patricio Manns, Isabel and Angel Parra, and Patricio Castillo. They were not the only Latin Americans forced from their country. Other **musician exiles** of the 1970s included Brazilian MPB singers Chico Buarque, Caetano Veloso and Gilberto Gil; Uruguay's nueva canción singer Daniel Viglietti; and Argentina's Mercedes Sosa.

In Chile, the first acts of musical defiance took place behind church walls, where a group of musicians who called themselves **Barroco Andino** started to play baroque music with Andean instruments within months of the coup.

It was a brave act, for the use of Andean or Amerindian instruments and culture was instinctively linked with the nueva canción movement. Chilean groups like **Quilapayún** and **Inti Illimani** wore the traditional ponchos of the peasant and played Andean instruments such as panpipes, bamboo flutes and the *charango*, and the maracas and shakers of Central America and the Caribbean. That these were the instruments of the communities who had managed

C

CONTEXTS | Chilean music: Nueva Canción

Discography

Nueva canción has had a raw deal on **CD** – it peaked in the decades before shiny discs – and for many classics, you'll need to search second-hand stores for vinyl. If you travel to Chile, you can also obtain **songbooks** for the music of Víctor Jara (the Fundación Víctor Jara publish his complete works), while most other songs of the period are featured in *Clásicos de la Música Popular Chilena Vol 11 1960–1973* (Ediciones Universidad Católica de Chile).

Compilations
Music of the Andes (Hemisphere EMI, UK).
Despite the title, this is essentially a nueva canción disc, with key Chilean groups Inti Illimani, Quilapayún and Illapu to the fore. There is also an instrumental recording of *Tinku* attributed to Víctor Jara.

Artists
Illapu
Illapu, with a track record stretching back over 25 years, and a big following in Chile, play Andean instruments – panpipes, *quenas* and *charangos* – along with saxophones, electric bass and Caribbean percussion. Their music is rooted in the north of the country where most of the band hails from.
Sereno (EMI, UK).
This enjoyable collection gives a pretty good idea of what Illapu have got up to over the years and includes strongly folkloric material, as well as dance pieces influenced by salsa, romantic ballads and the earlier styles of vocal harmony.

Inti Illimani
The foremost Chilean "new song" group, who began as students in 1967, bringing the Andean sound to Europe through their thousands of concerts in exile, and taking European influences back home again in the late 1980s. The original band, together for thirty years, featured the glorious-voiced José Séves.
Lejan'a (Xenophile, US).
The focus is on Andean themes in this celebration of their thirtieth anniversary and their original inspiration.
Arriesgaré la piel (Xenophile, US).
A celebration of the music the Intis grew up with, from creole-style tunes to Chilean *cuecas*, most lyrics by Patricio Manns with music by Salinas. This was the final album to be made with the core of the original band before Séves left.
Grandes Exitos (EMI, Chile).
A compilation of seventeen songs and instrumental pieces taken from the band's thirty-year history.

Quilapayún
This key Chilean new-song group worked closely in their early years with Víctor Jara and in 1973 – the year of the coup – they split into multiple groups in order to get

somehow to survive slavery, resist colonialism and its aftermath had a powerful symbolism. Both the "los Intis" and "los Quilas", as they became familiarly known, worked closely with Víctor Jara and also with popular classical composers Sergio Ortega and Luis Advis.

In 1973 both groups travelled to Europe as official cultural ambassadors of the Allende government, actively seeking support from governments in Europe at a time when the country was more or less besieged economically by a North American blockade, its economy being undermined by CIA activity. On September 11 when General Pinochet led the coup d'état in which Salvador

their message across on as many stages as possible. They co-authored, with Sergio Ortega, the street anthem *El Pueblo Unido Jamàs Sera Vencido* (the People United Will Never Be Defeated). Although they disbanded in the late 1990s, their influence lives on.

Santa Mar'a de Iquique (Dom Disque, France).
Chilean composer Luis Advis's ground-breaking Cantata, composed for Quilapaýun, tells the emblematic and heroic tale of the murder of unarmed nitrate workers and their families in 1907.

Víctor Jara
The leading singer-songwriter of his generation, Víctor Jara was murdered in his prime by Pinochet's forces in September 1973. His legacy is an extraordinary songbook, which can be heard in his original versions, as well as a host of Latin and Western covers.

Manifesto (Castle, UK).
Reissued to mark the 25th anniversary of his death, this is a key disc of nueva canción, with *Te recuerdo Amanda*, *Canto libre*, *La Plegaria a un labrador* and *Ay canto*, the final poem written in the Estadio Chile, before his death. Includes Spanish lyrics and English translations.

Vientos del Pueblo (Monitor, US).
A generous 22-song compilation that includes most of the Jara milestones, including *Te recuerdo Amanda* and *Preguntas por Puerto Montt*, plus the wonderful revolutionary romp of *A Cochabamba me voy*. Quilapaýun provide backing on half the album.

Víctor Jara Complete (Plane, Germany).
This four-CD box is the definitive Jara, featuring material from eight original LPs. Plane have also released an excellent single disc selection of highlights.

La Población (Alerce, Chile).
Classic Jara: a project involving other musicians, but including most of all the lives and experiences of those celebrated here, who lived in various shanty towns (*poblaciones*) including the one where Jara himself grew up.

Violeta Parra
One of South America's most significant folklorists and composers, Violeta Parra collected fragments of folklore from singers, teaching them to the next generation and influencing them with her own excellent compositions. Parra's songs have also been superbly recorded by Argentinian Mercedes Sosa.

Canto a mi América (Auvidis, France).
An excellent introduction to Parra's seminal songs.

Las Ultimas composiciones (Alerce, Chile).
A reissue of Parra's 1965 release which turned out to be her last as well as latest songs ("Ultimas" means both in Spanish).

Allende died, the Intis were in Italy and the Quilas in France. For the Intis, the tour ("the longest in history", as Intis member Jorge Coulon jokes) turned into a fifteen-year and fifty-four days European exile for the group, an exile which put nueva canción and Amerindian music firmly on Europe's agenda of Latin American music.

The groups were the heart and soul of a worldwide Chilean (and Latin American) solidarity movement, performing almost daily for the first ten years. Both also recorded albums of new songs, the Intis influenced by their many years in Italy, creating some beautiful songs of exile, including the seminal song *Vuelvo*, with key singer-songwriter and musician **Patricio Manns**.

The impact of their high-profile campaigning against the military meant that the Intis were turned back on the airport tarmac long after politicians and trade union leaders were repatriated. They eventually returned on September 18, 1988, Chile's National Day, the day of one of the biggest meetings of supporters of the "No" vote to the plebiscite called by Pinochet to determine whether he should stay in office. Going straight from the airport to sing on a huge open-air stage and to dance the traditional *cueca* (Chile's National Day dance), the group's homecoming was an emotional and timely one. In 1998, after ten years of rebuilding their lives, making music and supporting various projects, including the Víctor Jara Foundation, the group's personnel, almost unchanged since 1967, is now adapting to the amicable departure of Max Berri and Jose Séves to pursue other projects.

The Andean instruments and rhythms used by Quilapayún (who disbanded in the 1980s) and Inti Illimani have been skilfully used by many other groups whose music is equally interesting – groups like **Illapu**, who remained popular throughout the 1980s (with a number of years in forced exile) and 1990s.

The Future and Legacy

Times have changed in Chile and in Latin America generally, with revolutionary governments no longer in power, democracy restored after dictatorships, and even Pinochet placed under arrest. The nueva canción movement, tied to an era of ideals and struggle, and then the brutal years of survival under dictatorship, would seem to have lost its relevance.

Its musicians have moved on to more individual concerns in their (always poetic) songwriting. But the nueva canción form, the inspiration of the song as message, and the rediscovery of Andean music and instruments, continues to have resonance and influence. Among a new generation of singers inspired by the history of "new song" are **Carlos Varela** in Cuba and the Bolivian singer **Emma Junaro**.

And there will be others. For Latin America, nueva canción is not only music but history. As the Cuban press has said of the songs of Silvio Rodriguez: "We have here the great epic poems of our days." Or as the Dominican Republic's merengue superstar Juan Luis Guerra, put it, "they are the master songwriters – they have influenced everyone."

Books

Unfortunately, a number of the best and most evocative books written on Chile have long been out of print, but we include some of them – mainly travel narratives or general accounts – below (marked by o/p in the parentheses after the title), as they can often be found in public libraries. Modern publications are inevitably dominated by analyses and testimonies of the Pinochet years, much of which makes compelling reading. There are relatively few up-to-date general histories of Chile in English, with those available focusing more on the academic market than the general reader. Chilean fiction, meanwhile, is not very widely translated into English, with the exception of a handful of the country's more famous authors. Its poetry, or more specifically the poetry of its famous Nobel laureate, Pablo Neruda, has been translated into many languages and is widely available abroad. Note that in the list below, where two publishers are given, these refer to UK/ US publishers respectively. If just one publisher is listed, and no country is specified, the book is published in both the UK and the USA. Highly recommended books are preceded by ⚑. UP is University Press.

Impressions, travel and general accounts

General introductions

Stephen Clissold *Chilean Scrapbook* (Cresset; o/p). Beautifully and evocatively written, taking you from the top to the bottom of the country via a mixture of history, legend and anecdote.

Augustin Edwards *My Native Land* (Ernest Benn; o/p). Absorbing and vivid reflections on Chile's geography, history, folklore and literature;

particularly strong on landscape descriptions.

Benjamin Subercaseaux *Chile: A Geographic Extravaganza* (New York; o/p). This seductive, poetic meander through Chile's "mad geography" is still one of the most enjoyable general introductions to the country, if a little dated.

Recent travel/accounts

Tim Burford *Chile and Argentina: The Bradt Trekking Guide* (Bradt Travel Guides). Fantastically detailed account of how to access and climb the Andes from Atacama to Tierra del Fuego. Plenty of trail maps and practical advice from the original South American explorers.

Bruce Chatwin *In Patagonia* (Vintage/Penguin). The cult travel

book that single-handedly enshrined Patagonia as the ultimate edge-of-the-world destination. Witty and captivating, this is essential reading for visitors to Patagonia, though unfortunately concentrates far more on the Argentine side.

Ariel Dorfman *Desert Memories* (National Geographic). Vivid depiction of desert life gleaned from

Dorfman's travels through Chile's Norte Grande, which weaves past and present, memoir and meditation, history and family lore to provide an engaging chronicle of modern Chile.

Toby Green *Saddled with Darwin* (Phoenix). One hundred and sixty-five years after Charles Darwin embarked on the journey that produced the most radical theory of modern times, Green set out to retrace his footsteps on horseback. The result is an epic journey across six countries, including Chile, which paints an incisive portrait of change across the southern section of the continent.

Brian Keenan and **John McCarthy** *Between Extremes: A Journey Beyond Imagination* (Black Swan/Corgi/Transworld Pub Inc.). Five years after Keenan and McCarthy were released from captivity in Beirut, the pair set off to fulfil a dream they'd shared as hostages to journey down the spine of Chile, from Arica to Tierra del Fuego. This account of their journey, told in alternating narratives, is as much an homage to their friendship as it is a description of the landscapes and people of Chile.

John Pilkington *An Englishman in Patagonia* (Century; o/p). A fun-to-read and sympathetic portrayal of Patagonia and its people. Includes some wonderful black-and-white photographs.

Rosie Swale *Back to Cape Horn* (Collins; o/p). An extraordinary account of the author's epic 409-day journey on horseback from the Atacama Desert down to Cape Horn – which she'd last visited while sailing around the world ten years previously in 1972.

Patrick Symmes *Chasing Che* (Robinson/Vintage Books). The author undertakes an epic motorbike trip through South America – including hundreds of miles of Chile – following the route taken by a young Che Guevara back in 1952, as chronicled in *The Motorcycle Diaries* (see below). A great mix of biography, history, politics and travel anecdotes, this is a sharply written and highly entertaining read.

Sara Wheeler *Travels in a Thin Country* (Abacus/Modern Library). A pacy, amusing account of the author's six-month solo journey zigzagging the entire length of Chile in the early 1990s.

Nineteenth- and early twentieth-century accounts

John Arons and Claudio Vita-Finzi *The Useless Land* (Robert Hale; o/p). Four Cambridge geography students set out to explore the Atacama Desert in 1958 and relate their adventures along the way in this highly readable book.

Charles Darwin *Voyage of the Beagle* (Penguin/Wordsworth Editions Ltd). This eminently readable (abridged) book contains some superb, evocative descriptions of nineteenth-century Chile, from Tierra del Fuego right up to Iquique.

Maria Graham *Journal of a Residence in Chile During the Year 1822* (o/p). The classic nineteenth-century travel narrative on Chile, written by a spirited, perceptive and amusing British woman.

Che Guevara *The Motorcycle Diaries* (Fourth Estate/Verso Books). Comic, picaresque narrative taken from the diaries of the future revolutionary as he and his buddy, both just out of medical school, travelled around South America – including a large chunk of Chile – by motorbike.

Canning House Library 2 Belgrave Square, London SW1X 8PJ ☏0207/235 2303 (ext. 208),✉library@canninghouse.com, ⓦwww.canninghouse.com/library.htm. An exhaustive collection of books on Chile (and other Hispanic countries). Also produces a quarterly bulletin detailing new publications on Latin America and Brazil.

Latin American Bureau 1 Amwell St, London EC1R 1UL ☏0207/278 2829, ✉contactlab@lab.org.uk, ⓦwww.lab.org.uk. Publishers of books on Latin America, available by mail order along with a wide selection of titles produced by other publishers.

South American Explorer 126 Indian Creek Rd, Ithaca, NY 14850, US ☏607/277-0488, ✉explorer@saexplorers.org, ⓦwww.samexplo.org. Among its mountain of resources on South America, this long-established organization produces a free catalogue containing a wide choice of books available by mail order. The service can be used by members and non-members alike.

Auguste Guinnard *Three Years Slavery Among the Patagonians* (Tempus Publishing). This is the account of Guinnard's capture and often brutal enslavement by Tehuelche Indians at war with the European colonizers in 1859, his surprising enlightenment and eventual escape.

E. B. Herivel *We Farmed a Desert* (o/p). Entertaining account of the fifteen years spent by a British couple on a small farm in the Huasco Valley in the 1930s and 1940s.

Alistair Horne *Small Earthquake in Chile* (Macmillan; o/p). Wry description of a visit to Chile during the turbulent months leading up to the military coup, written by a British journalist.

Bea Howe *Child in Chile* (o/p). A charming description of the author's childhood in Valparaíso in the early 1900s, where her family formed part of the burgeoning British business community.

W. H. Hudson *Idle Days in Patagonia* (Tempus Publishing). Drawn by the variety of fauna and the remarkable birdlife, the novelist and naturalist W. H. Hudson travelled to Patagonia at the tail-end of the nineteenth century and wrote this series of charming, gentle observations.

George Musters *At Home with the Patagonians* (Tempus Publishing). Remarkable account of time spent living with the Tehuelche Indians at the end of the nineteenth century that explodes the myth of the "noble savage" and provides a historically important picture of their vanishing way of life.

History, politics and society

General

Leslie Bethell (ed) *Chile Since Independence* (Cambridge UP). Made up of four chapters taken from the *Cambridge History of Latin American History,* this is rather dry in parts, but rigorous, comprehensive and clear.

Nick Caistor *In Focus: Chile* (Latin American Bureau/Interlink Books).

Brief, potted introduction to Chile's history, politics and society, highlighting the social problems bequeathed by Pinochet's economic model.

🏃 **Simon Collier and William Sater** *A History of Chile, 1801–1994* (Cambridge UP). Probably the best single-volume history of Chile from independence to the 1990s; thoroughly academic but enlivened by colourful detail along with the authors' clear fondness for the country and its people.

John Hickman *News from the End of the Earth: A Portrait of Chile* (Hurst & Co./St Martin's Press). Written by a former British ambassador to Chile, this concise and highly readable book makes a good (if conservative) introduction to Chile's history, taking you from the conquest to the 1990s in some 250 pages.

Brian Loveman *Chile: the Legacy of Hispanic Capitalism* (Oxford UP). Solid analysis of Chile's history from the arrival of the Spanish in the 1540s to the 1973 military coup.

Sergio Villalobos *A Short History of Chile* (Editorial Universitaria, Chile). Clear, concise and sensible outline of Chile's history, from pre-Columbian cultures through to the past decade, aimed at the general reader with no prior knowledge of the subject. Available in Santiago.

The Pinochet years

Sheila Cassidy *Audacity to Believe* (Darton, Longman & Todd; o/p). Distressing account of the imprisonment and horrific torture of a British doctor (the author) after she'd treated a wounded anti-Pinochet activist.

🏃 **Pamela Constable** and **Arturo Valenzuela** *A Nation of Enemies* (W.W. Norton & Company). Written during the mid to late 1980s, this is a superb look at the terror of everyday life in Chile at that time and the state apparatus used to annihilate free thinking and initiative in Chile. Essential to understanding contemporary Chile.

Marc Cooper *Pinochet and Me: A Chilean Anti-Memoir* (Verso Books). First-hand account of life under Pinochet in the early days of the coup, written by a young American who served as Allende's translator and barely escaped the death squads. Followed up by accounts of his periodic visits to Chile over the next quarter century.

John Dinges *The Condor Years: How Pinochet and His Allies Brought Terror to Three Continents* (New Press). Exhaustively researched book that examines the creation and use of international hit squads by the Pinochet regime. The chilling accounts of multinational agreements to execute "enemies of the state" are recreated by author Dinges, an internationally recognized investigative reporter and professor at Columbia University.

Paul Drake (ed) *The Struggle for Democracy in Chile* (University of Nebraska Press). Excellent collection of ten essays examining the gradual breakdown of the military government's authority. The pieces, which offer contrasting views both in support of and opposition to the regime, were written in 1988, during the months around the plebiscite.

Diana Kay *Chileans in Exile: Private Struggles, Public Lives* (Longwood Academic). Although written in a somewhat dry, academic style, this is nonetheless a fascinating study of Chilean exiles in Scotland, with a strong focus on women. The author looks at their attempts to reconstruct their lives, their sense of dislocation, and the impact exile has had on their attitude to politics, marriage and the home.

Hugh O'Shaughnessy *Pinochet: The Politics of Torture* (Latin America Bureau; New York UP). Covering everything from the arrest of Pinochet in London to Pinochet's secret plans to distribute sarin nerve gas to Chilean consulates abroad, this book provides an overview of the most influential man in Chilean politics from 1973 to 1998.

Patricia Politzer *Fear in Chile, Lives Under Pinochet* (New Press). Award-winning account of the lives of Chileans during the dictatorship, another classic account of the repressive apparatus used to subdue Chileans.

Grino Rojo and John J Hasset (ed) *Chile, Dictatorship and the Struggle for Democracy* (Ediciones Hispamérica). A slim, accessible volume containing four essays written in the months approaching the 1988 plebiscite, in which the country would vote to reject or continue with military rule. Contains contrasting analyses of the impact of the dictatorship on the country and its people.

Jacobo Timerman *Chile: Death in the South* (Vintage Books; o/p). Reflections on the Pinochet years by an Argentine journalist, written thirteen years into the military regime. Particularly compelling are the short personal testimonies of torture victims that intersperse the narrative.

Thomas Wright and Rody Oñate *Flight from Chile: Voices of Exile* (University of New Mexico Press). Detailed and affecting account of the exodus after the 1973 coup, when over 200,000 Chileans fled their homeland.

Special-interest studies

George McBride *Chile: Land and Society* (Kennikat Press; o/p). A compelling and exhaustively researched examination of the impact of the hacienda system on Chilean society, and the relationship (up to the mid-twentieth century) between landowners and peasants.

Colin McEwan, Luis Borrero and Alfredo Prieto (eds) *Patagonia: Natural History, Prehistory and Ethnography at the Uttermost End of the Earth* (British Museum Press/Princeton UP). Brilliant account of the "human adaptation, survival and eventual extinction" of the native peoples of Patagonia, accompanied by dozens of haunting black-and-white photographs.

Nick Reding *The Last Cowboys at the End of the World: The Story of the Gauchos of Patagonia* (Crown). A brutally honest and at times brutal look at the end of the gaucho era in Patagonia. Excellent exploration of how in the mid-1990s the gaucho culture crashed headlong into the advance of modern society.

William Sater *The Heroic Image in Chile* (University of California Press; o/p). Fascinating, scholarly look at the reasons behind the near-deification of Arturo Prat, the naval officer who died futilely in battle in 1879, described by the author as "a secular saint".

Richard W Slatta *Cowboys of the Americas* (Yale UP). Exhaustively researched, highly entertaining and lavishly illustrated history of the cowboy cultures of the Americas, including detailed treatment of the Chilean *huaso*.

Chilean women

Marjorie Agosin (ed) *Scraps of Life: Chilean Arpilleras: Chilean Women and the Pinochet Dictatorship* (Zed Books/Red Sea Press). A sensitive portrayal of the women of Santiago's shanty towns who, during the dictatorship, scraped a living by sewing scraps of material together to make wall hangings, known as *arpilleras*, depicting scenes of violence and repression. The *arpilleras* became a symbol of their protest, and were later exhibited around the world.

Jo Fisher *Out of the Shadows* (Latin American Bureau/Monthly Review Press). Penetrating analysis of the emergence of the women's movement in Latin America, with a couple of chapters devoted to Chile.

Elizabeth Jelin (ed) *Women and Social Change in Latin America* (Zed Books). A series of intelligent essays examining the ways women's organizations have acted as mobilizing forces for social and political change in Latin America.

Fiction and poetry

Fiction

Marjorie Agosin (ed) *Landscapes of a New Land: Short Fiction by Latin American Women* (White Wine Press). This anthology includes four short stories by Chilean women authors, including the acclaimed Marta Brunet (1901–67) and María Luisa Bombal (1910–80). Overall, the book creates a poetic, at times haunting, evocation of female life in a patriarchal world. Also edited by Agosin, *Secret Weavers: Stories of the Fantastic by Women of Argentina and Chile* (White Wine Press; o/p) is a spellbinding collection of short stories interwoven with themes of magic, allegory, legend and fantasy.

Isabel Allende *The House of the Spirits* (Black Swan/Bantam Books). This baroque, fantastical and bestselling novel chronicles the fortunes of several generations of a rich, landowning family in an unnamed but thinly disguised Chile, culminating with a brutal military coup and the murder of the president. Allende's *Of Love and Shadows* (Black Swan/Bantam Books) is set against a background of disappearances and

dictatorship, including a fictional account of the real-life discovery of the bodies of fifteen executed workers in a Central Valley mine. The author is a relative of Salvador Allende.

José Donoso *Curfew* (Picador/Grove Atlantic). Gripping novel about an exiled folk singer's return to Santiago during the military dictatorship, by one of Chile's most outstanding twentieth-century writers. Other works by Donoso translated into English include *Hell Has No Limits* (Sun and Moon Press), about the strange existence of a transvestite and his daughter in a Central Valley brothel, and *The Obscene Bird of Night* (Godine), a dislocated, fragmented novel narrated by a deaf-mute old man as he retreats into madness.

Ariel Dorfman *Hard Rain* (Readers International). This complicated, thought-provoking novel is both an examination of the role of the writer in a revolutionary society, and a celebration of the "Chilean road to socialism" – not an easy read, but one that repays the effort. Dorfman later became internationally famous for his play *Death and the Maiden* (Penguin), made into a film by Roman Polanski. Dorfman has also written an account of the effort to prosecute Pinochet in *Exorcising Terror: The Incredible Unending Trial of Augusto Pinochet*.

Alberto Fuguet *Bad Vibes* (o/p; St Martin's Press). Two weeks in September 1980 as lived by a mixed-up Santiago rich kid. A sort of Chilean *Catcher In the Rye* set against the tensions of the military regime.

Alicia Partnoy (ed) *You Can't Drown the Fire: Latin American Women Writing in Exile* (Virago/Cleis Press). Excellent anthology bringing together a mixture of short stories, poems and essays by exiled Latin American women, including Veronica de Negri, Cecila Vicuña, Marjorie Agosin and Isabel Morel Letelier from Chile.

Luis Sepúlveda *The Name of a Bullfighter* (Allison & Busby Ltd). Fast-paced, rather macho thriller set in Hamburg, Santiago and Tierra del Fuego, by one of Chile's leading young novelists.

Antonio Skàrmeta *The Postman* (Hyperion), formerly *Burning Patience* (Minerva). Funny and poignant novel about a postman who delivers mail to the great poet Pablo Neruda, who helps him seduce the local beauty with the help of a few metaphors. It was also made into a successful film, *Il Postino*, with the action relocated to Capri. Also by Skàrmeta, *I Dreamt the Snow Was Burning* (Readers International) is a tense, dark novel evoking the suspicion and fear that permeated everyday life in the months surrounding the military coup, while *Watch Where the Wolf is Going* (Readers International) is a collection of short stories, some of them set in Chile.

Poetry

Vicente Huidobro *The Selected Poetry of Vicente Huidobro* (W.W. Norton & Co./New Directions). Intellectual, experimental and dynamic works by an early twentieth-century poet, highly acclaimed in his time (1893–1948) but often overlooked today.

Gabriela Mistral *Selected Poems* (Johns Hopkins UP). Mistral is far less widely translated than her fellow Nobel laureate, Neruda, but this collection serves as an adequate English-language introduction to her quietly passionate and bittersweet poetry, much of it inspired by the landscape of the Elqui Valley.

Pablo Neruda *Twenty Love Poems and a Song of Despair* (Jonathan Cape/

Penguin); *Canto General* (French & European Publications/University of California Press); *Captain's Verses* (New Directions). The doyenne of Chilean poetry seems to be one of those poets people love or hate – his work is extravagantly lyrical, frequently verbose, but often very tender, particularly his love poetry. Neruda has been translated into many languages, and is widely available.

Nicanor Parra *Emergency Poems* (W.W. Norton & Co./New Directions). Both a physicist and poet, Parra pioneered the "anti-poem" in Chile during the 1980s: bald, unlyrical, often satirical prose poems. A stimulating read.

Biography and memoirs

Isabel Allende *My Invented Country – A Nostalgic Journey Through Chile* (HarperCollins). A memoir that is an enthralling mix of fiction and biography and which describes her life in Chile up until the assassination of her uncle, president Salvador Allende. She provides a very personal view of her homeland and exhaustively examines the country, its terrain, people, customs and language.

Fernando Alegría *Allende: A Novel* (Stanford UP). Basically a biography, with fictional dialogue, of Salvador Allende, written by his former cultural attaché, who was busy researching the book while the president died in the coup. Also of note by Alegria is *The Chilean Spring*, a fictional diary of a young photographer coming to terms with the coup in Santiago.

Ariel Dorfman *Heading South, Looking North* (Hodder & Stoughton/Penguin). Memoir of one of Chile's most famous writers, in which he reflects on themes such as language, identity, guilt and politics. Intelligent and illuminating, with some interesting thoughts on the causes of the Unidad Popular's failures.

Joan Jara *Víctor: An Unfinished Song* (Bloomsbury; o/p). Poignant memoir written by the British wife of the famous Chilean folksinger Víctor Jara, describing their life together, the Nueva Canción movement (see p.615) and their optimism for Allende's new Chile. The final part, detailing Jara's imprisonment, torture and execution in Santiago's football stadium, is almost unbearably moving.

R. L. Mégroz *The Real Robinson Crusoe* (Cresset Press; o/p). Colourful biography of Alexander Selkirk, who spent four years and four months marooned on one of the Juan Fernández Islands, inspiring Daniel Defoe to write *The Adventures of Robinson Crusoe*.

Luis Muñoz *Being Luis* (Impress Books). Account of a childhood spent growing up in 1960s–70s Chile that reflects recent history and leads to Muñoz's development as a left-wing activist, his arrest and torture by the military regime and eventual exile to England.

Pablo Neruda *Memoirs* (Penguin). Though his occasional displays of vanity and compulsive name-dropping can be irritating, there's no doubt that this is an extraordinary man with a fascinating life. The book also serves as a useful outline of Chile's political movements from the 1930s to the 1970s.

Pacific Islands

Paul Bahn and John Flenley *Easter Island, Earth Island* (Thames & Hudson; o/p). Richly illustrated with glossy photographs, this scholarly but accessible book provides an up-to-date and comprehensive introduction to the island's history and archeology. Interestingly, it also suggests that Easter Island could be a microcosm representing a global dilemma – that of a land so despoiled by man that it could no longer support its civilization.

Sebastian Englert *Island at the Centre of the World* (Hale; o/p). Based on a series of lectures broadcast to the Chilean Navy serving in

Antarctica, this is perhaps the clearest and most accessible (though now somewhat dated) introduction to Easter Island, written by a genial German priest who lived there for 35 years from 1935.

Thor Heyerdahl *Aku Aku* (George Allen & Unwin; o/p). This account of Heyerdahl's famous expedition to Easter Island in 1955 makes a cracking read, with an acute sense of adventure and mystery. Dubious as the author's archeological theories are, it's hard not to get swept along by his enthusiasm. In contrast, his *Reports of the Norwegian Archeological Expedition to Easter Island and the East Pacific* is a rigorous and respected documentation of the expedition's findings.

Alfred Métraux *Easter Island* (André Deutsch; o/p). Key study of Easter Island's traditions, beliefs and customs by a Belgian anthropologist, based on exhaustive research carried out in the 1930s. Métraux's *The Ethnology of Easter Island*, published in periodical format, is available from Periodicals Service Company, 11 Main St, Germantown, NY, USA (☎518/537-5899).

Catherine and Michel Orliac *The Silent Gods: Mysteries of Easter Island* (Thames & Hudson; o/p). Pocket-sized paperback, densely packed with colour illustrations and surprisingly detailed background on the island's explorers, statues, myths and traditions.

Katherine Routledge *The Mystery of Easter Island* (Adventures Unlimited Press). Recently back in print, this compelling book chronicles one of the earliest archeological expeditions to the island, led by the author in 1914. Routledge interviewed many elderly islanders and recounts their oral testimonies as well as the discoveries of her excavations.

Diana Souhami *Selkirk's Island* (Phoenix/Harcourt) This gripping account of the misadventures of Alexander Selkirk – the real life Robinson Crusoe, who spent four years marooned on a Chilean Pacific island – includes some vivid and evocative descriptions of what's now known as Isla Robinson Crusoe. Deservedly won the Whitbread Biography Award in 2001.

Ralph Lee Woodward *Robinson Crusoe's Island* (University of North Carolina Press; o/p). There's a good deal more drama to the Juan Fernández Islands' history than the famous four-year marooning of Alexander Selkirk, all of it enthusiastically retold in this lively book.

Flora and fauna

Sharon R. Chester *Birds of Chile* (Wandering Albatross). First-rate, easy-to-carry guide with over 300 colour illustrations of the birds of mainland Chile.

Claudio Donoso Zegers *Chilean Trees Identification Guide/Arboles Nativos de Chile* (Marisa Cineo Ediciones, Chile). Handy pocket guide to Chile's main native trees, with commentary in Spanish and English. Produced for Conaf (Chile's national parks administration), and part of a series that includes *Chilean Bushes, Chilean Climber Plants* and *Chilean Terrestrial Mammals*. Available in Conaf's information office in Santiago (see p.95).

Language

Language

Language

R elatively few Chileans speak English, even in the tourist industry, though this is changing. Bus drivers, taxi drivers and shop assistants will almost certainly speak no English, so, to get by in Chile, you really need to equip yourself with a bit of basic Spanish. It's not a difficult language to pick up and there are numerous books, cassettes and CD-ROMs on the market, teaching to various levels – *Teach Yourself Latin American Spanish* is a very good book-cassette package for getting started, while for an old-fashioned, rigorous textbook, nothing beats H. Ramsden's *An Essential Course in Modern Spanish*, published in the UK by Nelson.

The snag is that Chilean Spanish does not conform to what you learn in the classroom or hear on a cassette, and even competent Spanish-speakers will find it takes a bit of getting used to. The first thing to contend with is the dizzying **speed** with which most Chileans speak; another is **pronunciation**, especially the habitual dropping of many consonants. In particular, "s" is frequently dropped from the end or middle of a word, so *dos* becomes *do*, *gracias* becomes *gracia*, and *fosforos* (matches) becomes *fohforo*. "D" has a habit of disappearing from past participles, so *comprado* is *comprao*, while the "gua" sound is commonly reduced to *wa*, making the city of Rancagua *Rancawa*. The –*as* ending of the second person singular of verbs (*estás*, *viajas*, and so on) is transformed into –*ai*: hence *¿cómo estás?* usually comes out as "comehtai"; the classic *"¿cachai?"* ("get it?") is the second person singular form of the slang verb *cachar*, meaning to understand.

Another way in which Chilean differs from classic Castilian Spanish is its borrowing of words from indigenous languages, mainly Quichoa, Aymara and Mapuche, but also from German (*küchen*, for cake) and even English ("plumber" in Chile is inexplicably *el gasfiter*). Adding to the confusion is a widespread use of **slang** and **idiom**, much of which is unique to Chile. None of this, however, should put you off attempting to speak Spanish in Chile – Chileans will really appreciate your efforts, and even faltering beginners will be complimented on their language skills.

Pronunciation

The rules of **pronunciation** are pretty straightforward and, once you get to know them, strictly observed. Unless there's an accent, words ending in d, l, r, and z are **stressed** on the last syllable, all others on the second last. All **vowels** are pure and short.

A somewhere between the "a" sound of back and that of father.
E as in get.
I as in police.
O as in hot.
U as in rule.

C is soft before E and I, hard otherwise: *cerca* is pronounced "*serka*".
G works the same way, a slightly guttural "h" sound (between an aspirate "h" and the ch in loch) before e or i, a hard G elsewhere – *gigante* becomes "higante".

H is always silent.
J is guttural: *jamon* is pronounced "hamon".
LL sounds like an English Y: *tortilla* is pronounced "torteeya".
N is as in English unless it has a tilde over it (ñ), when it becomes NY: *mañana* sounds like "manyana".
QU is pronounced like an English K (the "u" is silent).

R is rolled, RR doubly so.
V sounds more like B, *vino* becoming "beano".
X is slightly softer than in English – sometimes almost SH – except between vowels in place names where it has an "H" sound – for example México (Meh-Hee-Ko).
Z is the same as a soft C, so *cerveza* becomes "serbessa".

On the following page we've listed a few essential words and phrases, though if you're travelling for any length of time a dictionary or phrase book is obviously a worthwhile investment. If you're using a **dictionary**, bear in mind that in Spanish CH, LL, and Ñ count as separate letters and are traditionally listed in a special section after the Cs, Ls, and Ns respectively, though some new dictionaries do not follow this rule.

Words and phrases

The following should help you with your most basic day-to-day language needs; a menu reader and list of slang terms follows on.

Basics

sí, no	yes, no
por favor, gracias	please, thank you
dónde, cuando	where, when
qué, cuanto	what, how much
aquí, allí	here, there
este, eso	this, that
ahora, màs tarde	now, later
abierto/a, cerrado/a	open, closed
con, sin	with, without
buen(o)/a, mal(o)/a	good, bad
gran(de)	big
pequeño/a, chico	small
más, menos	more, less
hoy, mañana	today, tomorrow
ayer	yesterday

Greetings and responses

Hola, adiós (ciao/chau)	Hello, Goodbye
Buenos días	Good morning
Buenas tardes	Good afternoon
Buenas noches	Good evening/night
Hasta luego	See you later
Lo siento/discúlpeme (perdón)	Sorry

Con permiso/perdón	Excuse me
¿Como está (usted)?	How are you?
(No) Entiendo	I (don't) understand
De nada	Not at all/You're welcome
¿Habla (usted) inglés?	Do you speak English?
(No) Hablo español	I (don't) speak Spanish
Me llamo ...	My name is ...
¿Cómo se llama usted?	What's your name?
Soy inglés(a)	I am English
irlandés (a)	... Irish
escocés (a)	... Scottish
galés (a)	... Welsh
norte-americano(a)	... American
australiano (a)	... Australian
canadiense	... Canadian
neozelandés (a)	... New Zealander

Needs – accommodation and transport

Quiero...	I want
Quisiera...	I'd like
¿Sabe...?	Do you know...
No sé	I don't know

(¿) Hay…(?)	There is (is there)?
Deme…	Give me…
(uno así)	(one like that)
¿Tiene …?	Do you have…
la hora	the time
una habitación	a room
con dos camas/ cama matrimonial	with two beds/ double bed
con baño privado	with private bath
es para una persona	It's for one person
(dos personas)	(two people)
para una noche	for one night
(una semana)	(one week)
Está bien,	It's fine,
¿cuánto es?	how much is it?
Es demasiado caro	It's too expensive
¿No tiene algo más barato?	Don't you have anything cheaper?
¿Se puede..?	Can one…?
acampar aquí (cerca)?	camp (near) here?
¿Hay un hotel aquí cerca?	Is there a hotel nearby?
¿Por dónde se va a…?	How do I get to…?
Izquierda, derecha, derecho	Left, right, straight on
¿Dónde está…?	Where is…?
el terminal de buses	the bus station
la estación de ferrocarriles	the train station
el banco más cercano	the nearest bank
el correo	the post office
el baño	the toilet
¿De dónde sale el bus para…?	Where does the bus to… leave from?
¿Es éste el tren para Santiago?	Is this the train for Santiago?
¿Quisiera un pasaje (de ida y vuelta) para…	I'd like a (return) ticket to…
¿A qué hora sale (llega en…)?	What time does it leave (arrive in…)?
¿Cuánto tiempo demora el viaje?	How long does the journey take?
¿Qué hay para comer?	What is there to eat?
¿Qué es eso?	What's that?
¿Como se llama esto en español?	What's this called in Spanish?

Useful transport vocabulary

Pasaje	Ticket
Asiento	Seat
Pasillo	Aisle
Ventana	Window
Equipaje	Luggage
Custodia	Left luggage
Auto	Car
Rentacar	Car rental outlet
Arrendar	To rent
Doble tracción or cuatro por cuatro (4x4)	4WD
Tracción single or dos por dos (2x2)	Non-4WD
Kilometraje libre	Unlimited kilometres
Seguro	Insurance
Deducible	Damages excess
Bencina	Petrol
Estación de bencina	Petrol station
Bidon	Jerry can
Carretera	Highway
Camioneta (doble/simple cabina)	Pick-up truck (double/single

Chilean road signs

Peligro	Danger
Desvío	Detour
Resbaladizo	Slippery surface
No adelantar	No overtaking
Curva peligrosa	Dangerous bend
Reduzca velocidad	Reduce speed
Sin berma	No hard shoulder

Numbers and days

un/uno/una	1
dos	2
tres	3
cuatro	4
cinco	5
seis	6
siete	7
ocho	8
nueve	9
diez	10
once	11
doce	12

L

LANGUAGE | Words and phrases

637

trece	13	doscientos (as)	200
catorce	14	doscientos (as) uno	201
quince	15	quinientos (as)	500
dieciséis	16	mil	1000
diecisiete	17	dos mil	2000
dieciocho	18		
diecinueve	19	primer(o)a	first
veinte	20	segundo/a	second
veintiuno	21	tercer(o)/a	third
treinta	30		
cuarenta	40	lunes	Monday
cincuenta	50	martes	Tuesday
sesenta	60	miércoles	Wednesday
setenta	70	jueves	Thursday
ochenta	80	viernes	Friday
noventa	90	sábado	Saturday
cien(to)	100	domingo	Sunday
ciento uno	101		

Food: a Chilean menu reader

Basics

Aceite	Oil
Ají	Chilli
Ajo	Garlic
Arroz	Rice
Azúcar	Sugar
Huevos	Eggs
Leche	Milk
Mantequilla	Butter
Mermelada	Jam
Miel	Honey
Mostaza	Mustard
Pan	Bread
Pimienta	Pepper
Sal	Salt

Some common terms

A la parrilla	Grilled
A la plancha	Lightly fried
A lo pobre	Served with chips, onions and a fried egg
Ahumado	Smoked
Al horno	Oven-baked
Al vapor	Steamed
Asado	Roast or barbecued
Asado al palo	Spit-roasted, barbecued
Crudo	Raw
Frito	Fried
Pastel	Paste, purée, mince
Picante	Spicy hot
Pil-pil	Very spicy
Puré	Mashed (potato)
Relleno	Filled or stuffed

Meals

Agregado	Side order
Almuerzo	Lunch
Cena	Dinner
Comedor	Dining room
Cuchara	Spoon
Cuchillo	Knife
Desayuno	Breakfast
La carta	The menu
La cuenta	The bill
Menú del día	Fixed-price set meal (usually lunch)

Once	Afternoon tea
Plato vegetariano	Vegetarian dish
Tenedor	Fork

Meat (carne) and poultry (aves)

Bistec	Beef steak
Carne de vacuno	Beef
Cerdo	Pork
Chuleta	Cutlet, chop (usually pork)
Churrasco	Griddled beef, like a minute steak
Conejo	Rabbit
Cordero	Lamb steak
Escalopa Milanesa	Breaded veal escalope
Filete	Fillet steak
Jamón	Ham
Lechón, cochinillo	Suckling pig
Lomo	General term for steak of indiscriminate cut
Pato	Duck
Pavo	Turkey
Pollo	Chicken
Ternera	Veal
Vienesa	Hot dog sausage

Offal (menudos)

Chunchules	Intestines
Guatitas	Tripe
Pana	Liver
Lengua	Tongue
Patas	Feet, trotters
Picante de conejo	Curried rabbits' innards
Riñones	Kidneys

Fish (pescado)

Albacora	Albacore (a small, white-fleshed tuna)
Anchoveta	Anchovy
Atún	Tuna
Bonito	Pacific bonito, similar to tuna
Ceviche	Strips of fish "cooked" in lemon juice and onions

Congrio	A large, superior member of the cod family known as conger eel
Corvina	sea bass (not the same as Chilean sea bass, which is under boycott)
Lenguado	Sole
Merluza	Hake
Reineta	Similar to lemon sole
Salmón	Salmon
Trucha	Trout
Vidriola	Firm-fleshed white fish from the Juan Fernández archipelago

Seafood (mariscos)

Almeja	Clam, cockle
Calamar	Squid
Camarón	Prawn
Centolla	King crab
Choro, chorito	Mussel
Erizo	Sea urchin
Langosta	Lobster
Langosta de Isla de Pascua	Spiny lobster
Langosta de Juan Fernández	Crayfish, rock lobster
Langostino	Crayfish, red crab
Loco	Abalone
Macha	Razor clam
Mariscal	Mixed shellfish, served chilled
Mejillónes	Mussels
Ostiones	Scallops
Ostras	Oysters
Paila marina	Thick fish and seafood stew
Picoroco	Giant barnacle with a single crab-like claw
Piure	Scarlet-red, kidney-shaped animal with hair-like strands that lives inside a shell
Pulpo	Octopus

Vegetables (verduras)

Aceitunas	Olives
Alcachofa	Artichoke
Cebolla	Onion
Champiñón	Mushroom
Choclo	Maize, sweetcorn
Chucrút	Sauerkraut
Espinaca	Spinach
Lechuga	Lettuce
Palmito	Palm heart
Palta	Avocado
Papa	Potato
Papas fritas	Chips (French fries)
Poroto verde	Green, French, runner bean
Tomate	Tomato
Zapallo	Squash

Soups and stews

Caldillo	Vegetables cooked in meat stock; between a stew and a soup
Caldo	Quite bland, simple meat stock with loads of added salt
Charquicán	Meat stew with lots of vegetables
Chupe	Thick fish stew, topped with butter, breadcrumbs and gratinated cheese
Crema	Creamy soup thickened with flour or egg yolks
Zarzuela	Seafood stew (like bouillabaisse)

Salads (ensaladas)

Ensalada chilena	Tomatoes, shredded onion and vinaigrette
Ensalada primavera	Hard-boiled eggs, sweetcorn, peas, carrot, beetroot
Ensalada rusa	Diced vegetables and peas mixed in a thick mayonnaise
Ensalada surtida	Mixed salad
Palta reina	Avocado filled with tuna

Sandwiches (sanwiches)

Ave mayo	Chicken and mayonnaise
Ave sola	Chicken
Barros Jarpa	Ham and melted cheese
Barros Luco	Beef and melted cheese
Churrasco solo	Griddled beef, like a minute steak
Completo	Hot dog, sauerkraut, tomato, mayonnaise
Diplomático	Beef, egg and melted cheese
Especial	Hot dog with mayonnaise
Hamburguesa	Hamburger

Fruit (frutas)

Albaricoque	Apricot
Cereza	Cherry
Chirimoya	Custard apple
Ciruela	Plum
Durazno	Peach
Frambuesa	Raspberry
Frutilla	Strawberry
Higo	Fig
Limón	Lemon
Lúcuma	Native fruit often used in ice cream and cakes
Manzana	Apple
Membrillo	Quince
Mora	Mulberry
Naranja	Orange
Pera	Pear
Piña	Pineapple
Plátano	Banana
Pomelo	Grapefruit
Sandía	Watermelon
Tuna	Prickly pear
Uva	Grape(s)

Dessert (postres)

When fruit is described as being "in juice" (*al jugo*) or "in syrup" (*en almíbar*), it will be out of a tin.

Flan	Crème caramel	Manjar	Very sweet caramel, made from condensed milk
Helado	Ice cream		
Küchen	Cake		
Macedonia	Fruit salad	Panqueques	Pancakes
		Torta	Tart

Drinks and beverages

Note that, owing to the Chileans' compulsive use of the diminutive (*ito* and *ita*), you'll hardly ever be asked if you want a *té* or *café*, but rather a *tecito* or *cafecito*, which tends to throw people at first.

Alcoholic drinks

Cerveza	Beer
Champán	Champagne
Chicha (or sidra)	Cider
Vino (tinto/blanco/ rosado)	Wine (red/white/rosé)

Hot drinks

Café	Coffee
Descafeinado (rarely available)	Decaff
Chocolate caliente	Hot chocolate
Té de hierbas	Herbal tea
Té	Tea

Soft drinks

Bebida	Fizzy drink
(en lata/botella)	(in a can/bottle)
(de màquina)	(draught)
Jugo natural	Juice (pure)
Néctar	Juice (syrup)
Agua	Water
Agua mineral	Mineral water
(con gas)	(sparkling)
(sin gas)	(still)

Idiom and slang

As you travel through Chile you'll come across a lot of words and expressions that crop up again and again, many of which aren't in your dictionary, or, if they are, appear to have a different meaning from that given. Added to these day-to-day **chilenismos** is a very rich, exuberant and constantly expanding vocabulary of slang (*modismos*). This is near impossible to get to grips with, but mastering a few of the most common examples will help you get by and raise a smile if you drop them into the conversation.

Everyday words and expressions

Some of the words and expressions listed below are shared by neighbouring countries, while others are uniquely Chilean. As well as these peculiarities, we've listed a few other expressions you're likely to encounter very frequently.

Al tiro "right away", "immediately" – though this can mean anything up to several hours.

Boleto as Chilean law requires that customers must not leave shop premises without their *boleto* (receipt), you will frequently hear "*su*

boleta!" yelled at you as you try to leave without it.

Calefónt (pronounced "calefón"): "water heater" – not a real Chilean word, but one you'll need on a daily basis if you're staying in budget accommodation, where you'll have to remember to light the *calefónt* with *fósforos* (matches) before you take a shower.

Carné identity card.

Cédula interchangeable with *carné*.

Ciao (chau) by far the most common way of saying "goodbye" among friends; in slightly more formal situations, *hasta luego* is preferred over *adiós*.

Confort (pronounced "confor") A brand name but now the de facto word for toilet paper (which is correctly *papel higiénico*).

De repente in Spain this means "suddenly"; in Chile it means "maybe", "sometimes" or "occasionally".

Flojo "lazy", frequently invoked by northerners to describe southerners and southerners to describe northerners.

Guagua (pronounced "wawa") baby, derived from Quichoa.

Harto "loads of" (for example *harto trabajo*, loads of work); a more widely used and idiomatic alternative to *mucho*.

Listo literally "ready", and used as a response to indicate agreement, or that what's been said is understood; something like "sure" or "right".

Plata literally "silver" but meaning "money", used far more commonly than *dinero*, except in formal situations.

Qué le vaya (muy) bien "May everything go (very) well for you", frequently said when saying goodbye to someone you probably won't see again.

Rico "good", "delicious", "tasty", usually to describe food and drink.

Ya Chilean equivalent of the Spanish *vale*; used universally to convey "OK", "fine", "sure" or (depending on the tone) "Whatever", "Hmm, I see".

Slang

The few examples we give below barely scrape the surface of the living, constantly evolving lexicon of Chilean slang – for a crash course, get hold of the excellent *How to Survive in the Chilean Jungle* by John Brennan and Alvaro Baboada, published by Dolmen and available in the larger Santiago bookshops.

Buena onda "cool!"

Cachar "to understand"; hence "*¿cachai?*", "are you with me?", scattered ad nauseam through conversations.

Cocido drunk.

Cuico yuppie (especially in Santiago).

Huevón literally "huge testicle", meaning something like "asshole" or "fucker", but so commonly and enthusiastically used it's no longer particularly offensive. More like "jerk" or "idiot".

Los pacos the police.

Pololo/a boyfriend, girlfriend.

¡Sale! emphatically used to mean, "bullshit!" or "not a chance!"

Sí, po abbreviation of *sí*, *pues*, meaning "yeah", "sure" ("po" is tacked onto the end of just about every phrase, hence "*no po*", "*no sé po*").

Taco traffic jam.

Glossary

Adobe Sun-dried mud.

Altiplano High plateau region in the Andes of the far north.

Apu Mountain god.

Arriero Muleteer, or horseman.

Ayllu Kinship group or clan.

Barrio District, quarter or suburb.

Bofedal Spongy green grass or peat bog in the altiplano.

Camanchaca Coastal mist.

Casa patronal Hacienda-owner's house.

Chicha Cider; fermented grape or maize drink.

Colectivo Collective taxi.

Cordillera Mountain range.

Criollo "Creole": used historically to refer to a person of Spanish blood born in the American colonies, but nowadays as an adjective to describe something (such as food or music) as "typical" or "local".

Encomendero Possessor of an *encomienda*.

Encomienda A grant of indigenous labourers to landowners during colonial times.

Estancia Ranch, or large estate.

Fundo Estate or farm.

Hacienda Large estate.

Hoja de coca Coca-leaf.

Huaso Chilean "cowboy", or mounted farm worker.

Junta A ruling council; usually used to describe small groups who've staged a coup d'état.

Latifundio Huge estates.

Llareta Deep-green, rock-hard woody plant in the altiplano.

Local "Unit" or "shop" in shopping centre or mall.

Mayorazgo Entailment system of large estates.

Mestizo Person of mixed Spanish and indigenous blood.

Micro City bus.

Pampa Plain.

Peña Restaurant or nightclub where live folk music is performed.

Población Poor suburb.

Portazuela Mountain pass.

Pukará Fort.

Puna Quichoa word referring to barren Andean heights, sometimes used interchangeably with the Spanish word *altiplano*.

Quebrada Ravine, dried-out stream.

Soroche Altitude sickness.

Travel
store

TRAVEL

& MORE

www.roughguides.com

Chile

Tailor-made & small group tours to Latin America, Galapagos & Antarctica.

Specialists for over two decades.

ATOL No. 3760

020 7407 1478

select LatinAmerica

info@selectlatinamerica.com
www.selectlatinamerica.com

SOUTH AMERICAN SAFARIS

Overland Adventure Tours
From 3 to 24 weeks

Tel: +44 (0) 20 8767 9136
email: info@southamericansafaris.com
www.southamericansafaris.com

ADVENTURE. CULTURE. FUN

Small print and Index

A Rough Guide to Rough Guides

Published in 1982, the first Rough Guide – to Greece – was a student scheme that became a publishing phenomenon. Mark Ellingham, a recent graduate of English from Bristol University, had been travelling in Greece the previous summer and couldn't find the right guidebook. With a small group of friends he wrote his own guide, combining a highly contemporary, journalistic style with a thoroughly practical approach to travellers' needs.

The immediate success of the book spawned a series that rapidly covered dozens of destinations. And, in addition to impecunious backpackers, Rough Guides soon acquired a much broader and older readership that relished the guides' wit and inquisitiveness as much as their enthusiastic, critical approach and value-for-money ethos.

These days, Rough Guides include recommendations from shoestring to luxury and cover more than 200 destinations around the globe, including almost every country in the Americas and Europe, more than half of Africa and most of Asia and Australasia. Our ever-growing team of authors and photographers is spread all over the world, particularly in Europe, the USA, and Australia.

In the early 1990s, Rough Guides branched out of travel, with the publication of Rough Guides to World Music, Classical Music, and the Internet. All three have become benchmark titles in their fields, spearheading the publication of a wide range of books under the Rough Guide name.

SMALL PRINT

Including the travel series, Rough Guides now number more than 350 titles, covering: phrasebooks, waterproof maps, music guides from Opera to Heavy Metal, reference works as diverse as Conspiracy Theories and Shakespeare, and popular culture books from iPods to Poker. Rough Guides also produce a series of more than 120 World Music CDs in partnership with World Music Network.

Visit www.roughguides.com to see our latest publications.

Many Rough Guide travel images are available for commercial licensing at www.roughguidespictures.com

Rough Guide credits

Text editor: AnneLise Sorensen
Layout: Jessica Subramanian
Cartography: Maxine Repath, Rajesh Chhibber
Picture editor: Harriet Mills and Sarah Smithies
Production: Katherine Owers
Proofreader: Serena Stephenson
Cover design: Chloë Roberts
Editorial: London Kate Berens, Claire Saunders, Geoff Howard, Ruth Blackmore, Polly Thomas, Richard Lim, Clifton Wilkinson, Alison Murchie, Karoline Densley, Andy Turner, Keith Drew, Edward Aves, Nikki Birrell, Helen Marsden, Alice Park, Sarah Eno, David Paul, Lucy White, Joe Staines, Duncan Clark, Peter Buckley, Matthew Milton, Tracy Hopkins, Ruth Tidball; **New York** Andrew Rosenberg, Richard Koss, Steven Horak, Amy Hegarty, Hunter Slaton, April Isaacs, Sean Mahoney
Design & Pictures: London Simon Bracken, Dan May, Diana Jarvis, Mark Thomas, Jj Luck; **Delhi** Madhulita Mohapatra, Umesh Aggarwal, Ajay Verma, Amit Verma, Ankur Guha, Pradeep Thapliyal
Production: Sophie Hewat, Aimee Hampson

Cartography: London Ed Wright, Katie Lloyd-Jones, **Delhi** Manish Chandra, Jai Prakash Mishra, Ashutosh Bharti, Rajesh Mishra, Animesh Pathak, Jasbir Sandhu, Karobi Gogoi, Amod Singh
Online: New York Jennifer Gold, Suzanne Welles, Kristin Mingrone; **Delhi** Manik Chauhan, Narender Kumar, Shekhar Jha, Lalit K. Sharma, Rakesh Kumar, Chhandita Chakravarty
Marketing & Publicity: London Richard Trillo, Niki Hanmer, David Wearn, Demelza Dallow, Louise Maher, Jess Carter; **New York** Geoff Colquitt, Megan Kennedy, Katy Ball; **Delhi** Reem Khokhar
Custom publishing and foreign rights: Philippa Hopkins
Manager India: Punita Singh
Series editor: Mark Ellingham
Reference Director: Andrew Lockett
PA to Managing and Publishing Directors: Megan McIntyre
Publishing Director: Martin Dunford
Managing Director: Kevin Fitzgerald

Publishing information

This third edition published August 2006 by **Rough Guides Ltd,**
80 Strand, London WC2R 0RL, UK
345 Hudson St, 4th Floor,
New York, NY 10014, USA
14 Local Shopping Centre, Panchsheel Park,
New Delhi 110017, India
Distributed by the Penguin Group
Penguin Books Ltd,
80 Strand, London WC2R 0RL, UK
Penguin Putnam, Inc.
375 Hudson Street, NY 10014, USA
Penguin Group (Australia)
250 Camberwell Road, Camberwell,
Victoria 3124, Australia
Penguin Books Canada Ltd,
10 Alcorn Avenue, Toronto, Ontario,
M4V 1E4, Canada
Penguin Group (New Zealand)
Cnr Rosedale and Airborne Roads
Albany, Auckland, New Zealand
Cover concept by Peter Dyer.

Typeset in Bembo and Helvetica to an original design by Henry Iles.
Printed and bound in China

© Melissa Graham and Andrew Benson, 2006

No part of this book may be reproduced in any form without permission from the publisher except for the quotation of brief passages in reviews.

664pp includes index
A catalogue record for this book is available from the British Library
ISBN 13: 978-1-84353-549-2
ISBN 10: 1-84353-549-1

The publishers and authors have done their best to ensure the accuracy and currency of all the information in **The Rough Guide to Chile,** however, they can accept no responsibility for any loss, injury, or inconvenience sustained by any traveller as a result of information or advice contained in the guide.

1   3   5   7   9   8   6   4   2

SMALL PRINT

Help us update

We've gone to a lot of effort to ensure that the third edition of **The Rough Guide to Chile** is accurate and up to date. However, things change – places get "discovered", opening hours are notoriously fickle, restaurants and rooms raise prices or lower standards. If you feel we've got it wrong or left something out, we'd like to know, and if you can remember the address, the price, the time, the phone number, so much the better.

We'll credit all contributions, and send a copy of the next edition (or any other Rough Guide if you prefer) for the best letters. Everyone who writes to us and isn't already a subscriber will receive a copy of our full-colour thrice-yearly newsletter. Please mark letters: "**Rough Guide Chile Update**" and send to: Rough Guides, 80 Strand, London WC2R 0RL, or Rough Guides, 4th Floor, 345 Hudson St, New York, NY 10014. Or send an email to **mail@roughguides.com**

Have your questions answered and tell others about your trip at **www.roughguides.atinfopop.com**

Acknowledgements

Andrew Benson: Thanks to Ingrid, Adriana and Socorro, Manuel, and Jorge in Santiago; Charlie in Arica, Richard in Iquique, Jeannette, and everyone I met on Rapa Nui and Juan Fernández; Jason, Kyriakos and Roberto at the ESO; the staff for their special help at Sernatur offices in La Serena and Copiapó; David and Peter for material assistance from afar; Marjan, as ever, for special moments in BA; and everyone at Rough Guides involved in the whole project, in particular AnneLise for being patient, obliging and loyal. Very special thanks to Diego in La Serena. And I dedicate my research to the memory of Raúl Wünkhaus.

Alex Stewart: Thanks to all of the knowledgeable Sernatur staff and members of Conaf I encountered along the way who fielded my questions with patience and enthusiasm, providing answers and inspiration. Thanks also to all the folk I met in the course of my research who helped out with material or simply provided good company. Special mention goes to the staff at the Travellers Agency in Puerto Montt, Nadia and Armin for hospitality and cheese fondue,

Andreas for his generosity and for putting me up, Luisa for the use of her house and for some useful insider information and Christine Kossman at the Termas de Puyuhuapi for the kind invitation. Heartfelt thanks also go to Katie for her boundless support, tireless patience and enthusiasm on the road and to Joel and Kaz for their company and encouragement on foot. Finally, thanks to Andrew at Rough Guides for the opportunity, to AnneLise for scrupulous, diligent editing and to Melissa for her backing and support.

Melissa Graham thanks Martín Gubbins of Santiago for sharing his time and insight in the preparation of this book.

The editor would like to thank Andrew and Alex for their passion and perseverance; the RG Delhi team for top-notch typesetting; Harriet Mills for thorough picture research; Maxine Repath and Rajesh Chhibber for their mapmaking expertise; Serena Stephenson for her vigilant proofreading; Nicky Agate for a fine index; Richard Koss for his generous advice and assistance throughout; and Andrew Rosenberg for overall guidance.

SMALL PRINT

Readers' letters

Thanks to all those readers of the 2nd edition who took the trouble to write in with their amendments and additions. Apologies for any misspellings or omissions:

Patrick Reinquin, Monika Vetsch, Lorraine Byrne, Ajke Augustyns, Nicoletta Ravidà, Roberto Gilmozzi, Kiernan Rok, Sytske de Vries, Cristián Levy Cataldo, Paula Almeida, Jim & Jane Owens, Paul Cappon, Christian Asseburg, Richard and Catherine Ranger, Noel Burke, Iain Hayne, Avelyn Wong, Hung Dhong Lee, Heike Balzer, Elizabeth Ash, Ralph Holmes, Jeannette Croft.

Photo credits

Title page
Isla Negra © Paul Harris

Full page
Chilote church © South American Pictures

Introduction
p.5 Puerto Varas © Steve J Benbow/Axiom
p.6 Castro craft market © Sue Cunningham
Picture Library
p.7 Baqueanos, Torres del Paine © Paul Harris
p.8 Alpaca, Isluga National Park © Paul Harris
p.9 Aymara woman © Paul Harris
p.10 Lago Yelcho © Macduff Everton
p.11 Torres del Paine © Angus Oborn
p.12 Magellanic penguins © Dean Fox/
Superstock

Things not to miss
01 Parque Nacional Torres del Paine © Paul
Harris
02 Valparaíso © Katie Moore/South American
Pictures
03 Chinchorro mummy © Chris Sharp/South
American Pictures
04 Chilote church © John Warburton Lee
05 Punta Arenas cemetery © Hubert Stadler/
Corbis
06 Valle de la Luna © Robert McLeod/Robert
Harding
07 Bahía Inglesa © Chad Ehlers/Stone/Getty
Images
08 Lapis lazuli © Jose Manuel Sanchis Calvete/
Corbis
09 Penguins on Isla Magdalena © Andrew
Benson
10 Aerial view of Patagonia © Paul Harris
11 Mercado Central, Santiago © John Warburton
Lee
12 Moai statues on Easter Island © Sue Mann/
South American Pictures
13 Geoglyph at Cerro Unitas © Eric Lawrie
14 Pisco distillery, Elqui Valley © Gary Cook/
Alamy
15 Termas de Puyuhuapi © Sergio Pitamitz/
Superstock
16 San Rafael glacier © Rhonda Klevansky/
Stone/Getty Images
17 Huasos © Paul Harris
18 Sea lions in the Beagle Channel
© Paul Harris
19 Angler with catch © Paul Harris
20 Photo cut-out of Pablo Neruda, La Chascona,
Santiago © Corbis
21 Hikers ascending Volcán Villarrica © Robert
Francis/South American Pictures
22 Laguna Verde © Eric Lawrie
23 Cable cars over Santiago © Frans Lemmens/
Iconica/Getty Images
24 Pre-Colombian ceramic piece © Chris Sharp/
South American Pictures
25 Flowering desert © Peter Francis/South
American Pictures
26 Chile's northern skies © Corbis

Black and whites
p.88 Plaza de Armas, Santiago © John
Warburton-Lee
p.104 Correo Central © Tony Morrison/South
American Pictures
p.108 Palacio de la Moneda © Jason P. Howe/
South American Pictures
p.115 Cerro San Cristóbal © Sue Carpenter/
Axiom
p.133 Cajón del Maipó © Chris Barton Travel
Photography
p.144 Quinta Vergara © Chris Barton Travel
Photography
p.151 Valparaíso ascensor © Tony Morrison/
South American Pictures
p.168 Museo Francisco Fonck, Viña del Mar
© Chris Barton Travel Photography
p.173 Horcón © Jon Arnold Images/Alamy
p.180 Horse-riding in El Norte Chico © Paul
Harris
p.190 Fiesta Grande de la Virgen © Yadid Levy/
Alamy
p.197 Cerro Tololo observatory © NOAO/AURA/
NSF
p.217 Bahía Inglesa © Morya Photography
p.224 Valle de la Luna © Gala/Superstock
p.231 La Portada © Jason P Howe/South
American Pictures
p.240 Prehistoric mummy, San Pedro de Atacama
© Tony Morrison/South American Pictures
p.250 Teatro Municipal, Iquique © John
Warburton-Lee
p.262 Aymara festival © Rebecca Whitfield/South
American Pictures
p.275 Parinacota village © Paul Harris
p.280 Salto del Laja © Chris Sharp/ South
American Pictures
p.286 Rancagua rodeo © John Warburton-Lee
p.297 Curicó plaza © Tony Morrison/South
American Pictures
p.313 Termas de Chillán © Rebecca Whitfield/
South American Pictures
p.329 Araucaria tree © Paul Harris
p.336 Puerto Montt boat and flowers © Paul
Harris
p.355 Forest lakes around Pucón © Steven Horak
p.374 Mapuche girl © Danita Delimont/Alamy
p.392 Volcán Orsono © Paul Harris
p.402 Puerto Montt ferry © Andre Jenny/Alamy
p.414 Castro palafito, Chiloé © Tony Morrison/
South America Pictures
p.427 Castro fjord, Chiloé © Minden Pictures/
FLPA
p.430 Chilote church © John Warburton-Lee
p.444 Fern fronds in Parque Pumalín, © John
Warburton-Lee
p.455 Parque Pumalín rainforest © Paul Harris
p.462 Puyuhuapi © Sergio Pitamitz/Superstock
p.468 Hiking in Parque Nacional Queulat
© Sergio Pitamitz/Alamy
p.483 Magellanic penguins © Ingo Arndt
p.495 Statue of Ferdinand Magellan, Punta
Arenas © Kathy Jarvis/South America
Pictures
p.514 Gaucho, Torres del Paine © Paul Harris

SMALL PRINT

SMALL PRINT

Index

Map entries are in colour.

INDEX

I

655

I

INDEX

W

Y

Z

Map symbols

maps are listed in the full index using coloured text

-----	International boundary	♠	Guardería (ranger station)
----	Chapter boundary	♠	Refugio (mountain lodge)
▬▬▬	Motorway	⚲	Customs post
═══	Major road	⚡	Skiing area
═══	Minor road	✿	Wine
▬▬▬	Pedestrianized road	🏛	Monument
ⵏⵏⵏⵏⵏ	Steps	⚶	Swamp
------	Path	🏊	Swimming pool
———	Unpaved road	⚶	Church (regional maps)
▬●▬	Railway	⌂	Observatory
– – –	Ferry route	✗	Battle site
———	Waterway	⊼	Picnic area
═══	Tunnel	Ⓜ	Metro station
╰╯	Bridge	★	Bus stop
✈	International airport	⚿	Campsite
✈	Domestic airport	⊞	Hospital
♦	Point of interest	©	Telephone office
♯	Castle	ⓘ	Information office
∴	Ruins	✉	Post office
⚶	Viewpoint	◉	Hotel
⌒	Caves	▣	Restaurant
▲	Mountain peak	●–●	Cable car
⌂⌂	Mountain range	▪	Building
≈	Mountain passes	⊞	Church
ⵏⵏⵏⵏ	Cliffs	▢	Market
⋀	Volcano	◯	Stadium
⚶	Waterfall	▨	Park

MAP SYMBOLS

663

Travel Insurance

Wherever you are, wherever you are going,
we ve got you covered!
Visit our website at
www.roughguides.com/insurance
or call:

📞 UK: 0800 083 9507

📞 Spain: 900 997 149

📞 Australia: 1300 669 999

📞 New Zealand: 0800 55 99 11

📞 Worldwide: +44 870 890 2843

📞 USA, call toll free on: 1 800 749 4922

Please quote our ref: *Rough Guides Newsletter*

Cover for over 46 different nationalities and available in
4 different languages.